Microsoft® OFFICE 2010

INTRODUCTORY

Gary B. Shelly

Misty E. Vermaat

Contributing Authors

Raymond E. Enger

Steven M. Freund

Mary Z. Last

Philip J. Pratt

Jeffrey J. Quasney

Jill E. Romanoski

Susan L. Sebok

COURSE TECHNOLOGY
CENGAGE Learning™

SHELLY
CASHMAN
SERIES®

Australia • Brazil • Japan • Korea • Mexico • Singapore • Spain • United Kingdom • United States

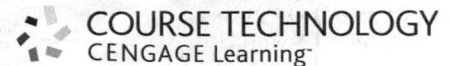
COURSE TECHNOLOGY
CENGAGE Learning

Microsoft Office 2010: Introductory
Gary B. Shelly, Misty E. Vermaat

Vice President, Publisher: Nicole Pinard

Executive Editor: Kathleen McMahon

Senior Product Manager: Mali Jones

Associate Product Manager: Aimee Poirier

Editorial Assistant: Lauren Brody

Director of Marketing: Cheryl Costantini

Marketing Manager: Tristen Kendall

Marketing Coordinator: Stacey Leasca

Print Buyer: Julio Esperas

Director of Production: Patty Stephan

Content Project Manager: Matthew Hutchinson

Development Editors: Jill Batistick, Amanda
    Brodkin, Deb Kaufmann, Lyn Markowicz,
    Lisa Ruffolo

Copyeditors: Foxxe Editorial and Troy Lilly

Proofreaders: Chris Clark and Karen Annett

Indexer: Rich Carlson

QA Manuscript Reviewers: Chris Scriver, John
    Freitas, Serge Palladino, Susan Pedicini,
    Danielle Shaw, Susan Whalen

Art Director: Marissa Falco

Cover Designer: Lisa Kuhn, Curio Press, LLC

Cover Photo: Tom Kates Photography

Text Design: Joel Sadagursky

Compositor: PreMediaGlobal

For product information and technology assistance, contact us at
Cengage Learning Customer & Sales Support, 1-800-354-9706

For permission to use material from this text or product,
submit all requests online at **cengage.com/permissions**
Further permissions questions can be emailed to
permissionrequest@cengage.com

Library of Congress Control Number: 2010929505

softcover binding:
ISBN-13: 978-1-4390-7838-9
ISBN-10: 1-4390-7838-6

hardcover spiral binding:
ISBN-13: 978-1-4390-7841-9
ISBN-10: 1-4390-7841-6

softcover spiral binding:
ISBN-13: 978-1-4390-7840-2
ISBN-10: 1-4390-7840-8

Course Technology
20 Channel Center Street
Boston, MA 02210
USA

Cengage Learning is a leading provider of customized learning solutions with
office locations around the globe, including Singapore, the United Kingdom,
Australia, Mexico, Brazil, and Japan. Locate your local office at:
international.cengage.com/region

Cengage Learning products are represented in Canada by Nelson Education, Ltd.

Visit our website **www.cengage.com/ct/shellycashman** to share and gain
ideas on our textbooks!

To learn more about Course Technology,
visit **www.cengage.com/coursetechnology**

Purchase any of our products at your local college store or at our preferred
online store **www.CengageBrain.com**

*We dedicate this book to the memory of James S. Quasney (1940 – 2009), who for 18 years co-authored
numerous books with Tom Cashman and Gary Shelly and provided extraordinary leadership to the Shelly
Cashman Series editorial team. As series editor, Jim skillfully coordinated, organized, and managed the
many aspects of our editorial development processes and provided unending direction, guidance, inspiration,
support, and advice to the Shelly Cashman Series authors and support team members. He was a trusted,
dependable, loyal, and well-respected leader, mentor, and friend. We are forever grateful to Jim for his faithful
devotion to our team and eternal contributions to our series.*

The Shelly Cashman Series Team

Printed in the United States of America
6 7 15 14 13 12

Microsoft OFFICE 2010
INTRODUCTORY

Contents

Microsoft Office 2010 and Windows 7

Office 2010 and Windows 7: Essential Concepts and Skills

Microsoft **Word 2010**

CHAPTER ONE
Creating, Formatting, and Editing a Word Document with Pictures

Microsoft **PowerPoint 2010**

Microsoft Excel 2010

CHAPTER ONE
Creating a Worksheet and an Embedded Chart

Microsoft Access 2010

CHAPTER ONE
Databases and Database Objects: An Introduction

Microsoft Outlook 2010

CHAPTER ONE
Managing E-Mail Messages with Outlook

CHAPTER TWO
Managing Calendars

Appendices

APPENDIX A
Project Planning Guidelines

APPENDIX B
Publishing Office 2010 Web Pages Online

APPENDIX C
Saving to the Web Using Windows Live DkyDrive

Capstone Projects

Capstone Project: Wee Ones Day Care

Preface

The Shelly Cashman Series® offers the finest textbooks in computer education. We are proud that since Microsoft Office 4.3, our series of Microsoft Office textbooks have been the most widely used books in education. With each new edition of our Office books, we make significant improvements based on the software and comments made by instructors and students. For this Microsoft Office 2010 text, the Shelly Cashman Series development team carefully reviewed our pedagogy and analyzed its effectiveness in teaching today's Office student. Students today read less, but need to retain more. They need not only to be able to perform skills, but to retain those skills and know how to apply them to different settings. Today's students need to be continually engaged and challenged to retain what they're learning.

With this Microsoft Office 2010 text, we continue our commitment to focusing on the user and how they learn best.

Objectives of This Textbook

Microsoft Office 2010: Introductory is intended for a first course on Office 2010 applications. No experience with a computer is assumed, and no mathematics beyond the high school freshman level is required. The objectives of this book are:

- To offer an introduction to Microsoft Windows 7, Microsoft Word 2010, Microsoft Excel 2010, Microsoft Access 2010, Microsoft PowerPoint 2010, and Microsoft Outlook 2010

- To expose students to practical examples of the computer as a useful tool

- To acquaint students with the proper procedures to create documents, worksheets, databases, and presentations suitable for coursework, professional purposes, and personal use

- To help students discover the underlying functionality of Office 2010 so they can become more productive

- To develop an exercise-oriented approach that allows learning by doing

New to This Edition

Microsoft Office 2010: Introductory offers a number of new features and approaches, which improve student understanding, retention, transference, and skill in using Office 2010 programs. The following enhancements will enrich the learning experience:

- Office 2010 and Windows 7: Essential Concepts and Skills chapter prevents repetitive coverage of basic skills in the application chapters.

- Streamlined first chapters for each application allow the ability to cover more advanced skills earlier.

- Chapter topic redistribution offers concise chapters that ensure complete skill coverage.

- Expanded coverage of PowerPoint and Outlook gives exposure to the numerous enhancements made to these applications.

- New pedagogical elements enrich material creating an accessible and user-friendly approach.

  - Break Points, a new boxed element, identify logical stopping points and give students instructions regarding what they should do before taking a break.

  - Within step instructions, Tab | Group Identifiers, such as (Home tab | Bold button), help students more easily locate elements in the groups and on the tabs on the Ribbon.

  - Modified step-by-step instructions tell the student what to do and provide the generic reason why they are completing a specific task, which helps students easily transfer given skills to different settings.

The Shelly Cashman Approach

A Proven Pedagogy with an Emphasis on Project Planning

Each chapter presents a practical problem to be solved, within a project planning framework. The project orientation is strengthened by the use of Plan Ahead boxes, which encourage critical thinking about how to proceed at various points in the project. Step-by-step instructions with supporting screens guide students through the steps. Instructional steps are supported by the Q&A, Experimental Step, and BTW features.

A Visually Engaging Book that Maintains Student Interest

The step-by-step tasks, with supporting figures, provide a rich visual experience for the student. Call-outs on the screens that present both explanatory and navigational information provide students with information they need when they need to know it.

Supporting Reference Materials (Appendices, Capstones, Quick Reference)

The appendices provide additional information about the Application at hand and include such topics and project planning guidelines and certification. With the Quick Reference, students can quickly look up information about a single task, such as keyboard short-cuts, and find page references of where in the book the task is illustrated. The Capstone Projects allow students to demonstrate mastery of skills across the Introductory content for Word, PowerPoint, Excel, and Access.

Integration of the World Wide Web

The World Wide Web is integrated into the Office 2010 learning experience by (1) BTW annotations; (2) BTW, Q&A, and Quick Reference Summary Web pages; and (3) the Learn It Online section for each chapter.

End-of-Chapter Student Activities

Extensive end-of-chapter activities provide a variety of reinforcement opportunities for students where they can apply and expand their skills.

Instructor Resources

The Instructor Resources include both teaching and testing aids and can be accessed via CD-ROM or at www.cengage.com/login.

Instructor's Manual Includes lecture notes summarizing the chapter sections, figures and boxed elements found in every chapter, teacher tips, classroom activities, lab activities, and quick quizzes in Microsoft Word files.

Syllabus Easily customizable sample syllabi that cover policies, assignments, exams, and other course information.

Figure Files Illustrations for every figure in the textbook in electronic form.

PowerPoint Presentations A multimedia lecture presentation system that provides slides for each chapter. Presentations are based on chapter objectives.

Solutions to Exercises Includes solutions for all end-of-chapter and chapter reinforcement exercises.

Test Bank & Test Engine Test Banks include 112 questions for every chapter, featuring objective-based and critical thinking question types, and including page number references and figure references, when appropriate. Also included is the test engine, ExamView, the ultimate tool for your objective-based testing needs.

Data Files for Students Includes all the files that are required by students to complete the exercises.

Additional Activities for Students Consists of Chapter Reinforcement Exercises, which are true/false, multiple-choice, and short answer questions that help students gain confidence in the material learned.

SAM: Skills Assessment Manager

SAM 2010 is designed to help bring students from the classroom to the real world. It allows students to train on and test important computer skills in an active, hands-on environment.

SAM's easy-to-use system includes powerful interactive exams, training, and projects on the most commonly used Microsoft Office applications. SAM simulates the Microsoft Office 2010 application environment, allowing students to demonstrate their knowledge and think through the skills by performing real-world tasks such as bolding word text or setting up slide transitions. Add in live-in-the-application projects, and students are on their way to truly learning and applying skills to business-centric documents.

Designed to be used with the Shelly Cashman Series, SAM includes handy page references so that students can print helpful study guides that match the Shelly Cashman textbooks used in class. For instructors, SAM also includes robust scheduling and reporting features.

Content for Online Learning

Course Technology has partnered with the leading distance learning solution providers and class-management platforms today. To access this material, instructors will visit our password-protected instructor resources available at www.cengage.com/coursetechnology. Instructor resources include the following: additional case projects, sample syllabi, PowerPoint presentations per chapter, and more. For additional information or for an instructor user name and password, please contact your sales representative. For students to access this material, they must have purchased a WebTutor PIN-code specific to this title and your campus platform. The resources for students may include (based on instructor preferences), but are not limited to: topic review, review questions, and practice tests.

Workbook for Microsoft Office 2010: Introductory Concepts and Techniques

This highly popular supplement (ISBN 1-4390-7844-0) includes a variety of activities that help students recall, review, and master the concepts presented. The Workbook complements the end-of-chapter material with an outline; a self-test consisting of true/false, multiple-choice, short answer, and matching questions; and activities calculated to help students develop a deeper understanding of the information presented.

CourseNotes

Course Technology's CourseNotes are six-panel quick reference cards that reinforce the most important and widely used features of a software application in a visual and user-friendly format. CourseNotes serve as a great reference tool during and after the student completes the course.

CourseNotes are available for software applications such as Microsoft Office 2010, Word 2010, PowerPoint 2010, Excel 2010, Access 2010, and Windows 7. Topic-based CourseNotes are available for Best Practices in Social Networking, Hot Topics in Technology, and Web 2.0. Visit www.cengage.com/ct/coursenotes to learn more!

A Guided Tour

Add excitement and interactivity to your classroom with "*A Guided Tour*" product line. Play one of the brief mini-movies to spice up your lecture and spark classroom discussion. Or, assign a movie for homework and ask students to complete the correlated assignment that accompanies each topic. "*A Guided Tour*" product line takes the prep work out of providing your students with information about new technologies and applications and helps keep students engaged with content relevant to their lives; all in under an hour!

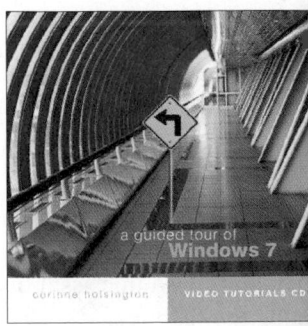

About Our Covers

The Shelly Cashman Series is continually updating our approach and content to reflect the way today's students learn and experience new technology. This focus on student success is reflected on our covers, which feature real students from Bentley University using the Shelly Cashman Series in their courses, and reflect the varied ages and backgrounds of the students learning with our books. When you use the Shelly Cashman Series, you can be assured that you are learning computer skills using the most effective courseware available.

Textbook Walk-Through

The Shelly Cashman Series Pedagogy: Project-Based — Step-by-Step — Variety of Assessments

Plan Ahead boxes prepare students to create successful projects by encouraging them to think strategically about what they are trying to accomplish before they begin working.

Step-by-step instructions now provide a context beyond the point-and-click. Each step provides information on why students are performing each task, or what will occur as a result.

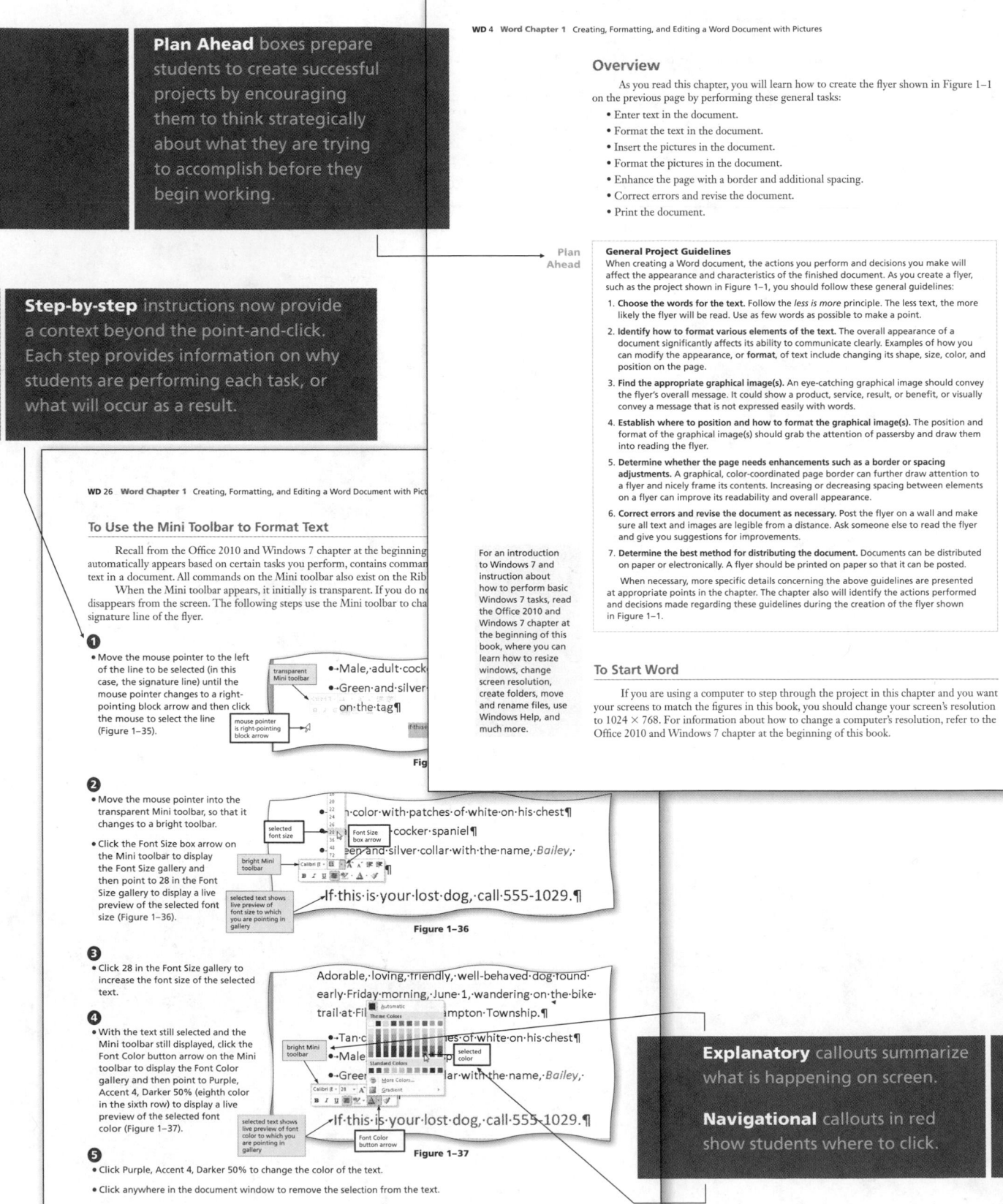

Overview

As you read this chapter, you will learn how to create the flyer shown in Figure 1–1 on the previous page by performing these general tasks:

- Enter text in the document.
- Format the text in the document.
- Insert the pictures in the document.
- Format the pictures in the document.
- Enhance the page with a border and additional spacing.
- Correct errors and revise the document.
- Print the document.

Plan Ahead

General Project Guidelines

When creating a Word document, the actions you perform and decisions you make will affect the appearance and characteristics of the finished document. As you create a flyer, such as the project shown in Figure 1–1, you should follow these general guidelines:

1. **Choose the words for the text.** Follow the *less is more* principle. The less text, the more likely the flyer will be read. Use as few words as possible to make a point.

2. **Identify how to format various elements of the text.** The overall appearance of a document significantly affects its ability to communicate clearly. Examples of how you can modify the appearance, or **format**, of text include changing its shape, size, color, and position on the page.

3. **Find the appropriate graphical image(s).** An eye-catching graphical image should convey the flyer's overall message. It could show a product, service, result, or benefit, or visually convey a message that is not expressed easily with words.

4. **Establish where to position and how to format the graphical image(s).** The position and format of the graphical image(s) should grab the attention of passersby and draw them into reading the flyer.

5. **Determine whether the page needs enhancements such as a border or spacing adjustments.** A graphical, color-coordinated page border can further draw attention to a flyer and nicely frame its contents. Increasing or decreasing spacing between elements on a flyer can improve its readability and overall appearance.

6. **Correct errors and revise the document as necessary.** Post the flyer on a wall and make sure all text and images are legible from a distance. Ask someone else to read the flyer and give you suggestions for improvements.

7. **Determine the best method for distributing the document.** Documents can be distributed on paper or electronically. A flyer should be printed on paper so that it can be posted.

When necessary, more specific details concerning the above guidelines are presented at appropriate points in the chapter. The chapter also will identify the actions performed and decisions made regarding these guidelines during the creation of the flyer shown in Figure 1–1.

For an introduction to Windows 7 and instruction about how to perform basic Windows 7 tasks, read the Office 2010 and Windows 7 chapter at the beginning of this book, where you can learn how to resize windows, change screen resolution, create folders, move and rename files, use Windows Help, and much more.

To Start Word

If you are using a computer to step through the project in this chapter and you want your screens to match the figures in this book, you should change your screen's resolution to 1024 × 768. For information about how to change a computer's resolution, refer to the Office 2010 and Windows 7 chapter at the beginning of this book.

To Use the Mini Toolbar to Format Text

Recall from the Office 2010 and Windows 7 chapter at the beginning automatically appears based on certain tasks you perform, contains comman text in a document. All commands on the Mini toolbar also exist on the Rib

When the Mini toolbar appears, it initially is transparent. If you do ne disappears from the screen. The following steps use the Mini toolbar to cha signature line of the flyer.

1
- Move the mouse pointer to the left of the line to be selected (in this case, the signature line) until the mouse pointer changes to a right-pointing block arrow and then click the mouse to select the line (Figure 1–35).

transparent Mini toolbar

- Male·adult·cock
- Green·and·silver on·the·tag¶

mouse pointer is right-pointing block arrow

Fig

2
- Move the mouse pointer into the transparent Mini toolbar, so that it changes to a bright toolbar.

- Click the Font Size box arrow on the Mini toolbar to display the Font Size gallery and then point to 28 in the Font Size gallery to display a live preview of the selected font size (Figure 1–36).

selected font size

Font Size box arrow

bright Mini toolbar

- n·color·with·patches·of·white·on·his·chest¶
- cocker·spaniel¶
- en·and·silver·collar·with·the·name,·*Bailey,*

selected text shows live preview of font size to which you are pointing in gallery

If·this·is·your·lost·dog,·call·555-1029.¶

Figure 1–36

3
- Click 28 in the Font Size gallery to increase the font size of the selected text.

4
- With the text still selected and the Mini toolbar still displayed, click the Font Color button arrow on the Mini toolbar to display the Font Color gallery and then point to Purple, Accent 4, Darker 50% (eighth color in the sixth row) to display a live preview of the selected font color (Figure 1–37).

Adorable,·loving,·friendly,·well-behaved·dog·found early·Friday·morning,·June·1,·wandering·on·the·bike trail·at·Fi   mpton·Township.¶

bright Mini toolbar

- Tan·c   es·of·white·on·his·chest¶
- Male
- Green   lar·with·the·name,·*Bailey,*

selected color

selected text shows live preview of font color to which you are pointing in gallery

Font Color button arrow

If·this·is·your·lost·dog,·call·555-1029.¶

Figure 1–37

5
- Click Purple, Accent 4, Darker 50% to change the color of the text.

- Click anywhere in the document window to remove the selection from the text.

Explanatory callouts summarize what is happening on screen.

Navigational callouts in red show students where to click.

&A boxes offer questions students may have hen working through the steps and provide dditional information about what they are oing right where they need it.

xperiment Steps within our step-by- ep instructions, encourage students explore, experiment, and take dvantage of the features of the Office 07 user interface. These steps are not ecessary to complete the projects, but e designed to increase the confidence th the software and build problem- lving skills.

eak Points identify logical eaks in the chapter if udents need to stop before mpleting the project.

1
- With the shape still selected, click the More button (shown in Figure 3–6) in the Shape Styles gallery (Drawing Tools Format tab | Shape Styles group) to expand the gallery.

Q&A What if my shape is no longer selected?

Click the shape to select it.

- Point to Intense Effect - Brown, Accent 4 in the Shape Styles gallery to display a live preview of that style applied to the shape in the document (Figure 3–7).

Experiment
- Point to various styles in the Shape Styles gallery and watch the style of the shape change in the document.

2
- Click Intense Effect - Brown, Accent 4 in the Shape Styles gallery to apply the selected style to the shape.

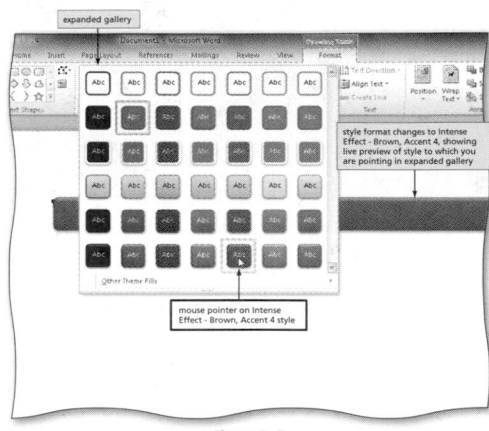

Figure 3–7

Other Ways
1. Click Format Shape Dialog Box Launcher (Drawing Tools Format tab | Shape Styles group), click Picture Color in left pane
2. Right-click shape, click Format Shape on

(Format Shape dialog box), select desired colors, click Close button

shortcut menu, click Picture Color in left pane (Format Shape dialog box), select desired colors, click Close button

---

WD 30 Word Chapter 1 Creating, Formatting, and Editing a Word Document with Pictures

Selecting Text

In many of the previous steps, you have selected text. Table 1–3 summarizes the techniques used to select various items.

Table 1 3 Techniques for Selecting Text		
Item to Select	**Mouse**	**Keyboard (where applicable)**
Block of text	Click at beginning of selection, scroll to end of selection, position mouse pointer at end of selection, hold down SHIFT key and then click; or drag through the text.	
Character(s)	Drag through character(s).	SHIFT+RIGHT ARROW or SHIFT+LEFT ARROW
Document	Move mouse to left of text until mouse pointer changes to a right-pointing block arrow and then triple-click.	CTRL+A
Graphic	Click the graphic.	
Line	Move mouse to left of line until mouse pointer changes to a right-pointing block arrow and then click.	HOME, then SHIFT+END; or END, then SHIFT+HOME
Lines	Move mouse to left of first line until mouse pointer changes to a right-pointing block arrow and then drag up or down.	HOME, then SHIFT+DOWN ARROW or END, then SHIFT+UP AROW
Paragraph	Triple-click paragraph; or move mouse to left of paragraph until mouse pointer changes to a right-pointing block arrow and then double-click.	CTRL+SHIFT+DOWN ARROW or CTRL+SHIFT+UP ARROW
Paragraphs	Move mouse to left of paragraph until mouse pointer changes to a right-pointing block arrow, double-click, and then drag up or down.	CTRL+SHIFT+DOWN ARROW or CTRL+SHIFT+UP ARROW repeatedly
Sentence	Press and hold down CTRL key and then click sentence.	
Word	Double-click the word.	CTRL+SHIFT+RIGHT ARROW or CTRL+SHIFT+LEFT ARROW
Words	Drag through words.	CTRL+SHIFT+RIGHT ARROW or CTRL+SHIFT+LEFT ARROW repeatedly

To Save an Existing Document with the Same File Name

You have made several modifications to the document since you last saved it. Thus, you should save it again. The following step saves the document again. For an example of the step listed below, refer to the Office 2010 and Windows 7 chapter at the beginning of this book.

1 Click the Save button on the Quick Access Toolbar to overwrite the previously saved file.

Break Point: If you wish to take a break, this is a good place to do so. You can quit Word now (refer to page WD 44 for instructions). To resume at a later time, start Word (refer to pages WD 4 and WD 5 for instructions), open the file called Found Dog Flyer (refer to page WD 45 for instructions), and continue following the steps from this location forward.

Inserting and Formatting Pictures in a Word Document

With the text formatted in the flyer, the next step is to insert digital pictures in the flyer and format the pictures. Flyers usually contain graphical images, such as a picture, to attract the attention of passersby. In the following pages, you will perform these tasks:

1. Insert the first digital picture into the flyer and then reduce its size.
2. Insert the second digital picture into the flyer and then reduce its size.
3. Change the look of the first picture and then the second picture.

Textbook Walk-Through

Chapter Summary A concluding paragraph, followed by a listing of the tasks completed within a chapter together with the pages on which the step-by-step, screen-by-screen explanations appear.

To Quit Word

The project now is complete. Thus, the following steps quit Word. For an example of the step listed below, refer to the Office 2010 and Windows 7 chapter at the beginning of this book.

1 If you have one Word document open, click the Close button on the right side of the title bar to close the document and quit Word; or if you have multiple Word documents open, click File on the Ribbon to open the Backstage view and then click Exit in the Backstage view to close all open documents and quit Word.

2 If a Microsoft Word dialog box appears, click the Save button to save any changes made to the document since the last save.

BTW

Printed Borders
If one or more of your borders do not print, click the Page Borders button (Page Layout tab | Page Background group), click the Options button (Borders and Shading dialog box), click the Measure from box arrow and click Text, change the four text boxes to 15 pt, and then click the OK button in each dialog box. Try printing the document again. If the borders still do not print, adjust the text boxes in the dialog box to a number smaller than 15 point.

Chapter Summary

In this chapter, you have learned how to enter text in a document, format text, insert a picture, format a picture, add a page border, and print a document. The items listed below include all the new Word skills you have learned in this chapter.

1. Start Word (WD 4)
2. Type Text (WD 6)
3. Display Formatting Marks (WD 7)
4. Insert a Blank Line (WD 7)
5. Wordwrap Text as You Type (WD 8)
6. Check Spelling and Grammar as You Type (WD 9)
7. Save a Document (WD 12)
8. Center a Paragraph (WD 14)
9. Select a Line (WD 15)
10. Change the Font Size of Selected Text (WD 16)
11. Change the Font of Selected Text (WD 17)
12. Change the Case of Selected Text (WD 18)
   (WD 19)

   (WD 26)

23. Bold Text (WD 28)
24. Change Theme Colors (WD 28)
25. Save an Existing Document with the Same File Name (WD 30)
26. Insert a Picture (WD 31)
27. Zoom the Document (WD 33)
28. Resize a Graphic (WD 34)
29. Resize a Graphic by Entering Exact Measurements (WD 36)
30. Apply a Picture Style (WD 37)
31. Apply Picture Effects (WD 38)
32. View One Page (WD 40)
33. Add a Page Border (WD 41)
34. Change Spacing before and after a Paragraph (WD 44)
35. Quit Word (WD 44)
36. Open a Document from Word (WD 45)
37. Insert Text in an Existing Document (WD 46)
38. Delete Text (WD 47)
39. Move Text (WD 47)
40. Change Document Properties (WD 49)
41. Print a Document (WD 51)

profile, your instructor may have assigned an autogradable f so, log into the SAM 2010 Web site at www.cengage.com/sam2010 and start files.

BTW

Quick Reference
For a table that lists how to complete the tasks covered in this book using the mouse, Ribbon, shortcut menu, and keyboard, see the Quick Reference Summary at the back of this book, or visit the Word 2010 Quick Reference Web page (scsite.com/wd2010/qr).

STUDENT ASSIGNMENTS

Learn It Online

Test your knowledge of chapter content and key terms.

Instructions: To complete the Learn It Online exercises, start your browser, click the Address bar, and then enter the Web address **scsite.com/wd2010/learn**. When the Word 2010 Learn It Online page is displayed, click the link for the exercise you want to complete and then read the instructions.

Chapter Reinforcement TF, MC, and SA
A series of true/false, multiple choice, and short answer questions that test your knowledge of the chapter content.

Flash Cards
An interactive learning environment where you identify chapter key terms associated with displayed definitions.

Practice Test
A series of multiple choice questions that test your knowledge of chapter content and key terms.

Who Wants To Be a Computer Genius?
An interactive game that challenges your knowledge of chapter content in the style of a television quiz show.

Wheel of Terms
An interactive game that challenges your knowledge of chapter key terms in the style of the television show *Wheel of Fortune*.

Crossword Puzzle Challenge
A crossword puzzle that challenges your knowledge of key terms presented in the chapter.

Apply Your Knowledge

Reinforce the skills and apply the concepts you learned in this chapter.

Modifying Text and Formatting a Document
Note: To complete this assignment, you will be required to use the Data Files for Students. See the inside back cover of this book for instructions on downloading the Data Files for Students, or contact your instructor for information about accessing the required files.

Instructions: Start Word. Open the document, Apply 1-1 Buffalo Photo Shoot Flyer Unformatted, from the Data Files for Students. The document you open is an unformatted flyer. You are to modify text, format paragraphs and characters, and insert a picture in the flyer.

Perform the following tasks:
1. Delete the word, single, in the sentence of body copy below the headline.
2. Insert the word, Creeks, between the words, Twin Buffalo, in the sentence of body copy below the headline.
3. At the end of the signature line, change the period to an exclamation point.
4. Center the headline and the signature line.
5. Change the theme colors to the Aspect color scheme.
6. Change the font and font size of the headline to 48-point Impact, or a similar font. Change the case of the headline text to all capital letters. Apply the text effect called Gradient Fill – Orange, Accent 1, Outline – White to the headline.
7. Change the font size of body copy between the headline and the signature line to 20 point.
8. Use the Mini toolbar to change the font size of the signature line to 26 point.
9. Select the words, hundreds of buffalo, in the paragraph below the headline and underline them.

Learn It Online Every chapter features a Learn It Online section that is comprised of six exercises. These exercises include True/False, Multiple Choice, Short Answer, Flash Cards, Practice Test, and Learning Games.

Apply Your Knowledge This exercise usually requires students to open and manipulate a file from the Data Files that parallels the activities learned in the chapter. To obtain a copy of the Data Files for Students, follow the instructions on the inside back cover of this text.

Extend Your Knowledge

Extend the skills you learned in this chapter and experiment with new skills. You may need to use Help to complete the assignment.

Modifying Text and Picture Formats and Adding Page Borders

Note: To complete this assignment, you will be required to use the Data Files for Students. See the inside back cover of this book for instructions on downloading the Data Files for Students, or contact your instructor for information about accessing the required files.

Instructions: Start Word. Open the document, Extend 1-1 TVC Cruises Flyer, from the Data Files for Students. You will enhance the look of the flyer shown in Figure 1–76. *Hint:* Remember, if you make a mistake while formatting the picture, you can reset it by clicking the Reset Picture button or Reset Picture button arrow (Picture Tools Format tab | Adjust group).

Perform the following tasks:

1. Use Help to learn about the following formats: remove bullets, grow font, shrink font, art page borders, decorative underline(s), picture bullets, picture border shading, shadow picture effects, and color saturation and tone.
2. Remove the bullet from the paragraph below the picture.

3. Select the text, 10 percent, and use the Grow Font button to increase its font size.
4. Add an art page border to the flyer. If the border is not in color, add color to it.
5. Change the solid underline below the word, cruises, to a decorative underline. Change

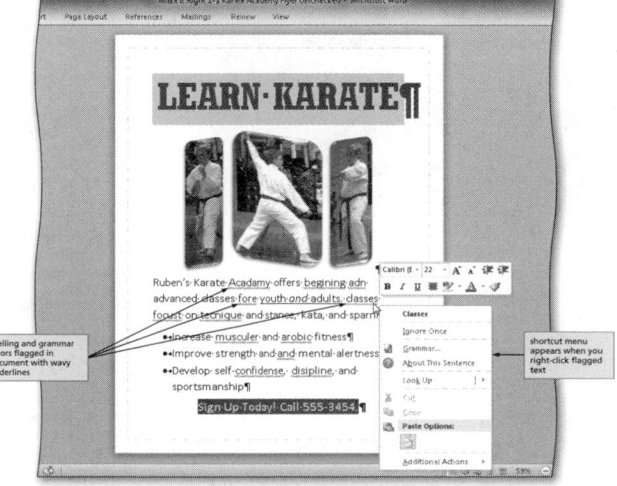

NEED AN ESCAPE?

change border color and add shadow effect; change color saturation and color tone

add art page border

remove bullet

use Grow Font button to increase font size

change to picture bullets

• **Tango Vacation Club members receive a 10 percent discount for cruises booked during May. Select from a variety of destinations.**

An experience of a lifetime awaits you!

- **Ultimate relaxation**
- **Endless fun and entertainment**
- **Breathtaking scenery**
- **Friendly, attentive staff**
- **Clean facilities**

Interested? Call TVC at 555-1029

Figure 1–76

Make It Right

Analyze a document and correct all errors and/or improve the design.

Correcting Spelling and Grammar Errors

Note: To complete this assignment, you will be required to use the Data Files for Students. See the inside back cover of this book for instructions on downloading the Data Files for Students, or contact your instructor for information about accessing the required files.

Instructions: Start Word. Open the document, Make It Right 1-1 Karate Academy Flyer Unchecked, from the Data Files for Students. The document is a flyer that contains spelling and grammar errors, as shown in Figure 1–77. You are to correct each spelling (red wavy underline) and grammar error (green and blue wavy underlines) by right-clicking the flagged text and then clicking the appropriate correction on the shortcut menu.

If your screen does not display the wavy underlines, click File on the Ribbon and then click Options in the Backstage view. When the Word Options dialog box is displayed, click Proofing in the left pane, be sure the 'Hide spelling errors in this document only' and 'Hide grammar errors in this document only' check boxes do not contain check marks, and then click the OK button. If your screen still does not display the wavy underlines, redisplay the Word Options dialog box, click Proofing, and then click the Recheck Document button.

Change the document properties, including keywords, as specified by your instructor. Save the revised document with the name, Make It Right 1-1 Karate Academy Flyer, and then submit it in the format specified by your instructor.

LEARN·KARATE¶

Ruben's·Karate·Acadamy·offers·begining·adn· advanced·classes·fore·youth·and·adults.·classes· focust·on·tecnique·and·stance,·kata,·and·sparri

- •Increase·musculer·and·arobic·fitness¶
- •Improve·strength·and·and·mental·alertness¶
- ••Develop·self-confidence,··disipline,·and· sportsmanship¶

Sign·Up·Today!·Call·555-3454¶

spelling and grammar errors flagged in document with wavy underlines

shortcut menu appears when you right-click flagged text

Figure 1–77

Textbook Walk-Through

STUDENT ASSIGNMENTS

In the Lab

Design and/or create a document using the guidelines, concepts, and skills presented in this chapter. Labs are listed in order of increasing difficulty.

Lab 1: Creating a Flyer with a Picture

Problem: As a part-time employee in the Student Services Center at school, you have been asked to prepare a flyer that advertises study habits classes. First, you prepare the unformatted flyer shown in Figure 1–78a, and then you format it so that it looks like Figure 1–78b. *Hint:* Remember, if you make a mistake while formatting the flyer, you can click the Undo button on the Quick Access Toolbar to undo your last action.

Note: To complete this assignment, you will be required to use the Data Files for Students. See the inside back cover of this book for instructions on downloading the Data Files for Students, or contact your instructor for information about accessing the required files.

Instructions: Perform the following tasks:
1. Start Word. Display formatting marks on the screen.
2. Type the flyer text, unformatted, as shown in Figure 1–78a, inserting a blank line between the headline and the body copy. If Word flags any misspelled words as you type, check their spelling and correct them.
3. Save the document using the file name, Lab 1-1 Study Habits Flyer.
4. Center the headline and the signature line.
5. Change the theme colors to Concourse.
6. Change the font size of the headline to 36 point and the font to Ravie, or a similar font. Apply the text effect called Gradient Fill – Dark Red, Accent 6, Inner Shadow.
7. Change the font size of body copy between the headline and the signature line to 20 point.
8. Change the font size of the signature line to 22 point. Bold the text in the signature line.

> **In the Lab** Three all new in-depth assignments per chapter require students to utilize the chapter concepts and techniques to solve problems on a computer.

Studying All Night?

blank line →

Let us help you! Our expert instructors teach effective stu[...]
energy-building techniques.

Classes are $15.00 per session

Sessions last four weeks

Classes meet in the Student Services Center twice a week

Call 555-2838 or stop by to sign up today!

Figure 1–78 (a) Unform[...]

Word Chapter 3

create a building block for Fair Grove Elementary School and insert the building block whenever you have to enter the school name. Resize table columns to fit contents. Check the spelling of the letter. Change the document properties, as specified by your instructor. Save the letter with Lab 3-3 Education Board Letter as the file name.

Cases and Places

Apply your creative thinking and problem solving skills to design and implement a solution.

Note: To complete these assignments, you may be required to use the Data Files for Students. See the inside back cover of this book for instructions on downloading the Data Files for Students, or contact your instructor for information about accessing the required files.

1: Create a Letter to a Potential Employer

Academic

As a student about to graduate, you are actively seeking employment in your field and have located an advertisement for a job in which you are interested. You decide to write a letter to the potential employer: Ms. Janice Tremont at Home Health Associates, 554 Mountain View Lane, Blue Dust, MO 64319.

The draft wording for the letter is as follows: I am responding to your advertisement for the nursing position in the *Blue Dust Press*. I have tailored my activities and education for a career in geriatric medicine. This month, I will graduate with concentrations in Geriatric Medicine (24 hours), Osteopathic Medicine (12 hours), and Holistic Nursing (9 hours). In addition to receiving my bachelor degree in nursing, I have enhanced my education by participating in the following activities: volunteered at Blue Dust's free health care clinic; attended several continuing education and career-specific seminars, including An Aging Populace, Care of the Homebound, and Special Needs of the Elderly; completed one-semester internship at Blue Dust Community Hospital in spring semester of 2012; completed Certified Nursing Assistant (CNA) program at Blue Dust Community College; and worked as nurse's aide for two years during college. I look forward to an interview so that we can discuss the position you offer and my qualifications. With my background and education, I am confident that I will make a positive contribution to Home Health Associates.

The letter should contain a letterhead that uses a shape and clip art, a table (use a table to present the areas of concentration), and a bulleted list (use a bulleted list to present the activities). Insert nonbreaking spaces in the newspaper name. Use the concepts and techniques presented in this chapter to create and format a letter according to the modified block style, creating appropriate paragraph breaks and rewording the draft as necessary. Use your personal information for contact information in the letter. Be sure to check the spelling and grammar of the finished letter. Submit your assignment in the format specified by your instructor.

2: Create a Letter Requesting Donations

Personal

As an alumnus of your historic high school, you are concerned that the building is being considered for demolition. You decide to write a letter to another graduate: Mr. Jim Lemon, 87 Travis Parkway, Vigil, CT 06802.

The draft wording for the letter is as follows: As a member of the class of 1988, you, like many others, probably have many fond memories of our alma mater, Vigil East High School. I recently learned that the building is being considered for demolition because of its age and structural integrity.

> **Cases & Places** exercises call on students to create open-ended projects that reflect academic, personal, and business settings.

Continued >

Microsoft® OFFICE 2010

INTRODUCTORY

Introduction to Computers

and How to Purchase Computers and Mobile Devices

What Is a Computer?

Computers are everywhere: at work, at school, and at home. In the workplace, employees use computers to create correspondence such as e-mail messages, memos, and letters; manage calendars; calculate payroll; track inventory; and generate invoices. At school, teachers use computers to assist with classroom instruction. Students use computers to complete assignments and research. People also spend hours of leisure time using a computer. They play games, communicate with friends and relatives online and using e-mail, purchase goods online, converse in chat rooms, listen to music or radio broadcasts, watch or create videos and movies, read books and magazines, share stories, research genealogy, retouch photos, and plan vacations. At work, at school, and at home, computers are helping people do their work faster, more accurately, and in some cases, in ways that previously would not have been possible.

A **computer** is an electronic device, operating under the control of instructions stored in its own memory, that can accept data (input), process the data according to specified rules (process), produce results (output), and store the results (storage) for future use. Generally, the term is used to describe a collection of electric, electronic, and mechanical components known as hardware. Figure 1 shows some common hardware components. These components are discussed in more depth later in this chapter.

☞ **Computers**

For more information, visit scsite.com/ic8/weblink and then click Computers.

Figure 1 Common computer hardware components include the keyboard, mouse, microphone, scanner, Web cam, printer, monitor, speakers, system unit, hard disk drive, external hard disk, optical disc drive(s), USB flash drive, card reader/writer, memory cards, and modem.

Computers perform four basic operations — input, process, output, and storage. These operations comprise the **information processing cycle**. Collectively, these operations process data into information and store it for future use.

A computer derives its power from its capability to perform the information processing cycle with amazing speed, reliability (low failure rate), and accuracy; its capacity to store huge amounts of data and information; and its capability to communicate with other computers.

For a computer to perform operations, it must be given a detailed set of instructions that tells it exactly what to do. These instructions are called a program, or software. Before processing for a specific activity begins, the program corresponding to that activity is stored in the computer. Once the program is stored, the computer can begin to execute the program's first instruction. The computer executes one program instruction after another until the activity is complete.

All computer processing requires data. **Data** is a collection of unprocessed items, which can include text, numbers, images, audio, and video. Computers manipulate data to create information. **Information** conveys meaning and is useful to people. During the output operation, the information that has been created is put into some form, such as a printed report, or it can be stored on the computer for future use. As shown in Figure 2, a computer processes several data items to produce a cash register receipt.

People who use the computer directly or use the information it provides are called **computer users**, **end users**, or sometimes, just **users**. Users and computer manufacturers can reduce the environmental impact of computers through green computing. **Green computing** involves reducing the electricity consumed and environmental waste generated when using a computer.

Programs

For more information, visit scsite.com/ic8/weblink and then click Computer Programs.

Information

For more information, visit scsite.com/ic8/weblink and then click Information.

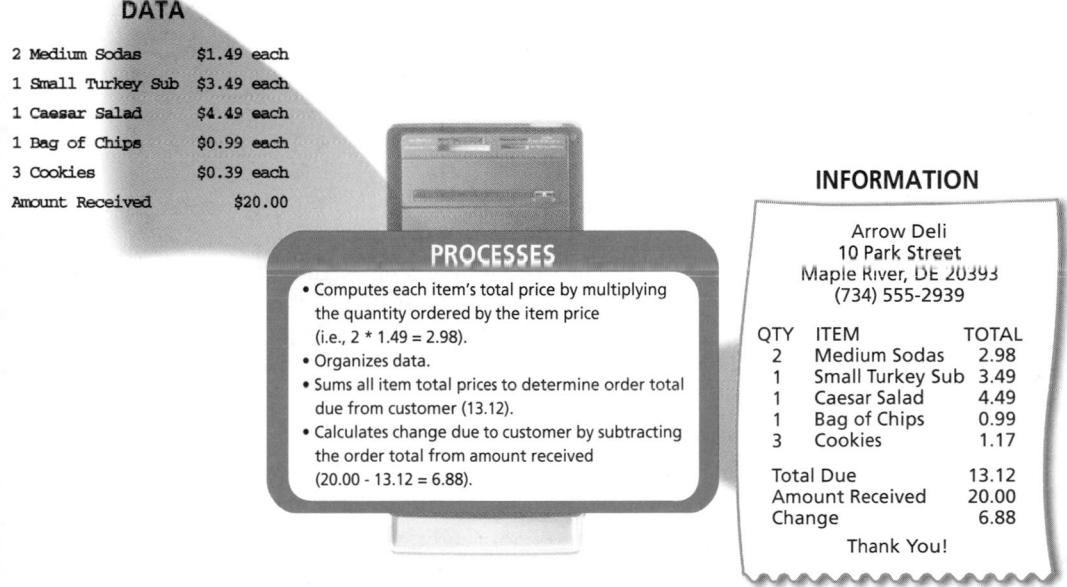

DATA

2 Medium Sodas	$1.49 each
1 Small Turkey Sub	$3.49 each
1 Caesar Salad	$4.49 each
1 Bag of Chips	$0.99 each
3 Cookies	$0.39 each
Amount Received	$20.00

PROCESSES

- Computes each item's total price by multiplying the quantity ordered by the item price (i.e., 2 * 1.49 = 2.98).
- Organizes data.
- Sums all item total prices to determine order total due from customer (13.12).
- Calculates change due to customer by subtracting the order total from amount received (20.00 - 13.12 = 6.88).

INFORMATION

Arrow Deli
10 Park Street
Maple River, DE 20393
(734) 555-2939

QTY	ITEM	TOTAL
2	Medium Sodas	2.98
1	Small Turkey Sub	3.49
1	Caesar Salad	4.49
1	Bag of Chips	0.99
3	Cookies	1.17

Total Due	13.12
Amount Received	20.00
Change	6.88

Thank You!

Figure 2   A computer processes data into information. In this simplified example, the item ordered, item price, quantity ordered, and amount received all represent data. The computer processes the data to produce the cash register receipt (information).

The Components of a Computer

The six primary components of a computer are input devices, the processor (control unit and arithmetic/logic unit), memory, output devices, storage devices, and communications devices. The processor, memory, and storage devices are housed in a box-like case called the system unit (shown in Figure 1). A **peripheral** is a device that connects to the system unit and is controlled by the processor in the computer. Peripherals can include input devices and output devices, as well as some storage devices and communications devices.

Figure 3 shows how the components of a computer interact to carry out a task. The following sections describe the types of personal computers and mobile devices, as well as their primary components (input devices, processor, memory, output devices, and communications devices).

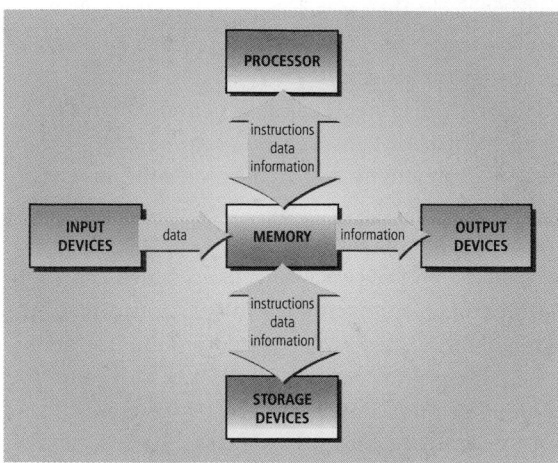

Figure 3　Most devices connected to the computer communicate with the processor to carry out a task. When a user starts a program, for example, its instructions transfer from a storage device to memory. Data needed by the program enters memory either from an input device or a storage device. The processor interprets and executes instructions in memory and also performs calculations on the data in memory. Resulting information is stored in memory, from which it can be sent to an output device or a storage device for future access, as needed.

Personal Computers and Mobile Devices

A **personal computer** is a computer that can perform all of its input, processing, output, and storage activities by itself. A personal computer contains a processor, memory, and one or more input, output, and storage devices. Personal computers also often contain a communications device. A **mobile computer** is a personal computer you can carry from place to place. Similarly, a **mobile device** is a computing device small enough to hold in your hand. The most popular type of mobile computer is the notebook computer.

Figure 4　A desktop computer.

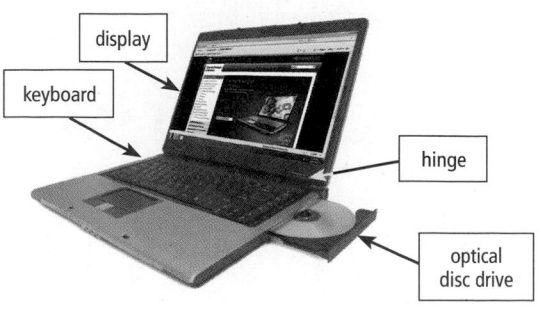

Figure 5　A traditional notebook computer.

Desktop Computers

A **desktop computer** is designed so that the system unit, input devices, output devices, and any other devices fit entirely on or under a desk or table (Figure 4). In some models, the monitor sits on top of the system unit, which is placed on the desk. The more popular style of system unit is the tall and narrow tower, which can sit on the floor vertically.

Notebook Computers

A **notebook computer**, also called a **laptop computer**, is a portable, personal computer often designed to fit on your lap (Figure 5). These computers are thin and lightweight, yet can be as powerful as the average desktop computer. A **netbook**, which is a type of notebook computer, is smaller, lighter, and often not as powerful as a traditional notebook computer. Resembling a letter-sized slate, the **Tablet PC** is a special type of notebook computer that allows you to write or draw on the screen using a digital pen.

Mobile Devices

Mobile devices, which are small enough to carry in a pocket, usually store programs and data permanently on memory inside the system unit or on small storage media such as memory cards. You often can connect a mobile device to a personal computer to exchange information. Three popular types of mobile devices are smart phones, portable media players, and digital cameras.

A **smart phone** is a phone that can connect to the Internet and usually also provides personal information management functions such as a calendar, an appointment book, an address book, a calculator, and a notepad (Figure 6). A **portable media player** is a mobile device on which you can store, organize, and play digital media (shown in Figure 1 on page COM 2). For example, you can listen to music; watch videos, movies, and television shows; and view photos on the device's screen. A **digital camera** is a device that allows users to take pictures and store the photographed images digitally, instead of on traditional film (shown in Figure 1). Digital cameras typically allow users to review, and sometimes modify, images while they are in the camera.

Figure 6 A smart phone is a popular mobile device.

Input Devices

An **input device** is any hardware component that allows you to enter data and instructions into a computer. Depending on your particular program and requirements, the input device you use may vary. Five widely used input devices are the keyboard, mouse, microphone, scanner, and Web cam (shown in Figure 1). The two primary input devices used are the keyboard and the mouse.

👆 **Input Devices**
For more information, visit scsite.com/ic8/weblink and then click Input Devices.

Keyboard

A **keyboard** is an input device that contains keys users press to enter data and instructions into the computer. All desktop computer keyboards have a typing area that includes the letters of the alphabet, numbers, punctuation marks, and other basic keys. Many desktop computer keyboards also have a numeric keypad on the right side of the keyboard. Most of today's desktop computer keyboards are enhanced keyboards. An enhanced keyboard has 12 or more function keys along the top and a set of arrow and additional keys between the typing area and the numeric keypad (Figure 7). Function keys are special keys programmed to issue instructions to a computer.

Figure 7 On a desktop computer keyboard, you type using keys in the typing area and on the numeric keypad.

A variety of options are available for typing on a smart phone (Figure 8). Many can display an on-screen keyboard, where you press the on-screen keys using your finger or a stylus. A **stylus** is a small metal or plastic device that looks like a tiny ink pen but uses pressure instead of ink. Some smart phones have one key for each letter of the alphabet, often called a mini-keyboard. Other phones have keypads that contain fewer keys than there are letters in the alphabet. For these phones, each key on the keypad represents multiple characters, which are identified on the key.

Figure 8   Users have a variety of options for typing on a phone.

Mouse and Other Pointing Devices

A **mouse** is a pointing device that fits comfortably under the palm of your hand (Figure 9). With a mouse, users control the movement of the **pointer**, which is a small symbol on the screen whose location and shape change as a user moves a pointing device. As you move a mouse, for example, the pointer on the screen also moves. Generally, you use the mouse to move the pointer on the screen to an object such as a button, a menu, an icon, a link, or text. Then, you press a mouse button to perform a certain action associated with that object. The bottom of a mouse is flat and contains a mechanism (ball, optical sensor, or laser sensor) that detects movement of the mouse.

Figure 9   This mouse uses a laser to detect movement of the mouse. It also includes buttons you push with your thumb that enable forward and backward navigation through Web pages.

Most notebook computers have a **touchpad**, a small, flat, rectangular pointing device near the keyboard that allows you to move the pointer by sliding a fingertip on the surface of the pad (Figure 10).

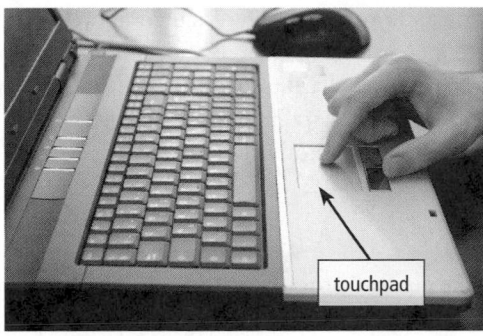

Figure 10   Most notebook computers have a touchpad that allows a user to control the movement of the pointer.

Other Input for Mobile Devices   Most mobile devices, such as smart phones and PDAs, and some notebook computers, such as Tablet PCs, use a variety of alternatives for entering data and instructions (Figure 11). One of the more popular input devices for mobile devices is the stylus. Some have touch screens, enabling you to touch the screen to perform tasks.

obtain maps and directions on the phone by attaching this navigation receiver to your vehicle's window

speak into the microphone that wirelessly communicates with the phone

take a picture using the digital camera built into the back of the phone

use one end of the stylus to write on the phone's screen and the other end as a ballpoint pen

transfer data and instructions to and from the computer and phone by connecting it to the computer with a cable

enter text messages via a wireless keyboard

Figure 11   Besides a touch screen and basic stylus, users have a variety of other options for entering data and instructions into a smart phone.

System Unit

The **system unit** is a case that contains electronic components of the computer used to process data (Figure 12). System units are available in a variety of shapes and sizes. The case of the system unit, also called the chassis, is made of metal or plastic and protects the internal components from damage. The **motherboard**, sometimes called a system board, is the main circuit board of the system unit. Many electronic components attach to the motherboard; others are built into it. The sound card and video card shown in Figure 12 are examples of adapter cards, which are circuit boards that provide connections and functions not built into the motherboard or expand on the capability of features integrated into the motherboard.

Processor

The **processor** (bottom of Figure 12), also called the **central processing unit** (**CPU**), interprets and carries out the basic instructions that operate a computer. Processors contain a control unit and an arithmetic/logic unit. The **control unit** directs and coordinates most of the operations in the computer. The **arithmetic/logic unit** (**ALU**) performs arithmetic, comparison, and other operations.

On a personal computer, all functions of the processor usually are on a single chip. A computer chip is a small piece of semiconducting material that contains many microscopic pathways capable of carrying electrical current. Today's processors can perform some operations in less than the time it takes to blink your eye.

Memory

Memory consists of electronic components that store instructions waiting to be executed and data needed by those instructions. Most memory keeps data and instructions temporarily, which means its contents are erased when the computer is shut off. When discussing computer memory, users typically are referring to RAM. Also called main memory, **RAM** (random access memory) consists of memory chips that can be read from and written to by the processor and other devices. These chips are placed on a memory module (lower left of Figure 12) that fits in a slot on the motherboard in the system unit.

The amount of memory in computers is measured in kilobytes, megabytes, gigabytes, or terabytes. A **byte** usually stores one character, such as the letter A. One **kilobyte** (**KB or K**) equals exactly 1,024 bytes, and one **megabyte** (**MB**) equals approximately one million bytes. One **gigabyte** (**GB**) equals approximately one billion bytes, and one **terabyte** (**TB**) equals approximately

Processor

For more information, visit scsite.com/ic8/weblink and then click Processor.

Memory

For more information, visit scsite.com/ic8/weblink and then click Memory.

Figure 12 The system unit on a typical personal computer consists of numerous electronic components, some of which are shown in this figure. The sound card and video card are two types of adapter cards.

one trillion bytes. A computer with 4 GB of RAM, therefore, can store approximately four billion characters. For reference, one megabyte can hold approximately 500 letter-size pages of text information, and one gigabyte can hold approximately 500,000 letter-size pages of text information.

Output Devices

Output devices are hardware components that convey information to one or more people. Commonly used output devices include display devices; printers; speakers, headphones, and earbuds; data projectors; and interactive whiteboards. When a computer is used for processing tasks such as creating documents, the two output devices widely used are the printer and a display device.

Output Devices
For more information, visit scsite.com/ic8/weblink and then click Output Devices.

Printers

A **printer** is an output device that produces text and graphics on a physical medium such as paper. Ink-jet printers and laser printers often are used with personal computers.

Ink-jet printers produce text and graphics in both black and white and color on a variety of paper types and sizes (Figure 13). Some ink-jet printers, called **photo printers,** produce photo-lab-quality pictures and are ideal for home or small-business use. The speed of an ink-jet printer is measured by the number of pages per minute (ppm) it can print. Most ink-jet printers print from 12 to 36 pages per minute. Graphics and colors print at the slower rate.

Figure 13   Ink-jet printers are a popular type of color printer used in the home.

A laser printer is a high-speed, high-quality printer that operates in a manner similar to a copy machine (Figure 14). Laser printers typically use individual sheets of paper stored in one or more removable trays that slide in the printer case. It creates images using a laser beam and powdered ink, called toner, on a special drum inside the printer, forming the images to be printed. Laser printers can cost from a couple hundred dollars to a few thousand dollars for the home and small office user, to several hundred thousand dollars for large business users. Generally, the more expensive the laser printer, the more pages it can print per minute.

A **multifunction peripheral**, also called an **all-in-one device**, is a single device that looks like a printer or copy machine but provides the functionality of a printer, scanner, copy machine, and perhaps a fax machine. Some use color ink-jet printer technology, while others include a black-and-white or color laser printer.

Figure 14   A color laser printer.

Display Devices

A **display device** is an output device that visually conveys text, graphics, and video information. A **monitor** is a display device that is packaged as a separate peripheral. A widely used monitor is an LCD monitor. The **LCD monitor** shown in

Figure 15 uses a liquid crystal display to produce images on the screen. The surface of the screen of an LCD monitor is composed of individual picture elements called **pixels**. **Resolution** is the number of horizontal and vertical pixels in a display device. For example, a screen set to a resolution of 1440 × 900 pixels displays up to 1440 pixels per horizontal row and 900 pixels per vertical row, for a total of 1,296,000 pixels to create a screen image. A higher resolution provides a smoother, sharper, clearer image.

Mobile computers such as notebook computers, including netbooks and Tablet PCs, and mobile devices such as smart phones, portable media players, PDAs, handheld game consoles, and digital cameras, have built-in LCD screens (Figure 16).

speakers

Figure 15 The LCD monitor is widely used with desktop computers.

notebook computer

PDA

smart phone

handheld game console

portable media player

digital camera

Figure 16 Notebook computers, PDAs, smart phones, handheld game consoles, portable media players, and digital cameras have color LCD screens.

Storage Devices

A **storage device** is the computer hardware that records and/or retrieves items to and from storage media. A **storage medium** (media is the plural) is the physical material on which a computer keeps data, instructions, and information. Three common types of storage media are hard disks, flash memory, and optical discs.

Hard Disks

A **hard disk** is a storage device that contains one or more inflexible, circular platters that use magnetic particles to store data, instructions, and information. The system unit on most personal computers contains at least one hard disk, sometimes called an internal hard disk because it is not portable. Users store documents, spreadsheets, presentations, databases, e-mail messages, Web pages, digital photos, music, videos, and software on hard disks.

Hard disks store data and instructions in tracks and sectors on a platter (Figure 17). A **track** is a narrow recording band that forms a full circle on the surface of the disk. The disk's storage locations consist of pie-shaped sections, which break the tracks into small arcs called **sectors**. On a hard disk, a sector typically stores up to 512 bytes of data. Storage capacities of internal hard disks for personal computers range from 160 GB to more than 2 TB.

On desktop computers, platters most often have a size of approximately 3.5 inches in diameter. On notebook computers and mobile devices, the diameter is 2.5 inches or less. A typical hard disk has multiple platters stacked on top of one another. Each platter has two read/write heads, one for each side. The hard disk has arms that move the read/write heads to the proper location on the platter (Figure 18). The hard disk platters spin at a high rate of speed, typically 5,400 to 15,000 revolutions per minute. On today's computers, the platters typically stop spinning or slow down after a specified time to save power.

When reading or writing, the read/write heads on a hard disk do not actually touch the surface of the disk. The distance between the read/write heads and the platters is about two millionths of one inch. This close clearance means that dirt, hair, dust, smoke, or other particles could cause the hard disk to have a **head crash**, when a read/write head touches a platter, usually resulting in loss of data or sometimes the entire disk. Although current hard disks are sealed tightly to keep out contaminants, head crashes do occur occasionally. Thus, it is crucial that you back up your hard disk regularly. A **backup** is a duplicate of a file, program, or disk placed on a separate storage medium that you can use in case the original is lost, damaged, or destroyed.

Figure 17 Tracks form circles on the surface of a hard disk platter. The disk's storage locations are divided into pie-shaped sections, which break the tracks into small arcs called sectors

How a Hard Disk Works

Step 1
The circuit board controls the movement of the head actuator and a small motor.

Step 2
A small motor spins the platters while the computer is running.

Step 3
When software requests a disk access, the read/write heads determine the current or new location of the data.

Step 4
The head actuator positions the read/write head arms over the correct location on the platters to read or write data.

Figure 18 This figure shows how a hard disk works.

Portable Hard Disks Some hard disks are portable. An **external hard disk** (Figure 19) is a separate freestanding hard disk that connects with a cable to a port on the system unit or communicates wirelessly. A **removable hard disk** (Figure 20) is a hard disk that you insert and remove from a drive. Both internal and external hard disks are available in miniature sizes to allow users to transport their data easily.

external hard disk

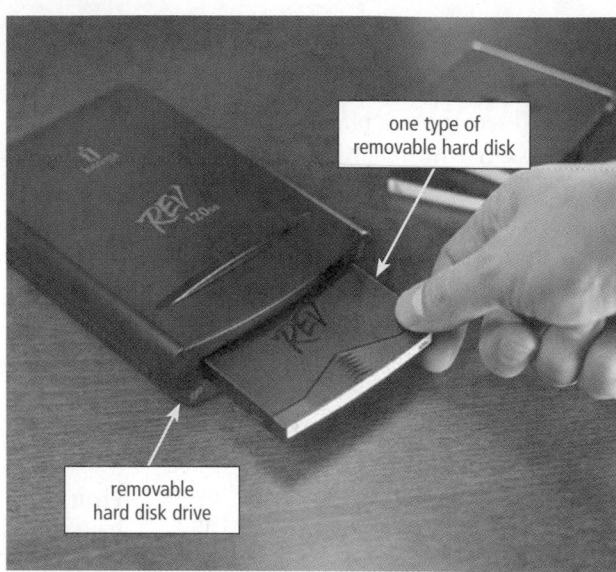

one type of removable hard disk

removable hard disk drive

Figure 19 An external hard disk.

Figure 20 A removable hard disk.

Flash Memory Storage

Flash memory is a type of memory that can be erased electronically and rewritten. Flash memory chips are a type of **solid state media**, which means they consist entirely of electronic components and contain no moving parts. Types of flash memory storage include solid state drives, memory cards, USB flash drives, and ExpressCard modules.

A **solid state drive** (**SSD**) is a storage device that typically uses flash memory to store data, instructions, and information (Figure 21). With available sizes of 3.5 inches, 2.5 inches, and 1.8 inches, SSDs are used in all types of computers, including desktop computers, mobile computers, and mobile devices such as portable media players and digital video cameras. Storage capacities of current SSDs range from 16 GB to 256 GB and more.

🖑 **Flash Memory Storage**

For more information, visit scsite.com/ic8/weblink and then click Flash Memory Storage.

Figure 21 As the price of SSDs drops, experts estimate that increasingly more users will purchase computers and devices that use this media.

A **memory card** is a removable flash memory device, usually no bigger than 1.5 inches in height or width, that you insert and remove from a slot in a computer, mobile device, or card reader/writer (Figure 22). Memory cards enable mobile users easily to transport digital photos, music, or files to and from mobile devices and computers or other devices.

card reader

digital camera

portable media player

smart phone

memory cards

photo printer

desktop computer

Figure 22 Many types of computers and devices have slots for memory cards.

Common types of memory cards include CompactFlash (CF), Secure Digital (SD), Secure Digital High Capacity (SDHC), microSD, microSDHC, xD Picture Card, Memory Stick PRO Duo, and Memory Stick Micro (M2) (Figure 23).

Various Memory Cards

Media Type		Storage Capacity	Use
CompactFlash (CF)		512 MB to 100 GB	Digital cameras, smart phones, PDAs, photo printers, portable media players, notebook computers, desktop computers
Secure Digital (SD)		512 MB to 8 GB	Digital cameras, digital video cameras, smart phones, PDAs, photo printers, portable media players
SDHC		4 to 32 GB	Digital cameras
microSD		1 to 2 GB	Smart phones, portable media players, handheld game consoles, handheld navigation devices
microSDHC		4 to 16 GB	Smart phones, portable media players, handheld game consoles, handheld navigation devices
xD Picture Card		256 MB to 2 GB	Digital cameras, photo printers
Memory Stick PRO Duo		1 to 16 GB	Digital cameras, smart phones, handheld game consoles
Memory Stick Micro (M2)		1 to 16 GB	Smart phones

Figure 23   A variety of memory cards.

A **USB flash drive**, sometimes called a thumb drive, is a flash memory storage device that plugs into a USB port on a computer or mobile device (Figure 24). USB flash drives are convenient for mobile users because they are small and light-weight enough to be transported on a keychain or in a pocket. Current USB flash drives have storage capacities ranging from 512 MB to 64 GB.

An **ExpressCard module** is a removable device, about 75 mm long and 34 mm wide or L-shaped with a width of 54 mm, that fits in an ExpressCard slot (Figure 25). ExpressCard modules can be used to add memory, storage, communications, multimedia, and security capabilities to a computer. ExpressCard modules commonly are used in notebook computers.

Figure 24 A close-up of the flash memory and circuitry inside a USB flash drive.

two sizes of
ExpressCard
modules

Figure 25 ExpressCard modules are available in two sizes.

Optical Discs

An **optical disc** is a flat, round, portable metal disc with a plastic coating. CDs, DVDs, and Blu-ray Discs are three types of optical discs. A CD can hold from 650 million to 1 billion characters. Some DVDs can store two full-length movies or 17 billion characters. Blu-ray Discs can store about 46 hours of standard video, or 100 billion characters. Optical discs used in personal computers are 4.75 inches in diameter and less than one-twentieth of an inch thick. Nearly every personal computer today has some type of optical disc drive installed in a drive bay. On some, you push a button to slide out a tray, insert the disc, and then push the same button to close the tray; others are slot loaded, which means you insert the disc in a narrow opening on the drive (Figure 26).

Figure 26 A slot-loaded optical disc drive.

Optical Disc Formats

Optical Disc	Read	Write	Erase
CD-ROM	Y	N	N
CD-R	Y	Y	N
CD-RW	Y	Y	Y
DVD-ROM BD-ROM	Y	N	N
DVD-R DVD+R BD-R	Y	Y	N
DVD-RW DVD+RW DVD-RAM BD-RE	Y	Y	Y

Figure 27 Manufacturers sell CD-ROM, DVD-ROM, and BD-ROM media prerecorded (written) with audio, video, and software. Users cannot change the contents of these discs. Users, however, can purchase the other formats of optical discs as blank media and record (write) their own data, instructions, and information on these discs.

🖑 **CDs**

For more information, visit scsite.com/ic8/weblink and then click CDs.

Many different formats of optical discs exist today. Figure 27 identifies a variety of optical disc formats and specifies whether a user can read from the disc, write on the disc, and/or erase the disc.

A **CD-ROM,** or compact disc read-only memory, is a type of optical disc that users can read but not write (record) or erase — hence, the name read-only. Manufacturers write the contents of standard CD-ROMs. A standard CD-ROM is called a single-session disc because manufacturers write all items on the disc at one time. Software manufacturers often distribute programs using CD-ROMs.

A typical CD-ROM holds from 650 MB to 1 GB of data, instructions, and information. To read a CD-ROM, insert the disc in a CD-ROM drive or a CD-ROM player. Because audio CDs and CD-ROMs use the same laser technology, you may be able to use a CD-ROM drive to listen to an audio CD while using the computer.

A **CD-R** (compact disc-recordable) is a multisession optical disc on which users can write, but not erase, their own items such as text, graphics, and audio. Multisession means you can write on part of the disc at one time and another part at a later time. Each part of a CD-R can be written on only one time, and the disc's contents cannot be erased.

A **CD-RW** (compact disc-rewritable) is an erasable multisession disc you can write on multiple times. To write on a CD-RW disc, you must have optical disc burning software and a CD-RW drive. Burning is the process of writing on an optical disc. A popular use of CD-RW and CD-R discs is to create audio CDs. For example, users can record their own music and save it on a CD, purchase and download songs from the Web to their computer and then burn the songs on a CD, or rearrange tracks on a purchased music CD. The process of copying audio and/or video data from a purchased disc and saving it on a storage medium is called ripping.

Although CDs have large storage capacities, even a CD cannot hold many of today's complex programs. Thus, some software companies have moved from CDs to the larger DVDs — a technology that can be used to store large amounts of text and even videos (Figure 28).

A **DVD-ROM** (digital versatile disk-read-only memory or digital video disc-read-only memory) is a high-capacity optical disc on which users can read but not write or erase. Manufacturers write the contents of DVD-ROMs and distribute them to consumers. DVD-ROMs store movies, music, huge databases, and complex software. To read a DVD-ROM, you need a **DVD-ROM drive** or DVD player. Most DVD-ROM drives also can read audio CDs, CD-ROMs, CD-Rs, and CD-RWs.

DVD drive

DVD

Figure 28 A DVD-ROM is a high-capacity optical disc.

A newer, more expensive DVD format is Blu-ray, which is a higher capacity and better quality than standard DVDs, especially for high-definition audio and video. A **Blu-ray Disc** (BD) has storage capacities of 100 GB, with expectations of exceeding 200 GB in the future.

Many types of recordable and rewritable DVD formats are available. DVD-R, DVD+R, and BD-R allow users to write on the disc once and read (play) it many times. **DVD-RW, DVD+RW, and DVD+RAM** are three competing rewritable DVD formats. Similarly, **BD-RE** is a high-capacity rewritable Blu-ray format. To write on these discs, you must have a compatible drive or recorder.

 DVDs
For more information, visit scsite.com/ic8/weblink and then click DVDs.

Cloud Storage

Cloud storage is an Internet service that provides hard disk storage to computer users (Figure 29). Fee arrangements vary. For example, one cloud storage service provides 25 GB of storage free to registered users; another charges $5 per month for 150 GB of storage. For organizations, cloud storage services typically charge for storage on a per gigabyte basis, such as 15 cents per gigabyte.

Types of services offered by cloud storage providers vary. Figure 30 identifies a variety of cloud storage providers.

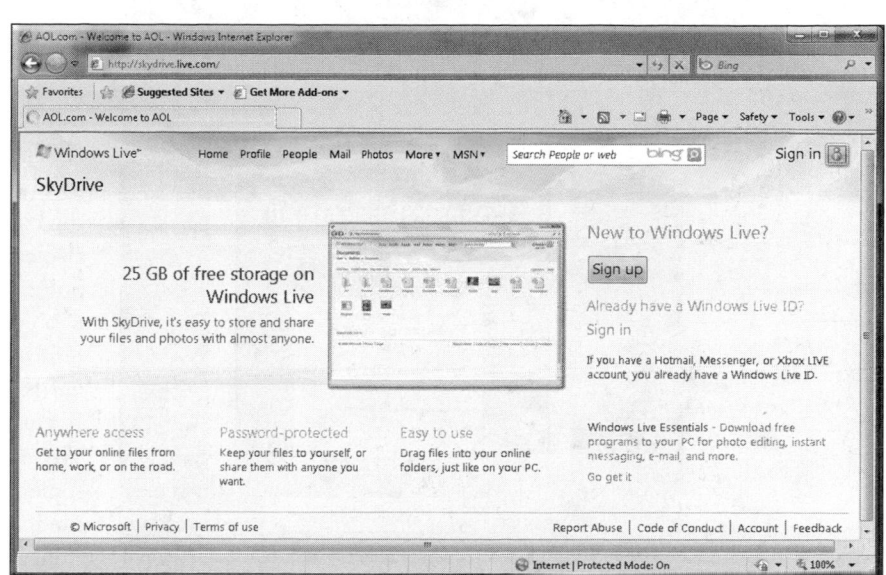

Figure 29   An example of one Web site advertising its storage service.

Cloud Storage Providers

Web Site Names	Type of Storage Provided
Box.net, IDrive, Windows Live SkyDrive	Backup or additional storage for any type of file
Flickr, Picasa	Digital photos
YouTube	Digital videos
Facebook, MySpace	Digital photos, digital videos, messages, and personal information
Google Docs	Documents, spreadsheets, presentations
Gmail, Windows Live Hotmail, Yahoo! Mail	E-mail messages
Amazon EC2, Amazon S3, Nirvanix	Enterprise-level storage

Figure 30   Some of the more widely used cloud storage providers.

Communications Devices

A **communications device** is a hardware component that enables a computer to send (transmit) and receive data, instructions, and information to and from one or more computers or mobile devices. A widely used communications device is a modem (Figure 1 on page COM 2).

Communications occur over **transmission media** such as cables, telephone lines, cellular radio networks, and satellites. Some transmission media, such as satellites and cellular radio networks, are **wireless**, which means they have no physical lines or wires. People around the world use computers and communications devices to communicate with each other using one or more transmission media.

Computer Software

Software, also called a **program,** consists of a series of related instructions, organized for a common purpose, that tells the computer what tasks to perform and how to perform them. You interact with a program through its user interface. The user interface controls how you enter data and instructions and how information is displayed on the screen. Software today often has a graphical user interface. With a **graphical user interface (GUI** pronounced gooey), you interact with the software using text, graphics, and visual images such as icons.

When you buy a computer, it usually has some software on its hard disk. This enables you to use the computer the first time you turn it on. Programs also can be installed after you purchase the computer. **Installing** is the process of adding software to a computer, and **uninstalling** is the process of removing programs and all associated files from the hard disk.

Much software is available at retail stores and on the Web for purchase and/or download. As an alternative, some people use a **Web application,** which is a Web site that allows users to access and interact with software from any computer or device that is connected to the Internet. Software can be divided into two categories: system software and application software (Figure 31).

Figure 31   Today's system software and application software usually have a graphical user interface.

System Software

System software consists of programs that control the operations of the computer and its devices. Two types of system software are operating systems and utility programs.

An **operating system** is a set of programs that coordinates all the activities among computer hardware devices. It provides a means for users to communicate with the computer and other software. Many of today's computers use Microsoft Windows, the latest version of which is shown in Figure 31, or Mac OS, Apple's operating system. When a user starts a computer, portions of the operating system are copied into memory from the computer's hard disk. These parts of the operating system remain in memory while the computer is on.

A **utility program** allows a user to perform maintenance-type tasks usually related to managing a computer, its devices, or its programs. For example, you can use a utility program to burn digital photos on an optical disc. Most operating systems include several utility programs for managing disk drives, printers, and other devices and media. You also can buy utility programs that allow you to perform additional computer management functions.

Application Software

Application software consists of programs designed to make users more productive and/or assist them with personal tasks. These include personal information management, note taking, project management, accounting, document management, computer-aided design, desktop publishing, paint/image editing, audio and video editing, multimedia authoring, Web page authoring, personal finance, legal, tax preparation, home design/landscaping, travel and mapping, education, reference, and entertainment (e.g., games or simulations). Software is available at stores that sell computer products and at many Web sites.

Computer users regularly use application software. Some of the more commonly used programs are word processing, presentation, spreadsheet, database, and e-mail. These programs often are sold together as a unit, called a business suite. When you purchase a collection of programs as a suite, the suite usually costs significantly less than purchasing them individually. Suites also provide ease of use because the programs in the suite normally use a similar interface and share features.

 Operating Systems

For more information, visit scsite.com/ic8/weblink and then click Operating Systems.

Word Processing **Word processing software** is used to create, edit, format, and print documents (Figure 32). A key advantage of word processing software is that users easily can make changes in documents, such as correcting spelling; changing margins; and adding, deleting, or relocating words, sentences, or entire paragraphs.

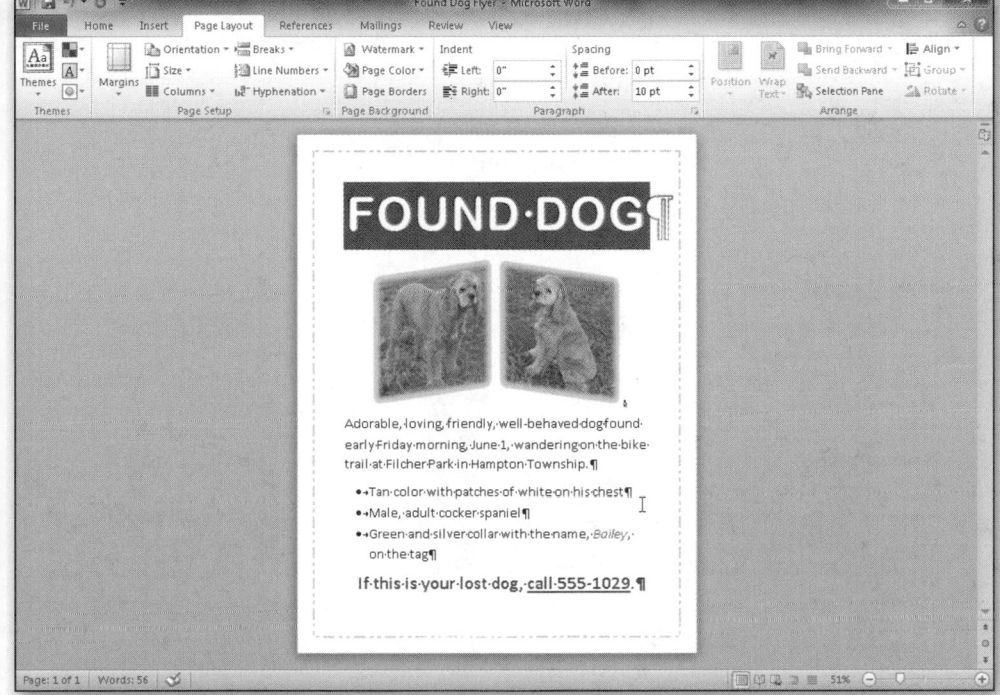

Word Processing Software

For more information, visit scsite.com/ic8/weblink and then click Word Processing Software.

Figure 32 Word processing software is used to create letters, memos, newsletters, and other documents.

Presentation **Presentation software** is application software that allows users to create visual aids for presentations to communicate ideas, messages, and other information to a group (Figure 33). The presentations can be viewed as slides, sometimes called a slide show, that are displayed on a large monitor or on a projection screen.

Presentation Software

For more information, visit scsite.com/ic8/weblink and then click Presentation Software.

Figure 33 Presentation software allows the user to produce professional-looking presentations.

Spreadsheet   **Spreadsheet software** allows users to organize data in rows and columns and perform calculations on the data (Figure 34). These rows and columns collectively are called a **worksheet**. Most spreadsheet software has basic features to help users create, edit, and format worksheets.

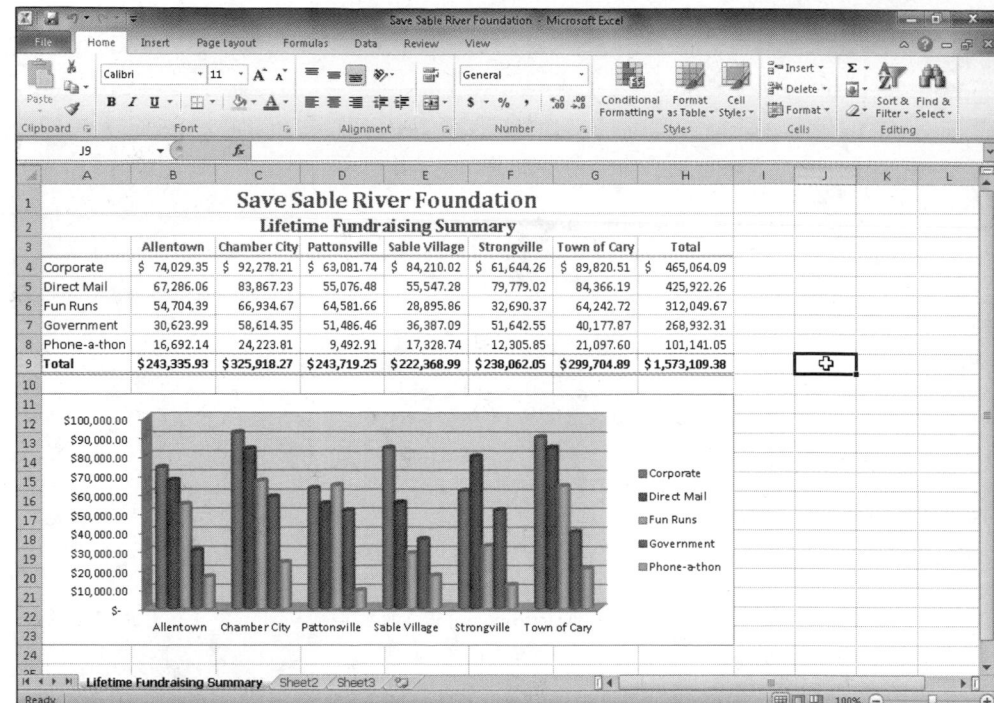

Spreadsheet Software

For more information, visit scsite.com/ic8/weblink and then click Spreadsheet Software.

Figure 34   With spreadsheet software, you create worksheets that contain data arranged in rows and columns, and you can perform calculations on the data in the worksheets.

Database   A **database** is a collection of data organized in a manner that allows access, retrieval, and use of that data. **Database software** is application software that allows users to create, access, and manage a database (Figure 35). Using database software, you can add, change, and delete data in a database; sort and retrieve data from the database; and create forms and reports using the data in the database.

Database Software

For more information, visit scsite.com/ic8/weblink and then click Database Software.

Figure 35   Database software allows the user to enter, retrieve, and update data in an organized and efficient manner.

E-Mail E-mail (short for electronic mail) is the transmission of messages and files via a computer network. Today, e-mail is a primary communications method for both personal and business use. You use an **e-mail program** to create, send, receive, forward, store, print, and delete e-mail messages (Figure 36). Outlook and Windows Live Mail are two popular desktop e-mail programs. Just as you address a letter when using the postal system, you address an e-mail message with the e-mail address of your intended recipient. Likewise, when someone sends you a message, he or she must have your e-mail address.

Networks and the Internet

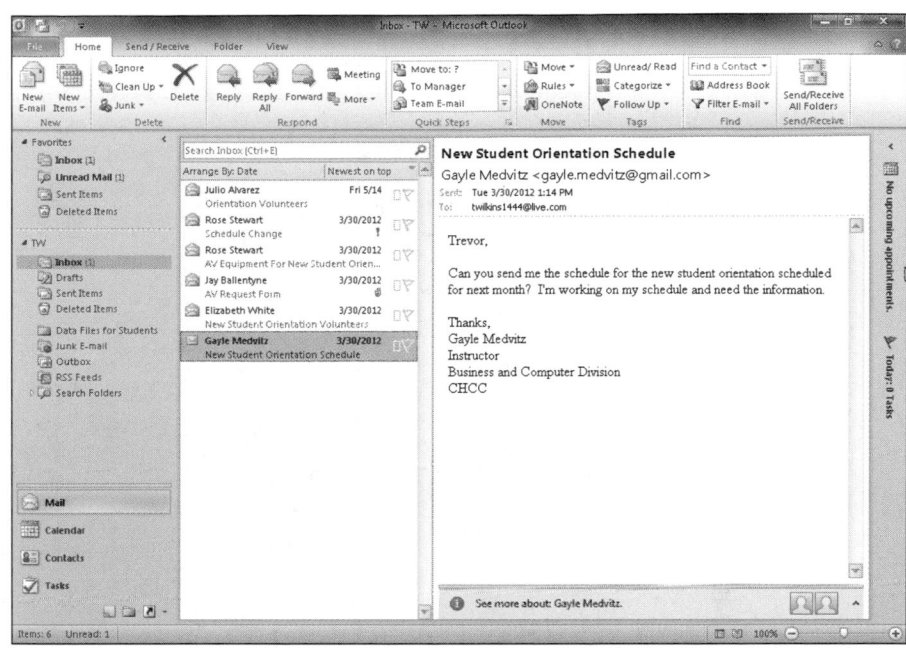

Figure 36 An e-mail program.

A **network** is a collection of computers and devices connected together, often wirelessly, via communications devices and transmission media. When a computer connects to a network, it is **online**. Networks allow users to share resources, such as hardware, software, data, and information. Sharing resources saves time and money. For example, instead of purchasing one printer for every computer in a company, the firm can connect a single printer and all computers via a network; the network enables all of the computers to access the same printer.

Most business computers are networked. These networks can be relatively small or quite extensive. A **local area network (LAN)** is a network that connects computers and devices in a limited geographical area such as a home, school computer laboratory, office building, or closely positioned group of buildings. A **wireless LAN (WLAN)** is a LAN that uses no physical wires. Often, a WLAN communicates with a wired LAN (Figure 37).

Figure 37 Computers and mobile devices on a wireless LAN often communicate via an access point with a wired LAN to access its software, printer, the Internet, and other resources.

A **wide area network** (**WAN**) is a network that covers a large geographic area (such as a city, country, or the world) using a communications channel that combines many types of media such as telephone lines, cables, and radio waves (Figure 38). The Internet is the world's largest WAN.

Figure 38   An example of a WAN.

The Internet

The **Internet** is a worldwide collection of networks that links millions of businesses, government agencies, educational institutions, and individuals. With an abundance of resources and data accessible via the Internet, more than one billion people around the world use the Internet for a variety of reasons, including the following (Figure 39):

- Communicating with and meeting other people
- Researching and accessing a wealth of information and news
- Shopping for goods and services
- Banking and investing
- Participating in online training
- Engaging in entertaining activities, such as planning vacations, playing online games, listening to music, watching or editing videos, and reading books and magazines
- Sharing information, photos, and videos
- Downloading music and videos
- Accessing and interacting with Web applications

An **access provider** is a business that provides individuals and organizations access to the Internet free or for a fee. Access providers are categorized as ISPs, online service providers, and wireless Internet service providers. An **ISP** (**Internet service provider**) is a regional or national access provider. A regional ISP usually provides Internet access to a specific geographic area.

Figure 39 Users access the Internet for a variety of reasons.

A national ISP is a business that provides Internet access in cities and towns nationwide. National ISPs usually offer more services and have a larger technical support staff than regional ISPs. Examples of national ISPs are AT&T and EarthLink. In addition to providing Internet access, an **online service provider** (**OSP**) also has many members-only features such as instant messaging or their own customized version of a Web browser. The two more popular OSPs are AOL (America Online) and MSN (Microsoft Network).

A **wireless Internet service provider**, sometimes called a wireless data provider, is a company that provides wireless Internet access to computers and mobile devices, such as smart phones and portable media players, with built-in wireless capability (such as Wi-Fi) or to computers using wireless modems or wireless access devices. Wireless modems usually are in the form of a USB flash drive or a card that inserts in a slot in a computer or mobile device. Examples of wireless Internet service providers include AT&T, Sprint Broadband Direct, T-Mobile, and Verizon Wireless.

The World Wide Web

One of the more popular services on the Internet is the **World Wide Web**, also called the **Web**, which contains billions of documents called Web pages. A **Web page** can contain text, graphics, animation, audio, and video, and has built-in connections, or links, to other documents, graphics, or other Web pages. Web pages are stored on computers throughout the world. A **Web site** is a collection of related Web pages. Visitors to a Web site access and view Web pages using a program called a **Web browser**. A Web page has a unique address, called a **Web address** or **URL** (**Uniform Resource Locator**).

As shown in Figure 40, a Web address consists of a protocol, a domain name, sometimes the path to a specific Web page or location in a Web page, and the Web page name. Many Web page addresses begin with **http://**, which stands for **Hypertext Transfer Protocol**, the set of rules that defines how pages transfer on the Internet. The domain name identifies the Web site, which is stored on a Web server. A **Web server** is a computer that delivers requested Web pages to your computer.

The term **Web 2.0** refers to Web sites that provide a means for users to share personal information (such as social networking Web sites), allow users to modify the Web site contents (such as some blogs), and/or have software built into the site for users to access (such as Web applications). A **social networking Web site** or **online social network** is an online community that encourages members to share their interests, ideas, stories, photos, music, and videos with other registered users. A **blog** is an informal Web site consisting of time-stamped articles in a diary or journal format. Examples of software available as Web applications include those that allow you to send and receive e-mail messages, prepare your taxes, organize digital photos, create documents, and play games.

World Wide Web

For more information, visit scsite.com/ic8/weblink and then click World Wide Web.

protocol	domain name	path	Web page name

http://www.nps.gov/grsm/planyourvist/wildlifeviewing.htm

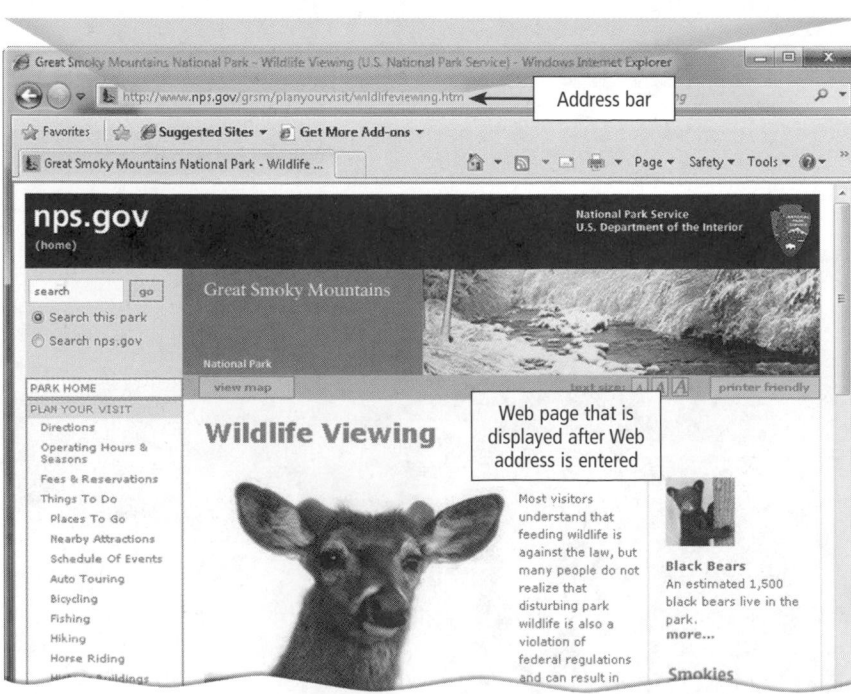

Figure 40   After entering http://www.nps.gov/grsm/planyourvisit/wildlifeviewing.htm as the Web address in the Address bar, this Web page at the United States National Park Service Web site is displayed.

E-commerce, short for electronic commerce, is a business transaction that occurs over an electronic network such as the Internet. Anyone with access to a computer or mobile device, an Internet connection, and a means to pay for purchased goods or services can participate in e-commerce.

Searching the Web

The Web is a worldwide resource of information. A primary reason that people use the Web is to search for specific information, including text, pictures, music, and video. The first step in successful searching is to identify the main idea or concept in the topic about which you are seeking information. Determine any synonyms, alternate spellings, or variant word forms for the topic. Then, use a search tool to locate the information.

Two types of search tools are search engines and subject directories. A **search engine** is a program that finds Web sites, Web pages, images, videos, news, maps, and other information related to a specific topic. A search engine is helpful in locating information for which you do not know an exact Web address or are not seeking a particular Web site. Search engines require that you enter a word or phrase, called **search text**, that describes the item you want to find. Figure 41 shows one way to use the Google search engine to search for the phrase, Aspen Colorado ski resorts. A **subject directory** classifies Web pages in an organized set of categories or groups, such as sports or

👆 **E-Commerce**

For more information, visit scsite.com/ic8/weblink and then click E-Commerce.

Step 1
Type the search engine's Web address (in this case, google.com) in the Address bar in the Web browser.

Step 2
Press the ENTER key. When the Google Web page is displayed, type Aspen Colorado ski resorts as the search text and then point to the Google Search button.

Step 4
Click the Aspen Snowmass link to display a Web page with a description and links to skiing in Aspen.

Step 3
Click the Google Search button. When the results of the search are displayed, scroll through the links and read the descriptions. Point to the Aspen Snowmass link.

Figure 41   This figure shows how to use a search engine.

shopping, and related subcategories. A subject directory provides categorized lists of links arranged by subject. Using this search tool, you locate a particular topic by clicking links through different levels, moving from the general to the specific.

Computer Viruses and Other Malware

Today, people rely on computers to create, store, and manage critical information. Thus, it is crucial users take measures to protect their computers and data from loss or damage, especially for information that is transmitted over networks. Every unprotected computer is susceptible to a computer virus, worm, Trojan horse, and/or rootkit.

- A computer **virus** is a potentially damaging computer program that affects, or infects, a computer negatively by altering the way the computer works without the user's knowledge or permission. Once the virus infects the computer, it can spread throughout and may damage files and system software, including the operating system.

- A **worm** is a program that copies itself repeatedly, for example in memory or on a network, using up resources and possibly shutting down the computer or network.

- A **Trojan horse** (named after the Greek myth) is a program that hides within or looks like a legitimate program. A certain condition or action usually triggers the Trojan horse. Unlike a virus or worm, a Trojan horse does not replicate itself to other computers.

- A **rootkit** is a program that hides in a computer and allows someone from a remote location to take full control of the computer. Once the rootkit is installed, the rootkit author can execute programs, change settings, monitor activity, and access files on the remote computer.

Computer viruses, worms, Trojan horses, and rootkits are classified as **malware** (short for malicious software), which are programs that act without a user's knowledge and deliberately alter the computer's operations. Users can take several precautions to protect their home and work computers and mobile devices from these malicious infections. For example, users should install an antivirus program and update it frequently. An **antivirus program** protects a computer against viruses by identifying and removing any computer viruses found in memory, on storage media, or on incoming files. Most antivirus programs also protect against other malware. When you purchase a new computer, it often includes antivirus software. The list in Figure 42 summarizes important tips for protecting your computer from viruses and other malware.

Tips for Preventing Viruses and Other Malware

1. Never start a computer with removable media inserted in the drives or plugged in the ports, unless the media are uninfected.

2. Never open an e-mail attachment unless you are expecting it *and* it is from a trusted source.

3. Set the macro security in programs so that you can enable or disable macros. Enable macros only if the document is from a trusted source and you are expecting it.

4. Install an antivirus program on all of your computers. Update the software and the virus signature files regularly.

5. Scan all downloaded programs for viruses and other malware.

6. If the antivirus program flags an e-mail attachment as infected, delete or quarantine the attachment immediately.

7. Before using any removable media, scan the media for malware. Follow this procedure even for shrink-wrapped software from major developers. Some commercial software has been infected and distributed to unsuspecting users.

8. Install a personal firewall program.

9. Stay informed about new virus alerts and virus hoaxes.

Figure 42   With the growing number of new viruses and other malware, it is crucial that users take steps to protect their computers.

Buyer's Guide:
How to Purchase Computers
and Mobile Devices

AT SOME POINT, perhaps while you are taking this course, you may decide to buy a computer or mobile device (Figure 43). The decision is an important one and will require an investment of both time and money. Like many buyers, you may have little experience with technology and find yourself unsure of how to proceed. You can start by talking to your friends, coworkers, and instructors about their computers and mobile devices. What type of computers and mobile devices did they buy? Why? For what purposes do they use their computers and mobile devices?

desktop computer

notebook computer

portable media
player

smart phone

digital camera

Figure 43   Computers and mobile devices.

How to Purchase a Desktop Computer

A desktop computer sits on or below a desk or table in a stationary location such as a home, office, or dormitory room. Desktop computers are a good option if you work mostly in one place and have plenty of space in a work area. Desktop computers generally provide more performance for your money. Today, manufacturers are placing more emphasis on style by offering bright colors, stylish displays, and theme-based displays so that the computer looks attractive if it is in an area of high visibility. Once you have decided that a desktop computer is most suited to your computing needs, the next step is to determine specific software, hardware, peripheral devices, and services to purchase, as well as where to buy the computer.

❶ Determine the specific software to use on your computer.

Before deciding to purchase software, be sure it contains the features necessary for the tasks you want to perform. Rely on the computer users in whom you have confidence to help you decide on the software to use. In addition, consider purchasing software that might help you perform tasks at home that you otherwise would perform at another location, such as at school or at work. The minimum requirements of the software you select may determine the operating system (Microsoft Windows, Mac OS, etc.) you need. If you decide to use a particular operating system that does not support software you want to use, you may be able to purchase similar software from other manufacturers.

Many Web sites and trade magazines provide reviews of software products. These Web sites frequently have articles that rate computers and software on cost, performance, and support.

Your hardware requirements depend on the minimum requirements of the software you will run on your computer. Some software requires more memory and disk space than others, as well as additional input, output, and storage devices. For example, suppose you want to run software that can copy one optical disc's contents directly to another optical disc, without first copying the data to the hard disk. To support that, you should consider a desktop computer or a high-end notebook computer, because the computer will need two optical disc drives: one that reads from an optical disc, and one that writes on an optical disc. If you plan to run software that allows your computer to function as an entertainment system, then you will need an optical disc drive, quality speakers, and an upgraded sound card.

❷ Know the system requirements of the operating system.

After determining the software you want to run on your new computer, the next step is to determine the operating system to use. If, however, you purchase a new computer, chances are it will have the latest version of your preferred operating system (Windows, Mac OS, etc.).

❸ Look for bundled software.

When you purchase a computer, it may include bundled software. Some sellers even let you choose which software you want. Remember, however, that bundled software has value only if you would have purchased the software even if it had not been included with the computer. At the very least, you probably will want word processing software and an antivirus program. If you need additional programs, such as a spreadsheet, a database, or presentation software, consider purchasing or downloading Microsoft Office, Microsoft Works, OpenOffice.org, or Sun StarOffice, which include several programs at a reduced price or at no cost.

❹ Avoid buying the least powerful computer available.

Once you know the application software you want to use, then consider the following important criteria about the computer's components: (1) processor speed, (2) size and types of memory (RAM) and storage, (3) types of input/output devices, (4) types of ports and adapter cards, and (5) types of communications devices. You also should consider if the computer is upgradeable and to what extent you are able to upgrade. For example, all manufacturers limit the amount of memory you can add. The information in Figure 44 on pages COM 29 and COM 30 can help you determine which computer components are best for you and outlines considerations for specific hardware components. For a sample Base Components worksheet that lists personal computer recommendations for various categories of users, see scsite.com/ic8/buyers.

Considerations for Hardware Components

Card Reader/Writer: A card reader/writer is useful for transferring data directly to and from a memory card, such as the type used in a digital camera, smart phone, or portable media player. Make sure the card reader/writer can read from and write on the memory cards that you use.

Digital Video Capture Device: A digital video (DV) capture device allows you to connect a computer to a video camera or VCR and record, edit, manage, and then write video back on an optical disc or VCR tape. To create quality video (true 30 frames per second, full-sized TV), the digital video capture device should have a USB or FireWire port.

External Hard Disk: An external hard disk can serve many purposes: it can serve as extra storage for your computer, provide a way to store and transport large files or large quantities of files, and provide a convenient way to back up data on other internal and external hard disks. External hard disks can be purchased with the same capacity as any internal disk. .

Fingerprint Reader: For added security, you may want to consider purchasing a fingerprint reader. It helps prevent unauthorized access to your computer and also allows you to log onto Web sites quickly via your fingerprint, rather than entering a user name and password each time you access the site. Most use a USB connection and require software installation.

Hard Disk: It is recommended that you buy a computer with at least a 320 GB hard disk if your primary interests are browsing the Web and using e-mail and Microsoft Office suite-type programs; 1 TB if you also want to edit digital photos or if you plan to edit digital video or manipulate large audio files even occasionally; and 2 TB if you will edit digital video, movies, or photos often; store audio files and music; or consider yourself to be a power user. Internal hard disk controllers are available with the RAID option for added data protection.

Joystick/Wheel: If you use the computer to play games, then you will want to purchase a joystick or a wheel. These devices, especially the more expensive ones, provide for realistic game play with force feedback, programmable buttons, and specialized levers and wheels.

Keyboard: The keyboard is one of the more important devices used to communicate with the computer. For this reason, make sure the keyboard you purchase has 101 to 105 keys, is comfortable and easy to use, and has a USB connection. A wireless keyboard should be considered, especially if you have a small desk area.

Microphone: If you plan to record audio or use speech recognition to enter text and commands, then purchase a close-talk headset with gain adjustment support.

Modem: Most computers include a modem so that you can use a telephone line to access the Internet. Some modems also have fax capabilities. Your modem should be rated at 56 Kbps.

Monitor: The monitor is where you will view documents, read e-mail messages, and view pictures. A minimum of a 19" LCD flat-panel monitor is recommended, but if you plan to use the computer for graphic design or game playing, then you may want to purchase a 22" or 27" monitor. Instead of a single large, widescreen monitor, you may want to consider a side-by-side monitor setup.

Mouse: While working with a desktop computer, you use the mouse constantly. Make sure the mouse has a wheel, which acts as a third button in addition to the top two buttons on the left and right. An ergonomic design also is important because your hand is on the mouse most of the time when you are using the computer. A wireless mouse should be considered to eliminate the cord and allow you to work at short distances from the computer.

Optical Disc Drives: Most computers include a DVD±RW combination drive and/or DVD/Blu-ray Disc drive. A DVD±RW or a Blu-ray Disc drive allows you to read optical discs and to write data on (burn) an optical disc. It also will allow you to store and share video files, digital photos, and other large files with other people who have access to a DVD/Blu-ray Disc drive. A Blu-ray Disc has a capacity of at least 25 GB, and a DVD has a capacity of at least 4.7 GB, versus the 650 MB capacity of a CD.

Figure 44 Hardware guidelines. *(continues)*

Considerations for Hardware Components

Ports: Depending on how you use the computer, you may need anywhere from 4 to 10 USB ports. USB ports have become the connection of choice in the computer industry. They offer an easy way to connect peripheral devices such as printers, digital cameras, and portable media players. Many computers intended for home or professional audio/video use have built-in FireWire ports. Most personal computers include a minimum of six USB ports, two FireWire ports, and an Ethernet port.

Printer: Your two basic printer choices are ink-jet and laser. Color ink-jet printers cost on average between $50 and $300. Laser printers cost from $200 to $2,000. In general, the less expensive the printer, the lower the resolution and speed, and the more often you are required to change the ink cartridges or toner. Laser printers print faster and with a higher quality than an ink-jet, and their toner on average costs less.

Processor: For a personal computer, an Intel Core i7 processor at 2.93 GHz is more than enough processor power for most home and small office/home office users. Higher-end users, such as large businesses or people who use the computer to play games, should upgrade to faster, more powerful processors.

RAM: RAM plays a vital role in the speed of a computer. Make sure the computer you purchase has at least 2 GB of RAM. If you have extra money to invest in a computer, consider increasing the RAM. The extra money for RAM will be well spent because more RAM typically translates into more speed.

Scanner: The most popular scanner purchased with a computer today is the flatbed scanner. When evaluating a flatbed scanner, check the color depth and resolution. Do not buy anything less than a color depth of 48 bits and a resolution of 1200 × 2400 dpi. The higher the color depth, the more accurate the color. A higher resolution picks up the more subtle gradations of color.

Sound Card: Many computers include a standard sound card that supports Dolby 5.1 surround and are capable of recording and playing digital audio. Make sure they are suitable in the event you decide to use the computer as an entertainment or gaming system.

Speakers: Once you have a good sound card, quality speakers and a separate subwoofer that amplifies the bass frequencies of the speakers can turn the computer into a premium stereo system.

USB Flash Drive: If you work on different computers and need access to the same data and information, then this portable flash memory device is ideal. USB flash drive capacity typically varies from 1 GB to 32 GB.

USB Hub: If you plan to connect several peripheral devices to the computer at the same time, then you need to be concerned with the number of ports available on the computer. If the computer does not have enough ports, then you should purchase a USB hub. A USB hub plugs into a single USB port and provides several additional ports.

Video Card: Most standard video cards satisfy the monitor display needs of most home and small office users. If you use your home computer to play games or if you are a graphic designer, you will want to upgrade to a higher quality video card. The higher refresh rates will further enhance the display of games, graphics, and movies.

Web Cam: A Web cam is a small digital video camera that can capture and display live video on a Web page. You also can capture, edit, and share video and still photos. Recommended minimum specifications include 640 × 480 resolution, a video with a rate of 30 frames per second, and a USB or FireWire port. Some Web cams are built into computer monitors.

Wireless LAN Access Point: A wireless LAN access point allows you to network several computers, so that multiple users can share files and access the Internet through a single Internet connection. Each device that you connect requires a wireless card or wireless capability. A wireless LAN access point can offer a range of operations up to several hundred feet, so be sure the device has a high-powered antenna.

Figure 44   Hardware guidelines. *(continued)*

Computer technology changes rapidly, meaning a computer that seems powerful enough today may not serve your computing needs in several years. In fact, studies show that many users regret not buying a more powerful computer. To avoid this, plan to buy a computer that will last for at least two to three years. You can help delay obsolescence by purchasing the fastest processor, the most memory, and the largest hard disk you can afford. If you must buy a less powerful computer, be sure you can upgrade it with additional memory, components, and peripheral devices as your computer requirements grow.

⑤ Consider upgrades to the mouse, keyboard, monitor, printer, microphone, and speakers.

You use these peripheral devices to interact with the computer, so make sure they are up to your standards. Review the peripheral devices listed in Figure 44 and then visit both local computer dealers and large retail stores to test the computers and devices on display. Ask the salesperson which input and output devices would be best for you and whether you should upgrade beyond the standard product. Consider purchasing a wireless keyboard and wireless mouse to eliminate wires on your desktop. A few extra dollars spent on these components when you initially purchase a computer can extend its usefulness by years.

⑥ Determine whether to use a broadband or dial-up connection to access the Internet.

If your computer has a modem, you can access the Internet using a standard telephone line. Ordinarily, you call a local or toll-free 800 number to connect to an Internet access provider. Using a dial-up Internet connection usually is relatively inexpensive but slow.

Broadband connections (cable, DSL, fiber, radio signals, or satellite) provide much faster Internet connections, which are ideal if you want faster file download speeds for software, digital photos, digital video, and music. As you would expect, they can be more expensive than a dial-up connection. If you want to use a broadband connection, your computer should have an Ethernet card installed, unless you are using a wireless broadband connection such as WiMax or 3G. If you will be using a dial-up connection, your computer should have a modem installed.

⑦ Use a worksheet to compare computers, services, and other considerations.

You can use a separate sheet of paper to take notes about each vendor's computer and then summarize the information on a worksheet. For a sample worksheet that compares prices for a PC or a Mac, see scsite.com/ic8/buyers. Most companies advertise a price for a base computer that includes components housed in the system unit (processor, RAM, sound card, video card, network card),

hard disks, optical disc drives, a keyboard, mouse, monitor, printer, speakers, and modem. Be aware, however, that some advertisements list prices for computers with only some of these components. Monitors and printers, for example, often are not included in a base computer's price. Depending on how you plan to use the computer, you may want to invest in additional or more powerful components. When comparing the prices of computers, make sure you are comparing identical or similar configurations.

⑧ If you are buying a new computer, you have several purchasing options: buying from a school bookstore, a local computer dealer, a local large retail store, or ordering by mail via telephone or the Web.

Each purchasing option has certain advantages. Many college bookstores, for example, sign exclusive pricing agreements with computer manufacturers and, thus, can offer student discounts. Local dealers and local large retail stores, however, more easily can provide hands-on support. Mail-order companies that sell computers by telephone or online via the Web (Figure 45) often provide the lowest prices, but extend less personal service. Some major mail-order companies, however, have started to provide next-business-day, on-site services. A credit card usually is required to buy from a mail-order company.

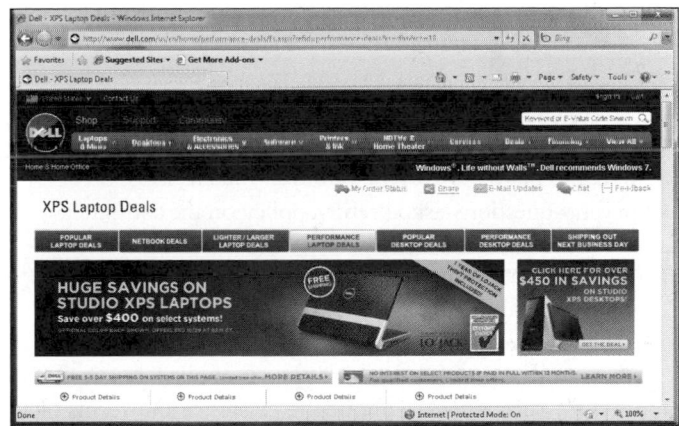

Figure 45 Mail-order companies, such as Dell, sell computers online.

⑨ If you are buying a used computer, stay with name brands such as Dell, Apple, HP, and Gateway.

Although brand-name equipment can cost more, most brand-name computers have longer, more comprehensive warranties, are better supported, and have more authorized centers for repair services. As with new computers, you can purchase a used computer from local computer dealers, local large retail stores, or mail order via the telephone or the Web. Classified ads and used computer sellers offer additional outlets for purchasing used computers.

⑩ If you have a computer and are upgrading to a new one, then consider selling or trading in the old one.

If you are a replacement buyer, your older computer still may have value. If you cannot sell the computer through the classified ads, via a Web site, or to a friend, then ask if the computer dealer will buy your old computer.

An increasing number of companies are taking trade-ins, but do not expect too much money for your old computer. Other companies offer to recycle your old computer free or for a fee.

⑪ Be aware of hidden costs.

Before purchasing, be sure to consider any additional costs associated with buying a computer, such as an additional telephone line, a broadband modem, an uninterruptible power supply (UPS), computer furniture, a USB flash drive, paper, and computer training classes you may want to take. Depending on where you buy the computer, the seller may be willing to include some or all of these in the computer purchase price.

⑫ Consider more than just price.

The lowest-cost computer may not be the best long-term buy. Consider such intangibles as the vendor's time in business, regard for quality, and reputation for support. If you need to upgrade a computer often, you may want to consider a leasing arrangement, in which you pay monthly lease fees, but can upgrade or add on to your computer as your equipment needs change. No matter what type of buyer you are, insist on a 30-day, no-questions-asked return policy on the computer.

⑬ Avoid restocking fees.

Some companies charge a restocking fee of 10 to 20 percent as part of their money-back return policy. In some cases, no restocking fee for hardware is applied, but it is applied for software. Ask about the existence and terms of any restocking policies before you buy.

⑭ Use a credit card to purchase a new computer.

Many credit cards offer purchase protection and extended warranty benefits that cover you in case of loss of or damage to purchased goods. Paying by credit card also gives you time to install and use the computer before you have to pay for it. Finally, if you are dissatisfied with the computer and are unable to reach an agreement with the seller, paying by credit card gives you certain rights regarding withholding payment until the dispute is resolved. Check your credit card terms for specific details.

⑮ Consider purchasing an extended warranty or service plan.

If you use your computer for business or require fast resolution to major computer problems, consider purchasing an extended warranty or a service plan through a local dealer or third-party company. Most extended warranties cover the repair and replacement of computer components beyond the standard warranty. Most service plans ensure that your technical support calls receive priority response from technicians. You also can purchase an on-site service plan that states that a technician will arrive at your home, work, or school within 24 hours. If your computer includes a warranty and service agreement for a year or less, consider extending the service for two or three years when you buy the computer.

How to Purchase a Notebook Computer

If you need computing capability when you travel or to use in lectures or meetings, you may find a notebook computer to be an appropriate choice. The guidelines mentioned in the previous section also apply to the purchase of a notebook computer. The following are additional considerations unique to notebook computers, including netbooks and Tablet PCs.

❶ Determine which computer fits your mobile computing needs.

Before purchasing a notebook computer, you need to determine whether a traditional notebook computer, netbook, or Tablet PC will meet your needs. If you spend most of your time working on spreadsheets, writing and/ or editing documents, sending and responding to e-mail messages, or using the Internet, then a traditional notebook computer will suffice. If your primary use will be to access the Internet while traveling and you are not concerned as much with processing power or hard disk capacity, consider a netbook. If you need a computer in class or you spend more time in meetings than in your office, then the Tablet PC may be the answer. Before you invest money in a Tablet PC, however, determine which programs you plan to use on it. You should not buy a Tablet PC simply because it is an interesting type of computer.

❷ Purchase a notebook computer with a sufficiently large screen.

Active-matrix screens display high-quality color that is viewable from all angles. Less expensive, passive-matrix screens sometimes are difficult to see in low-light conditions and cannot be viewed from an angle.

Notebook computers typically include a 12.1-inch, 13.3-inch, 14.1-inch, 15.4-inch, or 17-inch display. Netbooks have screens as small as 7 inches. For most users, a 14.1-inch display is satisfactory. If you intend to use the notebook computer as a desktop computer replacement, however, you may opt for a 15.4-inch or 17-inch display. The WSXGA+ standard (1680 × 1050) is popular with 17-inch displays, so if you intend to watch HD movies on the computer, take this into consideration. Some notebook computers with these larger displays weigh more than 10 pounds, however, so if you travel a lot and portability is essential, you might want a lighter computer with a smaller display. The lightest notebook computers, which weigh less than 3 pounds, are equipped with a 12.1-inch display.

Regardless of size, the resolution of the display should be at least 1024 × 768 pixels. To compare the screen size on various notebook computers, including netbooks and Tablet PCs, visit the company Web sites. Tablet PCs use a digitizer below a standard 10.4-inch motion-sensitive LCD display to make the writing experience on the screen feel like writing on paper. To ensure you experience the maximum benefits from the ClearType technology, make sure the LCD display has a resolution of 800 × 600 in landscape mode and a resolution of 600 × 800 in portrait mode.

❸ Experiment with different keyboards, pointing devices, and digital pens.

Notebook computer keyboards, especially netbook keyboards, are far less standardized than those for desktop computers. Some notebook computers, for example, have wide wrist rests, while others have none, and keyboard layouts on notebook computers often vary. Notebook computers also use a range of pointing devices, including touchpads, pointing sticks, trackballs, and, in the case of Tablet PCs, digital pens.

Before purchasing a notebook computer, try various types of keyboards and pointing devices to determine which is easiest for you to use. Regardless of the device you select, you also may want to purchase a standard mouse to use when you are working at a desk or other large surface. Figure 46 compares

Mouse and Digital Pen Operations

Mouse	Digital Pen
Point	Point
Click	Tap
Double-click	Double-tap
Right-click	Tap and hold
Click and drag	Drag

Figure 46 Standard point-and-click of a mouse compared with the gestures made with a digital pen.

the standard point-and-click of a mouse with the gestures made with a digital pen. Other gestures with the digital pen replicate some of the commonly used keys on a keyboard.

❹ Make sure the notebook computer you purchase has an optical disc drive.

Most mobile computers include an optical disc drive. Although DVD/Blu-ray Disc drives are slightly more expensive, they allow you to play CDs, DVDs, and Blu-ray Discs using your notebook computer and hear the sound through earbuds. If you decide to purchase a netbook, it might not include an optical disc drive. Instead, you might need to purchase an external optical disc drive.

❺ If necessary, upgrade the processor, memory, and disk storage at the time of purchase.

As with a desktop computer, upgrading a notebook computer's memory and disk storage usually is less expensive at the time of initial purchase. Some disk storage is custom designed for notebook computer manufacturers, meaning an upgrade might not be available in the future. If you are purchasing a lightweight notebook computer or Tablet PC, then it should include at least an Intel Core 2 Quad processor, 2 GB RAM, and 250 GB of storage. If you are purchasing a netbook, it should have an Intel Atom processor, at least 1 GB RAM, and 120 GB of storage.

❻ The availability of built-in ports and slots and a USB hub on a notebook computer is important.

A notebook computer does not have much room to add adapter cards. If you know the purpose for which you plan to use the notebook computer, then you can determine the ports you will need. Netbooks typically have fewer ports than traditional notebook computers and Tablet PCs. Most notebook computers include common ports, such as a video port, audio port, network port, FireWire port, and multiple USB ports. If you plan to connect the notebook computer to a television, however, then you will need a PC to TV port. To optimize television viewing, you may want to consider DisplayPort, DVI, or HDMI ports. If you want to connect to networks at school or in various offices via a network cable, make sure the notebook computer you purchase has a network port. If the notebook computer does not contain a network port, you will have to purchase an external network card that slides into an expansion slot in your computer, as well as a network cable. You also may want to consider adding a card reader.

7 **If you plan to use your notebook computer for note-taking at school or in meetings, consider a convertible Tablet PC.**

Some computer manufacturers have developed convertible Tablet PCs that allow the screen to rotate 180 degrees on a central hinge and then fold down to cover the keyboard (Figure 47). You then can use a digital pen to enter text or drawings into the computer by writing on the screen. Some notebook computers have wide screens for better viewing and editing, and some even have a screen on top of the unit in addition to the regular screen. If you spend much of your time attending lectures or meetings, then the slate Tablet PC is ideal. With a slate Tablet PC, users can attach a removable keyboard.

Figure 47 A convertible Tablet PC.

8 **If you purchase a Tablet PC, determine whether you require multi-touch technology.**

Newer operating systems now support hardware with multi-touch technology. If you choose an operating system that supports this technology, the Tablet PC also must support this technology.

9 **Purchase a notebook computer with an integrated Web cam.**

If you will be using a notebook computer to connect to the Internet and chat with friends online, consider purchasing one with an integrated Web cam.

10 **Check with your wireless carrier to see if it offers netbooks for sale.**

Most wireless carriers now offer wireless data plans allowing you to connect to the Internet from almost anywhere with a cell phone signal. Some wireless carriers now are selling netbooks with built-in capability to connect wirelessly to the Internet using a wireless data plan.

11 **Purchase a notebook computer with a built-in wireless network connection.**

A wireless network connection (Bluetooth, Wi-Fi a/b/g/n, WiMAX, etc.) can be useful when you travel or as part of a home network. Increasingly more airports, hotels, schools, and cafés have wireless networks that allow you to connect to the Internet. Many users today are setting up wireless home networks. With a wireless home network, your notebook computer can access the Internet, as well as other computers in the house, from any location to share files and hardware, such as a printer, and browse the Web. Most home wireless networks allow connections from distances of 150 to 800 feet.

12 **If you plan to use your notebook computer for long periods without access to an electrical outlet, purchase a second battery.**

The trend among notebook computer users today is power and size over battery life. Many notebook computer users today are willing to give up longer battery life for a larger screen, faster processor, and more storage. In addition, some manufacturers typically sell the notebook computer with the lowest capacity battery. For this reason, be careful in choosing a notebook computer if you plan to use it without access to electrical outlets for long periods, such as an airplane flight. You also might want to purchase a second battery as a backup. If you anticipate running the notebook computer on batteries frequently, choose a computer that uses lithium-ion batteries, which last longer than nickel cadmium or nickel hydride batteries.

13 **Purchase a well-padded and well-designed carrying case.**

An amply padded carrying case will protect your notebook computer from the bumps it will receive while traveling. A well-designed carrying case will have room for accessories such as spare optical discs, pens, and paperwork (Figure 48). Although a netbook may be small enough to fit in a handbag, make sure that the bag has sufficient padding to protect the computer.

Figure 48
A well-designed notebook computer carrying case.

⑭ If you plan to connect your notebook computer to a video projector, make sure the notebook computer is compatible with the video projector.

You should check, for example, to be sure that your notebook computer will allow you to display an image on the computer screen and projection device at the same time. Also, ensure that the notebook computer has the ports required to connect to the video projector. You also may consider purchasing a notebook computer with a built-in Web cam for video conferencing purposes.

⑮ For improved security and convenience, consider a fingerprint reader.

More than half a million notebook computers are stolen or lost each year. If you have critical information stored on your notebook computer, consider purchasing one with a fingerprint reader to protect the data if your computer is stolen or lost (Figure 49). Fingerprint security offers a level of protection that extends well beyond the standard password protection. If your notebook computer is stolen, the odds of recovering it improve dramatically with anti-theft tracking software. Manufacturers claim recovery rates of 90 percent or more for notebook computers using their product. For convenience, fingerprint readers also allow you to log onto several Web sites in lieu of entering user name and password information.

Figure 49 Fingerprint reader technology offers greater security than passwords.

⑯ Review the docking capabilities of the Tablet PC.

The Tablet Technology in the Windows operating system supports a grab-and-go form of docking, so that you can pick up and take a docked Tablet PC with you, just as you would pick up a notepad on your way to a meeting (Figure 50).

Figure 50 A Tablet PC docked to create a desktop computer with the Tablet PC as the monitor.

How to Purchase a Smart Phone

You probably will use a smart phone more often than other mobile devices. For this reason, it is important to choose a phone that is available through your preferred wireless carrier, available in your price range, and offers access to the features you will use most frequently. This section lists guidelines you should consider when purchasing a smart phone.

❶ Choose a wireless carrier and plan that satisfies your needs and budget.

Multiple wireless carriers exist today, and each one offers a different line of smart phones. For example, the Samsung Alias is available only through Verizon Wireless. Alternatively, some smart phones, such as the BlackBerry line of smart phones, are available from multiple wireless carriers. Before deciding on a smart phone, you first should research the wireless carriers in your area, and be sure to ascertain whether the coverage is acceptable. Additionally, compare the calling plans for the various carriers and determine which one best meets your needs. Once you have determined the wireless carrier to use, you then can choose from one of their available smart phones. Once you purchase a smart phone, most carriers allow you to perform a risk-free evaluation for 30 days. If you are not satisfied with the phone or its performance, you can return the phone and pay only for the service you have used.

❷ Decide on the size, style, and weight of the smart phone that will work best for you.

Smart phones are available in various sizes, weights, shapes, and colors. Some people prefer larger, heavier phones because they feel that they are more durable, while others prefer smaller, lightweight phones for easy portability. Some smart phones are flip phones, meaning that you have to open the phone (like a clamshell) to display the screen and keypad, some open by sliding the phone, and others do not need to be opened to use them. Figure 51 shows various smart phone styles.

Figure 51 Various smart phone styles.

❸ Determine whether you prefer a touch screen, keypad, or mini-keyboard.

Modern smart phones provide various ways to enter text. During the past several years, smart phones with touch screens as their primary input device have been penetrating the market. Some smart phone users prefer touch screens because the phone does not require additional space for a keypad or mini-keyboard, but others find it more difficult to type on a touch screen. Most newer smart phones with touch screens also include handwriting recognition. Smart phones with keypads might make it easier to type for some users, but others do not like the unfamiliar feeling of keys arranged in alphabetical order. In addition, you often have to press the keys multiple times before reaching the letter you want to type. Mini-keyboards are available on some smart phones, such as the BlackBerry and Samsung Alias. Mini-keyboards provide a key for each letter, but the keys are significantly smaller than those on a standard keyboard. Most smart phone users type on mini-keyboards using their thumbs.

❹ If you will be synchronizing your smart phone with a program on your computer, select a smart phone that is compatible with the program you wish to use.

Programs such as Microsoft Outlook allow you to synchronize your e-mail messages, contacts, and calendar with your smart phone. If you would like this functionality, purchase a smart phone that can synchronize with Microsoft Outlook. Similarly, if your company uses a BlackBerry Enterprise server or Microsoft Exchange server, you should consider purchasing a smart phone that can synchronize, either using wires or wirelessly, with those servers.

❺ Compare battery life.

Any smart phone is useful only if it has the power required to run. Talking and using the Internet on your smart phone will shorten battery life more quickly than when the phone is powered on but not in use. If you have a choice, be sure to purchase a battery that will allow the phone to function all day. Pay particular attention to the talk time and standby time. If you plan to talk on the phone more than the advertised talk time, you might consider purchasing a second battery or an extended battery if your phone supports it.

❻ Make sure your smart phone has enough memory and storage.

If you are using the smart phone to send and receive picture, video, and e-mail messages, and to store music, purchase a memory card that not only is compatible with your computer and smart phone, but also has adequate storage space for your messages and files. If you purchase a

memory card and eventually fill it, you easily can transfer the data to a larger memory card.

❼ Check out the accessories.

Determine which accessories you want for the smart phone. Accessories include carrying cases, screen protectors, synchronization cradles and cables, and car chargers.

How to Purchase a Portable Media Player

Portable media players are becoming the preferred device for listening to music and watching videos on the go. When choosing a portable media player, it is important to consider features and characteristics other than the physical size and amount of storage space. This section lists guidelines you should consider when purchasing a portable media player.

❶ Choose a device with sufficient storage capacity.

Audio and video files can consume a great deal of storage space, so be sure to purchase a portable media player that has enough capacity to store your audio and video files. You also should consider approximately how many media files you acquire each year, and make sure that your device has enough storage space to accommodate these files for years to come.

❷ Determine which file formats your new portable media player should support and how you will add files to your library.

Some portable media players are designed to accept new audio and video files only through a program installed on a computer. For example, it is easiest to add media files to an iPod using the iTunes program. Other portable media players connect to a computer using a cable and are displayed in Windows as a removable disk. You then can add files to the media player by dragging the files to the removable disk icon in Windows. The portable media player must support the file formats you are using. You can determine the file format by looking at the file extension on the media files you wish to transfer to your portable media player. Before purchasing a portable media player, make sure that it can support the file formats you are using.

❸ Consider a portable media player that can play video.

Some users prefer to watch videos on their portable media player in addition to playing music. You typically can download videos for portable media players less expensively than purchasing the movie on a DVD/Blu-ray Disc. Although the display on a portable media player is small, many still find entertainment value because they are able to watch videos while waiting for a bus, on an airplane, or at other locations where they otherwise might not have anything to occupy them.

❹ Read reviews about the sound quality on the portable media players you are considering.

Sound quality may vary greatly among portable media players. If you are unable to try the portable media player before buying it, read reviews and make sure that those reviewing the devices find the sound quality to be acceptable. You also may consider purchasing higher-quality earbuds or headphones to enhance the sound quality.

❺ Select a size and style that works best for you.

Portable media players are available in various shapes and styles. For example, Apple offers the iPod shuffle, iPod nano, iPod classic, and iPod touch (Figure 52). Each type of iPod varies in size and style, and some have capabilities (such as video) that others do not. Choose a size and style that meets your needs and fits your personality.

Figure 52 Portable media players are available in different shapes, styles, and colors.

❻ Check out additional memory cards.

Most portable media players have internal storage for your media files. If you wish to increase the available storage, consider purchasing a portable media player that allows you to increase storage capacity by inserting memory cards. Similar to most computers, it is less expensive initially to purchase the largest amount of storage that you can afford, but it is helpful to be able to increase your storage at a later date.

❼ Consider rechargeable batteries.

Although most portable media players include rechargeable batteries, some still use traditional alkaline batteries. Portable media players sometimes can last for only a few hours on alkaline batteries, and battery replacement can be costly. Rechargeable batteries often last longer and create less waste. If you are not near a power source, you are unable to recharge the batteries when they die. With alkaline batteries, you simply can insert new ones and continue enjoying your player.

❽ Stay within your budget.

As previously mentioned, portable media players are available in a variety of shapes and sizes, and they also are available with various storage capacities. When shopping for a portable media player, be realistic when you consider how you will use the device, as well as how much storage you require. Purchasing the latest and greatest device is not always the best option, and the cost can exceed what you care to spend.

How to Purchase a Digital Camera

Both amateur and professional photographers now are mostly purchasing digital cameras to meet their photography needs. Because digital cameras with new and improved features regularly are introduced to the marketplace, consumers should know how to compare the differences among the multiple cameras that are available. This section lists guidelines you should consider when purchasing a digital camera.

❶ Determine the type of digital camera that meets your needs.

Various types of digital cameras exist, including point-and-shoot cameras, field cameras, and studio cameras. Point-and-shoot cameras typically fit in your pocket and meet the needs of most general consumers. Field cameras, which often are used by photojournalists, are portable but flexible. Field cameras allow photographers to change lenses and use other attachments, and also are more customizable than point-and-shoot cameras. Studio cameras are used in photo studios and are stationary. These cameras give you the widest range of lenses and settings.

❷ The digital camera with the highest resolution is not always the best.

Many consumers mistakenly believe that the digital camera with the highest resolution is the best camera for their needs.

A higher resolution increases quality and clarity of your photos, as well as the size at which you can print the photos before noticing degradation in quality. If you never plan to print photos larger than 8" × 10", for example, you do not need a camera with a resolution greater than 5 megapixels. Many cameras available today advertise higher resolutions, but taking pictures at these high resolutions can use valuable storage space. Just because your camera can take a 10-megapixel photo does not mean that you always should set the resolution to 10 megapixels.

❸ Consider size and weight.

Digital cameras are available in various sizes and weights. Some people prefer smaller, lighter cameras because they are easier to transport and take up less space. Others prefer bulkier, heavier cameras because the weight helps steady them to take a clearer picture. Many digital cameras also include an image stabilization feature that reduces the possibility of a blurry picture if you move your hands slightly while taking the picture. Some also believe that heavier cameras are of better quality, although that seldom is true. When choosing a digital camera, practice taking pictures with it and select one that feels comfortable and natural.

❹ Different cameras require different memory cards.

When purchasing a digital camera, pay careful attention to the type of memory card the camera uses. Many use SD cards, some use xD Picture cards, and some use CompactFlash memory cards. Some memory cards are more expensive to replace than others, and some have a higher capacity than other cards. If you take a lot of pictures, purchase a camera that supports a memory card with a higher storage capacity so that you can avoid carrying multiple memory cards. You also might consider purchasing a camera that uses a memory card that is compatible with your other mobile devices.

❺ Photo editing features can save you time.

Some digital cameras have integrated tools that allow you to edit photos directly from the camera. For instance, you may be able to crop photos, change the brightness, or remove red-eye effects. Editing photos directly on the camera after taking them can save you from editing multiple photos at once when you transfer them to a computer. The photo editing capabilities available on digital cameras are limited when compared to photo editing programs, but in many cases they can edit a photo to your satisfaction.

❻ Make sure that you can see the LCD screen easily.

LCD screens on digital cameras allow you to configure the settings, frame a shot before taking it, and preview photos after taking them. LCD screens vary by inches, so select a camera with a screen that does not require you to strain your eyes to view. This is especially important if the camera

you are considering does not have a viewfinder, because you then will be required to use the display to frame your shots.

❼ Determine whether your pictures will require you to zoom.

If you plan to take pictures of people or objects that require you to zoom in, select a digital camera that has a high optical zoom. An optical zoom enlarges the subject by adjusting the camera lens, whereas a digital zoom uses formulas built into the camera to magnify images. Optical zooms, as opposed to digital zooms, often result in a higher quality photo. While a digital zoom might be capable of magnifying objects that are 100 feet away, the photo will suffer a loss of quality.

❽ Price is important.

As with all other devices, purchase a digital camera that does not exceed your budget. If you find a great camera that is available for more than you are willing to spend, consider locating a camera with a slightly lower resolution, an alternate brand, or a smaller screen. Digital cameras can last well beyond five years if properly maintained, so consider this a longer-term investment that will create memories lasting you a lifetime.

❾ Know your batteries.

Some digital cameras require replaceable alkaline or rechargeable batteries (often AA or AAA), and others have a rechargeable battery. Similar to batteries in portable media players, using disposable batteries in digital cameras can get expensive, and they may not last as long as rechargeable battery packs. Digital camera battery life is not measured in hours (as is the case with smart phones and portable media players); instead, it is measured in how many pictures can be taken on a single charge or set of batteries. Turning off the LCD screen and flash when you take pictures can help to extend battery life.

❿ Purchase accessories.

Accessories that are available for digital cameras include carrying cases, extra batteries and battery chargers, and extra memory cards (Figure 53). Carrying cases can help protect your digital camera, especially while traveling, and the extra batteries and chargers can stay inside your carrying case so that they are readily available should you need them. Screen protectors can help protect the LCD screen on your digital camera.

Figure 53   Digital camera accessories include memory cards, cases, batteries, and battery chargers.

Learn It Online

Instructions

To complete the Learn It Online exercises, start your browser, click the address bar, and then enter the Web address scsite.com/ic8/learn. When the Introduction to Computers Learn It Online page is displayed, click the link for the exercise you want to complete and then read the instructions.

1 Chapter Reinforcement TF, MC, and SA

A series of true/false, multiple choice, and short answer questions that test your knowledge of the chapter content.

2 Flash Cards

An interactive learning environment where you identify key terms associated with displayed definitions.

3 Practice Test

A series of multiple choice questions that test your knowledge of chapter content and key terms.

4 Who Wants To Be a Computer Genius?

An interactive game that challenges your knowledge of chapter content in the style of a television quiz show.

5 Wheel of Terms

An interactive game that challenges your knowledge of chapter key terms in the style of the television show *Wheel of Fortune*.

6 Crossword Puzzle Challenge

A crossword puzzle that challenges your knowledge of key terms presented in the chapter.

Case Studies

1. Computers are ubiquitous. Watching television, driving a car, using a credit card, ordering fast food, and the more obvious activity of typing a research paper all involve interaction with computers. Make a list of every computer you can recall that you encountered over the past week (be careful not to limit yourself just to the computers you see). Consider how each computer is used. How were the tasks the computers performed done before computers existed? Do you feel computers have a positive impact on people and organizations? Write a brief report and submit it to your instructor.

2. The Internet has had a tremendous impact on organizations. For some organizations, that influence has not been positive. For example, surveys suggest that as a growing number of people make their own travel plans online, travel agents are seeing fewer customers. Use the Web to research organizations that have been affected negatively by the Internet. What effect has the Internet had? How can the organization compete with the Internet? Do you feel that computers might replace humans entirely in the workforce? Why or why not? Write a brief report and submit it to your instructor.

3. As notebook computers become more affordable, an increasing number of college students are purchasing them to use instead of using computers available on campus. As a new college student, you also would like to purchase a notebook computer for your coursework. Shop online for a notebook computer that you believe will be sufficient for your major. Some schools have suggested notebook computer configurations that can assist in your search. Once you find a notebook computer, write a brief report describing the computer (include the brand, model, configuration information, and price), and submit it to your instructor.

4. Today, the functional lines among mobile devices seem blurred. Your cell phone has a digital camera; your portable media player has wireless Internet access; and your game console plays videos and connects to the Internet. These are examples of technological convergence, a process in which separate technologies merge in single products. Write a brief report on how your favorite mobile device is an example of convergence, listing the various technologies that it uses.

Index

Photo Credits

Office 2010 and Windows 7: Essential Concepts and Skills

Objectives

You will have mastered the material in this chapter when you can:

- Perform basic mouse operations
- Start Windows and log on to the computer
- Identify the objects on the Windows 7 desktop
- Identify the programs in and versions of Microsoft Office
- Start a program
- Identify the components of the Microsoft Office Ribbon

- Create folders
- Save files
- Change screen resolution
- Perform basic tasks in Microsoft Office programs
- Manage files
- Use Microsoft Office Help and Windows Help

Office 2010 and Windows 7: Essential Concepts and Skills

Office 2010 and Windows 7

This introductory chapter covers features and functions common to Office 2010 programs, as well as the basics of Windows 7.

Overview

As you read this chapter, you will learn how to perform basic tasks in Windows and Office programs by performing these general activities:

- Start programs using Windows.
- Use features common across Office programs.
- Organize files and folders.
- Change screen resolution.
- Quit Office programs.

Introduction to the Windows 7 Operating System

Windows 7 is the newest version of Microsoft Windows, which is the most popular and widely used operating system. An **operating system** is a computer program (set of computer instructions) that coordinates all the activities of computer hardware such as memory, storage devices, and printers, and provides the capability for you to communicat with the computer.

The Windows 7 operating system simplifies the process of working with document and programs by organizing the manner in which you interact with the computer. Windows 7 is used to run **application software**, which consists of programs designed to make users more productive and/or assist them with personal tasks, such as word processing.

Windows 7 has two interface variations, Windows 7 Basic and Windows 7 Aero. Computers with up to 1 GB of RAM display the Windows 7 Basic interface (Figure 1a). Computers with more than 1 GB of RAM also can display the Windows Aero interface (Figure 1b), which provides an enhanced visual appearance. The Windows 7 Professional, Windows 7 Enterprise, Windows 7 Home Premium, and Windows 7 Ultimate editions have the capability to use Windows Aero.

Using a Mouse

Windows users work with a mouse that has at least two buttons. For a right-handed user, the left button usually is the primary mouse button, and the right mouse button is the secondary mouse button. Left-handed people, however, can reverse the function of these buttons.

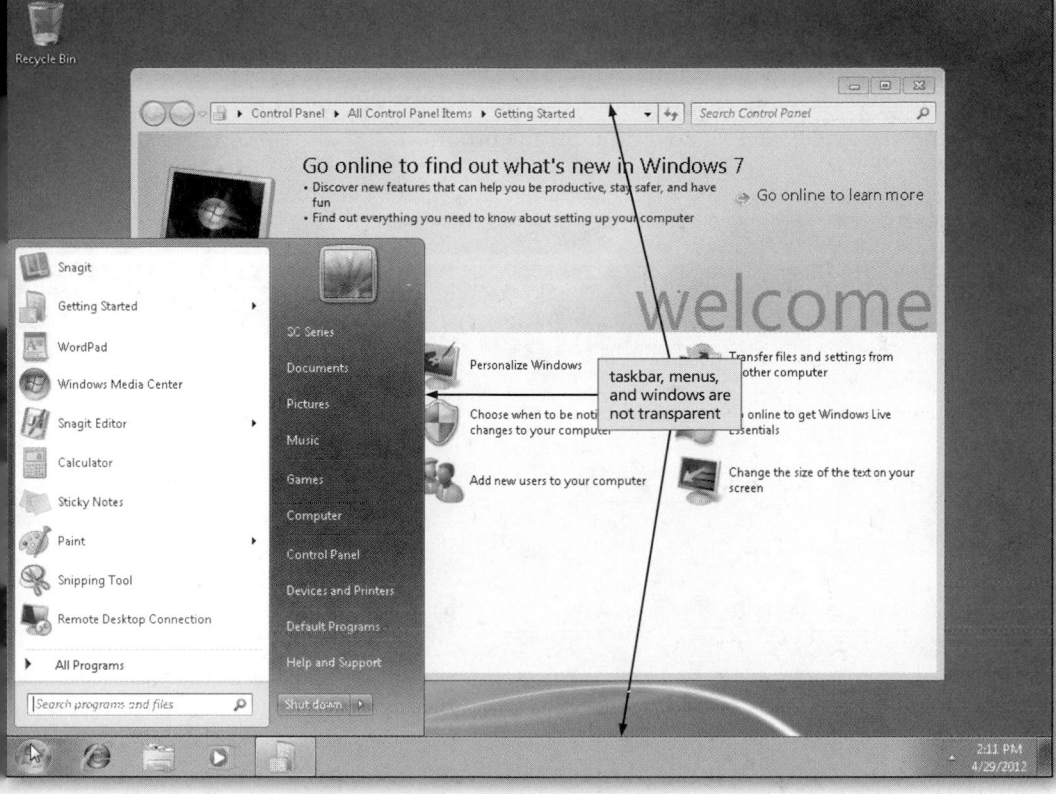

Figure 1(a) Windows 7 Basic interface

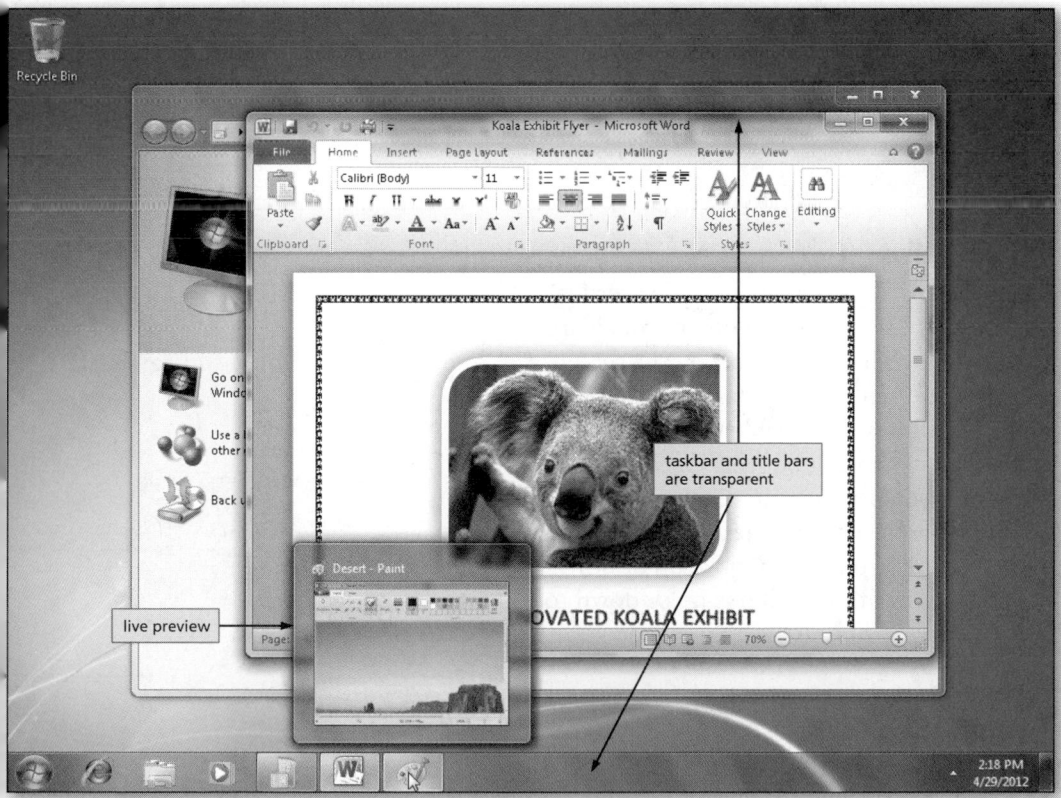

Figure 1(b) Windows 7 Aero interface

Table 1 explains how to perform a variety of mouse operations. Some programs also use keys in combination with the mouse to perform certain actions. For example, when you hold down the CTRL key while rolling the mouse wheel, text on the screen becomes larger or smaller based on the direction you roll the wheel. The function of the mouse buttons and the wheel varies depending on the program.

Table 1 Mouse Operations		
Operation	**Mouse Action**	**Example***
Point	Move the mouse until the pointer on the desktop is positioned on the item of choice.	Position the pointer on the screen.
Click	Press and release the primary mouse button, which usually is the left mouse button.	Select or deselect items on the screen or start a program or program feature.
Right-click	Press and release the secondary mouse button, which usually is the right mouse button.	Display a shortcut menu.
Double-click	Quickly press and release the left mouse button twice without moving the mouse.	Start a program or program feature.
Triple-click	Quickly press and release the left mouse button three times without moving the mouse.	Select a paragraph.
Drag	Point to an item, hold down the left mouse button, move the item to the desired location on the screen, and then release the left mouse button.	Move an object from one location to another or draw pictures.
Right-drag	Point to an item, hold down the right mouse button, move the item to the desired location on the screen, and then release the right mouse button.	Display a shortcut menu after moving an object from one location to another.
Rotate wheel	Roll the wheel forward or backward.	Scroll vertically (up and down).
Free-spin wheel	Whirl the wheel forward or backward so that it spins freely on its own.	Scroll through many pages in seconds.
Press wheel	Press the wheel button while moving the mouse.	Scroll continuously.
Tilt wheel	Press the wheel toward the right or left.	Scroll horizontally (left and right).
Press thumb button	Press the button on the side of the mouse with your thumb.	Move forward or backward through Web pages and/or control media, games, etc.

*Note: the examples presented in this column are discussed as they are demonstrated in this chapter.

Scrolling

A **scroll bar** is a horizontal or vertical bar that appears when the contents of an area may not be visible completely on the screen (Figure 2). A scroll bar contains **scroll arrows** and a **scroll box** that enable you to view areas that currently cannot be seen. Clicking the up and down scroll arrows moves the screen content up or down one line. You also can click above or below the scroll box to move up or down a section, or drag the scroll box up or down to move up or down to move to a specific location.

Shortcut Keys

In many cases, you can use the keyboard instead of the mouse to accomplish a task. To perform tasks using the keyboard, you press one or more keyboard keys, sometimes identified as

BTW

Minimize Wrist Injury
Computer users frequently switch between the keyboard and the mouse during a word processing session; such switching strains the wrist. To help prevent wrist injury, minimize switching. For instance, if your fingers already are on the keyboard, use keyboard keys to scroll. If your hand already is on the mouse, use the mouse to scroll.

Figure 2

shortcut key or **keyboard shortcut**. Some shortcut keys consist of a single key, such as the F1 key. For example, to obtain help about Windows 7, you can press the F1 key. Other shortcut keys consist of multiple keys, in which case a plus sign separates the key names, such as CTRL+ESC. This notation means to press and hold down the first key listed, press one or more additional keys, and then release all keys. For example, to display the Start menu, press CTRL+ESC, that is, hold down the CTRL key, press the ESC key, and then release both keys.

Starting Windows 7

It is not unusual for multiple people to use the same computer in a work, educational, recreational, or home setting. Windows 7 enables each user to establish a **user account**, which identifies to Windows 7 the resources, such as programs and storage locations, a user can access when working with a computer.

Each user account has a user name and may have a password and an icon, as well. A **user name** is a unique combination of letters or numbers that identifies a specific user to Windows 7. A **password** is a private combination of letters, numbers, and special characters associated with the user name that allows access to a user's account resources. A **user icon** is a picture associated with a user name.

When you turn on a computer, an introductory screen consisting of the Windows logo and copyright messages is displayed. The Windows logo is animated and glows as the Windows 7 operating system is loaded. After the Windows logo appears, depending on your computer's settings, you may or may not be required to log on to the computer. **Logging on** to a computer opens your user account and makes the computer available for use. If you are required to log on to the computer, the **Welcome screen** is displayed, which shows the user names of users on the computer (Figure 3). Clicking the user name or picture begins the process of logging on to the computer.

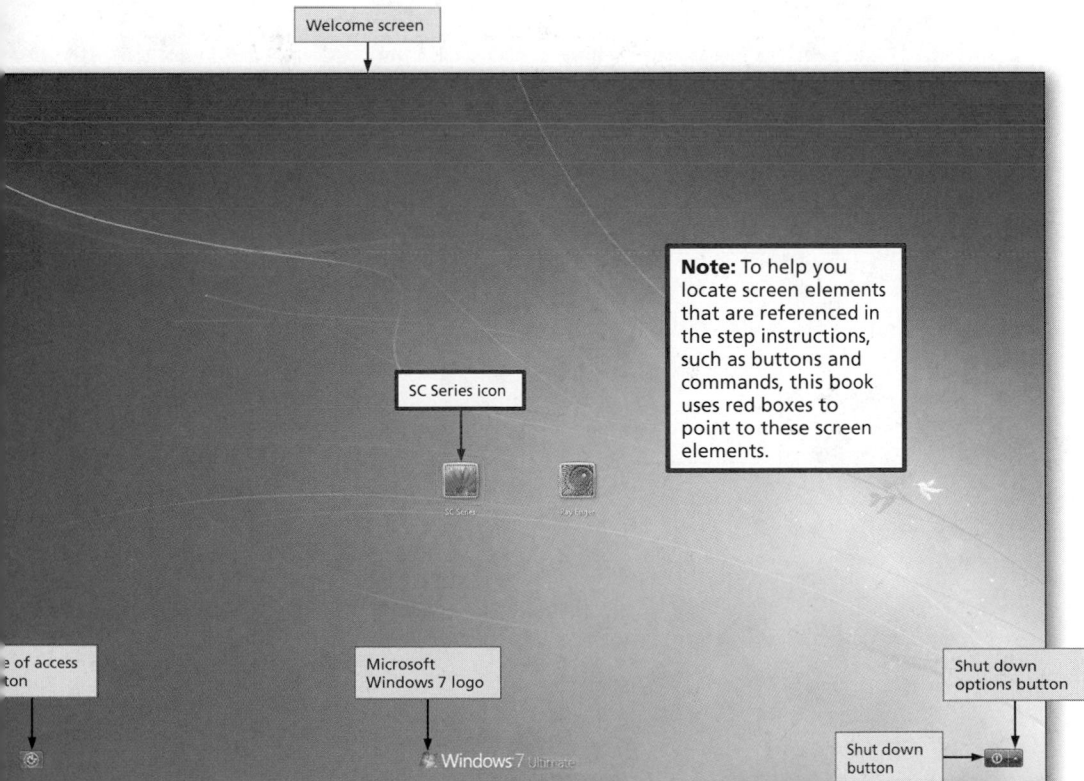

Note: To help you locate screen elements that are referenced in the step instructions, such as buttons and commands, this book uses red boxes to point to these screen elements.

Welcome screen

SC Series icon

e of access ton

Microsoft Windows 7 logo

Shut down options button

Shut down button

Figure 3

At the bottom of the Welcome screen is the 'Ease of access' button, Windows 7 logo, a Shut down button, and a 'Shut down options' button. The following list identifies the functions of the buttons and commands that typically appear on the Welcome screen:

- Clicking the 'Ease of access' button displays the Ease of Access Center, which provides tools to optimize your computer to accommodate the needs of the mobility, hearing, and vision impaired users.
- Clicking the Shut down button shuts down Windows 7 and the computer.
- Clicking the 'Shut down options' button, located to the right of the Shut down button, provides access to a menu containing commands that perform actions such as restarting the computer, putting the computer in a low-powered state, and shutting down the computer. The commands available on your computer may differ.
  - The **Restart command** closes open programs, shuts down Windows 7, and then restarts Windows 7 and displays the Welcome screen.
  - The **Sleep command** waits for Windows 7 to save your work and then turns off the computer fans and hard disk. To wake the computer from the Sleep state, press the power button or lift a notebook computer's cover, and log on to the computer.
  - The **Shut down command** shuts down and turns off the computer.

To Log On to the Computer

After starting Windows 7, you might need to log on to the computer. The following steps log on to the computer based on a typical installation. You may need to ask your instructor how to log on to your computer. This set of steps uses SC Series as the user name. The list of user names on your computer will be different.

1

- Click the user icon (SC Series, in this case) on the Welcome screen (shown in Figure 3 on the previous page); depending on settings, this either will display a password text box (Figure 4) or will log on to the computer and display the Windows 7 desktop.

Q&A Why do I not see a user icon?

Your computer may require you to type a user name instead of clicking an icon.

Q&A What is a text box?

A text box is a rectangular box in which you type text.

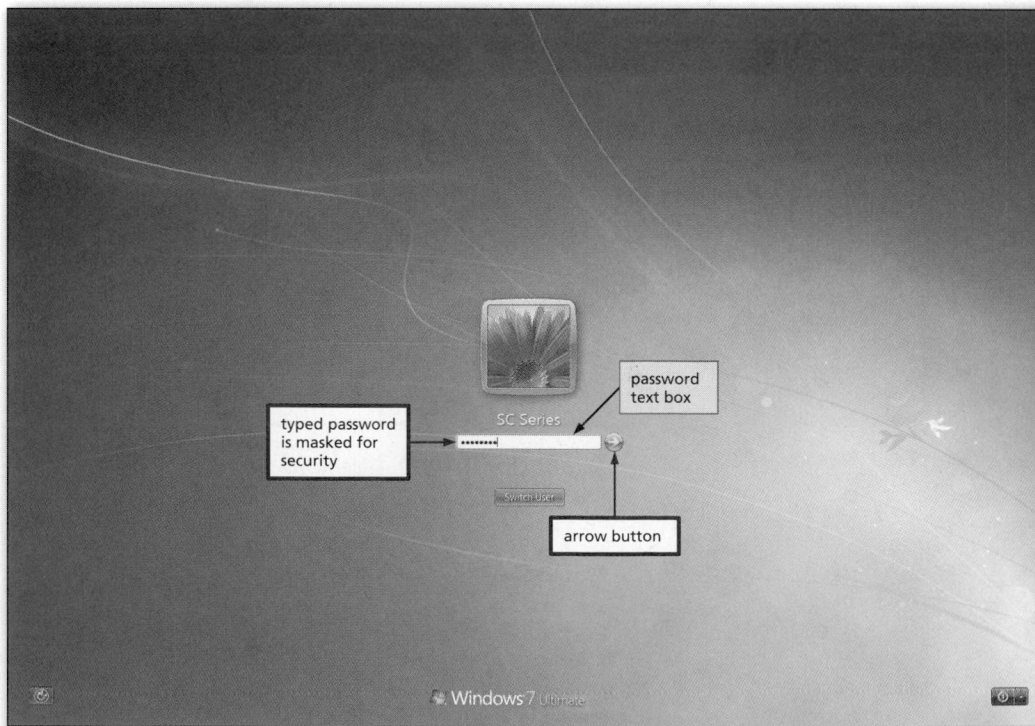

Figure 4

Q&A Why does my screen not show a password text box?

Your account does not require a password.

2

• If Windows 7 displays a password text box, type your password in the text box and then click the arrow button to log on to the computer and display the Windows 7 desktop (Figure 5).

Why does my desktop look different from the one in Figure 5?

The Windows 7 desktop is customizable, and your school or employer may have modified the desktop to meet its needs. Also, your screen resolution, which affects the size of the elements on the screen, may differ from the screen resolution used in this book. Later in this chapter, you learn how to change screen resolution.

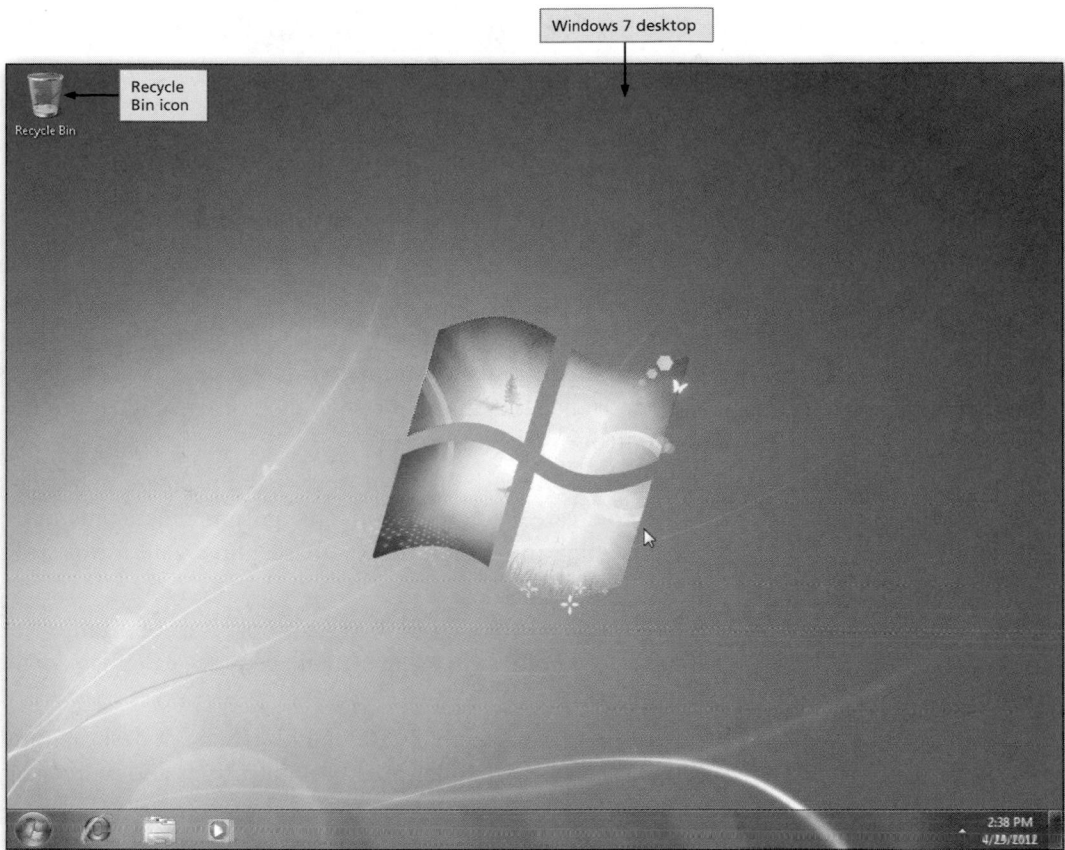

Figure 5

The Windows 7 Desktop

The Windows 7 desktop (Figure 5) and the objects on the desktop emulate a work area in an office. Think of the Windows desktop as an electronic version of the top of your desk. You can perform tasks such as placing objects on the desktop, moving the objects around the desktop, and removing items from the desktop.

When you start a program in Windows 7, it appears on the desktop. Some icons also may be displayed on the desktop. For instance, the icon for the **Recycle Bin**, the location of files that have been deleted, appears on the desktop by default. A **file** is a named unit of storage. Files can contain text, images, audio, and video. You can customize your desktop so that icons representing programs and files you use often appear on your desktop.

Introduction to Microsoft Office 2010

Microsoft Office 2010 is the newest version of Microsoft Office, offering features that provide users with better functionality and easier ways to work with the various files they create. These features include enhanced design tools, such as improved picture formatting tools and new themes, shared notebooks for working in groups, mobile versions of Office programs, broadcast presentation for the Web, and a digital notebook for managing and sharing multimedia information.

Microsoft Office 2010 Programs

Microsoft Office 2010 includes a wide variety of programs such as Word, PowerPoint, Excel, Access, Outlook, Publisher, OneNote, InfoPath, SharePoint Workspace, Communicator, and Web Apps:

- **Microsoft Word 2010**, or Word, is a full-featured word processing program that allows you to create professional-looking documents and revise them easily.
- **Microsoft PowerPoint 2010**, or PowerPoint, is a complete presentation program that allows you to produce professional-looking presentations.
- **Microsoft Excel 2010**, or Excel, is a powerful spreadsheet program that allows you to organize data, complete calculations, make decisions, graph data, develop professional-looking reports, publish organized data to the Web, and access real-time data from Web sites.
- **Microsoft Access 2010**, or Access, is a database management system that allows you to create a database; add, change, and delete data in the database; ask questions concerning the data in the database; and create forms and reports using the data in the database.
- **Microsoft Outlook 2010**, or Outlook, is a communications and scheduling program that allows you to manage e-mail accounts, calendars, contacts, and access to other Internet content.
- **Microsoft Publisher 2010**, or Publisher, is a desktop publishing program that helps you create professional-quality publications and marketing materials that can be shared easily.
- **Microsoft OneNote 2010**, or OneNote, is a note taking program that allows you to store and share information in notebooks with other people.
- **Microsoft InfoPath 2010**, or InfoPath, is a form development program that helps you create forms for use on the Web and gather data from these forms.
- **Microsoft SharePoint Workspace 2010**, or SharePoint, is collaboration software that allows you access and revise files stored on your computer from other locations.
- **Microsoft Communicator** is communications software that allows you to use different modes of communications such as instant messaging, video conferencing, and sharing files and programs.
- **Microsoft Web Apps** is a Web application that allows you to edit and share files on the Web using the familiar Office interface.

Microsoft Office 2010 Suites

A **suite** is a collection of individual programs available together as a unit. Microsoft offers a variety of Office suites. Table 2 lists the Office 2010 suites and their components.

Programs in a suite, such as Microsoft Office, typically use a similar interface and share features. In addition, Microsoft Office programs use **common dialog boxes** for performing actions such as opening and saving files. Once you are comfortable working with these elements and this interface and performing tasks in one program, the similarity can help you apply the knowledge and skills you have learned to another Office program(s). For example, the process for saving a file in Word is the same in PowerPoint, Excel, and the other Office programs. While briefly showing how to use several Office programs, this chapter illustrates some of the common functions across the programs and also identifies the characteristics unique to these programs.

Table 2 Microsoft Office 2010 Suites	Microsoft Office Professional Plus 2010	Microsoft Office Professional 2010	Microsoft Office Home and Business 2010	Microsoft Office Standard 2010	Microsoft Office Home and Student 2010
Microsoft Word 2010	✔	✔	✔	✔	✔
Microsoft PowerPoint 2010	✔	✔	✔	✔	✔
Microsoft Excel 2010	✔	✔	✔	✔	✔
Microsoft Access 2010	✔	✔	✗	✗	✗
Microsoft Outlook 2010	✔	✔	✔	✔	✗
Microsoft Publisher 2010	✔	✔	✗	✔	✗
Microsoft OneNote 2010	✔	✔	✔	✔	✔
Microsoft InfoPath 2010	✔	✗	✗	✗	✗
Microsoft SharePoint Workspace 2010	✔	✗	✗	✗	✗
Microsoft Communicator	✔	✗	✗	✗	✗

Starting and Using a Program

To use a program, you must instruct the operating system to start the program. Windows 7 provides many different ways to start a program, one of which is presented in this section (other ways to start a program are presented throughout this chapter). After starting a program, you can use it to perform a variety of tasks. The following pages use Word to discuss some elements of the Office interface and to perform tasks that are common to other Office programs.

Word

Word is a full-featured word processing program that allows you to create many types of personal and business documents, including flyers, letters, memos, resumes, reports, fax cover sheets, mailing labels, and newsletters. Word also provides tools that enable you to create Web pages and save these Web pages directly on a Web server. Word has many features designed to simplify the production of documents and add visual appeal. Using Word, you easily can change the shape, size, and color of text. You also can include borders, shading, tables, images, pictures, charts, and Web addresses in documents.

To Start a Program Using the Start Menu

Across the bottom of the Windows 7 desktop is the taskbar. The taskbar contains the **Start button**, which you use to access programs, files, folders, and settings on a computer. A **folder** is a named location on a storage medium that usually contains related documents. The taskbar also displays a button for each program currently running on a computer.

Clicking the Start button displays the Start menu. The **Start menu** allows you to access programs, folders, and files on the computer and contains commands that allow you to start programs, store and search for documents, customize the computer, and obtain help about thousands of topics. A **menu** is a list of related items, including folders, programs, and commands. Each **command** on a menu performs a specific action, such as saving a file or obtaining help.

The following steps, which assume Windows 7 is running, use the Start menu to start an Office program based on a typical installation. You may need to ask your instructor how to start Office programs for your computer. Although the steps illustrate starting the Word program, the steps to start any Office program are similar.

1

• Click the Start button on the Windows 7 taskbar to display the Start menu (Figure 6).

Q&A

Why does my Start menu look different?

It may look different depending on your computer's configuration. The Start menu may be customized for several reasons, such as usage requirements or security restrictions.

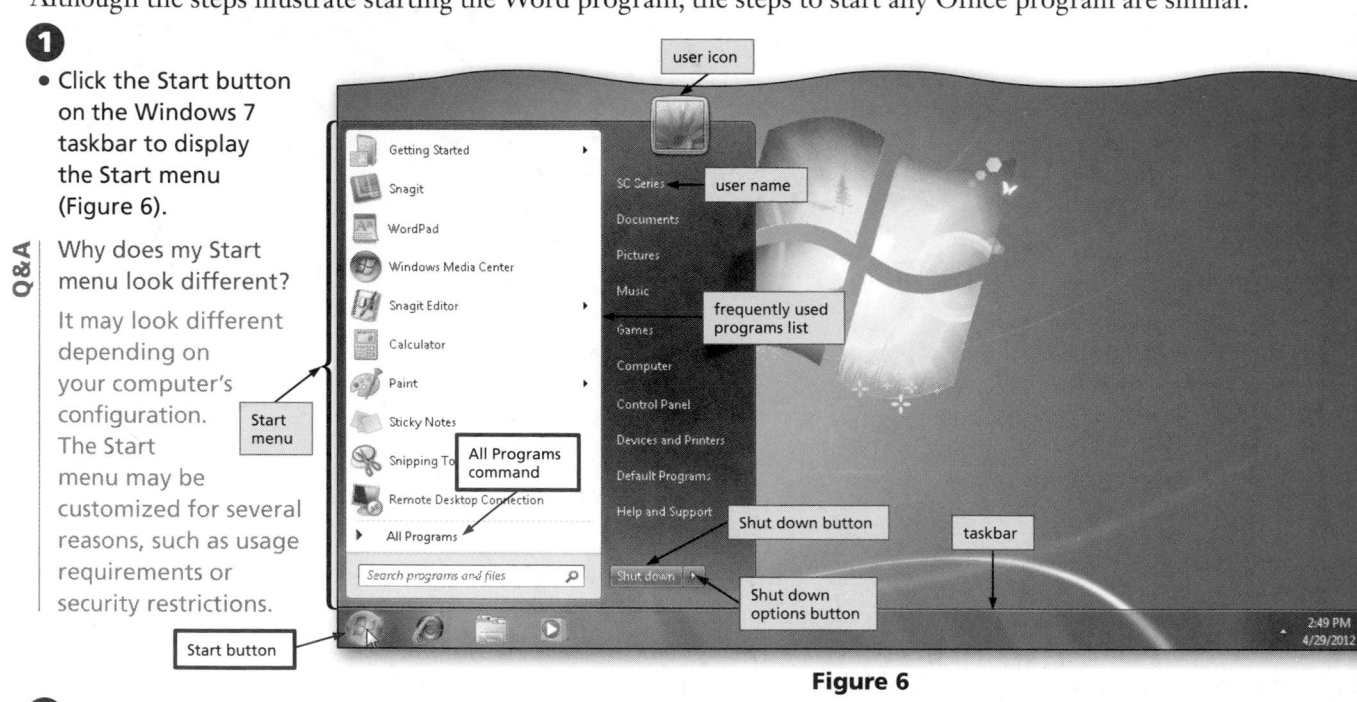

Figure 6

2

• Click All Programs at the bottom of the left pane on the Start menu to display the All Programs list (Figure 7).

Q&A

What is a pane?

A **pane** is an area of a window that displays related content. For example, the left pane on the Start menu contains a list of frequently used programs, as well as the All Programs command.

Q&A

Why might my All Programs list look different?

Most likely, the programs installed on your computer will differ from those shown in Figure 7. Your All Programs list will show the programs that are installed on your computer.

Figure 7

3

- If the program you wish to start is located in a folder, click or scroll to and then click the folder (Microsoft Office, in this case) in the All Programs list to display a list of the folder's contents (Figure 8).

Why is the Microsoft Office folder on my computer?

During installation of Microsoft Office 2010, the Microsoft Office folder was added to the All Programs list.

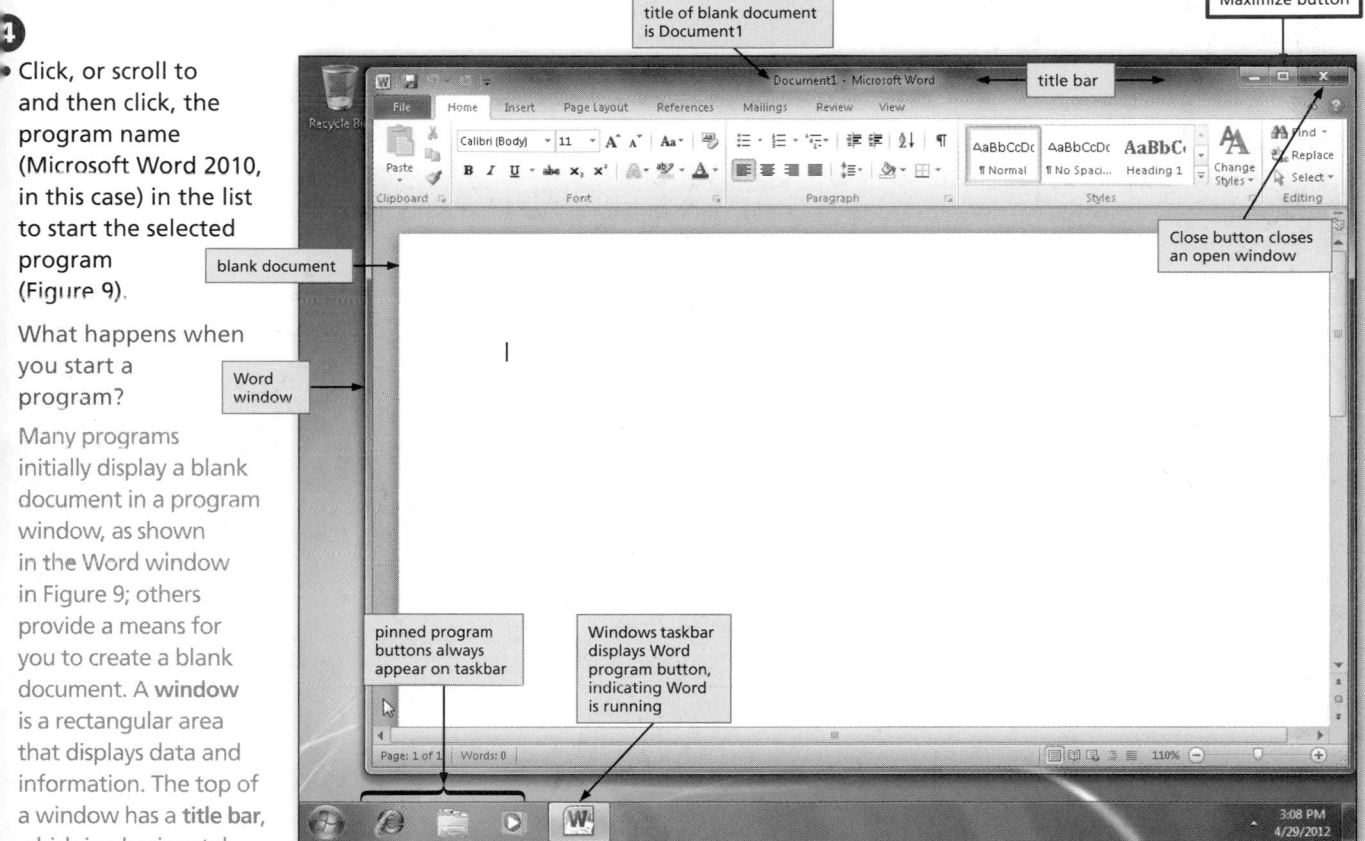

Figure 8

4

- Click, or scroll to and then click, the program name (Microsoft Word 2010, in this case) in the list to start the selected program (Figure 9).

What happens when you start a program?

Many programs initially display a blank document in a program window, as shown in the Word window in Figure 9; others provide a means for you to create a blank document. A **window** is a rectangular area that displays data and information. The top of a window has a **title bar**, which is a horizontal space that contains the window's name.

Figure 9

Why is my program window a different size?

The Word window shown in Figure 9 is not maximized. Your Word window already may be maximized. The next steps maximize a window.

Other Ways	
1. Double-click program icon on desktop, if one is present	3. Display Start menu, type program name in search box, click program name
2. Click program name in left pane of Start menu, if present	4. Double-click file created using program you want to start

To Maximize a Window

Sometimes content is not visible completely in a window. One method of displaying the entire contents of a window is to **maximize** it, or enlarge the window so that it fills the entire screen. The following step maximizes the Word window; however, any Office program's window can be maximized using this step.

1

- If the program window is not maximized already, click the Maximize button (shown in Figure 9 on the previous page) next to the Close button on the window's title bar (the Word window title bar, in this case) to maximize the window (Figure 10).

Q&A What happened to the Maximize button?

It changed to a Restore Down button, which you can use to return a window to its size and location before you maximized it.

Q&A How do I know whether a window is maximized?

A window is maximized if it fills the entire display area and the Restore Down button is displayed on the title bar.

Figure 10

Other Ways
1. Double-click title bar
2. Drag title bar to top of screen

The Word Document Window, Ribbon, and Elements Common to Office Programs

The Word window consists of a variety of components to make your work more efficient and documents more professional. These include the document window, Ribbon, Mini toolbar, shortcut menus, and Quick Access Toolbar. Most of these components are common to other Microsoft Office 2010 programs; others are unique to Word.

You view a portion of a document on the screen through a **document window** (Figure 11). The default (preset) view is **Print Layout view**, which shows the document on a mock sheet of paper in the document window.

Scroll Bars You use a scroll bar to display different portions of a document in the document window. At the right edge of the document window is a vertical scroll bar. If a document is too wide to fit in the document window, a horizontal scroll bar also appears at the bottom of the document window. On a scroll bar, the position of the scroll box reflects the location of the portion of the document that is displayed in the document window.

Figure 11

Status Bar   The **status bar**, located at the bottom of the document window above the Windows 7 taskbar, presents information about the document, the progress of current tasks, and the status of certain commands and keys; it also provides controls for viewing the document. As you type text or perform certain tasks, various indicators and buttons may appear on the status bar.

The left side of the status bar in Figure 11 shows the current page followed by the total number of pages in the document, the number of words in the document, and an icon to check spelling and grammar. The right side of the status bar includes buttons and controls you can use to change the view of a document and adjust the size of the displayed document.

Ribbon   The Ribbon, located near the top of the window below the title bar, is the control center in Word and other Office programs (Figure 12). The Ribbon provides easy, central access to the tasks you perform while creating a document. The Ribbon consists of tabs, groups, and commands. Each **tab** contains a collection of groups, and each **group** contains related functions. When you start an Office program, such as Word, it initially displays several main tabs, also called default tabs. All Office programs have a **Home tab**, which contains the more frequently used commands.

In addition to the main tabs, Office programs display **tool tabs**, also called contextual tabs (Figure 13), when you perform certain tasks or work with objects such as pictures or tables. If you insert a picture in a Word document, for example, the Picture Tools tab and its related subordinate Format tab appear, collectively referred to as the Picture Tools Format tab. When you are finished working with the picture, the Picture Tools Format tab disappears from the Ribbon. Word and other Office programs determine when tool tabs should appear and disappear based on tasks you perform. Some tool tabs, such as the Table Tools tab, have more than one related subordinate tab.

Items on the Ribbon include buttons, boxes (text boxes, check boxes, etc.), and galleries (Figure 12). A **gallery** is a set of choices, often graphical, arranged in a grid or in a list. You can scroll through choices in an in-Ribbon gallery by clicking the gallery's scroll arrows. Or, you can click a gallery's More button to view more gallery options on the screen at a time.

Figure 12

Some buttons and boxes have arrows that, when clicked, also display a gallery; others always cause a gallery to be displayed when clicked. Most galleries support **live preview**, which is a feature that allows you to point to a gallery choice and see its effect in the document — without actually selecting the choice (Figure 13).

Figure 13

Some commands on the Ribbon display an image to help you remember their function. When you point to a command on the Ribbon, all or part of the command glows in shades of yellow and orange, and an Enhanced ScreenTip appears on the screen. An **Enhanced ScreenTip** is an on-screen note that provides the name of the command, available keyboard shortcut(s), a description of the command, and sometimes instructions for how to obtain help about the command (Figure 14). Enhanced ScreenTips are more detailed than a typical ScreenTip, which usually displays only the name of the command.

Some groups on the Ribbon have a small arrow in the lower-right corner, called a **Dialog Box Launcher**, that when clicked, displays a dialog box or a task pane with additional options for the group (Figure 15). When presented with a dialog box, you make selections and must close the dialog box before returning to the document. A **task pane**, in contrast to a dialog box, is a window that can remain open and visible while you work in the document.

Figure 14

Mini Toolbar The **Mini toolbar**, which appears automatically based on tasks you perform, contains commands related to changing the appearance of text in a document. All commands on the Mini toolbar also exist on the Ribbon. The purpose of the Mini toolbar is to minimize mouse movement.

When the Mini toolbar appears, it initially is transparent (Figure 16a). If you do not use the transparent Mini toolbar, it disappears from the screen. To use the Mini toolbar, move the mouse pointer into the toolbar, which causes the Mini toolbar to change

Figure 15

from a transparent to bright appearance (Figure 16b). If you right-click an item in the document window, Word displays both the Mini toolbar and a shortcut menu, which is discussed in a later section in this chapter.

(a) transparent Mini toolbar

(b) bright Mini toolbar

Figure 16

Quick Access Toolbar   The **Quick Access Toolbar**, located initially (by default) above the Ribbon at the left edge of the title bar, provides convenient, one-click access to frequently used commands (Figure 14 on the previous page). The commands on the Quick Access Toolbar always are available, regardless of the task you are performing. The Quick Access Toolbar is discussed in more depth later in the chapter.

KeyTips   If you prefer using the keyboard instead of the mouse, you can press the ALT key on the keyboard to display **KeyTips**, or keyboard code icons, for certain commands (Figure 17). To select a command using the keyboard, press the letter or number displaye in the KeyTip, which may cause additional KeyTips related to the selected command to appear. To remove KeyTips from the screen, press the ALT key or the ESC key until all KeyTips disappear, or click the mouse anywhere in the program window.

Figure 17

To Display a Different Tab on the Ribbon

When you start Word, the Ribbon displays eight main tabs: File, Home, Insert, Page Layout, References, Mailings, Review, and View. The tab currently displayed is called the **active tab**.

The following step displays the Insert tab, that is, makes it the active tab.

1

• Click Insert on the Ribbon to display the Insert tab (Figure 18).

🔍 **Experiment**

• Click the other tabs on the Ribbon to view their contents. When you are finished, click the Insert tab to redisplay the Insert tab.

Q&A

If I am working in a different Office program, such as PowerPoint or Access, how do I display a different tab on the Ribbon?

Follow this same procedure; that is, click the desired tab on the Ribbon.

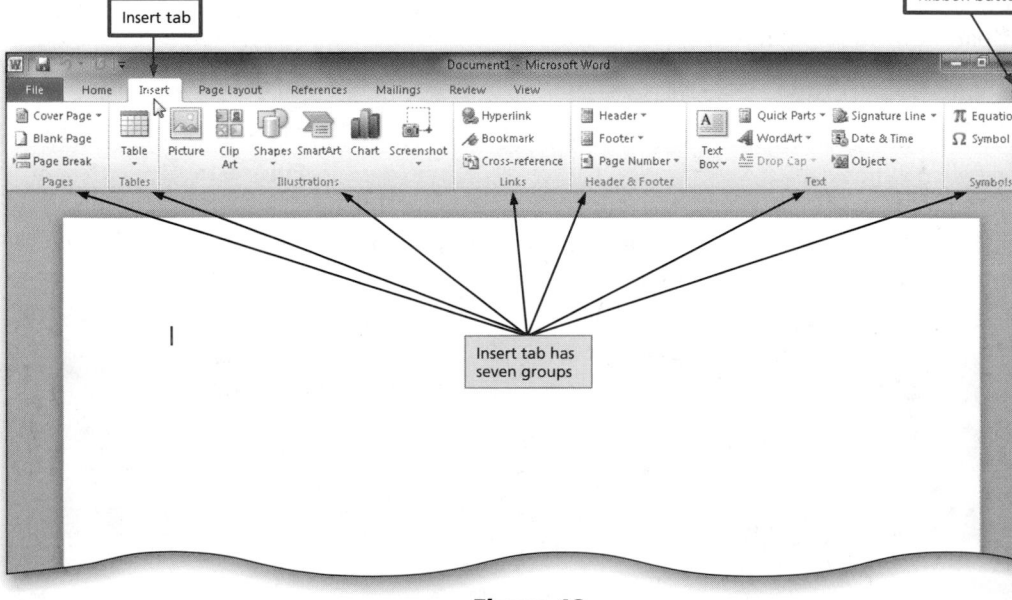

Figure 18

To Minimize, Display, and Restore the Ribbon

To display more of a document or other item in the window of an Office program, some users prefer to minimize the Ribbon, which hides the groups on the Ribbon and displays only the main tabs. Each time you start an Office program, the Ribbon appears the same way it did the last time you used that Office program. The chapters in this book, however, begin with the Ribbon appearing as it did at the initial installation of the software.

The following steps minimize, display, and restore the Ribbon in an Office program.

1

- Click the Minimize the Ribbon button on the Ribbon (shown in Figure 18) to minimize the Ribbon (Figure 19).

What happened to the groups on the Ribbon?

When you minimize the Ribbon, the groups disappear so that the Ribbon does not take up as much space on the screen.

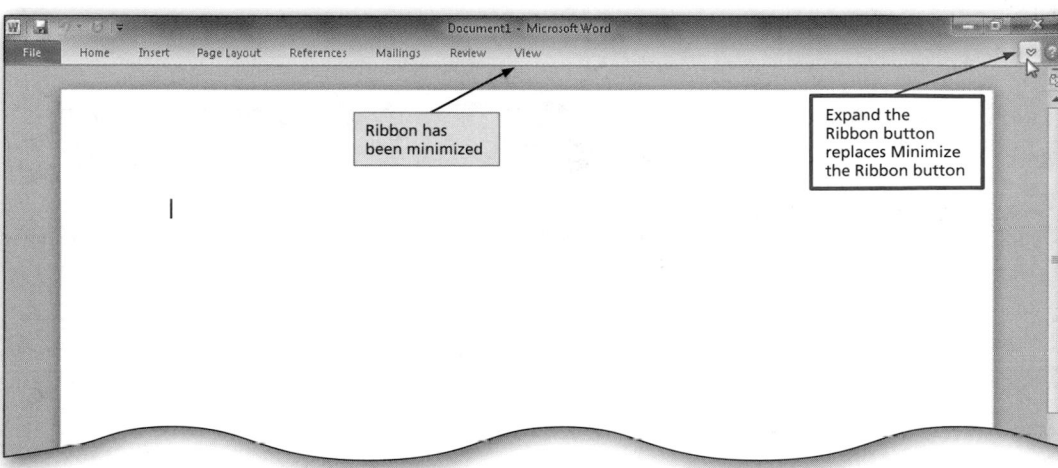

Figure 19

What happened to the Minimize the Ribbon button?

The Expand the Ribbon button replaces the Minimize the Ribbon button when the Ribbon is minimized.

2

- Click Home on the Ribbon to display the Home tab (Figure 20).

Why would I click the Home tab?

If you want to use a command on a minimized Ribbon, click the main tab to display the groups for that tab. After you select a command on the Ribbon, the groups will be hidden once again. If you decide not to use a command on the Ribbon, you can hide the groups by clicking the same main tab or clicking in the program window.

Figure 20

3

- Click Home on the Ribbon to hide the groups again (shown in Figure 19).

- Click the Expand the Ribbon button on the Ribbon (shown in Figure 19) to restore the Ribbon.

Other Ways

1. Double-click Home on the Ribbon
2. Press CTRL+F1

To Display and Use a Shortcut Menu

When you right-click certain areas of the Word and other program windows, a shortcut menu will appear. A **shortcut menu** is a list of frequently used commands that relate to the right-clicked object. When you right-click a scroll bar, for example, a shortcut menu appears with commands related to the scroll bar. When you right-click the Quick Access Toolbar, a shortcut menu appears with commands related to the Quick Access Toolbar. You can use shortcut menus to access common commands quickly. The following steps use a shortcut menu to move the Quick Access Toolbar, which by default is located on the title bar.

- Right-click the Quick Access Toolbar to display a shortcut menu that presents a list of commands related to the Quick Access Toolbar (Figure 21).

Figure 21

- Click Show Quick Access Toolbar Below the Ribbon on the shortcut menu to display the Quick Access Toolbar below the Ribbon (Figure 22).

Figure 22

- Right-click the Quick Access Toolbar to display a shortcut menu (Figure 23).

- Click Show Quick Access Toolbar Above the Ribbon on the shortcut menu to return the Quick Access Toolbar to its original position (shown in Figure 21).

Figure 23

To Customize the Quick Access Toolbar

The Quick Access Toolbar provides easy access to some of the more frequently used commands in Office programs. By default, the Quick Access Toolbar contains buttons for the Save, Undo, and Redo commands. You can customize the Quick Access Toolbar by changing its location in the window, as shown in the previous steps, and by adding more buttons to reflect commands you would like to access easily. The following steps add the Quick Print button to the Quick Access Toolbar.

• Click the Customize Quick Access Toolbar button to display the Customize Quick Access Toolbar menu (Figure 24).

Which commands are listed on the Customize Quick Access Toolbar menu?

It lists commands that commonly are added to the Quick Access Toolbar.

What do the check marks next to some commands signify?

Check marks appear next to commands that already are on the Quick Access Toolbar. When you add a button to the Quick Access Toolbar, a check mark will be displayed next to its command name.

Figure 24

• Click Quick Print on the Customize Quick Access Toolbar menu to add the Quick Print button to the Quick Access Toolbar (Figure 25).

How would I remove a button from the Quick Access Toolbar?

You would right-click the button you wish to remove and then click Remove from Quick Access Toolbar on the shortcut menu.

Figure 25

To Enter Text in a Document

The first step in creating a document is to enter its text by typing on the keyboard. By default, Word positions text at the left margin as you type. To begin creating a flyer, for example, you type the headline in the document window. The following steps type this first line of text, a headline, in a document.

- Type **SEE THE RENOVATED KOALA EXHIBIT** as the text (Figure 26).

Q&A What is the blinking vertical bar to the right of the text?

The insertion point. It indicates where text, graphics, and other items will be inserted in the document. As you type, the insertion point moves to the right, and when you reach the end of a line, it moves downward to the beginning of the next line.

Q&A What if I make an error while typing?

You can press the BACKSPACE key until you have deleted the text in error and then retype the text correctly.

Figure 26

- Press the ENTER key to move the insertion point to the beginning of the next line (Figure 27).

Q&A Why did blank space appear between the entered text and the insertion point?

Each time you press the ENTER key, Word creates a new paragraph and inserts blank space between the two paragraphs.

Figure 27

Saving and Organizing Files

While you are creating a document, the computer stores it in memory. When you save a document, the computer places it on a storage medium such as a hard disk, USB flash drive, or optical disc. A saved document is referred to as a file. A **file name** is the name assigned to a file when it is saved. It is important to save a document frequently for the following reasons:

- The document in memory might be lost if the computer is turned off or you lose electrical power while a program is running.
- If you run out of time before completing a project, you may finish it at a future time without starting over.

When saving files, you should organize them so that you easily can find them later. Windows 7 provides tools to help you organize files.

Organizing Files and Folders

A file contains data. This data can range from a research paper to an accounting spreadsheet to an electronic math quiz. You should organize and store these files in folders to avoid misplacing a file and to help you find a file quickly.

If you are a freshman taking an introductory computer class (CIS 101, for example), you may want to design a series of folders for the different subjects covered in the class. To accomplish this, you can arrange the folders in a hierarchy for the class, as shown in Figure 28.

Figure 28

The hierarchy contains three levels. The first level contains the storage device, in this case a USB flash drive. Windows 7 identifies the storage device with a letter, and, in some cases, a name. In Figure 28, the USB flash drive is identified as REMOVABLE (E:). The second level contains the class folder (CIS 101, in this case), and the third level contains seven folders, one each for a different Office program that will be covered in the class (Word, PowerPoint, Excel, Access, Outlook, Publisher, and OneNote).

When the hierarchy in Figure 28 is created, the USB flash drive is said to contain the CIS 101 folder, and the CIS 101 folder is said to contain the separate Office folders (i.e., Word, PowerPoint, Excel, etc.). In addition, this hierarchy easily can be expanded to include folders from other classes taken during additional semesters.

The vertical and horizontal lines in Figure 28 form a pathway that allows you to navigate to a drive or folder on a computer or network. A **path** consists of a drive letter (preceded by a drive name when necessary) and colon, to identify the storage device, and one or more folder names. Each drive or folder in the hierarchy has a corresponding path.

BTW

File Type
Depending on your Windows 7 settings, the file type .docx may be displayed immediately to the right of the file name after you save the file. The file type .docx is a Word 2010 document.

BTW

Saving Online
Instead of saving files on a USB flash drive, some people prefer to save them online so that they can access the files from any computer with an Internet connection. For more information, read Appendix C.

Table 3 shows examples of paths and their corresponding drives and folders.

Table 3 Paths and Corresponding Drives and Folders	
Path	**Drive and Folder**
Computer ▶ REMOVABLE (E:)	Drive E (REMOVABLE (E:))
Computer ▶ REMOVABLE (E:) ▶ CIS 101	CIS 101 folder on drive E
Computer ▶ REMOVABLE (E:) ▶ CIS 101 ▶ Word	Word folder in CIS 101 folder on drive E

The following pages illustrate the steps to organize the folders for this class and save a file in one of those folders:

1. Create the folder identifying your class.
2. Create the Word folder in the folder identifying your class.
3. Create the remaining folders in the folder identifying your class (one each for PowerPoint, Excel, Access, Outlook, Publisher, and OneNote).
4. Save a file in the Word folder.
5. Verify the location of the saved file.

To Create a Folder

When you create a folder, such as the CIS 101 folder shown in Figure 28 on the previous page, you must name the folder. A folder name should describe the folder and its contents. A folder name can contain spaces and any uppercase or lowercase characters, except a backslash (\), slash (/), colon (:), asterisk (*), question mark (?), quotation marks ("), less than symbol (<), greater than symbol (>), or vertical bar (|). Folder names cannot be CON, AUX, COM1, COM2, COM3, COM4, LPT1, LPT2, LPT3, PRN, or NUL. The same rules for naming folders also apply to naming files.

To store files and folders on a USB flash drive, you must connect the USB flash drive to an available USB port on a computer. The following steps create your class folder (CIS 101, in this case) on a USB flash drive.

- Connect the USB flash drive to an available USB port on the computer to open the AutoPlay window (Figure 29).

Q&A Why does the AutoPlay window not open?

Some computers are not configured to open an AutoPlay window. Instead, they might display the contents of the USB flash drive automatically, or you might need to access contents of the USB flash drive using the Computer window. To use the Computer window to display the USB flash drive's contents, click the Start button, click Computer on the Start menu, and then click the icon representing the USB flash drive.

Figure 29

Q&A Why does the AutoPlay window look different from the one in Figure 29?

The AutoPlay window that opens on your computer might display different options. The type of USB flash drive, its contents, and the next available drive letter on your computer all will determine which options are displayed in the AutoPlay window.

2

• Click the 'Open folder to view files' link in the AutoPlay window to open the USB flash drive window (Figure 30).

Why does Figure 30 show REMOVABLE (E:) for the USB flash drive?

REMOVABLE is the name of the USB flash drive used to illustrate these steps. The (E:) refers to the drive letter assigned by Windows 7 to the USB flash drive. The name and drive letter of your USB flash drive probably will be different.

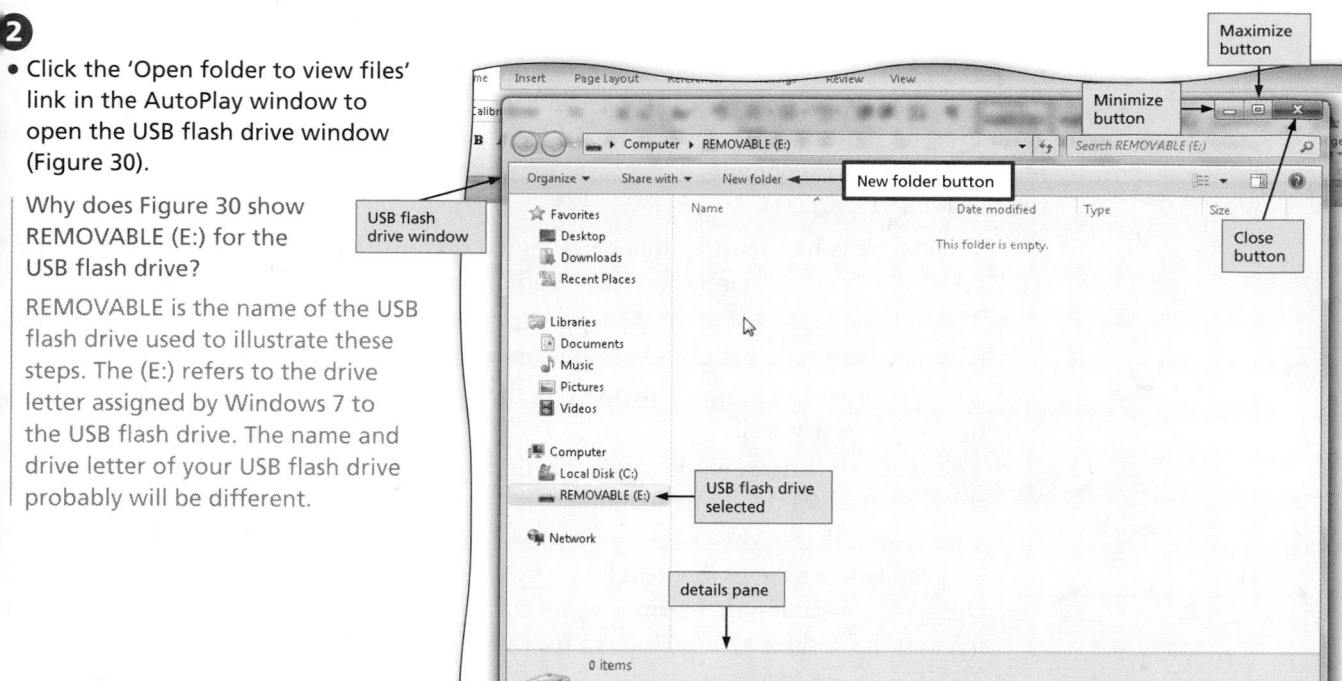

Figure 30

3

• Click the New folder button on the toolbar to display a new folder icon with the name, New folder, selected in a text box.

• Type CIS 101 (or your class code) in the text box to name the folder.

• Press the ENTER key to create a folder identifying your class on the selected drive (Figure 31). If the CIS 101 folder does not appear in the navigation pane, double-click REMOVABLE (E:) in the navigation pane to display the folder just added.

What happens when I press the ENTER key?

The class folder (CIS 101, in this case) is displayed in the File list, which contains the folder name, date modified, type, and size.

Why is the folder icon displayed differently on my computer?

Windows might be configured to display contents differently on your computer.

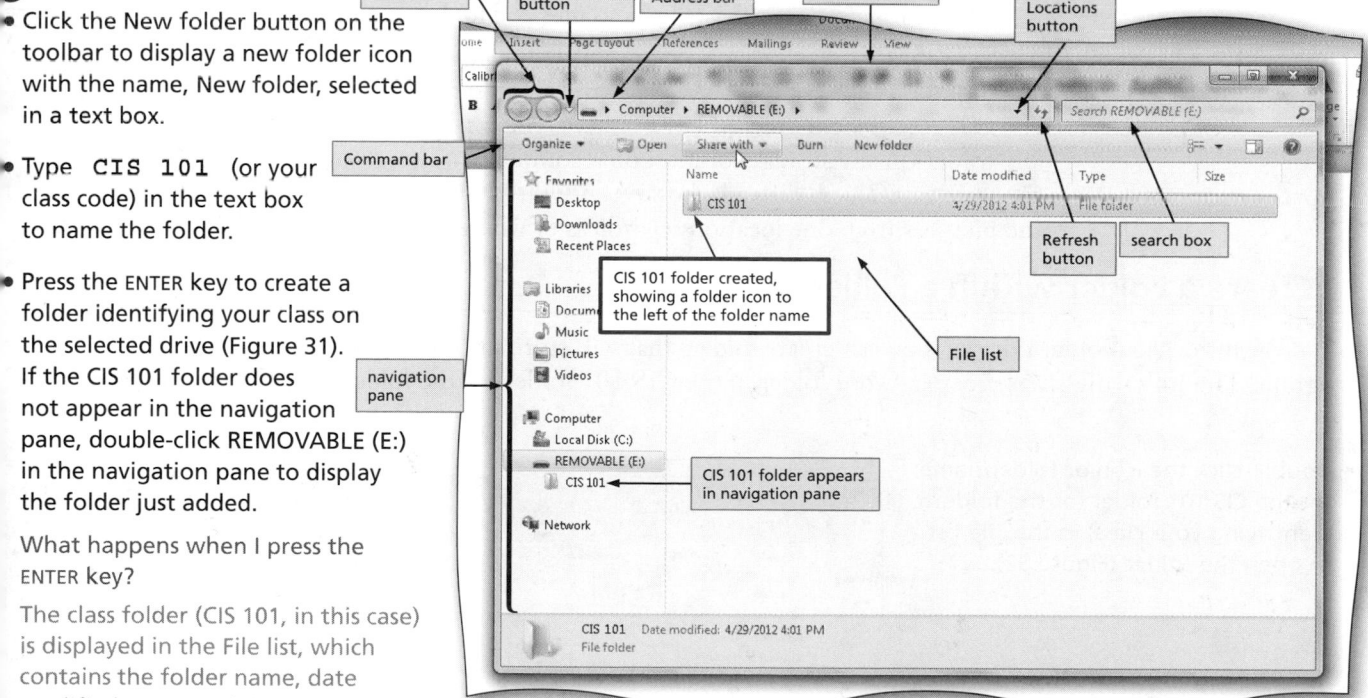

Figure 31

Folder Windows

The USB flash drive window (shown in Figure 31 on the previous page) is called a folder window. Recall that a folder is a specific named location on a storage medium that contains related files. Most users rely on **folder windows** for finding, viewing, and managing information on their computer. Folder windows have common design elements, including the following (Figure 31).

- The **Address bar** provides quick navigation options. The arrows on the Address bar allow you to visit different locations on the computer.
- The buttons to the left of the Address bar allow you to navigate the contents of the left pane and view recent pages. Other buttons allow you to specify the size of the window.
- The **Previous Locations button** saves the locations you have visited and displays the locations when clicked.
- The **Refresh button** on the right side of the Address bar refreshes the contents of the right pane of the folder window.
- The **search box** to the right of the Address bar contains the dimmed word, Search. You can type a term in the search box for a list of files, folders, shortcuts, and elements containing that term within the location you are searching. A **shortcut** is an icon on the desktop that provides a user with immediate access to a program or file.
- The **Command bar** contains five buttons used to accomplish various tasks on the computer related to organizing and managing the contents of the open window.
- The **navigation pane** on the left contains the Favorites area, Libraries area, Computer area, and Network area.
- The **Favorites area** contains links to your favorite locations. By default, this list contains only links to your Desktop, Downloads, and Recent Places.
- The **Libraries area** shows links to files and folders that have been included in a library.

A **library** helps you manage multiple folders and files stored in various locations on a computer. It does not store the files and folders; rather, it displays links to them so that you can access them quickly. For example, you can save pictures from a digital camera in any folder on any storage location on a computer. Normally, this would make organizing the different folders difficult; however, if you add the folders to a library, you can access all the pictures from one location regardless of where they are stored.

To Create a Folder within a Folder

With the class folder created, you can create folders that will store the files you create using each Office program. The following steps create a Word folder in the CIS 101 folder (or the folder identifying your class).

- Double-click the icon or folder name for the CIS 101 folder (or the folder identifying your class) in the File list to open the folder (Figure 32).

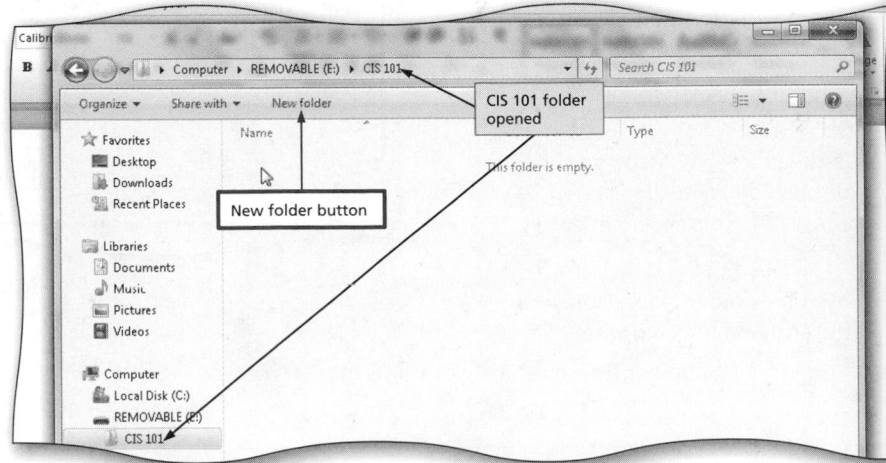

Figure 32

2

- Click the New folder button on the toolbar to display a new folder icon and text box for the folder.

- Type **Word** in the text box to name the folder.

- Press the ENTER key to create the folder (Figure 33).

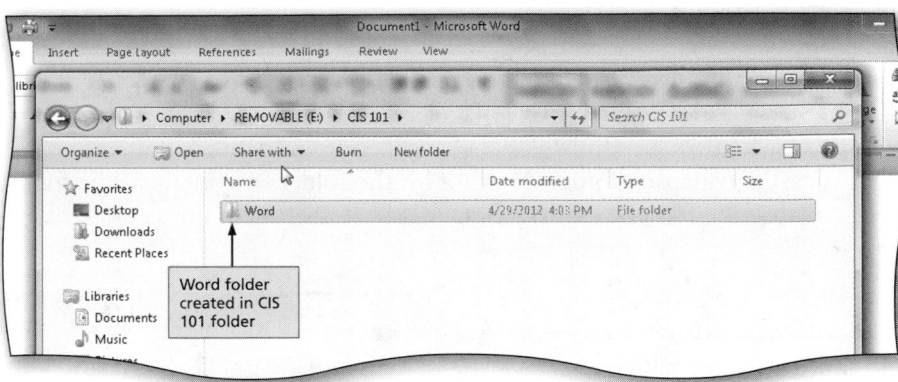

Figure 33

To Create the Remaining Folders

The following steps create the remaining folders in the folder identifying your class (in this case, CIS 101).

1 Click the New folder button on the toolbar to display a new folder icon and text box.

2 Type **PowerPoint** in the text box to name the folder.

3 Repeat Steps 1 and 2 to create each of the remaining folders, using the names Excel, Access, Outlook, Publisher, and OneNote as the folder names (Figure 34).

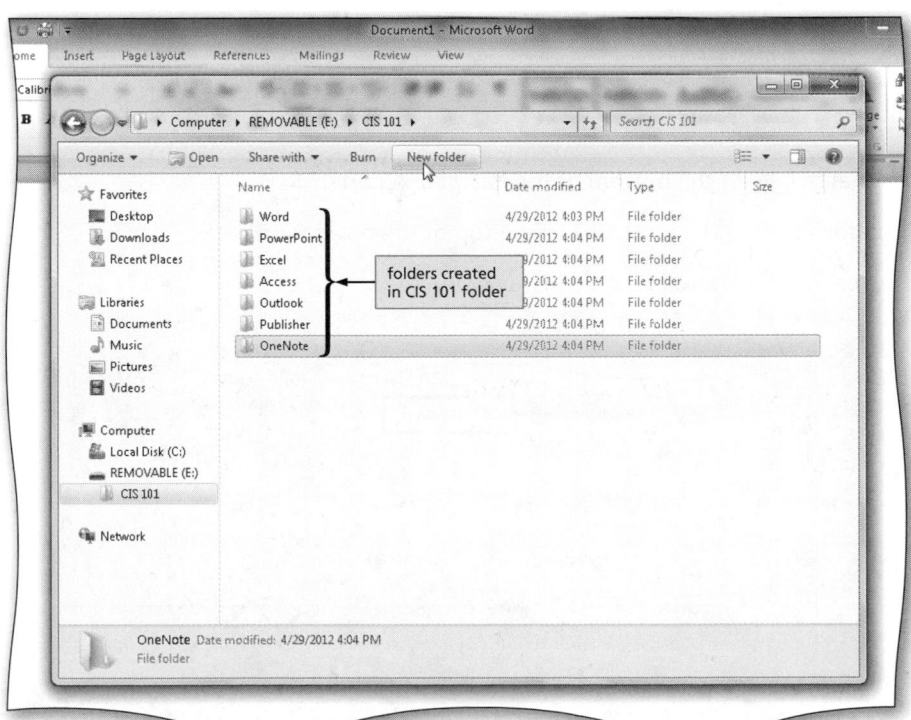

Figure 34

To Expand a Folder, Scroll through Folder Contents, and Collapse a Folder

Folder windows display the hierarchy of items and the contents of drives and folders in the right pane. You might want to expand a drive in the navigation pane to view its contents, scroll through its contents, and collapse it when you are finished viewing its contents. When a folder is expanded, it lists all the folders it contains. By contrast, a collapsed folder does not list the folders it contains. The following steps expand, scroll through, and then collapse the folder identifying your class (CIS 101, in this case).

- Double-click the folder identifying your class (CIS 101, in this case), which expands the folder to display its contents and displays a black arrow to the left of the folder icon (Figure 35).

Q&A
Why are the subject folders indented below the CIS 101 folder in the navigation pane?

It shows that the folders are contained within the CIS 101 folder.

Q&A
Why did a scroll bar appear in the navigation pane?

When all contents cannot fit in a window or pane, a scroll bar appears. As described earlier, you can view areas currently not visible by (1) clicking the scroll arrows, (2) clicking above or below the scroll bar, and (3) dragging the scroll box.

Figure 35

Experiment

- Click the down scroll arrow on the vertical scroll bar to display additional folders at the bottom of the navigation pane.

- Click the scroll bar above the scroll box to move the scroll box to the top of the navigation pane.

- Drag the scroll box down the scroll bar until the scroll box is halfway down the scroll bar.

2

- Double-click the folder identifying your class (CIS 101, in this case) to collapse the folder (Figure 36).

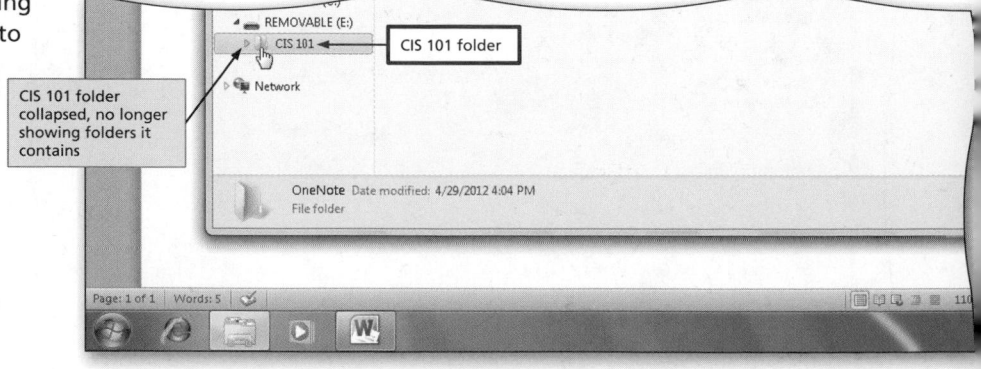

Figure 36

Other Ways
1. Point in navigation pane to display arrows, click white arrow to expand or click black arrow to collapse
2. Select folder to expand or collapse using arrow keys, press RIGHT ARROW to expand; press LEFT ARROW to collapse.

To Switch from One Program to Another

The next step is to save the Word file containing the headline you typed earlier. Word, however, currently is not the active window. You can use the program button on the taskbar and live preview to switch to Word and then save the document in the Word document window.

If Windows Aero is active on your computer, Windows displays a live preview window whenever you move your mouse on a button or click a button on the taskbar. If Aero is not supported or enabled on your computer, you will see a window title instead of a live preview. The steps below use the Word program; however, the steps are the same for any active Office program currently displayed as a program button on the taskbar.

The following steps switch to the Word window.

- Point to the Word program button on the taskbar to see a live preview of the open document(s) or the window title(s) of the open document(s), depending on your computer's configuration (Figure 37).

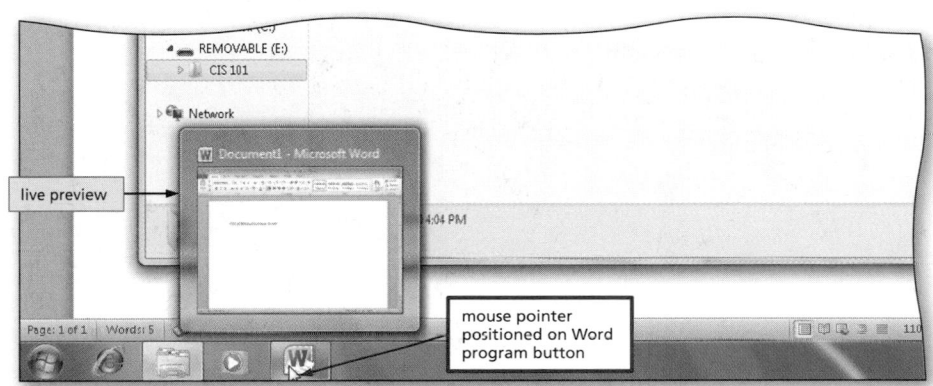

- Click the program button or the live preview to make the program associated with the program button the active window (shown in Figure 27 on page OFF 20).

Figure 37

What If multiple documents are open in a program?

If Aero is enabled on your computer, click the desired live preview. If Aero is not supported or not enabled, click the window title.

To Save a File in a Folder

Now that you have created the folders for storing files, you can save the Word document. The following steps save a file on a USB flash drive in the Word folder contained in your class folder (CIS 101, in this case) using the file name, Koala Exhibit.

- With a USB flash drive connected to one of the computer's USB ports, click the Save button on the Quick Access Toolbar to display the Save As dialog box (Figure 38).

Why does a file name already appear in the File name text box?

Word automatically suggests a file name the first time you save a document. The file name normally consists of the first few words contained in the document. Because the suggested file name is selected, you do not need to delete it; as soon as you begin typing, the new file name replaces the selected text.

Figure 38

2

- Type **Koala Exhibit** in the File name text box (Save As dialog box) to change the file name. Do not press the ENTER key after typing the file name because you do not want to close the dialog box at this time (Figure 39).

Q&A

What characters can I use in a file name?

The only invalid characters are the backslash (\), slash (/), colon (:), asterisk (*), question mark (?), quotation mark ("), less than symbol (<), greater than symbol (>), and vertical bar (|).

Figure 39

3

- Navigate to the desired save location (in this case, the Word folder in the CIS 101 folder [or your class folder] on the USB flash drive) by performing the tasks in Steps 3a, 3b, and 3c.

- If the navigation pane is not displayed in the dialog box, click the Browse Folders button to expand the dialog box.

- If Computer is not displayed in the navigation pane, drag the navigation pane scroll bar until Computer appears.

- If Computer is not expanded in the navigation pane, double-click Computer to display a list of available storage devices in the navigation pane.

- If necessary, scroll through the dialog box until your USB flash drive appears in the list of available storage devices in the navigation pane (Figure 40).

Figure 40

b

• If your USB flash drive is not expanded, double-click the USB flash drive in the list of available storage devices in the navigation pane to select that drive as the new save location and display its contents in the right pane.

c

• If your class folder (CIS 101, in this case) is not expanded, double-click the CIS 101 folder to select the folder and display its contents in the right pane.

What if I do not want to save in a folder?

Although storing files in folders is an effective technique for organizing files, some users prefer not to store files in folders. If you prefer not to save this file in a folder, skip all instructions in Step 3c and proceed to Step 4.

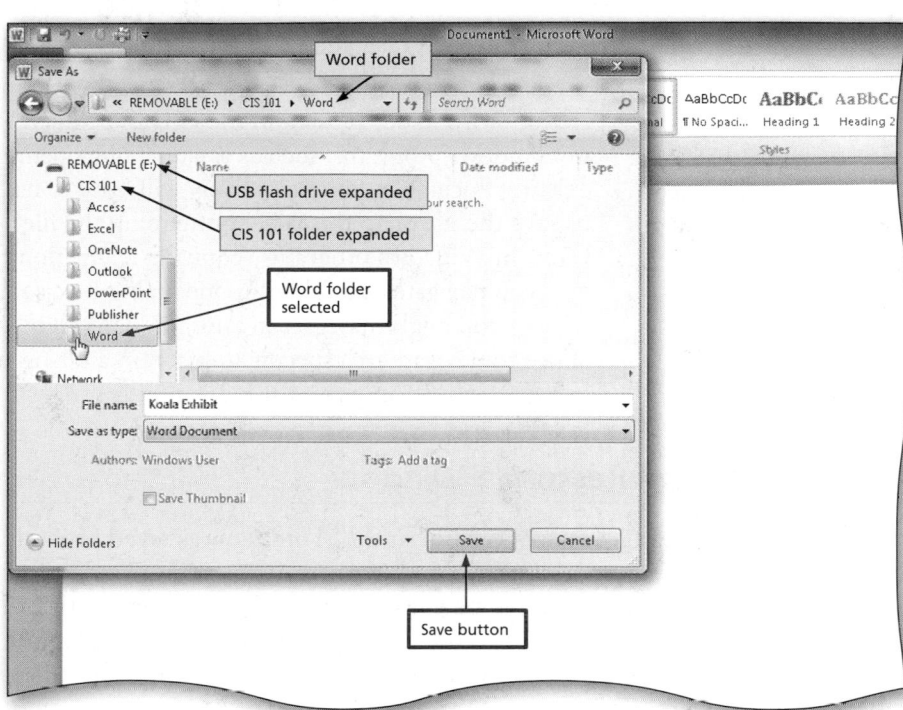

Figure 41

• Click the Word folder to select the folder and display its contents in the right pane (Figure 41).

4

• Click the Save button (Save As dialog box) to save the document in the selected folder on the selected drive with the entered file name (Figure 42).

How do I know that the file is saved?

While an Office program is saving a file, it briefly displays a message on the status bar indicating the amount of the file saved. In addition, the USB flash drive may have a light that flashes during the save process.

Figure 42

Other Ways
1. Click File on Ribbon, click Save, type file name, navigate to desired save location, click Save button   2. Press CTRL+S or press SHIFT+F12, type file name, navigate to desired save location, click Save button

Navigating in Dialog Boxes

Navigating is the process of finding a location on a storage device. While saving the Koala Exhibit file, for example, Steps 3a – 3c in the previous set of steps navigated to the Word folder located in the CIS 101 folder. When performing certain functions in Windows programs, such as saving a file, opening a file, or inserting a picture in an existing document, you most likely will have to navigate to the location where you want to save the file or to the folder containing the file you want to open or insert. Most dialog boxes in Windows programs requiring navigation follow a similar procedure; that is, the way you navigate to a folder in one dialog box, such as the Save As dialog box, is similar to how you might navigate in another dialog box, such as the Open dialog box. If you chose to navigate to a specific location in a dialog box, you would follow the instructions in Steps 3a – 3c on pages OFF 28 and OFF 29.

To Minimize and Restore a Window

Before continuing, you can verify that the Word file was saved properly. To do this, you will minimize the Word window and then open the USB flash drive window so that you can verify the file is stored on the USB flash drive. A **minimized window** is an open window hidden from view but that can be displayed quickly by clicking the window's program button on the taskbar.

In the following example, Word is used to illustrate minimizing and restoring windows; however, you would follow the same steps regardless of the Office program you are using.

The following steps minimize the Word window, verify that the file is saved, and then restore the minimized window.

1

- Click the Minimize button on the program's title bar (shown in Figure 42 on the previous page) to minimize the window (Figure 43).

Q&A

Is the minimized window still available?

The minimized window, Word in this case, remains available but no longer is the active window. It is minimized as a program button on the taskbar.

- If necessary, click the Windows Explorer program button on the taskbar to open the USB flash drive window.

Figure 43

2

- Double-click the Word folder to select the folder and display its contents (Figure 44).

Figure 44

Why does the Windows Explorer button on the taskbar change?

The button changes to reflect the status of the folder window (in this case, the USB flash drive window). A selected button indicates that the folder window is active on the screen. When the button is not selected, the window is open but not active.

3

- After viewing the contents of the selected folder, click the Word program button on the taskbar to restore the minimized window (as shown in Figure 42 on page OFF 29).

Other Ways	
1. Right-click title bar, click Minimize on shortcut menu, click taskbar button in taskbar button area	2. Press WINDOWS+M, press WINDOWS+SHIFT+M

Screen Resolution

Screen resolution indicates the number of pixels (dots) that the computer uses to display the letters, numbers, graphics, and background you see on the screen. When you increase the screen resolution, Windows displays more information on the screen, but the information decreases in size. The reverse also is true: as you decrease the screen resolution, Windows displays less information on the screen, but the information increases in size.

Screen resolution usually is stated as the product of two numbers, such as 1024 × 768 (pronounced "ten twenty-four by seven sixty-eight"). A 1024 × 768 screen resolution results in a display of 1,024 distinct pixels on each of 768 lines, or about

786,432 pixels. Changing the screen resolution affects how the Ribbon appears in Office programs. Figure 45 shows the Word Ribbon at screen resolutions of 1024×768 and 1280×800. All of the same commands are available regardless of screen resolution. Word, however, makes changes to the groups and the buttons within the groups to accommodate the various screen resolutions. The result is that certain commands may need to be accessed differently depending on the resolution chosen. A command that is visible on the Ribbon and available by clicking a button at one resolution may not be visible and may need to be accessed using its Dialog Box Launcher at a different resolution.

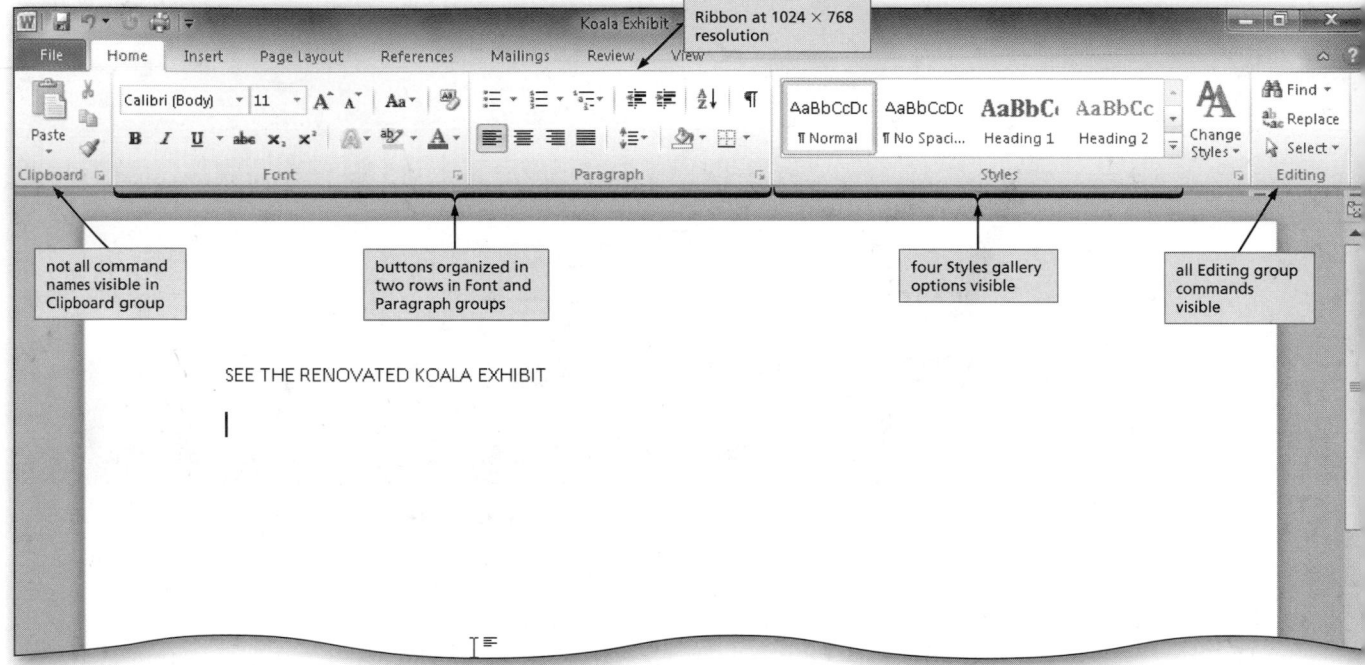

Figure 45 (a) Ribbon at Resolution of 1024 x 768

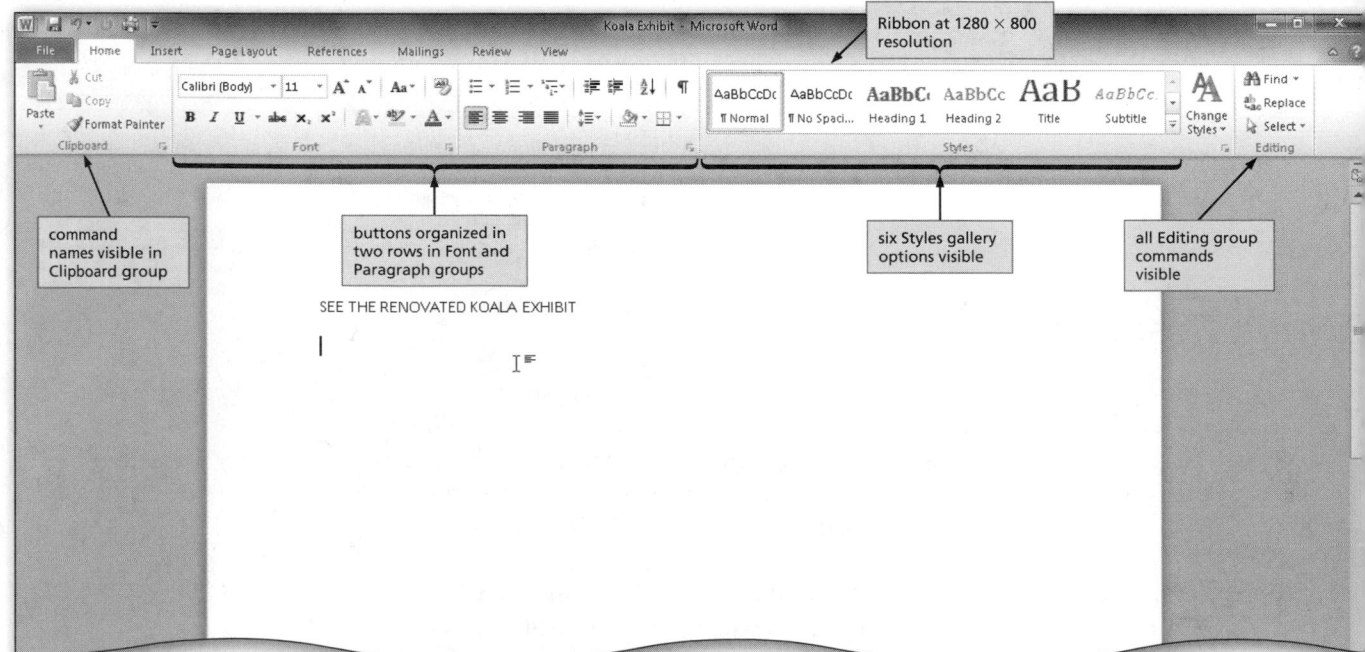

Figure 45 (b) Ribbon at Resolution of 1280 x 800

Comparing the two Ribbons in Figure 45, notice the changes in content and layout of the groups and galleries. In some cases, the content of a group is the same in each resolution, but the layout of the group differs. For example, the same gallery and buttons appear in the Styles groups in the two resolutions, but the layouts differ. In other cases, the content and layout are the same across the resolution, but the level of detail differs with the resolution. In the Clipboard group, when the resolution increases to 1280×800, the names of all the buttons in the group appear in addition to the buttons themselves. At the lower resolution, only the buttons appear.

To Change the Screen Resolution

If you are using a computer to step through the chapters in this book and you want your screen to match the figures, you may need to change your screen's resolution. The figures in this book use a screen resolution of 1024×768. The following steps change the screen resolution to 1024×768. Your computer already may be set to 1024×768 or some other resolution. Keep in mind that many computer labs prevent users from changing the screen resolution; in that case, read the following steps for illustration purposes.

1

- Click the Show desktop button on the taskbar to display the Windows 7 desktop.

- Right-click an empty area on the Windows 7 desktop to display a shortcut menu that displays a list of commands related to the desktop (Figure 46).

Why does my shortcut menu display different commands?

Depending on your computer's hardware and configuration, different commands might appear on the shortcut menu.

Figure 46

- Click Screen resolution on the shortcut menu to open the Screen Resolution window (Figure 47).

Figure 47

- Click the Resolution button in the Screen Resolution window to display the resolution slider.

Q&A

What is a slider?

A **slider** is an object that allows users to choose from multiple predetermined options. In most cases, these options represent some type of numeric value. In most cases, one end of the slider (usually the left or bottom) represents the lowest of available values, and the opposite end (usually the right or top) represents the highest available value.

- If necessary, drag the resolution slider until the desired screen resolution (in this case, 1024 × 768) is selected (Figure 48).

Q&A

What if my computer does not support the 1024 × 768 resolution?

Figure 48

Some computers do not support the 1024 × 768 resolution. In this case, select a resolution that is close to the 1024 × 768 resolution.

5

- Click an empty area of the Screen Resolution window to close the resolution slider.

- Click the OK button to change the screen resolution and display the Display Settings dialog box (Figure 49).

- Click the Keep changes button (Display Settings dialog box) to accept the new screen resolution.

Why does a message display stating that the image quality can be improved?

Some computer monitors are designed to display contents better at a certain screen resolution, sometimes referred to as an optimal resolution.

Figure 49

To Quit an Office Program with One Document Open

When you quit an Office program, such as Word, if you have made changes to a file since the last time the file was saved, the Office program displays a dialog box asking if you want save the changes you made to the file before it closes the program window. The dialog box contains three buttons with these resulting actions: the Save button saves the changes and then quits the Office program, the Don't Save button quits the Office program without saving changes, and the Cancel button closes the dialog box and redisplays the file without saving the changes.

If no changes have been made to an open document since the last time the file was saved, the Office program will close the window without displaying a dialog box.

The following steps quit an Office program. In the following example, Word is used to illustrate quitting an Office program; however, you would follow the same steps regardless of the Office program you were using.

1

- If necessary, click the Word program button on the taskbar to display the Word window on the desktop.

- Point to the Close button on the right side of the program's title bar, Word in this case (Figure 50).

Figure 50

2

- Click the Close button to close the document and quit Word.

What if I have more than one document open in an Office program?

You would click the Close button for each open document. When you click the last open document's Close button, the Office program also quits. As an alternative, you could click File on the Ribbon to open the Backstage view and then click Exit in the Backstage view to close all open documents and quit the Office program.

What is the Backstage view?

The **Backstage view** contains a set of commands that enable you to manage documents and data about the documents. The Backstage view is discussed in more depth later in this chapter.

3

- If a Microsoft Word dialog box appears, click the Save button to save any changes made to the document since the last save.

Other Ways
1. Right-click the Office program button on Windows 7 taskbar, click Close window or 'Close all windows' on shortcut menu
2. Press ALT + F4

Break Point: If you wish to take a break, this is a good place to do so. To resume at a later time, continue to follow the steps from this location forward.

Additional Microsoft Office Programs

The previous section used Word to illustrate common features of Office and some basic elements unique to Word. The following sections present elements unique to PowerPoint, Excel, and Access, as well as illustrate additional common features of Office.

In the following pages, you will learn how to do the following:

1. Start an Office program (PowerPoint) using the search box.
2. Create two small documents in the same Office program (PowerPoint).
3. Close one of the documents.
4. Reopen the document just closed.
5. Create a document in a different Office program (Excel).
6. Save the document with a new file name.
7. Create a file in a different Office program (Access).
8. Close the file and then open the file.

PowerPoint

PowerPoint is a complete presentation program that allows you to produce professional-looking presentations (Figure 51). A PowerPoint **presentation** also is called a **slide show**. PowerPoint contains several features to simplify creating a slide show. To make presentations more impressive, you can add diagrams, tables, pictures, video, sound, and animation effects. Additional PowerPoint features include the following:

- **Word processing** — Create bulleted lists, combine words and images, find and replace text, and use multiple fonts and font sizes.
- **Outlining** — Develop a presentation using an outline format. You also can import outlines from Microsoft Word or other word processing programs, including single-level and multilevel lists.
- **Charting** — Create and insert charts into presentations and then add effects and chart elements.
- **Drawing** — Create and modify diagrams using shapes such as arcs, arrows, cubes, rectangles, stars, and triangles. Then, customize and add effects to the diagrams, and arrange these objects by sizing, scaling, and rotating them.
- **Inserting multimedia** — Insert artwork and multimedia effects into a slide show. The Microsoft Clip Organizer, included with Office programs, contains hundreds of media files, including pictures, sounds, and movies.
- **Saving to the Web** — Save presentations or parts of a presentation so that they can be viewed in a Web browser. You can publish your slide show to the Internet or to an intranet.
- **E-mailing** — Send an entire slide show as an attachment to an e-mail message.
- **Collaborating** — Share a presentation with friends and coworkers. Ask them to review the slides and then insert comments that offer suggestions to enhance the presentation.
- **Preparing delivery** — Rehearse integrating PowerPoint slides into your speech by setting timings, using presentation tools, showing only selected slides in a presentation, and packaging the presentation for an optical disc.

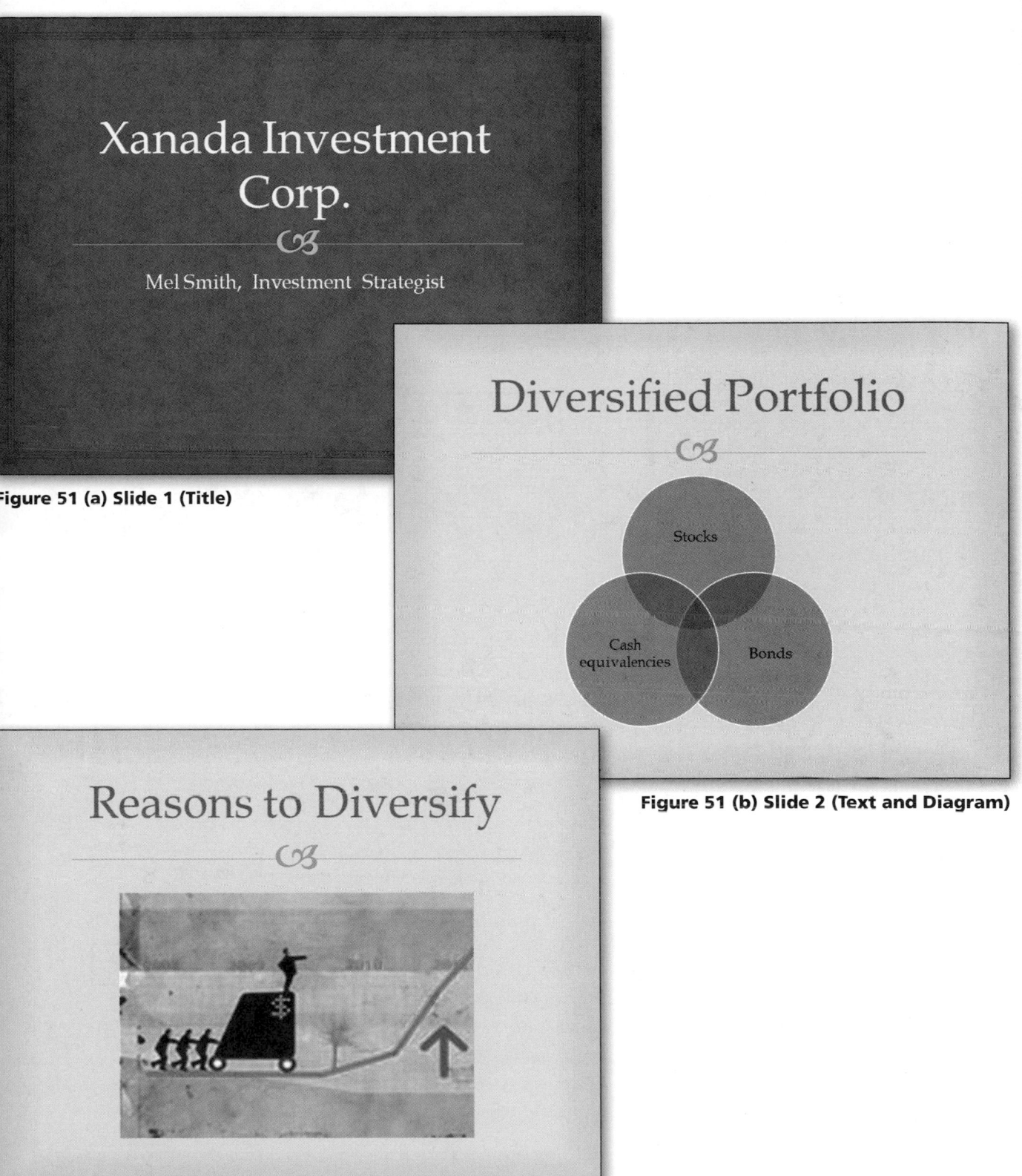

Figure 51 (a) Slide 1 (Title)

Figure 51 (b) Slide 2 (Text and Diagram)

Figure 51 (c) Slide 3 (Text and Picture)

To Start a Program Using the Search Box

The steps on the next page, which assume Windows 7 is running, use the search box to start the PowerPoint Office program based on a typical installation; however, you would follow similar steps to start any Office program. You may need to ask your instructor how to start programs for your computer.

- Click the Start button on the Windows 7 taskbar to display the Start menu.

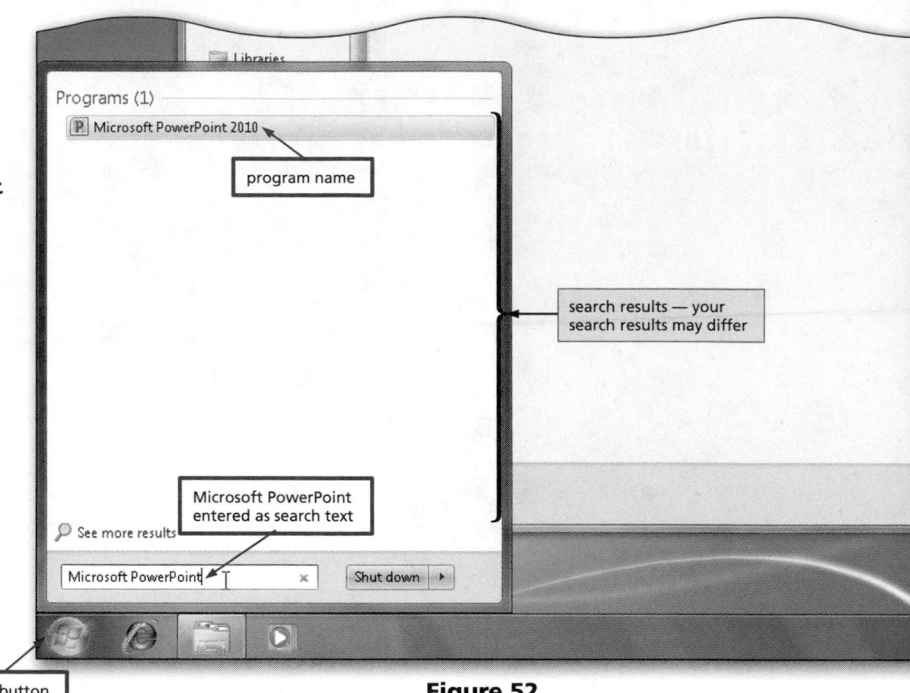

- Type **Microsoft PowerPoint** as the search text in the 'Search programs and files' text box and watch the search results appear on the Start menu (Figure 52).

Q&A
Do I need to type the complete program name or correct capitalization?

No, just enough of it for the program name to appear on the Start menu. For example, you may be able to type PowerPoint or powerpoint, instead of Microsoft PowerPoint.

Figure 52

- Click the program name, Microsoft PowerPoint 2010 in this case, in the search results on the Start menu to start PowerPoint and display a new blank presentation in the PowerPoint window.

- If the program window is not maximized, click the Maximize button on its title bar to maximize the window (Figure 53).

Figure 53

The PowerPoint Window and Ribbon

The PowerPoint window consists of a variety of components to make your work more efficient and documents more professional: the window, Ribbon, Mini toolbar, shortcut menus, and Quick Access Toolbar. Many of these components are common to other Office programs and have been discussed earlier in this chapter. Other components, discussed in the following paragraphs and later in subsequent chapters, are unique to PowerPoint.

The basic unit of a PowerPoint presentation is a **slide**. A slide may contain text and objects, such as graphics, tables, charts, and drawings. **Layouts** are used to position this content on the slide. When you create a new presentation, the default **Title Slide** layout appears (Figure 54). The purpose of this layout is to introduce the presentation to the audience. PowerPoint includes eight other built-in standard layouts.

The default slide layouts are set up in **landscape orientation**, where the slide width is greater than its height. In landscape orientation, the slide size is preset to 10 inches wide and 7.5 inches high when printed on a standard sheet of paper measuring 11 inches wide and 8.5 inches high.

BTW

Portrait Orientation
If your slide content is dominantly vertical, such as a skyscraper or a person, consider changing the slide layout to a portrait orientation. To change the orientation to portrait, click the Slide Orientation button (Design tab | Page Setup group) and then click Portrait. You can use both landscape and portrait orientation in the same slide show.

Figure 54

Placeholders **Placeholders** are boxes with dotted or hatch-marked borders that are displayed when you create a new slide. All layouts except the Blank slide layout contain placeholders. Depending on the particular slide layout selected, title and subtitle placeholders are displayed for the slide title and subtitle; a content text placeholder is displayed for text, art, or a table, chart, picture, graphic, or movie. The title slide in Figure 53 has two text placeholders for the main heading, or title, of a new slide and the subtitle.

Ribbon   The Ribbon in PowerPoint is similar to the one in Word and the other Microsoft Office programs. When you start PowerPoint, the Ribbon displays nine main tabs: File, Home, Insert, Design, Transitions, Animations, Slide Show, Review, and View.

To Enter Content in a Title Slide

With the exception of a blank slide and a slide with a picture and caption, PowerPoint assumes every new slide has a title. Many of PowerPoint's layouts have both a title text placeholder and at least one content placeholder. To make creating a presentation easier, any text you type after a new slide appears becomes title text in the title text placeholder. As you begin typing text in the title text placeholder, the title text also is displayed in the Slide 1 thumbnail in the Slides tab. The presentation title for this presentation is Xanada Investments. The following steps enter a presentation title on the title slide.

- Click the label 'Click to add title' located inside the title text placeholder (shown in Figure 53 on page OFF 38) to select the placeholder (Figure 55).

Figure 55

- Type **Xanada Investments** in the title text placeholder. Do not press the ENTER key because you do not want to create a new line of text (Figure 56).

What are the white squares and circles that appear around the title text placeholder as I type the presentation title?

The white squares and circles are sizing handles, which you can drag to change the size of the title text placeholder. Sizing handles also can be found around other placeholders and objects within a presentation.

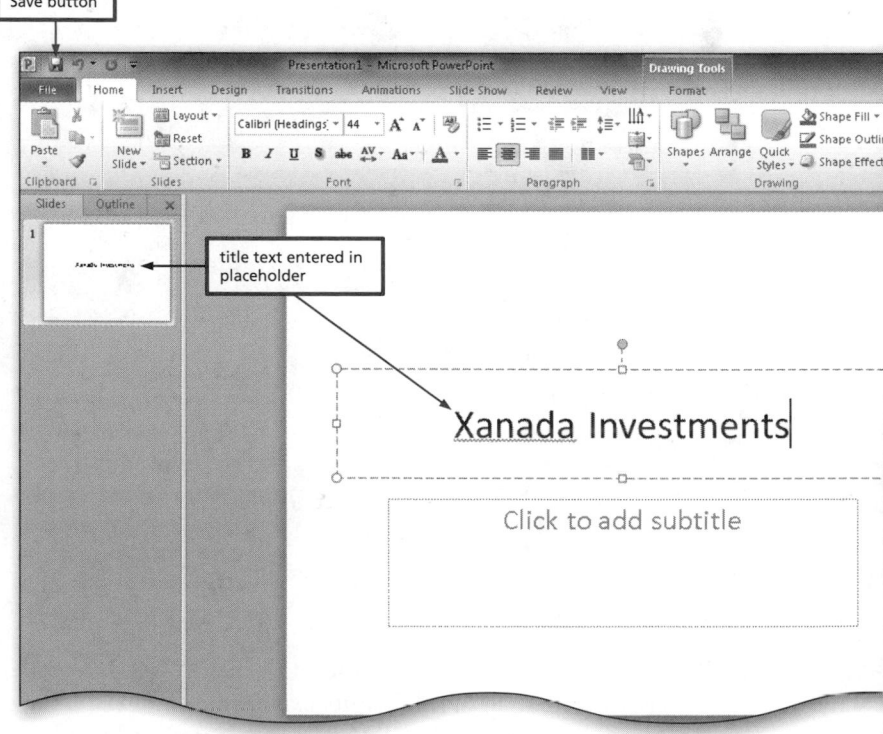

Figure 56

To Save a File in a Folder

The following steps save the presentation in the PowerPoint folder in the class folder (CIS 101, in this case) on a USB flash drive using the file name, Xanada Investments.

1 With a USB flash drive connected to one of the computer's USB ports, click the Save button on the Quick Access Toolbar to display the Save As dialog box.

2 If necessary, type `Xanada Investments` in the File name text box to change the file name. Do not press the ENTER key after typing the file name because you do not want to close the dialog box at this time.

3 Navigate to the desired save location (in this case, the PowerPoint folder in the CIS 101 folder [or your class folder] on the USB flash drive). For specific instructions, perform the tasks in Steps 3a through 3g.

3a If a navigation pane is not displayed in the Save As dialog box, click the Browse Folders button to expand the dialog box.

3b If Computer is not displayed in the navigation pane, drag the navigation pane scroll bar (Save As dialog box) until Computer appears.

3c If Computer is not expanded in the navigation pane, double-click Computer to display a list of available storage devices in the navigation pane.

3d If necessary, scroll through the Save As dialog box until your USB flash drive appears in the list of available storage devices in the navigation pane.

3e If your USB flash drive is not expanded, double-click the USB flash drive in the list of available storage devices in the navigation pane to select that drive as the new save location and display its contents in the right pane.

3f If your class folder (CIS 101, in this case) is not expanded, double-click the CIS 101 folder to select the folder and display its contents.

3g Click the PowerPoint folder to select it as the new save location and display its contents in the right pane.

4 Click the Save button (Save As dialog box) to save the presentation in the selected folder on the selected drive with the entered file name.

To Create a New Office Document from the Backstage View

As discussed earlier, the Backstage view contains a set of commands that enable you to manage documents and data about the documents. From the Backstage view in PowerPoint, for example, you can create, open, print, and save presentations. You also can share documents, manage versions, set permissions, and modify document properties. In other Office 2010 programs, the Backstage view may contain features specific to those programs. The steps on the following pages create a file, a blank presentation in this case, from the Backstage view.

1

- Click File on the Ribbon to open the Backstage view (Figure 57).

Q&A

What is the purpose of the File tab?

The **File** tab is used to display the Backstage view for each Office program.

Figure 57

2

- Click the New tab in the Backstage view to display the New gallery (Figure 58).

Q&A

Can I create documents through the Backstage view in other Office programs?

Yes. If the Office program has a New tab in the Backstage view, the New gallery displays various options for creating a new file.

Figure 58

3
- Click the Create button in the New gallery to create a new presentation (Figure 59).

Figure 59

To Enter Content in a Title Slide of a Second PowerPoint Presentation

The presentation title for this presentation is Koala Exhibit Gala. The following steps enter a presentation title on the title slide.

1 Click the title text placeholder (shown in Figure 59) to select it.

2 Type **Koala Exhibit Gala** in the title text placeholder. Do not press the ENTER key (Figure 60).

Figure 60

To Save a File in a Folder

The following steps save the second presentation in the PowerPoint folder in the class folder (CIS 101, in this case) on a USB flash drive using the file name, Koala Exhibit Gala.

1 With a USB flash drive connected to one of the computer's USB ports, click the Save button on the Quick Access Toolbar to display the Save As dialog box.

2 If necessary, type **Koala Exhibit Gala** in the File name text box to change the file name. Do not press the ENTER key after typing the file name because you do not want to close the dialog box at this time.

3 If necessary, navigate to the desired save location (in this case, the PowerPoint folder in the CIS 101 folder [or your class folder] on the USB flash drive).

4 Click the Save button (Save As dialog box) to save the presentation in the selected folder on the selected drive with the entered file name.

To Close an Office File Using the Backstage View

Sometimes, you may want to close an Office file, such as a PowerPoint presentation, entirely and start over with a new file. You also may want to close a file when you are finished working with it so that you can begin a new file. The following steps close the current active Office file, that is, the Koala Exhibit Gala presentation, without quitting the active program (PowerPoint in this case).

- Click File on the Ribbon to open the Backstage view (Figure 61).

- Click Close in the Backstage view to close the open file (Koala Exhibit Gala, in this case) without quitting the active program.

Q&A What if the Office program displays a dialog box about saving?

Click the Save button if you want to save the changes, click the Don't Save button if you want to ignore the changes since the last time you saved, and click the Cancel button if you do not want to close the document.

Q&A Can I use the Backstage view to close an open file in other Office programs, such as Word and Excel?

Yes.

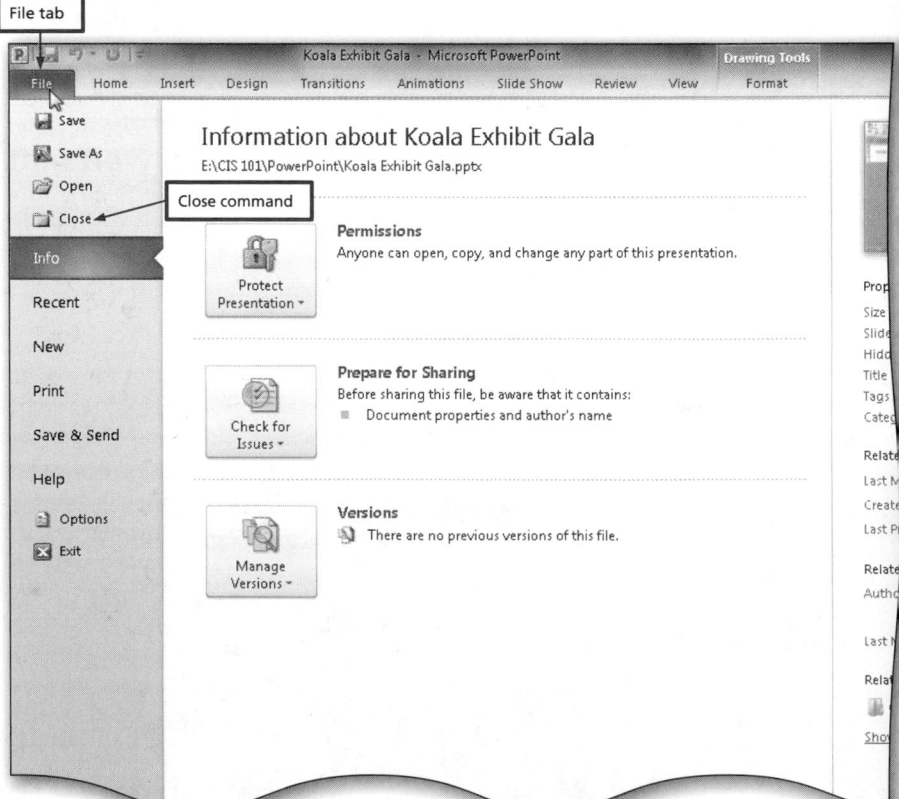

Figure 61

To Open a Recent Office File Using the Backstage View

You sometimes need to open a file that you recently modified. You may have more changes to make such as adding more content or correcting errors. The Backstage view allows you to access recent files easily. The following steps reopen the Koala Exhibit Gala file just closed.

1
- Click File on the Ribbon to open the Backstage view.

- Click the Recent tab in the Backstage view to display the Recent gallery (Figure 62).

2
- Click the desired file name in the Recent gallery, Koala Exhibit Gala in this case, to open the file (shown in Figure 60 on page OFF 43).

Can I use the Backstage view to open a recent file in other Office programs, such as Word and Excel?

Yes, as long as the file name appears in the list of recent files in the Recent gallery.

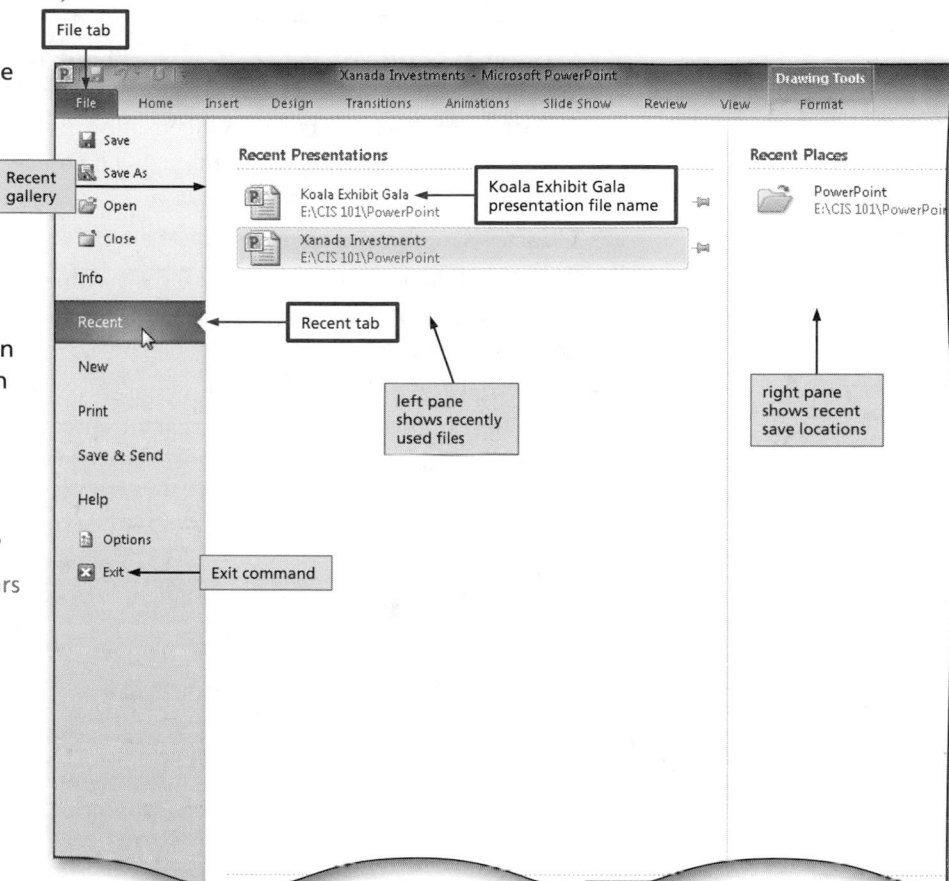

Figure 62

Other Ways

1. Click Start button, point to program name, click file name on submenu

2. Click File on Ribbon, click Open in Backstage view, navigate to file (Open dialog box), click Open button

To Quit an Office Program

You are finished using PowerPoint. Thus, you should quit this Office program. The following steps quit PowerPoint.

1 If you have one Office document open, click the Close button on the right side of the title bar to close the document and quit the Office program; or if you have multiple Office documents open, click File on the Ribbon to open the Backstage view and then click Exit in the Backstage view to close all open documents and quit the Office program.

2 If a dialog box appears, click the Save button to save any changes made to the document since the last save.

Excel

Excel is a powerful spreadsheet program that allows users to organize data, complete calculations, make decisions, graph data, develop professional-looking reports (Figure 63), publish organized data to the Web, and access real-time data from Web sites. The four major parts of Excel are:

- **Workbooks and Worksheets** - A **workbook** is like a notebook. Inside the workbook are sheets, each of which is called a **worksheet**. In other words, a workbook is a collection of worksheets. Worksheets allow users to enter, calculate, manipulate, and analyze data such as numbers and text. The terms worksheet and spreadsheet are interchangeable.

- **Charts** - Excel can draw a variety of charts.

- **Tables** - Tables organize and store data within worksheets. For example, once a user enters data into a worksheet, an Excel table can sort the data, search for specific data, and select data that satisfies defined criteria.

- **Web Support -** Web support allows users to save Excel worksheets or parts of a worksheet in HTML format, so that a user can view and manipulate the worksheet using a browser. Excel Web support also provides access to real-time data, such as stock quotes, using Web queries.

Figure 63

To Create a New Blank Office Document from Windows Explorer

Windows Explorer provides a means to create a blank Office document without ever starting an Office program. The following steps use Windows Explorer to create a blank Excel document.

①

- If necessary, click the Windows Explorer program button on the taskbar to make the folder window the active window in Windows Explorer.

- Double-click your class folder (CIS 101, in this case) in the navigation pane to display the contents of the selected folder.

- Double-click the Excel folder to display its contents in the right pane.

- With the Excel folder selected, right-click an open area in the right pane to display a shortcut menu.

- Point to New on the shortcut menu to display the New submenu (Figure 64).

Figure 64

②

- Click Microsoft Excel Worksheet on the New submenu to display an icon and text box for a new file in the current folder window (Figure 65).

③

- Type **Brain Busters** in the text box and then press the ENTER key to assign a name to the new file in the current folder (Figure 66).

Figure 65

Figure 66

To Start a Program from Windows Explorer and Open a File

Previously, you learned how to start an Office program using the Start menu and the search box. Another way start an Office program is to open an existing file from Windows Explorer, which causes the program in which the file was created to start and then open the selected file. The following steps, which assume Windows 7 is running, use Windows Explorer to start the Excel Office program based on a typical installation. You may need to ask your instructor how to start Office programs for your computer.

- If necessary, display the file to open in the folder window in Windows Explorer (shown in Figure 66 on the previous page).

- Right-click the file icon or file name (Brain Busters, in this case) to display a shortcut menu (Figure 67).

Figure 67

2

- Click Open on the shortcut menu to open the selected file in the program used to create the file, Microsoft Excel in this case (Figure 68).

- If the program window is not maximized, click the Maximize button on the title bar to maximize the window.

- For Excel users, if the worksheet window in Excel is not maximized, click the worksheet window Maximize button to maximize the worksheet window within Excel.

Figure 68

Q&A

Instead of using Windows Explorer, can I start Excel using the same method shown previously for Word and PowerPoint?

Yes, you can use any method of starting an Office program to start Excel.

Unique Features of Excel

The Excel window consists of a variety of components to make your work more efficient and worksheets more professional. These include the document window, Ribbon, Mini toolbar and shortcut menus, Quick Access Toolbar, and the Backstage view. Some of these components are common to other Microsoft Office 2010 programs; others are unique to Excel.

Excel opens a new workbook with three worksheets. If necessary, you can add additional worksheets as long as your computer has enough memory to accommodate them.

Each worksheet has a sheet name that appears on a **sheet tab** at the bottom of the workbook. For example, Sheet1 is the name of the active worksheet displayed in the Brain Busters workbook. If you click the sheet tab labeled Sheet2, Excel displays the Sheet2 worksheet.

The Worksheet   The worksheet is organized into a rectangular grid containing vertical columns and horizontal rows. A column letter above the grid, also called the **column heading**, identifies each column. A row number on the left side of the grid, also called the **row heading**, identifies each row. With the screen resolution set to 1024 × 768 and the Excel window maximized, Excel displays 15 columns (A through O) and 25 rows (1 through 25) of the worksheet on the screen, as shown in Figure 68.

The intersection of each column and row is a cell. A **cell** is the basic unit of a worksheet into which you enter data. Each worksheet in a workbook has 16,384 columns and 1,048,576 rows for a total of 17,179,869,180 cells. Only a small fraction of the active worksheet appears on the screen at one time.

A cell is referred to by its unique address, or **cell reference**, which is the coordinates of the intersection of a column and a row. To identify a cell, specify the column letter first, followed by the row number. For example, cell reference E2 refers to the cell located at the intersection of column E and row 2 (Figure 68).

One cell on the worksheet, designated the **active cell**, is the one into which you can enter data. The active cell in Figure 68 is A1. The active cell is identified in three ways. First, a heavy border surrounds the cell; second, the active cell reference shows immediately above column A in the Name box; and third, the column heading A and row heading 1 are highlighted so it is easy to see which cell is active (Figure 68).

The horizontal and vertical lines on the worksheet itself are called **gridlines**. Gridlines make it easier to see and identify each cell in the worksheet. If desired, you can turn the gridlines off so that they do not show on the worksheet, but it is recommended that you leave them on for now.

The mouse pointer in Figure 68 has the shape of a block plus sign. The mouse pointer appears as a block plus sign whenever it is located in a cell on the worksheet. Another common shape of the mouse pointer is the block arrow. The mouse pointer turns into the block arrow when you move it outside the worksheet or when you drag cell contents between rows or columns. The other mouse pointer shapes are described when they appear on the screen.

Ribbon   When you start Excel, the Ribbon displays eight main tabs: File, Home, Insert, Page Layout, Formulas, Data, Review, and View. The Formulas and Data tabs are specific to Excel. The Formulas tab allows you to work with Excel formulas, and the Data tab allows you to work with data processing features such as importing and sorting data.

BTW

The Worksheet Size and Window
The 16,384 columns and 1,048,576 rows in Excel make for a huge worksheet that – if you could imagine – takes up the entire side of a building to display in its entirety. Your computer screen, by comparison, is a small window that allows you to view only a minute area of the worksheet at one time. While you cannot see the entire worksheet, you can move the window over the worksheet to view any part of it.

BTW

Customizing the Ribbon
In addition to customizing the Quick Access Toolbar, you can add items to and remove items from the Ribbon. To customize the Ribbon, click File on the Ribbon to open the Backstage view, click Options in the Backstage view, and then click Customize Ribbon in the left pane of the Options dialog box. More information about customizing the Ribbon is presented in a later chapter.

Formula Bar The formula bar appears below the Ribbon (Figure 69). As you type, Exce displays the entry in the **formula bar**. You can make the formula bar larger by dragging the sizing handle at the bottom of the formula bar or clicking the expand button to the right of the formula bar. Excel also displays the active cell reference in the **Name box** on the left side of the formula bar.

Figure 69

To Enter a Worksheet Title

To enter data into a cell, you first must select it. The easiest way to select a cell (make it active) is to use the mouse to move the block plus sign mouse pointer to the cell and then click. An alternative method is to use the arrow keys that are located just to the right of the typewriter keys on the keyboard. An arrow key selects the cell adjacent to the active cell in the direction of the arrow on the key.

In Excel, any set of characters containing a letter, hyphen (as in a telephone number), or space is considered text. **Text** is used to place titles, such as worksheet titles, column titles, and row titles, on the worksheet. The following steps enter the worksheet title in cell A1.

- If it is not already the active cell, click cell A1 to make it the active cell (Figure 70).

Figure 70

2

• Type **Brain Buster Book Rentals** in cell A1 (Figure 71).

Why did the appearance of the formula bar change?

Excel displays the title in the formula bar and in cell A1. When you begin typing a cell entry, Excel displays two additional boxes in the formula bar: the Cancel box and the Enter box. Clicking the Enter box completes an entry. Clicking the Cancel box cancels an entry.

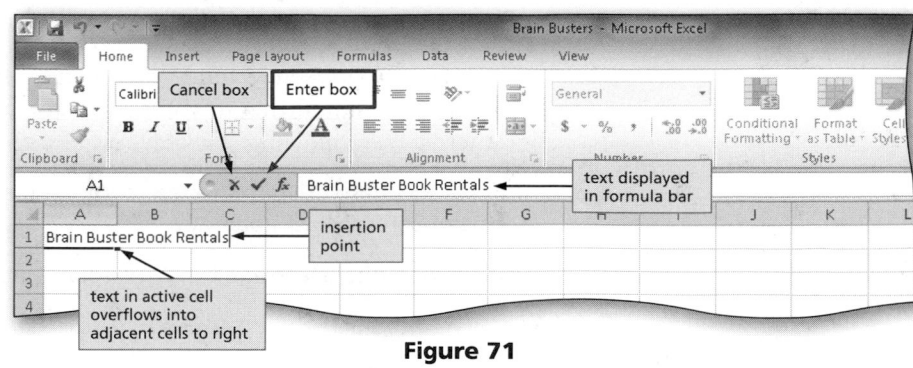

Figure 71

3

• Click the Enter box to complete the entry and enter the worksheet title in cell A1 (Figure 72).

Figure 72

Other Ways		
1. To complete entry, click any cell other than active cell	2. To complete entry, press ENTER, HOME, PAGE UP, PAGE DOWN, END,	UP, DOWN, LEFT ARROW, or RIGHT ARROW

To Save an Existing Office Document with the Same File Name

Saving frequently cannot be overemphasized. You have made modifications to the file (spreadsheet) since you created it. Thus, you should save again. Similarly, you should continue saving files frequently so that you do not lose your changes since the time you last saved the file. You can use the same file name, such as Brain Busters, to save the changes made to the document. The following step saves a file again.

1

• Click the Save button on the Quick Access Toolbar to overwrite the previously saved file (Brain Busters, in this case) on the USB flash drive (Figure 73).

Why did the Save As dialog box not appear?

Office programs, including Excel, overwrite the document using the setting specified the first time you saved the document.

Figure 73

Other Ways
1. Press CTRL+S or press SHIFT+F12

To Use Save As to Change the Name of a File

You might want to save a file with a different name and even to a different location. For example, you might start a homework assignment with a data file and then save it with a final file name for submitting to your instructor, saving it to a location designated by your instructor. The following steps save a file with a different file name.

1 With your USB flash drive connected to one of the computer's USB ports, click File on the Ribbon to open the Backstage view.

2 Click Save As in the Backstage view to display the Save As dialog box.

3 Type **Brain Busters Rental Summary** in the File name text box (Save As dialog box) to change the file name. Do not press the ENTER key after typing the file name because you do not want to close the dialog box at this time.

4 Navigate to the desired save location (the Excel folder in the CIS 101 folder [or your class folder] on the USB flash drive, in this case). For specific instructions, perform the tasks in steps 4a through 4g.

4a If a navigation pane is not displayed in the Save As dialog box, click the Browse Folders button to expand the dialog box.

4b If Computer is not displayed in the navigation pane, drag the navigation pane scroll bar (Save As dialog box) until Computer appears.

4c If Computer is not expanded in the navigation pane, double-click Computer to display a list of available storage devices in the navigation pane.

4d If necessary, scroll through the Save As dialog box until your USB flash drive appears in the list of available storage devices in the navigation pane.

4e If your USB flash drive is not expanded, double-click the USB flash drive in the list of available storage devices in the navigation pane to select that drive as the new save location and display its contents in the right pane.

4f If your class folder (CIS 101, in this case) is not expanded, double-click the CIS 101 folder to select the folder and display its contents.

4g Double-click the Excel folder to select it and display its contents in the right pane.

5 Click the Save button (Save As dialog box) to save the file in the selected folder on the selected drive with the new file name.

To Quit an Office Program

You are finished using Excel. The following steps quit Excel.

1 If you have one Office document open, click the Close button on the right side of the title bar to close the document and quit the Office program; or if you have multiple Office documents open, click File on the Ribbon to open the Backstage view and then click Exit in the Backstage view to close all open documents and quit the Office program.

2 If a dialog box appears, click the Save button to save any changes made to the file since the last save.

Access

The term **database** describes a collection of data organized in a manner that allows access, retrieval, and use of that data. **Microsoft Access 2010**, usually referred to as simply **Access,** is a database management system. A **database management system** is software that allows you to use a computer to create a database; add, change, and delete data in the database; create queries that allow you to ask questions concerning the data in the database; and create forms and reports using the data in the database.

To Start a Program

The following steps, which assume Windows 7 is running, start the Access program based on a typical installation. You may need to ask your instructor how to start programs for your computer.

● Click the Start button on the Windows 7 taskbar to display the Start menu.

● Type the name of the program, `Microsoft Access` in this case, as the search text in the 'Search programs and files' text box and watch the search results appear on the Start menu.

● Click the name of the program, Microsoft Access 2010 in this case, in the search results on the Start menu to start Access.

● If the program window is not maximized, click the Maximize button on its title bar to maximize the window (Figure 74).

◀ Do I have to start Access using these steps?

No. You can use any previously discussed method of starting an Office program to start Access.

Figure 74

Unique Elements in Access

You work on objects such as tables, forms, and reports in the **Access work area**. In Figure 74, the Access window contains no open objects. Figure 75 shows a work area with multiple objects open. **Object tabs** for the open objects appear at the top of the work area. You select an open object by clicking its tab. In the figure, the Suppliers Split Form is the selected object. To the left of the work area is the Navigation Pane, which contains a list of all the objects in the database. You use this pane to open an object. You also can customize the way objects are displayed in the Navigation Pane.

Because the Navigation Pane can take up space in the window, you may not have as much open space for working as you would with Word or Excel. You can use the Shutter Bar Open/Close button to minimize the Navigation Pane when you are not using it, which allows more space to work with tables, forms, reports, and other database elements.

Figure 75

Ribbon When you start Access, the Ribbon displays five main tabs: File, Home, Create, External Data, and Database Tools. Access has unique groupings such as Sort & Filter and Records that are designed specifically for working with databases. Many of the formatting options are reserved for the tool tabs that appear when you are working with forms and reports.

To Create an Access Database

Unlike the other Office programs, Access saves a database when you first create it. When working in Access, you will add data to an Access database. As you add data to a database, Access automatically saves your changes rather than waiting until you manually save the database or quit Access. Recall that in Word and Excel, you entered the data first and then saved it.

Because Access automatically saves the database as you add and change data, you do not have to always click the Save button. In fact, the Save button in Access is used for saving the objects (including tables, queries, forms, reports, and other database objects) a database contains. You can use either the Blank Database option or a template to create a new database. If you already know the organization of your database, you would use the Blank Database option. If not, you can use a template. Templates can guide you by suggesting some commonly used database organizations.

The following steps use the Blank Database option to create a database named Charmed Excursions in the Access folder in the class folder (CIS 101, in this case) on a USB flash drive.

1

- If necessary, click the Blank database button in the New gallery (shown in Figure 74 on page OFF 53) in the Backstage view to select the template type.

- Click the File Name text box to select the default database name.

- Type **Charmed Excursions** in the File Name text box to enter the new file name. Do not press the ENTER key after typing the file name because you do not want to create the database at this time (Figure 76).

Figure 76

Why is the Backstage view automatically open when you start Access?

Unlike other Office programs, you first must save a database before adding any data. For this reason, the Backstage view opens automatically when you start Access.

2

- Click the 'Browse for a location to put your database' button to display the File New Database dialog box.

- Navigate to the location for the database, that is, the USB flash drive, then to the folder identifying your class (CIS 101, in this case), and then to the Access folder (Figure 77). For detailed steps about navigating, see Steps 3a – 3c on pages OFF 28 and OFF 29.

Why does the 'Save as type' box say Microsoft Access 2007 Databases?

Microsoft Access database formats change with some new versions of Microsoft Access. The most recent format is the Microsoft Access 2007 Databases format, which was released with Access 2007.

Figure 77

- Click the OK button (File New Database dialog box) to select the Access folder as the location for the database and close the dialog box (Figure 78).

Figure 78

- Click the Create button in the Backstage view to create the database on the selected drive in the selected folder with the file name, Charmed Excursions. If necessary, click the Enable Content button (Figure 79).

Q&A

How do I know that the Charmed Excursions database is created?

The name of the database appears on the title bar.

Figure 79

To Close an Office File

Assume you need to close the Access database and return to it later. The following step closes an Office file.

1 Click File on the Ribbon to open the Backstage view and then click Close Database in the Backstage view to close the open file (Charmed Excursions, in this case) without quitting the active program.

Q&A

Why is Access still on the screen?

When you close a database, the program remains open.

To Open an Existing Office File

Assume you wish to continue working on an existing file, that is, a file you previously saved. Earlier in this chapter, you learned how to open a recently used file through the Backstage view. The following steps open a database, specifically the Charmed Excursions database, from the USB flash drive.

1

• With your USB flash drive connected to one of the computer's USB ports, if necessary, click File on the Ribbon to open the Backstage view.

• Click Open in the Backstage view to display the Open dialog box (Figure 80).

2

• Navigate to the location of the file to be opened (in this case, the USB flash drive, then to the CIS 101 folder [or your class folder], and then to the Access folder). For detailed steps about navigating, see Steps 3a – 3c on pages OFF 28 and OFF 29.

What if I did not save my file in a folder?

If you did not save your file in a folder, the file you wish to open should be displayed in the Open dialog box before navigating to any folders.

Figure 80

3

• Click the file to be opened, Charmed Excursions in this case, to select the file (Figure 81).

4

• Click the Open button (Open dialog box) to open the selected file and display the opened file in the current program window (shown in Figure 79).

Figure 81

Other Ways

1. Click File on the Ribbon, click Recent in Backstage view, double-click file

2. Press CTRL+O

3. Navigate to file in Windows Explorer, double-click file

To Quit an Office Program

You are finished using Access. The following step quits Access.

1 Click the Close button on the right side of the title bar to close the file and quit the Office program.

Other Office Programs

In addition to the Office programs discussed thus far, three other programs are useful when collaborating and communicating with others: Outlook, Publisher, and OneNote.

Outlook

Outlook is a powerful communications and scheduling program that helps you communicate with others, keep track of contacts, and organize your calendar. Personal information manager (PIM) programs such as Outlook provide a way for individuals and workgroups to organize, find, view, and share information easily. Outlook allows you to send and receive electronic mail (e-mail) and permits you to engage in real-time messaging with family, friends, or coworkers using instant messaging. Outlook also provides a means to organize contacts. Users can track e-mail messages, meetings, and notes related to a particular contact. Outlook's Calendar, Contacts, Tasks, and Notes components aid in this organization. Contact information readily is available from the Outlook Calendar, Mail, Contacts, and Task components by accessing the Find a Contact feature.

Electronic mail (e-mail) is the transmission of messages and files over a computer network. E-mail has become an important means of exchanging information and files between business associates, classmates and instructors, friends, and family. Businesses find that using e-mail to send documents electronically saves both time and money. Parents with students away at college or relatives who live across the country find that communicating by e-mail is an inexpensive and easy way to stay in touch with their family members. Exchanging e-mail messages is one of the more widely used features of the Internet.

The Outlook Window Figure 82 shows an Outlook window, which is divided into six panes: the Favorites folder pane, Mail folder pane, and Navigation Pane on the left side of the window, the Inbox message pane to the left of center, the Reading Pane to the right of center, and the People Pane just below the Reading Pane.

When an e-mail message is open in Outlook, it is displayed in a Message window (Figure 83). When you open a message, the Message window Ribbon displays the Message tab, which contains the more frequently used commands.

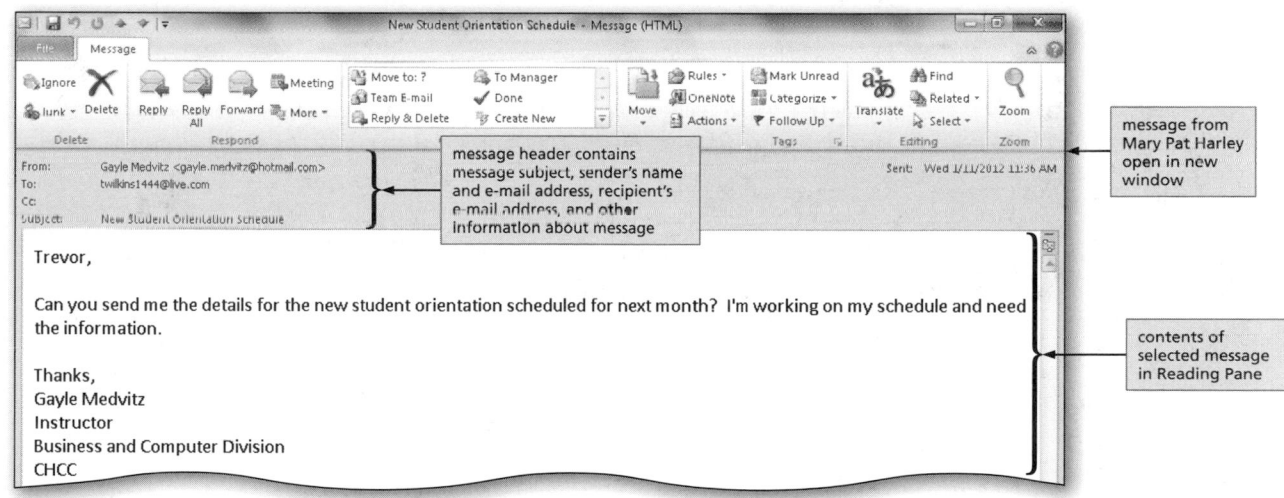

Figure 82

Inbox – Microsoft Outlook window

title bar

number of unread messages in blue

Favorites er pane

box folder

closed envelope icon indicates unread message

opened envelope icon indicates message that has been opened

folder

Mail button

Navigation Pane

Inbox message pane

To-Do Bar

Reading Pane

People Pane

Figure 83

message header contains message subject, sender's name and e-mail address, recipient's e-mail address, and other information about message

message from Mary Pat Harley open in new window

contents of selected message in Reading Pane

Publisher

Publisher is a powerful desktop publishing (DTP) program that assists you in designing and producing professional-quality documents that combine text, graphics, illustrations, and photos. DTP software provides additional tools beyond those typically found in word processing programs, including design templates, graphic manipulation tools, color schemes or libraries, advanced layout and printing tools, and Web components. For large jobs, businesses use DTP software to design publications that are camera ready, which means the files are suitable for outside commercial printing. In addition, DTP software can be used to create Web pages and interactive Web forms.

Publisher is used by people who regularly produce high-quality color publications, such as newsletters, brochures, flyers, logos, signs, catalogs, cards, and business forms. Saving publications as Web pages or complete Web sites is a powerful component of Publisher. All publications can be saved in a format that easily is viewed and manipulated using a browser.

Publisher has many features designed to simplify production and make publications visually appealing. Using Publisher, you easily can change the shape, size, and color of text and graphics. You can include many kinds of graphical objects, including mastheads, borders, tables, images, pictures, charts, and Web objects in publications, as well as integrate spreadsheets and databases.

BTW

Starting Publisher
When you first start Publisher, the New templates gallery usually is displayed in the Backstage view. If it is not displayed, click File on the Ribbon, click Options in the Backstage view, click General (Options dialog box), and then click Show the New template gallery when starting Publisher to select the check box in the General panel.

The Publisher Window On the right side of the Backstage view, Publisher displays the New template gallery, which includes a list of publication types. **Publication types** are typical publications used by desktop publishers. The more popular types are displayed in the center of the window. Each publication type is a link to display various templates and blank publications from which you may choose.

Once you select a publication type, the window changes to allow you to select a specific template (Figure 84). Some templates are installed with Publisher, and others are available online. Clicking a publication type causes template previews to be displayed in the center of the window. The templates are organized by purpose (for example, Sales) and then alphabetically by design type. On the right, Publisher will display a larger preview of the selected template, along with some customization options if the template is installed or a download option if the template is online. In Figure 84, the installed Arrows template is selected so that the customize options appear.

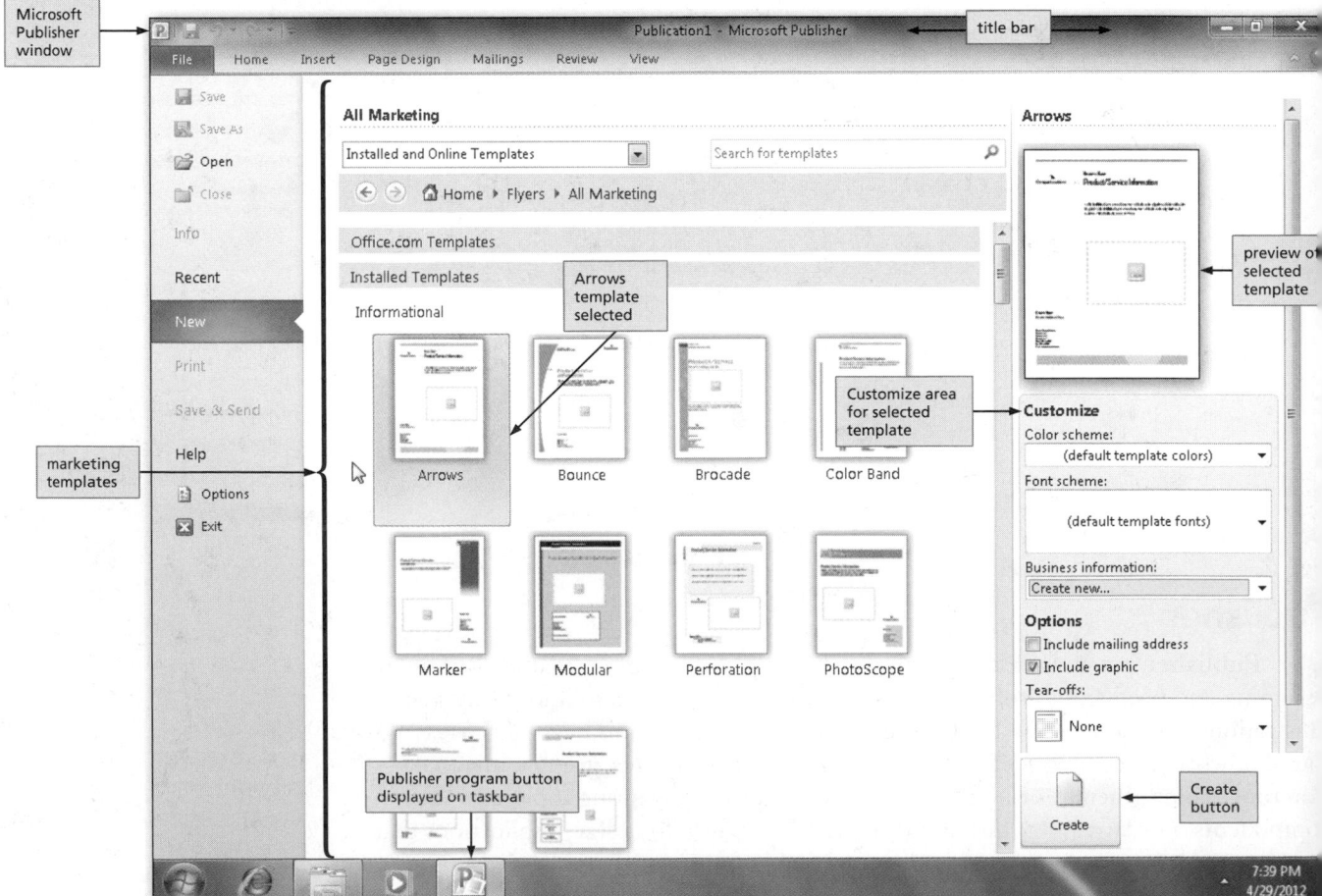

Figure 84

When you click the Create button, Publisher creates the document and sets it up for you to edit. Figure 85 shows the Arrows document that Publisher creates when default options are selected.

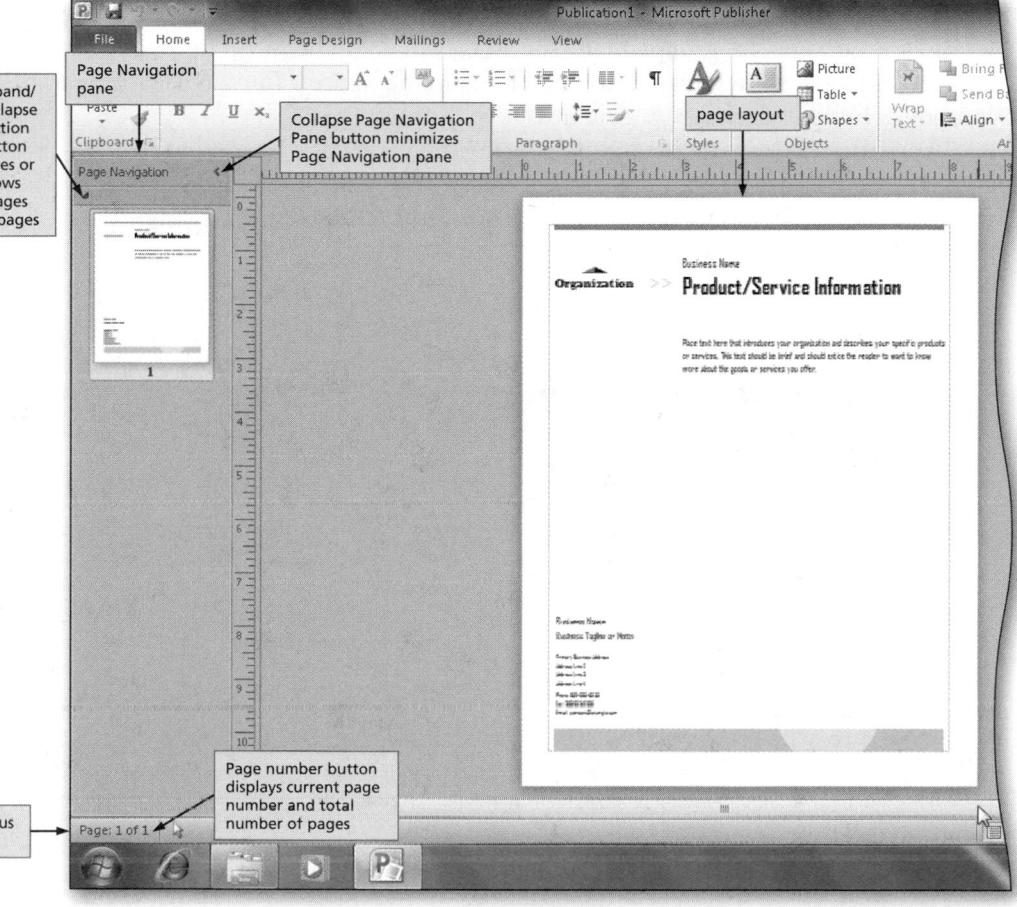

Figure 85

OneNote

OneNote is a note taking program that assists you in entering, saving, organizing, searching, and using notes. It enables you to create pages, which are organized in sections, just as in a physical notebook. In OneNote, you can type notes anywhere on a page and then easily move the notes around on the page. You can create lists and outlines, use handwriting to enter notes, and create drawings. If you use a Tablet PC to add handwritten notes to a document, OneNote can convert the handwriting to text. It also can perform searches on the handwritten entries. Pictures and data from other programs easily are incorporated in your notes.

In addition to typing and handwriting, you can take audio notes. For example, you could record conversations during a meeting or lecture. As you record, you can take additional notes. When you play back the audio notes, you can synchronize the additional notes you took; that is, OneNote will show you during playback the exact points at which you added the notes. A variety of note flags, which are symbols that call your attention to notes on a page, enable you to flag notes as being important. You then can use the Note Flags summary to view the flagged notes, which can be sorted in a variety of ways.

OneNote includes tools to assist you with organizing a notebook and navigating its contents. It also includes a search facility, making it easy to find the specific notes in which you are interested. For short notes that you always want to have available readily, you can use Side Notes, which are used much like the sticky notes that you might use in a physical notebook.

OneNote Window   All activity in OneNote takes place in the **notebook** (Figure 86). Like a physical notebook, the OneNote notebook consists of notes that are placed on **pages**. The pages are grouped into **sections**, which can be further grouped into **folders**. (No folders are shown in the notebook in the figure.) You can use the Search All Notebooks box to search for specific text in your notes.

You can add pages to the notebook using the New Page button in the Page Tabs pane. If Page Tabs are displayed, then you can switch to a page by clicking its tab. Figure 86 shows the Top Uses page being displayed for the General notebook.

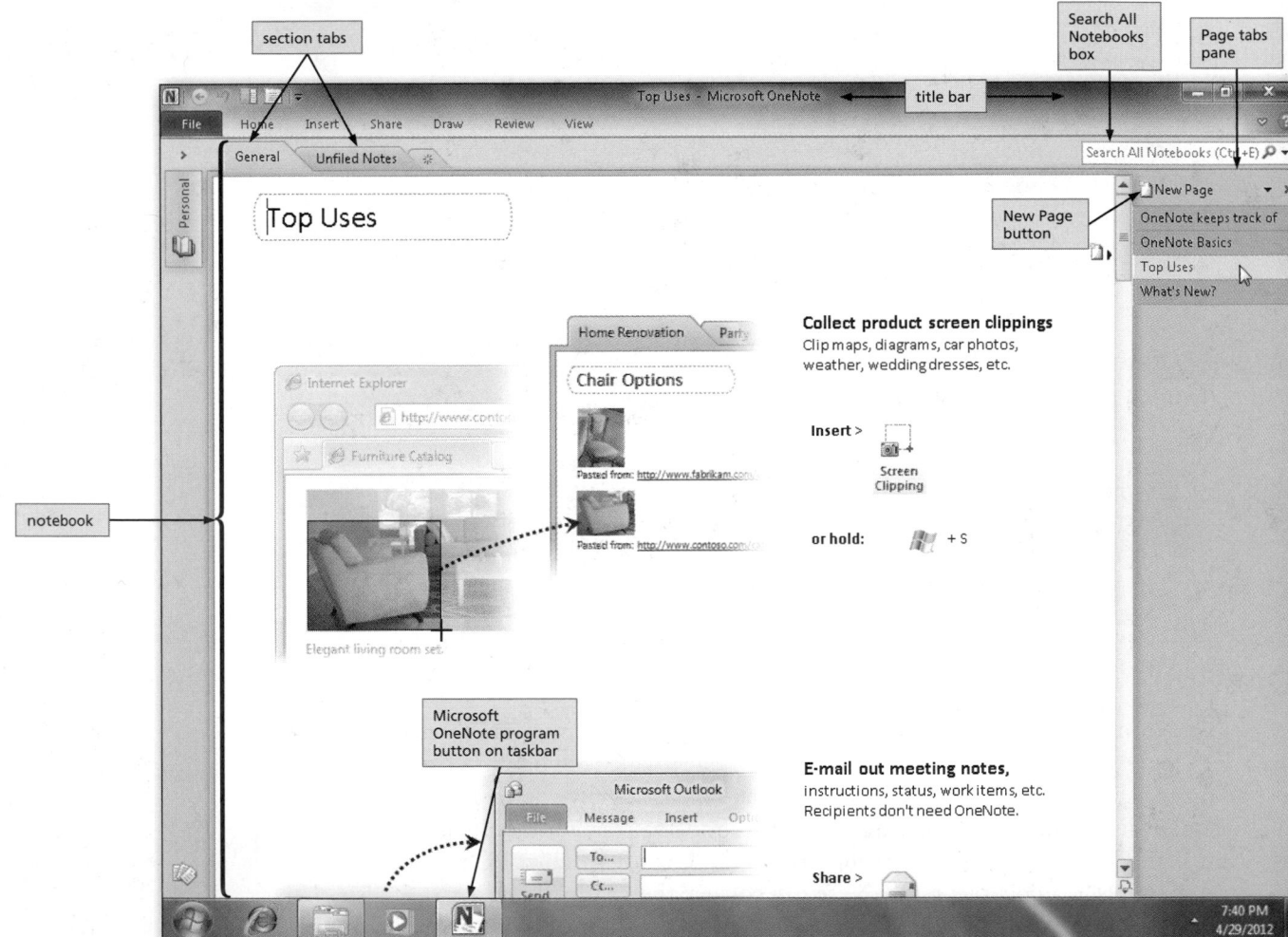

Figure 86

Break Point: If you wish to take a break, this is a good place to do so. To resume at a later time, continue to follow the steps from this location forward.

Moving, Renaming, and Deleting Files

Earlier in this chapter, you learned how to organize files in folders, which is part of a process known as **file management**. The following sections cover additional file management topics including renaming, moving, and deleting files.

To Rename a File

In some circumstances, you may want to change the name of, or rename, a file or a folder. For example, you may want to distinguish a file in one folder or drive from a copy of a similar file, or you may decide to rename a file to better identify its contents. The Word folder shown in Figure 87 contains the Word document, Koala Exhibit. The following steps change the name of the Koala Exhibit file in the Word folder to Koala Exhibit Flyer.

- If necessary, click the Windows Explorer program button on the taskbar to display the folder window in Windows Explorer.

- Navigate to the location of the file to be renamed (in this case, the Word folder in the CIS 101 [or your class folder] folder on the USB flash drive) to display the file(s) it contains in the right pane.

- Right-click the Koala Exhibit icon or file name in the right pane to select the Koala Exhibit file and display a shortcut menu that presents a list of commands related to files (Figure 87).

Figure 87

- Click Rename on the shortcut menu to place the current file name in a text box.

- Type **Koala Exhibit Flyer** in the text box and then press the ENTER key (Figure 88).

Are any risks involved in renaming files that are located on a hard disk?

If you inadvertently rename a file that is associated with certain programs, the programs may not be able to find the file and, therefore, may not execute properly. Always use caution when renaming files.

Can I rename a file when it is open?

No, a file must be closed to change the file name.

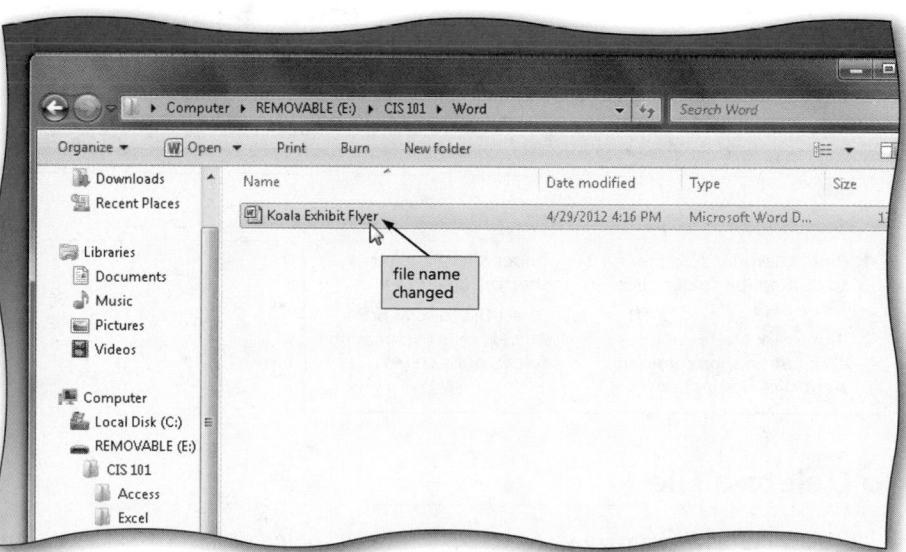

Figure 88

Other Ways
1. Select file, press F2, type new file name, press ENTER

To Move a File

At some time, you may want to move a file from one folder, called the source folder, to another, called the destination. When you move a file, it no longer appears in the original folder. If the destination and the source folders are on the same disk drive, you can move a file by dragging it. If the folders are on different disk drives, then you will need to right-drag the file. The following step moves the Brain Busters Rental Summary file from the Excel folder to the OneNote folder.

- In Windows Explorer, navigate to the location of the file to be moved (in this case, the Excel folder in the CIS 101 folder [or your class folder] on the USB flash drive).

- Click the Excel folder in the navigation pane to display the files it contains in the right pane (Figure 89).

- Drag the Brain Busters Rental Summary file in the right pane to the OneNote folder in the navigation pane.

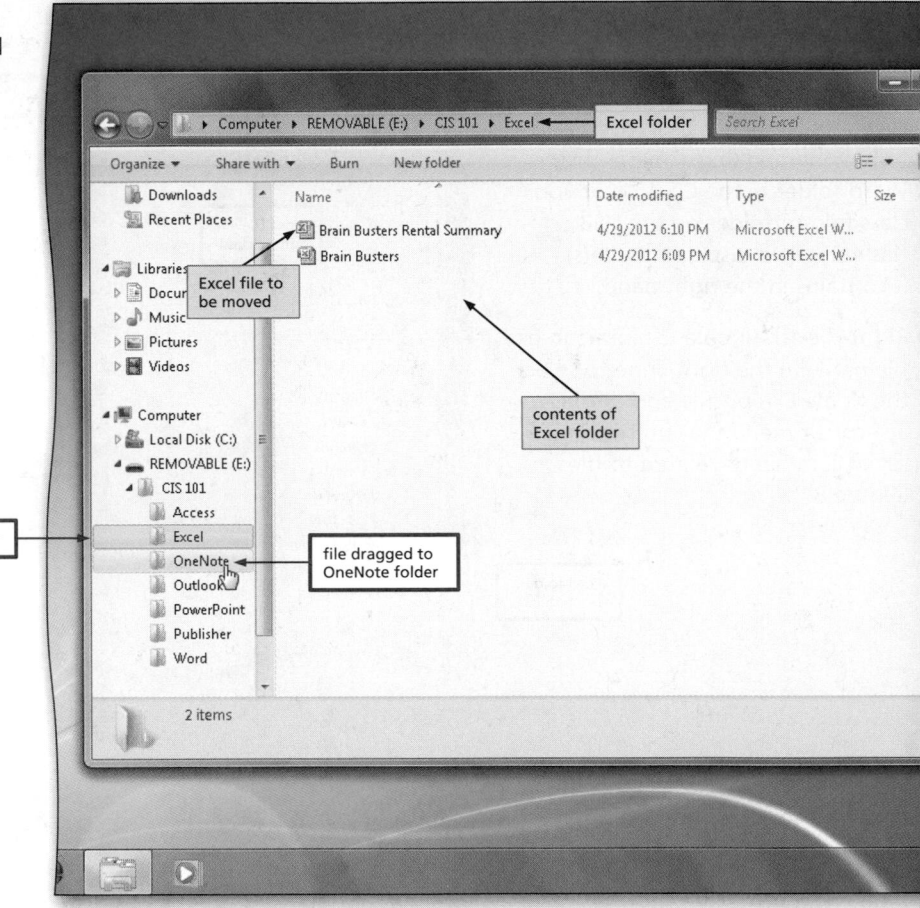

Figure 89

To Delete a File

A final task you may want to perform is to delete a file. Exercise extreme caution when deleting a file or files. When you delete a file from a hard disk, the deleted file is stored in the Recycle Bin where you can recover it until you empty the Recycle Bin. If you delete a file from removable media, such as a USB flash drive, the file is deleted permanently. The next steps delete the Koala Exhibit Gala file from the PowerPoint folder.

1

- In Windows Explorer, navigate to the location of the file to be deleted (in this case, the PowerPoint folder in the CIS 101 folder [or your class folder] on the USB flash drive).

- Click the PowerPoint folder in the navigation pane to display the files it contains in the right pane.

- Right-click the Koala Exhibit Gala icon or file name in the right pane to select the file and display a shortcut menu (Figure 90).

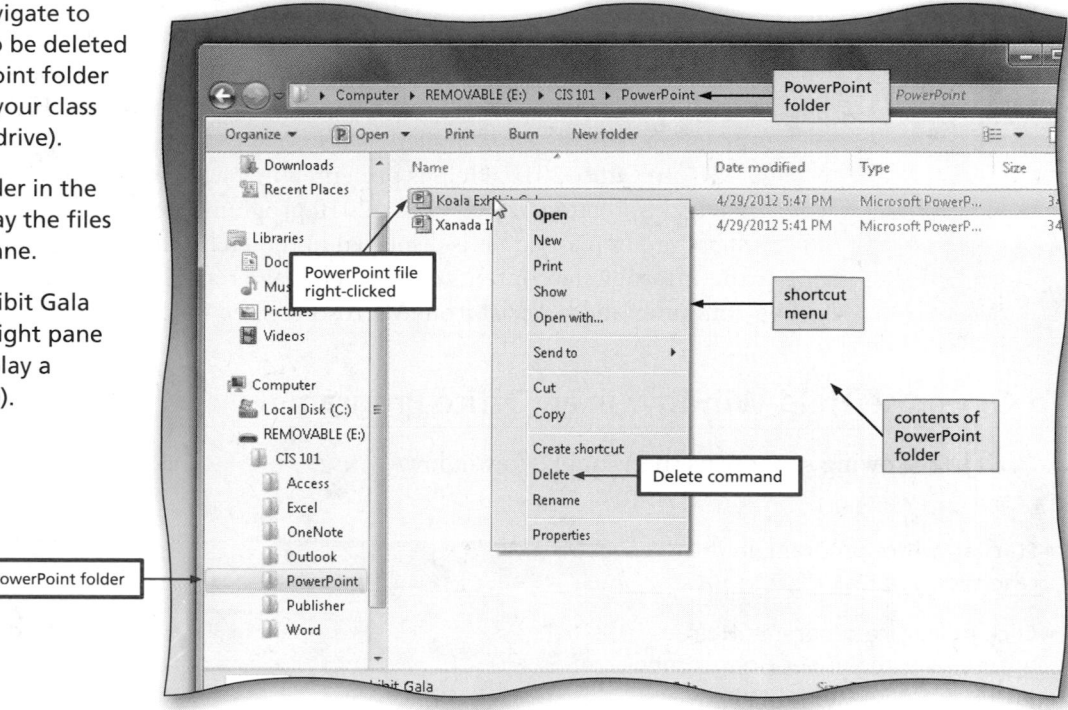

Figure 90

2

- Click Delete on the shortcut menu to display the Delete File dialog box (Figure 91).

- Click the Yes button (Delete File dialog box) to delete the selected file.

Can I use this same technique to delete a folder?

Yes. Right-click the folder and then click Delete on the shortcut menu. When you delete a folder, all of the files and folders contained in the folder you are deleting, together with any files and folders on lower hierarchical levels, are deleted as well.

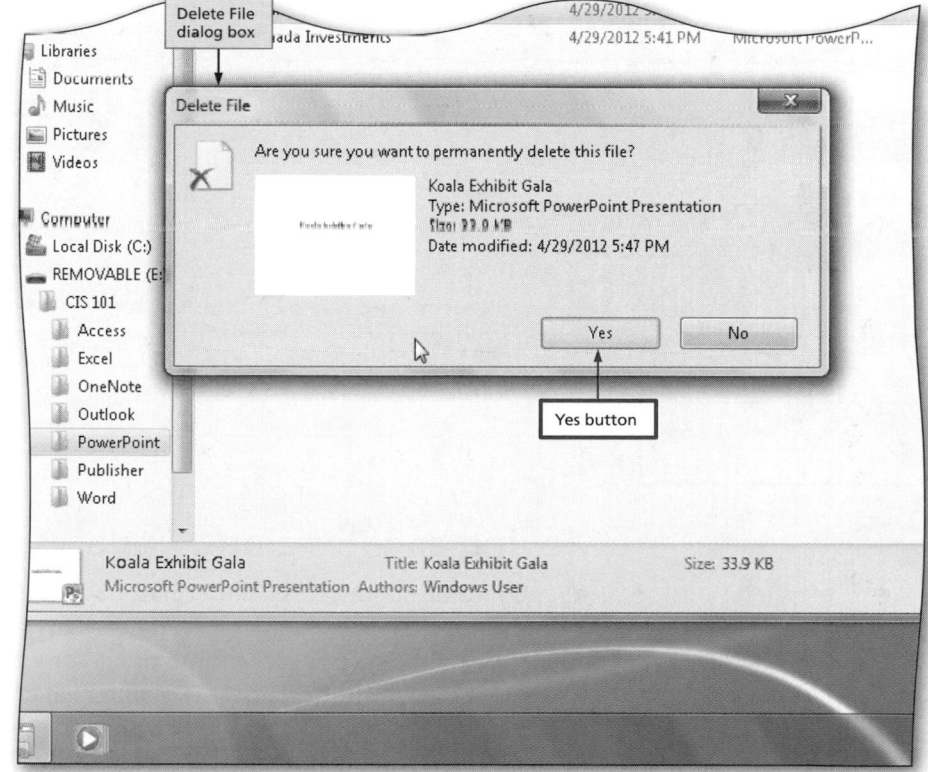

Figure 91

Other Ways

1. Select icon, press DELETE

Microsoft Office and Windows Help

At any time while you are using one of the Microsoft Office 2010 programs, you can use Office Help to display information about all topics associated with the program. To illustrate the use of Office Help, this section uses Word. Help in other Office 2010 programs operates in a similar fashion.

In Office 2010, Help is presented in a window that has Web-browser-style navigation buttons. Each Office 2010 program has its own Help home page, which is the starting Help page that is displayed in the Help window. If your computer is connected to the Internet, the contents of the Help page reflect both the local help files installed on the computer and material from Microsoft's Web site.

To Open the Help Window in an Office Program

The following step opens the Word Help window.

1

- Start an Office program, in this case Word.

- Click the Office program's Help button near the upper-right corner of the program window (the Microsoft Word Help button, in this case) to open the program's Help window (Figure 92).

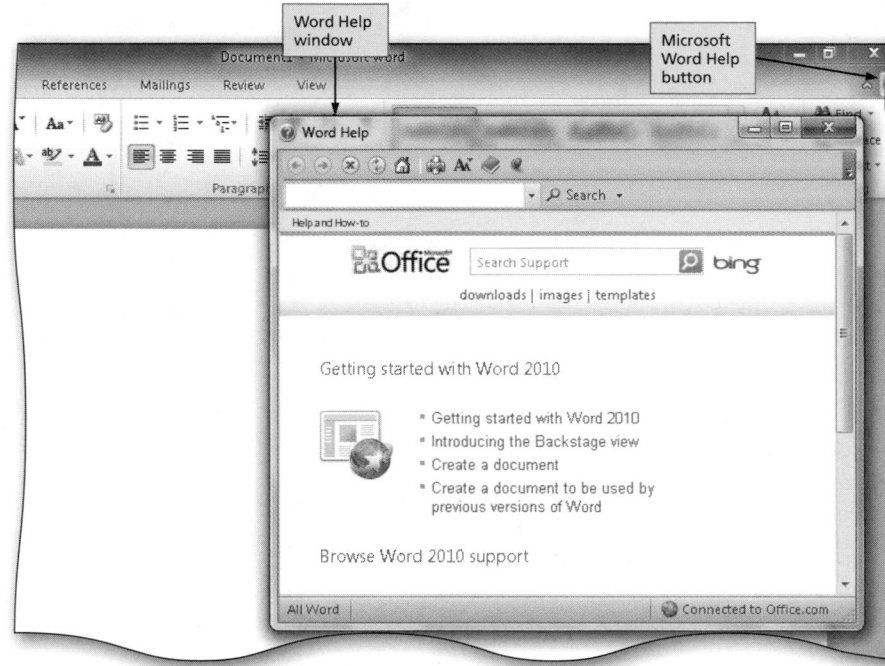

Figure 92

Other Ways

1. Press F1

Moving and Resizing Windows

Up to this point, this chapter has used minimized and maximized windows. At times, however, it is useful, or even necessary, to have more than one window open and visible on the screen at the same time. You can resize and move these open windows so that you can view different areas of and elements in the window. In the case of the Help window, for example, it could be covering document text in the Word window that you need to see.

To Move a Window by Dragging

You can move any open window that is not maximized to another location on the desktop by dragging the title bar of the window. The following step drags the Word Help window to the top left of the desktop.

• Drag the window title bar (the Word Help window title bar, in this case) so that the window moves to the top left of the desktop, as shown in Figure 93.

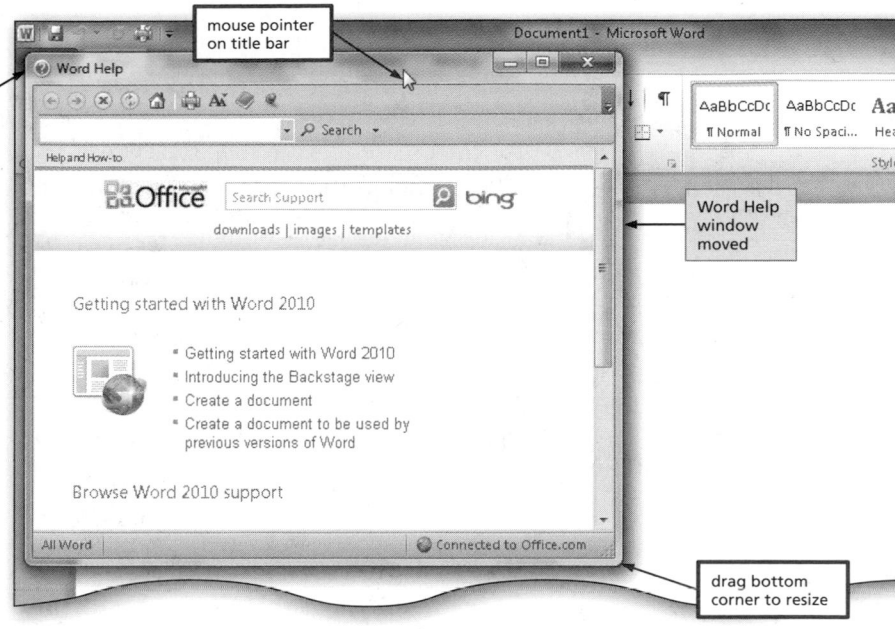

Figure 93

To Resize a Window by Dragging

Sometimes, information is not visible completely in a window. A method used to change the size of the window is to drag the window borders. The following step changes the size of the Word Help window by dragging its borders.

• Point to the lower-right corner of the window (the Word Help window, in this case) until the mouse pointer changes to a two-headed arrow.

• Drag the bottom border downward to display more of the active window (Figure 94).

Can I drag other borders on the window to enlarge or shrink the window?

Yes, you can drag the left, right, and top borders and any window corner to resize a window.

Will Windows 7 remember the new size of the window after I close it?

Yes. When you reopen the window, Windows 7 will display it at the same size it was when you closed it.

Figure 94

Using Office Help

Once an Office program's Help window is open, several methods exist for navigating Help. You can search for help by using any of the three following methods from the Help window:

1. Enter search text in the 'Type words to search for' text box
2. Click the links in the Help window
3. Use the Table of Contents

To Obtain Help Using the 'Type words to search for' Text Box

Assume for the following example that you want to know more about the Backstage view. The following steps use the 'Type words to search for' text box to obtain useful information about the Backstage view by entering the word, Backstage, as search text.

1

- Type **Backstage** in the 'Type words to search for' text box at the top of the Word Help window to enter the search text.

- Click the Search button arrow to display the Search menu (Figure 95).

- If it is not selected already, click All Word on the Search menu, so that Help performs the most complete search of the current program (Word, in this case). If All Word already is selected, click the Search button arrow again to close the Search menu.

Figure 95

Q&A

Why select All Word on the Search menu?

Selecting All Word on the Search menu ensures that Word Help will search all possible sources for information about your search term. It will produce the most complete search results.

2

• Click the Search button to display the search results (Figure 96).

Why do my search results differ?

If you do not have an Internet connection, your results will reflect only the content of the Help files on your computer. When searching for help online, results also can change as material is added, deleted, and updated on the online Help Web pages maintained by Microsoft.

Why were my search results not very helpful?

When initiating a search, be sure to check the spelling of the search text; also, keep your search specific, with fewer than seven words, to return the most accurate results.

Figure 96

3

• Click the Introducing Backstage link to open the Help document associated with the selected topic (Figure 97).

Figure 97

- Click the Home button on the toolbar to clear the search results and redisplay the Help home page (Figure 98).

Figure 98

To Obtain Help Using the Help Links

If your topic of interest is listed in the Browse area of the Help window, you can click the link to begin browsing the Help categories instead of entering search text. You browse Help just as you would browse a Web site. If you know which category contains your Help information, you may wish to use these links. The following step finds the Formatting Help information using the category links from the Word Help home page.

- Click the Formatting link on the Help home page (shown in Figure 98) to display the Formatting page (Figure 99).

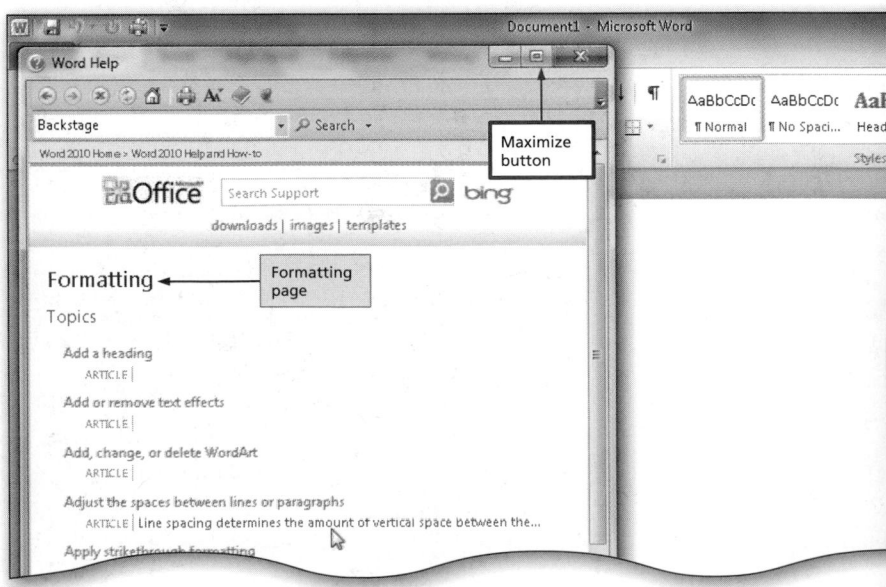

Figure 99

To Obtain Help Using the Help Table of Contents

A third way to find Help in Office programs is through the Help Table of Contents. You can browse through the Table of Contents to display information about a particular topic or to familiarize yourself with an Office program. The following steps access the Help information about themes by browsing through the Table of Contents.

1

● Click the Home button on the toolbar to display the Help home page.

● Click the Show Table of Contents button on the toolbar to display the Table of Contents pane on the left side of the Help window. If necessary, click the Maximize button on the Help title bar to maximize the window (Figure 100).

◀ Why does the appearance of the Show Table of Contents button change?

When the Table of Contents is displayed in the Help window, the Hide Table of Contents button replaces the Show Table of Contents button.

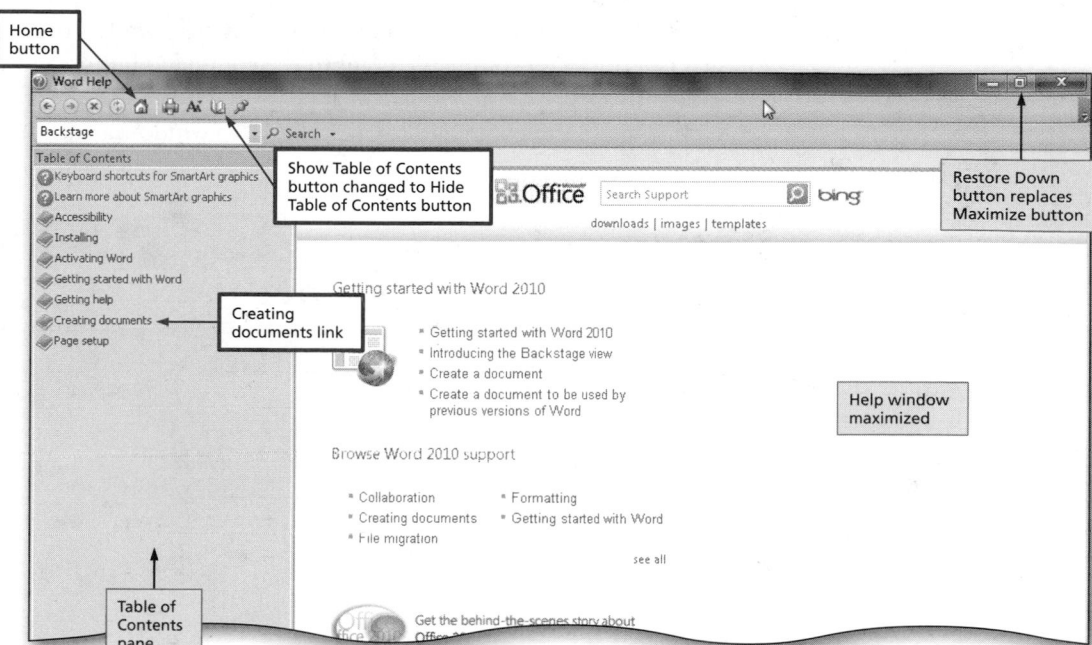

Figure 100

2

● Click the Creating documents link in the Table of Contents pane to view a list of Help subtopics.

● Click the Apply themes to Word documents link in the Table of Contents pane to view the selected Help document in the right pane (Figure 101).

● After reviewing the page, click the Close button to quit Help.

● Click the Office program's Close button (Word, in this case) to quit the Office program.

◀ How do I remove the Table of Contents pane when I am finished with it?

The Show Table of Contents button acts as a toggle. When the Table of Contents pane is visible, the button changes to Hide Table of Contents. Clicking it hides the Table of Contents pane and changes the button to Show Table of Contents.

Figure 101

Obtaining Help while Working in an Office Program

Help in the Office programs provides you with the ability to obtain help directly, without the need to open the Help window and initiate a search. For example, you may be unsure about how a particular command works, or you may be presented with a dialog box that you are not sure how to use.

Figure 102 shows one option for obtaining help while working in Word. If you want to learn more about a command, point to the command button and wait for the Enhanced ScreenTip to appear. If the Help icon appears in the Enhanced ScreenTip, press the F1 key while pointing to the command to open the Help window associated with that command.

Figure 102

Figure 103 shows a dialog box that contains a Help button. Pressing the F1 key while the dialog box is displayed opens a Help window. The Help window contains help about that dialog box, if available. If no help file is available for that particular dialog box, then the main Help window opens.

Figure 103

Using Windows Help and Support

One of the more powerful Windows 7 features is Windows Help and Support. **Windows Help and Support** is available when using Windows 7 or when using any Microsoft program running under Windows 7. This feature is designed to assist you in using Windows 7 or the various programs. Table 4 describes the content found in the Help and Support Center. The same methods used for searching Microsoft Office Help can be used in Windows Help and Support. The difference is that Windows Help and Support displays help for Windows 7, instead of for Microsoft Office.

Table 4 Windows Help and Support Center Content Areas	
Area	**Function**
Find an answer quickly	This area contains instructions about how to do a quick search using the search box.
Not sure where to start?	This area displays three topics to help guide a user: How to get started with your computer, Learn about Windows Basics, and Browse Help topics. Clicking one of the options navigates to corresponding Help and Support pages.
More on the Windows Website	This area contains links to online content from the Windows Web site. Clicking the links navigates to the corresponding Web pages on the Web site.

To Start Windows Help and Support

The following steps start Windows Help and Support and display the Windows Help and Support window, containing links to more information about Windows 7.

1

• Click the Start button on the taskbar to display the Start menu (Figure 104).

Why are the programs that are displayed on the Start menu different?

Windows adds the programs you have used recently to the left pane on the Start menu. You have started several programs while performing the steps in this chapter, so those programs now are displayed on the Start menu.

Figure 104

- Click Help and Support on the Start menu to open the Windows Help and Support window (Figure 105).

- After reviewing the Windows Help and Support window, click the Close button to quit Windows Help and Support.

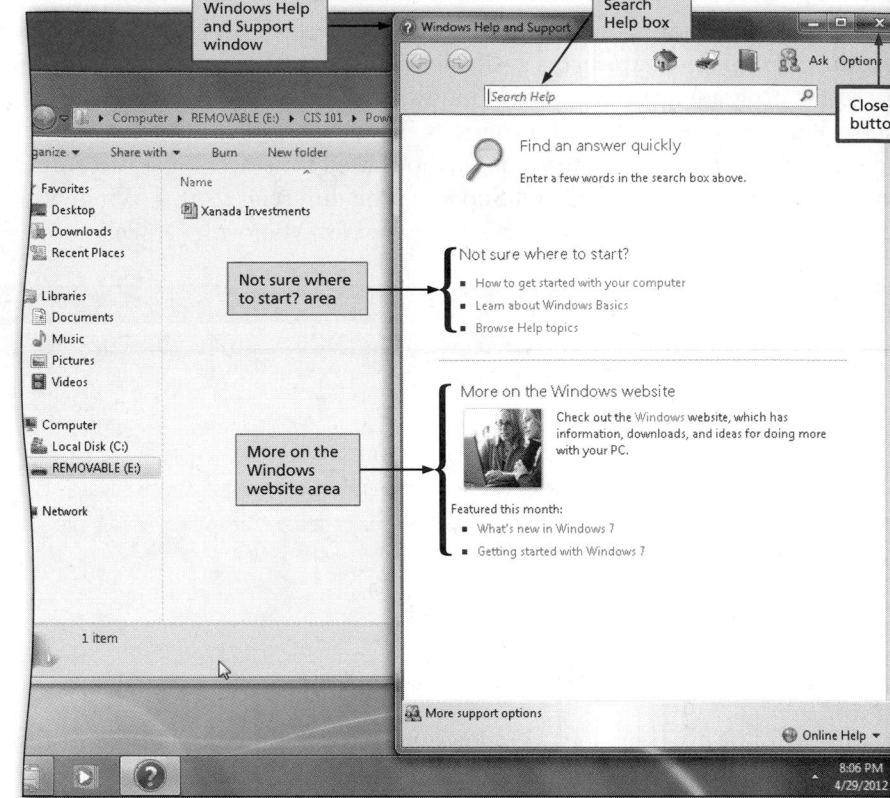

Figure 105

Other Ways

1. Press CTRL+ESC, press RIGHT ARROW, press UP ARROW, press ENTER
2. Press WINDOWS+F1

Chapter Summary

In this chapter, you learned about the Windows 7 interface. You started Windows 7, were introduced to the components of the desktop, and learned several mouse operations. You opened, closed, moved, resized, minimized, maximized, and scrolled a window. You used folder windows to expand and collapse drives and folders, display drive and folder contents, create folders, and rename and then delete a file.

You also learned some basic features of some Microsoft Office 2010 programs, including Word, PowerPoint, Excel, and Access. As part of this learning process, you discovered the common elements that exist among these different Office programs. You now can save basic document, presentation, spreadsheet, and database files. Additiona Office programs, including Outlook, Publisher, and OneNote also were discussed.

Microsoft Office Help was demonstrated, and you learned how to use the Office Help window. You were introduced to the Windows 7 Help and Support Center and learned how to use it to obtain more information about Windows 7.

The items listed below include all of the new Windows 7 and Office 2010 skills you have learned in this chapter

1. Log On to the Computer (OFF 6)
2. Start a Program Using the Start Menu (OFF 10)
3. Maximize a Window (OFF 12)
4. Display a Different Tab on the Ribbon (OFF 16)
5. Minimize, Display, and Restore the Ribbon (OFF 17)
6. Display and Use a Shortcut Menu (OFF 18)
7. Customize the Quick Access Toolbar (OFF 19)
8. Enter Text in a Document (OFF 20)

9. Create a Folder (OFF 22)
10. Create a Folder within a Folder (OFF 24)
11. Expand a Folder, Scroll through Folder Contents, and Collapse a Folder (OFF 26)
12. Switch from One Program to Another (OFF 27)
13. Save a File in a Folder (OFF 27)
14. Minimize and Restore a Window (OFF 30)
15. Change the Screen Resolution (OFF 33)

16. Quit an Office Program with One Document Open (OFF 35)
17. Start a Program Using the Search Box (OFF 37)
18. Enter Content in a Title Slide (OFF 40)
19. Create a New Office Document from the Backstage View (OFF 41)
20. Close an Office File Using the Backstage View (OFF 44)
21. Open a Recent Office File Using the Backstage View (OFF 45)
22. Create a New Blank Office Document from Windows Explorer (OFF 47)
23. Start a Program from Windows Explorer and Open a File (OFF 48)
24. Enter a Worksheet Title (OFF 50)
25. Save an Existing Document with the Same File Name (OFF 51)

26. Create an Access Database (OFF 55)
27. Open an Existing Office File (OFF 57)
28. Rename a File (OFF 63)
29. Move a File (OFF 64)
30. Delete a File (OFF 64)
31. Open the Help Window in an Office Program (OFF 66)
32. Move a Window by Dragging (OFF 66)
33. Resize a Window by Dragging (OFF 67)
34. Obtain Help Using the 'Type words to search for' Text Box (OFF 68)
35. Obtain Help Using the Help Links (OFF 70)
36. Obtain Help Using the Help Table of Contents (OFF 71)
37. Start Windows Help and Support (OFF 73)

If you have a SAM 2010 user profile, your instructor may have assigned an autogradable version of this assignment. If so, log into the SAM 2010 Web site at www.cengage.com/sam2010 to download the instruction and start files.

Learn It Online

Test your knowledge of chapter content and key terms.

Instructions: To complete the Learn It Online exercises, start your browser, click the Address bar, and then enter the Web address **scsite.com/office2010/learn**. When the Office 2010 Learn It Online page is displayed, click the link for the exercise you want to complete and then read the instructions.

Chapter Reinforcement TF, MC, and SA
A series of true/false, multiple choice, and short answer questions that test your knowledge of the chapter content.

Flash Cards
An interactive learning environment where you identify chapter key terms associated with displayed definitions.

Practice Test
A series of multiple choice questions that test your knowledge of chapter content and key terms.

Who Wants To Be a Computer Genius?
An interactive game that challenges your knowledge of chapter content in the style of a television quiz show.

Wheel of Terms
An interactive game that challenges your knowledge of chapter key terms in the style of the television show *Wheel of Fortune*.

Crossword Puzzle Challenge
A crossword puzzle that challenges your knowledge of key terms presented in the chapter.

Apply Your Knowledge

Reinforce the skills and apply the concepts you learned in this chapter.

Creating a Folder and a Document

Instructions: You will create a Word folder and then create a Word document and save it in the folder.

Perform the following tasks:

1. Connect a USB flash drive to an available USB port and then open the USB flash drive window.

2. Click the New folder button on the toolbar to display a new folder icon and text box for the folder name.

3. Type `Word` in the text box to name the folder. Press the ENTER key to create the folder on the USB flash drive.

4. Start Word.

5. Enter the text shown in Figure 106.

6. Click the Save button on the Quick Access Toolbar. Navigate to the Word folder on the USB flash drive and then save the document using the file name, Apply 1 Class List.

7. If your Quick Access Toolbar does not show the Quick Print button, add the Quick Print button to the Quick Access Toolbar. Print the document using the Quick Print button on the Quick Access Toolbar. When you are finished printing, remove the Quick Print button from the Quick Access Toolbar.

8. Submit the printout to your instructor.

9. Quit Word.

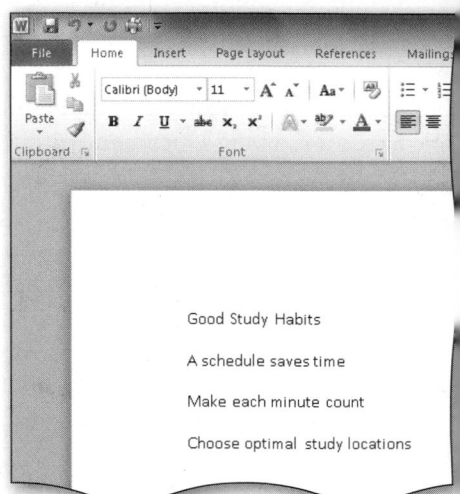

Good Study Habits

A schedule saves time

Make each minute count

Choose optimal study locations

Figure 106

Extend Your Knowledge

Extend the skills you learned in this chapter and experiment with new skills. You will use Help to complete the assignment.

Using Help

Instructions: Use Office Help to perform the following tasks.

Perform the following tasks:

1. Start Word.

2. Click the Microsoft Word Help button to open the Word Help window (Figure 107).

3. Search Word Help to answer the following questions.

   a. What are the steps to add a new group to the Ribbon?

   b. What are Quick Parts?

4. With the Word program still running, start PowerPoint.

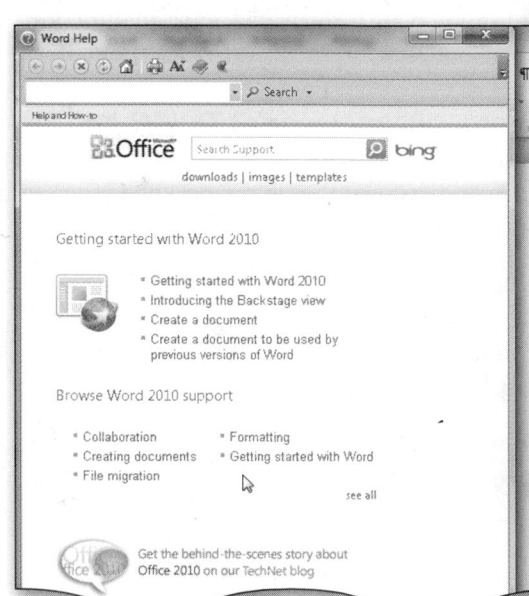

Figure 107

5. Click the Microsoft PowerPoint Help button on the title bar to open the PowerPoint Help window.

6. Search PowerPoint Help to answer the following questions.

   a. What is a slide master?

   b. How do you copy slides from another presentation into the existing presentation?

7. Quit PowerPoint.

8. Start Excel.

9. Click the Microsoft Excel Help button to open the Excel Help window.

10. Search Excel Help to answer the following questions.

   a. What are three different functions available in Excel?

   b. What are sparklines?

11. Quit Excel.

12. Start Access.

13. Click the Microsoft Access Help button to open the Access Help window.

14. Search Access Help to answer the following questions.

   a. What is SQL?

   b. What is a data macro?

15. Quit Access.

16. Type the answers from your searches in the Word document. Save the document with a new file name and then submit it in the format specified by your instructor.

17. Quit Word.

Make It Right

Analyze a file structure and correct all errors and/or improve the design.

Organizing Vacation Photos

Instructions: See the inside back cover of this book for instructions on downloading the Data Files for Students, or contact your instructor for information on accessing the required files.

Traditionally, you have stored photos from past vacations together in one folder. The photos are becoming difficult to manage, and you now want to store them in appropriate folders. You will create the folder structure shown in Figure 108. You then will move the photos to the folders so that they will be organized properly.

1. Connect a USB flash drive to an available USB port to open the USB flash drive window.

2. Using the techniques presented in the chapter, create the hierarchical folder structure shown in Figure 108.

3. Using the techniques presented in the chapter, move the vacation photos to their appropriate folders.

4. Submit your work in the format specified by your instructor.

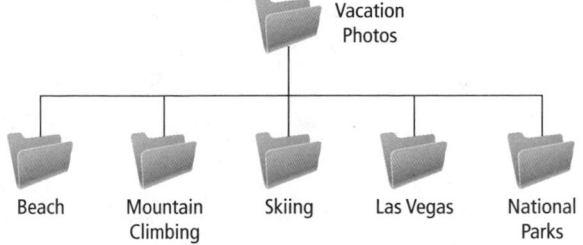

Figure 108

In the Lab

Use the guidelines, concepts, and skills presented in this chapter to increase your knowledge of Windows 7 and Office 2010. Labs are listed in order of increasing difficulty.

Lab 1: Using Windows Help and Support

Problem: You have a few questions about using Windows 7 and would like to answer these questions using Windows Help and Support.

Instructions: Use Windows Help and Support to perform the following tasks:

1. Display the Start menu and then click Help and Support to start Windows Help and Support.

2. Use the Help and Support Content page to answer the following questions.

   a. How do you reduce computer screen flicker?

   b. Which dialog box do you use to change the appearance of the mouse pointer?

   c. How do you minimize all windows?

   d. What is a VPN?

3. Use the Search Help text box in Windows Help and Support to answer the following questions.

   a. How can you minimize all open windows on the desktop?

   b. How do you start a program using the Run command?

   c. What are the steps to add a toolbar to the taskbar?

   d. What wizard do you use to remove unwanted desktop icons?

4. The tools to solve a problem while using Windows 7 are called **troubleshooters**. Use Windows Help and Support to find the list of troubleshooters (Figure 109), and answer the following questions.

   a. What problems does the HomeGroup troubleshooter allow you to resolve?

   b. List five Windows 7 troubleshooters that are not listed in Figure 109.

5. Use Windows Help and Support to obtain information about software licensing and product activation, and answer the following questions.

   a. What is genuine Windows?

   b. What is activation?

   c. What steps are required to activate Windows?

   d. What steps are required to read the Microsoft Software License Terms?

   e. Can you legally make a second copy of Windows 7 for use at home, work, or on a mobile computer or device?

   f. What is registration?

6. Close the Windows Help and Support window.

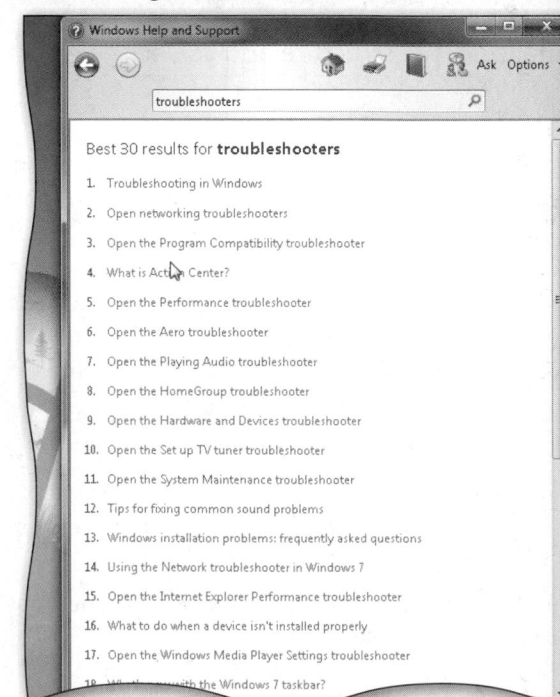

Figure 109

In the Lab

Lab 2: Creating Folders for a Pet Supply Store

Problem: Your friend works for Pete's Pet Supplies. He would like to organize his files in relation to the types of pets available in the store. He has five main categories: dogs, cats, fish, birds, and exotic. You are to create a folder structure similar to Figure 110.

Instructions: Perform the following tasks:

1. Connect a USB flash drive to an available USB port and then open the USB flash drive window.

2. Create the main folder for Pete's Pet Supplies.

3. Navigate to the Pete's Pet Supplies folder.

4. Within the Pete's Pet Supplies folder, create a folder for each of the following: Dogs, Cats, Fish, Birds, and Exotic.

5. Within the Exotic folder, create two additional folders, one for Primates and the second for Reptiles.

6. Submit the assignment in the format specified by your instructor.

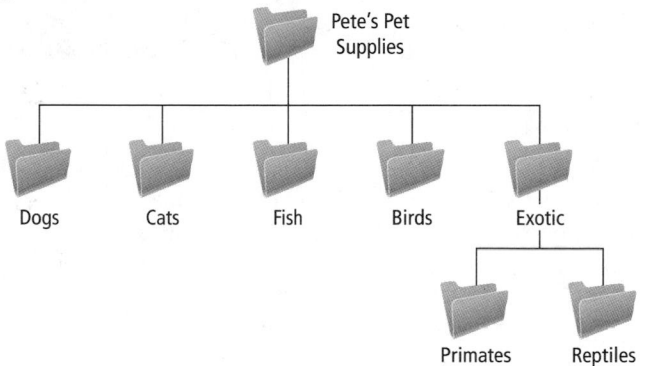

Figure 110

In the Lab

Lab 3: Creating Office Documents

Problem: You are taking a class that requires you to create a Word, PowerPoint, Excel, and Access file. You will save these files to folders named for four different Office programs (Figure 111).

Instructions: Create the folders shown in Figure 111. Then, using the respective Office program, create a small file to save in each folder (i.e., create a Word document to save in the Word folder, a PowerPoint presentation to save in the PowerPoint folder, and so on).

Figure 111

1. Connect a USB flash drive to an available USB port and then open the USB flash drive window.

2. Create the folder structure shown in Figure 111.

3. Navigate to the Word folder.

4. Create a Word document containing the text, My First Word Document, and then save it in the Word folder.

5. Navigate to the PowerPoint folder.

6. Create a PowerPoint presentation containing the title text, My First PowerPoint Presentation, and then save it in the PowerPoint folder.

7. Navigate to the Excel folder.

Continued >

In the Lab *continued*

8. Create an Excel spreadsheet containing the text, My First Excel Spreadsheet, in cell A1 and then save it in the Excel folder.

9. Navigate to the Access folder.

10. Save an Access database named, My First Database, in the Access folder.

11. Close all open Office programs.

12. Submit the assignment in the format specified by your instructor.

Cases and Places

Apply your creative thinking and problem solving skills to design and implement a solution.

Note: To complete these assignments, you may be required to use the Data Files for Students. See the inside back cover of this book for instructions on downloading the Data Files for Students, or contact your instructor for information about accessing the required files.

1: Creating Beginning Files for Classes

Academic

You are taking the following classes: Introduction to Engineering, Beginning Psychology, Introduction to Biology, and Accounting. Create folders for each of the classes. Use the following folder names: Engineering, Psychology, Biology, and Accounting, when creating the folder structure. In the Engineering folder, use Word to create a Word document with the name of the class and the class meeting location and time (MW 10:30 – 11:45, Room 317). In the Psychology folder, use PowerPoint to create your first lab presentation. It should begin with a title slide containing the text, Behavioral Observations. In the Biology folder, save a database named Research in the Biology folder. In the Accounting folder, create an Excel spreadsheet with the text, Tax Information, in cell A1. Use the concepts and techniques presented in this chapter to create the folders and files.

2: Using Help

Personal

Your parents enjoy working and playing games on their home computers. Your mother uses a notebook computer downstairs, and your father uses a desktop computer upstairs. They expressed interest in sharing files between their computers and sharing a single printer, so you offered to research various home networking options. Start Windows Help and Support, and search Help using the keywords, home networking. Use the link for installing a printer on a home network. Start Word and then type the main steps for installing a printer. Use the link for setting up a HomeGroup and then type the main steps for creating a HomeGroup in the Word document. Use the concepts and techniques presented in this chapter to use Help and create the Word document.

3: Creating Folders

Professional

Your boss at the bookstore where you work part-time has asked for help with organizing her files. After looking through the files, you decided upon a file structure for her to use, including the following folders: books, magazines, tapes, DVDs, and general merchandise. Within the books folder, create folders for hardback and paperback books. Within magazines, create folders for special issues and periodicals. In the tapes folder, create folders for celebrity and major release. In the DVDs folder, create a folder for book to DVD. In the general merchandise folder, create folders for novelties, posters, and games. Use the concepts and techniques presented in this chapter to create the folders.

1 | Creating, Formatting, and Editing a Word Document with Pictures

Objectives

You will have mastered the material in this chapter when you can:

- Enter text in a Word document
- Check spelling as you type
- Format paragraphs
- Format text
- Undo and redo commands or actions
- Change theme colors

- Insert digital pictures in a Word document
- Format pictures
- Add a page border
- Correct errors and revise a document
- Change document properties
- Print a document

1 | Creating, Formatting, and Editing a Word Document with Pictures

Introduction

To advertise a sale, promote a business, publicize an event, or convey a message to the community, you may want to create a flyer and hand it out in person or post it in a public location. Libraries, schools, religious organizations, grocery stores, coffee shops, and other places often provide bulletin boards or windows for flyers. These flyers announce personal items for sale or rent (car, boat, apartment); garage or block sales; services being offered (animal care, housecleaning, lessons); membership, sponsorship, or donation requests (club, religious organization, charity); and other messages such as a lost or found pet.

Project Planning Guidelines

The process of developing a document that communicates specific information requires careful analysis and planning. As a starting point, establish why the document is needed. Once the purpose is determined, analyze the intended readers of the document and their unique needs. Then, gather information about the topic and decide what to include in the document. Finally, determine the document design and style that will be most successful at delivering the message. Details of these guidelines are provided in Appendix A. In addition, each project in this book provides practical applications of these planning considerations.

Project — Flyer with Pictures

Individuals and businesses create flyers to gain public attention. Flyers, which usually are a single page in length, are an inexpensive means of reaching the community. Many flyers, however, go unnoticed because they are designed poorly.

The project in this chapter follows general guidelines and uses Word to create the flyer shown in Figure 1–1. This colorful, eye-catching flyer announces that a dog has been found. The pictures of the dog, taken with a camera phone, entice passersby to stop and look at the flyer. The headline on the flyer is large and colorful to draw attention into the text. The body copy below the pictures briefly describes where and when the dog was found, along with a bulleted list that concisely highlights important identifying information. The signature line of the flyer calls attention to the contact phone number. The dog's name, Bailey, and signature line are in a different color so that they stand apart from the rest of the text on the flyer. Finally, the graphical page border nicely frames and complements the contents of the flyer.

Figure 1–1

Overview

As you read this chapter, you will learn how to create the flyer shown in Figure 1–1 on the previous page by performing these general tasks:

- Enter text in the document.
- Format the text in the document.
- Insert the pictures in the document.
- Format the pictures in the document.
- Enhance the page with a border and additional spacing.
- Correct errors and revise the document.
- Print the document.

Plan Ahead

General Project Guidelines

When creating a Word document, the actions you perform and decisions you make will affect the appearance and characteristics of the finished document. As you create a flyer, such as the project shown in Figure 1–1, you should follow these general guidelines:

1. **Choose the words for the text.** Follow the *less is more* principle. The less text, the more likely the flyer will be read. Use as few words as possible to make a point.

2. **Identify how to format various elements of the text.** The overall appearance of a document significantly affects its ability to communicate clearly. Examples of how you can modify the appearance, or **format**, of text include changing its shape, size, color, and position on the page.

3. **Find the appropriate graphical image(s).** An eye-catching graphical image should convey the flyer's overall message. It could show a product, service, result, or benefit, or visually convey a message that is not expressed easily with words.

4. **Establish where to position and how to format the graphical image(s).** The position and format of the graphical image(s) should grab the attention of passersby and draw them into reading the flyer.

5. **Determine whether the page needs enhancements such as a border or spacing adjustments.** A graphical, color-coordinated page border can further draw attention to a flyer and nicely frame its contents. Increasing or decreasing spacing between elements on a flyer can improve its readability and overall appearance.

6. **Correct errors and revise the document as necessary.** Post the flyer on a wall and make sure all text and images are legible from a distance. Ask someone else to read the flyer and give you suggestions for improvements.

7. **Determine the best method for distributing the document.** Documents can be distributed on paper or electronically. A flyer should be printed on paper so that it can be posted.

When necessary, more specific details concerning the above guidelines are presented at appropriate points in the chapter. The chapter also will identify the actions performed and decisions made regarding these guidelines during the creation of the flyer shown in Figure 1–1.

For an introduction to Windows 7 and instruction about how to perform basic Windows 7 tasks, read the Office 2010 and Windows 7 chapter at the beginning of this book, where you can learn how to resize windows, change screen resolution, create folders, move and rename files, use Windows Help, and much more.

To Start Word

If you are using a computer to step through the project in this chapter and you want your screens to match the figures in this book, you should change your screen's resolution to 1024 × 768. For information about how to change a computer's resolution, refer to the Office 2010 and Windows 7 chapter at the beginning of this book.

The following steps, which assume Windows 7 is running, start Word based on typical installation. You may need to ask your instructor how to start Word for your computer. For a detailed example of the procedure summarized below, refer to the Office 2010 and Windows 7 chapter.

● Click the Start button on the Windows 7 taskbar to display the Start menu.

● Type **Microsoft Word** as the search text in the 'Search programs and files' text box and watch the search results appear on the Start menu.

● Click Microsoft Word 2010 in the search results on the Start menu to start Word and display a new blank document in the Word window.

● If the Word window is not maximized, click the Maximize button next to the Close button on its title bar to maximize the window.

● If the Print Layout button on the status bar is not selected (shown in Figure 1–2 on the next page), click it so that your screen is in Print Layout view.

What is Print Layout view?

The default (preset) view in Word is **Print Layout view**, which shows the document on a mock sheet of paper in the document window.

● If Normal (Home tab | Styles group) is not selected in the Quick Style gallery (shown in Figure 1–2), click it so that your document uses the Normal style.

What is the Normal style?

When you create a document, Word formats the text using a particular style. The default style in Word is called the **Normal style**, which is discussed later in this book.

What if rulers appear on my screen?

Click the View Ruler button above the vertical scroll bar to hide the rulers, or click View on the Ribbon to display the View tab and then place a check mark in the Ruler check box.

For an introduction to Office 2010 and instruction about how to perform basic tasks in Office 2010 programs, read the Office 2010 and Windows 7 chapter at the beginning of this book, where you can learn how to start a program, use the Ribbon, save a file, open a file, quit a program, use Help, and much more.

BTW **The Word Window**
The chapters in this book begin with the Word window appearing as it did at the initial installation of the software. Your Word window may look different depending on your screen resolution and other Word settings.

Entering Text

The first step in creating a document is to enter its text. With the projects in this book, you enter text by typing on the keyboard. By default, Word positions text you type at the left margin. In a later section of this chapter, you will learn how to format, or change the appearance of, the entered text.

Choose the words for the text.
The text in a flyer is organized into three areas: headline, body copy, and signature line.

• The **headline** is the first line of text on the flyer. It conveys the product or service being offered, such as a car for sale or personal lessons, or the benefit that will be gained, such as a convenience, better performance, greater security, higher earnings, or more comfort; or it can contain a message such as a lost or found pet.

• The **body copy** consists of all text between the headline and the signature line. This text highlights the key points of the message in as few words as possible. It should be easy to read and follow. While emphasizing the positive, the body copy must be realistic, truthful, and believable.

• The **signature line**, which is the last line of text on the flyer, contains contact information or identifies a call to action.

Plan
Ahead

BTW **Zooming**
If text is too small for you to read on the screen, you can zoom the document by dragging the Zoom slider on the status bar or clicking the Zoom Out or Zoom In buttons on the status bar. Changing the zoom has no effect on the printed document.

To Type Text

To begin creating the flyer in this chapter, type the headline in the document window. The following steps type this first line of text in the document.

1

- Type **Found Dog** as the headline (Figure 1–2).

Q&A What if I make an error while typing?

You can press the BACKSPACE key until you have deleted the text in error and then retype the text correctly.

Q&A Why did the Spelling and Grammar Check icon appear on the status bar?

When you begin typing text, the **Spelling and Grammar Check icon** appears on the status bar with an animated pencil writing on paper to indicate that Word is checking for spelling and grammar errors. When you stop typing, the pencil changes to a blue check mark (no errors) or a red X (potential errors found). Word flags potential errors in the document with a red, green, or blue wavy underline. Later in this chapter, you will learn how to fix flagged errors.

Home tab

document window

Normal style automatically selected when you first install Word

Styles group

View Ruler button shows or hides rulers

insertion point moves to the right as you type

Found Dog

text typed

mouse pointer's shape changes depending on task you are performing in Word and pointer's location on screen

Note: To help you locate screen elements that are referenced in the step instructions, such as buttons and commands, this book uses red boxes to point to these screen elements.

number of words in document

Spelling and Grammar Check icon contains a blue check mark, indicating the entered text contains no spelling or grammar errors

Print Layout button automatically selected when you first install Word

Zoom slider

Page: 1 of 1   Words: 2

Figure 1–2

2

- Press the ENTER key to move the insertion point to the beginning of the next line (Figure 1–3).

Q&A Why did blank space appear between the headline and the insertion point?

Each time you press the ENTER key, Word creates a new paragraph and inserts blank space between the two paragraphs. Later in this chapter, you will learn how to adjust the spacing between paragraphs.

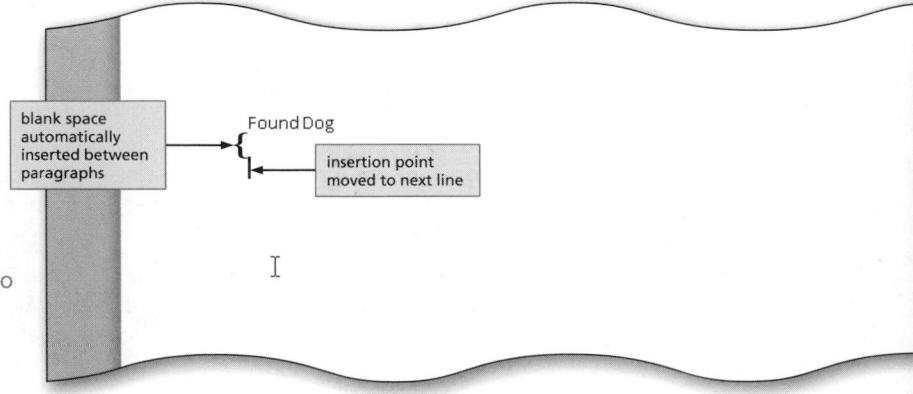

blank space automatically inserted between paragraphs

Found Dog

insertion point moved to next line

Figure 1–3

To Display Formatting Marks

To indicate where in a document you press the ENTER key or SPACEBAR, you may find it helpful to display formatting marks. A **formatting mark**, sometimes called a **nonprinting character**, is a character that Word displays on the screen but is not visible on a printed document. For example, the paragraph mark (¶) is a formatting mark that indicates where you press the ENTER key. A raised dot (·) shows where you press the SPACEBAR. Other formatting marks are discussed as they appear on the screen.

Depending on settings made during previous Word sessions, your Word screen already may display formatting marks (Figure 1–4). The following step displays formatting marks, if they do not show already on the screen.

1
- If the Home tab is not the active tab, click Home on the Ribbon to display the Home tab.

- If it is not selected already, click the Show/Hide ¶ button (Home tab | Paragraph group) to display formatting marks on the screen (Figure 1–4).

What if I do not want formatting marks to show on the screen?

You can hide them by clicking the Show/Hide ¶ button (Home tab | Paragraph group) again. It is recommended that you display formatting marks so that you visually can identify when you press the ENTER key, SPACEBAR, and other keys associated with nonprinting characters; therefore, most of the document windows presented in this book show formatting marks.

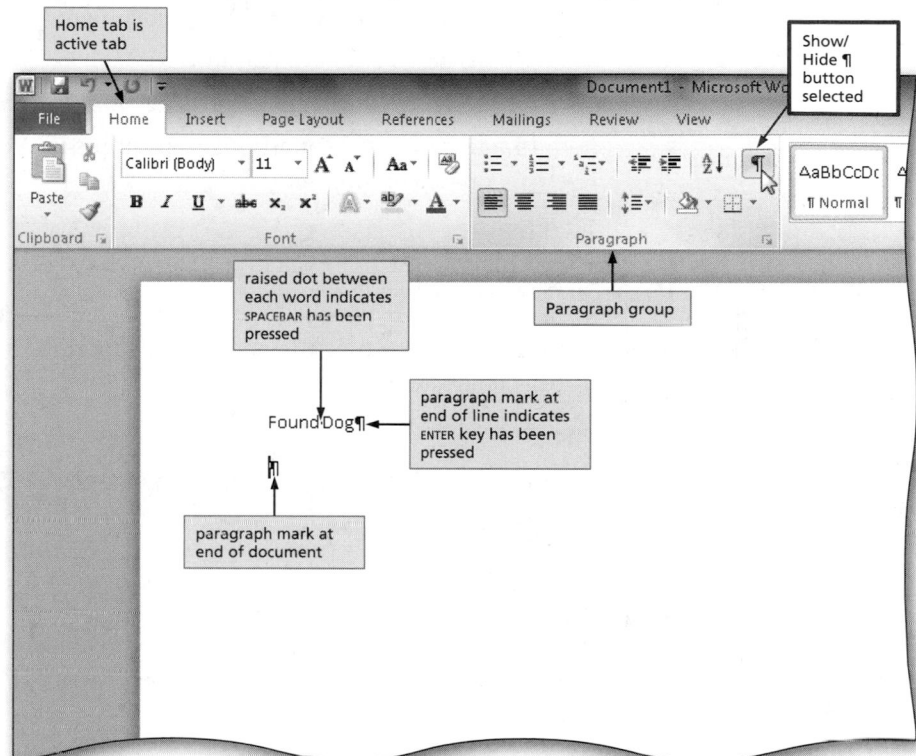

Figure 1–4

Other Ways
1. Press CTRL+SHIFT+*

To Insert a Blank Line

In the flyer, the digital pictures of the dog appear between the headline and body copy. You will not insert these pictures, however, until after you enter and format all text. Thus, you leave a blank line in the document as a placeholder for the pictures. To enter a blank line in a document, press the ENTER key without typing any text on the line. The following step inserts one blank line below the headline.

1
- Press the ENTER key to insert a blank line in the document (Figure 1–5).

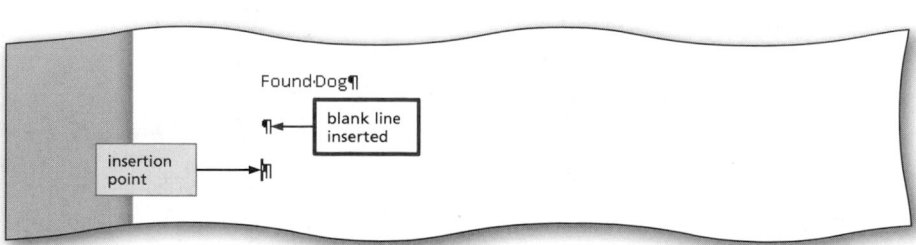

Figure 1–5

Wordwrap

Wordwrap allows you to type words in a paragraph continually without pressing the ENTER key at the end of each line. As you type, if a word extends beyond the right margin, Word also automatically positions that word on the next line along with the insertion point.

Word creates a new paragraph each time you press the ENTER key. Thus, as you type text in the document window, do not press the ENTER key when the insertion point reaches the right margin. Instead, press the ENTER key only in these circumstances:

1. To insert a blank line(s) in a document (as shown in the steps on the previous page)
2. To begin a new paragraph
3. To terminate a short line of text and advance to the next line
4. To respond to questions or prompts in Word dialog boxes, task panes, and other on-screen objects

BTW

The Ribbon and Screen Resolution
Word may change how the groups and buttons within the groups appear on the Ribbon, depending on the computer's screen resolution. Thus, your Ribbon may look different from the ones in this book if you are using a screen resolution other than 1024 × 768.

To Wordwrap Text as You Type

The next step in creating the flyer is to type the body copy. The following step illustrates how the body copy text wordwraps as you enter it in the document.

1

• Type the first sentence of the body copy: `Adorable, loving, friendly, well-behaved dog found early Friday morning, June 1, wandering on the bike trail at Filcher Park in Hampton Township.`

Q&A

Why does my document wrap on different words?

The printer connected to a computer is one factor that can control where wordwrap occurs for each line in a document. Thus, it is possible that the same document could wordwrap differently if printed on different printers.

• Press the ENTER key to position the insertion point on the next line in the document (Figure 1–6).

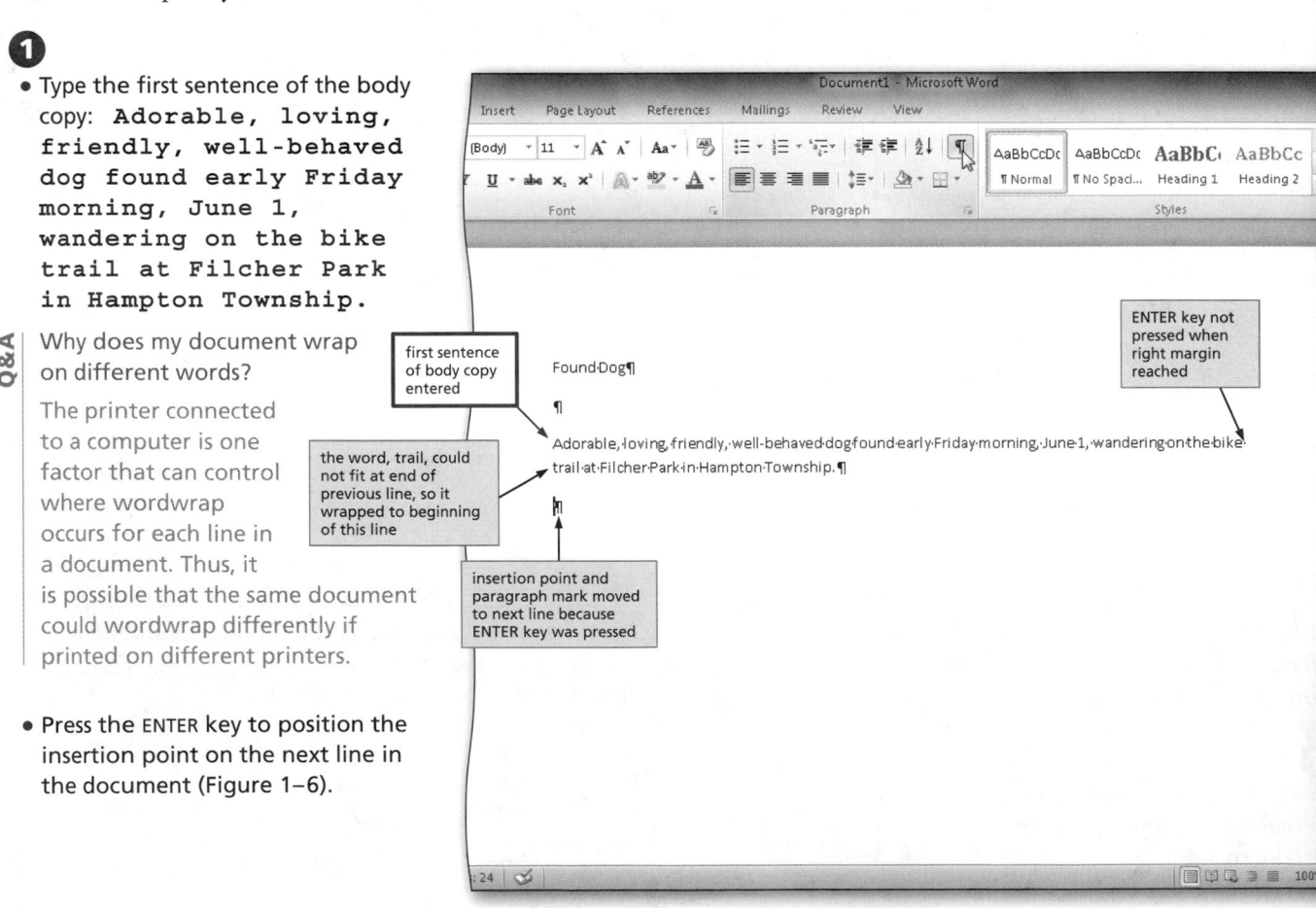

Figure 1–6

Spelling and Grammar Check

As you type text in a document, Word checks your typing for possible spelling and grammar errors. If all of the words you have typed are in Word's dictionary and your grammar is correct, as mentioned earlier, the Spelling and Grammar Check icon on the status bar displays a blue check mark. Otherwise, the icon shows a red X. In this case, Word flags the potential error in the document window with a red, green, or blue wavy underline. A red wavy underline means the flagged text is not in Word's dictionary (because it is a proper name or misspelled). A green wavy underline indicates the text may be incorrect grammatically. A blue wavy underline indicates the text may contain a contextual spelling error such as the misuse of homophones (words that are pronounced the same but that have different spellings or meanings, such as one and won). Although you can check the entire document for spelling and grammar errors at once, you also can check flagged errors as they appear on the screen.

A flagged word is not necessarily misspelled. For example, many names, abbreviations, and specialized terms are not in Word's main dictionary. In these cases, you can instruct Word to ignore the flagged word. As you type, Word also detects duplicate words while checking for spelling errors. For example, if your document contains the phrase, to the the store, Word places a red wavy underline below the second occurrence of the word, the.

BTW
Automatic Spelling Correction
As you type, Word automatically corrects some misspelled words. For example, if you type recieve, Word automatically corrects the misspelling and displays the word, receive, when you press the SPACEBAR or type a punctuation mark. To see a complete list of automatically corrected words, click File on the Ribbon to open the Backstage view, click Options in the Backstage view, click Proofing in the left pane (Word Options dialog box), click the AutoCorrect Options button, and then scroll through the list near the bottom of the dialog box.

To Check Spelling and Grammar as You Type

In the following steps, the word, patches, has been misspelled intentionally as paches to illustrate Word's check spelling as you type feature. If you are doing this project on a computer, your flyer may contain different misspelled words, depending on the accuracy of your typing.

Type **Tan color with paches** and then press the SPACEBAR so that a red wavy line appears below the misspelled word (Figure 1–7).

What if Word does not flag my spelling and grammar errors with wavy underlines?

To verify that the check spelling and grammar as you type features are enabled, click File on the Ribbon to open the Backstage view and then click Options in the Backstage view. When the Word Options dialog box is displayed, click Proofing in the left pane, and then ensure the 'Check spelling as you type' and 'Mark grammar errors as you type' check boxes contain check marks. Also ensure the 'Hide spelling errors in this document only' and 'Hide grammar errors in this document only' check boxes do not have check marks. Click the OK button.

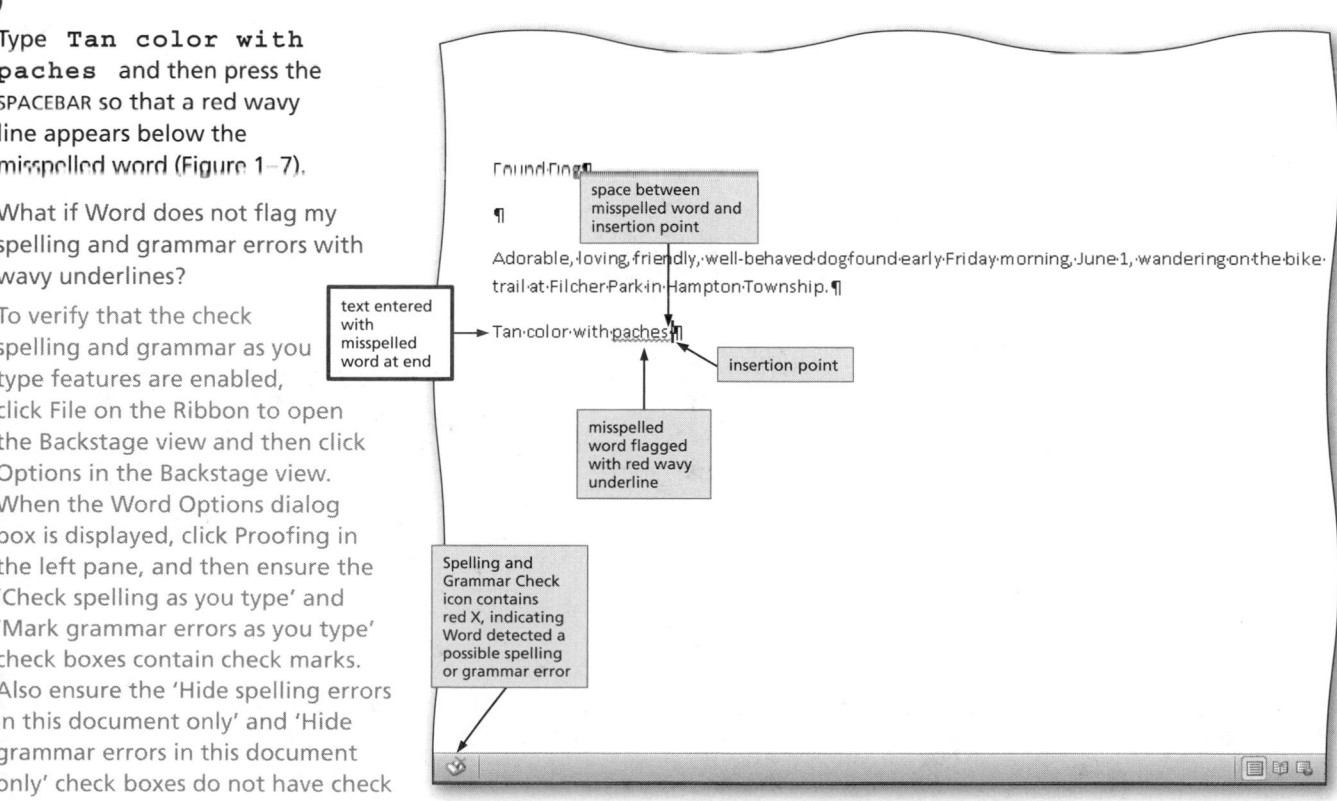

Figure 1–7

2

- Right-click the flagged word (paches, in this case) to display a shortcut menu that presents a list of suggested spelling corrections for the flagged word (Figure 1–8).

Q&A

What if, when I right-click the misspelled word, my desired correction is not in the list on the shortcut menu?

You can click outside the shortcut menu to close the shortcut menu and then retype the correct word, or you can click Spelling on the shortcut menu to display the Spelling dialog box. Chapter 2 discusses the Spelling dialog box.

Q&A

What if a flagged word actually is, for example, a proper name and spelled correctly?

Right-click it and then click Ignore All on the shortcut menu to instruct Word not to flag future occurrences of the same word in this document.

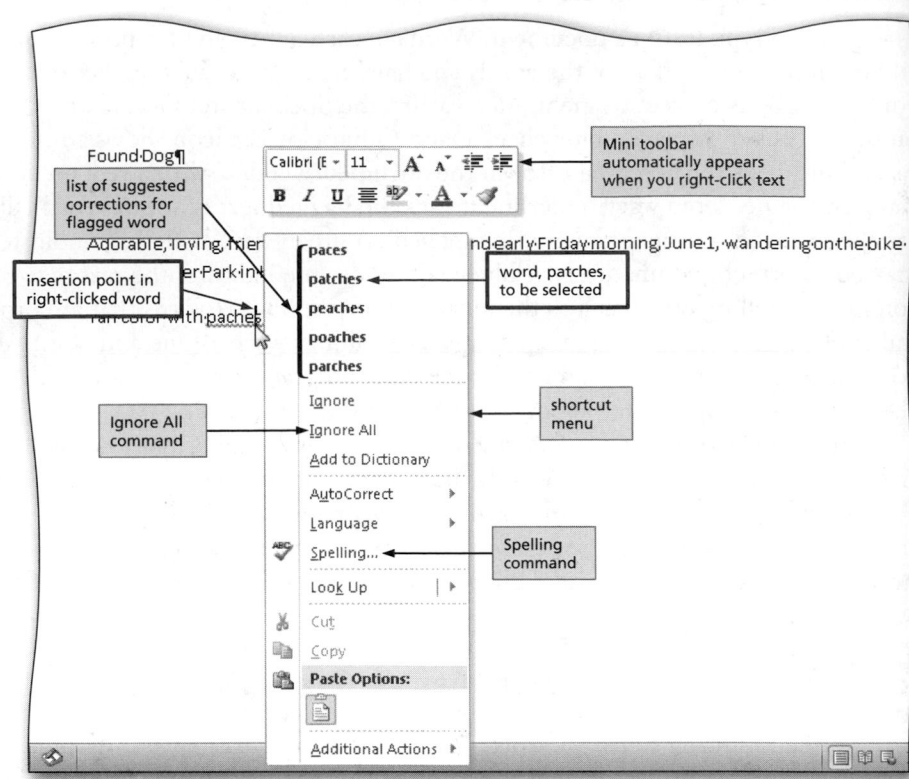

Figure 1–8

3

- Click patches on the shortcut menu to replace the misspelled word in the document with a correctly spelled word (Figure 1–9).

Figure 1–9

Other Ways

1. Click Spelling and Grammar Check icon on status bar, click desired word on shortcut menu

BTW

Character Widths
Many word processing documents use variable character fonts, where some characters are wider than others; for example, the letter w is wider than the letter i.

To Enter More Text

In the flyer, the text yet to be entered includes the remainder of the body copy, which will be formatted as a bulleted list, and the signature line. The next steps enter the remainder of text in the flyer.

Press the END key to move the insertion point to the end of the current line.

Type **of white on his chest** and then press the ENTER key.

Type **Male, adult cocker spaniel** and then press the ENTER key.

Type **Green and silver collar with the name, Bailey, on the tag** and then press the ENTER key.

Type the signature line in the flyer (Figure 1–10): **If this is your lost dog, call 555-1029.**

three paragraphs of body copy entered, which will be formatted as a bulleted list

Tan·color·with·patches·of·white·on·his·chest¶

Male,·adult·cocker·spaniel¶

Green·and·silver·collar·with·the·name,·Bailey,·on·the·tag¶

signature line entered

If·this·is·your·lost·dog,·call·555-1029.¶

Figure 1–10

Navigating a Document

You view only a portion of a document on the screen through the document window. At some point when you type text or insert graphics, Word probably will **scroll** the top or bottom portion of the document off the screen. Although you cannot see the text and graphics once they scroll off the screen, they remain in the document.

You can use either the keyboard or the mouse to scroll to a different location in a document and/or move the insertion point around a document. When you use the keyboard, the insertion point automatically moves when you press the desired keys. For example, the previous steps used the END key to move the insertion point to the end of the current line. Table 1–1 outlines various techniques to navigate a document using the keyboard.

With the mouse, you can use the scroll arrows or the scroll box on the scroll bar to display a different portion of the document in the document window and then click the mouse to move the insertion point to that location. Table 1–2 explains various techniques for using the scroll bar to scroll vertically with the mouse.

BTW

Minimize Wrist Injury
Computer users frequently switch between the keyboard and the mouse during a word processing session; such switching strains the wrist. To help prevent wrist injury, minimize switching. For instance, if your fingers already are on the keyboard, use keyboard keys to scroll. If your hand already is on the mouse, use the mouse to scroll.

Table 1–1 Moving the Insertion Point with the Keyboard

Insertion Point Direction	Key(s) to Press	Insertion Point Direction	Key(s) to Press
Left one character	LEFT ARROW	Up one paragraph	CTRL+UP ARROW
Right one character	RIGHT ARROW	Down one paragraph	CTRL+DOWN ARROW
Left one word	CTRL+LEFT ARROW	Up one screen	PAGE UP
Right one word	CTRL+RIGHT ARROW	Down one screen	PAGE DOWN
Up one line	UP ARROW	To top of document window	ALT+CTRL+PAGE UP
Down one line	DOWN ARROW	To bottom of document window	ALT+CTRL+PAGE DOWN
To end of line	END	To beginning of document	CTRL+HOME
To beginning of line	HOME	To end of document	CTRL+END

Table 1–2 Using the Scroll Bar to Scroll Vertically with the Mouse

Scroll Direction	Mouse Action	Scroll Direction	Mouse Action
Up	Drag the scroll box upward.	Down one screen	Click anywhere below the scroll box on the vertical scroll bar.
Down	Drag the scroll box downward.	Up one line	Click the scroll arrow at the top of the vertical scroll bar.
Up one screen	Click anywhere above the scroll box on the vertical scroll bar.	Down one line	Click the scroll arrow at the bottom of the vertical scroll bar.

BTW

Organizing Files and Folders
You should organize and store files in folders so that you easily can find the files later. For example, if you are taking an introductory computer class called CIS 101, a good practice would be to save all Word files in a Word folder in a CIS 101 folder. For a discussion of folders and detailed examples of creating folders, refer to the Office 2010 and Windows 7 chapter at the beginning of this book.

To Save a Document

You have performed many tasks while creating this flyer and do not want to risk losing work completed thus far. Accordingly, you should save the document.

The following steps assume you already have created folders for storing your files, for example, a CIS 101 folder (for your class) that contains a Word folder (for your assignments). Thus, these steps save the document in the Word folder in the CIS 101 folder on a USB flash drive using the file name, Found Dog Flyer. For a detailed example of the procedure summarized below, refer to the Office 2010 and Windows 7 chapter at the beginning of this book.

1 With a USB flash drive connected to one of the computer's USB ports, click the Save button on the Quick Access Toolbar to display the Save As dialog box.

2 Type **Found Dog Flyer** in the File name text box to change the file name. Do not press the ENTER key after typing the file name because you do not want to close the dialog box at this time.

3 Navigate to the desired save location (in this case, the Word folder in the CIS 101 folder [or your class folder] on the USB flash drive).

4 Click the Save button (Save As dialog box) to save the document in the selected folder on the selected drive with the entered file name.

Formatting Paragraphs and Characters

With the text for the flyer entered, the next step is to **format**, or change the appearance of, its text. A paragraph encompasses the text from the first character in the paragraph up to and including its paragraph mark (¶). **Paragraph formatting** is the process of changing the appearance of a paragraph. For example, you can center or add bullets to a paragraph. Characters include letters, numbers, punctuation marks, and symbols. **Character formatting** is the process of changing the way characters appear on the screen and in print. You use character formatting to emphasize certain words and improve readability of a document. For example, you can color or underline characters. Often, you apply both paragraph and character formatting to the same text. For example, you may center a paragraph (paragraph formatting) and underline some of the characters in the same paragraph (character formatting).

Although you can format paragraphs and characters before you type, many Word users enter text first and then format the existing text. Figure 1–11a shows the flyer in this chapter before formatting its paragraphs and characters. Figure 1–11b shows the flyer after formatting. As you can see from the two figures, a document that is formatted is easier to read and looks more professional. The following pages discuss how to format the flyer so that it looks like Figure 1–11b.

Characters that appear on the screen are a specific shape and size. The **font**, or typeface, defines the appearance and shape of the letters, numbers, and special characters. In Word, the default font usually is Calibri (shown in Figure 1–12 on page WD 14). You can leave characters in the default font or change them to a different font. **Font size** specifies the size of the characters and is determined by a measurement system called points. A single **point** is about 1/72 of one inch in height. The default font size in Word typically is 11 (Figure 1–12). Thus, a character with a font size of 11 is about 11/72 or a little less than 1/6 of one inch in height. You can increase or decrease the font size of characters in a document.

A document **theme** is a set of unified formats for fonts, colors, and graphics. Word includes a variety of document themes to assist you with coordinating these visual elements in a document. The default theme fonts are Cambria for headings and Calibri for body text. By changing the document theme, you quickly can give your document a new look. You also can define your own document themes.

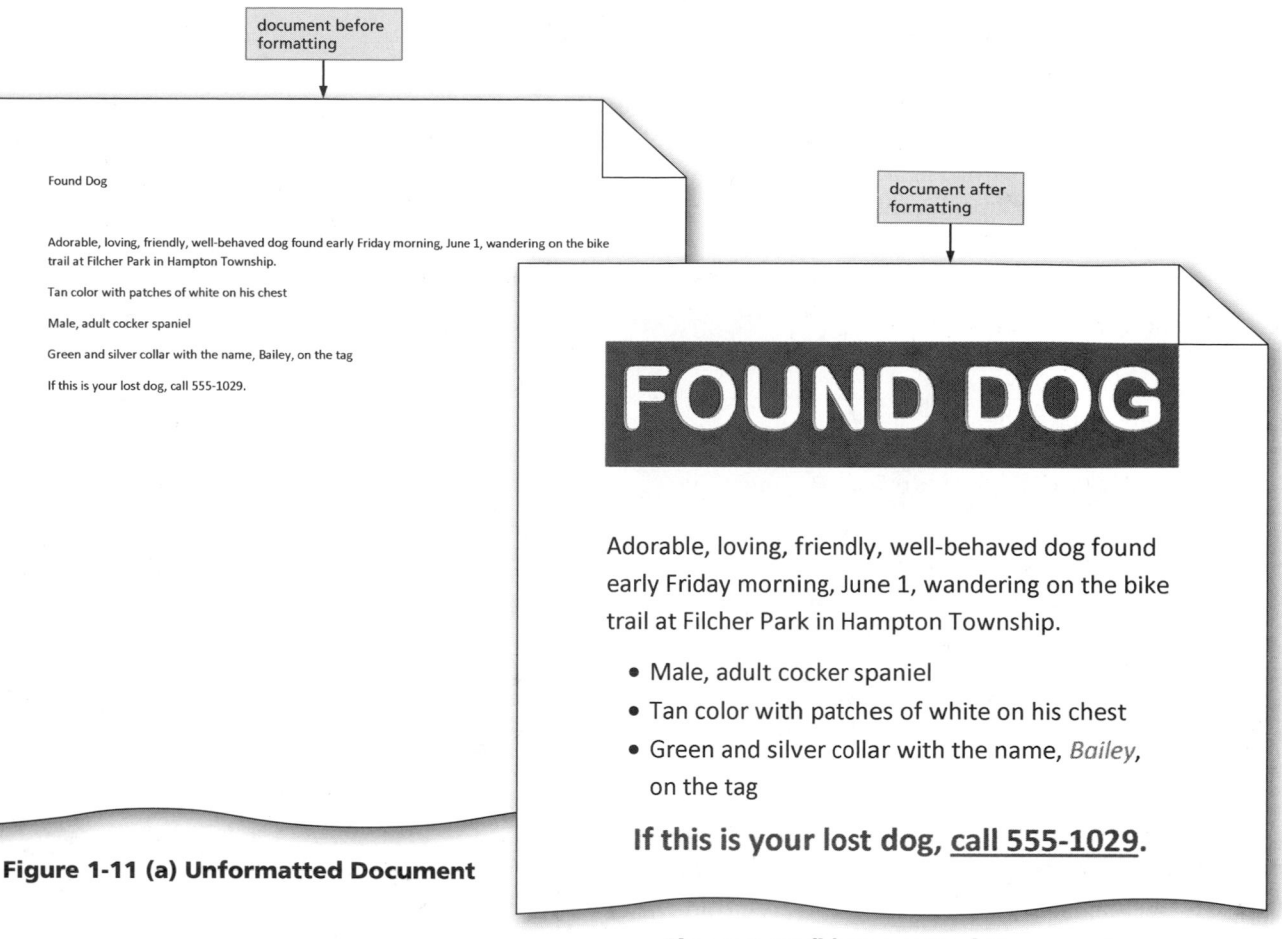

document before formatting

Found Dog

Adorable, loving, friendly, well-behaved dog found early Friday morning, June 1, wandering on the bike trail at Filcher Park in Hampton Township.

Tan color with patches of white on his chest

Male, adult cocker spaniel

Green and silver collar with the name, Bailey, on the tag

If this is your lost dog, call 555-1029.

document after formatting

FOUND DOG

Adorable, loving, friendly, well-behaved dog found early Friday morning, June 1, wandering on the bike trail at Filcher Park in Hampton Township.

- Male, adult cocker spaniel
- Tan color with patches of white on his chest
- Green and silver collar with the name, *Bailey*, on the tag

If this is your lost dog, <u>call 555-1029</u>.

Figure 1-11 (a) Unformatted Document

Figure 1-11 (b) Formatted Document

Identify how to format various elements of the text.

Plan Ahead

By formatting the characters and paragraphs in a document, you can improve its overall appearance. In a flyer, consider the following formatting suggestions.

- **Increase the font size of characters.** Flyers usually are posted on a bulletin board or in a window. Thus, the font size should be as large as possible so that passersby easily can read the flyer. To give the headline more impact, its font size should be larger than the font size of the text in the body copy. If possible, make the font size of the signature line larger than the body copy but smaller than the headline.

- **Change the font of characters.** Use fonts that are easy to read. Try to use only two different fonts in a flyer, for example, one for the headline and the other for all other text. Too many fonts can make the flyer visually confusing.

- **Change paragraph alignment.** The default alignment for paragraphs in a document is **left-aligned**, that is, flush at the left margin of the document with uneven right edges. Consider changing the alignment of some of the paragraphs to add interest and variety to the flyer.

- **Highlight key paragraphs with bullets.** A bulleted paragraph is a paragraph that begins with a dot or other symbol. Use bulleted paragraphs to highlight important points in a flyer.

- **Emphasize important words.** To call attention to certain words or lines, you can underline them, italicize them, or bold them. Use these formats sparingly, however, because overuse will minimize their effect and make the flyer look too busy.

- **Use color.** Use colors that complement each other and convey the meaning of the flyer. Vary colors in terms of hue and brightness. Headline colors, for example, can be bold and bright. Signature lines should stand out more than body copy but less than headlines. Keep in mind that too many colors can detract from the flyer and make it difficult to read.

To Center a Paragraph

The headline in the flyer currently is left-aligned (Figure 1–12). You want the headline to be **centered**, that is, positioned horizontally between the left and right margins on the page. Recall that Word considers a single short line of text, such as the two-word headline, a paragraph. Thus, you will center the paragraph containing the headline. The following steps center a paragraph.

1
- Click somewhere in the paragraph to be centered (in this case, the headline) to position the insertion point in the paragraph to be formatted (Figure 1–12).

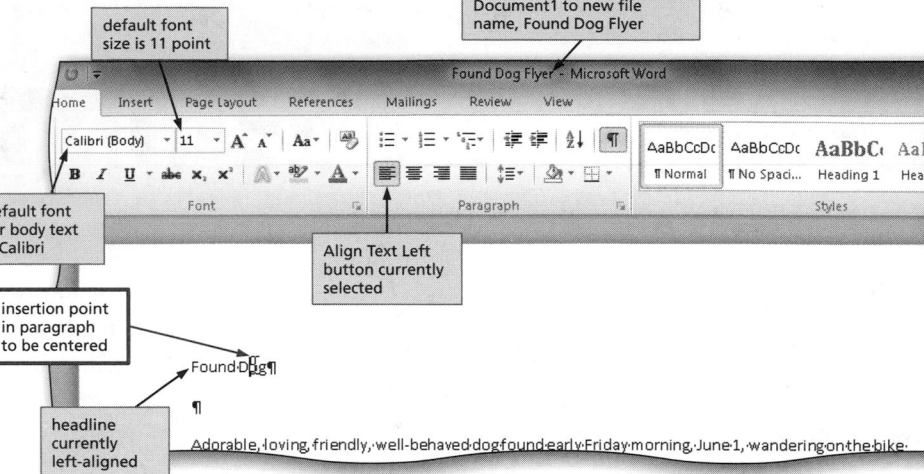

Figure 1–12

2
- Click the Center button (Home tab | Paragraph group) to center the paragraph containing the insertion point (Figure 1–13).

Q&A

What if I want to return the paragraph to left-aligned?

You would click the Center button again or click the Align Text Left button (Home tab | Paragraph group).

Figure 1–13

Other Ways

1. Right-click paragraph, click Center button on Mini toolbar

2. Right-click paragraph, click Paragraph on shortcut menu, click Indents and Spacing tab

3. Click Paragraph Dialog Box Launcher (Home tab or Page Layout tab | Paragraph group), click Indents and Spacing tab (Paragraph dialog box), click Alignment box arrow, click Centered, click OK button

(Paragraph dialog box), click Alignment box arrow, click Centered, click OK button

4. Press CTRL+E

BTW

File Type
Depending on your Windows settings, the file type .docx may be displayed on the title bar immediately to the right of the file name after you save the file. The file type .docx is a Word 2010 document.

To Center Another Paragraph

In the flyer, the signature line is to be centered to match the paragraph alignment of the headline. The following steps center the signature line.

1 Click somewhere in the paragraph to be centered (in this case, the signature line) to position the insertion point in the paragraph to be formatted.

2 Click the Center button (Home tab | Paragraph group) to center the paragraph containing the insertion point (shown in Figure 1–14).

Formatting Single versus Multiple Paragraphs and Characters

As shown on the previous pages, to format a single paragraph, simply move the insertion point in the paragraph, to make it the current paragraph, and then format the paragraph. Similarly, to format a single word, position the insertion point in the word, to make it the current word, and then format the word.

To format multiple paragraphs or words, however, you first must select the paragraphs or words you want to format and then format the selection. If your screen normally displays dark letters on a light background, which is the default setting in Word, then selected text displays light letters on a dark background.

BTW

Selecting Nonadjacent Items

In Word, you can select nonadjacent items, that is, items not next to each other. This is helpful when you are applying the same formatting to multiple items. To select nonadjacent items (text or graphics), select the first item, such as a word or paragraph, as usual; then, press and hold down the CTRL key. While holding down the CTRL key, select additional items.

To Select a Line

The default font size of 11 point is too small for a headline in a flyer. To increase the font size of the characters in the headline, you first must select the line of text containing the headline. The following steps select a line.

• Move the mouse pointer to the left of the line to be selected (in this case, the headline) until the mouse pointer changes to a right-pointing block arrow (Figure 1–14).

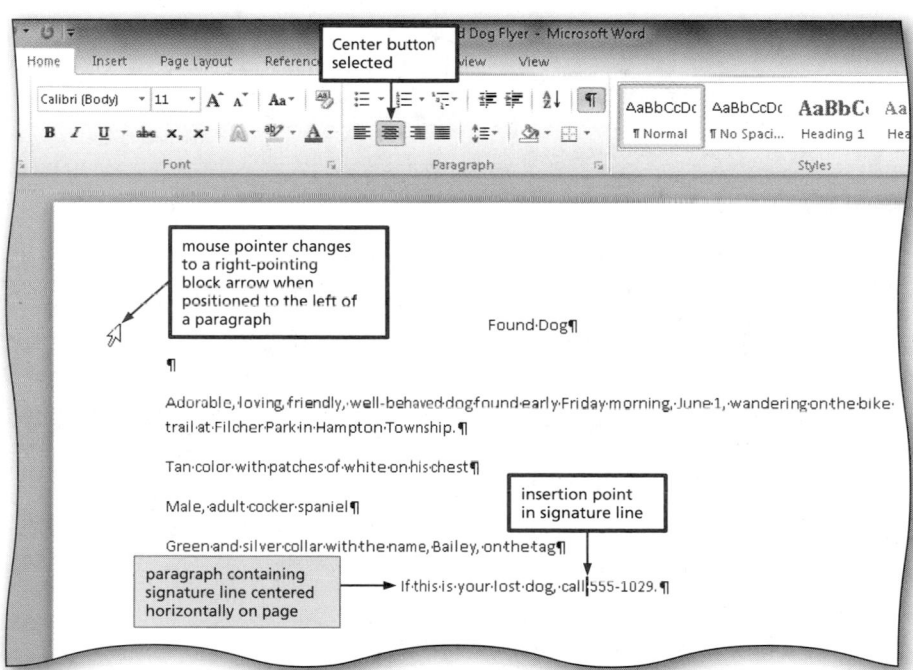

Figure 1–14

• While the mouse pointer is a right-pointing block arrow, click the mouse to select the entire line to the right of the mouse pointer (Figure 1–15).

Figure 1–15

Other Ways	
1. Drag mouse through line	2. With insertion point at beginning of desired line, press SHIFT+DOWN ARROW

To Change the Font Size of Selected Text

The next step is to increase the font size of the characters in the selected headline. You would like the headline to be as large as possible and still fit on a single line, which in this case is 72 point. The following steps increase the font size of the headline from 11 to 72 point.

1

● With the text selected, click the Font Size box arrow (Home tab | Font group) to display the Font Size gallery (Figure 1–16).

Q&A Why are the font sizes in my Font Size gallery different from those in Figure 1–16?

Font sizes may vary depending on the current font and your printer driver.

Q&A What happened to the Mini toolbar?

The Mini toolbar disappears if you do not use it. These steps use the Font Size box arrow on the Home tab instead of the Font Size box arrow on the Mini toolbar.

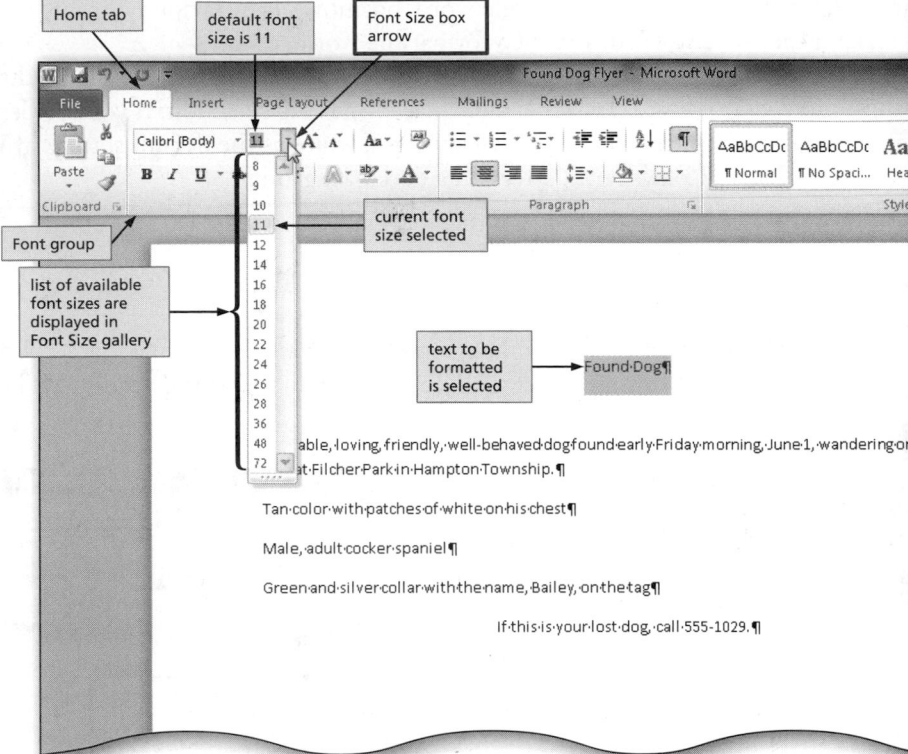

Figure 1–16

2

● Point to 72 in the Font Size gallery to display a live preview of the selected text at the selected point size (Figure 1–17).

🔍 **Experiment**

● Point to various font sizes in the Font Size gallery and watch the font size of the selected text change in the document window.

3

● Click 72 in the Font Size gallery to increase the font size of the selected text.

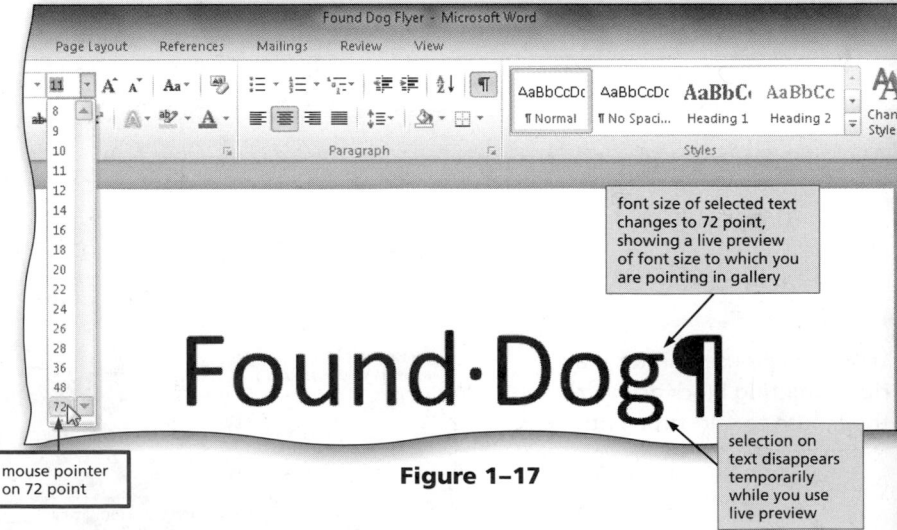

Figure 1–17

Other Ways

1. Click Font Size box arrow on Mini toolbar, click desired font size in Font Size gallery

2. Right-click selected text, click Font on shortcut menu, click Font tab (Font dialog box), select desired font size in Size list, click OK button

3. Click Font Dialog Box Launcher, click Font tab (Font dialog box), select desired font size in Size list, click OK button

4. Press CTRL+D, click Font tab (Font dialog box), select desired font size in Size list, click OK button

To Change the Font of Selected Text

The default theme font for headings is Cambria and for all other text, called body text in Word, is Calibri. Many other fonts are available, however, so that you can add variety to documents.

To draw more attention to the headline, you change its font so that it differs from the font of other text in the flyer. The following steps change the font of the headline from Calibri to Arial Rounded MT Bold.

1

- With the text selected, click the Font box arrow (Home tab | Font group) to display the Font gallery (Figure 1–18).

Will the fonts in my Font gallery be the same as those in Figure 1–18?

Your list of available fonts may differ, depending on the type of printer you are using and other settings.

What if the text is no longer selected?

Follow the steps on page WD 15 to select a line.

Figure 1–18

2

- Scroll through the Font gallery, if necessary, and then point to Arial Rounded MT Bold (or a similar font) to display a live preview of the selected text in the selected font (Figure 1–19).

Experiment

- Point to various fonts in the Font gallery and watch the font of the selected text change in the document window.

3

- Click Arial Rounded MT Bold (or a similar font) to change the font of the selected text.

Figure 1–19

Other Ways		
1. Click Font box arrow on Mini toolbar, click desired font in Font gallery 2. Right-click selected text, click Font on shortcut menu, click Font tab (Font dialog	box), select desired font in Font list, click OK button 3. Click Font Dialog Box Launcher (Home tab	Font group), click Font tab (Font dialog box), select desired	font in Font list, click OK button 4. Press CTRL+D, click Font tab (Font dialog box), select desired font in the Font list, click OK button

To Change the Case of Selected Text

The headline currently shows the first letter in each word capitalized, which sometimes is referred to as initial cap. To draw more attention to the headline, you would like the entire line of text to be capitalized, or in uppercase letters. The following steps change the headline to uppercase.

1

- With the text selected, click the Change Case button (Home tab | Font group) to display the Change Case gallery (Figure 1–20).

Figure 1–20

2

- Click UPPERCASE in the Change Case gallery to change the case of the selected text (Figure 1–21).

Q&A

What if a ruler appears on the screen or the mouse pointer shape changes?

Depending on the position of your mouse pointer and locations you click on the screen, a ruler may automatically appear or the mouse pointer shape may change. Simply move the mouse and the ruler should disappear and/or the mouse pointer shape will change.

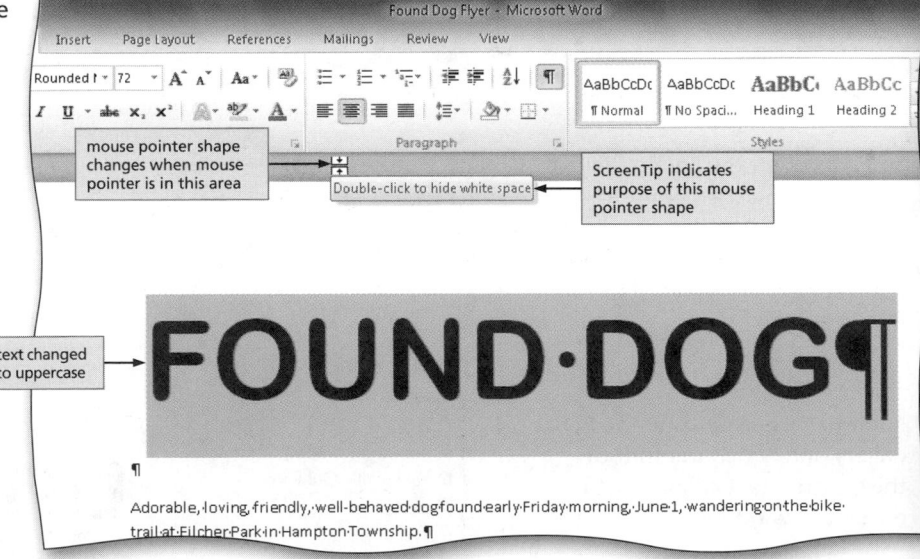

Figure 1–21

Other Ways

1. Right-click selected text, click Font on shortcut menu, click Font tab (Font dialog box), select All caps in Effects area, click OK button

2. Click Font Dialog Box Launcher (Home tab | Font group), click Font tab (Font dialog box), select All caps in Effects area, click OK button

3. Press SHIFT+F3 repeatedly until text is desired case

To Apply a Text Effect to Selected Text

You would like the text in the headline to be even more noticeable. Word provides many text effects to add interest and variety to text. The following steps apply a text effect to the headline.

- With the text selected, click the Text Effects button (Home tab | Font group) to display the Text Effects gallery (Figure 1–22).

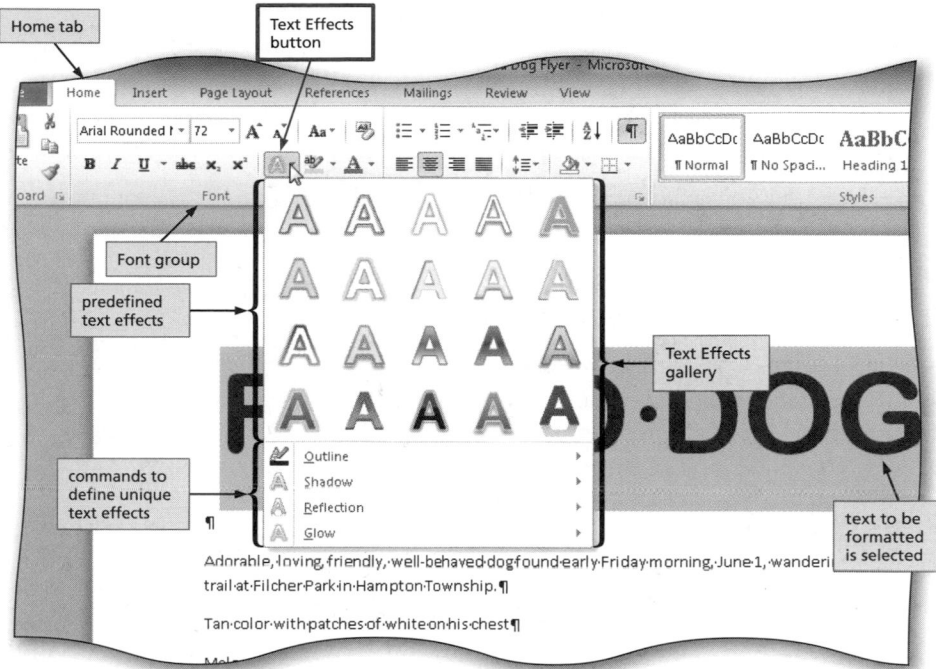

Figure 1–22

- Point to Fill – White, Gradient Outline – Accent 1 (first text effect in third row) to display a live preview of the selected text in the selected text effect (Figure 1–23).

Experiment

- Point to various text effects in the Text Effects gallery and watch the text effects of the selected text change in the document window.

- Click Fill – White, Gradient Outline – Accent 1 to change the text effect of the selected text.

- Click anywhere in the document window to remove the selection from the selected text.

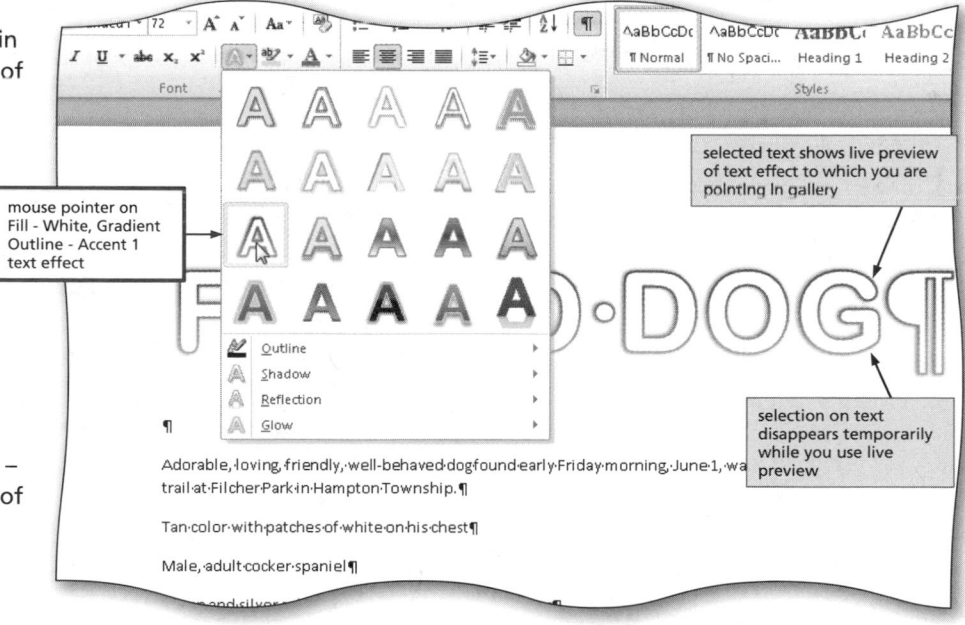

Figure 1–23

Other Ways

1. Right-click selected text, click Font on shortcut menu, click Font tab (Font dialog box), click Text Effects button, select desired text effects (Format Text Effects dialog box), click Close button, click OK button

2. Click Font Dialog Box Launcher (Home tab | Font group), click Font tab (Font dialog box), click Text Effects button, select desired text effects (Format Text Effects dialog box), click Close button, click OK button

To Shade a Paragraph

To make the headline of the flyer more eye-catching, you would like to shade it. When you **shade** text, Word colors the rectangular area behind any text or graphics. If the text to shade is a paragraph, Word shades the area from the left margin to the right margin of the current paragraph. To shade a paragraph, place the insertion point in the paragraph. To shade any other text, you must first select the text to be shaded. This flyer uses brown as the shading color for the headline. The following steps shade a paragraph.

1

- Click somewhere in the paragraph to be shaded (in this case, the headline) to position the insertion point in the paragraph to be formatted.

- Click the Shading button arrow (Home tab | Paragraph group) to display the Shading gallery (Figure 1–24).

Q&A What if I click the Shading button by mistake?

Click the Shading button arrow and proceed with Step 2.

Figure 1–24

2

- Point to Orange, Accent 6, Darker 50% (rightmost color in the sixth row) to display a live preview of the selected shading color (Figure 1–25).

 Experiment

- Point to various colors in the Shading gallery and watch the shading color of the current paragraph change.

Figure 1–25

3

- Click Orange, Accent 6, Darker 50% to shade the current paragraph.

Q&A What if I apply a dark shading color to dark text?

When the font color of text is Automatic, it usually is black. If you select a dark shading color, Word automatically may change the text color to white so that the shaded text is easier to read.

Other Ways
1. Click Border button arrow (Home tab | Paragraph group), click Borders and Shading, click Shading tab (Borders and Shading dialog box), click Fill box arrow, select desired color, click OK button

To Select Multiple Lines

The next formatting step for the flyer is to increase the font size of the characters between the headline and the signature line so that they are easier to read from a distance. To change the font size of the characters in multiple lines, you first must select all the lines to be formatted. The following steps select multiple lines.

1

- Move the mouse pointer to the left of the first paragraph to be selected until the mouse pointer changes to a right-pointing block arrow (Figure 1–26).

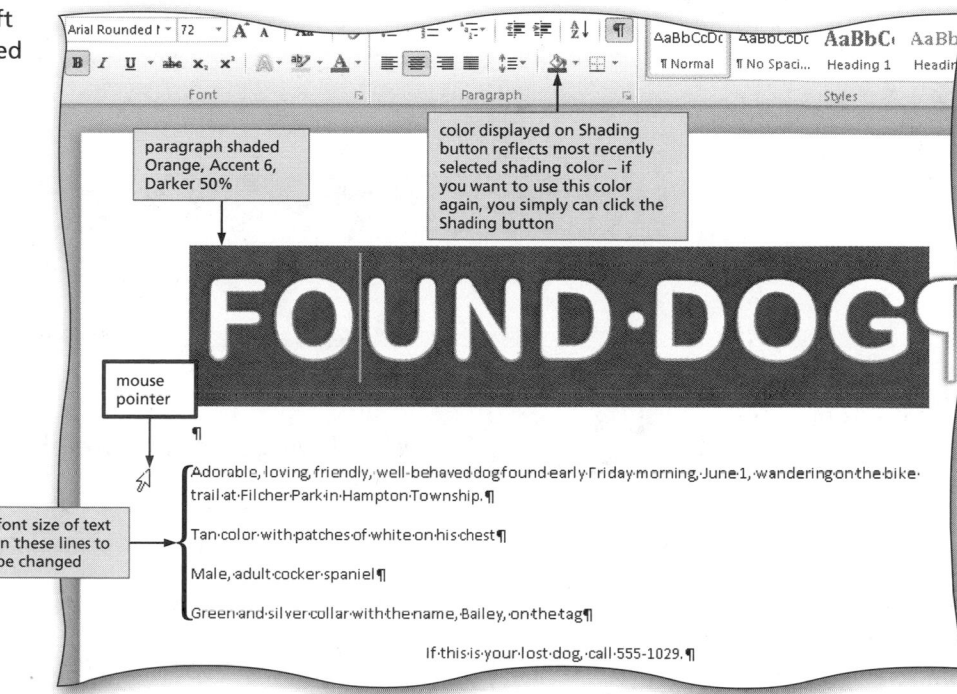

paragraph shaded Orange, Accent 6, Darker 50%

color displayed on Shading button reflects most recently selected shading color – if you want to use this color again, you simply can click the Shading button

mouse pointer

font size of text in these lines to be changed

Figure 1–26

2

- Drag downward to select all lines that will be formatted (Figure 1–27).

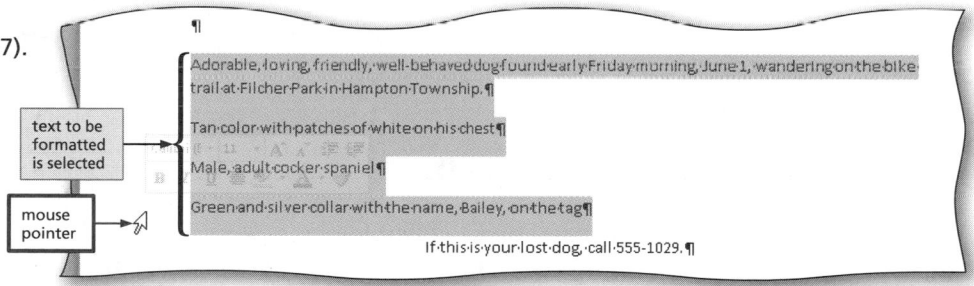

text to be formatted is selected

mouse pointer

Figure 1–27

Other Ways

1. With insertion point at beginning of desired line, press SHIFT+DOWN ARROW repeatedly until all lines are selected

To Change the Font Size of Selected Text

The characters between the headline and the signature line in the flyer currently are 11 point. To make them easier to read from a distance, this flyer uses 22 point for these characters. The steps on the next page change the font size of the selected text.

1 With the text selected, click the Font Size box arrow (Home tab | Font group) to display the Font Size gallery.

2 Click 22 in the Font Size gallery to increase the font size of the selected text.

3 Click anywhere in the document window to remove the selection from the text.

4 If necessary, scroll so that you can see all the text on the screen (Figure 1–28).

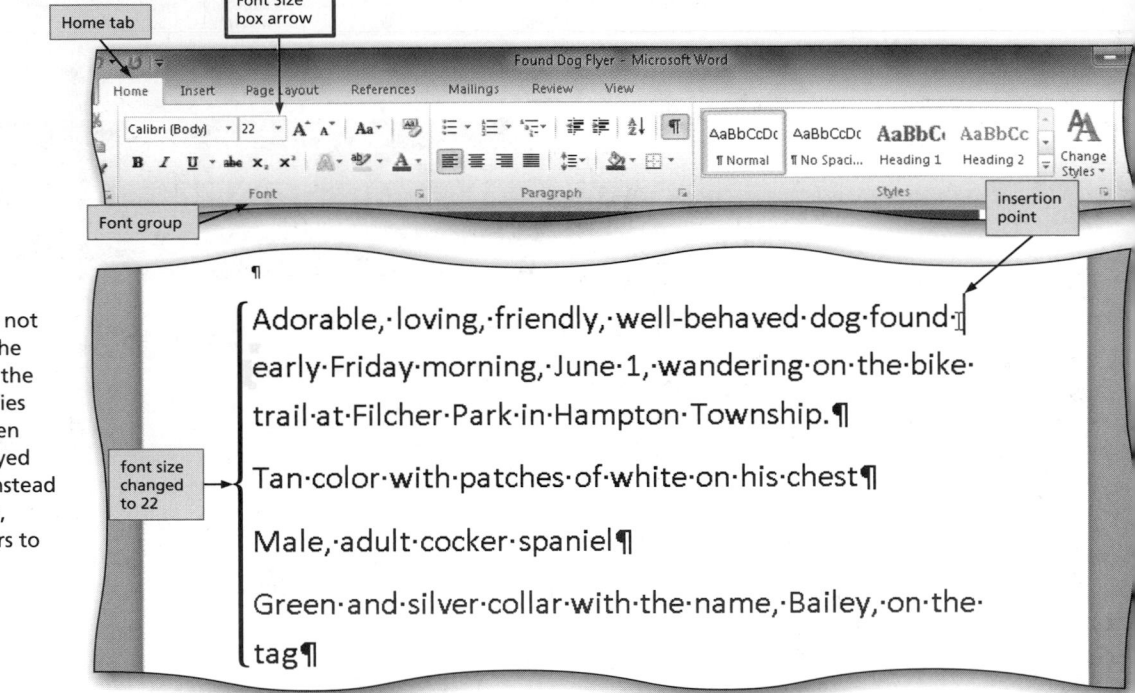

BTW

Formatting Marks
With some fonts, formatting marks do not display properly on the screen. For example, the raised dot that signifies a blank space between words may be displayed behind a character instead of in the blank space, causing the characters to look incorrect.

Figure 1–28

To Bullet a List of Paragraphs

The next step is to format as a bulleted list the three paragraphs of identifying information that are above the signature line in the flyer. A **bulleted list** is a series of paragraphs, each beginning with a bullet character.

To format a list of paragraphs with bullets, you first must select all the lines in the paragraphs. The following steps bullet a list of paragraphs.

1

- Move the mouse pointer to the left of the first paragraph to be selected until the mouse pointer changes to a right-pointing block arrow.

- Drag downward until all paragraphs that will be formatted with a bullet character are selected (Figure 1–29).

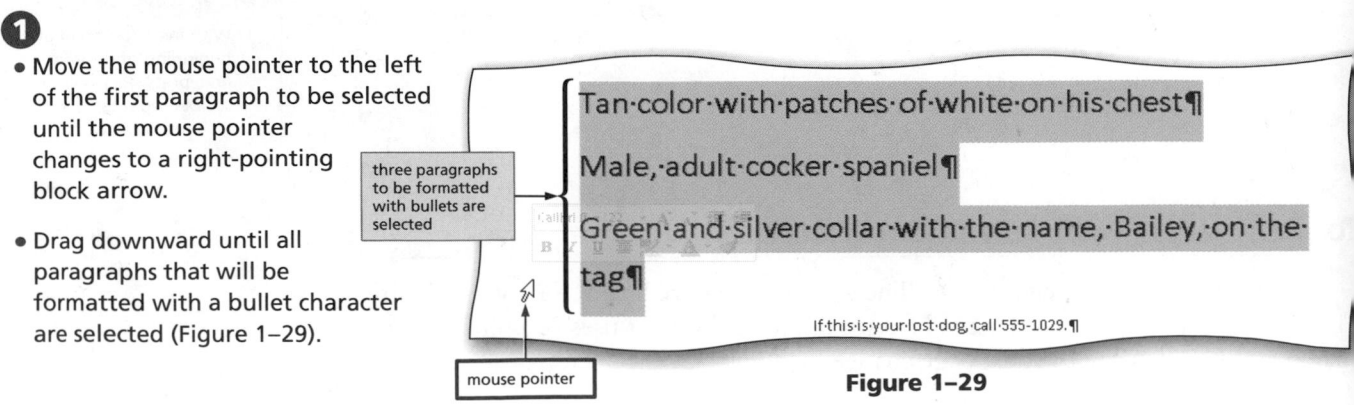

Figure 1–29

2

● Click the Bullets button (Home tab | Paragraph group) to place a bullet character at the beginning of each selected paragraph (Figure 1–30).

How do I remove bullets from a list or paragraph?

Select the list or paragraph and then click the Bullets button again.

What if I accidentally click the Bullets button arrow?

Press the ESCAPE key to remove the Bullets gallery from the screen and then repeat Step 2.

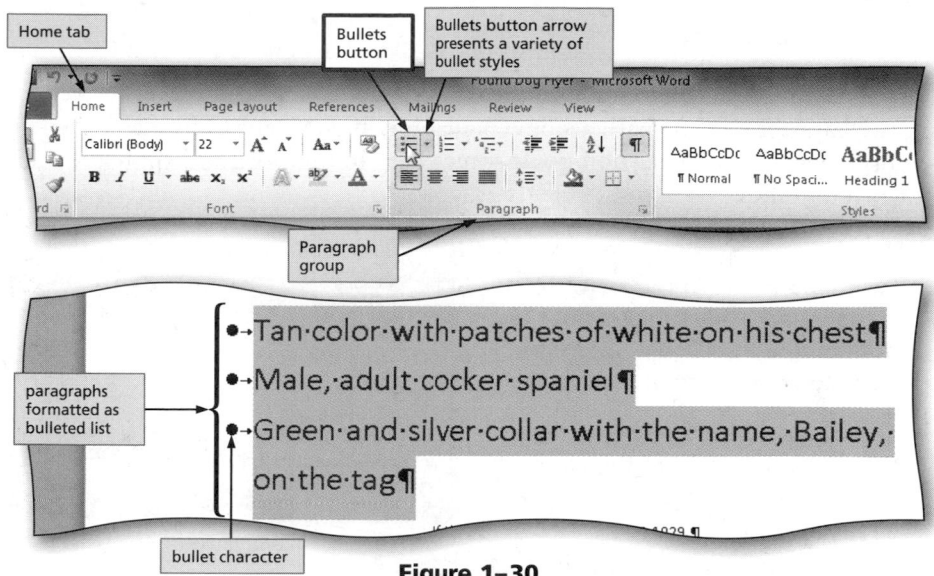

Figure 1–30

To Undo and Redo an Action

Word provides a means of canceling your recent command(s) or action(s). For example, if you format text incorrectly, you can undo the format and try it again. When you point to the Undo button, Word displays the action you can undo as part of a ScreenTip.

If, after you undo an action, you decide you did not want to perform the undo, you can redo the undone action. Word does not allow you to undo or redo some actions, such as saving or printing a document. The next steps undo the bullet format just applied and then redo the bullet format.

1

● Click the Undo button on the Quick Access Toolbar to reverse your most recent action (in this case, remove the bullets from the paragraphs) (Figure 1–31).

2

● Click the Redo button on the Quick Access Toolbar to reverse your most recent undo (in this case, place a bullet character on the paragraphs again) (shown in Figure 1–30).

Figure 1–31

To Italicize Text

The next step is to italicize the dog's name, Bailey, in the flyer to further emphasize it. **Italicized** text has a slanted appearance. As with a single paragraph, if you want to format a single word, you do not need to select it. Simply position the insertion point somewhere in the word and apply the desired format. The following step formats a word in italics.

- Click somewhere in the word to be italicized (Bailey, in this case) to position the insertion point in the word to be formatted.

- Click the Italic button (Home tab | Font group) to italicize the word containing the insertion point (Figure 1–32).

Q&A

How would I remove an italic format?

You would click the Italic button a second time, or you immediately could click the Undo button on the Quick Access Toolbar or press CTRL+Z.

Q&A

How can I tell what formatting has been applied to text?

The selected buttons and boxes on the Home tab show formatting characteristics of the location of the insertion point. With the insertion point in the word, Bailey, the Home tab shows these formats: 22-point Calibri italic font, bulleted paragraph.

Figure 1–32

Other Ways

1. Click Italic button on Mini toolbar

2. Right-click selected text, click Font on shortcut menu, click Font tab

3. Click Font Dialog Box Launcher (Home tab |

(Font dialog box), click Italic in Font style list, click OK button

Font group), click Font tab (Font dialog box), click Italic in Font style list, click OK button

4. Press CTRL+I

Plan Ahead

Use color.

When choosing color, associate the meaning of color to your message:

- Red expresses danger, power, or energy, and often is associated with sports or physical exertion.
- Brown represents simplicity, honesty, and dependability.
- Orange denotes success, victory, creativity, and enthusiasm.
- Yellow suggests sunshine, happiness, hope, liveliness, and intelligence.
- Green symbolizes growth, healthiness, harmony, blooming, and healing, and often is associated with safety or money.
- Blue indicates integrity, trust, importance, confidence, and stability.
- Purple represents wealth, power, comfort, extravagance, magic, mystery, and spirituality.
- White stands for purity, goodness, cleanliness, precision, and perfection.
- Black suggests authority, strength, elegance, power, and prestige.
- Gray conveys neutrality and thus often is found in backgrounds and other effects.

BTW

Q&As

For a complete list of the Q&As found in many of the step-by-step sequences in this book, visit the Word 2010 Q&A Web page (scsite.com/wd2010/qa).

To Color Text

To emphasize the dog's name even more, its color is changed to a shade of blue. The following steps change the color of the word, Bailey.

1

- With the insertion point in the word to format, click the Font Color button arrow (Home tab | Font group) to display the Font Color gallery (Figure 1–33).

What if I click the Font Color button by mistake?

Click the Font Color button arrow and then proceed with Step 2.

2

- Point to Blue, Accent 1, Darker 25% (fifth color in the fifth row) to display a live preview of the selected font color.

Experiment

- Point to various colors in the Font Color gallery and watch the color of the current word change.

Figure 1–33

3

- Click Blue, Accent 1, Darker 25% to change the color of the text (Figure 1–34).

How would I change the text color back to black?

You would position the insertion point in the word or select the text, click the Font Color button arrow (Home tab | Font group) again, and then click Automatic in the Font Color gallery.

Figure 1–34

Other Ways		
1. Click Font Color button arrow on Mini toolbar, click desired color	(Font dialog box), click Font color box arrow, click desired color, click OK button	Font group), click Font tab (Font dialog box), click Font color box arrow, click desired color, click OK button
2. Right-click selected text, click Font on shortcut menu, click Font tab	3. Click Font Dialog Box Launcher (Home tab		

To Use the Mini Toolbar to Format Text

Recall from the Office 2010 and Windows 7 chapter at the beginning of this book that the Mini toolbar, which automatically appears based on certain tasks you perform, contains commands related to changing the appearance of text in a document. All commands on the Mini toolbar also exist on the Ribbon.

When the Mini toolbar appears, it initially is transparent. If you do not use the transparent Mini toolbar, it disappears from the screen. The following steps use the Mini toolbar to change the color and font size of text in the signature line of the flyer.

1

- Move the mouse pointer to the left of the line to be selected (in this case, the signature line) until the mouse pointer changes to a right-pointing block arrow and then click the mouse to select the line (Figure 1–35).

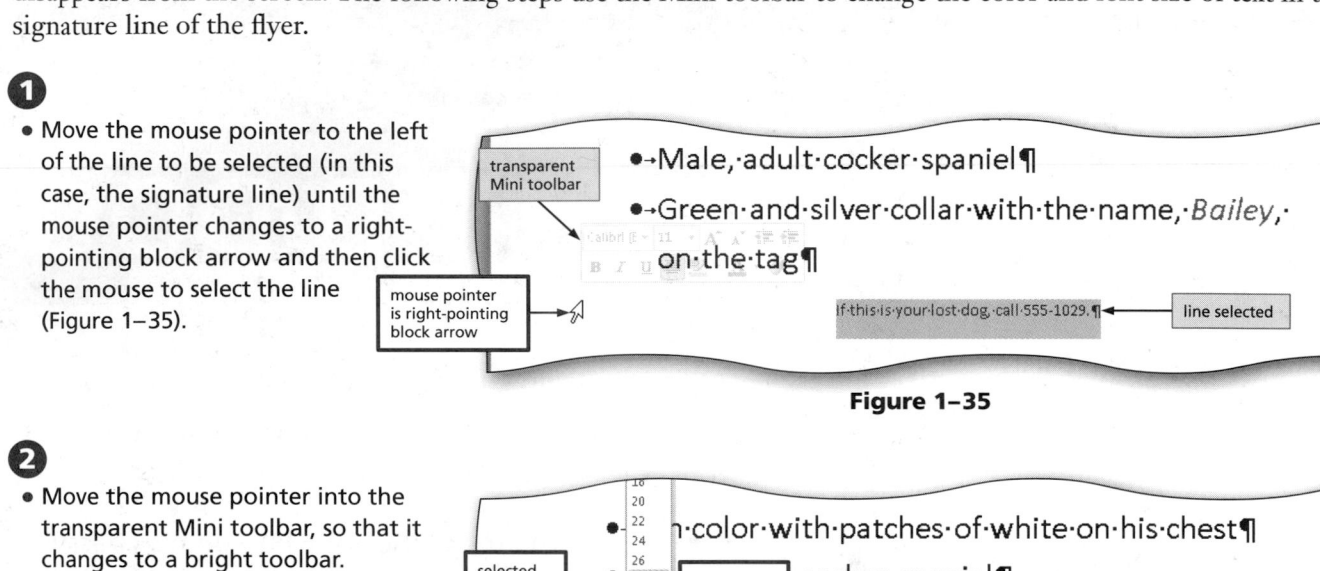

Figure 1–35

2

- Move the mouse pointer into the transparent Mini toolbar, so that it changes to a bright toolbar.

- Click the Font Size box arrow on the Mini toolbar to display the Font Size gallery and then point to 28 in the Font Size gallery to display a live preview of the selected font size (Figure 1–36).

Figure 1–36

3

- Click 28 in the Font Size gallery to increase the font size of the selected text.

4

- With the text still selected and the Mini toolbar still displayed, click the Font Color button arrow on the Mini toolbar to display the Font Color gallery and then point to Purple, Accent 4, Darker 50% (eighth color in the sixth row) to display a live preview of the selected font color (Figure 1–37).

Figure 1–37

5

- Click Purple, Accent 4, Darker 50% to change the color of the text.

- Click anywhere in the document window to remove the selection from the text.

To Select a Group of Words

To emphasize the contact information (call 555-1029), these words are underlined in the flyer. To format a group of words, you first must select them. The following steps select a group of words.

1

- Position the mouse pointer immediately to the left of the first character of the text to be selected, in this case, the c in call (Figure 1–38).

Why did the shape of the mouse pointer change?

The mouse pointer's shape is an I-beam when positioned in unselected text in the document window.

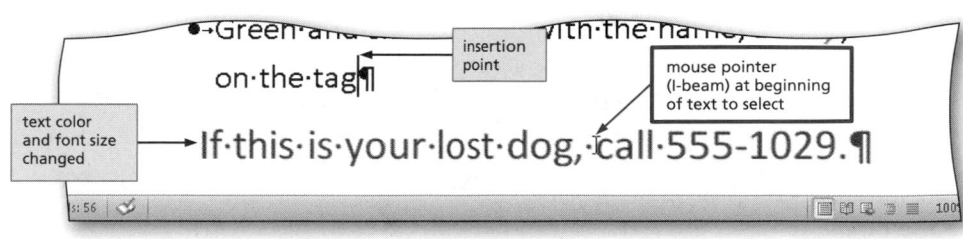

Figure 1–38

2

- Drag the mouse pointer through the last character of the text to be selected, in this case, the 9 in the phone number (Figure 1–39).

Why did the mouse pointer shape change again?

When the mouse pointer is positioned in selected text, its shape is a left-pointing block arrow.

Figure 1–39

Other Ways	
1. With insertion point at beginning of first word in group, press	CTRL+SHIFT+RIGHT ARROW repeatedly until all words are selected

To Underline Text

Underlines are used to emphasize or draw attention to specific text. **Underlined** text prints with an underscore (_) below each character. In the flyer, the contact information, call 555-1029, in the signature line is emphasized with an underline. The following step formats selected text with an underline.

1

- With the text selected, click the Underline button (Home tab | Font group) to underline the selected text (Figure 1–40).

How would I remove an underline?

You would click the Underline button a second time, or you immediately could click the Undo button on the Quick Access Toolbar.

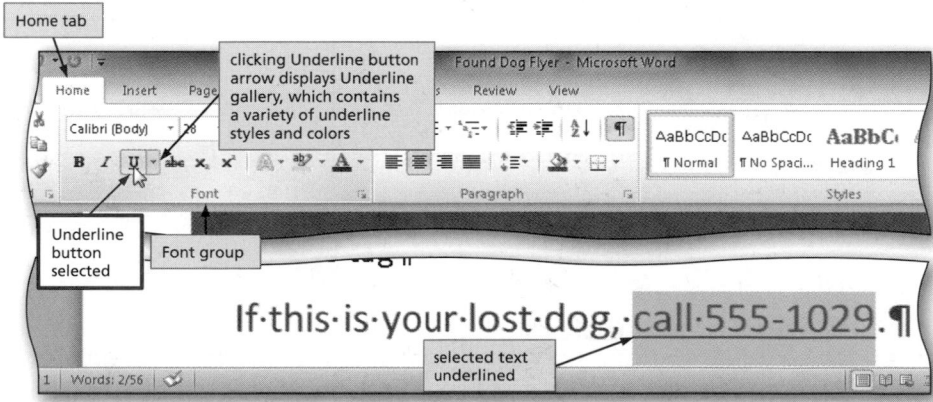

Figure 1–40

Other Ways		
1. Right-click text, click Font on shortcut menu, click Font tab (Font dialog box), click Underline style box arrow, click desired	underline style, click OK button 2. Click Font Dialog Box Launcher (Home tab | Font group), click Font tab	(Font dialog box), click Underline style box arrow, click desired underline style, click OK button 3. Press CTRL+U

To Bold Text

Bold characters appear somewhat thicker and darker than those that are not bold. To further emphasize the signature line, it is bold in the flyer. To format the line, as you have learned previously, you select the line first. The following steps format the signature line bold.

- Move the mouse pointer to the left of the line to be selected (in this case, the signature line) until the mouse pointer changes to a right-pointing block arrow and then click the mouse to select the text to be formatted.

- With the text selected, click the Bold button (Home tab | Font group) to bold the selected text (Figure 1–41).

Q&A

How would I remove a bold format?

You would click the Bold button a second time, or you immediately could click the Undo button on the Quick Access Toolbar.

- Click anywhere in the document window to remove the selection from the screen.

Figure 1–41

Other Ways

1. Click Bold button on Mini toolbar

2. Right-click selected text, click Font on shortcut menu, click Font tab (Font dialog box), click Bold in Font style list, click OK button

3. Click Font Dialog Box Launcher (Home tab | Font group), click Font tab (Font dialog box), click Bold in Font style list, click OK button

4. Press CTRL+B

To Change Theme Colors

A **color scheme** in Word is a document theme that identifies 12 complementary colors for text, background, accents, and links in a document. With more than 20 predefined color schemes, Word provides a simple way to select colors that work well together.

In the flyer, you want all the colors to convey honesty, dependability, and healing, that is, shades of browns and greens. In Word, the Aspect color scheme uses these colors. Thus, you will change the color scheme from the default, Office, to Aspect. The next steps change theme colors.

• Click the Change Styles button (Home tab | Styles group) to display the Change Styles menu.

• Point to Colors on the Change Styles menu to display the Colors gallery (Figure 1–42).

Experiment

• Point to various color schemes in the Colors gallery and watch the colors change in the document window.

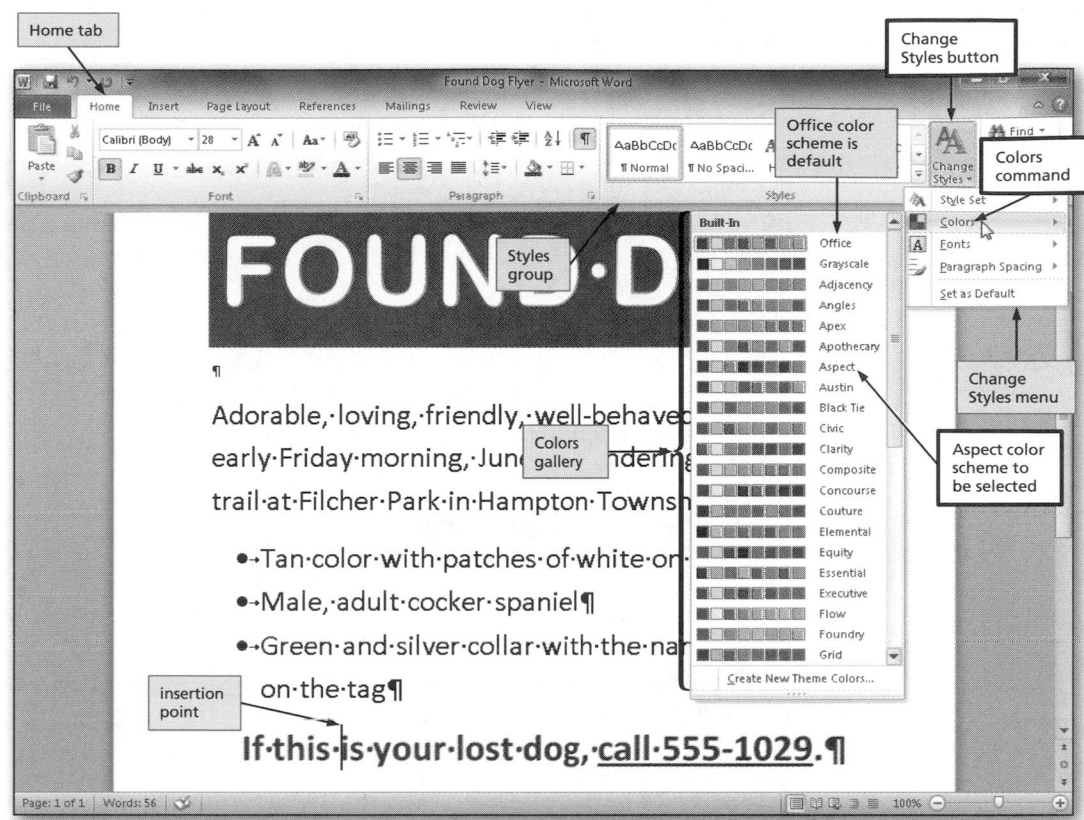

Figure 1–42

• Click Aspect in the Colors gallery to change the document theme colors (Figure 1–43).

What if I want to return to the original color scheme?

You would click the Change Styles button again, click Colors on the Change Styles menu, and then click Office in the Colors gallery.

Figure 1–43

Other Ways

1. Click Theme Colors button (Page Layout tab | Themes group), select desired color scheme

Selecting Text

In many of the previous steps, you have selected text. Table 1–3 summarizes the techniques used to select various items.

Table 1–3 Techniques for Selecting Text		
Item to Select	**Mouse**	**Keyboard (where applicable)**
Block of text	Click at beginning of selection, scroll to end of selection, position mouse pointer at end of selection, hold down SHIFT key and then click; or drag through the text.	
Character(s)	Drag through character(s).	SHIFT+RIGHT ARROW or SHIFT+LEFT ARROW
Document	Move mouse to left of text until mouse pointer changes to a right-pointing block arrow and then triple-click.	CTRL+A
Graphic	Click the graphic.	
Line	Move mouse to left of line until mouse pointer changes to a right-pointing block arrow and then click.	HOME, then SHIFT+END or END, then SHIFT+HOME
Lines	Move mouse to left of first line until mouse pointer changes to a right-pointing block arrow and then drag up or down.	HOME, then SHIFT+DOWN ARROW or END, then SHIFT+UP AROW
Paragraph	Triple-click paragraph; or move mouse to left of paragraph until mouse pointer changes to a right-pointing block arrow and then double-click.	CTRL+SHIFT+DOWN ARROW or CTRL+SHIFT+UP ARROW
Paragraphs	Move mouse to left of paragraph until mouse pointer changes to a right-pointing block arrow, double-click, and then drag up or down.	CTRL+SHIFT+DOWN ARROW or CTRL+SHIFT+UP ARROW repeatedly
Sentence	Press and hold down CTRL key and then click sentence.	
Word	Double-click the word.	CTRL+SHIFT+RIGHT ARROW or CTRL+SHIFT+LEFT ARROW
Words	Drag through words.	CTRL+SHIFT+RIGHT ARROW or CTRL+SHIFT+LEFT ARROW repeatedly

To Save an Existing Document with the Same File Name

You have made several modifications to the document since you last saved it. Thus, you should save it again. The following step saves the document again. For an example of the step listed below, refer to the Office 2010 and Windows 7 chapter at the beginning of this book.

 Click the Save button on the Quick Access Toolbar to overwrite the previously saved file.

Break Point: If you wish to take a break, this is a good place to do so. You can quit Word now (refer to page WD 44 for instructions). To resume at a later time, start Word (refer to pages WD 4 and WD 5 for instructions), open the file called Found Dog Flyer (refer to page WD 45 for instructions), and continue following the steps from this location forward.

Inserting and Formatting Pictures in a Word Document

With the text formatted in the flyer, the next step is to insert digital pictures in the flyer and format the pictures. Flyers usually contain graphical images, such as a picture, to attract the attention of passersby. In the following pages, you will perform these tasks:

1. Insert the first digital picture into the flyer and then reduce its size.
2. Insert the second digital picture into the flyer and then reduce its size.
3. Change the look of the first picture and then the second picture.

Find the appropriate graphical image.

To use a graphical image, also called a graphic, in a Word document, the image must be stored digitally in a file. Files containing graphical images are available from a variety of sources:

- Word includes a collection of predefined graphical images that you can insert in a document.
- Microsoft has free digital images on the Web for use in a document. Other Web sites also have images available, some of which are free, while others require a fee.
- You can take a picture with a digital camera or camera phone and **download** it, which is the process of copying the digital picture from the camera or phone to your computer.
- With a scanner, you can convert a printed picture, drawing, or diagram to a digital file.

    If you receive a picture from a source other than yourself, do not use the file until you are certain it does not contain a virus. A **virus** is a computer program that can damage files and programs on your computer. Use an antivirus program to verify that any files you use are virus free.

Plan Ahead

Establish where to position and how to format the graphical image.

The content, size, shape, position, and format of a graphic should capture the interest of passersby, enticing them to stop and read the flyer. Often, the graphic is the center of attraction and visually the largest element on a flyer. If you use colors in the graphical image, be sure they are part of the document's color scheme.

Plan Ahead

To Insert a Picture

The next step in creating the flyer is to insert one of the digital pictures of the dog so that it is centered on the blank line below the headline. The picture, which was taken with a camera phone, is available on the Data Files for Students. See the inside back cover of this book for instructions on downloading the Data Files for Students, or contact your instructor for information about accessing the required files.

The following steps insert a centered picture, which, in this example, is located in the Chapter 01 folder in the Word folder in the Data Files for Students folder on a USB flash drive.

1

- Position the insertion point on the blank line below the headline, which is the location where you want to insert the picture.

- Click the Center button (Home tab | Paragraph group) to center the paragraph that will contain the picture.

- Click Insert on the Ribbon to display the Insert tab (Figure 1–44).

Figure 1–44

2

- With your USB flash drive connected to one of the computer's USB ports, click the Insert Picture from File button (Insert tab | Illustrations group) (shown in Figure 1-44) to display the Insert Picture dialog box (shown in Figure 1-45 on the next page).

3

- Navigate to the picture location (in this case, the Chapter 01 folder in the Word folder in the Data Files for Students folder on a USB flash drive). For a detailed example of this procedure, refer to Steps 3a – 3c in the To Save a File in a Folder section in the Office 2010 and Windows 7 chapter at the beginning of this book.

- Click Dog Picture 1 to select the file (Figure 1–45).

Q&A | What if the picture is not on a USB flash drive?

Use the same process, but select the storage location containing the picture.

Insert Picture dialog box

Chapter 01 folder in Word folder in Data Files for Students folder selected

selected picture file

icons show pictures from Data Files for Students on USB flash drive (your list may differ)

USB flash drive is selected device

Data Files for Students folder selected

Insert button

Figure 1–45

4

- Click the Insert button (Insert Picture dialog box) to insert the picture at the location of the insertion point in the document (Figure 1–46).

Q&A | What are the symbols around the picture?

A selected graphic appears surrounded by a **selection rectangle**, which has small squares and circles, called **sizing handles**, at each corner and middle location.

Picture Tools Format tab automatically appears when graphic is selected in document

Shape Height and Shape Width boxes show height and width of currently selected graphic

inserted picture automatically selected

groups on Ribbon change to show commands related to formatting pictures, because Picture Tools Format tab now is the active tab

picture inserted in document at location of insertion point, which was in a centered paragraph

sizing handles

rest of picture and remaining text no longer fit in document window — your screen may scroll differently depending on your monitor and settings

Figure 1–46

To Zoom the Document

The next step is to reduce the size of the picture so that both pictures will fit side-by-side on the same line. With the current picture size, the flyer now has expanded to two pages. The final flyer, however, should fit on a single page. In Word, you can change the zoom so that you can see the entire document (that is, both pages) on the screen at once. Seeing the entire document at once helps you determine the appropriate size for the picture. The following step zooms the document.

①

Experiment

• Repeatedly click the Zoom Out and Zoom In buttons on the status bar and watch the size of the document change in the document window.

• Click the Zoom Out or Zoom In button as many times as necessary until the Zoom button on the status bar displays 50% on its face (Figure 1–47).

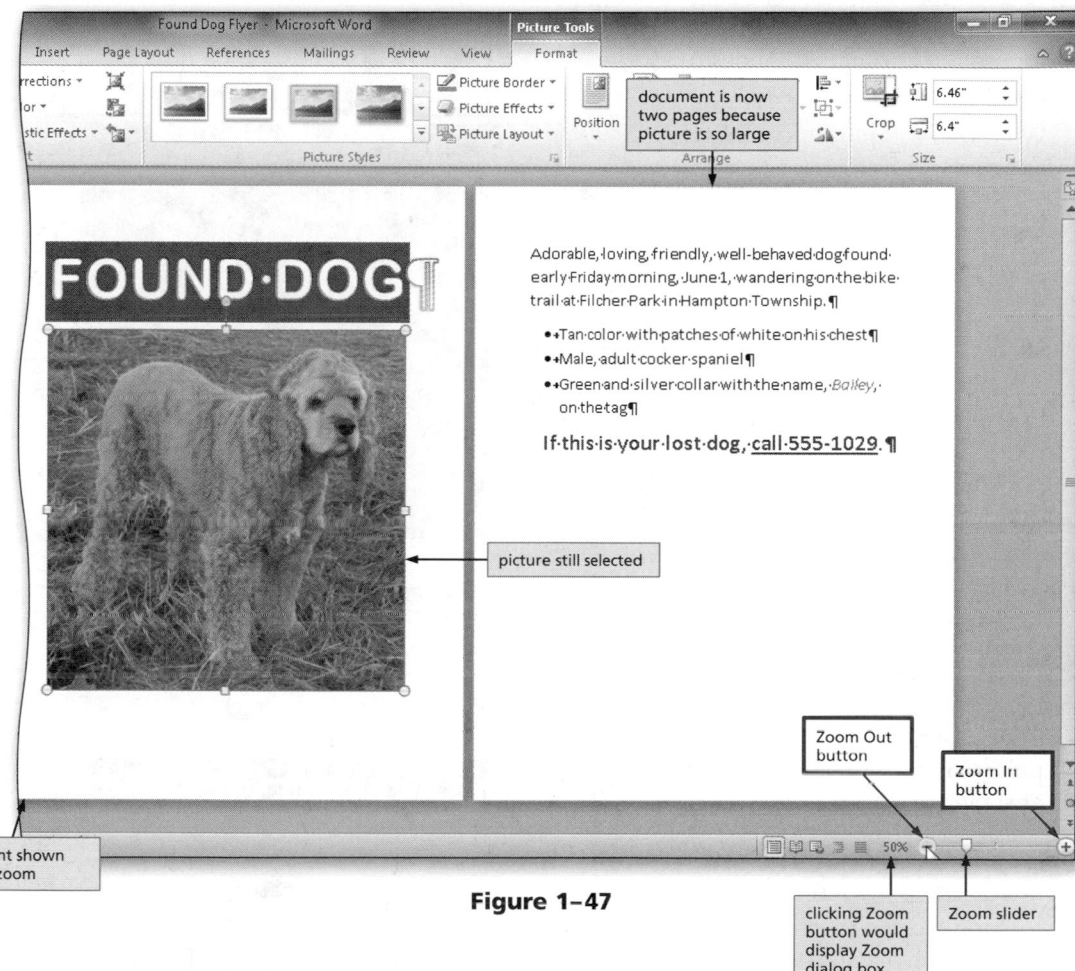

Figure 1–47

If I change the zoom percentage, will the document print differently?

Changing the zoom has no effect on the printed document.

Are there predefined zoom options?

Yes. Through the View tab | Zoom group or the Zoom dialog box, you can zoom to one page, two pages, many pages, page width, text width, and a variety of set percentages. Page width zoom places the edges of the page at the edges of the Word window, whereas Text width zoom places the contents of the page at the edges of the Word window.

Other Ways	
1. Drag Zoom slider on status bar	3. Click Zoom button (View tab | Zoom group), select desired zoom percent or type (Zoom dialog box), click OK button
2. Click Zoom button on status bar, select desired zoom percent or type (Zoom dialog box), click OK button	

To Resize a Graphic

The next step is to resize the picture so that both pictures will fit side-by-side on the same line below the headline. **Resizing** includes both enlarging and reducing the size of a graphic. In this flyer, you will reduce the size of the picture. With the entire document displayed in the document window, you will be able to see how the resized graphic will look on the entire page. The following steps resize a selected graphic.

- With the graphic still selected, point to the upper-right corner sizing handle on the picture so that the mouse pointer shape changes to a two-headed arrow (Figure 1–48).

Q&A What if my graphic (picture) is not selected?

To select a graphic, click it.

Figure 1–48

- Drag the sizing handle diagonally inward until the crosshair mouse pointer is positioned approximately as shown in Figure 1–49.

- Release the mouse button to resize the graphic, which in this case should have a height of about 2.74" and a width of about 2.73".

Q&A How can I see the height and width measurements?

Look in the Size group on the Picture Tools Format tab to see the height and width measurements of the currently selected graphic (shown in Figure 1–46 on page WD 32).

Q&A What if the graphic is the wrong size?

Repeat Steps 1, 2, and 3; or enter the desired height and width values in the Shape Height and Shape Width boxes (Picture Tools Format tab | Size group).

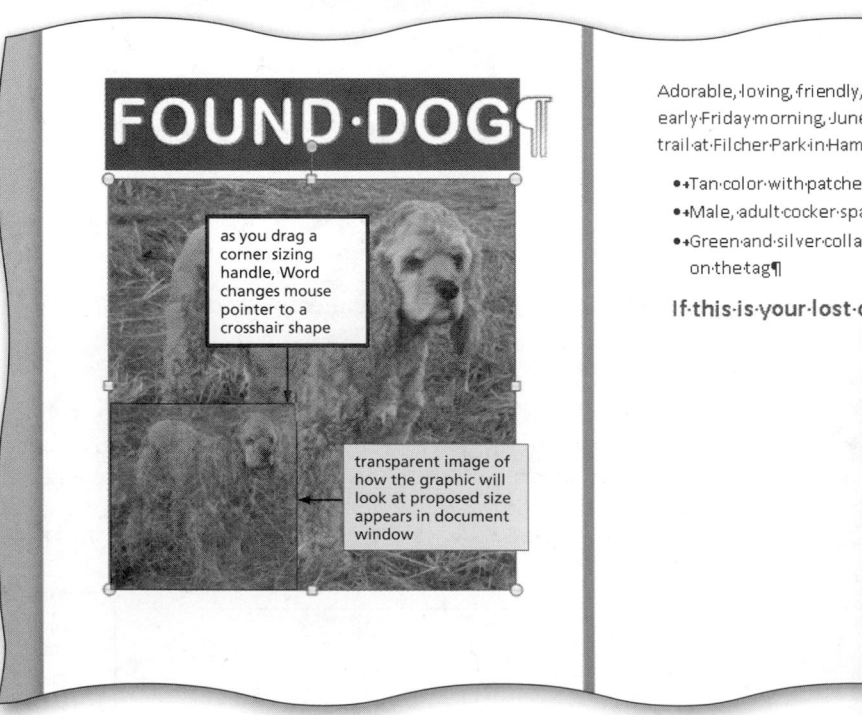

Figure 1–49

4
- Click to the right of the graphic to deselect it (Figure 1–50).

What happened to the Picture Tools Format tab?

When you click outside of a graphic or press a key to scroll through a document, Word deselects the graphic and removes the Picture Tools Format tab from the screen.

What if I want to return a graphic to its original size and start again?

With the graphic selected, click the Size Dialog Box Launcher (Picture Tools Format tab | Size group), click the Size tab (Layout dialog box), click the Reset button, and then click the OK button.

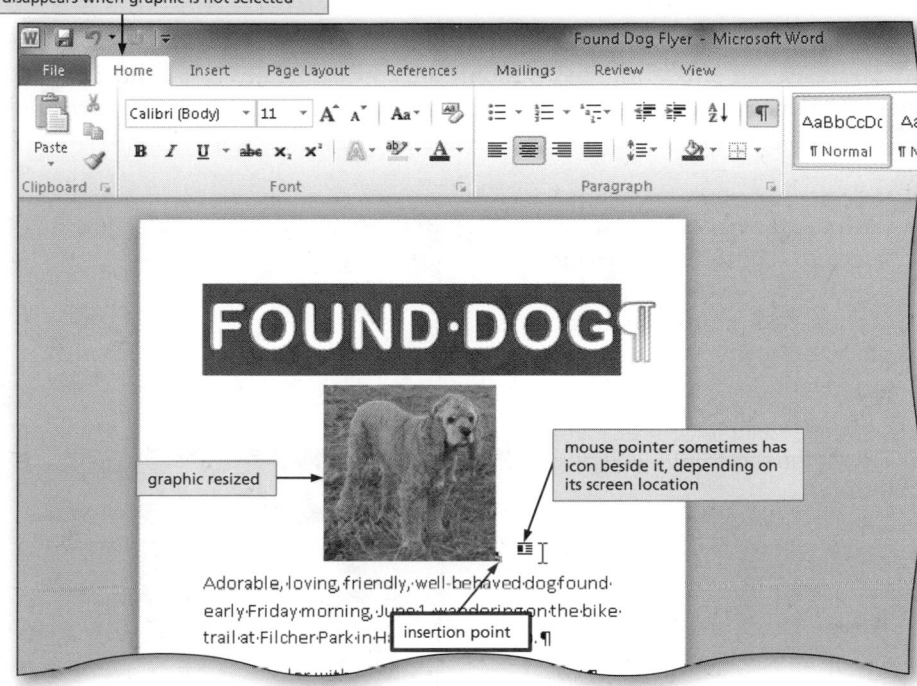

Figure 1–50

Other Ways

1. Enter height and width of graphic in Shape Height and Shape Width boxes (Picture Tools Format tab | Size group)	2. Click Size Dialog Box Launcher (Picture Tools Format tab | Size group), click Size tab (Layout dialog box), enter desired	height and width values in boxes, click OK button

To Insert Another Picture

The next step is to insert the other digital picture of the dog immediately to the right of the current picture. This second picture also is available on the Data Files for Students. See the inside back cover of this book for instructions on downloading the Data Files for Students, or contact your instructor for information about accessing the required files.

The following steps insert another picture immediately to the right of the current picture.

1 With the insertion point positioned as shown in Figure 1–50, click Insert on the Ribbon to display the Insert tab.

2 With your USB flash drive connected to one of the computer's USB ports, click the Insert Picture from File button (Insert tab | Illustrations group) to display the Insert Picture dialog box.

3 If necessary, navigate to the picture location (in this case, the Word folder in the CIS 101 folder [or your class folder] on the USB flash drive). For a detailed example of this procedure, refer to Steps 3a – 3c in the To Save a File in a Folder section in the Office 2010 and Windows 7 chapter at the beginning of this book.

4 Click Dog Picture 2 to select the file.

5 Click the Insert button (Insert Picture dialog box) to insert the picture at the location of the insertion point in the document.

To Resize a Graphic by Entering Exact Measurements

The next step is to resize the second picture so that it is the exact same size as the first picture. The height and width measurements of the first graphic are approximately 2.74" and 2.73", respectively. When a graphic is selected, its height and width measurements show in the Size group of the Picture Tools Format tab. The following steps resize a selected graphic by entering its desired exact measurements.

 1

- With the second graphic still selected, click the Shape Height box (Picture Tools Format tab | Size group) to select the contents in the box and then type **2.74** as the height.

Q&A What if the Picture Tools Format tab no longer is displayed on my Ribbon?

Double-click the picture to display the Picture Tools Format tab.

Q&A What if the contents of the Shape Height box are not selected?

Triple-click the Shape Height box.

2

- Click the Shape Width box to select the contents in the box, type **2.73** as the width, and then click the picture to apply the settings.

- If necessary, scroll up to display the entire document in the window (Figure 1–51).

Q&A Why did my measurements change slightly?

Depending on relative measurements, the height and width values entered may change slightly.

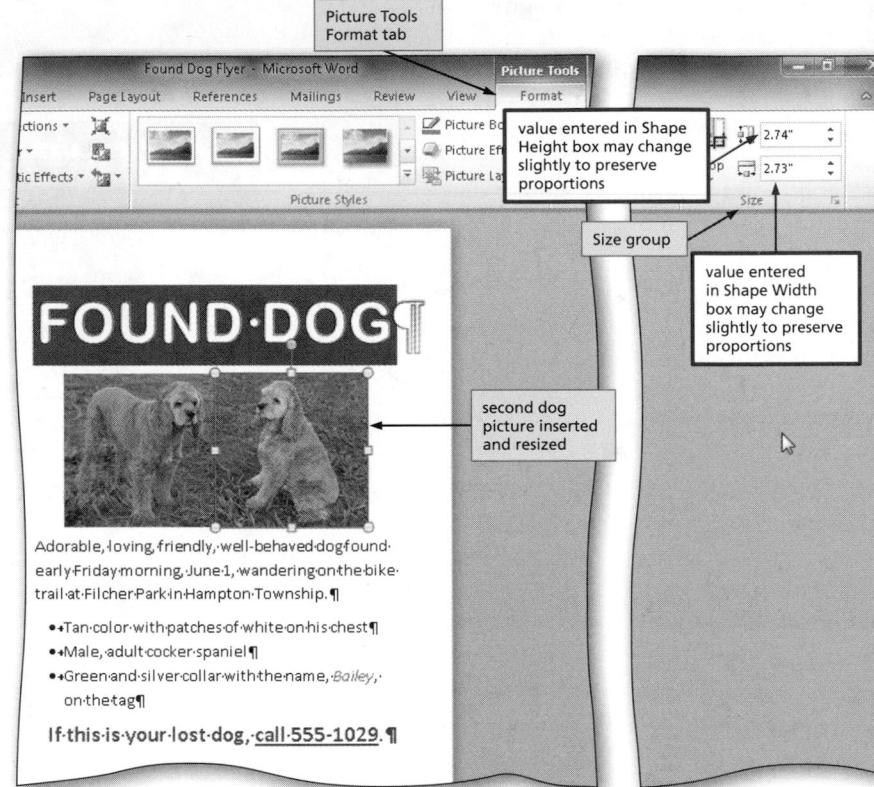

Figure 1–51

Other Ways		
1. Right-click picture, enter shape height and width values in boxes on shortcut menu	2. Right-click picture, click Size and Position on shortcut menu, click Size tab (Layout dialog box),	enter shape height and width values in boxes, click OK button

To Zoom the Document

You are finished resizing the graphics and no longer need to view the entire page in the document window. Thus, the following step changes the zoom back to 100 percent.

1 Click the Zoom In button on the status bar as many times as necessary until the Zoom button displays 100% on its face (shown in Figure 1–52).

o Apply a Picture Style

A **style** is a named group of formatting characteristics. Word provides more than 25 picture styles that enable ou easily to change a picture's look to a more visually appealing style, including a variety of shapes, angles, borders, nd reflections. The flyer in this chapter uses a style that applies soft edges to the picture. The following steps pply a picture style to a picture.

• Click the leftmost dog picture to select it (Figure 1–52).

What is the green circle attached to the selected graphic?

It is called a rotate handle. When you drag a graphic's rotate handle, the graphic moves in either a clockwise or counterclockwise direction.

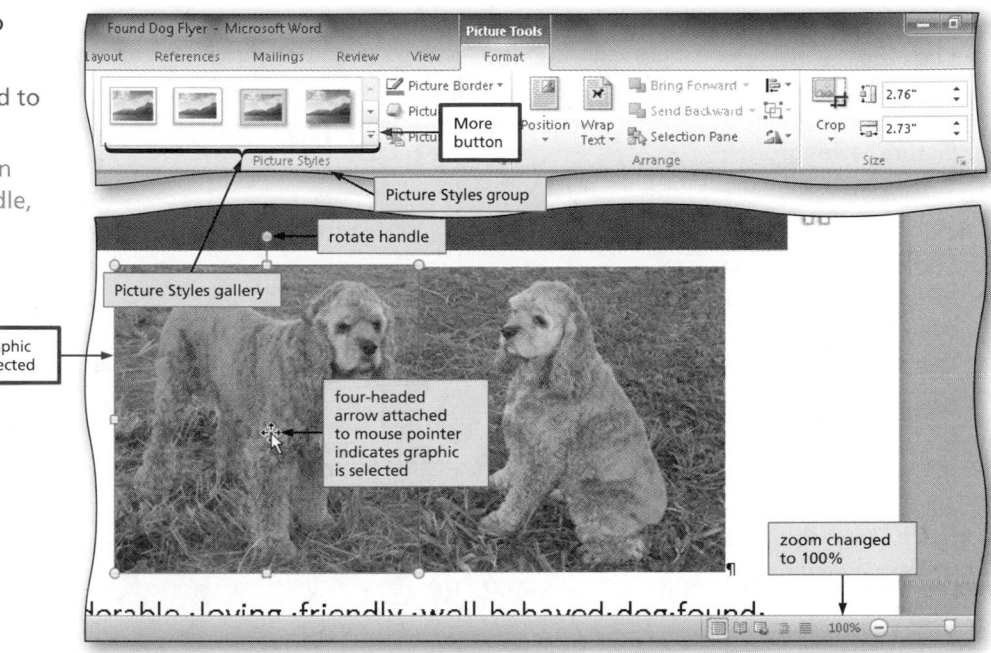

Figure 1–52

• Click the More button in the Picture Styles gallery (Picture Tools Format tab | Picture Styles group) (shown in Figure 1–52) to expand the gallery.

• Point to Soft Edge Rectangle in the Picture Styles gallery to display a live preview of that style applied to the picture in the document (Figure 1–53).

🔍 **Experiment**

• Point to various picture styles in the Picture Styles gallery and watch the style of the picture change in the document window.

• Click Soft Edge Rectangle in the Picture Styles gallery to apply the style to the selected picture.

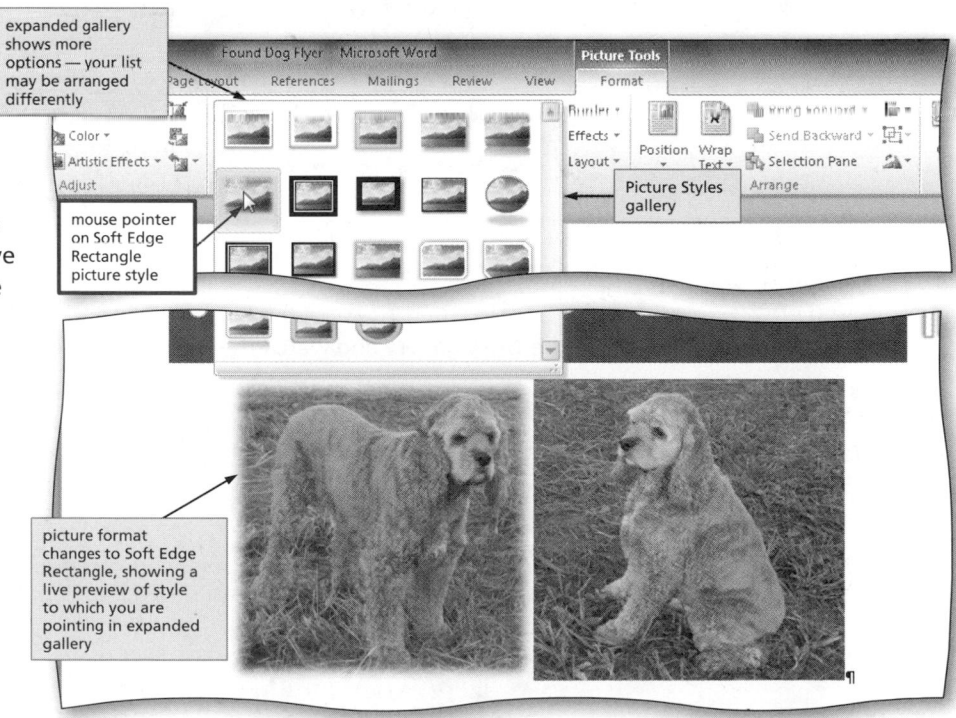

Figure 1–53

To Apply Picture Effects

Word provides a variety of picture effects so that you can further customize a picture. Effects include shadows, reflections, glow, soft edges, bevel, and 3-D rotation. The difference between the effects and the styles is that each effect has several options, providing you with more control over the exact look of the image.

In this flyer, the leftmost dog picture has a slight tan glow effect and is turned inward toward the center of the page. The following steps apply picture effects to the selected picture.

1

- Click the Picture Effects button (Picture Tools Format tab | Picture Styles group) to display the Picture Effects menu.

- Point to Glow on the Picture Effects menu to display the Glow gallery.

- Point to Tan, 5 pt glow, Accent color 6 in the Glow Variations area (rightmost glow in first row) to display a live preview of the selected glow effect applied to the picture in the document window (Figure 1–54).

Figure 1–54

 Experiment

- Point to various glow effects in the Glow gallery and watch the picture change in the document window.

2

- Click Tan, 5 pt glow, Accent color 6 in the Glow gallery to apply the selected picture effect.

Q&A

What if I wanted to discard formatting applied to a picture?

You would click the Reset Picture button (Picture Tools Format tab | Adjust group). To reset formatting and size, you would click the Reset Picture button arrow (Picture Tools Format tab | Adjust group) and then click Reset Picture & Size on the Reset Picture menu.

3

- Click the Picture Effects button (Picture Tools Format tab | Picture Styles group) to display the Picture Effects menu again.

- Point to 3-D Rotation on the Picture Effects menu to display the 3-D Rotation gallery.

- Point to Off Axis 1 Right in the Parallel area (second rotation in second row) to display a live preview of the selected 3-D effect applied to the picture in the document window (Figure 1–55).

Experiment

- Point to various 3-D rotation effects in the 3-D Rotation gallery and watch the picture change in the document window.

4

- Click Off Axis 1 Right in the 3-D Rotation gallery to apply the selected picture effect.

Figure 1–55

Other Ways		
1. Right-click picture, click Format Picture on shortcut menu, select desired options (Format Picture	dialog box), click Close button 2. Click Format Shape Dialog Box Launcher (Picture	Tools Format tab	Picture Styles group), select desired options (Format Picture dialog box), click Close button

To Apply a Picture Style and Effects to Another Picture

In this flyer, the rightmost dog picture also uses the soft edge picture style, has a light tan glow effect, and is turned inward toward the center of the page. The following steps apply the picture style and picture effects to the picture.

Click the rightmost dog picture to select it.

Click the More button in the Picture Styles gallery (Picture Tools Format tab | Picture Styles group) to expand the gallery and then click Soft Edge Rectangle in the Picture Styles gallery to apply the selected style to the picture.

Click the Picture Effects button (Picture Tools Format tab | Picture Styles group) to display the Picture Effects menu and then point to Glow on the Picture Effects menu to display the Glow gallery.

Click Tan, 5 pt glow, Accent color 6 (rightmost glow in first row) in the Glow gallery to apply the picture effect to the picture.

5 Click the Picture Effects button (Picture Tools Format tab | Picture Styles group) to display the Picture Effects menu again and then point to 3-D Rotation on the Picture Effects menu to display the 3-D Rotation gallery.

6 Click Off Axis 2 Left (rightmost rotation in second row) in the Parallel area in the 3-D Rotation gallery to apply the picture effect to the selected picture.

7 Click to the right of the picture to deselect it (Figure 1–56).

BTW

BTWs
For a complete list of the BTWs found in the margins of this book, visit the Word 2010 BTW Web page (scsite .com/wd2010/btw).

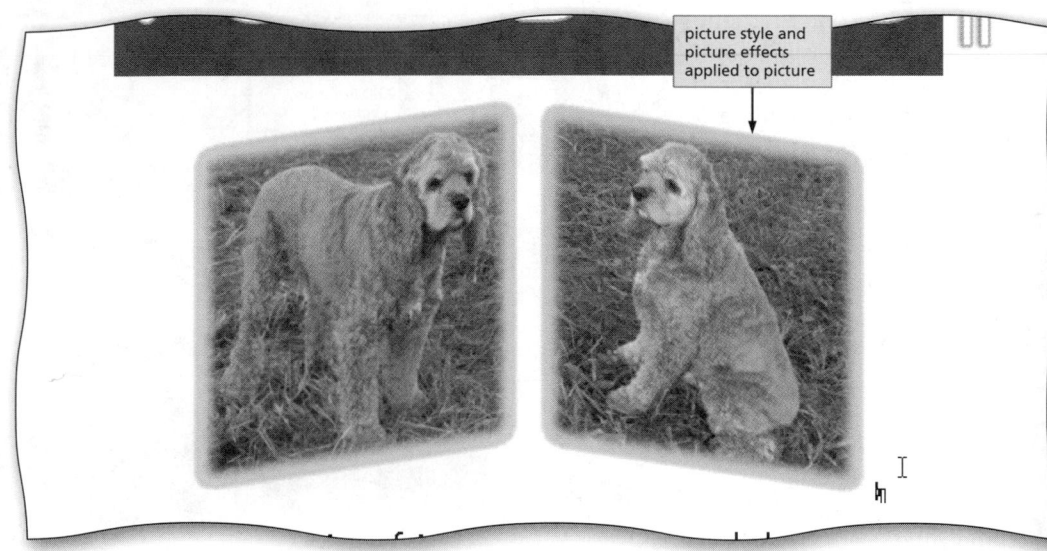

picture style and picture effects applied to picture

Figure 1–56

Enhancing the Page

BTW

Centering Page Contents Vertically
You can center page contents vertically between the top and bottom margins. To do this, click the Page Setup Dialog Box Launcher (Page Layout tab | Page Setup group), click the Layout tab (Page Setup dialog box), click the Vertical alignment box arrow, click Center in the list, and then click the OK button.

With the text and graphics entered and formatted, the next step is to look at the page as a whole and determine if it looks finished in its current state. As you review the page, answer these questions:

- Does it need a page border to frame its contents, or would a page border make it look too busy?
- Is the spacing between paragraphs and graphics on the page adequate? Do any sections of text or graphics look as if they are positioned too closely to the items above or below them?

You determine that a graphical, color-coordinated border would enhance the flyer. You also notice that the flyer would look more proportionate if it had a little more space above and below the pictures. The following pages make these enhancements to the flyer.

To View One Page

Earlier in this chapter, you changed the zoom using the Zoom Out and Zoom In buttons on the status bar. If you want to display an entire page as large as possible in the document window, Word can compute the correct zoom percentage for you. The next steps display a single page in its entirety in the document window as large as possible.

● Click View on the Ribbon to display
the View tab.

● Click the One Page button (View
tab | Zoom group) to display the
entire page in the document
window as large as possible
(Figure 1–57).

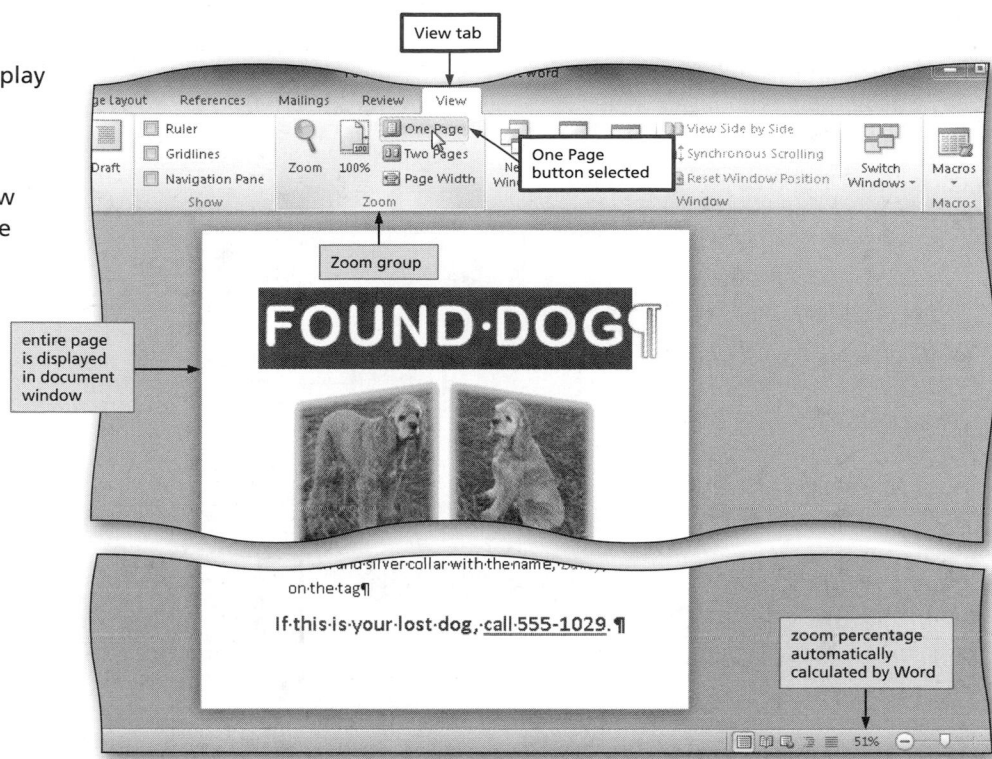

Figure 1–57

o Add a Page Border

In Word, you can add a border around the perimeter of an entire page. The flyer in this chapter has a light
reen dashed border. The following steps add a page border.

● Click Page Layout on the Ribbon to
display the Page Layout tab.

● Click the Page Borders button (Page
Layout tab | Page Background
group) to display the Borders and
Shading dialog box (Figure 1–58).

Figure 1–58

- Scroll through the Style list (Borders and Shading dialog box) and select the style shown in Figure 1–59.

- Click the Color box arrow to display a Color palette (Figure 1–59).

Figure 1–59

- Click Dark Green, Accent 4, Lighter 60% (eighth color in third row) in the Color palette to select the color for the page border.

- Click the Width box arrow and then click 3 pt to select the thickness of the page border (Figure 1–60).

Figure 1–60

• Click the OK button to add the border to the page (Figure 1–61).

What if I wanted to remove the border?

You would click None in the Setting list in the Borders and Shading dialog box.

Figure 1–61

o Change Spacing before and after a Paragraph

The default spacing above (before) a paragraph in Word is 0 points and below (after) is 10 points. In the flyer, ou want to increase the spacing above and below the paragraph containing the pictures. The following steps change he spacing above and below a paragraph.

• Position the insertion point in the paragraph to be adjusted, in this case, the paragraph containing the pictures.

• Click the Spacing Before box up arrow (Page Layout tab | Paragraph group) as many times as necessary until 24 pt is displayed in the Spacing Before box to increase the space above the current paragraph.

• Click the Spacing After box up arrow (Page Layout tab | Paragraph group) so that 12 pt is displayed in the Spacing After box to increase the space below the current paragraph (Figure 1–62).

If the text flows to two pages, reduce the spacing above and below paragraphs as necessary.

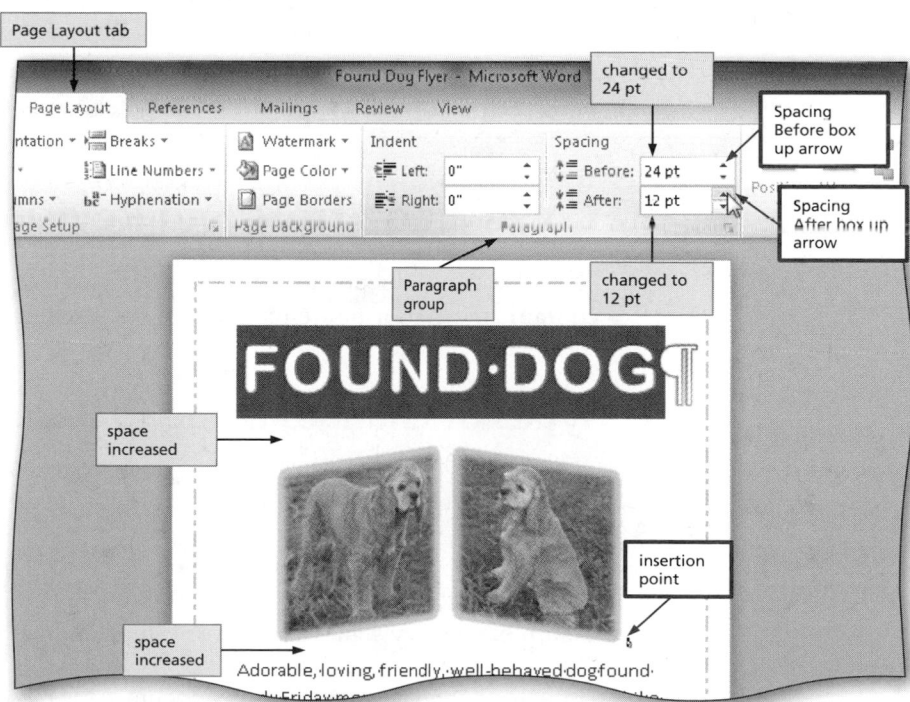

Figure 1–62

Other Ways

1. Right-click paragraph, click Paragraph on shortcut menu, click Indents and Spacing tab (Paragraph dialog box), enter spacing before and after values, click OK button

2. Click Paragraph Dialog Box Launcher (Home tab or Page Layout tab | Paragraph group), click Indents and Spacing tab (Paragraph dialog box), enter spacing before and after values, click OK button

To Save an Existing Document with the Same File Name

You have made several modifications to the document since you last saved it. Thus, you should save it again. The following step saves the document again. For an example of the step listed below, refer to the Office 2010 and Windows 7 chapter at the beginning of this book.

1 Click the Save button on the Quick Access Toolbar to overwrite the previously saved file.

To Quit Word

BTW

Certification
The Microsoft Office Specialist (MOS) program provides an opportunity for you to obtain a valuable industry credential — proof that you have the Word 2010 skills required by employers. For more information, visit the Word 2010 Certification Web page (scsite.com/wd2010/cert).

Although you still need to make some edits to this document, you want to quit Word and resume working on the project at a later time. Thus, the following steps quit Word. For a detailed example of the procedure summarized below, refer to the Office 2010 and Windows 7 chapter at the beginning of this book.

1 If you have one Word document open, click the Close button on the right side of the title bar to close the document and quit Word; or if you have multiple Word documents open, click File on the Ribbon to open the Backstage view and then click Exit in the Backstage view to close all open documents and quit Word.

2 If a Microsoft Word dialog box appears, click the Save button to save any changes made t the document since the last save.

Break Point: If you wish to take a break, this is a good place to do so. To resume at a later time, continue following the steps from this location forward.

Correcting Errors and Revising a Document

After creating a document, you may need to change it. For example, the document may contain an error, or new circumstances may require you to add text to the document.

Types of Changes Made to Documents

The types of changes made to documents normally fall into one of the three following categories: additions, deletions, or modifications.

Additions   Additional words, sentences, or paragraphs may be required in a document. Additions occur when you omit text from a document and want to insert it later. For example, you may want to add your e-mail address to the flyer.

Deletions   Sometimes, text in a document is incorrect or is no longer needed. For example, you may discover the dog's collar is just green. In this case, you would delete the words, and silver, from the flyer.

Modifications   If an error is made in a document or changes take place that affect the document, you might have to revise a word(s) in the text. For example, the dog may have been found in Hampton Village instead of Hampton Township.

To Start Word

Once you have created and saved a document, you may need to retrieve it from your storage medium. For example, you might want to revise the document or print it. The following steps, which assume Windows 7 is running, start Word so that you can open and modify the flyer. You may need to ask your instructor how to start Word for your computer. For a detailed example of the procedure summarized below, refer to the Office 2010 and Windows 7 chapter at the beginning of this book.

▶ Click the Start button on the Windows 7 taskbar to display the Start menu.

▶ Type **Microsoft Word** as the search text in the 'Search programs and files' text box and watch the search results appear on the Start menu.

▶ Click Microsoft Word 2010 in the search results on the Start menu to start Word and display a new blank document in the Word window.

▶ If the Word window is not maximized, click the Maximize button next to the Close button on its title bar to maximize the window.

To Open a Document from Word

Earlier in this chapter, you saved your project on a USB flash drive using the file name, Found Dog Flyer. The following steps open the Found Dog Flyer file from the Word folder in the CIS 101 folder on the USB flash drive. For a detailed example of the procedure summarized below, refer to the Office 2010 and Windows 7 chapter at the beginning of this book.

▶ With your USB flash drive connected to one of the computer's USB ports, click File on the Ribbon to open the Backstage view.

▶ Click Open in the Backstage view to display the Open dialog box.

▶ Navigate to the location of the file to be opened (in this case, the Word folder in the CIS 101 folder [or your class folder] on the USB flash drive). For a detailed example of this procedure, refer to Steps 3a – 3c in the To Save a File in a Folder section in the Office 2010 and Windows 7 chapter at the beginning of this book.

▶ Click Found Dog Flyer to select the file to be opened.

▶ Click the Open button (Open dialog box) to open the selected file and display the opened document in the Word window.

Could I have clicked the Recent tab to open the file?

Yes. Because the file was recently closed, it should appear in the Recent Documents list.

To Zoom the Document

While modifying the document, you prefer the document at 100 percent so that it is easier to read. Thus, the following step changes the zoom back to 100 percent.

▶ If necessary, click the Zoom In button on the status bar as many times as necessary until the Zoom button displays 100% on its face (shown in Figure 1–63 on the next page).

To Insert Text in an Existing Document

Word inserts text to the left of the insertion point. The text to the right of the insertion point moves to the right and downward to fit the new text. The following steps insert the word, very, to the left of the word, early, in the flyer.

- Scroll through the document and then click to the left of the location of text to be inserted (in this case, the e in early) to position the insertion point where text should be inserted (Figure 1–63).

Figure 1–63

- Type **very** and then press the SPACEBAR to insert the word to the left of the insertion point (Figure 1–64).

Q&A

Why did the text move to the right as I typed?

In Word, the default typing mode is **insert mode**, which means as you type a character, Word moves all the characters to the right of the typed character one position to the right.

Figure 1–64

Deleting Text from a Document

It is not unusual to type incorrect characters or words in a document. As discussed earlier in this chapter, you can click the Undo button on the Quick Access Toolbar to undo a command or action immediately — this includes typing. Word also provides other methods of correcting typing errors.

To delete an incorrect character in a document, simply click next to the incorrect character and then press the BACKSPACE key to erase to the left of the insertion point, or press the DELETE key to erase to the right of the insertion point.

To Delete Text

To delete a word or phrase, you first must select the word or phrase. The following steps select the word, very, that was just added in the previous steps and then delete the selection.

1 Position the mouse pointer somewhere in the word to be selected (in this case, very) and then double-click to select the word (Figure 1–65).

Adorable,·loving,·friendly,·well-behaved·dog·found·very·early·Friday·morning,·June·1,·wandering·on·the·bike·trail·at·Filcher·Park·in·Hampton·Township.¶

text to be deleted is selected

mouse pointer

Figure 1–65

2 With the text selected, press the DELETE key to delete the selected text (shown in Figure 1–63).

To Move Text

While proofreading the flyer, you realize that the body copy would read better if the first two bulleted paragraphs were reversed. An efficient way to move text a short distance, such as reversing two paragraphs, is drag-and-drop editing. With **drag-and-drop editing**, you select the text to be moved and then drag the selected item to the new location and then *drop*, or insert, it there. Another technique for moving text is the cut-and-paste technique, which is discussed in the next chapter. The following steps use drag-and-drop editing to move text.

1 Position the mouse pointer in the paragraph to be moved (in this case, the second bulleted item) and then triple-click to select the paragraph.

With the mouse pointer in the selected text, press and hold down the mouse button, which displays a dotted insertion point and a small dotted box with the mouse pointer (Figure 1–66).

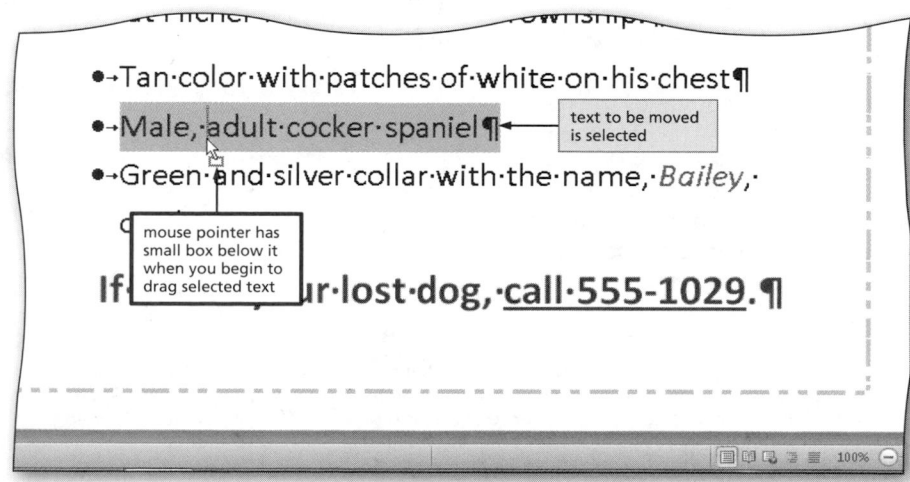

•→Tan·color·with·patches·of·white·on·his·chest¶

•→Male,·adult·cocker·spaniel¶

text to be moved is selected

•→Green·and·silver·collar·with·the·name,·*Bailey*,·

mouse pointer has small box below it when you begin to drag selected text

If ... ur·lost·dog,·call·555-1029.¶

100%

Figure 1–66

2

- Drag the dotted insertion point to the location where the selected text is to be moved, as shown in Figure 1–67.

selected text to be dropped at location of dotted insertion point

Adorable, loving, friendly, well-behaved dog found early Friday morning, June 1, wandering on the bike trail at Filcher Park in Hampton Township.¶

- → Tan color with patches of white on his chest¶
- → Male, adult cocker spaniel¶
- → Green and silver collar with the name, *Bailey*, on the tag¶

If this is your lost dog, call 555-1029.¶

Figure 1–67

3

- Release the mouse button to move the selected text to the location of the dotted insertion point (Figure 1–68).

Q&A What if I accidentally drag text to the wrong location?

Click the Undo button on the Quick Access Toolbar and try again.

Q&A Can I use drag-and-drop editing to move any selected item?

Yes, you can select words, sentences, phrases, and graphics and then use drag-and-drop editing to move them.

Q&A What is the purpose of the Paste Options button?

If you click the Paste Options button, a menu appears that allows you to change the format of the item that was moved. The next chapter discusses the Paste Options menu.

- Click anywhere in the document window to remove the selection from the bulleted item.

selected text moved

Paste Options button automatically appears when you drag and drop text or other objects

Adorable, loving, friendly, well-behaved dog found early Friday morning, June 1, wandering on the bike trail at Filcher Park in Ha... ...o.¶

- → Male, adult cocker spaniel¶
- → Tan color with patches of white on his chest¶
- → Green and silver collar with the name, *Bailey*, on the tag¶

If this is your lost dog, call 555-1029.¶

Figure 1–68

Other Ways

1. Click Cut button (Home tab | Clipboard group), click where text or object is to be pasted, click Paste button (Home tab | Clipboard group)

2. Right-click selected text, click Cut on shortcut menu, right-click where text or object is to be pasted, click Keep Source Formatting on shortcut menu

3. Press CTRL+X, position insertion point where text or object is to be pasted, press CTRL+V

Changing Document Properties

Word helps you organize and identify your files by using **document properties**, which are the details about a file. Document properties, also known as **metadata**, can include information such as the project author, title, subject, and keywords. A **keyword** is a word or phrase that further describes the document. For example, a class name or document topic can describe the file's purpose or content.

Document properties are valuable for a variety of reasons:

• Users can save time locating a particular file because they can view a document's properties without opening the document.

• By creating consistent properties for files having similar content, users can better organize their documents.

• Some organizations require Word users to add document properties so that other employees can view details about these files.

Five different types of document properties exist, but the more common ones used in this book are standard and automatically updated properties. **Standard properties** are associated with all Microsoft Office documents and include author, title, and subject. **Automatically updated properties** include file system properties, such as the date you create or change a file, and statistics, such as the file size.

BTW

Printing Document Properties
To print document properties, click File on the Ribbon to open the Backstage view, click the Print tab in the Backstage view to display the Print gallery, click the first button in the Settings area to display a list of options specifying what you can print, click Document Properties in the list to specify you want to print the document properties instead of the actual document, and then click the Print button in the Print gallery to print the document properties on the currently selected printer.

To Change Document Properties

The **Document Information Panel** contains areas where you can view and enter document properties. You can view and change information in this panel at any time while you are creating a document. Before saving the flyer again, you want to add your name and course information as document properties. The following steps use the Document Information Panel to change document properties.

1

• Click File on the Ribbon to open the Backstage view.

• If necessary, click the Info tab to display the Info gallery (Figure 1–69).

How do I close the Backstage view?

Click File on the Ribbon or click the preview of the document in the Info gallery to return to the Word document window.

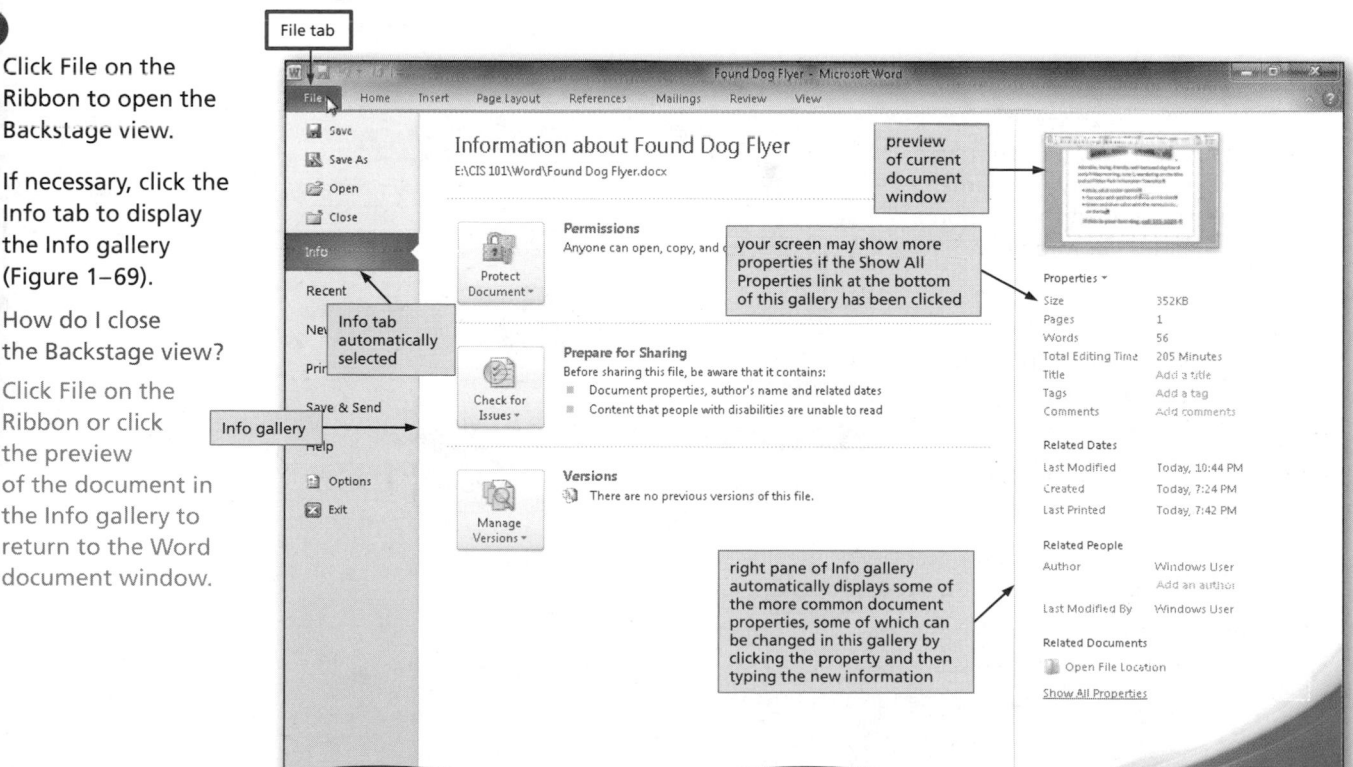

Figure 1–69

2
- Click the Properties button in the right pane of the Info gallery to display the Properties menu (Figure 1–70).

Figure 1–70

3
- Click Show Document Panel on the Properties menu to close the Backstage view and display the Document Information Panel in the Word document window (Figure 1–71).

Q&A

Why are some of the document properties in my Document Information Panel already filled in?

The person who installed Microsoft Office 2010 on your computer or network may have set or customized the properties.

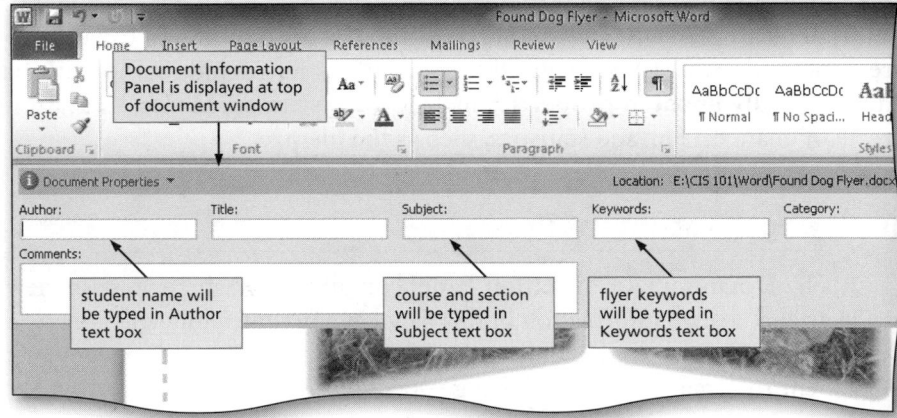

Figure 1–71

4
- Click the Author text box, if necessary, and then type your name as the Author property. If a name already is displayed in the Author text box, delete it before typing your name.

- Click the Subject text box, if necessary delete any existing text, and then type your course and section as the Subject property.

- If an AutoComplete dialog box appears, click its Yes button.

Figure 1–72

- Click the Keywords text box, if necessary delete any existing text, and then type **cocker spaniel** as the Keywords property (Figure 1–72).

Q&A

What types of document properties does Word collect automatically?

Word records details such as time spent editing a document, the number of times a document has been revised, and the fonts and themes used in a document.

5
- Click the Close the Document Information Panel button so that the Document Information Panel no longer is displayed.

Other Ways

1. Click File on Ribbon, click Info in Backstage view, if necessary click Show All Properties link in Info gallery, click property to change and then type new information, close Backstage view

To Save an Existing Document with the Same File Name

You are finished editing the flyer. Thus, you should save it again. The following step saves the document again. For an example of the step listed below, refer to the Office 2010 and Windows 7 chapter at the beginning of this book.

Click the Save button on the Quick Access Toolbar to overwrite the previously saved file.

Printing a Document

After creating a document, you may want to print it. Printing a document enables you to distribute the document to others in a form that can be read or viewed but typically not edited. It is a good practice to save a document before printing it, in the event you experience difficulties printing.

Determine the best method for distributing the document.
The traditional method of distributing a document uses a printer to produce a hard copy. A **hardcopy** or **printout** is information that exists on a physical medium such as paper. For users that can receive fax documents, you can elect to print a hard copy on a remote fax machine. Hard copies can be useful for the following reasons:

- Many people prefer proofreading a hard copy of a document rather than viewing it on the screen to check for errors and readability.
- Hard copies can serve as reference material if your storage medium is lost or becomes corrupted and you need to recreate the document.

Instead of distributing a hard copy of a document, users can choose to distribute the document as an electronic image that mirrors the original document's appearance. The electronic image of the document can be e-mailed, posted on a Web site, or copied to a portable storage medium such as a USB flash drive. Two popular electronic image formats, sometimes called fixed formats, are PDF by Adobe Systems and XPS by Microsoft. In Word, you can create electronic image files through the Print tab in the Backstage view, the Send & Save tab in the Backstage view, and the Save As dialog box. Electronic images of documents, such as PDF and XPS, can be useful for the following reasons:

- Users can view electronic images of documents without the software that created the original document (e.g., Word). Specifically, to view a PDF file, you use a program called Acrobat Reader, which can be downloaded free from Adobe's Web site. Similarly, to view an XPS file, you use a program called an XPS Viewer, which is included in the latest versions of Windows and Internet Explorer.
- Sending electronic documents saves paper and printer supplies. Society encourages users to contribute to **green computing**, which involves reducing the environmental waste generated when using a computer.

BTW

Conserving Ink and Toner
If you want to conserve ink or toner, you can instruct Word to print draft quality documents by clicking File on the Ribbon to open the Backstage view, clicking Options in the Backstage view to display the Word Options dialog box, clicking Advanced in the left pane (Word Options dialog box), scrolling to the Print area in the right pane, placing a check mark in the 'Use draft quality' check box, and then clicking the OK button. Then, use the Backstage view to print the document as usual.

To Print a Document

With the completed document saved, you may want to print it. Because this flyer is being posted, you will print a hard copy on a printer. The steps on the next page print a hard copy of the contents of the saved Found Dog Flyer document.

- Click File on the Ribbon to open the Backstage view.

- Click the Print tab in the Backstage view to display the Print gallery (Figure 1–73).

Q&A How can I print multiple copies of my document?

Increase the number in the Copies box in the Print gallery.

Q&A What if I decide not to print the document at this time?

Click File on the Ribbon to close the Backstage view and return to the Word document window.

Figure 1–73

- Verify the printer name that appears on the Printer Status button will print a hard copy of the document. If necessary, click the Printer Status button to display a list of available printer options and then click the desired printer to change the currently selected printer.

- Click the Print button in the Print gallery to print the document on the currently selected printer.

- When the printer stops, retrieve the hard copy (Figure 1–74).

Q&A Do I have to wait until my document is complete to print it?

No, you can follow these steps to print a document at any time while you are creating it.

Q&A What if I want to print an electronic image of a document instead of a hard copy?

You would click the Printer Status button in the Print gallery and then select the desired electronic image option such as a Microsoft XPS Document Writer, which would create an XPS file.

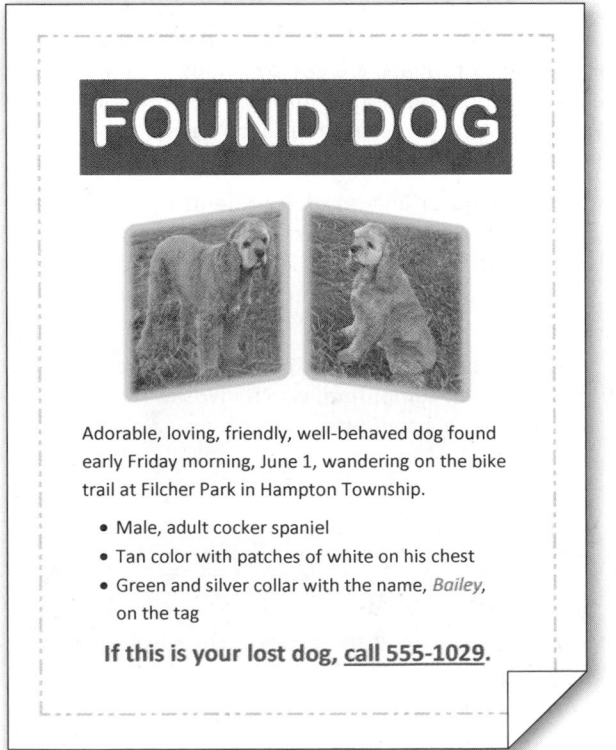

Figure 1–74

Other Ways

1. Press CTRL+P, press ENTER

To Quit Word

The project now is complete. Thus, the following steps quit Word. For an example of the step listed below, refer to the Office 2010 and Windows 7 chapter at the beginning of this book.

1 If you have one Word document open, click the Close button on the right side of the title bar to close the document and quit Word; or if you have multiple Word documents open, click File on the Ribbon to open the Backstage view and then click Exit in the Backstage view to close all open documents and quit Word.

2 If a Microsoft Word dialog box appears, click the Save button to save any changes made to the document since the last save.

BTW

Printed Borders
If one or more of your borders do not print, click the Page Borders button (Page Layout tab | Page Background group), click the Options button (Borders and Shading dialog box), click the Measure from box arrow and click Text, change the four text boxes to 15 pt, and then click the OK button in each dialog box. Try printing the document again. If the borders still do not print, adjust the text boxes in the dialog box to a number smaller than 15 point.

Chapter Summary

In this chapter, you have learned how to enter text in a document, format text, insert a picture, format a picture, add a page border, and print a document. The items listed below include all the new Word skills you have learned in this chapter.

1. Start Word (WD 4)
2. Type Text (WD 6)
3. Display Formatting Marks (WD 7)
4. Insert a Blank Line (WD 7)
5. Wordwrap Text as You Type (WD 8)
6. Check Spelling and Grammar as You Type (WD 9)
7. Save a Document (WD 12)
8. Center a Paragraph (WD 14)
9. Select a Line (WD 15)
10. Change the Font Size of Selected Text (WD 16)
11. Change the Font of Selected Text (WD 17)
12. Change the Case of Selected Text (WD 18)
13. Apply a Text Effect to Selected Text (WD 19)
14. Shade a Paragraph (WD 20)
15. Select Multiple Lines (WD 21)
16. Bullet a List of Paragraphs (WD 22)
17. Undo and Redo an Action (WD 23)
18. Italicize Text (WD 24)
19. Color Text (WD 25)
20. Use the Mini Toolbar to Format Text (WD 26)
21. Select a Group of Words (WD 27)
22. Underline Text (WD 27)
23. Bold Text (WD 28)
24. Change Theme Colors (WD 28)
25. Save an Existing Document with the Same File Name (WD 30)
26. Insert a Picture (WD 31)
27. Zoom the Document (WD 33)
28. Resize a Graphic (WD 34)
29. Resize a Graphic by Entering Exact Measurements (WD 36)
30. Apply a Picture Style (WD 37)
31. Apply Picture Effects (WD 38)
32. View One Page (WD 40)
33. Add a Page Border (WD 41)
34. Change Spacing before and after a Paragraph (WD 44)
35. Quit Word (WD 44)
36. Open a Document from Word (WD 45)
37. Insert Text in an Existing Document (WD 46)
38. Delete Text (WD 47)
39. Move Text (WD 47)
40. Change Document Properties (WD 49)
41. Print a Document (WD 51)

 If you have a SAM 2010 user profile, your instructor may have assigned an autogradable version of this assignment. If so, log into the SAM 2010 Web site at www.cengage.com/sam2010 to download the instruction and start files.

BTW

Quick Reference
For a table that lists how to complete the tasks covered in this book using the mouse, Ribbon, shortcut menu, and keyboard, see the Quick Reference Summary at the back of this book, or visit the Word 2010 Quick Reference Web page (scsite.com/wd2010/qr).

Learn It Online

Test your knowledge of chapter content and key terms.

Instructions: To complete the Learn It Online exercises, start your browser, click the Address bar, and then enter the Web address `scsite.com/wd2010/learn`. When the Word 2010 Learn It Online page is displayed, click the link for the exercise you want to complete and then read the instructions.

Chapter Reinforcement TF, MC, and SA
A series of true/false, multiple choice, and short answer questions that test your knowledge of the chapter content.

Flash Cards
An interactive learning environment where you identify chapter key terms associated with displayed definitions.

Practice Test
A series of multiple choice questions that test your knowledge of chapter content and key terms.

Who Wants To Be a Computer Genius?
An interactive game that challenges your knowledge of chapter content in the style of a television quiz show.

Wheel of Terms
An interactive game that challenges your knowledge of chapter key terms in the style of the television show *Wheel of Fortune*.

Crossword Puzzle Challenge
A crossword puzzle that challenges your knowledge of key terms presented in the chapter.

Apply Your Knowledge

Reinforce the skills and apply the concepts you learned in this chapter.

Modifying Text and Formatting a Document
Note: To complete this assignment, you will be required to use the Data Files for Students. See the inside back cover of this book for instructions on downloading the Data Files for Students, or contact your instructor for information about accessing the required files.

Instructions: Start Word. Open the document, Apply 1-1 Buffalo Photo Shoot Flyer Unformatted, from the Data Files for Students. The document you open is an unformatted flyer. You are to modify text, format paragraphs and characters, and insert a picture in the flyer.

Perform the following tasks:
1. Delete the word, single, in the sentence of body copy below the headline.
2. Insert the word, Creeks, between the words, Twin Buffalo, in the sentence of body copy below the headline.
3. At the end of the signature line, change the period to an exclamation point.
4. Center the headline and the signature line.
5. Change the theme colors to the Aspect color scheme.
6. Change the font and font size of the headline to 48-point Impact, or a similar font. Change the case of the headline text to all capital letters. Apply the text effect called Gradient Fill – Orange, Accent 1, Outline – White to the headline.
7. Change the font size of body copy between the headline and the signature line to 20 point.
8. Use the Mini toolbar to change the font size of the signature line to 26 point.
9. Select the words, hundreds of buffalo, in the paragraph below the headline and underline them.

10. Italicize the word, every, in the paragraph below the headline. Undo this change and then redo the change.

11. Select the three lines (paragraphs) of text above the signature line and add bullets to the selected paragraphs.

12. Switch the last two bulleted paragraphs. That is, select the Questions bullet and move it so that it is the last bulleted paragraph.

13. Bold the first word of each bulleted paragraph. Change the font color of these same three words to Dark Green, Accent 4, Darker 50%.

14. Bold the text in the signature line. Shade the signature line Dark Green, Accent 4, Darker 50%. If the font color does not automatically change to a lighter color, change it to a shade of white.

15. Change the zoom so that the entire page is visible in the document window.

16. Insert the picture of the buffalo centered on the blank line below the headline. The picture is called Buffalo and is available on the Data Files for Students. Apply the Snip Diagonal Corner, White picture style to the inserted picture. Apply the glow called Dark Green, 5 pt glow, Accent color 4 to the picture.

17. Change the spacing after the headline paragraph to 6 point.

18. The entire flyer now should fit on a single page. If it flows to two pages, resize the picture or decrease spacing before and after paragraphs until the entire flyer text fits on a single page.

19. Change the zoom to text width, then page width, then 100% and notice the differences.

20. Enter the text, Twin Creeks, as the keywords in the document properties. Change the other document properties, as specified by your instructor.

21. Click File on the Ribbon and then click Save As. Save the document using the file name, Apply 1-1 Buffalo Photo Shoot Flyer Formatted.

22. Print the document. Submit the revised document, shown in Figure 1–75, in the format specified by your instructor.

23. Quit Word.

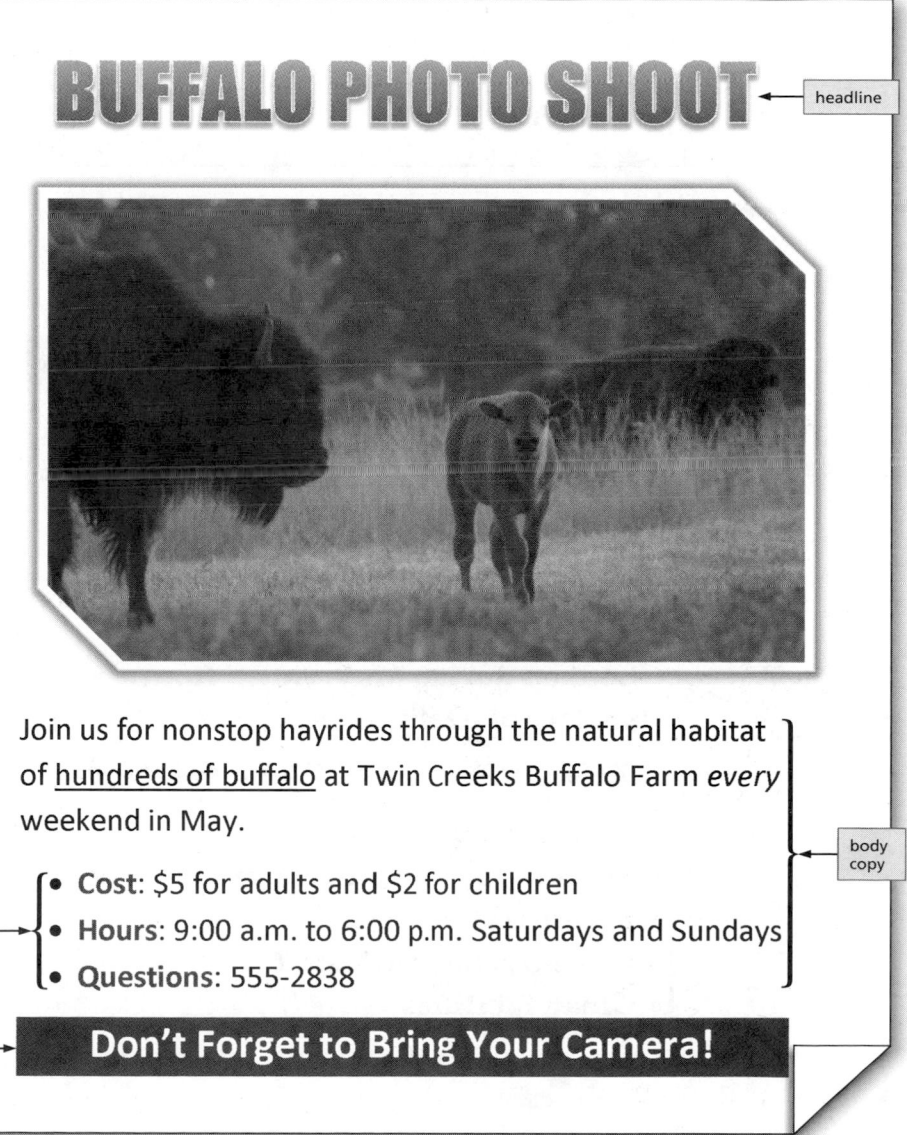

Figure 1–75

Extend Your Knowledge

Extend the skills you learned in this chapter and experiment with new skills. You may need to use Help to complete the assignment.

Modifying Text and Picture Formats and Adding Page Borders

Note: To complete this assignment, you will be required to use the Data Files for Students. See the inside back cover of this book for instructions on downloading the Data Files for Students, or contact your instructor for information about accessing the required files.

Instructions: Start Word. Open the document, Extend 1-1 TVC Cruises Flyer, from the Data Files for Students. You will enhance the look of the flyer shown in Figure 1–76. *Hint:* Remember, if you make a mistake while formatting the picture, you can reset it by clicking the Reset Picture button or Reset Picture button arrow (Picture Tools Format tab | Adjust group).

Perform the following tasks:

1. Use Help to learn about the following formats: remove bullets, grow font, shrink font, art page borders, decorative underline(s), picture bullets, picture border shading, shadow picture effects, and color saturation and tone.
2. Remove the bullet from the paragraph below the picture.

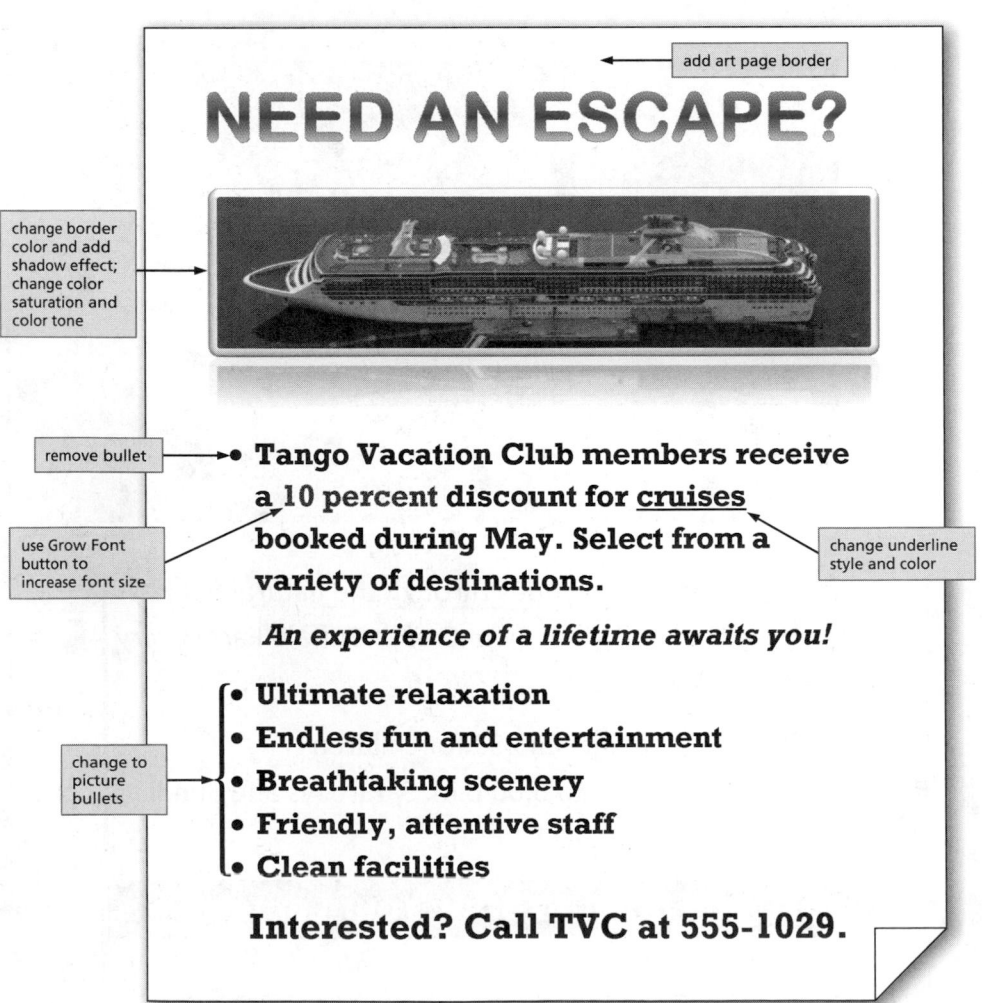

3. Select the text, 10 percent, and use the Grow Font button to increase its font size.
4. Add an art page border to the flyer. If possible, add color to the border.
5. Change the solid underline below the word, cruises, to a decorative underline. Change the color of the underline.
6. Change the style of the bullets to picture bullet(s).
7. Change the color of the picture border. Add a shadow picture effect to the picture.
8. Change the color saturation and color tone of the picture.
9. Change the document properties, including keywords, as specified by your instructor. Save the revised document with a new file name and then submit it in the format specified by your instructor.

Figure 1–76

Make It Right

Analyze a document and correct all errors and/or improve the design.

Correcting Spelling and Grammar Errors

Note: To complete this assignment, you will be required to use the Data Files for Students. See the inside back cover of this book for instructions on downloading the Data Files for Students, or contact your instructor for information about accessing the required files.

Instructions: Start Word. Open the document, Make It Right 1-1 Karate Academy Flyer Unchecked, from the Data Files for Students. The document is a flyer that contains spelling and grammar errors, as shown in Figure 1–77. You are to correct each spelling (red wavy underline) and grammar error (green and blue wavy underlines) by right-clicking the flagged text and then clicking the appropriate correction on the shortcut menu.

If your screen does not display the wavy underlines, click File on the Ribbon and then click Options in the Backstage view. When the Word Options dialog box is displayed, click Proofing in the left pane, be sure the 'Hide spelling errors in this document only' and 'Hide grammar errors in this document only' check boxes do not contain check marks, and then click the OK button. If your screen still does not display the wavy underlines, redisplay the Word Options dialog box, click Proofing, and then click the Recheck Document button.

Change the document properties, including keywords, as specified by your instructor. Save the revised document with the name, Make It Right 1-1 Karate Academy Flyer, and then submit it in the format specified by your instructor.

Figure 1–77

In the Lab

Design and/or create a document using the guidelines, concepts, and skills presented in this chapter. Labs are listed in order of increasing difficulty.

Lab 1: Creating a Flyer with a Picture

Problem: As a part-time employee in the Student Services Center at school, you have been asked to prepare a flyer that advertises study habits classes. First, you prepare the unformatted flyer shown in Figure 1–78a, and then you format it so that it looks like Figure 1–78b. *Hint:* Remember, if you make a mistake while formatting the flyer, you can click the Undo button on the Quick Access Toolbar to undo your last action.

Note: To complete this assignment, you will be required to use the Data Files for Students. See the inside back cover of this book for instructions on downloading the Data Files for Students, or contact your instructor for information about accessing the required files.

Instructions: Perform the following tasks:

1. Start Word. Display formatting marks on the screen.
2. Type the flyer text, unformatted, as shown in Figure 1–78a, inserting a blank line between the headline and the body copy. If Word flags any misspelled words as you type, check their spelling and correct them.
3. Save the document using the file name, Lab 1-1 Study Habits Flyer.
4. Center the headline and the signature line.
5. Change the theme colors to Concourse.
6. Change the font size of the headline to 36 point and the font to Ravie, or a similar font. Apply the text effect called Gradient Fill – Dark Red, Accent 6, Inner Shadow.
7. Change the font size of body copy between the headline and the signature line to 20 point.
8. Change the font size of the signature line to 22 point. Bold the text in the signature line.

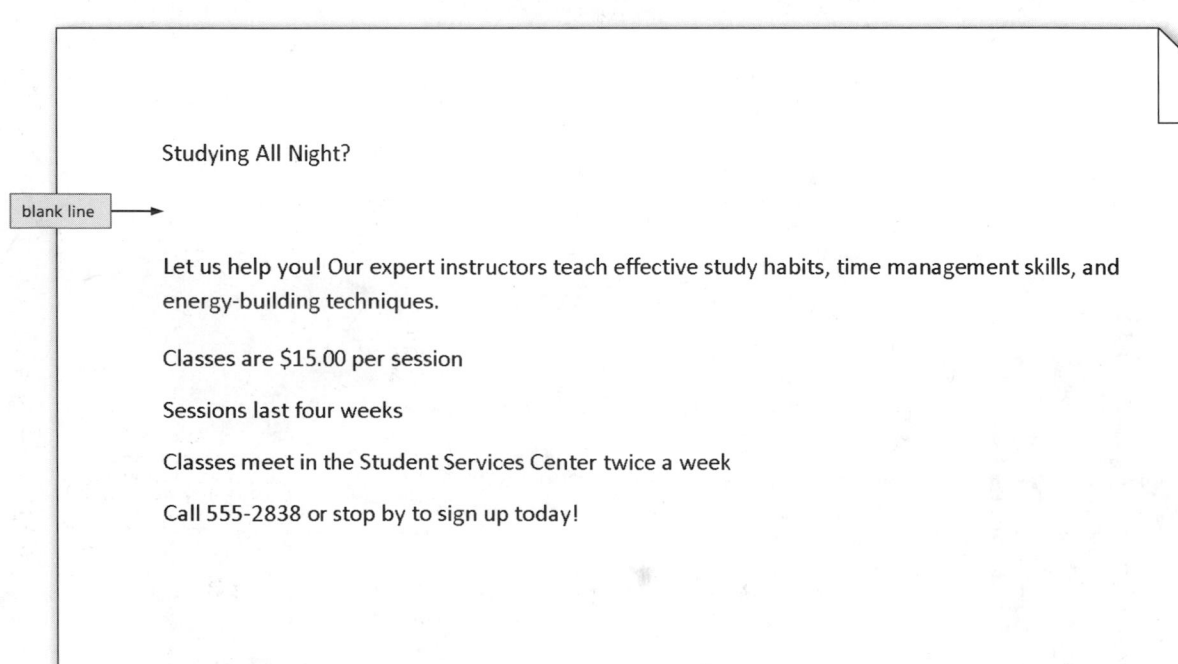

Figure 1–78 (a) Unformatted Flyer

9. Change the font of the body copy and signature line to Rockwell, and change the color of the signature line to Dark Red, Accent 6.

10. Bullet the three lines (paragraphs) of text above the signature line.

11. Bold and capitalize the text, Let us help you!, and change its color to Dark Red, Accent 6.

12. Italicize the word, or, in the signature line.

13. Underline the text, Student Services Center, in the third bulleted paragraph.

14. Change the zoom so that the entire page is visible in the document window.

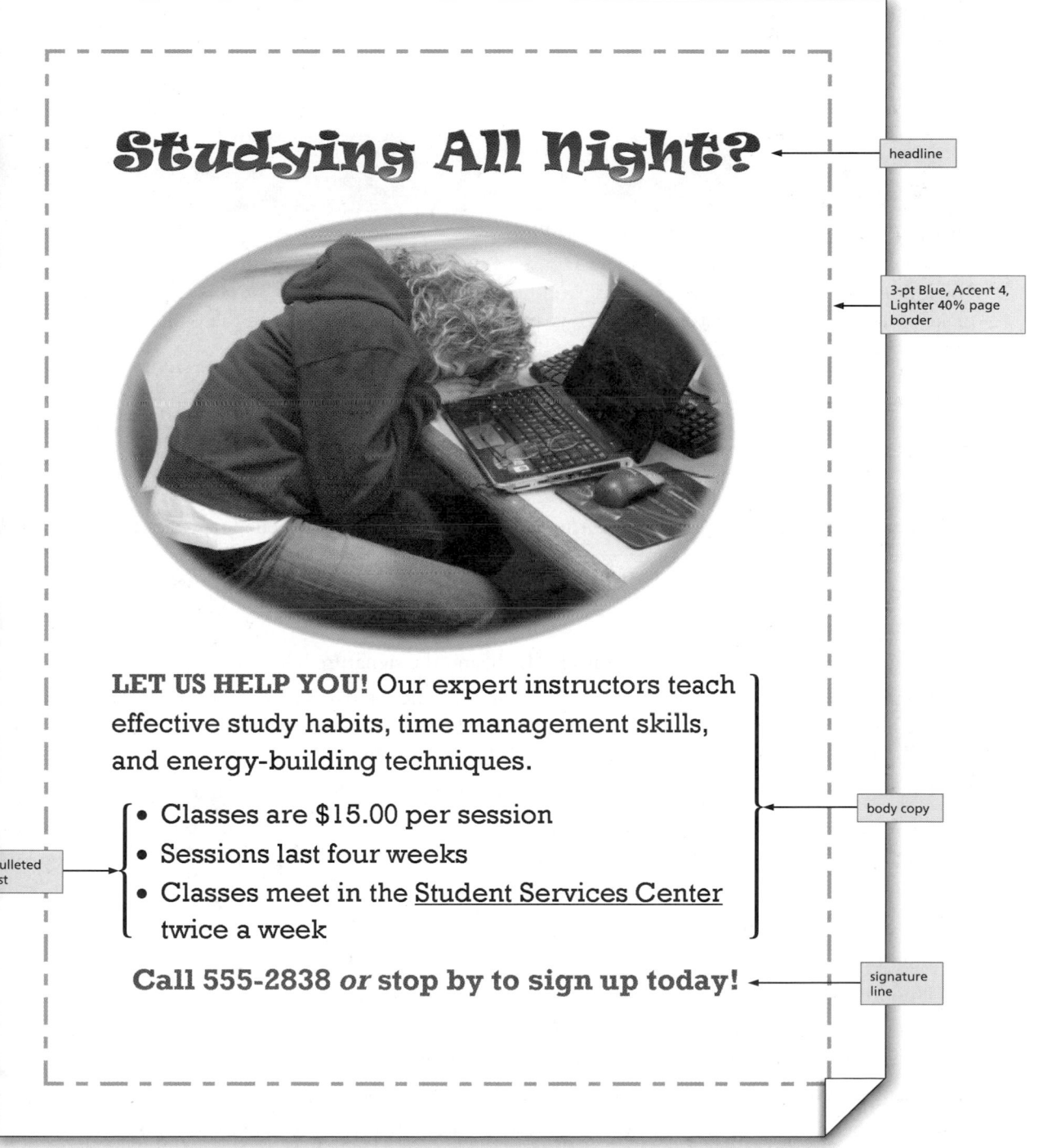

Figure 1–78 (b) Formatted Flyer

Continued >

In the Lab *continued*

15. Insert the picture centered on a blank line below the headline. The picture is called Sleeping and is available on the Data Files for Students.

16. Apply the Soft Edge Oval picture style to the inserted picture. Apply the glow effect called Blue, 5 pt glow, Accent color 4 to the picture.

17. The entire flyer should fit on a single page. If it flows to two pages, resize the picture or decrease spacing before and after paragraphs until the entire flyer text fits on a single page.

18. Add the page border shown in Figure 1–78b on the previous page.

19. Change the document properties, including keywords, as specified by your instructor. Save the flyer again with the same file name. Submit the document, shown in Figure 1–78b, in the format specified by your instructor.

In the Lab

Lab 2: Creating a Flyer with a Resized Picture

Problem: Your boss at Granger Camera House has asked you to prepare a flyer that announces the upcoming photography contest. You prepare the flyer shown in Figure 1–79. *Hint:* Remember, if you make a mistake while formatting the flyer, you can click the Undo button on the Quick Access Toolbar to undo your last action.

Note: To complete this assignment, you will be required to use the Data Files for Students. See the inside back cover of this book for instructions on downloading the Data Files for Students, or contact your instructor for information about accessing the required files.

Instructions: Perform the following tasks:

1. Start Word. Type the flyer text, unformatted. If Word flags any misspelled words as you type, check their spelling and correct them.

2. Save the document using the file name, Lab 1-2 Photography Contest Flyer.

3. Change the theme colors to the Apex color scheme.

4. Center the headline, the line that says RULES, and the signature line.

5. Change the font size of the headline to 36 point and the font to Stencil, or a similar font. Shade the headline paragraph Lavender, Background 2, Darker 50%. Apply the text effect called Fill – Lavender, Accent 6, Outline – Accent 6, Glow – Accent 6.

6. Change the font size of body copy between the headline and the signature line to 18 point.

7. Change the font size of the signature line to 24 point and the font to Stencil. Bold the text in the signature line. Change the font color of the text in the signature line to Gray-50%, Text 2.

8. Bullet the three paragraphs of text above the signature line.

9. Italicize the word, not.

10. Bold the word, landscape.

11. Underline the text, August 31.

12. Shade the line that says RULES to the Gray-50%, Text 2 color. If the font color does not automatically change to a lighter color, change it to White, Background 1.

13. Change the zoom so that the entire page is visible in the document window.

14. Insert the picture on a blank line below the headline. The picture is called Wind Power and is available on the Data Files for Students.

15. Resize the picture so that it is approximately 3.5" × 5.25". Apply the Rotated, White picture style to the inserted picture. Apply the glow effect called Lavender, 5 pt glow, Accent color 6 to the picture.

16. The entire flyer should fit on a single page. If it flows to two pages, resize the picture or decrease spacing before and after paragraphs until the entire flyer text fits on a single page.

17. Add the page border shown in Figure 1–79.

18. Change the document properties, including keywords, as specified by your instructor. Save the flyer again with the same file name. Submit the document, shown in Figure 1–79, in the format specified by your instructor.

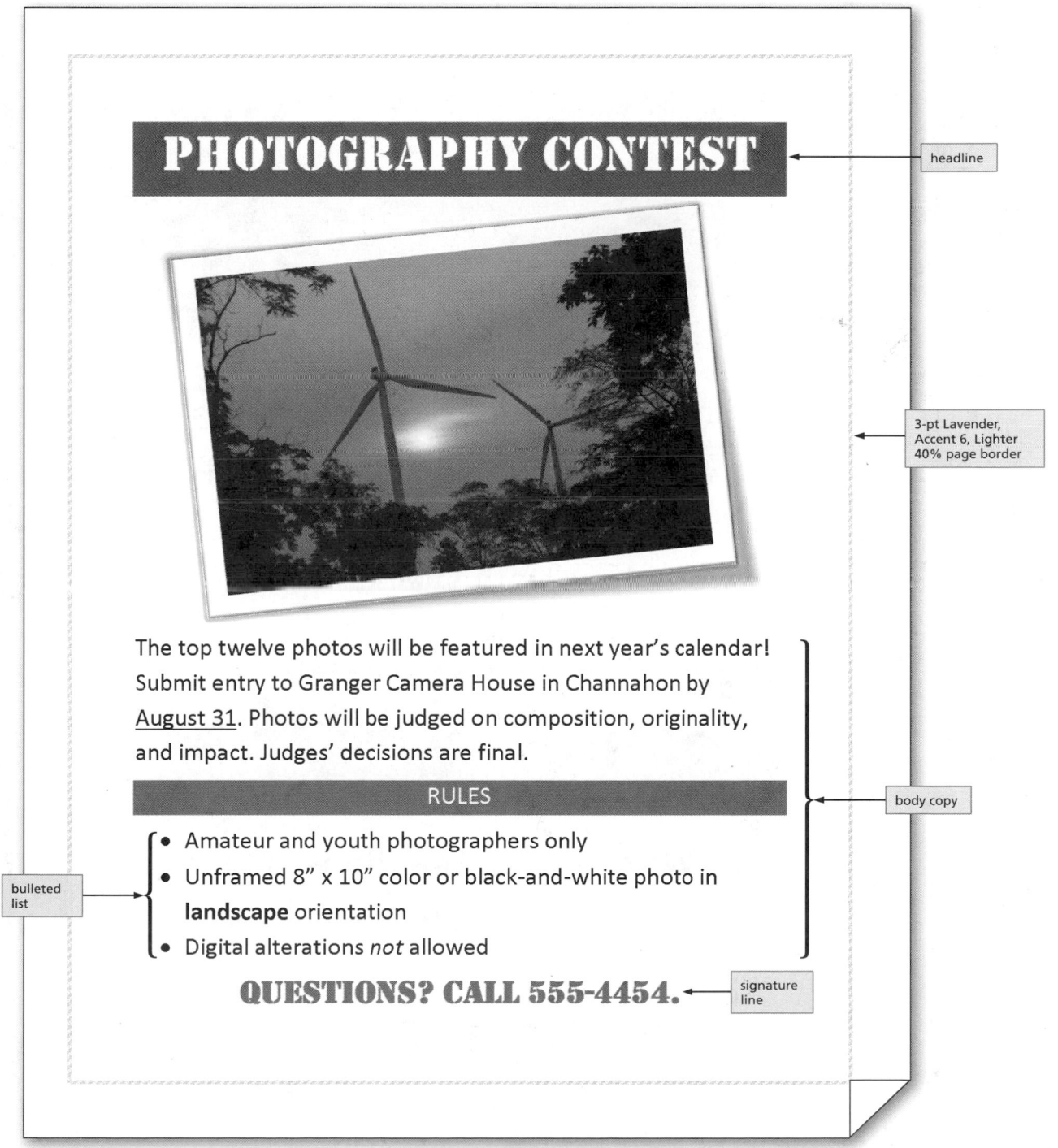

Figure 1–79

In the Lab

Lab 3: Creating a Flyer with Pictures

Problem: Your boss at Warner Depot has asked you to prepare a flyer that advertises its scenic train ride. You prepare the flyer shown in Figure 1–80.

3-pt Tan, Accent 6, Darker 50% page border

48-point Algerian font; uppercase; centered; Fill - Tan, Text 2, Outline - Background 2 text effect

Aspect theme colors

Bevel Rectangle picture style; Perspective Diagonal Upper Left Shadow picture effect; Perspective Le 3-D Rotation picture effect

26-point Dark Blue, Accent 3, Darker 50% Rockwell font; centered

Tan Accent 6 shading; White, Background 1 font color

underlined

bulleted list; left-aligned

Bevel Rectangle pict style; Perspective Diagonal Upper Righ Shadow picture effe Perspective Right 3-I Rotation picture effe

28-point Dark Blue, Accent 3, Darker 50% Rockwell font; centered

bold, italic, Tan, Accent 6, Darker 50% font

Figure 1–80

Note: To complete this assignment, you will be required to use the Data Files for Students. See the inside back cover of this book for instructions on downloading the Data Files for Students, or contact your instructor for information about accessing the required files.

Instructions: Start Word. Enter the text in the flyer, checking spelling as you type, and then format it as shown in Figure 1–80. The pictures to be inserted are called Train and Scenery and are available on the Data Files for Students. Adjust spacing before and after paragraphs and resize pictures as necessary so that the flyer fits on a single page.

Change the document properties, including keywords, as specified by your instructor. Save the document using the file name, Lab 1-3 Train Ride Flyer. Submit the document, shown in Figure 1–80, in the format specified by your instructor.

Cases and Places

Apply your creative thinking and problem solving skills to design and implement a solution.

Note: To complete these assignments, you may be required to use the Data Files for Students. See the inside back cover of this book for instructions on downloading the Data Files for Students, or contact your instructor for information about accessing the required files.

1: Design and Create a Spring Break Flyer

Academic

As secretary of your school's Student Government Association, you are responsible for creating and distributing flyers for spring break group outings. This year, you have planned a trip to Settlers Resort. The flyer should contain two digital pictures appropriately resized; the Data Files for Students contains two pictures called Cabin 1 and Cabin 2, or you can use your own digital pictures if they are appropriate for the topic of the flyer. The flyer should contain the headline, Feeling Adventurous?, and this signature line: Call Lyn at 555-9901 to sign up. The body copy consists of the following, in any order: Spring Break – Blast to the Past. Settlers Resort is like a page right out of a history textbook! Spend five days living in the 1800s. The bulleted list in the body copy is as follows: One-room cabins with potbelly stoves, Campfire dining with authentic meals, and Horseback riding and much more.

Use the concepts and techniques presented in this chapter to create and format this flyer. Be sure to check spelling and grammar. Submit your assignment in the format specified by your instructor.

2: Design and Create a Yard Sale Flyer

Personal

You are planning a yard sale and would like to create and post flyers around town advertising the upcoming sale. The flyer should contain two digital pictures appropriately resized; the Data Files for Students contains two pictures called Yard Sale 1 and Yard Sale 2, or you can use your own digital pictures if they are appropriate for the topic of the flyer. The flyer should contain the headline, Yard Sale!, and this signature line: Questions? Call 555-9820. The body copy consists of the following, in any order: Hundreds of items for sale. After 20 years, we are moving to a smaller house and are selling anything that won't fit. Everything for sale must go! The bulleted list in the body copy is as follows: When: August 7, 8, 9 from 9:00 a.m. to 7:00 p.m.; Where: 139 Ravel Boulevard; and What: something for everyone – from clothing to collectibles.

Use the concepts and techniques presented in this chapter to create and format this flyer. Be sure to check spelling and grammar. Submit your assignment in the format specified by your instructor.

Continued >

Cases and Places *continued*

3: Design and Create a Village Fireworks Flyer

Professional

As a part-time employee at the Village of Crestwood, your boss has asked you to create and distribute flyers for the upcoming fireworks extravaganza. The flyer should contain two digital pictures appropriately resized; the Data Files for Students contains two pictures called Fireworks 1 and Fireworks 2, or you can use your own digital pictures if they are appropriate for the topic of the flyer. The flyer should contain the headline, Light Up The Sky, and this signature line: Call 555-2983 with questions. The body copy consists of the following, in any order: Join Us! The Village of Crestwood will present its tenth annual Light Up The Sky fireworks extravaganza on August 8 at 9:00 p.m. during the end of summer celebration in Douglas Park. The bulleted list in the body copy is as follows: Pork chop dinners will be sold for $3.00 beginning at 6:00 p.m., Bring chairs and blankets, and Admission is free.

Use the concepts and techniques presented in this chapter to create and format this flyer. Be sure to check spelling and grammar. Submit your assignment in the format specified by your instructor.

2 Creating a Research Paper with Citations and References

Objectives

You will have mastered the material in this chapter when you can:

- Describe the MLA documentation style for research papers
- Change line and paragraph spacing in a document
- Modify a style
- Use a header to number pages of a document
- Apply formatting using shortcut keys
- Modify paragraph indentation

- Insert and edit citations and their sources
- Add a footnote to a document
- Insert a manual page break
- Create a bibliographical list of sources
- Cut, copy, and paste text
- Find text and replace text
- Find a synonym
- Use the Research task pane to look up information

2 | Creating a Research Paper with Citations and References

Introduction

In both academic and business environments, you will be asked to write reports. Business reports range from proposals to cost justifications to five-year plans to research findings. Academic reports focus mostly on research findings.

A **research paper** is a document you can use to communicate the results of research findings. To write a research paper, you learn about a particular topic from a variety of sources (research), organize your ideas from the research results, and then present relevant facts and/or opinions that support the topic. Your final research paper combines properly credited outside information along with personal insights. Thus, no two research papers — even if about the same topic — will or should be the same.

Project — Research Paper

When preparing a research paper, you should follow a standard documentation style that defines the rules for creating the paper and crediting sources. A variety of documentation styles exists, depending on the nature of the research paper. Each style requires the same basic information; the differences in styles relate to requirements for presenting the information. For example, one documentation style uses the term bibliography for the list of sources, whereas another uses references, and yet a third prefers the title works cited. Two popular documentation styles for research papers are the **Modern Language Association of America (MLA)** and **American Psychological Association (APA)** styles. This chapter uses the MLA documentation style because it is used in a wide range of disciplines.

The project in this chapter follows research paper guidelines and uses Word to create the short research paper shown in Figure 2–1. This paper, which discusses triangulation, follows the MLA documentation style. Each page contains a page number. The first two pages present the name and course information (student name, instructor name, course name, and paper due date), paper title, an introduction with a thesis statement, details that support the thesis, and a conclusion. This section of the paper also includes references to research sources and a footnote. The third page contains a detailed, alphabetical list of the sources referenced in the research paper. All pages include a header at the upper-right edge of the page.

BTW

APA Appendix
If your version of this book includes the Word APA Appendix and you are required to create a research paper using the APA documentation style instead of the MLA documentation style, the appendix shows the steps required to create the research paper in this chapter using the APA guidelines. If your version of this book does not include the Word APA Appendix, see print publications or search the Web for the APA guidelines.

Figure 2–1

Overview

As you read through this chapter, you will learn how to create the research paper shown in Figure 2–1 on the previous page by performing these general tasks:

- Change the document settings.
- Type the research paper.
- Save the research paper.
- Create an alphabetical list of sources.
- Proof and revise the research paper.
- Print the research paper.

Plan Ahead

General Project Guidelines

When creating a Word document, the actions you perform and decisions you make will affect the appearance and characteristics of the finished document. As you create a research paper, such as the project shown in Figure 2–1, you should follow these general guidelines:

1. **Select a topic.** Spend time brainstorming ideas for a topic. Choose one you find interesting. For shorter papers, narrow the scope of the topic; for longer papers, broaden the scope. Identify a tentative thesis statement, which is a sentence describing the paper's subject matter.

2. **Research the topic and take notes.** Gather credible, relevant information about the topic that supports the thesis statement. Sources of research include books, magazines, newspapers, and the Internet. As you record facts and ideas, list details about the source: title, author, place of publication, publisher, date of publication, etc. When taking notes, be careful not to **plagiarize**. That is, do not use someone else's work and claim it to be your own. If you copy information directly, place it in quotation marks and identify its source.

3. **Organize your ideas.** Classify your notes into related concepts. Make an outline from the categories of notes. In the outline, identify all main ideas and supporting details.

4. **Write the first draft, referencing sources.** From the outline, compose the paper. Every research paper should include an introduction containing the thesis statement, supporting details, and a conclusion. Follow the guidelines identified in the required documentation style. Reference all sources of information.

5. **Create the list of sources.** Using the formats specified in the required documentation style, completely list all sources referenced in the body of the research paper in alphabetical order.

6. **Proofread and revise the paper.** If possible, proofread the paper with a fresh set of eyes, that is, at least one to two days after completing the first draft. Proofreading involves reading the paper with the intent of identifying errors (spelling, grammar, etc.) and looking for ways to improve the paper (wording, transitions, flow, etc.). Try reading the paper out loud, which helps to identify unclear or awkward wording. Ask someone else to proofread the paper and give you suggestions for improvements.

When necessary, more specific details concerning the above guidelines are presented at appropriate points in the chapter. The chapter also will identify the actions performed and decisions made regarding these guidelines during the creation of the research paper shown in Figure 2–1.

MLA Documentation Style

The research paper in this project follows the guidelines presented by the MLA. To follow the MLA documentation style, use 12-point Times New Roman, or a similar, font. Double-space text on all pages of the paper using one-inch top, bottom, left, and right margins. Indent the first word of each paragraph one-half inch from the left margin. At the right margin of each page, place a page number one-half inch from the top margin. On each page, precede the page number by your last name.

The MLA documentation style does not require a title page. Instead, place your name and course information in a block at the left margin beginning one inch from the top of the page. Center the title one double-spaced line below your name and course information.

In the text of the paper, place author references in parentheses with the page number(s) of the referenced information. The MLA documentation style uses in-text **parenthetical references** instead of noting each source at the bottom of the page or at the end of the paper. In the MLA documentation style, notes are used only for optional content or bibliographic notes.

If used, content notes elaborate on points discussed in the paper, and bibliographic notes direct the reader to evaluations of statements in a source or provide a means for identifying multiple sources. Use a superscript (raised number) both to signal that a note exists and to sequence the notes (shown in Figure 2-1 on page WD 67). Position notes at the bottom of the page as footnotes or at the end of the paper as endnotes. Indent the first line of each note one-half inch from the left margin. Place one space following the superscripted number before beginning the note text. Double-space the note text (shown in Figure 2–1).

The MLA documentation style uses the term **works cited** to refer to the bibliographic list of sources at the end of the paper. The works cited page alphabetically lists sources that are referenced directly in the paper. Place the list of sources on a separate numbered page. Center the title, Works Cited, one inch from the top margin. Double-space all lines. Begin the first line of each source at the left margin, indenting subsequent lines of the same source one-half inch from the left margin. List each source by the author's last name, or, if the author's name is not available, by the title of the source.

BTW

APA Documentation Style
In the APA documentation style, a separate title page is required instead of placing name and course information on the paper's first page. Double-space all pages of the paper with one-inch top, bottom, left, and right margins. Indent the first word of each paragraph one-half inch from the left margin. In the upper-right margin of each page, including the title page, place a running head that consists of the page number preceded by a brief summary of the paper title.

Changing Document Settings

The MLA documentation style defines some global formats that apply to the entire research paper. Some of these formats are the default in Word. For example, the default left, right, top, and bottom margin settings in Word are one inch, which meets the MLA documentation style. You will modify, however, the font, font size, line and paragraph spacing, and header formats as required by the MLA documentation style.

To Start Word

If you are using a computer to step through the project in this chapter and you want your screens to match the figures in this book, you should change your screen's resolution to 1024 × 768. For information about how to change a computer's resolution, refer to the Office 2010 and Windows 7 chapter at the beginning of this book.

For an introduction to Windows 7 and instruction about how to perform basic Windows 7 tasks, read the Office 2010 and Windows 7 chapter at the beginning of this book, where you can learn how to resize windows, change screen resolution, create folders, move and rename files, use Windows Help, and much more.

BTW

New Document Window
If you wanted to open a new blank document window, you could press CTRL+N or click File on the Ribbon to open the Backstage view, click the New tab to display the New gallery, click the Blank document button, and then click the Create button.

The following steps, which assume Windows 7 is running, start Word based on a typical installation. You may need to ask your instructor how to start Word for your computer. For a detailed example of the procedure summarized below, refer to the Office 2010 and Windows 7 chapter.

1 Click the Start button on the Windows 7 taskbar to display the Start menu.

2 Type `Microsoft Word` as the search text in the 'Search programs and files' text box and watch the search results appear on the Start menu.

3 Click Microsoft Word 2010 in the search results on the Start menu to start Word and display a new blank document in the Word window.

4 If the Word window is not maximized, click the Maximize button next to the Close button on its title bar to maximize the window.

5 If the Print Layout button on the status bar is not selected (shown in Figure 2–2), click it so that your screen is in Print Layout view.

6 If Normal (Home tab | Styles group) is not selected in the Quick Style gallery (shown in Figure 2–2), click it so that your document uses the Normal style.

7 If your zoom percent is not 100, click the Zoom Out or Zoom In button as many times as necessary until the Zoom button displays 100% on its face (shown in Figure 2–2).

BTW

Style Formats
To see the formats assigned to a particular style in a document, click the Styles Dialog Box Launcher (Home tab | Styles group) and then click the Style Inspector button in the Styles task pane. Position the insertion point in the style in the document and then point to the Paragraph formatting or Text level formatting areas in the Style Inspector task pane to display an Enhanced ScreenTip describing formats assigned to the location of the insertion point. You also can click the Reveal Formatting button in the Style Inspector task pane to display the Reveal Formatting task pane.

To Display Formatting Marks

As discussed in Chapter 1, it is helpful to display formatting marks that indicate where in the document you press the ENTER key, SPACEBAR, and other keys. The following steps display formatting marks.

1 If the Home tab is not the active tab, click Home on the Ribbon to display the Home tab.

2 If the Show/Hide ¶ button (Home tab | Paragraph group) is not selected already, click it to display formatting marks on the screen.

Styles

When you create a document, Word formats the text using a particular style. A **style** is a named group of formatting characteristics, including font and font size. The default style in Word is called the **Normal style**, which most likely uses 11-point Calibri font. If you do not specify a style for text you type, Word applies the Normal style to the text. In addition to the Normal style, Word has many other built-in, or predefined, styles that you can use to format text. Styles make it easy to apply many formats at once to text. You can modify existing styles and create your own styles. Styles are discussed as they are used in this book.

To Modify a Style

The MLA documentation style requires that all text in the research paper use 12-point Times New Roman, or a similar, font. If you change the font and font size using buttons on the Ribbon, you will need to make the change many times during the course of creating the paper because Word formats different areas of a document using the Normal style, which uses 11-point Calibri font. For example, body text, headers, and bibliographies all display text based on the Normal style. Thus, instead of changing the font and font size for each of these document elements, a more efficient technique would be to change the Normal style for this document to 12-point Times New Roman. By changing the Normal style, you ensure that all text in the document will use the format required by the MLA. The next steps change the Normal style.

1

• Right-click Normal in the Quick Style gallery (Home tab | Styles group) to display a shortcut menu related to styles (Figure 2–2).

default font and font size for Normal style

What if I am in a lab environment and cannot modify the Normal style?

Use the buttons on the Ribbon to change the font to Times New Roman and the font size to 12.

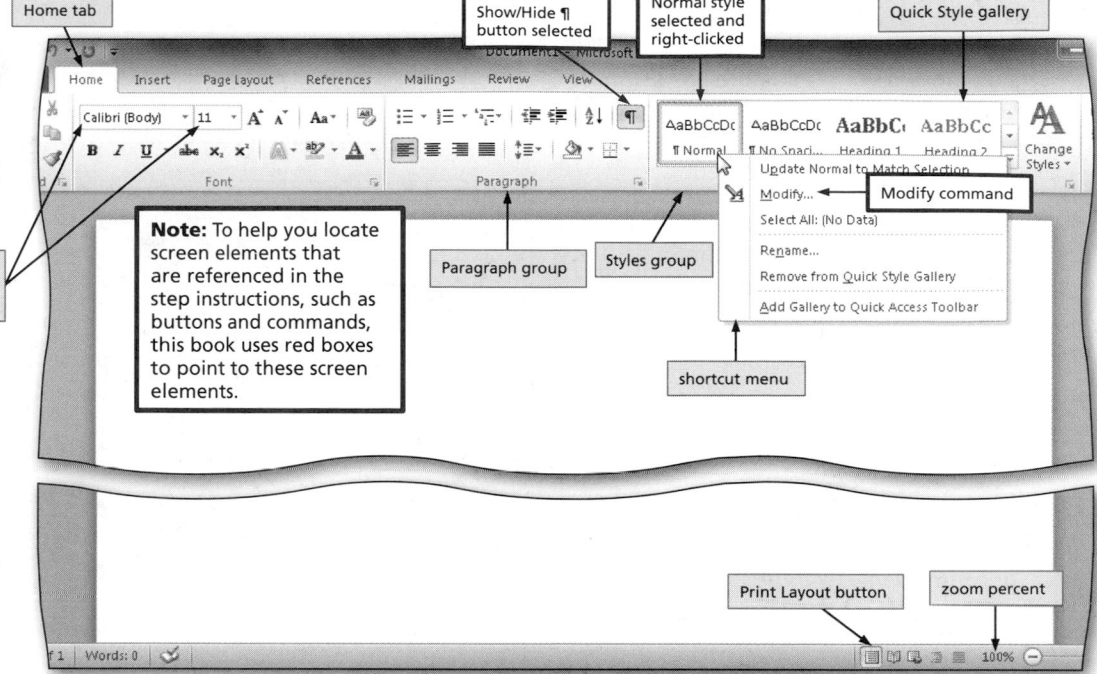

Home tab

Show/Hide ¶ button selected

Normal style selected and right-clicked

Quick Style gallery

Note: To help you locate screen elements that are referenced in the step instructions, such as buttons and commands, this book uses red boxes to point to these screen elements.

Paragraph group

Styles group

Update Normal to Match Selection

Modify...

Modify command

Select All: (No Data)

Rename...

Remove from Quick Style Gallery

Add Gallery to Quick Access Toolbar

shortcut menu

Print Layout button

zoom percent

Figure 2–2

2

• Click Modify on the shortcut menu to display the Modify Style dialog box (Figure 2–3).

Modify Style dialog box

style name

Modify Style

Properties

Name: Normal

Style type: Paragraph

Style based on: (no style)

Style for following paragraph: ¶ Normal

Formatting

current font for Normal style is Calibri

Calibri (Body)   11   **B** *I* U   Automatic

current font size for Normal style is 11 point

Previous Paragraph Previous Paragraph Previous Paragraph Previous Paragraph Previous Paragraph Previous Paragraph Previous Paragraph Previous Paragraph Previous Paragraph Previous Paragraph

Sample Text Sample Text Sample Text Sample Text Sample Text Sample Text Sample Text
Sample Text Sample Text Sample Text Sample Text Sample Text Sample Text Sample Text
Sample Text Sample Text Sample Text Sample Text Sample Text

Following Paragraph Following Paragraph Following Paragraph Following Paragraph Following Paragraph
Following Paragraph Following Paragraph Following Paragraph Following Paragraph Following Paragraph
Following Paragraph Following Paragraph Following Paragraph Following Paragraph Following Paragraph
Following Paragraph Following Paragraph Following Paragraph Following Paragraph Following Paragraph

Font: (Default) +Body (Calibri), Left
   Line spacing: Multiple 1.15 li, Space
   After: 10 pt, Widow/Orphan control, Style: Quick Style

☑ Add to Quick Style list
◉ Only in this document   ◯ New documents based on this template

Format ▾   OK   Cancel

Figure 2–3

3

- Click the Font box arrow (Modify Style dialog box) to display the Font list. Scroll to and then click Times New Roman in the list to change the font for the style being modified.

- Click the Font Size box arrow (Modify Style dialog box) and then click 12 in the Font Size list to change the font size for the style being modified.

- Ensure that the 'Only in this document' option button is selected (Figure 2-4).

Will all future documents use the new font and font size?

No, because the 'Only in this document' option button is selected. If you want all future documents to use a new setting, you would select the 'New documents based on this template' option button.

4

- Click the OK button (Modify Style dialog box) to update the Normal style to the specified settings.

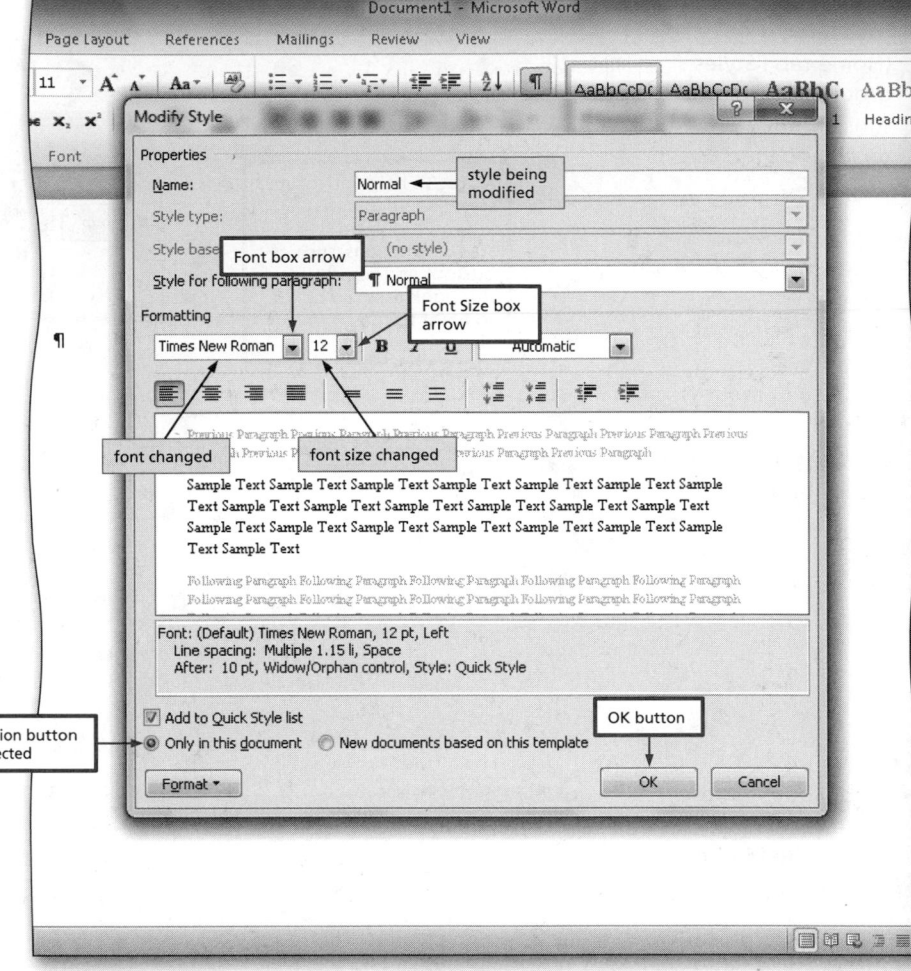

Figure 2-4

Other Ways

1. Click Styles Dialog Box Launcher, click box arrow next to style name, click Modify on menu, change settings (Modify Style dialog box), click OK button

2. Press ALT+CTRL+SHIFT+S, click box arrow next to style name, click Modify on menu, change settings (Modify Style dialog box), click OK button

---

Adjusting Line and Paragraph Spacing

Line spacing is the amount of vertical space between lines of text in a paragraph. **Paragraph spacing** is the amount of space above and below a paragraph. By default, the Normal style places 10 points of blank space after each paragraph and inserts a vertical space equal to 1.15 lines between each line of text. It also automatically adjusts line height to accommodate various font sizes and graphics.

The MLA documentation style requires that you **double-space** the entire research paper. That is, the amount of vertical space between each line of text and above and below paragraphs should be equal to one blank line. The next sets of steps adjust line spacing and paragraph spacing according to the MLA documentation style.

To Change Line Spacing

The lines of the research paper should be double-spaced, according to the MLA documentation style. In Word, you change the line spacing to 2.0 to double-space lines in a paragraph. The following steps change the line spacing to double.

• Click the Line and Paragraph Spacing button (Home tab | Paragraph group) to display the Line and Paragraph Spacing gallery (Figure 2–5).

What do the numbers in the Line and Paragraph Spacing gallery represent?

The default line spacing is 1.15 lines. The options 1.0, 2.0, and 3.0 set line spacing to single, double, and triple, respectively. Similarly, the 1.5 and 2.5 options set line spacing to 1.5 and 2.5 lines. All these options adjust line spacing automatically to accommodate the largest font or graphic on a line.

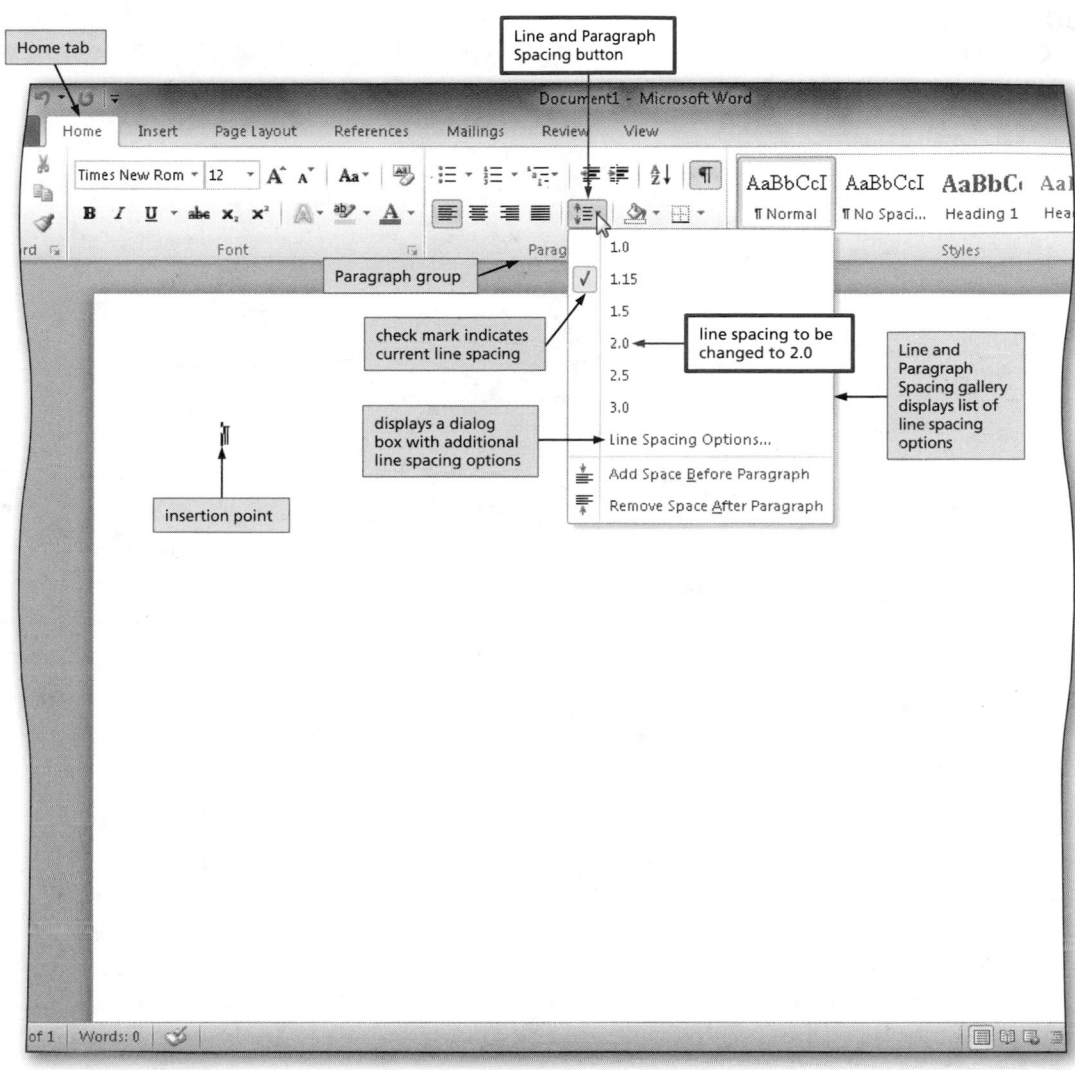

Figure 2–5

• Click 2.0 in the Line and Paragraph Spacing gallery to change the line spacing at the location of the insertion point.

Can I change the line spacing of existing text?

Yes. Select the text first and then change the line spacing as described in these steps.

Other Ways

1. Right-click paragraph, click Paragraph on shortcut menu, click Indents and Spacing tab (Paragraph dialog box), click Line spacing box arrow, click desired spacing, click OK button

2. Click Paragraph Dialog Box Launcher (Home tab or Page Layout tab | Paragraph group), click Indents and Spacing tab (Paragraph dialog box), click Line spacing box arrow, click desired spacing, click OK button

3. Press CTRL+2 for double-spacing

To Remove Space after a Paragraph

The research paper should not have additional blank space after each paragraph. The following steps remove space after a paragraph.

- Click the Line and Paragraph Spacing button (Home tab | Paragraph group) to display the Line and Paragraph Spacing gallery (Figure 2–6).

- Click Remove Space After Paragraph in the Line and Paragraph Spacing gallery so that no blank space appears after paragraphs.

Q&A

Can I remove space after existing paragraphs?

Yes. Select the paragraphs first and then remove the space as described in these steps.

Figure 2–6

Other Ways

1. Click Spacing After box arrows (Page Layout tab | Paragraph group) until 0 pt is displayed

2. Right-click paragraph, click Paragraph on shortcut menu, click

Indents and Spacing tab (Paragraph dialog box), click After box arrows until 0 pt is displayed, click OK button

3. Click Paragraph Dialog Box Launcher (Home

tab or Page Layout tab | Paragraph group), click Indents and Spacing tab (Paragraph dialog box), click After box arrows until 0 pt is displayed, click OK button

To Update a Style to Match a Selection

To ensure that all paragraphs in the paper will be double-spaced and do not have space after the paragraphs, you want the Normal style to include the line and paragraph spacing changes made in the previous two sets of steps. You can update a style to reflect the settings of the location of the insertion point or selected text. Because no text has yet been typed in the research paper, you do not need to select text prior to updating the Normal style. The following steps update the Normal style.

- Right-click Normal in the Quick Style gallery (Home tab | Styles group) to display a shortcut menu (Figure 2–7).

- Click Update Normal to Match Selection on the shortcut menu to update the selected (or current) style to reflect the settings at the location of the insertion point.

Other Ways

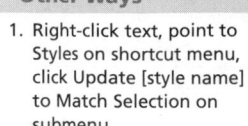

1. Right-click text, point to Styles on shortcut menu, click Update [style name] to Match Selection on submenu

Figure 2–7

Headers and Footers

A **header** is text and graphics that print at the top of each page in a document. Similarly, a **footer** is text and graphics that print at the bottom of every page. In Word, headers print in the top margin one-half inch from the top of every page, and footers print in the bottom margin one-half inch from the bottom of each page, which meets the MLA documentation style. In addition to text and graphics, headers and footers can include document information such as the page number, current date, current time, and author's name.

In this research paper, you are to precede the page number with your last name placed one-half inch from the upper-right edge of each page. The procedures on the following pages enter your name and the page number in the header, as specified by the MLA documentation style.

BTW

The Ribbon and Screen Resolution
Word may change how the groups and buttons within the groups appear on the Ribbon, depending on the computer's screen resolution. Thus, your Ribbon may look different from the ones in this book if you are using a screen resolution other than 1024 x 768.

To Switch to the Header

To enter text in the header, you instruct Word to edit the header. The following steps switch from editing the document text to editing the header.

1

- Click Insert on the Ribbon to display the Insert tab.

- Click the Header button (Insert tab | Header & Footer group) to display the Header gallery (Figure 2–8).

Can I use a built-in header for this research paper?

None of the built-in headers adheres to the MLA documentation style. Thus, you enter your own header content, instead of using a built-in header, for this research paper.

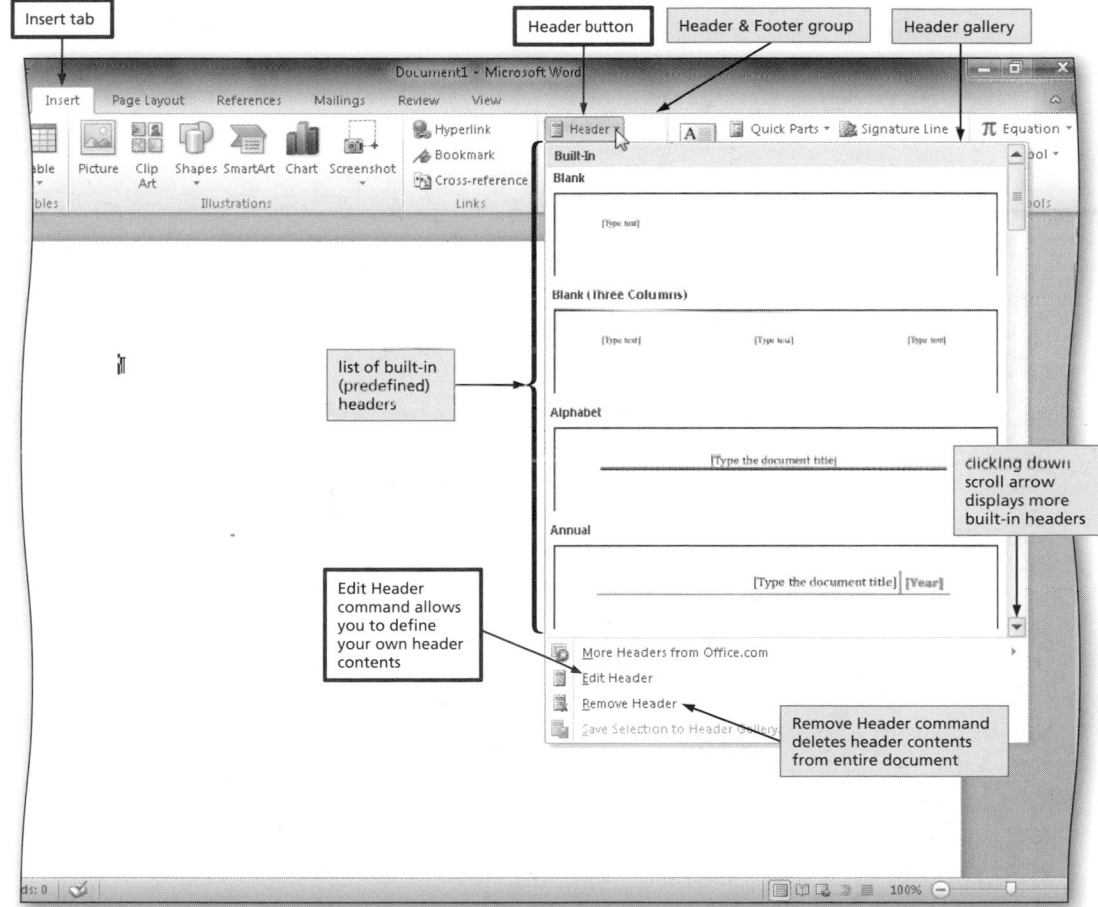

Figure 2–8

How would I remove a header from a document?

You would click Remove Header in the Header gallery (shown in Figure 2–8). Similarly, to remove a footer, you would click Remove Footer in the Footer gallery.

 Experiment

- Click the down scroll arrow in the Header gallery to see the available built-in headers.

2

- Click Edit Header in the Header gallery to switch from the document text to the header, which allows you to edit the contents of the header (Figure 2–9).

Q&A

How do I remove the Header & Footer Tools Design tab from the Ribbon?

When you are finished editing the header, you will close it, which removes the Header & Footer Tools Design tab.

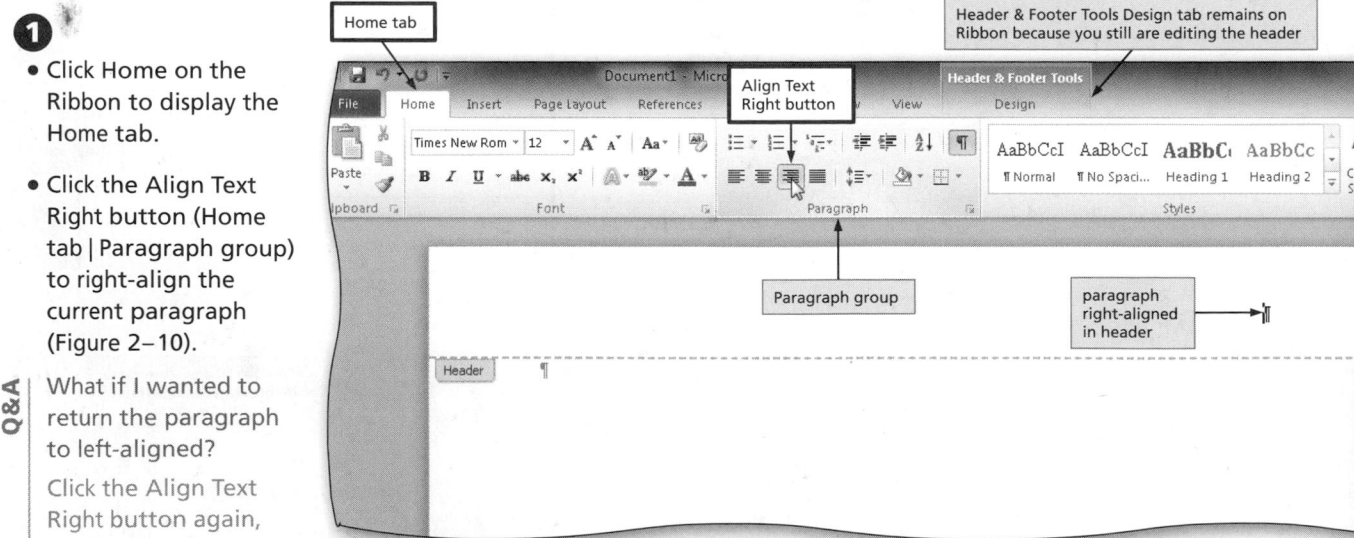

Header & Footer Tools Design tab automatically appears because you are editing the header

header

paragraph left-aligned

document text is dimmed while you edit header

bottom of header

Header

indicates header is being edited

Figure 2–9

Other Ways

1. Double-click dimmed header

2. Right-click header in document, click Edit Header button that appears

To Right-Align a Paragraph

The paragraph in the header currently is left-aligned (Figure 2–9). Your last name and the page number should print **right-aligned**, that is, at the right margin. The following step right-aligns a paragraph.

1

- Click Home on the Ribbon to display the Home tab.

- Click the Align Text Right button (Home tab | Paragraph group) to right-align the current paragraph (Figure 2–10).

Q&A

What if I wanted to return the paragraph to left-aligned?

Click the Align Text Right button again, or click the Align Text Left button.

Home tab

Header & Footer Tools Design tab remains on Ribbon because you still are editing the header

Align Text Right button

Paragraph group

paragraph right-aligned in header

Header

Figure 2–10

Other Ways

1. Right-click paragraph, click Paragraph on shortcut menu, click Indents and Spacing tab (Paragraph dialog box), click Alignment box arrow, click Right, click OK button

2. Click Paragraph Dialog Box Launcher (Home tab or Page Layout tab | Paragraph group), click Indents and Spacing tab (Paragraph dialog box), click Alignment box arrow, click Right, click OK button

3. Press CTRL+R

To Enter Text

The following steps enter your last name right-aligned in the header area.

1 Click Design on the Ribbon to display the Header & Footer Tools Design tab.

2 Type `Marino` and then press the SPACEBAR to enter the last name in the header.

BTW

Footers
If you wanted to create a footer, you would click the Footer button (Insert tab | Header & Footer group) and then select the desired built-in footer or click Edit Footer to create a customized footer; you also could double-click the dimmed footer, or right-click the footer and then click the Edit Footer button that appears.

To Insert a Page Number

The next task is to insert the current page number in the header. The following steps insert a page number at the location of the insertion point.

1

• Click the Insert Page Number button (Header & Footer Tools Design tab | Header & Footer group) to display the Insert Page Number menu.

• Point to Current Position on the Insert Page Number menu to display the Current Position gallery (Figure 2–11).

Experiment

• Click the down scroll arrow in the Current Position gallery to see the available page number formats.

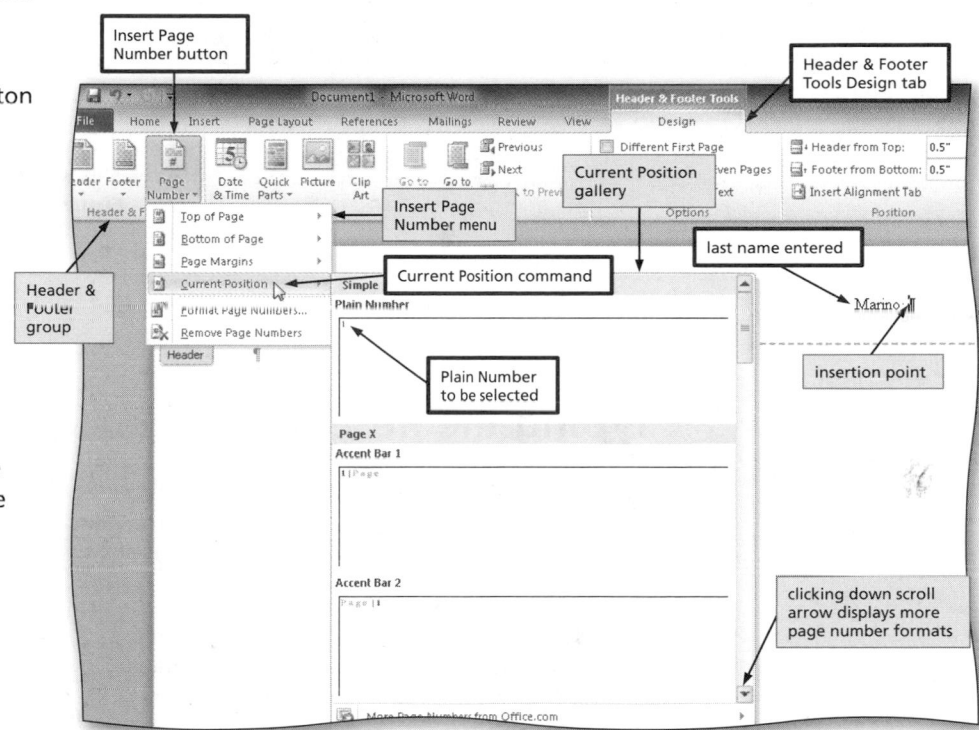

Figure 2–11

2

• If necessary, scroll to the top of the Current Position gallery. Click Plain Number in the Current Position gallery to insert an unformatted page number at the location of the insertion point (Figure 2–12).

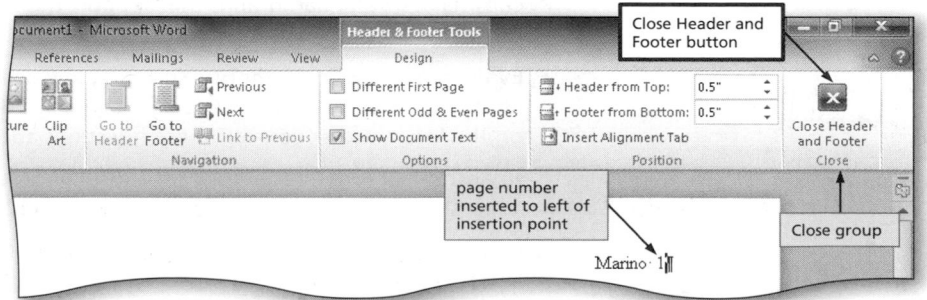

Figure 2–12

Other Ways		
1. Click Insert Page Number button (Insert tab | Header & Footer group)	2. Click Quick Parts button (Insert tab | Text group or Header & Footer Tools Design tab | Insert group),	click Field on Quick Parts menu, select Page in Field names list (Field dialog box), click OK button

To Close the Header

You are finished entering text in the header. Thus, the next task is to switch back to the document text. The following step closes the header.

- Click the Close Header and Footer button (Header & Footer Tools Design tab | Close group) (shown in Figure 2–12 on the previous page) to close the header and switch back to the document text (Figure 2–13).

Q&A

How do I make changes to existing header text?

Switch to the header using the steps described on pages WD 75 and WD 76, edit the header as you would edit text in the document window, and then switch back to the document text.

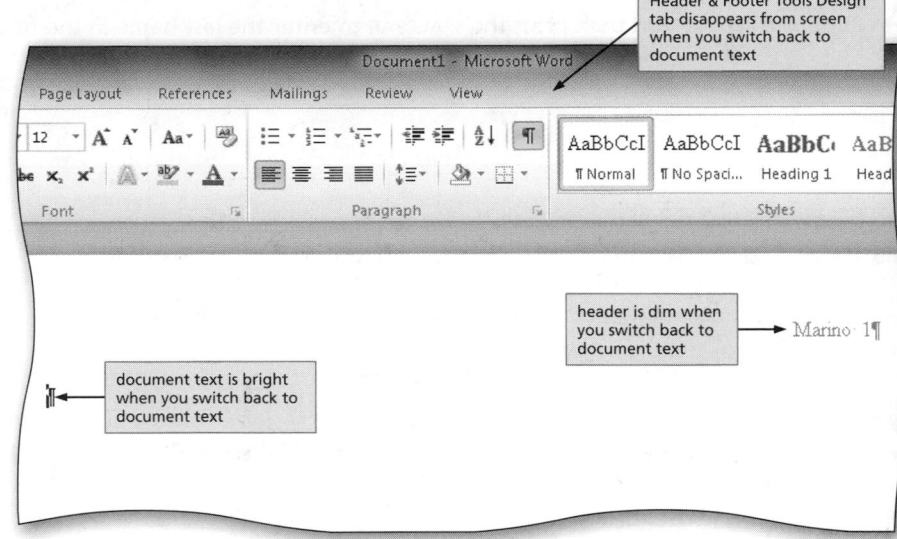

Figure 2–13

Other Ways

1. Double-click dimmed document text

Typing the Research Paper Text

The text of the research paper in this chapter encompasses the first two pages of the paper. You will type the text of the research paper and then modify it later in the chapter, so that it matches Figure 2–1 on page WD 67.

Plan Ahead

Write the first draft, referencing sources.
As you write the first draft of a research paper, be sure it includes the proper components, uses credible sources, and does not contain any plagiarized material.

- **Include an introduction, body, and conclusion.** The first paragraph of the paper introduces the topic and captures the reader's attention. The body, which follows the introduction, consists of several paragraphs that support the topic. The conclusion summarizes the main points in the body and restates the topic.

- **Evaluate sources for authority, currency, and accuracy.** Be especially wary of information obtained from the Web. Any person, company, or organization can publish a Web page on the Internet. Ask yourself these questions about the source:

  - Authority: Does a reputable institution or group support the source? Is the information presented without bias? Are the author's credentials listed and verifiable?

  - Currency: Is the information up to date? Are dates of sources listed? What is the last date revised or updated?

  - Accuracy: Is the information free of errors? Is it verifiable? Are the sources clearly identified?

(continued)

(continued)

- **Acknowledge all sources of information; do not plagiarize.** Not only is plagiarism unethical, but it is considered an academic crime that can have severe punishments such as failing a course or being expelled from school.

  When you summarize, paraphrase (rewrite information in your own words), present facts, give statistics, quote exact words, or show a map, chart, or other graphical image, you must acknowledge the source. Information that commonly is known or accessible to the audience constitutes common knowledge and does not need to be acknowledged. If, however, you question whether certain information is common knowledge, you should document it — just to be safe.

o Enter Name and Course Information

As discussed earlier in this chapter, the MLA documentation style does not require separate title page for research papers. Instead, place your name and course information a block at the top of the page, below the header, at the left margin. The following steps ter the name and course information in the research paper.

- Type **Annalisa Marino** as the student name and then press the ENTER key.

- Type **Mr. Winters** as the instructor name and then press the ENTER key.

- Type **English 101** as the course name and then press the ENTER key.

- Type **April 4, 2012** as the paper due date and then press the ENTER key (Figure 2–14).

BTW

Date Formats
The MLA documentation style prefers the day-month-year (4 April 2012) or month-day-year (April 4, 2012) format.

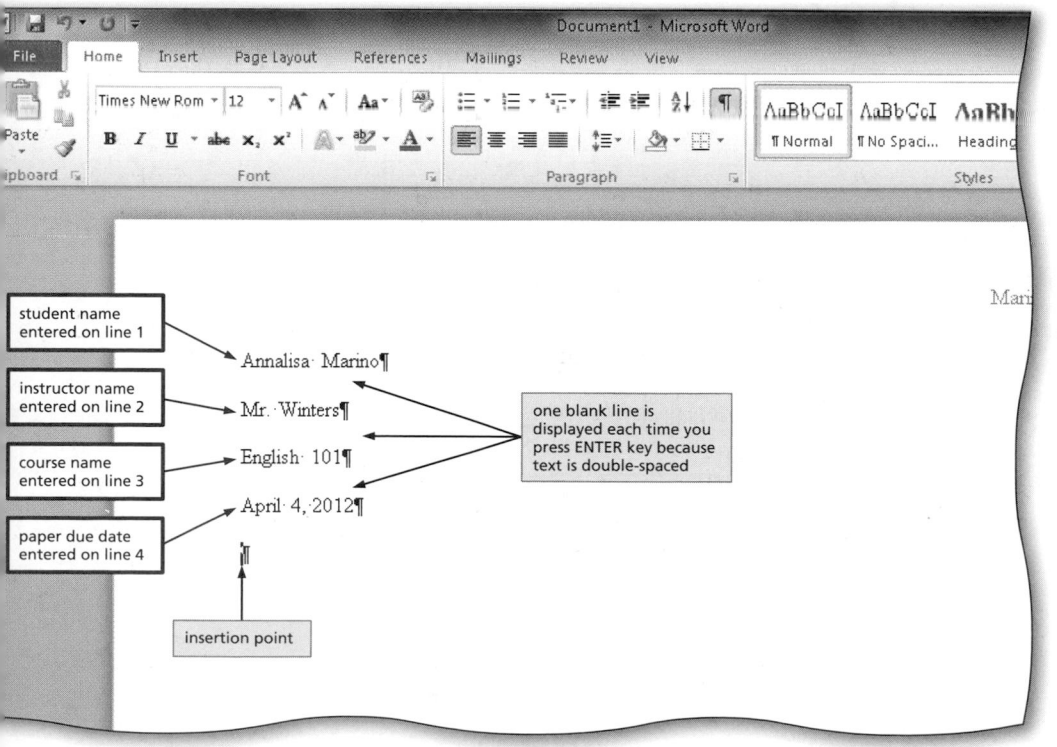

Figure 2–14

To Click and Type

The next step is to enter the title of the research paper centered between the page margins. In Chapter 1, you used the Center button (Home tab | Paragraph group) to center text and graphics. As an alternative, you can use Word's **Click and Type** feature to format and enter text, graphics, and other items. To use Click and Type, you double-click a blank area of the document window. Word automatically formats the item you type or insert according to the location where you double-clicked. The following steps use Click and Type to center and then type the title of the research paper.

Experiment

- Move the mouse pointer around the document below the entered name and course information and observe the various icons that appear with the I-beam.

- Position the mouse pointer in the center of the document at the approximate location for the research paper title until a center icon appears below the I-beam (Figure 2–15).

Q&A

What are the other icons that appear in the Click and Type pointer?

A left-align icon appears to the right of the I-beam when the Click and Type pointer is in certain locations on the left side of the document window. A right-align icon appears to the left of the I-beam when the Click and Type pointer is in certain locations on the right side of the document window.

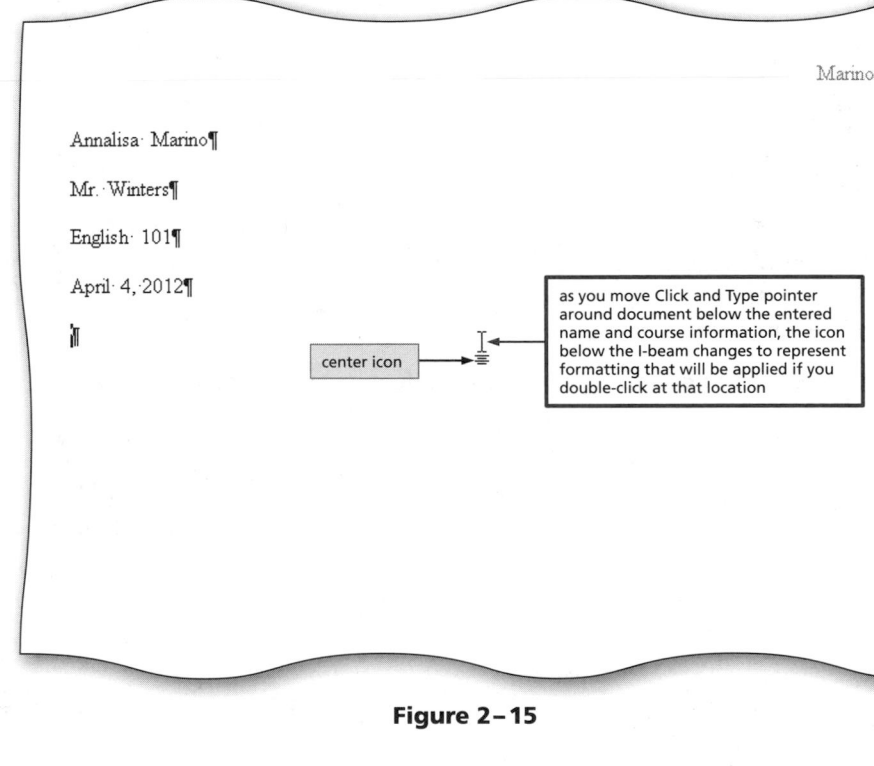

Figure 2–15

- Double-click to center the paragraph mark and insertion point between the left and right margins.

- Type **Can You Find Me Now?** as the paper title and then press the ENTER key to position the insertion point on the next line (Figure 2–16).

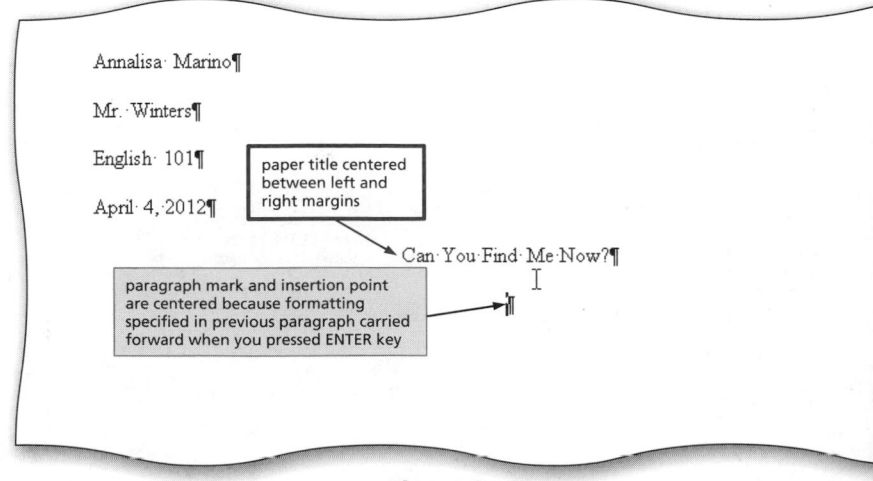

Figure 2–16

Shortcut Keys

Word has many **shortcut keys**, or keyboard key combinations, for your convenience while typing. Table 2–1 lists the common shortcut keys for formatting characters. Table 2–2 lists common shortcut keys for formatting paragraphs.

Table 2–1 Shortcut Keys for Formatting Characters

Character Formatting Task	Shortcut Keys	Character Formatting Task	Shortcut Keys
All capital letters	CTRL+SHIFT+A	Italic	CTRL+I
Bold	CTRL+B	Remove character formatting (plain text)	CTRL+SPACEBAR
Case of letters	SHIFT+F3	Small uppercase letters	CTRL+SHIFT+K
Decrease font size	CTRL+SHIFT+<	Subscript	CTRL+EQUAL SIGN
Decrease font size 1 point	CTRL+[	Superscript	CTRL+SHIFT+PLUS SIGN
Double-underline	CTRL+SHIFT+D	Underline	CTRL+U
Increase font size	CTRL+SHIFT+>	Underline words, not spaces	CTRL+SHIFT+W
Increase font size 1 point	CTRL+]		

Table 2–2 Shortcut Keys for Formatting Paragraphs

Paragraph Formatting	Shortcut Keys	Paragraph Formatting	Shortcut Keys
1.5 line spacing	CTRL+5	Justify paragraph	CTRL+J
Add/remove one line above paragraph	CTRL+0 (zero)	Left-align paragraph	CTRL+L
Center paragraph	CTRL+E	Remove hanging indent	CTRL+SHIFT+T
Decrease paragraph indent	CTRL+SHIFT+M	Remove paragraph formatting	CTRL+Q
Double-space lines	CTRL+2	Right-align paragraph	CTRL+R
Hanging indent	CTRL+T	Single-space lines	CTRL+1
Increase paragraph indent	CTRL+M		

To Format Text Using Shortcut Keys

The paragraphs below the paper title should be left-aligned, instead of centered. Thus, the next step is to left-align the paragraph below the paper title. When your fingers are already on the keyboard, you may prefer using shortcut keys to format text as you type it. The following step left-aligns a paragraph using the shortcut keys CTRL+L. (Recall from Chapter 1 that a notation such as CTRL+L means to press the letter L on the keyboard while holding down the CTRL key.)

Press CTRL+L to left-align the current paragraph, that is, the paragraph containing the insertion point (shown in Figure 2–17 on the next page).

Why would I use a keyboard shortcut instead of the Ribbon to format text?

Switching between the mouse and the keyboard takes time. If your hands are already on the keyboard, use a shortcut key. If your hand is on the mouse, use the Ribbon.

BTW

Shortcut Keys
To print a complete list of shortcut keys in Word, click the Microsoft Word Help button near the upper-right corner of the Word window, type **shortcut keys** in the 'Type words to search for' text box at the top of the Word Help window, press the ENTER key, click the Keyboard shortcuts for Microsoft Word link, click the Show All link in the upper-right corner of the Help window, click the Print button in the Help window, and then click the Print button in the Print dialog box.

For an introduction to Office 2010 and instruction about how to perform basic tasks in Office 2010 programs, read the Office 2010 and Windows 7 chapter at the beginning of this book, where you can learn how to start a program, use the Ribbon, save a file, open a file, quit a program, use Help, and much more.

To Save a Document

You have performed many tasks while creating this research paper and do not want to risk losing work completed thus far. Accordingly, you should save the document. The following steps assume you already have created folders for storing your files, for example, a CIS 101 folder (for your class) that contains a Word folder (for your assignments). Thus, these steps save the document in the Word folder in the CIS 101 folder on a USB flash drive using the file name, Triangulation Paper.

1 With a USB flash drive connected to one of the computer's USB ports, click the Save button on the Quick Access Toolbar to display the Save As dialog box.

2 Type `Triangulation Paper` in the File name text box to change the file name. Do not press the ENTER key after typing the file name because you do not want to close the dialog box at this time.

3 Navigate to the desired save location (in this case, the Word folder in the CIS 101 folder [or your class folder] on the USB flash drive).

4 Click the Save button (Save As dialog box) to save the document in the selected folder on the selected drive with the entered file name.

To Display the Rulers

According to the MLA documentation style, the first line of each paragraph in the research paper is to be indented one-half inch from the left margin. Although you can use a dialog box to indent paragraphs, Word provides a quicker way through the **horizontal ruler**. This ruler is displayed at the top edge of the document window just below the Ribbon. Word also provides a **vertical ruler** that is displayed along the left edge of the Word window. The following step displays the rulers because you want to use the ruler to indent paragraphs.

1

Experiment

• Repeatedly click the View Ruler button on the vertical scroll bar to see the how this button is used to both show and hide the rulers.

• If the rulers are not displayed, click the View Ruler button on the vertical scroll bar to display the horizontal and vertical rulers on the screen (Figure 2–17).

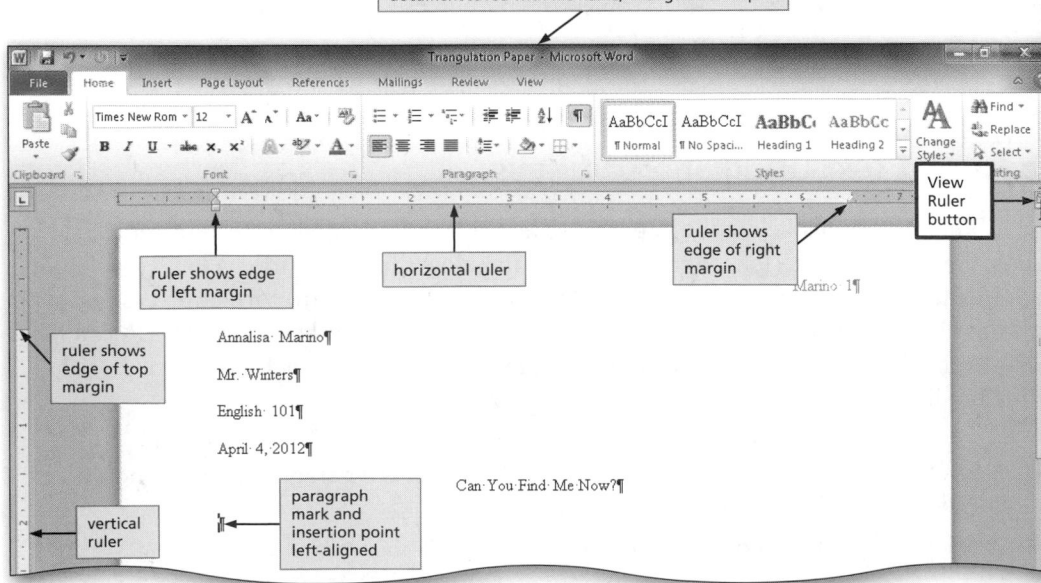

Figure 2–17

Q&A

For what tasks would I use the rulers?

You can use the rulers to indent paragraphs, set tab stops, change page margins, and adjust column widths.

Other Ways

1. Click View Ruler check box (View tab | Show group)

To First-Line Indent Paragraphs

The first line of each paragraph in the research paper is to be indented one-half inch from the left margin. You can use the horizontal ruler, usually simply called the **ruler**, to indent just the first line of a paragraph, which is called **first-line indent**.

The left margin on the ruler contains two triangles above a square. The **First Line Indent marker** is the top triangle at the 0" mark on the ruler (Figure 2–18). The bottom triangle is discussed later in this chapter. The small square at the 0" mark is the Left Indent marker. The **Left Indent marker** allows you to change the entire left margin, whereas the First Line Indent marker indents only the first line of the paragraph. The following steps first-line indent paragraphs in the research paper.

With the insertion point on the paragraph mark below the research paper title, point to the First Line Indent marker on the ruler (Figure 2–18).

Figure 2–18

Drag the First Line Indent marker to the .5" mark on the ruler to display a vertical dotted line in the document window, which indicates the proposed location of the first line of the paragraph (Figure 2–19).

Figure 2–19

3

- Release the mouse button to place the First Line Indent marker at the .5" mark on the ruler, or one-half inch from the left margin (Figure 2–20).

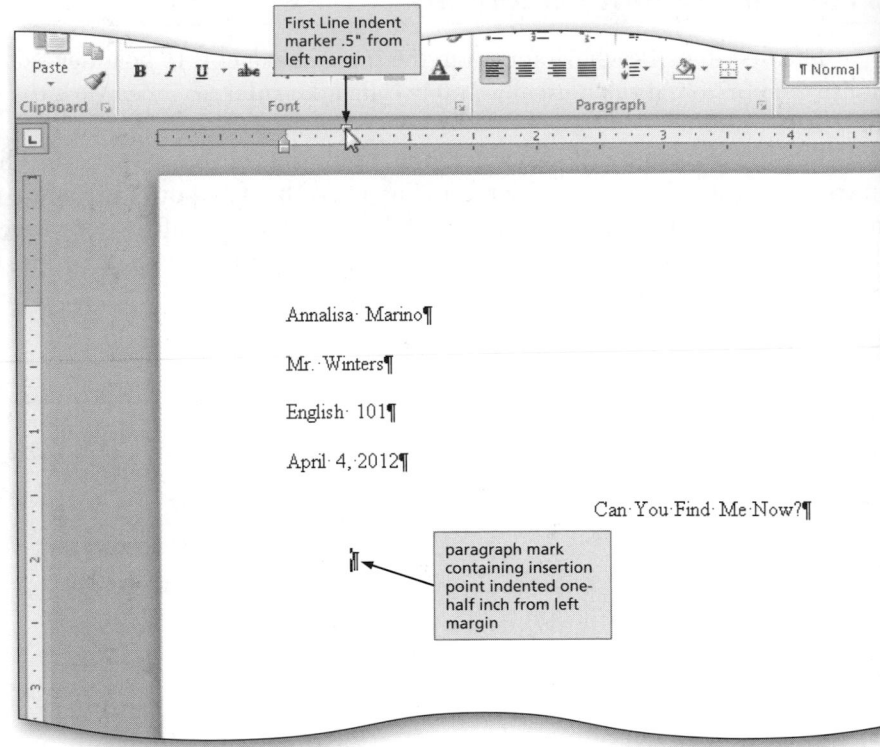

Figure 2–20

4

- Type **How is a Nintendo Wii console able to determine the location of a Wii Remote while a player interacts with a game?** and notice that Word automatically indented the first line of the paragraph by one-half inch (Figure 2–21).

Q&A

Will I have to set a first-line indent for each paragraph in the paper?

No. Each time you press the ENTER key, paragraph formatting in the previous paragraph carries forward to the next paragraph. Thus, once you set the first-line indent, its format carries forward automatically to each subsequent paragraph you type.

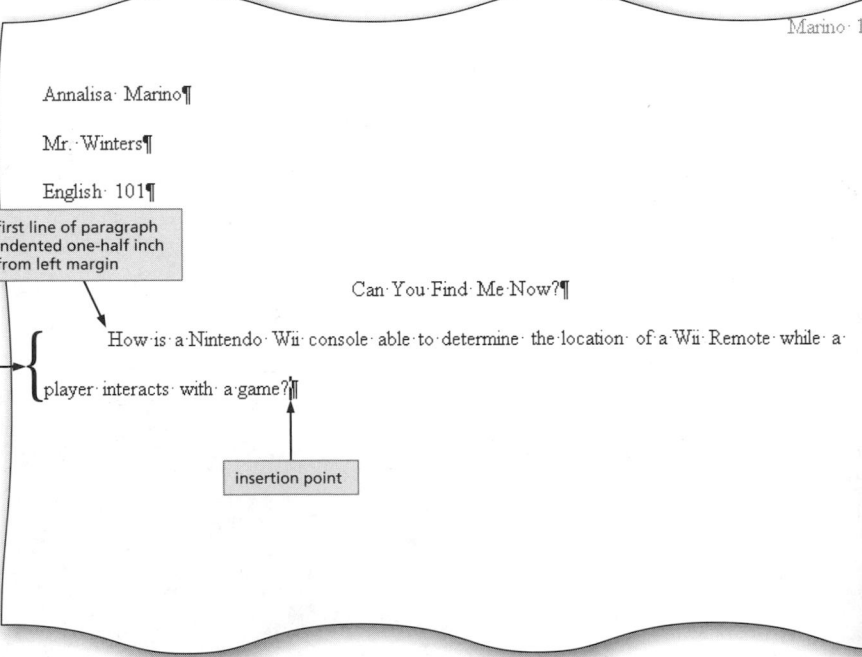

Figure 2–21

Other Ways

1. Right-click paragraph, click Paragraph on shortcut menu, click Indents and Spacing tab (Paragraph dialog box), click Special box arrow, click First line, click OK button

2. Click Paragraph Dialog Box Launcher (Home tab or Page Layout tab | Paragraph group), click Indents and Spacing tab (Paragraph dialog box), click Special box arrow, click First line, click OK button

3. Press TAB key at beginning of paragraph

To AutoCorrect as You Type

As you type, you may make typing, spelling, capitalization, or grammar errors. For this reason, Word provides an **AutoCorrect** feature that automatically corrects these kinds of errors as you type them in the document. For example, if you type ahve, Word automatically changes it to the correct spelling, have, when you press the SPACEBAR or a punctuation mark key such as a period or comma.

Word has predefined many commonly misspelled words, which it automatically corrects for you. The following steps intentionally misspell the word, the, as teh to illustrate the AutoCorrect feature.

1

- Press the SPACEBAR.

- Type the beginning of the next sentence, misspelling the word, the, as follows: **The answer is triangulation, a process that determines teh** (Figure 2–22).

Figure 2–22

2

- Press the SPACEBAR and watch Word automatically correct the misspelled word.

- Type the rest of the sentence (Figure 2–23): **location of an object by measuring the angles from two or more fixed points.**

Figure 2–23

To Use the AutoCorrect Options Button

When you position the mouse pointer on text that Word automatically corrected, a small blue box appears below the text. If you point to the small blue box, Word displays the AutoCorrect Options button. When you click the **AutoCorrect Options button**, Word displays a menu that allows you to undo a correction or change how Word handles future automatic corrections of this type. The steps on the next page illustrate the AutoCorrect Options button and menu.

● Position the mouse pointer in the text automatically corrected by Word (the word, the, in this case) to display a small blue box below the automatically corrected word (Figure 2–24).

mouse pointer in automatically corrected text

How is a Nintendo Wii console able to determine the location of a Wii Remote while a

player interacts with a game? The answer is triangulation, a process that determines the location

of an object by measuring the angles from two or more fixed points.

pointing to small blue box will display AutoCorrect Options button

Figure 2–24

● Point to the small blue box to display the AutoCorrect Options button.

● Click the AutoCorrect Options button to display the AutoCorrect Options menu (Figure 2–25).

AutoCorrect Options button

AutoCorrect Options menu

player interacts with a game? The answer is triangulation, a process that determines the location

of an object by measuring the angles from two or more fixed points.

Change back to "teh"

Stop Automatically Correcting "teh"

Control AutoCorrect Options...

insertion point

clicking this command displays AutoCorrect dialog box

Figure 2–25

● Press the ESCAPE key to remove the AutoCorrect Options menu from the screen.

Q&A

Do I need to remove the AutoCorrect Options button from the screen?

No. When you move the mouse pointer, the AutoCorrect Options button will disappear from the screen. If, for some reason, you wanted to remove the AutoCorrect Options button from the screen, you could press the ESCAPE key a second time.

To Create an AutoCorrect Entry

In addition to the predefined list of AutoCorrect spelling, capitalization, and grammar errors, you can create your own AutoCorrect entries to add to the list. For example, if you tend to mistype the word sensor as senser, you should create an AutoCorrect entry for it. The following steps create an AutoCorrect entry.

● Click File on the Ribbon to open the Backstage view (Figure 2–26).

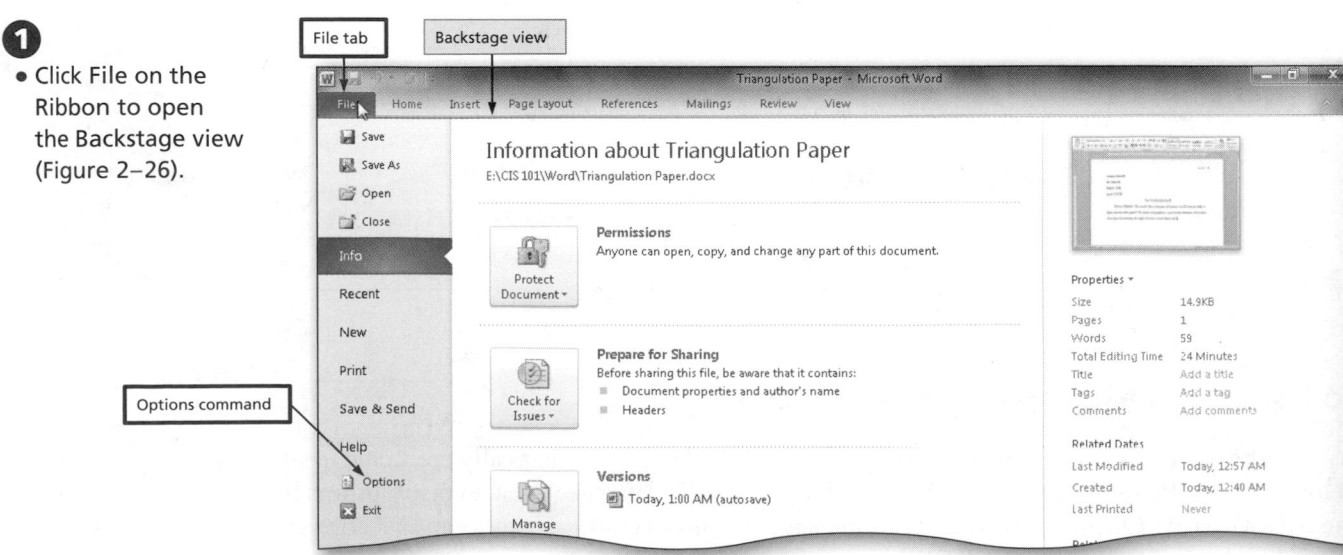

File tab

Backstage view

Options command

Triangulation Paper - Microsoft Word

File | Home | Insert | Page Layout | References | Mailings | Review | View

Save
Save As
Open
Close
Info
Recent
New
Print
Save & Send
Help
Options
Exit

Information about Triangulation Paper
E:\CIS 101\Word\Triangulation Paper.docx

Permissions
Anyone can open, copy, and change any part of this document.

Protect Document ▾

Prepare for Sharing
Before sharing this file, be aware that it contains:
■ Document properties and author's name
■ Headers

Check for Issues ▾

Versions
📄 Today, 1:00 AM (autosave)

Manage

Properties ▾
Size   14.9KB
Pages   1
Words   59
Total Editing Time 24 Minutes
Title   Add a title
Tags   Add a tag
Comments   Add comments

Related Dates
Last Modified Today, 12:57 AM
Created   Today, 12:40 AM
Last Printed   Never

Figure 2–26

2

• Click Options in the Backstage view to display the Word Options dialog box.

• Click Proofing in the left pane (Word Options dialog box) to display proofing options in the right pane.

• Click the AutoCorrect Options button in the right pane to display the AutoCorrect dialog box.

• When Word displays the AutoCorrect dialog box, type **senser** in the Replace text box.

• Press the TAB key and then type **sensor** in the With text box (Figure 2–27).

Figure 2–27

How would I delete an existing AutoCorrect entry?

You would select the entry to be deleted in the list of defined entries in the AutoCorrect dialog box and then click the Delete button.

3

• Click the Add button (AutoCorrect dialog box) to add the entry alphabetically to the list of words to correct automatically as you type. (If your dialog box displays a Replace button instead, click it and then click the Yes button in the Microsoft Word dialog box to replace the previously defined entry.)

• Click the OK button (AutoCorrect dialog box) to close the dialog box.

• Click the OK button (Word Options dialog box) to close the dialog box.

The AutoCorrect Dialog Box

In addition to creating AutoCorrect entries for words you commonly misspell or mistype, you can create entries for abbreviations, codes, and so on. For example, you could create an AutoCorrect entry for asap, indicating that Word should replace this text with the phrase, as soon as possible.

If, for some reason, you do not want Word to correct automatically as you type, you can turn off the 'Replace text as you type' feature by clicking Options in the Backstage view, clicking Proofing in the left pane (Word Options dialog box), clicking the AutoCorrect Options button in the right pane (Figure 2–27), removing the check mark from the 'Replace text as you type' check box, and then clicking the OK button in each open dialog box.

The AutoCorrect sheet in the AutoCorrect dialog box (Figure 2–27) contains other check boxes that correct capitalization errors if the check boxes are selected. If you

BTW

Automatic Corrections
If you do not want to keep a change automatically made by Word and you immediately notice the automatic correction, you can undo the change by clicking the Undo button on the Quick Access Toolbar or pressing CTRL+Z. You also can undo a correction through the AutoCorrect Options button, which was shown above.

type two capital letters in a row, such as TH, Word makes the second letter lowercase, Th. If you begin a sentence with a lowercase letter, Word capitalizes the first letter of the sentence. If you type the name of a day in lowercase letters, such as tuesday, Word capitalizes the first letter in the name of the day, Tuesday. If you leave the CAPS LOCK key on and begin a new sentence, such as aFTER, Word corrects the typing, After, and turns off the CAPS LOCK key. If you do not want Word to automatically perform any of these corrections, simply remove the check mark from the appropriate check box in the AutoCorrect dialog box.

Sometimes you do not want Word to AutoCorrect a particular word or phrase. For example, you may use the code WD. in your documents. Because Word automatically capitalizes the first letter of a sentence, the character you enter following the period will be capitalized (in the previous sentence, it would capitalize the letter i in the word, in). To allow the code WD. to be entered into a document and still leave the AutoCorrect feature turned on, you would set an exception. To set an exception to an AutoCorrect rule, click Options in the Backstage view, click Proofing in the left pane (Word Options dialog box), click the AutoCorrect Options button in the right pane, click the Exceptions button (Figure 2–27 on the previous page), click the appropriate tab in the AutoCorrect Exceptions dialog box, type the exception entry in the text box, click the Add button, click the Close button (AutoCorrect Exceptions dialog box), and then click the OK button in each of the remaining dialog boxes.

To Enter More Text

The next step is to continue typing text in the research paper up to the location of the in-text parenthetical reference. The following steps enter this text.

1 With the insertion point positioned at the end of the first paragraph in the paper, as shown in Figure 2–25 on page WD 86, press the ENTER key, so that you can begin typing the text in the second paragraph.

2 Type `Surveyors often use triangulation to measure distance. Starting at a known location and elevation, surveyors measure a length to create a base line and then use a theodolite to measure an angle to an unknown point from each side of the base line` and then press the SPACEBAR.

Citations

Both the MLA and APA guidelines suggest the use of in-text parenthetical references (placed at the end of a sentence), instead of footnoting each source of material in a paper. These parenthetical references, called citations in Word, guide the reader to the end of the paper for complete information about the source.

BTW

Spacing after Punctuation
Because word processing documents use variable character fonts, it often is difficult to determine in a printed document how many times someone has pressed the SPACEBAR between sentences. Thus, the rule is to press the SPACEBAR only once after periods, colons, and other punctuation marks.

Plan Ahead

Reference all sources.
During your research, be sure to record essential publication information about each of your sources. Following is a sample list of types of required information for the MLA documentation style.

- Book: full name of author(s), complete title of book, edition (if available), volume (if available), publication city, publisher name, publication year, publication medium

- Magazine: full name of author(s), complete title of article, magazine title, issue number (if available), date of magazine, page numbers of article, publication medium

- Web site: full name of author(s), title of Web site, Web site publisher or sponsor (if none, write N.p.), publication date (if none, write n.d.), publication medium, date viewed

Word provides tools to assist you with inserting citations in a paper and later generating a list of sources from the citations. With a documentation style selected, Word automatically formats the citations and list of sources according to that style. The process for adding citations in Word is as follows:

1. Modify the documentation style, if necessary.
2. Insert a citation placeholder.
3. Enter the source information for the citation.

You can combine Steps 2 and 3, where you insert the citation placeholder and enter the source information at once. Or, you can insert the citation placeholder as you write and then enter the source information for the citation at a later time. While creating the research paper in this chapter, you will use both methods.

To Change the Bibliography Style

The first step in inserting a citation is to be sure the citations and sources will be formatted using the correct documentation style, called the bibliography style in Word. The following steps change the specified documentation style.

1
- Click References on the Ribbon to display the References tab.

- Click the Bibliography Style box arrow (References tab | Citations & Bibliography group) to display a gallery of predefined documentation styles (Figure 2–28).

2
- Click MLA Sixth Edition in the Bibliography Style gallery to change the documentation style to MLA.

What if I am using a different edition of a documentation style shown in the Bibliography Style gallery?

Select the closest one and then, if necessary, perform necessary edits before submitting the paper.

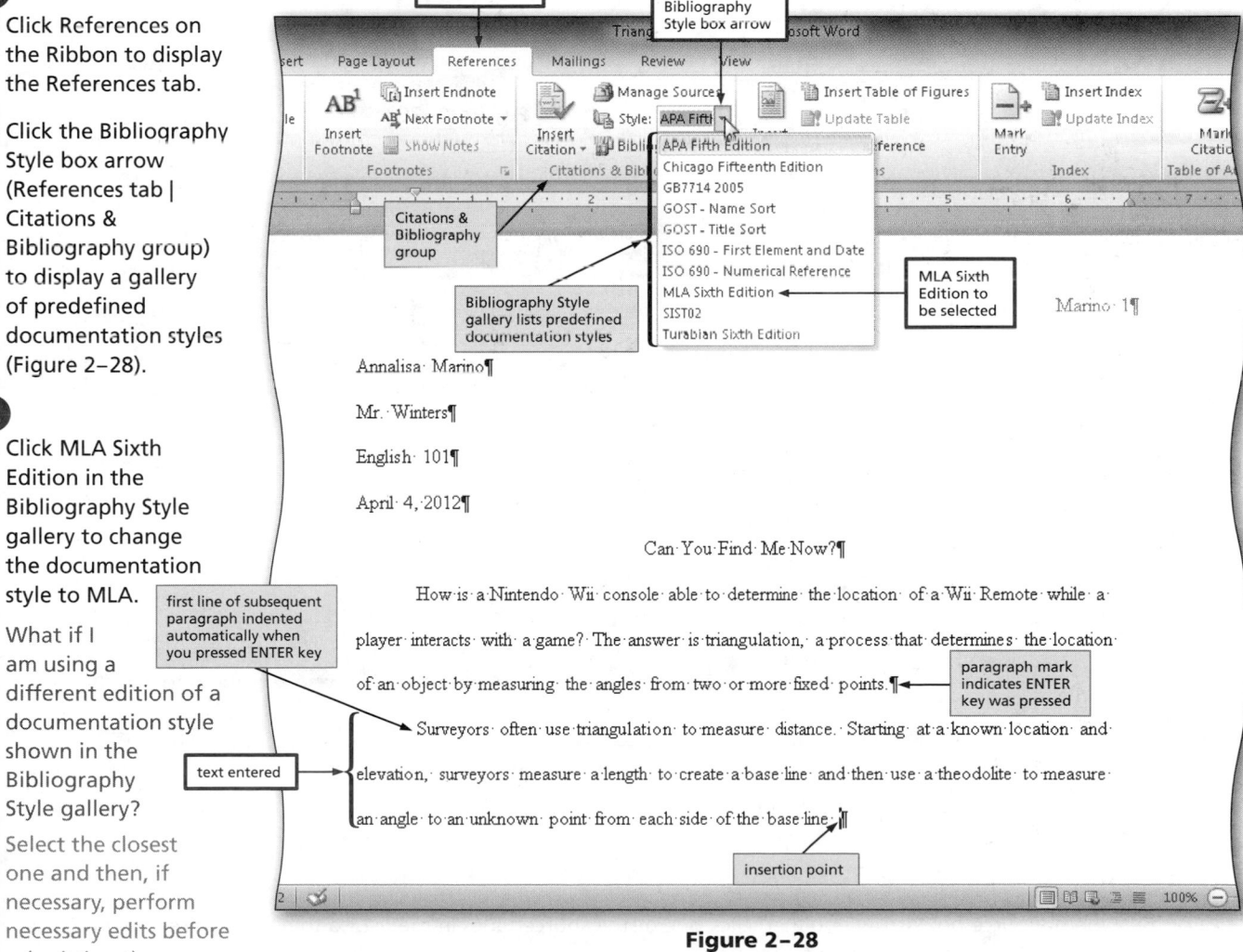

Figure 2–28

To Insert a Citation and Create Its Source

With the documentation style selected, the next task is to insert a citation placeholder and enter the source information for the citation. You can accomplish these steps at once by instructing Word to add a new source. The following steps add a new source for a magazine (periodical) article.

• Click the Insert Citation button (References tab | Citations & Bibliography group) to display the Insert Citation menu (Figure 2–29).

Figure 2–29

• Click Add New Source on the Insert Citation menu to display the Create Source dialog box (Figure 2–30).

What are the Bibliography Fields in the Create Source dialog box?

A **field** is a placeholder for data whose contents can change. You enter data in some fields; Word supplies data for others. In this case, you enter the contents of the fields for a particular source, for example, the author name in the Author field.

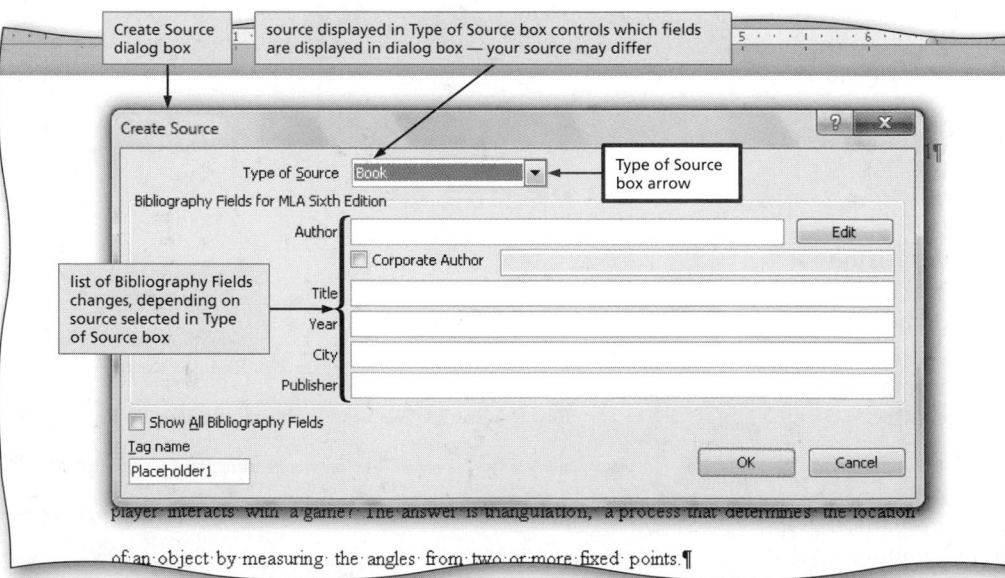

Figure 2–30

Experiment

• Click the Type of Source box arrow and then click one of the source types in the list, so that you can see how the list of fields changes to reflect the type of source you selected.

3

- If necessary, click the Type of Source box arrow (Create Source dialog box) and then click Article in a Periodical, so that the list shows fields required for a magazine (periodical).

- Click the Author text box. Type `Jains, Malila` as the author.

- Click the Title text box. Type `How Surveyors Measure and Calculate Angles` as the article title.

- Press the TAB key and then type `Today's Modern Surveyor` as the periodical title.

- Press the TAB key and then type `2012` as the year.

- Press the TAB key and then type `Mar.` as the month.

- Press the TAB key twice and then type `30-48` as the pages (Figure 2–31).

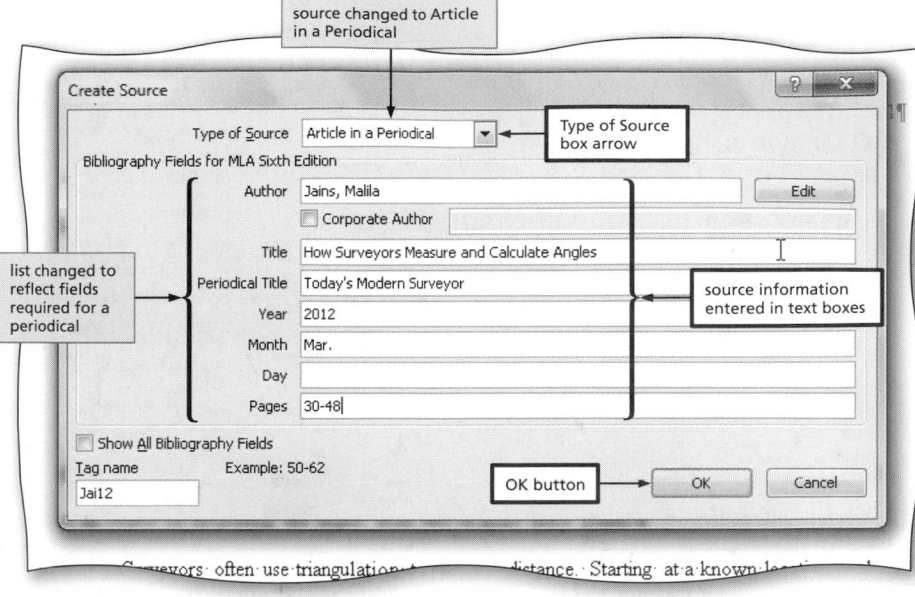

Figure 2–31

4

- Click the OK button to close the dialog box, create the source, and insert the citation in the document at the location of the insertion point (Figure 2–32).

Figure 2–32

To Edit a Citation

In the MLA documentation style, if a source has page numbers, you should include them in the citation. Thus, Word provides a means to enter the page numbers to be displayed in the citation. The following steps edit a citation, so that the page numbers appear in it.

1

- Click somewhere in the citation to be edited, in this case somewhere in (Jains), which selects the citation and displays the Citation Options box arrow.

- Click the Citation Options box arrow to display the Citation Options menu (Figure 2–33).

What is the purpose of the tab to the left of the selected citation?

If, for some reason, you wanted to move a citation to a different location in the document, you would select the citation and then drag the citation tab to the desired location.

Figure 2–33

2

- Click Edit Citation on the Citation Options menu to display the Edit Citation dialog box.

- Type **30-48** in the Pages text box (Edit Citations dialog box) (Figure 2–34).

Figure 2–34

3

- Click the OK button to close the dialog box and add the page numbers to the citation in the document (Figure 2–35).

Figure 2–35

4

- Press the END key to move the insertion point to the end of the line, which also deselects the citation.

- Press the PERIOD key to end the sentence.

BTW

Edit a Source
To edit a source, click somewhere in the citation, click the Citation Options box arrow, and then click Edit Source on the Citation Options menu to display the Edit Source dialog box (which resembles the Create Source dialog box). Make necessary changes and then click the OK button.

To Enter More Text

The next step is to continue typing text in the research paper up to the location of the footnote. The following steps enter this text.

1 Press the SPACEBAR.

2 Type the next sentence (Figure 2–36): **The length of the base line and the two known angles allow a computer or person to determine the location of a third point.**

Figure 2–36

To Save an Existing Document with the Same File Name

You have made several modifications to the document since you last saved it. Thus, you should save it again. The following step saves the document again.

● Click the Save button on the Quick Access Toolbar to overwrite the previously saved file.

Footnotes

As discussed earlier in this chapter, notes are optional in the MLA documentation style. If used, content notes elaborate on points discussed in the paper, and bibliographic notes direct the reader to evaluations of statements in a source or provide a means for identifying multiple sources. The MLA documentation style specifies that a superscript (raised number) be used for a **note reference mark** to signal that a note exists either at the bottom of the page as a **footnote** or at the end of the document as an **endnote**.

In Word, **note text** can be any length and format. Word automatically numbers notes sequentially by placing a note reference mark both in the body of the document and to the left of the note text. If you insert, rearrange, or remove notes, Word renumbers any subsequent note reference marks according to their new sequence in the document.

To Insert a Footnote Reference Mark

The following step inserts a footnote reference mark in the document at the location of the insertion point and at the location where the footnote text will be typed.

● With the insertion point positioned as shown in Figure 2–36, click the Insert Footnote button (References tab | Footnotes group) to display a note reference mark (a superscripted 1) in two places: (1) in the document window at the location of the insertion point and (2) at the bottom of the page where the footnote will be positioned, just below a separator line (Figure 2–37).

What if I wanted notes to be positioned as endnotes instead of as footnotes?

You would click the Insert Endnote button (References tab | Footnotes group), which places the separator line and the endnote text at the end of the document, instead of the bottom of the page containing the reference.

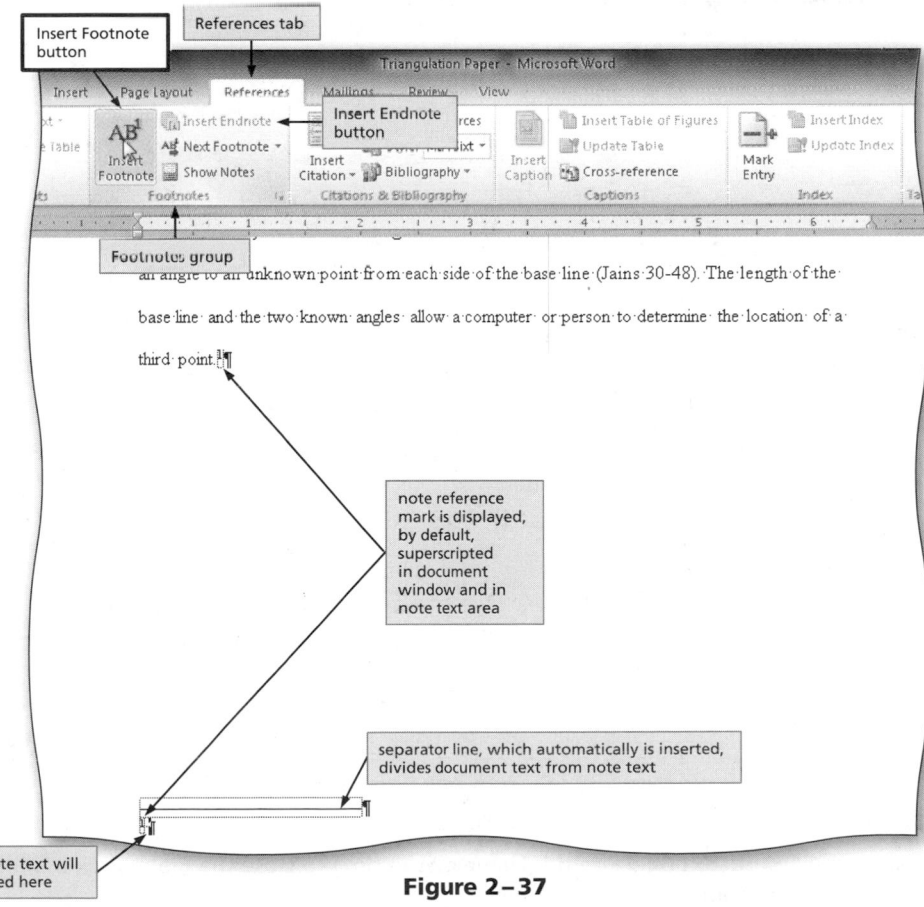

Figure 2–37

Other Ways
1. Press CTRL+ALT+F

To Enter Footnote Text

The following step types the footnote text to the right of the note reference mark below the separator line.

1 Type the footnote text up to the citation: `Cordoba and Sarkis state that electronic theodolites calculate angles automatically and then send the calculated angles to a computer for analysis` and then press the SPACEBAR.

To Insert a Citation Placeholder

Earlier in this chapter, you inserted a citation and its source at once. Sometimes, you may not have the source information readily available and would prefer entering it at a later time.

In the footnote, you will insert a placeholder for the citation and enter the source information later. The following steps insert a citation placeholder.

1
- With the insertion point positioned as shown in Figure 2–38, click the Insert Citation button (References tab | Citations & Bibliography group) to display the Insert Citation menu (Figure 2–38).

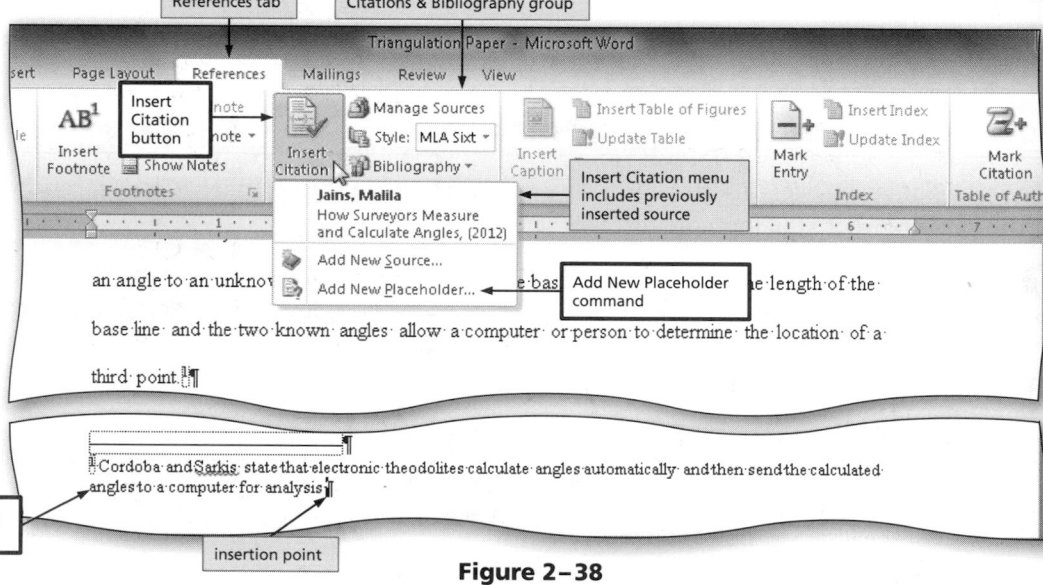

Figure 2–38

2
- Click Add New Placeholder on the Insert Citation menu to display the Placeholder Name dialog box.

- Type `Cordoba` as the tag name for the source (Figure 2–39).

Q&A What is a tag name?

A tag name is an identifier that links a citation to a source. Word automatically creates a tag name when you enter a source. When you create a citation placeholder, enter a meaningful tag name, which will appear in the citation placeholder until you edit the source.

Figure 2–39

3
- Click the OK button (Placeholder Name dialog box) to close the dialog box and insert the entered tag name in the citation placeholder in the document.

- Press the PERIOD key to end the sentence.

Footnote Text Style

When you insert a footnote, Word formats it using the Footnote Text style, which does not adhere to the MLA documentation style. For example, notice in Figure 2–38 that the footnote text is single-spaced, left-aligned, and a smaller font size than the text in the research paper. According to the MLA documentation style, notes should be formatted like all other paragraphs in the paper.

You could change the paragraph formatting of the footnote text to first-line indent and double-spacing and then change the font size from 10 to 12 point. If you use this technique, however, you will need to change the format of the footnote text for each footnote you enter into the document.

A more efficient technique is to modify the format of the Footnote Text style so that every footnote you enter in the document will use the formats defined in this style.

To Modify a Style Using a Shortcut Menu

The Footnote Text style specifies left-aligned single-spaced paragraphs with a 10-point font size for text. To meet MLA documentation style, the footnotes should be double-spaced with a first line indent and a 12-point font size for text. The following steps modify the Footnote Text style.

1

• Right-click the note text in the footnote to display a shortcut menu related to footnotes (Figure 2–40).

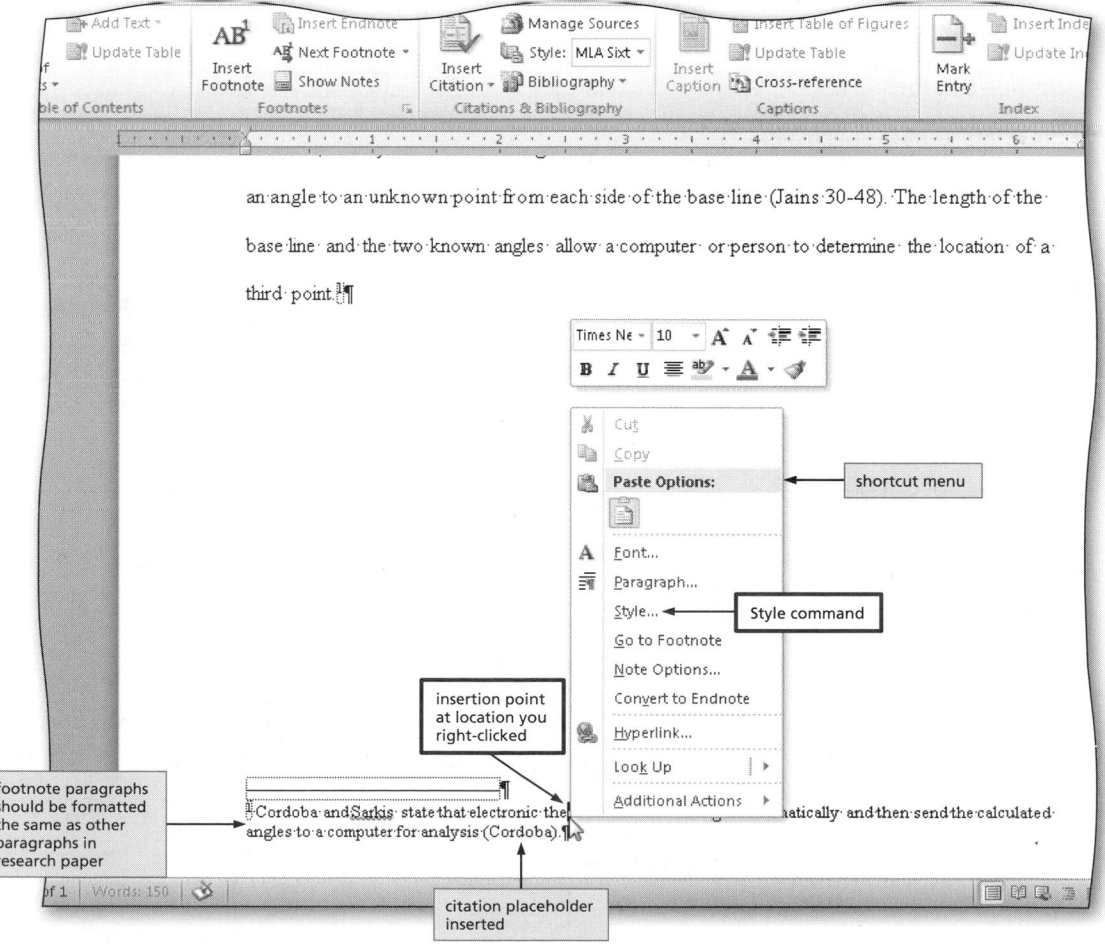

Figure 2–40

2

- Click Style on the shortcut menu to display the Style dialog box. If necessary, click the Category box arrow, click All styles in the Cagetory list, and then click Footnote Text in the Styles list.

- Click the Modify button (Style dialog box) to display the Modify Style dialog box.

- Click the Font Size box arrow (Modify Style dialog box) to display the Font Size list and then click 12 in the Font Size list to change the font size.

- Click the Double Space button to change the line spacing.

- Click the Format button to display the Format menu (Figure 2–41).

Style dialog box

Modify Style dialog box

Category box arrow

Styles list

Footnote Text style selected

changed to 12

Modify button

Font Size box arrow

Double Space button

Paragraph command

Preview area lists formats assigned to selected style (your level of detail may differ depending on previous settings)

Format menu

Format button

Figure 2–41

3

- Click Paragraph on the Format menu (Modify Style dialog box) to display the Paragraph dialog box.

- Click the Special box arrow (Paragraph dialog box) and then click First line (Figure 2–42).

Paragraph dialog box

Special box arrow

changed to First line

Apply button

OK button

OK button

Figure 2–42

4

- Click the OK button (Paragraph dialog box) to close the dialog box.

- Click the OK button (Modify Style dialog box) to close the dialog box.

- Click the Apply button (Style dialog box) to apply the style changes to the footnote text (Figure 2–43).

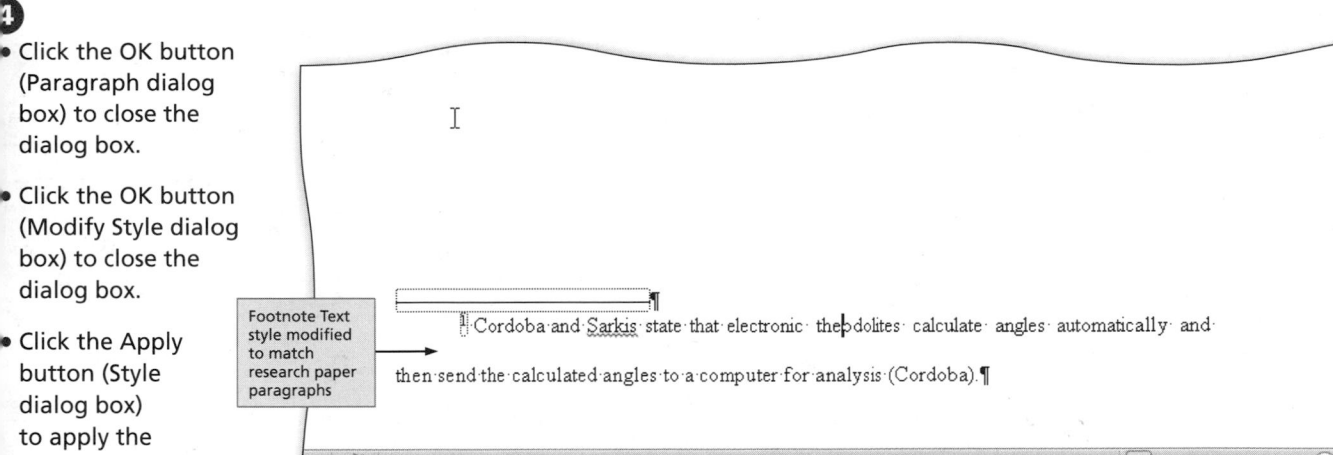

Footnote Text style modified to match research paper paragraphs

¶ Cordoba and Sarkis state that electronic theodolites calculate angles automatically and then send the calculated angles to a computer for analysis (Cordoba).¶

Figure 2–43

Will all footnotes use this modified style?

Yes. Any future footnotes entered in the document will use a 12-point font with the paragraphs first-line indented and double-spaced.

Other Ways

1. Click Styles Dialog Box Launcher (Home tab | Styles group), point to style name in list, click style name box arrow, click Modify, change settings

(Modify Style dialog box), click OK button

2. Click Styles Dialog Box Launcher (Home tab | Styles group), click Manage Styles button

in task pane, select style name in list, click Modify button, change settings (Modify Style dialog box), click OK button in each dialog box

To Edit a Source

When you typed the footnote text for this research paper, you inserted a citation placeholder for the source. Assume you now have the source information and are ready to enter it. The following steps edit a source.

1

- Click somewhere in the citation placeholder to be edited, in this case (Cordoba), to select the citation placeholder.

- Click the Citation Options box arrow to display the Citation Options menu (Figure 2–44).

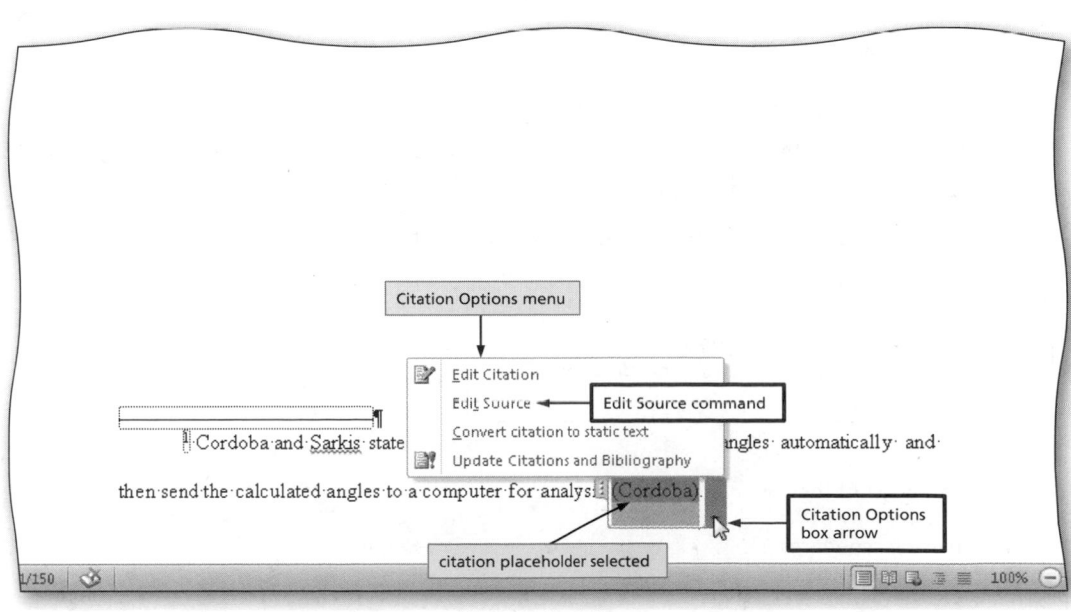

Citation Options menu

Edit Citation
Edit Source ← Edit Source command
Convert citation to static text
Update Citations and Bibliography

¶ Cordoba and Sarkis state ... angles automatically and then send the calculated angles to a computer for analysis (Cordoba)

Citation Options box arrow

citation placeholder selected

Figure 2–44

2

- Click Edit Source on the Citation Options menu to display the Edit Source dialog box.

- If necessary, click the Type of Source box arrow (Edit Source dialog box) and then click Book, so that the list shows fields required for a book.

- Click the Author text box. Type **Cordoba, Nicolas E.,; Sarkis, Kara A.** as the author.

Q&A

What if I do not know how to punctuate the author entry so that Word formats it properly?

Click the Edit button (Edit Source dialog box) to the right of the Author entry for assistance. For example, you should separate multiple author names with a semicolon as shown in this figure.

Figure 2–45

- Click the Title text box. Type **The Surveyor's Theodolite Formula** as the book title.

- Press the TAB key and then type **2012** as the year.

- Press the TAB key and then type **Orlando** as the city.

- Press the TAB key and then type **Orange County Press** as the publisher (Figure 2–45).

3

- Click the OK button to close the dialog box and create the source.

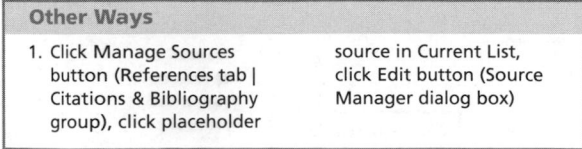

Other Ways	
1. Click Manage Sources button (References tab | Citations & Bibliography group), click placeholder	source in Current List, click Edit button (Source Manager dialog box)

BTW

Q&As
For a complete list of the Q&As found in many of the step-by-step sequences in this book, visit the Word 2010 Q&A Web page (scsite.com/wd2010/qa).

To Edit a Citation

In the MLA documentation style, if you reference the author's name in the text, you should not list it again in the parenthetical citation. Instead, just list the page number in the citation. To do this, you instruct Word to suppress author and title. The following steps edit the citation, suppressing the author and title but displaying the page numbers.

1 If necessary, click somewhere in the citation to be edited, in this case (Cordoba), to select the citation and display the Citation Options box arrow.

2 Click the Citation Options box arrow to display the Citation Options menu.

3 Click Edit Citation on the Citation Options menu to display the Edit Citation dialog box.

4 Type 2 5 in the Pages text box (Edit Citation dialog box).

5 Click the Author check box to place a check mark in it.

6 Click the Title check box to place a check mark in it (Figure 2–46).

7 Click the OK button to close the dialog box, remove the author name from the citation in the footnote, suppress the title from showing, and add a page number to the citation (shown in Figure 2-47 on page WD 101).

Figure 2–46

BTW

Footnote and Endnote Location
You can change the location of footnotes from the bottom of the page to the end of the text by clicking the Footnotes and Endnote Dialog Box Launcher (References tab | Footnotes group), clicking the Footnotes box arrow (Footnote and Endnote dialog box), and then clicking Below text. Similarly, clicking the Endnotes box arrow (Footnote and Endnote dialog box) enables you to change the location of endnotes from the end of the document to the end of a section. If you wanted to print just the footnotes or endnotes, you could position them at the end of the document on a separate page and then print that page.

BTW

Sending Footnotes or Endnotes to a PowerPoint Presentation
If you wanted footnotes and endnotes, or other headings, to be presented in a PowerPoint slide show, you would perform the following steps. Click the Customize Quick Access Toolbar button on the Quick Access Toolbar. Click More Commands on the Customize Quick Access Toolbar menu. Click the 'Choose commands from' box arrow (Word Options dialog box) and then click All Commands in the list. Scroll through the list of commands and then click Send to Microsoft PowerPoint to select the command. Click the Add button to add the selected command to the Customize Quick Access Toolbar list. Click the OK button to add the button to the Quick Access Toolbar. Then, click the Send to Microsoft PowerPoint button on the Quick Access Toolbar to create a PowerPoint presentation containing the endnotes and footnotes (it may also contain a few additional headings, which you can delete as needed).

Working with Footnotes and Endnotes

You edit footnote text just as you edit any other text in the document. To delete or move a note reference mark, however, the insertion point must be in the document text (not in the footnote text).

To delete a note, select the note reference mark in the document text (not in the footnote text) by dragging through the note reference mark and then click the Cut button (Home tab | Clipboard group). Or, click immediately to the right of the note reference mark in the document text and then press the BACKSPACE key twice, or click immediately to the left of the note reference mark in the document text and then press the DELETE key twice.

To move a note to a different location in a document, select the note reference mark in the document text (not in the footnote text), click the Cut button (Home tab | Clipboard group), click the location where you want to move the note, and then click the Paste button (Home tab | Clipboard group). When you move or delete notes, Word automatically renumbers any remaining notes in the correct sequence.

If you position the mouse pointer on the note reference mark in the document text, the note text is displayed above the note reference mark as a ScreenTip. To remove the ScreenTip, move the mouse pointer.

If, for some reason, you wanted to change the format of note reference marks in footnotes or endnotes (i.e., from 1, 2, 3, to A, B, C), you would click the Footnote & Endnote Dialog Box Launcher (References tab | Footnotes group) to display the Footnote and Endnote dialog box, click the Number format box arrow (Footnote and Endnote dialog box), click the desired number format in the list, and then click the Apply button.

If, for some reason, you wanted to convert footnotes to endnotes, you would click the Footnote & Endnote Dialog Box Launcher (References tab | Footnotes group) to display the Footnote and Endnote dialog box, click the Convert button (Footnote and Endnote dialog box), select the 'Convert all footnotes to endnotes' option button, click the OK button, and then click the Close button (Footnote and Endnote dialog box).

To Enter More Text

The next step is to continue typing text in the body of the research paper. The following steps enter this text.

1 Position the insertion point after the note reference mark in the document and then press the ENTER key.

2 Type the third paragraph of the research paper (Figure 2–47): `Similarly, the Nintendo Wii console uses triangulation to determine the location of a Wii Remote. A player places a sensor bar, which contains two infrared transmitters, near or on top of a television. While the player uses the Wii Remote, the Wii console determines the remote's location by calculating the distance and angles between the Wii Remote and the two transmitters on the sensor bar. Determining the location of a Wii Remote is relatively simple because the sensor bar contains only two fixed points: the transmitters.`

To Count Words

Often when you write papers, you are required to compose the papers with a minimum number of words. The minimum requirement for the research paper in this chapter is 325 words. You can look on the status bar and see the total number of words thus far in a document. For example, Figure 2–47 shows the research paper as 236 words, but you are not sure if that count includes the words in your footnote. The following steps display the Word Count dialog box, so that you can verify the footnote text is included in the count.

1

• Click the Word Count indicator on the status bar to display the Word Count dialog box.

• If necessary, place a check mark in the 'Include textboxes, footnotes and endnotes' check box (Word Count dialog box) (Figure 2–47).

Why do the statistics in my Word Count dialog box differ from Figure 2–47?

Depending on the accuracy of your typing, your statistics may differ.

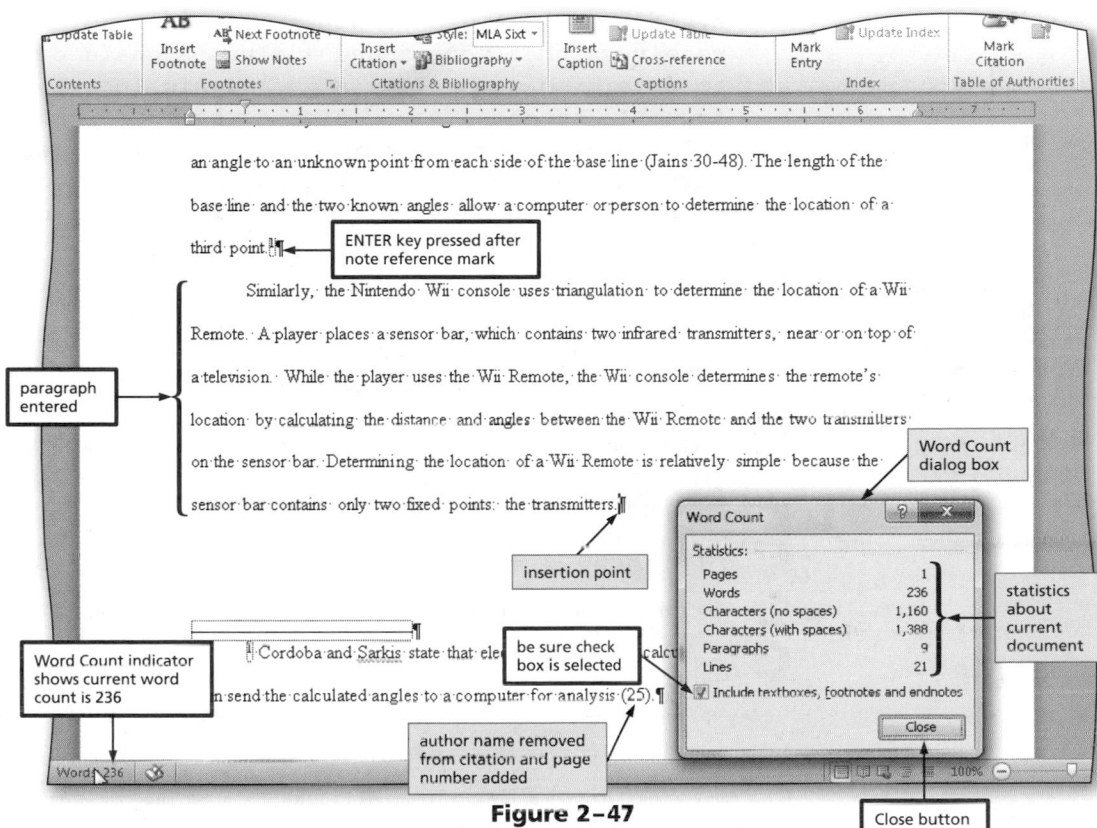

Figure 2–47

2

• Click the Close button to close the dialog box.

Can I display statistics for just a section of the document?

Yes. Select the section and then click the Word Count indicator on the status bar to display statistics about the selected text.

Other Ways

1. Click Word Count button (Review tab | Proofing group)
2. Press CTRL+SHIFT+G

Automatic Page Breaks

As you type documents that exceed one page, Word automatically inserts page breaks, called **automatic page breaks** or **soft page breaks**, when it determines the text has filled one page according to paper size, margin settings, line spacing, and other settings. If you add text, delete text, or modify text on a page, Word recomputes the location of automatic page breaks and adjusts them accordingly.

Word performs page recomputation between the keystrokes, that is, in between the pauses in your typing. Thus, Word refers to the automatic page break task as **background repagination**. The steps on the next page illustrate Word's automatic page break feature.

To Enter More Text and Insert a Citation Placeholder

The next task is to type the fourth paragraph in the body of the research paper. The following steps enter this text and a placeholder.

1 With the insertion point positioned at the end of the third paragraph as shown in Figure 2–47 on the previous page, press the ENTER key.

2 Type the fourth paragraph of the research paper (Figure 2–48): **A more complex application of triangulation occurs in a global positioning system (GPS). A GPS consists of one or more earth-based receivers that accept and analyze signals sent by satellites to determine a receiver's geographic location. GPS receivers, found in handheld navigation devices and many vehicles, use triangulation to determine their location relative to at least three geostationary satellites. According to Sanders, the satellites are the fixed points in the triangulation formula** and then press the SPACEBAR.

BTW

Page Break Locations
As you type, your page break may occur at different locations depending on Word settings and the type of printer connected to the computer.

Q&A

Why does the text move from the second page to the first page as I am typing?

Word, by default, will not allow the first line of a paragraph to be by itself at the bottom of a page (an orphan) or the last line of a paragraph to be by itself at the top of a page (a widow). As you type, Word adjusts the placement of the paragraph to avoid orphans and widows.

3 Click the Insert Citation button (References tab | Citations & Bibliography group) to display the Insert Citation menu. Click Add New Placeholder on the Insert Citation menu to display the Placeholder Name dialog box.

4 Type **Sanders** as the tag name for the source.

5 Click the OK button to close the dialog box and insert the tag name in the citation placeholder.

6 Press the PERIOD key to end the sentence.

Figure 2–48

To Edit a Source

When you typed the fourth paragraph of the research paper, you inserted a citation placeholder, Sanders, for the source. You now have the source information, which is for a Web site, and are ready to enter it. The following steps edit the source for the Sanders citation placeholder.

- Click somewhere in the citation placeholder to be edited, in this case (Sanders), to select the citation placeholder.

- Click the Citation Options box arrow to display the Citation Options menu.

- Click Edit Source on the Citation Options menu to display the Edit Source dialog box.

- If necessary, click the Type of Source box arrow (Edit Source dialog box); scroll to and then click Web site, so that the list shows fields required for a Web site.

- Place a check mark in the Show All Bibliography Fields check box to display more fields related to Web sites.

- Click the Author text box. Type **Sanders, Gregory B.** as the author.

- Click the Name of Web Page text box. Type **Understanding Satellites and Global Positioning Systems** as the Web page name.

- Click the Production Company text box. Type **Course Technology** as the production company.

- Click the Year Accessed text box. Type **2012** as the year accessed.

- Press the TAB key and then type **Feb.** as the month accessed.

Q&A What if some of the text boxes disappear as I enter the Web site fields?

With the Show All Bibliography Fields check box selected, the dialog box may not be able to display all Web site fields at the same time. In this case, some may scroll up.

- Press the TAB key and then type **27** as the day accessed (Figure 2–49).

Q&A Do I need to enter a Web address (URL)?

The latest MLA documentation style update does not require the Web address in the source.

- Click the OK button to close the dialog box and create the source.

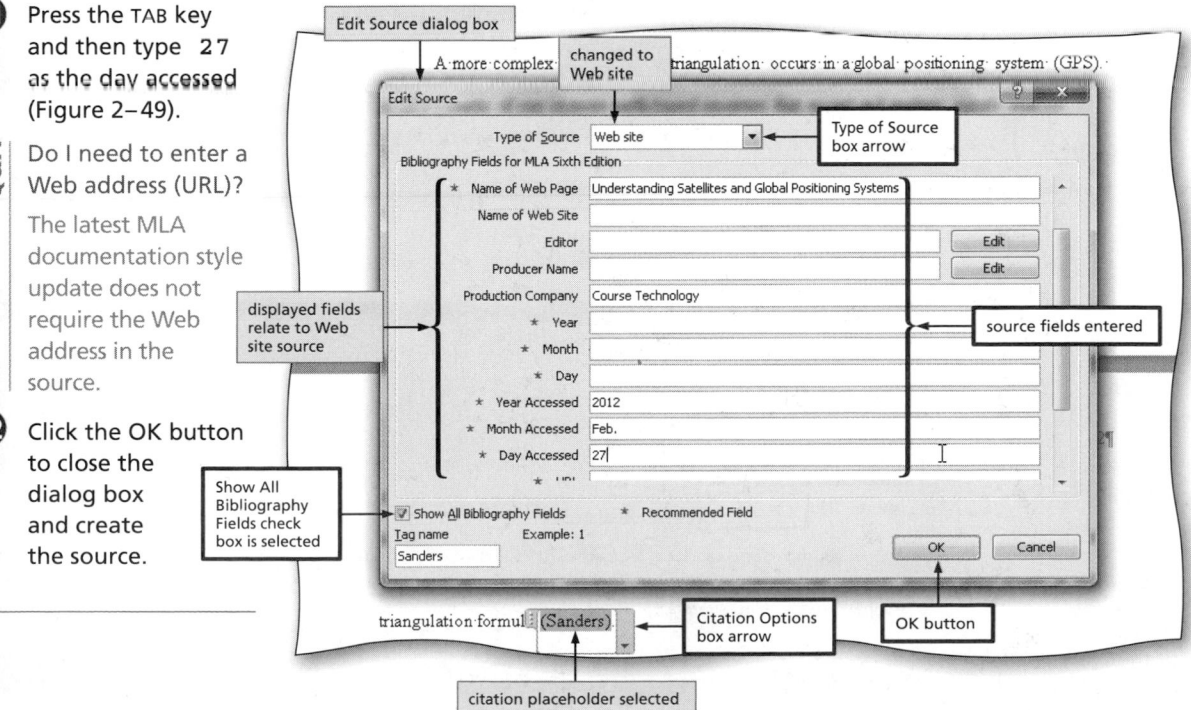

Figure 2–49

To Edit a Citation

As mentioned earlier, if you reference the author's name in the text, you should not list it again in the parenthetical citation. For Web site citations, when you suppress the author's name, the citation shows the Web site name because page numbers do not apply. The following steps edit the citation, suppressing the author and displaying the name of the Web site instead.

1 If necessary, click somewhere in the citation to be edited, in this case (Sanders), to select the citation and display the Citation Options box arrow.

2 Click the Citation Options box arrow and then click Edit Citation on the Citation Options menu to display the Edit Citation dialog box.

3 Click the Author check box (Edit Citation dialog box) to place a check mark in it (Figure 2–50).

4 Click the OK button to close the dialog box, remove the author name from the citation, and show the name of the Web site in the citation (shown in Figure 2–51).

Figure 2–50

To Enter More Text

The next step is to type the last paragraph of text in the research paper. The following steps enter this text.

1 Press the END key to position the insertion point at the end of the fourth paragraph and then press the ENTER key.

2 Type the last paragraph of the research paper (Figure 2–51): `The next time you pass a surveyor, play a Nintendo Wii, or follow a route prescribed by a vehicle's navigation system, keep in mind that none of it might have been possible without the concept of triangulation.`

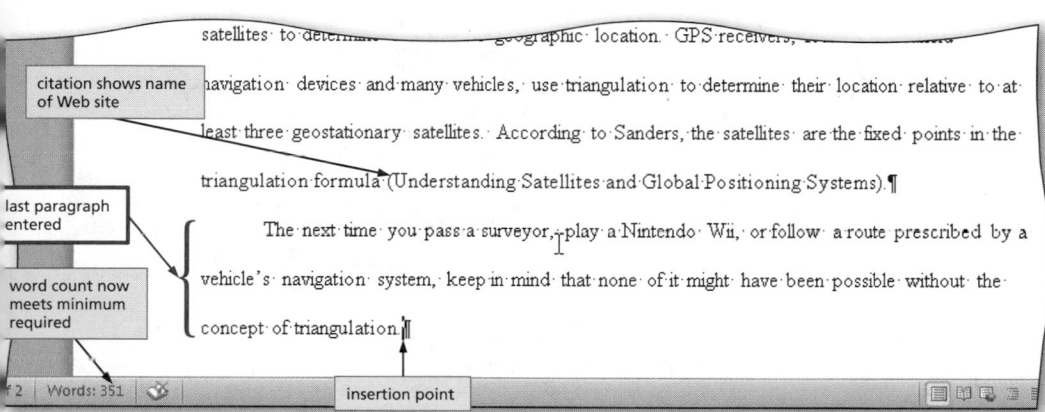

satellites to determine geographic location. GPS receivers, navigation devices and many vehicles, use triangulation to determine their location relative to at least three geostationary satellites. According to Sanders, the satellites are the fixed points in the triangulation formula (Understanding Satellites and Global Positioning Systems).¶

The next time you pass a surveyor, play a Nintendo Wii, or follow a route prescribed by a vehicle's navigation system, keep in mind that none of it might have been possible without the concept of triangulation.¶

citation shows name of Web site

last paragraph entered

word count now meets minimum required

insertion point

2 | Words: 351

Figure 2–51

To Save an Existing Document with the Same File Name

You have made several modifications to the document since you last saved it. Thus, you should save it again. The following step saves the document again.

1 Click the Save button on the Quick Access Toolbar to overwrite the previously saved file.

Break Point: If you wish to take a break, this is a good place to do so. You can quit Word now (refer to page WD 125 for instructions). To resume at a later time, start Word (refer to page WD 70 for instructions), open the file called Triangulation Paper (refer to page WD 45 for instructions), and continue following the steps from this location forward.

Creating an Alphabetical Works Cited Page

According to the MLA documentation style, the **works cited page** is a list of sources that are referenced directly in a research paper. You place the list on a separate numbered page with the title, Works Cited, centered one inch from the top margin. The works are to be alphabetized by the author's last name or, if the work has no author, by the work's title. The first line of each entry begins at the left margin. Indent subsequent lines of the same entry one-half inch from the left margin.

Plan
Ahead

Create the list of sources.

A **bibliography** is an alphabetical list of sources referenced in a paper. Whereas the text of the research paper contains brief references to the source (the citations), the bibliography lists all publication information about the source. Documentation styles differ significantly in their guidelines for preparing a bibliography. Each style identifies formats for various sources, including books, magazines, pamphlets, newspapers, Web sites, television programs, paintings, maps, advertisements, letters, memos, and much more. You can find information about various styles and their guidelines in printed style guides and on the Web.

To Page Break Manually

The works cited are to be displayed on a separate numbered page. Thus, you must insert a manual page break following the body of the research paper so that the list of sources is displayed on a separate page. A **manual page break**, or **hard page break**, is one that you force into the document at a specific location.

Word never moves or adjusts manual page breaks. Word, however, does adjust any automatic page breaks that follow a manual page break. Word inserts manual page breaks immediately above or to the left of the location of the insertion point. The following step inserts a manual page break after the text of the research paper.

- Verify that the insertion point is positioned at the end of the text of the research paper, as shown in Figure 2–51 on the previous page.

- Click Insert on the Ribbon to display the Insert tab.

- Click the Page Break button (Insert tab | Pages group) to insert a manual page break immediately to the left of the insertion point and position the insertion point immediately below the manual page break (Figure 2–52).

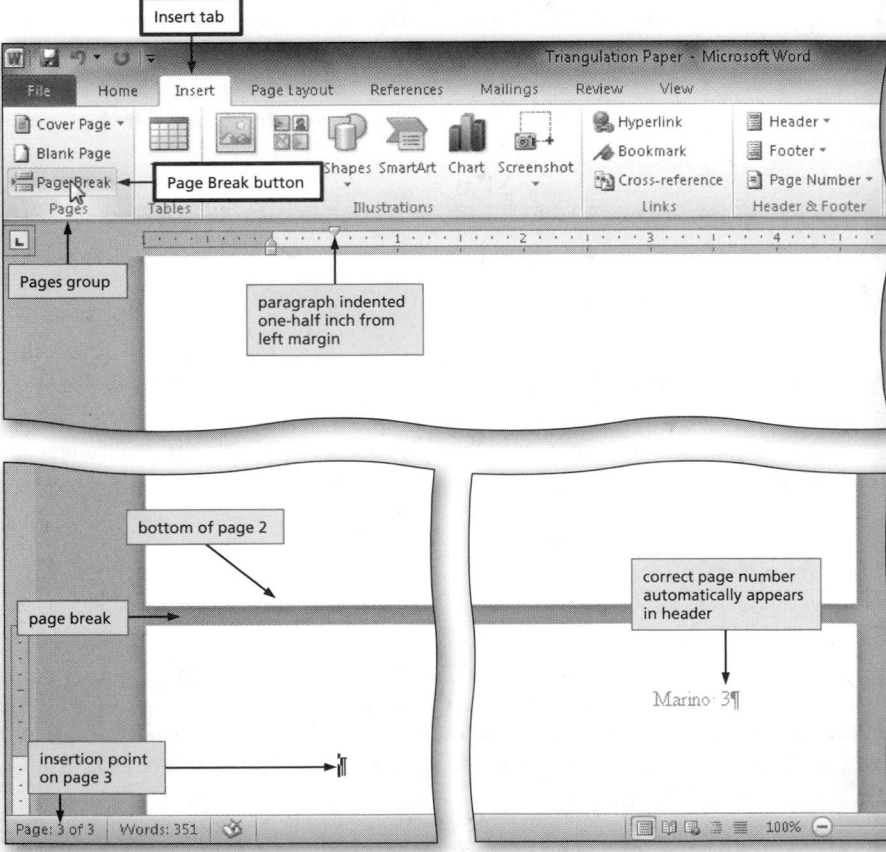

Figure 2–52

To Apply a Style

The works cited title is to be centered between the margins of the paper. If you simply issue the Center command, the title will not be centered properly. Instead, it will be one-half inch to the right of the center point because earlier you set the first-line indent for paragraphs to one-half inch.

To properly center the title of the works cited page, you could drag the First Line Indent marker back to the left margin before centering the paragraph, or you could apply the Normal style to the location of the insertion point. Recall that you modified the Normal style for this document to 12-point Times New Roman with double-spaced, left-aligned paragraphs that have no space after the paragraphs.

To apply a style to a paragraph, first position the insertion point in the paragraph and then apply the style. The following step applies the modified Normal style to the location of the insertion point.

1

- Click Home on the Ribbon to display the Home tab.

- With the insertion point on the paragraph mark at the top of page 3 (as shown in Figure 2–52) even if Normal is selected, click Normal in the Quick Style gallery (Home tab | Styles group) to apply the Normal style to the paragraph containing the insertion point (Figure 2–53).

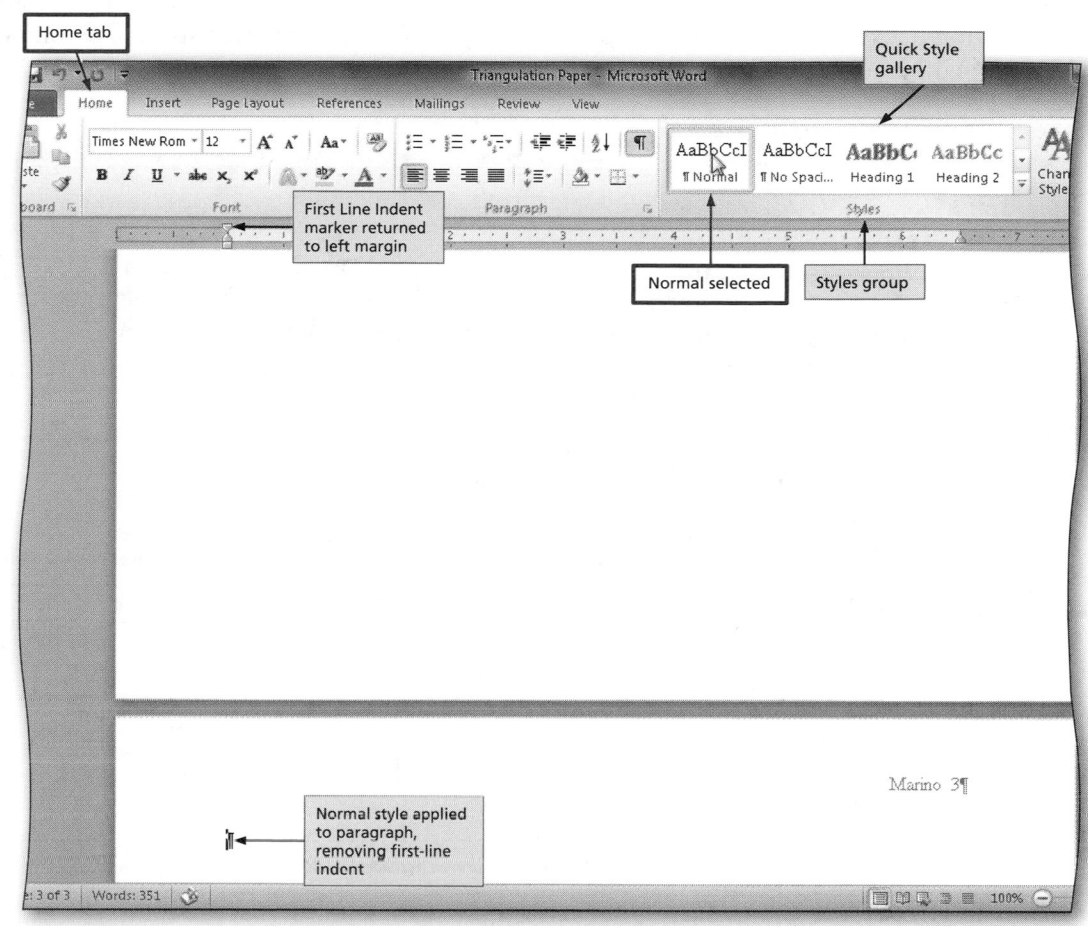

Figure 2–53

Other Ways	
1. Click Styles Dialog Box Launcher (Home tab | Styles group), click desired style in Styles task pane	2. Press CTRL+SHIFT+S, click Style Name box arrow in Apply Styles task pane, click desired style in list

To Center Text

The next step is to enter the title, Works Cited, centered between the margins of the paper. The following steps use shortcut keys to format the title.

1 Press CTRL+E to center the paragraph mark.

2 Type **Works Cited** as the title.

3 Press the ENTER key.

4 Press CTRL+L to left-align the paragraph mark (shown in Figure 2–54 on the next page).

BTW

BTWs
For a complete list of the BTWs found in the margins of this book, visit the Word 2010 BTW Web page (scsite.com/wd2010/btw).

To Create the Bibliographical List

While typing the research paper, you created several citations and their sources. Word can format the list of sources and alphabetize them in a **bibliographical list**, saving you time looking up style guidelines. That is, Word will create a bibliographical list with each element of the source placed in its correct position with proper punctuation, according to the specified style. For example, in this research paper, the book source will list, in this order, the author name(s), book title, publisher city, publishing company name, and publication year with the correct punctuation between each element according to the MLA documentation style. The following steps create an MLA-styled bibliographical list from the sources previously entered.

- Click References on the Ribbon to display the References tab.

- With the insertion point positioned as shown in Figure 2–54, click the Bibliography button (References tab | Citations & Bibliography group) to display the Bibliography gallery (Figure 2–54).

Q&A

Will I select the Works Cited option from the Bibliography gallery?

No. The title it inserts is not formatted according to the MLA documentation style. Thus, you will use the Insert Bibliography command instead.

Figure 2–54

- Click Insert Bibliography in the Bibliography gallery to insert a list of sources at the location of the insertion point.

- If necessary, scroll to display the entire list of sources in the document window (Figure 2–55).

Q&A

What is the n.d. in the last work?

The MLA documentation style uses the abbreviation n.d. for no date, for example, no date on the Web page.

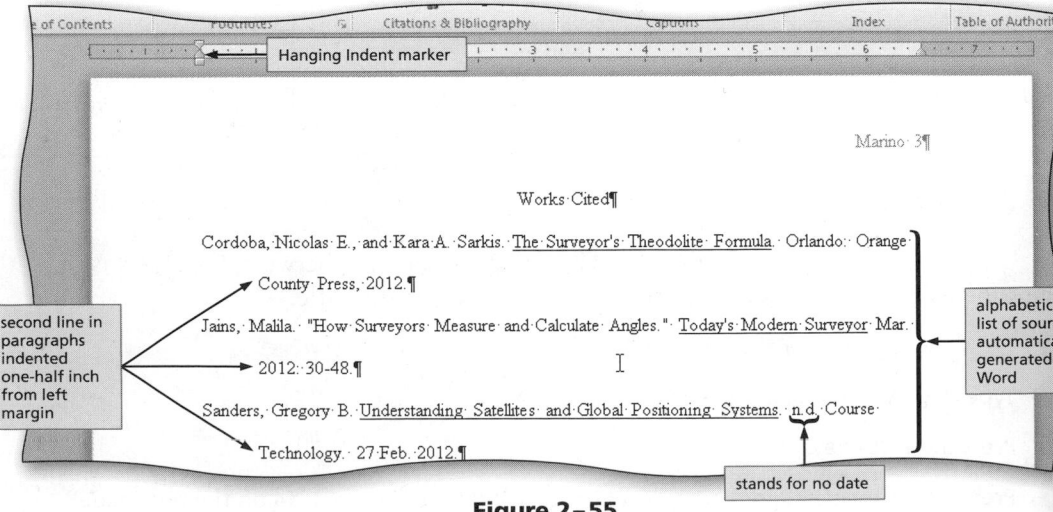

Figure 2–55

TO FORMAT PARAGRAPHS WITH A HANGING INDENT

Notice in Figure 2–55 that the first line of each source entry begins at the left margin, and subsequent lines in the same paragraph are indented one-half inch from the left margin. In essence, the first line hangs to the left of the rest of the paragraph; thus, this type of paragraph formatting is called a **hanging indent**. The Bibliography style in Word automatically formats the works cited paragraphs with a hanging indent.

If you wanted to format paragraphs with a hanging indent, you would use one of the following techniques.

- With the insertion point in the paragraph to format, drag the **Hanging Indent marker** (the bottom triangle) on the ruler to the desired mark on the ruler (i.e., .5") to set the hanging indent at that location from the left margin.

or

- Right-click the paragraph to format, click Paragraph on shortcut menu, click Indents and Spacing tab (Paragraph dialog box), click Special box arrow, click Hanging, and then click the OK button.

or

- Click the Paragraph Dialog Box Launcher (Home tab or Page Layout tab | Paragraph group), click Indents and Spacing tab (Paragraph dialog box), click Special box arrow, click Hanging, and then click the OK button.

or

- With the insertion point in the paragraph to format, press CTRL+T.

To Modify a Source and Update the Bibliographical List

If you modify the contents of any source, the list of sources automatically updates because the list is a field. The following steps modify the title of the magazine article.

1

- Click the Manage Sources button (References tab | Citations & Bibliography group) to display the Source Manager dialog box.

- Click the source you wish to edit in the Current List, in this case the article by Jains, to select the source.

- Click the Edit button (Source Manager dialog box) to display the Edit Source dialog box.

- In the Title text box, insert the word, Distance, between the words, Measure and, in the title (Figure 2–56).

Figure 2–56

- Click the OK button (Edit Source dialog box) to close the dialog box.

- If a Microsoft Word dialog box appears, click its Yes button to update all occurrences of the source.

- Click the Close button (Source Manager dialog box) to update the list of sources in the document and close the dialog box (Figure 2–57).

Q&A What if the list of sources in the document is not updated automatically?

Click in the list of sources and then press the F9 key, which is the shortcut key to update a field.

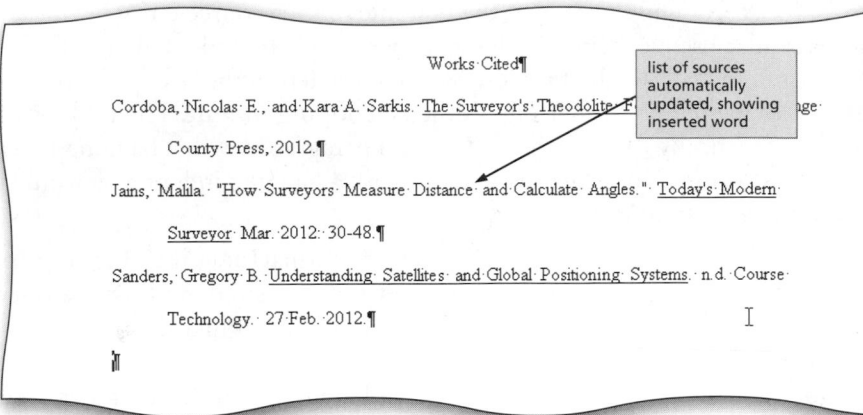

Figure 2–57

To Convert a Field to Regular Text

Word may use an earlier version of the MLA documentation style to format the bibliography. The latest guidelines for the MLA documentation style, for example, state that titles should be italicized instead of underlined, and each work should identify the source's publication medium (e.g., Print for printed media, Web for online media, etc.). If you format or add text to the bibliography, Word automatically will change it back to the Bibliography style's predetermined formats when the bibliography field is updated. To preserve modifications you make to the format of the bibliography, you can convert the bibliography field to regular text. Keep in mind, though, once you convert the field to regular text, it no longer is a field that can be updated. The following step converts a field to regular text.

- Click somewhere in the field to select it, in this case, somewhere in the bibliography (Figure 2–58).

Q&A What if the bibliography field is not shaded gray?

Click File on the Ribbon to open the Backstage view, click Options in the Backstage view, click Advanced in the left pane (Word Options dialog box), scroll to the 'Show document content' area, click the Field shading box arrow, click When selected, and then click the OK button.

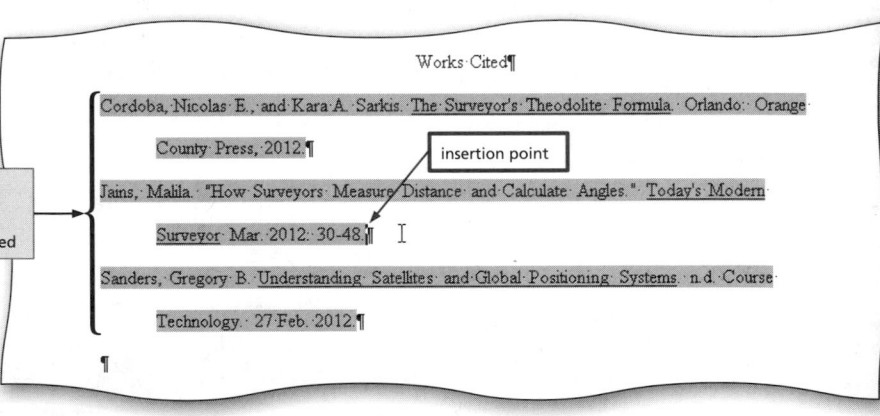

Figure 2–58

Q&A Why are all the words in the bibliography shaded?

The bibliography field consists of all text in the bibliography.

- Press CTRL+SHIFT+F9 to convert the selected field to regular text.

Q&A Why did the gray shading disappear?

The bibliography no longer is a field, so it is not shaded gray.

- Click anywhere in the document to remove the selection from the text.

To Format the Works Cited to the Latest MLA Documentation Style

As mentioned earlier, the latest the MLA documentation style guidelines state that titles should be italicized instead of underlined, and each work should identify the source's publication medium (e.g., Print, Web, Radio, Television, CD, DVD, Film, etc.). The following steps format and modify the Works Cited as specified by the latest MLA guidelines, if yours are not already formatted this way.

1 Drag through the book title, The Surveyor's Theodolite Formula, to select it.

2 Click Home on the Ribbon to display the Home tab. Click the Underline button (Home tab | Font group) to remove the underline from the selected text and then click the Italic button (Home tab | Font group) to italicize the selected text.

3 Select the magazine title, Today's Modern Surveyor. Remove the underline from the selected title and then italicize the selected title.

4 Select the Web page title, Understanding Satellites and Global Positioning Systems. Remove the underline from the selected title and then italicize the selected title.

5 After the period following the year in the first work, press the SPACEBAR and then type **Print.**

6 After the period following the page range in the second work, press the SPACEBAR and then type **Print.**

7 Before the date in the third work, type **Web.** and then press the SPACEBAR (Figure 2–59).

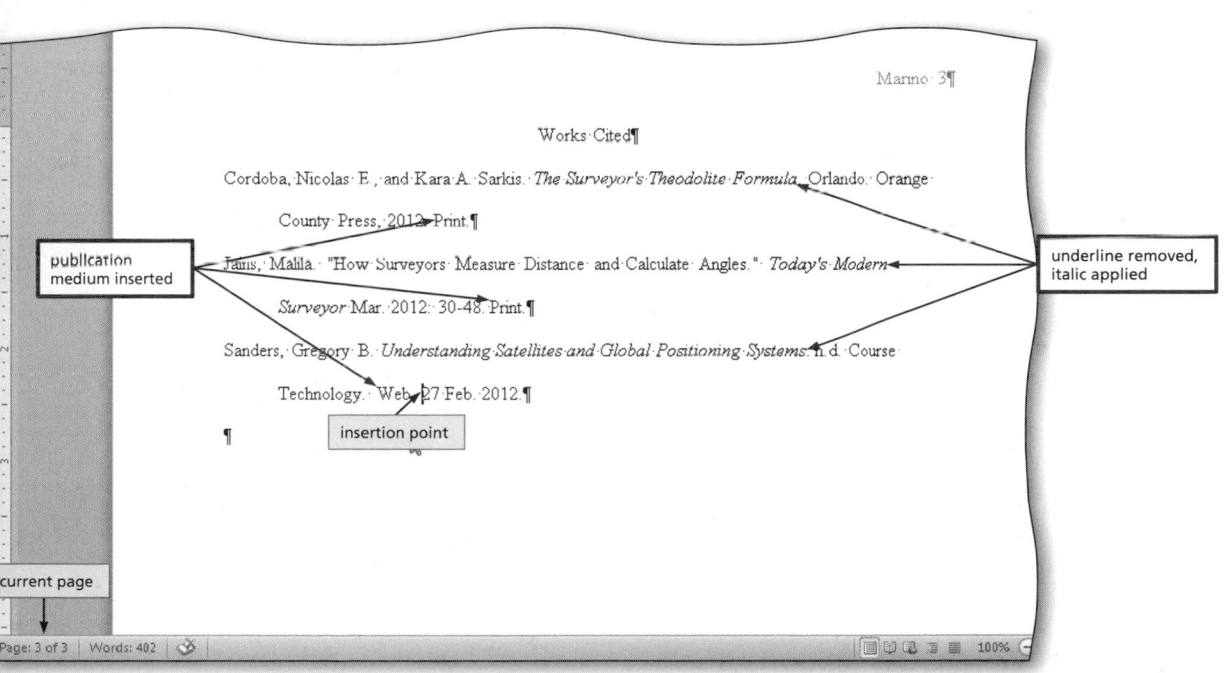

Figure 2–59

To Save an Existing Document with the Same File Name

You have made several modifications to the document since you last saved it. Thus, you should save it again. The following step saves the document again.

1 Click the Save button on the Quick Access Toolbar to overwrite the previously saved file.

Proofing and Revising the Research Paper

As discussed in Chapter 1, once you complete a document, you might find it necessary to make changes to it. Before submitting a paper to be graded, you should proofread it. While **proofreading**, look for grammatical errors and spelling errors. You also should ensure the transitions between sentences flow smoothly and the sentences themselves make sense.

Plan Ahead

Proofread and revise the paper.

As you proofread the paper, look for ways to improve it. Check all grammar, spelling, and punctuation. Be sure the text is logical and transitions are smooth. Where necessary, add text, delete text, reword text, and move text to different locations. Ask yourself these questions:

- Does the title suggest the topic?
- Is the thesis clear?
- Is the purpose of the paper clear?
- Does the paper have an introduction, body, and conclusion?
- Does each paragraph in the body relate to the thesis?
- Is the conclusion effective?
- Are all sources acknowledged?

To assist you with the proofreading effort, Word provides several tools. You can browse through pages, copy text, find text, replace text, insert a synonym, check spelling and grammar, and look up information. The following pages discuss these tools.

To Scroll Page by Page through a Document

The next step is to modify text on the second page of the paper. Currently, the third page is the active page (Figure 2–59 on the previous page). The following step scrolls up one page in the document.

1
- With the insertion point on the third page of the paper, click the Previous Page button on the vertical scroll bar to position the insertion point at the top of the previous page (Figure 2–60).

Q&A The button on my screen shows a ScreenTip different from Previous Page. Why?

By default, the functions of the buttons above and below the Select Browse Object button are Previous Page and Next Page, respectively. You can change the commands associated with these buttons by clicking the Select Browse Object button and then clicking the desired browse object. The Browse by Page command on the Select Browse Object menu, for example, changes the buttons back to Previous Page and Next Page.

Q&A How do I display the next page?
Click the Next Page button on the vertical scroll bar.

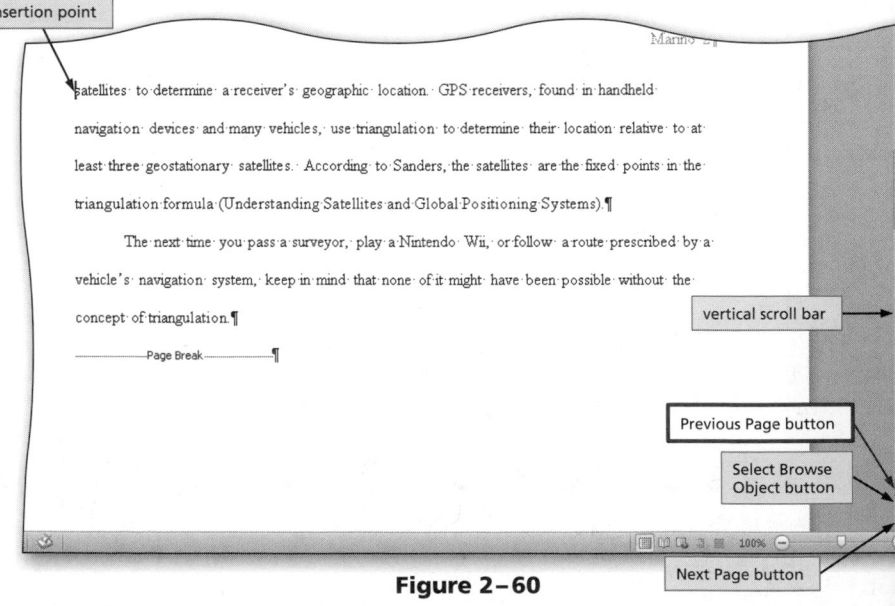

Figure 2–60

Other Ways

1. Click Page Number indicator on status bar, click Page in 'Go to what' list (Find and Replace dialog box), type desired page number in 'Enter page number' text box, click Go To button
2. Press CTRL+PAGE UP or CTRL+PAGE DOWN

Copying, Cutting, and Pasting

While proofreading the research paper, you decide it would read better if the word, geostationary, appeared in front of the word, satellites, in the last sentence of the fourth paragraph. You could type the word at the desired location, but because this is a difficult word to spell, you decide to use the Office Clipboard. The **Office Clipboard** is a temporary storage area that holds up to 24 items (text or graphics) copied from any Office program.

Copying is the process of placing items on the Office Clipboard, leaving the item in the document. **Cutting**, by contrast, removes the item from the document before placing it on the Office Clipboard. **Pasting** is the process of copying an item from the Office Clipboard into the document at the location of the insertion point.

To Copy and Paste

In the research paper, you copy a word from one sentence to another. The following steps copy and paste a word.

1
- Select the item to be copied (the word, geostationary, in this case).

- Click the Copy button (Home tab | Clipboard group) to copy the selected item in the document to the Office Clipboard (Figure 2–61).

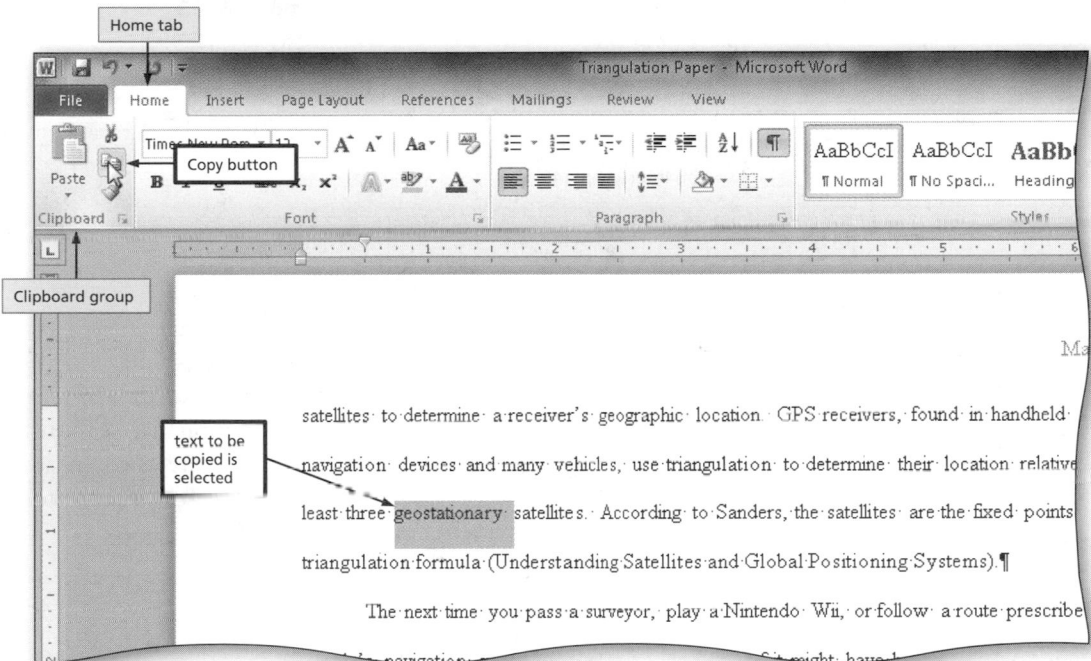

Figure 2–61

2
- Position the insertion point at the location where the item should be pasted (immediately to the left of the word, satellites, in this case) (Figure 2–62).

Figure 2–62

3

- Click the Paste button (Home tab | Clipboard group) to paste the copied item in the document at the location of the insertion point (Figure 2–63).

Q&A

What if I click the Paste button arrow by mistake?

Click the Paste button arrow again to remove the Paste menu.

Figure 2–63

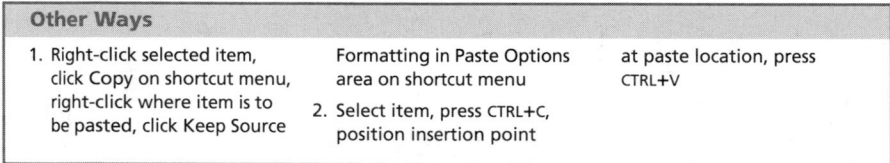

Other Ways

1. Right-click selected item, click Copy on shortcut menu, right-click where item is to be pasted, click Keep Source Formatting in Paste Options area on shortcut menu

2. Select item, press CTRL+C, position insertion point at paste location, press CTRL+V

To Display the Paste Options Menu

When you paste an item or move an item using drag-and-drop editing, which was discussed in the previous chapter, Word automatically displays a Paste Options button near the pasted or moved text (Figure 2–63). The Paste Options button allows you to change the format of a pasted item. For example, you can instruct Word to format the pasted item the same way as where it was copied, or format it the same way as where it is being pasted. The following steps display the Paste Options menu.

- Click the Paste Options button to display the Paste Options menu (Figure 2–64).

Q&A

What are the functions of the buttons on the Paste Options menu?

In general, the left button indicates the pasted item should look the same as it did in its original location. The second button formats the pasted text to match the rest of the item where it was pasted. The third button removes all formatting from the pasted item. The Set Default Paste command displays the Word Options dialog box. Keep in mind that the buttons shown on a Paste Options menu will vary, depending on the item being pasted.

Figure 2–64

- Press the ESCAPE key to remove the Paste Options menu from the window.

To Find Text

While proofreading the paper, you would like to locate all occurrences of Wii console because you are contemplating changing this text to Wii game console. The following steps find all occurrences of specific text in a document.

1

• Click the Find button (Home tab | Editing group) to display the Navigation Pane (Figure 2–65).

What is the Navigation Pane?

The **Navigation Pane** is a window that enables you to search for text in a document, browse through pages in a document, or browse through headings in a document.

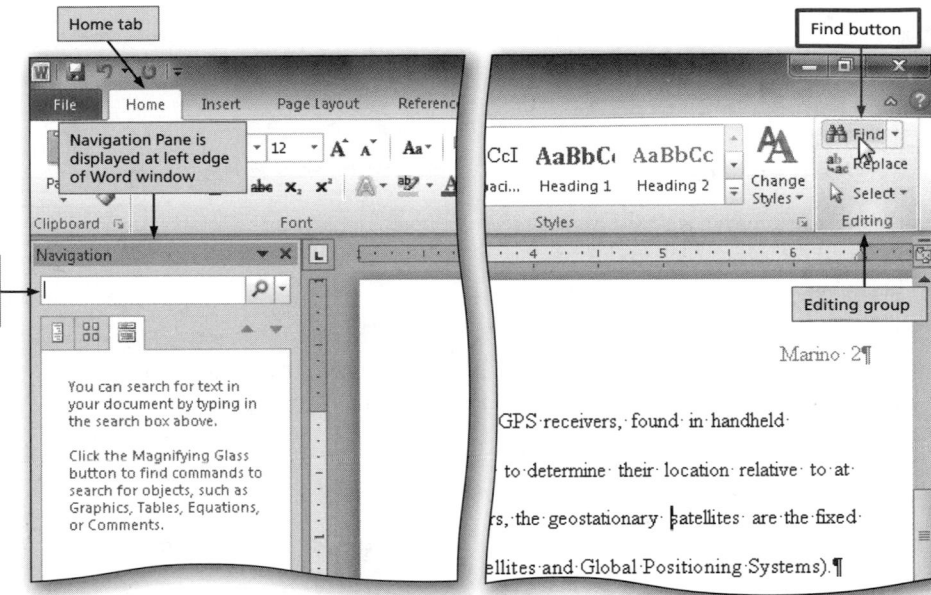

Figure 2–65

2

• Type **Wii console** in the Navigation Pane text box to display all occurrences of the typed text, called the search text, in the Navigation Pane and to highlight the occurrences of the search text in the document window (Figure 2–66).

3

 Experiment

• Type various search text in the Navigation Pane text box, and watch Word both list matches in the Navigation Pane and highlight matches in the document window. When you are finished experimenting, repeat Step 2.

Figure 2–66

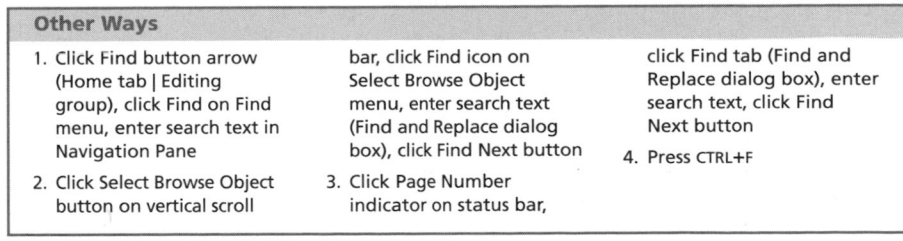

Other Ways

1. Click Find button arrow (Home tab | Editing group), click Find on Find menu, enter search text in Navigation Pane

2. Click Select Browse Object button on vertical scroll bar, click Find icon on Select Browse Object menu, enter search text (Find and Replace dialog box), click Find Next button

3. Click Page Number indicator on status bar, click Find tab (Find and Replace dialog box), enter search text, click Find Next button

4. Press CTRL+F

To Replace Text

You decide to change all occurrences of Wii console to Wii game console. To do this, you can use Word's find and replace feature, which automatically locates each occurrence of a word or phrase and then replaces it with specified text. The following steps replace all occurrences of Wii console with Wii game console.

- Click the Replace button (Home tab | Editing group) to display the Replace sheet in the Find and Replace dialog box.

- If necessary, type **Wii console** in the Find what text box (Find and Replace dialog box).

- Press the TAB key. Type **Wii game console** in the Replace with text box (Figure 2–67).

Figure 2–67

- Click the Replace All button to instruct Word to replace all occurrences of the Find what text with the Replace with text (Figure 2–68). If Word displays a dialog box asking if you want to continue searching from the beginning of the document, click the Yes button.

Q&A Does Word search the entire document?

If the insertion point is at the beginning of the document, Word searches the entire document; otherwise, Word searches from the location of the insertion point to the end of the document and then displays a dialog box asking if you want to continue searching from the beginning. You also can search a section of text by selecting the text before clicking the Replace button.

Figure 2–68

- Click the OK button (Microsoft Word dialog box) to close the dialog box.

- Click the Close button (Find and Replace dialog box) to close the dialog box.

Other Ways
1. Click Select Browse Object button on vertical scroll bar, click Find icon on Select Browse Object menu, click Replace tab   2. Click Page Number indicator on status bar, click Replace tab (Find and Replace dialog box)   3. Press CTRL+H

Find and Replace Dialog Box

The Replace All button (Find and Replace dialog box) replaces all occurrences of the Find what text with the Replace with text. In some cases, you may want to replace only certain occurrences of a word or phrase, not all of them. To instruct Word to confirm each change, click the Find Next button (Find and Replace dialog box) (Figure 2–68), instead of the Replace All button. When Word locates an occurrence of the text, it pauses and waits for you to click either the Replace button or the Find Next button. Clicking the Replace button changes the text; clicking the Find Next button instructs Word to disregard the replacement and look for the next occurrence of the Find what text.

If you accidentally replace the wrong text, you can undo a replacement by clicking the Undo button on the Quick Access Toolbar. If you used the Replace All button, Word undoes all replacements. If you used the Replace button, Word undoes only the most recent replacement.

BTW

Finding Formatting
To search for formatting or a special character, click the More button (shown in Figure 2–67) to expand the Find dialog box. To find formatting, use the Format button in the expanded Find dialog box. To find a special character, use the Special button.

To Go to a Page

The next step in revising the paper is to change a word on the second page of the document. You could scroll to the location in the document, or as mentioned earlier, you can use the Navigation Pane to browse through pages in a document. The following steps display the top of the second page in the document window and position the insertion point at the beginning of that page.

①

- Click the 'Browse the pages in your document' tab in the Navigation Pane to display thumbnail images of the pages in the document (Figure 2–69).

    What if the Navigation Pane is not on the screen anymore?

    Click View on the Ribbon to display the View tab and then click Navigation Pane (View tab | Show group) to select the check box.

②

- Click the thumbnail of the second page, even if the second page already is selected, to display the top of the selected page in the top of the document window (shown in Figure 2–70 on the next page).

③

- Click the Close button in the Navigation Pane to close the pane.

Figure 2–69

Other Ways

1. Click Find button arrow (Home tab | Editing group), click Go To on Find menu, click Go To tab (Find and Replace dialog box), enter page number, click Go To button

2. Click Select Browse Object button on vertical scroll bar, click Go To icon on Select Browse Object menu, enter page number (Find and Replace dialog box), click Go To button

3. Click Page Number indicator on status bar, click Go To tab (Find and Replace dialog box), enter page number, click Go To button

4. Press CTRL+G

To Find and Insert a Synonym

When writing, you may discover that you used the same word in multiple locations or that a word you used was not quite appropriate. In these instances, you will want to look up a **synonym**, or a word similar in meaning, to the duplicate or inappropriate word. A **thesaurus** is a book of synonyms. Word provides synonyms and a thesaurus for your convenience.

In this project, you would like a synonym for the word, prescribed, in the fourth paragraph of the research paper. The following steps find a suitable synonym.

1

- Locate and then right-click the word for which you want to find a synonym (in this case, prescribed) to display a shortcut menu related to the word you right-clicked.

- Point to Synonyms on the shortcut menu to display a list of synonyms for the word you right-clicked (Figure 2–70).

Figure 2–70

2

- Click the synonym you want (in this case, suggested) on the Synonyms submenu to replace the selected word in the document with the selected synonym (Figure 2–71).

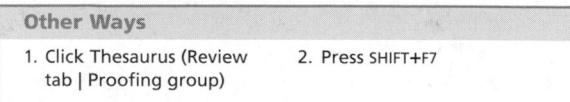

Figure 2–71

Q&A

What if the synonyms list on the shortcut menu does not display a suitable word?

You can display the thesaurus in the Research task pane by clicking Thesaurus on the Synonyms submenu. The Research task pane displays a complete thesaurus, in which you can look up synonyms for various meanings of a word. You also can look up an **antonym,** or word with an opposite meaning. The Research task pane is discussed later in this chapter.

Other Ways	
1. Click Thesaurus (Review tab | Proofing group)	2. Press SHIFT+F7

To Check Spelling and Grammar at Once

As discussed in Chapter 1, Word checks spelling and grammar as you type and places a wavy underline below possible spelling or grammar errors. Chapter 1 illustrated how to check these flagged words immediately. As an alternative, you can wait and check the entire document for spelling and grammar errors at once. The next steps check spelling and grammar at once.

Note: In the following steps, the word, theodolite, has been misspelled intentionally as theadalight to illustrate the use of Word's check spelling and grammar at once feature. If you are completing this project on a personal computer, your research paper may contain different misspelled words, depending on the accuracy of your typing.

1
- Press CTRL+HOME because you want the spelling and grammar check to begin from the top of the document.

- Click Review on the Ribbon to display the Review tab.

- Click the Spelling & Grammar button (Review tab | Proofing group) to begin the spelling and grammar check at the location of the insertion point, which in this case, is at the beginning of the document.

- Click the desired spelling in the Suggestions list (theodolite, in this case) (Figure 2–72).

Figure 2–72

2
- With the word, theodolite, selected in the Suggestions list, click the Change button (Spelling and Grammar dialog box) to change the flagged word to the selected suggestion and then continue the spelling and grammar check until the next error is identified or the end of the document is reached (Figure 2–73).

3
- Click the Ignore All button (Spelling and Grammar dialog box) to ignore this and future occurrences of the flagged proper noun and then continue the spelling and grammar check until the next error is identified or the end of the document is reached.

4
- When the spelling and grammar check is finished and Word displays a dialog box, click its OK button.

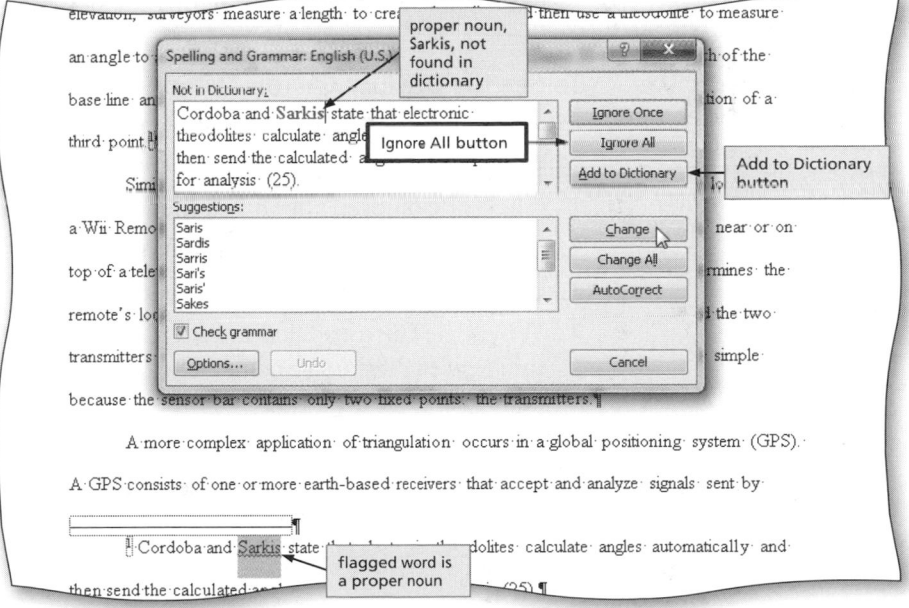

Figure 2–73

Can I check spelling of just a section of a document?

Yes, select the text before starting the spelling and grammar check.

Other Ways

1. Click Spelling and Grammar Check icon on status bar, click Spelling on shortcut menu

2. Right-click flagged word, click Spelling on shortcut menu

3. Press F7

Readability Statistics
You can instruct Word to display readability statistics when it has finished a spelling and grammar check on a document. Three readability statistics presented are the percent of passive sentences, the Flesch Reading Ease score, and the Flesch-Kincaid Grade Level score. The Flesch Reading Ease score uses a 100-point scale to rate the ease with which a reader can understand the text in a document. A higher score means the document is easier to understand. The Flesch-Kincaid Grade Level score rates the text in a document on a U.S. school grade level. For example, a score of 10.0 indicates a student in the tenth grade can understand the material. To show readability statistics when the spelling and grammar check is complete, open the Backstage view, click Options in the Backstage view, click Proofing in the left pane (Word Options dialog box), place a check mark in the 'Show readability statistics' check box, and then click the OK button. Readability statistics will be displayed the next time you check spelling and grammar at once in the document.

The Main and Custom Dictionaries

As shown in the steps on the previous page, Word may flag a proper noun as an error because the proper noun is not in its main dictionary. To prevent Word from flagging proper nouns as errors, you can add the proper nouns to the custom dictionary. To add a correctly spelled word to the custom dictionary, click the Add to Dictionary button (Spelling and Grammar dialog box) or right-click the flagged word and then click Add to Dictionary on the shortcut menu. Once you have added a word to the custom dictionary, Word no longer will flag it as an error.

TO VIEW OR MODIFY ENTRIES IN A CUSTOM DICTIONARY

To view or modify the list of words in a custom dictionary, you would follow these steps.

1. Click File on the Ribbon and then click Options in the Backstage view.
2. Click Proofing in the left pane (Word Options dialog box).
3. Click the Custom Dictionaries button.
4. When Word displays the Custom Dictionaries dialog box, place a check mark next to the dictionary name to view or modify. Click the Edit Word List button (Custom Dictionaries dialog box). (In this dialog box, you can add or delete entries to and from the selected custom dictionary.)
5. When finished viewing and/or modifying the list, click the OK button in the dialog box.
6. Click the OK button (Custom Dictionaries dialog box).
7. If the 'Suggest from main dictionary only' check box is selected in the Word Options dialog box, remove the check mark. Click the OK button (Word Options dialog box).

TO SET THE DEFAULT CUSTOM DICTIONARY

If you have multiple custom dictionaries, you can specify which one Word should use when checking spelling. To set the default custom dictionary, you would follow these steps.

1. Click File on the Ribbon and then click Options in the Backstage view.
2. Click Proofing in the left pane (Word Options dialog box).
3. Click the Custom Dictionaries button.
4. When the Custom Dictionaries dialog box is displayed, place a check mark next to the desired dictionary name. Click the Change Default button (Custom Dictionaries dialog box).
5. Click the OK button (Custom Dictionaries dialog box).
6. If the 'Suggest from main dictionary only' check box is selected in the Word Options dialog box, remove the check mark. Click the OK button (Word Options dialog box).

To Use the Research Task Pane to Look Up Information

From within Word, you can search through various forms of reference information. Earlier, this chapter discussed the Research task pane with respect to looking up a synonym in a thesaurus. Other services available in the Research task pane include a dictionary and, if you are connected to the Web, a search engine and other Web sites that provide information such as stock quotes, news articles, and company profiles.

Assume you want to know more about the word, geostationary. The following steps use the Research task pane to look up a definition of a word.

1

• Locate the word you want to look up.

• While holding down the ALT key, click the word you want to look up (in this case, geostationary) to open the Research task pane and display a dictionary entry for the ALT+clicked word. Release the ALT key.

2

• Click the Search for box arrow in the Research task pane to display a list of search locations (Figure 2–74).

Why does my Research task pane look different?

Depending on your settings and Microsoft's Web site search settings, your Research task pane may appear different from the figures shown here.

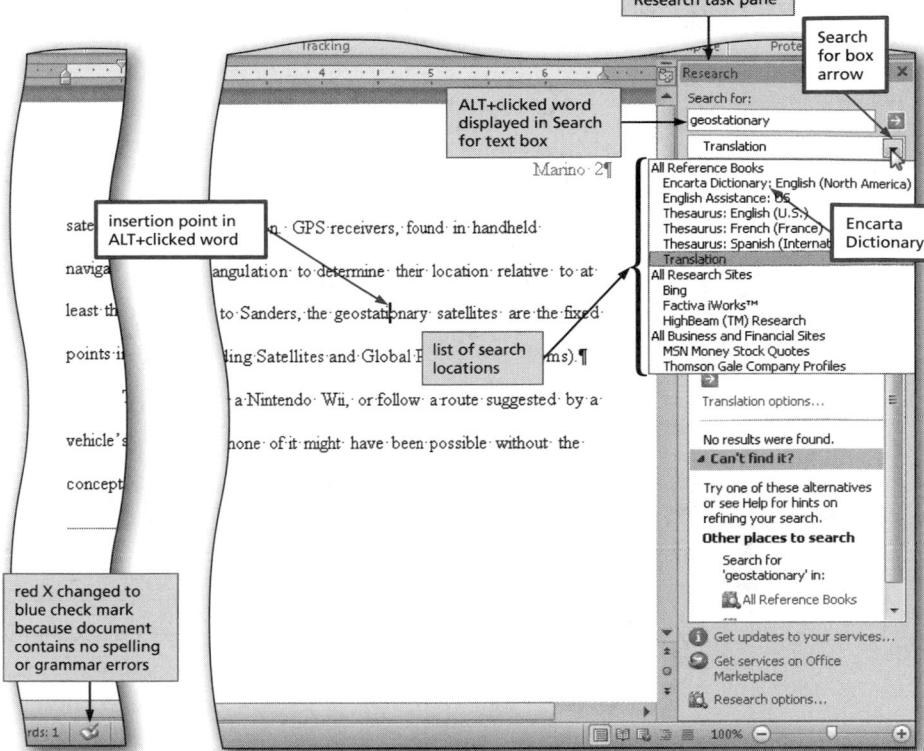

Figure 2–74

• Click Encarta Dictionary in the list to display a definition for the ALT+clicked word (Figure 2–75).

Can I copy information from the Research task pane into my document?

Yes, you can use the Copy and Paste commands. When using Word to insert material from the Research task pane or any other online reference, however, be careful not to plagiarize.

3

• Click the Close button in the Research task pane.

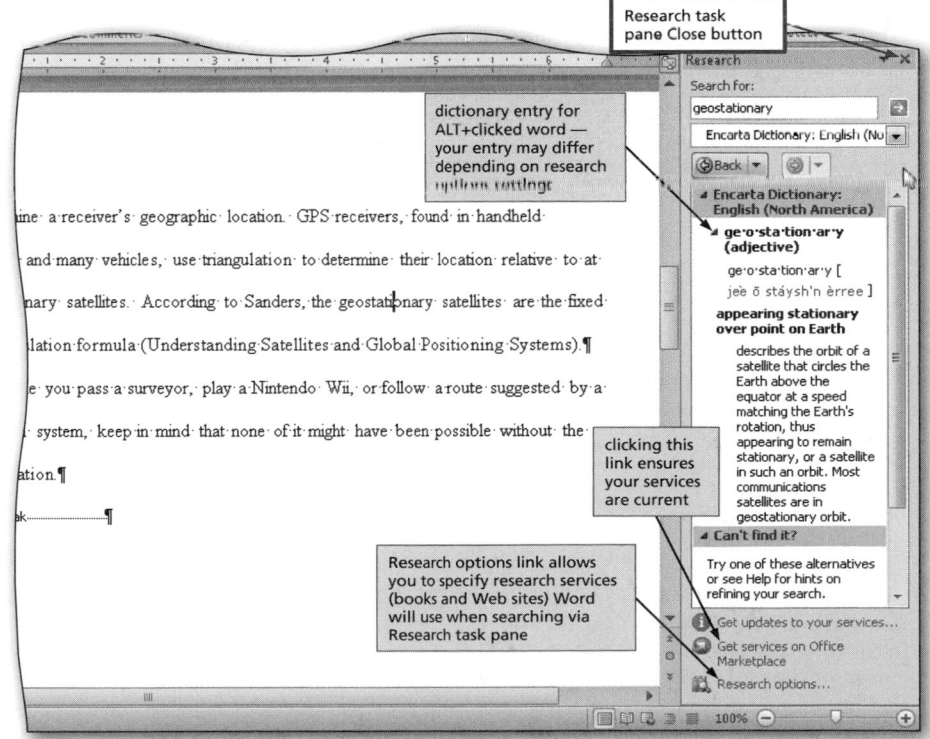

Figure 2–75

Other Ways

1. Click Research button (Review tab | Proofing group)

BTW

Grammar and Style Options
To set grammar and writing style options, click File on the Ribbon to open the Backstage view, click the Options button, and then click Proofing in the left pane (Word Options dialog box) to display a variety of spelling and grammar options that you can select or deselect by placing or removing check marks. To specify how Word checks grammar, click the Settings button in the right pane (Word Options dialog box) and then select the desired settings in the Grammar Settings dialog box.

Research Task Pane Options

When you install Word, it selects a series of services (reference books and Web sites) that it searches through when you use the Research task pane. You can view, modify, and update the list of services at any time.

Clicking the Research options link at the bottom of the Research task pane (shown in Figure 2–75 on the previous page) displays the Research Options dialog box, where you can view or modify the list of installed services. You can view information about any installed service by clicking the service in the list and then clicking the Properties button. To activate an installed service, click the check box to its left; likewise, to deactivate a service, remove the check mark. To add a particular Web site to the list, click the Add Services button, enter the Web address in the Address text box, and then click the Add button (Add Services dialog box). To update or remove services, click the Update/Remove button, select the service in the list, click the Update (or Remove) button (Update or Remove Services dialog box), and then click the Close button. You also can install parental controls through the Parental Control button (Research Options dialog box), for example, if you want to prevent minor children who use Word from accessing the Web.

To Change Document Properties

Before saving the research paper again, you want to add your name, course information, and some keywords as document properties. The following steps use the Document Information Panel to change document properties.

1 Click File on the Ribbon to open the Backstage view and, if necessary, select the Info tab.

2 Click the Properties button in the right pane of the Info gallery to display the Properties menu and then click Show Document Panel on the Properties menu to close the Backstage view and display the Document Information Panel in the Word document window.

3 Click the Author text box, if necessary, and then type your name as the Author property. If a name already is displayed in the Author text box, delete it before typing your name.

4 Click the Subject text box, if necessary delete any existing text, and then type your course and section as the Subject property.

5 Click the Keywords text box, if necessary delete any existing text, and then type **surveyor, Wii, GPS** as the Keywords property.

6 Click the Close the Document Information Panel button so that the Document Information Panel no longer is displayed.

To Save an Existing Document with the Same File Name

You have made several modifications to the document since you last saved it. Thus, you should save it again. The following step saves the document again.

1 Click the Save button on the Quick Access Toolbar to overwrite the previously saved file.

BTW

Conserving Ink and Toner
If you want to conserve ink or toner, you can instruct Word to print draft quality documents by clicking File on the Ribbon to open the Backstage view, clicking Options in the Backstage view to display the Word Options dialog box, clicking Advanced in the left pane (Word Options dialog box), scrolling to the Print area in the right pane, placing a check mark in the 'Use draft quality' check box, and then clicking the OK button. Then, use the Backstage view to print the document as usual.

To Print Document Properties

With the document properties entered and the completed document saved, you may want to print the document properties along with the document. The following steps print the document properties for the Triangulation Paper.

1

- Click File on the Ribbon to open the Backstage view and then click the Print tab in the Backstage view to display the Print gallery.

- Verify the printer name that appears on the Printer Status button will print a hard copy of the document. If necessary, click the Printer Status button to display a list of available printer options and then click the desired printer to change the currently selected printer.

- Click the first button in the Settings area to display a list of options specifying what you can print (Figure 2–76).

2

- Click Document Properties in the list to specify you want to print the document properties instead of the actual document.

- Click the Print button in the Print gallery to print the document properties on the currently selected printer (Figure 2–77).

What if the currently updated document properties do not print on the hard copy?

Try closing the document, reopening the document, and then repeating these steps.

Figure 2–76

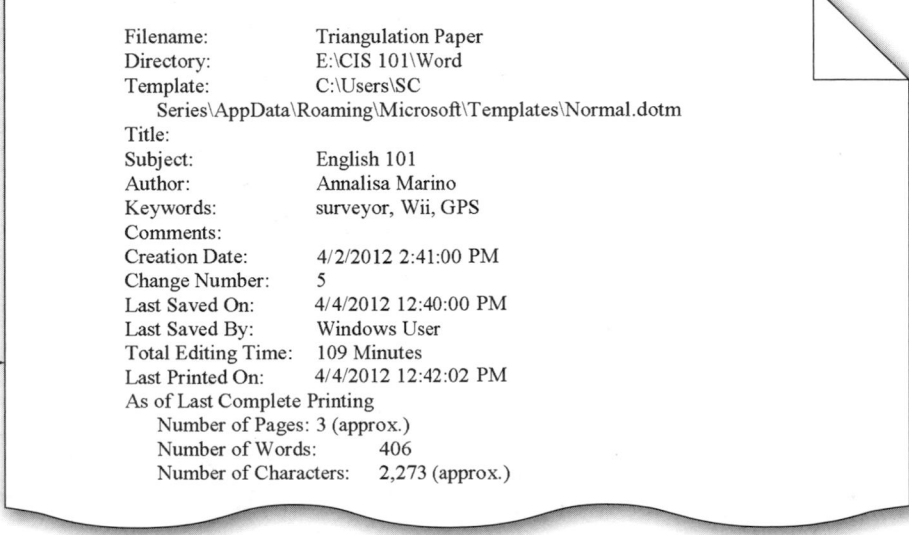

Filename:	Triangulation Paper
Directory:	E:\CIS 101\Word
Template:	C:\Users\SC
	Series\AppData\Roaming\Microsoft\Templates\Normal.dotm
Title:	
Subject:	English 101
Author:	Annalisa Marino
Keywords:	surveyor, Wii, GPS
Comments:	
Creation Date:	4/2/2012 2:41:00 PM
Change Number:	5
Last Saved On:	4/4/2012 12:40:00 PM
Last Saved By:	Windows User
Total Editing Time:	109 Minutes
Last Printed On:	4/4/2012 12:42:02 PM
As of Last Complete Printing	
Number of Pages:	3 (approx.)
Number of Words:	406
Number of Characters:	2,273 (approx.)

Figure 2–77

Other Ways
1. Press CTRL+P, press ENTER

To Preview the Document and Then Print It

Before printing the research paper, you want to verify the page layouts. The following steps change the print option to print the document (instead of the document properties), preview the printed pages in the research paper, and then print the document.

- Position the insertion point at the top of the document because you want initially to view the first page in the document.

- Click File on the Ribbon to open the Backstage view and then click the Print tab in the Backstage view to display the Print gallery.

- Verify the printer name that appears on the Printer Status button will print a hard copy of the document. If necessary, select a different printer.

- Click the first button in the Settings area to display a list of options specifying what you can print (Figure 2–78).

Figure 2–78

- Click Print All Pages in the list to specify you want to print all pages in the actual document.

- Click the Next Page button in the Print gallery to preview the second page of the research paper in the Print gallery.

- Click the Next Page button again to preview the third page of the research paper in the Print gallery (Figure 2–79).

- Click the Print button in the Print gallery to print the research paper on the currently selected printer (shown in Figure 2–1 on page WD 67).

Figure 2–79

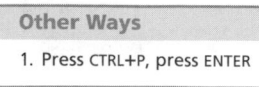

Other Ways

1. Press CTRL+P, press ENTER

To Quit Word

This project now is complete. The following steps quit Word. For a detailed example of the procedure summarized below, refer to the Office 2010 and Windows 7 chapter at the beginning of this book.

1 If you have one Word document open, click the Close button on the right side of the title bar to close the document and quit Word; or if you have multiple Word documents open, click File on the Ribbon to open the Backstage view and then click Exit in the Backstage view to close all open documents and quit Word.

2 If a Microsoft Word dialog box appears, click the Save button to save any changes made to the document since the last save.

BTW

Quick Reference
For a table that lists how to complete the tasks covered in this book using the mouse, Ribbon, shortcut menu, and keyboard, see the Quick Reference Summary at the back of this book, or visit the Word 2010 Quick Reference Web page (scsite.com/wd2010/qr).

Chapter Summary

In this chapter, you have learned how to change document settings, use headers to number pages, modify a style, insert and edit citations and their sources, add footnotes, create a bibliographical list of sources, and use the Research task pane. The items listed below include all the new Word skills you have learned in this chapter.

1. Modify a Style (WD 70)
2. Change Line Spacing (WD 73)
3. Remove Space after a Paragraph (WD 74)
4. Update a Style to Match a Selection (WD 74)
5. Switch to the Header (WD 75)
6. Right-Align a Paragraph (WD 76)
7. Insert a Page Number (WD 77)
8. Close the Header (WD 78)
9. Click and Type (WD 80)
10. Display the Rulers (WD 82)
11. First-Line Indent Paragraphs (WD 83)
12. AutoCorrect as You Type (WD 85)
13. Use the AutoCorrect Options Button (WD 85)
14. Create an AutoCorrect Entry (WD 86)
15. Change the Bibliography Style (WD 89)
16. Insert a Citation and Create Its Source (WD 90)
17. Edit a Citation (WD 91)
18. Insert a Footnote Reference Mark (WD 93)
19. Insert a Citation Placeholder (WD 94)
20. Modify a Style Using a Shortcut Menu (WD 95)
21. Edit a Source (WD 97)
22. Count Words (WD 101)
23. Page Break Manually (WD 106)
24. Apply a Style (WD 106)
25. Create the Bibliographical List (WD 108)
26. Format Paragraphs with a Hanging Indent (WD 109)
27. Modify a Source and Update the Bibliographical List (WD 109)
28. Convert a Field to Regular Text (WD 110)
29. Scroll Page by Page through a Document (WD 112)
30. Copy and Paste (WD 113)
31. Display the Paste Options Menu (WD 114)
32. Find Text (WD 115)
33. Replace Text (WD 116)
34. Go to a Page (WD 117)
35. Find and Insert a Synonym (WD 118)
36. Check Spelling and Grammar at Once (WD 118)
37. View or Modify Entries in a Custom Dictionary (WD 120)
38. Set the Default Custom Dictionary (WD 120)
39. Use the Research Task Pane to Look Up Information (WD 120)
40. Print Document Properties (WD 123)
41. Preview the Document and Then Print It (WD 124)

 If you have a SAM 2010 user profile, your instructor may have assigned an autogradable version of this assignment. If so, log into the SAM 2010 Web site at www.cengage.com/sam2010 to download the instruction and start files.

Learn It Online

Test your knowledge of chapter content and key terms.

Instructions: To complete the Learn It Online exercises, start your browser, click the Address bar, and then enter the Web address **scsite.com/wd2010/learn**. When the Word 2010 Learn It Online page is displayed, click the link for the exercise you want to complete and then read the instructions.

Chapter Reinforcement TF, MC, and SA
A series of true/false, multiple choice, and short answer questions that test your knowledge of the chapter content.

Flash Cards
An interactive learning environment where you identify chapter key terms associated with displayed definitions.

Practice Test
A series of multiple choice questions that test your knowledge of chapter content and key terms.

Who Wants To Be a Computer Genius?
An interactive game that challenges your knowledge of chapter content in the style of a television quiz show.

Wheel of Terms
An interactive game that challenges your knowledge of chapter key terms in the style of the television show *Wheel of Fortune*.

Crossword Puzzle Challenge
A crossword puzzle that challenges your knowledge of key terms presented in the chapter.

Apply Your Knowledge

Reinforce the skills and apply the concepts you learned in this chapter.

Revising Text and Paragraphs in a Document

Note: To complete this assignment, you will be required to use the Data Files for Students. See the inside back cover of this book for instructions on downloading the Data Files for Students, or contact your instructor for information about accessing the required files.

Instructions: Start Word. Open the document, Apply 2-1 Space Paragraph Draft, from the Data Files for Students. The document you open contains a paragraph of text. You are to revise the document as follows: move a word, move another word and change the format of the moved word, change paragraph indentation, change line spacing, find all occurrences of a word, replace all occurrences of a word with another word, locate a synonym, and edit the header.

Perform the following tasks:
1. Copy the word, exploration, from the first sentence and paste it in the last sentence after the word, space, so that it is the eighth word in the sentence.
2. Select the underlined word, safe, in the paragraph. Use drag-and-drop editing to move the selected word, safe, so that it is before the word, mission, in the same sentence. Click the Paste Options button that displays to the right of the moved word, safe. Remove the underline format from the moved sentence by clicking Keep Text Only on the Paste Options menu.
3. Display the ruler, if necessary. Use the ruler to indent the first line of the paragraph one-half inch.
4. Change the line spacing of the paragraph to double.
5. Use the Navigation Pane to find all occurrences of the word, sensors. How many are there?
6. Use the Find and Replace dialog box to replace all occurrences of the word, issues, with the word, problems. How many replacements were made?

7. Use Word to find the word, height. Use Word's thesaurus to change the word, height, to the word, altitude.

8. Switch to the header so that you can edit it. In the first line of the header, change the word, Draft, to the word, Modified, so that it reads: Space Paragraph Modified.

9. In the second line of the header, insert the page number (with no formatting) one space after the word, Page.

10. Change the alignment of both lines of text in the header from left-aligned to right-aligned. Switch back to the document text.

11. Change the document properties, as specified by your instructor.

12. Click File on the Ribbon and then click Save As. Save the document using the file name, Apply 2-1 Space Paragraph Modified.

13. Print the document properties and then print the revised document, shown in Figure 2–80.

14. Use the Research task pane to look up the definition of the word, NASA, in the paragraph. Handwrite the definition of the word on your printout, as well as your response to the question in #6.

15. Change the Search for box to All Research Sites. Print an article from one of the sites.

16. Display the Research Options dialog box and, on your printout, handwrite the currently active Reference Books, Research Sites, and Business and Financial Sites. If your instructor approves, activate one of the services.

Figure 2–80

Extend Your Knowledge

Extend the skills you learned in this chapter and experiment with new skills. You may need to use Help to complete the assignment.

Working with References and Proofing Tools

Note: To complete this assignment, you will be required to use the Data Files for Students. See the inside back cover of this book for instructions on downloading the Data Files for Students, or contact your instructor for information about accessing the required files.

Instructions: Start Word. Open the document, Extend 2-1 Digital Camera Paper Draft, from the Data Files for Students. You will add another footnote to the paper, use the thesaurus, convert the document from MLA to APA documentation style, convert the footnotes to endnotes, modify the Endnote Text style, change the format of the note reference marks, and translate the document to another language (Figure 2–81).

Figure 2–81

Perform the following tasks:

1. Use Help to learn more about footers, footnotes and endnotes, bibliography styles, AutoCorrect, and the Mini Translator.

2. Delete the footer from the document.

3. Insert a second footnote at an appropriate place in the research paper. Use the following footnote text: For instance, Adams states that you may be able to crop photos, change the brightness, or remove red eye effects.

4. Change the location of the footnotes from bottom of page to below text.

5. Use the Find and Replace dialog box to find the word, small, in the document and then replace it with a word of your choice.

6. Save the document with a new file name and then print it. On the printout, write the number of words, characters without spaces, characters with spaces, paragraphs, and lines in the document. Be sure to include footnote text in the statistics.

7. Select the entire document and then change the documentation style of the citations and bibliography from MLA to APA. Save the APA version of the document with a new file name and then print it. Compare the two versions. Circle the differences between the two documents.

8. Convert the footnotes to endnotes.

9. Modify the Endnote Text style to 12-point Times New Roman font, double-spaced text with a hanging-line indent.

0. Change the format of the note reference marks to capital letters (A, B, etc.).

1. Add an AutoCorrect entry that replaces the word, camora, with the word, camera. Add this sentence, A field camora usually is more than sufficient for most users., to the end of the second paragraph, misspelling the word camera to test the AutoCorrect entry. Delete the AutoCorrect entry that replaces camora with the word, camera.

2. Display readability statistics. What are the Flesch-Kincaid Grade Level, the Flesch Reading Ease score, and the percent of passive sentences?

3. Save the revised document with endnotes with a new file name and then print it. On the printout, write your response to the question in #12.

4. If you have an Internet connection, translate the research paper into a language of your choice using the Translate button (Review tab | Language group). Submit the translated document in the format specified by your instructor. Use the Mini Translator to hear how to pronounce three words in your paper.

Make It Right

Analyze a document and correct all errors and/or improve the design.

Inserting Missing Elements in an MLA-Styled Research Paper

Note: To complete this assignment, you will be required to use the Data Files for Students. See the inside back cover of this book for instructions on downloading the Data Files for Students, or contact your instructor for information about accessing the required files.

Instructions: Start Word. Open the document, Make It Right 2-1 Biometrics Paper Draft, from the Data Files for Students. The document is a research paper that is missing several elements. You are to insert these missing elements, all formatted according to the MLA documentation style: header with a page number, name and course information, paper title, footnote, and source information for a citation.

Perform the following tasks:

1. Insert a header with a page number (use your own last name). Also, insert name and course information (your name, your instructor name, your course name, and today's date), and an appropriate paper title, all formatted according to the MLA documentation style.

2. The Jenkins citation placeholder is missing its source information (Figure 2–82). Use the following source information to edit the source: magazine article titled "Fingerprint Readers" written by Arthur D. Jenkins and Marissa K. Weavers, magazine name is *Security Today*, publication date is February 2012, article is on pages 55–60. Edit the citation so that it displays the author name and the page numbers of 55–56 for this reference.

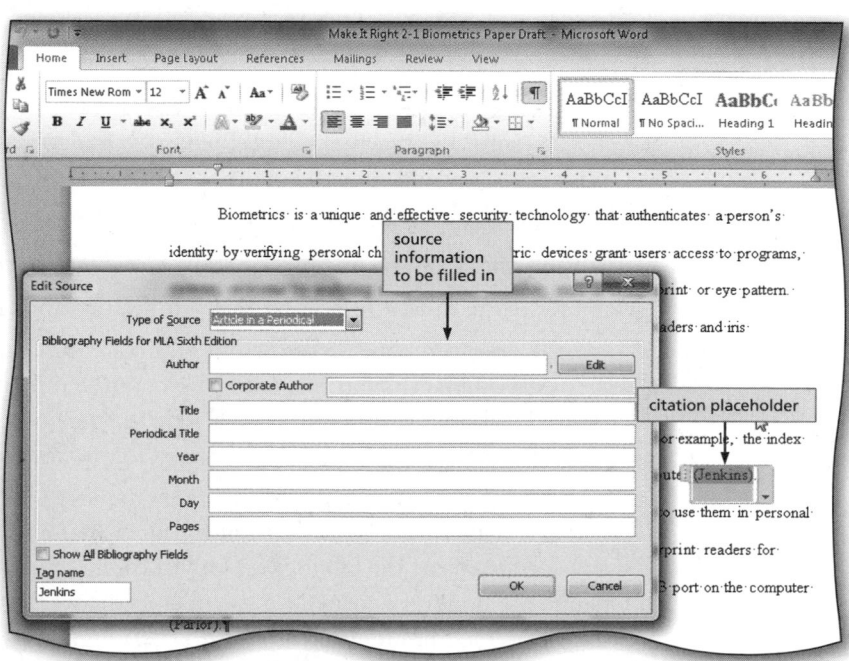

Figure 2–82

Continued >

STUDENT ASSIGNMENTS

Make It Right *continued*

3. Modify the source of the book authored by Carolina Doe, so that the publisher city is Chicago instead of Dallas.

4. Change the Footnote Text style to 12-point Times New Roman, double-spaced paragraphs with a first-line indent.

5. Insert the following footnote with the note reference at an appropriate place in the paper, formatted according to the MLA documentation style: Parlor states that one use of fingerprint readers is for users to log on to programs and Web sites via their fingerprint instead of entering a user name and password.

6. Use the Navigation Pane to display page 3. Use Word to insert the bibliographical list (bibliography). Convert the works cited to regular text. Change the underline format on the titles of the works to the italic format, and insert the correct publication medium for each work.

7. Change the document properties, as specified by your instructor. Save the revised document with the file name, Make It Right 2-1 Biometrics Paper Modified, and then submit it in the format specified by your instructor.

In the Lab

Design and/or create a document using the guidelines, concepts, and skills presented in this chapter. Labs are listed in order of increasing difficulty.

Lab 1: Preparing a Short Research Paper

Problem: You are a college student currently enrolled in an introductory business class. Your assignment is to prepare a short research paper (275–300 words) about video or computer games. The requirements are that the paper be presented according to the MLA documentation style and have three references. One of the three references must be from the Web. You prepare the paper shown in Figure 2–83 on pages WD 131 and WD 132, which discusses game controllers.

Instructions: Perform the following tasks:

1. Start Word. If necessary, display formatting marks on the screen.

2. Modify the Normal style to 12-point Times New Roman font.

3. Adjust line spacing to double.

4. Remove space below (after) paragraphs.

5. Update the Normal style to reflect the adjusted line and paragraph spacing.

6. Create a header to number pages.

7. Type the name and course information at the left margin. Center and type the title.

8. Set a first-line indent to one-half inch for paragraphs in the body of the research paper.

9. Type the research paper as shown in Figures 2–83a and 2–83b. Change the bibliography style to MLA. As you insert citations, enter their source information (shown in Figure 2–83c). The first citation is a book; the second is an article in a periodical; and the third is a Web site. Edit the citations so that they are displayed according to Figures 2–83a and 2–83b.

10. At the end of the research paper text, press the ENTER key and then insert a manual page break so that the Works Cited page begins on a new page. Enter and format the works cited title (Figure 2–83c). Use Word to insert the bibliographical list (bibliography). Convert the bibliography field to text. Change the underline format on the titles of the works to the italic format and insert the correct publication medium for each work (shown in Figure 2–83c).

(b) Page 2

Kimble 2

Game controllers are used primarily to direct movement and actions of on-screen objects. Two popular types are gamepads and motion-sensing game controllers. Games become more enjoyable every day with the use of new and exciting game controllers. What will be next?

a) Page 1

Kimble 1

Harley Kimble

Ms. Longherst

English 101

April 30, 2012

From One Controller to Another

Video games and computer games use a game controller as the input device that directs movements and actions of on-screen objects. Two commonly used game controllers are gamepads and motion-sensing game controllers (Joyce). Game controllers not only enrich the gaming experience but also aid in the movements and actions of players.

A gamepad is held by the player with both hands, allowing the player to control the movement or actions of the objects in the video or computer games. Players press buttons on the gamepad, often with their thumbs, to carry out actions. Some gamepads have swiveling sticks that also can trigger events during game play (Cortez 20-24). Some gamepads include wireless capabilities; others connect via a cable directly to the game console or a personal computer.

Motion-sensing game controllers allow the user to guide on-screen elements or trigger events by moving a handheld input device in predetermined directions through the air. These controllers communicate with a game console or personal computer via wired or wireless technology. A variety of games, from sports to simulations, use motion-sensing game controllers. Some of these controllers, such as baseball bats and golf clubs, are designed for only one specific kind of game; others are general purpose. A popular, general-purpose, motion-sensing game controller is Nintendo's Wii Remote. Shaped like a television remote control and operated with one hand, the Wii Remote uses Bluetooth wireless technology to communicate with the Wii game console (Bloom 56-59).

Figure 2–83

Continued >

(c) Page 3

Kimble 3

Works Cited

Bloom, June. *The Gaming Experience*. New York: Buffalo Works Press, 2012. Print.

Cortez, Domiciano Isachar. "Today's Game Controllers." *Gaming, Gaming, Gaming* Jan. 2012:

12-34. Print.

Joyce, Andrea D. *What Gamers Want*. 15 Feb. 2012. Web. 28 Mar. 2012.

11. Check the spelling and grammar of the paper at once.

12. Change the document properties, as specified by your instructor. Save the document using Lab 2-1
    Game Controllers Paper as the file name.

13. Print the research paper. Handwrite the number of words, paragraphs, and characters in the
    research paper above the title of your printed research paper.

In the Lab

Lab 2: Preparing a Research Report with a Footnote

Problem: You are a college student enrolled in an introductory English class. Your assignment is to
prepare a short research paper in any area of interest to you. The requirements are that the paper
be presented according to the MLA documentation style, contain at least one note positioned as
a footnote, and have three references. One of the three references must be from the Internet. You
prepare a paper about trends in agriculture (Figure 2–84).

Instructions: Perform the following tasks:
  1. Start Word. Modify the Normal style to 12-point Times New Roman font. Adjust line spacing to
     double and remove space below (after) paragraphs. Update the Normal style to include the adjusted
     line and paragraph spacing. Create a header to number pages. Type the name and course information
     at the left margin. Center and type the title. Set a first-line indent for paragraphs in the body of the
     research paper.
  2. Type the research paper as shown in Figures 2–84a and 2–84b. Insert the footnote as shown in
     Figure 2–84a. Change the Footnote Text style to the format specified in the MLA documentation
     style. Change the bibliography style to MLA. As you insert citations, use the source information
     listed below and on page WD 134:
     a. Type of Source: Article in a Periodical
        Author: Barton, Blake
        Title: Computers in Agriculture
        Periodical Title: Agriculture Today and Tomorrow
        Year: 2012
        Month: Feb.
        Pages 53–86
        Publication Medium: Print

(b) Page 2

Gander 2

Brewster, the discovery of pests might trigger a pesticide to discharge in the affected area

automatically (Agriculture: Expanding and Growing).

Many farmers use technology on a daily basis to regulate soil moisture and to keep their

crops pest free. With technology, farming can be much more convenient and efficient.

(a) Page 1

Gander 1

Samuel Gander

Mr. Dunham

English 102

April 25, 2012

Farming on a Whole New Level

Although people have worked in agriculture for more than 10,000 years, advances in

technology assist with maintaining and protecting land, crops, and animals. The demand to keep

food prices affordable encourages those working in the agriculture industry to operate as

efficiently as possible (Newman and Ruiz 33-47).

Almost all people and companies in this industry have many acres of land they must

maintain, and it is not always feasible for farmers to take frequent trips around the property to

perform basic tasks such as watering soil in the absence of rain. The number of people-hours

required to water soil manually on several thousand acres of land might result in businesses

spending thousands of dollars in labor and utility costs. If the irrigation process is automated,

sensors detect how much rain has fallen recently, as well as whether the soil is in need of

watering. The sensors then send this data to a computer that processes it and decides when and

how much to water.[1]

In addition to keeping the soil moist and reducing maintenance costs, computers also can

utilize sensors to analyze the condition of crops in the field and determine whether pests or

diseases are affecting the crops. If sensors detect pests and/or diseases, computers send a

notification to the appropriate individual to take corrective action. In some cases, according to

_____

[1] Barton states that many automated home irrigation systems also are programmable and

use rain sensors (67-73).

Figure 2–84

Continued >

In the Lab *continued*

    b. Type of Source: Book
       Author: Newman, Albert D., and Carmen W. Ruiz
       Title: The Agricultural Industry Today
       Year: 2012
       City: New York
       Publisher: Alabama Press
       Publication Medium: Print

    c. Type of Source: Web site
       Author: Brewster, Letty
       Name of Web page: Agriculture: Expanding and Growing
       Year: 2012
       Month: Jan.
       Day: 3
       Publication Medium: Web
       Year Accessed: 2012
       Month Accessed: Feb.
       Day Accessed: 9

3. At the end of the research paper text, press the ENTER key once and insert a manual page break so that the Works Cited page begins on a new page. Enter and format the works cited title. Use Word to insert the bibliographical list. Convert the bibliography field to text. Change the underline format on the titles of the works to the italic format, and insert the correct publication medium for each work.

4. Check the spelling and grammar of the paper.

5. Save the document using Lab 2-2 Agriculture Paper as the file name.

6. Print the research paper. Handwrite the number of words, including the footnotes, in the research paper above the title of your printed research paper.

In the Lab

Lab 3: Composing a Research Paper from Notes

Problem: You have drafted the notes shown in Figure 2–85. Your assignment is to prepare a short research paper from these notes.

Instructions: Perform the following tasks:

1. Start Word. Review the notes in Figure 2–85 and then rearrange and reword them. Embellish the paper as you deem necessary. Present the paper according to the MLA documentation style.

    Create an AutoCorrect entry that automatically corrects the spelling of the misspelled word, digtal, to the correct spelling, digital. Set an AutoCorrect exception for CD., so that Word does not lowercase the next typed letter.

    Insert a footnote that refers the reader to the Web for more information. Enter citations and their sources as shown.

    Create the works cited page (bibliography) from the listed sources. Convert the bibliography field to text. Change the underline format on the titles of the works to the italic format, and insert the correct publication medium for each work.

2. If necessary, set the default dictionary. Add the word, Flickr, to the dictionary. Check the spelling and grammar of the paper.

3. Use the Research task pane to look up a definition of a word in the paper. Copy and insert the definition into the document as a footnote. Be sure to quote the definition and cite the source. *Hint:* Use a Web site as the type of source.

4. Save the document using Lab 2-3 Cloud Storage Paper as the file name. Print the research paper. Handwrite the number of words, including the footnotes, in the research paper above the title of the printed research paper.

Cloud Storage:

- When storing data using cloud storage, the user must locate the appropriate Web site. Some sites support only certain file types. Other sites provide more than just storage.
- Cloud storage is one of the many different features available on the Internet.
- Cloud storage allows users to store files on Web sites.
- Computer users may use this type of storage if they do not want to store their data locally on a hard disk or other type of media.

Different Web sites provide different types of cloud storage. Three are Google's Gmail, YouTube, and Windows Live SkyDrive (source: "Cloud Storage and the Internet," an article on pages 23-37 in March 2012 issue of *Internet Usage and Trends* by Leona Carter).

- Google's e-mail program, Gmail, is cloud storage that stores e-mail messages.
- YouTube is different from Gmail, however, because it stores only digital videos (source: pages 22-24 in a book called *Working with the Internet: Cloud Storage* by Robert M. Gaff, published at Jane Lewis Press in New York in 2012).
- Windows Live SkyDrive is a cloud storage provider that accepts any type of file. This type of Web site is used mainly for backup or additional storage space.

Some cloud storage Web sites also provide other services (source: a Web site titled *The Internet: Cloud Storage* by Rebecca A. Ford and Harry I. Garland of Course Technology dated January 2, 2012, viewed on March 7, 2012).

- Flickr provides cloud storage for digital photos and also enables users to manage their photos and share them with others.
- Facebook provides cloud storage for a number of different file types including digital photos, digital videos, messages, and personal information. Facebook also provides a means of social networking.
- Google Docs not only stores documents, spreadsheets, and presentations in its cloud, it also enables its users to create these documents.

Figure 2–85

Cases and Places

Apply your creative thinking and problem solving skills to design and implement a solution.

Note: To complete these assignments, you may be required to use the Data Files for Students. See the inside back cover of this book for instructions on downloading the Data Files for Students, or contact your instructor for information about accessing the required files.

1: Create a Research Paper about Preparing for a Career in the Computer Industry

Academic

As a student in an introductory computer class, your instructor has assigned a research paper that discusses educational options available for students pursuing a career in the computer industry. The source for the text in your research paper is in a file called Preparing for a Career in the Computer Industry, which is located on the Data Files for Students. In addition to this source, if your instructor requests, use the Research task pane to obtain information from another source. Include a note positioned as a footnote. Add an AutoCorrect entry to correct a word you commonly mistype.

Using the concepts and techniques presented in this chapter, along with the text in the file on the Data Files for Students, create and format this research paper according to the MLA documentation style. Be sure to check spelling and grammar of the finished paper. Submit your assignment in the format specified by your instructor.

2: Create a Research Paper about Computer Viruses

Personal

The computer you recently purchased included an antivirus program. Because you need practice writing research papers and you want to learn more about computer viruses, you decide to write a paper about computer viruses. The source for the text in your research paper is in a file called Computer Viruses, which is located on the Data Files for Students. In addition to this source, if your instructor requests, use the Research task pane to obtain information from another source. Include a note positioned as a footnote. Add an AutoCorrect entry to correct a word you commonly mistype.

Using the concepts and techniques presented in this chapter, along with the text in the file on the Data Files for Students, create and format this research paper according to the MLA documentation style. Be sure to check spelling and grammar of the finished paper. Submit your assignment in the format specified by your instructor.

3: Create a Research Paper about a Disaster Recovery Plan

Professional

Your boss has asked you to research the components of a disaster recovery plan. Because you learned in college how to write research papers, you decide to present your findings in a research paper. The source for the text in your research paper is in a file called Disaster Recovery Plan, which is located on the Data Files for Students. In addition to this source, if your instructor requests, use the Research task pane to obtain information from another source. Include a note positioned as a footnote. Add an AutoCorrect entry to correct a word you commonly mistype.

Using the concepts and techniques presented in this chapter, along with the text in the file on the Data Files for Students, create and format this research paper according to the MLA documentation style. Be sure to check spelling and grammar of the finished paper. Submit your assignment in the format specified by your instructor.

3 | Creating a Business Letter with a Letterhead and Table

Objectives

You will have mastered the material in this chapter when you can:

- Change margins
- Insert and format a shape
- Change text wrapping
- Insert and format a clip art image
- Insert a symbol
- Add a border to a paragraph
- Clear formatting
- Convert a hyperlink to regular text

- Create a file from an existing file
- Apply a Quick Style
- Set and use tab stops
- Insert the current date
- Create, insert, and modify a building block
- Insert a Word table, enter data in the table, and format the table
- Address and print an envelope

3 | Creating a Business Letter with a Letterhead and Table

Introduction

In a business environment, people use documents to communicate with others. Business documents can include letters, memos, newsletters, proposals, and resumes. An effective business document clearly and concisely conveys its message and has a professional, organized appearance. You can use your own creative skills to design and compose business documents. Using Word, for example, you can develop the content and decide on the location of each item in a business document.

Project — Business Letter with a Letterhead and Table

At some time, you will prepare some type of business letter. Contents of business letters include requests, inquiries, confirmations, acknowledgements, recommendations, notifications, responses, invitations, offers, referrals, complaints, and more.

The project in this chapter follows generally accepted guidelines for writing letters and uses Word to create the business letter shown in Figure 3–1. This business letter to a potential advertiser (Wilcox Tractor Restorations) includes a custom letterhead, as well as all essential business letter components: date line, inside address, salutation, body, complimentary close, and signature block. To easily present the advertisement rates, this information appears in a table, and the discounts are in a bulleted list.

Overview

As you read through this chapter, you will learn how to create the business letter in Figure 3–1 by performing these general tasks:

- Design and create a letterhead.
- Compose a business letter.
- Print the business letter.
- Address and print an envelope.

business letter

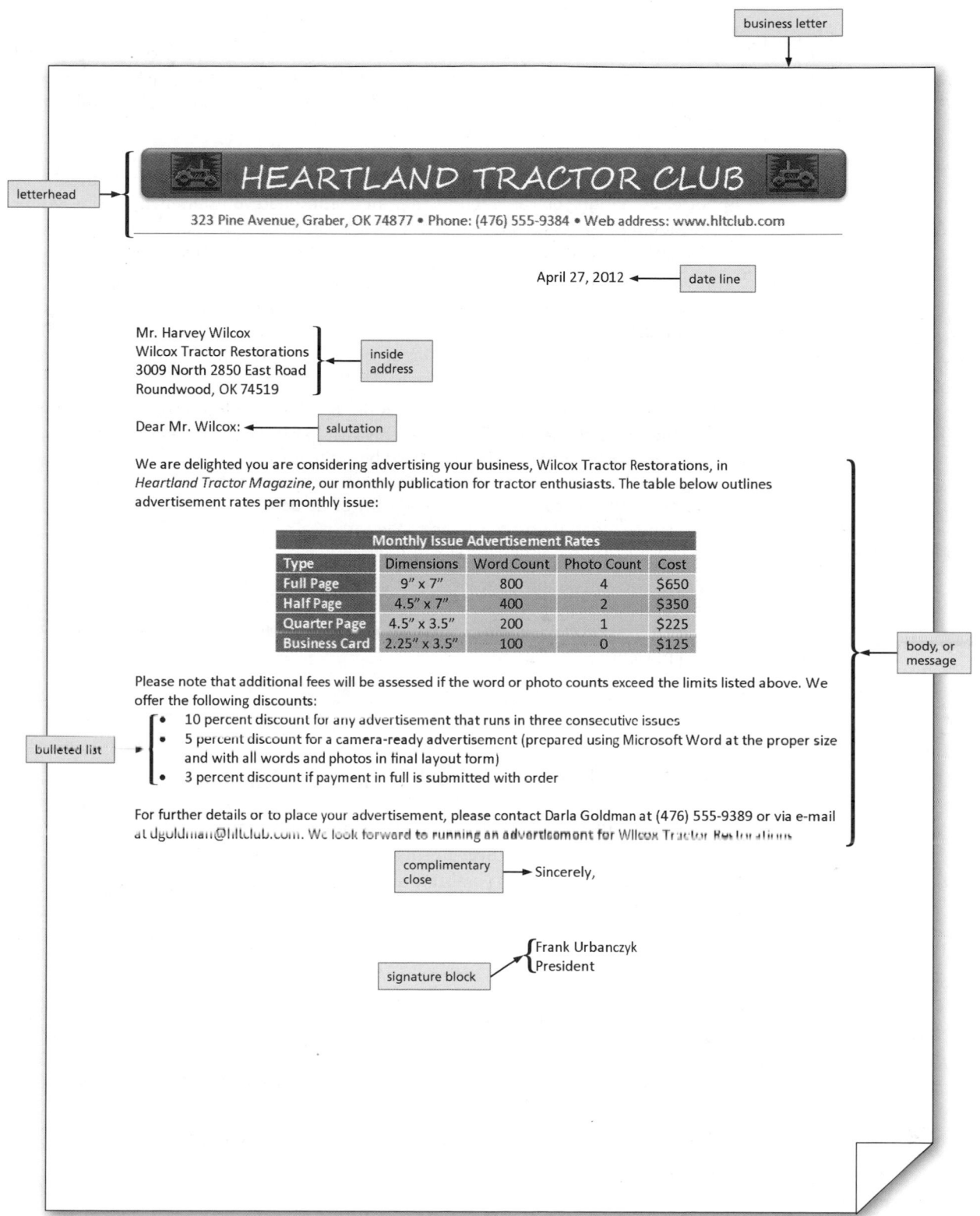

letterhead

HEARTLAND TRACTOR CLUB

323 Pine Avenue, Graber, OK 74877 • Phone: (476) 555-9384 • Web address: www.hltclub.com

April 27, 2012   ◄   date line

Mr. Harvey Wilcox
Wilcox Tractor Restorations   inside
3009 North 2850 East Road   address
Roundwood, OK 74519

Dear Mr. Wilcox: ◄   salutation

We are delighted you are considering advertising your business, Wilcox Tractor Restorations, in *Heartland Tractor Magazine*, our monthly publication for tractor enthusiasts. The table below outlines advertisement rates per monthly issue:

Monthly Issue Advertisement Rates				
Type	Dimensions	Word Count	Photo Count	Cost
Full Page	9" x 7"	800	4	$650
Half Page	4.5" x 7"	400	2	$350
Quarter Page	4.5" x 3.5"	200	1	$225
Business Card	2.25" x 3.5"	100	0	$125

body, or message

Please note that additional fees will be assessed if the word or photo counts exceed the limits listed above. We offer the following discounts:

bulleted list

- 10 percent discount for any advertisement that runs in three consecutive issues
- 5 percent discount for a camera-ready advertisement (prepared using Microsoft Word at the proper size and with all words and photos in final layout form)
- 3 percent discount if payment in full is submitted with order

For further details or to place your advertisement, please contact Darla Goldman at (476) 555-9389 or via e-mail at dgoldman@hltclub.com. We look forward to running an advertisement for Wilcox Tractor Restorations.

complimentary
close   ►   Sincerely,

Frank Urbanczyk
President
signature block

Figure 3–1

Plan Ahead

General Project Guidelines

When creating a Word document, the actions you perform and decisions you make will affect the appearance and characteristics of the finished document. As you create a business letter, such as the project shown in Figure 3–1 on the previous page, you should follow these general guidelines:

1. **Determine how to create a letterhead.** A **letterhead** is the section of a letter that identifies an organization or individual. Often, the letterhead appears at the top of a letter. Although you can design and print a letterhead yourself, many businesses pay an outside firm to design and print their letterhead, usually on higher-quality paper. They then use the professionally preprinted paper for external business communications.

2. **If you do not have preprinted letterhead paper, design a creative letterhead.** Use text, graphics, formats, and colors that reflect the organization or individual. Include the organization's or individual's name, postal mailing address, and telephone number. If the organization or individual has an e-mail address and Web address, you may include those as well.

3. **Compose an effective business letter.** A finished business letter should look like a symmetrically framed picture with evenly spaced margins, all balanced below an attractive letterhead. The letter should be well-written, properly formatted, logically organized, and use visuals where appropriate. The content of a letter should contain proper grammar, correct spelling, logically constructed sentences, flowing paragraphs, and sound ideas. If possible, keep the length of a business letter to one page. Be sure to proofread the finished letter carefully.

When necessary, more specific details concerning the above guidelines are presented at appropriate points in the chapter. The chapter also will identify the actions performed and decisions made regarding these guidelines during the creation of the business letter shown in Figure 3–1.

For an introduction to Windows 7 and instruction about how to perform basic Windows 7 tasks, read the Office 2010 and Windows 7 chapter at the beginning of this book, where you can learn how to resize windows, change screen resolution, create folders, move and rename files, use Windows Help, and much more.

To Start Word and Display Formatting Marks

If you are using a computer to step through the project in this chapter and you want your screens to match the figures in this book, you should change your screen's resolution to 1024 × 768. For information about how to change a computer's resolution, refer to the Office 2010 and Windows 7 chapter at the beginning of this book.

The following steps start Word and display formatting marks.

1 Start Word. If necessary, maximize the Word window.

2 If the Print Layout button on the status bar is not selected (shown in Figure 3–2), click it so that your screen is in Print Layout view.

3 Change your zoom to 110% (or a percent where the document is large enough for you easily to see its contents).

4 If the Show/Hide ¶ button (Home tab | Paragraph group) is not selected already, click it to display formatting marks on the screen.

For an introduction to Office 2010 and instruction about how to perform basic tasks in Office 2010 programs, read the Office 2010 and Windows 7 chapter at the beginning of this book, where you can learn how to start a program, use the Ribbon, save a file, open a file, quit a program, use Help, and much more.

To Change Theme Colors

Recall that Word provides document themes that contain a variety of color schemes to assist you in selecting complementary colors in a document. In a letter, select a color scheme that adequately reflects the organization or person. The letter in this chapter uses the Executive color scheme. The following steps change theme colors.

1. Click the Change Styles button (Home tab | Styles group) to display the Change Styles menu and then point to Colors on the Change Styles menu to display the Colors gallery.

2. Click Executive in the Colors gallery to change the document theme colors to the selected color scheme.

To Change Margin Settings

Word is preset to use standard 8.5-by-11-inch paper, with 1-inch top, bottom, left, and right margins. If you change the default (preset) margin settings, the new margin settings affect every page in the document. If you wanted the margins to affect just a portion of the document, you would divide the document into sections (discussed in a later chapter), which enables you to specify different margin settings for each section.

The business letter in this chapter uses .75-inch left and right margins and 1-inch top and bottom margins, so that more text can fit from left to right on the page. The following steps change margin settings.

1
- Display the Page Layout tab.
- Click the Margins button (Page Layout tab | Page Setup group) to display the Margins gallery (Figure 3–2).

2
- Click Moderate in the Margins gallery to change the margins to the specified settings.

What if the margin settings I want are not in the Margins gallery?

You can click Custom Margins in the Margins gallery and then enter your desired margin values in the top, bottom, left, and right text boxes in the dialog box.

Figure 3–2

Creating a Letterhead

The cost of preprinted letterhead can be high. Thus, an alternative is to create your own letterhead and save it in a file. When you want to create a letter at a later time using the letterhead, simply create a new document from the letterhead file. In this chapter, you create a letterhead and then save it in a file for future use.

<table>
<tr><td>Plan
Ahead</td><td>

Design a creative letterhead.
A letterhead often is the first section a reader notices on a letter. Thus, it is important the letterhead appropriately reflect the essence of the business or individual (i.e., formal, technical, creative, etc.). The letterhead should leave ample room for the contents of the letter. When designing a letterhead, consider its contents, placement, and appearance.

• **Contents of letterhead.** A letterhead should contain these elements:

  • Complete legal name of the individual, group, or company

  • Complete mailing address: street address including building, room, suite number, or post office box, along with city, state, and postal code

  • Telephone number(s) and fax number, if one exists

  Many letterheads also include a Web address, an e-mail address, and a logo or other image. If you use an image, select one that expresses your personality or goals.

• **Placement of elements in the letterhead.** Many letterheads center their elements across the top of the page. Others align some or all of the elements with the left or right margins. Sometimes, the elements are split between the top and bottom of the page. For example, a name and logo may be at the top of the page with the address at the bottom of the page.

• **Appearance of letterhead elements.** Use fonts that are easy to read. Give the organization or individual name impact by making its font size larger than the rest of the text in the letterhead. For additional emphasis, consider formatting the name in bold, italic, or a different color. Choose colors that complement each other and convey the goals of the organization or individual.

  When finished designing the letterhead, determine if a divider line would help to visually separate the letterhead from the remainder of the letter.

</td></tr>
</table>

The letterhead for the business letter in this chapter consists of the organization name, appropriate graphics, postal address, telephone number, and Web address. The name and graphics are enclosed in a rectangular shape (Figure 3–1 on page WD 139), and the contact information is below the shape. You will follow these general steps to create the letterhead for the business letter:

1. Insert and format a shape.
2. Enter and format the organization name in the shape.
3. Insert, format, and position the images in the shape.
4. Enter the contact information below the shape.
5. Add a border below the contact information.

To Insert a Shape

The first step is in creating the letterhead in this chapter is to draw a rectangular shape. Word has a variety of predefined shapes, which are a type of drawing object, that you can insert in documents. A **drawing object** is a graphic that you create using Word. Examples of shape drawing objects include rectangles, circles, triangles, arrows, flowcharting symbols, stars, banners, and callouts. The next steps insert a rounded rectangle shape.

1

- Display the Insert tab.

- Click the Shapes button (Insert tab | Illustrations group) to display the Shapes gallery (Figure 3–3).

Figure 3–3

2

- Click the Rounded Rectangle shape in the Rectangles area of the Shapes gallery, which removes the gallery and changes the mouse pointer to the shape of a crosshair.

- Position the mouse pointer (a crosshair) by the insertion point in the document window, as shown in Figure 3–4, which is the location for the upper-left corner of the desired shape.

What is the purpose of the crosshair mouse pointer?

In the document window, you will drag the crosshair mouse pointer from the upper-left corner to the lower-right corner to form the desired location and size of the shape.

Figure 3–4

- Drag the mouse to the right and downward to form the boundaries of the shape, as shown in Figure 3–5. Do not release the mouse button.

Figure 3–5

- Release the mouse button so that Word draws the shape according to your drawing in the document window.

- Verify your shape is the same approximate height and width as the one in this project by clicking the Size button (Drawing Tools Format tab | Size group) and then, if necessary, changing the values in the Shape Height box and Shape Width boxes to 0.5" and 7", respectively (Figure 3–6). When finished, click the Size button again to remove the Shape Height and Shape Width boxes.

Figure 3–6

Q&A

What is the purpose of the rotate and adjustment handles?

When you drag an object's **rotate handle**, which is the green circle, Word rotates the object in the direction you drag the mouse. When you drag an object's **adjustment handle**, which is the yellow diamond, Word changes the object's shape.

Q&A

What if I wanted to delete a shape and start over?

With the shape selected, you would press the DELETE key.

To Apply a Shape Style

Word provides a Shape Styles gallery, allowing you to change the appearance of the shape. Because the organization in this project, Heartland Tractor Club, supports many different tractor manufacturers, its letterhead should use a color that is not commonly associated with a particular tractor manufacturer. The next steps apply a shape style that uses a shade of brown.

- With the shape still selected, click the More button (shown in Figure 3–6) in the Shape Styles gallery (Drawing Tools Format tab | Shape Styles group) to expand the gallery.

What if my shape is no longer selected?

Click the shape to select it.

- Point to Intense Effect - Brown, Accent 4 in the Shape Styles gallery to display a live preview of that style applied to the shape in the document (Figure 3–7).

Experiment

- Point to various styles in the Shape Styles gallery and watch the style of the shape change in the document.

- Click Intense Effect - Brown, Accent 4 in the Shape Styles gallery to apply the selected style to the shape.

Figure 3–7

Other Ways

1. Click Format Shape Dialog Box Launcher (Drawing Tools Format tab | Shape Styles group), click Picture Color in left pane

(Format Shape dialog box), select desired colors, click Close button

2. Right-click shape, click Format Shape on

shortcut menu, click Picture Color in left pane (Format Shape dialog box), select desired colors, click Close button

To Add Text to a Shape

The next step is to add the organization name to the shape. The following steps add text to a shape.

- Right-click the shape to display a shortcut menu and the Mini toolbar (Figure 3–8).

Figure 3–8

- Click Add Text on the shortcut menu to place an insertion point centered in the shape.

- Type **HEARTLAND TRACTOR CLUB** as the organization name in the shape (Figure 3–9).

text entered and automatically formatted according to the selected style

HEARTLAND·TRACTOR·CLUB¶

Figure 3–9

To Use the Grow Font Button to Increase Font Size

You want the font size of the organization name to be much larger in the shape. In previous chapters, you used the Font Size box arrow (Home tab | Font group) to change the font size of text. Word also provides a Grow Font button (Home tab | Font group), which increases the font size of selected text each time you click the button. The following steps use the Grow Font button to increase the font size of the organization name to 22 point.

1

- Drag through the organization name in the shape to select the text to be formatted.

2

- Display the Home tab.

- Repeatedly click the Grow Font button (Home tab | Font group) until the Font Size box displays 22 to increase the font size of the selected text (Figure 3–10).

Q&A

What if I click the Grow Font button (Home tab | Font group) too many times, causing the font size to be too big?

Click the Shrink Font button (Home tab | Font group) until the desired font size is displayed.

Grow Font button

Shrink Font button

Home tab

current font

Calibri (Body)   22

Font box arrow

Font group

Font Size box displays 22

Font

AaBbCcDc   AaBbCcD

¶ Normal   ¶ No Spaci

Paragraph

document text (paragraph mark) hidden behind shape because shape is formatted as In Front of Text

HEARTLAND·TRACTOR·CLUB¶

selected text changed to 22 point

Experiment

- Repeatedly click the Grow Font and Shrink Font buttons (Home tab | Font group) and watch the font size of the selected name change in the document window. When you are finished experimenting with these two buttons, set the font size to 22.

Figure 3–10

Other Ways

1. Press CTRL+SHIFT+>

To Change the Font of Selected Text

The font of the organization name currently is Calibri. To make the organization name stand out even more, change the font of the name in the letterhead to a font different from the rest of the letter. The following steps change the font of the selected text.

1 With the text selected, click the Font box arrow (Home tab | Font group) to display the Font gallery.

2 Scroll to and then click Segoe Script in the Font gallery to change the font of the selected text (shown in Figure 3–11 on the next page).

3 Click anywhere in the text in the shape to remove the selection and place the insertion point in the shape.

Floating versus Inline Objects

When you insert an object, such as a shape, in a document, Word inserts it as either an inline object or a floating object. An **inline object** is an object that is part of a paragraph. With inline objects, you change the location of the object by setting paragraph options, such as centered, right-aligned, and so on. A **floating object** is an object that can be positioned at a specific location in a document or in a layer over or behind text in a document. You have more flexibility with floating objects because you can position a floating object anywhere on the page.

In addition to changing an object from inline to floating and vice versa, Word provides several floating options. All of these options affect how text wraps with the object. Table 3–1 lists the various text wrapping options and explains the function of each one.

Table 3–1 Text Wrapping Options

Text Wrapping Option	Object Type	How It Works
In Line with Text	Inline	Object positioned according to paragraph formatting; for example, if paragraph is centered, object will be centered with any text in the paragraph.
Square	Floating	Text wraps around object, with text forming a box around the object.
Tight	Floating	Text wraps around object, with text forming to shape of the object.
Through	Floating	Object appears at beginning, middle, or end of text. Moving object changes location of text.
Top and Bottom	Floating	Object appears above or below text. Moving object changes location of text.
Behind Text	Floating	Object appears behind text.
In Front of Text	Floating	Object appears in front of text and may cover the text.

BTW

Positioning Objects
If you want to use the Square text wrapping option, you can specify where the object should be positioned on the page. To specify the position, select the object, click the Object Position button (Picture Tools Format tab | Arrange group), and then click the desired location in the Object Position gallery.

To Change an Object's Text Wrapping

When you insert a shape in a Word document, the default text wrapping is In Front of Text, which means the object will cover any text behind it. Because you want the letterhead above the contents of the letter, instead of covering the contents of the letter, you change the text wrapping for the shape to Top and Bottom. The following steps change a shape's text wrapping.

- Click the edge of the shape to select the shape.

- Display the Drawing Tools Format tab.

- Click the Wrap Text button (Drawing Tools Format tab | Arrange group) to display the Wrap Text gallery (Figure 3–11).

Figure 3–11

Experiment

- Point to various text wrapping options in the Wrap Text gallery and watch the shape configure to the selected wrapping option, which in this case, moves the paragraph mark to different locations in the document.

- Click Top and Bottom in the Wrap Text gallery so that the object does not cover the document text.

Other Ways
1. Right-click object, point to Wrap Text on shortcut menu, click desired wrapping style

To Insert Clip Art

Files containing graphical images, or graphics, are available from a variety of sources. In the Chapter 1 document, you inserted a digital picture taken with a camera phone. In this project, you insert **clip art**, which is a predefined graphic. In Microsoft Office programs, clip art is located in the **Clip Organizer**, which contains a collection of clip art, photos, animations, sounds, and videos.

The letterhead in this project contains clip art of a tractor (Figure 3–1 on page WD 139). Thus, the next steps insert a clip art image on the line below the shape in the document.

1

- Click the paragraph mark below the shape to position the insertion point where you want to insert the clip art image.

- Display the Insert tab.

- Click the Clip Art button (Insert tab | Illustrations group) to display the Clip Art pane (Figure 3–12).

  What is a pane?

  Recall from the Office 2010 and Windows 7 chapter at the beginning of this book that a pane, or task pane, is a separate window that enables you to carry out some Word tasks more efficiently.

Figure 3–12

2

- If the Search for text box displays text, drag through the text to select it.

- Type **tractor** in the Search for text box to specify the search text, which in this case indicates the type of image you wish to locate.

- Click the Go button to display a list of clips that match the entered search text (Figure 3–13).

  Why is my list of clips different from Figure 3–13?

  If your Include Office.com content check box is selected and you are connected to the Internet, the Clip Art pane displays clips from the Web as well as those installed on your hard disk.

Figure 3–13

- Click the clip art of the yellow tractor to insert this clip art image in the document at the location of the insertion point (Figure 3–14).

- Click the Close button on the Clip Art pane title bar to close the task pane.

Figure 3–14

To Resize a Graphic to a Percent of the Original

In this project, the graphic is 35 percent of its original size. Instead of dragging a sizing handle to change the graphic's size, as you learned in Chapter 1, you can set exact size percentages. The following steps resize a graphic to a percent of the original.

- With the graphic still selected, click the Advanced Layout: Size Dialog Box Launcher (Picture Tools Format tab | Size group) to display the Layout dialog box.

Q&A

What if the graphic is not selected or the Picture Tools Format tab is not on the Ribbon?

Click the graphic to select it or double-click the graphic to make the Picture Tools Format tab the active tab.

- In the Scale area (Layout dialog box), double-click the current value in the Height box to select it.

- Type 35 in the Height box and then press the TAB key to display the same percent value in the Width box (Figure 3–15).

Figure 3–15

Why did Word automatically fill in the value in the Width box?

When the 'Lock aspect ratio' check box (Layout dialog box) is selected, Word automatically maintains the size proportions of the graphic.

How do I know to use 35 percent for the resized graphic?

The larger graphic consumed too much room on the page. Try various percentages to determine the size that works best in the letterhead design.

❸
• Click the OK button to close the dialog box and resize the selected graphic (Figure 3–16).

> graphic selected and resized to 35% of its original size

> HEARTLAND·TRACTOR·CLUB¶

Figure 3–16

Other Ways
1. Right-click graphic, click Size and Position on shortcut menu, enter values (Layout dialog box), click OK button

To Change the Color of a Graphic

In Word, you can change the color of a graphic. The clip art currently consists of shades of yellow and brown. Because the clip art in this project will be placed in a rectangle shape, you prefer to use colors that blend better with the current color scheme. The following steps change the color of the graphic to a shade in the current color scheme that matches the color of the shape.

❶
• With the graphic still selected (shown in Figure 3–16), click the Color button (Picture Tools Format tab | Adjust group) to display the Color gallery.

• Point to Orange, Accent color 3 Dark in the Color gallery (fourth color in second row) to display a live preview of that color applied to the selected graphic in the document (Figure 3–17).

🔍 Experiment
• Point to various colors in the Color gallery and watch the color of the graphic change in the document.

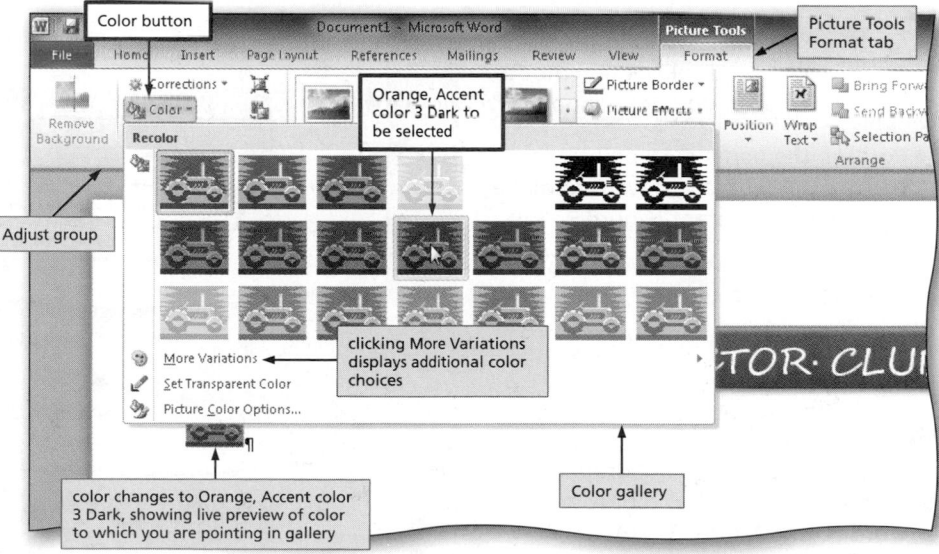

> Color button

> Picture Tools Format tab

> Orange, Accent color 3 Dark to be selected

> Adjust group

> clicking More Variations displays additional color choices

> color changes to Orange, Accent color 3 Dark, showing live preview of color to which you are pointing in gallery

> Color gallery

Figure 3–17

❷
• Click Orange, Accent color 3 Dark in the Color gallery to change the color of the selected graphic.

How would I change a graphic back to its original colors?

With the graphic selected, you would click No Recolor in the Color gallery (upper-left color).

Other Ways
1. Right-click graphic, click Format Picture on shortcut menu, click Picture Color button in left pane (Format Picture dialog box), select color, click Close button

To Set a Transparent Color in a Graphic

In Word, you can make one color in a graphic transparent, that is, remove the color. You would make a color transparent if you wanted to remove part of a graphic or see text or colors behind a graphic. In this project, you will remove the lighter brown from the edges of the tractor graphic so that when you move the graphic on the rectangular shape, the color of the shape can be seen in the transparent locations. The following steps set a transparent color in a graphic.

1

- With the graphic still selected, click the Color button (Picture Tools Format tab | Adjust group) to display the Color gallery (Figure 3–18).

Figure 3–18

2

- Click Set Transparent Color in the Color gallery to display a pen mouse pointer in the document window.

- Position the pen mouse pointer in the graphic where you want to make the color transparent (Figure 3–19).

Q&A Can I make multiple colors in a graphic transparent?

No, you can make only one color transparent.

Figure 3–19

3

- Click the location in the graphic where you want the color to be transparent (Figure 3–20).

Q&A What if I make the wrong color transparent?

Click the Undo button on the Quick Access Toolbar, or press CTRL+Z, and then repeat these steps.

Figure 3–20

To Adjust the Brightness and Contrast of a Graphic

In Word, you can adjust the lightness (brightness) of a graphic and also contrast, which is the difference between the lightest and darkest areas of the graphic. The following steps decrease the brightness and contrast of the tractor graphic, each by 20%.

1

- With the graphic still selected (shown in Figure 3–20), click the Corrections button (Picture Tools Format tab | Adjust group) to display the Corrections gallery (Figure 3–21).

Does live preview work in this gallery?

Yes, but the graphic is covered by the gallery in this case. To see the live preview, you would need to position the graphic so that you can see it while the gallery is displayed.

Figure 3–21

2

- Click Brightness: −20% Contrast: −20% in the Corrections gallery (second image in second row) to change the brightness and contrast of the selected graphic (Figure 3–22).

Can I remove all formatting applied to a graphic and start over?

Yes. With the graphic selected, you would click the Reset Picture button (Picture Tools Format tab | Adjust group).

Figure 3–22

Other Ways

1. Right-click graphic, click Format Picture on shortcut menu, click Picture Corrections button in left pane (Format Picture dialog box), adjust settings, click Close button

To Change the Border Color on a Graphic

The tractor graphic currently has no border (outline). You would like the graphic to have a brown border. The following steps change the border color on a graphic.

- Click the Picture Border button arrow (Picture Tools Format tab | Picture Styles group) to display the Picture Border gallery.

- Point to Brown, Accent 4, Darker 50% (eighth theme color from left in the sixth row) in the Picture Border gallery to display a live preview of that border color around the picture (Figure 3–23).

- Point to various colors in the Picture Border gallery and watch the border color on the picture change in the document window.

Figure 3–23

- Click Brown, Accent 4, Darker 50% in the Picture Border gallery to change the picture border color.

Q&A How would I remove a border from a graphic?

With the graphic selected, you would click the No Outline in the Picture Border gallery.

To Change an Object's Text Wrapping

The tractor graphic is to be positioned to the left of the organization name in the shape. Clip art, by default, is formatted as an inline graphic, which cannot be moved into a shape. To move the graphic in the shape so that it is not covered by any text, you format it as a floating object with In Front of Text wrapping. The following steps change a graphic's text wrapping.

1. If necessary, click the graphic to select it. If necessary, display the Picture Tools Format tab.

2. Click the Wrap Text button (Picture Tools Format tab | Arrange group) to display the Wrap Text gallery.

Q&A Do both the Picture Tools Format and Drawing Tools Format tabs have a Wrap Text button?

Yes. You can specify how to wrap text with both pictures and drawings.

3. Click In Front of Text in the Wrap Text gallery so that you can position the object on top of any item in the document, in this case, on top of the rectangular shape.

To Move a Graphic

The next step is to move the tractor graphic up so that it is positioned to the left of the text on the rectangle shape. The following steps move a graphic.

1
● Position the mouse pointer in the graphic so that the mouse pointer has a four-headed arrow attached to it (Figure 3–24).

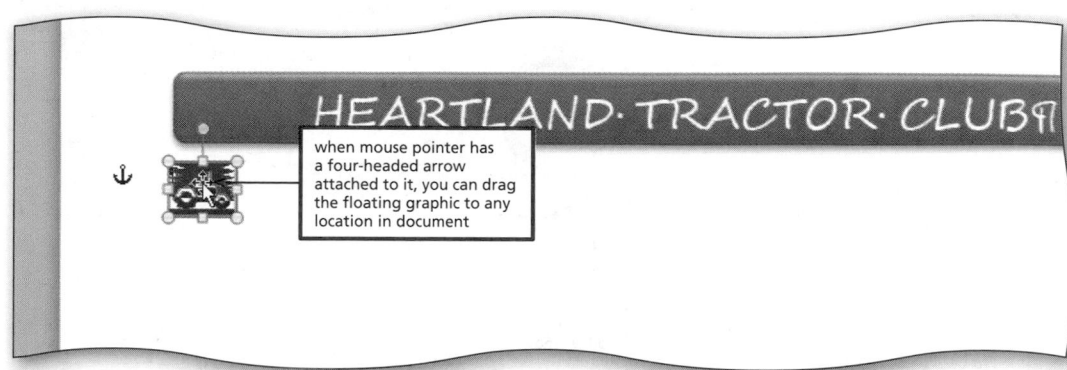

Figure 3–24

2
● Drag the graphic to the location shown in Figure 3–25.

What if I moved the graphic to the wrong location?

Repeat these steps. You can drag a floating graphic to any location in a document.

Figure 3–25

To Copy a Graphic

In this project, the same tractor graphic is to be placed to the right of the organization name in the shape. Instead of performing the same steps to insert and format another tractor graphic, you can copy the graphic to the Office Clipboard, paste the graphic from the Office Clipboard, and then move the graphic to the desired location.

You use the same steps to copy a graphic as you used in Chapter 2 to copy text. The following steps copy a graphic.

● If necessary, click the graphic to select it.

● Display the Home tab.

● Click the Copy button, shown in Figure 3–26 on the next page, (Home tab | Clipboard group) to copy the selected item to the Office Clipboard.

To Use Paste Options

The next step is to paste the copied graphic in the document. The following steps paste a graphic using the Paste Options gallery.

1
- Click the Paste button arrow (Home tab | Clipboard group) to display the Paste gallery.

Q&A What if I accidentally click the Paste button?

Click the Paste Options button below the graphic pasted in the document to display a Paste Options gallery.

- Point to the Keep Source Formatting button in the Paste gallery to display a live preview of that paste option (Figure 3–26).

Experiment
- Point to the two buttons in the Paste gallery and watch the appearance of the pasted graphic change.

Figure 3–26

Q&A What do the buttons in the Paste gallery mean?

The Keep Source Formatting button indicates the pasted graphic should have the same formats as it did in its original location. The second button removes all formatting from the graphic.

Q&A Why are these paste buttons different from the ones in Chapter 2?

The buttons that appear in the Paste gallery differ depending on the item you are pasting. Use live preview to see how the pasted object will look in the document.

2
- Click the Keep Source Formatting button in the Paste gallery to paste the object using the same formatting as the original.

To Move a Graphic

The next step is to move the second tractor graphic so that it is positioned to the right of the text in the rectangle shape. The following step moves a graphic.

1 Position the mouse pointer in the graphic so that the mouse pointer has a four-headed arrow attached to it and then drag the graphic to the location shown in Figure 3–27.

Q&A Why does my graphic not look like it is positioned the same as the graphic on the left?

The paragraph mark at the end of the organization name may be obstructing your view. To determine if the graphic is positioned properly, you can temporarily turn off formatting marks by clicking the Show/Hide ¶ button (Home tab | Paragraph group).

Figure 3–27

To Flip a Graphic

The next step is to flip the clip art image on the right so that the tractor is facing the opposite direction. The following steps flip a graphic horizontally.

1

- If necessary, display the Picture Tools Format tab.

- With the graphic still selected, click the Rotate button (Picture Tools Format tab | Arrange group) to display the Rotate gallery.

- Point to Flip Horizontal in the Rotate gallery to display a live preview of the selected rotate option applied to the selected graphic (Figure 3–28).

🔎 **Experiment**

- Point to the rotate options in the Rotate gallery and watch the picture rotate in the document window.

Figure 3–28

2

- Click Flip Horizontal in the Rotate gallery, so that Word flips the graphic to display its mirror image.

Can I flip a graphic vertically?

Yes, you would click Flip Vertical in the Rotate gallery. You also can rotate a graphic clockwise or counterclockwise by clicking the Rotate Right 90° and Rotate Left 90° commands, respectively, in the Rotate gallery.

To Specify Formatting before Typing and Then Enter Text

The contact information for the organization in this project is located on the line below the organization name. The following steps format and then enter the postal address in the letterhead.

- Position the insertion point on the line below the shape containing the organization name.

- If necessary, display the Home tab. Click the Center button (Home tab | Paragraph group) to center the paragraph.

- Click the Font Color button arrow (Home tab | Font group) to display the Font Color gallery and then click Orange, Accent 3, Darker 50% (seventh color in sixth row) in the Font Color gallery to change the font color.

- Type **323 Pine Avenue, Graber, OK 74877** and then press the SPACEBAR (shown in Figure 3–29 on the next page).

BTW

Q&As
For a complete list of the Q&As found in many of the step-by-step sequences in this book, visit the Word 2010 Q&A Web page (scsite.com/wd2010/qa).

To Insert a Symbol from the Symbol Dialog Box

In the letterhead in this chapter, a small round dot separates the postal address and phone number, and the same type of dot separates the phone number and Web address information. This special symbol (the round dot) is not on the keyboard. Thus, Word provides a method of inserting dots and other symbols, such as letters in the Greek alphabet and mathematical characters.

The following steps insert a dot symbol, called a bullet symbol, between the postal address and phone number in the letterhead.

- If necessary, position the insertion point as shown in Figure 3–29.

- Display the Insert tab.

- Click the Insert Symbol button (Insert tab | Symbols group) to display the Insert Symbol gallery (Figure 3–29).

Q&A What if the symbol I want to insert already appears in the Symbol gallery?

You can click any symbol shown in the Symbol gallery to insert it in the document.

Figure 3–29

- Click More Symbols in the Insert Symbol gallery to display the Symbol dialog box.

- If the font in the Font box is not (normal text), click the Font box arrow (Symbol dialog box) and then scroll to (normal text) and click it to select this font.

- If the subset in the Subset box is not General Punctuation, click the Subset box arrow and then scroll to General Punctuation and click it to select this subset.

- In the list of symbols, if necessary, scroll to the bullet symbol shown in Figure 3–30 and then click the symbol to select it.

Figure 3–30

- Click the Insert button (Symbol dialog box) to place the selected symbol in the document to the left of the insertion point (Figure 3–30).

Q&A Why is the Symbol dialog box still open?

The Symbol dialog box remains open, allowing you to insert additional symbols.

- Click the Close button (Symbol dialog box) to close the dialog box.

To Insert a Symbol from the Symbol Gallery

In the letterhead, another bullet symbol separates the phone number from the Web address information. Once you insert a symbol using the Symbol dialog box, Word adds that symbol to the Symbol gallery so that it is more readily available. The following steps use the Symbol gallery to insert a bullet symbol between the phone number and Web address.

1
- Press the SPACEBAR, type **Phone: (476) 555-9384** and then press the SPACEBAR.

2
- Click the Insert Symbol button (Insert tab | Symbols group) to display the Insert Symbol gallery (Figure 3–31).

Why is the bullet symbol now in the Insert Symbol gallery?

When you insert a symbol from the Symbol dialog box, Word automatically adds the symbol to the Insert Symbol gallery.

Figure 3–31

3
- Click the bullet symbol in the Insert Symbol gallery to insert the symbol at the location of the insertion point (shown in Figure 3–32).

To Enter Text

The following steps enter the Web address in the letterhead.

- Press the SPACEBAR.

- Type **Web address: www.hltclub.com** to finish the text in the letterhead (Figure 3–32).

BTW

Inserting Special Characters
In addition to symbols, you can insert a variety of special characters including dashes, hyphens, spaces, apostrophes, and quotation marks. Click the Special Characters tab in the Symbols dialog box (Figure 3–30), click the desired character in the Character list, click the Insert button, and then click the Close button.

Figure 3–32

To Bottom Border a Paragraph

The letterhead in this project has a horizontal line that extends from the left margin to the right margin immediately below the address, phone, and Web address information, which separates the letterhead from the rest of the letter. In Word, you can draw a solid line, called a **border**, at any edge of a paragraph. That is, borders may be added above or below a paragraph, to the left or right of a paragraph, or in any combination of these sides. The following steps add a bottom border to the paragraph containing address, phone, and Web information.

- Display the Home tab.

- With the insertion point in the paragraph to border, click the Border button arrow (Home tab | Paragraph group) to display the Border gallery (Figure 3–33).

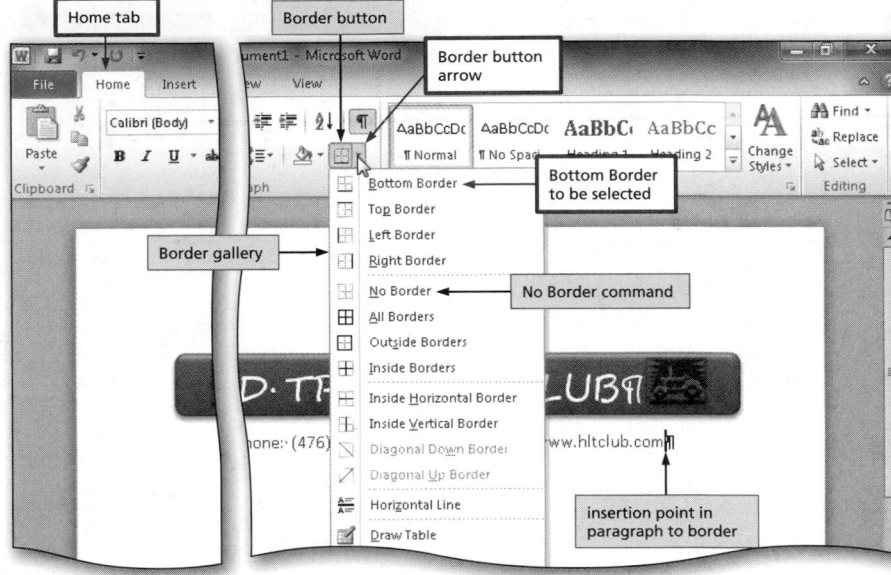

Figure 3–33

2

- Click Bottom Border in the Border gallery to place a border below the paragraph containing the insertion point (Figure 3–34).

Q&A If the face of the Border button displays the border icon I want to use, can I click the Border button instead of using the Border button arrow?

Yes.

Q&A How would I remove an existing border from a paragraph?

If, for some reason, you wanted to remove a border from a paragraph, you would position the insertion point in the paragraph, click the Border button arrow (Home tab | Paragraph group), and then click No Border in the Border gallery.

Figure 3–34

Other Ways

1. Click Page Borders button (Page Layout tab | Page Background group), click Borders tab (Borders and Shading dialog box), select desired border options, click OK button

To Clear Formatting

The next step is to position the insertion point below the letterhead, so that you can type the contents of the letter. When you press the ENTER key at the end of a paragraph containing a border, Word moves the border forward to the next paragraph. The paragraph also retains all current settings, such as the center format. Instead, you want the paragraph and characters on the new line to use the Normal style: black font with no border.

In Word, the term, **clear formatting**, refers to returning the formatting to the Normal style. The following steps clear formatting at the location of the insertion point.

1

- With the insertion point between the Web address and paragraph mark at the end of the line (as shown in Figure 3–34), press the ENTER key to move the insertion point and paragraph to the next line (Figure 3–35).

Figure 3–35

2

- Click the Clear Formatting button (Home tab | Font group) to apply the Normal style to the location of the insertion point (Figure 3–36).

Figure 3–36

Other Ways

1. Click More button in Styles gallery (Home tab | Styles group), click Clear Formatting
2. Click Styles Dialog Box Launcher (Home tab | Styles group), click Clear All in Styles task pane
3. Select text, press CTRL+SPACEBAR, press CTRL+Q

AutoFormat as You Type

As you type text in a document, Word automatically formats some of it for you. For example, when you press the ENTER key or SPACEBAR after typing an e-mail address or Web address, Word automatically formats the address as a hyperlink, that is, colored blue and underlined. In Figure 3–35 on the previous page, for example, Word formatted the Web address as a hyperlink because you pressed the ENTER key at the end of the line. Table 3–2 outlines commonly used AutoFormat As You Type options and their results.

Table 3–2 Commonly Used AutoFormat As You Type Options

Typed Text	AutoFormat Feature	Example
Quotation marks or apostrophes	Changes straight quotation marks or apostrophes to curly ones	"the" becomes "the"
Text, a space, one hyphen, one or no spaces, text, space	Changes the hyphen to an en dash	ages 20 - 45 becomes ages 20 – 45
Text, two hyphens, text, space	Changes the two hyphens to an em dash	Two types--yellow and red becomes Two types—yellow and red
Web or e-mail address followed by SPACEBAR or ENTER key	Formats Web or e-mail address as a hyperlink	www.scsite.com becomes www.scsite.com
Three hyphens, underscores, equal signs, asterisks, tildes, or number signs and then ENTER key	Places a border above a paragraph	--- This line becomes _____ This line

Number followed by a period, hyphen, right parenthesis, or greater than sign and then a space or tab followed by text	Creates a numbered list	1. Word
		2. PowerPoint
		
		becomes
		
		  1. Word
		  2. PowerPoint

Asterisk, hyphen, or greater than sign and then a space or tab followed by text	Creates a bulleted list	* Home tab
		* Insert tab
		
		becomes
		
		  • Home tab
		  • Insert tab

Fraction and then a space or hyphen	Condenses the fraction entry so that it consumes one space instead of three	1/2 becomes ½
Ordinal and then a space or hyphen	Makes part of the ordinal a superscript	3rd becomes 3rd

BTW

AutoFormat Settings
Before you can use them, AutoFormat options must be enabled. To check if an AutoFormat option is enabled, click File on the Ribbon to open the Backstage view, click Options in the Backstage view, click Proofing in the left pane (Word Options dialog box), click the AutoCorrect Options button, click the AutoFormat As You Type tab, select the appropriate check boxes, and then click the OK button in each open dialog box.

To Convert a Hyperlink to Regular Text

The Web address in the letterhead should be formatted as regular text; that is, it should not be blue or underlined. Thus, the following steps remove the hyperlink format from the Web address in the letterhead.

1

- Right-click the hyperlink (in this case, the Web address) to display the Mini toolbar and a shortcut menu (Figure 3–37).

Figure 3–37

2

- Click Remove Hyperlink on the shortcut menu to remove the hyperlink format from the text.

- Position the insertion point on the paragraph mark below the border because you are finished with the letterhead (Figure 3–38).

Figure 3–38

Could I have used the AutoCorrect Options button instead of the Remove Hyperlink command?

Yes. Alternatively, you could have pointed to the small blue box at the beginning of the hyperlink, clicked the AutoCorrect Options button, and then clicked Undo Hyperlink on the AutoCorrect Options menu.

Other Ways
1. With insertion point in hyperlink, click Hyperlink button (Insert tab | Links group), click Remove Link button

BTW

Saving a Template
As an alternative to saving the letterhead as a Word document, you could save it as a template. To do so, click File on the Ribbon to open the Backstage view, click the Save & Send tab to display the Save & Send gallery, click Change File Type, click Template in the right pane, click the Save As button, enter the template name (Save As dialog box), if necessary select the Templates folder, and then click the Save button in the dialog box. To use the template, click File on the Ribbon to open the Backstage view, click the New tab to display the New gallery, click My templates, and then double-click the template icon or name.

To Change Document Properties, Then Save and Close a File

The letterhead now is complete. Thus, you should save it in a file. The following steps assume you already have created folders for storing your files, for example, a CIS 101 folder (for your class) that contains a Word folder (for your assignments). Thus, these steps change document properties, save the file in the Word folder in the CIS 101 folder on a USB flash drive using the file name, Heartland Letterhead, and then close the file.

1 Click File on the Ribbon to open the Backstage view and then, if necessary, select the Info tab. Display the Properties menu and then click Show Document Panel on the Properties menu to close the Backstage view and display the Document Information Panel in the Word document window.

2 Enter your name in the Author property, and enter your course and section in the Subject property. Close the Document Information Panel.

3 With a USB flash drive connected to one of the computer's USB ports, click the Save button on the Quick Access Toolbar to display the Save As dialog box.

4 Type `Heartland Letterhead` in the File name text box to change the file name. Do not press the ENTER key after typing the file name because you do not want to close the dialog box at this time.

5 Navigate to the desired save location (in this case, the Word folder in the CIS 101 folder [or your class folder] on the USB flash drive).

6 Click the Save button (Save As dialog box) to save the file in the selected folder on the selected drive with the entered file name.

7 Click File on the Ribbon to open the Backstage view and then click Close in the Backstage view to close the document.

Break Point: If you wish to take a break, this is a good place to do so. To resume at a later time, start Word and continue following the steps from this location forward.

Creating a Business Letter

You have created a letterhead for the business letter. The next step is to compose the rest of the content in the business letter. The following pages use Word to create a business letter that contains a table and a bulleted list.

Plan Ahead

> **Compose an effective business letter.**
> When composing a business letter, you need to be sure to include all essential elements and to decide which letter style to use.
>
> - **Include all essential letter elements, properly spaced and sized.** All business letters contain the same basic elements, including the date line, inside address, message, and signature block (shown in Figure 3–1 on page WD 139). If a business letter does not use a letterhead, then the top of the letter should include return address information in a heading.
>
> - **Use proper spacing and formats for the contents of the letter below the letterhead.** Use a font that is easy to read, in a size between 8 and 12 point. Add emphasis with bold, italic, and bullets where appropriate, and use tables to present numeric information. Paragraphs should be single-spaced, with double-spacing between paragraphs.
>
> - **Determine which letter style to use.** You can follow many different styles when creating business letters. A letter style specifies guidelines for the alignment and spacing of elements in the business letter.

To Create a New File from an Existing File

The top of the business letter in this chapter contains the letterhead, which you saved in a separate file. You could open the letterhead file and then save it with a new name, so that the letterhead file remains intact for future use. A more efficient technique is to create a new file from the letterhead file. Doing this enables you to save the document the first time using the Save button on the Quick Access Toolbar instead of requiring you to use the Save As command in the Backstage view. The following steps create a new file from an existing file.

1

- Click File on the Ribbon to open the Backstage view.

- Click the New tab in the Backstage view to display the New gallery (Figure 3–39).

What are the templates in the New gallery?

A template is a document that includes prewritten text and/or formatting common to documents of the specified type. Word provides many templates to simplify the task of creating documents.

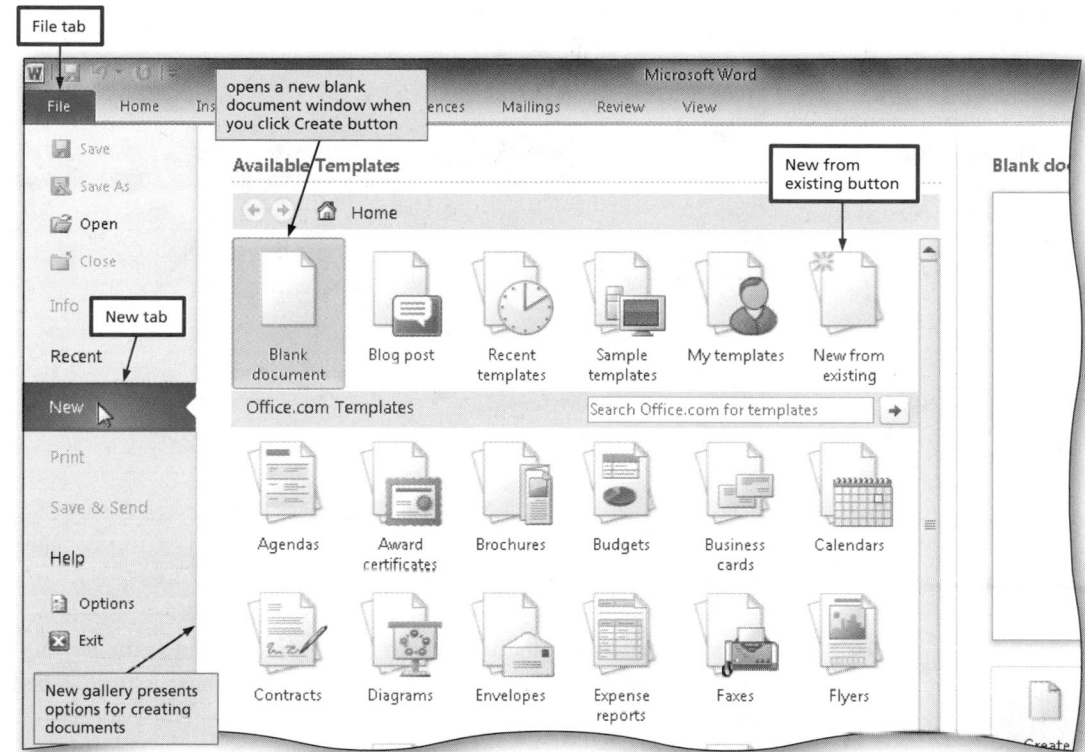

Figure 3–39

2

- Click the 'New from existing' button in the New gallery to display the New from Existing Document dialog box.

- If necessary, navigate to the location of the saved Heartland Letterhead file (in this case, the Word folder in the CIS 101 folder on the USB flash drive).

- Click Heartland Letterhead to select the file (Figure 3–40).

Figure 3–40

3

- Click the Create New button (New from Existing Document dialog box) to open a new document window that contains the contents of the selected file.

- If necessary, click the paragraph mark below the letterhead to position the insertion point at that location (Figure 3–41).

Figure 3–41

BTW

New Document Window
If you wanted to open a new blank document window, you could press CTRL+N or click File on the Ribbon to open the Backstage view, click the New tab to display the New gallery, click the Blank document button, and then click the Create button.

To Save a Document

Because you do not want to lose the letterhead at the top of this document, you should save the letter before continuing. The following steps assume you already have created folders for storing your files, for example, a CIS 101 folder (for your class) that contains a Word folder (for your assignments). Thus, these steps save the document in the Word folder in the CIS 101 folder on a USB flash drive using the file name, Heartland Advertisement Letter.

1 With a USB flash drive connected to one of the computer's USB ports, click the Save button on the Quick Access Toolbar to display the Save As dialog box.

2 Type **Heartland Advertisement Letter** in the File name text box to change the file name. Do not press the ENTER key after typing the file name because you do not want to close the dialog box at this time.

3 If necessary, navigate to the desired save location (in this case, the Word folder in the CIS 101 folder [or your class folder] on the USB flash drive).

4 Click the Save button (Save As dialog box) to save the document in the selected folder on the selected drive with the entered file name.

To Apply a Quick Style

Recall that the Normal style in Word places 10 points of blank space after each paragraph and inserts a vertical space equal to 1.15 lines between each line of text. The business letter should use single spacing for paragraphs and double spacing between paragraphs. Thus, you will modify the spacing for the paragraphs.

Word has many built-in, or predefined, styles called Quick Styles that you can use to format text. The No Spacing style, for example, defines line spacing to single and does not insert any additional blank space between lines when you press the ENTER key. To apply a quick style to a paragraph, you first position the insertion point in the paragraph and then apply the style. The next step applies the No Spacing quick style to a paragraph.

1

- With the insertion point positioned in the paragraph to be formatted, click No Spacing in the Quick Style gallery (Home tab | Styles group) to apply the selected style to the current paragraph (Figure 3–42).

Will this style be used in the rest of the document?

Yes. The paragraph formatting, which includes the style, will carry forward to subsequent paragraphs each time you press the ENTER key.

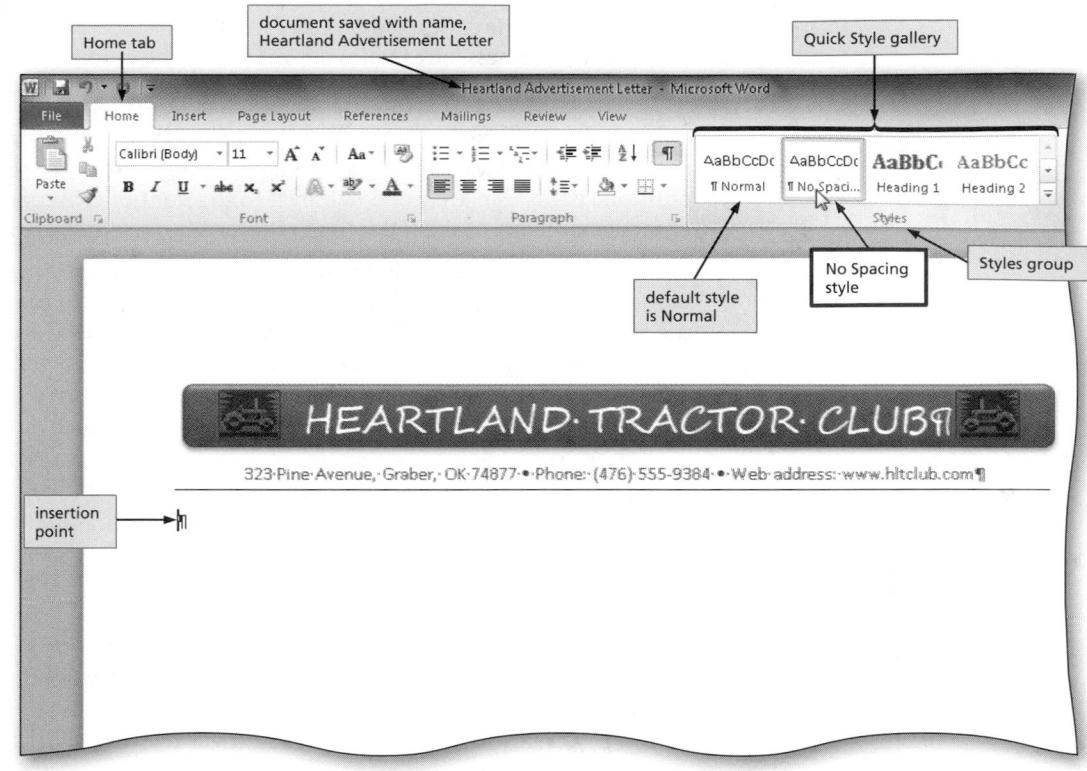

Figure 3–42

Other Ways	
1. Click Styles Dialog Box Launcher (Home tab | Styles group), click desired style in Styles task pane	2. Press CTRL+SHIFT+S, click Style Name box arrow in Apply Styles task pane, click desired style in list

Include all essential letter elements.

Be sure to include all essential business letter elements, properly spaced, in your letter.

- The **date line**, which consists of the month, day, and year, is positioned two to six lines below the letterhead.

- The **inside address**, placed three to eight lines below the date line, usually contains the addressee's courtesy title plus full name, job title, business affiliation, and full geographical address.

- The **salutation**, if present, begins two lines below the last line of the inside address. If you do not know the recipient's name, avoid using the salutation "To whom it may concern" — it is impersonal. Instead, use the recipient's title in the salutation, e.g., Dear Personnel Director. In a business letter, use a colon (:) at the end of the salutation; in a personal letter, use a comma.

- The body of the letter, the **message**, begins two lines below the salutation. Within the message, paragraphs are single-spaced with one blank line between paragraphs.

- Two lines below the last line of the message, the **complimentary close** is displayed. Capitalize only the first word in a complimentary close.

- Type the **signature block** at least four blank lines below the complimentary close, allowing room for the author to sign his or her name.

Plan
Ahead

Plan
Ahead

Determine which letter style to use.
Three common business letter styles are the block, the modified block, and the modified semi-block. Each style specifies different alignments and indentations.

- In the block letter style, all components of the letter begin flush with the left margin.

- In the modified block letter style, the date, complimentary close, and signature block are positioned approximately one-half inch to the right of center or at the right margin. All other components of the letter begin flush with the left margin.

- In the modified semi-block letter style, the date, complimentary close, and signature block are centered, positioned approximately one-half inch to the right of center or at the right margin. The first line of each paragraph in the body of the letter is indented one-half to one inch from the left margin. All other components of the letter begin flush with the left margin.

The business letter in this project follows the modified block style.

Using Tab Stops to Align Text

A **tab stop** is a location on the horizontal ruler that tells Word where to position the insertion point when you press the TAB key on the keyboard. Word, by default, places a tab stop at every one-half inch mark on the ruler. These default tab stops are indicated at the bottom of the horizontal ruler by small vertical tick marks (shown in Figure 3–43). You also can set your own custom tab stops. Tab settings are a paragraph format. Thus, each time you press the ENTER key, any custom tab stops are carried forward to the next paragraph.

To move the insertion point from one tab stop to another, press the TAB key on the keyboard. When you press the TAB key, a **tab character** formatting mark appears in the empty space between the tab stops.

When you set a custom tab stop, you specify how the text will align at a tab stop. The tab marker on the ruler reflects the alignment of the characters at the location of the tab stop. Table 3–3 shows types of tab stop alignments in Word and their corresponding tab markers.

BTW

Tabs Dialog Box
You can use the Tabs dialog box to set, change the alignment of, and remove custom tab stops. To display the Tabs dialog box, click the Paragraph Dialog Box Launcher (Home tab or Page Layout tab | Paragraph group) and then click the Tabs button (Paragraph dialog box), or double-click a tab marker on the ruler. To set a custom tab stop, enter the desired position (Tabs dialog box) and then click the Set button. To change the alignment of a custom tab stop, click the tab stop position to be changed, click the new alignment, and then click the Set button. To remove an existing tab stop, click the tab stop position to be removed and then click the Clear button. To remove all tab stops, click the Clear All button in the Tabs dialog box.

Table 3–3 Types of Tab Stop Alignments

Tab Stop Alignment	Tab Marker	Result of Pressing TAB Key	Example
Left Tab	⌞	Left-aligns text at the location of the tab stop	toolbar ruler
Center Tab	⊥	Centers text at the location of the tab stop	toolbar ruler
Right Tab	⌟	Right-aligns text at the location of the tab stop	toolbar ruler
Decimal Tab	⊥.	Aligns text on decimal point at the location of the tab stop	45.72 223.75
Bar Tab	∣	Aligns text at a bar character at the location of the tab stop	toolbar ruler

To Display the Ruler

One way to set custom tab stops is by using the horizontal ruler. Thus, the following step displays the ruler in the document window.

1 If the rulers are not displayed already, click the View Ruler button on the vertical scroll bar (shown in Figure 3–43).

Q&A What if the View Ruler button is not visible on the vertical scroll bar?

Display the View tab and then place a check mark in the Ruler check box.

To Set Custom Tab Stops

The first required element of the business letter is the date line, which in this letter is positioned two lines below the letterhead. The date line contains the month, day, and year, and begins four inches from the left margin, which is approximately one-half inch to the right of center. Thus, you should set a custom tab stop at the 4" mark on the ruler. The following steps set a left-aligned tab stop.

1

- With the insertion point on the paragraph mark below the border (shown in Figure 3–42 on page WD 167), press the ENTER key so that a blank line appears above the insertion point.

- If necessary, click the tab selector at the left edge of the horizontal ruler until it displays the type of tab you wish to use, which is the Left Tab icon in this case.

- Position the mouse pointer on the 4" mark on the ruler, which is the location of the desired custom tab stop (Figure 3–43).

Figure 3–43

What is the purpose of the tab selector?

Before using the ruler to set a tab stop, ensure the correct tab stop icon appears in the tab selector. Each time you click the tab selector, its icon changes. The Left Tab icon is the default. For a list of the types of tab stops, see Table 3–3.

2

- Click the 4" mark on the ruler to place a tab marker at that location (Figure 3–44).

What if I click the wrong location on the ruler?

You can move a custom tab stop by dragging the tab marker to the desired location on the ruler. Or, you can remove an existing custom tab stop by pointing to the tab marker on the ruler and then dragging the tab marker down and out of the ruler.

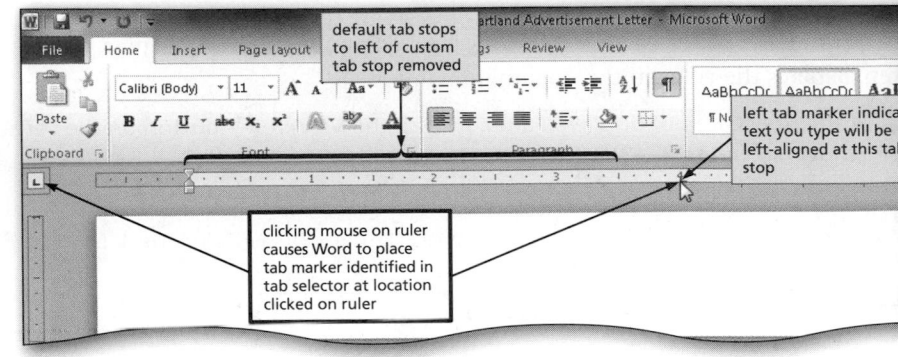

Figure 3–44

What happened to all the default tab stops on the ruler?

When you set a custom tab stop, Word clears all default tab stops to the left of the newly set custom tab stop on the ruler.

Other Ways

1. Click Paragraph Dialog Box Launcher (Home tab or Page Layout tab | Paragraph group), click Tabs button (Paragraph dialog box), type tab stop position (Tabs dialog box), click Set button, click OK button

To Insert the Current Date in a Document

The next step is to enter the current date at the 4" tab stop in the document, as specified in the guidelines for a modified block style letter. In Word, you can insert a computer's system date in a document. The following steps insert the current date in the letter.

1

- Press the TAB key to position the insertion point at the location of the tab stop in the current paragraph.

- Display the Insert tab.

- Click the Insert Date and Time button (Insert tab | Text group) to display the Date and Time dialog box.

- Select the desired format (Date and Time dialog box), in this case April 27, 2012.

- If the Update automatically check box is selected, click the check box to remove the check mark (Figure 3–45).

Figure 3–45

Why should the Update automatically check box not be selected?

In this project, the date at the top of the letter always should show today's date (for example, April 27, 2012). If, however, you wanted the date always to change to reflect the current computer date (for example, showing the date you open or print the letter), then you would place a check mark in this check box.

2

- Click the OK button to insert the current date at the location of the insertion point (Figure 3–46).

Figure 3-46

To Enter the Inside Address and Salutation

The next step in composing the business letter is to type the inside address and salutation. The following steps enter this text.

1 With the insertion point at the end of the date (shown in Figure 3–46), press the ENTER key three times.

2 Type **Mr. Harvey Wilcox** and then press the ENTER key.

3 Type **Wilcox Tractor Restorations** and then press the ENTER key.

4 Type **3009 North 2850 East Road** and then press the ENTER key.

5 Type **Roundwood, OK 74519** and then press the ENTER key twice.

6 Type **Dear Mr. Wilcox:** to complete the inside address and salutation entries (Figure 3–47).

Figure 3-47

To Create a Building Block

If you use the same text or graphic frequently, you can store the text or graphic as a **building block** and then insert the stored building block entry in the open document, as well as in future documents. That is, you can create the entry once as a building block and then insert the building block when you need it. In this way, you avoid entering the text or graphics inconsistently or incorrectly in different locations throughout the same or multiple documents.

The steps on the next page create a building block for the prospective advertiser's name, Wilcox Tractor Restorations. Later, you will insert the building block in the document instead of typing the advertiser's name.

1

- Select the text to be a building block, in this case Wilcox Tractor Restorations. Do not select the paragraph mark at the end of the text because you do not want the paragraph to be part of the building block.

Q&A

Why is the paragraph mark not part of the building block?

Select the paragraph mark only if you want to store paragraph formatting, such as indentation and line spacing, as part of the building block.

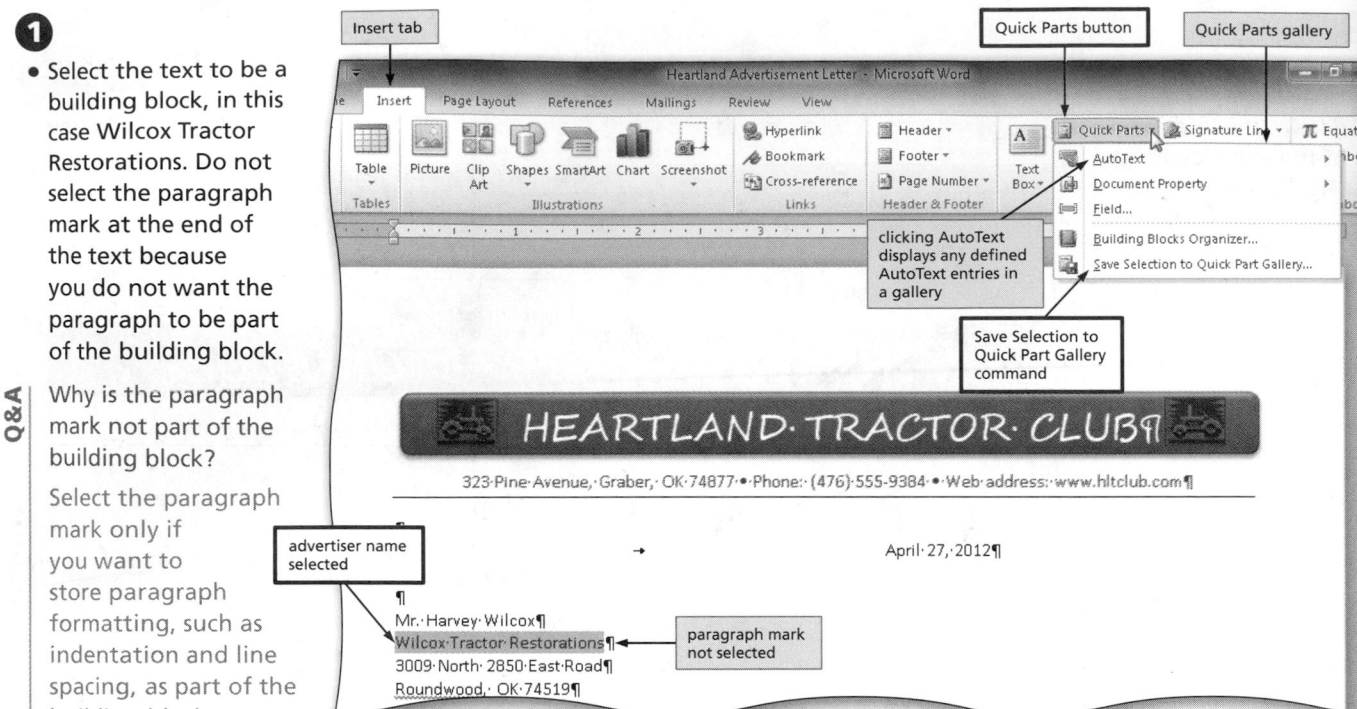

Figure 3–48

- Click the Quick Parts button (Insert tab | Text group) to display the Quick Parts gallery (Figure 3–48).

2

- Click Save Selection to Quick Part Gallery in the Quick Parts gallery to display the Create New Building Block dialog box.

- Type **wtr** in the Name text box (Create New Building Block dialog box) to replace the proposed building block name (Wilcox Tractor, in this case) with a shorter building block name (Figure 3–49).

3

- Click the OK button to store the building block entry and close the dialog box.

- If Word displays another dialog box, click the Yes button, to save changes to the building blocks.

Figure 3–49

Q&A

Will this building block be available in future documents?

When you quit Word, a dialog box may appear asking if you want to save changes to the "Building Blocks". Click the Save button if you want to use the new building block in future documents.

Other Ways

1. Select text, press ALT+F3

To Modify a Building Block

When you save a building block in the Quick Parts gallery, it is displayed at the top of the Quick Parts gallery. If the building block is a text entry, you can place it in the AutoText gallery instead, which also is accessible through the Quick Parts gallery.

When you point to the building block in the Quick Parts gallery, a ScreenTip displays the building block name. If you want to display more information when the user points to the building block, you can include a description as an Enhanced ScreenTip. The following steps modify a building block to include a description and change its category to AutoText.

1

- Click the Quick Parts button (Insert tab | Text group) to display the Quick Parts gallery.

- Right-click the Wilcox Tractor Restorations building block to display a shortcut menu (Figure 3–50).

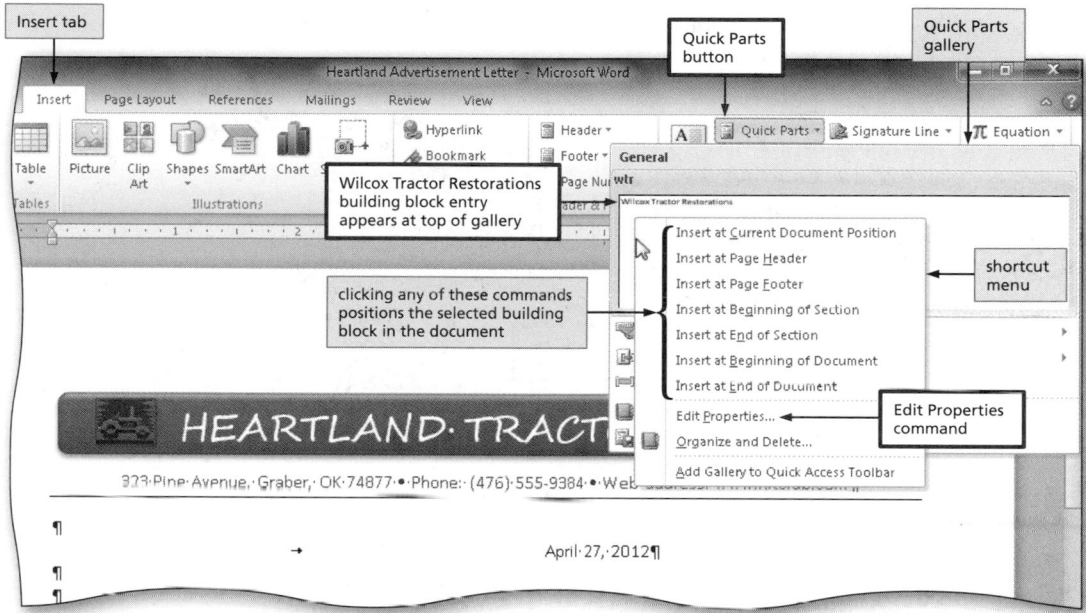

Figure 3–50

2

- Click Edit Properties on the shortcut menu to display the Modify Building Block dialog box, filled in with information related to the selected building block.

- Click the Gallery box arrow (Modify Building Block dialog box) and then click AutoText to change the gallery in which the building block will be displayed.

- Type **Potential Advertiser** in the Description text box (Figure 3–51).

Figure 3–51

3

- Click the OK button to store the building block entry and close the dialog box.

- Click the Yes button when asked if you want to redefine the building block entry.

To Insert a Building Block

In the first sentence in the body of the letter, you want the prospective advertiser name, Wilcox Tractor Restorations, to be displayed. Recall that you stored a building block name of wtr for Wilcox Tractor Restorations. Thus, you will type the building block name and then instruct Word to replace a building block name with the stored building block entry. The following steps insert a building block.

- Click to the right of the colon in the salutation and then press the ENTER key twice to position the insertion point one blank line below the salutation.
- Type the beginning of the first sentence as follows, entering the building block name as shown: **We are delighted you are considering advertising your business, wtr** (Figure 3–52).

Figure 3–52

- Press the F3 key to instruct Word to replace the building block name (wtr) with the stored building block entry (Wilcox Tractor Restorations) (Figure 3–53).

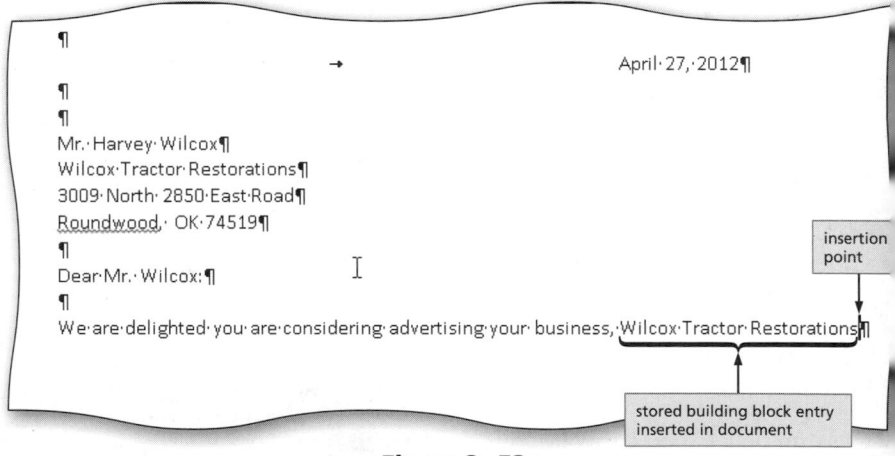

Figure 3–53

Other Ways

1. Click Quick Parts button (Insert tab | Text group), if necessary point to AutoText, click desired building block

Building Blocks versus AutoCorrect

In Project 2, you learned how to use the AutoCorrect feature, which enables you to insert and create AutoCorrect entries, similarly to how you created and inserted building blocks in this chapter. The difference between an AutoCorrect entry and a building block entry is that the AutoCorrect feature makes corrections for you automatically as soon as you press the SPACEBAR or type a punctuation mark, whereas you must instruct Word to insert a building block. That is, you enter the building block name and then press the F3 key, or click the Quick Parts button and select the building block from one of the galleries.

To Insert a Nonbreaking Space

Some compound words, such as proper nouns, dates, units of time and measure, abbreviations, and geographic destinations, should not be divided at the end of a line. These words either should fit as a unit at the end of a line or be wrapped together to the next line.

Word provides two special characters to assist with this task: the nonbreaking space and the nonbreaking hyphen. A **nonbreaking space** is a special space character that prevents two words from splitting if the first word falls at the end of a line. Similarly, a **nonbreaking hyphen** is a special type of hyphen that prevents two words separated by a hyphen from splitting at the end of a line.

The following steps insert a nonbreaking space between the words in the magazine name.

1

• With the insertion point at the end of the building block entry in the document (as shown in Figure 3–53), press the COMMA key and then press the SPACEBAR.

• Type `in` and then press the SPACEBAR. Press CTRL+I to turn on italics because magazine names should be italicized.

• Type `Heartland` as the first word in the magazine name and then press CTRL+SHIFT+SPACEBAR to insert a nonbreaking space after the entered word (Figure 3–54).

Figure 3–54

2

• Type `Tractor` and then press CTRL+SHIFT+SPACEBAR to insert another nonbreaking space after the entered word.

• Type `Magazine` and then press CTRL+I to turn off italics (Figure 3–55).

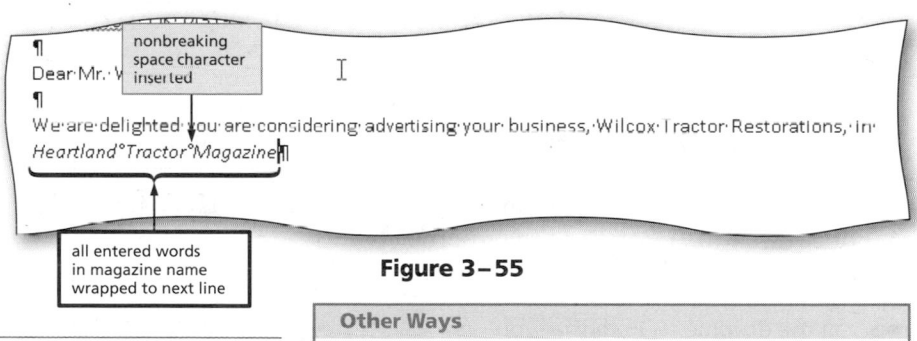

Figure 3–55

Other Ways
1. Click Symbol button (Insert tab | Symbols group), click More Symbols, click Special Characters tab (Symbol dialog box), click Nonbreaking Space in Character list, click Insert button, click Close button

To Enter Text

The next step in creating the letter is to enter the rest of the text in the first paragraph. The following steps enter this text.

1 Press the COMMA key and then press the SPACEBAR.

2 Type this text: `our monthly publication for tractor enthusiasts. The table below outlines advertisement rates per monthly issue:`

3 Press the ENTER key twice to place a blank line between paragraphs (shown in Figure 3–56 on the next page).

Why does my document wrap on different words?

Differences in wordwrap may relate to the printer connected to your computer. Thus, it is possible that the same document could wordwrap differently if associated with a different printer.

BTW

Nonbreaking Hyphen
If you wanted to insert a nonbreaking hyphen, you would press CTRL+SHIFT+HYPHEN.

To Save an Existing Document with the Same File Name

You have made several modifications to the document since you last saved it. Thus, you should save it again. The following step saves the document again.

1 Click the Save button on the Quick Access Toolbar to overwrite the previously saved file.

Break Point: If you wish to take a break, this is a good place to do so. You can quit Word now. To resume at a later time, start Word, open the file called Heartland Advertisement Letter, and continue following the steps from this location forward.

Tables

The next step in composing the business letter is to place a table listing the rates for various types of advertisements (shown in Figure 3–1 on page WD 139). A Word **table** is a collection of rows and columns. The intersection of a row and a column is called a **cell**, and cells are filled with data.

The first step in creating a table is to insert an empty table in the document. When inserting a table, you must specify the total number of rows and columns required, which is called the **dimension** of the table. The table in this project has five columns. You often do not know the total number of rows in a table. Thus, many Word users create one row initially and then add more rows as needed. In Word, the first number in a dimension is the number of columns, and the second is the number of rows. For example, in Word, a 5 × 1 (pronounced "five by one") table consists of five columns and one row.

To Insert an Empty Table

The next step is to insert an empty table in the letter. The following steps insert a table with five columns and one row at the location of the insertion point.

1

• Scroll the document up so that you will be able to see the table in the document window.

• With the insertion point positioned as shown in Figure 3–56, click the Table button (Insert tab | Tables group) to display the Table gallery (Figure 3–56).

Experiment

• Point to various cells on the grid to see a preview of various table dimensions in the document window.

Figure 3–56

2

● Position the mouse pointer on the cell in the first row and fifth column of the grid to preview the desired table dimension (Figure 3–57).

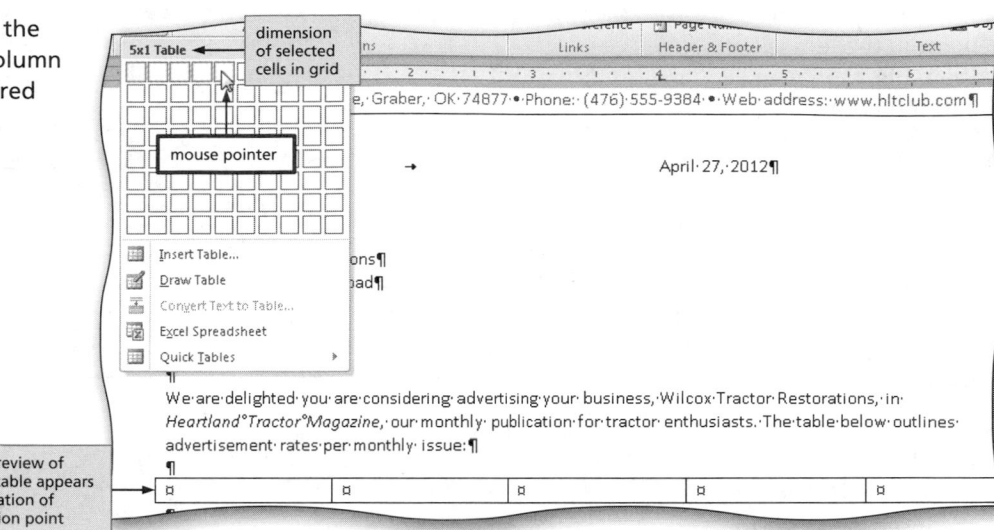

Figure 3–57

3

● Click the cell in the first row and fifth column of the grid to insert an empty table with one row and five columns in the document.

● If necessary, scroll the table up in the document window (Figure 3–58).

What are the small circles in the table cells?

Each table cell has an **end-of-cell mark**, which is a formatting mark that assists you with selecting and formatting cells. Similarly, each row has an **end-of-row mark**, which you can use to add columns to the right of a table. Recall that formatting marks do not print on a hard copy. The end-of-cell marks currently are left-aligned, that is, positioned at the left edge of each cell.

Figure 3–58

Other Ways
1. Click Table (Insert tab | Tables group), click Insert Table in Table gallery, enter number of columns and rows (Insert Table dialog box), click OK button

To Enter Data in a Table

The next step is to enter data in the cells of the empty table. The data you enter in a cell wordwraps just as text wordwraps between the margins of a document. To place data in a cell, you click the cell and then type.

To advance rightward from one cell to the next, press the TAB key. When you are at the rightmost cell in a row, press the TAB key to move to the first cell in the next row; do not press the ENTER key. The ENTER key is used to begin a new paragraph within a cell. One way to add new rows to a table is to press the TAB key when the insertion point is positioned in the bottom-right corner cell of the table. The step on the next page enters data in the first row of the table and then inserts a blank second row.

1

- With the insertion point in the left cell of the table, type **Type** and then press the TAB key to advance the insertion point to the next cell.

- Type **Dimensions** and then press the TAB key to advance the insertion point to the next cell.

- Type **Word Count** and then press the TAB key to advance the insertion point to the next cell.

- Type **Photo Count** and then press the TAB key to advance the insertion point to the next cell.

Figure 3–59

- Type **Cost** and then press the TAB key to insert a second row at the end of the table and position the insertion point in the first column of the new row (Figure 3–59).

How do I edit cell contents if I make a mistake?

Click in the cell and then correct the entry.

To Enter Data in a Table

The following steps enter the remaining data in the table.

1 Type **Full Page** and then press the TAB key to advance the insertion point to the next cell. Type **9" x 7"** and then press the TAB key to advance the insertion point to the next cell. Type **800** and then press the TAB key to advance the insertion point to the next cell. Type **4** and then press the TAB key to advance the insertion point to the next cell. Type **$650** and then press the TAB key to insert a row at the end of the table and position the insertion point in the first column of the new row.

2 In the third row, type **Half Page** in the first column, **4.5" x 7"** as the dimensions, **400** as the word count, **2** as the photo count, and **$350** as the cost. Press the TAB key to position the insertion point in the first column of a new row.

3 In the fourth row, type **Quarter Page** in the first column, **4.5" x 3.5"** as the dimensions, **200** as the word count, **1** as the photo count, and **$225** as the cost. Press the TAB key.

4 In the fifth row, type **Business Card** in the first column, **2.25" x 3.5"** as the dimensions, **100** as the word count, **0** as the photo count, and **$125** as the cost (Figure 3–60).

BTW

Tables
For simple tables, such as the one just created, Word users often select the table dimension in the Table gallery to create the table. For a more complex table, such as one with a varying number of columns per row, Word has a Draw Table feature that allows users to draw a table in the document using a pencil pointer. To use this feature, click the Table button (Insert tab | Tables group) and then click Draw Table.

Figure 3–60

To Apply a Table Style

The next step is to apply a table style to the table. Word provides a Table Styles gallery, allowing you to change the basic table format to a more visually appealing style. Word provides a gallery of more than 90 table styles, which include a variety of colors and shading. The following steps apply a table style to the table in the letter.

1

- With the insertion point in the table, be sure the check marks match those in the Table Style Options group (Table Tools Design tab) as shown in Figure 3–60.

What if the Table Tools Design tab no longer is the active tab?

Click in the table and then display the Table Tools Design tab.

What do the options in the Table Style Options group mean?

When you apply table styles, if you want the top row of the table (header row), a row containing totals (total row), first column, or last column to be formatted differently, select those check boxes. If you want the rows or columns to alternate with colors, select Banded Rows or Banded Columns, respectively.

2

- Click the More button in the Table Styles gallery (shown in Figure 3–60) (Table Tools Design tab | Table Styles group) to expand the gallery.

- Scroll and then point to Medium Grid 3 - Accent 4 in the Table Styles gallery to display a live preview of that style applied to the table in the document (Figure 3–61).

Experiment

- Point to various table styles in the Table Styles gallery and watch the format of the table change in the document window.

Figure 3–61

- Click Medium Grid 3 - Accent 4 in the Table Styles gallery to apply the selected style to the table (Figure 3–62).

🔍 **Experiment**

- Select and remove check marks from various check boxes in the Table Style Options group and watch the format of the table change in the document window. When finished experimenting, be sure the check marks match those shown in Figure 3–62.

Figure 3–62

To Resize Table Columns to Fit Table Contents

The table in this project currently extends from the left margin to the right margin of the document. You want each column to be only as wide as the longest entry in the table. That is, the first column must be wide enough to accommodate the words, Business Card, and the second column should be only as wide as the title, Dimensions, and so on. The following steps instruct Word to fit the width of the columns to the contents of the table automatically.

- With the insertion point in the table, display the Table Tools Layout tab.

- Click the AutoFit button (Table Tools Layout tab | Cell Size group) to display the AutoFit menu (Figure 3–63).

Q&A

What causes the table move handle and table resize handle to appear and disappear from the table?

They appear whenever you position the mouse pointer in the table.

Figure 3–63

- Click AutoFit Contents on the AutoFit menu, so that Word automatically adjusts the widths of the columns based on the text in the table (Figure 3–64).

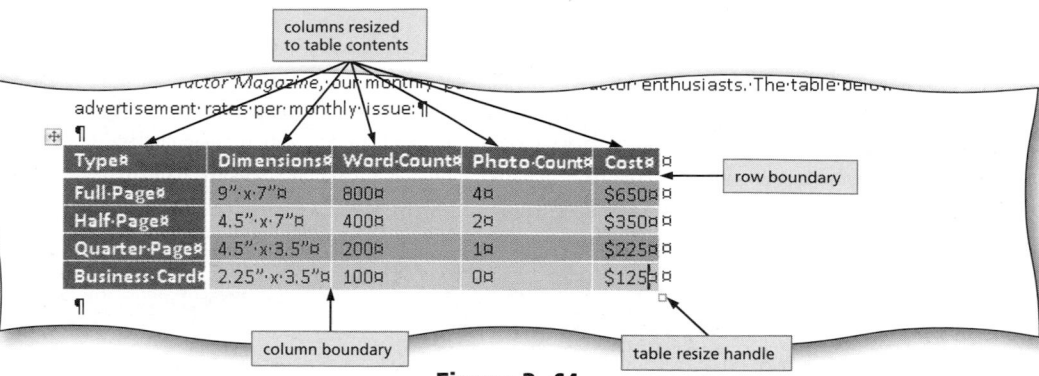

Figure 3–64

Can I resize columns manually?

Yes, you can drag a **column boundary**, the border to the right of a column, until the column is the desired width. Similarly, you can resize a row by dragging the **row boundary**, the border at the bottom of a row, until the row is the desired height. You also can resize the entire table by dragging the **table resize handle**, which is a small square that appears when you point to a corner of the table (shown in Figure 3–63).

Other Ways

1. Right-click table, point to AutoFit on shortcut menu, click AutoFit to Contents
2. Double-click column boundary

Selecting Table Contents

When working with tables, you may need to select the contents of cells, rows, columns, or the entire table. Table 3–4 identifies ways to select various items in a table.

Table 3–4 Selecting Items in a Table

Item to Select	Action
Cell	Point to left edge of cell and click when the mouse pointer changes to a small solid upward angled pointing arrow
	Or, position insertion point in cell, click Select button (Table Tools Layout tab | Table group), and then click Select Cell on the Select menu.
Column	Point to border at top of column and click when the mouse pointer changes to a small solid downward-pointing arrow.
	Or, position insertion point in column, click Select button (Table Tools Layout tab | Table group), and then click Select Column on the Select menu.
Row	Point to the left of the row and click when mouse pointer changes to a right-pointing block arrow.
	Or, position insertion point in row, click Select button (Table Tools Layout tab | Table group), and then click Select Row on the Select menu.
Multiple cells, rows, or columns adjacent to one another	Drag through cells, rows, or columns.
Multiple cells, rows, or columns not adjacent to one another	Select first cell, row, or column (as described above) and then hold down CTRL key while selecting next cell, row, or column.
Next cell	Press TAB key.
Previous cell	Press SHIFT+TAB.
Table	Point somewhere in table and then click table move handle that appears in upper-left corner of table.
	Or, position insertion point in table, click Select button (Table Tools Layout tab | Table group), and then click Select Table on the Select menu.

To Align Data in Cells

The next step is to change the alignment of the data in cells in the second, third, fourth, and fifth columns of the table. In addition to aligning text horizontally in a cell (left, center, or right), you can align it vertically within a cell (top, center, bottom). When the height of the cell is close to the same height as the text, however, differences in vertical alignment are not readily apparent, which is the case for this table. The following steps center data in cells.

- Select the cells in the second, third, fourth, and fifth columns using one of the techniques described in Table 3–4 on the previous page (Figure 3–65).

Figure 3–65

- Click the Align Top Center button (Table Tools Layout tab | Alignment group) to center the contents of the selected cells.

- Click in the table to remove the selection (Figure 3–66).

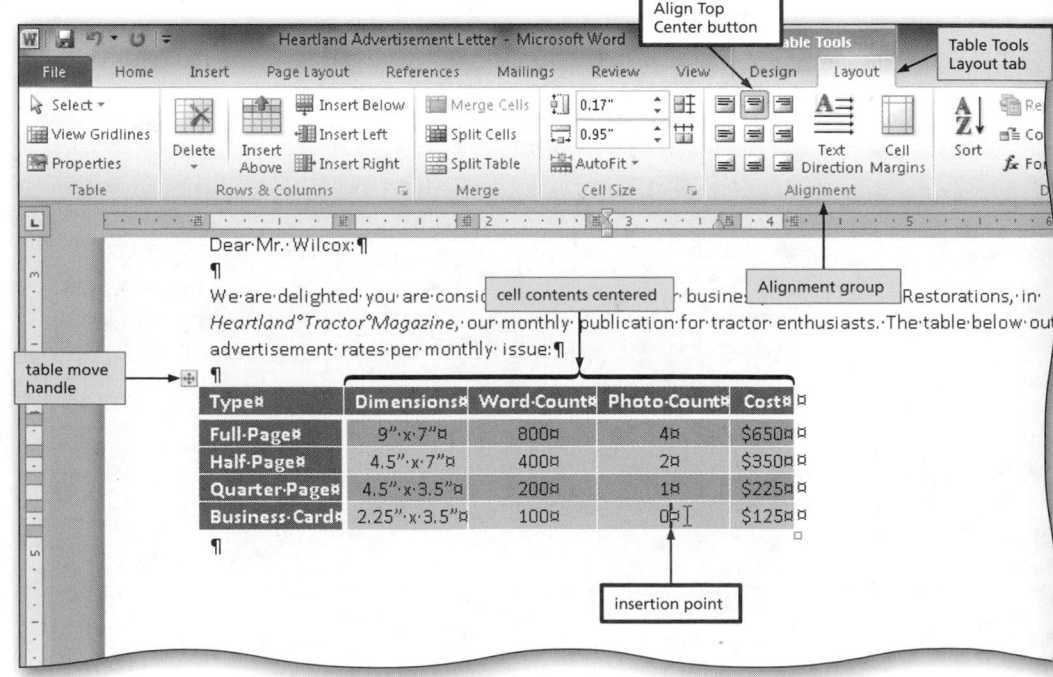

Figure 3–66

To Center a Table

When you first create a table, it is left-aligned, that is, flush with the left margin. In this letter, the table should e centered between the margins. To center a table, you first select the entire table. The following steps select and enter a table using the Mini toolbar.

- Position the mouse pointer in the table so that the table move handle appears (shown in Figure 3–66).

What if the table move handle does not appear?

You also can select a table by clicking the Select button (Table Tools Layout tab | Table group) and then clicking Select Table on the menu.

- Click the table move handle to select the entire table (Figure 3–67).

Figure 3–67

- Move the mouse pointer into the Mini toolbar, so that the toolbar changes to a bright toolbar. Click the Center button on the Mini toolbar to center the selected table between the left and right margins (Figure 3–68).

Could I have clicked the Center button on the Home tab?

Yes. If the command you want to use is

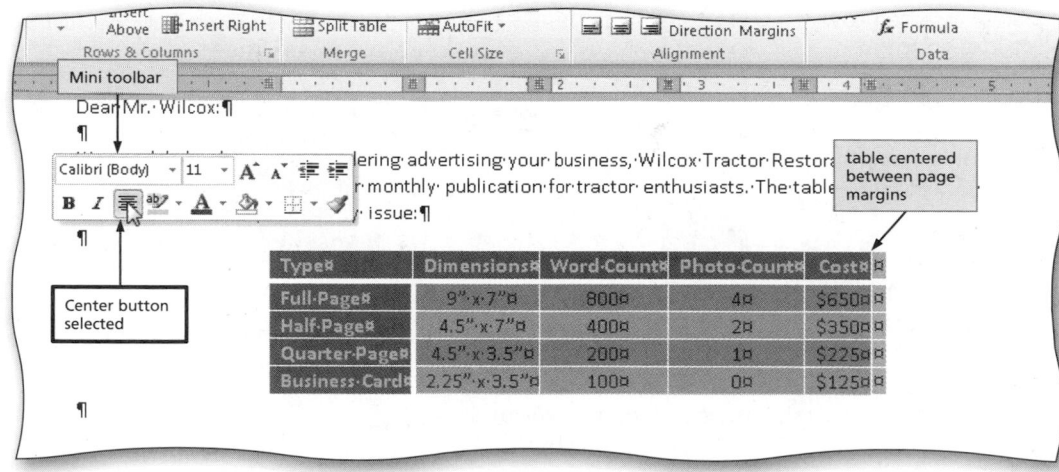

Figure 3–68

not on the currently displayed tab on the Ribbon and it is available on the Mini toolbar, use the Mini toolbar instead of switching to a different tab. This technique minimizes mouse movement.

To Insert a Row in a Table

The next step is to insert a row at the top of the table because you want to place a title on the table. As discussed earlier, you can insert a row at the end of a table by positioning the insertion point in the bottom-right corner cell and then pressing the TAB key. You cannot use the TAB key to insert a row at the beginning or middle of a table. Instead, you use the Insert Rows Above or Insert Rows Below command. The following steps insert a row in a table.

- Position the mouse pointer somewhere in the first row of the table because you want to insert a row above this row (Figure 3–69).

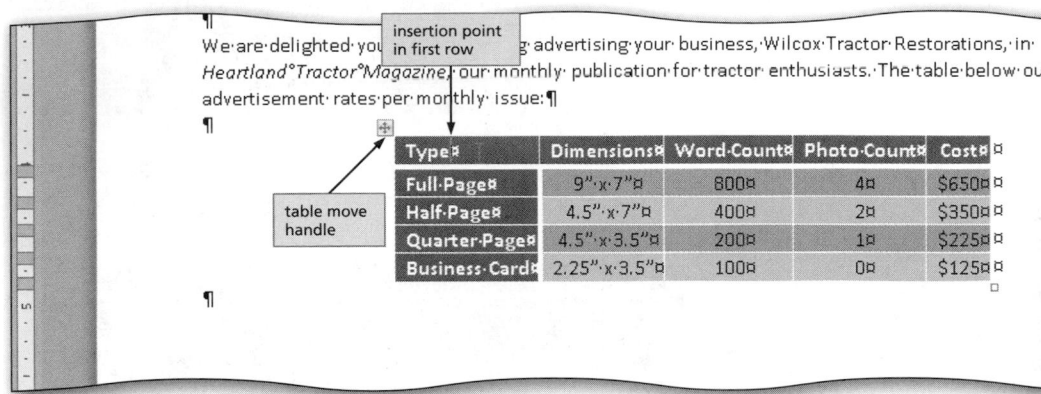

Figure 3–69

❷

- Click the Insert Rows Above button (Table Tools Layout tab | Rows & Columns group) to insert a row above the row containing the insertion point and then select the newly inserted row (Figure 3–70).

Q&A

Do I have to insert rows above the row containing the insertion point?

No. You can insert below the row containing the insertion point by clicking the Insert Rows Below button (Table Tools Layout tab | Rows & Columns group).

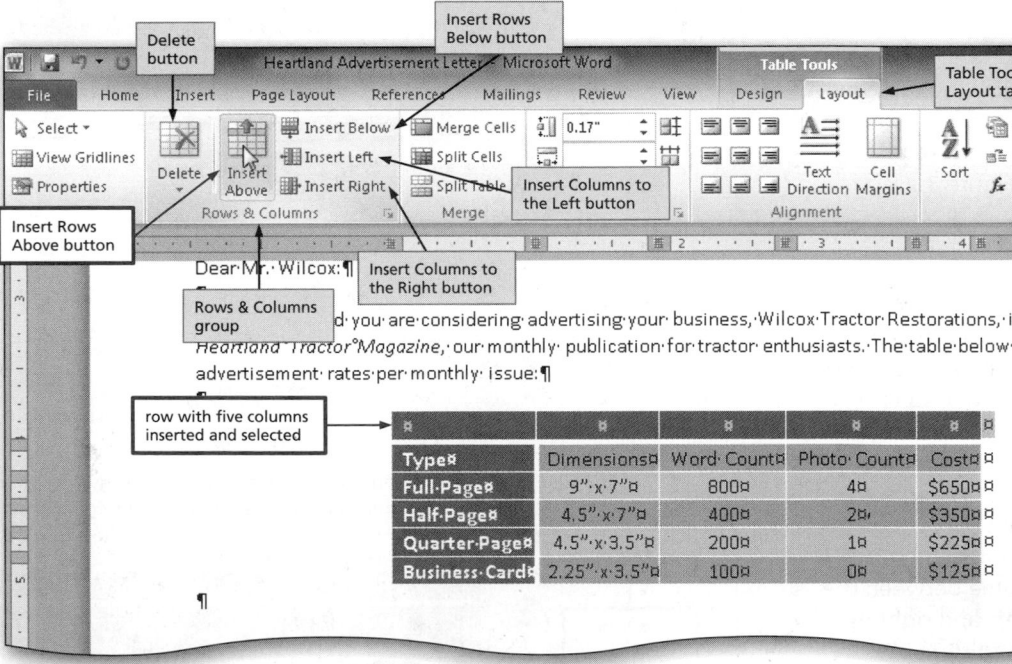

Figure 3–70

Q&A

Why did the colors in the second row change?

The table style specifies to format the Header row differently, which is the first row.

Other Ways

1. Right-click row, point to Insert on shortcut menu, click desired command on Insert submenu

TO INSERT A COLUMN IN A TABLE

If, instead of inserting rows, you wanted to insert a column in a table, you would perform the following steps.

1. Position the insertion point in the column to the left or right of where you want to insert the column.

2. Click the Insert Columns to the Left button (Table Tools Layout tab | Rows & Columns group) to insert a column to the left of the current column, or click the Insert Columns to the Right button (Table Tools Layout tab | Rows & Columns group) to insert a column to the right of the current column. Or you could right-click the table, point to Insert on the shortcut menu, and click Insert Columns to the Left or Insert Columns to the Right on the Insert submenu.

Deleting Table Data

If you want to delete row(s) or delete column(s) from a table, position the insertion point in the row(s) or column(s) to delete, click the Delete button (Table Tools Layout tab | Rows & Columns group), and then click Delete Rows or Delete Columns on the Delete menu. Or, select the row or column to delete, right-click the selection, and then click Delete Rows or Delete Columns on the shortcut menu.

To delete the contents of a cell, select the cell contents and then press the DELETE or BACKSPACE key. You also can drag and drop or cut and paste the contents of cells. To delete an entire table, select the table, click the Delete button (Table Tools Layout tab | Rows & Columns group), and then click Delete Table on the Delete menu. To delete the contents of a table and leave an empty table, you would select the table and then press the DELETE key.

To Merge Cells

The top row of the table is to contain the table title, which should be centered above the columns of the table. The row just inserted has one cell for each column, in this case, five cells (shown in Figure 3–70). The title of the table, however, should be in a single cell that spans all rows. Thus, the following steps merge the five cells into a single cell.

With the cells to merge selected (as shown in Figure 3–70), click the Merge Cells button (Table Tools Layout tab | Merge group) to merge the five cells into one cell (Figure 3–71).

Type	Dimensions	Word Count	Photo Count	Cost
Full-Page	9" x 7"	800	4	$650
Half-Page	4.5" x 7"	400	2	$350
Quarter-Page	4.5" x 3.5"	200	1	$225
Business-Card	2.25" x 3.5"	100	0	$125

Figure 3–71

- Position the insertion point in the first row and then type **Monthly Issue Advertisement Rates** as the table title (Figure 3–72).

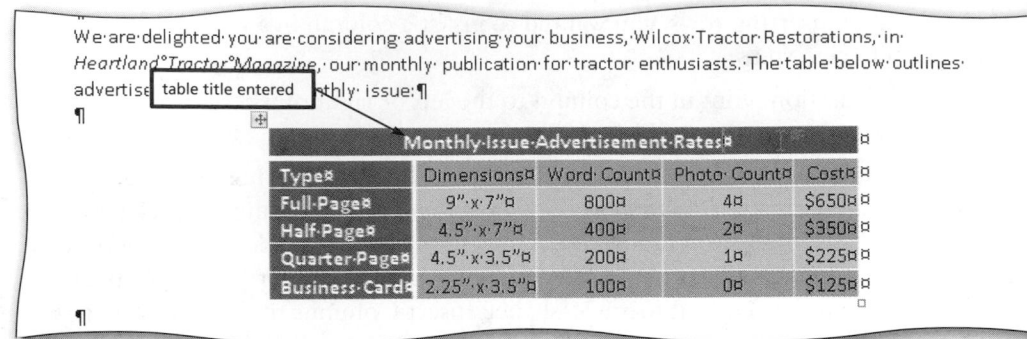

We·are·delighted·you·are·considering·advertising·your·business,·Wilcox·Tractor·Restorations,·in·
Heartland°Tractor°Magazine,·our·monthly·publication·for·tractor·enthusiasts.·The·table·below·outlines·
advertise [table title entered] thly·issue:¶

Monthly·Issue·Advertisement·Rates¤				
Type¤	Dimensions¤	Word·Count¤	Photo·Count¤	Cost¤
Full·Page¤	9"·x·7"¤	800¤	4¤	$650¤
Half·Page¤	4.5"·x·7"¤	400¤	2¤	$350¤
Quarter·Page¤	4.5"·x·3.5"¤	200¤	1¤	$225¤
Business·Card¤	2.25"·x·3.5"¤	100¤	0¤	$125¤

Figure 3–72

To Split Table Cells

Instead of merging multiple cells into a single cell, sometimes you want to split a single cell into multiple cells. If you wanted to split cells, you would perform the following steps.

1. Position the insertion point in the cell to split.
2. Click the Split Cells button (Table Tools Layout tab | Merge group), or right-click the cell and then click Split Cells on the shortcut menu, to display the Split Cells dialog box.
3. Enter the number of columns and rows into which you want the cell split (Split Cells dialog box).
4. Click the OK button.

To Add More Text

The table now is complete. The next step is to enter text below the table. The following steps enter text.

1 Position the insertion point on the paragraph mark below the table and then press the ENTER key.

2 Type **Please note that additional fees will be assessed if the word or photo counts exceed the limits listed above. We offe:** **the following discounts:** and then press the ENTER key (shown in Figure 3–73)

To Bullet a List as You Type

In Chapter 1, you learned how to apply bullets to existing paragraphs. If you know before you type that a list should be bulleted, you can use Word's AutoFormat As You Type feature to bullet the paragraphs as you type them (see Table 3–2 on page WD 162). The following steps add bullets to a list as you type.

1

- Press the ASTERISK key (*) as the first character on the line (Figure 3–73).

Half·Page¤	4.⟨		2¤	$350¤
Quarter·Page¤	4.5"·x·3.5"¤	200¤	1¤	$225¤
Business·Card¤	2.25"·x·3.5"¤	100¤	0¤	$125¤

[blank line] ¶

[text entered] Please·note·that·additional·fees·will·be·assessed·if·the·word·or·photo·counts·exceed·the·limits·listed·above.··We·
offer·the·following·discounts:¶

*¶

asterisk entered at beginning of line

Figure 3–73

2

● Press the SPACEBAR to convert the asterisk to a bullet character.

What if I did not want the asterisk converted to a bullet character?

You could undo the AutoFormat by clicking the Undo button, pressing CTRL+Z, clicking the AutoCorrect Options button that appears to the left of the bullet character as soon as you press the SPACEBAR, and then clicking Undo Automatic Bullets on the AutoCorrect Options menu, or by clicking the Bullets button (Home tab | Paragraph group).

● Type **10 percent discount for any advertisement that runs in three consecutive issues** as the first bulleted item.

● Press the ENTER key to place another bullet character at the beginning of the next line (Figure 3–74).

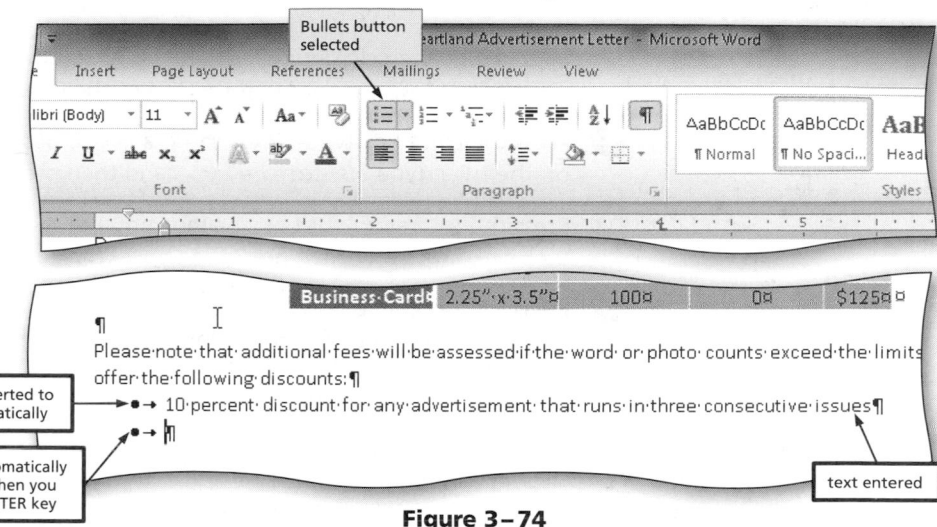

Figure 3–74

3

● Type **5 percent discount for a camera-ready advertisement (prepared using Microsoft Word at the proper size and with all words and photos in final layout form)** and then press the ENTER key.

● Type **3 percent discount if payment in full is submitted with order** and then press the ENTER key.

● Press the ENTER key to turn off automatic bullets as you type (Figure 3–75).

Why did automatic bullets stop?

When you press the ENTER key without entering any text after the automatic bullet character, Word turns off the automatic bullets feature.

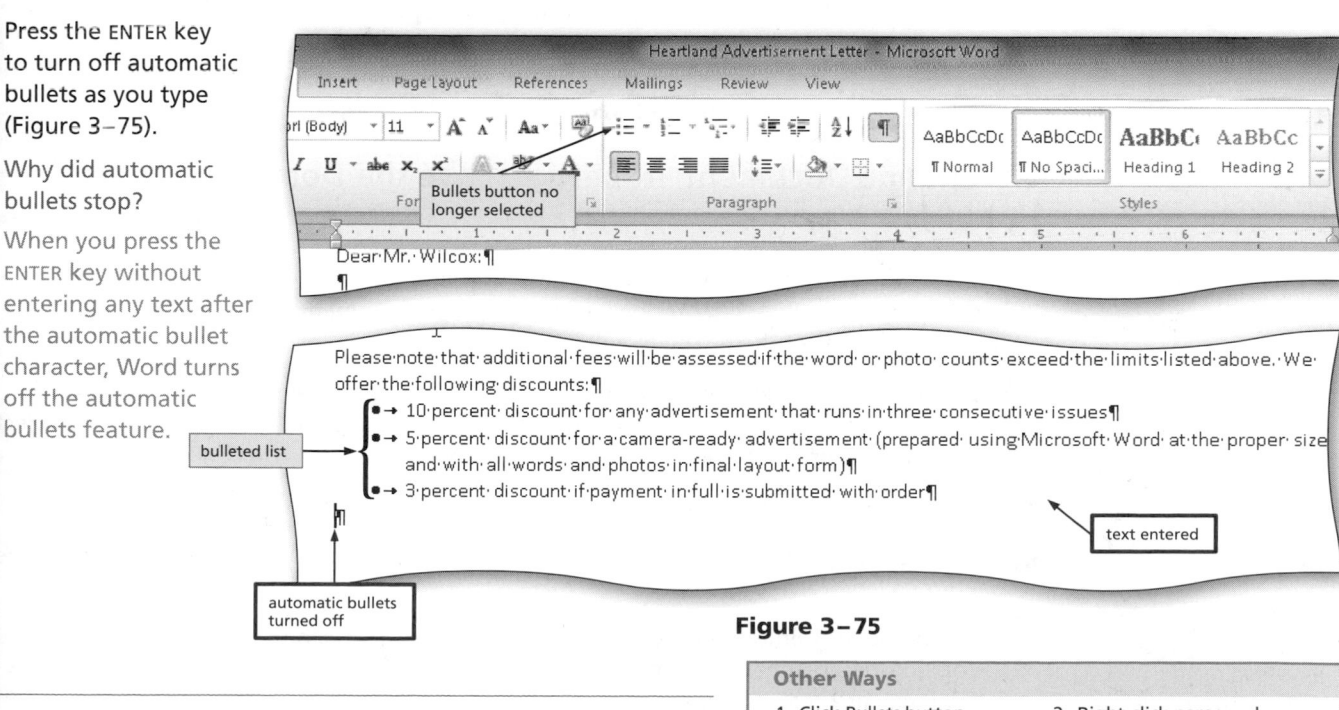

Figure 3–75

Other Ways	
1. Click Bullets button (Home tab | Paragraph group)	2. Right-click paragraph to be bulleted, point to Bullets on shortcut menu, click desired bullet style

BTW

Certification
The Microsoft Office Specialist (MOS) program provides an opportunity for you to obtain a valuable industry credential — proof that you have the Word 2010 skills required by employers. For more information, visit the Word 2010 Certification Web page (scsite.com/wd2010/cert).

To Enter More Text

The following steps enter the remainder of text in the letter.

① Press the ENTER key and then type the paragraph shown in Figure 3–76, making certain you use the building block name, wtr, to insert the advertiser name.

② If necessary, remove the hyperlink from the e-mail address by right-clicking the e-mail address and then clicking Remove Hyperlink on the shortcut menu. Press the END key to position the insertion point at the end of the line.

③ Press the ENTER key twice. Press the TAB key to position the insertion point at the 4" mark on the ruler. Type `Sincerely,` and then press the ENTER key four times.

④ Press the TAB key to position the insertion point at the 4" mark on the ruler. Type `Frank Urbanczyk` and then press the ENTER key.

⑤ Press the TAB key to position the insertion point at the 4" mark on the ruler. Type `President` as the final text in the business letter (Figure 3–76).

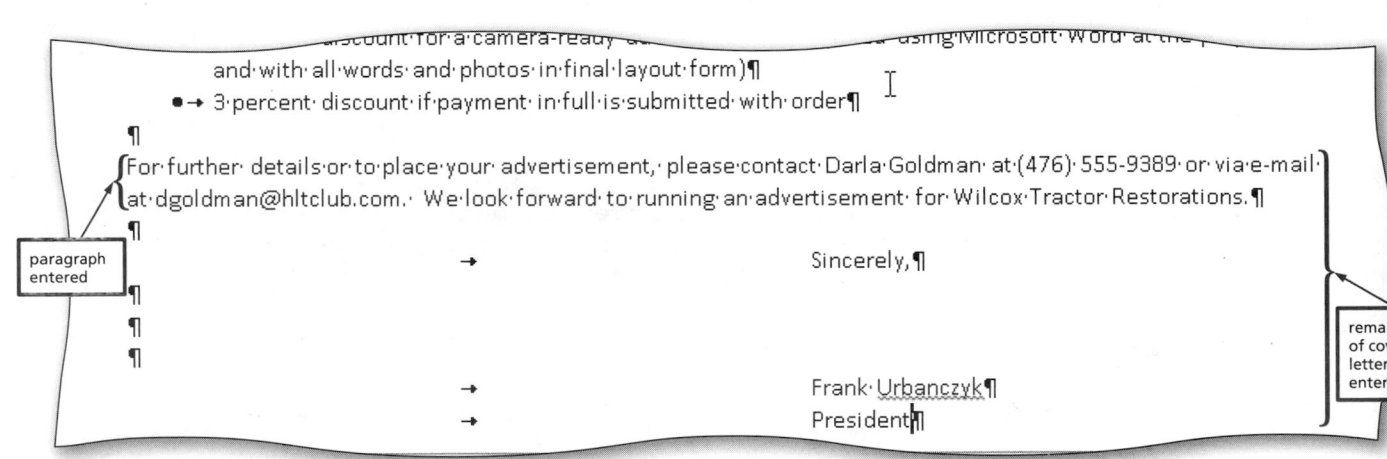

Figure 3–76

To Change Document Properties, Save the Document Again, and Print It

BTW

Conserving Ink and Toner
If you want to conserve ink or toner, you can instruct Word to print draft quality documents by clicking File on the Ribbon to open the Backstage view, clicking Options in the Backstage view to display the Word Options dialog box, clicking Advanced in the left pane (Word Options dialog box), scrolling to the Print area in the right pane, placing a check mark in the 'Use draft quality' check box, and then clicking the OK button. Then, use the Backstage view to print the document as usual.

Before saving the letter again, you want to add your name and course and section as document properties. The following steps change document properties, save the document again, and then print the document.

① Display the Document Information Panel in the Word document window. If necessary, enter your name in the Author property, and enter your course and section in the Subject property. Close the Document Information Panel.

② Click the Save button on the Quick Access Toolbar to overwrite the previously saved file.

③ Open the Backstage view and then click the Print tab in the Backstage view to display the Print gallery.

④ Verify the printer name that appears on the Printer Status button will print a hard copy of the document. If necessary, click the Printer Status button to display a list of available printer options and then click the desired printer to change the currently selected printer.

⑤ Click the Print button in the Print gallery to print the letter on the currently selected printer (shown in Figure 3–1 on page WD 139).

Addressing and Printing Envelopes and Mailing Labels

BTW

BTWs
For a complete list of the BTWs found in the margins of this book, visit the Word 2010 BTW Web page (scsite.com/wd2010/btw).

With Word, you can print address information on an envelope or on a mailing label. Computer-printed addresses look more professional than handwritten ones.

To Address and Print an Envelope

The following steps address and print an envelope. If you are in a lab environment, check with your instructor before performing these steps.

1
- Scroll through the letter to display the inside address in the document window.
- Drag through the inside address to select it (Figure 3–77).

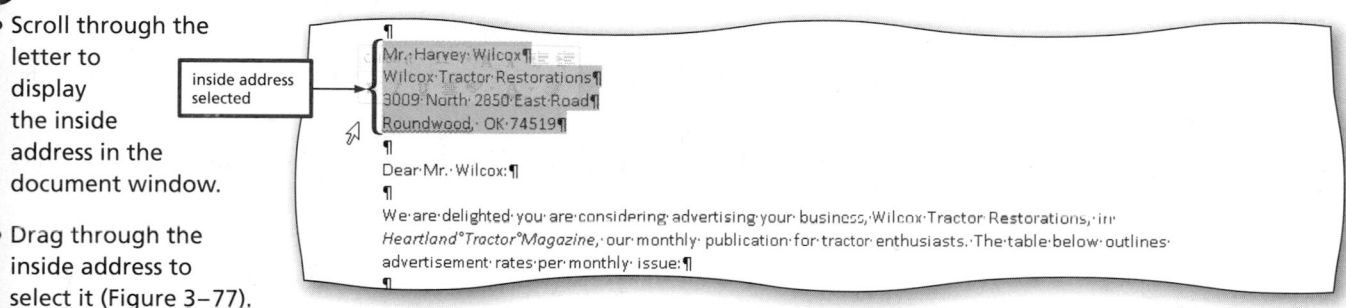

Figure 3–77

2
- Display the Mailings tab.
- Click the Create Envelopes button (Mailings tab | Create group) to display the Envelopes and Labels dialog box.
- If necessary, click the Envelopes tab (Envelopes and Labels dialog box) (Figure 3–78).

3
- Insert an envelope in your printer, as shown in the Feed area of the dialog box (your Feed area may be different depending on your printer).

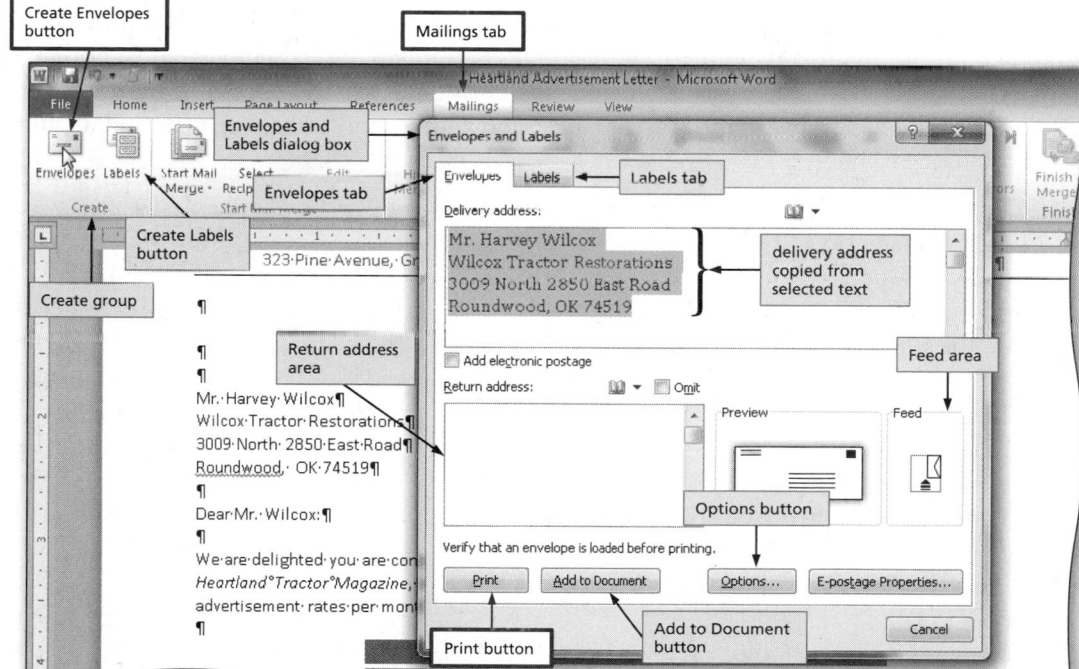

Figure 3–78

- Click the Print button (Envelopes and Labels dialog box) to print the envelope.

Envelopes and Labels

Instead of printing the envelope immediately, you can add it to the document by clicking the Add to Document button (Envelopes and Labels dialog box). To specify a different envelope or label type (identified by a number on the box of envelopes or labels), click the Options button (Envelopes and Labels dialog box).

Instead of printing an envelope, you can print a mailing label. To do this, click the Create Labels button (Mailings tab | Create group) (shown in Figure 3–78 on the previous page). Type the delivery address in the Delivery address box. To print the same address on all labels on the page, click 'Full page of the same label' in the Print area. Click the Print button (Envelopes and Labels dialog box) to print the label(s).

To Quit Word

This project now is complete. The following steps quit Word.

BTW

Quick Reference
For a table that lists how to complete the tasks covered in this book using the mouse, Ribbon, shortcut menu, and keyboard, see the Quick Reference Summary at the back of this book, or visit the Word 2010 Quick Reference Web page (scsite.com/wd2010/qr).

1 If you have one Word document open, click the Close button on the right side of the title bar to close the document and quit Word; or if you have multiple Word documents open, click File on the Ribbon to open the Backstage view and then click Exit in the Backstage view to close all open documents and quit Word.

2 If a Microsoft Word dialog box appears, click the Save button to save any changes made to the document since the last save.

3 If Word displays a dialog box asking if you want to save modified "Building Blocks", click the Save button.

Chapter Summary

In this chapter, you have learned how to use Word to change margins, insert and format a shape, change text wrapping, insert and format clip art, move and copy graphics, insert symbols, add a border, clear formatting, convert a hyperlink to regular text, create a file from an existing file, set and use tab stops, insert the current date, create and insert building blocks, insert and format tables, and address and print envelopes and mailing labels. The items listed below include all the new Word skills you have learned in this chapter.

1. Change Margin Settings (WD 141)
2. Insert a Shape (WD 142)
3. Apply a Shape Style (WD 144)
4. Add Text to a Shape (WD 145)
5. Use the Grow Font Button to Increase Font Size (WD 146)
6. Change an Object's Text Wrapping (WD 148)
7. Insert Clip Art (WD 148)
8. Resize a Graphic to a Percent of the Original (WD 150)
9. Change the Color of a Graphic (WD 151)
10. Set a Transparent Color in a Graphic (WD 152)
11. Adjust the Brightness and Contrast of a Graphic (WD 153)
12. Change the Border Color on a Graphic (WD 154)
13. Move a Graphic (WD 155)
14. Use Paste Options (WD 156)
15. Flip a Graphic (WD 157)
16. Insert a Symbol from the Symbol Dialog Box (WD 158)
17. Insert a Symbol from the Symbol Gallery (WD 159)
18. Bottom Border a Paragraph (WD 160)
19. Clear Formatting (WD 161)
20. Convert a Hyperlink to Regular Text (WD 163)
21. Create a New File from an Existing File (WD 165)
22. Apply a Quick Style (WD 166)
23. Set Custom Tab Stops (WD 169)
24. Insert the Current Date in a Document (WD 170)
25. Create a Building Block (WD 171)
26. Modify a Building Block (WD 173)
27. Insert a Building Block (WD 174)
28. Insert a Nonbreaking Space (WD 175)
29. Insert an Empty Table (WD 176)
30. Enter Data in a Table (WD 177)
31. Apply a Table Style (WD 179)
32. Resize Table Columns to Fit Table Contents (WD 180)
33. Align Data in Cells (WD 182)
34. Center a Table (WD 183)
35. Insert a Row in a Table (WD 184)
36. Insert a Column in a Table (WD 185)
37. Merge Cells (WD 185)
38. Split Table Cells (WD 186)
39. Bullet a List as You Type (WD 186)
40. Address and Print an Envelope (WD 189)

 If you have a SAM 2010 user profile, your instructor may have assigned an autogradable version of this assignment. If so, log into the SAM 2010 Web site at www.cengage.com/sam2010 to download the instruction and start files.

Learn It Online

Test your knowledge of chapter content and key terms.

Instructions: To complete the Learn It Online exercises, start your browser, click the Address bar, and then enter the Web address `scsite.com/wd2010/learn`. When the Word 2010 Learn It Online page is displayed, click the link for the exercise you want to complete and then read the instructions.

Chapter Reinforcement TF, MC, and SA

A series of true/false, multiple choice, and short answer questions that test your knowledge of the chapter content.

Flash Cards

An interactive learning environment where you identify chapter key terms associated with displayed definitions.

Practice Test

A series of multiple choice questions that test your knowledge of chapter content and key terms.

Who Wants To Be a Computer Genius?

An interactive game that challenges your knowledge of chapter content in the style of a television quiz show.

Wheel of Terms

An interactive game that challenges your knowledge of chapter key terms in the style of the television show *Wheel of Fortune*.

Crossword Puzzle Challenge

A crossword puzzle that challenges your knowledge of key terms presented in the chapter.

Apply Your Knowledge

Reinforce the skills and apply the concepts you learned in this chapter.

Working with Tabs and a Table

Note: To complete this assignment, you will be required to use the Data Files for Students. See the inside back cover of this book for instructions on downloading the Data Files for Students, or contact your instructor for information about accessing the required files.

Instructions: Start Word. Create a new document from the file called Apply 3-1 Projected College Expenses Draft, located on the Data Files for Students. The document is a Word table that you are to edit and format. The revised table is shown in Figure 3–79.

Projected College Expenses

	Freshman	Sophomore	Junior	Senior
Room & Board	3390.00	3627.30	3881.21	4152.90
Tuition & Books	4850.50	5189.50	5552.72	5941.46
Entertainment	635.00	679.45	727.01	777.90
Cell Phone	359.88	365.78	372.81	385.95
Miscellaneous	325.00	347.75	372.09	398.14
Clothing	540.25	577.80	618.29	661.52
Total	$10,100.63	$10,787.58	$11,524.13	$12,317.87

Figure 3–79

Continued >

Apply Your Knowledge *continued*

Perform the following tasks:

1. In the line containing the table title, Projected College Expenses, remove the tab stop at the 1" mark on the ruler.

2. Set a centered tab at the 3" mark on the ruler.

3. Bold the characters in the title. Use the Grow Font button to increase their font size to 14. Change their color to Dark Blue, Text 2, Darker 25%.

4. In the table, delete the row containing the Food expenses.

5. Insert a new row at the bottom of the table. In the first cell of the new row, enter Total in the cell. Enter these values in the next three cells: Freshman – $10,100.63; Sophomore – $10,787.58; Senior – $12,317.87.

6. Insert a column between the Sophomore and Senior columns. Fill in the column as follows: Column Title – Junior; Room & Board – 3881.21; Tuition & Books – 5552.72; Entertainment – 727.01; Cell Phone – 372.81; Miscellaneous – 372.09; Clothing – 618.29; Total – $11,524.13.

7. In the Table Style Options group (Table Tools Design tab), these check boxes should have check marks: Header Row, Total Row, Banded Rows, and First Column. The Last Column and Banded Columns check boxes should not be selected.

8. Apply the Medium Grid 3 - Accent 2 style to the table.

9. Make all columns as wide as their contents (AutoFit Contents).

10. Center the cells containing the column headings.

11. Right-align all cells containing numbers in the table.

12. Center the table between the left and right margins of the page.

13. Change the document properties, as specified by your instructor.

14. Save the document using the file name, Apply 3-1 Projected College Expenses Modified and submit it in the format specified by your instructor.

Extend Your Knowledge

Extend the skills you learned in this chapter and experiment with new skills. You may need to use Help to complete the assignment.

Working with Formulas, Clip Art, Sorting, Picture Bullets, Tabs, and Mailing Labels

Note: To complete this assignment, you will be required to use the Data Files for Students. See the inside back cover of this book for instructions on downloading the Data Files for Students, or contact your instructor for information about accessing the required files.

Instructions: Start Word. Create a new document from the file called Extend 3-1 Herbals Letter Draft, located on the Data Files for Students. You will enter formulas in the table, change the clip art to Web clip art, change the table style, sort paragraphs, use picture bullets, move tabs, print mailing labels, and work with the Clip Organizer.

Perform the following tasks:

1. Use Help to learn about entering formulas, clip art from the Web, sorting, picture bullets, and printing mailing labels.

2. Use the Formula dialog box (Figure 3–80) to add formulas to the last column in the table so that the total due displays for each item; be sure to enter a number format so that the products are

displayed with dollar signs. Then, add formulas to the last row in the table so that the total quantity and total due are displayed, also with dollar signs. Write down the formulas that Word uses to find the product of values in the rows and to sum the values in a column.

3. Delete the current clip art images in the letterhead. Use the Clip Art pane to locate appropriate clip art from the Web, make the clip available offline, and insert an image on each side of the business name in the letterhead.

4. Change the table style. One at a time, select and deselect each check box in the Table Style Options group. Write down the function of each check box: Header Row, Total Row, Banded Rows, First Column, Last Column, and Banded Columns. Select the check boxes you prefer for the table.

5. Sort the paragraphs in the bulleted list.

6. Change the bullets in the bulleted list to picture bullets.

7. Move the tab stops in the date line, complimentary close, and signature block from the 3.5" mark to the 4" mark on the ruler.

8. Change the document properties, as specified by your instructor. Save the revised document and then submit it in the format specified by your instructor.

9. Print a single mailing label for the letter.

10. Print a full page of mailing labels, each containing the address shown in Figure 3–80.

11. If your instructor approves, start the Clip Organizer. How many collections appear? Expand the Office Collections. Copy one of the Academic clips to the Favorites folder in the My Collections folder. Locate the clip you made available offline in Step 3 and then preview it. What are five of its properties? Add a keyword to the clip. Delete the clip you made available offline.

Figure 3–80

Make It Right

Analyze a document and correct all errors and/or improve the design.

Formatting a Business Letter

Note: To complete this assignment, you will be required to use the Data Files for Students. See the inside back cover of this book for instructions on downloading the Data Files for Students, or contact your instructor for information about accessing the required files.

Instructions: Start Word. Create a new document from the file called Make It Right 3-1 Scholarship Letter Draft, located on the Data Files for Students. The document is a business letter that is missing elements and is formatted poorly or incorrectly (Figure 3–81). You are to insert and format clip art in the letterhead, change the color of the text and graphic(s), insert symbols, remove a hyperlink, change the letter style from block to modified block, and format the table.

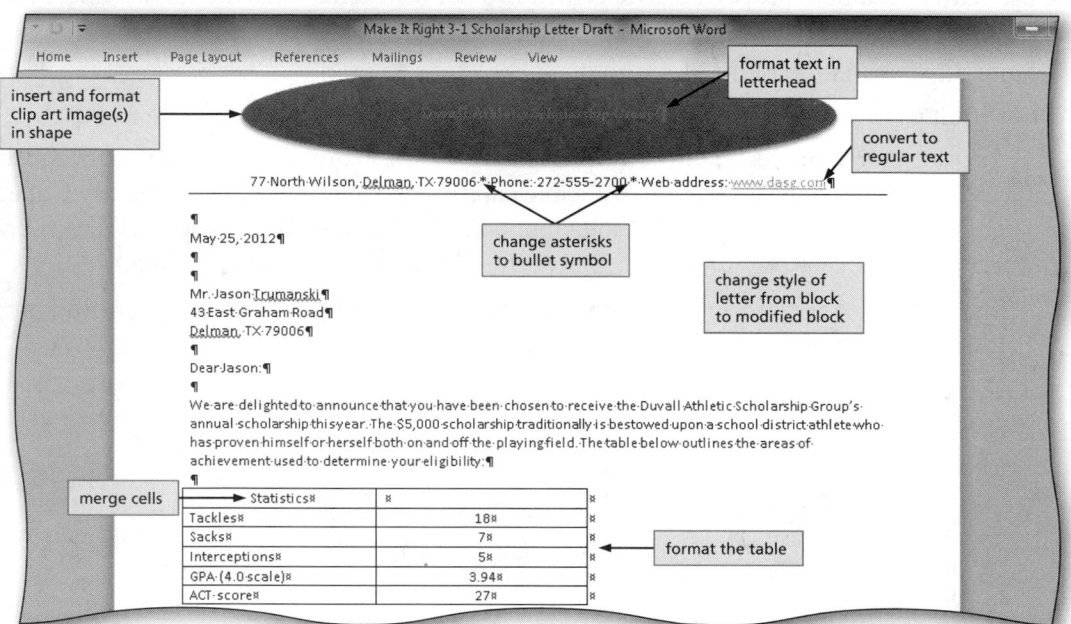

Figure 3–81

Perform the following tasks:

1. Increase the font size of the text in the letterhead. Change the color of the text in the letterhead.

2. Locate and insert at least one appropriate clip art image in the letterhead. If necessary, resize the graphic(s). Move the graphic(s) into the shape.

3. Change the color of the graphic to match the color of the text or shape. Adjust the brightness and contrast of the graphic. Format one color in the graphic as transparent. Change the picture border color.

4. Change the asterisks in the contact information to the dot symbol. Convert the Web address hyperlink to regular text.

5. The letter currently is the block letter style. It should be the modified block letter style. Format the appropriate paragraphs by setting custom tab stops and then positioning those paragraphs at the tab stops. Be sure to position the insertion point in the paragraph before setting the tab stop.

6. Merge the two cells in the first row of the table to one cell and then center the title in the cell. Center the entire table between the page margins. Apply a table style of your choice.

7. Change the document properties, as specified by your instructor. Save the revised document using the file name, Make It Right 3-1 Scholarship Letter Modified, and then submit it in the format specified by your instructor.

n the Lab

Design and/or create a document using the guidelines, concepts, and skills presented in this chapter. Labs are listed in order of increasing difficulty.

Lab 1: Creating a Letter with a Letterhead

Problem: As a consultant for DataLock Storage, you respond to queries from potential customers. One letter you prepare is shown in Figure 3–82.

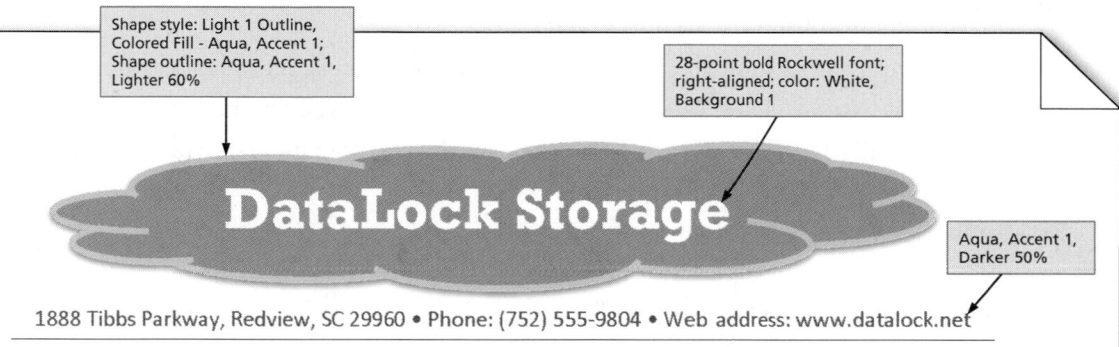

Shape style: Light 1 Outline, Colored Fill - Aqua, Accent 1; Shape outline: Aqua, Accent 1, Lighter 60%

28-point bold Rockwell font; right-aligned; color: White, Background 1

Aqua, Accent 1, Darker 50%

DataLock Storage

1888 Tibbs Parkway, Redview, SC 29960 • Phone: (752) 555-9804 • Web address: www.datalock.net

April 6, 2012

Ms. Shannon Kates
922 West Court Street
Redview, SC 29960

Dear Ms. Kates:

Thank you for your recent inquiry regarding our cloud storage service. Our basic plan provides 50 GB of storage space at a monthly rate of $5.95, and our elite plan provides 500 GB of storage space at a monthly rate of $25.95.

Please note that additional storage plans and services are available, depending upon your storage needs. In addition to secure data storage, we offer the following:

- Robust encryption techniques
- Automatic backups
- Specialized technical support 24/7/365
- Remote access

For further details or to develop a monthly plan tailored to your specific storage needs, please contact me at (752) 555-9804 or via e-mail at ageorge@datalock.net. We look forward to working with you to solve your data storage needs.

Sincerely,

Andy George
Consultant

Figure 3–82

Continued >

In the Lab *continued*

Perform the following tasks:

1. Change the theme colors to Technic.

2. Create the letterhead shown at the top of Figure 3–82 on the previous page, following these guidelines:

   a. Insert the cloud shape at an approximate height of 0.95" and width of 5.85". Change text wrapping for the shape to Top and Bottom. Add the company name, DataLock Storage, to the shape. Format the shape and its text as indicated in the figure.

   b. Insert the bullet symbols as shown in the contact information. Remove the hyperlink format from the Web address. If necessary, clear formatting after entering the bottom border.

   c. Save the letterhead with the file name, Lab 3-1 Cloud Storage Letterhead.

3. Create the letter shown in Figure 3–82 using the modified block letter style, following these guidelines:

   a. Apply the No Spacing Quick Style to the document text (below the letterhead).

   b. Set a left-aligned tab stop at the 3.5" mark on the ruler for the date line, complimentary close, and signature block. Insert the current date.

   c. Bullet the list as you type it.

   d. Convert the e-mail address to regular text.

   e. Check the spelling of the letter. Change the document properties, as specified by your instructor. Save the letter with Lab 3-1 Cloud Storage Letter as the file name.

4. If your instructor permits, address and print an envelope or a mailing label for the letter.

In the Lab

Lab 2: Creating a Letter with a Letterhead and Table

Problem: As head librarian at Jonner Public Library, you are responsible for sending confirmation letters for class registrations. You prepare the letter shown in Figure 3–83.

Perform the following tasks:

1. Change the theme colors to Trek. Change the margins to 1" top and bottom and .75" left and right.

2. Create the letterhead shown at the top of Figure 3–83, following these guidelines:

   a. Insert the down ribbon shape at an approximate height of 1" and width of 7". Change text wrapping for the shape to Top and Bottom. Add the library name to the shape. Format the shape and its text as indicated in the figure.

   b. Insert the clip art image, resize it, change text wrapping to Top and Bottom, move it to the left of the shape, and format it as indicated in the figure. Copy the clip art image and move the copy of the image to the right of the shape, as shown in the figure. Flip the copied image horizontally.

   c. Insert the black small square symbols as shown in the contact information. Remove the hyperlink format from the Web address. If necessary, clear formatting after entering the bottom border.

   d. Save the letterhead with the file name, Lab 3-2 Library Letterhead.

3. Create the letter shown in Figure 3–83, following these guidelines:

   a. Apply the No Spacing Quick Style to the document text (below the letterhead).

   b. Set a left-aligned tab stop at the 4" mark on the ruler for the date line, complimentary close, and signature block. Insert the current date.

   c. Insert and center the table. Format the table as specified in the figure.

   d. Bullet the list as you type it. Convert the e-mail address to regular text.

   e. Check the spelling of the letter. Change the document properties, as specified by your instructor. Save the letter with Lab 3-2 Library Letter as the file name.

4. If your instructor permits, address and print an envelope or a mailing label for the letter.

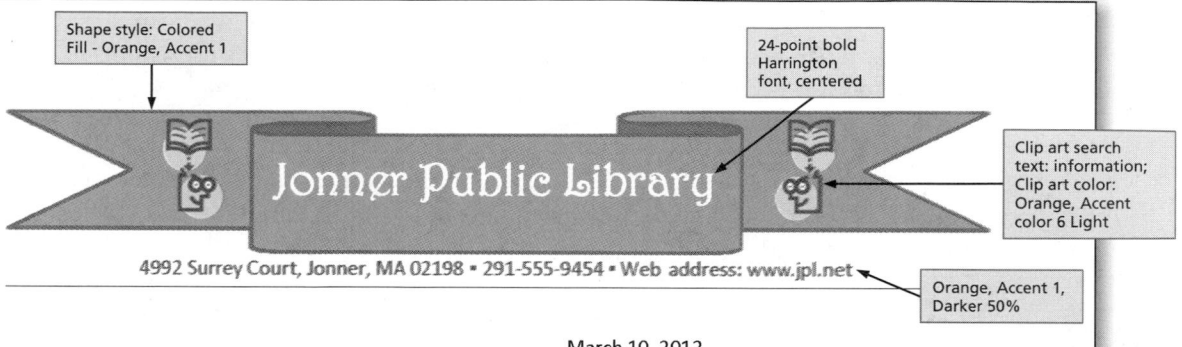

Shape style: Colored Fill - Orange, Accent 1

24-point bold Harrington font, centered

Clip art search text: information; Clip art color: Orange, Accent color 6 Light

Orange, Accent 1, Darker 50%

March 10, 2012

Mr. Brent Jackson
5153 Anlyn Drive
Jonner, MA 02198

Dear Mr. Jackson:

Thank you for registering online for our spring classes. As a library patron, you are aware that we offer a great deal more than books and magazines. The table below outlines the classes for which you have registered, along with the dates and locations:

Table style: Medium Grid 3 - Accent 1; Table style options: Header Row and Banded Columns

Class	Date	Location
Intro to Windows 7	April 10	Room 10B
eBay Basics	April 18	Room 24C
Genealogy Searches	April 24	Room 10B
Overview of Office 2010	April 28	Room 22A

Note that all classes, regardless of date, begin at 10:00 a.m. and last four hours. Although no materials or textbooks are required for the classes, you are strongly encouraged to bring the following items:

- Pens, pencils, or other writing implements
- Blank CD or DVD to store documents and notes created during class
- Notebook or loose-leaf binder for handwritten notes
- Your valid library card to verify enrollment eligibility

Please note that no food or drinks are allowed in any of our computer facilities. If you have any questions or would like to register for additional courses, please contact me at (291) 555-9454 or via e-mail at mtlawrence@jpl.net.

Again, thank you for your interest in and continued patronage of Jonner Public Library. We look forward to seeing you when your first class begins.

Sincerely,

Marcia Lawrence
Head Librarian

Figure 3–83

STUDENT ASSIGNMENTS

In the Lab

Lab 3: Creating a Letter with a Letterhead and Table

Problem: As president of the County Education Board, you communicate with schools in your district
One of the schools has just been awarded a four-star rating.

Instructions: Prepare the letter shown in Figure 3–84. Change the theme colors to Pushpin. Change
the margins to 1" top and bottom and .75" left and right. Follow the guidelines in the modified semi-
block letter style. Use proper spacing between elements of the letter. After entering the inside address,

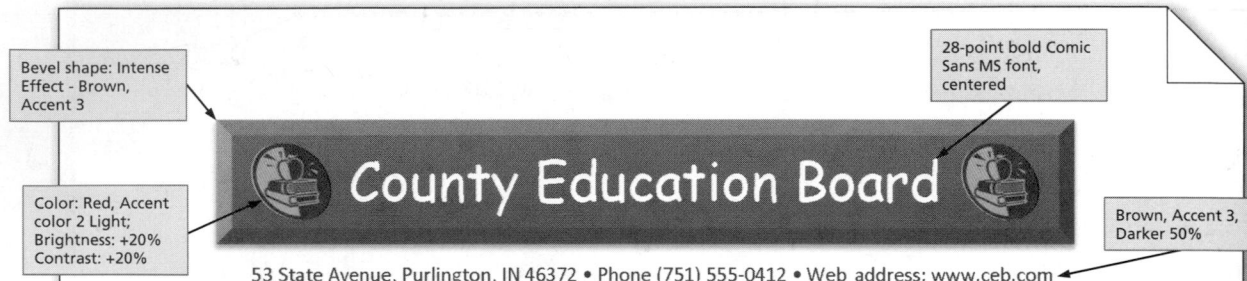

Bevel shape: Intense
Effect - Brown,
Accent 3

28-point bold Comic
Sans MS font,
centered

Color: Red, Accent
color 2 Light;
Brightness: +20%
Contrast: +20%

Brown, Accent 3,
Darker 50%

53 State Avenue, Purlington, IN 46372 • Phone (751) 555-0412 • Web address: www.ceb.com

March 31, 2012

Ms. Sarah Rosen, Principal
Fair Grove Elementary School
3373 Sherman Boulevard
Purlington, IN 46372

Dear Ms. Rosen:

We are delighted to announce that a four-star rating has been granted to Fair Grove Elementary School
for the fifth consecutive year. As you know, this rating is the highest distinction a county school can receive. The
table below outlines the county requirements compared with Fair Grove's overall figures:

Table style: Medium
Grid 3 - Accent 3; Table
style options: Header
Row and First Column

Four-Star Ranking Requirements		
Area	Minimum Requirement	Fair Grove Figure
Attendance	95%	97.2%
Language Proficiency	90%	91.1%
Math Proficiency	90%	90.7%

To earn a four-star rating, schools must rank in the top 20 percent of the three areas shown in the table.
Fair Grove Elementary School is one of only ten county schools to achieve this distinction. In addition to the
academic performance and attendance figures, we recognize your other achievements, as follows:

- Nearly 80 percent of Fair Grove students are involved in extracurricular activities
- Operating expenses and budget are kept to a minimum, with no additional funds requested from county
  budget last year
- High rate of teacher retention and satisfaction
- Parental involvement and inclusion in coursework, volunteer projects, and unpaid positions (i.e.,
  recreational sports league coaches, cafeteria monitors, chaperones, etc.)

The County Education Board extends its congratulations to you for a job well done. Please accept our
thanks for your continuing role in shaping our county's future citizens.

Sincerely,

Walt Andreas
President

Figure 3–84

create a building block for Fair Grove Elementary School and insert the building block whenever you have to enter the school name. Resize table columns to fit contents. Check the spelling of the letter. Change the document properties, as specified by your instructor. Save the letter with Lab 3-3 Education Board Letter as the file name.

Cases and Places

Apply your creative thinking and problem solving skills to design and implement a solution.

Note: To complete these assignments, you may be required to use the Data Files for Students. See the inside back cover of this book for instructions on downloading the Data Files for Students, or contact your instructor for information about accessing the required files.

1: Create a Letter to a Potential Employer
Academic
As a student about to graduate, you are actively seeking employment in your field and have located an advertisement for a job in which you are interested. You decide to write a letter to the potential employer: Ms. Janice Tremont at Home Health Associates, 554 Mountain View Lane, Blue Dust, MO 64319.

The draft wording for the letter is as follows: I am responding to your advertisement for the nursing position in the *Blue Dust Press*. I have tailored my activities and education for a career in geriatric medicine. This month, I will graduate with concentrations in Geriatric Medicine (24 hours), Osteopathic Medicine (12 hours), and Holistic Nursing (9 hours). In addition to receiving my bachelor degree in nursing, I have enhanced my education by participating in the following activities: volunteered at Blue Dust's free health care clinic; attended several continuing education and career-specific seminars, including An Aging Populace, Care of the Homebound, and Special Needs of the Elderly; completed one-semester internship at Blue Dust Community Hospital in spring semester of 2012; completed Certified Nursing Assistant (CNA) program at Blue Dust Community College; and worked as nurse's aide for two years during college. I look forward to an interview so that we can discuss the position you offer and my qualifications. With my background and education, I am confident that I will make a positive contribution to Home Health Associates.

The letter should contain a letterhead that uses a shape and clip art, a table (use a table to present the areas of concentration), and a bulleted list (use a bulleted list to present the activities). Insert nonbreaking spaces in the newspaper name. Use the concepts and techniques presented in this chapter to create and format a letter according to the modified block style, creating appropriate paragraph breaks and rewording the draft as necessary. Use your personal information for contact information in the letter. Be sure to check the spelling and grammar of the finished letter. Submit your assignment in the format specified by your instructor.

2: Create a Letter Requesting Donations
Personal
As an alumnus of your historic high school, you are concerned that the building is being considered for demolition. You decide to write a letter to another graduate: Mr. Jim Lemon, 87 Travis Parkway, Vigil, CT 06802.

The draft wording for the letter is as follows: As a member of the class of 1988, you, like many others, probably have many fond memories of our alma mater, Vigil East High School. I recently learned that the building is being considered for demolition because of its age and structural integrity.

Continued >

Cases and Places *continued*

As a result, I have decided to call upon the many graduating classes of the school to band together and save the historic building from demolition. According to the documents I have reviewed and information from meetings I have attended, a minimum of $214,000 is necessary to save the school and bring it up to code. Once the repairs are made, I plan to start the process of having it declared an historic landmark. You can help by donating your time, skills, or money. We need skilled tradesmen, including carpenters, roofers, plumbers, and electricians, as well as laborers. In addition, we are asking for monetary donations, as follows, although donations in any amount will be accepted gladly: a donation of $100 categorizes you as a Save Our School Friend, $250 a Patron, and $500 a Benefactor. Once our monetary goal has been reached, the necessary repairs and replacements will be made as follows: Phase I: roof and exterior, Phase II: electrical and plumbing, and Phase III: interior walls, trim, flooring, and fixtures. I hope you will join our conservation efforts so that Vigil East High School will continue to stand proudly for many more years. If you have questions, please contact me at the phone number or e-mail address above. I hope to hear from you soon.

The letter should contain a letterhead that uses a shape and clip art, a table (use a table to present the Save Our School donor categories), and a bulleted list (use a bulleted list to present the phases). Use the concepts and techniques presented in this chapter to create and format a letter according to the modified block style, creating appropriate paragraph breaks and rewording the draft as necessary. Use your personal information for contact information in the letter and Save Our School as the text in the letterhead. Be sure to check spelling and grammar of the finished letter. Submit your assignment in the format specified by your instructor.

3: Create a Confirmation Letter

Professional

As coordinator for Condor Parks and Recreation, you send letters to confirm registration for activities. You write a confirmation letter to this registrant: Ms. Tracey Li, 52 West 15th Street, Harpville, KY 42194. Condor Parks and Recreation is located at 2245 Community Place, Harpville, KY 42194; phone number is (842) 555-0444; and Web address is www.condorparks.com.

The draft wording for the letter is as follows: Thank you for your interest in our new spring activities recently listed in the *Condor Daily Press*. The courses for which you have enrolled, along with their dates and times are Introductory Golf Clinic on May 5 – 6 from 4:00 – 6:00 p.m. at a cost of $25, Recreational League Volleyball on April 30 – May 28 from 7:30 – 9:00 p.m. at a cost of $130, Pilates on May 30 – June 27 from 8:00 – 9:00 p.m. at a cost of $75, and Intermediate Golf Clinic on June 9 – 10 from 12:00 – 2:00 p.m. at a cost of $30. By paying your annual $25 parks and recreation fee, you also are entitled to the following benefits: free access to racquetball and tennis courts, on a first-come-first-served basis; attendance at any park-sponsored events, including plays, musical performances, and festivals; and free parking at any parks and recreation facility. Please confirm your registration by calling me at [enter your phone number here] or via e-mail at [enter your e-mail address here]. Thank you for your interest in Condor Parks and Recreation offerings. We look forward to seeing you at upcoming events.

The letter should contain a letterhead that uses a shape and clip art, a table (use a table to present the courses enrolled), and a bulleted list (use a bulleted list to present the benefits). Insert nonbreaking spaces in the newspaper name. Use the concepts and techniques presented in this chapter to create and format a letter according to the modified block style, creating appropriate paragraph breaks and rewording the draft as necessary. Be sure to check spelling and grammar of the finished letter. Submit your assignment in the format specified by your instructor.

1 Creating and Editing a Presentation with Clip Art

Objectives

You will have mastered the material in this chapter when you can:

- Select a document theme
- Create a title slide and a text slide with a multi-level bulleted list
- Add new slides and change slide layouts
- Insert clips and pictures into a slide with and without a content placeholder
- Move and size clip art

- Change font size and color
- Bold and italicize text
- Duplicate a slide
- Arrange slides
- Select slide transitions
- View a presentation in Slide Show view
- Print a presentation

1 | Creating and Editing a Presentation with Clip Art

Introduction

A PowerPoint **presentation**, also called a **slide show**, can help you deliver a dynamic, professional-looking message to an audience. PowerPoint allows you to produce slides to use in an academic, business, or other environment. One of the more common uses of these slides is to enhance an oral presentation. A speaker may desire to convey information, such as urging students to volunteer at a fund-raising event, explaining changes in employee compensation packages, or describing a new laboratory procedure. The PowerPoint slides should reinforce the speaker's message and help the audience retain the information presented. Custom slides can fit your specific needs and contain diagrams, charts, tables, pictures, shapes, video, sound, and animation effects to make your presentation more effective. An accompanying handout gives audience members reference notes and review material for your presentation.

Project Planning Guidelines

> The process of developing a presentation that communicates specific information requires careful analysis and planning. As a starting point, establish why the presentation is needed. Next, analyze the intended audience for the presentation and its unique needs. Then, gather information about the topic and decide what to include in the presentation. Finally, determine the presentation design and style that will be most successful at delivering the message. Details of these guidelines are provided in Appendix A. In addition, each project in this book provides practical applications of these planning considerations.

BTW

Energy-Saving Information
The U.S. Department of Energy's Web site has myriad information available on the topics of energy efficiency and renewable energy. These features can provide news and product research that you can share with audiences with the help of a PowerPoint presentation.

Project — Presentation with Bulleted Lists and Clip Art

In this chapter's project, you will follow proper design guidelines and learn to use PowerPoint to create, save, and print the slides shown in Figures 1–1a through 1–1e. The objective is to produce a presentation, called It Is Easy Being Green, to help consumers understand basic steps they can take to save energy in their homes. This slide show has a variety of clip art and visual elements to add interest and illustrate energy-cutting measures. Some of the text has formatting and color enhancements. Transitions help one slide flow gracefully into the next during a slide show. In addition, you will print a handout of your slides to distribute to audience members.

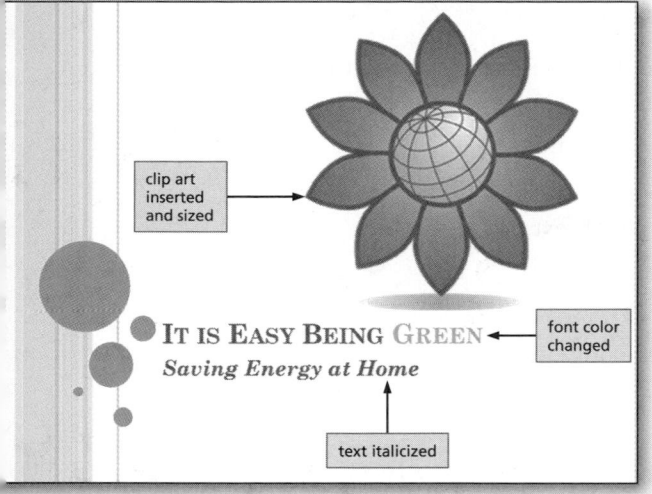

(a) Slide 1 (Title Slide with Clip Art)

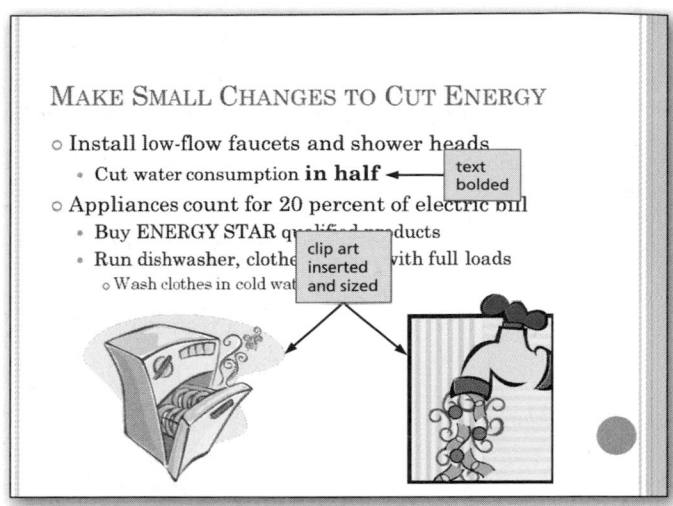

(b) Slide 2 (Multi-Level Bulleted List with Clip Art)

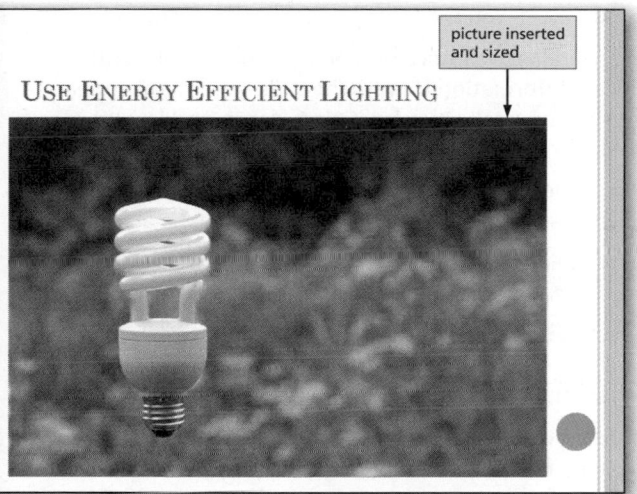

(c) Slide 3 (Title and Photograph)

(d) Slide 4 (Comparison Layout and Clip Art)

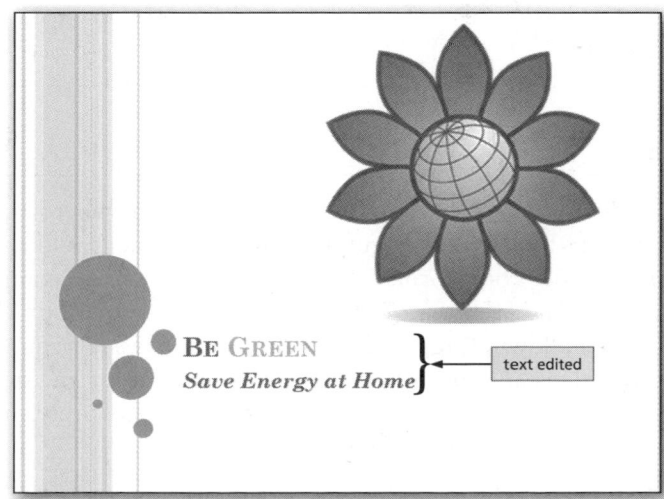

(e) Slide 5 (Closing Slide)

Figure 1–1

Overview

As you read this chapter, you will learn how to create the presentation shown in Figure 1–1 on the previous page by performing these general tasks:

- Select an appropriate document theme.
- Enter titles and text on slides.
- Change the size, color, and style of text.
- Insert clips and a photograph.
- Add a transition to each slide.
- View the presentation on your computer.
- Print your slides.

Plan Ahead

> **General Project Guidelines**
>
> When creating a PowerPoint document, the actions you perform and decisions you make will affect the appearance and characteristics of the finished document. As you create a presentation such as the project shown in Figure 1–1, you should follow these general guidelines:
>
> 1. **Find the appropriate theme.** The overall appearance of a presentation significantly affects its capability to communicate information clearly. The slides' graphical appearance should support the presentation's overall message. Colors, fonts, and layouts affect how audience members perceive and react to the slide content.
>
> 2. **Choose words for each slide.** Use the less is more principle. The less text, the more likely the slides will enhance your speech. Use the fewest words possible to make a point.
>
> 3. **Format specific elements of the text.** Examples of how you can modify the appearance, or **format**, of text include changing its shape, size, color, and position on the slide.
>
> 4. **Determine where to save the presentation.** You can store a document permanently, or **save** it, on a variety of storage media, including a hard disk, USB flash drive, or CD. You also can indicate a specific location on the storage media for saving the document.
>
> 5. **Determine the best method for distributing the presentation.** Presentations can be distributed on paper or electronically. You can print a hard copy of the presentation slides for proofing or reference, or you can distribute an electronic image in various formats.
>
> When necessary, more specific details concerning the above guidelines are presented at appropriate points in the chapter. The chapter also will identify the actions performed and decisions made regarding these guidelines during the creation of the slides shown in Figure 1–1.

To Start PowerPoint

If you are using a computer to step through the project in this chapter and you want your screens to match the figures in this book, you should change your screen's resolution to 1024 × 768. For information about how to change a computer's resolution, refer to the Office 2010 and Windows 7 chapter at the beginning of this book.

The following steps, which assume Windows 7 is running, start PowerPoint based on a typical installation. You may need to ask your instructor how to start PowerPoint for your computer. For a detailed example of the procedure summarized below, refer to the Office 2010 and Windows 7 chapter.

1 Click the Start button on the Windows 7 taskbar to display the Start menu.

2 Type `Microsoft PowerPoint` as the search text in the 'Search programs and files' text box and watch the search results appear on the Start menu.

3 Click Microsoft PowerPoint 2010 in the search results on the Start menu to start PowerPoint and display a new blank document in the PowerPoint window.

4 If the PowerPoint window is not maximized, click the Maximize button next to the Close button on its title bar to maximize the window.

Choosing a Document Theme

You can give a presentation a professional and integrated appearance easily by using a document theme. A **document theme** provides consistency in design and color through-out the entire presentation by setting the color scheme, font set, and layout of a presentation. This collection of formatting choices includes a set of colors (the Theme Colors group), a set of heading and content text fonts (the Theme Fonts group), and a set of lines and fill effects (the Theme Effects group). These groups allow you to choose and change the appearance of all the slides or individual slides in your presentation. The left edge of the status bar in Figure 1–2 shows the current slide number followed by the total number of slides in the document and a document theme identifier.

Find the appropriate theme.
In the initial steps of this project, you will select a document theme by locating a particular built-in theme in the Themes group. You could, however, apply a theme at any time while creating the presentation. Some PowerPoint slide show designers create presentations using the default Office Theme. This blank design allows them to concentrate on the words being used to convey the message and does not distract them with colors and various text attributes. Once the text is entered, the designers then select an appropriate document theme.

Plan Ahead

To Choose a Document Theme

The document theme identifier shows the theme currently used in the slide show. PowerPoint initially uses the **Office Theme** until you select a different theme. The following steps change the theme for this presentation from the Office Theme to the Oriel document theme.

1

• Click Design on the Ribbon to display the Design tab (Figure 1–2).

Figure 1–2

2

• Click the More button (Design tab | Themes group) to expand the gallery, which shows more Built-In theme gallery options (Figure 1–3).

Experiment

• Point to various document themes in the Themes gallery and watch the colors and fonts change on the title slide.

Q&A Are the themes displayed in a specific order?

Yes. They are arranged in alphabetical order running from left to right. If you point to a theme, a ScreenTip with the theme's name appears on the screen.

Figure 1–3

Q&A What if I change my mind and do not want to select a new theme?

Click anywhere outside the All Themes gallery to close the gallery.

3

• Click the Oriel theme to apply this theme to Slide 1 (Figure 1–4).

Q&A If I decide at some future time that this design does not fit the theme of my presentation, can I apply a different design?

Yes. You can repeat these steps at any time while creating your presentation.

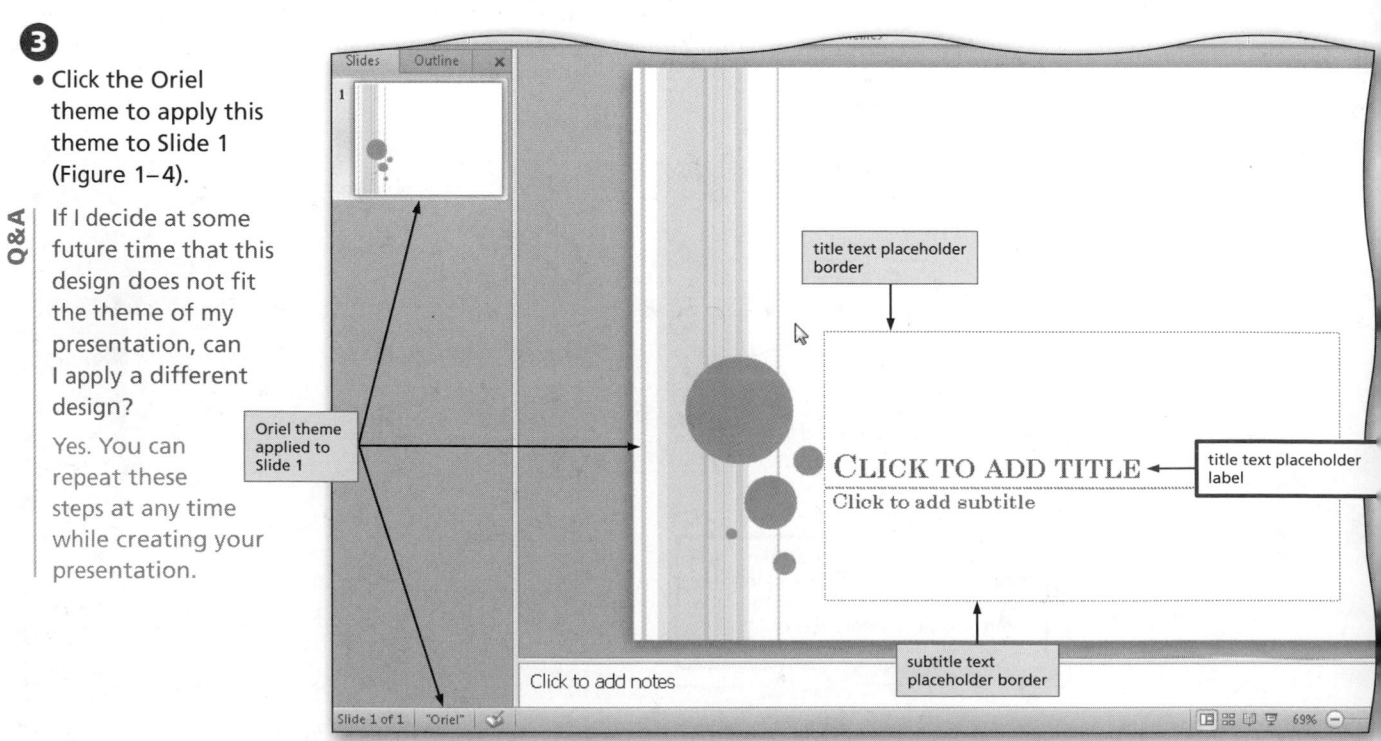

Figure 1–4

Creating a Title Slide

When you open a new presentation, the default **Title Slide** layout appears. The purpose of this layout is to introduce the presentation to the audience. PowerPoint includes eight other built-in standard layouts. The default (preset) slide layouts are set up in **landscape orientation**, where the slide width is greater than its height. In landscape orientation, the slide size is preset to 10 inches wide and 7.5 inches high when printed on a standard sheet of paper measuring 11 inches wide and 8.5 inches high.

Placeholders are boxes with dotted or hatch-marked borders that are displayed when you create a new slide. Most layouts have both a title text placeholder and at least one content placeholder. Depending on the particular slide layout selected, title and sub-title placeholders are displayed for the slide title and subtitle; a content text placeholder is displayed for text, art, or a table, chart, picture, graphic, or movie. The title slide has two text placeholders where you can type the main heading, or title, of a new slide and the subtitle.

With the exception of a blank slide, PowerPoint assumes every new slide has a title. To make creating a presentation easier, any text you type after a new slide appears becomes title text in the title text placeholder. The following steps create the title slide for this presentation.

To Enter the Presentation Title

The presentation title for Project 1 is It Is Easy Being Green. This title creates interest by introducing the concept of simple energy conservation tasks. The following step creates the slide show's title.

1
- Click the label, Click to add title, located inside the title text placeholder to select the placeholder (Figure 1–5).

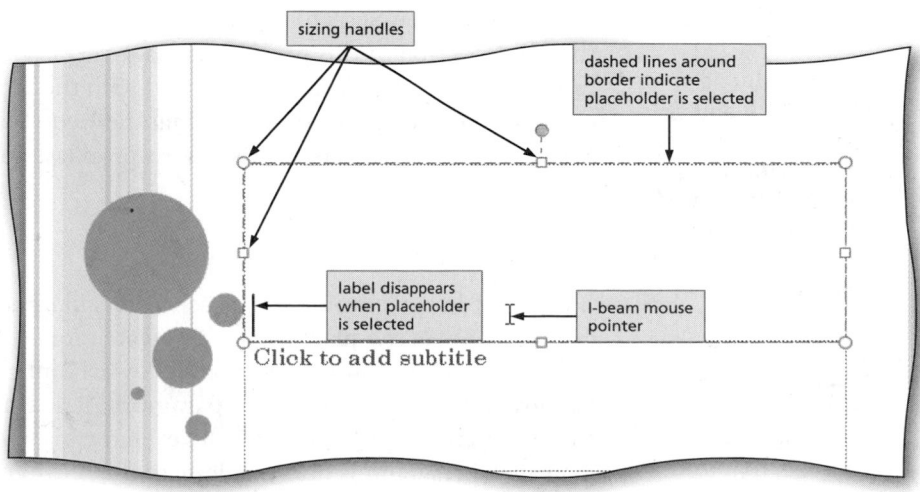

Figure 1–5

2

- Type **It Is Easy Being Green** in the title text placeholder. Do not press the ENTER key (Figure 1–6).

Q&A

Why does the text display with capital letters despite the fact I am typing uppercase and lowercase letters?

The Oriel theme uses the Small Caps effect for the title text. This effect converts lowercase letters to uppercase and reduces their size.

Figure 1–6

Correcting a Mistake When Typing

If you type the wrong letter, press the BACKSPACE key to erase all the characters back to and including the one that is incorrect. If you mistakenly press the ENTER key after typing the title and the insertion point is on the new line, simply press the BACKSPACE key to return the insertion point to the right of the letter n in the word, Green.

When you install PowerPoint, the default setting allows you to reverse up to the last 20 changes by clicking the Undo button on the Quick Access Toolbar. The ScreenTip that appears when you point to the Undo button changes to indicate the type of change just made. For example, if you type text in the title text placeholder and then point to the Undo button, the ScreenTip that appears is Undo Typing. For clarity, when referencing the Undo button in this project, the name displaying in the ScreenTip is referenced. You can reapply a change that you reversed with the Undo button by clicking the Redo button on the Quick Access Toolbar. Clicking the Redo button reverses the last undo action. The ScreenTip name reflects the type of reversal last performed.

For an introduction to Office 2010 and instruction about how to perform basic tasks in Office 2010 programs, read the Office 2010 and Windows 7 chapter at the beginning of this book, where you can learn how to start a program, use the Ribbon, save a file, open a file, quit a program, use Help, and much more.

Paragraphs

Text in the subtitle text placeholder supports the title text. It can appear on one or more lines in the placeholder. To create more than one subtitle line, you press the ENTER key after typing some words. PowerPoint creates a new line, which is the second paragraph in the placeholder. A **paragraph** is a segment of text with the same format that begins when you press the ENTER key and ends when you press the ENTER key again. This new paragraph is the same level as the previous paragraph. A **level** is a position within a structure, such as an outline, that indicates the magnitude of importance. PowerPoint allows for five paragraph levels.

To Enter the Presentation Subtitle Paragraph

The first subtitle paragraph links to the title by giving further detail that the presentation will focus on energy-saving measures at home. The following steps enter the presentation subtitle.

1
- Click the label, Click to add subtitle, located inside the subtitle text placeholder to select the placeholder (Figure 1–7).

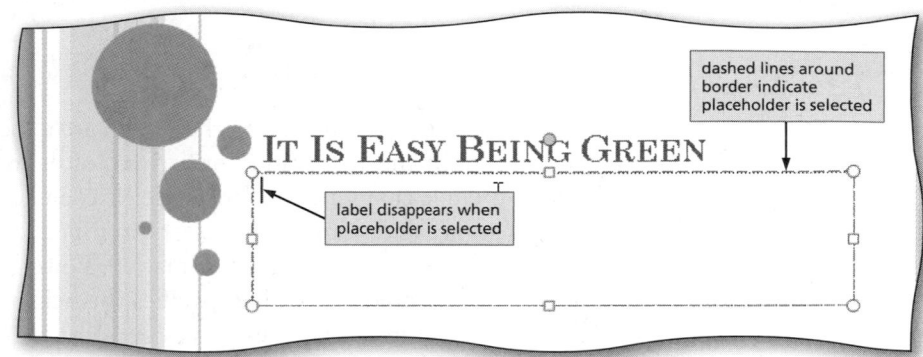

Figure 1–7

2
- Type `Saving Energy at Home` but do not press the ENTER key (Figure 1–8).

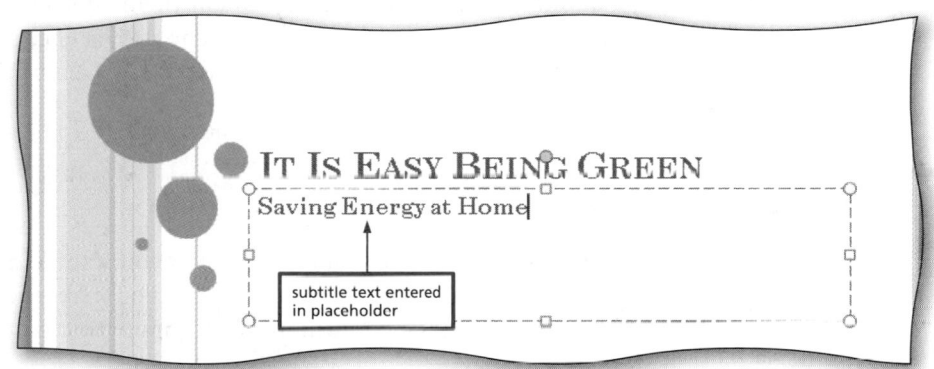

Figure 1–8

Identify how to format specific elements of the text.

Plan
Ahead

Most of the time, you use the document theme's text attributes, color scheme, and layout. Occasionally, you may want to change the way a presentation looks, however, and still keep a particular document theme. PowerPoint gives you that flexibility.

Graphic designers use several rules when formatting text.

- Avoid all capital letters, if possible. Audiences have difficulty comprehending sentences typed in all capital letters, especially when the lines exceed seven words. All capital letters leaves no room for emphasis or inflection, so readers get confused about what material deserves particular attention. Some document themes, however, have a default title text style of all capital letters.

- Avoid text with a font size less than 30 point. Audience members generally will sit a maximum of 50 feet from a screen, and at this distance 30-point type is the smallest size text they can read comfortably without straining.

- Make careful color choices. Color evokes emotions, and a careless color choice may elicit the incorrect psychological response. PowerPoint provides a color gallery with hundreds of colors. The built-in document themes use complementary colors that work well together. If you stray from these themes and add your own color choices, without a good reason to make the changes, your presentation is apt to become ineffective.

Formatting Characters in a Presentation

Recall that each document theme determines the color scheme, font set, and layout of a presentation. You can use a specific document theme and then change the characters' formats any time before, during, or after you type the text.

BTW

Q&As
For a complete list of the Q&As found in many of the step-by-step sequences in this book, visit the PowerPoint 2010 Q&A Web page (scsite.com/ppt2010/qa).

Fonts and Font Styles

Characters that appear on the screen are a specific shape and size. Examples of how you can modify the appearance, or **format**, of these typed characters on the screen and in print include changing the font, style, size, and color. The **font**, or typeface, defines the appearance and shape of the letters, numbers, punctuation marks, and symbols. **Style** indicates how the characters are formatted. PowerPoint's text font styles include regular, italic, bold, and bold italic. **Size** specifies the height of the characters and is gauged by a measurement system that uses points. A **point** is 1/72 of an inch in height. Thus, a character with a font size of 36 is 36/72 (or 1/2) of an inch in height. **Color** defines the hue of the characters.

This presentation uses the Oriel document theme, which uses particular font styles and font sizes. The Oriel document theme default title text font is named Century Schoolbook. It has a bold style with no special effects, and its size is 30 point. The Oriel document theme default subtitle text font also is Century Schoolbook with a font size of 18 point.

To Select a Paragraph

You can use many techniques to format characters. When you want to apply the same formats to multiple words or paragraphs, it is efficient to select the desired text and then make the desired changes to all the characters simultaneously. The first formatting change you will make will apply to the title slide subtitle. The following step selects this paragraph.

1
- Triple-click the paragraph, Saving Energy at Home, in the subtitle text placeholder to select the paragraph (Figure 1–9).

Q&A
Can I select the paragraph using a technique other than triple-clicking?

Yes. You can move your mouse pointer to the left of the first paragraph and then drag to the end of the line.

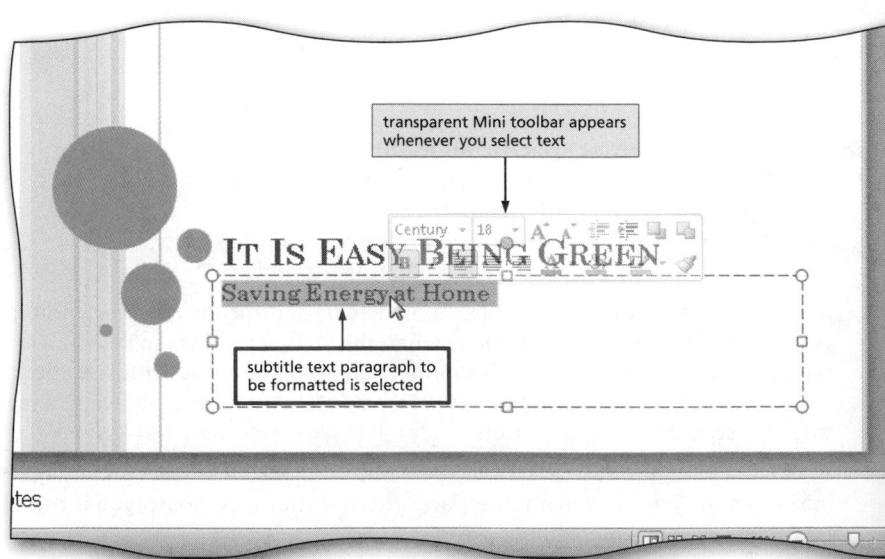

Figure 1–9

To Italicize Text

Different font styles often are used on slides to make them more appealing to the reader and to emphasize particular text. **Italicized** text has a slanted appearance. Used sparingly, it draws the readers' eyes to these characters. The following step adds emphasis to the second line of the subtitle text by changing regular text to italic text.

1

• With the subtitle text still selected, click the Italic button on the Mini toolbar to italicize that text on the slide (Figure 1–10).

If I change my mind and decide not to italicize the text, how can I remove this style?

Click the Italic button a second time or immediately click the Undo button on the Quick Access Toolbar or press CTRL+Z.

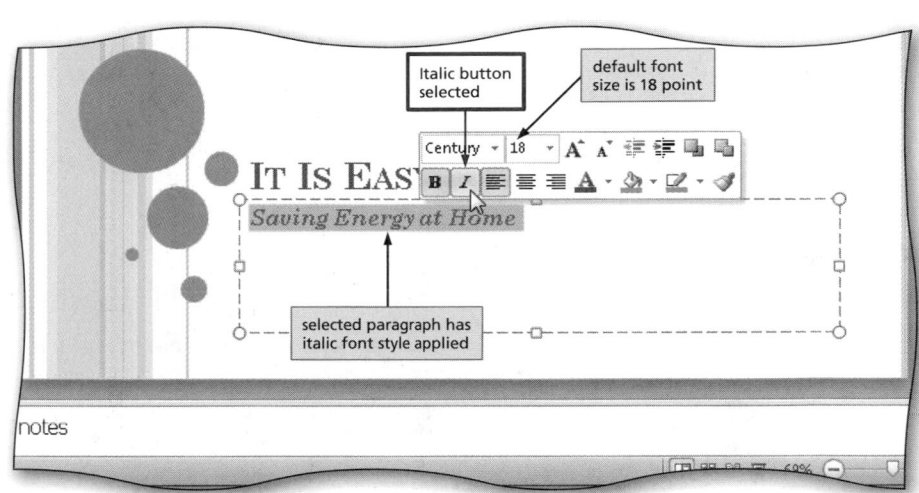

Figure 1–10

Other Ways		
1. Right-click selected text, click Font on shortcut menu, click Font tab (Font dialog box), click Italic in Font style list, click OK button	2. Select text, click Italic button (Home tab | Font group) 3. Click Font Dialog Box Launcher (Home tab | Font	group), click Font tab (Font dialog box), click Italic in Font style list, click OK button 4. Select text, press CTRL+I

To Increase Font Size

To add emphasis, you increase the font size for the subtitle text. The Increase Font Size button on the Mini toolbar increases the font size in preset increments. The following step uses this button to increase the font size.

1

• Click the Increase Font Size button on the Mini toolbar twice to increase the font size of the selected text from 18 to 24 point (Figure 1–11).

Figure 1–11

Other Ways		
1. Click Font Size box arrow on Mini toolbar, click desired font size in Font Size gallery	2. Click Increase Font Size button (Home tab | Font group) 3. Click Font Size box arrow (Home tab | Font group),	click desired font size in Font size gallery 4. Press CTRL+SHIFT+>

To Select a Word

PowerPoint designers use many techniques to emphasize words and characters on a slide. To add emphasis to the energy-saving concept of your slide show, you want to increase the font size and change the font color to green for the word, Green, in the title text. You could perform these actions separately, but it is more efficient to select the word and then change the font attributes. The following steps select a word.

- Position the mouse pointer somewhere in the word to be selected (in this case, in the word, Green) (Figure 1–12).

Figure 1–12

- Double-click the word to select it (Figure 1–13).

Figure 1–13

Other Ways

1. Position mouse pointer before first character, press CTRL+SHIFT+RIGHT ARROW

Plan Ahead

Format text colors.
When selecting text colors, try to limit using red. This color often is associated with dangerous or alarming situations. In addition, at least 15 percent of men have difficulty distinguishing varying shades of green or red. They also often see the color purple as blue and the color brown as green. This problem is more pronounced when the colors appear in small areas, such as slide paragraphs or line chart bars.

To Change the Text Color

PowerPoint allows you to use one or more text colors in a presentation. To add more emphasis to the word, Green, in the title slide text, you decide to change the color. The following steps add emphasis to this word by changing the font color from black to green.

● With the word, Green, selected, click the Font Color arrow on the Mini toolbar to display the gallery of Theme Colors and Standard Colors (Figure 1–14).

If the Mini toolbar disappears from the screen, how can I display it once again?

Right-click the text, and the Mini toolbar should appear.

Experiment

● Point to various colors in the gallery and watch the word's font color change.

Figure 1–14

● Click the Green button in the Standard Colors row on the Mini toolbar (sixth color) to change the font color to green (Figure 1–15).

Why did I select the color Green?

Green is one of the 10 standard colors associated with every document theme, and it is a universal color to represent respecting natural resources. The color will emphasize the fact that the presentation focuses on green conservation measures.

Figure 1–15

What is the difference between the colors shown in the Theme Colors area and the Standard Colors?

The 10 colors in the top row of the Theme Colors area are two text, two background, and six accent colors in the Oriel theme; the five colors in each column under the top row display different transparencies. These colors are available in every document theme.

● Click outside the selected area to deselect the word.

Other Ways	
1. Right-click selected text, click Font on shortcut menu, click Font Color button, click Green in Standard Colors row	2. Click Font Color arrow (Home tab | Font group), click Green in Standard Colors row

BTW

Organizing Files and Folders
You should organize and store files in folders so that you easily can find the files later. For example, if you are taking an introductory computer class called CIS 101, a good practice would be to save all PowerPoint files in a PowerPoint folder in a CIS 101 folder. For a discussion of folders and detailed examples of creating folders, refer to the Office 2010 and Windows 7 chapter at the beginning of this book.

To Save a Presentation

You have performed many tasks while creating this slide and do not want to risk losing work completed thus far. Accordingly, you should save the document.

The following steps assume you already have created folders for storing your files, for example, a CIS 101 folder (for your class) that contains a PowerPoint folder (for your assignments). Thus, these steps save the document in the PowerPoint folder in the CIS 101 folder on a USB flash drive using the file name, Saving Energy. For a detailed example of the procedure summarized below, refer to the Office 2010 and Windows 7 chapter at the beginning of this book.

1 With a USB flash drive connected to one of the computer's USB ports, click the Save button on the Quick Access Toolbar to display the Save As dialog box.

2 Type `Saving Energy` in the File name text box to change the file name. Do not press the ENTER key after typing the file name because you do not want to close the dialog box at this time.

3 Navigate to the desired save location (in this case, the PowerPoint folder in the CIS 101 folder [or your class folder] on the USB flash drive).

4 Click the Save button (Save As dialog box) to save the document in the selected folder on the selected drive with the entered file name.

Adding a New Slide to a Presentation

With the text for the title slide for the presentation created, the next step is to add the first text slide immediately after the title slide. Usually, when you create a presentation, you add slides with text, clip art, graphics, or charts. Some placeholders allow you to double-click the placeholder and then access other objects, such as media clips, charts, diagrams, and organization charts. You can change the layout for a slide at any time during the creation of a presentation.

To Add a New Text Slide with a Bulleted List

When you add a new slide, PowerPoint uses the Title and Content slide layout. This layout provides a title placeholder and a content area for text, art, charts, and other graphics. A vertical scroll bar appears in the Slide pane when you add the second slide so that you can move from slide to slide easily. A thumbnail of this slide also appears in the Slides tab. The following steps add a new slide with the Title and Content slide layout.

1
- Click Home on the Ribbon to display the Home tab (Figure 1–16).

Figure 1–16

2

● Click the New Slide button (Home tab | Slides group) to insert a new slide with the Title and Content layout (Figure 1–17).

Why does the bullet character display an orange circle?

The Oriel document theme determines the bullet characters. Each paragraph level has an associated bullet character.

I clicked the New Slide arrow instead of the New Slide button. What should I do?

Click the Title and Content slide thumbnail in the layout gallery.

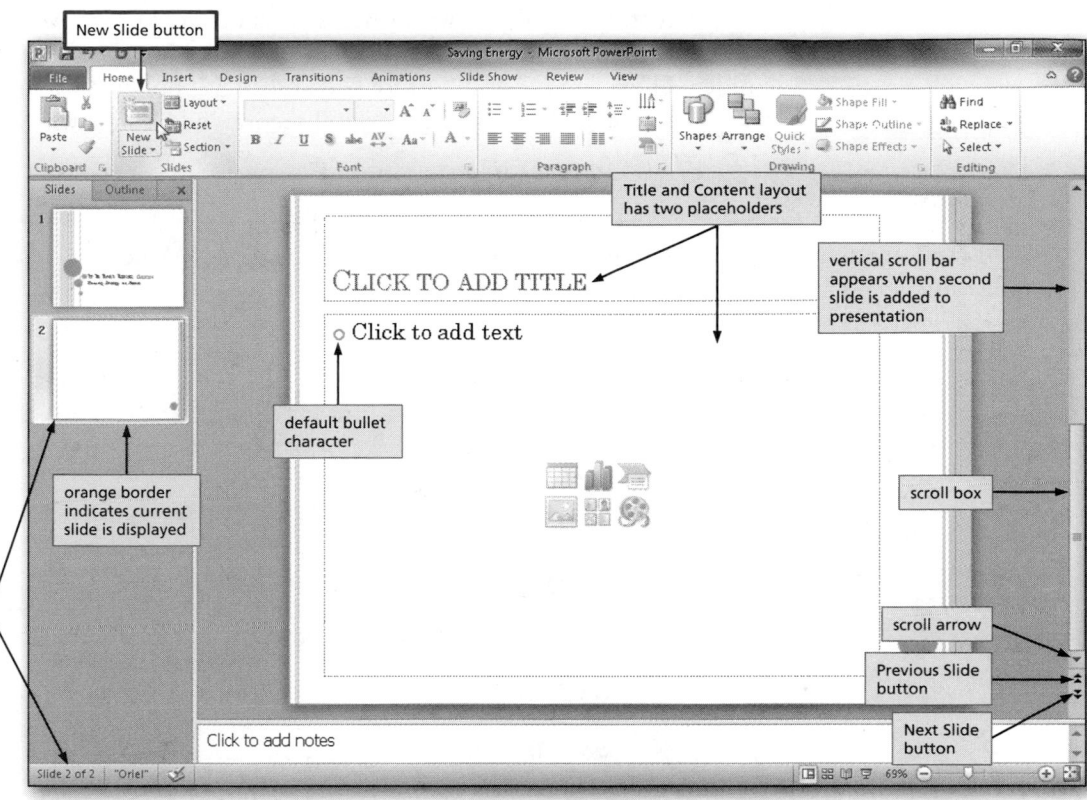

Figure 1–17

Choose the words for the slide.

All presentations should follow the 7 × 7 rule, which states that each slide should have a maximum of seven lines, and each line should have a maximum of seven words. PowerPoint designers must choose their words carefully and, in turn, help viewers read the slides easily.

Avoid line wraps. Your audience's eyes want to stop at the end of a line. Thus, you must plan your words carefully or adjust the font size so that each point displays on only one line.

Plan Ahead

Creating a Text Slide with a Multi-Level Bulleted List

The information in the Slide 2 text placeholder is presented in a bulleted list with three levels. A **bulleted list** is a list of paragraphs, each of which is preceded by a bullet. A slide that consists of more than one level of bulleted text is called a **multi-level bulleted list slide**. In a multi-level bulleted list, a lower-level paragraph is a subset of a higher-level paragraph. It usually contains information that supports the topic in the paragraph immediately above it.

Two of the Slide 2 bullets appear at the same paragraph level, called the first level: Install low-flow faucets and shower heads, and Appliances count for 20 percent of electric bill. Beginning with the second level, each paragraph indents to the right of the preceding level and is pushed down to a lower level. For example, if you increase the indent of a first-level paragraph, it becomes a second-level paragraph. The second, fourth, and fifth paragraphs on Slide 2 are second-level paragraphs. The last paragraph, Wash clothes in cold water, is a third-level paragraph.

BTW

The Ribbon and Screen Resolution
PowerPoint may change how the groups and buttons within the groups appear on the Ribbon, depending on the computer's screen resolution. Thus, your Ribbon may look different from the ones in this book if you are using a screen resolution other than 1024 x 768.

Creating a text slide with a multi-level bulleted list requires several steps. Initially, you enter a slide title in the title text placeholder. Next, you select the content text placeholder. Then, you type the text for the multi-level bulleted list, increasing and decreasing the indents as needed. The next several sections add a slide with a multi-level bulleted list

To Enter a Slide Title

PowerPoint assumes every new slide has a title. The title for Slide 2 is Make Small Changes to Cut Energy. The following step enters this title.

- Click the label, Click to add title, to select it and then type **Make Small Changes to Cut Energy** in the placeholder. Do not press the ENTER key (Figure 1–18).

Q&A

What are those six icons grouped in the middle of the slide?

You can click one of the icons to insert a specific type of content: table, chart, SmartArt graphic, picture, clip art, or media clip.

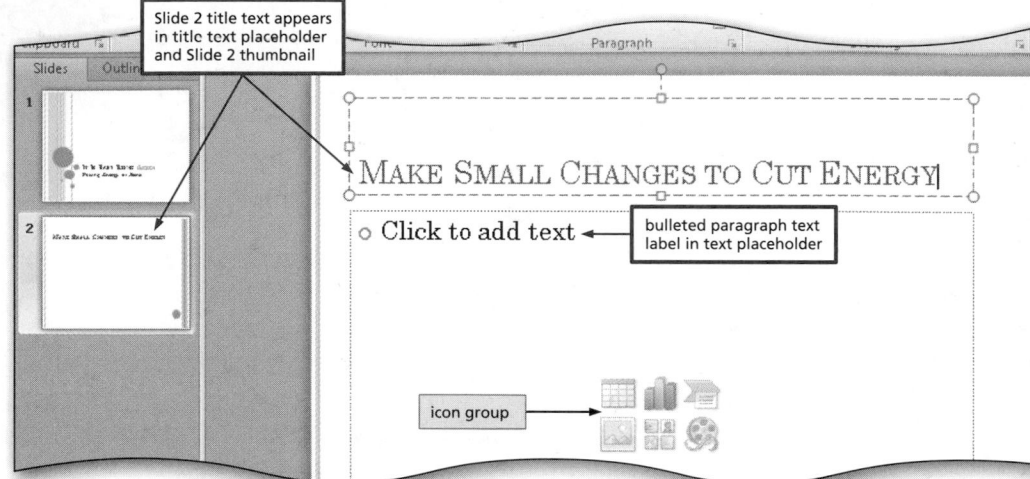

Figure 1–18

To Select a Text Placeholder

Before you can type text into the text placeholder, you first must select it. The following step selects the text placeholder on Slide 2.

- Click the label, Click to add text, to select the text placeholder (Figure 1–19).

Q&A

Why does my mouse pointer have a different shape?

If you move the mouse pointer away from the bullet, it will change shape.

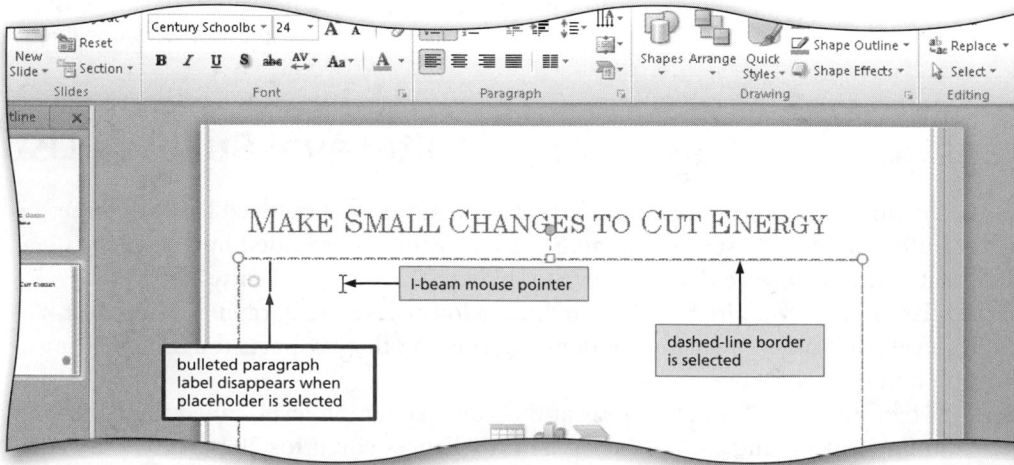

Figure 1–19

Other Ways

1. Press CTRL+ENTER

To Type a Multi-Level Bulleted List

The content placeholder provides an area for the text characters. When you click inside a placeholder, you then can type or paste text. As discussed previously, a bulleted list is a list of paragraphs, each of which is preceded by a bullet. A paragraph is a segment of text ended by pressing the ENTER key.

The content text placeholder is selected, so the next step is to type the multi-level bulleted list that consists of six paragraphs, as shown in Figure 1–1b on page PPT 3. Creating a lower-level paragraph is called **demoting** text; creating a higher-level paragraph is called **promoting** text. The following steps create a multi-level bulleted list consisting of three levels.

1

- Type `Install low-flow faucets and shower heads` and then press the ENTER key (Figure 1–20).

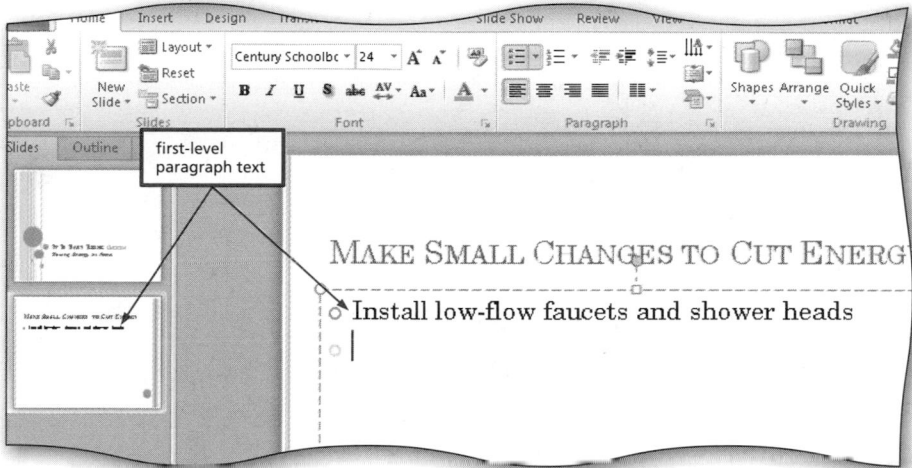

Figure 1–20

2

- Click the Increase List Level button (Home tab | Paragraph group) to indent the second paragraph below the first and create a second-level paragraph (Figure 1–21).

Why does the bullet for this paragraph have a different size and color?

A different bullet is assigned to each paragraph level.

Figure 1–21

3

- Type `Cut water consumption in half` and then press the ENTER key (Figure 1–22).

Figure 1–22

● Click the Decrease List Level button (Home tab | Paragraph group) so that the second-level paragraph becomes a first-level paragraph (Figure 1–23).

Q&A

Can I delete bullets on a slide?

Yes. If you do not want bullets to display in a particular paragraph, click the Bullets button (Home tab | Paragraph group) or right-click the paragraph and then click the Bullets button on the shortcut menu.

Other Ways

1. Press TAB to promote paragraph; press SHIFT+TAB to demote paragraph

Figure 1–23

To Type the Remaining Text for Slide 2

The following steps complete the text for Slide 2.

1 Type `Appliances count for 20 percent of electric bill` and then press the ENTER key.

2 Click the Increase List Level button (Home tab | Paragraph group) to demote the paragraph to the second level.

3 Type `Buy ENERGY STAR qualified products` and then press the ENTER key to add a new paragraph at the same level as the previous paragraph.

4 Type `Run dishwasher, clothes washer with full loads` and then press the ENTER key.

5 Click the Increase List Level button (Home tab | Paragraph group) to demote the paragraph to the third level.

6 Type `Wash clothes in cold water` but do not press the ENTER key (Figure 1–24).

Q&A

I pressed the ENTER key in error, and now a new bullet appears after the last entry on this slide. How can I remove this extra bullet?

Press the BACKSPACE key twice.

Figure 1–24

To Select a Group of Words

PowerPoint designers use many techniques to emphasize words and characters on a slide. To add emphasis to your slide show's concept of saving natural resources, you want to bold and increase the font size of the words, in half, in the body text. You could perform these actions separately, but it is more efficient to select the words and then change the font attributes. The following steps select two words.

- Position the mouse pointer immediately to the left of the first character of the text to be selected (in this case, the i in the word, in) (Figure 1–25).

Figure 1–25

- Drag the mouse pointer through the last character of the text to be selected (in this case, the f in half) (Figure 1–26).

Figure 1–26

Other Ways
1. Press CTRL+SHIFT+RIGHT ARROW

To Bold Text

Bold characters display somewhat thicker and darker than those that display in a regular font style. Clicking the Bold button on the Mini toolbar is an efficient method of bolding text. To add more emphasis to the amount of water savings that can occur by installing low-flow faucets and shower heads, you want to bold the words, in half. The following step bolds this text.

1

- With the words, in half, selected, click the Bold button on the Mini toolbar to bold the two words (Figure 1–27).

Figure 1–27

Other Ways

1. Click Bold button (Home tab | Font group)
2. Press CTRL+B

BTW

Formatting Words
To format one word, position the insertion point anywhere in the word. Then make the formatting changes you desire. The entire word does not need to be selected for the change to occur.

To Increase Font Size

To add emphasis, you increase the font size for the words, in half. The following step increases the font size from 21 to 24 point.

1 With the words, in half, still selected, click the Increase Font Size button on the Mini toolbar once (Figure 1–28).

Figure 1–28

Adding New Slides and Changing the Slide Layouts

Slide 3 in Figure 1–1c on page PPT 3 contains a photograph and does not contain a bulleted list. When you add a new slide, PowerPoint applies the Title and Content layout. This layout along with the Title Slide layout for Slide 1 are the default styles. A **layout** specifies the arrangement of placeholders on a slide. These placeholders are arranged in various configurations and can contain text, such as the slide title or a bulleted list, or they can contain content, such as SmartArt graphics, pictures, charts, tables, shapes, and clip art. The placement of the text, in relationship to content, depends on the slide layout. You can specify a particular slide layout when you add a new slide to a presentation or after you have created the slide.

Using the **Layout gallery**, you can choose a slide layout. The nine layouts in this gallery have a variety of placeholders to define text and content positioning and formatting. Three layouts are for text: Title Slide, Section Header, and Title Only. Five are for text and content: Title and Content, Two Content, Comparison, Content with Caption, and Picture with Caption. The Blank layout has no placeholders. If none of these standard layouts meets your design needs, you can create a **custom layout**. A custom layout specifies the number, size, and location of placeholders, background content, and optional slide and placeholder-level properties.

When you change the layout of a slide, PowerPoint retains the text and objects and repositions them into the appropriate placeholders. Using slide layouts eliminates the need to resize objects and the font size because PowerPoint automatically sizes the objects and text to fit the placeholders.

To Add a Slide with the Title Only Layout

The following steps add Slide 3 to the presentation with the Title Only slide layout style.

If necessary, click Home on the Ribbon to display the Home tab.

Click the New Slide arrow (Home tab | Slides group) to display the Layout gallery (Figure 1–29).

Figure 1–29

2

• Click Title Only to add a new slide and apply that layout to Slide 3 (Figure 1–30).

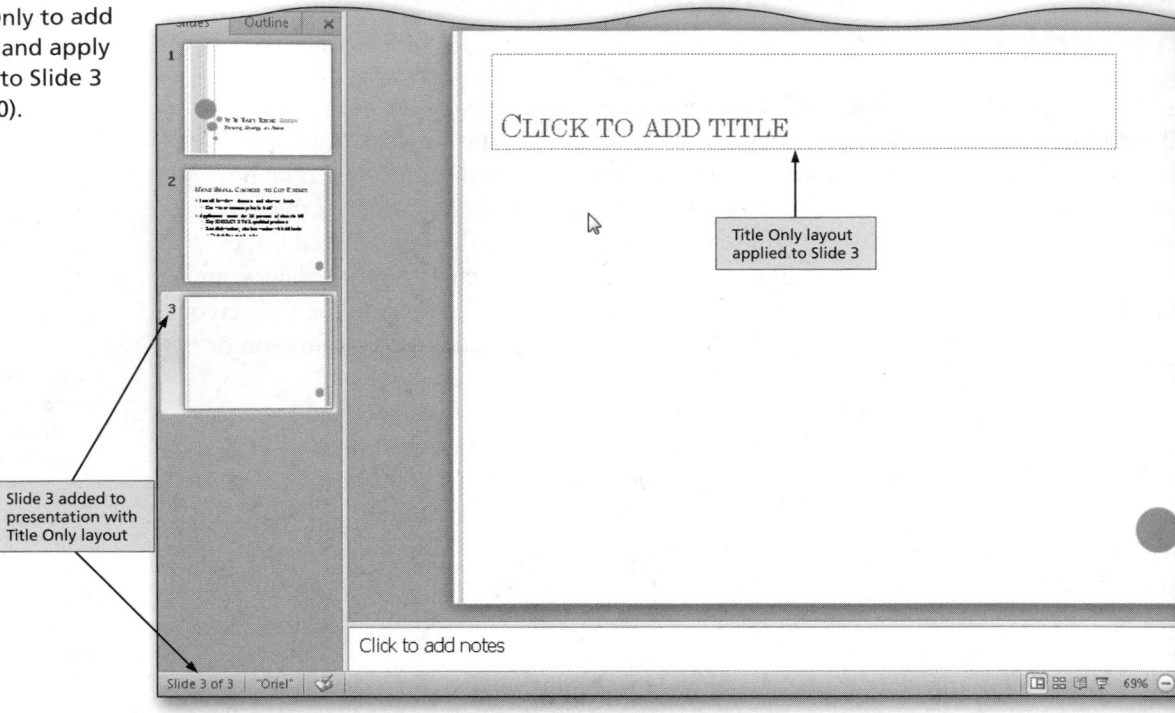

Figure 1–30

To Enter a Slide Title

The only text on Slide 3 is the title. The following step enters the title text for this slide.

1 Type `Use Energy Efficient Lighting` as the title text but do not press the ENTER key (Figure 1–31).

BTW

Portrait Page Orientation
If your slide content is dominantly vertical, such as a skyscraper or a person, consider changing the slide layout to a portrait page orientation. To change the orientation, click the Slide Orientation button (Design tab | Page Setup group) and then click the desired orientation.

CLICK TO ADD TITLE

USE ENERGY EFFICIENT LIGHTING

Slide 3 title text

Figure 1–31

To Add a New Slide and Enter a Slide Title and Headings

The text on Slide 4 in Figure 1–1d on page PPT 3 consists of a title and two headings. The appropriate layout for this slide is named Comparison. The following steps add Slide 4 to the presentation with the Comparison layout and then enter the title and heading text for this slide.

- Click the New Slide arrow in the Slides group to display the Layout gallery (Figure 1–32).

Figure 1–32

- Click Comparison to add Slide 4 and apply that layout.

- Type **Adjust Your Thermostats** in the title text placeholder but do not press the ENTER key.

- Click the left orange heading placeholder with the label, Click to add text, to select this placeholder (Figure 1–33).

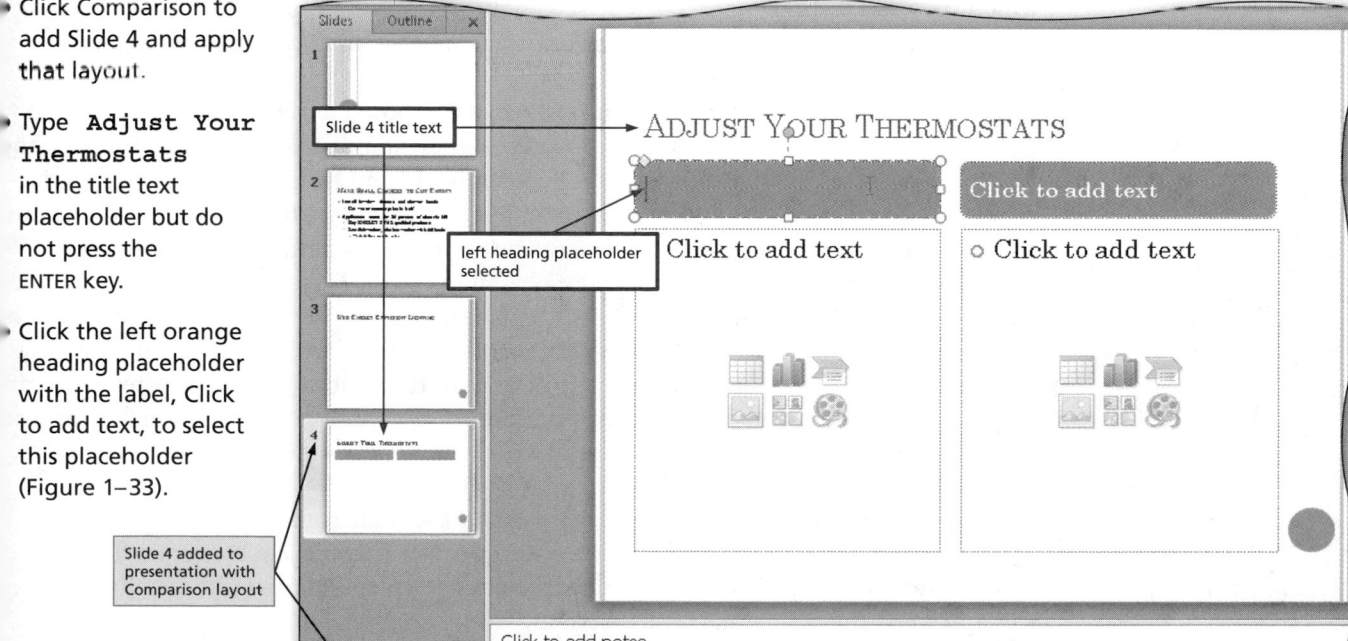

Figure 1–33

3

- Type `Furnace: 68 degrees` but do not press the ENTER key.

- Click the right orange heading placeholder and then type `Water heater: 120 degrees` but do not press the ENTER key (Figure 1–34).

Figure 1–34

Break Point: If you wish to take a break, this is a good place to do so. You can quit PowerPoint now (refer to page PPT 50 for instructions). To resume at a later time, start PowerPoint (refer to pages PPT 4 and PPT 5 for instructions), open the file called Saving Energy (refer to pages PPT 50 and PPT 51 for instructions), and continue following the steps from this location forward.

PowerPoint Views

The PowerPoint window display varies depending on the view. A **view** is the mode in which the presentation appears on the screen. PowerPoint has four main views: Normal, Slide Sorter, Reading, and Slide Show. It also has another view, called Notes Page view, used for entering information about a slide.

The default view is **Normal view**, which is composed of three working areas that allow you to work on various aspects of a presentation simultaneously. The left side of the screen has a Tabs pane that consists of a **Slides tab** and an **Outline tab**. These tabs alternate between views of the presentation in a thumbnail, or miniature, view of the slides and an outline of the slide text. You can type the text of the presentation on the Outline tab and easily rearrange bulleted lists, paragraphs, and individual slides. As you type, you can view this text in the **Slide pane**, which shows a large view of the current slide on the right side of the window. You also can enter text, graphics, animations, and hyperlinks directly in the Slide pane. The **Notes pane** at the bottom of the window is an area where you can type notes and additional information. This text can consist of notes to yourself or remarks to share with your audience. If you want to work with your notes in full page format, you can display them in **Notes Page view**.

In Normal view, you can adjust the width of the Slide pane by dragging the **splitter bar** and the height of the Notes pane by dragging the pane borders. After you have created at least two slides, a scroll bar containing **scroll arrows** and **scroll boxes** will appear on the right edge of the window.

To Move to Another Slide in Normal View

When creating or editing a presentation in Normal view (the view you are currently using), you often want to display a slide other than the current one. Before continuing with developing this project, you want to display the title slide by dragging the scroll box on the vertical scroll bar. When you drag the scroll box, the **slide indicator** shows the number and title of the slide you are about to display. Releasing the mouse button shows the slide. The following steps move from Slide 4 to Slide 1 using the scroll box on the Slide pane.

- Position the mouse pointer on the scroll box.

- Press and hold down the mouse button so that Slide: 4 of 4 Adjust Your Thermostats appears in the slide indicator (Figure 1–35).

Figure 1–35

- Drag the scroll box up the vertical scroll bar until Slide: 1 of 4 It Is Easy Being Green appears in the slide indicator (Figure 1–36).

Figure 1–36

3

- Release the mouse button so that Slide 1 appears in the Slide pane and the Slide 1 thumbnail has an orange border in the Slides tab (Figure 1–37).

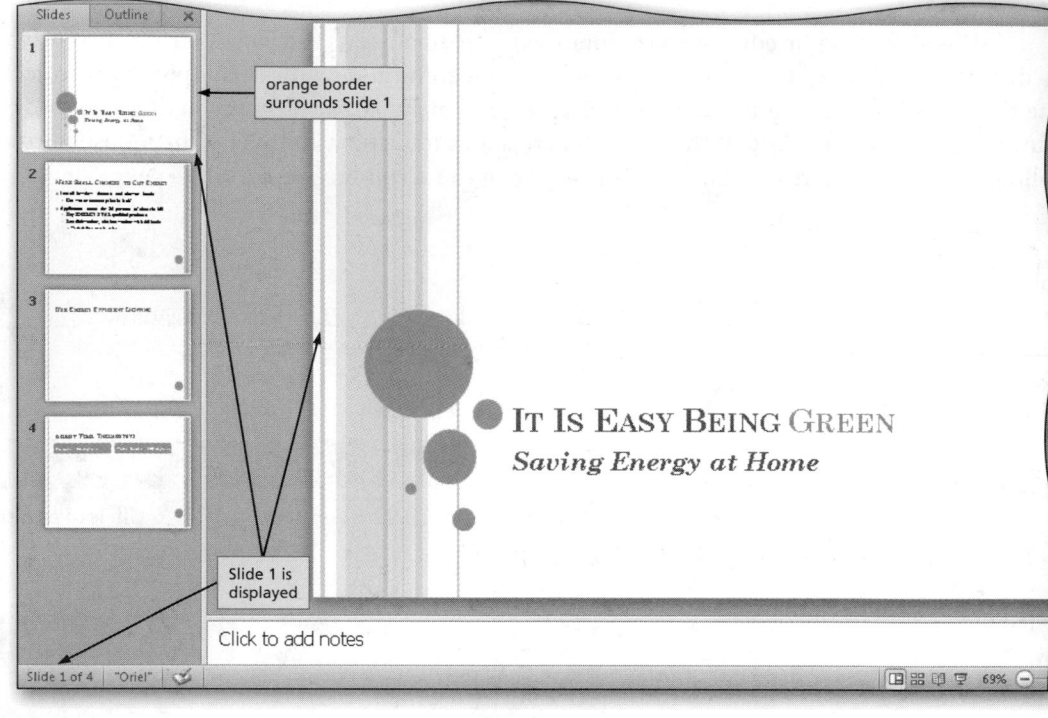

Figure 1–37

Other Ways

1. Click Next Slide button or Previous Slide button to move forward or back one slide

2. Click slide thumbnail on Slides tab

3. Press PAGE DOWN or PAGE UP to move forward or back one slide

Today's Clip
Each day, Microsoft features "today's clip," which reflects events or themes specific to this time. For example, the pictures, illustrations, and clip art have back-to-school images, winter scenes, and holiday characters.

Inserting Clip Art and Photographs into Slides

A **clip** is a single media file that can include art, sound, animation, or movies. Adding a clip can help increase the visual appeal of many slides and can offer a quick way to add professional-looking graphic images and sounds to a presentation without creating these files yourself. This art is contained in the **Microsoft Clip Organizer**, a collection of drawings, photographs, sounds, videos, and other media files shared among Microsoft Office applications. The **Office Collections** contains all these media files included with Microsoft Office.

You also can add your own clips to slides. You can insert these files directly from a storage medium, such as a USB flash drive. In addition, you can add them to the other files in the Clip Organizer so that you can search for and reuse these images, sounds, animations, and movies. When you create these media files, they are stored on your hard disk in **My Collections**. The Clip Organizer will find these files and create a new collection with these files. Two other locations for clips are Shared Collections and Web Collections. Files in the **Shared Collections** typically reside on a shared network file server and are accessible to multiple users. The **Web Collections** clips reside on the Microsoft Clip Art and Media Home page on the Microsoft Office Online Web site. They are available only if you have an active Internet connection.

The Clip Art Task Pane

You can add clips to your presentation in two ways. One way is by selecting one of the slide layouts that includes a content placeholder with a Clip Art button. A second method is by clicking the Clip Art button in the Images area on the Insert tab. Clicking the Clip Art button opens the Clip Art task pane. The **Clip Art task pane** allows you to search for clips by using descriptive keywords, file names, media file formats, and clip collections. Specific file formats could be for clip art, photographs, movies, and sounds.

Clips are organized in hierarchical **clip collections** that combine topic-related clips into categories, such as Academic, Business, and Technology.

Clips have one or more keywords associated with various entities, activities, labels, and emotions. In most instances, the keywords give the name of the clip and related categories. For example, an image of a cow in the Animals category has the keywords animals, cattle, cows, dairies, farms, and Holsteins. You can enter these keywords in the Search for text box to find clips when you know one of the words associated with the image. Otherwise, you might find it necessary to scroll through several categories to find an appropriate clip.

Depending on the installation of the Microsoft Clip Organizer on your computer, you might not have the clip art used in this chapter. Contact your instructor if you are missing clips used in the following steps. If you have an active connection to the Internet, clips from the Microsoft Office Online Web site will display automatically as the result of your search results.

Adhere to copyright regulations.

You have permission to use the clips from the Microsoft Clip Organizer. If you want to use a clip from another source, be certain you have the legal right to insert this file in your presentation. Read the copyright notices that may accompany the clip and may be posted on the Web site where you obtained the clip. The owners of these images and files often ask you to give them credit for using their work, which may be satisfied by stating where you obtained the images.

Plan
Ahead

To Insert a Clip from the Clip Organizer into the Title Slide

Slide 1 uses the Title Slide layout, which has two placeholders for text but none for graphical content. You desire to place a graphic on Slide 1, so you will locate a clip art image of a green globe and flower and then insert it in this slide. Later in this chapter, you will size and position it in an appropriate location. The following steps add a clip to Slide 1.

Click Insert on the Ribbon to display the Insert tab.

Click the Clip Art button (Insert tab | Images group) to display the Clip Art task pane.

Click the Search for text box in the Clip Art task pane, if necessary delete any letters that are present, and then type **green globe** in the Search for text box.

If necessary, click the 'Include Office.com content' check box to select it (Figure 1–38).

Figure 1–38

- Click the Go button so that the Microsoft Clip Organizer will search for and display all clips having the keywords, green globe.

- If necessary, click the Yes button if a Microsoft Clip Organizer dialog box appears asking if you want to include additional clip art images from Office.com.

- If necessary, scroll down the list to display the globe clip shown in Figure 1–39.

- Click the clip to insert it into the slide (Figure 1–39).

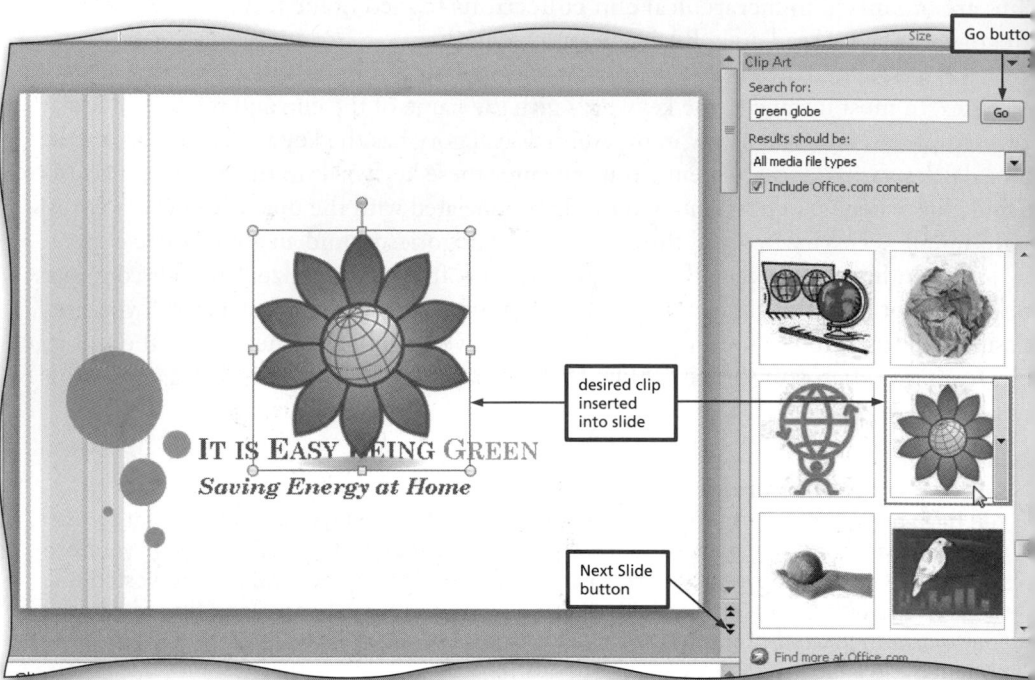

Figure 1–39

Q&A What if the globe image displayed in Figure 1–39 is not shown in my Clip Art task pane?

Select a similar clip. Your clips may be different depending on the clips installed on your computer and if you have an active connection to the Internet.

Q&A What is the yellow star image that displays in the lower-right corner of some clips in the Clip Art task pane?

The star indicates the image is animated and will move when the slide containing this clip is displayed during a slide show.

Q&A Why is this globe clip displayed in this location on the slide?

The slide layout does not have a content placeholder, so PowerPoint inserts the clip in the center of the slide.

To Insert a Clip from the Clip Organizer into a Slide without a Content Placeholder

The next step is to add two clips to Slide 2. Slide 2 has a bulleted list in the text placeholder, so the icon group does not display in the center of the placeholder. Later in this chapter, you will resize the inserted clips. The Clip Art task pane is displayed and will remain open until you close it. The following steps add one clip to Slide 2.

1 Click the Next Slide button to display Slide 2.

2 Click the Search for text box in the Clip Art task pane and then delete the letters in the Search for text box.

3 Type `faucets` and then click the Go button.

4 If necessary, scroll down the list to display the faucet clip shown in Figure 1–40 and then click the clip to insert it into Slide 2 (Figure 1–40).

Figure 1–40

To Insert a Second Clip from the Clip Organizer into a Slide without a Content Placeholder

The following steps add a second clip to Slide 2. PowerPoint inserts this clip on top of the faucet clip in the center of the slide. Both clips will be moved and resized later in this project.

1 Click the Search for text box in the Clip Art task pane and then delete the letters in the text box.

2 Type **dishwasher**, click the Go button, locate the clip shown in Figure 1–41, and then click the clip to insert it into Slide 2 (Figure 1–41).

BTW

Clip Properties
Each clip has properties that identify its characteristics. When you right-click a clip in the Microsoft Clip Organizer, you will see details of the clip's name, file type, size, dimensions, keywords, and creation date. You also can preview the clip and edit its assigned keywords.

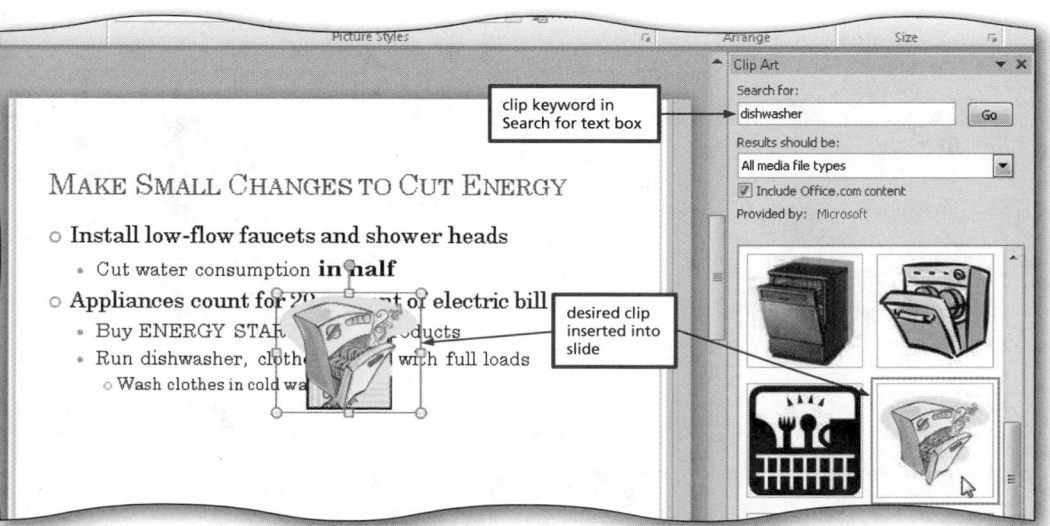

Figure 1–41

To Insert a Clip from the Clip Organizer into a Content Placeholder

Slide 4 uses the Comparison layout, which has a content placeholder below each of the two headings. You desire to insert clip art into both content placeholders to reinforce the concept that consumers should adjust the heating temperatures of their furnace and water heater. The following steps insert clip art of a furnace into the left content placeholder and a water heater into the right content placeholder on Slide 4.

- Click the Close button in the Clip Art task pane so that it no longer is displayed.

- Click the Next Slide button twice to display Slide 4.

- Click the Clip Art button in the left content placeholder to select that placeholder and to open the Clip Art task pane (Figure 1–42).

Q&A

Do I need to close the Clip Art task pane when I am finished inserting the two clips into Slide 2?

No. You can leave the Clip Art task pane open and then display Slide 4. It is often more convenient, however, to open this pane when you are working with a layout that has a content placeholder so that the clip is inserted in the desired location.

Figure 1–42

- Click the Search for text box in the Clip Art task pane, delete any letters that are present, type **furnace** in the Search for text box, and then click the Go button to search for and display all pictures having the keyword, furnace.

- If necessary, scroll down the list to display the furnace clip shown in Figure 1–43.

- Click the clip to insert it into the left content placeholder (Figure 1–43).

Figure 1–43

3

- Click anywhere in the right placeholder except one of the six icons to select the placeholder.

I clicked the Clip Art icon by mistake, which closed the Clip Art task pane. How do I open it?

Click the Clip Art icon.

4

- Click the Search for text box in the Clip Art task pane, delete any letters that are present, type **water heater** in the Search for text box, and then click the Go button.

- If necessary, scroll down the list to display the water heater clip shown in Figure 1–44 and then click the clip to insert it into the right content placeholder (Figure 1–44).

Figure 1–44

Photographs and the Clip Organizer

In addition to clip art, you can insert pictures into a presentation. These may include scanned photographs, line art, and artwork from storage media, such as USB flash drives, hard disks, optical discs, and memory cards. To insert a picture into a presentation, the picture must be saved in a format that PowerPoint can recognize. Table 1–1 identifies some of the formats PowerPoint recognizes.

Table 1–1 Primary File Formats PowerPoint Recognizes	
Format	**File Extension**
Computer Graphics Metafile	.cgm
CorelDRAW	.cdr, .cdt, .cmx, and .pat
Encapsulated PostScript	.eps
Enhanced Metafile	.emf
FlashPix	.fpx
Graphics Interchange Format	.gif
Hanako	.jsh, .jah, and .jbh
Joint Photographic Experts Group (JPEG)	.jpg
Kodak PhotoCD	.pcd
Macintosh PICT	.pct
PC Paintbrush	.pcx
Portable Network Graphics	.png
Tagged Image File Format	.tif
Windows Bitmap	.bmp, .rle, .dib
Microsoft Windows Metafile	.wmf
WordPerfect Graphics	.wpg

BTW

Compressing File Size
When you add a picture to a presentation, PowerPoint automatically compresses this image. Even with this compression applied, a presentation that contains pictures usually has a large file size. To reduce this size, you can compress a picture further without affecting the quality of how it displays on the slide. To compress a picture, select the picture and then click the Compress Pictures button (Picture Tools Format tab | Adjust group). You can restore the picture's original settings by clicking the Reset Picture button (Picture Tools Format tab | Adjust group).

BTW

Wrapping Text around a Picture
PowerPoint 2010 does not allow you to wrap text around a picture or other graphics, such as tables, shapes, charts, or graphics. This feature, however, is available in Word 2010.

You can import files saved with the .emf, .gif, .jpg, .png, .bmp, .rle, .dib, and .wmf formats directly into PowerPoint presentations. All other file formats require separate filters that are shipped with the PowerPoint installation software and must be installed separately. You can download additional filters from the Microsoft Office Online Web site.

To Insert a Photograph from the Clip Organizer into a Slide without a Content Placeholder

Next, you will add a photograph to Slide 3. You will not insert this picture into a content placeholder, so it will display in the center of the slide. Later in this chapter, you will resize this picture. To start the process of locating this photograph, you do not need to click the Clip Art button in the content placeholder because the Clip Art task pane already is displayed. The following steps add a photograph to Slide 3.

1 Click the Previous Slide button to display Slide 3.

2 Click the Search for text box in the Clip Art task pane, delete the letters in the text box, type CFL, and then click the Go button.

3 If necessary, scroll down the list to display the picture of a light bulb shown in Figure 1–45, and then click the photograph to insert it into Slide 2 (Figure 1–45).

Q&A Why is my photograph a different size from the one shown in Figure 1–1c on page PPT 3?

The photograph was inserted into the slide and not into a content placeholder. You will resize the picture later in this chapter.

Figure 1–45

Break Point: If you wish to take a break, this is a good place to do so. You can quit PowerPoint now (refer to page PPT 50 for instructions). To resume at a later time, start PowerPoint (refer to pages PPT 4 and PPT 5 for instructions), open the file called Saving Energy (refer to pages PPT 50 and PPT 51 for instructions), and continue following the steps from this location forward.

Resizing Clip Art and Photographs

Sometimes it is necessary to change the size of clip art. **Resizing** includes enlarging or reducing the size of a clip art graphic. You can resize clip art using a variety of techniques. One method involves changing the size of a clip by specifying exact dimensions in a dialog box. Another method involves dragging one of the graphic's sizing handles to the desired location. A selected graphic appears surrounded by a **selection rectangle**, which has small squares and circles, called **sizing handles** or move handles, at each corner and middle location.

To Resize Clip Art

On Slides 1, 2, and 4, much space appears around the clips, so you can increase their sizes. Likewise, the photograph on Slide 3 can be enlarged to fill more of the space below the slide title. To change the size, drag the corner sizing handles to view how the clip will look on the slide. Using these corner handles maintains the graphic's original proportions. Dragging the square sizing handles alters the proportions so that the graphic's height and width become larger or smaller. The following steps increase the size of the Slide 1 clip using a corner sizing handle.

1
• Click the Close button in the Clip Art task pane so that it no longer is displayed.

• Click the Previous Slide button two times to display Slide 1.

• Click the globe clip to select it and display the selection rectangle.

• Point to the lower-left corner sizing handle on the clip so that the mouse pointer changes to a two-headed arrow (Figure 1–46).

Figure 1–46

2

- Drag the sizing handle diagonally toward the lower-left corner of the slide until the mouse pointer is positioned approximately as shown in Figure 1–47.

Q&A

What if the clip is not the same size as the one shown in Figure 1–47?

Repeat Steps 1 and 2.

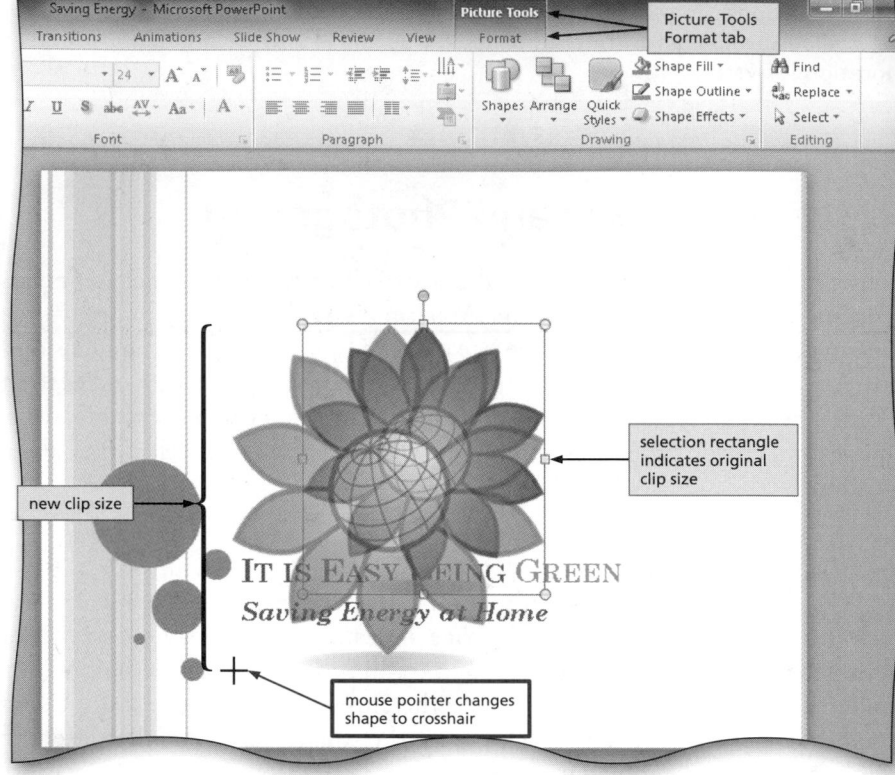

Figure 1–47

3

- Release the mouse button to resize the clip.
- Click outside the clip to deselect it (Figure 1–48).

Q&A

What happened to the Picture Tools Format tab?

When you click outside the clip, PowerPoint deselects the clip and removes the Picture Tools Format tab from the screen.

Q&A

What if I want to return the clip to its original size and start again?

With the graphic selected, click the Reset Picture button (Picture Tools Format tab | Adjust group).

Figure 1–48

To Resize Clips on Slide 4

   The two clip art images on Slide 4 also can be enlarged to fill much of the white space below the headings. You will reposition the clips in a later step. The following steps resize these clips using a sizing handle.

- Click the Next Slide button three times to display Slide 4.

- Click the furnace clip to select it.

- Drag the lower-left corner sizing handle on the clip diagonally outward until the clip is resized approximately as shown in Figure 1–49.

- Click the water heater clip to select it.

- Drag the lower-right corner sizing handle on the clip diagonally outward until the clip is resized approximately as shown in Figure 1–49.

Figure 1–49

To Resize a Photograph

   The light bulb picture in Slide 3 can be enlarged slightly to fill much of the space below the slide title. You resize a photograph in the same manner that you resize clip art. The following steps resize this photograph using a sizing handle.

- Click the Previous Slide button to display Slide 3.

- Click the light bulb photograph to select it.

3 Drag the lower-left corner sizing handle on the photograph diagonally outward until the photograph is resized approximately as shown in Figure 1–50.

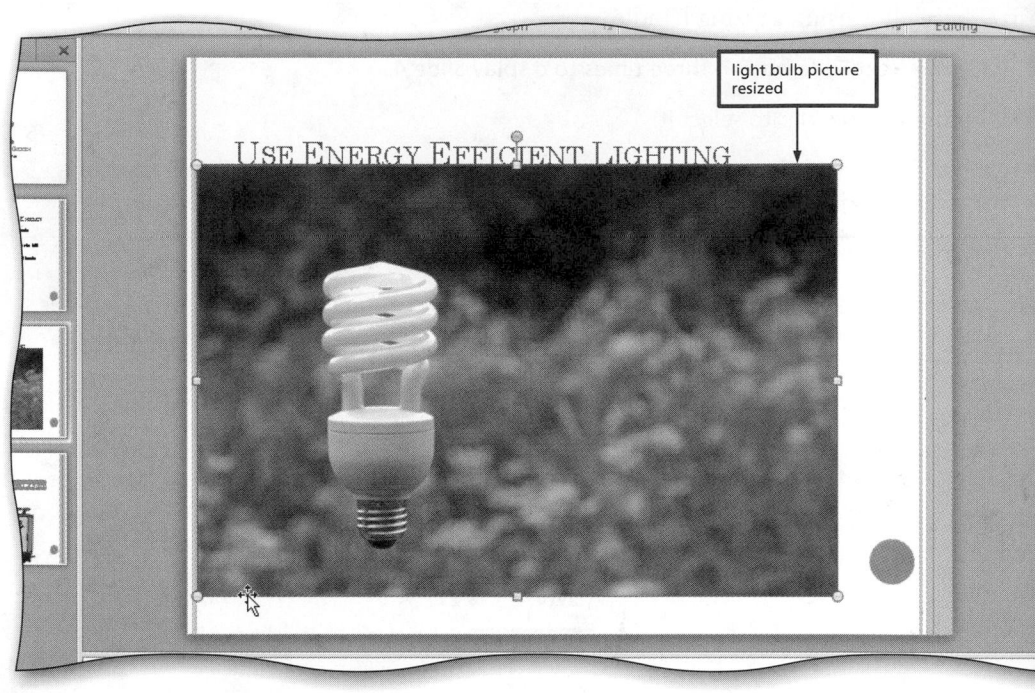

Figure 1–50

To Move Clips

After you insert clip art or a photograph on a slide, you might want to reposition it. The light bulb photograph on Slide 3 could be centered in the space between the slide title and the left and right edges of the slide. The clip on Slide 1 could be positioned in the upper-right corner of the slide. On Slide 4, the furnace and water heater clips could be centered under each heading. The following steps move these graphics.

1

• If necessary, click the light bulb photograph on Slide 3 to select it.

• Press and hold down the mouse button and then drag the photograph diagonally downward below the title text (Figure 1–51).

• If necessary, select the photograph and then use the ARROW keys to position it precisely as shown in Figure 1–51.

The photograph still is not located exactly where I want it to display. What can I do to align the photograph?

Press the CTRL key while you press the ARROW keys. This key combination moves the clip in smaller increments than when you press only an ARROW key.

Figure 1–51

2

- Click the Next Slide button to display Slide 4.

- Click the furnace clip to select it, press and hold down the mouse button, and then drag the clip to center it under the furnace heading.

- Click the water heater clip and then drag the clip to center it under the water heater heading (Figure 1–52).

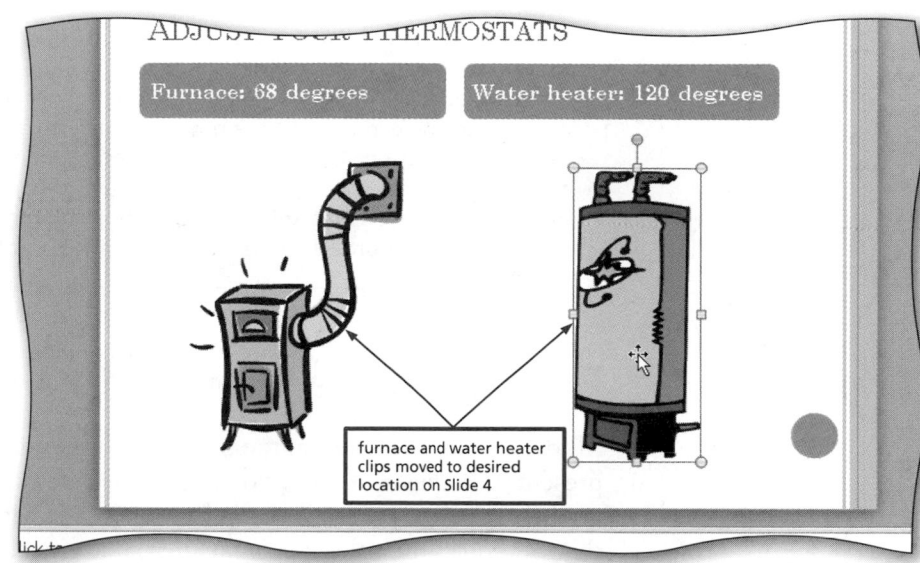

Figure 1–52

3

- Click the Previous Slide button twice to display Slide 2.

- Click the dishwasher clip, which is on top of the faucet clip, and then drag the clip to center it under the last bulleted paragraph, Wash clothes in cold water.

- Click the faucet clip and then drag the clip so that the faucet handle is centered under the words, full loads.

- Drag a corner sizing handle on the faucet clip diagonally outward until the clip is resized approximately as shown in Figure 1–53. You may need to drag the clip to position it in the desired location.

Figure 1–53

- Select the dishwasher clip and then resize and move it so that the clip displays approximately as shown in Figure 1–53.

4

- Click the Previous Slide button to display Slide 1.

- Click the globe clip and then drag it to the upper-right corner of the slide. You may want to adjust its size by selecting it and then dragging the corner sizing handles.

- Click outside the clip to deselect it (Figure 1–54).

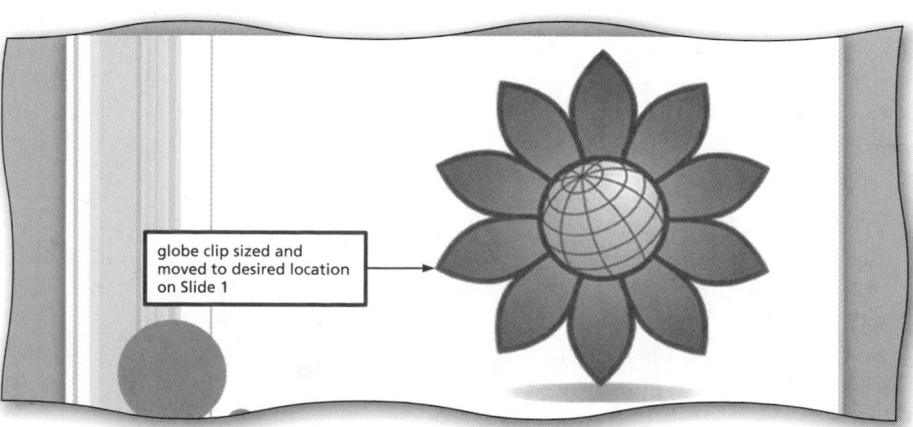

Figure 1–54

Plan
Ahead

Choose a closing slide.
After the last slide appears during a slide show, the default PowerPoint setting is to end the presentation with a **black slide**. This black slide appears only when the slide show is running and concludes the slide show, so your audience never sees the PowerPoint window. It is a good idea, however, to end the presentation with a final closing slide to display at the end of the presentation. This slide ends the presentation gracefully and should be an exact copy, or a very similar copy, of your title slide. The audience will recognize that the presentation is drawing to a close when this slide appears. It can remain on the screen when the audience asks questions, approaches the speaker for further information, or exits the room.

Ending a Slide Show with a Closing Slide

All the text for the slides in the Saving Energy slide show has been entered. This presentation thus far consists of a title slide, one text slide with a multi-level bulleted list, a third slide for a photograph, and a fourth slide with a Comparison layout. A closing slide that resembles the title slide is the final slide to create.

To Duplicate a Slide

When two slides contain similar information and have the same format, duplicating one slide and then making minor modifications to the new slide saves time and increases consistency.

Slide 5 will have the same layout and design as Slide 1. The most expedient method of creating this slide is to copy Slide 1 and then make minor modifications to the new slide. The following steps duplicate the title slide.

- With Slide 1 selected, click the New Slide arrow (Home tab | Slides group) to display the Oriel layout gallery (Figure 1–55).

Figure 1–55

2
• Click Duplicate
Selected Slides in the
Oriel layout gallery
to create a new
Slide 2, which is a
duplicate of Slide 1
(Figure 1–56).

Figure 1–56

Break Point: If you wish to take a break, this is a good place to do so. You can quit PowerPoint now (refer to page PPT 50 for instructions). To resume at a later time, start PowerPoint (refer to pages PPT 4 and PPT 5 for instructions), open the file called Saving Energy (refer to pages PPT 50 and PPT 51 for instructions), and continue following the steps from this location forward.

To Arrange a Slide

The new Slide 2 was inserted directly below Slide 1 because Slide 1 was the selected slide. This duplicate slide needs to display at the end of the presentation directly after the final title and content slide.

Changing slide order is an easy process and is best performed in the Slides pane. When you click the slide thumbnail and begin to drag it to a new location, a line indicates the new location of the selected slide. When you release the mouse button, the slide drops into the desired location. Hence, this process of dragging and then dropping the thumbnail in a new location is called **drag and drop**. You can use the drag-and-drop method to move any selected item, including text and graphics. The following step moves the new Slide 2 to the end of the presentation so that it becomes a closing slide.

1

- With Slide 2 selected, drag the Slide 2 slide thumbnail in the Slides pane below the last slide thumbnail (Figure 1–57).

Q&A

The Slide 2 thumbnail is not visible in the Slides pane when I am dragging the thumbnail downward. How do I know it will be positioned in the desired location?

A blue horizontal bar indicates where the slide will move.

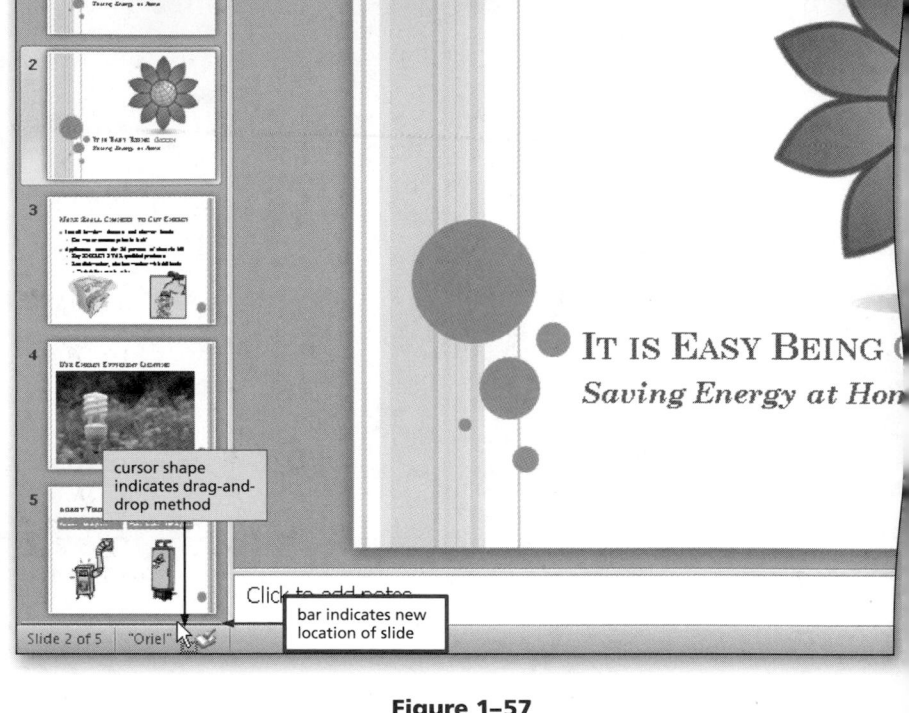

Figure 1–57

Other Ways

1. Click slide icon on Outline tab, drag icon to new location
2. Click Slide Sorter (View tab | Presentation Views group), click slide thumbnail, drag thumbnail to new location

Making Changes to Slide Text Content

After creating slides in a presentation, you may find that you want to make changes to the text. Changes may be required because a slide contains an error, the scope of the presentation shifts, or the style is inconsistent. This section explains the types of changes that commonly occur when creating a presentation.

You generally make three types of changes to text in a presentation: additions, replacements, and deletions.

- Additions are necessary when you omit text from a slide and need to add it later. You may need to insert text in the form of a sentence, word, or single character. For example, you may want to add the presenter's middle name on the title slide.

- Replacements are needed when you want to revise the text in a presentation. For example, you may want to substitute the word *their* for the word *there*.

- Deletions are required when text on a slide is incorrect or no longer is relevant to the presentation. For example, a slide may look cluttered. Therefore, you may want to remove one of the bulleted paragraphs to add more space.

Editing text in PowerPoint basically is the same as editing text in a word processing program. The following sections illustrate the most common changes made to text in a presentation.

Replacing Text in an Existing Slide

When you need to correct a word or phrase, you can replace the text by selecting the text to be replaced and then typing the new text. As soon as you press any key on the keyboard, the selected text is deleted and the new text is displayed.

PowerPoint inserts text to the left of the insertion point. The text to the right of the insertion point moves to the right (and shifts downward if necessary) to accommodate the added text.

Deleting Text

You can delete text using one of three methods. One is to use the BACKSPACE key to remove text just typed. The second is to position the insertion point to the left of the text you want to delete and then press the DELETE key. The third method is to drag through the text you want to delete and then press the DELETE or BACKSPACE key. Use the third method when deleting large sections of text.

To Delete Text in a Placeholder

To keep the ending slide clean and simple, you want to delete a few words in the slide show title and subtitle text. The following steps change It Is Easy Being Green to Be Green and then change Saving Energy at Home to Save Energy.

1
- With Slide 5 selected, position the mouse pointer immediately to the left of the first character of the text to be selected (in this case, the I in the word, It).

- Drag the mouse pointer through the last character of the text to be selected (in this case, the space after the y in Easy) (Figure 1–58).

Figure 1–58

- Click the Cut button (Home tab | Clipboard group) to delete all the selected text (Figure 1–59).

Figure 1–59

- Select the letters, ing, in the word, Being.
- Click the Cut button (Figure 1–60).

Figure 1–60

- Select the letters, ing, in the word, Saving, and then click the Cut button.
- Type e to change the word to Save (Figure 1–61).

Other Ways

1. Right-click selected text, click Cut on shortcut menu
2. Select text, press DELETE or BACKSPACE key
3. Select text, press CTRL+X

Figure 1–61

Adding a Transition

PowerPoint provides many animation effects to add interest and make a slide show presentation look professional. **Animation** includes special visual and sound effects applied to text or content. A **slide transition** is a special animation effect used to progress from one slide to the next in a slide show. You can control the speed of the transition effect and add a sound.

PowerPoint provides a variety of transitions arranged into three categories that describe the types of effects: Subtle, Exciting, and Dynamic Content.

To Add a Transition between Slides

In this presentation, you apply the Doors transition in the Exciting category to all slides and change the transition speed from 1.40 seconds to 2 seconds. The following steps apply this transition to the presentation.

1
- Click the Transitions tab on the Ribbon and then point to the More button (Transitions tab | Transition to This Slide group) (Figure 1–62).

Is a transition applied now?

No. The first slide icon in the Transitions group has an orange border, which indicates no transition has been applied.

Figure 1–62

2
- Click the More button to expand the Transitions gallery.

- Point to the Doors transition in the Exciting category in the Transitions gallery (Figure 1–63).

Can I add a sound to play during this transition?

Yes. Click the Sound arrow (Transitions tab | Timing group) to display the Sound list and then select a sound from this list. You also can use your own sound if you select Other Sound in the list, select the desired sound (Add Audio dialog box), and then click the OK button.

Figure 1–63

3

- Click Doors in the Exciting category in the Transitions gallery to apply this transition to the closing slide.

Q&A Why does a star appear next to Slide 5 in the Slides tab?

The star indicates that a transition animation effect is applied to that slide.

- Click the Duration up arrow (Transitions tab | Timing group) three times to change the transition speed from 01.40 seconds to 02.00 seconds (Figure 1–64).

Q&A Why did the time change?

Each transition has a default duration time. The Doors transition time is 1:40 seconds.

Figure 1–64

4

- Click the Preview Transitions button (Transitions tab | Preview area) to view the transition and the new transition time (Figure 1–65).

 Can I adjust the duration time I just set?

Yes. Click the Duration up or down arrows or type a speed in the Duration text box and preview the transition until you find the time that best fits your presentation.

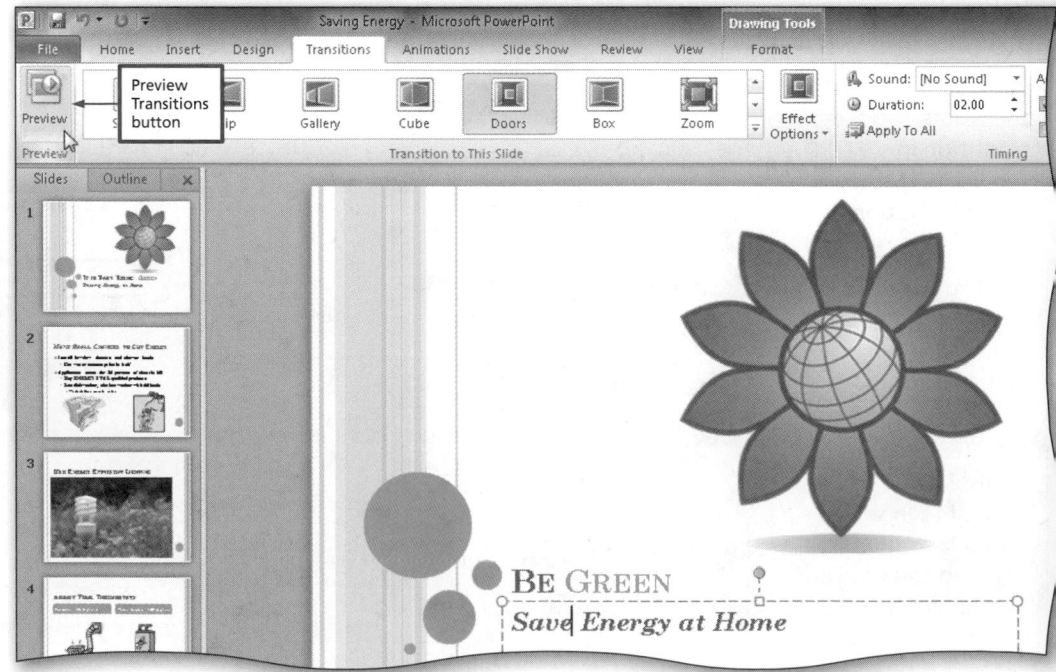

Figure 1–65

5
- Click the Apply To All button (Transitions tab | Timing group) to apply the Doors transition and the increased transition time to Slides 1 through 4 in the presentation (Figure 1–66).

What if I want to apply a different transition and duration to each slide in the presentation?

Repeat Steps 2 and 3 for each slide individually.

Figure 1–66

Changing Document Properties

PowerPoint helps you organize and identify your files by using **document properties**, which are the details about a file. Document properties, also known as **metadata**, can include information such as the project author, title, subject, and keywords. A **keyword** is a word or phrase that further describes the document. For example, a class name or document topic can describe the file's purpose or content.

Document properties are valuable for a variety of reasons:

- Users can save time locating a particular file because they can view a document's properties without opening the document.

- By creating consistent properties for files having similar content, users can better organize their documents.

- Some organizations require PowerPoint users to add document properties so that other employees can view details about these files.

Five different types of document properties exist, but the more common ones used in this book are standard and automatically updated properties. **Standard properties** are associated with all Microsoft Office documents and include author, title, and subject. **Automatically updated properties** include file system properties, such as the date you create or change a file, and statistics, such as the file size.

BTW

PowerPoint Help
At any time while using PowerPoint, you can find answers to questions and display information about various topics through PowerPoint Help. Used properly, this form of assistance can increase your productivity and reduce your frustrations by minimizing the time you spend learning how to use PowerPoint. For instruction about PowerPoint Help and exercises that will help you gain confidence in using it, read the Office 2010 and Windows 7 chapter at the beginning of this book.

To Change Document Properties

The **Document Information Panel** contains areas where you can view and enter document properties. You can view and change information in this panel at any time while you are creating a document. Before saving the presentation again, you want to add your name and course information as document properties. The following steps use the Document Information Panel to change document properties.

1

- Click File on the Ribbon to open the Backstage view.

- If necessary, click the Info tab in the Backstage view to display the Info gallery (Figure 1–67).

Q&A

How do I close the Backstage view?

Click File on the Ribbon or click the preview of the document in the Info gallery to return to the PowerPoint document window.

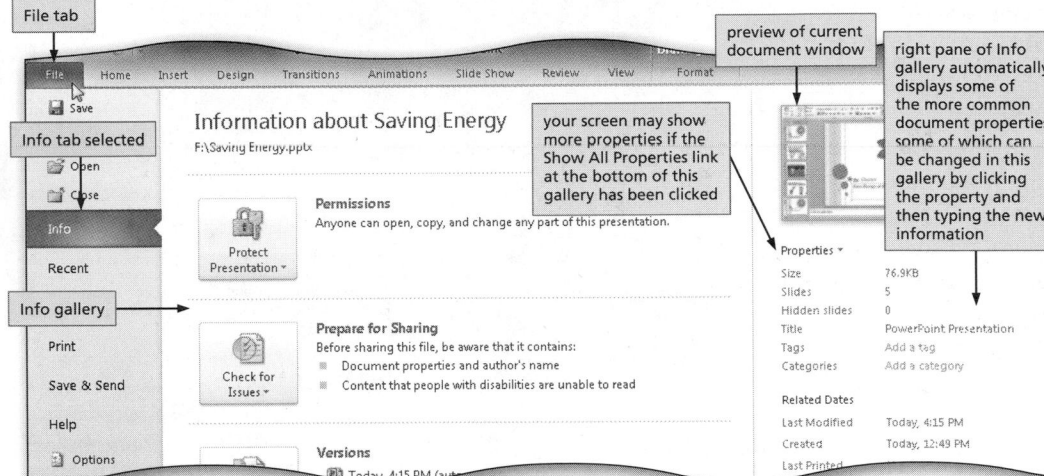

Figure 1–67

2

- Click the Properties button in the right pane of the Info gallery to display the Properties menu (Figure 1–68).

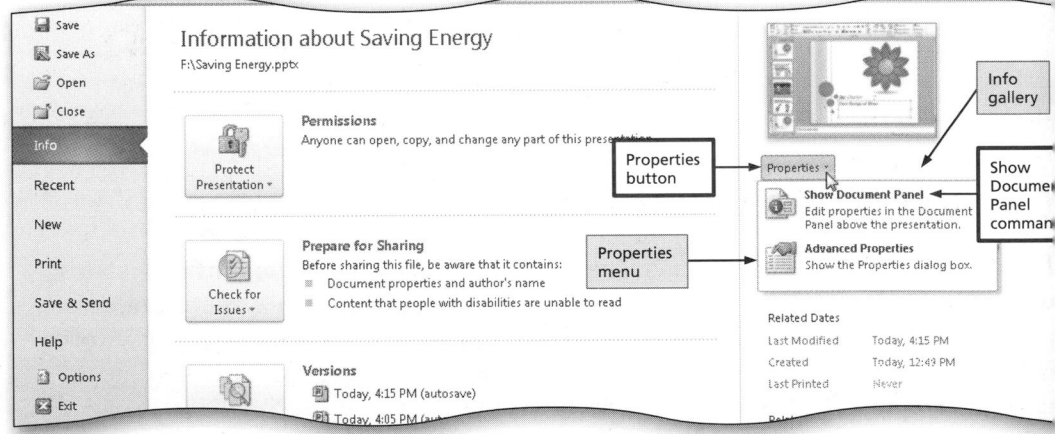

Figure 1–68

3

- Click Show Document Panel on the Properties menu to close the Backstage view and display the Document Information Panel in the PowerPoint document window (Figure 1–69).

Figure 1–69

Q&A

Why are some of the document properties in my Document Information Panel already filled in?

The person who installed Microsoft Office 2010 on your computer or network may have set or customized the properties.

4

- Click the Author text box, if necessary, and then type your name as the Author property. If a name already is displayed in the Author text box, delete it before typing your name.

Figure 1–70

- Click the Subject text box, if necessary delete any existing text, and then type your course and section as the Subject property.

- If an AutoComplete dialog box appears, click its Yes button.

- Click the Keywords text box, if necessary delete any existing text, and then type **energy savings** as the Keywords property (Figure 1–70).

What types of document properties does PowerPoint collect automatically?

PowerPoint records details such as time spent editing a document, the number of times a document has been revised, and the fonts and themes used in a document.

5

- Click the Close the Document Information Panel button so that the Document Information Panel no longer is displayed.

Other Ways

1. Click File on Ribbon, click Info in Backstage view, if necessary click Show All Properties link in Info gallery, click property to change and type new information, close Backstage view

To Save an Existing Presentation with the Same File Name

You have made several modifications to the presentation since you last saved it. Thus, you should save it again. The following step saves the document again. For an example of the step listed below, refer to the Office 2010 and Windows 7 chapter at the beginning of this book.

1 Click the Save button on the Quick Access Toolbar to overwrite the previously saved file.

BTW

Saving in a Previous PowerPoint Format
To ensure that your presentation will open in PowerPoint 2003 or older versions of this software, you must save your file in PowerPoint 97-2003 format. These files will have the .ppt extension.

Viewing the Presentation in Slide Show View

The Slide Show button, located in the lower-right corner of the PowerPoint window above the status bar, allows you to show a presentation using a computer. The computer acts like a slide projector, displaying each slide on a full screen. The full-screen slide hides the toolbars, menus, and other PowerPoint window elements.

To Start Slide Show View

When making a presentation, you use **Slide Show view**. You can start Slide Show view from Normal view or Slide Sorter view. Slide Show view begins when you click the Slide Show button on the lower-right corner of the status bar. PowerPoint then shows the current slide on the full screen without any of the PowerPoint window objects, such as the menu bar or toolbars. The following steps start Slide Show view.

- Click the Slide 1 thumbnail in the Slides pane to select and display Slide 1.

- Point to the Slide Show button in the lower-right corner of the PowerPoint window on the status bar (Figure 1–71).

Q&A Why did I need to select Slide 1?

When you run a slide show, PowerPoint begins the show with the currently displayed slide. If you had not selected Slide 1, then only Slide 5 would have displayed in the slide show.

Figure 1–71

- Click the Slide Show button to display the title slide (Figure 1–72).

Q&A Where is the PowerPoint window?

When you run a slide show, the PowerPoint window is hidden. It will reappear once you end your slide show.

Other Ways

1. Click Slide Show From Beginning button (Slide Show tab | Start Slide Show group)
2. Press F5

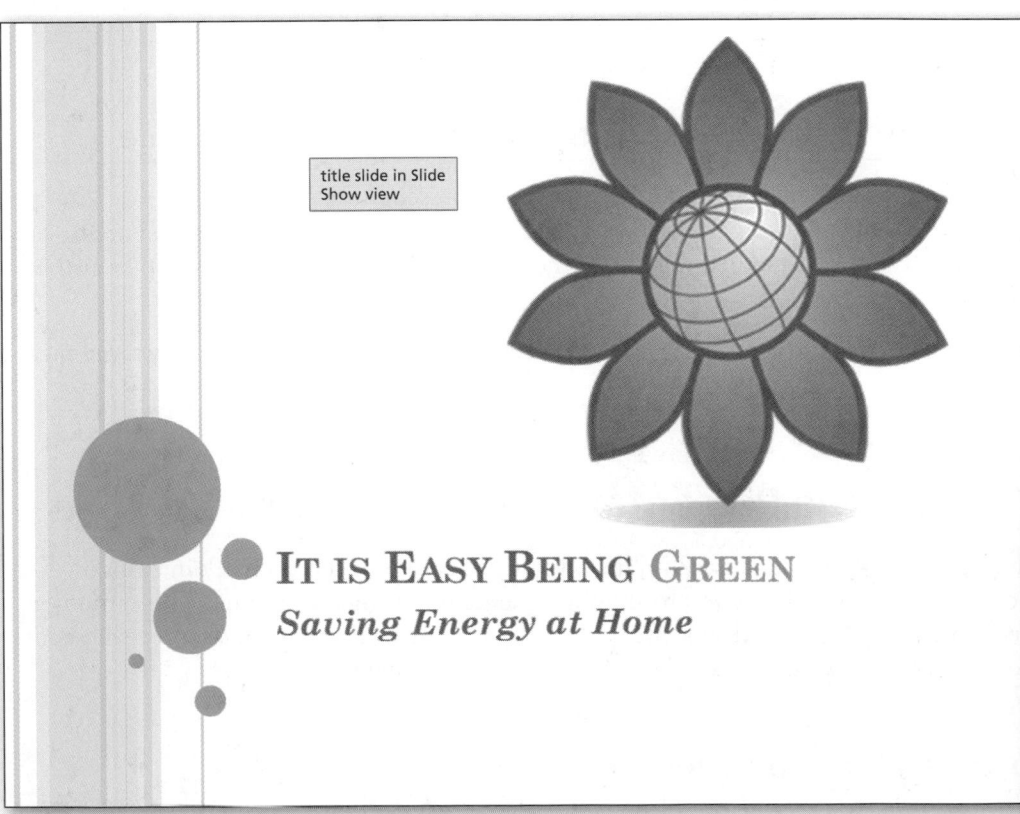

Figure 1–72

To Move Manually through Slides in a Slide Show

After you begin Slide Show view, you can move forward or backward through the slides. PowerPoint allows you to advance through the slides manually or automatically. During a slide show, each slide in the presentation shows on the screen, one slide at a time. Each time you click the mouse button, the next slide appears. The following steps move manually through the slides.

• Click each slide until Slide 5 (Be Green) is displayed (Figure 1–73).

I see a small toolbar in the lower-left corner of my slide. What is this toolbar?

The Slide Show toolbar appears when you begin running a slide show and then move the mouse pointer. The buttons on this toolbar allow you to navigate to the next slide, the previous slide, to mark up the current slide, or to change the current display.

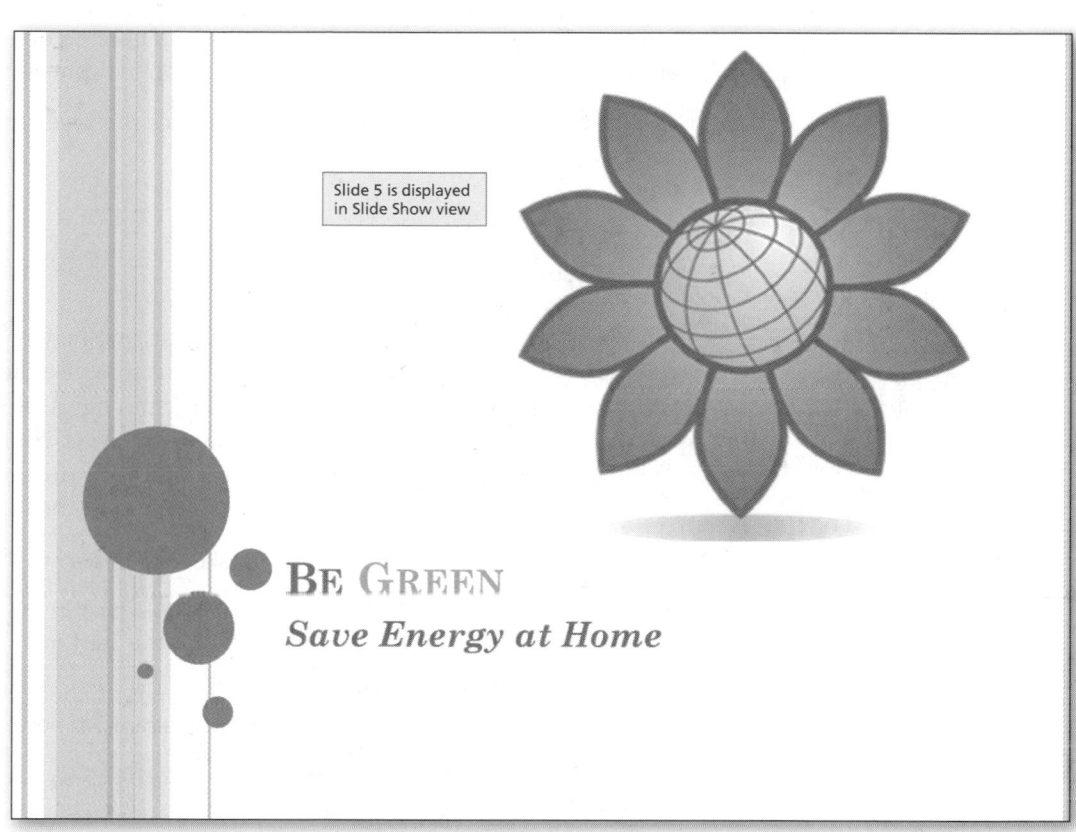

Figure 1–73

• Click Slide 5 so that the black slide appears with a message announcing the end of the slide show (Figure 1–74).

How can I end the presentation at this point?

Click the black slide to return to Normal view in the PowerPoint window or press the ESC key.

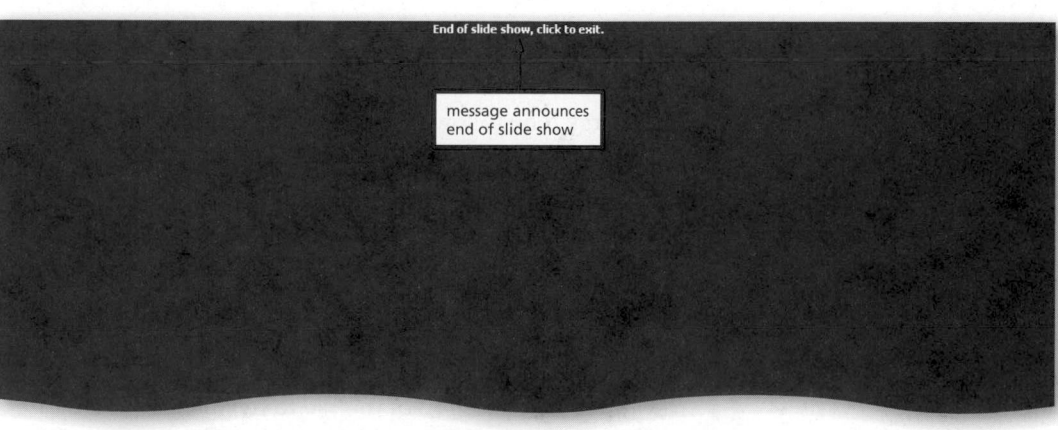

Figure 1–74

Other Ways

1. Press PAGE DOWN to advance one slide at a time, or press PAGE UP to go back one slide at a time

2. Press RIGHT ARROW or DOWN ARROW to advance one slide at a time, or press LEFT ARROW or UP ARROW to go back one slide at a time

3. If Slide Show toolbar is displayed, click Next Slide or Previous Slide button on toolbar

To Quit PowerPoint

This project now is complete. The following steps quit PowerPoint. For a detailed example of the procedure summarized below, refer to the Office 2010 and Windows 7 chapter at the beginning of this book.

1 If you have one PowerPoint presentation open, click the Close button on the right side of the title bar to close the document and quit PowerPoint; or if you have multiple PowerPoint presentations open, click File on the Ribbon to open the Backstage view and then click Exit in the Backstage view to close all open documents and quit PowerPoint.

2 If a Microsoft PowerPoint dialog box appears, click the Save button to save any changes made to the document since the last save.

To Start PowerPoint

Once you have created and saved a document, you may need to retrieve it from your storage medium. For example, you might want to revise the presentation or print it. The following steps, which assume Windows 7 is running, start PowerPoint so that you can open and modify the presentation. You may need to ask your instructor how to start PowerPoint for your computer. For a detailed example of the procedure summarized below, refer to the Office 2010 and Windows 7 chapter at the beginning of this book.

1 Click the Start button on the Windows 7 taskbar to display the Start menu.

2 Type **Microsoft PowerPoint** as the search text in the 'Search programs and files' text box and watch the search results appear on the Start menu.

3 Click Microsoft PowerPoint 2010 in the search results on the Start menu to start PowerPoint and display a new blank document in the PowerPoint window.

4 If the PowerPoint window is not maximized, click the Maximize button next to the Close button on its title bar to maximize the window.

To Open a Document from PowerPoint

Earlier in this chapter you saved your project on a USB flash drive using the file name Saving Energy. The following steps open the Saving Energy file from the PowerPoint folder in the CIS 101 folder on the USB flash drive. For a detailed example of the procedure summarized below, refer to the Office 2010 and Windows 7 chapter at the beginning of this book.

1 With your USB flash drive connected to one of the computer's USB ports, click File on the Ribbon to open the Backstage view.

2 Click Open in the Backstage view to display the Open dialog box.

3 Navigate to the location of the file to be opened (in this case, the USB flash drive, then to the CIS 101 folder [or your class folder], and then to the PowerPoint folder).

4 Click Saving Energy to select the file to be opened.

5 Click the Open button (Open dialog box) to open the selected file and display the opened document in the PowerPoint window.

Printing a Presentation

After creating a presentation, you may want to print the slides. Printing a presentation enables you to distribute the document to others in a form that can be read or viewed but typically not edited. It is a good practice to save a presentation before printing it, in the event you experience difficulties printing.

Determine the best method for distributing the presentation.

The traditional method of distributing a presentation uses a printer to produce a hard copy. A **hardcopy** or **printout** is information that exists on a physical medium such as paper. For users who can receive fax documents, you can elect to print a hard copy on a remote fax machine. Hard copies can be useful for the following reasons:

* Many people prefer proofreading a hard copy of a document rather than viewing it on the screen to check for errors and readability.

* Hard copies can serve as reference material if your storage medium is lost or becomes corrupted and you need to recreate the document.

Instead of distributing a hard copy of a presentation slides, users can choose to distribute the presentation as an electronic image that mirrors the original document's appearance. The electronic image of the document can be e-mailed, posted on a Web site, or copied to a portable storage medium such as a USB flash drive. Two popular electronic image formats, sometimes called fixed formats, are PDF by Adobe Systems and XPS by Microsoft. In PowerPoint, you can create electronic image files through the Print tab in the Backstage view, the Save & Send tab in the Backstage view, and the Save As dialog box. Electronic images of documents, such as PDF and XPS, can be useful for the following reasons.

* Users can view electronic images of documents without the software that created the original document (e.g., PowerPoint). Specifically, to view a PDF file, you use a program called Acrobat Reader, which can be downloaded free from Adobe's Web site. Similarly, to view an XPS file, you use a program called an XPS Viewer, which is included in the latest versions of Windows and Internet Explorer.

* Sending electronic documents saves paper and printer supplies. Society encourages users to contribute to **green computing**, which involves reducing the environmental waste generated when using a computer.

Plan
Ahead

To Print a Presentation

With the completed presentation saved, you may want to print it. If copies of the presentation are being distributed to audience members, you will print a hard copy of each individual slide on a printer. The following steps print a hard copy of the contents of the saved Saving Energy presentation.

- Click File on the Ribbon to open the Backstage view.

- Click the Print tab in the Backstage view to display the Print gallery (Figure 1–75).

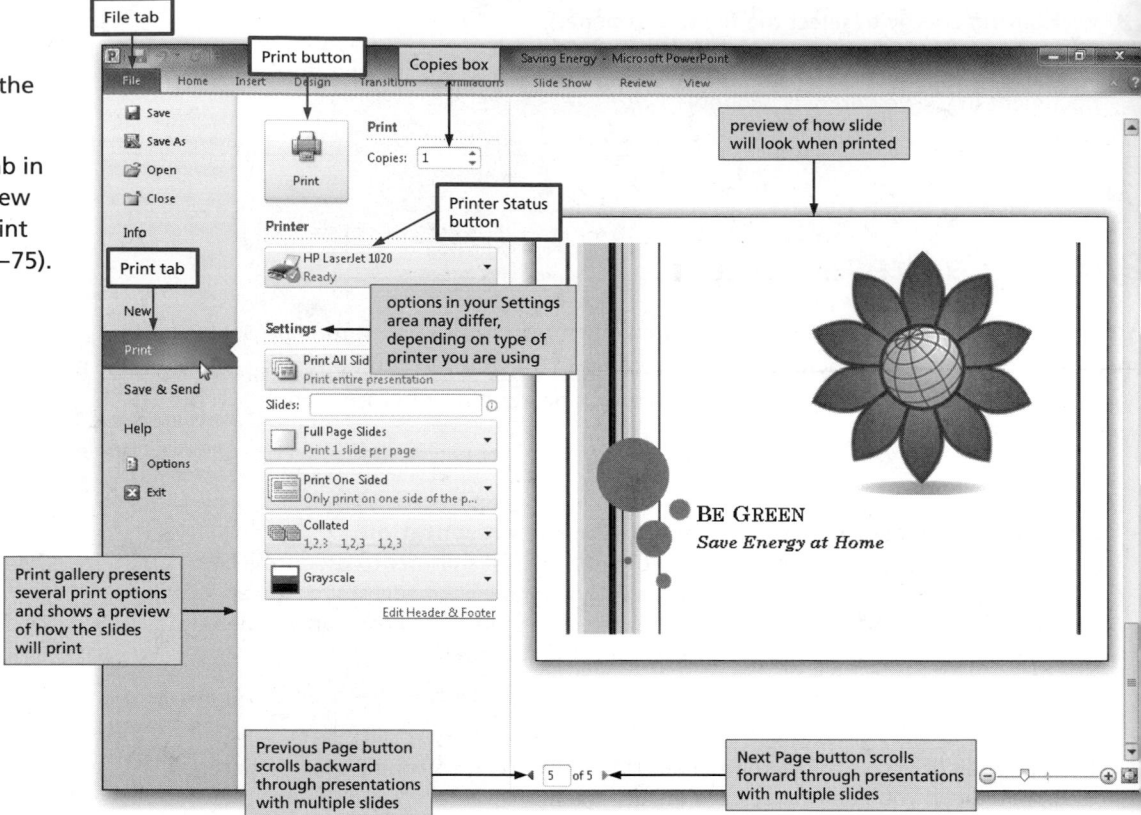

Figure 1–75

Q&A How do I preview Slides 2 through 5?

Click the Next Page button in the Print gallery to scroll forward through pages in the document; similarly, click the Previous Page button to scroll backward through pages.

Q&A How can I print multiple copies of my slides?

Increase the number in the Copies box in the Print gallery.

Q&A What if I decide not to print the document at this time?

Click File on the Ribbon to close the Backstage view and return to the PowerPoint document window.

- Verify the printer name that appears on the Printer box Status button will print a hard copy of the document. If necessary, click the Printer Status button to display a list of available printer options and then click the desired printer to change the currently selected printer.

BTW

Quick Reference
For a table that lists how to complete the tasks covered in this book using the mouse, Ribbon, shortcut menu, and keyboard, see the Quick Reference Summary at the back of this book, or visit the PowerPoint 2010 Quick Reference Web page (scsite.com/ppt2010/qr).

3

- Click the Print button in the Print gallery to print the document on the currently selected printer.

- When the printer stops, retrieve the hard copy (Figure 1–76).

Do I have to wait until my document is complete to print it?

No, you can follow these steps to print a document at any time while you are creating it.

What if I want to print an electronic image of a document instead of a hard copy?

You would click the Printer Status button in the Print gallery and then select the desired electronic image option such as a Microsoft XPS Document Writer, which would create an XPS file.

(a) Slide 1

(b) Slide 2

(c) Slide 3

(d) Slide 4

(e) Slide 5

Figure 1–76

Other Ways
1. Press CTRL+P, press ENTER

To Quit PowerPoint

The project now is complete. The following steps quit PowerPoint. For a detailed example of the procedure summarized below, refer to the Office 2010 and Windows 7 chapter at the beginning of this book.

1 If you have one PowerPoint document open, click the Close button on the right side of the title bar to close the document and quit PowerPoint; or if you have multiple PowerPoint documents open, click File on the Ribbon to open the Backstage view and then click Exit in the Backstage view to close all open documents and quit PowerPoint.

2 If a Microsoft Office PowerPoint dialog box appears, click the Save button to save any changes made to the document since the last save.

Chapter Summary

In this chapter you have learned how to apply a document theme, create a title slide and text slides with a bulleted list, clip art, and a photograph, size and move clip art and a photograph, format and edit text, add a slide transition, view the presentation in Slide Show view, and print slides as handouts. The items listed below include all the new PowerPoint skills you have learned in this chapter.

1. Start PowerPoint (PPT 4)
2. Choose a Document Theme (PPT 5)
3. Enter the Presentation Title (PPT 7)
4. Enter the Presentation Subtitle Paragraph (PPT 9)
5. Select a Paragraph (PPT 10)
6. Italicize Text (PPT 11)
7. Increase Font Size (PPT 11)
8. Select a Word (PPT 12)
9. Change the Text Color (PPT 13)
10. Save a Presentation (PPT 14)
11. Add a New Text Slide with a Bulleted List (PPT 14)
12. Enter a Slide Title (PPT 16)
13. Select a Text Placeholder (PPT 16)
14. Type a Multi-Level Bulleted List (PPT 17)
15. Select a Group of Words (PPT 19)
16. Bold Text (PPT 19)
17. Add a Slide with the Title Only Layout (PPT 21)
18. Add a New Slide and Enter a Slide Title and Headings (PPT 23)
19. Move to Another Slide in Normal View (PPT 25)
20. Insert a Clip from the Clip Organizer into the Title Slide (PPT 27)
21. Insert a Clip from the Clip Organizer into a Content Placeholder (PPT 30)
22. Insert a Photograph from the Clip Organizer into a Slide without a Content Placeholder (PPT 32)
23. Resize Clip Art (PPT 33)
24. Move Clips (PPT 36)
25. Duplicate a Slide (PPT 38)
26. Arrange a Slide (PPT 39)
27. Delete Text in a Placeholder (PPT 41)
28. Add a Transition between Slides (PPT 43)
29. Change Document Properties (PPT 46)
30. Save an Existing Presentation with the Same File Name (PPT 47)
31. Start Slide Show View (PPT 47)
32. Move Manually through Slides in a Slide Show (PPT 49)
33. Quit PowerPoint (PPT 50)
34. Open a Document from PowerPoint (PPT 50)
35. Print a Presentation (PPT 51)

 If you have a SAM 2010 user profile, your instructor may have assigned an autogradable version of this assignment. If so, log into the SAM 2010 Web site at www.cengage.com/sam2010 to download the instruction and start files.

Learn It Online

Test your knowledge of chapter content and key terms.

Instructions: To complete the Learn It Online exercises, start your browser, click the Address bar, and then enter the Web address   `scsite.com/ppt2010/learn`.   When the PowerPoint 2010 Learn It Online page is displayed, click the link for the exercise you want to complete and then read the instructions.

Chapter Reinforcement TF, MC, and SA

A series of true/false, multiple choice, and short answer questions that test your knowledge of the chapter content.

Flash Cards

An interactive learning environment where you identify chapter key terms associated with displayed definitions.

Practice Test

A series of multiple choice questions that test your knowledge of chapter content and key terms.

Who Wants To Be a Computer Genius?

An interactive game that challenges your knowledge of chapter content in the style of a television quiz show.

Wheel of Terms

An interactive game that challenges your knowledge of chapter key terms in the style of the television show *Wheel of Fortune*.

Crossword Puzzle Challenge

A crossword puzzle that challenges your knowledge of key terms presented in the chapter.

Apply Your Knowledge

Reinforce the skills and apply the concepts you learned in this chapter.

Modifying Character Formats and Paragraph Levels and Moving a Clip

Note: To complete this assignment, you will be required to use the Data Files for Students. See the inside back cover of this book for instructions on downloading the Data Files for Students, or contact your instructor for information about accessing the required files.

Instructions: Start PowerPoint. Open the presentation, Apply 1-1 Flu Season, from the Data Files for Students.

The two slides in the presentation discuss ways to avoid getting or spreading the flu. The document you open is an unformatted presentation. You are to modify the document theme, indent the paragraphs, resize and move the clip art, and format the text so the slides look like Figure 1–77 on the next page.

Continued >

Apply Your Knowledge *continued*

Perform the following tasks:

1. Change the document theme to Urban. On the title slide, use your name in place of Student Name and bold and italicize your name. Increase the title text font size to 60 point. Resize and position the clip as shown in Figure 1–77a.

2. On Slide 2, increase the indent of the second, third, and fifth paragraphs (Cover mouth and nose with a tissue; No tissue? Use your elbow or sleeve; Use soap, warm water for 20 seconds) to second-level paragraphs. Then combine paragraphs six and seven (Drink fluids; Get plenty of rest) to read, Drink fluids and get plenty of rest, as shown in Figure 1–77b.

3. Change the document properties, as specified by your instructor. Save the presentation using the file name, Apply 1–1 Avoid the Flu. Submit the revised document in the format specified by your instructor.

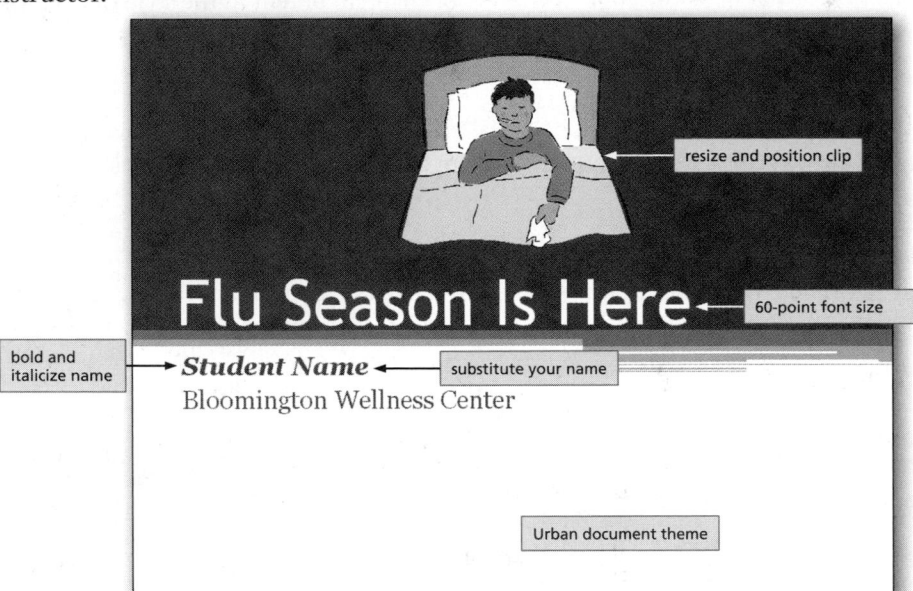

(a) Slide 1 (Title Slide with Clip Art)

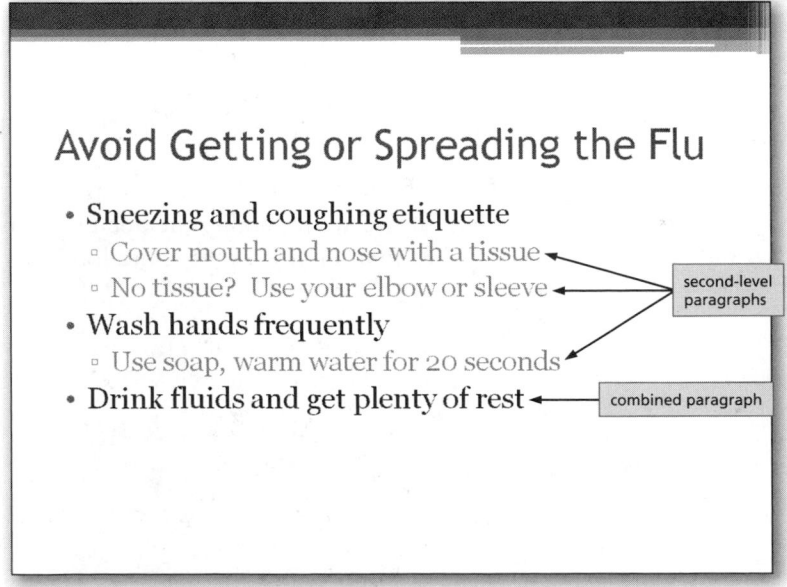

(b) Slide 2 (Multi-Level Bulleted List)

Figure 1–77

Extend Your Knowledge

Extend the skills you learned in this chapter and experiment with new skills. You may need to use Help to complete the assignment.

Changing Slide Theme, Layout, and Text

Note: To complete this assignment, you will be required to use the Data Files for Students. See the inside back cover of this book for instructions on downloading the Data Files for Students, or contact your instructor for information about accessing the required files.

Instructions: Start PowerPoint. Open the presentation that you are going to prepare for your dental hygiene class, Extend 1–1 Winning Smile, from the Data Files for Students.

You will choose a theme, format slides, and create a closing slide.

Perform the following tasks:

1. Apply an appropriate document theme.

2. On Slide 1, use your name in place of Student Name. Format the text on this slide using techniques you learned in this chapter, such as changing the font size and color and also bolding and italicizing words.

3. On Slide 2, change the slide layout and adjust the paragraph levels so that the lines of text are arranged under two headings: Discount Dental and Dental Insurance (Figure 1–78).

4. On Slide 3, create paragraphs and adjust the paragraph levels to create a bulleted list. Edit the text so that the slide meets the 7 × 7 rule, which states that each line should have a maximum of seven words, and each slide should have a maximum of seven lines.

5. Create an appropriate closing slide using the title slide as a guide.

6. The slides contain a variety of clips downloaded from the Microsoft Clip Organizer. Size and move them when necessary.

7. Apply an appropriate transition to all slides.

8. Change the document properties, as specified by your instructor. Save the presentation using the file name, Extend 1–1 Dental Plans.

9. Submit the revised document in the format specified by your instructor.

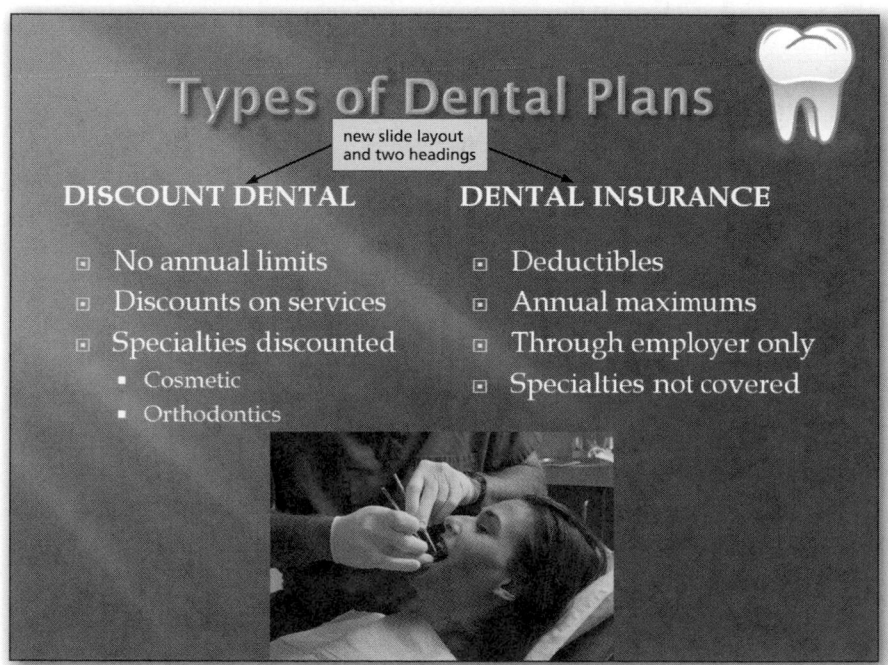

Figure 1–78

Make It Right

Analyze a presentation and correct all errors and/or improve the design.

Correcting Formatting and List Levels

Note: To complete this assignment, you will be required to use the Data Files for Students. See the inside back cover of this book for instructions on downloading the Data Files for Students, or contact your instructor for information about accessing the required files.

Instructions: Start PowerPoint. Open the presentation, Make It Right 1–1 Air Ducts, from the Data Files for Students.

Members of your homeowners' association are having their semiannual meeting, and each member of the board is required to give a short presentation on the subject of energy savings. You have decided to discuss the energy-saving benefits of maintaining the air ducts in your home. Correct the formatting problems and errors in the presentation while keeping in mind the guidelines presented in this chapter.

Perform the following tasks:

1. Change the document theme from Origin, shown in Figure 1–79, to Module.
2. On Slide 1, replace the words, Student Name, with your name. Format your name so that it displays prominently on the slide.
3. Increase the size of the clip on Slide 1 and move it to the upper-right corner.
4. Move Slide 2 to the end of the presentation so that it becomes the new Slide 3.
5. On Slide 2, correct the spelling errors and then increase the font size of the Slide 2 title text, Check Hidden Air Ducts, to 54 point. Increase the size of the clip and move it up to fill the white space on the right of the bulleted list.
6. On Slide 3, correct the spelling errors and then change the font size of the title text, Energy Savings, to 54 point. Increase the indent levels for paragraphs 2 and 4. Increase the size of the clips. Center the furnace clip at the bottom of the slide.
7. Change the document properties, as specified by your instructor. Save the presentation using the file name, Make It Right 1–1 Ducts Presentation.
8. Apply the same transition and duration to all slides.
9. Submit the revised document in the format specified by your instructor.

Figure 1–79

n the Lab

Design and/or create a presentation using the guidelines, concepts, and skills presented in this chapter. Labs 1, 2, and 3 are listed in order of increasing difficulty.

Lab 1: Creating a Presentation with Bulleted Lists, a Closing Slide, and Clips

Problem: You are working with upper-level students to host a freshmen orientation seminar. When you attended this seminar, you received some helpful tips on studying for exams. Your contribution to this year's seminar is to prepare a short presentation on study skills. You develop the outline shown in Figure 1–80 and then prepare the PowerPoint presentation shown in Figures 1–81a through 1–81d.

Hit the Books
Studying for an Exam
Sarah Jones

Prepare in Advance
Location
Quiet, well-lit
Timing
15-minute breaks every hour
Material
Quiz yourself

Exam Time
Day of Exam
Rest properly
Eat a good meal
Wear comfy clothes
Be early
Be confident

Figure 1–80

Perform the following tasks:

1. Create a new presentation using the Aspect document theme.

2. Using the typed notes illustrated in Figure 1–80, create the title slide shown in Figure 1–81a, using your name in place of Sarah Jones. Italicize your name and increase the font size to 24 point. Increase the font size of the title text paragraph, Hit the Books, to 48 point. Increase the font size of the first paragraph of the subtitle text, Studying for an Exam, to 28 point.

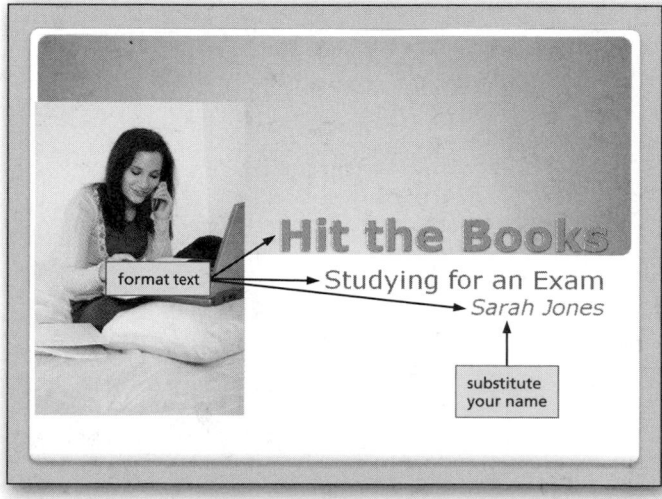

(a) Slide 1 (Title Slide)
Figure 1–81

Continued >

In the Lab continued

STUDENT ASSIGNMENTS

3. Using the typed notes in Figure 1–80, create the two text slides with bulleted lists and find and insert clips from the Microsoft Clip Organizer, as shown in Figures 1–81b and 1–81c.

4. Create a closing slide by duplicating Slide 1, deleting your name, replacing the photograph with the photograph shown in Figure 1–81d, and moving the slide to the end of the presentation.

5. On Slide 3, change the font color of the words, Be confident, to Yellow (fourth color in the Standard Colors row) and then bold this text.

6. Apply the Uncover transition in the Subtle category to all slides. Change the duration to 1.25 seconds.

7. Drag the scroll box to display Slide 1. Click the Slide Show button to start Slide Show view. Then click to display each slide.

8. Change the document properties, as specified by your instructor. Save the presentation using the file name, Lab 1–1 Study Skills.

9. Submit the document in the format specified by your instructor.

(b) Slide 2

(c) Slide 3

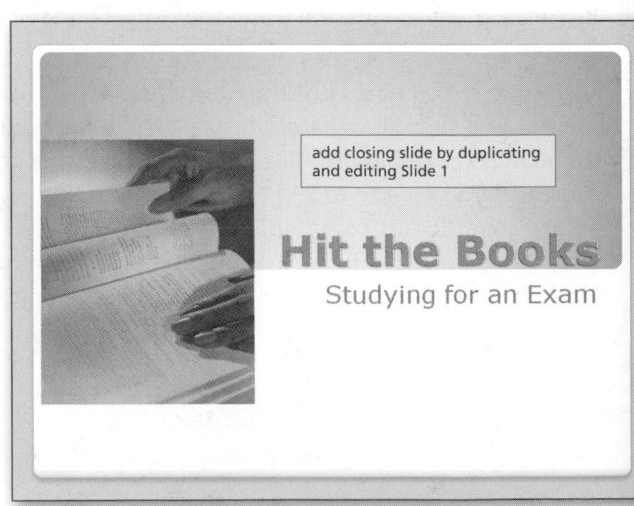

(d) Slide 4 (Closing Slide)

Figure 1–81 (continued)

In the Lab

Lab 2: Creating a Presentation with Bulleted Lists and Clips

Problem: Your health class instructor has assigned every student a different vitamin to research. She hands you the outline shown in Figure 1–82 and asks you to create the presentation about Vitamin D shown in Figures 1–83a through 1–83d on pages PPT 62 and PPT 63.

Vitamin D

The Sunshine Vitamin
Are You D-ficient?
Presented by Jim Warner

Why Is Vitamin D Important?
We need Vitamin D
Vital to our bodies
Promotes absorption of calcium and magnesium
For healthy teeth and bones
Maintains calcium and phosphorus in blood

Daily Requirements
How much do we need?
Child: 5 mcg (200 IU)
Adult: 10-20 mcg (400-600 IU)

Vitamin D Sources
Sunshine
Is our primary source
Vitamin manufactured by our body after exposure
Three times a week
For 10-15 minutes
Foods and Supplements
Contained in few foods
Some fish liver oils
Flesh of fatty fish
Fortified products
Milk and cereals
Available as supplement

Vitamin D History
Research began in 1924
Found to prevent rickets
United States and Canada
Instituted policy of fortifying foods with Vitamin D
Milk – food of choice
Other countries
Fortified cereal, bread, margarine

Figure 1–82

Continued >

In the Lab *continued*

Perform the following tasks:

1. Create a new presentation using the Solstice document theme.

2. Using the typed notes illustrated in Figure 1–82, create the title slide shown in Figure 1–83a, using your name in place of Jim Warner. Italicize the title, The Sunshine Vitamin, and increase the font size to 48 point. Change the font size of the first line of the subtitle text, Are You D-ficient?, to 36 point. Change the font color of the title text to Orange (third color in the Standard Colors row) and both lines of the subtitle text to Light Blue (seventh color in the Standard Colors row).

3. Using the typed notes in Figure 1–82, create the three text slides with bulleted lists shown in Figures 1–83b through 1–83d. Change the color of the title text on all slides and the text above the bulleted lists on Slides 2 and 3 to Orange.

4. Add the photographs and clip art shown in Figures 1–83a through 1–83d from the Microsoft Clip Organizer. Adjust the clip sizes when necessary.

5. Apply the Ripple transition in the Exciting category to all slides. Change the duration to 2.00 seconds.

6. Drag the scroll box to display Slide 1. Click the Slide Show button to start Slide Show view. Then click to display each slide.

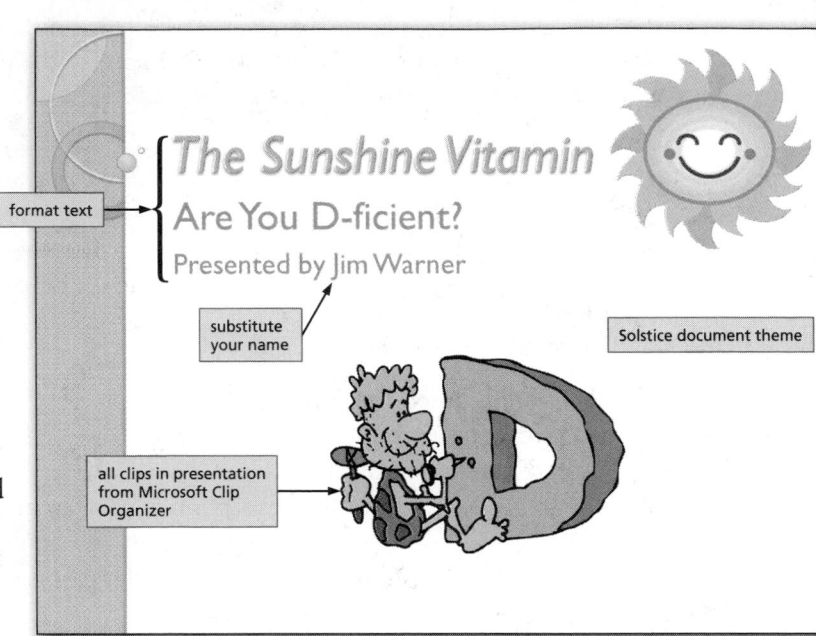

(a) Slide 1 (Title Slide)

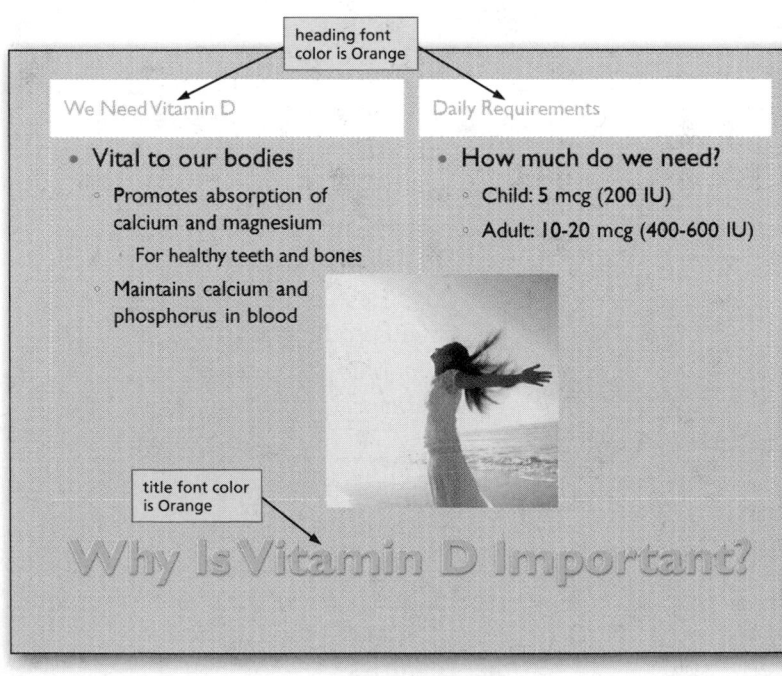

(b) Slide 2

Figure 1–83

7. Change the document properties, as specified by your instructor. Save the presentation using the file name, Lab 1–2 Vitamin D.

8. Submit the revised document in the format specified by your instructor.

(c) Slide 3

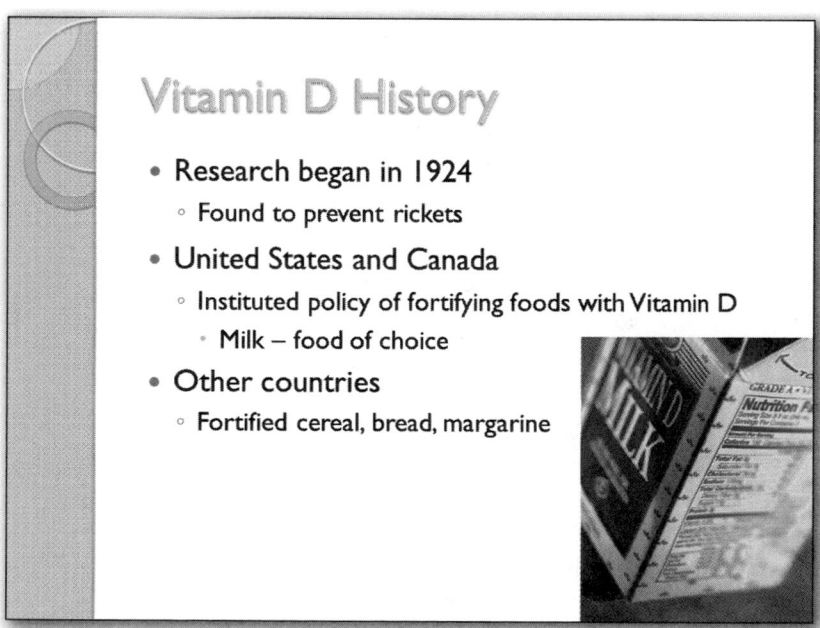

(d) Slide 4

Figure 1–83 (continued)

In the Lab

Lab 3: Creating and Updating Presentations with Clip Art

Problem: You are employed part time at your health club, and the Child Care Center director has asked you to put together a presentation for her to use at the next open house. The club has a large playroom that is perfect for children's parties.

Instructions Part 1: Using the outline in Figure 1–84, create the presentation shown in Figure 1–85. Use the Office Theme document theme. On the title slide shown in Figure 1–85a, increase the font size of the title paragraph, Make It a Party!, to 48, change the font color to Red, and change the text font style to italic. Decrease the font size of the entire subtitle paragraph to 28, and change the font color to Blue.

Make It a Party!
   Host Your Child's
   Next Birthday Party
   at the Oaks Health Club

We Do the Work
You Enjoy the Moment
   Two-hour party
   Two chaperones
   Lunch & cake provided
   Game or craft activity available
   Decorations

Two Party Packages
   Package No. 1 - $8/child
      Lunch
         Hot Dogs
         Pizza
   Package No. 2 - $12/child
      Lunch including beverage
         Hot Dogs
         Pizza
      Game
      Craft (age appropriate)

Reserve Your Party Date
   Reserve 2 weeks in advance
   Deposit required
   Party room can hold 20 children
   Sign up in the Child Care Center

Figure 1–84

Create the three text slides with multi-level bulleted lists, photographs, and clip art shown in Figures 1–85b through 1–85d on the next page. Adjust the clip sizes when necessary. Apply the Vortex transition in the Exciting category to all slides and decrease the duration to 3.00 seconds. Change the document properties, as specified by your instructor. Save the presentation using the file name, Lab 1–3 Part One Child Party.

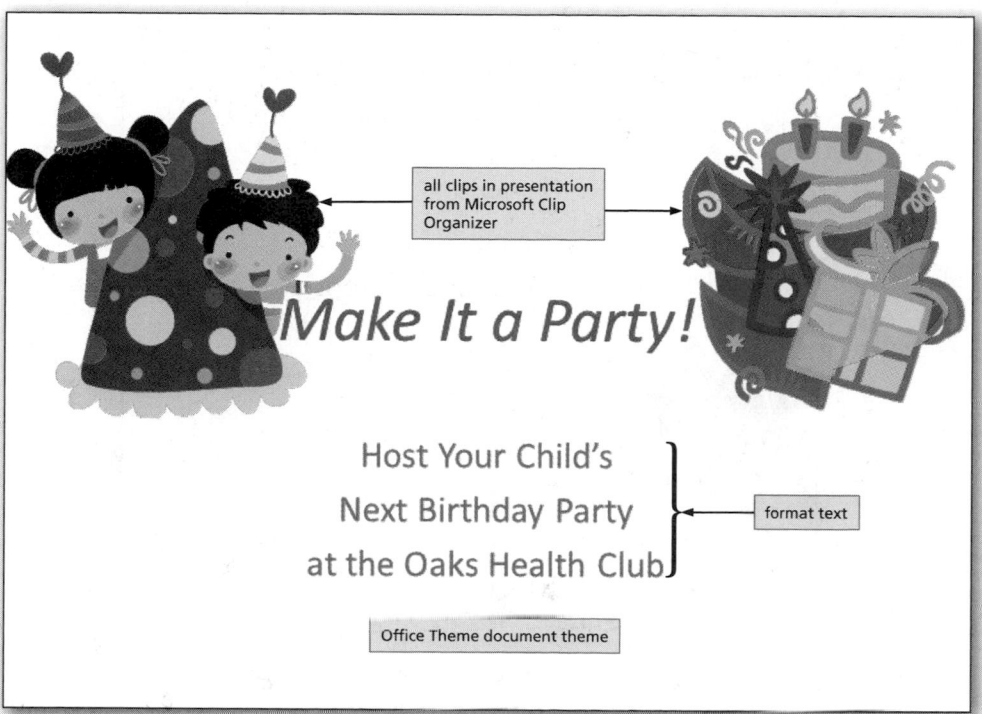

(a) Slide 1 (Title Slide)

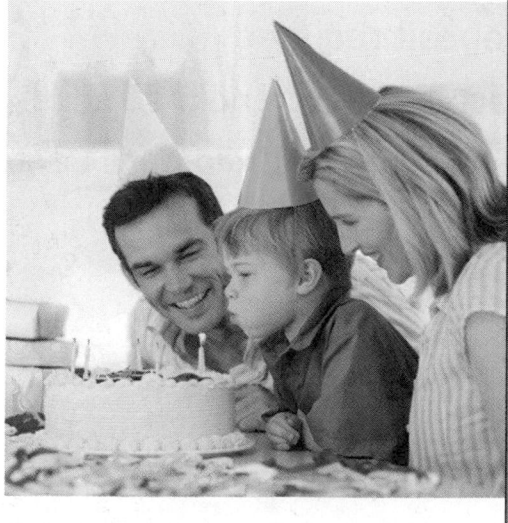

(b) Slide 2

Figure 1–85

Continued >

In the Lab *continued*

Two Party Packages

Package No. 1 - $8/child

- Lunch
  - Hot Dogs
  - Pizza

Package No. 2 - $12/child

- Lunch including beverage
  - Hot Dogs
  - Pizza
- Game
- Craft (age appropriate)

(c) Slide 3

Reserve Your Party Date

- Reserve 2 weeks in advance
- Deposit required
- Party room can hold 20 children
- Sign up in the Child Care Center

(d) Slide 4
Figure 1–85 (continued)

Instructions Part 2:   The children's parties have proved to be a great perk for members of the health club. A large group of older adults work out at the club and also meet socially once a month. These members have asked about renting the playroom to hold a retirement party for some of their friends. You decide to modify the children's party presentation to promote retirement parties. Use the outline in Figure 1–86 to modify the presentation created in Part 1 to create the presentation shown in Figure 1–87 on the next page. Required changes are indicated by a yellow highlight.

To begin, save the current presentation with the new file name, Lab 1–3 Part Two Retirement Party. Change the document theme to Flow. On Slide 3, change the pianist's name from Ms. Winn to your name. Apply the Fade transition in the Subtle category to all slides and change the duration speed to 2.25 seconds. View the slide show. Change the document properties, as specified by your instructor. Submit both Part One and Part Two documents in the format specified by your instructor.

Make It a Party!
Host Your
Retirement Party
at the Oaks Health Club

We Do the Work
You Enjoy the Moment
Two-hour party

Lunch & cake provided

Decorations
Music

Two Party Packages
Package No. 1 - $9/person
Lunch
Lasagna
Salad & bread
Package No. 2 - $20/person
Lunch including beverage
Lasagna
Salad & bread
Ms. Winn on piano
Photo booth

Reserve Your Party Date
Reserve 2 weeks in advance
Deposit required
Party room can hold 15 adults
Sign up at the main desk

Figure 1–86

Continued >

In the Lab *continued*

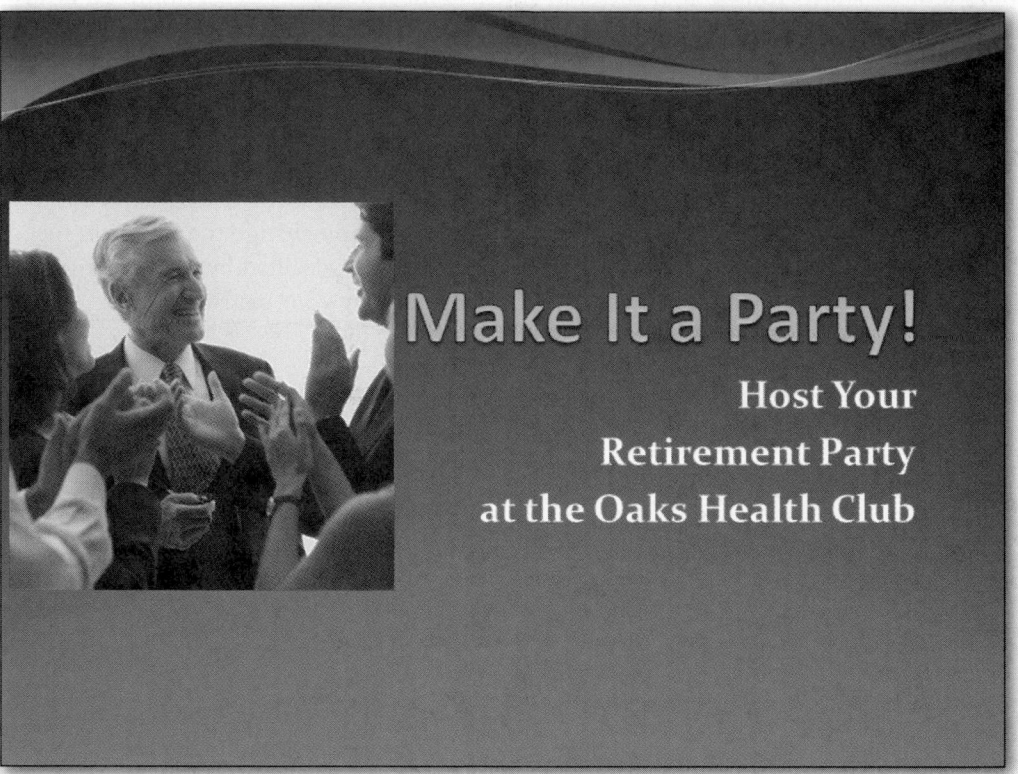

(a) Slide 1 (Title Slide)

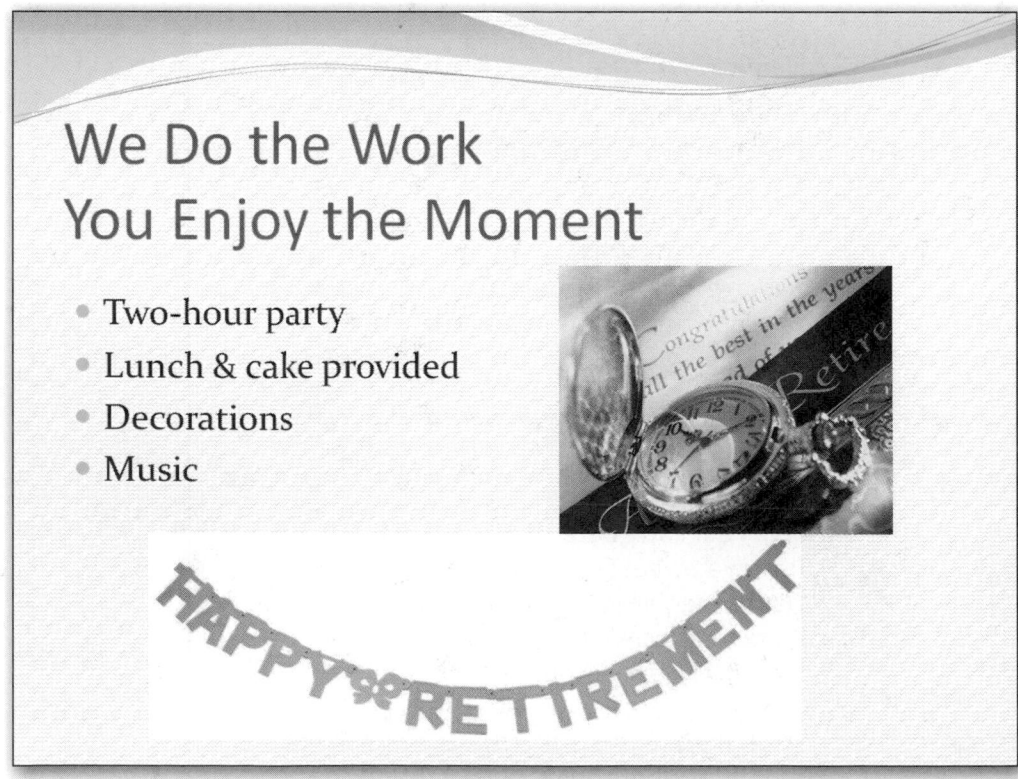

(b) Slide 2
Figure 1–87

(c) Slide 3

(d) Slide 4
Figure 1–87 (continued)

Cases and Places

Apply your creative thinking and problem-solving skills to design and implement a solution.

Note: To complete these assignments, you may be required to use the Data Files for Students. See the inside back cover of this book for instructions on downloading the Data Files for Students, or contact your instructor for information about accessing the required files.

As you design the presentations, remember to use the 7 × 7 rule: a maximum of seven words on a line and a maximum of seven lines on one slide.

1: Design and Create a Presentation about Galileo

Academic

Italian-born Galileo is said to be the father of modern science. After the invention of the telescope by a Dutch eyeglass maker named Hans Lippershey, Galileo made his own telescope and made many discoveries. You decide to prepare a PowerPoint presentation to accompany a speech that is required in your Astronomy class. You create the outline shown in Figure 1–88 about Galileo. Use this outline, along with the concepts and techniques presented in this chapter, to develop and format a slide show with a title slide and three text slides with bulleted lists. Add photographs and clip art from the Microsoft Clip Organizer and apply a transition. Submit your assignment in the format specified by your instructor.

Galileo Galilei
  Father of Modern Science
  Astronomy 201
  Sandy Wendt

Major Role in Scientific Revolution
February 15, 1564 - January 8, 1642
  Physicist
  Mathematician
  Astronomer
  Philosopher

Galileo's Research Years
  1581 - Studied medicine
  1589-1592 - Studied math and physics
  1592-1607 - Padua University
    Developed Law of Inertia
  1609 - Built telescope
    Earth's moon
    Jupiter's moons

Galileo's Later Years
  Dialogue - Two Chief World Systems
    Controversy develops
  1633 - Rome
    Heresy trial
    Imprisoned
  1642 - Dies

Figure 1–88

2: Design and Create a Presentation Promoting Hiking for Family Fitness

Personal

A great way for the entire family to get exercise is by participating in a hiking adventure. Employees at the local forest preserve district near your home have remodeled the nature center, and you have volunteered to give a presentation at the open house to help families plan their hikes. Use the outline shown in Figure 1–89 and then create an accompanying PowerPoint presentation. Use the concepts and techniques presented in this chapter to develop and format this slide show with a title slide, three text slides with bulleted lists, and clip art. Add photographs and clip art from the Microsoft Clip Organizer and apply a transition. Submit your assignment in the format specified by your instructor.

Take a Hike
 An Adventure with Kids
 Presented by Joshua Lind
 Pines Nature Center

Planning the Adventure
 Trail length — varies by child's age
  Ages 2 to 4: 1 to 2 miles
  Ages 5 to 7: 3 to 4 miles
  Ages 8 to 12: 5 to 7 miles
 Backpack — limit to 20 percent of child's weight

Packing Supplies
 Snacks and Drinks
  Child's favorite healthy foods
   Fruit and nuts
  Water
 Miscellaneous
  Sunscreen
  Insect repellent
  First-aid kit

Wearing the Right Clothes
 Dress in layers
  Children get cold quicker than adults
 Wear long pants and long-sleeved shirt
  Protect against insects and cuts
 Wear a hat and comfortable shoes
  Keep body warm

Figure 1–89

Continued >

Cases and Places *continued*

3: Design and Create a Landscaping Service Presentation

Professional

The home and garden center where you work is hosting weekend clinics for customers. The owner asks you to give a presentation about the center's new landscaping division and hands you the outline shown in Figure 1–90. Use the concepts and techniques presented in this chapter to develop and format a PowerPoint presentation with a title slide, three text slides with bulleted lists, and clip art. Add photographs and clip art from the Microsoft Clip Organizer and apply a transition. Submit your assignment in the format specified by your instructor.

Barry's Landscaping Service
Bensenville, Indiana

Full-Service Landscaping
Initial design
Installation
Maintenance

Scope of Services
Landscape design
Irrigation
Lighting
Lawn-care programs
Tree/shrub maintenance
Masonry, carpentry
Water features

Our Promise to You
Deliver on-time service
Provide highest level of workmanship
Give maximum value for your dollar
Install high-quality plants and materials
Respond quickly to your needs

Figure 1–90

2 Enhancing a Presentation with Pictures, Shapes, and WordArt

Objectives

You will have mastered the material in this chapter when you can:

- Change theme colors
- Insert a picture to create a background
- Format slide backgrounds
- Insert and size a shape
- Add text to a shape

- Apply effects to a shape
- Change the font and add a shadow
- Format pictures
- Apply a WordArt style
- Format WordArt
- Format text using the Format Painter

2 | Enhancing a Presentation with Pictures, Shapes, and WordArt

Introduction

In our visually oriented culture, audience members enjoy viewing effective graphics. Whether reading a document or viewing a PowerPoint presentation, people increasingly want to see photographs, artwork, graphics, and a variety of typefaces. Researchers have known for decades that documents with visual elements are more effective than those that consist of only text because the illustrations motivate audiences to study the material. People remember at least one-third more information when the document they are seeing or reading contains visual elements. These graphics help clarify and emphasize details so they appeal to audience members with differing backgrounds, reading levels, attention spans, and motivations.

Project — Presentation with Pictures, Shapes, and WordArt

BTW

Yoga's Origins
The term, yoga, is derived from the Sanskrit word yuj, meaning to join or unite. Yogis have been practicing this system of exercises and philosophy of mental control for more than 26,000 years.

The project in this chapter follows graphical guidelines and uses PowerPoint to create the presentation shown in Figure 2–1. This slide show, which discusses yoga and meditation, has a variety of illustrations and visual elements. For example, pictures have particular shapes and effects. The enhanced type has a style that blends well with the background and illustrations. Pictures and type are formatted using Quick Styles and WordArt, which give your presentation a professional look.

Overview

As you read through this chapter, you will learn how to create the presentation shown in Figure 2–1 by performing these general tasks:

- Format slide backgrounds.
- Insert and format pictures by applying styles and effects.
- Insert and format shapes.
- Format text using WordArt.
- Print a handout of your slides.

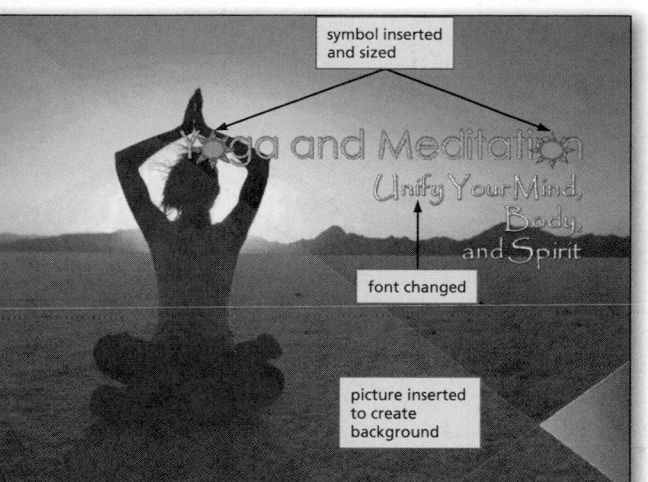

a) Slide 1 (Title Slide with Picture Background and Shapes)

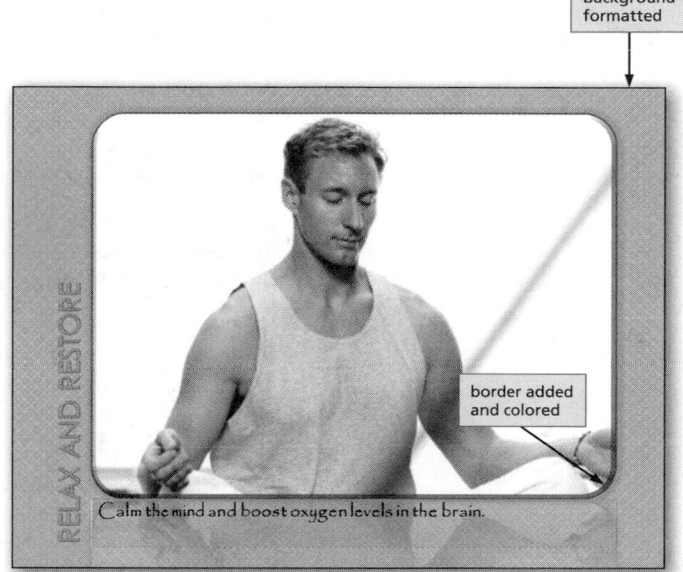

(b) Slide 2 (Formatted Picture)

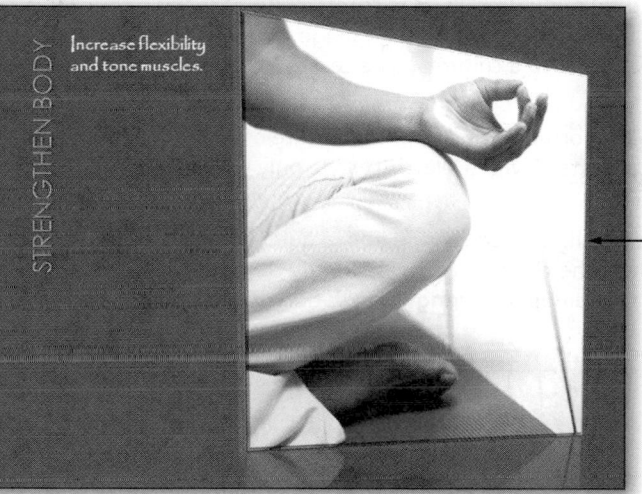

(c) Slide 3 (Formatted Picture)

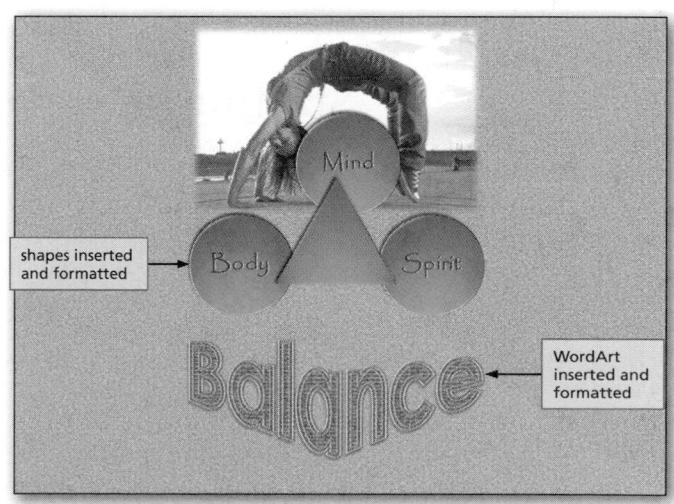

(d) Slide 4 (Inserted and Formatted Shapes)

Figure 2–1

Plan
Ahead

General Project Guidelines

When creating a PowerPoint presentation, the actions you perform and decisions you make will affect the appearance and characteristics of the finished document. As you create a presentation with illustrations, such as the project shown in Figure 2–1, you should follow these general guidelines:

1. **Focus on slide text content.** Give some careful thought to the words you choose. Some graphic designers advise starting with a blank screen so that the document theme does not distract from or influence the words.

2. **Apply style guidelines.** Many organizations and publishers establish guidelines for writing styles. These rules apply to capitalization, punctuation, word usage, and document formats. Ask your instructor or manager for a copy of these guidelines or use popular writing guides, such as the *The Chicago Manual of Style*, *The Associated Press Stylebook*, and *The Elements of Style*.

3. **Use color effectively.** Your audience's eyes are drawn to color on a slide. Used appropriately, color can create interest by emphasizing material and promoting understanding. Be aware of symbolic meanings attached to colors, such as red generally representing danger, electricity, and heat.

4. **Adhere to copyright regulations.** Copyright laws apply to printed and electronic materials. You can copy an existing photograph or artwork if it is in the public domain, if your company owns the graphic, or if you have obtained permission to use it. Be certain you have the legal right to use a desired graphic in your presentation.

5. **Consider graphics for multicultural audiences.** In today's intercultural society, your presentation might be viewed by people whose first language is different from yours. Some graphics have meanings specific to a culture, so be certain to learn about your intended audience and their views.

6. **Use WordArt in moderation.** Used correctly, the graphical nature of WordArt can add interest and set a tone. Format text with a WordArt style only when needed for special emphasis.

When necessary, more specific details concerning the above guidelines are presented at appropriate points in the chapter. The chapter also will identify the actions you perform and decisions made regarding these guidelines during the creation of the presentation shown in Figure 2–1.

Starting PowerPoint

For an introduction to Windows 7 and instruction about how to perform basic Windows 7 tasks, read the Office 2010 and Windows 7 chapter at the beginning of this book, where you can learn how to resize windows, change screen resolution, create folders, move and rename files, use Windows Help, and much more.

Chapter 1 introduced you to starting PowerPoint, selecting a document theme, creating slides with clip art and a bulleted list, and printing a presentation. The following steps, which assume Windows 7 is running, start PowerPoint. You may need to ask your instructor how to start PowerPoint for your computer. For a detailed example of the procedure summarized on the next page, refer to pages OFF 33 through OFF 35 in the Office 2010 and Windows 7 chapter.

To Start PowerPoint and Apply a Document Theme

1 Click the Start button on the Windows 7 taskbar to display the Start menu.

2 Type `Microsoft PowerPoint` as the search text in the 'Search programs and files' text box.

3 Click Microsoft PowerPoint 2010 in the search results on the Start menu to start PowerPoint and display a new blank document.

4 If the PowerPoint window is not maximized, click the Maximize button.

5 Apply the Verve document theme.

Focus on slide text content.
Once you have researched your presentation topic, many methods exist to begin developing slide content.

- Select a document theme and then enter text, illustration, and tables.
- Open an existing presentation and modify the slides and theme.
- Import an outline created in Microsoft Word.
- Start with a blank presentation that uses the default Office Theme. Consider this practice similar to an artist who begins creating a painting with a blank, white canvas.

    Experiment using different methods of developing the initial content for slides. Experienced PowerPoint users sometimes find one technique works better than another to stimulate creativity or help them organize their ideas in a particular circumstance.

Plan Ahead

For an introduction to Office 2010 and instruction about how to perform basic tasks in Office 2010 programs, read the Office 2010 and Windows 7 chapter at the beginning of this book, where you can learn how to start a program, use the Ribbon, save a file, open a file, quit a program, use Help, and much more.

Creating Slides and Changing Font Colors and Background Style

In Chapter 1, you selected a document theme and then typed the content for the title and text slides. In this chapter, you will type the slide content for the title and text slides, select a background, insert and format pictures and shapes, and then insert and format WordArt. To begin creating the four slides in this presentation, you will enter text in four different layouts, change the theme colors, and then change the background style.

Apply style guidelines.
A good stylebook is useful to decide when to use numerals or words to represent numbers, as in the sentence, More than 25 students are waiting for the bus to arrive. Stylebooks also offer rules on forming possessives, capitalizing titles, and using commas. Once you decide on a style to use in your presentation, apply it consistently throughout your presentation.

Plan Ahead

To Create a Title Slide

Recall from Chapter 1 that the title slide introduces the presentation to the audience. In addition to introducing the presentation, this project uses the title slide to capture the audience's attention by using title text and a background picture. The following steps create the slide show's title slide.

1 Type `Yoga and Meditation` in the title text placeholder.

2 Type `Unify Your Mind,` in the subtitle text placeholder.

3 Press the ENTER key and then type `Body,` as the second line in the subtitle text placeholder.

4 Press the ENTER key and then type `and Spirit` as the third line in the subtitle text placeholder. Change the capital letter 'A' in the word, And, at the beginning of this line to a lowercase 'a' (Figure 2–2).

Q&A Some stylebooks recommend using lowercase letters when using coordinating conjunctions (for, and, nor, but, or, yet, so) and also when using articles (a, an, the). Why is the case of the word, and, changed in the subtitle text?

By default, PowerPoint capitalizes the first word of each paragraph. For consistency, you can decide to lowercase this word to apply a particular style rule so that the word, and, is lowercase in both the title and subtitle text.

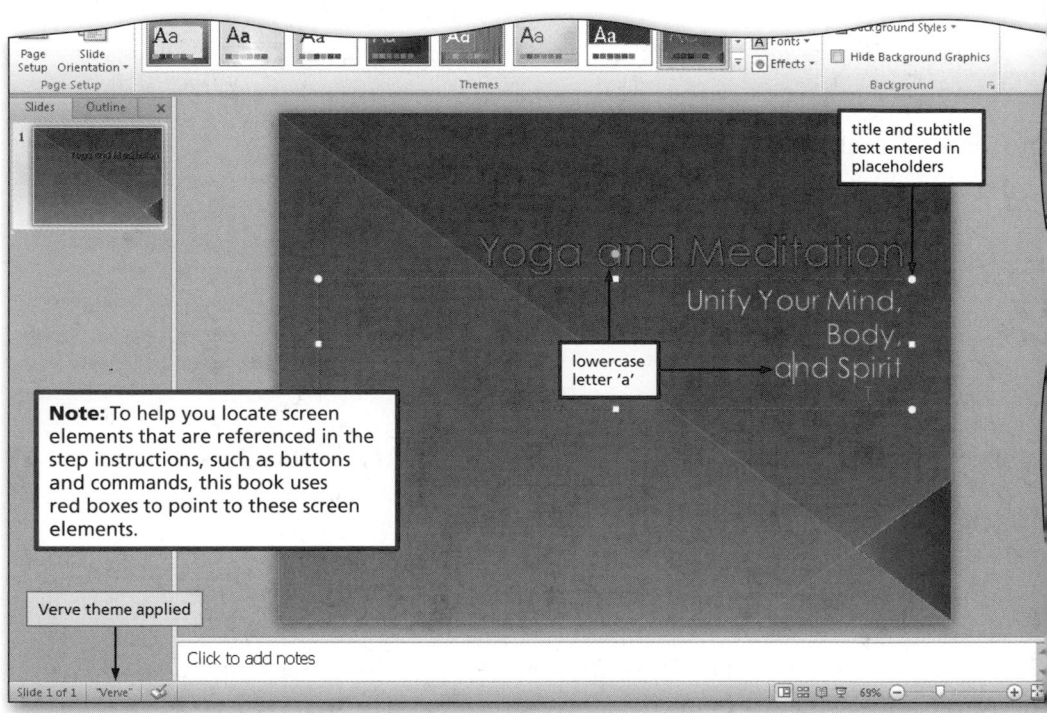

Note: To help you locate screen elements that are referenced in the step instructions, such as buttons and commands, this book uses red boxes to point to these screen elements.

Figure 2–2

BTW

Q&As
For a complete list of the Q&As found in many of the step-by-step sequences in this book, visit the PowerPoint 2010 Q&A Web page (scsite.com/ppt2010/qa).

To Create the First Text Slide

The first text slide you create in Chapter 2 emphasizes the relaxation and restoration benefits derived from practicing yoga and meditation. The following steps add a new slide (Slide 2) and then create a text slide using the Picture with Caption layout.

1 Click Home on the Ribbon to display the Home tab, click the New Slide button arrow, and then click Picture with Caption in the Layout gallery to add a new slide with this layout.

2 Type `Relax and Restore` in the title text placeholder.

3 Press CTRL+ENTER to move to the caption placeholder and then type `Calm the mind and boost oxygen levels in the brain.` in this placeholder (Figure 2–3).

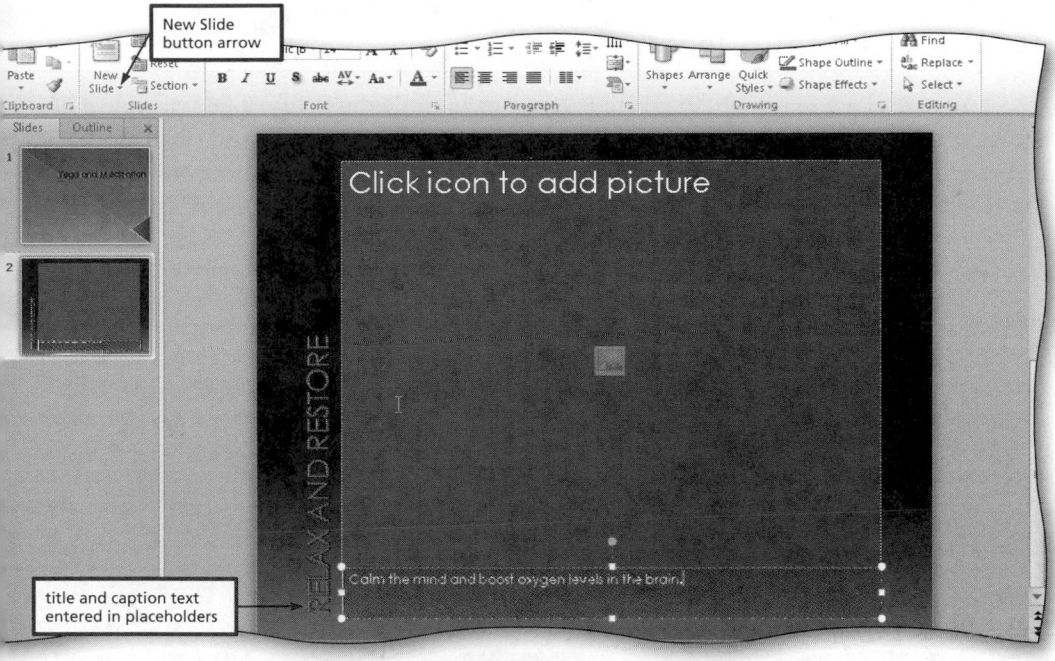

Figure 2–3

To Create the Second Text Slide

The second text slide you create stresses the fact that yoga and meditation strengthen the body in multiple ways. The following steps add a new text slide (Slide 3) that uses the Content with Caption layout.

1 Click the New Slide button arrow and then click Content with Caption in the Layout gallery to add a new slide with this layout.

2 Type **Strengthen Body** in the title text placeholder.

3 Press CTRL+ENTER and then type **Increase flexibility and tone muscles.** in the caption placeholder (Figure 2– 4).

Why does the text display with capital letters despite the fact I am typing uppercase and lowercase letters?

The Verve theme uses the All Caps effect for the title text. This effect converts lowercase letters to uppercase.

BTW

BTWs
For a complete list of the BTWs found in the margins of this book, visit the PowerPoint 2010 BTW Web page (scsite.com/ppt2010/btw).

Figure 2–4

To Create the Third Text Slide

Yoga and meditation help create balance in an individual's life. The last slide you create uses graphics to depict the connection among the mind, body, and spirit. You will insert symbols later in this project to create this visual element. For now, you want to create the basic slide. The following step adds a new text slide (Slide 4) that uses the Blank layout.

1 Click the New Slide button arrow and then click Blank in the Layout gallery. (Figure 2–5).

Figure 2–5

BTW

The Ribbon and Screen Resolution
PowerPoint may change how the groups and buttons within the groups appear on the Ribbon, depending on the computer's screen resolution. Thus, your Ribbon may look different from the ones in this book if you are using a screen resolution other than 1024 × 768.

Presentation Template Color Scheme

Each presentation template has 12 complementary colors, which collectively are called the **color scheme**. You can apply these colors to all slides, an individual slide, notes pages, or audience handouts. A color scheme consists of four colors for a background and text, six accent colors, and two hyperlink colors. The Theme Colors button on the Design tab contains a square with four colors; the top two colors indicate the primary text and background colors, and the bottom two colors indicate the accent colors. You also can customize the theme colors to create your own set and give them a unique name. Table 2–1 explains the components of a color scheme.

Table 2–1 Color Scheme Components

Component	Description
Background color	The background color is the fundamental color of a PowerPoint slide. For example, if the background color is black, you can place any other color on top of it, but the fundamental color remains black. The black background shows everywhere you do not add color or other objects.
Text color	The text color contrasts with the background color of the slide. As a default, the text border color is the same as the text color. Together with the background color, the text and border colors set the tone for a presentation. For example, a gray background with black text and border sets a dramatic tone. In contrast, a red background with yellow text and border sets a vibrant tone.
Accent colors	Accent colors are designed as colors for secondary features on a slide. They often are used as fill colors on graphs and as shadows.
Hyperlink colors	The default hyperlink color is set when you type the text. When you click the hyperlink text during a presentation, the color changes to the Followed Hyperlink color.

To Change the Presentation Theme Colors

The first modification to make is to change the color scheme throughout the presentation. The following steps change the color scheme for the template from a gray title slide background with pink text and accents to a blue background with pink and orange accents.

- Click Design on the Ribbon and then click the Theme Colors button (Design tab | Themes group) to display the Theme Colors gallery.

- Scroll down and then point to the Oriel built-in theme to display a live preview of this color scheme (Figure 2–6).

Experiment

- Point to various themes in the Theme Colors gallery and watch the colors change on Slide 4.

Why does a gold line surround the Verve color scheme in the Theme Colors gallery?

It shows the Verve document theme is applied, and those eight colors are associated with that theme.

Figure 2–6

- Click Oriel in the Theme Colors gallery to change the presentation theme colors to Oriel (Figure 2–7).

What if I want to return to the original theme color?

You would click the Theme Colors button and then click Verve in the Theme Colors gallery.

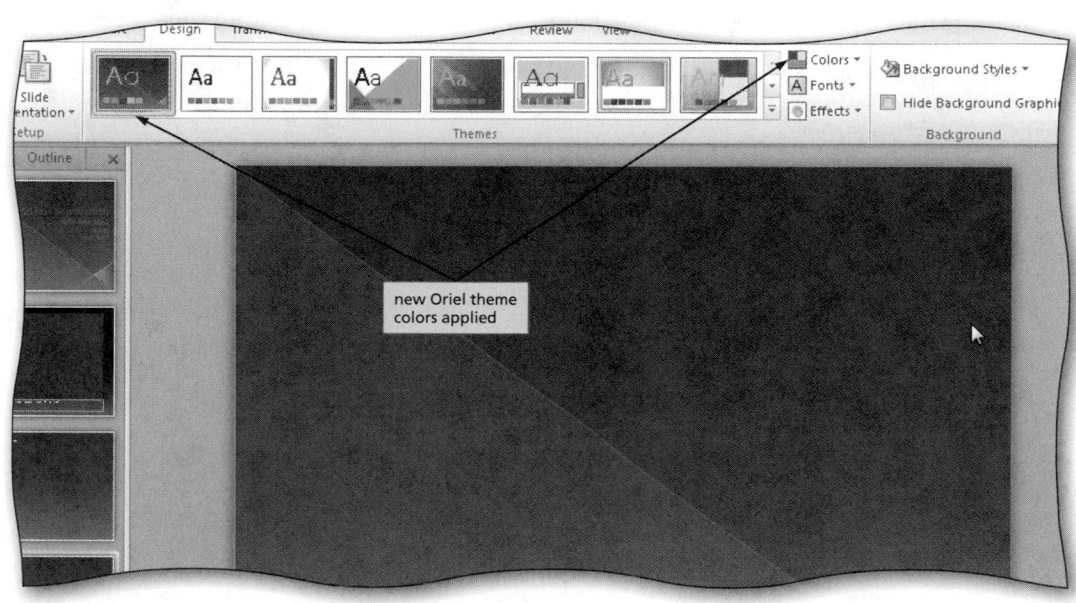

Figure 2–7

BTW

Showing the Quick Access Toolbar below the Ribbon
By default, the Quick Access Toolbar is displayed in the upper-left corner of the PowerPoint window next to the PowerPoint icon. You can move this toolbar below the Ribbon in two ways: clicking the Customize Quick Access Toolbar button and then clicking Show Below the Ribbon in the list; or clicking the Show Quick Access Toolbar below the Ribbon check box in the Customize the Quick Access Toolbar pane (File tab | Options | Quick Access Toolbar | PowerPoint Options dialog box) to place a check mark in it. If you want to relocate the toolbar back to its original location, either click the Customize Quick Access toolbar button and then click Show Above the Ribbon or click the Show Quick Access Toolbar below the Ribbon check box to remove the check mark.

BTW

Inserting Watermarks
Checks, currency, business cards, and legal documents use watermarks to verify their authenticity. These semi-transparent images are visible when you hold this paper up to a light. You, likewise, can insert a clip art image or a picture as a watermark behind all or part of your slide to identify your unique PowerPoint presentation.

To Save a Presentation

You have performed many tasks while creating this slide and do not want to risk losing work completed thus far. Accordingly, you should save the document.

The following steps assume you already have created folders for storing your files, for example, a CIS 101 folder (for your class) that contains a PowerPoint folder (for your assignments). Thus, these steps save the document in the PowerPoint folder in the CIS 101 folder on a USB flash drive using the file name, Yoga. For a detailed example of the procedure summarized below, refer to pages OFF 27 through OFF 29 in the Office 2010 and Windows 7 chapter at the beginning of this book.

1 With a USB flash drive connected to one of the computer's USB ports, click the Save button on the Quick Access Toolbar to display the Save As dialog box.

2 Type `Yoga` in the File name text box to change the file name. Do not press the ENTER key after typing the file name because you do not want to close the dialog box at this time.

3 Navigate to the desired save location (in this case, the PowerPoint folder in the CIS 101 folder [or your class folder] on the USB flash drive).

4 Click the Save button (Save As dialog box) to save the document in the selected folder on the selected drive with the entered file name.

Inserting and Formatting Pictures in a Presentation

With the text entered and background formatted in the presentation, the next step is to insert digital pictures into the placeholders on Slides 2 and 3 and then format the pictures. These graphical images draw the viewers' eyes to the slides and help them retain the information presented.

In the following pages, you will perform these tasks:

1. Insert the first digital picture into Slide 3.
2. Insert the second digital picture into Slide 2.
3. Change the look of the first picture.
4. Change the look of the second picture.
5. Resize the second picture.
6. Insert a digital picture into the Slide 1 background.
7. Format slide backgrounds.

Adhere to copyright regulations.
You have permission to use the clips from the Microsoft Clip Organizer. If you want to use a clip from another source, be certain you have the legal right to insert this file in your presentation. Read the copyright notices that accompany the clip and are posted on the Web site. The owners of these images and files often ask you to give them credit for using their work, which may be satisfied by stating where you obtained the images.

Plan
Ahead

To Insert a Picture

The next step in creating the presentation is to insert one of the digital yoga pictures in the picture placeholder on Slide 3. The picture is available on the Data Files for Students. See the inside back cover of this book for instructions on downloading the Data Files for Students, or contact your instructor for information about accessing the required files.

The following steps insert a picture, which, in this example, is located in the PowerPoint Chapter 02 folder on the same USB flash drive that contains the saved presentation, into Slide 3.

• With your USB flash drive connected to one of the computer's USB ports, click the Previous Slide button to display Slide 3.

• Click the Insert Picture from File button in the content placeholder to display the Insert Picture dialog box.

• If Computer is not displayed in the navigation pane, drag the navigation pane scroll bar (Insert Picture dialog box) until Computer appears.

Figure 2–8

• Click Computer in the navigation pane to display a list of available storage devices in the Insert Picture dialog box. If necessary, scroll through the dialog box until your USB flash drive appears in the list of available storage devices.

• Double-click your USB flash drive in the list of available storage devices to display a list of files and folders on the selected USB flash drive. Double-click the Data Files for Students folder, double-click the PowerPoint folder, and then double-click the Chapter 02 folder to display a list of files in that folder.

• Scroll down and then click Hands Yoga to select the file name (Figure 2–8).

What if the picture is not on a USB flash drive?
Use the same process, but select the drive containing the picture.

3

- Click the Insert button (Insert Picture dialog box) to insert the picture into the content placeholder in Slide 3 (Figure 2–9).

Q&A

What are the symbols around the picture?

A selected graphic appears surrounded by a **selection rectangle**, which has small squares and circles, called **sizing handles**, at each corner and middle location.

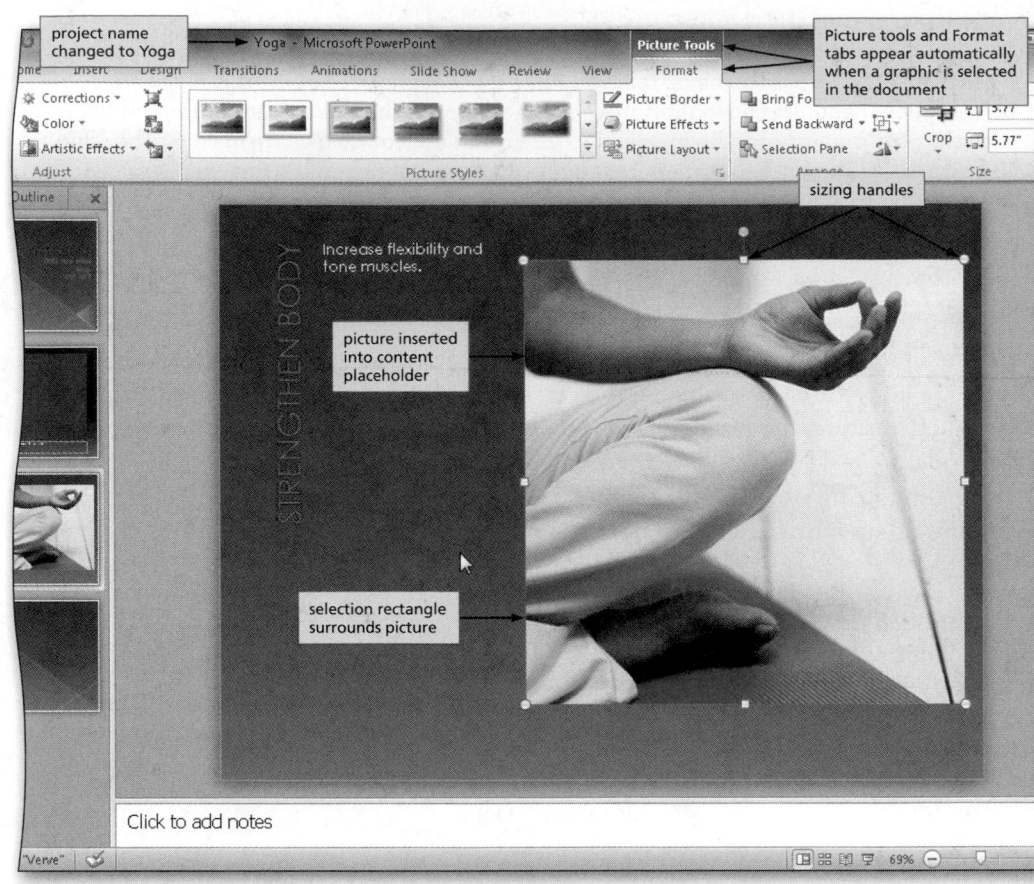

Figure 2 – 9

To Insert Another Picture into a Content Placeholder

BTW

Modernism's Effect on Graphic Design
The modernist movement of the late nineteenth and twentieth centuries influenced the design principles in use today. Artists and architects of that era simplified the world in terms of legible fonts, abstract shapes, and balanced layouts. Modernists sought to create works independent of language so their message could reach people throughout the world.

The next step is to insert another digital yoga picture into the Slide 2 content placeholder. This second picture also is available on the Data Files for Students. See the inside back cover of this book for instructions on downloading the Data Files for Students, or contact your instructor for information about accessing the required files.

The following steps insert a picture into Slide 2.

1 Click the Previous Slide button to display Slide 2.

2 With your USB flash drive connected to one of the computer's USB ports, click the Insert Picture from File icon in the content placeholder to display the Insert Picture dialog box.

3 If the list of files and folders on the selected USB flash drive are not displayed in the Insert Picture dialog box, double-click your USB flash drive to display them and then navigate to the PowerPoint Chapter 02 folder.

4 Scroll down and then click Green Tank Meditation to select the file name.

5 Click the Insert button (Insert Picture dialog box) to insert the picture into the Slide 2 content placeholder (Figure 2–10).

Figure 2–10

To Insert a Picture into a Slide without a Content Placeholder

In Chapter 1, you inserted a clip into a slide without a content placeholder. You also can insert a picture into a slide that does not have a content placeholder. The picture for Slide 4 is available on the Data Files for Students. See the inside back cover of this book for instructions on downloading the Data Files for Students, or contact your instructor for information about accessing the required files. The following steps insert a picture into Slide 4.

- Click the Next Slide button two times to display Slide 4.

- With your USB flash drive connected to one of the computer's USB ports, click Insert on the Ribbon (Figure 2–11).

Figure 2–11

- Click Insert Picture from File (Insert tab | Images group) to display the Insert Picture dialog box. If the list of files and folders on the selected USB flash drive are not displayed in the Insert Picture dialog box, double-click your USB flash drive to display them and then navigate to the PowerPoint Chapter 02 folder.

- Click Arch Yoga to select the file name (Figure 2–12).

Figure 2–12

- Click the Insert button (Insert Picture dialog box) to insert the picture into the Slide 4 content placeholder.

- Move the picture so that it displays approximately as shown in Figure 2–13.

Figure 2–13

Q&A

What is the green circle attached to the selected graphic?

The green circle is a rotate handle. When you drag a graphic's rotate handle, the graphic moves in either a clockwise or counter clockwise direction.

To Correct a Picture

A photograph's color intensity can be modified by changing the brightness and contrast. **Brightness** determines the overall lightness or darkness of the entire image, whereas **contrast** is the difference between the darkest and lightest areas of the image. The brightness and contrast are changed in predefined percentage increments. The following step increases the brightness and decreases the contrast to intensify the picture colors.

- With the Arch Yoga picture on Slide 4 still selected, click the Corrections button (Picture Tools Format tab | Adjust group) to display the Corrections gallery.

- Point to Brightness: +20% Contrast: −40% (fourth picture in first row of Brightness and Contrast area) to display a live preview of these corrections on the picture (Figure 2–14).

 Experiment

- Point to various pictures in the Brightness and Contrast area and watch the brightness and contrast change on the picture in Slide 4.

Figure 2–14

Why is a yellow border surrounding the picture in the center of the gallery?

The image on Slide 4 currently has normal brightness and contrast (0%), which is represented by this center image in the gallery.

- Click Brightness: +20% Contrast: −40% to apply this correction to the yoga picture.

How can I remove all effects from the picture?

Click the Reset Picture button (Picture Tools Format tab | Adjust group).

Other Ways
1. Click Picture Corrections Options, move Brightness or Contrast sliders or enter   number in box next to slider (Format Picture dialog box)

To Apply a Picture Style

The pictures on Slides 2, 3, and 4 grasp the audience's attention, but you can increase their visual appeal by applying a style. A **style** is a named group of formatting characteristics. PowerPoint provides more than 25 picture styles that enable you easily to change a picture's look to a more visually appealing style, including a variety of shapes, angles, borders, and reflections. The photos in Slides 2, 3, and 4 in this chapter use styles that apply soft edges, reflections, or angled perspectives to the pictures. The following steps apply a picture style to the Slide 4 picture.

• With the Slide 4 picture selected, click the Picture Tools Format tab and then click the More button in the Picture Styles gallery (Picture Tools Format tab | Picture Styles group) (shown in Figure 2–14 on the previous page) to expand the gallery.

• Point to Soft Edge Rectangle in the Picture Styles gallery to display a live preview of that style applied to the picture in the document (Figure 2–15).

Experiment

• Point to various picture styles in the Picture Styles gallery and watch the style of the picture change in the document window.

Figure 2–15

• Click Soft Edge Rectangle in the Picture Styles gallery to apply the style to the selected picture (Figure 2–16).

Figure 2–16

To Apply Other Picture Styles

The next step is to apply picture styles to the yoga pictures in Slides 3 and 2. To provide continuity, both of these styles will have a reflection. The following steps apply other picture styles to the Slide 3 and Slide 2 pictures.

1 Click the Previous Slide button to display Slide 3.

2 Click the Slide 3 picture to select it, click the Picture Tools Format tab, and then click the More button in the Picture Styles gallery to expand the gallery.

3 Click Reflected Perspective Right in the Picture Styles gallery to apply this style to the picture in Slide 3.

4 Click the Previous Slide button to display Slide 2.

5 Click the Slide 2 picture to select it, click the Picture Tools Format tab, and then click the More button in the Picture Styles gallery to expand the gallery.

6 Click Reflected Rounded Rectangle in the Picture Styles gallery to apply this style to the picture in Slide 2 (Figure 2–17).

Figure 2–17

To Apply Picture Effects

PowerPoint provides a variety of picture effects so that you can further customize a picture. Effects include shadows, reflections, glow, soft edges, bevel, and 3-D rotation. The difference between the effects and the styles is that each effect has several options, providing you with more control over the exact look of the image.

In this presentation, the photos on Slides 2 and 3 have an orange glow effect and have a bevel applied to their edges. The following steps apply picture effects to the selected picture.

- With the Slide 2 picture selected, click the Picture Effects button (Picture Tools Format tab | Picture Styles group) to display the Picture Effects menu.

  What if the Picture Tools Format tab no longer is displayed on my Ribbon?

  Double-click the picture to display the Picture Tools and Format tabs.

- Point to Glow on the Picture Effects menu to display the Glow gallery.

Figure 2–18

- Point to Orange, 11 pt glow, Accent color 1 in the Glow Variations area (leftmost glow in third row) to display a live preview of the selected glow effect applied to the picture in the document window (Figure 2–18).

 Experiment

- Point to various glow effects in the Glow gallery and watch the picture change in the document window.

- Click Orange, 11 pt glow, Accent color 1 in the Glow gallery to apply the selected picture effect.

3

- Click the Picture Effects button (Picture Tools Format tab | Picture Styles group) to display the Picture Effects menu again.

- Point to Bevel on the Picture Effects menu to display the Bevel gallery.

- Point to Angle (leftmost bevel in second row) to display a live preview of the selected bevel effect applied to the Slide 2 picture (Figure 2–19).

Experiment

- Point to various bevel effects in the Bevel gallery and watch the picture change in the slide.

Figure 2–19

4

- Click Angle in the Bevel gallery to apply the selected picture effect.

Other Ways

1. Right-click picture, click Format Picture on shortcut menu, select desired options (Format Picture dialog box), click Close button

2. Click Format Shape dialog box launcher (Picture

   Tools Format tab | Picture Styles group), select desired options (Format Picture dialog box), click Close button

To Apply a Picture Style and Effect to Another Picture

In this presentation, the Slide 3 picture also has orange glow and bevel effects. The following steps apply the picture style and picture effects to the picture.

1 Click the Next Slide button to display Slide 3 and then click the picture to select it.

2 Click the Picture Effects button (Picture Tools Format tab | Picture Styles group) to display the Picture Effects menu and then point to Glow on the Picture Effects menu to display the Glow gallery.

3 Click Orange, 11 pt glow, Accent color 1 (leftmost glow in third row) in the Glow gallery to apply the picture effect to the picture.

4 Click the Picture Effects button (Picture Tools Format tab | Picture Styles group) to display the Picture Effects menu again and then point to Bevel on the Picture Effects menu to display the Bevel gallery.

5 Click Convex (third bevel in second row) in the Bevel area to apply the picture effect to the selected picture (Figure 2–20).

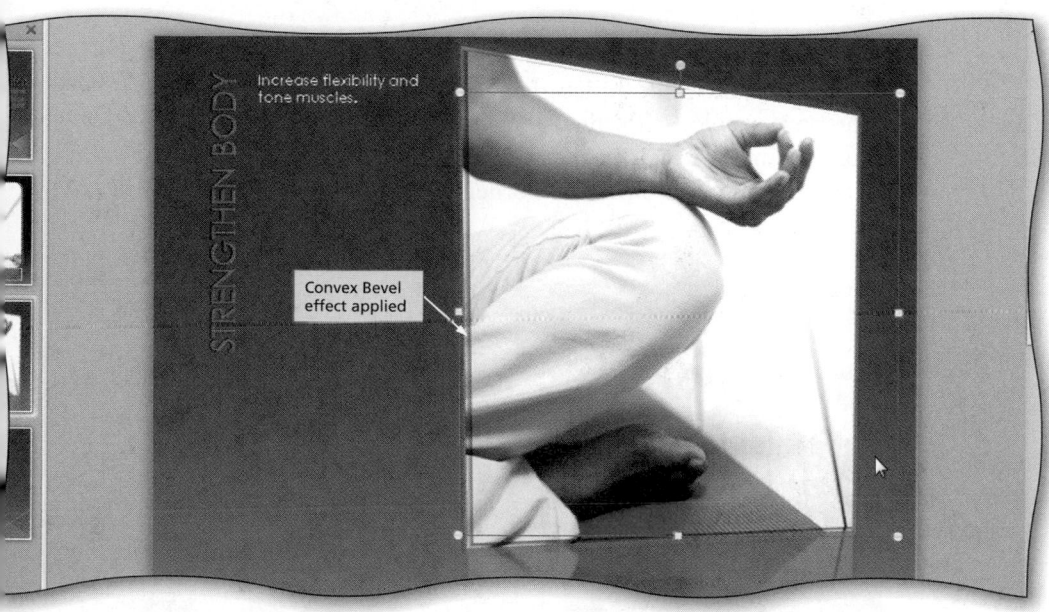

Figure 2–20

o Add a Picture Border

The next step is to add a small border to the Slide 3 picture. Some picture styles provide a border, but the Reflected ounded Rectangle style you applied to this picture does not. The following steps add a border to the Slide 3 picture.

With the Slide 3 picture still selected, click the Picture Border button (Picture Tools Format tab | Picture Styles group) to display the Picture Border gallery.

What if the Picture Tools Format tab no longer is displayed on my Ribbon?

Double-click the picture to display the Picture Tools and Format tabs.

Point to Weight on the Picture Border gallery to display the Weight list.

Point to 1½ pt to display a live preview of this line weight on the picture (Figure 2–21).

⊘ Experiment

Point to various line weights in the Weight list and watch the line thickness change.

Can I make the line width more than 6 pt?

Yes. Click More Lines and then increase the amount in the Width box.

Figure 2–21

Click 1½ pt to add this line weight to the picture.

To Change a Picture Border Color

The default color for the border you added to the Slide 3 picture is White. Earlier in this chapter, you changed the color scheme to Oriel. To coordinate the border color with the title text color and other elements of this theme, you will use a shade of red in the Oriel color scheme. Any color galleries you display show colors defined in this current color scheme. The following steps change the Slide 3 picture border color.

1
- With the Slide 3 photo still selected, click the Picture Border button (Picture Tools Format tab | Picture Styles group) to display the Picture Border gallery.

Q&A
What if the Picture Tools Format tab no longer is displayed on my Ribbon?

Double-click the picture to display the Picture Tools and Format tabs.

2
- Point to Red, Accent 3 (seventh theme color from left in first row) in the Picture Border gallery to display a live preview of that border color on the picture (Figure 2–22).

 Experiment
- Point to various colors in the Picture Border gallery and watch the border on the picture change in the slide.

Figure 2–22

3
- Click Red, Accent 3 in the Picture Border gallery to change the picture border color.

To Add a Picture Border and Color to Another Picture

In this presentation, the Slide 2 picture does not have a border as part of the Reflected Perspective Right picture style. The following steps add a border to Slide 2 and change the color.

1 Click the Previous Slide button to display Slide 2 and then click the picture to select it.

2 Click the Picture Border button (Picture Tools Format tab | Picture Styles group) to display the Picture Border gallery.

3 Point to Weight on the Picture Border gallery to display the Weight list and then point to 1½ pt to display a live preview of this line weight on the picture.

4 Click 1½ pt to add this line weight to the picture.

5 Click the Picture Border button (Picture Tools Format tab | Picture Styles group) to display the Picture Border gallery again and then click Red, Accent 3 in the Picture Border gallery to change the picture border color (Figure 2–23).

Figure 2–23

o Resize a Graphic by Entering Exact Measurements

The next step is to resize the Slide 3 picture so that it fills much of the empty space in the slide. In Chapter 1, ou resized clips by dragging the sizing handles. This technique also applies to changing the size of photos. You also an resize graphics by specifying exact height and width measurements. The yoga picture can be enlarged so that its eight and width measurements are 6.0". When a graphic is selected, its height and width measurements show in he Size group of the Picture Tools Format tab. The following steps resize the Slide 3 picture by entering its desired xact measurements.

Click the Next Slide button to display Slide 3 and then select the picture. Click the Shape Height text box (Picture Tools Format tab | Size group) to select the contents in the text box and then type   6 as the height (Figure 2–24).

Figure 2–24

What if the contents of the Shape Height text box are not selected?

Triple-click the Shape Height text box.

Why did the width size also change?

PowerPoint kept the photo in proportion so that the width changed the same amount as the height changed.

• Click the Shape Width text box (Picture Tools Format tab | Size group) to select the contents in the text box and then type   6   as the width if this number does not display automatically.

• If necessary, move the photo to the location shown in Figure 2–25.

Q&A What if I want to return a graphic to its original size and start again?

With the graphic selected, click the Size and Position dialog box launcher (Picture Tools Format tab | Size group), if necessary click the Size tab (Format Picture dialog box), click the Reset button, and then click the Close button.

Other Ways

1. Right-click picture, enter shape height and width values in text boxes on shortcut menu
2. Right-click picture, click Format Picture

   on shortcut menu, click Size (Format Picture dialog box), enter shape height and width values in text boxes, click Close button

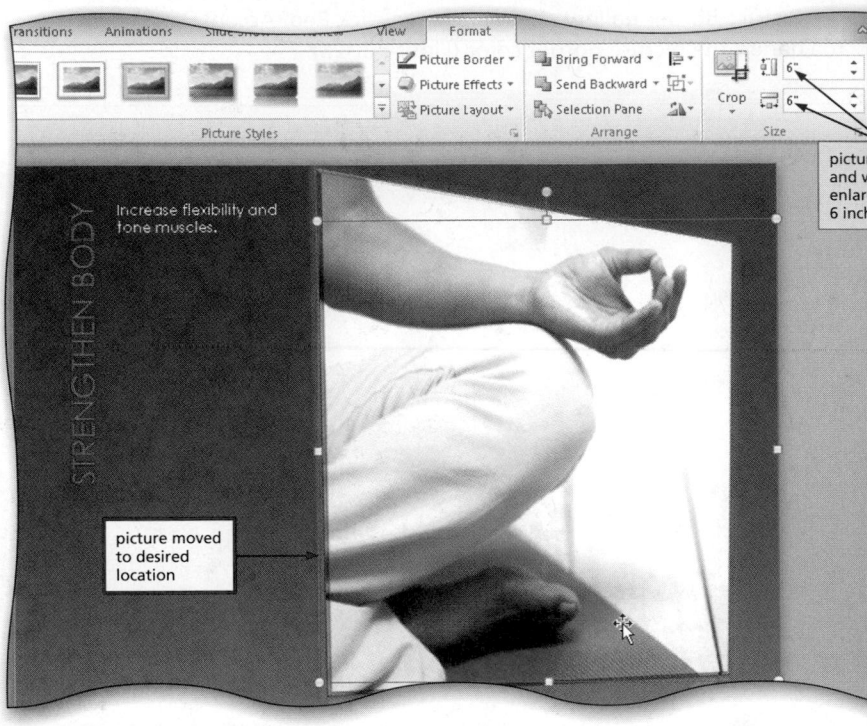

Figure 2–25

To Resize Another Graphic Using Exact Measurements

The Arch Yoga picture on Slide 4 also can be enlarged to fill space at the top of the slide. The yoga picture can be enlarged so that its height and width measurements are 3" and 4.48", respectively. The following steps resize the Slide 4 picture.

1 Click the Next Slide button to display Slide 4 and then select the picture. Click the Shape Height text box (Picture Tools Format tab | Size group) to select the contents in the text box and type   3   as the height.

2 Move the photo to the location shown in Figure 2–26.

Figure 2–26

To Save an Existing Document with the Same File Name

You have made several modifications to the document since you last saved it. Thus, you should save it again. The following step saves the document again. For an example of the step listed below, refer to page OFF 51 in the Office 2010 and Windows 7 chapter at the beginning of this book.

Click the Save button on the Quick Access Toolbar to overwrite the previously saved file.

Break Point: If you wish to take a break, this is a good place to do so. You can quit PowerPoint now. To resume at a later time, start PowerPoint, open the file called Yoga, and continue following the steps from this location forward.

Formatting Slide Backgrounds

A slide's background is an integral part of a presentation because it can generate audience interest. Every slide can have the same background, or different backgrounds can be used in a presentation. This background is considered **fill**, which is the content that makes up the interior of a shape, line, or character. Three fills are available: solid, gradient, and picture or texture. **Solid fill** is one color used throughout the entire slide. **Gradient fill** is one color shade gradually progressing to another shade of the same color or one color progressing to another color. **Picture or texture fill** uses a specific file or an image that simulates a material, such as cork, granite, marble, or canvas.

Once you add a fill, you can adjust its appearance. For example, you can adjust its **transparency**, which allows you to see through the background, so that any text on the slide is visible. You also can select a color that is part of the theme or a custom color. You can use **offsets**, another background feature, to move the background from the slide borders in varying distances by percentage. **Tiling options** repeat the background image many times vertically and horizontally on the slide; the smaller the tiling percentage, the greater the number of times the image is repeated.

BTW

Resetting Backgrounds
If you have made many changes to the background and want to start the process over, click the Reset Background button in the Format Background dialog box.

To Insert a Texture Fill

A wide variety of texture fills are available to give your presentation a unique look. The 24 pictures in the Textures gallery give the appearance of a physical object, such as water drops, sand, tissue paper, and a paper bag. You also can use your own texture pictures for custom backgrounds. When you insert a fill, PowerPoint assumes you want this custom background on only the current slide displayed. To make this background appear on all slides in the presentation, click the Apply to All button in the Format Background dialog box. The following steps insert the Sand fill on Slide 4 in the presentation.

• Right-click anywhere on the Slide 4 blue background to display the shortcut menu (Figure 2-27).

Figure 2-27

- Click Format Background on the shortcut menu to display the Format Background dialog box.

- With the Fill pane displaying, click 'Picture or texture fill' to expand the fill options (Figure 2–28).

Q&A Why did the background change to a yellow texture?

This texture is the Papyrus background, which is the default texture fill.

Figure 2–28

- Click the Texture arrow to display the Texture gallery (Figure 2–29).

Q&A Is a live preview available to see the various textures on this slide?

No. Live preview is not an option with the background textures and fills.

Q&A How does a texture fill differ from a gradient fill?

A texture fill can have the appearance of paper goods or a natural material, such as sand, water, or marble. A gradient fill blends two or more fill colors. PowerPoint includes several built-in gradient fills, and you also can create your own blend of desired colors. When you click the Gradient fill option, you can select a fill

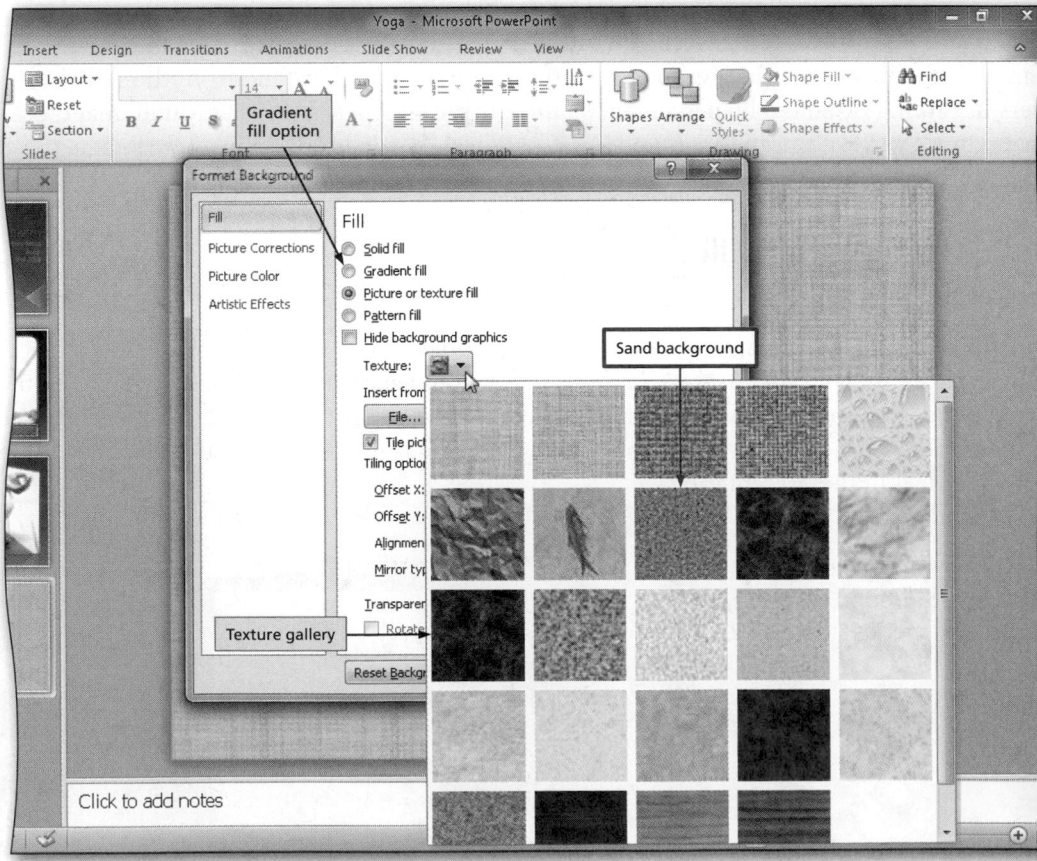

Figure 2–29

from the Light Variations and Dark Variations areas. If you click More Gradients, you can select the custom colors, the location or stop, where the blending ends, the direction and angle of the blend, and the percentage of brightness and transparency.

④

- Click the Sand background (third texture in second row) to insert this background on Slide 4 (Figure 2–30).

The Format Background dialog box is covering part of the slide. Can I move this box?

Yes. Click the dialog box title and drag it to a different location so that you can view the slide.

Could I insert this background on all four slides simultaneously?

Yes. You would click the Apply to All button to insert the Sand background on all slides.

Figure 2–30

To Insert a Picture to Create a Background

For variety and interest, you want to use another yoga picture as the Slide 1 background. This picture is stored on the Data Files for Students. PowerPoint will stretch the height and width of this picture to fill the slide area. The following steps insert the picture, Sunrise Yoga, on only Slide 1.

❶

- Click the Previous Slide button three times to display Slide 1.

- With the Fill pane displaying (Format Background dialog box), click 'Picture or texture fill'.

- Click the File button in the Insert from area (shown in Figure 2–30) to display the Insert Picture dialog box.

- If necessary, double-click your USB flash drive in the list of available storage devices to display a list of files and folders on the selected USB flash drive and then navigate to the PowerPoint Chapter 02 folder.

- Scroll down and then click Sunrise Yoga to select the file name (Figure 2–31).

What if the picture is not on a USB flash drive?

Use the same process, but select the drive containing the picture.

Figure 2–31

- Click the Insert button (Insert Picture dialog box) to insert the Sunrise Yoga picture as the Slide 1 background (Figure 2–32).

Q&A

What if I do not want to use this picture?

Click the Undo button on the Quick Access Toolbar.

Q&A

Why do the Left and Right offsets in the Stretch options area show a −6% value?

PowerPoint automatically reduced the photograph slightly so that it fills the entire slide.

Q&A

Can I move the Format Background dialog box to the left so that I can see more of the subtitle text?

Yes. Click the dialog box title and then drag the box to the desired location on the slide.

Figure 2–32

To Format a Background Picture Fill Transparency

The Sunrise Yoga picture on Slide 1 is a rich color and conflicts with the title and subtitle text. One method of reducing this richness is to change the transparency. The **Transparency slider** indicates the amount of opaqueness. The default setting is 0, which is fully opaque. The opposite extreme is 100%, which is fully transparent. To change the transparency, you can move the Transparency slider or enter a number in the text box next to the slider. The following step adjusts the transparency to 10%.

1

- Click the Transparency slider and drag it to the right until 10% is displayed in the Transparency text box (Figure 2–33).

Q&A

Can I move the slider in small increments so that I can get a precise percentage easily?

Yes. Press the RIGHT ARROW or LEFT ARROW key to move the slider in one-percent increments.

Figure 2–33

To Format a Background Texture Fill Transparency

The Sand texture on Slide 4 is dark and may not offer sufficient contrast with the symbols and text you are going to insert on this slide. You can adjust the transparency of slide texture in the same manner that you change a picture transparency. The following steps adjust the texture transparency to 50%.

1
- Click the Next Slide button three times to display Slide 4.

- Click the Transparency slider and drag it to the right until 50% is displayed in the Transparency text box (Figure 2–34).

2
- Click the Close button (Format Background dialog box).

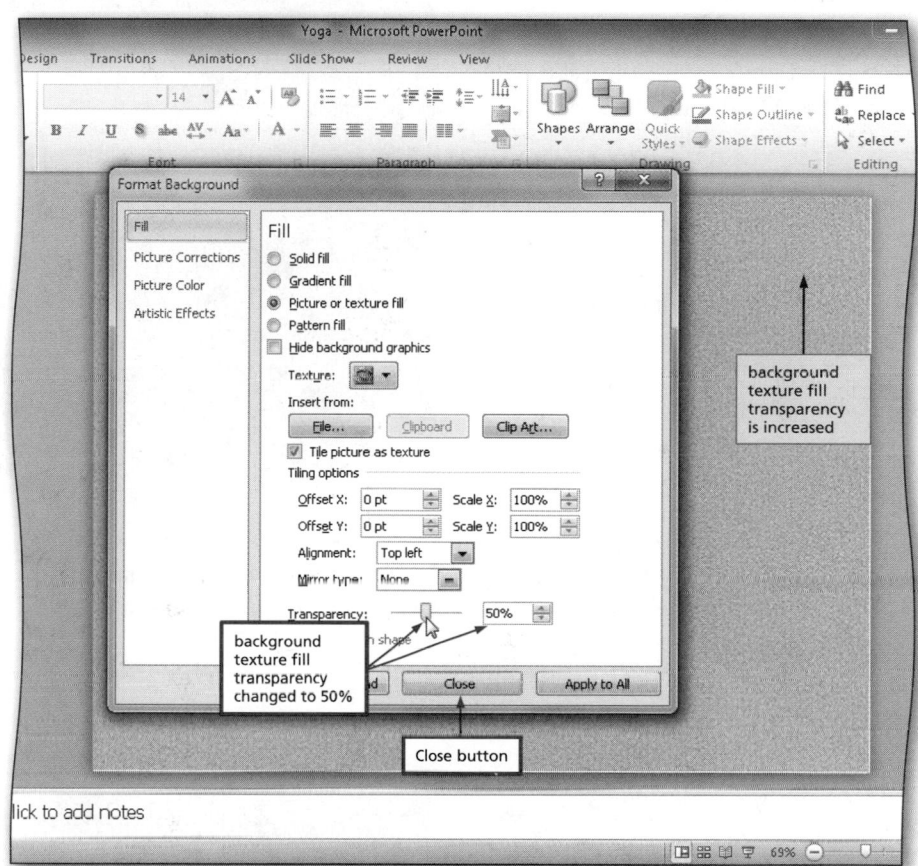

Figure 2–34

To Choose a Background Style

Now that the backgrounds for Slides 1 and 4 are set, and the title and text paragraphs for the presentation have been entered, you need to make design decisions for Slides 2 and 3. In this project, you will choose a background for these slides. For each theme, PowerPoint provides 12 **background styles** with designs that may include color, shading, patterns, and textures. **Fill effects** add pattern and texture to a background, which add depth to a slide. The following steps add a background style to Slides 2 and 3 in the presentation.

- Click the Previous Slide button once to display Slide 3 and then click the Design tab on the Ribbon.

- Click the Background Styles button (Design tab | Background group) to display the Background Styles gallery.

- Right-click Style 11 (third style in third row) to display the shortcut menu (Figure 2–35).

- Point to various styles themes in the Background Styles gallery and watch the backgrounds change on the slide.

Q&A Are the backgrounds displayed in a specific order?

Yes. They are arranged in order from light to dark running from left to right. The first row has solid backgrounds; the middle row has darker fills at the top and bottom; the bottom row has fill patterns. If you point to a background, a ScreenTip with the background's name appears on the screen.

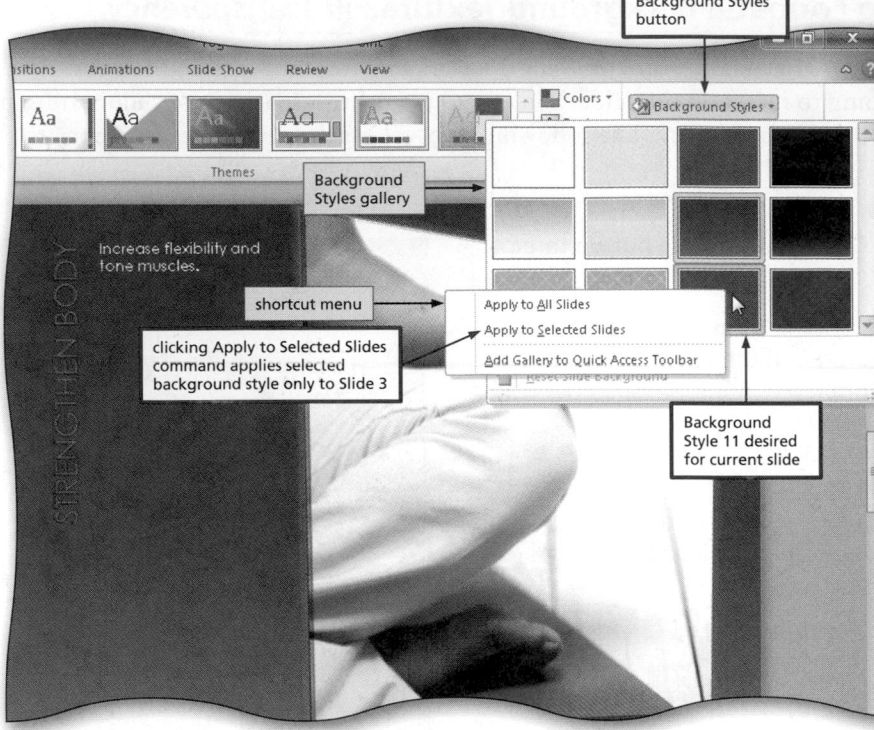

Figure 2–35

2

- Click Apply to Selected Slides to apply Style 11 to Slide 3 (Figure 2–36).

Q&A If I decide later that this background style does not fit the theme of my presentation, can I apply a different background?

Yes. You can repeat these steps at any time while creating your presentation.

Q&A What if I want to apply this background style to all slides in the presentation?

Click the desired style or click Apply to All Slides in the shortcut menu.

Other Ways

1. Click Background Styles, right-click desired background, press s

Figure 2–36

To Choose Another Background Style

In this presentation, the Slide 2 background can have a coordinating background to complement the yoga picture. The following steps add a background to Slide 2.

1 Click the Previous Slide button to display Slide 2. Click the Background Styles button (Design tab | Background group) and then right-click Style 10 (second style in third row) to display the shortcut menu.

2 Click Apply to Selected Slides to apply this background style to Slide 2 (Figure 2–37).

Background Style 10 applied to Slide 2

RELAX AND RESTORE

Calm the mind and boost oxygen levels in the brain.

Figure 2–37

Formatting Title and Content Text

Choosing well-coordinated colors and styles for text and objects in a presentation is possible. Once you select a particular Quick Style and make any other font changes, you then can copy these changes to other text using the **Format Painter**. The Format Painter allows you to copy all formatting changes from one object to another.

To Change the Subtitle and Caption Font

The default Verve theme heading, subtitle, and caption text font is Century Gothic. To draw more attention to subtitle and caption text and to help differentiate these slide elements from the title text, you want to change the font from Century Gothic to Papyrus. To change the font, you must select the letters you want to format. In Chapter 1, you selected a paragraph and then formatted the characters. To format the text in multiple paragraphs quickly and simultaneously, you can select all the paragraphs to be formatted and then apply formatting changes. The following steps change the subtitle and caption font.

BTW

Introducing the Presentation
Before your audience enters the room, start the presentation and then display Slide 1. This slide should be visually appealing and provide general interest in the presentation. An effective title slide gives a good first impression.

• Click the Previous Slide button to display Slide 1. Move the mouse pointer to the left of the first subtitle paragraph, Unify Your Mind, until the mouse pointer changes to an I-beam (Figure 2–38).

Figure 2–38

• Drag downward to select all three subtitle lines that will be formatted (Figure 2–39).

Figure 2–39

• With the text selected, click Home on the Ribbon and then click the Font box arrow (Home tab | Font group) to display the Font gallery (Figure 2–40).

Q&A

Will the fonts in my Font gallery be the same as those shown in Figure 2–40?

Your list of available fonts may differ, depending on what fonts you have installed and the type of printer you are using.

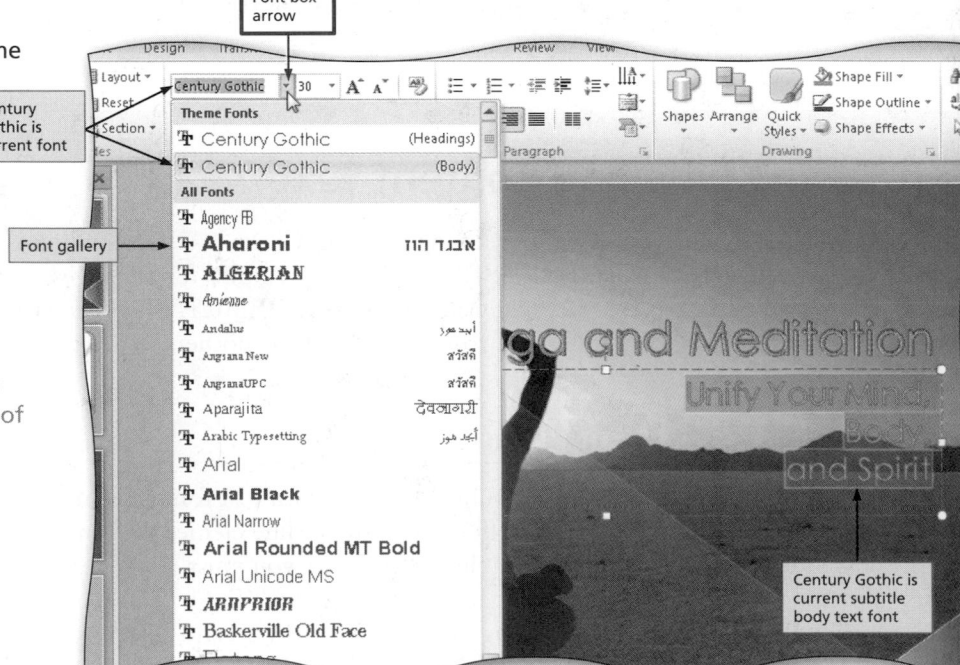

Figure 2–40

- Scroll through the Font gallery and then point to Papyrus (or a similar font) to display a live preview of the title text in the Papyrus font (Figure 2–41).

  Experiment

- Point to various fonts in the Font gallery and watch the subtitle text font change on the slide.

- Click Papyrus (or a similar font) to change the font of the selected text to Papyrus.

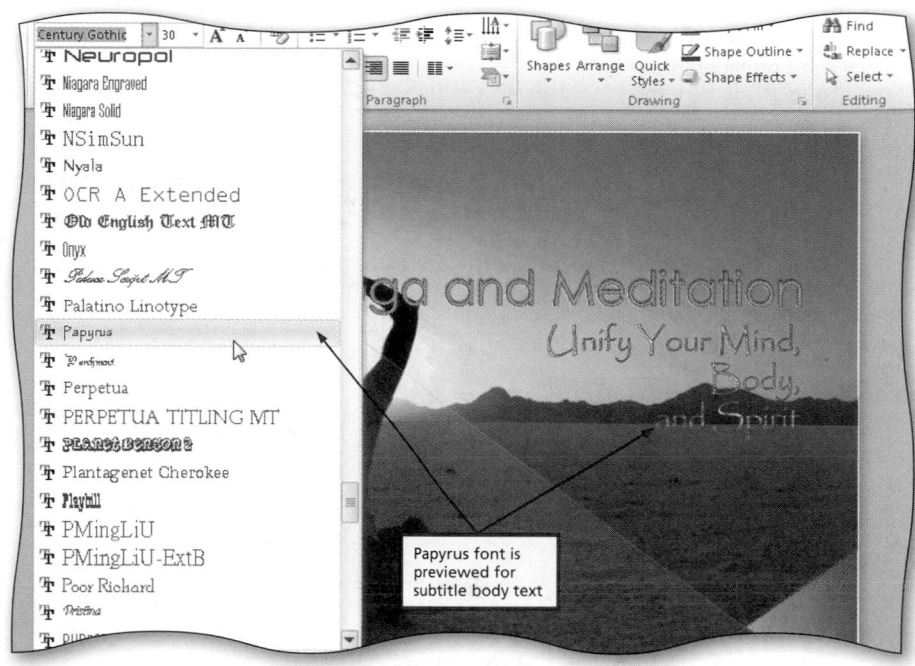

Figure 2–41

Other Ways

1. Click Font box arrow on Mini toolbar, click desired font in Font gallery	Font tab, select desired font in Font list, click OK button	desired font in Font list, click OK button
2. Right-click selected text, click Font on shortcut menu (Font dialog box), click	3. Click Font dialog box launcher (Home tab | Font group), click Font tab (Font dialog box), select	4. Press CTRL+SHIFT+F, click Font tab (Font dialog box), select desired font in the Font list, click OK button

To Shadow Text

A **shadow** helps letters display prominently by adding a shadow behind the text. The following step adds a shadow to the selected subtitle text, Unify Your Mind, Body, and Spirit.

- With the subtitle text selected, click the Text Shadow button (Home tab | Font group) to add a shadow to the selected text (Figure 2–42).

  How would I remove a shadow?

  You would click the Shadow button a second time, or you immediately could click the Undo button on the Quick Access Toolbar.

Figure 2–42

Formatting Text Effects
Text Shadow is one of a variety of effects PowerPoint provides in the Font group. If you click the Font dialog box launcher, you can select additional effects, such as Small Caps and Superscript, in the Font dialog box. In addition, you can format the letters by adding glow, reflection, 3-D, and other effects by selecting the text, clicking the Text Effects button (Drawing Tools Format tab | WordArt Styles group), pointing to an effect in the Text Effects menu, and then selecting an effect in the gallery.

To Format the Subtitle Text

To increase readability, you can format the Slide 1 subtitle text by bolding the characters and changing the font color to yellow. The following steps format the Slide 1 subtitle text.

1 With the subtitle text selected, click the Bold button (Home tab | Font group) to bold the text.

2 Click the Font Color arrow and change the color to Light Yellow, Text 2 (fourth color in first row) (Figure 2–43).

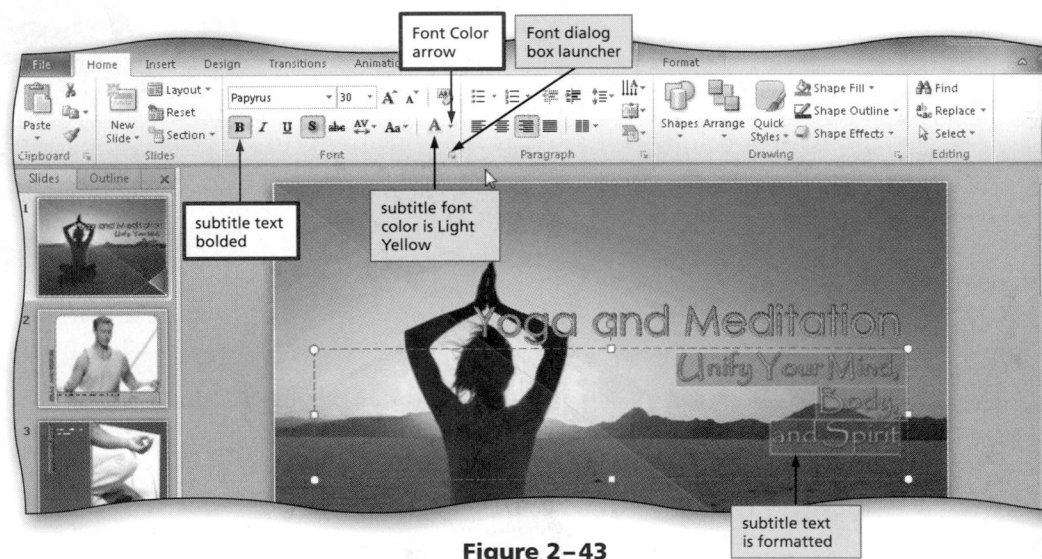

Figure 2–43

Decreasing Font Size
The Increase Font Size buttons on the Mini toolbar and in the Font group (Home tab) enlarge the selected characters in predetermined amounts. The Decrease Font Size buttons, which appear to the right of the Increase Font Size buttons, reduce the characters' size in the same predetermined point sizes.

To Format the Slide 2 Caption

The caption on a slide should be large enough for audience members to read easily and should coordinate with the font styles in other parts of the presentation. The caption on Slide 2 can be enhanced by changing the font, the font color, and the font size. The following steps format the Slide 2 caption text.

1 Click the Next Slide button to display Slide 2. Triple-click the caption text to select all the characters, click the Font box arrow on the Mini toolbar, and then scroll down and click Papyrus.

2 Click the Increase Font Size button on the Mini toolbar three times to increase the font size to 20 point.

3 Click the Bold button on the Mini toolbar to bold the text (Figure 2–44).

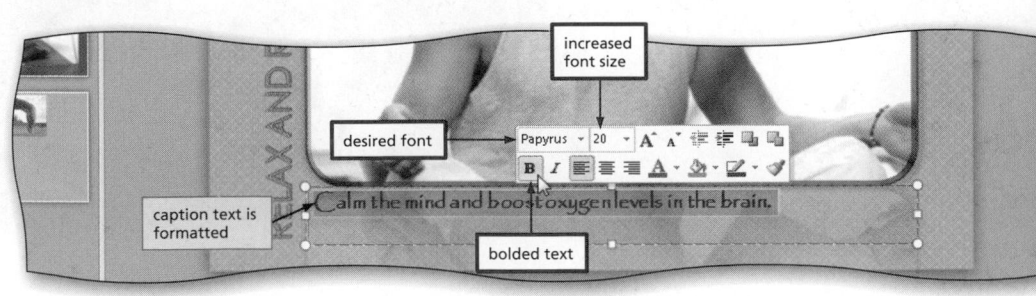

Figure 2–44

Format Painter

To save time and avoid formatting errors, you can use the Format Painter to apply custom formatting to other places in your presentation quickly and easily. You can use this feature in three ways:

- To copy only character attributes, such as font and font effects, select text that has these qualities.
- To copy both paragraph attributes, such as alignment and indentation and character attributes, select the entire paragraph.
- To apply the same formatting to multiple words, phrases, or paragraphs, double-click the Format Painter button and then select each item you want to format. You then can press the ESC key or click the Format Painter button to turn off this feature.

To Format Text Using the Format Painter

To save time and duplicated effort, you quickly can use the Format Painter to copy formatting attributes from the Slide 2 caption text and apply them to Slide 3. The following steps use the Format Painter to copy formatting features.

- With the Slide 2 caption text still selected, double-click the Format Painter button (Home tab | Clipboard group).
- Move the mouse pointer off the Ribbon (Figure 2–45).

Why did my mouse pointer change shape?

The mouse pointer changed shape by adding a paintbrush to indicate that the Format Painter function is active.

Figure 2–45

- Click the Next Slide button to display Slide 3. Triple-click the caption placeholder to apply the format to all the caption text (Figure 2–46).
- Press the ESC key to turn off the Format Painter feature.

Figure 2–46

Other Ways

1. Click Format Painter button on Mini toolbar

Break Point: If you wish to take a break, this is a good place to do so. Be sure to save the Yoga file again and then you can quit PowerPoint. To resume at a later time, start PowerPoint, open the file called Yoga, and continue following the steps from this location forward.

Sizing Shapes
PowerPoint's Shapes gallery provides a wide variety of symbols that can help emphasize your major points on each slide. As you select the shapes and then size them, keep in mind that your audience will focus on the largest shapes first. The most important information, therefore, should be placed in or near the shapes with the most visual size.

Adding and Formatting a Shape

One method of getting the audience's attention and reinforcing the major concepts being presented is to have graphical elements on the title slide. PowerPoint provides a wide variety of predefined shapes that can add visual interest to a slide. Shape elements include lines, basic geometrical shapes, arrows, equation shapes, flowchart symbols, stars, banners, and callouts. After adding a shape to a slide, you can change its default characteristics by adding text, bullets, numbers, and styles. You also can combine multiple shapes to create a more complex graphic.

Slides 1 and 4 in this presentation are enhanced in a variety of ways. First, a sun shape is added to the Slide 1 title text in place of the letter o. Then a circle shape is inserted on Slide 4 and copied twice, and text is added to each circle and then formatted. Finally, a triangle is inserted on top of the three circle shapes on Slide 4.

To Add a Shape

Many of the shapes included in the Shapes gallery can direct the viewer to important aspects of the presentation. For example, the sun shape helps emphasize the presentation's theme of practicing yoga and meditation, and it complements the Sunrise Yoga background picture. The following steps add the Sun shape to Slide 1.

- Click the Previous Slide button two times to display Slide 1. Click the Shapes button (Home tab | Drawing group) to display the Shapes gallery (Figure 2–47).

Figure 2–47

I do not see a Shapes button in the Drawing group. Instead, I have three rows of the shapes I have used recently in presentations. Why?

Monitor dimensions and resolution affect how buttons display on the Ribbon. Click the Shapes More button to display the entire Shapes gallery.

2

● Click the Sun shape in the Basic Shapes area of the Shapes gallery.

Why did my pointer change shape?

The pointer changed to a plus shape to indicate the Sun shape has been added to the Clipboard.

● Position the mouse pointer (a crosshair) above the person's hands in the picture, as shown in Figure 2–48.

Figure 2–48

3

● Click Slide 1 to insert the Sun shape (Figure 2–49).

Figure 2–49

Other Ways
1. Click More button (Drawing Tools Format tab | Insert Shapes group)

To Resize a Shape

The next step is to resize the Sun shape. The shape should be reduced so that it is approximately the same size as the letter o in the words Yoga and Meditation. The following steps resize the selected Sun shape.

1

● With the mouse pointer appearing as a two-headed arrow, drag a corner sizing handle on the picture diagonally inward until the Sun shape is resized approximately as shown in Figure 2–50.

What if my shape is not selected?

To select a shape, click it.

What if the shape has changed proportions?

To maintain a shape's proportions, hold down the SHIFT key when you drag a corner sizing handle.

Figure 2–50

- Release the mouse button to resize the shape.

- Drag the Sun shape on top of the letter o in the word, Yoga (Figure 2–51).

Q&A What if I want to move the shape to a precise location on the slide?

With the shape selected, press the ARROW keys or the CTRL+ARROW keys to move the shape to the desired location.

Figure 2–51

Other Ways

1. Enter shape height and width in Height and Width text boxes (Drawing Tools Format tab | Size group)

(Drawing Tools Format tab | Size group), click Size tab, enter desired height and width values in text boxes, click Close button

2. Click Size and Position dialog box launcher

To Copy and Paste a Shape

The next step is to copy the Sun shape. The duplicate shape will be placed over the letter 'o' in the word, Meditation. The following steps copy and move the identical second Sun shape.

- With the Sun shape still selected, click the Copy button (Home tab | Clipboard group) (Figure 2–52).

Q&A What if my shape is not selected?

To select a shape, click it.

Q&A How does the Copy button differ from the Cut button?

Clicking the Copy button leaves the shape in the slide while placing the same shape on the Office Clipboard. Clicking the Cut button removes the shape from the slide and then places it on the Office Clipboard.

Figure 2–52

2
- Click the Paste button on the Home tab to insert a duplicate Sun shape on Slide 1.

- Drag the Sun shape on top of the letter o in the word, Meditation, and release the mouse button when a dashed line connects this Sun shape to the Sun shape that is displaying in the word, Yoga (Figure 2–53).

What does the dashed line represent?

PowerPoint displays this Smart Guide when two shapes are aligned precisely. In this case, the two Sun shapes are centered horizontally.

Figure 2–53

Other Ways

1. Right-click selected shape, click Copy on shortcut menu, right click, click Paste on shortcut menu

2. Select shape, press CTRL+C, press CTRL+V

BTW

Copying and Pasting Text
The process of copying text is similar to copying a shape. When you copy text, you place the word, phrase, sentence, or other letters on the Office Clipboard. When you paste this text, you copy the letters from the Office Clipboard into another location on a slide. To copy and paste text, select the text to be copied, click the Copy button (Home tab | Clipboard group), position the insertion point at the location where the text should be pasted, and then click the Paste button (Home tab | Clipboard group) to paste the copied text at the location of the insertion point.

To Add Other Shapes

Circles, squares, and triangles are among the geometric shapes included in the Shapes gallery. These shapes can be combined to show relationships among the elements, and they can help illustrate the basic concepts presented in your slide show. The following steps add the Oval and Isosceles Triangle shapes to Slide 4.

1
- Click the Next Slide button three times to display Slide 4 and then click the Shapes button (Home tab | Drawing group) to display the Shapes gallery (Figure 2–54).

Figure 2–54

- Click the Oval shape in the Basic Shapes area of the Shapes gallery.

- Position the mouse pointer in the center of Slide 4 and then click to insert the Oval shape.

- Press and hold down the SHIFT key and then drag a corner sizing handle until the Oval shape forms a circle and is the size shown in Figure 2–55.

Q&A

Why did I need to press the SHIFT key while enlarging the shape?

Holding down the SHIFT key while dragging draws a perfect circle.

- Move the shape so it is positioned approximately as shown in the figure.

Oval shape inserted, sized, and moved to desired location on slide

Figure 2–55

- Click the Shapes button (Home tab | Drawing group) and then click the Isosceles Triangle shape in the Basic Shapes area of the Shapes gallery.

- Position the mouse pointer in the right side of Slide 4 and then click to insert the Isosceles Triangle shape.

- Resize the shape so that it displays approximately as shown in Figure 2–56.

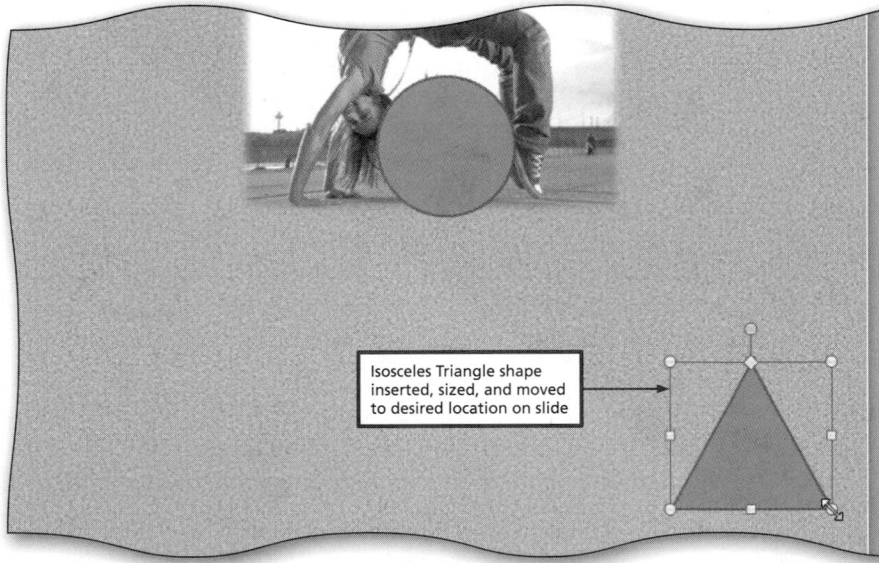

Isosceles Triangle shape inserted, sized, and moved to desired location on slide

Figure 2–56

To Apply a Shape Style

Formatting text in a shape follows the same techniques as formatting text in a placeholder. You can change font, font color and size, and alignment. The next step is to apply a shape style to the oval so that it appears to have depth. The Shape Styles gallery has a variety of styles that change depending upon the theme applied to the presentation. The following steps apply a style to the Oval shape.

1

- Click the Oval shape to select it and then display the Drawing Tools Format tab (Figure 2–57).

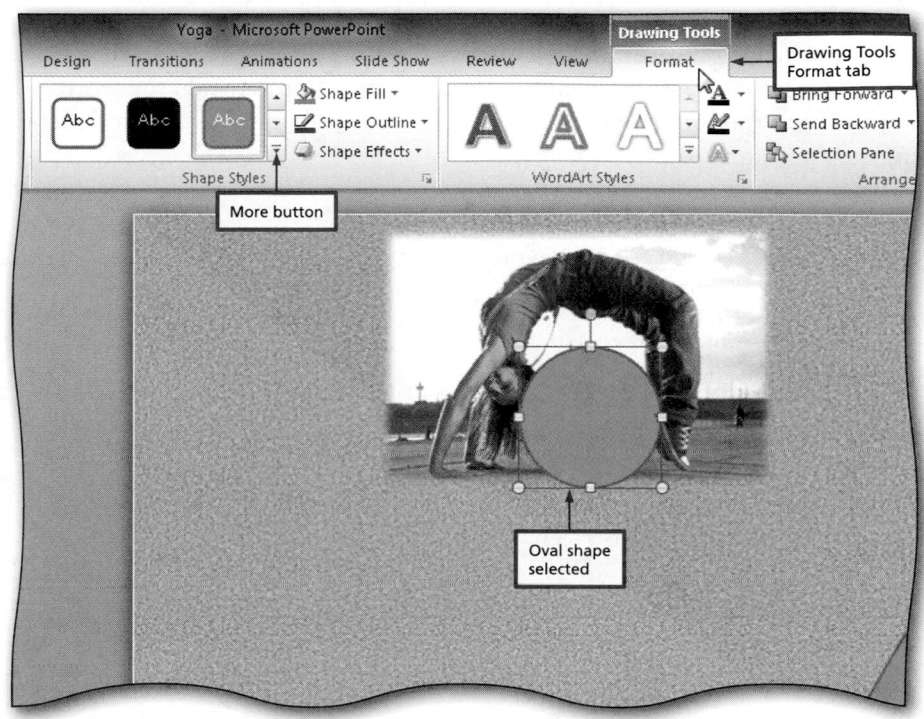

Figure 2–57

2

- Click the More button in the Shape Styles gallery (Drawing Tools Format tab | Shape Styles group) to expand the Shape Styles gallery.

- Point to Intense Effect – Orange, Accent 1 in the Shape Styles gallery (second shape in last row) to display a live preview of that style applied to the shape in the slide (Figure 2–58).

🔎 **Experiment**

- Point to various styles in the Shape Styles gallery and watch the style of the shape change.

3

- Click Intense Effect – Orange, Accent 1 in the Shape Styles gallery to apply the selected style to the Oval shape.

Figure 2–58

Other Ways	
1. Click Format Shape dialog box launcher (Drawing Tools Format tab | Shape Styles group), select desired colors (Format Shape dialog box), click Close button	2. Right-click shape, click Format Shape on shortcut menu, select desired colors (Format Shape dialog box), click Close button

To Add Formatted Text to a Shape

Formatting text in a shape follows the same techniques as formatting text in a placeholder. You can change font, font color and size, and alignment. The next step is to add the word, Mind, to the shape, change the font to Papyrus and the font color to Blue-Gray, center and bold the text, and increase the font size to 24 point. The following step adds text to the Oval shape.

- With the Oval shape selected, type **Mind** in the shape.

- Change the font to Papyrus.

- Change the font color to Blue-Gray, Background 2 (third color in first Theme Colors row).

- Change the font size to 24 point and bold the text (Figure 2–59).

Figure 2–59

BTW

Drawing a Square
Holding down the SHIFT key while dragging a Rectangle shape draws a square.

To Copy a Shape

Your presentation emphasizes that mind, body, and spirit are equal components in finding balance in life. Each of these elements can be represented by an oval. The following steps copy the Oval shape.

1 Click Home on the Ribbon. Click the edge of the Oval shape so that it is a solid line.

2 Click the Copy button (Home tab | Clipboard group).

3 Click the Paste button (Home tab | Clipboard group) two times to insert two duplicate Oval shapes on Slide 4.

4 Move the Oval shapes so they appear approximately as shown in Figure 2–60.

5 In the left oval, select the word, Mind, and then type the word, **Body**, in the oval.

6 In the right oval, select the word, Mind, and then type the word, **Spirit**, in the oval (Figure 2–60). You may need to enlarge the size of the oval shapes slightly so that each word is displayed on one line.

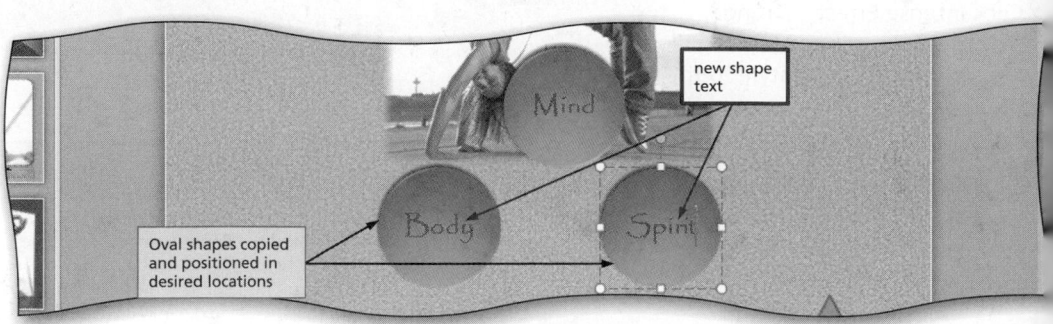

Figure 2–60

To Apply Another Style

The triangle shape helps show the unity among body, mind, and spirit. You can apply a coordinating shape style to the isosceles triangle and then place it on top of the three ovals. The following steps apply a style to the Isosceles Triangle shape.

1 Display the Drawing Tools Format tab. Click the Isosceles Triangle shape on Slide 4 to select it.

2 Click the More button in the Shape Styles gallery (Drawing Tools Format tab | Shape Styles group) to expand the Shape Styles gallery and then click Intense Effect – Blue, Accent 2 (third style in last row) to apply that style to the triangle.

3 Move the triangle shape to the center of the Ovals.

4 Click the Bring Forward button twice (Drawing Tools Format tab | Arrange group) to display the triangle on top of the ovals. Resize the triangle if necessary so that it displays as shown in Figure 2–61.

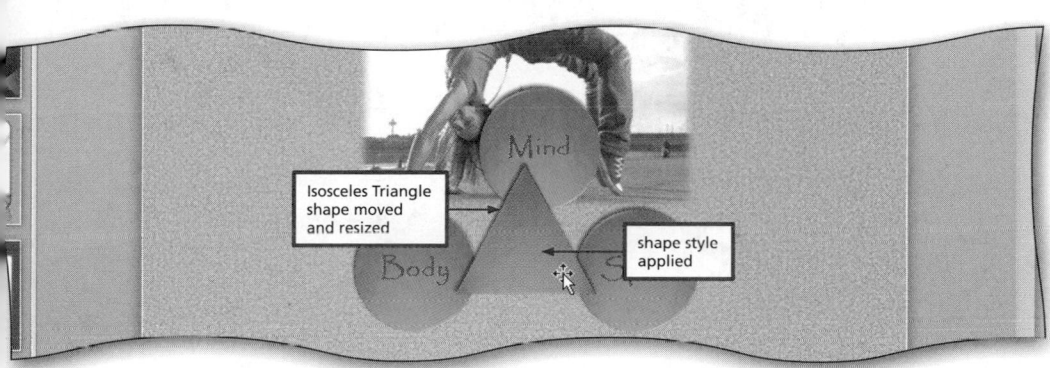

Figure 2–61

Break Point: If you wish to take a break, this is a good place to do so. Be sure to save the Yoga file again and then you can quit PowerPoint. To resume at a later time, start PowerPoint, open the file called Yoga, and continue following the steps from this location forward.

Using WordArt

One method of adding appealing visual elements to a presentation is by using **WordArt** styles. This feature is found in other Microsoft Office applications, including Word and Excel. This gallery of decorative effects allows you to type new text or convert existing text to WordArt. You then can add elements such as fills, outlines, and effects.

As with slide backgrounds, WordArt fill in the interior of a letter can consist of a solid color, texture, picture, or gradient. The WordArt **outline** is the exterior border surrounding each letter or symbol. PowerPoint allows you to change the outline color, weight, and style. You also can add an **effect**, which helps add emphasis or depth to the characters. Some effects are shadows, reflections, glows, bevels, and 3-D rotations.

BTW

Creating Logos
Many companies without graphic arts departments create their logos using WordArt. The bevels, glows, and shadows allow corporate designers to develop unique images with 3-D effects that give depth to their companies' emblems.

Plan Ahead

Use WordArt in moderation.
Some WordArt styles are bold and detailed, and they can detract from the message you are trying to present if not used carefully. Select a WordArt style when needed for special emphasis, such as a title slide that audience members will see when they enter the room. WordArt can have a powerful effect, so do not overuse it.

To Insert WordArt

Yoga and meditation can help individuals find balance among the mind, body, and spirit. The symbols on Slide 4 emphasize this relationship, and you want to call attention to the concept. You quickly can add a visual element to the slide by selecting a WordArt style from the WordArt Styles gallery and then applying it to a word. The following steps insert WordArt.

- With Slide 4 displaying, click Insert on the Ribbon.
- Click the WordArt button (Insert tab | Text group) to display the WordArt gallery (Figure 2–62).

Figure 2–62

- Click Fill – Blue, Accent 2, Double Outline – Accent 2 (last letter A in third row) to display the WordArt text box (Figure 2–63).

Q&A What is a matte bevel style that is part of some of the styles in the gallery?

A matte finish gives a dull and rough effect. A bevel edge is angled or sloped and gives the effect of a three-dimensional object.

Figure 2–63

- Type **Balance** in the text box, as the WordArt text (Figure 2–64).

Q&A Why did the Format tab appear automatically in the Ribbon?

It appears when you select text to which you could add a WordArt style or other effect.

Figure 2–64

To Change a WordArt Shape

The WordArt text is useful to emphasize the harmony among the mind, body, and spirit. You can further emphasize this word by changing its shape. PowerPoint provides a variety of graphical shapes that add interest to text. The following steps change the WordArt to Triangle Down shape.

- With the Slide 4 text still selected, click the Text Effects button (Drawing Tools Format tab | WordArt Styles group) to display the Text Effects menu (Figure 2–65).

Figure 2–65

- Point to Transform in the Text Effects menu to display the WordArt Transform gallery (Figure 2–66).

Experiment

- Point to various styles in the Transform gallery and watch the format of the text and borders change.

How can I see the preview of a Transform effect if the gallery is overlaying the WordArt letters?

Move the WordArt text box to the left or right side of the slide and then repeat Steps 1 and 2.

Figure 2–66

• Click the Triangle Down shape in the Warp area to apply the Triangle Down shape to the WordArt text (Figure 2–67).

Q&A

Can I change the shape I applied to the WordArt?

Yes. Position the insertion point in the text box and then repeat Steps 1 and 2.

Figure 2–67

• Drag the WordArt downward until it is positioned approximately as shown in Figure 2–68.

• Drag a corner sizing handle diagonally outward until the WordArt is resized approximately as shown in the figure.

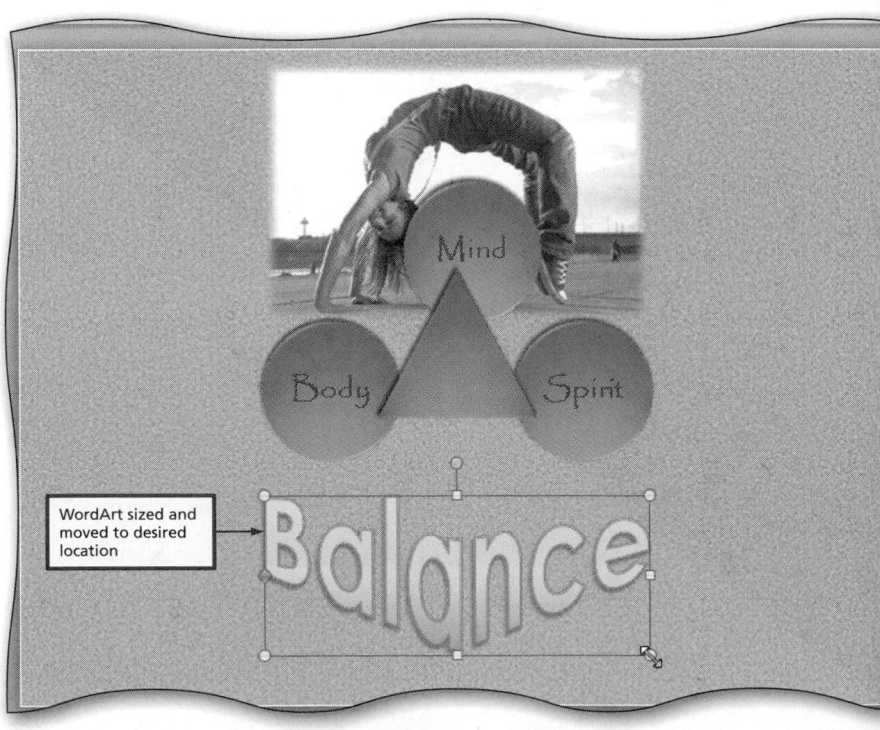

Figure 2–68

To Apply a WordArt Text Fill

The Slide 4 background has a Sand texture for the background, and you want to coordinate the WordArt fill with a similar texture. The following steps add the Denim texture as a fill for the WordArt characters.

• With the WordArt text selected, click the Text Fill button arrow (Drawing Tools Format tab | WordArt Styles group) to display the Text Fill gallery.

The Text Fill gallery did not display. Why not?

Be sure you click the Text Fill button arrow, which is to the right of the Text Fill button. If you mistakenly click the Text Fill button, PowerPoint places the default fill in the WordArt instead of displaying the Text Fill gallery.

• Point to Texture in the Text Fill gallery to display the Texture gallery (Figure 2–69).

Figure 2–69

Experiment

• Point to various styles in the Text Fill gallery and watch the fill change.

How can I see the preview of a fill if the gallery is overlaying the WordArt letters?

Move the WordArt text box to the left or right side of the slide and then repeat Step 1.

• Click the Denim texture (third texture in first row) to apply this texture as the fill for the WordArt.

Can I apply this texture simultaneously to text that appears in more than one place on my slide?

Yes. Select one area of text, press and then hold the CTRL key while you select the other text, and then apply the texture.

To Change the Weight of a WordArt Outline

The letters in the WordArt style applied have a double outline around the edges. To emphasize this characteristic, you can increase the width of the lines. As with font size, lines also are measured in point size, and PowerPoint gives you the option to change the line **weight**, or thickness, starting with ¼ point (pt) and increasing in one-fourth–point increments. Other outline options include modifying the color and the line style, such as changing to dots or dashes or a combination of dots and dashes. The following steps change the WordArt outline weight to 6 pt.

- With the WordArt still selected, click the Text Outline button arrow (Drawing Tools Format tab | WordArt Styles group) to display the Text Outline gallery.

- Point to Weight in the gallery to display the Weight list.

- Point to 6 pt to display a live preview of this line weight on the WordArt text outline (Figure 2–70).

 Experiment

- Point to various line weights in the Weight list and watch the line thickness change.

Q&A Can I make the line width more than 6 pt?

Yes. Click More Lines and increase the amount in the Width box.

Figure 2–70

- Click 6 pt to apply this line weight to the title text outline.

Q&A Must my text have an outline?

No. To delete the outline, click No Outline in the Text Outline gallery.

To Change the Color of a WordArt Outline

The WordArt outline color is similar to the Denim fill color. To add variety, you can change the outline color. The following steps change the WordArt outline color.

- With the WordArt still selected, click the Text Outline button arrow (Drawing Tools Format tab | WordArt Styles group) to display the Text Outline gallery.

- Point to Orange, Accent 1 (fifth color in first row) to display a live preview of this outline color (Figure 2–71).

🔍 **Experiment**

- Point to various colors in the gallery and watch the outline colors change.

- Click Orange, Accent 1 to apply this color to the WordArt outline.

Figure 2–71

To Add a Transition between Slides

A final enhancement you will make in this presentation is to apply the Rotate transition in the Dynamic Content category to all slides and change the transition speed to Slow. The following steps apply this transition to the presentation.

- Click Transitions on the Ribbon. Click the More button (Transitions tab | Transition to This Slide group) to expand the Transitions gallery.

- Click the Rotate transition in the Dynamic Content category to apply this transition to Slide 4.

- Click the Duration up arrow in the Timing group four times to change the transition speed from 02.00 to 03.00.

- Click the Preview Transitions button (Transitions tab | Preview area) to view the new transition time.

- Click the Apply To All button (Transitions tab | Timing group) to apply this transition and speed to all four slides in the presentation (Figure 2–72 on the next page).

BTW

Selecting Effect Options
Many PowerPoint transitions have options that you can customize to give your presentation a unique look. When you click the Effect Options button (Transitions tab | Transition to This Slide group), you can, for example, select the option to have a slide appear on the screen from the left or the right, or the screen can fade to black before the next slide is displayed.

Figure 2–72

To Change Document Properties

Before saving the presentation again, you want to add your name, class name, and some keywords as document properties. The following steps use the Document Information Panel to change document properties.

1 Click File on the Ribbon to open the Backstage view. If necessary, click the Info tab.

2 Click the Properties button in the right pane of the Info gallery.

3 Click Show Document Panel on the Properties menu to close the Backstage view and display the Document Information Panel.

4 Click the Author box, if necessary, and then type your name as the Author property.

5 Click the Subject text box and then type your course and section as the Subject property.

6 Click the Keywords text box and then type `yoga, meditation` as the Keywords property.

7 Click the Close the Document Information Panel button so that the Document Information Panel no longer is displayed.

BTW

Certification
The Microsoft Office Specialist (MOS) program provides an opportunity for you to obtain a valuable industry credential — proof that you have the PowerPoint 2010 skills required by employers. For more information, visit the PowerPoint 2010 Certification Web page (scsite.com/ppt2010/cert).

To Print a Presentation

With the completed presentation saved, you may want to print it. If copies of the presentation are being distributed to audience members, you will print a hard copy of each individual slide on a printer. The following steps print a hard copy of the contents of the saved Yoga presentation.

1 Click File on the Ribbon to open the Backstage view. Click the Print tab in the Backstage view to display the Print gallery.

2 Verify the printer name in the Printer box will print a hard copy of the document. If necessary, click the Printer box arrow to display a list of available Printer options and then click the desired printer to change the currently selected printer.

3 Click the Print button in the Print gallery to print the document on the currently selected printer. When the printer stops, retrieve the hard copy (Figure 2–73).

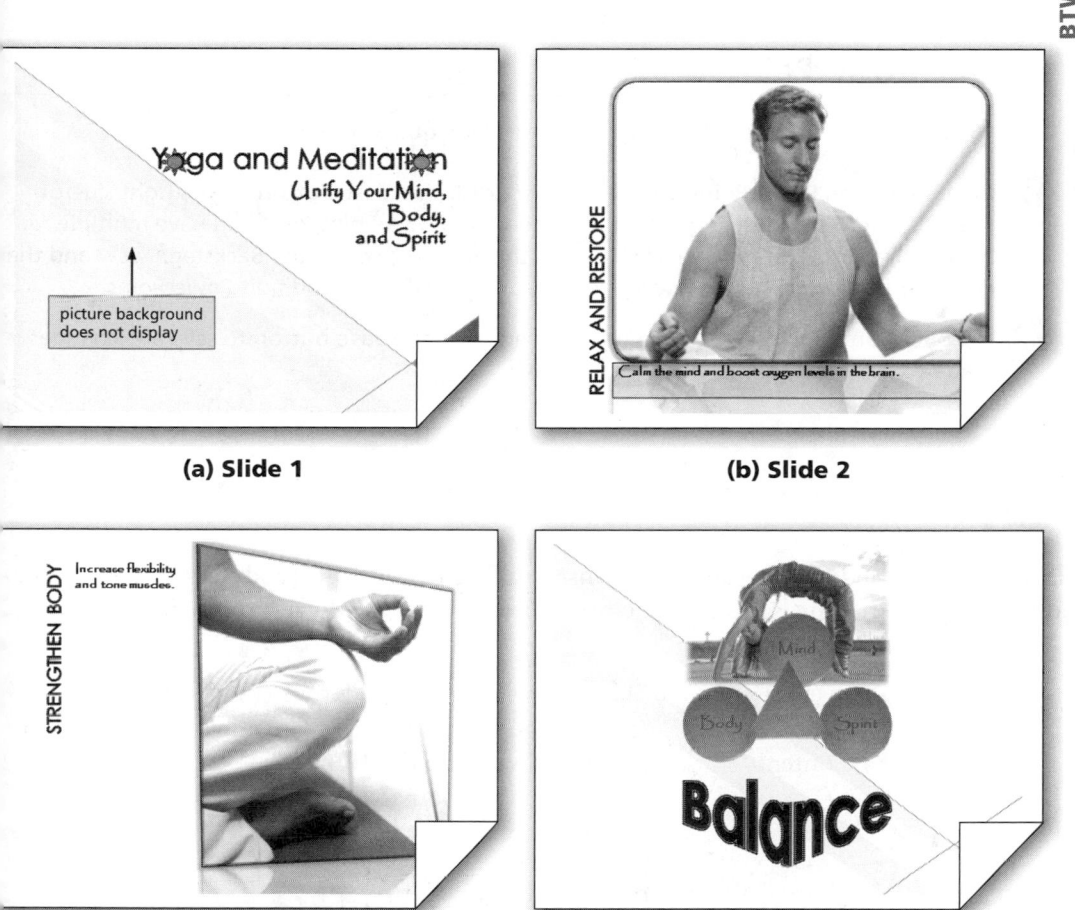

(a) Slide 1

(b) Slide 2

(c) Slide 3

(d) Slide 4

Figure 2–73 (Handouts printed using a black-and-white printer)

To Save an Existing Presentation with the Same File Name

You have made several changes to the presentation since you last saved it. Thus, you should save it again. The following step saves the document again.

1 Click the Save button on the Quick Access Toolbar to overwrite the previously saved file.

To Run an Animated Slide Show

All changes are complete, and the presentation is saved. You now can view the Yoga presentation. The following steps start Slide Show view.

1 Click the Slide 1 thumbnail in the Slides tab to select and display Slide 1.

2 Click the Slide Show button to display the title slide and then click each slide to view the transition effect and slides.

To Quit PowerPoint

This project is complete. The following steps quit PowerPoint.

1 If you have one PowerPoint document open, click the Close Button on the right side of the title bar to close the document and then quit PowerPoint; or if you have multiple PowerPoint documents open, click File on the Ribbon to open the Backstage view and then click Exit in the Backstage view to close all open documents and quit PowerPoint.

2 If a Microsoft PowerPoint dialog box appears, click the Save button to save any changes made to the presentation since the last save.

Chapter Summary

In this chapter you have learned how to add a background style, insert and format pictures, add shapes, size graphic elements, apply styles, and insert WordArt. The items listed below include all the new PowerPoint skills you have learned in this chapter.

1. Change the Presentation Theme Colors (PPT 81)
2. Insert a Picture (PPT 83)
3. Insert a Picture into a Slide without a Content Placeholder (PPT 85)
4. Correct a Picture (PPT 86)
5. Apply a Picture Style (PPT 87)
6. Apply Picture Effects (PPT 89)
7. Add a Picture Border (PPT 91)
8. Change a Picture Border Color (PPT 92)
9. Resize a Graphic by Entering Exact Measurements (PPT 93)
10. Insert a Texture Fill (PPT 95)
11. Insert a Picture to Create a Background (PPT 97)
12. Format a Background Picture Fill Transparency (PPT 98)
13. Format a Background Texture Fill Transparency (PPT 99)
14. Choose a Background Style (PPT 99)
15. Change the Subtitle and Caption Font (PPT 101)
16. Shadow Text (PPT 103)
17. Format Caption Text Using the Format Painter (PPT 105)
18. Add a Shape (PPT 106)
19. Resize a Shape (PPT 107)
20. Copy and Paste a Shape (PPT 108)
21. Add Other Shapes (PPT 109)
22. Apply a Shape Style (PPT 110)
23. Add Formatted Text to a Shape (PPT 112)
24. Insert WordArt (PPT 114)
25. Change the WordArt Shape (PPT 115)
26. Apply a WordArt Text Fill (PPT 117)
27. Change the Weight of a WordArt Outline (PPT 118)
28. Change the Color of a WordArt Outline (PPT 118)

Learn It Online

Test your knowledge of chapter content and key terms.

Instructions: To complete the Learn It Online exercises, start your browser, click the Address bar, and then enter the Web address **scsite.com/ppt2010/learn**. When the PowerPoint 2010 Learn It Online page is displayed, click the link for the exercise you want to complete and then read the instructions.

Chapter Reinforcement TF, MC, and SA

A series of true/false, multiple choice, and short answer questions that test your knowledge of the chapter content.

Flash Cards

An interactive learning environment where you identify chapter key terms associated with displayed definitions.

Practice Test

A series of multiple choice questions that test your knowledge of chapter content and key terms.

Who Wants To Be a Computer Genius?

An interactive game that challenges your knowledge of chapter content in the style of a television quiz show.

Wheel of Terms

An interactive game that challenges your knowledge of chapter key terms in the style of the television show *Wheel of Fortune*.

Crossword Puzzle Challenge

A crossword puzzle that challenges your knowledge of key terms presented in the chapter.

Apply Your Knowledge

Reinforce the skills and apply the concepts you learned in this chapter.

Changing the Background and Adding Photographs, WordArt, and a Shape Quick Style

Note: To complete this assignment, you will be required to use the Data Files for Students. See the inside back cover of this book for instructions on downloading the Data Files for Students, or contact your instructor for information about accessing the required files.

Instructions: Start PowerPoint. Open the presentation, Apply 2-1 Lab Procedures, from the Data Files for Students.

The four slides in the presentation present laboratory safety procedures for your chemistry class. The document you open is an unformatted presentation. You are to add pictures, which are available in the Data Files for Students. You also will change the background style, change slide layouts, apply a transition, and use the Format Painter so the slides look like Figure 2–74.

Perform the following tasks:

1. Change the background style to Style 5 (row 2, column 1).

2. On the title slide (Figure 2–74a), create a background by inserting the picture called Lab Assistant. Change the transparency to 30%.

3. Apply the WordArt style, Fill – Red, Accent 2, Matte Bevel (row 6, column 3) to the title text and increase the font size to 54 point. Also, apply the WordArt Transform text effect, Chevron Up (row 2, column 1 in the Warp area) to this text.

4. In the Slide 1 subtitle area, replace the words, Student Name, with your name. Bold and italicize your name and the words, Presented by, and then apply the WordArt style, Fill – Red, Accent 2, Warm Matte Bevel (row 5, column 3). Position this subtitle text and the title text as shown in Figure 2–74a.

Continued >

Apply Your Knowledge *continued*

5. On Slide 2, change the layout to Two Content and insert the pictures shown in Figure 2–74b called Female in Lab Coat and Female with Goggles. In the left placeholder, apply the Rotated, White picture style to the inserted picture. In the right placeholder, apply the Reflected Bevel, Black picture style to the inserted picture and then change the picture border color to Purple.

6. On Slide 3, change the layout to Two Content and insert the Fire Extinguisher picture shown in Figure 2–74c. Apply the Soft Edge Oval picture style and change the picture brightness to +20% (row 3, column 4 in the Brightness and Contrast area).

7. On Slide 4, change the layout to Picture with Caption and then insert the picture, Hand Washing shown in Figure 2–74d. Increase the subtitle text font size to 18 point. Change the title text font size to 28 point, add a shadow, change font to Algerian, and change the font color to Purple.

8. Use the Format Painter to format the title text on Slides 2 and 3 with the same features as the title text on Slide 4.

9. Apply the Wipe transition in the Subtle category to all slides. Change the duration to 2.00 seconds

(a) Slide 1

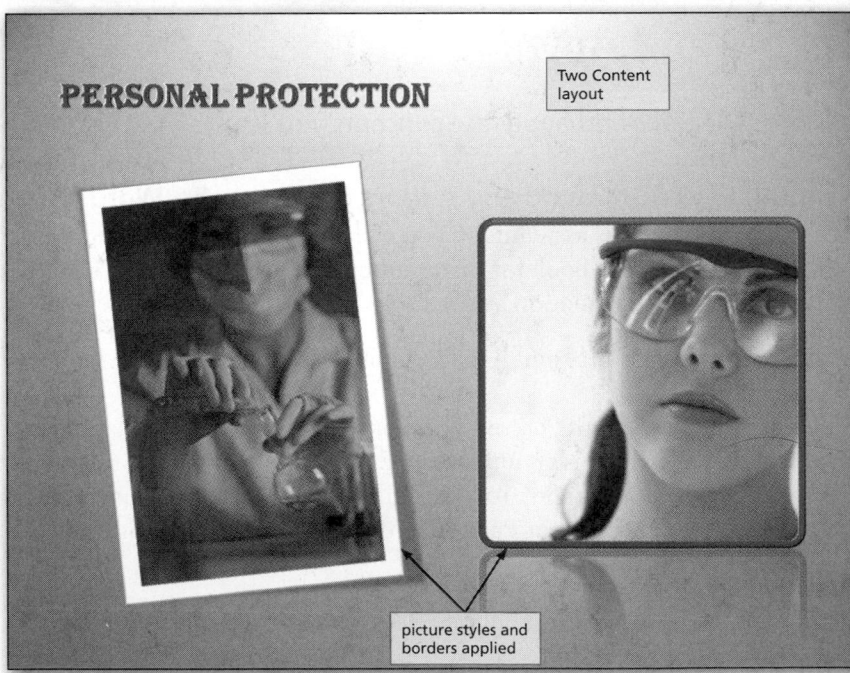

(b) Slide 2

Figure 2–74

10. Change the document properties, as specified by your instructor. Save the presentation using the file name, Apply 2-1 Chemistry Lab Safety. Submit the revised document in the format specified by your instructor.

(c) Slide 3

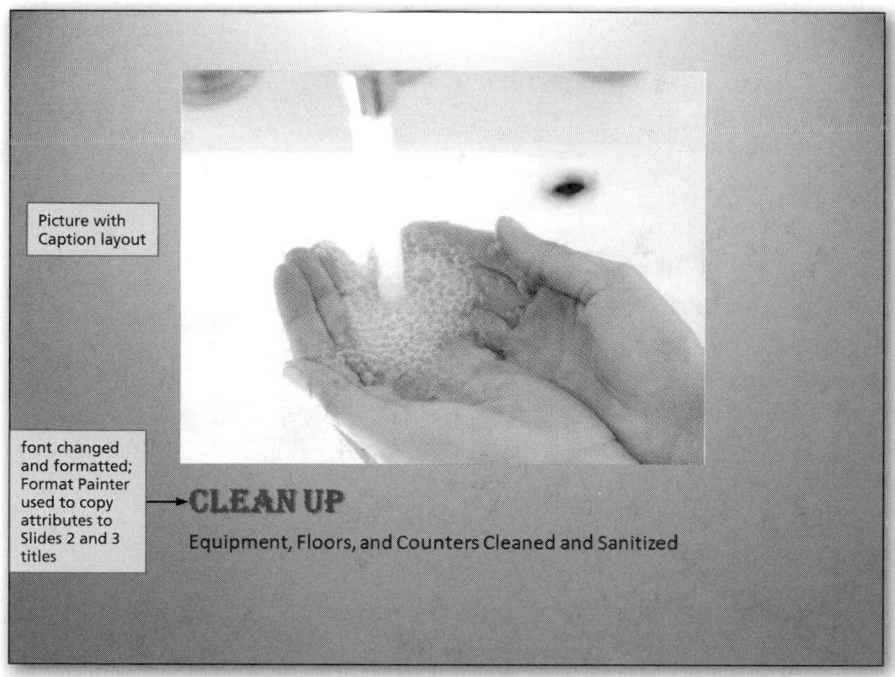

(d) Slide 4

Figure 2 – 74 (Continued)

Extend Your Knowledge

Extend the skills you learned in this chapter and experiment with new skills. You may need to use Help to complete the assignment.

Changing Slide Backgrounds and Picture Contrast, and Inserting Shapes and WordArt

Note: To complete this assignment, you will be required to use the Data Files for Students. See the inside back cover of this book for instructions on downloading the Data Files for Students, or contact your instructor for information about accessing the required files.

Instructions: Start PowerPoint. Open the presentation, Extend 2-1 Smith Family Reunion, from the Data Files for Students.

You will create backgrounds including inserting a picture to create a background, apply a WordArt Style and Effect, and add shapes to create the presentation shown in Figure 2–75.

Perform the following tasks:

1. Change the background style to Denim (row 1, column 3) and change the transparency to 48%. On Slides 2 through 5, change the title text to bold.

2. On the title slide (Figure 2–75a), create a background by inserting the picture called Tree, which is available on the Data Files for Students. Change the transparency to 40%.

3. Apply the WordArt style, Gradient Fill – Blue, Accent 1, to the title text and increase the font size to 66 point. Also, apply the WordArt Transform text effect, Arch Up (row 1, column 1 in the Follow Path area), to this text.

4. In the Slide 1 subtitle area, insert the Wave shape in the Stars and Banners area. Also, apply the Shape Style, Subtle Effect – Orange, Accent 6 to the Wave shape. Type **Highlights From Our Last Reunion** and increase the font size to 40 point, change the text to bold italic and change the color to Green. Position the shape as shown in Figure 2–75a.

(a) Slide 1

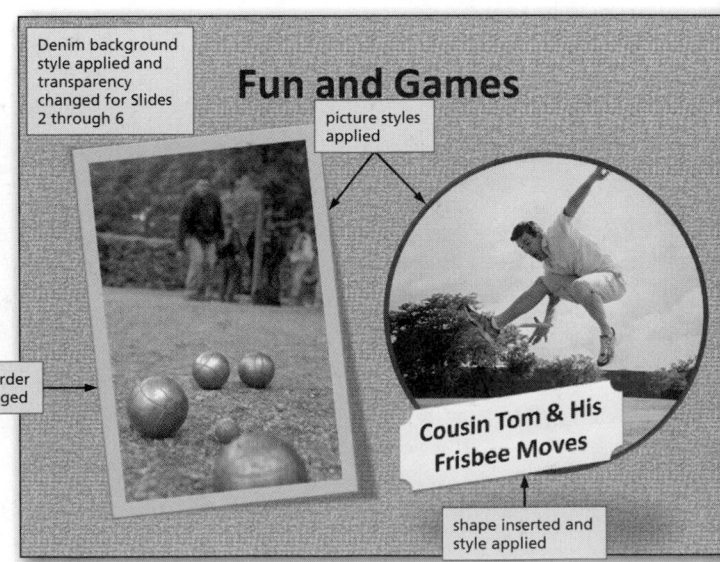

(b) Slide 2

Figure 2–75

5. On Slide 2, change the layout to Two Content and insert the pictures shown in Figure 2–75b. The pictures to be inserted are called Bocce Ball and Frisbee Catcher and are available on the Data Files for Students. In the left placeholder, apply the Rotated White picture style to the inserted picture and change the picture border to Light Green. In the right placeholder, apply the Beveled Oval Black picture style to the inserted picture.

6. Insert the Plaque shape in the Basic Shapes area. Also, apply the Shape Style, Subtle Effect, Olive Green, Accent 3 and apply the Shape Effect, 3-D Rotation, Parallel, Off Axis 1 Right. Type **Cousin Tom & His Frisbee Moves** and increase the font size to 28 point. Move the shape as shown in Figure 2–75b.

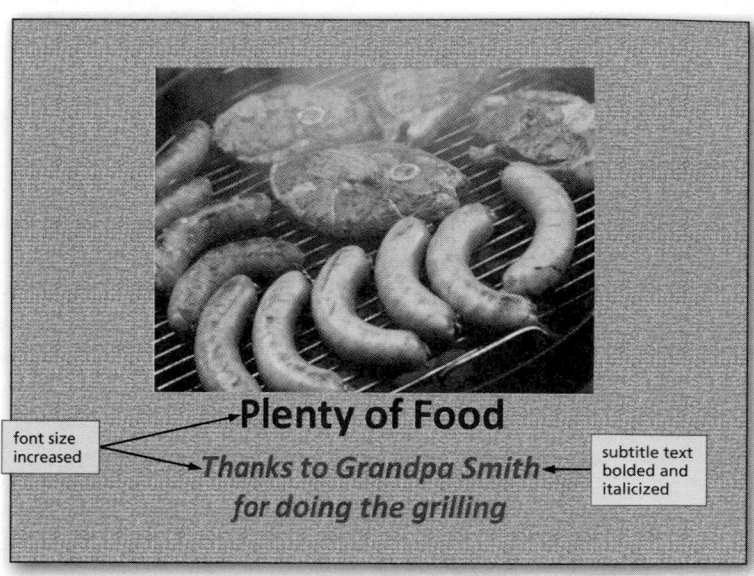

(c) Slide 3

7. On Slide 3, change the layout to Picture with Caption and insert the picture shown in Figure 2–75c. The picture to be inserted is called BBQ Grill. Increase the title font size to 44 point. Also, increase the subtitle font size to 32 point, and then bold and italicize this text.

8. On Slide 4, change the layout to Two Content and insert the pictures shown in Figure 2–75d. The pictures to be inserted are called Reunion Boys and Reunion Toddler. In the left placeholder, apply the Rotated, White picture effect to the picture. In the right placeholder, apply the Bevel Perspective picture effect. Move the pictures as shown in Figure 2–75d.

(d) Slide 4

Figure 2 – 75 (Continued)

Continued >

Extend Your Knowledge *continued*

9. On Slide 5, change the layout to Title and Content and insert the picture shown in Figure 2–75e. The picture to be inserted is called Reunion. Enlarge the picture as shown.

10. Insert the Oval Callout and Cloud Callout shapes in the Callouts area. In the Oval Callout shape, type **I hope Grandma makes cookies!** and change the font size to 24 point bold italic. Also add a Shape Style, Moderate Effect – Olive Green Accent 3 to this shape. In the Cloud Callout shape, type **I'm looking forward to our next reunion!** and change the font size to 24 point and the style to bold italic. Move the shapes as shown in Figure 2–75e. Use the adjustment handles (the yellow diamond below each shape) to move the callout arrows as shown in Figure 2–75e. You may need to use Help to learn how to move these arrows.

11. On Slide 6, change the layout to Picture with Caption and insert the picture shown in Figure 2–75f and change the picture contrast to +20. The picture to be inserted is called Reunion Tree.

(e) Slide 5

(f) Slide 6

Figure 2 – 75 (Continued)

12. Insert the Up Ribbon shape in the Stars and Banners area and type the words **Announcing Our Next Reunion**. Change the font color to Green, the font size to 32 point, and the style to bold italic. Also, apply the Shape Style, Subtle Effect – Orange Accent 6. In the title placeholder, type **Save the date – June 20, 2012** and change the font size to 28 point. Bold this text.

13. Add the Orbit transition under the Dynamic Content section to Slide 6 only. You may need to use Help to learn how to apply the transition to only one slide. Change the duration to 2.00 seconds.

14. Change the document properties, as specified by your instructor. Save the presentation using the file name, Extend 2-1 Smith Reunion.

15. Submit the revised document in the format specified by your instructor.

Make It Right

Analyze a presentation and correct all errors and/or improve the design.

Changing a Theme and Background Style

Note: To complete this assignment, you will be required to use the Data Files for Students. See the inside back cover of this book for instructions on downloading the Data Files for Students, or contact your instructor for information about accessing the required files.

Instructions: Start PowerPoint. Open the presentation, Make It Right 2-1 New Aerobics Classes, from the Data Files for Students.

   Correct the formatting problems and errors in the presentation while keeping in mind the guidelines presented in this chapter.

Perform the following tasks:

1. Change the document theme from Flow, shown in Figure 2–76, to Waveform. Apply the Background Style 10 (row 3, column 2) to Slide 5 only.

2. On the title slide, change the title from New Aerobics Classes to New Pool Programs. Type your name in place of Northlake Fitness Center and change the font to bold italic.

3. Move Slide 2 to the end of the presentation so that it becomes the new Slide 5.

4. Adjust the picture sizes, font sizes, and shapes so they do not overlap text and are the appropriate dimensions for the slide content.

5. Apply the Ripple transition to all slides. Change the duration to 02.00.

6. Change the document properties, as specified by your instructor. Save the presentation using the file name, Make It Right 2-1 New Pool Programs.

7. Submit the revised document in the format specified by your instructor.

Figure 2 – 76

In the Lab

Design and/or create a presentation using the guidelines, concepts, and skills presented in this chapter. Labs 1, 2, and 3 are listed in order of increasing difficulty.

Lab 1: Creating a Presentation Inserting Pictures and Applying Picture Styles

Problem: You are studying German operas in your Music Appreciation class. Wilhelm Richard Wagner (pronounced 'va:gner') lived from 1813 to 1883 and was a composer, conductor, theatre director, and essayist known for his operas. Wagner wrote and composed many operas, and King Ludwig II of Bavaria was one of his biggest supporters. Because you recently visited southern Germany and toured King Ludwig's castles, you decide to create a PowerPoint presentation with some of your photos to accompany your class presentation. These pictures are available on the Data Files for Students. Create the slides shown in Figure 2–77 from a blank presentation using the Office Theme document theme.

Note: To complete this assignment, you will be required to use the Data Files for Students. See the inside back cover of this book for instructions on downloading the Data Files for Students, or contact your instructor for information about accessing the required files.

Instructions: Perform the following tasks:
 1. On Slide 1, create a background by inserting the picture called Castle 1, which is available on the Data Files for Students.
 2. Type **Fairy Tale Trip to Germany** as the Slide 1 title text. Apply the WordArt style, Fill – Tan, Text 2, Outline – Background 2, and increase the font size to 60 point. Change the text fill to the Papyrus texture, and then change the text outline weight to 1½ pt. Also, apply the Transform text effect, Arch Up (in the Follow Path area), to this text. Position this WordArt as shown in Figure 2–77a.
 3. Type the title and content for the four text slides shown in Figure 2–77. Apply the Two Content layout to Slides 2 and 3 and the Picture with Caption layout to Slides 4 and 5.
 4. On Slide 2, insert the picture called Castle 2 from the Data Files for Students in the right placeholder. Apply the Bevel Perspective picture style. Resize the picture so that it is approximately 4.5" × 6", change the border color to Purple, change the border weight to 6 pt, and then move the picture, as shown in Figure 2–77b.
 5. On Slide 3, insert the picture called Castle 3 from the Data Files for Students. Apply the Reflected Bevel, Black picture style and then change the border color to Green. Do not change the border weight.
 6. On Slide 4, insert the picture called Castle 4 from the Data Files for Students. Apply the Beveled Oval, Black picture style, change the border color to Blue, and then change the border weight to 6 pt.
 7. On Slide 5, insert the picture called Castle 5 from the Data Files for Students. Apply the Moderate Frame, Black picture style, change the border color to Purple, and then change the border weight to 6 pt.
 8. For both Slides 4 and 5, increase the title text size to 28 point and the caption text size to 24 point.
 9. On Slide 2, change the title text font to Algerian, change the color to purple, and bold this text. Use the Format Painter to apply these formatting changes to the Slide 3 title text. In Slide 3, insert the Vertical Scroll shape located in the Stars and Banners area, apply the Subtle Effect – Purple, Accent 4 shape style, and change the shape outline weight to 3 pt. Type the text, **Inspiration for Disney's Sleeping Beauty Castle**, and then change the font to Curlz MT, or a similar font. Bold this text, change the color to Dark Blue, and then change the size to 28 point. Increase the scroll shape size, as shown in Figure 2–77c.
10. On Slides 2, 3, 4, and 5, change the background style to the White marble fill texture (row 2, column 5) and change the transparency to 35%. Apply the Glitter transition to all slides. Change the duration to 04.50.

11. Change the document properties, as specified by your instructor. Save the presentation using the file name, Lab 2-1 Trip to Germany.

12. Submit the revised document in the format specified by your instructor.

picture inserted as background

WordArt style, texture fill, and effect applied

(a) Slide 1

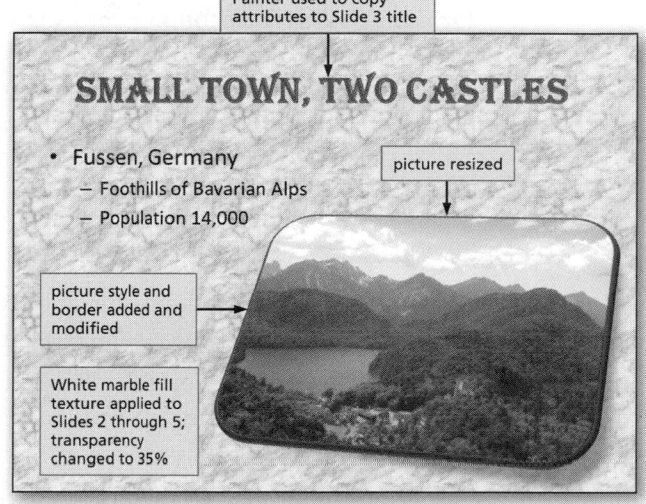

font changed and formatted; Format Painter used to copy attributes to Slide 3 title

picture resized

picture style and border added and modified

White marble fill texture applied to Slides 2 through 5; transparency changed to 35%

(b) Slide 2

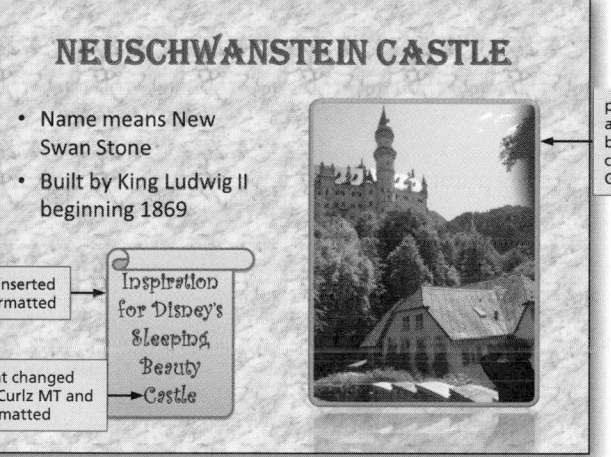

picture style applied and border color changed to Green

e inserted ormatted

ont changed o Curlz MT and ormatted

(c) Slide 3

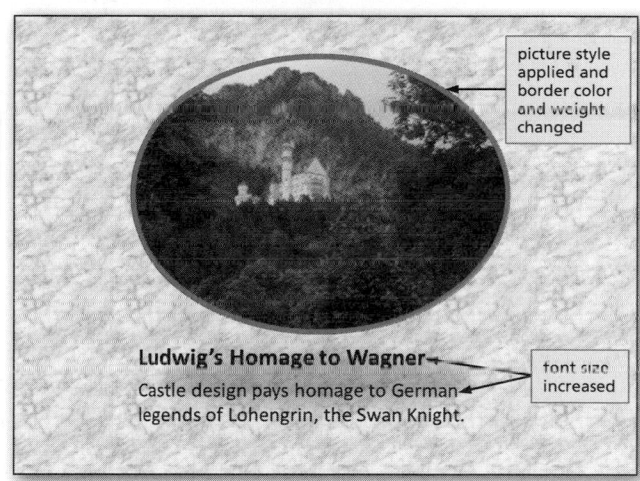

picture style applied and border color and weight changed

font size increased

(d) Slide 4

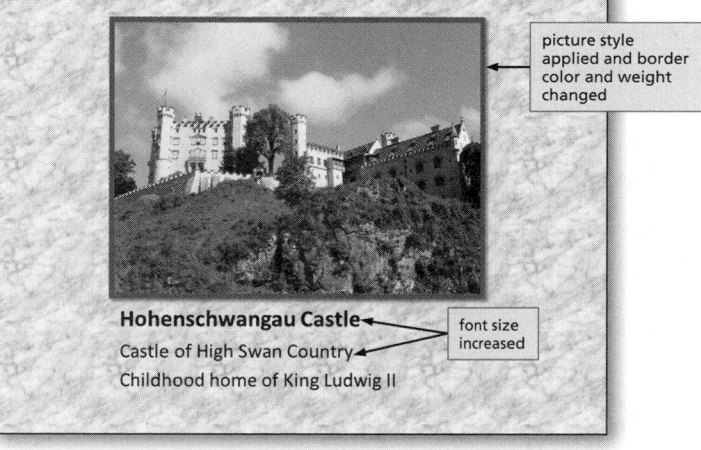

picture style applied and border color and weight changed

font size increased

(e) Slide 5

Figure 2 – 77

In the Lab

Lab 2: Creating a Presentation with a Shape and with WordArt

Problem: With the economy showing some improvement, many small businesses are approaching lending institutions for loans to expand their businesses. You work part-time for Loans Are Us, and your manager asked you to prepare a PowerPoint presentation for the upcoming Small Business Fair in your community. The pictures for this presentation are available on the Data Files for Students.

Note: To complete this assignment, you will be required to use the Data Files for Students. See the inside back cover of this book for instructions on downloading the Data Files for Students, or contact your instructor for information about accessing the required files.

Instructions: Perform the following tasks:

1. Create a new presentation using the Austin document theme.

2. Type the title and content for the title slide and the three text slides shown in Figure 2–78a–d. Apply the Title Only layout to Slide 2, the Two Content layout to Slide 3, and the Picture with Caption layout to Slide 4.

3. On both Slides 2 and 4, create a background by inserting the picture called Money. Change the transparency to 35%.

4. On Slide 1, insert the picture called Meeting. Apply the Reflected Bevel, White picture style. Resize the picture so that it is approximately 3.76" × 4.7", change the border color to Dark Blue, change the border weight to 3 pt, and then move the picture, as shown in Figure 2–78a. Increase the title text font size to 60 point, and then apply the WordArt style, Fill – Orange, Accent 6, Warm Matte Bevel.

5. Increase the subtitle text, Loans Are Us, font size to 28 point and then bold and italicize this text. Apply the WordArt style, Fill – Green, Accent 1, Metal Bevel, Reflection.

6. On Slide 2, bold the title text. Insert the pictures called Doc1, Doc2, and Doc3. Resize these pictures so they are approximately 3" × 2.7" and then move them to the locations shown in Figure 2–78b. Insert the Flowchart: Decision shape located in the Flowchart area, apply the Subtle Effect – Orange, Accent 6 shape style, and then resize the shape so that it is approximately 1.5" × 5.83". Change the shape outline weight to 6 pt. Type **Assets, Liabilities & Sales Reports** as the shape text, change the font to Aharoni, or a similar font, change the color to Dark Blue, and then change the size to 24 point.

7. On Slide 3, bold the title text. Insert the picture called Presentation into the right placeholder, apply the Beveled Oval, Black shape picture style, resize the picture so that it is approximately 3.5" × 5.25", and then sharpen the picture 50%.

8. On Slide 4, insert the picture called Cash and Credit Card. Change the title text font size to 36 point and bold this text. Change the subtitle text font size to 24 point and then bold and italicize these words.

9. Apply the Shape transition to all slides. Change the duration to 01.25.

10. Change the document properties, as specified by your instructor. Save the presentation using the file name, Lab 2-2 Small Business Loans.

11. Submit the document in the format specified by your instructor.

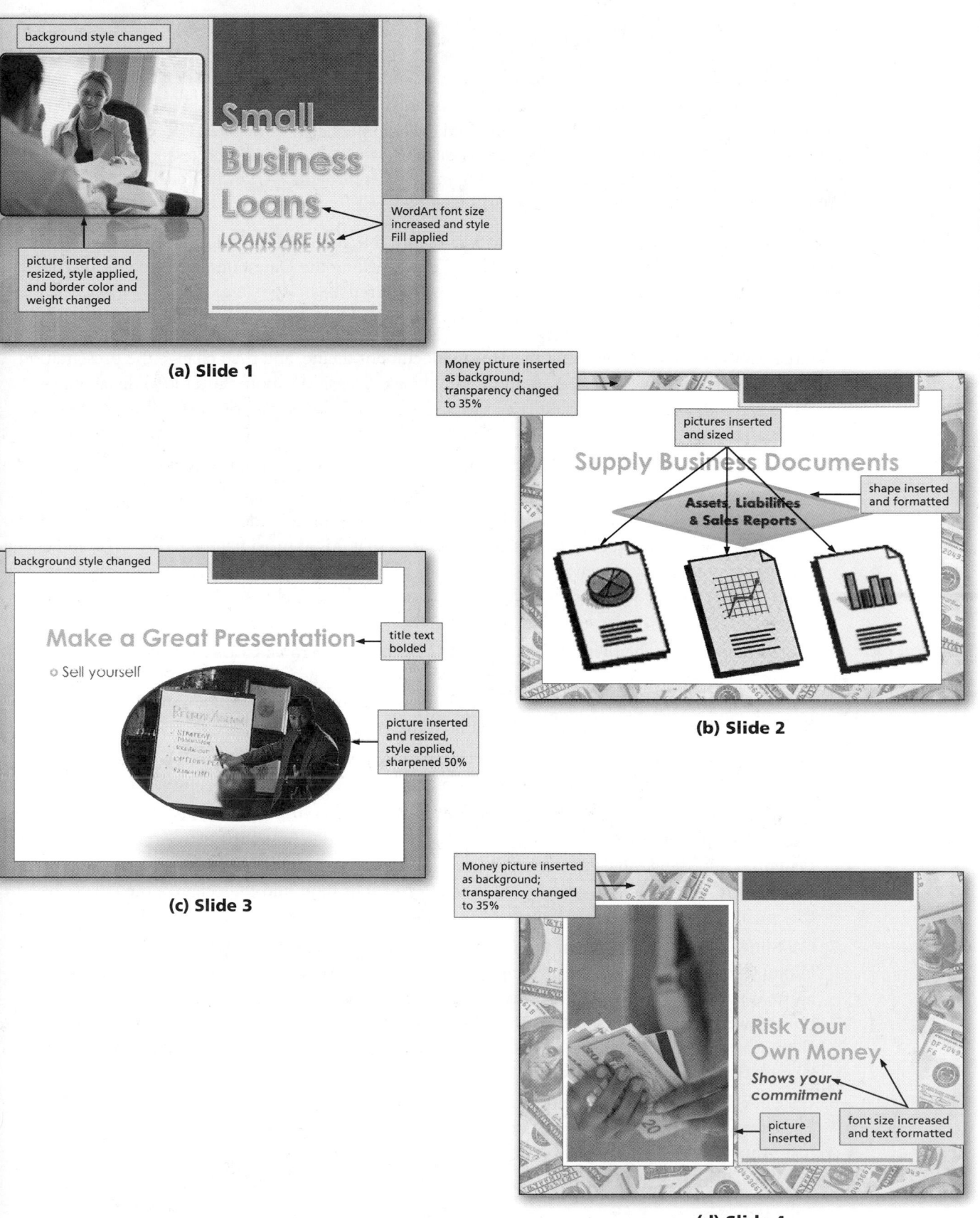

(a) Slide 1

(b) Slide 2

(c) Slide 3

(d) Slide 4

Figure 2–78

In the Lab

Lab 3: Creating a Presentation with Pictures and Shapes

Problem: One of your assignments in your child development class is to give a speech about teaching children the value of money, so you decide to create a PowerPoint presentation to add a little interest to your speech. Prepare the slides shown in Figures 2–79a through 2–79e. The pictures for this presentation are available on the Data Files for Students.

Note: To complete this assignment, you will be required to use the Data Files for Students. See the inside back cover of this book for instructions on downloading the Data Files for Students, or contact your instructor for information about accessing the required files.

Instructions: Perform the following tasks:

1. Create a new presentation using the Median document theme, and then change the presentation theme colors to Flow. This presentation should have five slides; apply the Title Slide layout to Slide 1, the Picture with Caption layout to Slides 2 and 5, the Comparison layout to Slide 3, and the Blank layout to Slide 4.

2. Type the title and content text for the title slide and the four text slides shown in Figure 2–79a–d.

3. On Slide 1, change the title text font size to 54 point. To make the letter 's' appear smaller than the other letters in the first word of the title slide title text placeholder, change the font size of this letter to 44 point. Insert the Oval shape, resize it so that it is approximately 0.5" × 0.5", and change the shape fill to white, which is the second color in the first row of the Theme Colors gallery. Type $, increase the font size to 48 point, change the color to green, and bold this dollar sign. Cover the letter 'o' in the word, Do, with this shape.

4. Insert the picture called Piggy Bank. Apply the Rounded Diagonal Corner, White picture style. Resize the picture so that it is approximately 4.4" × 5.03", change the border color to Light Blue, change the border weight to 3 pt, and then move the picture, as shown in Figure 2–79a. Change the subtitle font size to 32 point and then bold this text.

5. On Slide 2, insert the picture called Child Doing Dishes and then decrease the picture's contrast to −20%. Change the title text size to 36 point and bold this text. Change the caption text size to 32 point.

6. On Slide 3, change the background style to Style 6. Bold the title text. Change the heading title text size in both placeholders to 32 point. In the right placeholder, insert the picture called Father and Daughter and then apply the Reflected Bevel, White picture style. Resize the picture so that it is approximately 3" × 4", change the border color to Light Blue, and then change the border weight to 3 pt, as shown in Figure 2–79c.

7. On Slide 4, create a background by inserting the picture called Piggy Bank and Coins. Insert the Cloud shape located in the Basic Shapes area and then increase the cloud shape size so that it is approximately 3" × 5.6". Change the shape outline color to Yellow and then change the shape outline weight to 3 pt. Type **Teach your children to save for a big purchase.** as the shape text, and then change the font to Comic Sans MS. Bold and italicize this text and then change the font size to 32 point.

8. On Slide 5, create a background by inserting the picture called Coins. Insert the picture called Father and Child Shopping and then decrease the picture's brightness to −20%. Change the title text font size to 36 point and bold this text.

9. Apply the Box transition to all slides. Change the duration to 02.00. Check the spelling and correct any errors.

10. Change the document properties, as specified by your instructor. Save the presentation using the file name, Lab 2-3 ABCs of Money.

11. Submit the revised document in the format specified by your instructor.

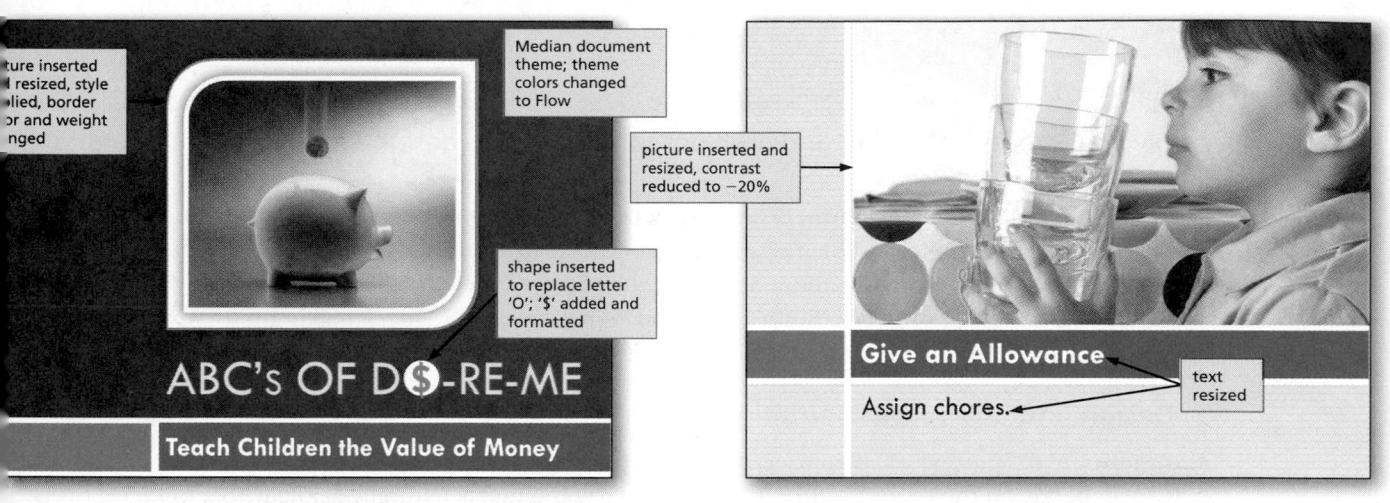

(a) Slide 1   (b) Slide 2

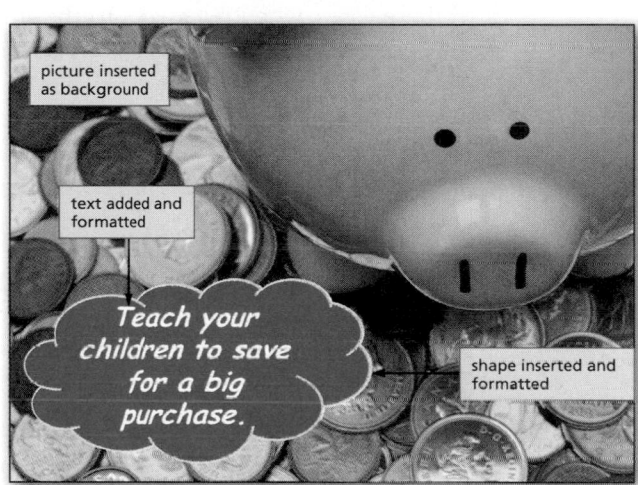

(c) Slide 3   (d) Slide 4

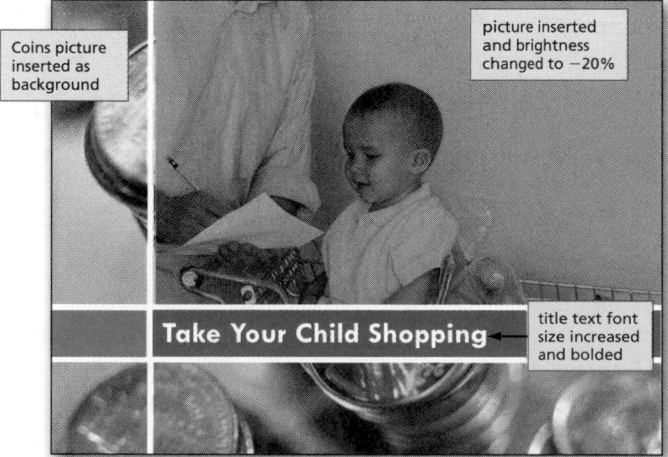

(e) Slide 5

Figure 2–79

Cases and Places

Apply your creative thinking and problem-solving skills to design and implement a solution.

Note: To complete these assignments, you may be required to use the Data Files for Students. See the inside back cover of this book for instructions on downloading the Data Files for Students, or contact your instructor for information about accessing the required files.

As you design the presentations, remember to use the 7 × 7 rule: a maximum of seven words on a line and a maximum of seven lines on one slide.

1: Design and Create a Presentation about Acid Rain

Academic

Nature depends on the correct pH balance. Although some rain is naturally acidic with a pH level of around 5.0, human activities have increased the amount of acid in this water. Burning fossil fuels, including coal, oil, and natural gas, produces sulfur dioxide. Exhaust from vehicles releases nitrogen oxides. Both of these gases, when released into the atmosphere, mix with water droplets, forming acid rain. In your science class, you are studying about the causes and effects of acid rain. Create a presentation to show what causes acid rain and what effects it can have on humans, animals, plant life, lakes, and rivers. The presentation should contain at least three pictures appropriately resized. The Data Files for Students contains five pictures called Factory, Rain, Soil, Tree and Clouds, and Vehicles; you can use your own digital pictures or pictures from Office.com if they are appropriate for this topic. These pictures also should have appropriate styles and border colors. Use shapes such as arrows to show what gases are released into the atmosphere. Apply at least three objectives found at the beginning of this chapter to develop the presentation. Add a title slide with a shape and a closing slide. Be sure to check spelling.

2: Design and Create a Presentation about Tutoring

Personal

You have been helping some of your classmates with their schoolwork, and you have decided that you should start a small tutoring business. In the student center, there is a kiosk where students can find out about programs and activities on campus. The student center manager gave you permission to submit a short PowerPoint presentation promoting your tutoring business; this presentation will be added to the kiosk. The presentation should contain pictures appropriately resized. The Data Files for Students contains four pictures called Tutoring 1, Tutoring 2, Tutoring 3, and Tutoring 4, or you can use your own digital pictures or pictures from Office.com if they are appropriate for this topic. Change the contrast and brightness for at least one picture. Insert shapes and WordArt to enhance your presentation. Apply a transition in the Subtle area to all slides and increase the duration. Be sure to check spelling.

3: Design and Create a Presentation on Setting Up Children's Fish Tanks

Professional

Fish make great pets for young children, but there is a lot to learn before they can set up a fish tank properly. The owner of the pet store where you work has asked you to create a presentation for the store to give parents an idea of what they need to purchase and consider when setting up a fish tank. He would like you to cover the main points such as the appropriate size bowl or tank, setup procedures, filtration, water quality, types of fish, care, and feeding. The presentation should contain pictures appropriately resized. The Data Files for Students contains five pictures called Fish 1, Fish 2, Fish 3, Fish 4, and Fish 5, or you can use your own digital pictures or pictures from Office.com if they are appropriate for this topic. Add a title slide and closing slide to complete your presentation. Format the title slide with a shape and change the theme color scheme. Change the title text font on the title slide. Format the background with at least one picture and apply a background texture to at least one slide. This presentation is geared to parents of young children, so keep it colorful, simple, and fun.

3 | Reusing a Presentation and Adding Media

Objectives

You will have mastered the material in this chapter when you can:

- Color a picture
- Add an artistic effect to a picture
- Delete and move placeholders
- Align paragraph text
- Copy a slide element from one slide to another

- Ungroup, change the color, and regroup a clip
- Insert and edit a video clip
- Insert audio
- Control audio and video clips
- Check for spelling errors
- Print a presentation as a handout

3 | Reusing a Presentation and Adding Media

Introduction

At times, you will need to revise a PowerPoint presentation. Changes may include inserting and adding effects to pictures, altering the colors of clips and pictures, and updating visual elements displayed on a slide. Applying a different theme, changing fonts, and substituting graphical elements can give a slide show an entirely new look. Adding media, including sounds, video, and music, can enhance a presentation and help audience members retain the information being presented.

Project — Presentation with Video, Audio, and Pictures with Effects

The project in this chapter follows graphical guidelines and uses PowerPoint to create the presentation shown in Figure 3–1. The slides in this revised presentation, which discusses Bird Migration, have a variety of audio and visual elements. For example, the pictures have artistic effects applied that soften the pictures and help the audience focus on other elements on the slides. The bird clip has colors that blend well with the background. The video has been edited to play only the portion with Bird Migration and has effects to add audience interest. Bird calls integrate with the visual elements. Overall, the slides have myriad media elements and effects that are exciting for your audience to watch and hear.

Overview

As you read through this chapter, you will learn how to create the presentation shown in Figure 3–1 by performing these general tasks:

- Format pictures by recoloring and adding artistic effects.
- Insert and format video and audio clips.
- Modify clip art.
- Vary paragraph alignment.
- Check a presentation for spelling errors.
- Print a handout of your slides.

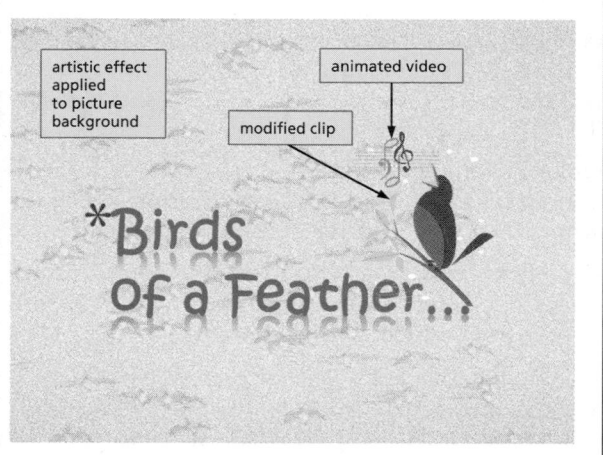

(a) Slide 1 (Title Slide with Picture Background, Modified Clip, and Animated Clip)

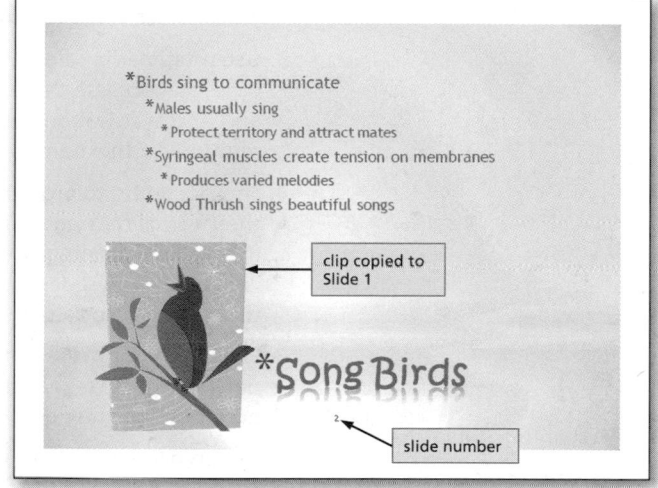

(b) Slide 2 (Bulleted List)

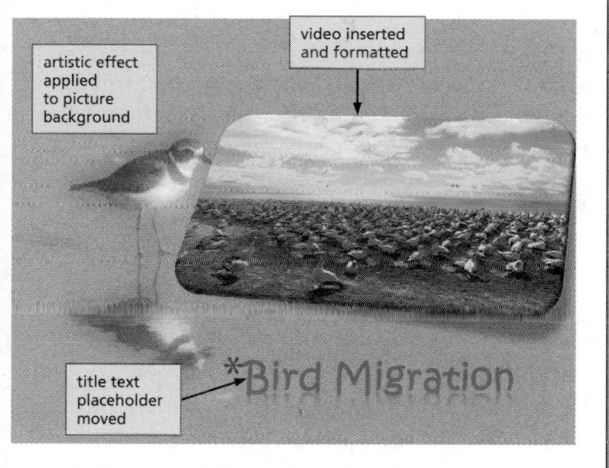

(c) Slide 3 (Picture Background and Video Clip)

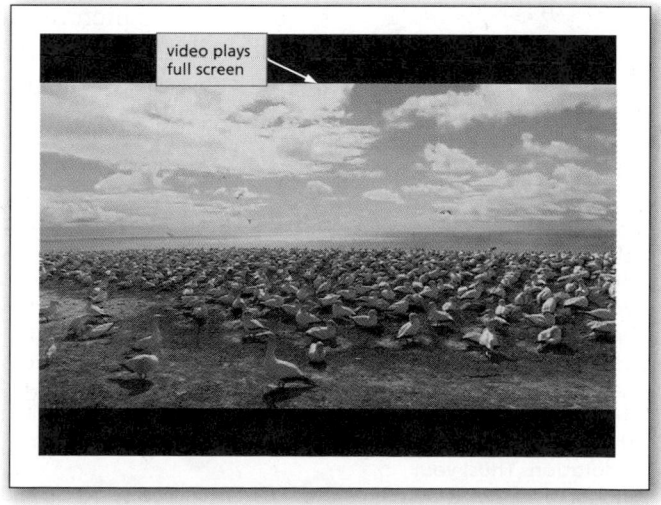

(d) Slide 4 (Video Playing Full Screen)

Figure 3–1

Plan Ahead

General Project Guidelines

When creating a PowerPoint presentation, the actions you perform and the decisions you make will affect the appearance and characteristics of the finished document. As you create a presentation with illustrations, such as the project shown in Figure 3–1, you should follow these general guidelines:

1. **Use the color wheel to determine color choices.** Warm colors and cool colors evoke opposite effects on audience members. As you make decisions to color pictures, consider the emotions you want to generate and choose colors that match these sentiments.

2. **Vary paragraph alignment.** Different effects are achieved when text alignment shifts in a presentation. Themes dictate whether paragraph text is aligned left, center, or right in a placeholder, but you can modify these design decisions when necessary.

3. **Use multimedia selectively.** Video, music, and sound files can add interest to your presentation. Use these files only when necessary, however, because they draw the audience's attention away from the presenter and toward the slides. Using too many multimedia files can be overwhelming.

4. **Use handouts to organize your speech.** Effective speakers take much time to prepare their verbal message that will accompany each slide. They practice their speeches and decide how to integrate the material displayed. Viewing the thumbnails, or miniature versions of the slides, will help you associate the slide image with the script. These thumbnails also can be cut out and arranged when organizing the presentation.

5. **Evaluate your presentation.** As soon as you finish your presentation, critique your performance. You will improve your communication skills by eliminating the flaws and accentuating the positives.

When necessary, more specific details concerning the above guidelines are presented at appropriate points in the chapter. The chapter also will identify the actions performed and decisions made regarding these guidelines during the creation of the presentation shown in Figure 3–1.

For an introduction to Windows 7 and instruction about how to perform basic Windows 7 tasks, read the Office 2010 and Windows 7 chapter at the beginning of this book, where you can learn how to resize windows, change screen resolution, create folders, move and rename files, use Windows Help, and much more.

Starting PowerPoint

Chapter 1 introduced you to starting PowerPoint, selecting a document theme, creating slides with clip art and a bulleted list, and printing a presentation. Chapter 2 enhanced slides by adding pictures, shapes, and WordArt. The following steps, which assume Windows 7 is running, start PowerPoint and open the Birds presentation. For a detailed example of the procedure summarized below, refer to the Office 2010 and Windows 7 chapter at the beginning of this book.

BTW

The Ribbon and Screen Resolution
PowerPoint may change how the groups and buttons within the groups appear on the Ribbon, depending on the computer's screen resolution. Thus, your Ribbon may look different from the ones in this book if you are using a screen resolution other than 1024 × 768.

To Start PowerPoint and Open and Save a Presentation

1 Click the Start button on the Windows 7 taskbar to display the Start menu, type **Microsoft PowerPoint** as the search text in the 'Search programs and files' text box, and then click Microsoft PowerPoint 2010 in the search results on the Start menu to start PowerPoint and display a new blank document.

2 If the PowerPoint window is not maximized, click the Maximize button.

3 Open the presentation, Birds, from the Data Files for Students. See the inside back cover of this book for instructions on downloading the Data Files for Students, or contact your instructor for more information on accessing the required files.

4 Save the presentation using the file name, Bird Migration.

Inserting Pictures and Adding Effects

The Bird Migration presentation consists of four slides that have some text, a clip art image, a formatted background, and a transition applied to all slides. You will insert pictures into two slides and then modify them by adding artistic effects and recoloring. You also will copy the clip art from Slide 2 to Slide 1 and modify the objects in this clip. In Chapter 2, you inserted pictures, made corrections, and added styles and effects; the new effects you apply in this chapter will add to your repertoire of picture enhancements that increase interest in your presentation.

In the following pages, you will perform these tasks:

1. Insert the first digital picture into Slide 1.
2. Insert the second digital picture into Slide 3.
3. Recolor the Slide 3 picture.
4. Recolor and add an artistic effect to the Slide 1 picture.
5. Add an artistic effect to the Slide 3 picture.
6. Send the Slide 3 picture back behind all other slide objects.
7. Send the Slide 1 picture back behind all other slide objects.

For an introduction to Office 2010 and instruction about how to perform basic tasks in Office 2010 programs, read the Office 2010 and Windows 7 chapter at the beginning of this book, where you can learn how to start a program, use the Ribbon, save a file, open a file, quit a program, use Help, and much more.

To Insert and Resize Pictures into Slides without Content Placeholders

The next step is to insert digital pictures into Slides 1 and 3. These pictures are available on the Data Files for Students. See the inside back cover of this book for instructions on downloading the Data Files for Students, or contact your instructor for information about accessing the required files.

The following steps insert pictures into Slides 1 and 3.

1 With Slide 1 displaying and your USB flash drive connected to one of the computer's USB ports, click Insert on the Ribbon to display the Insert tab and then click the Picture button (Insert tab | Images group) to display the Insert Picture dialog box.

2 If necessary, navigate to the picture location (in this case, the PowerPoint folder in the CIS 101 folder [or your class folder] on the USB flash drive). For a detailed example of this procedure, refer to Steps 3a–3c on pages OFF 28 and OFF 29 in the Office 2010 and Windows 7 chapter at the beginning of this book.

3 Click Birds in Sky to select the file.

4 Click the Insert button (Insert Picture dialog box) to insert the picture into Slide 1.

5 Resize the picture so that it covers the entire slide (approximately 7.5" × 10").

6 Display Slide 3, display the Insert tab, click the Picture button to display the Insert Picture dialog box, and then insert the Bird Reflect picture into Slide 3.

7 Resize the picture so that it covers the entire slide (approximately 7.5" × 10") (Figure 3–2).

How do I resize the picture so that it maintains its proportions?
Press and hold the SHIFT key while dragging a sizing handle away from or toward the center of the picture. To maintain the picture's proportions and keep its center in the same location, press and hold down both the CTRL and SHIFT keys while you drag a sizing handle.

BTW

Inserting Text Boxes
If you want to add text in an area of the slide where a content placeholder is not located, you can insert a text box. This object allows you to emphasize or set off text that you consider important for your audience to read. To create a text box, click the Text Box button (Insert tab | Text group), click the slide, and then drag this object to the desired location on the slide. Click inside the text box to add or paste text. You also can change the look and style of the text box characters by using formatting features (Home tab | Font group).

Figure 3–2

Plan Ahead

Use the color wheel to determine color choices.

The color wheel is one of designers' basic tools. Twelve colors on the wheel are arranged in a specific order, with the three primary colors — red, yellow, and blue — forming a triangle. Between the primary colors are the secondary colors that are formed when the primary colors are mixed. For example, red and yellow mixed together form orange; red and blue form purple; and yellow and blue form green. The six other colors on the wheel are formed when the primary colors are mixed with the secondary colors.

Red, orange, and yellow are considered warm colors, and they display adjacent to each other on one side of the wheel. They are bold and lively, so you should use them when your message is intended to invigorate an audience and create a pleasing effect. Opposite the warm colors are the cool colors: green, blue, and purple. They generate a relaxing, calming atmosphere.

If you put a primary and secondary color together, such as red and purple, your slide will make a very bold and vivid statement. Be certain that effect is one you intend when planning your message.

Adjusting Picture Colors

BTW

Q&As
For a complete list of the Q&As found in many of the step-by-step sequences in this book, visit the PowerPoint 2010 Q&A Web page (scsite.com/ppt2010/qa).

PowerPoint allows you to adjust colors to match or add contrast to slide elements by coloring pictures. The Color Picture gallery has a wide variety of preset formatting combinations. The thumbnails in the gallery display the more common color saturation, color tone, and recolor adjustments. **Color saturation** changes the intensity of colors. High saturation produces vivid colors; low saturation produces gray tones. **Color tone** affects the coolness, called blue, or the warmness, called orange, of pictures. When a digital camera does not measure the tone correctly, a **color cast** occurs, and, as a result, one color dominates the picture. **Recolor** effects convert the picture into a wide variety of hues. The more common are **grayscale**, which changes the color picture into black, white, and shades of gray, and **sepia**, which changes the picture colors into brown, gold, and yellow, reminiscent of a faded photo. You also can fine-tune the color adjustments by clicking Picture Color Options and More Variations commands in the Color gallery.

To Color a Picture

The Slipstream theme and text on Slides 1 and 3 have many shades of blue. The inserted pictures, in addition, have blue backgrounds. The following steps recolor the Slide 3 picture to coordinate with the blue colors on the slide.

1

• With Slide 3 displaying and the Bird Reflect picture selected, click the Color button (Picture Tools Format tab | Adjust group) to display the Color gallery (Figure 3–3).

Why does the Adjust group look different on my screen?

Your monitor is set to a different resolution. See Chapter 1 for an explanation of screen resolution and the appearance of the Ribbon.

Why are yellow borders surrounding the thumbnails in the Color Saturation and Color Tone areas in the gallery?

The image on Slide 3 currently has normal color saturation and a normal color tone.

Figure 3–3

2

• Point to Blue, Accent color 1 Light (second picture in last row of Recolor area) to display a live preview of this adjustment on the picture.

🔎 **Experiment**

• Point to various thumbnails in the Recolor area and watch the hues change on the picture in Slide 3.

• Click Blue, Accent color 1 Light to apply this correction to the Bird Reflect picture (Figure 3–4).

Could I have applied this correction to the picture if it had been a background instead of a file inserted into the slide?

No. Artistic effects cannot be applied to backgrounds.

Figure 3–4

To Color a Second Picture

The Slide 1 picture has rich hues and is very prominent on the slide. To soften its appearance and to provide continuity with the Slide 3 picture, you can color this picture. The following steps color the picture on the title slide.

1 Display Slide 1 and then click the picture to select it. Click the Color button (Picture Tools Format tab | Adjust group) to display the Color gallery.

2 Click Washout (fourth picture in first row of Recolor area) to apply this correction to the Bird Reflect picture (Figure 3–5).

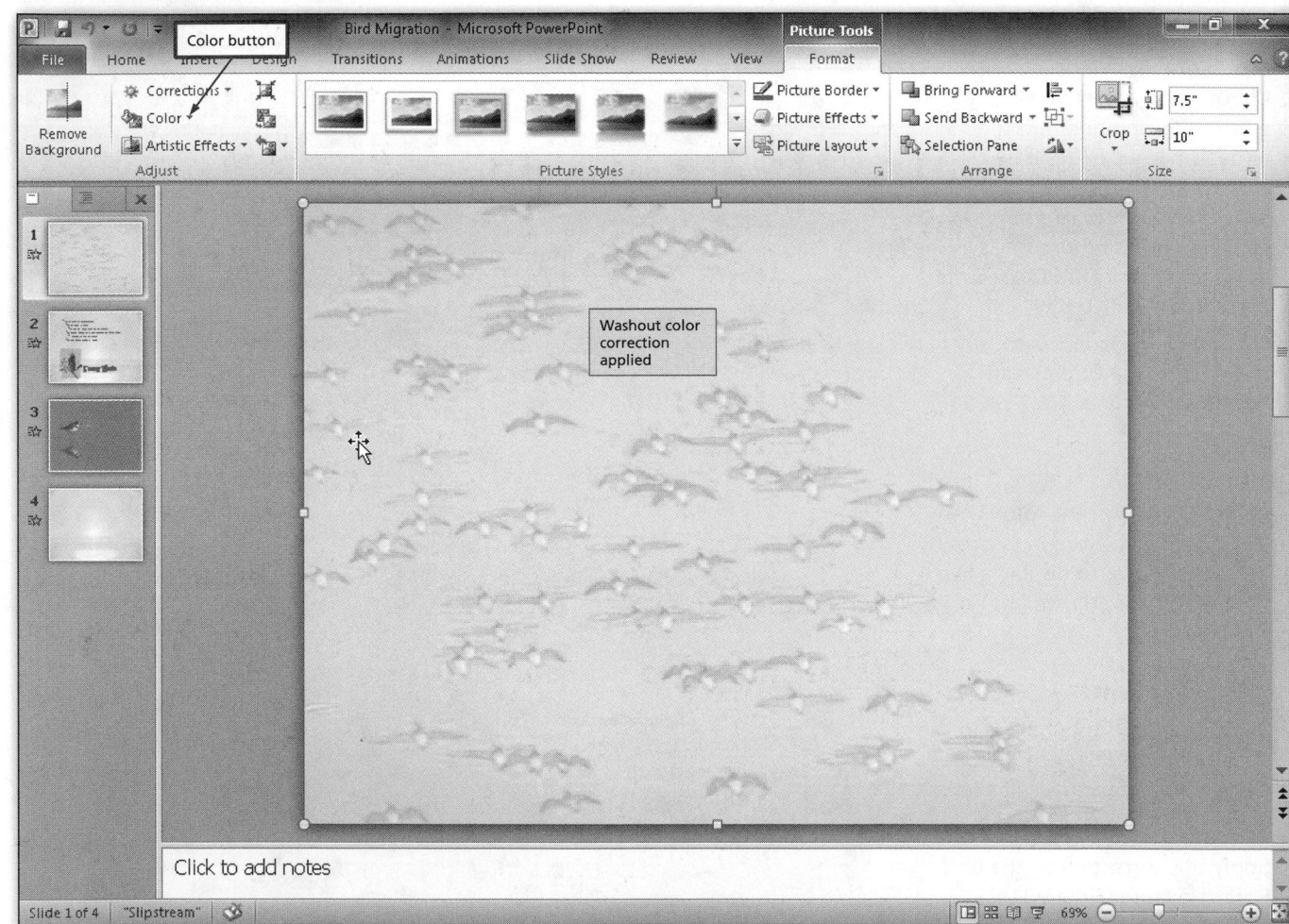

Figure 3–5

To Add an Artistic Effect to a Picture

Artists use a variety of techniques to create effects in their paintings. For example, they can vary the amount of paint on their brushstroke, use fine bristles to add details, mix colors to increase or decrease intensity, and smooth their paints together to blend the colors. You, likewise, can add similar effects to your pictures using PowerPoint's built-in artistic effects. The following steps add an artistic effect to the Slide 3 picture.

• With the Birds in Sky picture selected in Slide 1, click the Artistic Effects button (Picture Tools Format tab | Adjust group) to display the Artistic Effects gallery (Figure 3–6).

Why does the Adjust group look different on my screen?

Your monitor is set to a different resolution. See Chapter 1 for an explanation of screen resolution and the appearance of the Ribbon.

Why is a yellow border surrounding the first thumbnail in the gallery?

The first thumbnail shows a preview of the image on Slide 1 with no artistic effect applied.

Figure 3–6

• Point to Film Grain (third picture in third row) to display a live preview of this adjustment on the picture.

🔎 **Experiment**

• Point to various thumbnails and watch the hues change on the picture in Slide 1.

• Click Film Grain to apply this correction to the Birds in Sky picture (Figure 3–7).

Must I adjust a picture by recoloring and applying an artistic effect?

No. You can apply either a color or an effect. You may prefer at times to mix these adjustments to create a unique image.

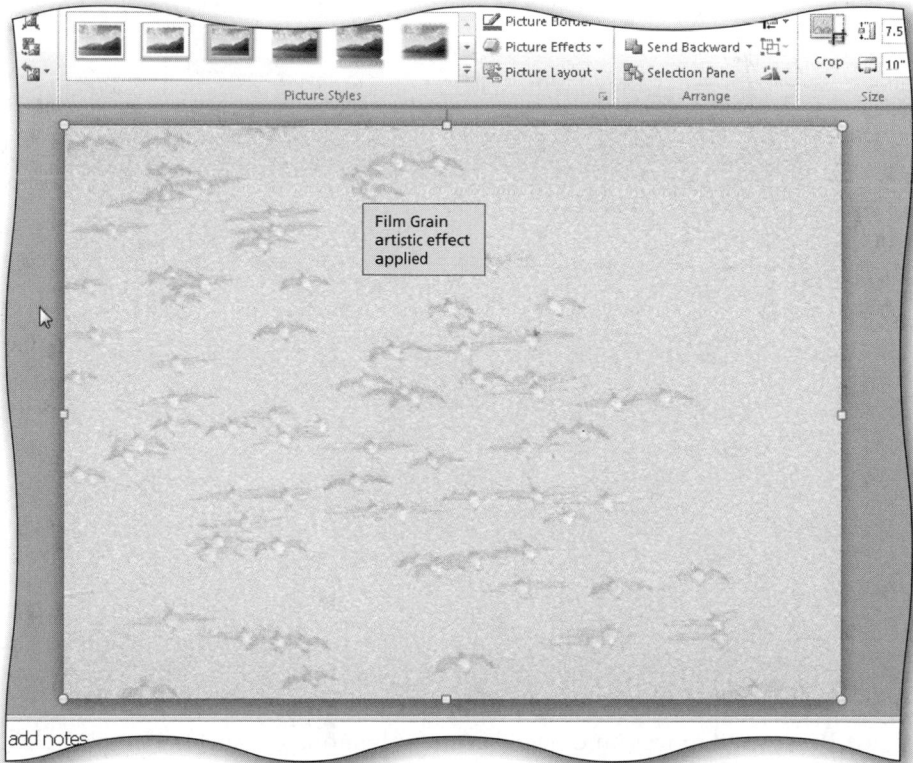

Figure 3–7

To Add an Artistic Effect to a Second Picture

The Slide 3 picture was softened when you applied a blue accent color. You can further change the images and provide continuity with the Slide 1 picture by applying an artistic effect. The following steps add an artistic effect to the Slide 3 picture.

1 Display Slide 3 and then click the picture to select it. If necessary, click the Picture Tools Format tab and then click the Artistic Effects button (Picture Tools Format tab | Adjust group) to display the Artistic Effects gallery.

2 Click Glow Diffused (fourth picture in second row) to apply this effect to the Bird Reflect picture (Figure 3–8).

Figure 3–8

To Change the Stacking Order

The objects on a slide stack on top of each other, much like individual cards in a deck. On Slides 1 and 3, the pictures you inserted are on top of text placeholders. To change the order of these objects, you use the Bring Forward and Send Backward commands. **Bring Forward** moves an object toward the top of the stack, and **Send Backward** moves an object underneath another object. When you click the Bring Forward button arrow, PowerPoint displays a menu with an additional command, **Bring to Front**, which moves a selected object to the top of the stack. Likewise, when you click the Send Backward button arrow, the **Send to Back** button moves the selected object underneath all objects on the slide. The following steps arrange the Slide 3 and Slide 1 pictures by sending them to the bottom of the stack on each slide.

● With the Bird Reflect picture selected in Slide 3, click the Send Backward button arrow (Picture Tools Format tab | Arrange group) to display the Send Backward menu (Figure 3–9).

How can I see objects that are not on the top of the stack?

Press TAB or SHIFT+TAB to display each slide object.

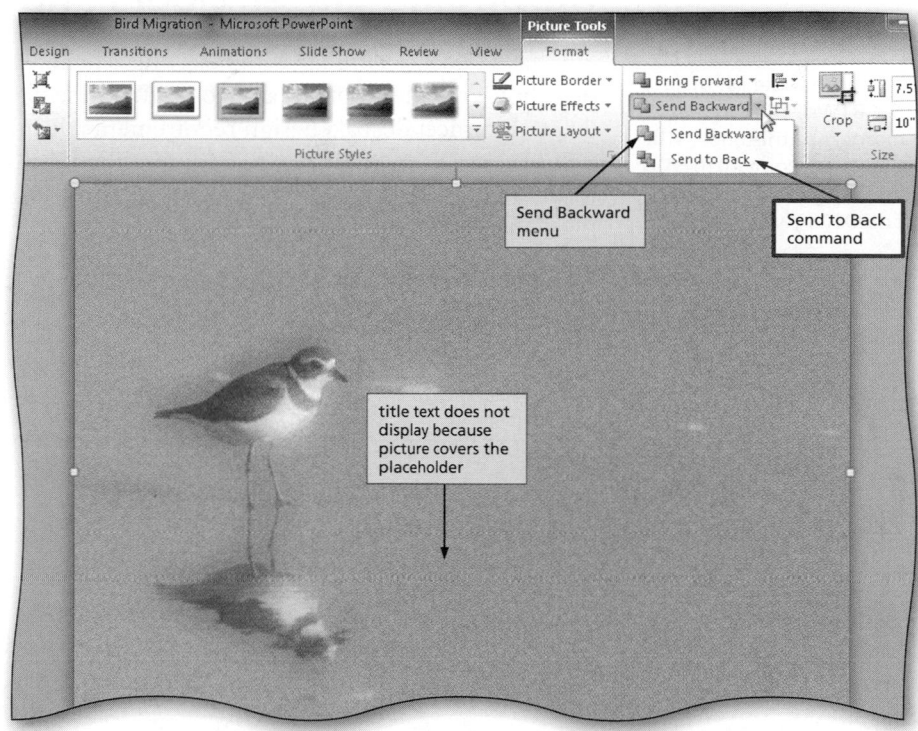

Figure 3–9

● Click Send to Back to move the picture underneath all slide objects (Figure 3–10).

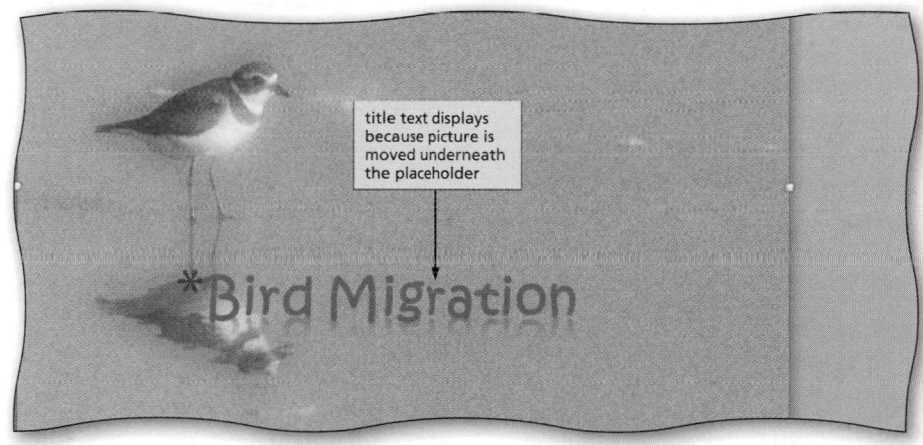

Figure 3–10

● Display Slide 1, select the Birds in Sky picture, and then click the Send Backward button arrow (Picture Tools Format tab | Arrange group).

● Click Send to Back to move the picture underneath all slide objects (Figure 3–11).

Figure 3–11

Other Ways

1. Click Send to Back (Picture Tools Format tab | Arrange group), press K

2. Point to Send to Back on shortcut menu, click Send to Back

Modifying Placeholders and Deleting a Slide

BTW

BTWs
For a complete list of the BTWs found in the margins of this book, visit the PowerPoint 2010 BTW Web page (scsite.com/ppt2010/btw).

You have become familiar with inserting text and graphical content in the three types of placeholders: title, subtitle, and content. These placeholders can be moved, resized, and deleted to meet desired design requirements. In addition, placeholders can be added to a slide when needed. After you have modified the placeholder locations, you can view thumbnails of all your slides simultaneously by changing views.

In the following pages, you will perform these tasks:

1. Resize and move the Slide 1 title text placeholder.
2. Delete the Slide 1 subtitle text placeholder.
3. Align the Slide 1 and Slide 3 paragraph text.
4. Delete Slide 4.
5. Change views.

To Resize a Placeholder

The AutoFit button displays on the left side of the Slide 1 title text placeholder because the two lines of text exceed the placeholder's borders. PowerPoint attempts to reduce the font size when the text does not fit, and you can click this button to resize the existing text in the placeholder so the spillover text will fit within the borders. You also can resize the placeholder so that the letters fit within the rectangle. The following step increases the Slide 1 title text placeholder.

- With Slide 1 displaying, click somewhere in the title text paragraph to position the insertion point in the paragraph. Click the border of the title text placeholder to select it. Point to the bottom-middle sizing handle so that the mouse pointer changes to a two-headed arrow.

- Drag the bottom border downward to enlarge the text placeholder (Figure 3–12).

Q&A Can I drag other sizing handles to enlarge or shrink the placeholder?

Yes, you also can drag the left, right, top, and corner sizing handles to resize a placeholder.

Q&A How do the square sizing handles differ from circle sizing handles?

Dragging a square handle alters the shape of the text box so that it is wider or taller. Dragging a circle handle keeps the box in the same proportion and simply enlarges the overall shape.

Figure 3–12

To Move a Placeholder

The theme layouts determine where the text and content placeholders display on the slide. If you desire to have a placeholder appear in a different area of the slide, you can move it to a new location. The Slide 1 title text placeholder currently displays in the upper third of the slide, but the text in this placeholder would be more aesthetically pleasing if it were moved toward the center of the slide. The following step moves the Slide 1 title text placeholder.

- With the Slide 1 title text placeholder border displaying as a solid line, point to an area of the bottom border between two sizing handles so that the mouse pointer changes to a four-headed arrow.

What if the placeholder border displays as a dotted line?

Click the border to change the line from dotted to solid.

Can I click any part of the border, or do I need to click the bottom edge?

You can click any of the four border lines.

Figure 3–13

- Drag the placeholder downward so that it overlaps part of the subtitle text placeholder (Figure 3–13).

- Click to set the placeholder in its new location.

To Delete a Placeholder

When you run a slide show, empty placeholders do not display. You may desire to delete unused placeholders from a slide so that they are not a distraction when you are designing slide content. The subtitle text placeholder on Slide 1 is not required for this presentation, so you can remove it. The following steps remove the Slide 1 subtitle text placeholder.

Click a border of the subtitle text placeholder so that it displays as a solid line or fine dots (Figure 3–14).

Q&A What if the placeholder border is displaying as a dotted line?

Click the border to change the line from dotted to solid or fine dots.

Press the DELETE key to remove the placeholder.

Q&A Can I click the Cut button (Home tab | Clipboard group) to delete the placeholder?

Yes. Clicking the Cut button deletes the placeholder if it does not contain any text.

Figure 3–14

<table>
<tr><td>Plan
Ahead</td><td>**Vary paragraph alignment.**
Designers use alignment within paragraphs to aid readability and to indicate relationships among slide elements. English language readers are accustomed to seeing paragraphs that are aligned left. When paragraphs are aligned right, the viewer's eyes are drawn to this unexpected text design. If your paragraph is short, consider centering or right-aligning the text for emphasis.</td></tr>
</table>

To Align Paragraph Text

The presentation theme determines the formatting characteristics of fonts and colors. It also establishes paragraph formatting, including the alignment of text. Some themes center the text paragraphs between the left and right placeholder borders, while others **left-align** the paragraph so that the first character of a text line is near the left border or **right-align** the paragraph so that the last character of a text line is near the right border. The paragraph also can be **justified** so that the text is aligned to both the left and right borders. When PowerPoint justifies text, it adds extras spaces between the words to fill the entire line.

The words, Birds of a Feather, are centered in the Slide 1 title text placeholder. Later, you will add clip art above the word, Feather, so you desire to left-align the paragraph to make room for this art. In addition, the words in the Slide 3 title text placeholder, Bird Migration, are covering the bird in the picture. You can right-align these words to uncover the bird in the lower-left corner. The following steps change the alignment of the Slide 1 and Slide 3 title placeholders.

1
- With the Home tab displayed, click somewhere in the title text paragraph of Slide 1 to position the insertion point in the paragraph to be formatted (Figure 3–15).

Figure 3–15

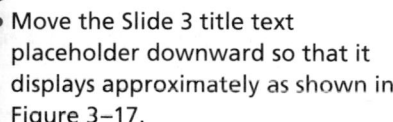

• Click the Align Text Left button (Home tab | Paragraph group) to left-align the paragraph (Figure 3–16).

What if I want to return the paragraph to center alignment?

Click the Center button (Home tab | Paragraph group).

• Display Slide 3. Click somewhere in the title text paragraph to position the insertion point in the paragraph to be formatted.

• Click the Align Text Right button (Home tab | Paragraph group) to right-align the paragraph.

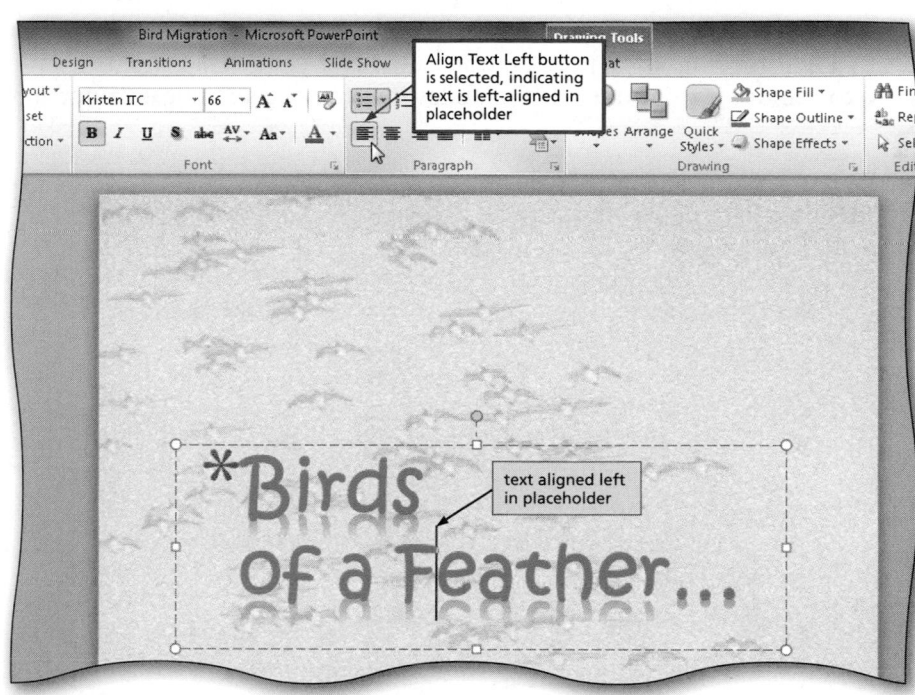

Figure 3–16

• Move the Slide 3 title text placeholder downward so that it displays approximately as shown in Figure 3–17.

Can I align text vertically in a text box?

Yes. You can align paragraphs vertically in the top, middle, or bottom of a text box. Position the insertion point in a paragraph and then click the Align Text button (Home tab | Paragraph group) to display the Align Text gallery. You can experiment with the alignment by pointing to each of these three options and watching the paragraphs in the text box change position. If you click More Options at the bottom of the gallery, you can made additional alignment changes in the Format Text Effects dialog box.

Figure 3–17

Other Ways
1. Right-click paragraph, click Align Text Right button on Mini toolbar 2. Right-click paragraph, click Paragraph on shortcut menu, click Indents and	Spacing tab (Paragraph dialog box), click Alignment box arrow, click Right, click OK button 3. Click Paragraph Dialog Box Launcher (Home tab | | Paragraph group), click Indents and Spacing tab (Paragraph dialog box), click Alignment box arrow, click Right, click OK button 4. Press CTRL+R

To Delete a Slide

The Bird Migration presentation has a blank slide at the end. You decide that you will not use this slide, so you need to remove it from the file. The following steps delete Slide 4 from the presentation.

1

• Right-click the Slide 4 thumbnail in the Slides tab to display the shortcut menu (Figure 3–18).

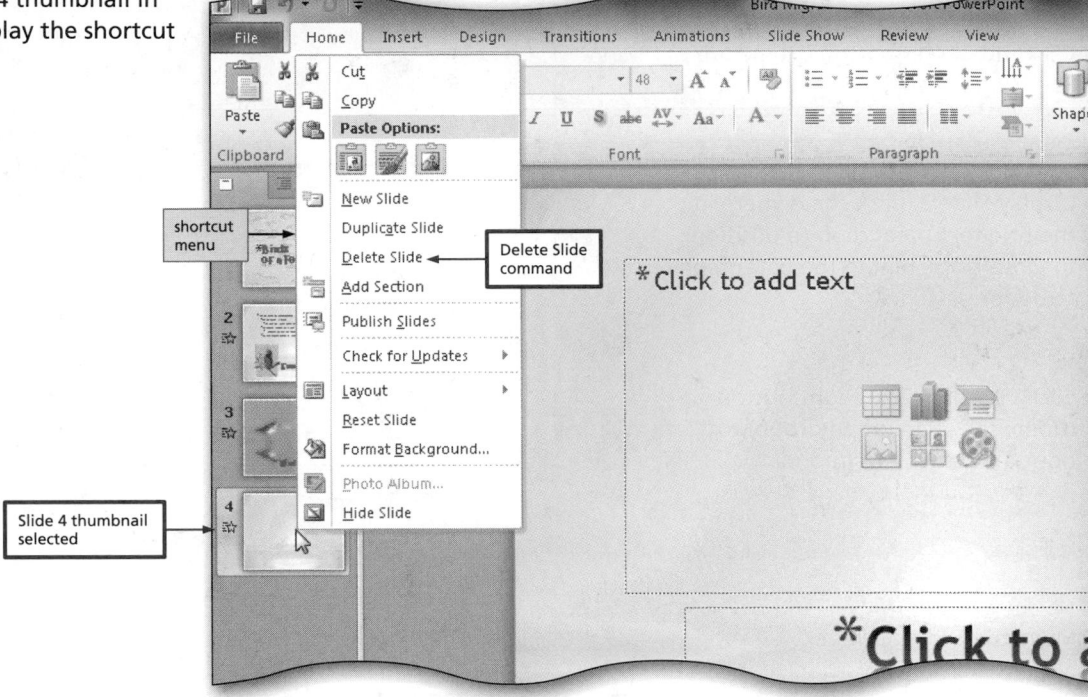

Figure 3–18

2

• Click Delete Slide to delete Slide 4 from the presentation (Figure 3–19).

Figure 3–19

Q&A Can I delete multiple slides simultaneously?

Yes. If the slides are sequential, click the first slide you want to delete, press and hold the SHIFT key, click the last slide that you want to delete, right-click any selected slide, and then click Delete Slide on the shortcut menu. If the slides are not sequential, press and hold the CTRL key while you click each slide that you want to delete, right-click any selected slide, and then click Delete Slide on the shortcut menu.

Changing Views

You have been using Normal view to create and edit your slides. Once you completed your slides, you reviewed the final products by displaying each slide in Slide Show view, which occupies the full computer screen. You were able to view how the transitions, graphics, and effects will display in an actual presentation before an audience.

PowerPoint has other views to help review a presentation for content, organization, and overall appearance. Slide Sorter view allows you to look at several slides at one time. Reading view is similar to Slide Show view because each slide displays individually, but the slides do not fill the entire screen. Using this view, you easily can control the progression through the slides forward or backward with simple controls at the bottom of the window. Switching between Slide Sorter view, Reading view, and Normal view helps you review your presentation, assess whether the slides have an attractive design and adequate content, and make sure they are organized for the most impact. After reviewing the slides, you can change the view to Normal so that you may continue working on the presentation.

BTW

Using the Ribbon to Adjust Views

While it is convenient to change views by clicking the controls on the bar at the bottom of the PowerPoint Window, you also can change views by using the Ribbon. The Presentation Views group on the View tab has four buttons that allow you to change to Normal, Slide Sorter, Reading, and Slide Show views.

To Change Views

You have made several modifications to the slides, so you should check for balance and consistency. The following steps change the view from Normal view to Slide Sorter view, then Reading view, and back to Normal view.

• Click the Slide Sorter view button in the lower right of the PowerPoint window to display the presentation in Slide Sorter view (Figure 3–20).

Can I view only the slide title text in Slide Sorter View?

Yes. Press and hold the ALT key while you press and hold the mouse button. Each slide title will display against a white background.

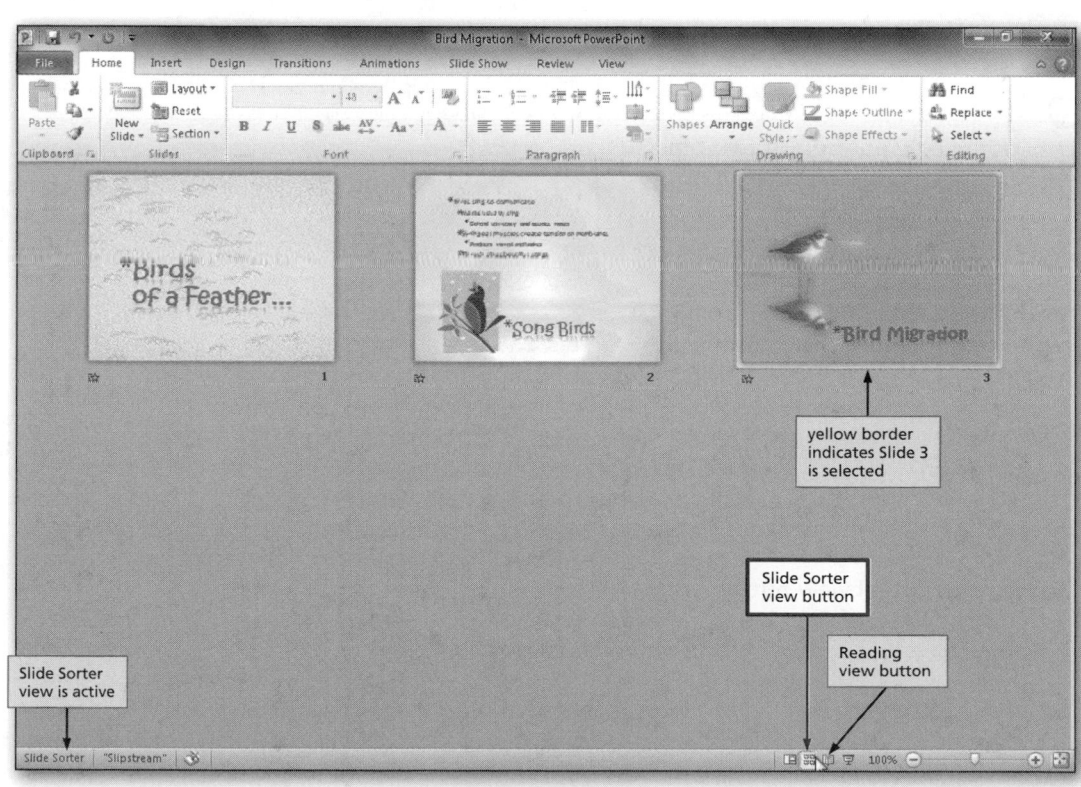

Figure 3–20

Why is Slide 3 selected?

It is the current slide in the Slide pane.

- Click the Reading view button in the lower right of the PowerPoint window to display Slide 3 of the presentation in Reading view (Figure 3–21).

Figure 3–21

- Click the Previous button two times to display Slide 2 and then Slide 1.

- Click the Next button two times to advance through the presentation.

- Click the Menu button to display a menu of commonly used commands (Figure 3–22).

- Click End Show to return to Slide Sorter view, which is the view you were using before Reading view.

- Click the Normal view button to display the presentation in Normal view.

Figure 3–22

Other Ways

1. Click desired view button (View tab | Presentation Views group)

Copying and Modifying a Clip

Slide 1 (shown in Figure 3–1a on PPT 139) contains a modified version of a songbird. You may want to modify a clip art picture for various reasons. Many times, you cannot find a clip art picture that precisely illustrates your topic. For example, you want a picture of a red sports car, but the only available clip art picture is painted black.

Occasionally, you may want to remove or change a portion of a clip art picture or you might want to combine two or more clip art pictures. For example, you can use one clip art picture for the background and another picture as the foreground. Other times, you may want to combine a clip art picture with another type of object. In this presentation, the bird picture has a yellow background that is not required to display on the slide, so you will ungroup the clip art picture and remove the background.

Modifying the clip on Slide 1 requires several steps. You first must copy it using the Office Clipboard and then paste it in the desired location. The **Office Clipboard** is a temporary storage location that can hold a maximum of 24 text or graphics items copied from any Office program. The same procedure of copying and pasting objects works for copying and pasting text from one placeholder to another. In the following pages, you will perform these tasks:

1. Copy the clip from Slide 2 to Slide 1.
2. Zoom Slide 1 to examine the clip.
3. Ungroup the clip.
4. Edit and change the clip colors.
5. Delete a clip object.
6. Regroup the clip.

To Copy a Clip from One Slide to Another

The bird clip on Slide 2 also can display in a modified form on the title slide. The following steps copy this slide element from Slide 2 to Slide 1.

- Display Slide 2. With the Home tab displayed, click the bird clip to select it and then click the Copy button (Home tab | Clipboard group) (Figure 3–23).

Why are some words on Slide 2 underlined with red wavy lines?

Those words are not in PowerPoint's main or custom dictionaries, so PowerPoint indicates that they may be misspelled. For example, the word, Syringeal, is spelled correctly, but is not in PowerPoint's dictionaries.

- Display Slide 1 and then click the Paste button (Home tab | Clipboard group) to insert the bird clip into the title slide.

Is the clip deleted from the Office Clipboard when I paste it into the slide?

No.

Figure 3–23

• Decrease the clip size by dragging one of the corner sizing handles inward until the clip is the size shown in Figure 3–24. Drag the clip to the location shown in this figure.

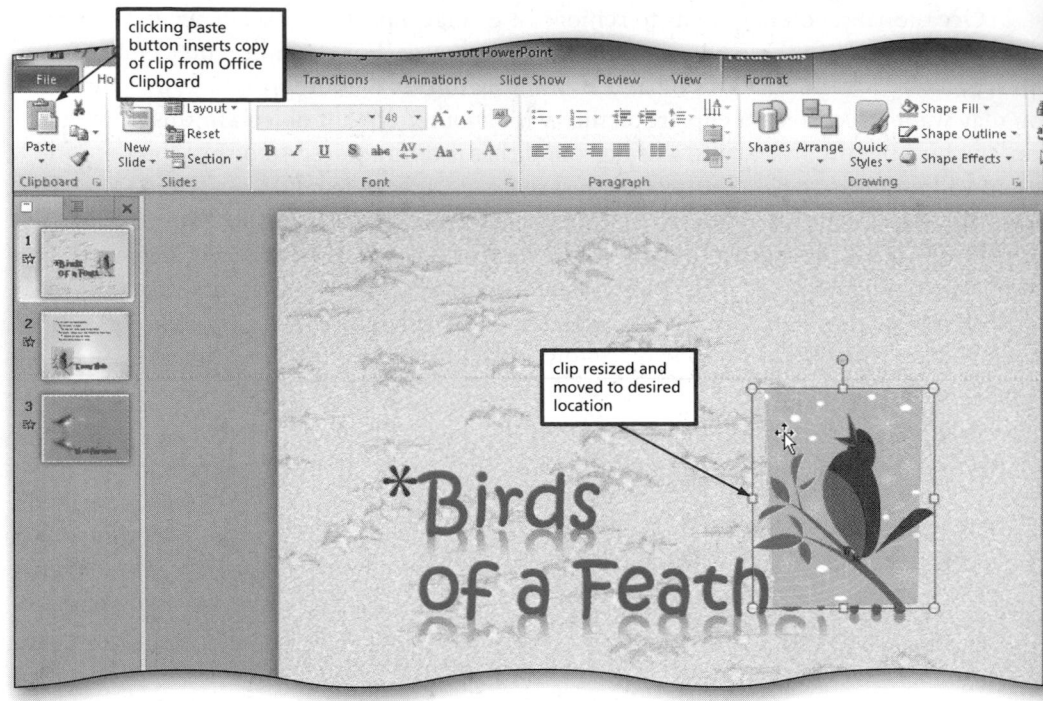

Figure 3–24

To Zoom a Slide

You will be modifying small areas of the clip, so it will help you select the relevant pieces if the graphic is enlarged. The following step changes the zoom to 150 percent.

• Drag the Zoom slider to the right to change the zoom level to 150% (Figure 3–25).

Figure 3–25

Other Ways

1. Click Zoom button (View tab | Zoom group), change percentage in Percent text box (Zoom dialog box), click OK button

2. Click Zoom In button at end of slider

3. Click Zoom level on left side of slider, change percentage in Percent text box (Zoom dialog box), click OK button

To Ungroup a Clip

The next step is to ungroup the bird clip on Slide 1. When you **ungroup** a clip art picture, PowerPoint breaks it into its component objects. A clip may be composed of a few individual objects or several complex groups of objects. These groups can be ungrouped repeatedly until they decompose into individual objects. Because a clip art picture is a collection of complex groups of objects, you may need to ungroup a complex object into less complex objects before being able to modify a specific object. When you ungroup a clip and click the Yes button in the Microsoft PowerPoint dialog box, PowerPoint converts the clip to a PowerPoint object. The following steps ungroup a clip.

- With the bird clip selected, click Format on the Ribbon to display the Picture Tools Format tab.

- Click the Group button (Picture Tools Format tab | Arrange group) to display the Group menu (Figure 3–26).

Why does the Group button look different on my screen?

Your monitor is set to a different resolution. See Chapter 1 for an explanation of screen resolution and the appearance of the Ribbon.

Figure 3–26

- Click Ungroup on the Group menu to display the Microsoft PowerPoint dialog box (Figure 3–27).

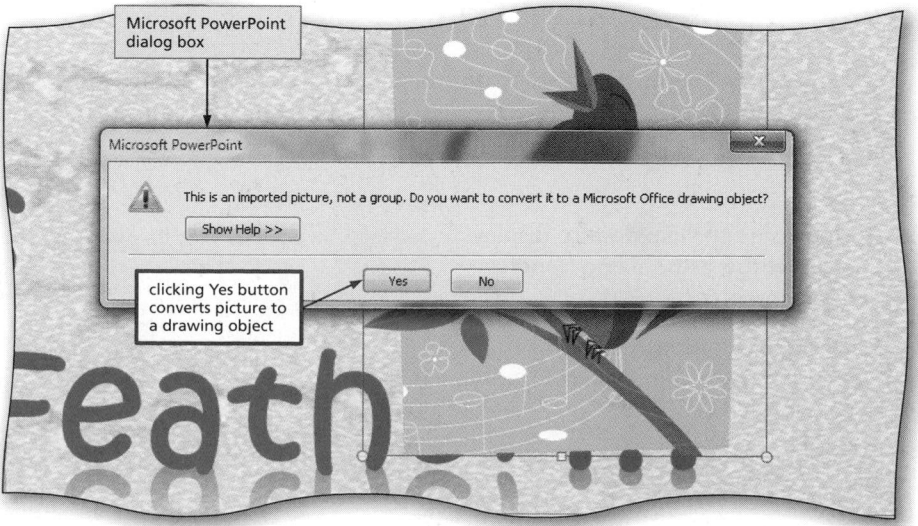

Figure 3–27

3

- Click the Yes button (Microsoft PowerPoint dialog box) to convert the clip to a Microsoft Office drawing.

Q&A What happens if I click the No button?

The clip will remain displayed on the slide as a clip art picture and will not ungroup.

- Click Format on the Ribbon to display the Drawing Tools Format tab. Click the Group button (Drawing Tools Format tab | Arrange group) and then click Ungroup again.

Q&A Why does the Drawing Tools Format tab show different options this time?

The clip has become a drawing object, so tools related to drawing now display.

- With the Drawing Tools Format tab displayed, click the Group button (Drawing Tools Format tab | Arrange group), and then click Ungroup a third time to display the objects that constitute the bird clip (Figure 3–28).

Figure 3–28

Q&A Why do all those circles and squares display in the clip?

The circles and squares are sizing handles for each of the clip's objects, which resemble pieces of a jigsaw puzzle.

To Change the Color of a Clip Object

Now that the bird picture is ungrouped, you can change the color of the objects. The clip is composed of hundreds of objects, so you must exercise care when selecting the correct object to modify. The following steps change the color of the bird's mouth and the leaves.

- Click outside the clip area to display the clip without the sizing handles around the objects.

- Click the bird's mouth to display sizing handles around the colored area (Figure 3–29).

Q&A What if I selected a different area by mistake?

Click outside the clip and retry.

Figure 3–29

- Click the Shape Fill button arrow (Drawing Tools Format tab | Shape Styles group) to display the Shape Fill gallery.

- Point to Yellow in the Standard Colors area (fourth color) to display a live preview of the mouth color (Figure 3–30).

 Experiment

- Point to various colors and watch the bird's mouth color change.

Figure 3–30

- Click the color Yellow to change the bird's mouth color.

Why is the bar under the Shape Fill button now yellow?

The button displays the last fill color selected.

- Click a leaf on the branch to display the sizing handles around the colored area (Figure 3–31).

Figure 3–31

- Click the Shape Fill button arrow (Drawing Tools Format tab | Shape Styles group) and then point to Green, Accent 3 in the Theme Colors area (seventh color in first row) to display a live preview of the color of the selected leaf in the graphic (Figure 3–32).

 Experiment

- Point to various colors and watch the leaf color change.

Figure 3–32

5

- Click the Green, Accent 3 color to change the leaf color.

6

- Click another leaf on the branch to select it.

- Click the Shape Fill button to change the leaf color to Green, Accent 3 (Figure 3–33).

Q&A
Why did I not need to click the Shape Fill button arrow to select this color?

PowerPoint uses the last fill color selected. This color displays in the bar under the bucket icon on the button.

Figure 3–33

7

- Repeat Step 6 until all the leaves have been recolored (Figure 3–34).

Q&A
Can I open the Microsoft Clip Organizer when I am not using PowerPoint?

Yes. On the Start menu, point to All Programs, point to Microsoft Office, point to Microsoft Office 2010 Tools, and then click Microsoft Clip Organizer.

Figure 3–34

Other Ways

1. Right-click object, click Format Shape on shortcut menu, click Color button

To Delete a Clip Object

With the bird mouth and leaf colors changed, you want to delete the gold background object. The following steps delete this object.

1

• Click the background in any area where the gold color displays to select this object (Figure 3–35).

Can I select multiple objects so I can delete them simultaneously?

Yes. While pressing the SHIFT key, click the unwanted elements to select them.

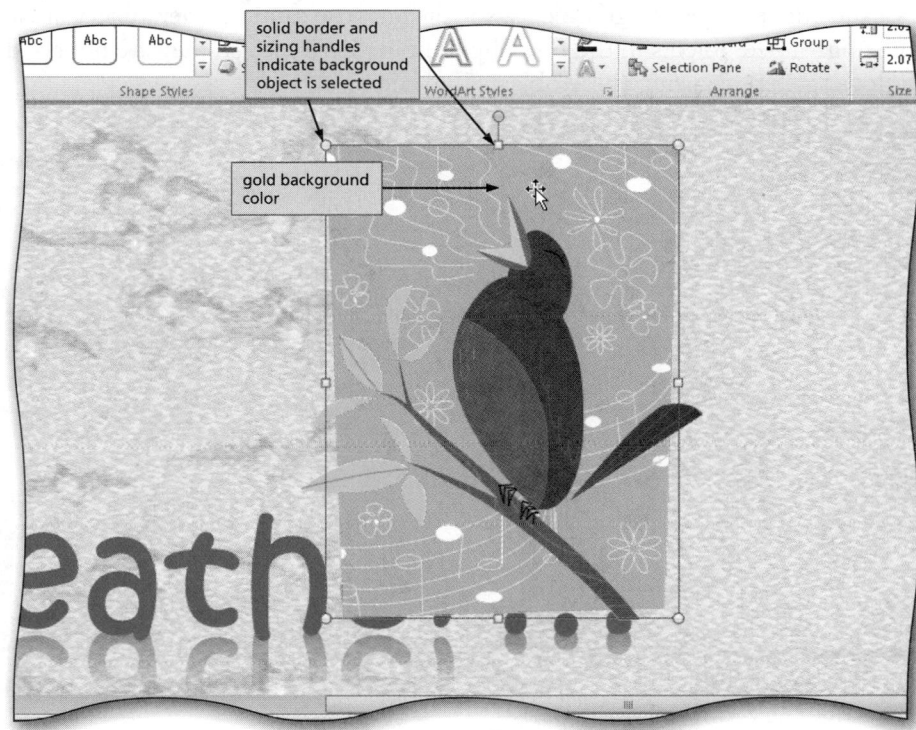

Figure 3–35

2

• Press the DELETE key to delete this object (Figure 3–36).

Should the white musical staff display on the slide?

Yes. It is part of the bird clip.

Figure 3–36

To Regroup Objects

When you ungrouped the bird clip, you eliminated the embedding data or linking information that tied all the individual pieces together. If you attempt to move or size this clip now, you might encounter difficulties because it consists of hundreds of objects and is no longer one unified piece. Dragging or sizing affects only a selected object, not the entire collection of objects, so you must use caution when objects are not completely regrouped. All of the ungrouped objects in the bird clip must be regrouped so they are not accidentally moved or manipulated. The following steps regroup these objects into one object.

- With the clip selected, click the Drawing Tools Format tab and then click the Group button (Drawing Tools Format tab | Arrange group) to display the Group menu (Figure 3–37).

- Click Regroup to combine all the objects.

- Use the Zoom slider to change the zoom level to 69%.

Figure 3–37

Other Ways
1. Right-click clip, point to Group on shortcut menu, click Regroup
2. Press CTRL+G

Plan Ahead

Use multimedia selectively.
PowerPoint makes it easy to insert multimedia into a presentation. Well-produced video clips add value when they help explain a procedure or show movement that cannot be captured in a photograph. Music can help calm or energize an audience, when appropriate. A sound, such as applause when a correct answer is given, can emphasize an action. Before you insert these files on a slide, however, consider whether they really add any value to your overall slide show. If you are inserting them just because you can, you might want to reconsider your decision. Audiences quickly tire of extraneous sounds and movement on slides, and they will find these media clips annoying. Keep in mind that the audience's attention should focus primarily on the presenter; extraneous or inappropriate media files may divert their attention and, in turn, decrease the quality of the presentation.

Break Point: If you wish to take a break, this is a good place to do so. Be sure to save the Bird Migration file again and then you can quit PowerPoint. To resume at a later time, start PowerPoint, open the file called Bird Migration, and continue following the steps from this location forward.

Adding Media to Slides

Media files can enrich a presentation if they are used correctly. Movies files can have two formats: digital video produced with a camera and editing software or animated GIF (Graphics Interchange Format) files composed of multiple images combined into a single file. Sound files can be from the Microsoft Clip Organizer, files stored on your computer, or an audio track on a CD. To hear the sounds, you need a sound card and speakers on your system.

In the following pages, you will perform these tasks:

1. Insert a video file into Slide 3.
2. Trim the video file so only the final few seconds play.
3. Add video options that determine the clip's appearance and playback.
4. Insert audio files.
5. Add audio options that determine the clips' appearance and playback.
6. Add a video style to the Slide 3 clip.
7. Resize the video.
8. Insert a movie clip into Slide 1.

To Insert a Video File

Slide 3 has the title, Bird Migration, and you have a video clip that is composed of many scenes featuring various animals and birds. A short segment of this clip shows a flock of birds on a beach, and you want to use only this part of the clip in your presentation. PowerPoint allows you to insert this clip into your slide and then trim the file so that just a portion will play when you preview the clip or run the slide show. This clip is available on the Data Files for Students. See the inside back cover of this book for instructions on downloading the Data Files for Students, or contact your instructor for more information about accessing the required file. The following steps insert this video clip into Slide 3.

- Display Slide 3 and then display the Insert tab. With your USB flash drive connected to one of the computer's USB ports, click the Insert Video button (Insert tab | Media group) to display the Insert Video dialog box.

- If the list of files and folders on the selected USB flash drive are not displayed in the Insert Video dialog box, double-click your USB flash drive to display them.

- Click Wildlife to select the file (Figure 3–38).

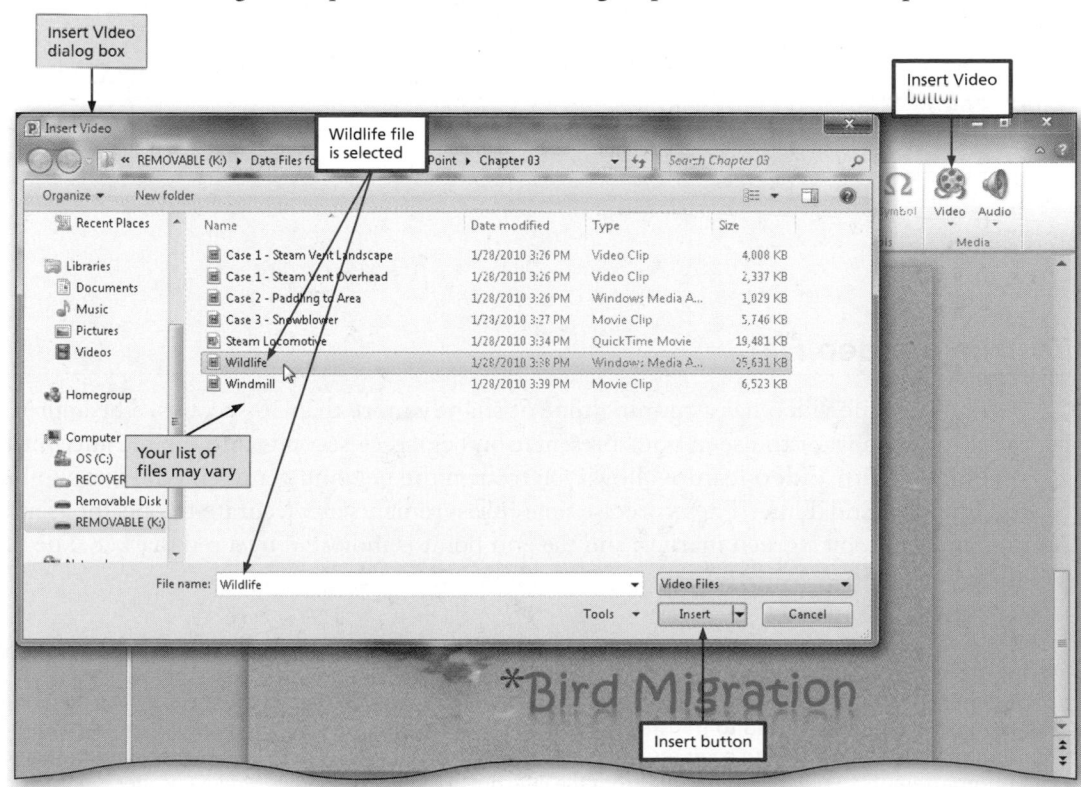

Figure 3–38

2

- Click the Insert button (Insert Video dialog box) to insert the movie clip into Slide 3 (Figure 3–39).

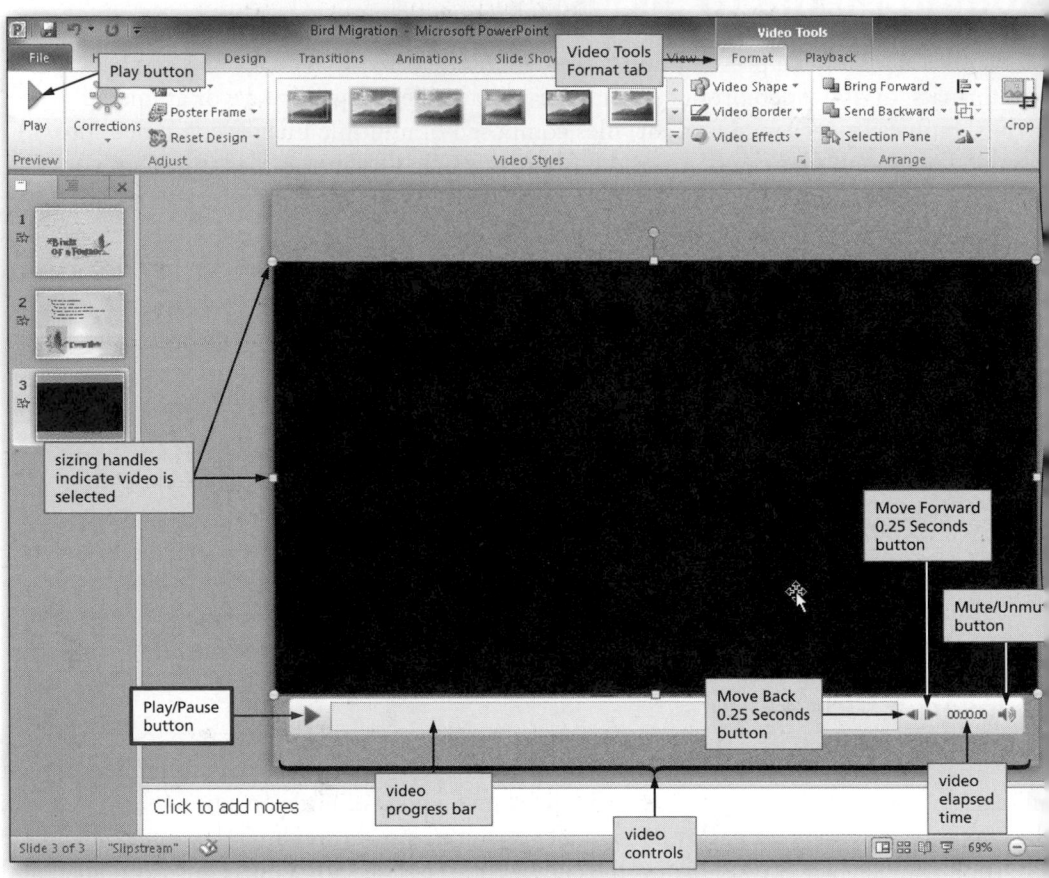

Figure 3–39

Can I adjust the color of a video clip?

Yes. You correct the brightness and contrast, and you also recolor a video clip using the same methods you learned in this chapter to color a picture.

To Trim a Video File

The Wildlife video has a running time of slightly more than 30 seconds. The approximately six-second segment that you want to use in your presentation begins 24 seconds into the file and finishes at the end of the clip. PowerPoint's **Trim Video** feature allows you to trim the beginning and end of your clip by designating your desired Start Time and End Time. These precise time measurements are accurate to one-thousandth of a second. The start point is indicated by a green marker, and the end point is indicated by a red marker. The following steps trim the Wildlife video clip.

Using Codecs

Digital media file sizes often are quite large, so video and audio content developers use a codec (**co**mpressor/**dec**ompressor) to reduce the required storage space and to transfer the files across the Internet quickly and smoothly. Your computer can play any compressed file if the specific codec used to compress the file is available on your computer. If the codec is not installed or is not recognized, your computer attempts to download this file from the Internet. Microsoft Windows Media Encoder is a free program that makes some media files compatible with PowerPoint.

1

- With the video clip selected on Slide 3, click the Play/Pause button to play the entire video.

  Can I play the video by clicking the Play button in the Preview group?

  Yes. This Play button plays the entire clip. You may prefer to click the Play/Pause button displayed in the Video Controls to stop the video and examine one of the frames.

- Click Playback on the Ribbon to display the Video Tools Playback tab. Click the Trim Video button (Editing group) to display the Trim Video dialog box (Figure 3–40).

Figure 3–40

2

- Point to the start point, which is indicated by the green marker on the left side, so that the mouse pointer changes to a two-headed arrow.

- Drag the green marker to the right until the Start Time is 00:24:634 (Figure 3–41).

  Can I specify the start or end times without dragging the markers?

  Yes. You can enter the time in the Start Time or End Time boxes, or you can click the Start Time or End Time box arrows. You also can click the Next Frame and Previous Frame buttons (Trim Video dialog box).

  How would I indicate an end point if I want the clip to end at a time other than at the end of the clip?

  You would drag the red marker to the left until the desired end time displays.

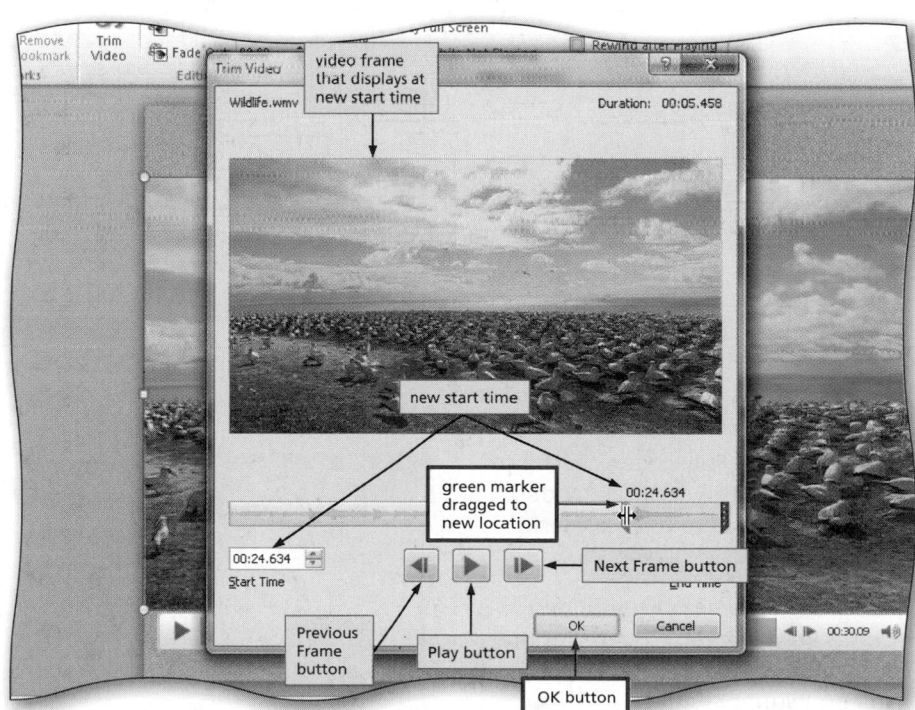

Figure 3–41

3

- Click the Play button (Trim Video dialog box) to review the shortened video clip.

- Click the OK button to set the Start Time and End Time and to close the Trim Video dialog box.

Other Ways

1. Right-click clip, click Trim Video on shortcut menu

To Add Video Options

Once the video clip is inserted into Slide 3, you can specify options that affect how the file is displayed and played. For example, you can have the video play automatically when the slide is displayed, or you can click the slide when you are ready to start the playback. You also can have the video fill the entire slide, which is referred to as **full screen**. If you decide to play the slide show automatically and have it display full screen, you can drag the video frame to the gray area off the slide so that it does not display briefly before going to full screen. You can select the Loop until Stopped option to have the video repeat until you click the next slide, or you can choose to not have the video frame display on the slide until you click the slide.

If your video clip has recorded sounds, the volume controls give you the option to set how loudly this audio will play. They also allow you to mute the sound so that your audience will hear no background noise or music.

The following steps add the options of playing the video full screen automatically when Slide 3 is displayed and also mutes the background music recorded on the video clip.

- If necessary, click Playback on the Ribbon to display the Video Tools Playback tab. Click the Start box (Video Tools Playback tab | Video Options group) to view the Start menu (Figure 3–42).

Q&A

What does the On Click option do?

The video clip would begin playing when a presenter clicks the slide during the slide show.

Figure 3–42

- Click Automatically in the Start menu (Figure 3–43).

Figure 3–43

- Click the Play Full Screen check box (Video Tools Playback tab | Video Options group) to place a check mark in it.

- Click the Volume button (Video Tools Playback tab | Video Options group) to display the Volume menu (Figure 3–44).

④

- Click Mute in the Volume menu.

Figure 3–44

To Insert an Audio File

Avid bird watchers listen to the songs and calls birds make to each other. The Microsoft Clip Organizer and Office.com have several of these sounds in audio files that you can download and insert into your presentation. Once these audio files are inserted into a slide, you can add options that specify how long and how loudly the clip will play; these options are similar to the video options you just selected for the Wildlife video clip. The following steps insert an audio clip into Slide 3.

• With Slide 3 displaying, click Insert on the Ribbon to display the Insert tab and then click the Insert Audio button arrow (Insert tab | Media group) to display the Insert Audio menu (Figure 3–45).

Figure 3–45

• Click Clip Art Audio in the Insert Audio menu to open the Clip Art task pane.

• If necessary, click the 'Results should be' box arrow, click the 'All media types' check box to remove the check mark from each of the four types of media files, and then click the Audio check box to place a check mark in it (Figure 3–46).

Can I use this technique to search solely for videos, photographs, or illustrations?

Yes. You also can search for a combination of these file types, such as both video and audio files.

Figure 3–46

- If necessary, delete any letters that are present in the Search for text box and then type **Glade Birds** in the Search for text box. If necessary, click the 'Include Office.com content' check box to select it.

- Click the Go button so that the Microsoft Clip Organizer will search for and display all clips having the keyword or title, Glade Birds.

- Point to the Glade Birds clip to display the properties of this file (Figure 3–47).

Q&A What if the Glade Birds audio clip is not shown in my Clip Art task pane?

Select a similar clip. Your clips may be different depending on the clips installed on your computer and if you have an active Internet connection.

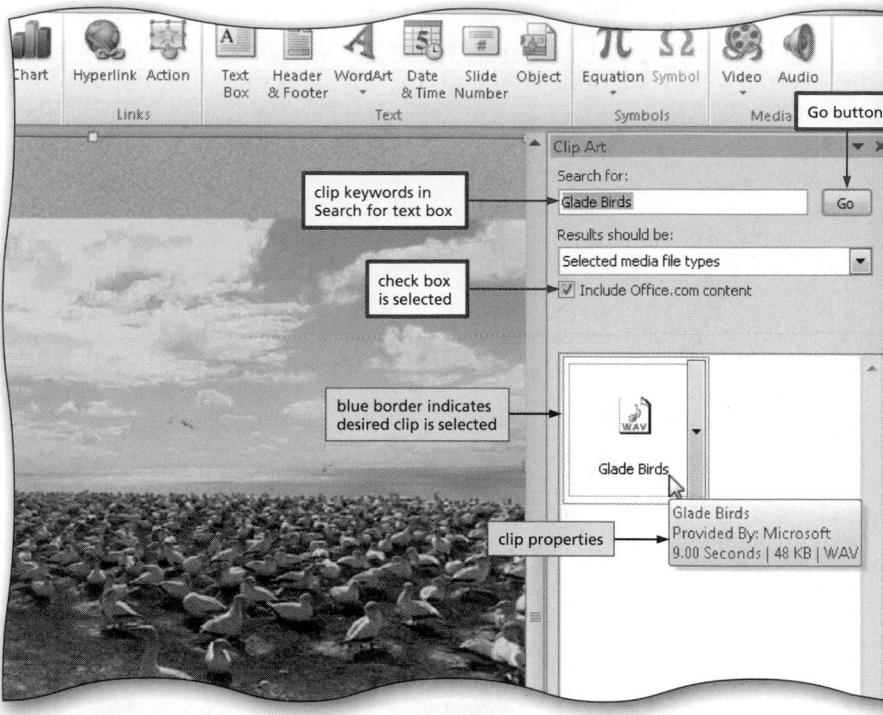

Figure 3–47

Q&A What are the properties associated with this clip?

The properties include the number of seconds of playing time, the file size, and the type of audio file. This file is a **Windows waveform (.wav)** file, which uses a standard format to encode and communicate music and sound between computers, music synthesizers, and instruments.

- Right-click the Glade Birds clip to select the clip and to display the Edit menu (Figure 3–48).

Figure 3–48

• Click Preview/
Properties to display
the Preview/Properties
dialog box and to hear
the clip (Figure 3–49).

What are the
words listed in the
Keywords box?

Those words are the
search terms associated
with the file. If you
enter any of those
words in the Search for
text box, this audio file
would display in the
results list.

Can I preview the clip
again?

Yes. Click the Play
button in the Preview/
Properties dialog box.

Figure 3–49

• Click the Close button
(Preview/Properties
dialog box) to close
the dialog box.

• Click Glade Birds in
the results list (Clip Art
task pane) to insert
that file into Slide 3
(Figure 3–50).

Why does a sound icon
display in the video?

The icon indicates an
audio file is inserted.

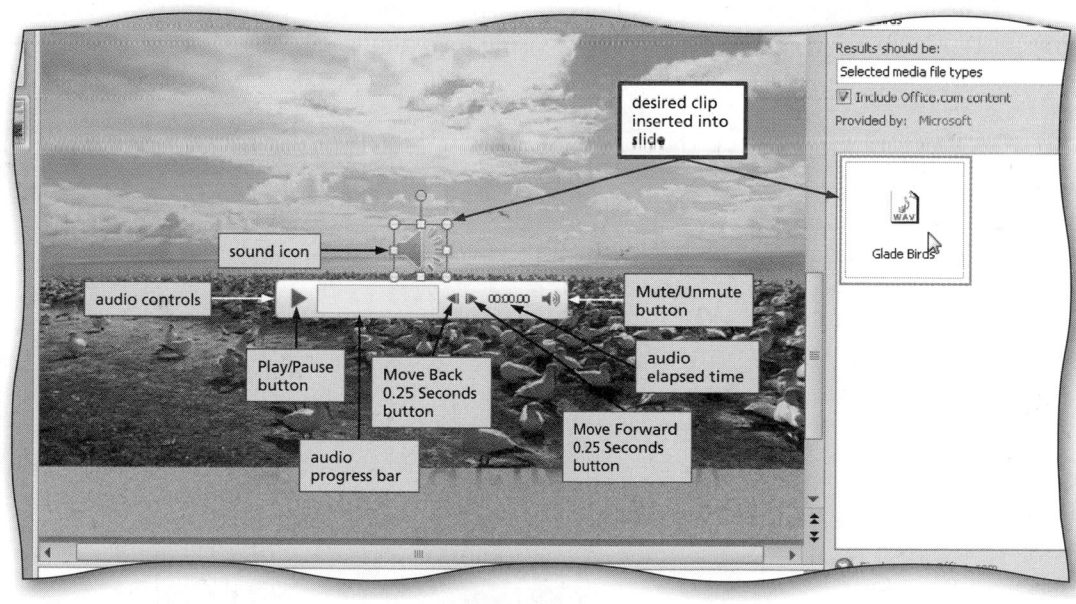

Figure 3–50

Do the Audio Controls buttons have the same functions as the Video Controls buttons that
displayed when I inserted the Wildlife clip?

Yes. The controls include playing and pausing the sound, moving back or forward 0.25
seconds, audio progress, elapsed time, and muting or unmuting the sound.

- Drag the sound icon to the upper-left corner of the slide (Figure 3–51).

Q&A

Must I move the icon on the slide?

No. Although your audience will not see the icon when you run the slide show, it is easier for you to see the media elements when they are separated on the slide rather than stacked on top of each other.

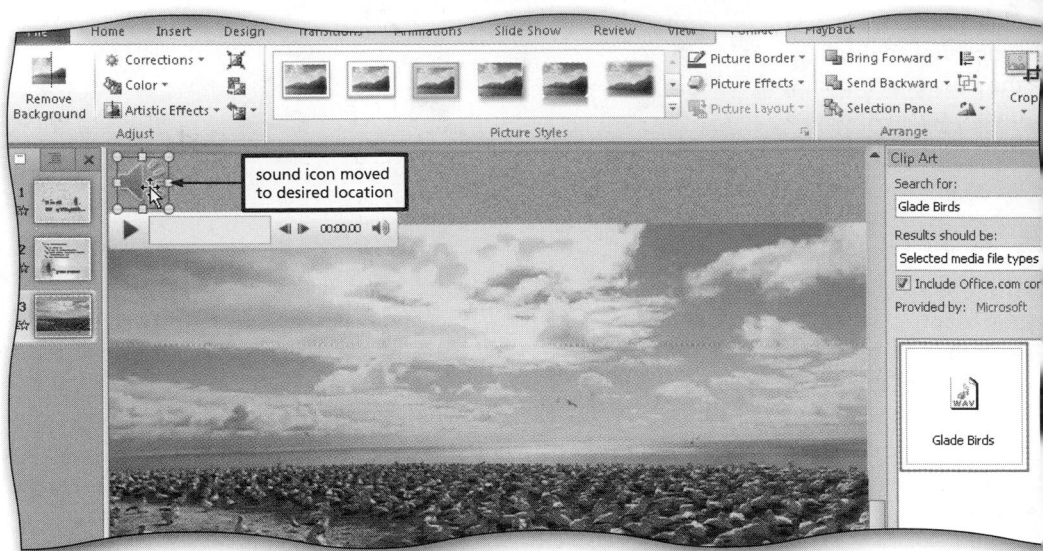

Figure 3–51

To Add Audio Options

Once an audio clip is inserted into a slide, you can specify options that control playback and appearance. As wit the video options you applied to the Wildlife clip, the audio clip can play either automatically or when clicked, it can repeat the clip while a particular slide is displayed, and you can drag the sound icon off the slide and set the volume.

The following steps add the options of starting automatically and playing until the slide no longer is displayed hiding the sound icon on the slide, and increasing the volume.

- Click Playback on the Ribbon to display the Audio Tools Playback tab. Click the Start box (Audio Tools Playback tab | Audio Options group) to display the Start box menu (Figure 3–52).

- Click Automatically in the Start menu.

Q&A

Does the On Click option function the same way for an audio clip as On Click does for a video clip?

Yes. If you were to select On Click, the sound would begin playing only after the presenter clicks Slide 1 during a presentation.

Figure 3–52

- Click the Loop until Stopped check box (Audio Tools Playback tab | Audio Options group) to place a check mark in it.

What is the difference between the Loop until Stopped option and the Play across slides option?

The audio clip in the Loop until Stopped option repeats for as long as one slide is displayed. In contrast, the Play across slides option clip would play only once, but it would continue to play while other slides in the presentation are displayed. Once the end of the clip is reached, the sound would end and not repeat.

- Click the Hide During Show check box (Video Tools Playback tab | Audio Options group) to place a check mark in it (Figure 3–53).

Why would I want the icon to display during the show?

If you had selected the On Click start option, you would need to find this icon on the slide and click it to start playing the clip.

Figure 3–53

To Insert an Additional Audio File and Set Options

Having an audio clip play when Slide 1 is displayed would add interest and help set the tone of the presentation. Only one bird appears on that slide, and it appears to be singing heartily. A single bird singing would coordinate nicely with this clip art image. The following steps insert a songbird audio clip into Slide 1 and set playback options.

- Display Slide 1, delete any letters that are present in the Search for text box, and then type **Birds at dawn** in the Search for text box (Clip Art task pane), and search for this audio clip.

- Insert the Birds at dawn clip into Slide 1 and then drag the sound icon to the lower-left corner of the slide.

- Close the Clip Art task pane.

- Display the Audio Tools Playback tab. Click the Start box (Audio Tools Playback tab | Audio Options group) and then click Automatically in the Start menu.

- Click the Loop until Stopped check box (Audio Tools Playback tab | Audio Options group) to place a check mark in it.

BTW

Playing Audio Continuously
You can play one audio file throughout an entire presentation instead of only when one individual slide is displayed. When you select the 'Play across slides' option in the Start box (Audio Tools Playback tab | Audio Options group), the audio clip will play continuously as you advance through the slides in your presentation. If you select this option, be certain the length of the clip exceeds the total time you will display all slides in your slide show.

BTW

Using Bookmarks in Audio and Video Clips
While delivering a presentation, bookmarks are useful in helping you find specific locations in an audio or video clip. They can start an animation or jump to a specific location in the audio or video file. To add a bookmark to an audio clip as it is playing, click the Audio Tools Playback tab and then click the Add Bookmark button (Audio Tools Playback tab | Bookmarks group) at the time when you want to add the bookmark. To add a bookmark to a video clip as it is playing, click the Video Tools Playback tab and then click the Add Bookmark button (Video Tools Playback tab | Bookmarks group) when you see the frame where you want to add the bookmark.

BTW

Trimming an Audio Clip
You can shorten an audio clip to play only a specific part of the file. The steps for trimming an audio file are similar to those used for trimming a video file. Select the clip, click the Play/Pause button, and

⑥ Click the Hide During Show check box (Audio Tools Playback tab | Audio Options group).

⑦ Click the Volume button (Audio Tools Playback tab | Audio Options group) and then change the volume to Medium (Figure 3–54).

Figure 3–54

then click the Trim Audio button (Audio Tools Playback tab | Editing group). When the Trim Audio dialog box is displayed, you then can drag the green start point marker to the desired starting position and the red end point marker to the desired ending position.

To Add a Video Style

The Wildlife video clip on Slide 3 displays full screen when it is playing, but you can increase the visual appea of the clip when it is not playing by applying a video style. The video styles are similar to the picture styles you applied in Chapter 2 and include various shapes, angles, borders, and reflections. The following steps apply a video style to the Wildlife clip on Slide 3.

• Display Slide 3 and select the video. Click Format on the Ribbon to display the Video Tools Format tab (Figure 3–55).

Figure 3–55

2

- With the video selected, click the More button in the Video Styles gallery (Video Tools Format tab | Video Styles group) (shown in Figure 3–55) to expand the gallery.

- Point to Bevel Perspective in the Intense area of the Video Styles gallery to display a live preview of that style applied to the video on the slide (Figure 3–56).

Experiment

- Point to various picture styles in the Video Styles gallery and watch the style of the video frame change in the document window.

Figure 3–56

3

- Click Bevel Perspective in the Video Styles gallery to apply the style to the selected video (Figure 3–57).

Can I preview the movie clip?

Yes. Point to the clip and then click the Play/Pause button on the Video Controls below the video.

Can I add a border to a video style?

Yes. You add a border using the same method you learned in Chapter 2 to add a border to a picture. Click the Video Border button (Video Tools Format tab | Video Styles gallery) and then select a border line weight and color.

Figure 3–57

To Resize a Video

The Wildlife video size can be decreased to fill the space on the right side of the slide. You resize a video clip in the same manner that you resize clip art and pictures. The following steps resize this video using a sizing handle.

- With the video clip selected, drag the lower-left corner sizing handle on the photograph diagonally inward until the photograph is resized to approximately 3.9″ × 6.93″.

- Drag the clip to the location shown in Figure 3–58.

Q&A

Can I rearrange the order in which video and audio clips play during a slide show?

Yes. You can change the sequence by clicking the Animation Pane button (Animations tab | Advanced Animation group) to open the Animation Pane, selecting one of the clips in the list, and then clicking the up or down Re-Order arrows at the bottom of the task pane. You also can select one of the clips and then click the Move Earlier or Move Later buttons (Animations tab | Timing group).

Figure 3–58

TO SHOW MEDIA CONTROLS

When you are running a slide show, slide show controls display by default when you move your mouse pointer over audio and video clips. These controls allow you to pause, play, mute, unmute, and move the clip forward and backward.

To hide these controls during a slide show, you would perform the following step.

1. Click the Show Media Controls check box (Slide Show tab | Set Up group) to remove the check mark.

If you want to show the hidden media controls, you would perform the following step.

1. Click the Show Media Controls check box (Slide Show tab | Set Up group) to place a check mark in it.

To Insert a Movie Clip

PowerPoint classifies animated GIF files as a type of video or movie because the clips have movement or action. These files are commonplace on Web sites. They also are found in PowerPoint presentations when you want to call attention to material on a particular slide. You can insert them into a PowerPoint presentation in the same manner that you insert video and audio files. They play automatically when the slide is displayed. The following steps insert a music notes video clip into Slide 1.

1

- Display Slide 1 and then display the Insert tab.

- Click the Picture button (Insert tab | Images group) to display the Insert Picture dialog box.

- If necessary, navigate to the Chapter 3 files on your USB drive.

- Click Music Notes to select the file (Figure 3–59).

  Why does my list of files look different?

  The list of picture files can vary depending upon the contents of your USB drive and the organization of those files into folders for each chapter.

  Can I search for animated GIF files in the Microsoft Clip Organizer?

  Yes. Click the Video button arrow (Insert tab | Media group), click Clip Art Video, click the Videos check box (Clip Art task pane), type the search text, and then click the Go button.

Figure 3–59

2

- Click the Insert button (Insert Picture dialog box) to insert the Music Notes animated GIF clip into Slide 1.

- Resize the clip so that it is approximately 1" × 1.47".

- Drag the clip to the location shown in Figure 3–60.

  Why is the animation not showing?

  Animated GIF files move only in Slide Show view and Reading view.

Figure 3–60

Break Point: If you wish to take a break, this is a good place to do so. Be sure to save the Bird Migration file again and then you can quit PowerPoint. To resume at a later time, start PowerPoint, open the file called Bird Migration, and continue following the steps from this location forward.

BTW

Revising Your Text
Generating ideas, revising slides, editing graphics and text, and then proofreading all slide text are required as part of the development process. A good PowerPoint developer has the ability to write and then revise slide content. Multiple drafts generally are needed to complete a successful presentation. PowerPoint's Find and Replace feature is useful if you need to change all instances of a word throughout a large presentation when you are revising slides.

Reviewing and Revising Individual Slides

The text and graphics for all slides in the Bird Migration presentation have been entered. Once you complete a slide show, you might decide to change elements. PowerPoint provides several tools to assist you with making changes. They include finding and replacing text, inserting a synonym, and checking spelling. The following pages discuss these tools.

Replace Dialog Box

At times, you might want to change all occurrences of a word or phrase to another word or phrase. For example, an instructor may have one slide show to accompany a lecture for several introductory classes, and he wants to update slides with the particular class name and section that appear on several slides. He manually could change the characters, but PowerPoint includes an efficient method of replacing one word with another. The Find and Replace feature automatically locates specific text and then replaces it with desired text.

In some cases, you may want to replace only certain occurrences of a word or phrase, not all of them. To instruct PowerPoint to confirm each change, click the Find Next button in the Replace dialog box instead of the Replace All button. When PowerPoint locates an occurrence of the text, it pauses and waits for you to click either the Replace button or the Find Next button. Clicking the Replace button changes the text; clicking the Find Next button instructs PowerPoint to disregard that particular instance and look for the next occurrence of the Find what text.

To Find and Replace Text

While reviewing your slides, you realize that you could give more specific information regarding the type of thrush discussed in Slide 2. The Wood Thrush's songs especially are melodic and beautiful, so you decide to add the word, Wood, to the bird's name. In addition, you want to capitalize the word, Thrush, because it is a specific type of thrush. To perform this action, you can use PowerPoint's Find and Replace feature, which automatically locates each occurrence of a word or phrase and then replaces it with specified text. The word, thrush, displays twice on Slide 2. The following steps use Find and Replace to replace all occurrences of the word, thrush, with the words, Wood Thrush.

BTW

Matching Case and Finding Whole Words
Two options in the Replace dialog box are useful when revising slides. Match case maintains the upper- or lowercase letters within a word, such as a capitalized word at the beginning of a sentence. In addition, the 'Find whole words only' option specifies that PowerPoint makes replacements only when the word typed in the Find what box is a complete word and is not embedded within another word. For example, if you want to change the word 'diction' to 'pronunciation,' clicking the 'Find whole words only' option prevents PowerPoint from changing the word, dictionary, to 'pronunciationary.'

- Display the Home tab and then display Slide 2. Click the Replace button (Home tab | Editing group) to display the Replace dialog box.

- Type **thrush** in the Find what text box (Replace dialog box).

- Press the TAB key. Type **Wood Thrush** in the Replace with text box (Figure 3–61).

  Do I need to display the slide that contains the words for which I want to search?

  No. But to allow you to see the results of this search and replace action, you can display the slide where the changes will occur.

Figure 3–61

- Click the Replace All button (Replace dialog box) to instruct PowerPoint to replace all occurrences of the Find what word, thrush, with the Replace with words, Wood Thrush (Figure 3–62).

  If I accidentally replaced the wrong text, can I undo this replacement?

  Yes. Click the Undo button on the Quick Access Toolbar to undo all replacements. If you had clicked the Replace button instead of the Replace All button, PowerPoint would undo only the most recent replacement.

Figure 3–62

- Click the OK button (Microsoft PowerPoint dialog box).

- Click the Close button (Replace dialog box).

Other Ways

1. Press CTRL+H

To Find and Insert a Synonym

When reviewing your slide show, you may decide that a particular word does not express the exact usage you intended or that you used the same word on multiple slides. In these cases, you could find a **synonym**, or word similar in meaning, to replace the inappropriate or duplicate word. PowerPoint provides a **thesaurus**, which is a list of synonyms and antonyms, to help you find a replacement word.

In this project, you want to find a synonym to replace the word, Defend, on Slide 2. The following steps locate an appropriate synonym and replace the word.

- With Slide 2 displaying, right-click the word, Defend, to display a shortcut menu.

- Point to Synonyms on the shortcut menu to display a list of synonyms for this word (Figure 3–63).

Figure 3–63

- Click the synonym you want (Protect) on the Synonyms submenu to replace the word, Defend, in the presentation with the word, Protect (Figure 3–64).

Figure 3–64

Q&A

What if a suitable word does not display in the Synonyms submenu?

You can display the thesaurus in the Research task pane by clicking Thesaurus on the Synonyms submenu. A complete thesaurus with synonyms displays in the Research task pane along with an **antonym**, which is a word with an opposite meaning.

Other Ways

1. Click Thesaurus (Review tab | Proofing group)
2. Press SHIFT+F7

BTW

Foreign Language Synonyms
The thesaurus contains synonyms for languages other than English. To look up words in the thesaurus of another language, click the Thesaurus button (Review tab | Proofing group), click Research options (Research task pane), select the desired languages in the Reference Books area, and then click the OK button.

To Add Notes

As you create slides, you may find material you want to state verbally and do not want to include on the slide. You can type and format notes in the **Notes pane** as you work in Normal view and then print this information as **notes pages**. After adding comments, you can print a set of speaker notes. These notes will print below a small image of the slide. Charts, tables, and pictures added to the Notes pane also print on these pages. In this project, comments were included on Slide 2 when you opened that file. The following steps add text to the Notes pane on Slides 1 and 3.

1

• Display Slide 1, click the Notes pane, and then type `More than 10,000 species of birds exist in the world. The largest bird is the ostrich, and the smallest is the hummingbird. They generally live in small groups, but some form huge flocks with thousands of members and a variety of species. Flocks help keep the birds safe while they search for food.` (Figure 3–65).

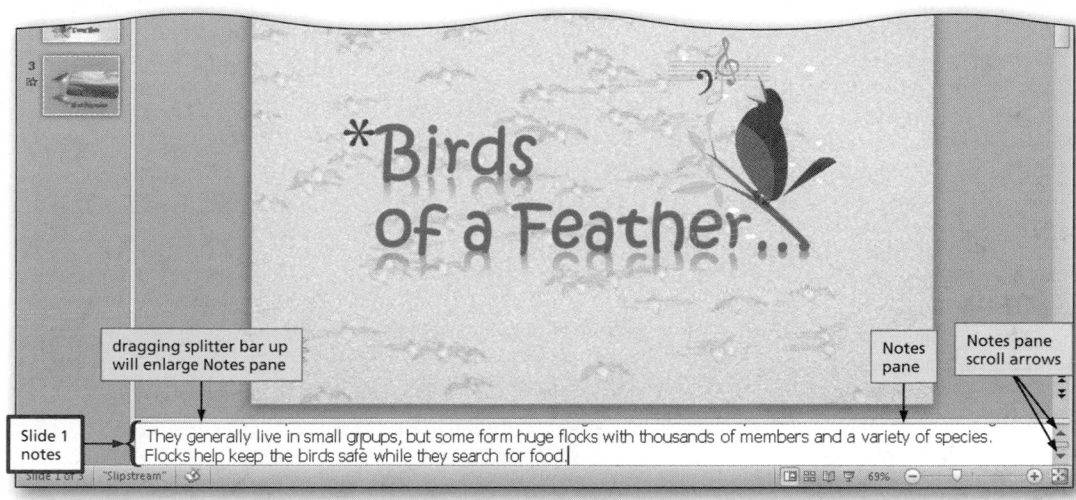

Figure 3–65

What if I cannot see all the lines I typed?

You can drag the splitter bar up to enlarge the Notes pane. Clicking the Notes pane scroll arrows allows you to view the entire text.

2

• Display Slide 3, click the Notes pane, and then type `Birds migrate to benefit from warm weather. Some can fly more than 6,000 miles without stopping. We can help bird migration by providing food, shelters, nest sites, and water.` (Figure 3–66).

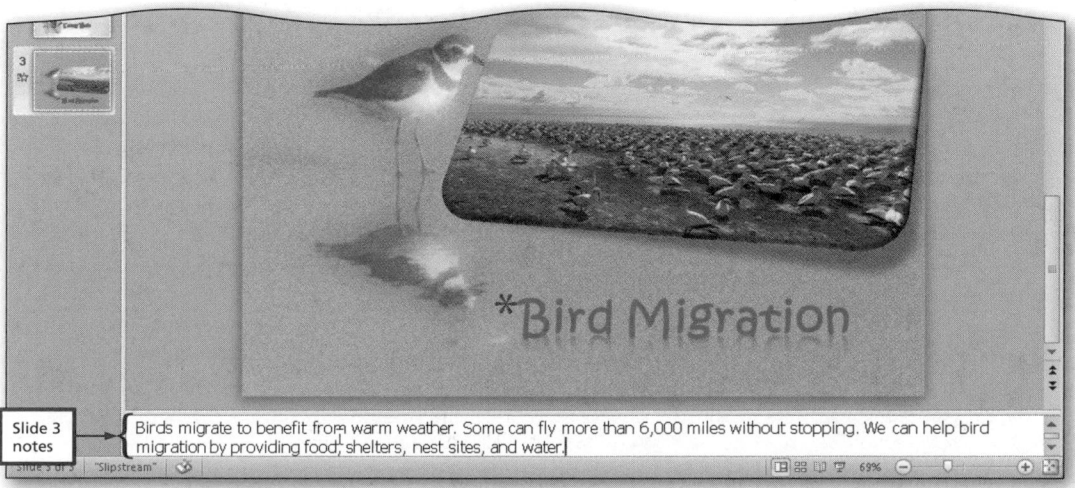

Figure 3–66

BTW

Using AutoCorrect Features

Microsoft Office programs use the AutoCorrect feature to correct typing mistakes and commonly misspelled words. When you install Microsoft Office, a default list of typical misspellings is created. To view this list, click File on the Ribbon to open the Backstage view, under Help click Options, click Proofing in left pane (PowerPoint Options dialog box), and then click the AutoCorrect Options button. If necessary, click the AutoCorrect tab (AutoCorrect dialog box). The first column of this list contains the word that you often mistype, and the second column contains the replacement text. You can modify the AutoCorrect list with words you are apt to misspell. The AutoCorrect feature also inserts symbols, such as replacing (c) with the copyright symbol, ©.

Checking Spelling

After you create a presentation, you should check it visually for spelling errors and style consistency. In addition, you use PowerPoint's Spelling tool to identify possible misspellings on the slides and in the notes. Do not rely on the spelling checker to catch all your mistakes. Although PowerPoint's spelling checker is a valuable tool, it is not infallible. You should proofread your presentation carefully by pointing to each word and saying it aloud as you point to it. Be mindful of commonly misused words such as its and it's, through and though, and to and too.

PowerPoint checks the entire presentation for spelling mistakes using a standard dictionary contained in the Microsoft Office group. This dictionary is shared with the other Microsoft Office applications such as Word and Excel. A **custom dictionary** is available if you want to add special words such as proper names, cities, and acronyms. When checking a presentation for spelling errors, PowerPoint opens the standard dictionary and the custom dictionary file, if one exists. When a word appears in the Spelling dialog box, you can perform one of several actions, as described in Table 3–1.

Table 3–1 Spelling Dialog Box Buttons and Actions

Button Name	When To Use	Action
Ignore	Word is spelled correctly but not found in dictionaries	PowerPoint continues checking rest of the presentation but will flag that word again if it appears later in document.
Ignore All	Word is spelled correctly but not found in dictionaries	PowerPoint ignores all occurrences of the word and continues checking rest of presentation.
Change	Word is misspelled	Click proper spelling of the word in Suggestions list. PowerPoint corrects word, continues checking rest of presentation, but will flag that word again if it appears later in document.
Change All	Word is misspelled	Click proper spelling of word in Suggestions list. PowerPoint changes all occurrences of misspelled word and continues checking rest of presentation.
Add	Add word to custom dictionary	PowerPoint opens custom dictionary, adds word, and continues checking rest of presentation.
Suggest	Correct spelling is uncertain	Lists alternative spellings. Click the correct word from the Suggestions box or type the proper spelling. Corrects the word and continues checking the rest of the presentation.
AutoCorrect	Add spelling error to AutoCorrect list	PowerPoint adds spelling error and its correction to AutoCorrect list. Any future misspelling of word is corrected automatically as you type.
Close	Stop spelling checker	PowerPoint closes spelling checker and returns to PowerPoint window.

The standard dictionary contains commonly used English words. It does not, however, contain many proper names, abbreviations, technical terms, poetic contractions, or antiquated terms. PowerPoint treats words not found in the dictionaries as misspellings.

To Check Spelling

The following steps check the spelling on all slides in the Bird Migration presentation.

- Click Review on the Ribbon to display the Review tab.

- Click the Spelling button (Review Tab | Proofing group) to start the spelling checker and display the Spelling dialog box (Figure 3–67).

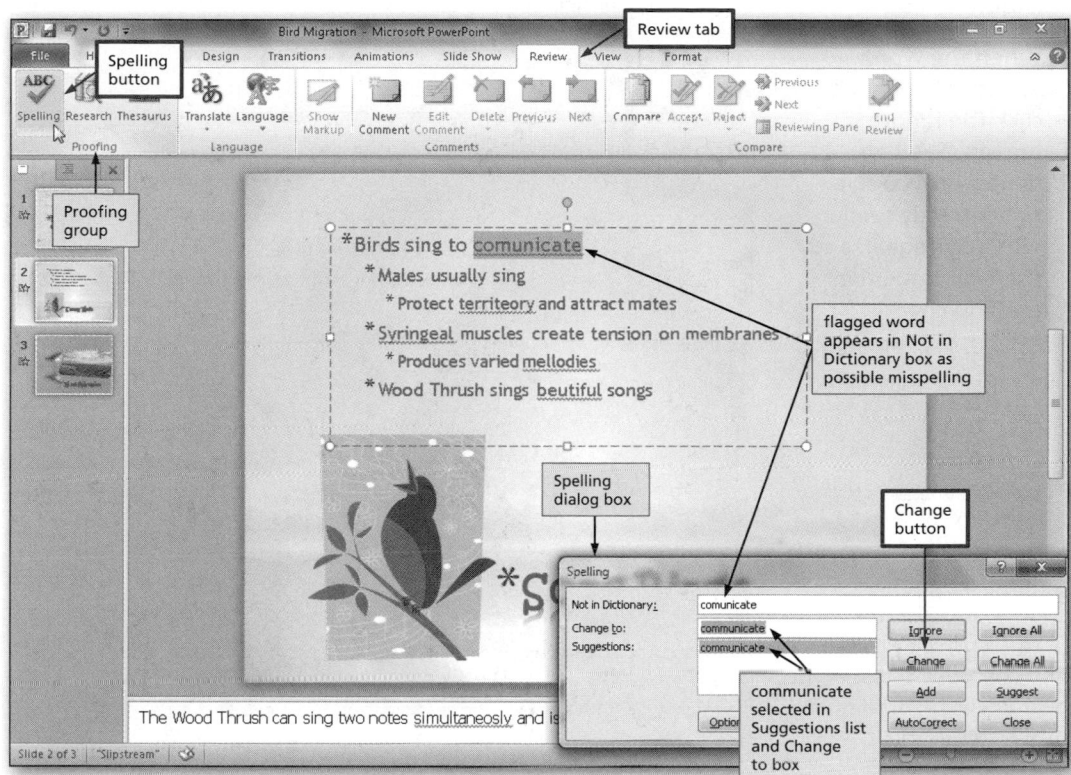

Figure 3–67

- With the word, communicate, selected in the Suggestions list, click the Change button (Spelling dialog box) to replace the misspelled flagged word, comunicate, with the selected correctly spelled word, communicate, and then continue the spelling check (Figure 3–68).

Could I have clicked the Change All button instead of the Change button?

Yes. When you click the Change All button, you change the current and future occurrences of the misspelled word.

The misspelled word, comunicate, appears only once in the presentation, so clicking the Change or the Change All button in this instance produces identical results.

Figure 3–68

- Replace the misspelled word, territeory, with the word, territory (Figure 3–69).

- When the word, Syringeal, is flagged, click the Ignore button (Spelling dialog box) to skip the correctly spelled word, Syringeal, and then continue the spelling check.

Syringeal is flagged as a possible misspelled word. Why?

Your custom dictionary does not contain the word, so it is recognized as spelled incorrectly. You can add this word to a custom dictionary to prevent the spelling checker from flagging it as a mistake.

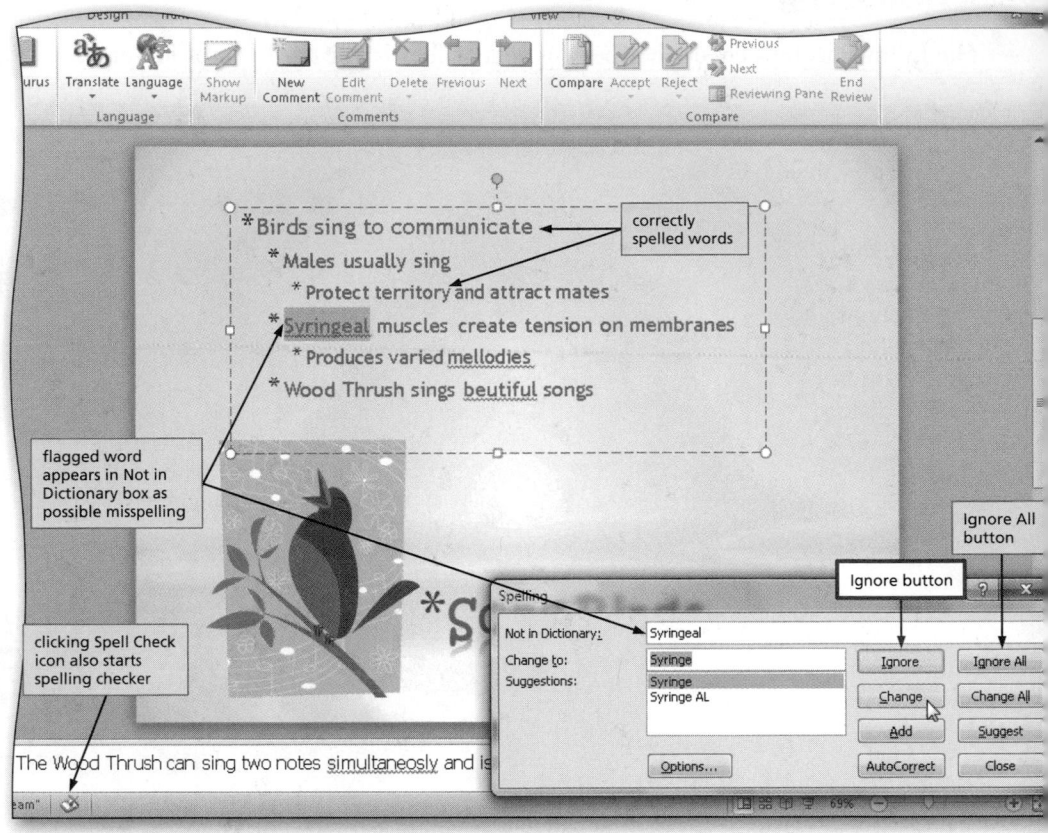

Figure 3–69

Could I have clicked the Ignore All button instead of the Ignore button?

Yes. When you click the Ignore All button, you ignore the current and future occurrences of the word.

- Continue checking all flagged words in the presentation. When the Microsoft PowerPoint dialog box appears, click the OK button (Microsoft PowerPoint dialog box) to close the spelling checker and return to the current slide, Slide 2, or to the slide where a possible misspelled word appeared.

Other Ways
1. Click Spell Check icon on status bar, click Spelling on shortcut menu 2. Right-click flagged word, click correct word or	click Spelling on shortcut menu 3. Press F7

To Insert a Slide Number

PowerPoint can insert the slide number on your slides automatically to indicate where the slide is positioned within the presentation. The number location on the slide is determined by the presentation theme. You have the option to not display this slide number on the title slide. The following steps insert the slide number on all slides except the title slide.

- If a word in the Notes pane is selected, click the Slide 2 Slide pane. Display the Insert tab and then click the Insert Slide Number button (Insert tab | Text group) to display the Header and Footer dialog box (Figure 3–70).

Why did I need to click the Slide pane?

The page number would have been inserted in the Notes pane instead of on the slide.

Figure 3–70

- Click the Slide number check box (Header and Footer dialog box) to place a check mark in it.

- Click the 'Don't show on title slide' check box (Header and Footer dialog box) to place a check mark in it (Figure 3–71).

Where does the slide number display on the slide?

Each theme determines where the slide number is displayed in the footer. In the Slipstream theme, the slide number location is the center of the footer, as indicated by the black box at the bottom of the Preview area.

Figure 3–71

- Click the Apply to All button (Header and Footer dialog box) to close the dialog box and insert the slide number on all slides except Slide 1 (Figure 3–72).

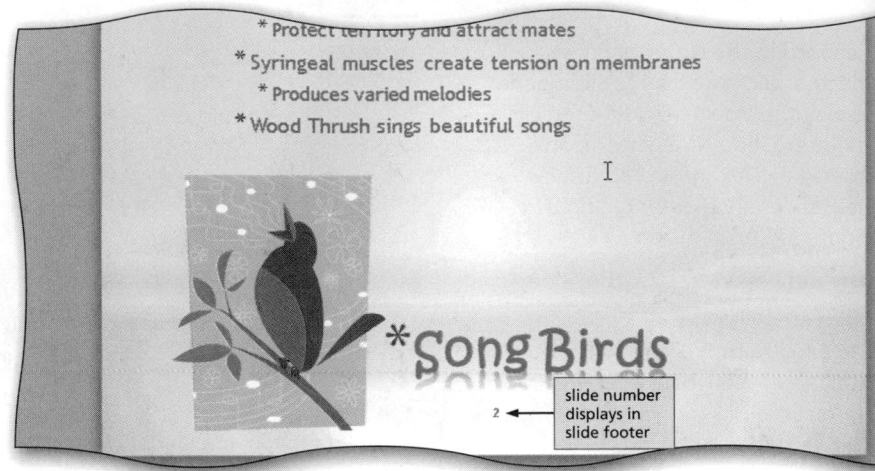

slide number displays in slide footer

Figure 3–72

How does clicking the Apply to All button differ from clicking the Apply button?

The Apply button inserts the slide number only on the currently displayed slide whereas the Apply to All button inserts the slide number on every slide.

Other Ways

1. Click Header & Footer button (Insert tab | Text group), click Slide Number box (Header and Footer dialog box), click 'Slide number' and 'Don't show on title slide' boxes, click Apply to All button

Plan Ahead

Use handouts to organize your speech.

As you develop a lengthy presentation with many visuals, handouts may help you organize your material. Print handouts with the maximum number of slides per page. Use scissors to cut each thumbnail and then place these miniature slide images adjacent to each other on a flat surface. Any type on the thumbnails will be too small to read, so the images will need to work with only the support of the verbal message you provide. You can rearrange these thumbnails as you organize your speech. When you return to your computer, you can rearrange the slides on your screen to match the order of your thumbnail printouts. Begin speaking the actual words you want to incorporate in the body of the talk. This process of glancing at the thumbnails and hearing yourself say the key ideas of the speech is one of the best methods of organizing and preparing for the actual presentation. Ultimately, when you deliver your speech in front of an audience, the images on the slides or on your note cards should be sufficient to remind you of the accompanying verbal message.

To Preview and Print a Handout

Printing handouts is useful for reviewing a presentation because you can analyze several slides displayed simultaneously on one page. Additionally, many businesses distribute handouts of the slide show before or after a presentation so attendees can refer to a copy. Each page of the handout can contain reduced images of one, two, three, four, six, or nine slides. The three-slides-per-page handout includes lines beside each slide so that your audience can write notes conveniently. The following steps preview and print a presentation handout.

- Click File on the Ribbon to open the Backstage view and then click the Print tab to display Slide 2 in the Print gallery.

- Click Full Page Slides in the Settings area to display the Full Page Slides gallery (Figure 3–73).

Why does the preview of my slide appear in color?

Your printer determines how the preview appears. If your printer is not capable of printing color images, the preview will not appear in color.

Figure 3–73

- Click 2 Slides in the Handouts area to select this option and display a preview of the handout (Figure 3–74).

The current date displays in the upper-right corner of the handout, and the page number displays in the lower-right corner of the footer. Can I change their location or add other information to the header and footer?

Yes. Click the Edit Header & Footer link at the bottom of the Print gallery, click the Notes and Handouts tab (Header and Footer dialog box), and then decide what content to include on the handout page.

Figure 3–74

• Click the Next Page and Previous Page buttons to display previews of the two pages in the presentation.

• Click the Print button in the Print gallery to print the handout.

• When the printer stops, retrieve the printed handout (Figure 3–75).

current date

5/3/2012

*Birds of a Feather...

*Birds sing to communicate
*Males usually sing
*Protect territory and attract mates
*Syringeal muscles create tension on membranes
*Produces varied melodies
*Wood Thrush sings beautiful songs

*Song Birds

page number

1

current date

5/3/2012

(a) Page 1

*Bird Migration

page number

2

(b) Page 2

Figure 3–75

To Print Speaker Notes

Comments added to slides in the Notes pane give the speaker information that supplements the text on the slide. They will print with a small image at the top and the comments below the slide. The following steps print the speaker notes.

- Click the Print tab in the Backstage view and then click 2 Slides in the Settings area to display the gallery (Figure 3–76).

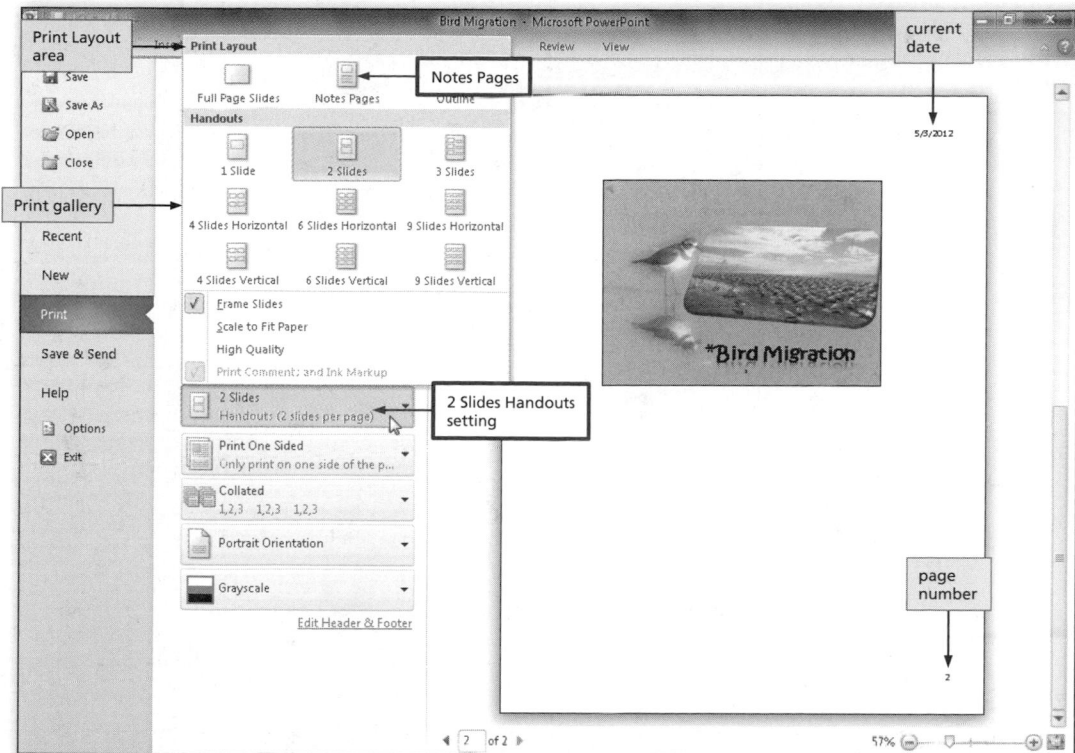

Figure 3–76

- Click Notes Pages in the Print Layout area to selcct this option and display a preview of the current page (Figure 3–77).

- Click the Previous Page and Next Page buttons to display previews of other pages in the presentation.

Figure 3–77

- Click the Print button in the Print gallery to print the notes.

- When the printer stops, retrieve the printed pages (Figure 3–78).

(a) Page 1

(b) Page 2

(c) Page 3

Figure 3–78

Evaluate your presentation.

One of the best methods of improving your communication skills is to focus on what you learned from the experience. Respond to these questions:

- How successfully do you feel you fulfilled your assignment?
- What strategies did you use to develop your slides and the accompanying oral presentation?
- What revisions did you make?
- If you could go back to the speaking engagement and change one thing, what would it be?
- What feedback did you receive from your instructor or audience?

Plan
Ahead

To Change Document Properties

Before saving the presentation again, you want to add your name, class name, and some keywords as document properties. The following steps use the Document Information Panel to change document properties.

- In the Backstage view, click the Properties button in the right pane of the Info gallery, and then click Show Document Panel on the Properties menu to close the Backstage view and display the Document Information Panel.

- Enter your name in the Author text box. Enter your course and section in the Subject text box. Enter the text, **bird, migration, singing** in the Keywords text box.

- Close the Document Information Panel.

- Click the Save button on the Quick Access Toolbar to overwrite the previous Bird Migration file on the USB flash drive.

BTW

Quick Reference
For a table that lists how to complete the tasks covered in this book using the mouse, Ribbon, shortcut menu, and keyboard, see the Quick Reference Summary at the back of this book, or visit the PowerPoint 2010 Quick Reference Web page (scsite.com/ppt2010/qr).

To Run a Slide Show with Media

All changes are complete, and the presentation is saved. You now can view the Bird Migration presentation. The following steps start Slide Show view.

- Click the Slide 1 thumbnail in the Slide pane to select and display Slide 1.

- Click the Slide Show button to display the title slide, watch the animations, and listen to the bird calls. Allow the audio clip to repeat several times.

- Press the SPACEBAR to display Slide 2.

- Press the SPACEBAR to display Slide 3. Listen to the audio clip, watch the video clip, and then allow the audio clip to repeat several times.

- Press the SPACEBAR to end the slide show and click to exit the slide show.

BTW

Certification
The Microsoft Office Specialist (MOS) program provides an opportunity for you to obtain a valuable industry credential — proof that you have the PowerPoint 2010 skills required by employers. For more information, visit the PowerPoint 2010 Certification Web page (scsite.com/ppt2010/cert).

To Quit PowerPoint

This project is complete. The following steps quit PowerPoint.

- Click the Close button on the right side of the title bar to close the document and then quit PowerPoint.

- If a Microsoft PowerPoint dialog box appears, click the Save button to save any changes made to the presentation since the last save.

Chapter Summary

In this chapter you have learned how to enhance an existing presentation by adding video, audio, and pictures with effects. You also learned to modify placeholders, align text, and review a presentation by checking spelling and creating handouts. The items listed below include all the new PowerPoint skills you have learned in this chapter.

1. Color a Picture (PPT 143)
2. Add an Artistic Effect to a Picture (144)
3. Change the Stacking Order (PPT 146)
4. Resize a Placeholder (PPT 148)
5. Move a Placeholder (PPT 148)
6. Delete a Placeholder (PPT 149)
7. Align Paragraph Text (PPT 150)
8. Delete a Slide (PPT 152)
9. Change Views (PPT 153)
10. Copy a Clip from One Slide to Another (PPT 155)
11. Zoom a Slide (PPT 156)
12. Ungroup a Clip (PPT 157)
13. Change the Color of a Clip Object (PPT 158)
14. Delete a Clip Object (PPT 161)
15. Regroup Objects (PPT 162)
16. Insert a Video File (PPT 163)
17. Trim a Video File (PPT 164)
18. Add Video Options (PPT 166)
19. Insert an Audio File (PPT 167)
20. Add Audio Options (PPT 170)
21. Add a Video Style (PPT 172)
22. Resize a Video (PPT 174)
23. Insert a Movie Clip (PPT 174)
24. Find and Replace Text (PPT 176)
25. Find and Insert a Synonym (PPT 178)
26. Add Notes (PPT 179)
27. Check Spelling (PPT 181)
28. Insert a Slide Number (PPT 182)
29. Preview and Print a Handout (PPT 184)
30. Print Speaker Notes (PPT 187)

If you have a SAM 2010 user profile, your instructor may have assigned an autogradable version of this assignment. If so, log into the SAM 2010 Web site at www.cengage.com/sam2010 to download the instruction and start files.

Learn It Online

Test your knowledge of chapter content and key terms.

Instructions: To complete the Learn It Online exercises, start your browser, click the Address bar, and then enter the Web address **scsite.com/ppt2010/learn**. When the PowerPoint 2010 Learn It Online page is displayed, click the link for the exercise you want to complete and then read the instructions.

Chapter Reinforcement TF, MC, and SA

A series of true/false, multiple choice, and short answer questions that test your knowledge of the chapter content.

Flash Cards

An interactive learning environment where you identify chapter key terms associated with displayed definitions.

Practice Test

A series of multiple choice questions that test your knowledge of chapter content and key terms.

Who Wants To Be a Computer Genius?

An interactive game that challenges your knowledge of chapter content in the style of a television quiz show.

Wheel of Terms

An interactive game that challenges your knowledge of chapter key terms in the style of the television show *Wheel of Fortune*.

Crossword Puzzle Challenge

A crossword puzzle that challenges your knowledge of key terms presented in the chapter.

Apply Your Knowledge

Reinforce the skills and apply the concepts you learned in this chapter.

Adding Artistic Effects to Pictures, Moving a Placeholder, and Inserting and Controlling Audio Clips

Note: To complete this assignment, you will be required to use the Data Files for Students. See the inside back cover of this book for instructions on downloading the Data Files for Students, or contact your instructor for information about accessing the required files.

Instructions: Start PowerPoint. Open the presentation, Apply 3-1 SAD, from the Data Files for Students.

The five slides in the presentation, shown in Figure 3–79, present information about Seasonal Affective Disorder, also known as SAD, which is a mood disorder that occurs generally during the winter months. The document you open is composed of slides containing pictures and clip art, and you will apply artistic effects or modify some of these graphic elements. You also will insert audio clips from Office.com. In addition, you will move the placeholder on the final slide.

Perform the following tasks:

1. Insert the audio clip, Sad Piano Music, into Slide 1 (Figure 3–79a). Change the volume to Medium, start the clip automatically, and hide the sound icon during the slide show. Then copy this audio clip to Slides 2, 3, and 4 with the same options. Insert the audio clip, Variety Hour, into Slide 5, change the volume to Medium, start the clip automatically, and hide the sound icon during the slide show.

2. On Slide 2, color the picture by selecting Yellow, Accent color 2 Dark from the Recolor area, as shown in Figure 3–79b.

3. On Slide 3, apply the Watercolor Sponge artistic effect to the picture, as shown in Figure 3–79c.

4. On Slide 4, select the lamp clip and then change the Zoom level to 120%. Ungroup the lamp clip and then recolor the arms to Dark Teal, Text 2, Lighter 10% (last color in fourth Theme Colors column), as shown in Figure 3–79d. Regroup the clip. Change the Zoom level to 69%.

5. On Slide 5, move the WordArt placeholder above the bird in the picture, as shown in Figure 3–79e.

6. On Slide 1, type `Up to 9 percent of U.S. adults may suffer from SAD.` in the Notes pane.

7. Check the slides for spelling errors and then run the revised presentation.

8. Change the document properties, as specified by your instructor. Save the presentation using the file name, Apply 3-1 Seasonal Affective Disorder.

9. Submit the revised document in the format specified by your instructor.

(a) Slide 1

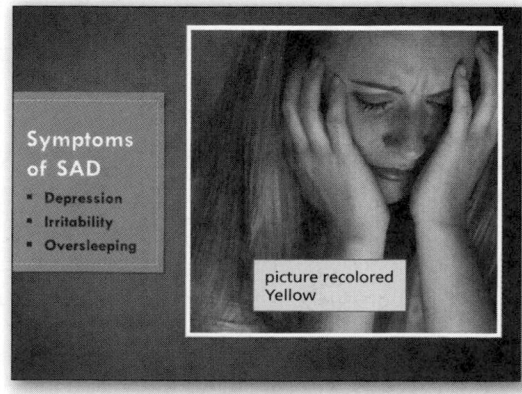

(b) Slide 2

Figure 3–79

Continued >

STUDENT ASSIGNMENTS

(c) Slide 3

(d) Slide 4

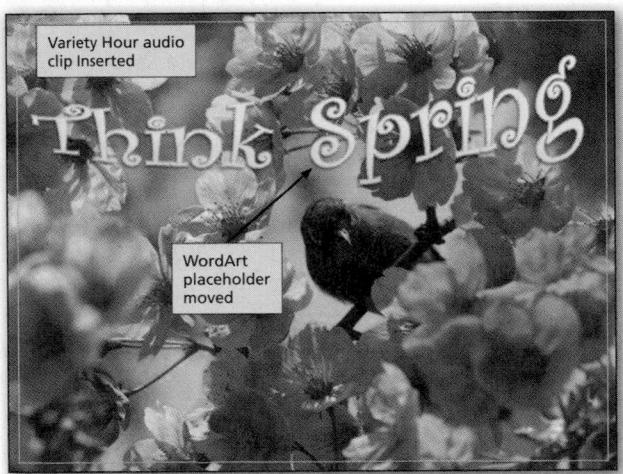

(e) Slide 5

Figure 3–79 (Continued)

Extend Your Knowledge

Extend the skills you learned in this chapter and experiment with new skills. You may need to use Help to complete the assignment.

Formatting a Video Border, Deleting Audio, Adding a Font Effect, and Pausing and Resuming Video Playback

Note: To complete this assignment, you will be required to use the Data Files for Students. See the inside back cover of this book for instructions on downloading the Data Files for Students, or contact your instructor for information about accessing the required files.

Instructions: Start PowerPoint. Open the presentation, Extend 3-1 Nature, from the Data Files for Students.
You will add the Small Caps font effect to the title text on the title slide, delete an audio clip, and format a video border, as shown in Figure 3–80a. While the slide show is running, you will adjust the video playback to pause and then resume playing the clip.

Perform the following tasks:

1. On Slide 1, move the title text placeholder up so that it is positioned in the upper-right corner of the slide, as shown in Figure 3–80a. Right-align the title text and then add the Small Caps font effect to these letters. *Hint:* Font effects are located in the Font dialog box (Home tab | Font group).

2. On the title slide, delete the audio clip positioned in the upper-left corner of the slide. The three audio clips on the right side of the slide will remain.

3. Change the video style from Soft Edge Oval to Beveled Oval, Black (in the Moderate area). Then change the video border color to Gold, Accent 2 and change the border weight to 10 pt. *Hint:* Click More Lines in the Video Border Weight gallery and then change the Border Style Width.

4. On Slide 2, add a border to each of the six pictures that surround the center deer video frame, and then change the border colors and the border weights. Use Figure 3–80b as a guide. Add the Compound Frame, Black video style (in the Moderate area) to the bird feeder clip.

5. Change the document properties, as specified by your instructor. Save the presentation using the file name, Extend 3-1 Observing Nature.

6. Start the slide show. When a few seconds of the video have elapsed, pause the video and then move your mouse pointer to an area other than the video and listen to the bird audio clips. Then move the mouse pointer over the video clip to display the Video Controls. Resume the video playback.

7. Submit the revised document in the format specified by your instructor.

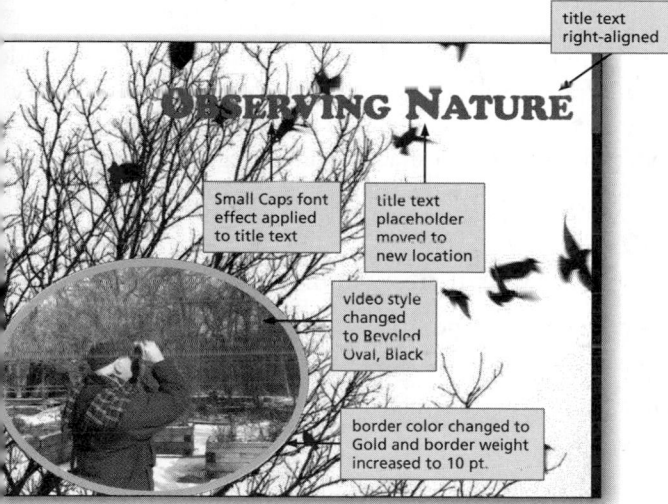

title text right-aligned

Small Caps font effect applied to title text

title text placeholder moved to new location

video style changed to Beveled Oval, Black

border color changed to Gold and border weight increased to 10 pt.

(a) Slide 1

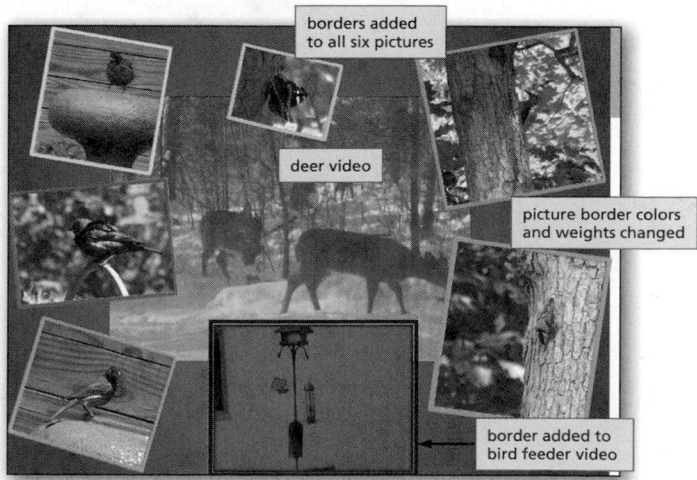

borders added to all six pictures

deer video

picture border colors and weights changed

border added to bird feeder video

(b) Slide 2

Figure 3–80

Make It Right

Analyze a presentation and correct all errors and/or improve the design.

Editing Clips, Finding and Replacing Text, and Correcting Spelling

Note: To complete this assignment, you will be required to use the Data Files for Students. See the inside back cover of this book for instructions on downloading the Data Files for Students, or contact your instructor for information about accessing the required files.

Instructions: Start PowerPoint. Open the presentation, Make It Right 3-1 Flamingos, from the Data Files for Students.

Correct the formatting problems and errors in the presentation while keeping in mind the guidelines presented in this chapter.

Perform the following tasks:

1. On Slide 1 (Figure 3–81), change the audio clip volume to High and hide the sound icon during the show. Loop this clip for the duration of the slide show.

2. On Slide 2, add the Reflection video effect located in the Reflection Variations area, Tight Reflection 4 pt offset (first reflection in second row) to the video.

3. Trim the Slide 2 video so that the Start Time is 00:21.087 and the End Time is 01:44.273. The duration should be 01:23.186 minutes.

4. Copy the flamingo clip from Slide 4 to Slide 3 and then delete Slide 4. Place this clip on the left side of the picture frame and then adjust the picture frame size so it is the appropriate dimension for the slide content. Ungroup the flamingo clip and then recolor the flamingo to match the color of its legs, the palm tree leaves to a shade of green, and the bird to a shade of blue. Regroup the clip.

5. Find the word, Antarctica, in the Slide 1 Notes pane, and then replace it with the words, South America. Then find the number, 14, and replace it with the number, 4.

6. Check the slides for spelling errors and then run the revised presentation.

7. Change the document properties, as specified by your instructor. Save the presentation using the file name, Make It Right 3-1 Chilean Flamingos.

8. Submit the revised document in the format specified by your instructor.

Figure 3–81

In the Lab

Design and/or create a presentation using the guidelines, concepts, and skills presented in this chapter. Labs 1, 2, and 3 are listed in order of increasing difficulty.

Lab 1: Inserting Audio Clips, Coloring a Picture, and Applying Artistic Effects to Pictures

Note: To complete this assignment, you will be required to use the Data Files for Students. See the inside back cover of this book for instructions on downloading the Data Files for Students, or contact your instructor for information about accessing the required files.

Problem: Start PowerPoint. Open the presentation, Lab 3-1 Cooking, from the Data Files for Students. Your college has an outstanding culinary program, and you are preparing a PowerPoint presentation to promote an upcoming seafood cooking class. The slides will feature audio clips and graphics with applied effects. Create the slides shown in Figure 3–82.

Instructions: Perform the following tasks.

1. On Slide 1, insert the Mr. Light music audio clip from Office.com. Change the volume to Low, play across slides, and hide the sound icon during the show. Move the subtitle text placeholder downward to the location shown in Figure 3–82a and center both paragraphs.

2. On Slide 2, insert the picture called Blackboard and Chef, which is available on the Data Files for Students. Change the color of the picture to Gold, Accent color 3 Dark (Recolor area). Add a border to this picture using Dark Red, Accent 5, and then change the border weight to 6 pt., as shown in Figure 3–82b.

(a) Slide 1

(b) Slide 2

Figure 3–82

Continued >

STUDENT ASSIGNMENTS

In the Lab *continued*

3. On Slide 3, right-align all the text. Insert the Chef video clip from Office.com and resize this clip so that it is approximately 4.08" × 3.99", as shown in Figure 3–82c. Insert the Pepper Grinder video clip from Office.com and resize this clip so that it is approximately 3.81" × 2.25". Move the Pepper Grinder video clip to the lower-left corner of the slide. Insert the audio clips, Pepper Grinder and Cartoon Crash, from Office.com. Start these clips automatically, hide the sound icons during the show, and loop until stopped.

4. On Slide 4, apply the Watercolor Sponge artistic effect to the lobster picture in the left content placeholder and the Plastic Wrap artistic effect to the paella picture in the right content placeholder, as shown in Figure 3–82d.

5. On Slide 5, insert the Bottle Open audio clip from Office.com. Move the sound icon to the lower-right corner of the slide. Start this clip on click. Center the text in the caption placeholder and then move this placeholder downward to the location shown in Figure 3–82e.

6. Review the slides in Slide Sorter view to check for consistency, and then change the view to Normal.

7. Drag the scroll box to display Slide 1. Start Slide Show view and display each slide.

8. Change the document properties, as specified by your instructor. Save the presentation using the file name, Lab 3-1 Cooking Classes.

9. Submit the revised document in the format specified by your instructor.

(c) Slide 3

(d) Slide 4

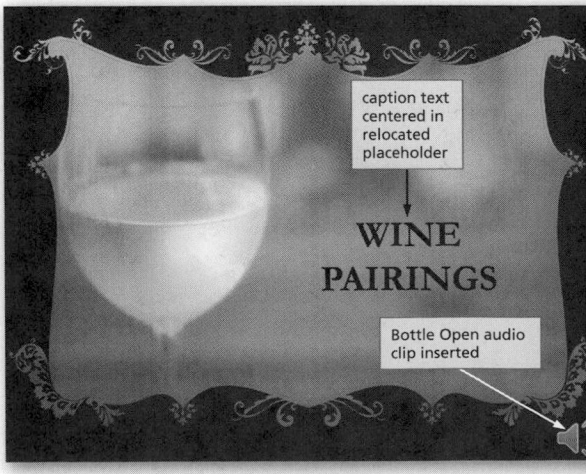

(e) Slide 5

Figure 3–82 (Continued)

In the Lab

Lab 2: Adding Slide Numbers, Applying Artistic Effects to Pictures, and Recoloring a Video

Note: To complete this assignment, you will be required to use the Data Files for Students. See the inside back cover of this book for instructions on downloading the Data Files for Students, or contact your instructor for information about accessing the required files.

Problem: The Dutch tradition is continuing with Klompen dancers, who take their name from their traditional wooden clog shoes. You attended an annual festival this past spring and captured some video clips of teenagers dancing a traditional dance. In addition, you have some video of a hand-built windmill. In your speech class, you desire to inform your classmates of a few aspects of Dutch life, so you prepare the presentation shown in Figure 3–83.

Instructions: Perform the following tasks.

1. Start PowerPoint. Open the presentation, Lab 3-2 Dancers, from the Data Files for Students. On Slide 1, apply the Mosaic Bubbles artistic effect to the tulips picture, as shown in Figure 3–83a. Insert the audio clip, Spring Music, from Office.com. Start this clip automatically, hide the sound icon during the show, and change the volume to Medium.

2. On Slide 2, apply the Marker artistic effect to the wooden shoe picture, as shown in Figure 3–83b. Change the Start option for the video clip from On Click to Automatically. Apply the Rotated, Gradient video style (Moderate area) to the video clip, change the video border color to Tan, Accent 6, and then change the border width to 20 pt.

3. On Slide 2, type `Many dancers wear traditional, hand-sewn Dutch costumes. Dancers wear thick socks to make the wooden shoes comfortable during this annual event.` in the Notes pane.

(a) Slide 1

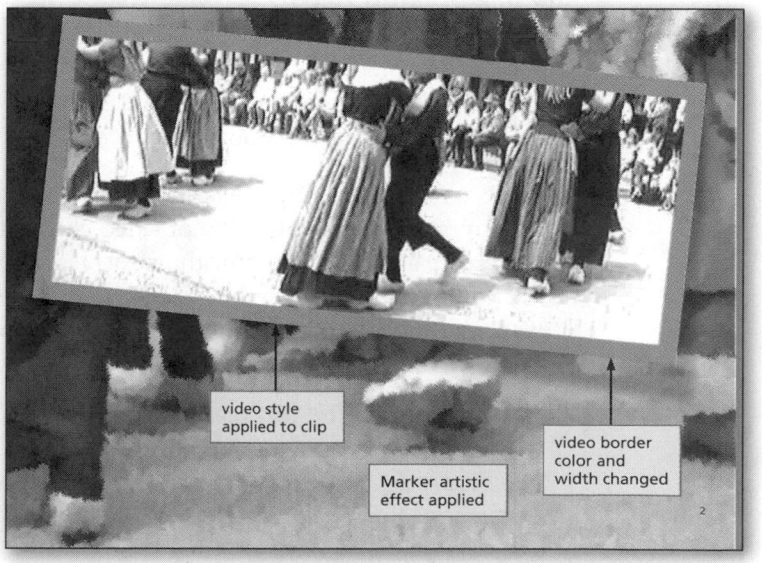

(b) Slide 2

Figure 3–83

Continued >

In the Lab continued

4. On Slide 3, insert the video clip called Windmill from the Data Files for Students. Apply the Reflected Bevel, White video style (Intense area). Change the color of the video to Dark Blue, Accent color 3 Dark (Recolor area). Start this clip automatically and loop until stopped. Center the text in the title placeholder, as shown in Figure 3–83c.

5. Use the thesaurus to change the word, Custom, to Tradition. Check the slides for spelling errors.

6. Add the slide number to all slides except the title slide.

7. Review the slides in Slide Sorter view to check for consistency. Then click the Reading view button to display the current slide and click the Next and Previous buttons to display each slide. Change the view to Normal.

8. Change the document properties, as specified by your instructor. Save the presentation using the file name, Lab 3-2 Klompen Dancers.

9. Submit the revised document in the format specified by your instructor.

(c) Slide 3

Figure 3–83 (Continued)

In the Lab

Lab 3: Applying Artistic Effects to and Recoloring Pictures, Inserting Audio, and Trimming Video

Note: To complete this assignment, you will be required to use the Data Files for Students. See the inside back cover of this book for instructions on downloading the Data Files for Students, or contact your instructor for information about accessing the required files.

Problem: Your Uncle Barney is an avid railroad buff, and he especially is interested in viewing steam locomotives. He has a collection of video clips and photographs of historic steam engines, and he asks you to create a presentation for the next Hessville Train Club meeting he is planning to attend. Start PowerPoint and then open the presentation, Lab 3-3 Locomotives, from the Data Files for Students. Prepare the slides shown in Figures 3–84a through 3–84c.

Instructions: Perform the following tasks.

1. Delete the subtitle text placeholder on Slide 1. Then insert the picture, Steamer 624, from the Data Files for Students and apply the Glow Diffused artistic effect. Position the picture as shown in Figure 3–84a. Center the title text. Insert the audio clip, Train Whistle By, from Office.com. Start this clip automatically, hide the sound icon during the show, and loop until stopped.

2. On Slide 2, insert the picture, Locomotive, from the Data Files for Students and resize it so that it fills the entire slide height and width (approximately 7.5" × 10"). Change the color of the picture to Tan, Accent color 1 Light (Recolor area), as shown in Figure 3–84b.

3. Insert the video clip, Steam Locomotive, from the Data Files for Students. Resize this clip to approximately 4.54" × 8.07" and move the clip to the location shown in Figure 3–84b. Apply the Metal Rounded Rectangle video style (Intense area). Change the color of the border to Olive Green, Accent 2. Trim the Slide 2 video so that the Start Time is 00:06.186 and the End Time is 00:23.432. The duration should be 00:17.246 seconds. Start this clip automatically and loop until stopped.

4. On Slide 3, insert the picture, Railroad Track Border, and the video clip, Red Locomotive, from the Data Files for Students. Resize the Red Locomotive clip to approximately 2.78" × 5.36" and move it to the location shown in Figure 3–84c. Also, insert the audio clip, Steam Train Pass, from Office.com, and move this sound icon to the lower-left corner of the slide. Copy the audio clip, Train Whistle By, from Slide 1 and then move the sound icon to the upper-right corner of the slide. Start both audio clips automatically, hide the sound icons during the show, and loop until stopped.

5. Review the slides in Slide Sorter view. Then click the Reading view button to display the current slide and click the Next and Previous buttons to display each slide. Change the view to Normal.

6. Change the document properties, as specified by your instructor. Save the presentation using the file name, Lab 3-3 Steam Locomotives.

7. Submit the revised document in the format specified by your instructor.

(a) Slide 1

(b) Slide 2

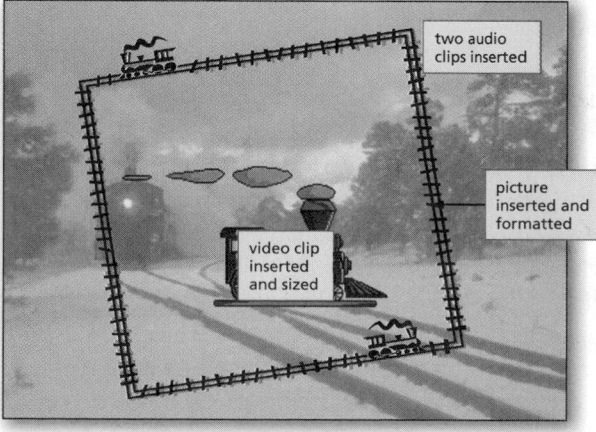

(c) Slide 3

Figure 3–84

Cases and Places

Apply your creative thinking and problem-solving skills to design and implement a solution.

Note: To complete these assignments, you will be required to use the Data Files for Students. See the inside back cover of this book for instructions on downloading the Data Files for Students, or contact your instructor for information about accessing the required files.

As you design the presentations, remember to use the 7 × 7 rule: a maximum of seven words on a line and a maximum of seven lines on one slide.

1: Design and Create a Presentation about Kilauea Volcano

Academic

Most of the volcanic eruptions in Hawaii have occurred within Hawaii Volcanoes National Park. One of these volcanoes, Kilauea, has been erupting since 1983, and visitors to the National Park can drive on two roads to see lava tubes, steam vents, and plants returning to the barren landscape. Rainwater drains through cracks in the ground, is heated, and then is released through fissures and condenses in the cool air. Lava flows in underground tubes, and vents release volcanic gases that consist mainly of carbon dioxide, steam, and sulfur dioxide. During your recent trip to Hawaii Volcanoes National Park, you drove on these roads and captured these geological wonders with your video and digital cameras. You want to share your experience with your Geology 101 classmates. Create a presentation to show the pictures and video clips, which are located in the Data Files for Students and begin with the file name, Case 1. You also can use pictures from Office.com if they are appropriate for this topic. Apply appropriate styles and effects, and use at least three objectives found at the beginning of this chapter to develop the presentation. Be sure to check spelling.

2: Design and Create a Presentation about Surfing

Personal

During your summer vacation, you took surfing lessons and enjoyed the experience immensely. You now want to share your adventure with friends, so you decide to create a short PowerPoint presentation with video clips of the surf and of your paddling on your surfboard to the instruction area in the ocean. You also have pictures of your introductory lesson on shore and of your first successful run catching a wave. The Data Files for Students contains these media files that begin with the file name, Case 2. You also can use your own digital pictures or pictures from Office.com if they are appropriate for this topic. Use the clip, Case 2 - Yellow and Green Surfboard, on one slide, but ungroup this clip and then change the surfboard's colors to your school's team colors. Trim the video clips and apply appropriate styles and effects. Use at least three objectives found at the beginning of this chapter to develop the presentation. Be sure to check spelling.

3: Design and Create a Presentation to Promote Your Snow Removal Business

Professional

Record snowfalls have wreaked havoc in your neighborhood, so you have decided to earn tuition money by starting a snow removal business. You are willing to clear sidewalks and driveways when snowfall exceeds three inches. To promote your business, you desire to create a PowerPoint presentation to run behind the counter at the local hardware store. The Data Files for Students contains pictures and a video clip that begin with the file name, Case 3. You also can use your own digital pictures or pictures from Office.com if they are appropriate for this topic. Use the clip, Case 3 - Man Shoveling, on one slide, but ungroup this clip and then zoom in and delete the white area of the clip depicting the man's breath. Also recolor at least one picture and apply an artistic effect. Be sure to check spelling.

1 | Creating a Worksheet and an Embedded Chart

Objectives

You will have mastered the material in this chapter when you can:

- Describe the Excel worksheet
- Enter text and numbers
- Use the Sum button to sum a range of cells
- Copy the contents of a cell to a range of cells using the fill handle
- Apply cell styles
- Format cells in a worksheet

- Create a Clustered Cylinder chart
- Change a worksheet name and worksheet tab color
- Change document properties
- Preview and print a worksheet
- Use the AutoCalculate area to display statistics
- Correct errors on a worksheet

1 | Creating a Worksheet and an Embedded Chart

Introduction

Almost any organization collects vast amounts of data. Often, data is consolidated into a summary so that people in the organization better understand the meaning of the data. A Excel worksheet allows data easily to be summarized and charted. A chart conveys a visual representation of data. In this chapter, you will create a worksheet that includes a chart. The data in the worksheet and chart includes data for donations made to a not-for-profit organization that operates in several cities.

Project Planning Guidelines

The process of developing a worksheet that communicates specific information requires careful analysis and planning. As a starting point, establish why the worksheet is needed. Once the purpose is determined, analyze the intended users of the worksheet and their unique needs. Then, gather information about the topic and decide what to include in the worksheet. Finally, determine the worksheet design and style that will be most successful at delivering the message. Details of these guidelines are provided in Appendix A. In addition, each project developed in this book provides practical applications of these planning considerations.

Project — Worksheet with an Embedded Chart

The project in this chapter follows proper design guidelines and uses Excel to create the worksheet shown in Figure 1–1. The worksheet contains fundraising data for the Save Sable River Foundation. The Save Sable River Foundation raises funds to care for the environment and preserve the usability of a river that flows through six cities. The foundation raises funds by using five different fundraising activities. Through a concentrated marketing campaign and providing visible results to the communities, the Save Sable River Foundation quickly became a popular local institution. After several years of successful fundraising, senior management requested an easy-to-read worksheet that shows lifetime fundraising amounts for each fundraising technique by city. In addition, they asked for a chart showing lifetime fundraising amounts because the president of the foundation likes to have a graphical representation that allows him quickly to identify stronger and weaker fundraising activities by city.

Figure 1–1

The first step in creating an effective worksheet is to make sure you understand what is required. The person or persons requesting the worksheet should supply their requirements in a requirements document. A **requirements document** includes a needs statement, a source of data, a summary of calculations, and any other special requirements for the worksheet, such as charting and Web support. Figure 1–2 on the following page shows the requirements document for the new workbook to be created in this chapter.

BTW

Excel 2010 Features
With its what-if analysis tools, research capabilities, collaboration tools, streamlined user interface, smart tags, charting features, Web capabilities, hundreds of functions, and enhanced formatting capabilities, Excel 2010 is one of the easier and more powerful spreadsheet programs available. Its dynamic analytical features make it possible to answer complicated what-if questions and its Web capabilities allow you to create, publish, view, share, and analyze data on an intranet or the World Wide Web.

requirements
document

BTW

Worksheet Development Cycle
Spreadsheet specialists do not sit down and start entering text, formulas, and data into a blank Excel worksheet as soon as they have a spreadsheet assignment. Instead, they follow an organized plan, or methodology, that breaks the development cycle into a series of tasks. The recommended methodology for creating worksheets includes: (1) analyze requirements (supplied in a requirements document); (2) design solution; (3) validate design; (4) implement design; (5) test solution; and (6) document solution.

REQUEST FOR NEW WORKBOOK

Date Submitted:	March 22, 2012
Submitted By:	Kevin Li
Worksheet Title:	Save Sable River Foundation Lifetime Fundraising Summary
Needs:	An easy-to-read worksheet that shows a summary of the Save Sable River Foundation's lifetime fundraising efforts for each city in which we operate (Allentown, Chamber City, Pattonsville, Sable Village, Strongville, and the Town of Cary). The worksheet also should include total funds raised for each city, total funds raised for each fundraising activity, and total lifetime funds raised.
Source of Data:	The data for the worksheet is available from the chief financial officer (CFO) of the Save Sable River Foundation.
Calculations:	The following calculations must be made for the worksheet: (a) total lifetime funds raised for each of the six cities; (b) total lifetime funds raised for each of the five fundraising activities; and (c) total lifetime funds raised for the organization.
Chart Requirements:	Below the data in the worksheet, construct a Clustered Cylinder chart that compares the total funds raised for each city within each type of fundraising activity.

Approvals

Approval Status:	X	Approved
		Rejected
Approved By:	Marsha Davis	
Date:	March 29, 2012	
Assigned To:	J. Quasney, Spreadsheet Specialist	

Figure 1–2

Overview

As you read this chapter, you will learn how to create the worksheet shown in Figure 1–1 on the previous page by performing these general tasks:

- Enter text in the worksheet
- Total data in the worksheet
- Format the text in the worksheet
- Insert a chart into the worksheet
- Identify the worksheet with a worksheet name
- Preview and print the worksheet

Plan Ahead

BTW

BTWs
For a complete list of the BTWs found in the margins of this book, visit the Excel 2010 BTW Web page (scsite.com/ex2010/btw).

General Project Guidelines
While creating an Excel worksheet, you need to make several decisions that will determine the appearance and characteristics of the finished worksheet. As you create the worksheet shown in Figure 1–1, you should follow these general guidelines:

1. **Select titles and subtitles for the worksheet.** Follow the *less is more* guideline. The less text in the titles and subtitles, the more impact the titles and subtitles will have. Use the fewest words possible to specify the information presented in the worksheet to the intended audience.

(continued)

(continued)

2. **Determine the contents for rows and columns.** Rows typically contain information that is analogous to items in a list, such as the fundraising techniques used by an organization. Columns typically contain descriptive information about items in rows or contain information that helps to group the data in the worksheet, such as the locations in which the organization operates. Row headings and column headings are usually placed in alphabetical sequence, unless an alternative order is recommended in the requirements document.

3. **Determine the calculations that are needed.** You can decide to total data in a variety of ways, such as across rows or in columns. You also can include a grand total.

4. **Determine where to save the workbook.** You can store a workbook permanently, or **save** it, on a variety of storage media including a hard disk, USB flash drive, CD, or DVD. You also can indicate a specific location on the storage media for saving the workbook.

5. **Identify how to format various elements of the worksheet.** The overall appearance of a worksheet significantly affects its ability to communicate clearly. Examples of how you can modify the appearance, or format, of text include changing its shape, size, color, and position on the worksheet.

6. **Decide on the type of chart needed.** Excel can create many different types of charts, such as cylinder charts and pie charts. Each type of chart relays a different message about the data in the worksheet. Choose a type of chart that relays the message that you want to convey.

7. **Establish where to position and how to format the chart.** The position and format of the chart should command the attention of the intended audience. If possible, position the chart so that it prints with the worksheet data on a single page.

8. **Choose a name for the worksheet.** Each worksheet in a workbook should be named to clarify its purpose. A good worksheet name is succinct, unique to the workbook, and meaningful to any user of the workbook.

9. **Determine the best method for distributing the workbook.** Workbooks and worksheets can be distributed on paper or electronically. The decision regarding how to distribute workbooks and worksheets greatly depends on your intended audience. For example, a worksheet may be printed for inclusion in a report, or a workbook may be distributed using e-mail if the recipient intends to update the workbook.

When necessary, more specific details concerning the above guidelines are presented at appropriate points in the chapter. The chapter also will identify the actions performed and decisions made regarding these guidelines during the creation of the worksheet shown in Figure 1–1 on page EX 3.

Plan Ahead

BTW

Worksheet Development
The key to developing a useful worksheet is careful planning. Careful planning can reduce your effort significantly and result in a worksheet that is accurate, easy to read, flexible, and useful. When analyzing a problem and designing a worksheet solution, you should follow these steps: (1) define the problem, including need, source of data, calculations, charting, and Web or special requirements; (2) design the worksheet; (3) enter the data and formulas; and (4) test the worksheet.

After carefully reviewing the requirements document (Figure 1–2) and making the necessary decisions, the next step is to design a solution or draw a sketch of the worksheet based on the requirements, including titles, column and row headings, the location of data values, and the Clustered Cylinder chart, as shown in Figure 1–3 on the following page. The dollar signs, 9s, and commas that you see in the sketch of the worksheet indicate formatted numeric values.

Save Sable River Foundation
Lifetime Fundraising Summary

	Allentown	Chamber City	Pattonsville	Sable Village	Strongville	Town of Cary	Total
Corporate Direct Mail Fun Runs Government Phone-a-thon	$99,999.99	$99,999.99	$99,999.99	$99,999.99	$99,999.99	$99,999.99	$99,999.99
Total	$999,999.99	$999,999.99	$999,999.99	$999,999.99	$999,999.99	$999,999.99	$9,999,999.99

sketch of worksheet

Legend of Fundraising Types

Allentown   Chamber City   Pattonsville   Sable Village   Strongville   Town of Cary

Figure 1–3

With a good understanding of the requirements document, an understanding of the necessary decisions, and a sketch of the worksheet, the next step is to use Excel to create the worksheet and chart.

To Start Excel

If you are using a computer to step through the project in this chapter and you want your screens to match the figures in this book, you should change your screen's resolution to 1024 × 768. For information about how to change a computer's resolution, refer to the Office 2010 and Windows 7 chapter at the beginning of this book.

The following steps, which assume Windows 7 is running, start Excel based on a typical installation. You may need to ask your instructor how to start Excel for your computer. For a detailed example of the procedure summarized below, refer to the Office 2010 and Windows 7 chapter.

1 Click the Start button on the Windows 7 taskbar to display the Start menu.

2 Type **Microsoft Excel** as the search text in the 'Search programs and files' text box and watch the search results appear on the Start menu.

3 Click Microsoft Excel 2010 in the search results on the Start menu to start Excel and display a new blank workbook in the Excel window.

4 If the Excel window is not maximized, click the Maximize button next to the Close button on its title bar to maximize the window.

Selecting a Cell

To enter data into a cell, you first must select it. The easiest way **to select a cell** (make it active) is to use the mouse to move the block plus sign mouse pointer to the cell and then click.

An alternative method is to use the arrow keys that are located just to the right of the alphanumeric keys on a standard keyboard. An arrow key selects the cell adjacent to the active cell in the direction of the arrow on the key.

You know a cell is selected, or active, when a heavy border surrounds the cell and the active cell reference appears in the Name box on the left side of the formula bar. Excel also changes the active cell's column heading and row heading to a gold color.

Entering Text

In Excel, any set of characters containing a letter, hyphen (as in a telephone number), or space is considered text. **Text** is used to place titles, such as worksheet titles, column titles, and row titles, on the worksheet.

Plan Ahead

Select titles and subtitles for the worksheet.
Worksheet titles and subtitles should be as brief and meaningful as possible. A worksheet title could include the name of the organization, department, or a description of the content of the worksheet. A worksheet subtitle, if included, could include a more detailed description of the content of the worksheet. Examples of worksheet titles are December 2010 Payroll and Year 2011 Projected Budget, and examples of subtitles are Marketing Department and Rent and Utilities, respectively.

Plan Ahead

Determine the contents of rows and columns.
As shown in Figure 1–4, data in a worksheet often is identified by row and column titles so that the user of a worksheet easily can identify the meaning of the data. Rows typically contain information that is similar to items in a list. Columns typically contain descriptive information about items in rows or contain information that helps to group the data in the worksheet. Examples of row titles are Product and Total, and examples of column titles are Name and Address.

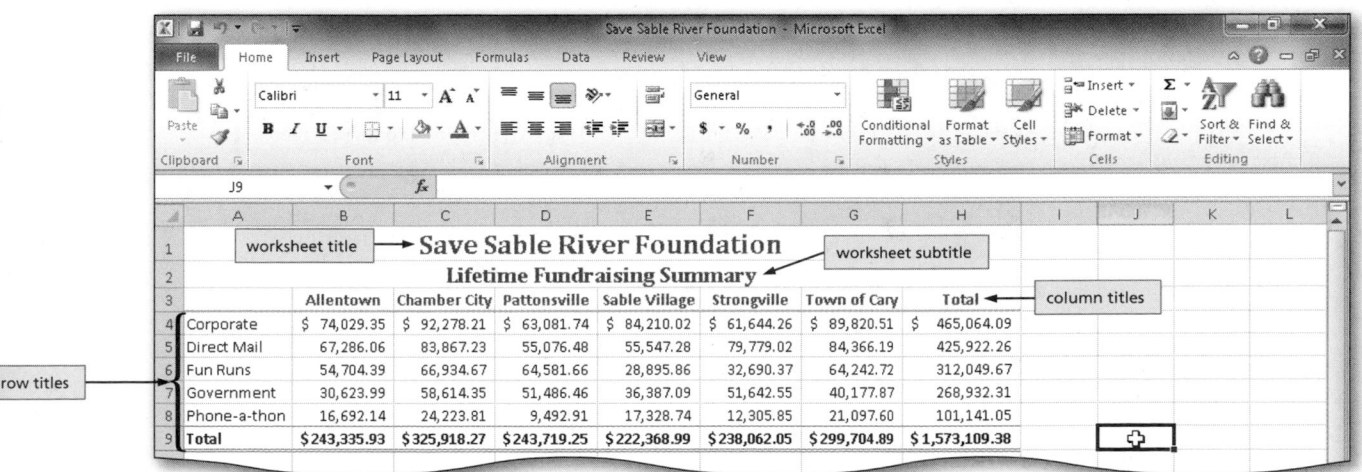

Figure 1–4

To Enter the Worksheet Titles

As shown in Figure 1–4 on the previous page, the worksheet title, Save Sable River Foundation, identifies the organization for which the worksheet is being created in Chapter 1. The worksheet subtitle, Lifetime Fundraising Summary, identifies the type of report.

The following steps enter the worksheet titles in cells A1 and A2. Later in this chapter, the worksheet titles will be formatted so they appear as shown in Figure 1–4.

- If necessary, click cell A1 to make cell A1 the active cell (Figure 1–5).

Q&A What if I make a mistake while typing?

If you type the wrong letter and notice the error before clicking the Enter box or pressing the ENTER key, use the BACKSPACE key to delete all the characters back to and including the incorrect letter. To cancel the entire entry before entering it into the

Figure 1–5

cell, click the Cancel box in the formula bar or press the ESC key. If you see an error in a cell after entering the text, select the cell and retype the entry.

- Type **Save Sable River Foundation** in cell A1 and then point to the Enter box in the formula bar to prepare to enter text in the active cell (Figure 1–6).

Q&A Why did the appearance of the formula bar change?

Excel displays the title in the formula bar and in cell A1. When you begin typing a cell entry, Excel displays two additional boxes in the formula bar:

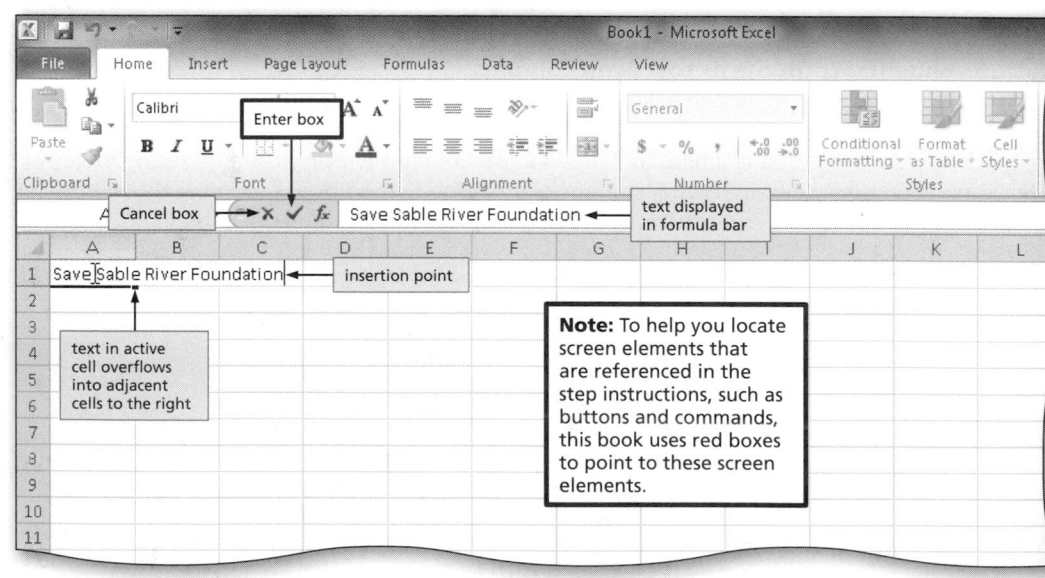

Figure 1–6

the Cancel box and the Enter box. Clicking the **Enter box** completes an entry. Clicking the **Cancel box** cancels an entry.

Q&A What is the vertical line in cell A1?

The text in cell A1 is followed by the insertion point. The **insertion point** is a blinking vertical line that indicates where the next typed character will appear.

• Click the Enter box to complete the entry and enter a worksheet title (Figure 1–7).

Why does the entered text appear in three cells?

When the text is longer than the width of a column, Excel displays the overflow characters in adjacent cells to the right as long as those adjacent cells contain no data. If the adjacent cells contain data, Excel would hide the overflow characters. Excel displays the overflow characters in the formula bar whenever that cell is the active cell.

Figure 1–7

• Click cell A2 to select it.

• Type **Lifetime Fundraising Summary** as the cell entry.

• Click the Enter box to complete the entry and enter a worksheet subtitle (Figure 1–8).

What happens when I click the Enter box?

When you complete an entry by clicking the Enter box, the insertion point disappears and the cell in which the text is entered remains the active cell.

Figure 1–8

Other Ways		
1. To complete entry, click any cell other than active cell	3. To complete entry, press HOME, PAGE UP, PAGE DOWN, or END	LEFT ARROW, or RIGHT ARROW.
2. To complete entry, press ENTER	4. To complete entry, press UP ARROW, DOWN ARROW,	

AutoCorrect

The **AutoCorrect feature** of Excel works behind the scenes, correcting common mistakes when you complete a text entry in a cell. AutoCorrect makes three types of corrections for you:

1. Corrects two initial capital letters by changing the second letter to lowercase.

2. Capitalizes the first letter in the names of days.

3. Replaces commonly misspelled words with their correct spelling. For example, it will change the misspelled word *recieve* to *receive* when you complete the entry. AutoCorrect will correct the spelling of hundreds of commonly misspelled words automatically.

BTW

Q&As
For a complete list of the Q&As found in many of the step-by-step sequences in this book, visit the Excel 2010 Q&A Web page (scsite.com/ex2010/qa).

To Enter Column Titles

The column titles in row 3 (Allentown, Chamber City, Pattonsville, Sable Village, Strongville, Town of Cary, and Total) identify the numbers in each column. In the case of the Save the Sable River Foundation data, the cities identify the funds raised using each fundraising type. The cities, therefore, are placed in columns. To enter the column titles in row 3, select the appropriate cell and then enter the text. The following steps enter the column titles in row 3.

- Click cell B3 to make it the active cell (Figure 1–9).

Figure 1–9

- Type **Allentown** to begin entry of a column title in the active cell (Figure 1–10).

Figure 1–10

● Press the RIGHT ARROW key to enter a column title and make the cell to the right the active cell (Figure 1–11).

Why is the RIGHT ARROW key used to complete the entry in the cell?

If the next entry you want to enter is in an adjacent cell, use the arrow keys to complete the entry in a cell. When you press an arrow key to complete an entry, the adjacent cell in the direction of the arrow (up, down, left, or right) becomes the active cell. If the next entry is in a nonadjacent cell, complete the current entry by clicking the next cell in which you plan to enter data. You also can click the Enter box or press the ENTER key and then click the appropriate cell for the next entry.

Figure 1–11

● Repeat Steps 2 and 3 to enter the remaining column titles; that is, enter **Chamber City** in cell C3, **Pattonsville** in cell D3, **Sable Village** in cell E3, **Strongville** in cell F3, **Town of Cary** in cell G3, and **Total** in cell H3 (complete the last entry in cell H3 by clicking the Enter box in the formula bar) (Figure 1–12).

Figure 1–12

To Enter Row Titles

The next step in developing the worksheet for this project is to enter the row titles in column A. For the Save Sable River Foundation data, the list of fundraising activities meets the criterion that information that identifies columns be in a list. It is more likely that in the future, the organization will add more fundraising activities as opposed to more cities. Each fundraising activity, therefore, should be placed in its own row. The row titles in column A (Corporate, Direct Mail, Fun Runs, Government, Phone-a-thon, and Total) identify the numbers in each row.

This process for entering row titles is similar to the process for entering column titles. The following steps enter the row titles in the worksheet.

1

- Click cell A4 to select it.

- Type **Corporate** and then press the DOWN ARROW key to enter a row title and to make the cell below the current cell the active cell (Figure 1–13).

Figure 1–13

2

- Repeat Step 1 to enter the remaining row titles in column A; that is, enter **Direct Mail** in cell A5, **Fun Runs** in cell A6, **Government** in cell A7, **Phone-a-thon** in cell A8, and **Total** in cell A9 (Figure 1–14).

Q&A

Why is the text left-aligned in the cells?

When you enter text, Excel automatically left-aligns the text in the cell. Excel treats any combination of numbers, spaces, and nonnumeric characters as text. For example, Excel recognizes the following entries as text:

401AX21, 921–231, 619 321, 883XTY

You can change the text alignment in a cell by realigning it. Other alignment techniques are discussed later in this chapter.

Figure 1–14

Entering Numbers

In Excel, you can enter numbers into cells to represent amounts. A **number** can contain only the following characters:

0 1 2 3 4 5 6 7 8 9 + - ( ) , / . $ % E e

If a cell entry contains any other keyboard character (including spaces), Excel interprets the entry as text and treats it accordingly. The use of the special characters is explained when they are used in this book.

To Enter Numbers

The Save Sable River Foundation Lifetime Fundraising Summary numbers used in Chapter 1 are summarized in Table 1–1. These numbers, which represent lifetime fundraising amounts for each of the fundraising activities and cities, must be entered in rows 4, 5, 6, 7, and 8.

Table 1–1 Save Sable River Foundation Lifetime Fundraising Summary

	Allentown	Chamber City	Pattonsville	Sable Village	Strongville	Town of Cary
Corporate	74029.35	92278.21	63081.74	84210.02	61644.26	89820.51
Direct Mail	67286.06	83867.23	55076.48	55547.28	79779.02	84366.19
Fun Runs	54704.39	66934.67	64581.66	28895.86	32690.37	64242.72
Government	30623.99	58614.35	51486.46	36387.09	51642.55	40177.87
Phone-a-thon	10092.14	24223.81	9492.91	17328.74	12305.85	21097.60

The following steps enter the numbers in Table 1–1 one row at a time.

- Click cell B4 to select it.

- Type 74029.35 and then press the RIGHT ARROW key to enter the data in the selected cell and make the cell to the right the active cell (Figure 1–15).

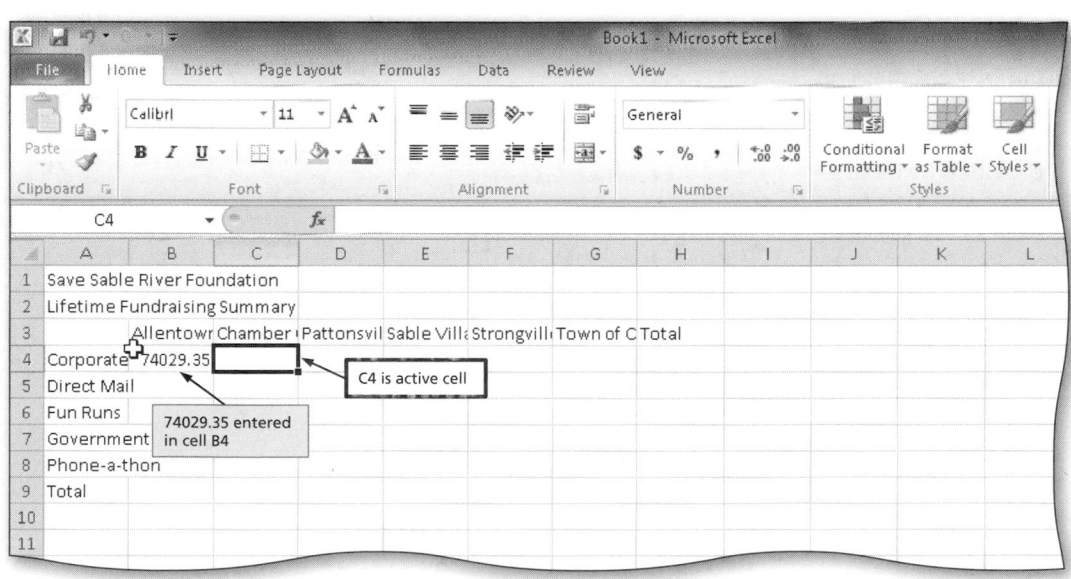

Figure 1–15

Do I need to enter dollar signs, commas, or trailing zeros for the fundraising summary amounts?

You are not required to type dollar signs, commas, or trailing zeros. When you enter a dollar value that has cents, however, you must add the decimal point and the numbers representing the cents. Later in this chapter, the numbers will be formatted to use dollar signs, commas, and trailing zeros to improve the appearance and readability of the numbers.

2

- Enter 92278.21 in cell C4, 63081.74 in cell D4, 84210.02 in cell E4, 61644.26 in cell F4, and 89820.51 in cell G4 to complete the first row of numbers in the worksheet (Figure 1–16).

Q&A

Why are the numbers right-aligned?

When you enter numeric data in a cell, Excel recognizes the values as numbers and right-aligns the values in order to properly vertically align decimal and integer values. For example, values entered below those entered in this step automatically will be right-aligned as well so that the decimals of the values properly align.

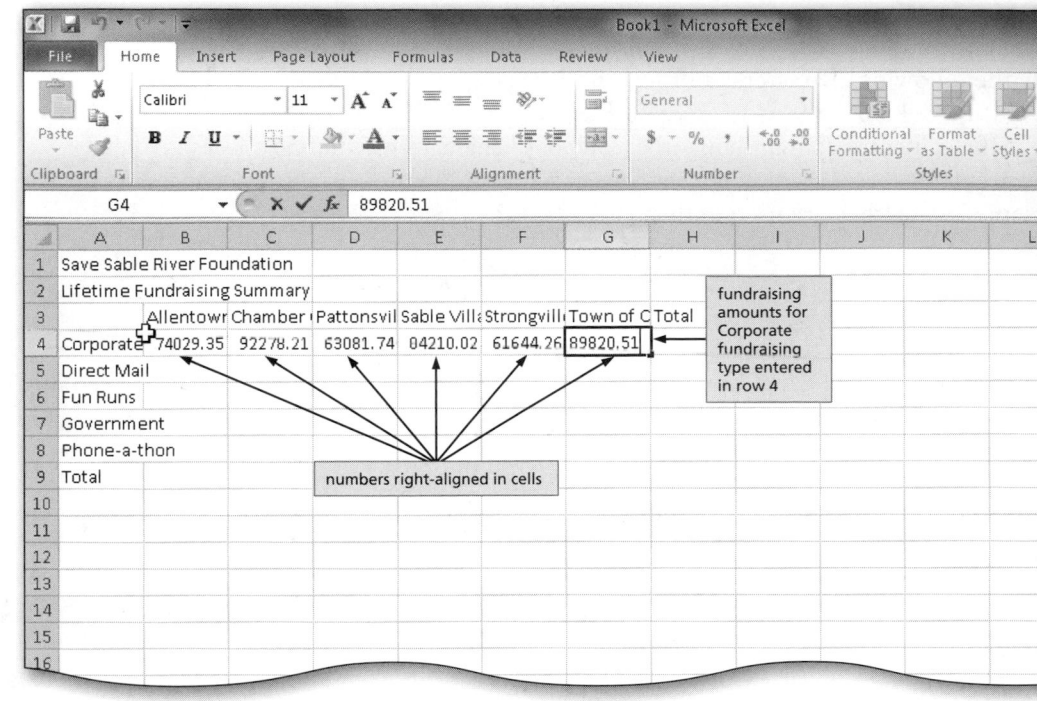

Figure 1–16

3

- Click cell B5 to select it and complete the entry in the previously selected cell.

- Enter the remaining lifetime fundraising summary numbers provided in Table 1–1 on page EX 13 for each of the four remaining fundraising activities in rows 5, 6, 7, and 8 to finish entering numbers in the worksheet (Figure 1–17).

Q&A

Why did clicking cell B5 complete the entry in cell G4?

Selecting another cell completes the entry in the previously selected cell in the same way as pressing the ENTER key, pressing an arrow key, or clicking the Enter box on the formula bar. In the next set of steps, the entry of the number in cell G4 will be completed by selecting another cell.

Figure 1–17

Calculating a Sum

The next step in creating the worksheet is to perform any necessary calculations, such as calculating the column and row totals.

To Sum a Column of Numbers

As stated in the requirements document in Figure 1–2 on page EX 4, totals are required for each city, each fundraising activity, and the organization. The first calculation is to determine the fundraising total for the fundraising activities in the city of Allentown in column B. To calculate this value in cell B9, Excel must add, or sum, the numbers in cells B4, B5, B6, B7, and B8. Excel's **SUM function**, which adds all of the numbers in a range of cells, provides a convenient means to accomplish this task.

A **range** is a series of two or more adjacent cells in a column or row or a rectangular group of cells. For example, the group of adjacent cells B4, B5, B6, B7, and B8 is called a range. Many Excel operations, such as summing numbers, take place on a range of cells.

After the total lifetime fundraising amount for the fundraising activities in the city of Allentown in column B is determined, the totals for the remaining cities and totals for each fundraising activity will be determined. The following steps sum the numbers in column B.

Click cell B9 to make it the active cell and complete the entry in the previously selected cell.

Click the Sum button (Home tab | Editing group) to display a formula in the formula bar and in the active cell (Figure 1–18).

Figure 1–18

How does Excel know which cells to sum?

When you enter the SUM function using the Sum button, Excel automatically selects what it considers to be your choice of the range to sum. When proposing the range to sum, Excel first looks for a range of cells with numbers above the active cell and then to the left. If Excel proposes the wrong range, you can correct it by dragging through the correct range before pressing the ENTER key. You also can enter the correct range by typing the beginning cell reference, a colon (:), and the ending cell reference.

BTW

Calculating Sums
Excel calculates sums for a variety of data types. For example, Boolean values, such as TRUE and FALSE, can be summed. Excel treats the value of TRUE as 1 and the value of FALSE as 0. Times also can be summed. For example, Excel treats the sum of 1:15 and 2:45 as 4:00.

2

- Click the Enter box in the formula bar to enter a sum in the active cell (Figure 1–19).

Q&A

What is the purpose of the Sum button arrow?

If you click the Sum button arrow on the right side of the Sum button (Home tab | Editing group) (Figure 1–19), Excel displays a list of often used functions from which you can choose. The list includes functions that allow you to determine the average, the number of items in the selected range, the maximum value, or the minimum value of a range of numbers.

Figure 1–19

Other Ways

1. Click Insert Function button in the formula bar, select SUM in Select a function list, click OK button, select range, click OK button

2. Click Sum button arrow (Home tab | Editing group), click More Functions, select SUM (Insert Function dialog box), click OK button, select range, click OK button

3. Type = s in cell, select SUM from list, select range

4. Press ALT + EQUAL SIGN (=) twice

BTW

Entering Numbers as Text
Sometimes, you will want Excel to treat numbers, such as postal codes and telephone numbers, as text. To enter a number as text, start the entry with an apostrophe (').

Using the Fill Handle to Copy a Cell to Adjacent Cells

Excel also must calculate the totals for Chamber City in cell C9, Pattonsville in cell D9, Sable Village in cell E9, Strongville in cell F9, and the Town of Cary in cell G9. Table 1–illustrates the similarities between the entry in cell B9 and the entries required to sum th totals in cells C9, D9, E9, F9 and G9.

Table 1–2 Sum Function Entries in Row 9		
Cell	**Sum Function Entries**	**Remark**
B9	=SUM(B4:B8)	Sums cells B4, B5, B6, B7, and B8
C9	=SUM(C4:C8)	Sums cells C4, C5, C6, C7, and C8
D9	=SUM(D4:D8)	Sums cells D4, D5, D6, D7, and D8
E9	=SUM(E4:E8)	Sums cells E4, E5, E6, E7, and E8
F9	=SUM(F4:F8)	Sums cells F4, F5, F6, F7, and F8
G9	=SUM(G4:G8)	Sums cells G4, G5, G6, G7, and G8

To place the SUM functions in cells C9, D9, E9, F9, and G9, you could follow the same steps shown previously in Figures 1–18 on page EX 15 and 1–19. A second, more efficient method, however, is to copy the SUM function from cell B9 to the range C9:G9. The cell being copied is called the **source area** or **copy area**. The range of cells receiving the copy is called the **destination area** or **paste area**.

Although the SUM function entries in Table 1–2 are similar, they are not exact copies. The range in each SUM function entry uses cell references that are one column to the right of the previous column. When you copy formulas that include cell references, Excel automatically adjusts them for each new position, resulting in the SUM function entries illustrated in Table 1–2. Each adjusted cell reference is called a **relative reference**.

To Copy a Cell to Adjacent Cells in a Row

The easiest way to copy the SUM formula from cell B9 to cells C9, D9, E9, F9, and G9 is to use the fill handle. The **fill handle** is the small black square located in the lower-right corner of the heavy border around the active cell. The following steps use the fill handle to copy cell B9 to the adjacent cells C9:G9.

1
• With cell B9 active, point to the fill handle to activate it (Figure 1–20).

Figure 1–20

2
• Drag the fill handle to select the destination area, range C9:G9, to display a shaded border around the source area and the destination area (Figure 1–21). Do not release the mouse button.

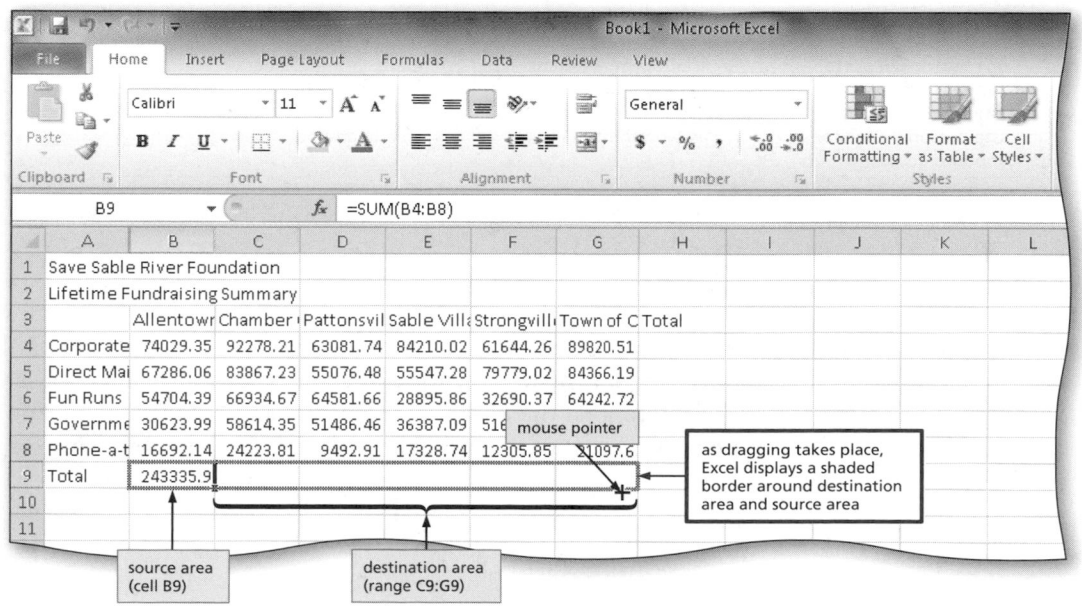

Figure 1–21

3

- Release the mouse button to copy the SUM function from the active cell to the destination area and calculate the sums (Figure 1–22).

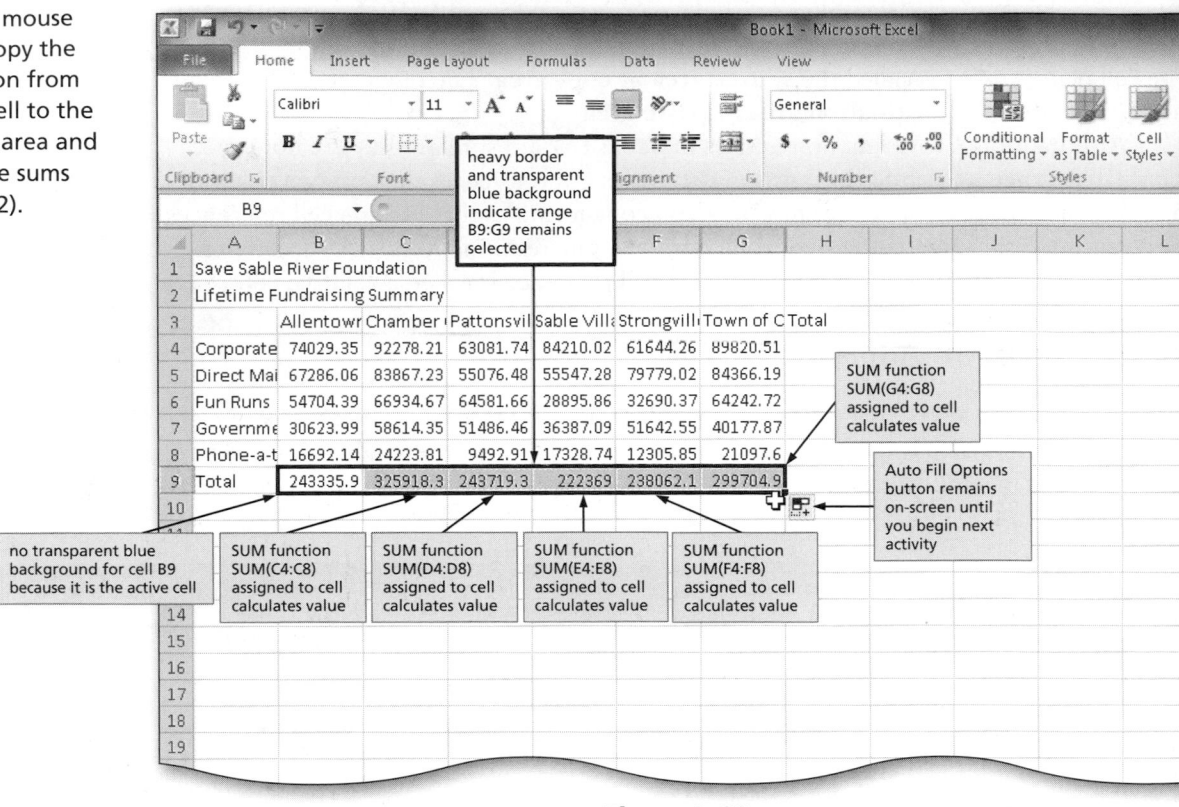

Figure 1–22

Q&A

What is the purpose of the Auto Fill Options button?

When you copy one range to another, Excel displays an Auto Fill Options button (Figure 1–22). The Auto Fill Options button allows you to choose whether you want to copy the values from the source area to the destination area with formatting, do so without formatting, or copy only the format. To view the available fill options, click the Auto Fill Options button. The Auto Fill Options button disappears when you begin another activity in Excel, such as typing data in another cell or applying formatting to a cell or range of cells.

Other Ways

1. Select source area, click Copy button (Home tab | Clipboard group), select destination area, click Paste button (Home tab | Clipboard group)

2. Right-click source area, click Copy on shortcut menu, right-click destination area, click Paste on shortcut menu

3. Select source area and then point to border of range; while holding down CTRL, drag source area to destination area

To Determine Multiple Totals at the Same Time

The next step in building the worksheet is to determine the lifetime fundraising totals for each fundraising activity and total lifetime fundraising for the organization in column H. To calculate these totals, you can use the SUM function much as it was used to total the lifetime fundraising amounts by city in row 9. In this example, however, Excel will determine totals for all of the rows at the same time. The following steps sum multiple totals at once.

• Click cell H4 to make it the active cell (Figure 1–23).

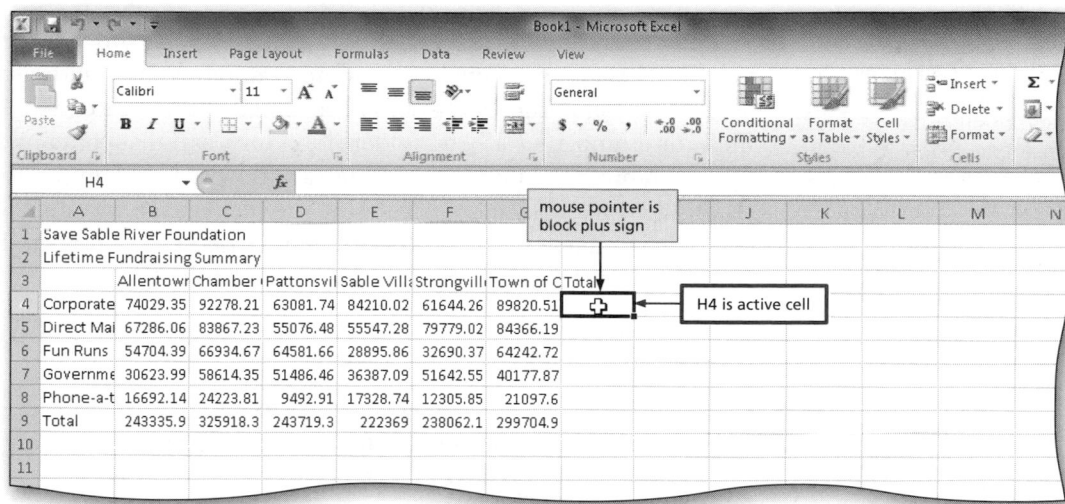

Figure 1–23

With the mouse pointer in cell H4 and in the shape of a block plus sign, drag the mouse pointer down to cell H9 to highlight the range with a transparent view (Figure 1–24).

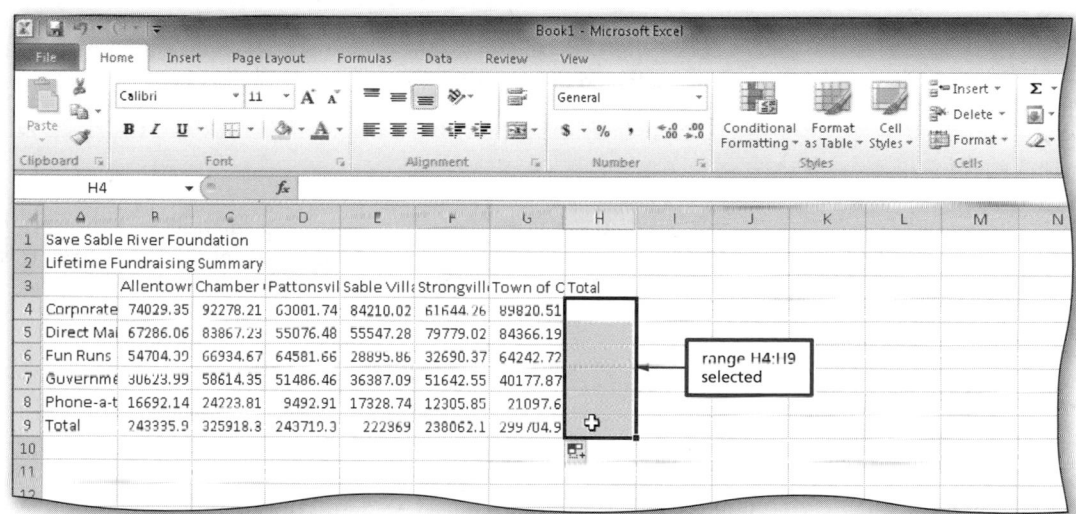

Figure 1–24

• Click the Sum button (Home tab | Editing group) to calculate and display the sums of the corresponding rows (Figure 1–25).

Select cell A10 to deselect the selected range.

How does Excel create unique totals for each row?

If each cell in a selected range is next to a row of numbers, Excel assigns the SUM function to each cell when you click the Sum button.

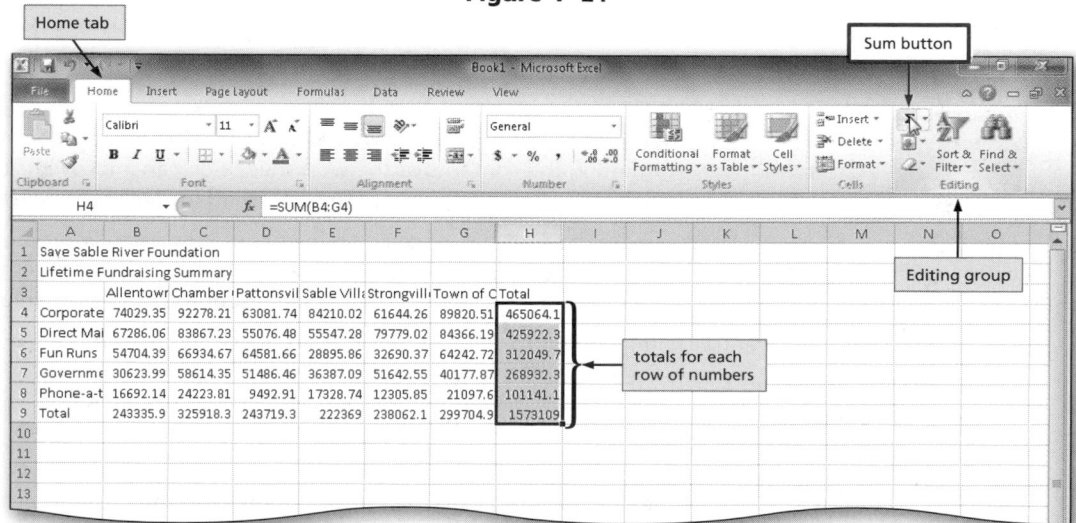

Figure 1–25

BTW

Organizing Files and Folders
You should organize and store files in folders so that you easily can find the files later. For example, if you are taking an introductory computer class called CIS 101, a good practice would be to save all Excel files in an Excel folder in a CIS 101 folder. For a discussion of folders and detailed examples of creating folders, refer to the Office 2010 and Windows 7 chapter at the beginning of this book.

To Save a Workbook

You have performed many tasks while creating this workbook and do not want to risk losing work completed thus far. Accordingly, you should save the workbook.

The following steps assume you already have created folders for storing your files, for example, a CIS 101 folder (for your class) that contains an Excel folder (for your assignments). Thus, these steps save the workbook in the Excel folder in the CIS 101 folder on a USB flash drive using the file name, Save Sable River Foundation. For a detailed example of the procedure summarized below, refer to the Office 2010 and Windows 7 chapter at the beginning of this book.

1 With a USB flash drive connected to one of the computer's USB ports, click the Save button on the Quick Access Toolbar to display the Save As dialog box.

2 Type `Save Sable River Foundation` in the File name text box to change the file name. Do not press the ENTER key after typing the file name because you do not want to close the dialog box at this time.

3 Navigate to the desired save location (in this case, the Excel folder in the CIS 101 folder [or your class folder] on the USB flash drive).

4 Click the Save button (Save As dialog box) to save the document in the selected folder on the selected drive with the entered file name.

Break Point: If you wish to take a break, this is a good place to do so. You can quit Excel. To resume at a later time, start Excel, open the file called Save Sable River Foundation, and continue following the steps from this location forward.

BTW

AutoRecover
The AutoRecover feature of Excel, sometimes called AutoSave, allows you to specify how often and where Excel automatically saves workbooks. If your computer loses power, becomes unusable while you are interacting with a workbook, or you forget to save a workbook before closing it, Excel notifies you if there are workbooks that were automatically saved when one of these events occurred. You view and change AutoRecover options by clicking the Options button in the Backstage view and then clicking Save in the left panel of the Excel Options dialog box.

Formatting the Worksheet

The text, numeric entries, and functions for the worksheet now are complete. The next step is to format the worksheet. You **format** a worksheet to emphasize certain entries and make the worksheet easier to read and understand.

Figure 1–26a shows the worksheet before formatting. Figure 1–26b shows the worksheet after formatting. As you can see from the two figures, a worksheet that is formatted not only is easier to read but also looks more professional.

Plan Ahead

Identify how to format various elements of the worksheet.
By formatting the contents of the worksheet, you can improve its overall appearance. When formatting a worksheet, consider the following formatting suggestions:

- **Increase the font size of cells.** An increased font size gives more impact to the text in a cell. In order to indicate their relative importance, worksheet titles should have the largest font size, followed by worksheet subtitles, and then column and row headings.

- **Change the font color of cells.** Different cell colors help the reader of a worksheet quickly differentiate between the sections of a worksheet. Worksheet titles and subtitles easily should be identifiable from column and row headings. The overuse of too many colors, however, may be distracting to the reader of a worksheet.

- **Center the worksheet titles, subtitles, and column headings.** Centering text in worksheet titles and subtitles over the portion of the worksheet that they represent helps the reader of a worksheet quickly to identify the information that is of interest to them.

(continued)

(continued)

- **Modify column widths to best fit text in cells.** Make certain that text in a cell does not overflow into another cell. A column's width should be adjusted to accommodate the largest amount of text used in a cell in the column. Columns that contain data that is similar in nature to other columns should share the same column width.

- **Change the font style of cells.** Use a bold font style to make worksheet titles, worksheet subtitles, column headings, row headings, and totals stand out. Use italics and underline font styles judiciously, as specific rules of grammar apply to their use.

Figure 1–26 (a) Before Formatting

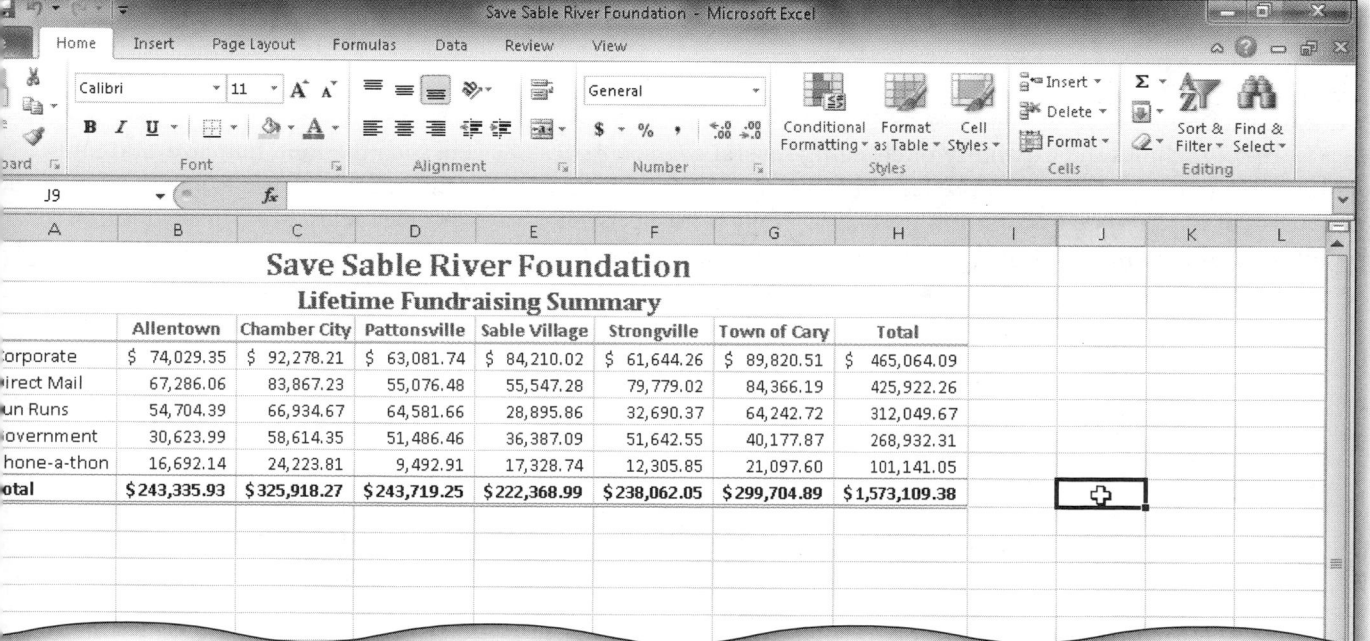

Figure 1–26 (b) After Formatting

To change the unformatted worksheet in Figure 1–26a on the previous page to the formatted worksheet in Figure 1–26b on the previous page, the following tasks must be completed:

1. Change the font, change the font style to bold, increase the font size, and change the font color of the worksheet titles in cells A1 and A2.
2. Center the worksheet titles in cells A1 and A2 across columns A through H.
3. Format the body of the worksheet. The body of the worksheet, range A3:H9, includes the column titles, row titles, and numbers. Formatting the body of the worksheet changes the numbers to use a dollars-and-cents format, with dollar signs in the first row (row 4) and the total row (row 9); adds underlining that emphasizes portions of the worksheet; and modifies the column widths to fit the text in the columns and make the text and numbers readable.

The remainder of this section explains the process required to format the worksheet. Although the formatting procedures are explained in the order described above, you should be aware that you could make these format changes in any order. Modifying the column widths, however, usually is done last because other formatting changes may affect the size of data in the cells in the column.

Font, Style, Size, and Color

The characters that Excel displays on the screen are a specific font, style, size, and color. The **font**, or font face, defines the appearance and shape of the letters, numbers, and special characters. Examples of fonts include Calibri, Cambria, Times New Roman, Arial, and Courier. **Font style** indicates how the characters are emphasized. Common font styles include regular, bold, underline, and italic. The **font size** specifies the size of the character on the screen. Font size is gauged by a measurement system called points. A single point is about 1/72 of one inch in height. Thus, a character with a **point size** of 10 is about 10/72 of one inch in height. The **font color** defines the color of the characters. Excel can display characters in a wide variety of colors, including black, red, orange, and blue.

When Excel begins, the preset font for the entire workbook is Calibri, with a font size, font style, and font color of 11–point regular black. Excel allows you to change the font characteristics in a single cell, a range of cells, the entire worksheet, or the entire workbook.

To Change a Cell Style

Excel includes the capability of changing several characteristics of a cell, such the font, font size, and font color, all at once by assigning a predefined cell style to a cell. Using the predefined styles that Excel includes provides a consistent appearance to common portions of your worksheets, such as worksheet titles, worksheet subtitles, column headings, and total rows. The following steps assign the Title cell style to the worksheet title in cell A1.

Click cell A1 to make cell A1 the active cell.

Click the Cell Styles button (Home tab | Styles group) to display the Cell Styles gallery (Figure 1–27).

Figure 1–27

Point to the Title cell style in the Titles and Headings area of the Cell Styles gallery to see a live preview of the cell style in the active cell (Figure 1–28).

Experiment

Point to several other cell styles in the Cell Styles gallery to see a live preview of other cell styles in cell A1.

Figure 1–28

Click the Title cell style to apply the cell style to the active cell (Figure 1–29).

Why do several items in the Font group on the Ribbon change?

The changes to the Font box, Bold button, and Font Size box indicate the font changes applied to the active cell, cell A1, as a result of applying the Title cell style.

Figure 1–29

To Change the Font

Different fonts often are used in a worksheet to make it more appealing to the reader and to relate or distinguish data in the worksheet. The following steps change the worksheet subtitle's fonts from Calibri to Cambria.

1
- Click cell A2 to make it the active cell.

- Click the Font box arrow (Home tab | Font group) to display the Font gallery (Figure 1–30).

Q&A Which fonts are displayed in the Font gallery?

Because many programs supply additional fonts beyond what comes with the Windows 7 operating system, the number of fonts available on your computer will depend on the programs installed. This book uses only fonts that come with the Windows 7 operating system and Microsoft Office 2010.

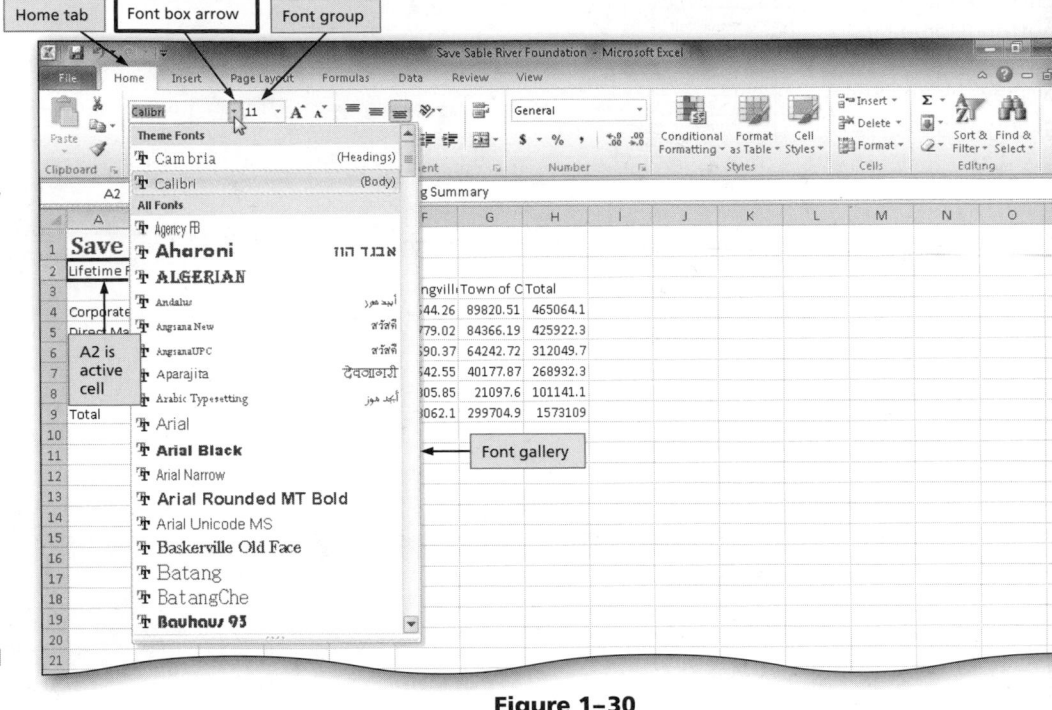

Figure 1–30

2
- Point to Cambria in the Theme Fonts area of the Font gallery to see a live preview of the selected font in the active cell (Figure 1–31).

Experiment
- Point to several other fonts in the Font gallery to see a live preview of other fonts in the selected cell.

Q&A What is the Theme Fonts area?

Excel applies the same default theme to any new workbook that you start. A **theme** is a collection of cell styles and other styles that have common characteristics, such as a color scheme and font. The default theme for an Excel workbook is the Office theme. The Theme Fonts area of the Font gallery includes the fonts included in the default Office theme. Cambria is recommended for headings and Calibri is recommended by Microsoft for cells in the body of the worksheet (Figure 1–31).

Figure 1–31

Click Cambria in the Theme Fonts area to change the font of the worksheet subtitle to Cambria (Figure 1–32).

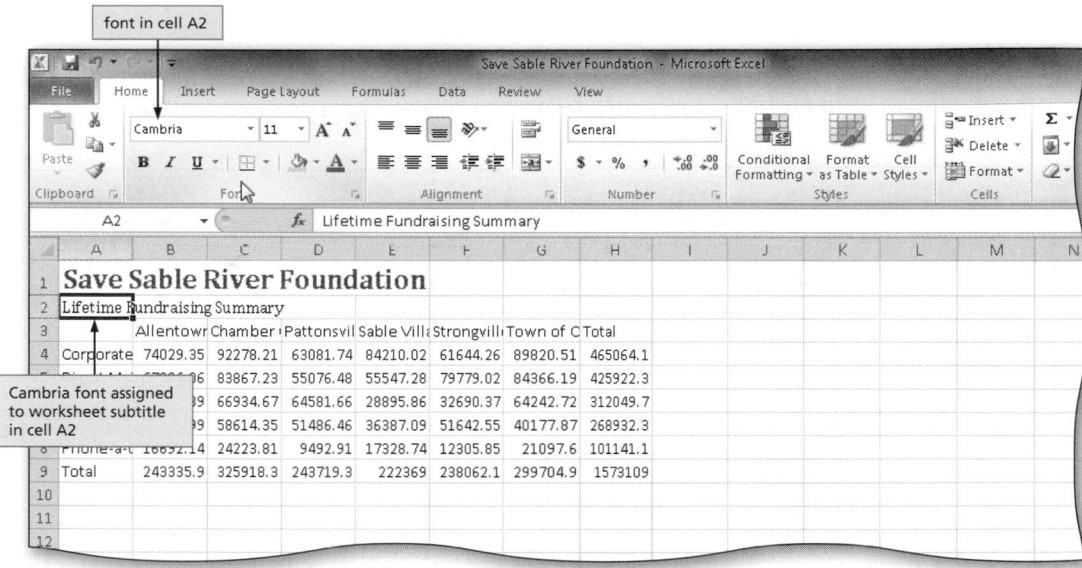

Figure 1–32

To Bold a Cell

You **bold** an entry in a cell to emphasize it or make it stand out from the rest of the worksheet. The following step bolds the worksheet subtitle in cell A2.

With cell A2 active, click the Bold button (Home tab | Font group) to change the font style of the active cell to bold (Figure 1–33).

What if a cell already includes a bold style?

If the active cell is already bold, then Excel displays the Bold button with a transparent orange background.

How do I remove the bold style from a cell?

Clicking the Bold button (Home tab | Font group) a second time removes the bold font style.

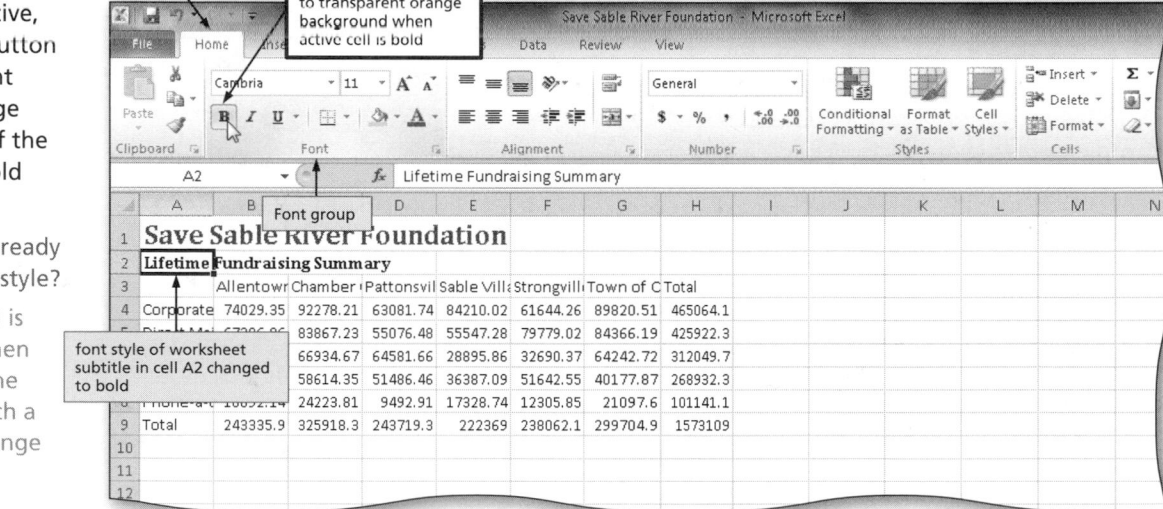

Figure 1–33

To Increase the Font Size of a Cell Entry

Increasing the font size is the next step in formatting the worksheet subtitle. You increase the font size of a cell so that the entry stands out and is easier to read. The following steps increase the font size of the worksheet subtitle in cell A2.

- With cell A2 selected, click the Font Size box arrow (Home tab | Font group) to display the Font Size list.

- Point to 14 in the Font Size list to see a live preview of the active cell with the selected font size (Figure 1–34).

Experiment

- Point to several other font sizes in the Font Size list to see a live preview of other font sizes in the selected cell.

Figure 1–34

- Click 14 in the Font Size list to change the font size in the active cell (Figure 1–35).

Q&A

Can I assign a font size that is not in the Font Size list?

Yes. An alternative to clicking a font size in the Font Size list is to click the Font Size box (Home tab | Font group), type the font size, and then press the ENTER key. This procedure allows you to assign a font size not available in the Font Size list to a selected cell entry.

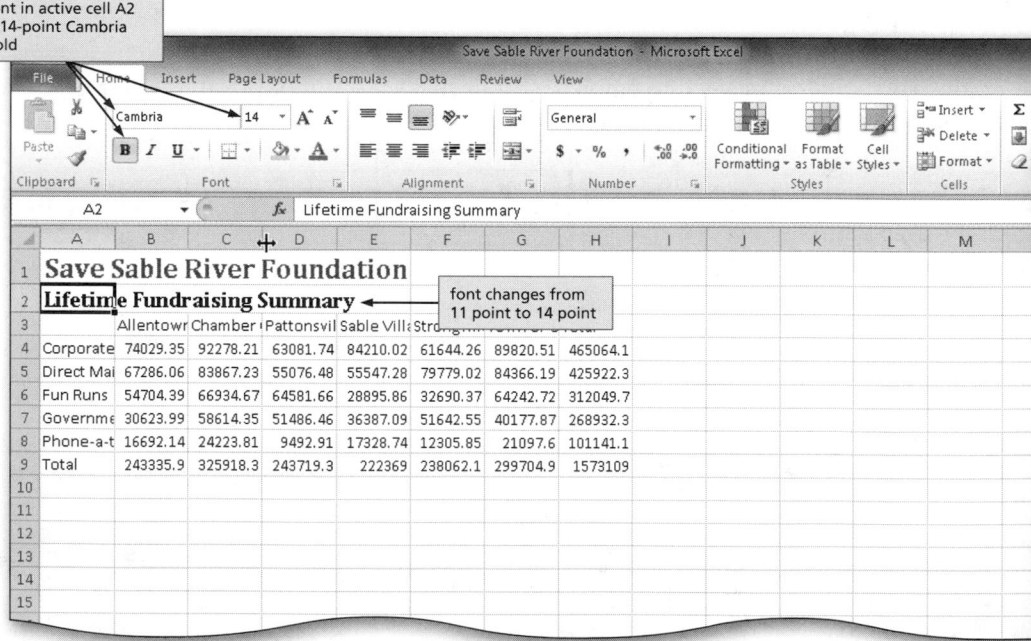

Figure 1–35

Other Ways

1. Click Increase Font Size button (Home tab | Font group) or Decrease Font Size button (Home tab | Font group)

2. Click Font Size box arrow on Mini toolbar, click desired font size in Font Size gallery

3. Right-click cell, click Format Cells on shortcut menu, click Font tab (Format Cells dialog box), select font size in Size box, click OK button

To Change the Font Color of a Cell Entry

The next step is to change the color of the font in cell A2 from black to dark blue. The following steps change the font color of a cell entry.

- With cell A2 selected, click the Font Color button arrow (Home tab | Font group) to display the Font Color gallery.

- Point to Dark Blue, Text 2 (dark blue color in column 4, row 1) in the Theme Colors area of the Font Color gallery to see a live preview of the font color in the active cell (Figure 1–36).

Experiment

- Point to several other colors in the Font Color gallery to see a live preview of other font colors in the active cell.

Which colors does Excel make available on the Font Color gallery?

You can choose from more than 60 different font colors on the Font Color gallery (Figure 1–36). Your Font Color gallery may have more or fewer colors, depending on color settings of your operating system. The Theme Colors area includes colors that are included in the current workbook's theme.

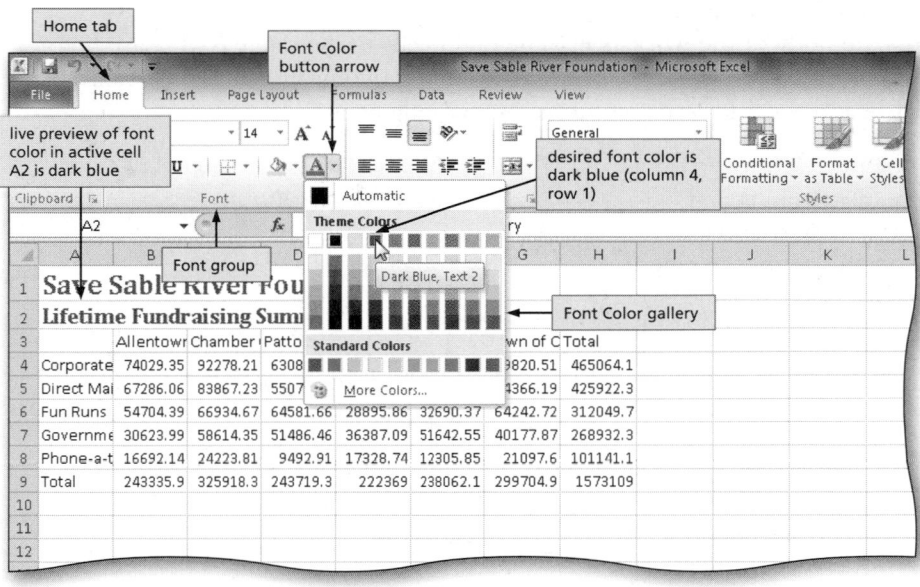

Figure 1–36

- Click Dark Blue, Text 2 (column 4, row 1) on the Font Color gallery to change the font of the worksheet subtitle in the active cell (Figure 1–37).

Why does the Font Color button change after I select the new font color?

When you choose a color on the Font Color gallery, Excel changes the Font Color button (Home tab | Font group) to the chosen color. Thus, to change the font color of the cell entry in another cell to the same color, you need only to select the cell and then click the Font Color button (Home tab | Font group).

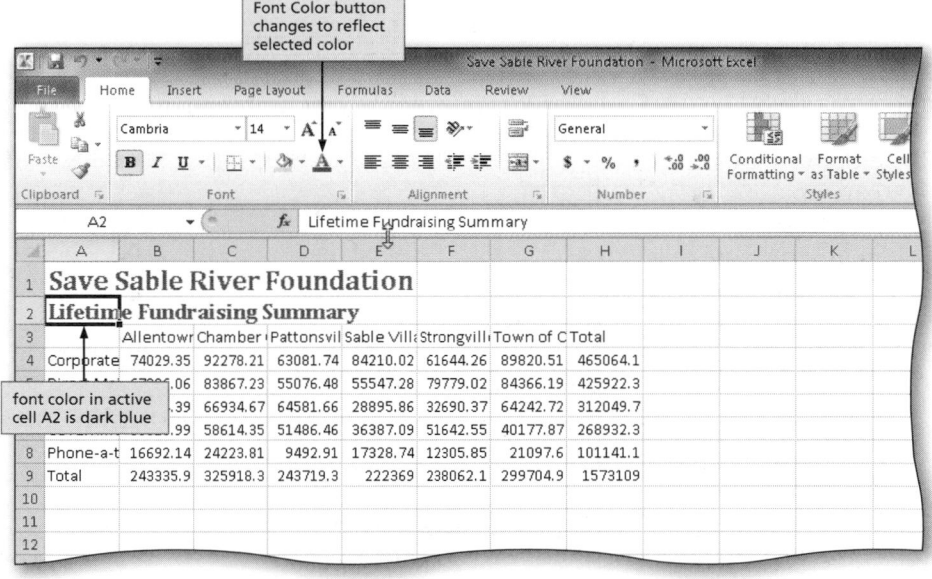

Figure 1–37

<table>
<tr><td>**Other Ways**</td></tr>
</table>

1. Click Font Color box arrow on Mini toolbar, click desired font color in the Font Color gallery

2. Right-click cell, click Format Cells on shortcut menu, click Font tab (Format Cells dialog box), select color in Font Color gallery, click OK button

To Center Cell Entries Across Columns by Merging Cells

The final step in formatting the worksheet title and subtitle is to center them across columns A through H. Centering a title across the columns used in the body of the worksheet improves the worksheet's appearance. To do this, the eight cells in the range A1:H1 are combined, or merged, into a single cell that is the width of the columns in the body of the worksheet. The eight cells in the range A2:H2 are merged in a similar manner. **Merging cells** involves creating a single cell by combining two or more selected cells. The following steps center the worksheet title and subtitle across columns by merging cells.

1

• Select cell A1 and then drag to cell H1 to highlight the range to be merged and centered (Figure 1–38).

Q&A

What if a cell in the range B1:H1 contains data?

For the Merge & Center button (Home tab | Alignment group) to work properly, all the cells except the leftmost cell in the selected range must be empty.

Figure 1–38

2

• Click the Merge & Center button (Home tab | Alignment group) to merge cells A1 through H1 and center the contents of the leftmost cell across the selected columns (Figure 1–39).

Q&A

What happened to cells B1 through H1?

After the merge, cells B1 through H1 no longer exist. The new cell A1 now extends across columns A through H.

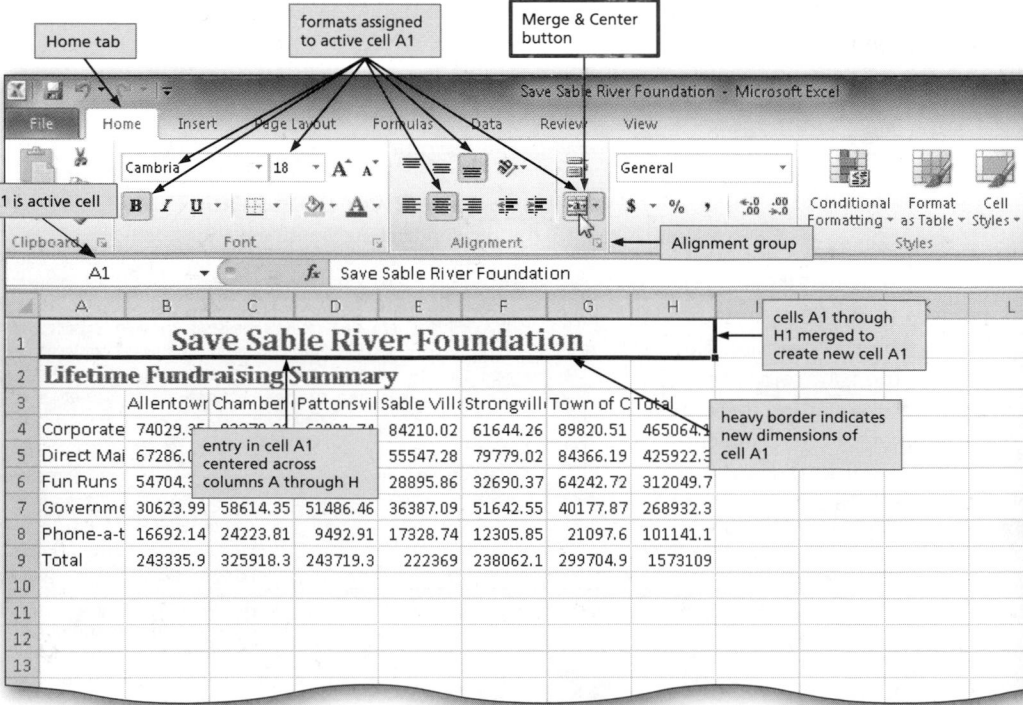

Figure 1–39

● Repeat Steps 1 and 2 to merge and center the worksheet subtitle across cells A2 through H2 (Figure 1–40).

Are cells B1 through H1 and B2 through H2 lost forever?

No. The opposite of merging cells is **splitting a merged cell**. After you have merged multiple cells to create one merged cell, you can unmerge, or split, the merged cell to display the original cells on the worksheet. You split a merged cell by selecting it and clicking the Merge & Center button. For example, if you click the Merge & Center button a second time in Step 2, it will split the merged cell A1 into cells A1, B1, C1, D1, E1, F1, G1, and H1.

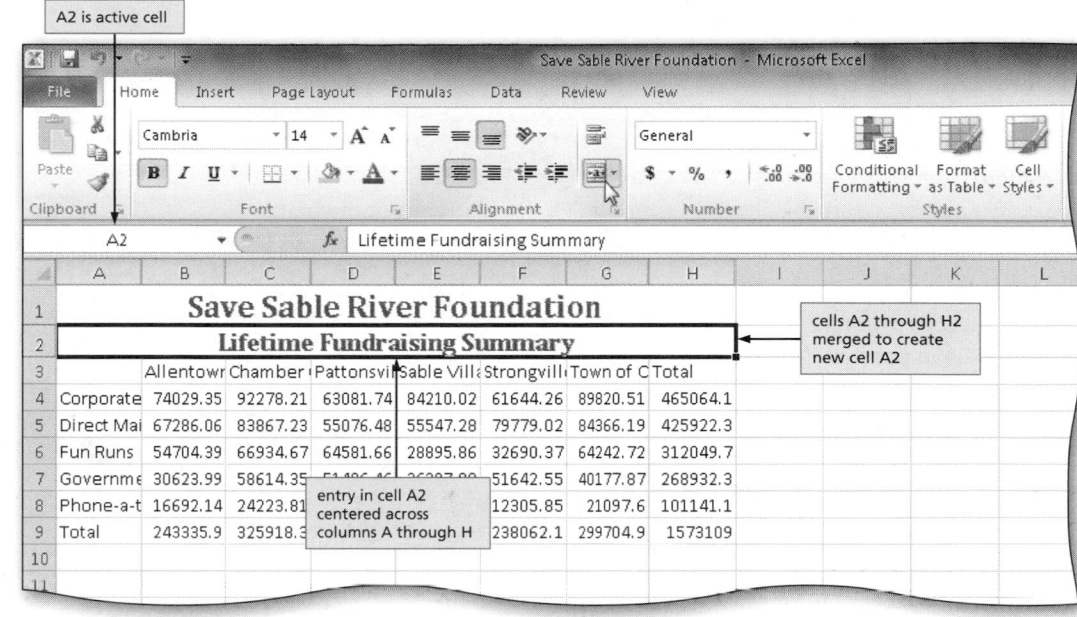

Figure 1–40

To Format Column Titles and the Total Row

The next step to format the worksheet is to format the column titles in row 3 and the total values in row 9. Column titles and the total row should be formatted so anyone who views the worksheet quickly can distinguish the column titles and total row from the data in the body of the worksheet. The following steps format the column titles and total row using cell styles in the default worksheet theme.

● Click cell A3 and then drag the mouse pointer to cell H3 to select a range (Figure 1–41).

Why is cell A3 selected in the range for the column headings?

The style to be applied to the column headings includes an underline that will help to distinguish the column headings from the rest of the worksheet. Including cell A3 in the range ensures that the cell will include the underline, which is visually appealing and further helps to separate the data in the worksheet.

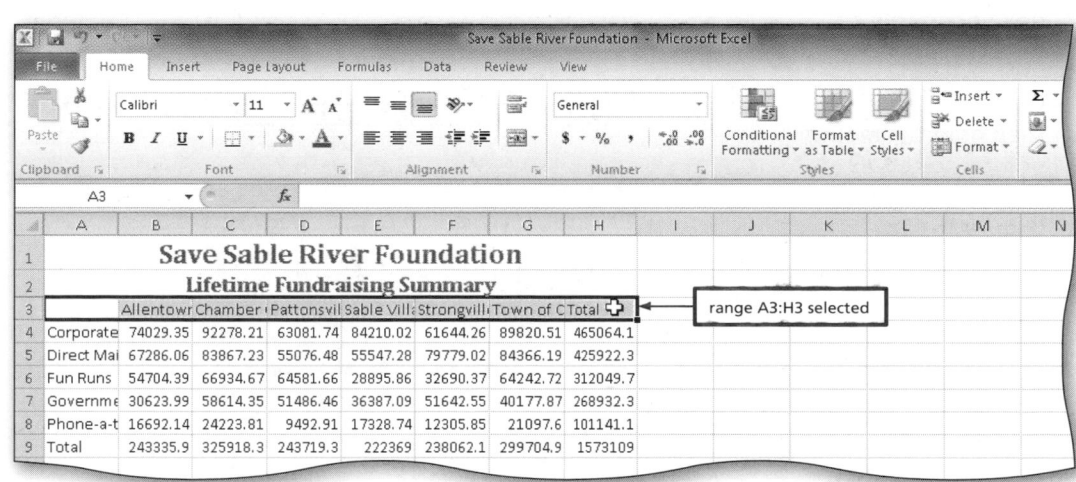

Figure 1–41

2

- Click the Cell Styles button (Home tab | Styles group) to display the Cell Styles gallery.

- Point to the Heading 3 cell style in the Titles and Headings area of the Cell Styles gallery to see a live preview of the cell style in the selected range (Figure 1–42).

Figure 1–42

 Experiment

- Point to other cell styles in the Titles and Headings area of the Cell Styles gallery to see a live preview of other cell styles in the selected range, A3:H3.

3

- Click the Heading 3 cell style to apply the cell style to the selected range.

- Click the Center button (Home tab | Alignment group) to center the column headings in the selected range.

- Click cell A9 and then drag the mouse pointer to cell H9 to select a range (Figure 1–43).

Figure 1–43

Q&A Why should I choose Heading 3 instead of another heading cell style?

Excel includes many types of headings, such as Heading 1 and Heading 2, because worksheets often include many levels of headings above columns. In the case of the worksheet created for this project, the Heading 3 title includes formatting that makes the column titles' font size smaller than the title and subtitle and makes the column titles stand out from the data in the body of the worksheet.

4
- Click the Cell Styles button (Home tab | Styles group) to display the Cell Styles gallery and then click the Total cell style in the Titles and Headings area to apply the selected cell style to the cells in the selected range.

- Click cell A11 to select it (Figure 1–44).

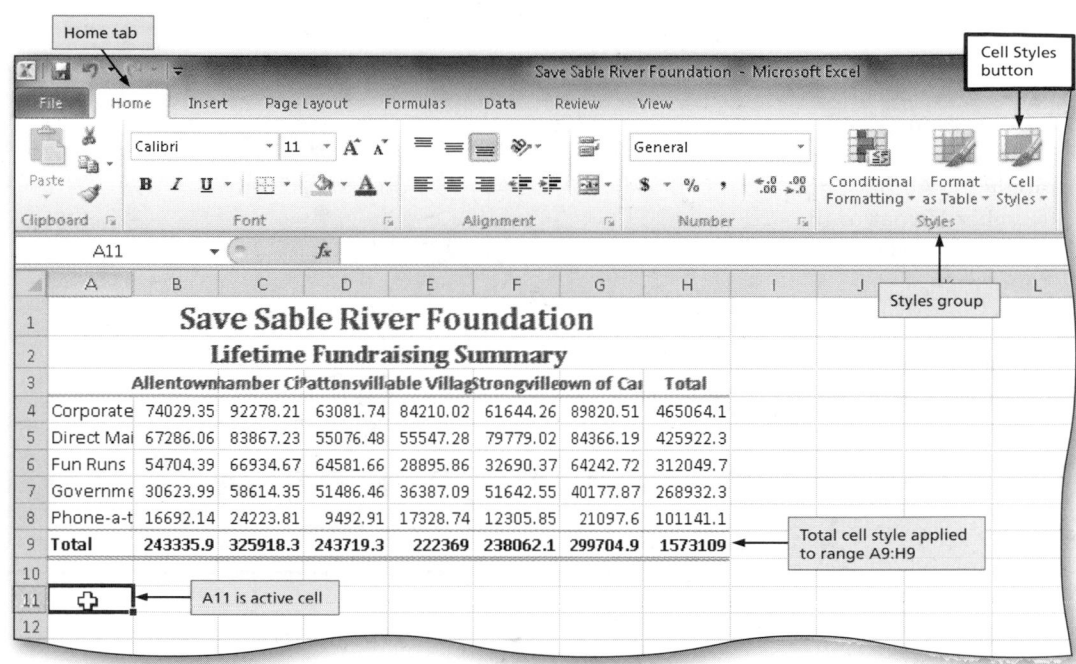

Figure 1–44

To Format Numbers in the Worksheet

As previously noted, the numbers in the worksheet should be formatted to use a dollar-and-cents format, with dollar signs in the first row (row 4) and the total row (row 9). Excel allows you to format numbers in a variety of ways, and these methods are discussed in other chapters in this book. The following steps use buttons on the Ribbon to format the numbers in the worksheet.

1
- Select cell B4 and drag the mouse pointer to cell H4 to select a range (Figure 1–45).

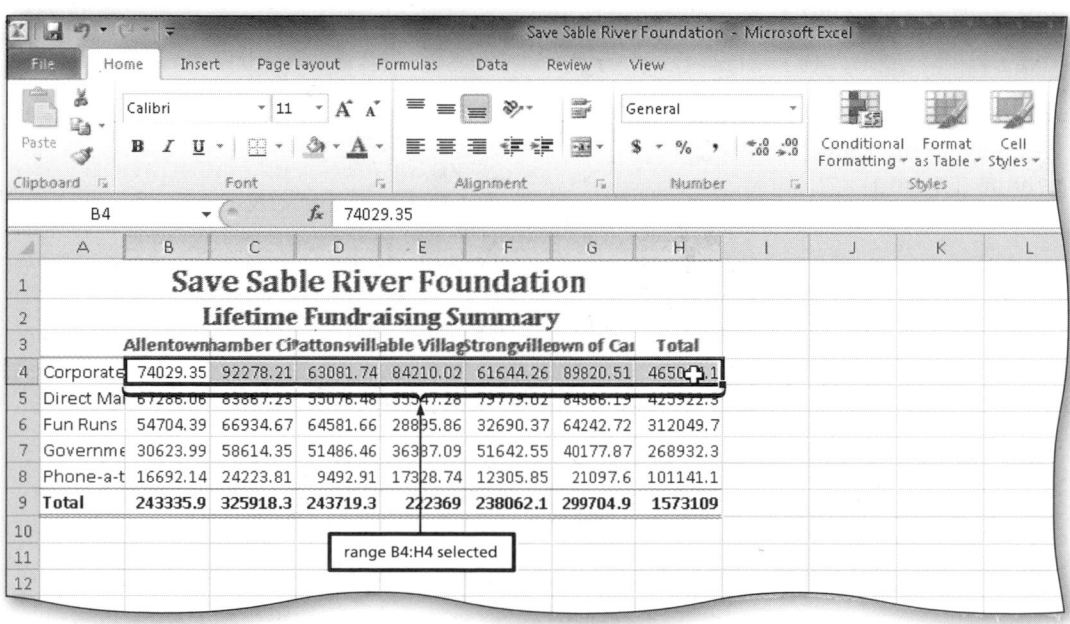

Figure 1–45

2

- Click the Accounting Number Format button (Home tab | Number group) to apply the Accounting Number format to the cells in the selected range.

- Select the range B5:H8 (Figure 1–46).

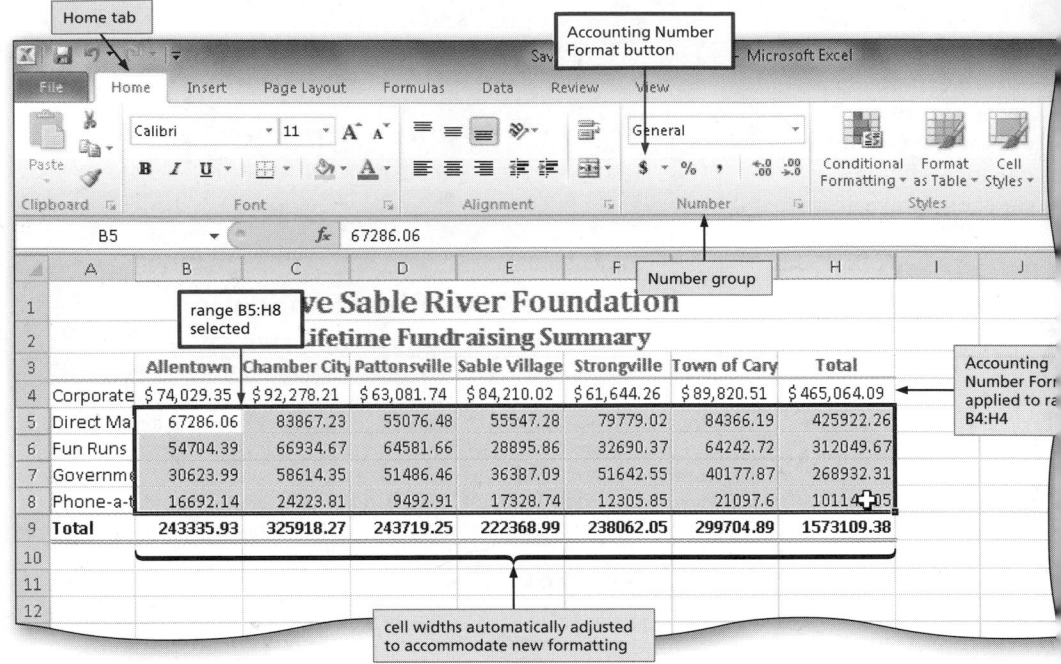

Figure 1–46

Q&A What effect does the Accounting Number format have on the selected cells?

The Accounting Number format causes the cells to be displayed with two decimal places so that decimal places in cells below the selected cells align vertically. Cell widths are adjusted automatically to accommodate the new formatting.

3

- Click the Comma Style button (Home tab | Number group) to apply the Comma Style format to the selected range.

- Select the range B9:H9 to make it the active range (Figure 1–47).

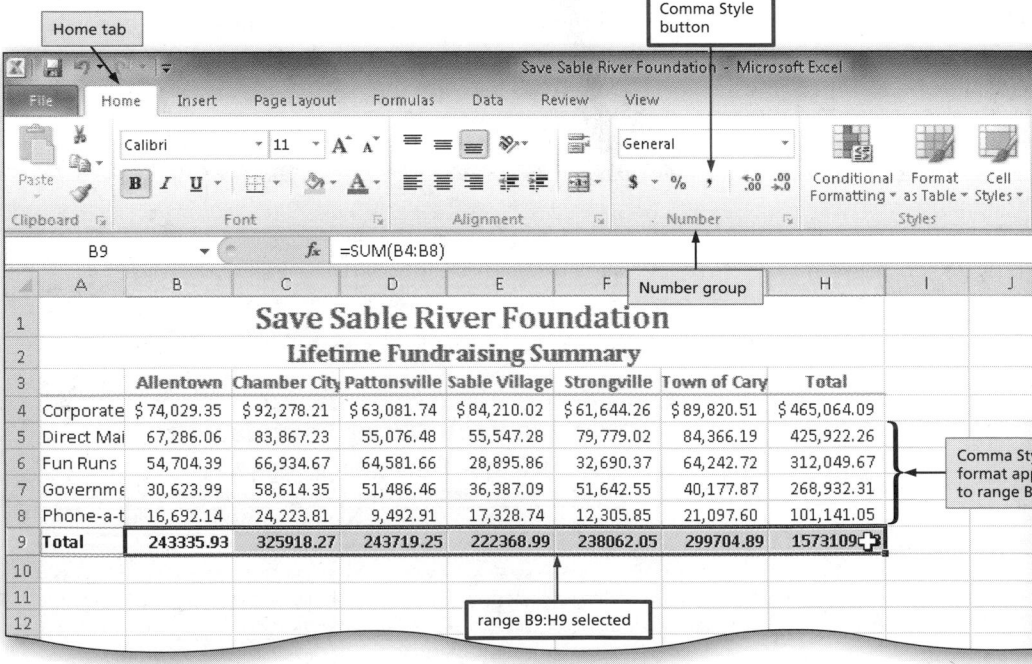

Figure 1–47

Q&A What effect does the Comma Style format have on the selected cells?

The Comma Style format causes the cells to be displayed with two decimal places and commas as thousands separators.

4
- Click the Accounting Number Format button (Home tab | Number group) to apply the Accounting Number format to the cells in the selected range.

- Select cell A11 (Figure 1–48).

Why did the column widths automatically adjust again?

Because the total row contains larger numbers, the Accounting Number format again causes the cell widths automatically to adjust to accommodate the new formatting just as occurred in Step 2.

Figure 1–48

To Adjust the Column Width

The last step in formatting the worksheet is to adjust the width of column A so that the word Phone-a-thon in cell A8 is shown in its entirety in the cell. Excel includes several methods for adjusting cell widths and row heights, and these methods are discussed later in this book. The following steps adjust the width of column A so that the contents of cell A8 are displayed in the cell.

1
- Point to the boundary on the right side of the column A heading above row 1 to change the mouse pointer to a split double arrow (Figure 1–49).

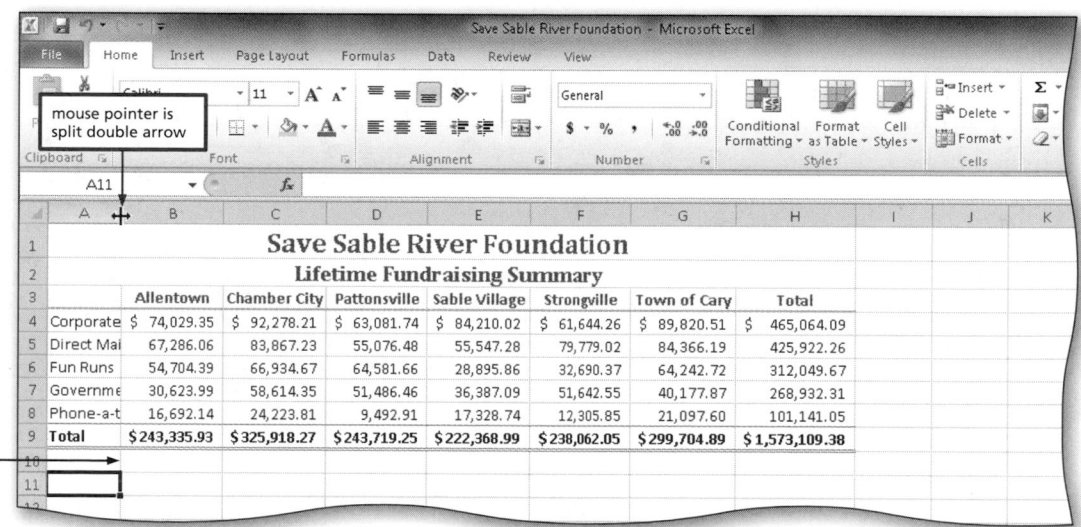

Figure 1–49

②

- Double-click on the boundary to adjust the width of the column to the width of the largest item in the column (Figure 1–50).

Q&A

What if none of the items in column A extends through the entire width of the column?

If all of the items in column A were shorter in length than the width of the column when you double-click the right side of the column A heading, then Excel still would adjust the column width to the largest item in the column. That is, Excel would reduce the width of the column to the largest item.

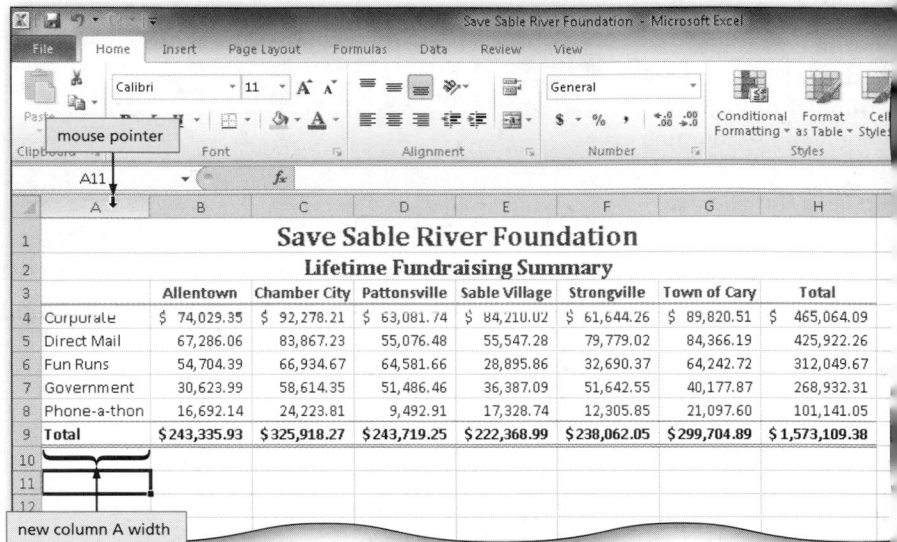

Figure 1–50

Using the Name Box to Select a Cell

The next step is to chart the lifetime fundraising amounts for the five fundraising activities used by the organization. To create the chart, you first must select the cell in the upper-left corner of the range to chart (cell A3). Rather than clicking cell A3 to select it, the next section describes how to use the Name box to select the cell.

To Use the Name Box to Select a Cell

The Name box is located on the left side of the formula bar. To select any cell, click the Name box and enter the cell reference of the cell you want to select. The following steps select cell A3 using the Name box.

①

- Click the Name box in the formula bar and then type a3 as the cell you wish to select (Figure 1–51).

Q&A

Why is cell A11 still selected?

Even though cell A11 is the active cell, Excel displays the typed cell reference a3 in the Name box until you press the ENTER key.

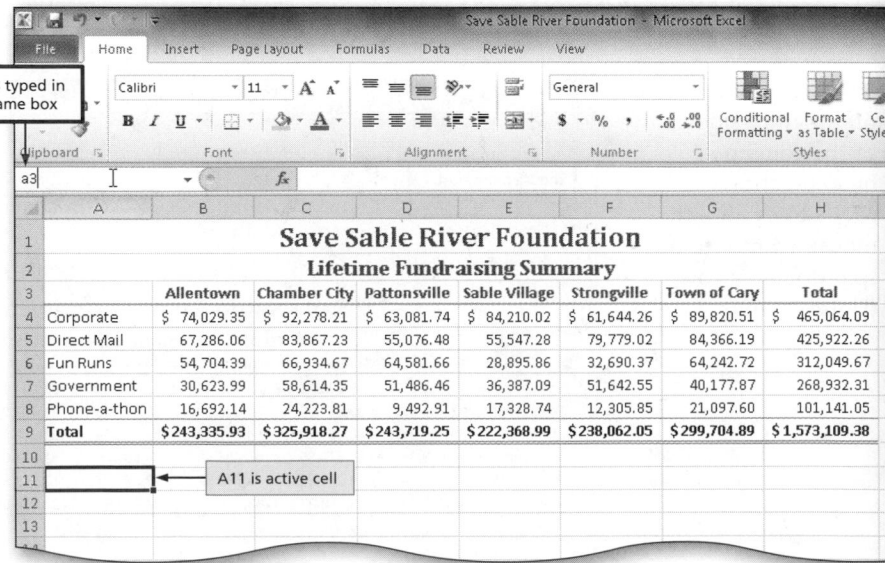

Figure 1–51

2

• Press the ENTER key to change the active cell in the Name box (Figure 1–52).

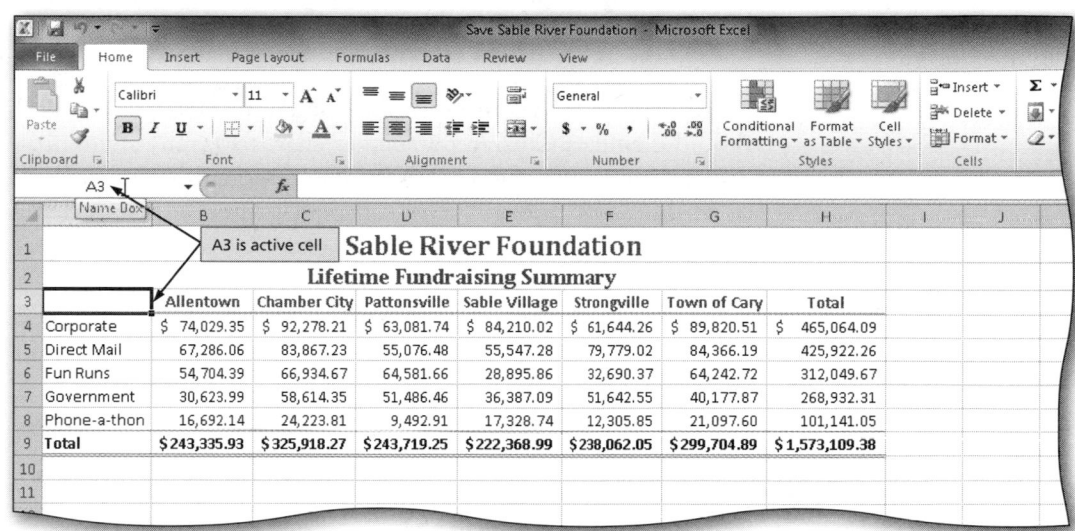

Figure 1–52

Other Ways to Select Cells

As you will see in later chapters, in addition to using the Name box to select any cell in a worksheet, you also can use it to assign names to a cell or range of cells. Excel supports several additional ways to select a cell, as summarized in Table 1–3.

Table 1–3 Selecting Cells in Excel	
Key, Box, or Command	**Function**
ALT+PAGE DOWN	Selects the cell one worksheet window to the right and moves the worksheet window accordingly.
ALT+PAGE UP	Selects the cell one worksheet window to the left and moves the worksheet window accordingly.
ARROW	Selects the adjacent cell in the direction of the arrow on the key.
CTRL+ARROW	Selects the border cell of the worksheet in combination with the arrow keys and moves the worksheet window accordingly. For example, to select the rightmost cell in the row that contains the active cell, press CTRL+RIGHT ARROW. You also can press the END key, release it, and then press the appropriate arrow key to accomplish the same task.
CTRL+HOME	Selects cell A1 or the cell one column and one row below and to the right of frozen titles and moves the worksheet window accordingly.
Find command on Find and Select menu or SHIFT+F5	Finds and selects a cell that contains specific contents that you enter in the Find and Replace dialog box. If necessary, Excel moves the worksheet window to display the cell. You also can press CTRL+F to display the Find dialog box.
Go To command on Find and Select menu or F5	Selects the cell that corresponds to the cell reference you enter in the Go To dialog box and moves the worksheet window accordingly. You also can press CTRL+G to display the Go To dialog box.
HOME	Selects the cell at the beginning of the row that contains the active cell and moves the worksheet window accordingly.
Name box	Selects the cell in the workbook that corresponds to the cell reference you enter in the Name box.
PAGE DOWN	Selects the cell down one worksheet window from the active cell and moves the worksheet window accordingly.
PAGE UP	Selects the cell up one worksheet window from the active cell and moves the worksheet window accordingly.

Break Point: If you wish to take a break, this is a good place to do so. Be sure to save the Save Sable River Foundation file again and then you can quit Excel. To resume at a later time, start Excel, open the file called Save Sable River Foundation, and continue following the steps from this location forward.

Adding a Clustered Cylinder Chart to the Worksheet

As outlined in the requirements document in Figure 1–2 on page EX 4, the worksheet should include a Clustered Cylinder chart to graphically represent the lifetime fundraisin for each fundraising activity in which the organization engages. The Clustered Cylinder chart shown in Figure 1–53 is called an **embedded chart** because it is drawn on the same worksheet as the data.

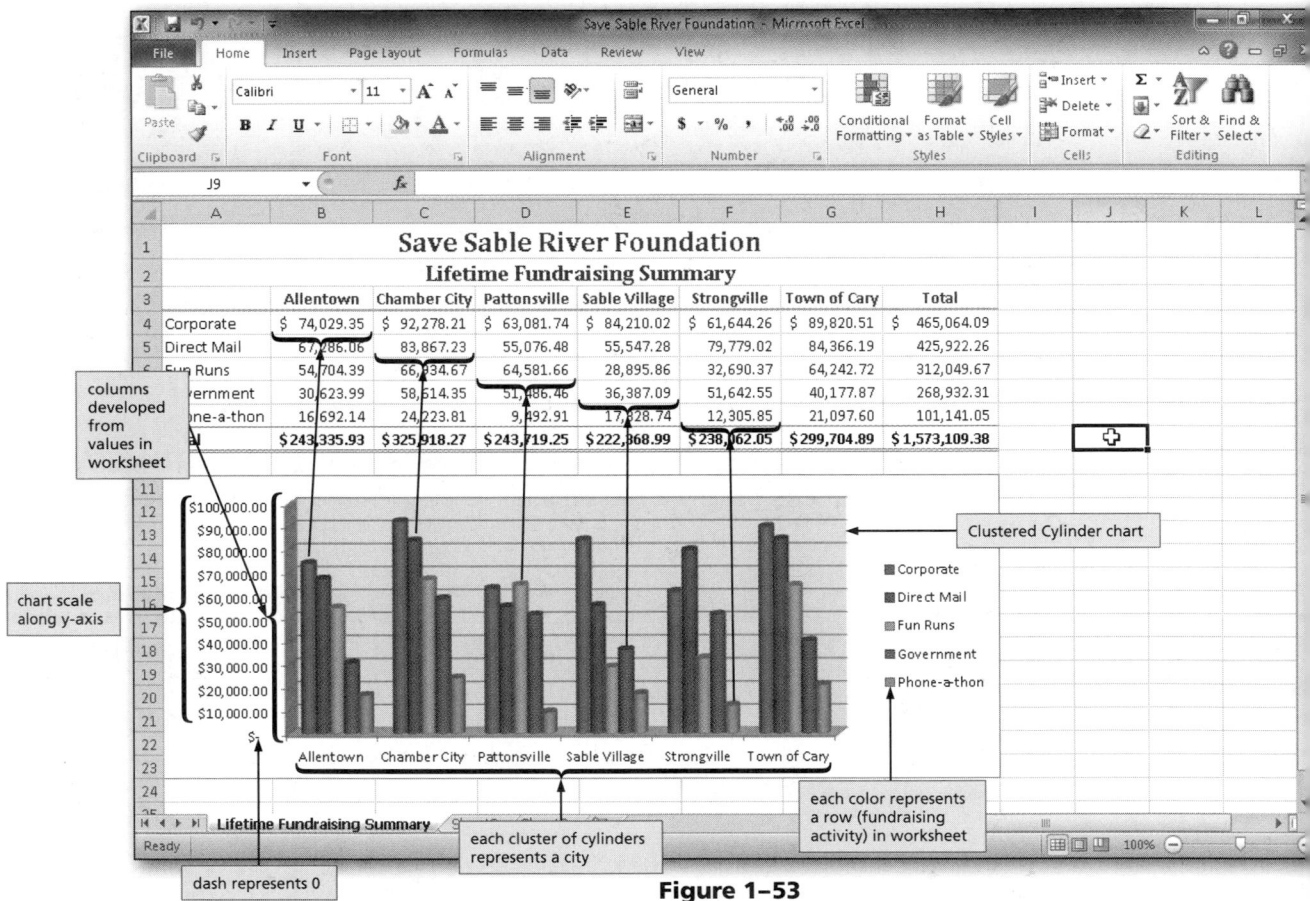

Figure 1–53

Plan Ahead

Decide on the type of chart needed.
Excel includes 11 chart types from which you can choose, including column, line, pie, bar, area, X Y (scatter), stock, surface, doughnut, bubble, and radar. The type of chart you choose depends on the type of data that you have, how much data you have, and the message you want to convey.

A line chart often is used to illustrate changes in data over time. Pie charts show the contribution of each piece of data to the whole, or total, of the data. Area charts, like line charts, illustrate changes over time, but often are used to compare more than one set of data and the area under the lines is filled in with a different color for each set of data. An X Y (scatter) chart is used much line a line chart, but each piece of data is represented by a dot and is not connected with a line. A stock chart provides a number of methods commonly

(continued)

(continued)

used in the financial industry to show stock market data. A surface chart compares data from three columns and/or rows in a three-dimensional manner. A doughnut chart is much like a pie chart, but a doughnut chart allows for comparing more than one set of data, resulting in a chart that looks like a doughnut, with each subsequent set of data surrounding the previous set. A bubble chart is much like an X Y (scatter) chart, but a third set of data results indicates how large each individual dot, or bubble, is on the chart. A radar chart can compare several sets of data in a manner that resembles a radar screen, with each set of data represented by a different color. A column or cylinder chart is a good way to compare values side by side. A Clustered Cylinder chart can go even further in comparing values across categories.

Establish where to position and how to format the chart.

- When possible, try to position charts so that both the data and chart appear on the screen on the worksheet together and so that the data and chart can be printed in the most readable manner possible.

- When choosing/selecting colors for a chart, consider the color scheme of the rest of the worksheet. The chart should not present colors that are in stark contrast to the rest of the worksheet. If the chart will be printed in color, minimize the amount of dark colors on the chart so that the chart both prints quickly and conserves ink.

In the case of the Save Sable River Foundation Lifetime Fundraising Summary, comparisons of fundraising activities within each city can be made side by side with a Clustered Cylinder chart. The chart uses differently colored cylinders to represent amounts raised for different fundraising activities. Each city uses the same color scheme for identifying fundraising activities, which allows for easy identification and comparison.

- For the city of Allentown, for example, the dark blue cylinder representing Corporate donations shows lifetime donations of $74,029.35

- For Chamber City, the maroon cylinder representing Direct Mail donations shows lifetime donations of $83,867.23

- For the city of Pattonsville, the lime green cylinder representing donations for Fun Runs shows lifetime donations of $64,581.66

- For Sable Village, the purple cylinder representing Government donations shows lifetime donations of $36,387.09

- For the city of Strongville, the light blue cylinder representing Phone-a-thon donations shows lifetime donations of $12,305.85

Because the same color scheme is used in each city to represent the five fundraising activities, you easily can compare funds raised by each fundraising activity among the cities. The totals from the worksheet are not represented, because the totals are not in the range specified for charting.

Excel derives the chart scale based on the values in the worksheet and then displays the scale along the vertical axis (also called the **y-axis** or **value axis**) of the chart. For example, no value in the range B4:G8 is less than 0 or greater than $100,000.00, so the scale ranges from 0 to $100,000.00. Excel also determines the $10,000.00 increments of the scale automatically. For the numbers along the y-axis, Excel uses a format that includes representing the 0 value with a dash (Figure 1–53).

Plan Ahead

BTW

Cell Values and Charting
When you change a cell value on which a chart is dependent, Excel redraws the chart instantaneously, unless automatic recalculation is disabled. If automatic recalculation is disabled, then you must press the F9 key to redraw the chart. To enable or disable automatic recalculation, click the Calculations Options button (Formulas tab | Calculation group).

BTW

Using Dual Axes on a Chart
Figure 1–53 shows a chart with a y-axis along the left side of the chart. If you have additional data to chart for each city, you can overlay a second chart with a different y-axis on top of the first chart. The second y-axis is displayed on the right side of the chart. In this case, the chart is said to have dual axes. Additionally, a different type of chart usually is laid over the first chart. For example, if a second y-axis were added to the chart shown in Figure 1–53, a good choice for the second chart would be a line chart. To add a second y-axis to a chart, click the data series to plot on the new axis, click Format Selection (Chart Tools Format tab | Current Selection group), click the Secondary Axis option button (Format Data Series dialog box), and then click the Close button.

To Add a Clustered Cylinder Chart to the Worksheet

The area on the worksheet where the chart appears is called the chart location. As shown in Figure 1–53 on page EX 36, the chart location in this worksheet is the range A11:G23; this range is immediately below the worksheet data. Placing the chart below the data on the Save Sable River Foundation Lifetime Fundraising Summary worksheet makes it easier to read the chart along with the data, and the chart and data easily can be printed on one sheet of paper.

The following steps draw a Clustered Cylinder chart that compares the funds raised by fundraising activity for the six cities.

- Click cell A3 and then drag the mouse pointer to cell G8 to select the range to be charted (Figure 1–54).

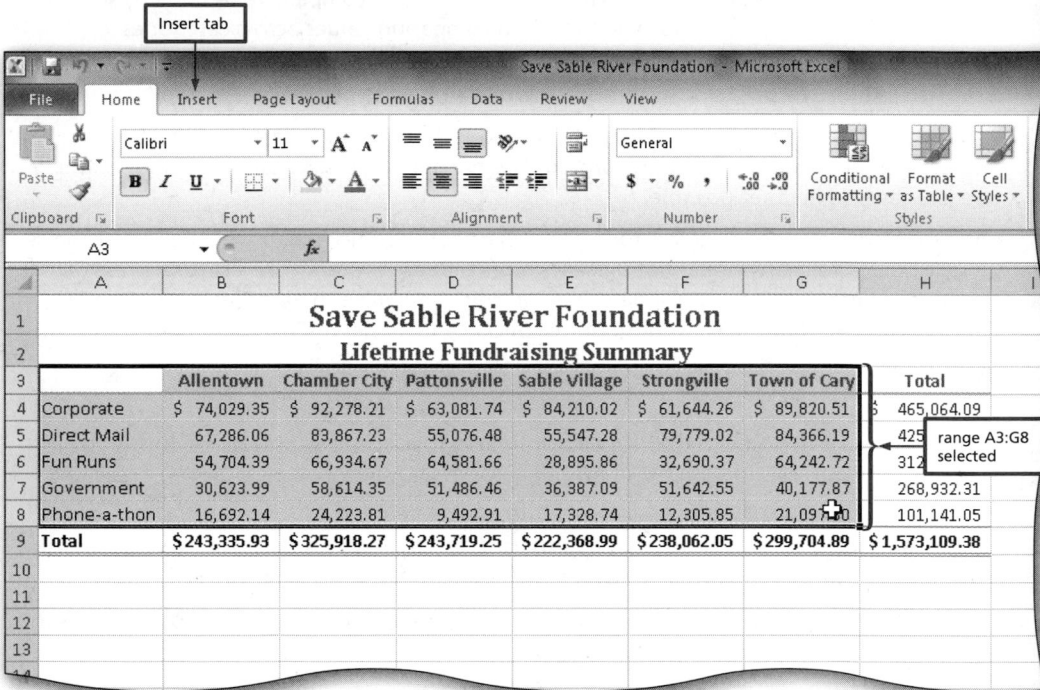

Figure 1–54

2

- Click Insert on the Ribbon to display the Insert tab (Figure 1–55).

Q&A

What tasks can I perform with the Insert tab?

The Insert tab includes commands that allow you to insert various objects, such as shapes, tables, illustrations, and charts, into a worksheet. These objects will be discussed as they are used throughout this book.

Figure 1–55

3

- Click the Column button (Insert tab | Charts group) to display the Column gallery (Figure 1–56).

Figure 1–56

4

- Click the Clustered Cylinder chart type in the Cylinder area of the Column gallery to add the selected chart type to the middle of the worksheet in a selection rectangle.

- Press and hold down the mouse button while pointing to the upper-right edge of the selection rectangle to change the mouse pointer to a double two-headed arrow (Figure 1–57).

Why is a new tab displayed on the Ribbon?

When you select objects such as shapes or charts, Excel displays contextual tabs that include special commands that are used to work

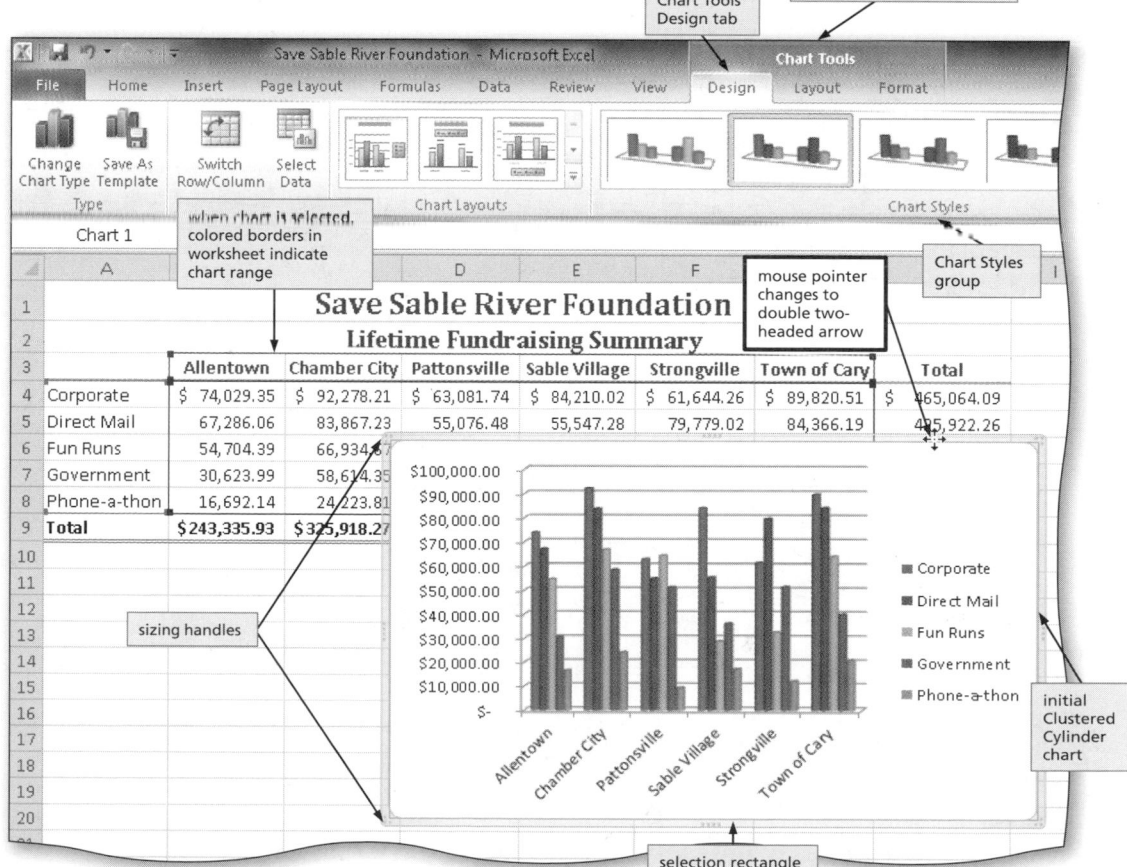

Figure 1–57

with the type of object selected. Because a chart is selected, Excel displays the Chart Tools contextual tab. The three tabs below the Chart Tools contextual tab, Design, Layout, and Format, are tabs that include commands to work with charts.

5

- Drag the chart down and to the left to position the upper-left corner of the dotted line rectangle over the upper-left corner of cell A11.

- Press and hold down the mouse button while pointing to the middle sizing handle on the right edge of the chart (Figure 1–58).

Q&A

How does Excel know which data to use to create the chart?

Excel automatically selects the entries in the topmost row of the chart range (row 3) as the titles for the horizontal axis (also called the **x-axis** or **category axis**) and draws a column for each of the 30 cells in the range containing numbers.

Figure 1–58

6

- While continuing to hold down the mouse button, press the ALT key and drag the right edge of the chart to the right edge of column H and then release the mouse button to resize the chart.

- Press and hold down the mouse button while pointing to the middle sizing handle on the bottom edge of the selection rectangle and do not release the mouse button (Figure 1–59).

Q&A

Why should I hold the ALT key down while I resize a chart?

Holding down the ALT key while you drag a chart **snaps** (aligns) the edge of the chart area to the worksheet gridlines. If you do not hold down the ALT key, then you can place an edge of a chart in the middle of a column or row.

Figure 1–59

7

• While continuing to hold down the mouse button, press the ALT key and drag the bottom edge of the chart up to the bottom edge of row 23 and then release the mouse button to resize the chart.

• If necessary, scroll the worksheet so that row 1 displays at the top of the worksheet.

• Click the More button in the Chart Styles gallery (Chart Tools Design tab | Chart Styles group) to expand the gallery (Figure 1–60).

Figure 1–60

8

• Click Style 34 in the Chart Styles gallery (column 2, row 5) to apply the chart style to the chart.

• Click cell J9 to deselect the chart and complete the worksheet (Figure 1–61).

What is the purpose of the items on the right side of the chart?

The items to the right of the column chart in Figure 1–61 are the **legend**, which identifies the colors assigned to each bar in the chart. Excel automatically selects the entries in the leftmost column of the chart range (column A) as titles within the legend.

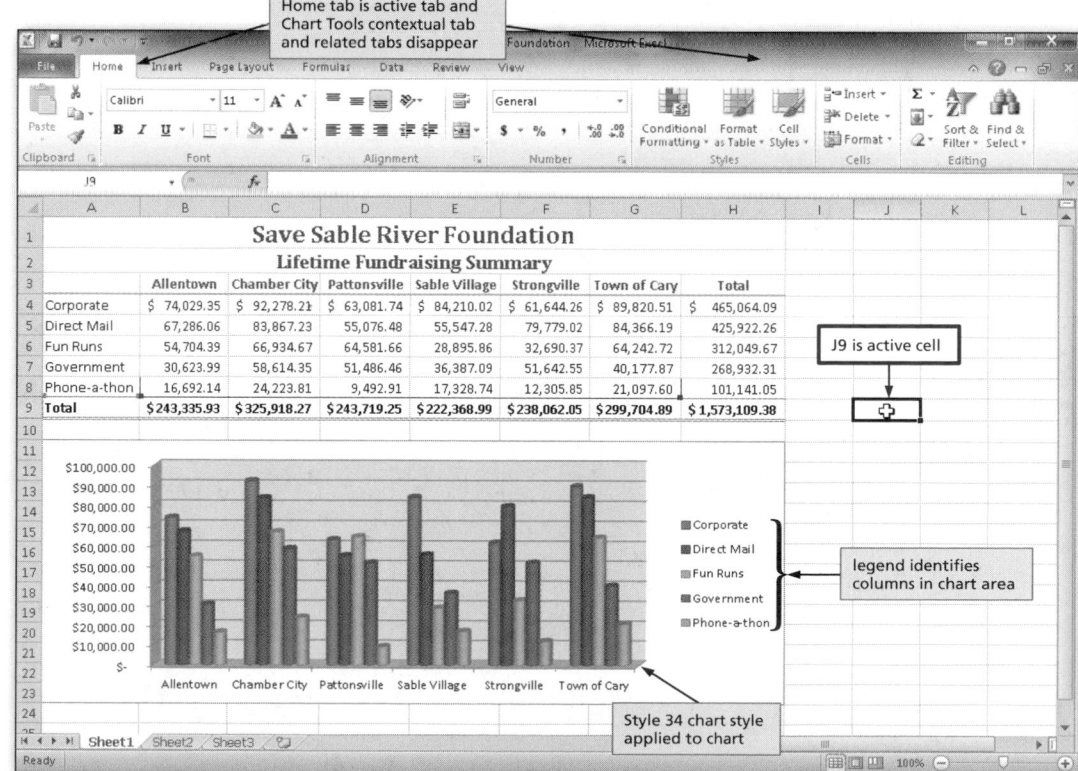

Figure 1–61

Changing the Worksheet Names

The sheet tabs at the bottom of the window allow you to view any worksheet in the workbook. You click the sheet tab of the worksheet you want to view in the Excel window. By default, Excel presets the names of the worksheets to Sheet1, Sheet2, and so on. The worksheet names become increasingly important as you move toward more sophisticated workbooks, especially workbooks in which you reference cells between worksheets.

Plan Ahead

> **Choose a name for the worksheet.**
> Use simple, meaningful names for each worksheet. Worksheet names often match the worksheet title. If a worksheet includes multiple titles in multiple sections of the worksheet, use a name that encompasses the meaning of all of the sections.

To Change the Worksheet Names

Lifetime Fundraising Summary is a meaningful name for the Save Sable River Foundation Lifetime Fundraising Summary worksheet. The following steps rename worksheets by double-clicking the sheet tabs.

1
- Double-click the sheet tab labeled Sheet1 in the lower-left corner of the window.

- Type **Lifetime Fundraising Summary** as the worksheet name and then press the ENTER key to display the new worksheet name on the sheet tab (Figure 1–62).

Figure 1–62

Q&A
What is the maximum length for a worksheet tab?

Worksheet names can be up to 31 characters (including spaces) in length. Longer worksheet names, however, mean that fewer sheet tabs will show. To view more sheet tabs, you can drag the tab split box (Figure 1–62) to the right. This will reduce the size of the scroll bar at the bottom of the screen. Double-click the tab split box to reset it to its normal position.

2
- Right-click the sheet tab labeled Lifetime Fundraising Summary in the lower-left corner of the window to display a shortcut menu.

- Point to Tab Color on the shortcut menu to display the color gallery (Figure 1–63).

Figure 1–63

Q&A
How can I quickly move between worksheet tabs?

You can use the tab scrolling buttons to the left of the sheet tabs (Figure 1–63) to move between worksheets. The leftmost and rightmost scroll buttons move to the first or last worksheet in the workbook. The two middle scroll buttons move one worksheet to the left or right.

3
- Click Red, Accent 2 (column 6, row 1) in the Theme Colors area to change the color of the tab (Figure 1–64)

4
- If necessary, click Home on the Ribbon to display the Home tab.

Figure 1–64

Changing Document Properties

Excel helps you organize and identify your files by using **document properties**, which are the details about a file. Document properties, also known as **metadata**, can include information such as the project author, title, subject, and keywords. A **keyword** is a word or phrase that further describes the document. For example, a class name or document topic can describe the file's purpose or content.

Document properties are valuable for a variety of reasons:

- Users can save time locating a particular file because they can view a document's properties without opening the document.
- By creating consistent properties for files having similar content, users can better organize their documents.
- Some organizations require Excel users to add document properties so that other employees can view details about these files.

Five different types of document properties exist, but the more common ones used in this book are standard and automatically updated properties. **Standard properties** are associated with all Microsoft Office documents and include author, title, and subject. **Automatically updated properties** include file system properties, such as the date you create or change a file, and statistics, such as the file size.

To Change Document Properties

The **Document Information Panel** contains areas where you can view and enter document properties. You can view and change information in this panel at any time while you are creating a workbook. Before saving the workbook again, you want to add your name and course information as document properties. The following steps use the Document Information Panel to change document properties.

1
- Click File on the Ribbon to open the Backstage view. If necessary, click the Info tab in the Backstage view to display the Info gallery (Figure 1–65).

How do I close the Backstage view?

Click File on the Ribbon or click the preview of the document in the Info gallery to return to the Excel document window.

Figure 1–65

2

- Click the Properties button in the right pane of the Info gallery to display the Properties menu (Figure 1–66).

Figure 1–66

3

- Click Show Document Panel on the Properties menu to close the Backstage view and display the Document Information Panel in the Excel workbook window (Figure 1–67).

Q&A

Why are some of the document properties in my Document Information Panel already filled in?

The person who installed Microsoft Office 2010 on your computer or network may have set or customized the properties.

Figure 1–67

4

- Click the Author text box, if necessary, and then type your name as the Author property. If a name already is displayed in the Author text box, delete it before typing your name.

- Click the Subject text box, if necessary delete any existing text, and then type your course and section as the Subject property.

- If an AutoComplete dialog box appears, click its Yes button.

- Click the Keywords text box, if necessary delete any existing text, and then type **Lifetime Fundraising Summary** as the Keywords property (Figure 1–68).

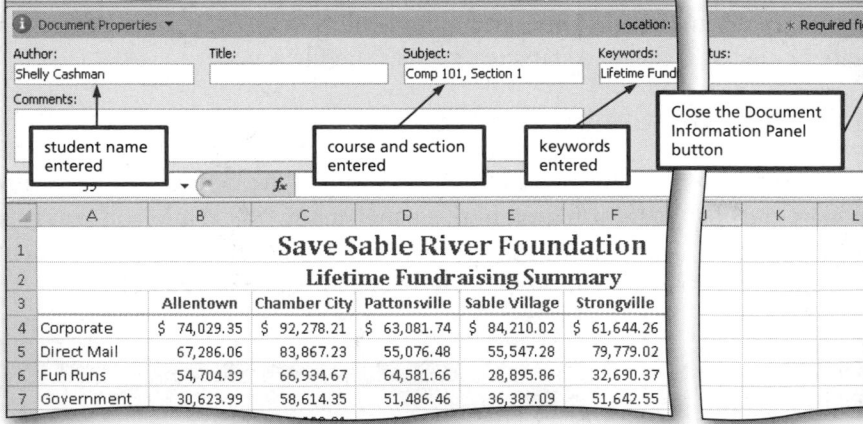

Figure 1–68

Q&A

What types of document properties does Excel collect automatically?

Excel records details such as time spent editing a workbook, the number of times a workbook has been revised, and the fonts and themes used in a workbook.

5

- Click the Close the Document Information Panel button so that the Document Information Panel no longer is displayed. If a dialog box is displayed, click the No button to close it.

Other Ways

1. Click File on Ribbon, cl¯ Info in the Backstage view, if necessary click Show All Properties link in Info gallery, clic property to change an¯ type new information, close the Backstage vie

To Save an Existing Workbook with the Same File Name

You have made several modifications to the workbook since you last saved it. Thus, you should save it again. The following step saves the workbook again. For an example of the step listed below, refer to the Introduction to Office 2010 and Windows 7 chapter at the beginning of this book.

● Click the Save button on the Quick Access Toolbar to overwrite the previously saved file.

Previewing and Printing a Worksheet

After creating a worksheet, you may want to print it. Printing a worksheet enables you to distribute the worksheet to others in a form that can be read or viewed but typically not edited. It is a good practice to save a workbook before printing a worksheet, in the event you experience difficulties printing.

Determine the best method for distributing the worksheet.
The traditional method of distributing a worksheet uses a printer to produce a hard copy. A **hardcopy or printout** is information that exists on a physical medium such as paper. For users that can receive fax documents, you can elect to print a hard copy on a remote fax machine. Hard copies can be useful for the following reasons:

- Many people prefer proofreading a hard copy of a worksheet rather than viewing it on the screen to check for errors and readability.

- Hard copies can serve as reference material if your storage medium is lost or becomes corrupted and you need to re-create the worksheet.

Instead of distributing a hard copy of a worksheet, users can choose to distribute the worksheet as an electronic image that mirrors the original worksheet's appearance. The electronic image of the worksheet can be e-mailed, posted on a Web site, or copied to a portable storage medium such as a USB flash drive. Two popular electronic image formats, sometimes called fixed formats, are PDF by Adobe Systems and XPS by Microsoft. In Excel, you can create electronic image files through the Print tab in the Backstage view, the Save & Send tab in the Backstage view, and the Save As dialog box. Electronic images of worksheets, such as PDF and XPS, can be useful for the following reasons:

- Users can view electronic images of worksheets without the software that created the original worksheet (e.g., Excel). Specifically, to view a PDF file, you use a program called Acrobat Reader, which can be downloaded free from Adobe's Web site. Similarly, to view an XPS file, you use a program called an XPS Viewer, which is included in the latest versions of Windows and Internet Explorer.

- Sending electronic documents saves paper and printer supplies. Society encourages users to contribute to **green computing**, which involves reducing the environmental waste generated when using a computer.

To Preview and Print a Worksheet in Landscape Orientation

With the completed workbook saved, you may want to print it. Because the worksheet is included in a report, you will print a hard copy on a printer. The following steps print a hard copy of the contents of the Save Sable River Foundation Lifetime Fundraising Summary worksheet.

1

• Click File on the Ribbon to open the Backstage view.

• Click the Print tab in the Backstage view to display the Print gallery (Figure 1–69).

Q&A

How can I print multiple copies of my worksheet?

Increase the number in the Copies box in the Print gallery.

Q&A

What if I decide not to print the worksheet at this time?

Click File on the Ribbon to close the Backstage view and return to the Excel workbook window.

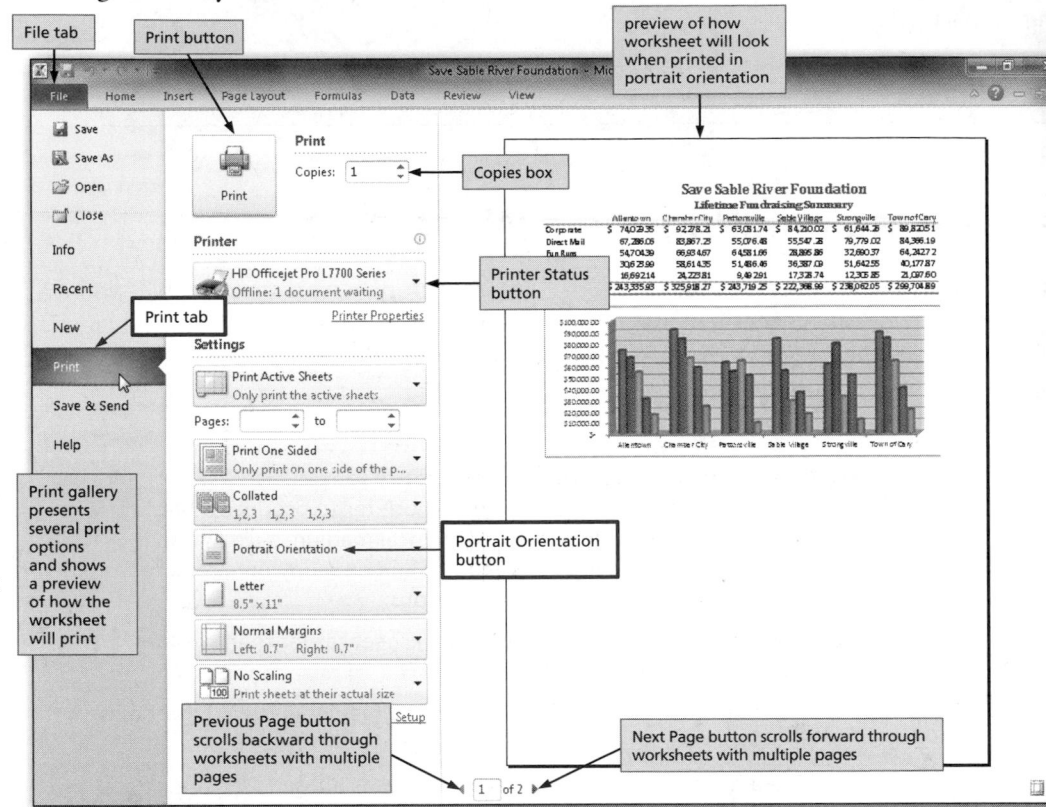

Figure 1–69

2

• Verify the printer name that appears on the Printer Status button will print a hard copy of the document. If necessary, click the Printer Status button to display a list of available printer options and then click the desired printer to change the currently selected printer.

3

• Click the Portrait Orientation button in the Settings area and then select Landscape Orientation to change the orientation of the page to landscape and view the entire worksheet on one page (Figure 1–70).

Figure 1–70

4

- Click the Print button in the Print gallery to print the worksheet in landscape orientation on the currently selected printer.

- When the printer stops, retrieve the hard copy (Figure 1–71).

Do I have to wait until my worksheet is complete to print it?

No, you can follow these steps to print a document at any time while you are creating it.

What if I want to print an electronic image of a worksheet instead of a hard copy?

You would click the Printer Status button in the Print gallery and then select the desired electronic image option such as a Microsoft XPS Document Writer, which would create an XPS file.

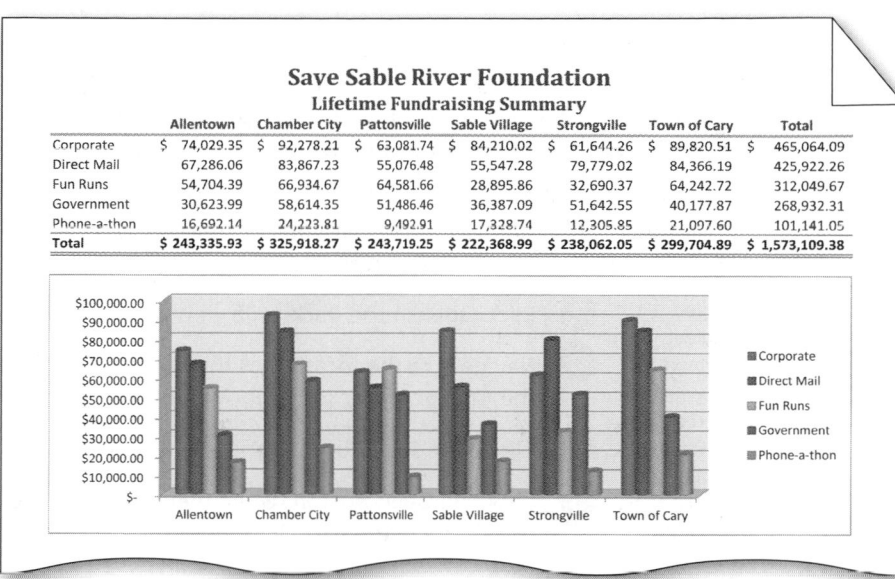

Figure 1–71

To Quit Excel

This Save Sable River Foundation workbook now is complete. The following steps quit Excel if only one workbook is open. For a detailed example of the procedure summarized below, refer to the Office 2010 and Windows 7 chapter at the beginning of this book.

- If you have one Excel workbook open, click the Close button on the right side of the title bar to close the document and quit Excel; or if you have multiple Excel workbooks open, click File on the Ribbon to open the Backstage view and then click the Exit button to close all open workbooks and quit Excel.

- If a Microsoft Office Excel dialog box appears, click the Save button to save any changes made to the workbook since the last save.

Starting Excel and Opening a Workbook

Once you have created and saved a workbook, you may need to retrieve it from your storage medium. For example, you might want to revise a worksheet or reprint it. Opening a workbook requires that Excel is running on your computer.

To Start Excel

- Click the Start button on the Windows 7 taskbar to display the Start menu.

- Type **Microsoft Excel** as the search text in the 'Search programs and files' text box and watch the search results appear on the Start menu.

- Click Microsoft Excel 2010 in the search results on the Start menu to start Excel and display a new blank workbook in the Excel window.

- If the Excel window is not maximized, click the Maximize button next to the Close button on its title bar to maximize the window.

Managing Versions
Excel automatically saves your work, even when you have not saved a file. If you inadvertently close a file without saving it, you can recover your work by clicking Info in the Backstage view and then clicking the Manage Versions button. On the Manage Versions list, click Recover Unsaved Workbooks to display the Open dialog box. Select the file you want to recover and then click the Open button (Open dialog box) to display the file. You also can click the file to recover in the Versions list next to the Manage Versions button. To delete recent copies of unsaved files, click Delete All Unsaved Workbooks on the Manage Versions list.

To Open a Workbook from Excel

Earlier in this chapter you saved your project on a USB flash drive using the file name Save Sable River Foundation. The following steps open the Save Sable River Foundation file from the Excel folder in the CIS 101 folder on the USB flash drive. For a detailed example of the procedure summarized below, refer to page OFF 57 in the Office 2010 and Windows 7 chapter at the beginning of this book.

1 With your USB flash drive connected to one of the computer's USB ports, click File on the Ribbon to open the Backstage view.

2 Click Open in the Backstage view to display the Open dialog box.

3 Navigate to the location of the file to be opened (in this case, the USB flash drive, then to the CIS 101 folder [or your class folder], and then to the Excel folder).

4 Click Save Sable River Foundation to select the file to be opened.

5 Click the Open button (Open dialog box) to open the selected file and display the opened workbook in the Excel window.

AutoCalculate

You easily can obtain a total, an average, or other information about the numbers in a range by using the **AutoCalculate area** on the status bar. First, select the range of cells containing the numbers you want to check. Next, right-click the AutoCalculate area to display the Status Bar Configuration shortcut menu (Figure 1–72). The check mark to the left of the active functions (Average, Count, and Sum) indicates that the sum, count, and average of the selected range are displayed in the AutoCalculate area on the status bar. The functions of the AutoCalculate commands on the Status Bar Configuration shortcut menu are described in Table 1–4.

AutoCalculate
Use the AutoCalculate area on the status bar to check your work as you enter data in a worksheet. If you enter large amounts of data, you select a range of data and then check the AutoCalculate area to provide insight into statistics about the data you entered. Often, you will have an intuitive feel for whether the numbers are accurate or if you may have made a mistake while entering the data.

Table 1–4 AutoCalculate Shortcut Menu Commands	
Command	**Function**
Average	AutoCalculate area displays the average of the numbers in the selected range
Count	AutoCalculate area displays the number of nonblank cells in the selected range
Numerical Count	AutoCalculate area displays the number of cells containing numbers in the selected range
Minimum	AutoCalculate area displays the lowest value in the selected range
Maximum	AutoCalculate area displays the highest value in the selected range
Sum	AutoCalculate area displays the sum of the numbers in the selected range

To Use the AutoCalculate Area to Determine a Maximum

The following steps display the largest amounts of funds raised for any city for the Fun Runs fundraising activity.

- Select the range B6:G6 and then right-click the AutoCalculate area on the status bar to display the Customize Status Bar shortcut menu (Figure 1–72).

What is displayed on the Customize Status Bar shortcut menu?

This shortcut menu includes several commands that allow you to control the items displayed on the Customize Status Bar shortcut menu. The AutoCalculate area includes six commands as well as the result of the associated calculation on the right side of the menu.

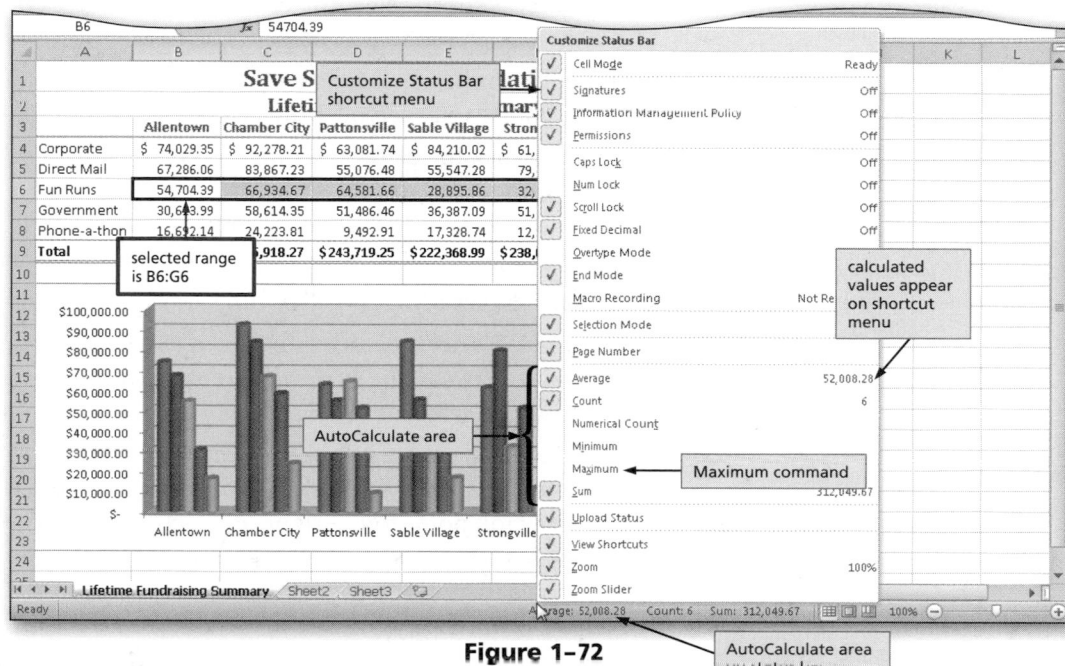

Figure 1–72

- Click Maximum on the shortcut menu to display the Maximum value in the range B6:G6 in the AutoCalculate area of the status bar.

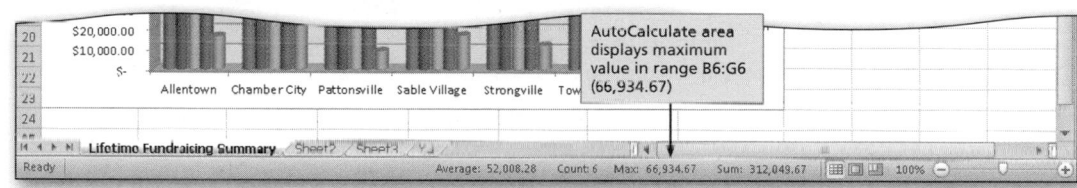

Figure 1–73

- Click anywhere on the worksheet to cause the shortcut menu to disappear (Figure 1–73).

- Right-click the AutoCalculate area and then click Maximum on the shortcut menu to cause the Maximum value to no longer appear in the AutoCalculate area.

- Click anywhere on the worksheet to cause the shortcut menu to disappear.

Correcting Errors

You can correct errors on a worksheet using one of several methods. The method you choose will depend on the extent of the error and whether you notice it while typing the data or after you have entered the incorrect data into the cell.

Correcting Errors While You Are Typing Data into a Cell

If you notice an error while you are typing data into a cell, press the BACKSPACE key to erase the incorrect characters and then type the correct characters. If the error is a major one, click the Cancel box in the formula bar or press the ESC key to erase the entire entry and then reenter the data from the beginning.

Correcting Errors After Entering Data into a Cell

If you find an error in the worksheet after entering the data, you can correct the error in one of two ways:

1. If the entry is short, select the cell, retype the entry correctly, and then click the Enter box or press the ENTER key. The new entry will replace the old entry.

2. If the entry in the cell is long and the errors are minor, using Edit mode may be a better choice than retyping the cell entry. Use the Edit mode as described below.

   a. Double-click the cell containing the error to switch Excel to Edit mode. In **Edit mode**, Excel displays the active cell entry in the formula bar and a flashing insertion point in the active cell (Figure 1–74). With Excel in Edit mode, you can edit the contents directly in the cell — a procedure called **in-cell editing**.

   b. Make changes using in-cell editing, as indicated below.

      (1) To insert new characters between two characters, place the insertion point between the two characters and begin typing. Excel inserts the new characters at the location of the insertion point.

      (2) To delete a character in the cell, move the insertion point to the left of the character you want to delete and then press the DELETE key or place the insertion point to the right of the character you want to delete and then press the BACKSPACE key. You also can use the mouse to drag through the character or adjacent characters you want to delete and then press the DELETE key or click the Cut button (Home tab | Clipboard group).

      (3) When you are finished editing an entry, click the Enter box or press the ENTER key.

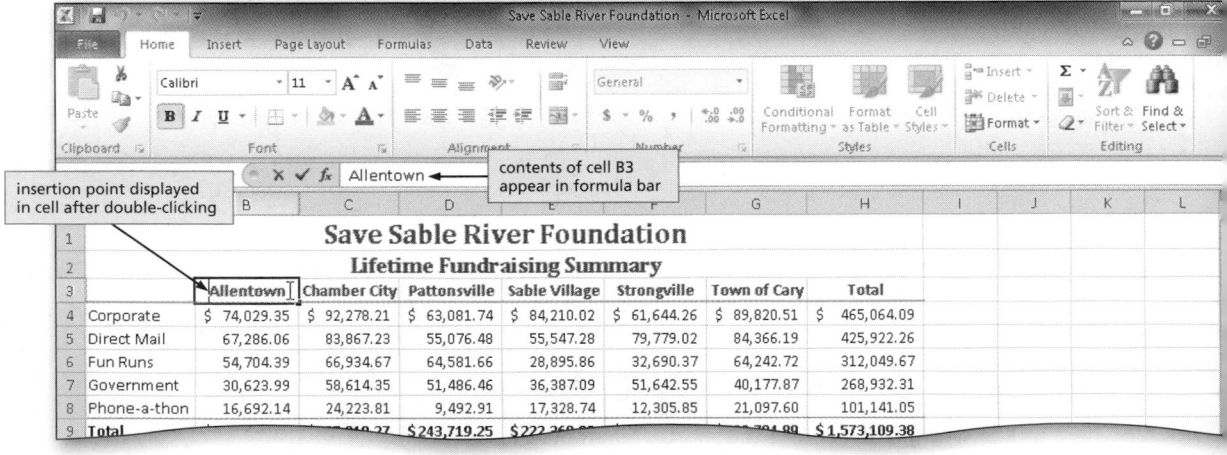

Figure 1–74

When Excel enters the Edit mode, the keyboard usually is in Insert mode. In **Insert mode**, as you type a character, Excel inserts the character and moves all characters to the right of the typed character one position to the right. You can change to Overtype mode by pressing the INSERT key. In **Overtype mode**, Excel overtypes, or replaces, the character to the right of the insertion point. The INSERT key toggles the keyboard between Insert mode and Overtype mode.

While in Edit mode, you may have reason to move the insertion point to various points in the cell, select portions of the data in the cell, or switch from inserting characters to overtyping characters. Table 1–5 summarizes the more common tasks performed during in-cell editing.

Table 1–5 Summary of In-Cell Editing Tasks

	Task	Mouse	Keyboard
1	Move the insertion point to the beginning of data in a cell.	Point to the left of the first character and click.	Press HOME
2	Move the insertion point to the end of data in a cell.	Point to the right of the last character and click.	Press END
3	Move the insertion point anywhere in a cell.	Point to the appropriate position and click the character.	Press RIGHT ARROW or LEFT ARROW
4	Highlight one or more adjacent characters.	Drag the mouse pointer through adjacent characters.	Press SHIFT+RIGHT ARROW or SHIFT+LEFT ARROW
5	Select all data in a cell.	Double-click the cell with the insertion point in the cell if there are no spaces in the data in the cell.	
6	Delete selected characters.	Click the Cut button (Home tab | Clipboard group)	Press DELETE
7	Delete characters to the left of the insertion point.		Press BACKSPACE
8	Delete characters to the right of the insertion point.		Press DELETE
9	Toggle between Insert and Overtype modes.		Press INSERT

BTW

Excel Help
At any time while using Excel, you can find answers to questions and display information about various topics through Excel Help. Used properly, this form of assistance can increase your productivity and reduce your frustrations by minimizing the time you spend learning how to use Excel. For instruction about Excel Help and exercises that will help you gain confidence in using it, read the Office 2010 and Windows 7 chapter at the beginning of this book.

Undoing the Last Cell Entry

Excel provides the Undo command on the Quick Access Toolbar (Figure 1–75), which allows you to erase recent cell entries. Thus, if you enter incorrect data in a cell and notice it immediately, click the Undo button and Excel changes the cell entry to what it was prior to the incorrect data entry.

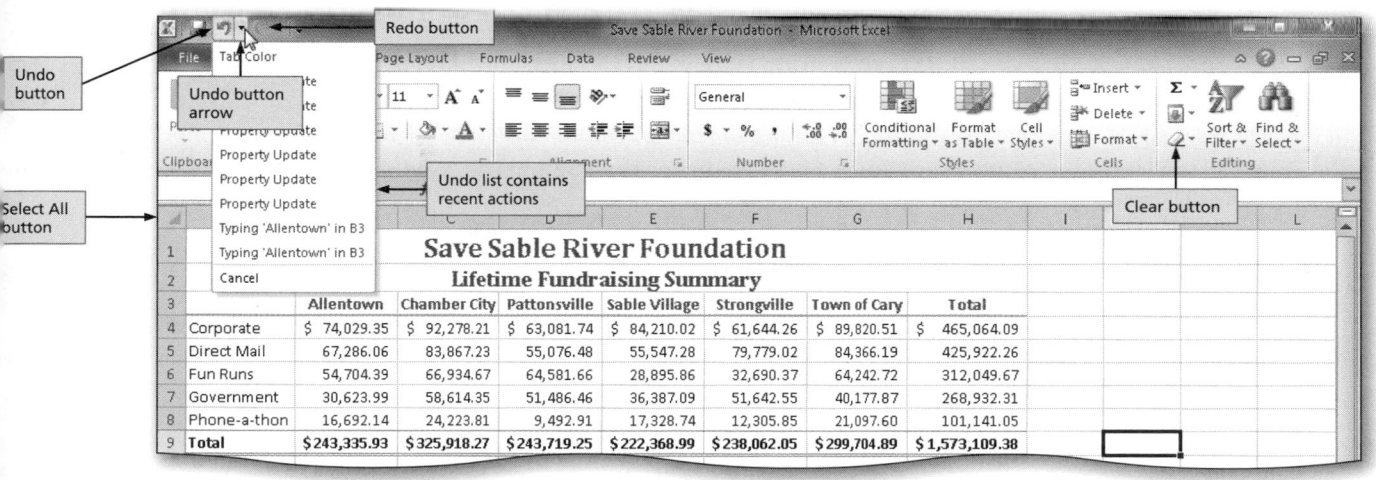

Figure 1–75

Excel remembers the last 100 actions you have completed. Thus, you can undo up to 100 previous actions by clicking the Undo button arrow to display the Undo list and then clicking the action to be undone (Figure 1–75). You can drag through several actions in the Undo list to undo all of them at once. If no actions are available for Excel to undo, then the Undo button is dimmed and inoperative.

The Redo button, next to the Undo button on the Quick Access Toolbar, allows you to repeat previous actions.

Clearing a Cell or Range of Cells

If you enter data into the wrong cell or range of cells, you can erase, or clear, the data using one of the first four methods listed below. The fifth method clears the formatting from the selected cells.

TO CLEAR CELL ENTRIES USING THE FILL HANDLE

1. Select the cell or range of cells and then point to the fill handle so the mouse pointer changes to a crosshair.
2. Drag the fill handle back into the selected cell or range until a shadow covers the cell or cells you want to erase. Release the mouse button.

TO CLEAR CELL ENTRIES USING THE SHORTCUT MENU

1. Select the cell or range of cells to be cleared.
2. Right-click the selection.
3. Click Clear Contents on the shortcut menu.

TO CLEAR CELL ENTRIES USING THE DELETE KEY

1. Select the cell or range of cells to be cleared.
2. Press the DELETE key.

TO CLEAR CELL ENTRIES AND FORMATTING USING THE CLEAR BUTTON

1. Select the cell or range of cells to be cleared.
2. Click the Clear button (Home tab | Editing group) (Figure 1–75 on the previous page)
3. Click Clear Contents on the menu.

TO CLEAR FORMATTING USING THE CELL STYLES BUTTON

1. Select the cell or range of cells from which you want to remove the formatting.
2. Click the Cell Styles button (Home tab | Styles group) and point to Normal.
3. Click Normal in the Cell Styles Gallery.

The Clear button (Home tab | Editing group) is the only command that clears both the cell entry and the cell formatting. As you are clearing cell entries, always remember that you should *never press the* SPACEBAR *to clear a cell*. Pressing the SPACEBAR enters a blank character. A blank character is text and is different from an empty cell, even though the cell may appear empty.

Clearing the Entire Worksheet

If the required worksheet edits are extremely extensive, you may want to clear the entire worksheet and start over. To clear the worksheet or delete an embedded chart, you would use the following steps.

TO CLEAR THE ENTIRE WORKSHEET

1. Click the Select All button on the worksheet (Figure 1–75).
2. Click the Clear button (Home tab | Editing group) and then click Clear All on the Clear menu to delete both the entries and formats.

The Select All button selects the entire worksheet. Instead of clicking the Select All button, you can press CTRL+A. To clear an unsaved workbook, click the workbook's Close Window button or click the Close button in the Backstage view. Click the No button if the Microsoft Excel dialog box asks if you want to save changes. To start a new, blank workbook, click the New button in the Backstage view.

BTW

Getting Back to Normal
If you accidentally assign unwanted formats to a range of cells, you can use the Normal cell style selection in the Cell Styles gallery. Click Cell Styles (Home tab | Styles group) and then click Normal in the Cell Styles gallery. Doing so changes the format to Normal style. To view the characteristics of the Normal style, right-click the style in the Cell Styles gallery and then click Modify or press ALT+APOSTROPHE (').

BTW

Certification
The Microsoft Office Specialist (MOS) program provides an opportunity for you to obtain a valuable industry credential — proof that you have the Excel 2010 skills required by employers. For more information, visit the Excel 2010 Certification Web page (scsite.com/ex2010/cert).

To delete an embedded chart, you would complete the following steps.

To Delete an Embedded Chart

. Click the chart to select it.

. Press the DELETE key.

o Quit Excel

The project now is complete. The following steps quit Excel. For a detailed example f the procedure summarized below, refer to the Office 2010 and Windows 7 chapter at the eginning of this book.

● If you have one Excel workbook open, click the Close button on the right side of the title bar to close the document and quit Excel; or if you have multiple Excel workbooks open, click File on the Ribbon to open the Backstage view and then click Exit in the Backstage view to close all open workbooks and quit Excel.

● If a Microsoft Office Excel dialog box appears, click the Save button to save any changes made to the document since the last save.

Chapter Summary

n this chapter you have learned how to enter text and numbers to create a worksheet, how to select a range, how to se the Sum button, format cells, insert a chart, and preview and print a worksheet. The items listed below include l the new Excel skills you have learned in this chapter.

1. To Start Excel (EX 6)
2. Enter the Worksheet Titles (EX 8)
3. Enter Column Titles (EX 10)
4. Enter Row Titles (EX 12)
5. Enter Numbers (EX 13)
6. Sum a Column of Numbers (EX 15)
7. Copy a Cell to Adjacent Cells in a Row (EX 17)
8. Determine Multiple Totals at the Same Time (EX 18)
9. Save a Workbook (EX 20)
10. Change a Cell Style (EX 22)
11. Change the Font (EX 24)
12. Bold a Cell (EX 25)
13. Increase the Font Size of a Cell Entry (EX 26)
14. Change the Font Color of a Cell Entry (EX 27)
15. Center Cell Entries Across Columns by Merging Cells (EX 28)
16. Format Column Titles and the Total Row (EX 29)
17. Format Numbers in the Worksheet (EX 31)
18. Adjust the Column Width (EX 33)
19. Use the Name Box to Select a Cell (EX 34)
20. Add a Clustered Cylinder Chart to the Worksheet (EX 38)

21. Change the Worksheet Names (EX 42)
22. Change Document Properties (EX 43)
23. Save an Existing Workbook with the Same File Name (EX 45)
24. Preview and Print a Worksheet in Landscape Orientation (EX 46)
25. Quit Excel (EX 47)
26. Start Excel (EX 47)
27. Open a Workbook from Excel (EX 48)
28. Use the AutoCalculate Area to Determine a Maximum (EX 49)
29. Clear Cell Entries Using the Fill Handle (EX 52)
30. Clear Cell Entries Using the Shortcut Menu (EX 52)
31. Clear Cell Entries Using the DELETE Key (EX 52)
32. Clear Cell Entries and Formatting Using the Clear Button (EX 52)
33. Clear Formatting Using the Cell Styles Button (EX 52)
34. Clear the Entire Worksheet (EX 52)
35. Delete an Embedded Chart (EX 53)

If you have a SAM 2010 user profile, your instructor may have assigned an autogradable version of this assignment. If so, log into the SAM 2010 Web site at www.cengage.com/sam2010 to download the instruction and start files.

Learn It Online

Test your knowledge of chapter content and key terms.

Instructions: To complete the Learn It Online exercises, start your browser, click the Address bar, and then enter the Web address `scsite.com/ex2010/learn`. When the Excel 2010 Learn It Online page is displayed, click the link for the exercise you want to complete and then read the instructions.

Chapter Reinforcement TF, MC, and SA
A series of true/false, multiple choice, and short answer questions that test your knowledge of the chapter content.

Who Wants To Be a Computer Genius?
An interactive game that challenges your knowledge of chapter content in the style of a television quiz show.

Flash Cards
An interactive learning environment where you identify chapter key terms associated with displayed definitions.

Wheel of Terms
An interactive game that challenges your knowledge of chapter key terms in the style of the television show *Wheel of Fortune*.

Practice Test
A series of multiple choice questions that test your knowledge of chapter content and key terms.

Crossword Puzzle Challenge
A crossword puzzle that challenges your knowledge of key terms presented in the chapter.

Apply Your Knowledge

Reinforce the skills and apply the concepts you learned in this chapter.

Changing the Values in a Worksheet

Instructions: Start Excel. Open the workbook Apply 1–1 Clothes Campus Third Quarter Expenses (Figure 1–76a). See the inside back cover of this book for instructions for downloading the Data Files for Students, or see your instructor for information on accessing the files required in this book.

1. Make the changes to the worksheet described in Table 1–6 so that the worksheet appears as shown in Figure 1–76b. As you edit the values in the cells containing numeric data, watch the totals in row 7, the totals in column F, and the chart change.

2. Change the worksheet title in cell A1 to the Title cell style and then merge and center it across columns A through F. Use buttons in the Font group on the Home tab on the Ribbon to change the worksheet subtitle in cell A2 to 16-point Cambria red, bold font and then center it across columns A through F. Use the Red, Accent 2 theme color (column 6, row 1 on the Font gallery) for the red font color.

3. Apply the worksheet name, Third Quarter Expenses, to the sheet tab and apply the Red, Accent 2 theme color to the sheet tab.

4. Change the document properties as specified by your instructor. Save the workbook using the file name, Apply 1–1 Clothed for Campus Third Quarter Expenses. Submit the revised workbook as specified by your instructor.

Table 1–6 New Worksheet Data	
Cell	**Change Cell Contents To**
A1	Clothed for Campus
B4	7829.50
C4	19057.83
D5	24217.92
E5	25859.62
E6	35140.84

Before

After

Figure 1–76

Extend Your Knowledge

Extend the skills you learned in this chapter and experiment with new skills. You may need t
use Help to complete the assignment.

Formatting a Worksheet and Adding Additional Charts

Instructions: Start Excel. Open the workbook Extend 1–1 Pack Right Moving Supplies. See the insid
back cover of this book for instructions for downloading the Data Files for Students, or see your
instructor for information on accessing the files required in this book. Perform the following tasks
to format cells in the worksheet and to add two charts to the worksheet.

1. Use the commands in the Font group on the Home tab on the Ribbon to change the font of the
   title in cell A1 to 22-point Arial Black, green, bold, and the subtitle of the worksheet to 14-point
   Arial, red, bold.

2. Select the range A3:G8, click the Insert tab on the Ribbon, and then click the Dialog Box Launch●
   in the Charts group on the Ribbon to open the Insert Chart dialog box. If necessary, drag the
   lower-right corner of the Insert Chart dialog box to expand it (Figure 1–77).

Figure 1–77

3. Insert a Stacked Area in 3-D chart by clicking the Stacked Area in 3-D chart in the gallery and the
   clicking the OK button. You may need to use the scroll box on the right side of the Insert Chart
   dialog box to view the Area charts in the gallery. Move the chart either below or to the right of th●
   data in the worksheet. Click the Design tab and apply a chart style of your choice to the chart.

4. Deselect the chart and reselect the range A3:G8, and then follow Step 3 above to insert a Cluster●
   Horizontal Cone chart in the worksheet. Move the chart either below or to the right of the data s●
   that each chart does not overlap the Stacked Area in 3-D chart. Make sure to make the values on
   the horizontal axis readable by expanding the size of the chart. Choose a different chart style for
   this chart than the one you selected for the Stacked Area in 3-D chart.

5. Resize each chart so that each snaps to the worksheet gridlines. You may need to scroll the worksheet to resize and view the charts. Preview the worksheet.

6. Apply a worksheet name to the sheet tab and apply a color of your choice to the sheet tab.

7. Change the document properties as specified by your instructor. Save the workbook using the file name, Extend 1–1 Pack Right Moving Supplies Charts. Submit the revised workbook as specified by your instructor.

Make It Right

Analyze a workbook and correct all errors and/or improve the design.

Fixing Formatting Problems and Data Errors in a Worksheet

Instructions: Start Excel. Open the workbook Make It Right 1–1 Pets. See the inside back cover of this book for instructions for downloading the Data Files for Students, or see your instructor for information on accessing the files required for this book. Correct the following formatting problems and data errors (Figure 1–78) in the worksheet, while keeping in mind the guidelines presented in this chapter.

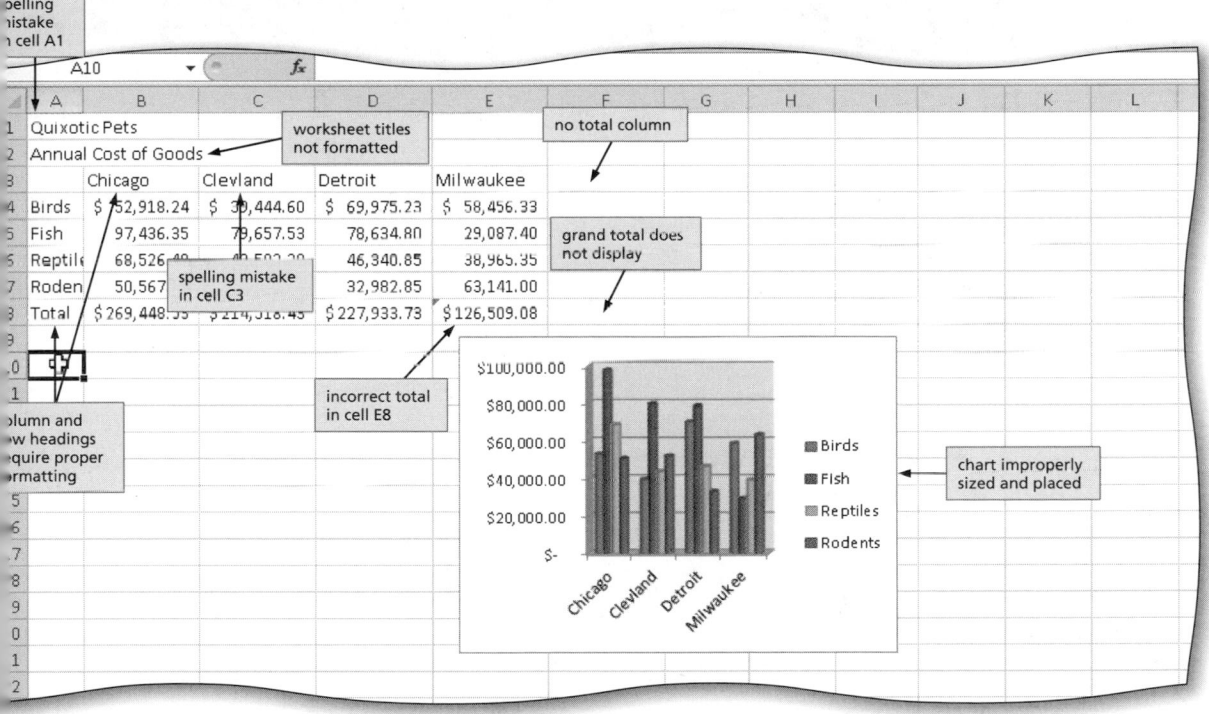

Figure 1–78

1. Merge and center the worksheet title and subtitle appropriately.

2. Format the worksheet title with a cell style appropriate for a worksheet title.

3. Format the subtitle using commands in the Font group on the Home tab on the Ribbon and apply the Red, Accent 2 color to the subtitle.

4. Correct the spelling mistake in cell A1 by changing Quixotic to Exotic. Correct the spelling mistake in cell C3 by changing Clevland to Cleveland.

Continued >

Make It Right *continued*

5. Add a column header for totals in column F, create the necessary totals in column E, and create t necessary totals in row 8 and column F.

6. Apply proper formatting to the column headers and total row, including centering the column head

7. Adjust the column sizes so that all data in each column is visible.

8. Create the grand total for the annual cost of goods.

9. The SUM function in cell E8 does not sum all of the numbers in the column. Correct this error by editing the range for the SUM function in the cell.

10. Resize and move the chart so that it is below the worksheet data and does not extend past the rig edge of the worksheet data. Be certain to snap the chart to the worksheet gridlines by holding do the ALT key as you resize the chart to the right edge of column F and the bottom of row 22.

11. Apply a worksheet name to the sheet tab and apply the Aqua, Accent 5 color to the sheet tab.

12. Change the document properties as specified by your instructor. Save the workbook using the file name, Make It Right 1–1 Exotic Pets Annual Cost of Goods. Submit the revised workbook as specified by your instructor.

In the Lab

Design and/or create a workbook using the guidelines, concepts, and skills presented in thi chapter. Labs 1, 2, and 3 are listed in order of increasing difficulty.

Lab 1: Annual Revenue Analysis Worksheet

Problem: You work as a spreadsheet specialist for A Healthy Body Shop, a high-end total fitness cen franchise. Your manager has asked you to develop an annual revenue analysis worksheet similar to th one shown in Figure 1–79.

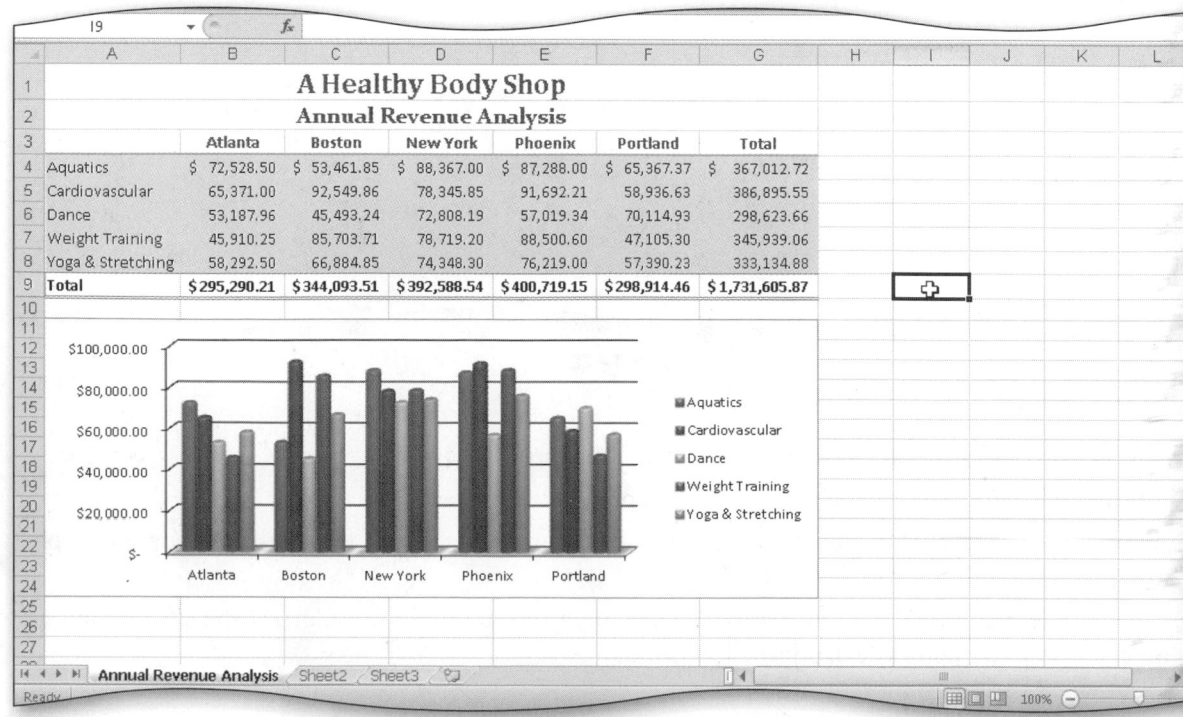

Figure 1–79

Instructions: Perform the following tasks.

1. Start Excel. Enter the worksheet title, A Healthy Body Shop, in cell A1 and the worksheet subtitle, Annual Revenue Analysis, in cell A2. Beginning in row 3, enter the franchise locations, fitness activities, and annual revenues shown in Table 1–7.

Table 1–7 A Healthy Body Shop Annual Revenues

	Atlanta	Boston	New York	Phoenix	Portland
Aquatics	72528.50	53461.85	88367.00	87288.00	65367.37
Cardiovascular	65371.00	92549.86	78345.85	91692.21	58936.63
Dance	53187.96	45493.24	72808.19	57019.34	70114.93
Weight Training	45910.25	85703.71	78719.20	88500.60	47105.30
Yoga & Stretching	58292.50	66884.85	74348.30	76219.00	57390.23

2. Create totals for each franchise location, fitness activity, and company grand total.

3. Format the worksheet title with the Title cell style. Center the title across columns A through G. Do not be concerned if the edges of the worksheet title are not displayed.

4. Format the worksheet subtitle to 14-point Constantia dark blue, bold font, and center it across columns A through G.

5. Use Cell Styles to format the range A3:G3 with the Heading 3 cell style, the range A4:G8 with the 40% - Accent 6 cell style, and the range A9:G9 with the Total cell style. Center the column headers in row 3. Apply the Accounting Number format to the range B4:G4 and the range B9:G9. Apply the Comma Style to the range B5:G8. Adjust any column widths to the widest text entry in each column.

6. Select the range A3:F8 and then insert a Clustered Cylinder chart. Apply the Style 26 chart style to the chart. Move and resize the chart so that it appears in the range A11:G24. If the labels along the horizontal axis (x-axis) do not appear as shown in Figure 1–79, then drag the right side of the chart so that it is displayed in the range A11:G24.

7. Apply the worksheet name, Annual Revenue Analysis, to the sheet tab and apply the Orange, Accent 6, Darker 25% color to the sheet tab. Change the document properties, as specified by your instructor.

8. Save the workbook using the file name Lab 1-1 A Healthy Body Shop Annual Revenue Analysis.

9. Preview and print the worksheet in landscape orientation.

10. Make the following two corrections to the sales amounts: 62,675.45 for New York Weight Training (cell D7), 67,238.56 for Portland Cardiovascular (cell F5). After you enter the corrections, the company totals in cell G9 should equal $1,723,864.05.

11. Preview and print the revised worksheet in landscape orientation. Close the workbook without saving the changes.

12. Submit the assignment as specified by your instructor.

In the Lab

Lab 2: Semiannual Sales Analysis Worksheet

Problem: As the chief accountant for Play 'em Again, a reseller of cell phones, DVDs, electronic games, MP3 players, and accessories, you have been asked by the vice president to create a worksheet to analyze the semiannual sales for the company by products across sales channels (Figure 1–80 on the following page). The sales channels and corresponding revenue by product for the year are shown in Table 1–8.

Continued >

In the Lab *continued*

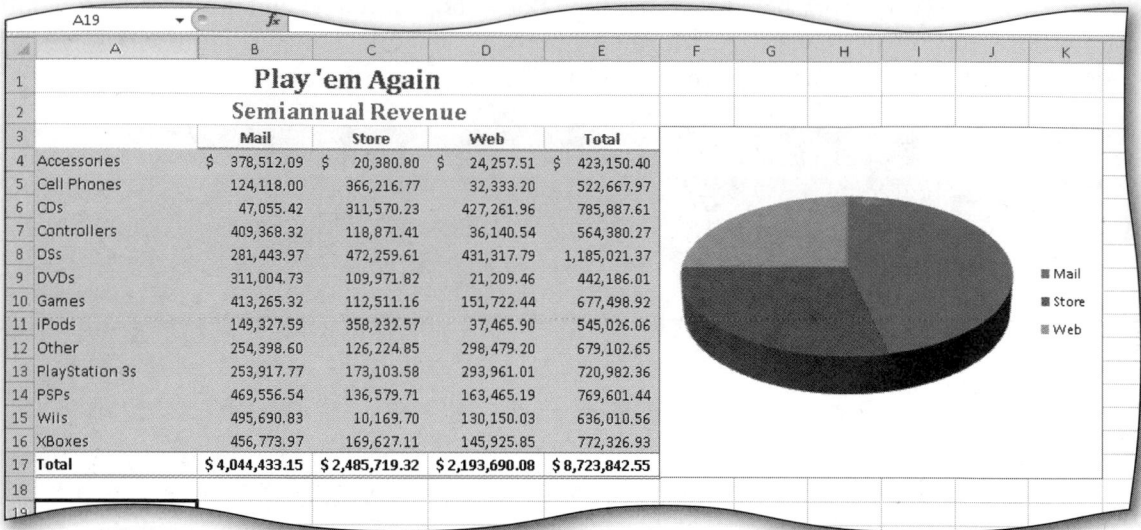

Figure 1–80

Instructions: Perform the following tasks.

1. Create the worksheet shown in Figure 1–80 using the data in Table 1–8.

2. Use the SUM function to determine total revenue for the three sales channels, the totals for each product, and the company total. Add column and row headings for the totals row and totals column, as appropriate.

Table 1–8 Play 'em Again Semiannual Revenue			
	Mail	**Store**	**Web**
Accessories	378512.09	20380.80	24257.51
Cell Phones	124118.00	366216.77	32333.20
CDs	47055.42	311570.23	427261.96
Controllers	409368.32	118871.41	36140.54
DSs	281443.97	472259.61	431317.79
DVDs	311004.73	109971.82	21209.46
Games	413265.32	112511.16	151722.44
iPods	149327.59	358232.57	37465.90
Other	254398.60	126224.85	298479.20
PlayStation 3s	253917.77	173103.58	293961.01
PSPs	469556.54	136579.71	163465.19
Wiis	495690.83	10169.70	130150.03
XBoxes	456773.97	169627.11	145925.85

3. Format the worksheet title with the Title cell style and center it across columns A through E. Use the Font group on the Ribbon to format the worksheet subtitle to 16-point Cambria red, bold fon Center the title across columns A through E.

4. Format the range B3:E3 with the Heading 3 cell style and center the text in the cells. Format the range A4:E16 with the 20% - Accent 4 cell style, and the range B17:E17 with the Total cell style. Format cells B4:E4 and B17:E17 with the Accounting Number Format and cells B5:E16 with the Comma Style numeric format.

Create a pie chart that shows the revenue contributions of each sales channel. Chart the sales channel names (B3:D3) and corresponding totals (B17:D17). That is, select the range B3:D3, and then while holding down the CTRL key, select the range B17:D17. Insert the Pie in 3-D chart, as shown in Figure 1–80, by using the Pie button (Insert tab | Charts group). Use the chart location F3: K17.

Apply the worksheet name, Semiannual Revenue, to the sheet tab and apply the Purple, Accent 4, Lighter 80% color to the sheet tab. Change the document properties, as specified by your instructor.

Save the workbook using the file name, Lab 1-2 Play 'em Again Semiannual Revenue. Print the worksheet in landscape orientation.

Two corrections to the figures were sent in from the accounting department. The correct revenue is $118,124.45 for Cell Phones sold through the mail (cell B5) and $43,573.67 for iPods sold over the Web (cell D11). After you enter the two corrections, the company total in cell E17 should equal $8,723,956.77. Print the revised worksheet in landscape orientation.

Use the Undo button to change the worksheet back to the original numbers in Table 1–8. Use the Redo button to change the worksheet back to the revised state.

Close Excel without saving the latest changes. Start Excel and open the workbook saved in Step 7. Double-click cell C14 and use in-cell editing to change the Store PSPs revenue to $128,857.32. Write the company total in cell E17 at the top of the first printout. Click the Undo button.

Click cell A1 and then click the Merge & Center button on the Home tab on the Ribbon to split cell A1 into cells A1, B1, C1, D1, and E1. To merge the cells into one again, select the range A1:E1 and then click the Merge & Center button.

Close the workbook without saving the changes. Submit the assignment as specified by your instructor.

the Lab

3: Projected College Cash Flow Analysis Worksheet

oblem: Attending college is an expensive proposition and your resources are limited. To plan for ur four-year college career, you have decided to organize your anticipated resources and expenses a worksheet. The data required to prepare your worksheet is shown in Table 1–9.

ble 1–9 College Cost and Resources

sources	Freshman	Sophomore	Junior	Senior
9 Plans	2700.00	2889.00	3091.23	3307.62
ancial Aid	5250.00	5617.50	6010.73	6431.48
ɔ	3100.00	3317.00	3549.19	3797.63
ents	3700.00	3959.00	4236.13	4532.66
vings	4250.00	4547.50	4865.83	5206.43
her	1100.00	1177.00	1259.39	1347.55
penses	Freshman	Sophomore	Junior	Senior
tivities Fee	500.00	535.00	572.45	612.52
oks	650.00	695.50	744.19	796.28
othes	750.00	802.50	858.68	918.78
tertainment	1650.00	1765.50	1889.09	2021.32
om & Board	7200.00	7704.00	8243.28	8820.31
ition	8250.00	8827.50	9445.43	10106.60
scellaneous	1100.00	1177.00	1259.39	1347.55

Continued >

In the Lab *continued*

Instructions Part 1: Using the numbers in Table 1–9, create the worksheet shown in columns A through F in Figure 1–81. Format the worksheet title as Calibri 24-point bold purple. Merge and center the worksheet title in cell A1 across columns A through F. Format the worksheet subtitles in cells A2 and A11 as Calibri 16-point bold red. Format the ranges A3:F3 and A12:F12 with the Heading 2 cell style and center the text in the cells. Format the ranges A4:F9 and A13:F19 with the 20% - Accent 2 cell style, and the ranges A10:F10 and A20:F20 with the Total cell style.

Change the name of the sheet tab and apply the Purple color from the Standard Colors area to the sheet tab. Update the document properties, including the addition of at least one keyword to the properties, and save the workbook using the file name, Lab 1-3 Part 1 College Resources and Expenses. Print the worksheet. Submit the assignment as specified by your instructor.

Figure 1–81

After reviewing the numbers, you realize you need to increase manually each of the Sophomore-year expenses in column C by $400, except for the Activities Fee. Change the Sophomore-year expenses to reflect this change. Manually change the Parents resources for the Sophomore year by the amount required to cover the increase in costs. The totals in cells F10 and F20 should equal $91,642.87. Print the worksheet. Close the workbook without saving changes.

Instructions Part 2: Open the workbook Lab 1-3 Part 1 College Resources and Expenses and then save the workbook using the file name, Lab 1-3 Part 2 College Resources and Expenses. Insert an Exploded pie in 3-D chart in the range G3:K10 to show the contribution of each category of resources for the Sophomore year. Chart the ranges A4:A9 and C4:C9 and apply the Style 26 chart style to the chart. Add the Pie chart title as shown in cell G2 in Figure 1–81. Insert an Exploded pie in 3-D chart in the range G12:K20 to show the contribution of each category of expenses for the Sophomore year. Chart the ranges A13:A19 and C13:C19 and apply the Style 26 chart style to the chart. Add the Pie chart title shown in cell G11 in Figure 1–81. Save the workbook. Print the worksheet in landscape orientation. Submit the assignment as specified by your instructor.

Instructions Part 3: Open the workbook Lab 1-3 Part 2 College Resources and Expenses and then save the workbook using the file name, Lab 1-3 Part 3 College Resources and Expenses. A close inspection of Table 1–9 shows that both cost and financial support figures increase 7% each year. Use Excel Help to learn how to enter the data for the last three years using a formula and the Copy and Paste buttons (Home tab | Clipboard group). For example, the formula to enter in cell C4 is =B4*1.07. Enter formulas to replace all the numbers in the range C4:E9 and C13:E19. If necessary, reformat the tables, as described in Part 1. The worksheet should appear as shown in Figure 1–81, except that some of the totals will be off by approximately 0.01 due to rounding errors. Save the workbook. Submit the assignment as specified by your instructor. Close the workbook without saving changes.

Cases and Places

Apply your creative thinking and problem solving skills to design and implement a solution.

1: Analyzing Quarterly Expenses

Academic

To estimate the funds needed by your school's Travel Club to make it through the upcoming quarter, you decide to create a report for the club itemizing the expected quarterly expenses. The anticipated expenses are listed in Table 1–10. Use the concepts and techniques presented in this chapter to create the worksheet and an embedded Clustered Cylinder chart. Be sure to use an appropriate chart style that compares the quarterly cost of each expense. Total each expense item and each quarter. Include a grand total for all of the expenses. Use the AutoCalculate area to determine the average amount spent per quarter on each expense. Manually insert the averages with appropriate titles in an appropriate area on the worksheet.

Table 1–10 Travel Club Quarterly Expenses

	1st Quarter	2nd Quarter	3rd Quarter	4th Quarter
Copies and Supplies	75	50	80	150
Meeting Room Rent	400	425	400	425
Miscellaneous	150	100	175	70
Refreshments	130	155	150	225
Speaker Fees	200	200	400	500
Travel	450	375	500	375

2: Create an Exploded Pie in 3-D Chart to Summarize Property Values

Personal

Your wealthy Aunt Nicole owns several properties of varying value. She would like to see the values of the properties in a worksheet and chart that helps her to better understand her investments. She has asked you to develop a worksheet totaling the values of the properties and also to include other relevant statistics. The property values are: Property 1, $56,671.99; Property 2, $82,276.58; Property 3, $60,135.45; Property 4, $107,373.39; and Property 5, $87,512.82. Create an Exploded pie in 3-D chart to illustrate the relative property values. Use the AutoCalculate area to find the average, maximum, and minimum property values and manually enter them and their corresponding identifiers in an appropriate area of the worksheet. Use the Sum button to total the property values.

Continued >

Cases and Places *continued*

3: Analyzing Historical Yearly Sales

Business

You are working part-time for Noble's Mobile Services. Your manager has asked you to prepare a worksheet to help her analyze historical yearly sales by type of product (Table 1–11). Use the concepts and techniques presented in this chapter to create the worksheet and an embedded 3-D Clustered Column chart that includes proper numerical formatting, totaling, and formatting of the worksheet.

Table 1–11 Noble's Mobile Services Historical Yearly Sales				
	2008	2009	2010	2011
Camera Phones	92598	10487	136791	176785
Headsets	9035	8909	4886	6512
Music Phones	57942	44923	54590	67696
Other Accessories	27604	38793	24483	33095
Satellite Radios	17161	19293	30763	44367
Standard Mobile Phones	8549	9264	7600	6048
Wireless PDAs	57963	68059	103025	87367

2 Formulas, Functions, and Formatting

Objectives

You will have mastered the material in this chapter when you can:

- Enter formulas using the keyboard
- Enter formulas using Point mode
- Apply the AVERAGE, MAX, and MIN functions
- Verify a formula using Range Finder
- Apply a theme to a workbook
- Apply a date format to a cell or range

- Add conditional formatting to cells
- Change column width and row height
- Check the spelling in a worksheet
- Set margins, headers, and footers in Page Layout view
- Preview and print versions of a worksheet

2 | Formulas, Functions, and Formatting

Introduction

In Chapter 1, you learned how to enter data, sum values, format a worksheet to make it easier to read, and draw a chart. This chapter continues to highlight these topics and presents some new ones.

The new topics covered in this chapter include using formulas and functions to create a worksheet. A **function** is a prewritten formula that is built into Excel. Other new topics include option buttons, verifying formulas, applying a theme to a worksheet, adding borders, formatting numbers and text, using conditional formatting, changing the widths of columns and heights of rows, spell checking, using alternative types of worksheet displays and printouts, and adding page headers and footers to a worksheet. One alternative worksheet display and printout shows the formulas in the worksheet instead of the values. When you display the formulas in the worksheet, you see exactly what text, data, formulas, and functions you have entered into it.

Project — Worksheet with Formulas and Functions

The project in this chapter follows proper design guidelines and uses Excel to create the worksheet shown in Figure 2–1. The Mobile Masses Store opened its doors when consumer demand for mobile devices, such as mobile phones and PDAs, had just begun. The store's owners pay each employee on a biweekly basis. Before the owners pay the employees, they summarize the hours worked, pay rate, and tax information for each employee to ensure that the business properly compensates its employees. This summary includes information such as the employee names, hire dates, number of dependents, hours worked, hourly pay rate, net pay, and tax information. As the complexity of the task of creating the summary increases, the owners want to use Excel to create a biweekly payroll report.

Figure 2–1

Recall that the first step in creating an effective worksheet is to make sure you understand what is required. The people who will use the worksheet usually provide the requirements. The requirements document for The Mobile Masses Store Biweekly Payroll Report worksheet includes the following needs: source of data, summary of calculations, and other facts about its development (Figure 2–2 on the following page).

REQUEST FOR NEW WORKSHEET

Date Submitted:	April 16, 2012
Submitted By:	Samuel Snyder
Worksheet Title:	The Mobile Masses Store Biweekly Payroll Report
Needs:	An easy-to-read worksheet that summarizes the company's biweekly payroll (Figure 2-3). For each employee, the worksheet is to include the employee's name, hire date, dependents, hours worked, hourly pay rate, gross pay, federal tax, state tax, net pay, and total tax percent. The worksheet also should include totals and the average, highest value, and lowest value for column of numbers specified below.
Source of Data:	The data supplied by Samuel includes the employee names, hire dates, hours worked, and hourly pay rates. This data is shown in Table 2-1 on page EX 72.
Calculations:	The following calculations must be made for each of the employees: 1. Gross Pay = Hours Worked × Hourly Pay Rate 2. Federal Tax = 0.22 × (Gross Pay − Dependents * 24.32) 3. State Tax = 0.04 × Gross Pay 4. Net Pay = Gross Pay − (Federal Tax + State Tax) 5. Tax % = (Federal Tax + State Tax) / Gross Pay 6. Compute the totals for hours worked, gross pay, federal tax, state tax, and net pay. 7. Compute the total tax percent. 8. Use the AVERAGE function to determine the average for dependents, hours worked, hourly pay rate, gross pay, federal tax, state tax, and net pay. 9. Use the MAX and MIN functions to determine the highest and lowest values for dependents, hours worked, hourly pay rate, gross pay, federal tax, state tax, net pay, and total tax percent.

Approvals

Approval Status:	X	Approved
		Rejected
Approved By:	Julie Adams	
Date:	April 23, 2012	
Assigned To:	J. Quasney, Spreadsheet Specialist	

Figure 2–2

Overview

As you read this chapter, you will learn how to create the worksheet shown in Figure 2–1 by performing these general tasks:

- Enter formulas and apply functions in the worksheet
- Add conditional formatting to the worksheet
- Apply a theme to the worksheet
- Set margins, and add headers and footers to a worksheet
- Work with the worksheet in Page Layout view
- Change margins on the worksheet
- Print a section of the worksheet

Plan
Ahead

General Project Decisions
While creating an Excel worksheet, you need to make several decisions that will determine the appearance and characteristics of the finished worksheet. As you create the worksheet necessary to meet the requirements shown in Figure 2–2, you should follow these general guidelines:

1. **Plan the layout of the worksheet.** Rows typically contain items analogous to items in a list. A name could serve as an item in a list, and, therefore, each name could be placed in a row. As a list grows, such as a list of employees, the number of rows in the worksheet will increase. Information about each item in the list and associated calculations should appear in columns.

2. **Determine the necessary formulas and functions needed.** Calculations result from known values. Formulas for such calculations should be known in advance of creating a worksheet. Values such as the average, highest, and lowest values can be calculated using Excel functions as opposed to relying on complex formulas.

3. **Identify how to format various elements of the worksheet.** The appearance of the worksheet affects its ability to express information clearly. Numeric data should be formatted in generally accepted formats, such as using commas as thousands separators and parentheses for negative values.

4. **Establish rules for conditional formatting.** Conditional formatting allows you to format a cell based on the contents of the cell. Decide under which circumstances you would like a cell to stand out from related cells and determine in what way the cell will stand out.

5. **Specify how the hard copy of a worksheet should appear.** When it is possible that a person will want to create a hard copy of a worksheet, care should be taken in the development of the worksheet to ensure that the contents can be presented in a readable manner. Excel prints worksheets in landscape or portrait orientation, and margins can be adjusted to fit more or less data on each page. Headers and footers add an additional level of customization to the printed page.

When necessary, more specific details concerning the above guidelines are presented at appropriate points in the chapter. The chapter also will identify the actions performed and decisions made regarding these guidelines during the creation of the worksheet shown in Figure 2–1 on page EX 67.

In addition, using a sketch of the worksheet can help you visualize its design. The sketch for The Mobile Masses Store Biweekly Payroll Report worksheet includes a title, a subtitle, column and row headings, and the location of data values (Figure 2–3 on the following page). It also uses specific characters to define the desired formatting for the worksheet, as follows:

1. The row of Xs below the leftmost column defines the cell entries as text, such as employee names.
2. The rows of Zs and 9s with slashes, dollar signs, decimal points, commas, and percent signs in the remaining columns define the cell entries as numbers. The Zs indicate that the selected format should instruct Excel to suppress leading 0s. The 9s indicate that the selected format should instruct Excel to display any digits, including 0s.
3. The decimal point means that a decimal point should appear in the cell entry and indicates the number of decimal places to use.
4. The slashes in the second column identify the cell entry as a date.
5. The dollar signs that are not adjacent to the Zs in the first row below the column headings and in the total row signify a fixed dollar sign. The dollar signs that are adjacent to the Zs below the total row signify a floating dollar sign, or one that appears next to the first significant digit.

BTW

Aesthetics versus Function
The function, or purpose, of a worksheet is to provide a user with direct ways to accomplish tasks. In designing a worksheet, functional considerations should come before visual aesthetics. Avoid the temptation to use flashy or confusing visual elements within the worksheet. One exception to this guideline occurs when you may need to draw the user's attention to an area of a worksheet that will help the user more easily complete a task.

The Mobile Masses Store
Biweekly Payroll Report

Employee	Hire Date	Dependents	Hours Worked	Hourly Pay Rate	Gross Pay	Federal Tax	State Tax	Net Pay	Tax %
xxxxxxxxx	99/99/99	99	99.99	$ ZZ9.99	$ ZZ,ZZ9.99	$ ZZ9.99	$ ZZ,ZZ9.99	$ ZZ,ZZ9.99	Z9.99%
Totals			999.99		$ ZZZ,ZZ9.99	$ ZZZ,ZZ9.99	$ ZZZ,ZZ9.99	$ ZZZ,ZZ9.99	Z9.99%
Average		99	99.99	$ZZ9.99	$ZZZ,ZZ9.99	$ZZZ,ZZ9.99	$ZZZ,ZZ9.99	$ZZZ,ZZ9.99	Z9.99%
Highest		99							
Lowest		99							

Xs indicate text data

9s indicate numeric data

Zs indicate numeric data with 0s suppressed

$ adjacent to Z indicates floating dollar sign

$ not adjacent to Z indicates a fixed dollar sign

Figure 2–3

6. The commas indicate that the selected format should instruct Excel to display a comma separator only if the number has enough digits to the left of the decimal point.

7. The percent sign (%) in the far-right column indicates a percent sign should appear after the number.

With a good comprehension of the requirements document, an understanding of the necessary decisions, and a sketch of the worksheet, the next step is to use Excel to create the worksheet.

To Start Excel

If you are using a computer to step through the project in this chapter and you wa your screens to match the figures in this book, you should change your screen's resolutio to 1024 × 768. For information about how to change a computer's resolution, refer to th Office 2010 and Windows 7 chapter at the beginning of this book.

The following steps, which assume Windows 7 is running, start Excel based on a typical installation. You may need to ask your instructor how to start Excel for your computer. For a detailed example of the procedure summarized below, refer to the Office 2010 and Windows 7 chapter.

1 Click the Start button on the Windows 7 taskbar to display the Start menu.

2 Type `Microsoft Excel` as the search text in the 'Search programs and files' text box, and watch the search results appear on the Start menu.

3 Click Microsoft Excel 2010 in the search results on the Start menu to start Excel and displa a new blank workbook in the Excel window.

4 If the Excel window is not maximized, click the Maximize button next to the Close buttor on its title bar to maximize the window.

Entering the Titles and Numbers into the Worksheet

The first step in creating the worksheet is to enter the titles and numbers into the worksheet. The following sets of steps enter the worksheet title and subtitle and then the biweekly payroll report data shown in Table 2–1.

To Enter the Worksheet Title and Subtitle

The following steps enter the worksheet title and subtitle into cells A1 and A2.

1 If necessary, select cell A1. Type **The Mobile Masses Store** in the selected cell and then press the DOWN ARROW key to enter the worksheet title.

2 Type **Biweekly Payroll Report** in cell A2 and then press the DOWN ARROW key to enter the worksheet subtitle (Figure 2–4 on page 73).

The employee names and the row titles Totals, Average, Highest, and Lowest in the leftmost column begin in cell A4 and continue down to cell A16. The employee data is entered into rows 4 through 12 of the worksheet. The remainder of this section explains the steps required to enter the column titles, payroll data, and row titles, as shown in Figure 2–4, and then save the workbook.

To Enter the Column Titles

The column titles in row 3 begin in cell A3 and extend through cell J3. Some of the column titles in Figure 2–3 include multiple lines of text, such as Hours Worked in cell D3. To start a new line in a cell, press ALT+ENTER after each line, except for the last line, which is completed by clicking the Enter box, pressing the ENTER key, or pressing one of the arrow keys. When you see ALT+ENTER in a step, press the ENTER key while holding down the ALT key and then release both keys. The following steps enter the column titles.

1 With cell A3 selected, type **Employee** and then press the RIGHT ARROW key to enter the column heading.

2 Type **Hire Date** in cell B3 and then press the RIGHT ARROW key to enter the column heading.

3 Type **Dependents** and then press the RIGHT ARROW key to enter the column heading.

4 In cell D3, type **Hours** and then press ALT+ENTER to enter the first line of the column heading. Type **Worked** and then press the RIGHT ARROW key to enter the column heading.

5 Type **Hourly** and then press ALT+ENTER to begin a new line in the cell. Type **Pay Rate** and then press the RIGHT ARROW key to enter the column heading.

6 Type **Gross Pay** in cell F3 and then press the RIGHT ARROW key to enter the column heading.

7 Type **Federal Tax** in cell G3 and then press the RIGHT ARROW key to enter the column heading.

8 Type **State Tax** in cell H3 and then press the RIGHT ARROW key to enter the column heading.

9 Type **Net Pay** in cell I3 and then press the RIGHT ARROW key to enter the column heading.

10 Type **Tax %** in cell J3 to enter the column heading.

For an introduction to Office 2010 and instruction about how to perform basic tasks in Office 2010 programs, read the Office 2010 and Windows 7 chapter at the beginning of this book, where you can learn how to start a program, use the Ribbon, save a file, open a file, quit a program, use Help, and much more.

BTW

The Ribbon and Screen Resolution
Excel may change how the groups and buttons within the groups appear on the Ribbon, depending on the computer's screen resolution. Thus, your Ribbon may look different from the ones in this book if you are using a screen resolution other than 1024 × 768.

BTW

BTWs
For a complete list of the BTWs found in the margins of this book, visit the Excel 2010 BTW Web page (scsite.com/ex2010/btw).

To Enter the Biweekly Payroll Data

The biweekly payroll data in Table 2–1 includes a hire date for each employee. Excel considers a date to be a number and, therefore, it displays the date right-aligned in the cell. The following steps enter the data for each employee: name, hire date, dependents, hours worked, and hourly pay rate.

1 Select cell A4, type **Charvat, Emily**, and then press the RIGHT ARROW key to enter the employee name.

2 Type **3/3/09** in cell B4 and then press the RIGHT ARROW key to enter a date in the selected cell.

3 Type **1** in cell C4 and then press the RIGHT ARROW key to enter a number in the selected cell.

4 Type **65.25** in cell D4 and then press the RIGHT ARROW key to enter a number in the selected cell.

5 Type **20.50** in cell E4 and then click cell A5 to enter a number in the selected cell.

6 Enter the payroll data in Table 2–1 for the eight remaining employees in rows 5 through 12 (Figure 2–4).

Q&A

In step 2, why did the date that was entered change from 3/3/09 to 3/3/2009?

When Excel recognizes that you entered a date in mm/dd/yy format, it automatically formats the date as mm/dd/yyyy for you. Most professionals prefer to view dates in mm/dd/yyyy format as opposed to mm/dd/yy format because the latter can cause confusion regarding the intended year. For example, a date displayed as 3/3/50 could imply a date of 3/3/1950 or 3/3/2050. The use of a four-digit year eliminates this confusion.

Table 2–1 The Mobile Masses Store Biweekly Payroll Report Data				
Employee	**Hire Date**	**Dependents**	**Hours Worked**	**Hourly Pay Rate**
Charvat, Emily	3/3/09	1	65.25	20.50
Chen, Bin	6/14/10	2	80.00	25.85
Felski, Noah	10/11/08	0	64.50	12.60
Kersey, Jane	3/4/11	1	68.50	21.45
Merna, Thomas	1/15/10	3	78.25	22.60
Pollitt, Sherry	11/15/08	2	49.25	18.25
Prasad, Rao	2/15/08	0	33.50	9.35
Washington, Yolanda	5/11/06	2	79.25	23.75
Zica, James	4/14/11	1	80.00	19.65

To Enter the Row Titles

The following steps add row titles for the rows that will contain the totals, average, highest, and lowest amounts.

1 Select cell A13. Type **Totals** and then press the DOWN ARROW key to enter a row header.

2 Type **Average** in cell A14 and then press the DOWN ARROW key to enter a row header.

3 Type **Highest** in cell A15 and then press the DOWN ARROW key to enter a row header.

4 Type **Lowest** in cell A16 and then press the ENTER key to enter a row header. Select cell F4 to prepare to enter a formula in the cell (Figure 2–4).

Figure 2–4

To Change Document Properties

As discussed in Chapter 1, the first time you save a workbook, you should change the document properties. The following steps change the document properties.

1 Click File on the Ribbon to open the Backstage view. If necessary, click the Info tab in the Backstage view to display the Info gallery.

2 Click the Properties button in the right pane of the Info gallery to display the Properties menu.

3 Click Show Document Panel on the Properties menu to close the Backstage view and display the Document Information Panel in the Excel workbook window.

4 Click the Author text box, if necessary, and then type your name as the Author property. If a name already is displayed in the Author text box, delete it before typing your name.

5 Click the Subject text box, if necessary delete any existing text, and then type your course and section as the Subject property.

6 If an AutoComplete dialog box appears, click its Yes button.

7 Click the Keywords text box, if necessary delete any existing text, and then type **Biweekly Payroll Report** as the Keywords property.

8 If an AutoComplete dialog box appears, click its Yes button.

9 Click the Close the Document Information Panel button so that the Document Information Panel no longer is displayed.

To Change the Sheet Name and Save the Workbook

The following steps change the sheet name to Biweekly Payroll Report, change the sheet tab color, and save the workbook on a USB flash drive in the Excel folder (for your assignments) using the file name, The Mobile Masses Biweekly Payroll Report.

1 Double-click the Sheet1 tab and then enter `Biweekly Payroll Report` as the sheet name and then press the ENTER key.

2 Right-click the tab to display the shortcut menu and then click Tab Color on the shortcut menu to display the Color gallery. Click Orange, Accent 1, Darker 25% (column 5, row 5) the Theme Colors area to apply a new color to the sheet tab.

3 With a USB flash drive connected to one of the computer's USB ports, click the Save button on the Quick Access Toolbar to display the Save As dialog box.

4 Type `The Mobile Masses Biweekly Payroll Report` in the File name text box to change the file name. Do not press the ENTER key after typing the file name because you do not want to close the dialog box at this time.

5 Navigate to the desired save location (in this case, the Excel folder in the CIS 101 folder [or your class folder] on the USB flash drive).

6 Click the Save button (Save As dialog box) to save the document in the selected folder or the selected drive with the entered file name.

BTW

Entering Numbers in a Range
An efficient way to enter data into a range of cells is to select a range and then enter the first number in the upper-left cell of the range. Excel responds by accepting the value and moving the active cell selection down one cell. When you enter the last value in the first column, Excel moves the active cell selection to the top of the next column.

Entering Formulas

One of the reasons Excel is such a valuable tool is that you can assign a **formula** to a cell and Excel will calculate the result. Consider, for example, what would happen if you had to multiply 65.25 by 20.5 and then manually enter the product for Gross Pay, 1,337.625, in cell F4. Every time the values in cells D4 or E4 changed, you would have to recalculate the product and enter the new value in cell F4. By contrast, if you enter a formula in cell F4 to multiply the values in cells D4 and E4, Excel recalculates the product whenever new values are entered into those cells and displays the result in cell F4.

Plan Ahead

Determine the formulas and functions needed.
As you have learned, formulas and functions simplify the creation and maintenance of worksheets because Excel performs calculations for you. When formulas and functions are used together properly, the amount of data that a user manually must enter in a worksheet greatly can be diminished:

- **Utilize proper algebraic notation.** Most Excel formulas are the result of algebraic calculations. A solid understanding of algebraic operators and the order of operations is important to writing sound formulas.

- **Utilize the fill handle and copy and paste operations to copy formulas.** The fill handle and the Excel copy and paste functionality help to minimize errors caused by retyping formulas. When possible, if a similar formula will be used repeatedly in a worksheet, avoid retyping the formula and instead use the fill handle.

- **Be careful about using invalid and circular cell references.** An invalid reference occurs when Excel does not understand a cell reference used in a formula, resulting in Excel displaying a #REF! error message in the cell.

(Continued)

(Continued)

A formula in a cell that contains a reference back to itself is called a **circular reference**. Excel often warns you when you create a circular reference. In almost all cases, circular references are the result of an incorrect formula. A circular reference can be direct or indirect. For example, placing the formula =A1 in cell A1 results in a direct circular reference. An indirect circular reference occurs when a formula in a cell refers to another cell or cells that include a formula that refers back to the original cell.

- **Employ the Excel built-in functions whenever possible.** Excel includes prewritten formulas called **functions** to help you compute a range of values and statistics. A function takes a value or values, performs an operation, and returns a result to the cell. The values that you use with a function are called **arguments**. All functions begin with an equal sign and include the arguments in parentheses after the function name. For example, in the function =AVERAGE(C4:C12), the function name is AVERAGE, and the argument is the range C4:C12. Become familiar with the extensive number of built-in functions. When you have the choice, always use built-in functions instead of writing and typing a formula version of your mathematical expression. Such a practice reduces the possibility of errors and simplifies the formula used in a cell, resulting in improved readability.

Plan Ahead

BTW

Automatic Recalculation
Every time you enter a value into a cell in the worksheet, Excel automatically recalculates all formulas. You can change to manual recalculation by clicking the Calculation Options button (Formulas tab | Calculation group) and then clicking Manual. In manual calculation mode, pressing the F9 key instructs Excel to recalculate all formulas.

To Enter a Formula Using the Keyboard

The formulas needed in the worksheet are noted in the requirements document as follows:

1. Gross Pay (column F) = Hours Worked × Hourly Pay Rate
2. Federal Tax (column G) = 0.22 × (Gross Pay − Dependents × 24.32)
3. State Tax (column H) = 0.04 × Gross Pay
4. Net Pay (column I) = Gross Pay − (Federal Tax + State Tax)
5. Tax% (column J) = (Federal Tax + State Tax) / Gross Pay

The gross pay for each employee, which appears in column F, is equal to hours worked in column D times hourly pay rate in column E. Thus, the gross pay for Emily Charvat in cell F4 is obtained by multiplying 65.25 (cell D4) by 20.50 (cell E4) or =D4*E4. The following steps enter the initial gross pay formula in cell F4 using the keyboard.

1

- With cell F4 selected, type **=d4*e4** in the cell to display the formula in the formula bar and in the current cell and to display colored borders around the cells referenced in the formula (Figure 2–5).

What occurs on the worksheet as I enter the formula?

The **equal sign** (=) preceding d4*e4 alerts Excel that you are entering a formula or function and not text. Because the most common error when entering a formula is to reference the wrong cell in a formula mistakenly, Excel colors the borders of the cells referenced in the formula. The coloring helps in the reviewing process to ensure the cell references are correct. The **asterisk** (*) following d4 is the arithmetic operator that directs Excel to perform the multiplication operation.

Figure 2–5

2

• Press the RIGHT ARROW key to complete the arithmetic operation indicated by the formula, to display the result in the worksheet, and to select the cell to the right (Figure 2–6). The number of decimal places shown in cell F4 may be different, but these values will be adjusted later in this chapter.

Figure 2–6

Arithmetic Operations

Table 2–2 describes multiplication and other valid Excel arithmetic operators.

Table 2–2 Summary of Arithmetic Operators			
Arithmetic Operator	**Meaning**	**Example of Usage**	**Meaning**
–	Negation	–78	Negative 78
%	Percentage	=23%	Multiplies 23 by 0.01
^	Exponentiation	=3 ^ 4	Raises 3 to the fourth power
*	Multiplication	=61.5 * C5	Multiplies the contents of cell C5 by 61.5
/	Division	=H3 / H11	Divides the contents of cell H3 by the contents of cell H11
+	Addition	=11 + 9	Adds 11 and 9
–	Subtraction	=22 – F15	Subtracts the contents of cell F15 from 22

Order of Operations

When more than one arithmetic operator is involved in a formula, Excel follows the same basic order of operations that you use in algebra. Moving from left to right in a formula, the **order of operations** is as follows: first negation (−), then all percentages (%), then all exponentiations (^), then all multiplications (*) and divisions (/), and finally, all additions (+) and subtractions (−).

As in algebra, you can use parentheses to override the order of operations. For example, if Excel follows the order of operations, 8 * 3 + 2 equals 26. If you use parentheses, however, to change the formula to 8 * (3 + 2), the result is 40, because the parentheses instruct Excel to add 3 and 2 before multiplying by 8. Table 2–3 illustrates several examples of valid Excel formulas and explains the order of operations.

Table 2–3 Examples of Excel Formulas	
Formula	**Meaning**
=G15	Assigns the value in cell G15 to the active cell.
=2^4 + 7	Assigns the sum of 16 + 7 (or 23) to the active cell.
=100 + D2 or =D2 +100 or =(100 + D2)	Assigns 100 plus the contents of cell D2 to the active cell.
=25% * 40	Assigns the product of 0.25 times 40 (or 10) to the active cell.
− (K15 * X45)	Assigns the negative value of the product of the values contained in cells K15 and X45 to the active cell. You do not need to type an equal sign before an expression that begins with minus signs, which indicates a negation.
=(U8 − B8) * 6	Assigns the product of the difference between the values contained in cells U8 and B8 times 6 to the active cell.
=J7 / A5 + G9 * M6 − Z2 ^ L7	Completes the following operations, from left to right: exponentiation (Z2 ^ L7), then division (J7 / A5), then multiplication (G9 * M6), then addition (J7 / A5) + (G9 * M6), and finally subtraction (J7 / A5 + G9 * M6) − (Z2 ^ L7). If cells A5 = 6, G9 = 2, J7 = 6, L7 = 4, M6 = 5, and Z2 = 2, then Excel assigns the active cell the value −5; that is, 6 / 6 + 2 * 5 − 2 ^ 4 = −5.

To Enter Formulas Using Point Mode

The sketch of the worksheet in Figure 2–3 on page EX 70 calls for the federal tax, state tax, net pay, and tax % for each employee to appear in columns G, H, I, and J, respectively. All four of these values are calculated using formulas in row 4:

Federal Tax (cell G4) = 0.22 × (Gross Pay − Dependents × 24.32) or =0.22*(F4−C4*24.32)
State Tax (cell H4) = 0.04 × Gross Pay or = 0.04* F4
Net Pay (cell I4) = Gross Pay − (Federal Tax + State Tax) or =F4-(G4+H4)
Tax % (cell J4) = (Federal Tax + State Tax) / Gross Pay or =(G4+H4)/F4

An alternative to entering the formulas in cells G4, H4, I4, and J4 using the keyboard is to enter the formulas using the mouse and Point mode. **Point mode** allows you to select cells for use in a formula by using the mouse. The steps on the following pages enter formulas using Point mode.

1

- With cell G4 selected type =0.22*(to begin the formula and then click cell F4 to add a cell reference in the formula (Figure 2–7).

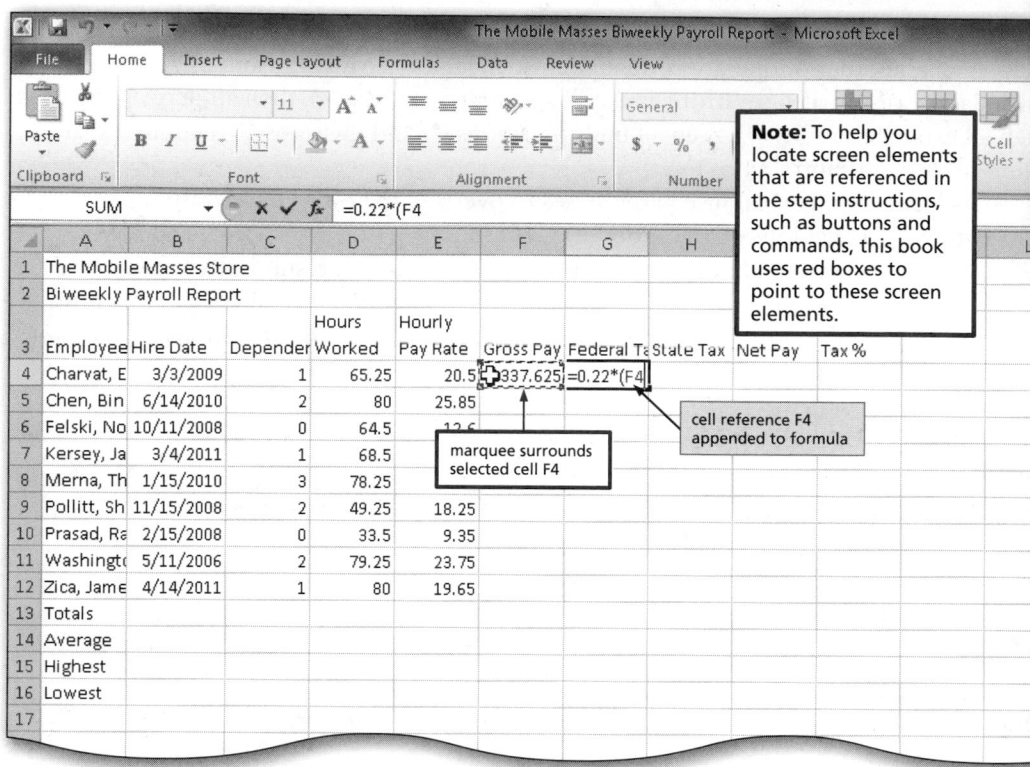

Figure 2–7

2

- Type – (minus sign) and then click cell C4 to add a subtraction operator and a reference to another cell to the formula.

- Type *24.32) to complete the formula (Figure 2–8).

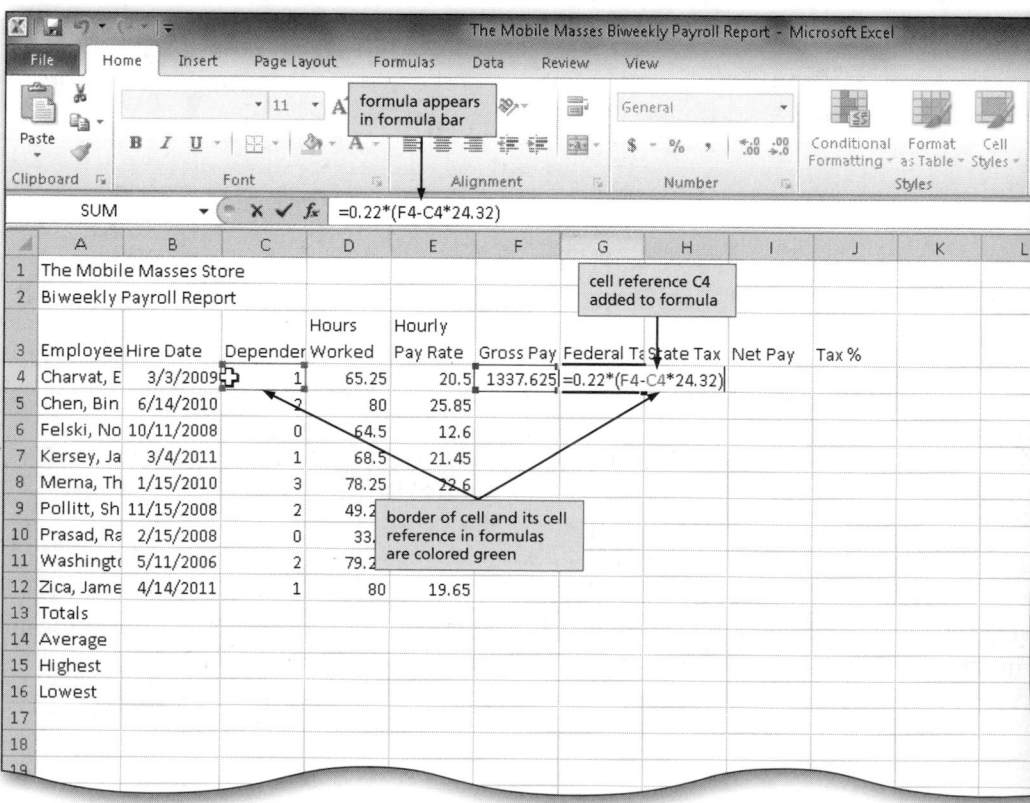

Figure 2–8

3

- Click the Enter box in the formula bar and then select cell H4 to prepare to enter the next formula.

- Type **=0.04*** and then click cell F4 to add a cell reference to the formula (Figure 2–9).

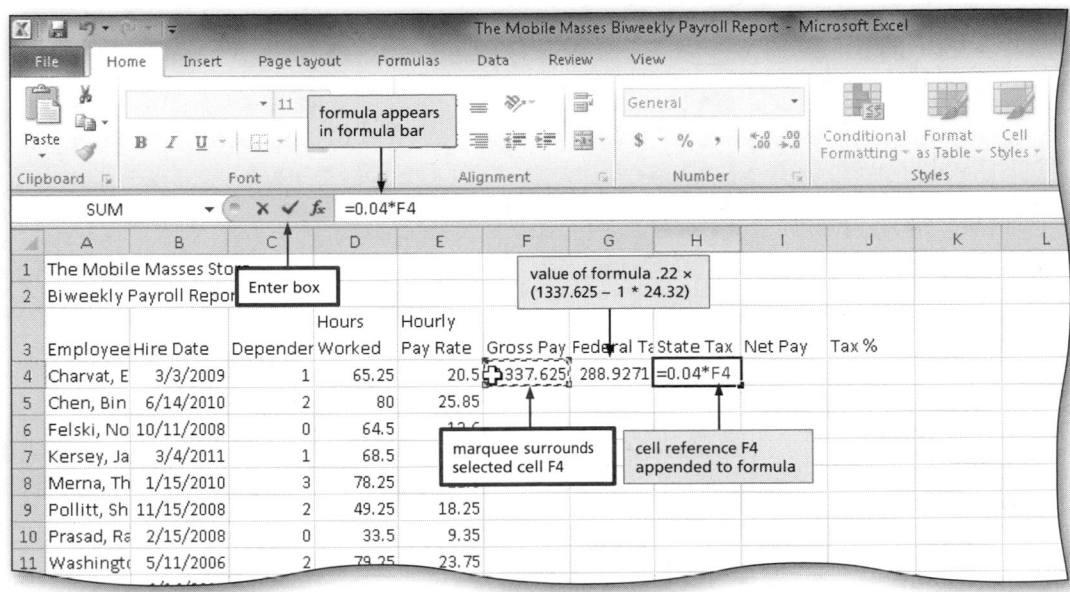

Figure 2–9

Why should I use Point mode to enter formulas?

Using Point mode to enter formulas often is faster and more accurate than using the keyboard to type the entire formula when the cell you want to select does not require you to scroll. In many instances, as in these steps, you may want to use both the keyboard and mouse when entering a formula in a cell. You can use the keyboard to begin the formula, for example, and then use the mouse to select a range of cells.

4

- Click the Enter box in the formula bar and then select cell I4 to prepare to enter the next formula.

- Type **=** (equal sign) and then click cell F4 to begin the formula and add a cell reference to the formula.

- Type **– (** (minus sign followed by an open parenthesis) and then click cell G4 to add a subtraction operator, open parenthesis, and cell reference to the formula.

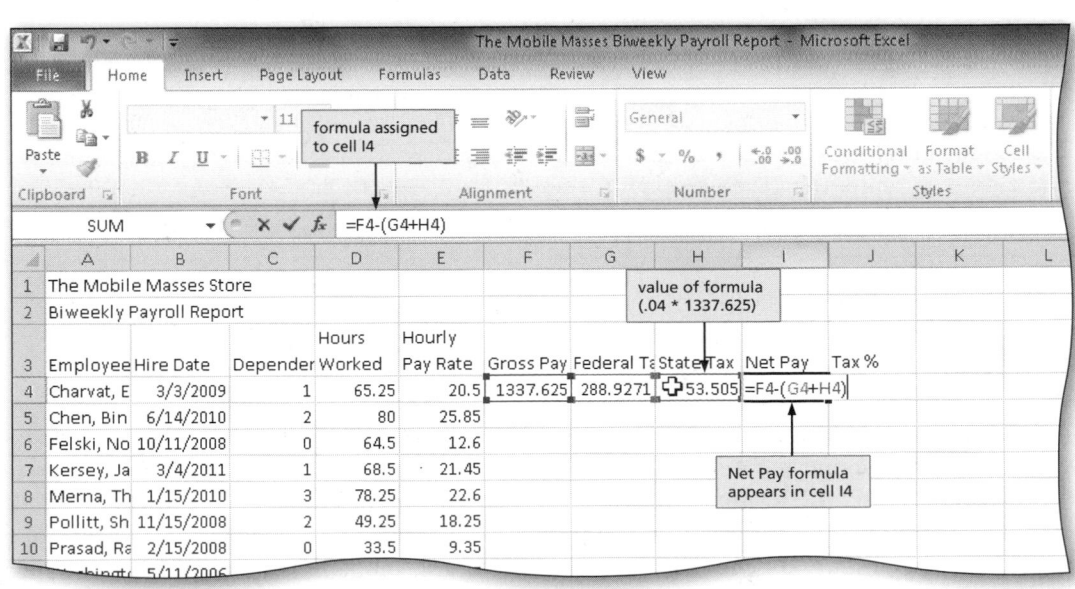

Figure 2–10

- Type **+** (plus sign) and then click cell H4 to add an addition operator and cell reference to the formula.

- Type **)** (close parenthesis) to complete the formula (Figure 2–10).

5

- Click the Enter box in the formula bar to enter the formula in cell I4.

- Select cell J4. Type = ((equal sign followed by an open parenthesis) and then click cell G4 to add a reference to the formula.

- Type + (plus sign) and then click cell H4 to add a cell reference to the formula.

- Type) / (close parenthesis followed by a forward slash), and then click cell F4 to add a cell reference to the formula.

- Click the Enter box in the formula bar to enter the formula in cell J4 (Figure 2–11).

Figure 2–11

Q&A

Why do three decimal places show in cell J4?

The actual value assigned by Excel to cell J4 from the division operation in step 5 is 0.256000075. While not all the decimal places appear in Figure 2–11, Excel maintains all of them for computational purposes. Thus, if referencing cell J4 in a formula, the value used for computational purposes is 0.256000075, not 0.256. The cell formatting is set to display six digits after the decimal point, but the formatting also suppresses trailing zeroes. If the cell formatting were set to display six digits and show trailing zeroes, then Excel would display 0.256000 in cell J4. If you change the cell formatting of column J to display nine digits after the decimal point, then Excel displays the true value 0.256000075.

To Copy Formulas Using the Fill Handle

The five formulas for Emily Charvat in cells F4, G4, H4, I4, and J4 now are complete. You could enter the same five formulas one at a time for the eight remaining employees. A much easier method of entering the formulas, however, is to select the formulas in row 4 and then use the fill handle to copy them through row 12. When performing copying operations in Excel, the source area is the cell, or range, from which data or formulas are being copied. When a range is used as a source, sometimes it is called the source range. The destination area is the cell, or range, to which data or formulas are being copied. When a range is used as a destination, sometimes it is called the destination range. Recall from Chapter 1 that the fill handle is a small rectangle in the lower-right corner of the active cell or active range. The following steps copy the formulas using the fill handle.

1

- Select the source range, F4:J4 in this case, and then point to the fill handle.

- Drag the fill handle down through cell J12 and continue to hold the mouse button to select the destination range (Figure 2–12).

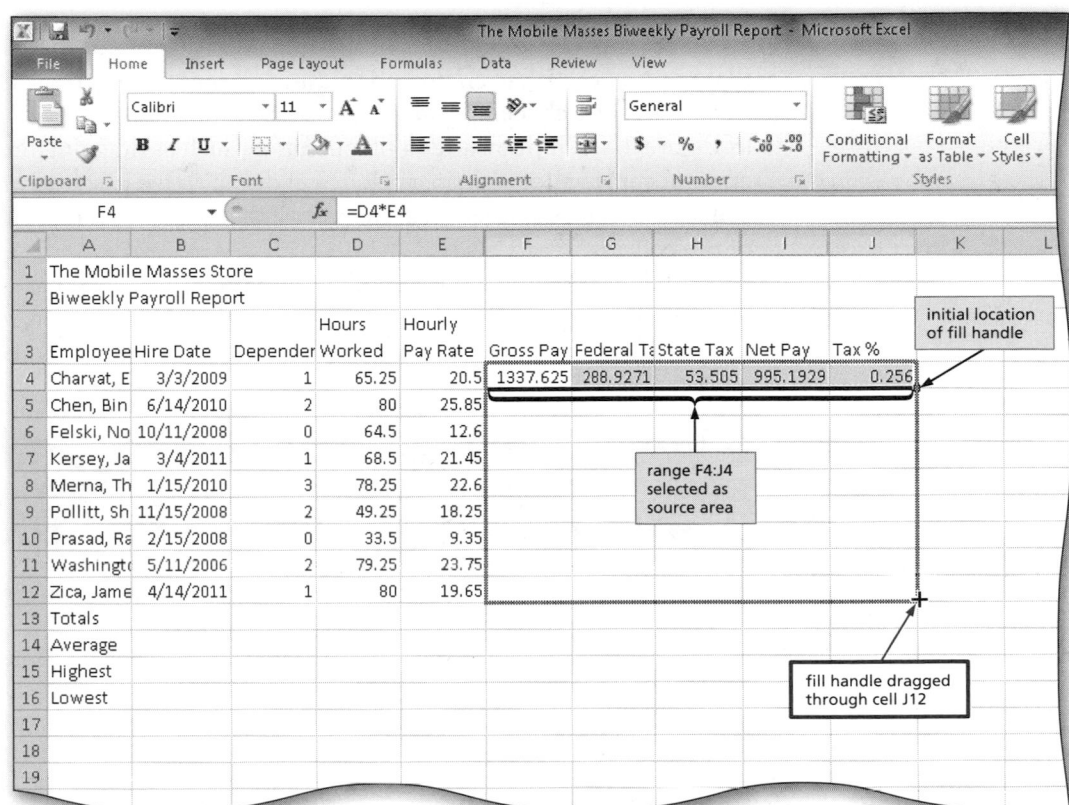

Figure 2–12

2

- Release the mouse button to copy the formulas to the destination range (Figure 2–13).

How does Excel adjust the cell references in the formulas in the destination area?

Recall that when you copy a formula, Excel adjusts the cell references so that the new formulas contain references corresponding to the new location and perform calculations using the appropriate values. Thus, if you copy downward, Excel adjusts the row portion of cell references. If you copy across, then Excel adjusts the column portion of cell references. These cell references are called **relative cell references**.

Figure 2–13

Other Ways

1. Select source area, click Copy button (Home tab | Clipboard group), select destination area, click Paste button (Home tab | Clipboard group)

2. Right-click source area, click Copy on shortcut menu, right-click destination area, click Paste icon on shortcut menu

3. Select source area and then point to border of range; while holding down CTRL, drag source area to destination area

Option Buttons

Excel displays Option buttons in a workbook while you are working on it to indicate that you can complete an operation using automatic features such as AutoCorrect, Auto Fill, error checking, and others. For example, the Auto Fill Options button shown in Figure 2–13 appears after a fill operation, such as dragging the fill handle. When an error occurs in a formula in a cell, Excel displays the Trace Error button next to the cell and identifies the cell with the error by placing a green triangle in the upper left of the cell.

Table 2–4 summarizes the Option buttons available in Excel. When one of these buttons appears on your worksheet, click the button arrow to produce the list of options for modifying the operation or to obtain additional information.

BTW

The Paste Options Button
The Paste Options button provides powerful functionality. When performing copy and paste operations, the button allows you great freedom in specifying what it is you want to paste. For example, you could choose to paste an exact copy of what you copied, including the cell contents and formatting. You also could copy just formulas, just formatting, just the cell values, a combination of these options, or a picture of what you copied.

Table 2–4 Options Buttons in Excel

Button	Name	Menu Function
	Auto Fill Options	Gives options for how to fill cells following a fill operation, such as dragging the fill handle.
	AutoCorrect Options	Undoes an automatic correction, stops future automatic corrections of this type, or causes Excel to display the AutoCorrect Options dialog box.
	Insert Options	Lists formatting options following an insertion of cells, rows, or columns.
(Ctrl) ▾	Paste Options	Specifies how moved or pasted items should appear (for example, with original formatting, without formatting, or with different formatting).
	Trace Error	Lists error-checking options following the assignment of an invalid formula to a cell.

BTW

Selecting a Range
You can select a range using the keyboard. Press the F8 key and then use the arrow keys to select the desired range. After you are finished, make sure to press the F8 key to turn off the selection process or you will continue to select ranges.

To Determine Totals Using the Sum Button

The next step is to determine the totals in row 13 for the hours worked in column D, gross pay in column F, federal tax in column G, state tax in column H, and net pay in column I. To determine the total hours worked in column D, the values in the range D4 through D12 must be summed. To do so, enter the function =sum(d4:d12) in cell D13 or select cell D13, click the Sum button (Home tab | Editing group), and then press the ENTER key. Recall that a function is a prewritten formula that is built into Excel. Similar SUM functions can be used in cells F13, G13, H13, and I13 to total gross pay, federal tax, state tax, and net pay, respectively. The following steps determine totals in cell D13 and the range F13:I13.

1 Select cell to contain the sum, cell D13 in this case. Click the Sum button (Home tab | Editing group) to sum the contents of the range D4:D12 in cell D13 and then click the Enter box to display a total in the selected cell.

2 Select the range to contain the sums, range F13:I13 in this case. Click the Sum button (Home tab | Editing group) to display totals in the selected range (Figure 2–14).

Figure 2–14

o Determine the Total Tax %

With the totals in row 13 determined, the next step is to copy the tax % formula in ell J12 to cell J13 as performed in the following steps.

Select the cell to be copied, J12 in this case, and then point to the fill handle.

Drag the fill handle down through cell J13 to copy the formula (Figure 2–15).

Why was the formula I13/F13 not copied to cell J13 earlier?

The formula, I13/F13, was not copied to cell J13 when cell J4 was copied to the range J5:J12 because both cells involved in the computation (I13 and F13) were blank, or zero, at the time. A **blank cell** in Excel has a numerical value of zero, which would have resulted in an error message in cell J13. Once the totals were determined, both cells I13 and F13 (especially F13, because it is the divisor) had nonzero numerical values.

rsey, Ja	3/4/2011	1	68.5	21.45	1469.325	317.9011	58.773	1092.651	0.256359
erna, Th	1/15/2010	3	78.25	22.6	1768.45	373.0078	70		0.250924
llitt, Sh	11/15/2008	2	49.25	18.25	898.8125	187.038	35.		0.248095
asad, Ra	2/15/2008	0	33.5	9.35	313.225	68.9095	12		0.26
ashingt	5/11/2006	2	79.25	23.75	1882.188	403.3805	75.2875	1403.52	0.254315
a, Jame	4/14/2011	1	80	19.65	1572	340.489		1168.63	0.256596
tals			598.5		12122.33	2602.70		034.725	0.254704
erage									
ghest									

formula is =(G12+H12)/ F12

formula is =(G13+H13)/ F13

Auto Fill Options button appears after copying cell J12 to cell J13

Figure 2–15

Using the AVERAGE, MAX, and MIN Functions

The next step in creating The Mobile Masses Biweekly Payroll Report worksheet is to compute the average, highest value, and lowest value for the number of dependents listed in the range C4:C12 using the AVERAGE, MAX, and MIN functions in the range C14:C16. Once the values are determined for column C, the entries can be copied across to the other columns.

With Excel, you can enter functions using one of five methods: (1) the keyboard or mouse, (2) the Insert Function box in the formula bar, (3) the Sum menu, (4) the Sum command (Formulas tab | Function Library group), and (5) the Name box area in the formula bar (Figure 2–16). The method you choose will depend on your typing skills and whether you can recall the function name and required arguments.

In the following pages, each of the first three methods will be used. The keyboard and mouse method will be used to determine the average number of dependents (cell C14). The Insert Function button in the formula bar method will be used to determine the highest number of dependents (cell C15). The Sum menu method will be used to determine the lowest number of dependents (cell C16).

BTW

Statistical Functions
Excel usually considers a blank cell to be equal to 0. The statistical functions, however, ignore blank cells. Excel thus calculates the average of three cells with values of 10, blank, and 8 to be 9 [(10 + 8) / 2] and not 6 [(10 + 0 + 8) / 3].

To Determine the Average of a Range of Numbers Using the Keyboard and Mouse

The **AVERAGE function** sums the numbers in the specified range and then divides the sum by the number of cells with numeric values in the range. The following steps use the AVERAGE function to determine the average of the numbers in the range C4:C12.

1

- Select the cell to contain the average, cell C14 in this case.

- Type =av in the cell to display the Formula AutoComplete list. Press the DOWN ARROW key to highlight the required formula (Figure 2–16).

Q&A

What is happening as I type?

As you type the equal sign followed by the characters in the name of a function, Excel displays the Formula AutoComplete list. This list contains those functions that alphabetically match the letters you have typed. Because you typed =av, Excel displays all the functions that begin with the letters av.

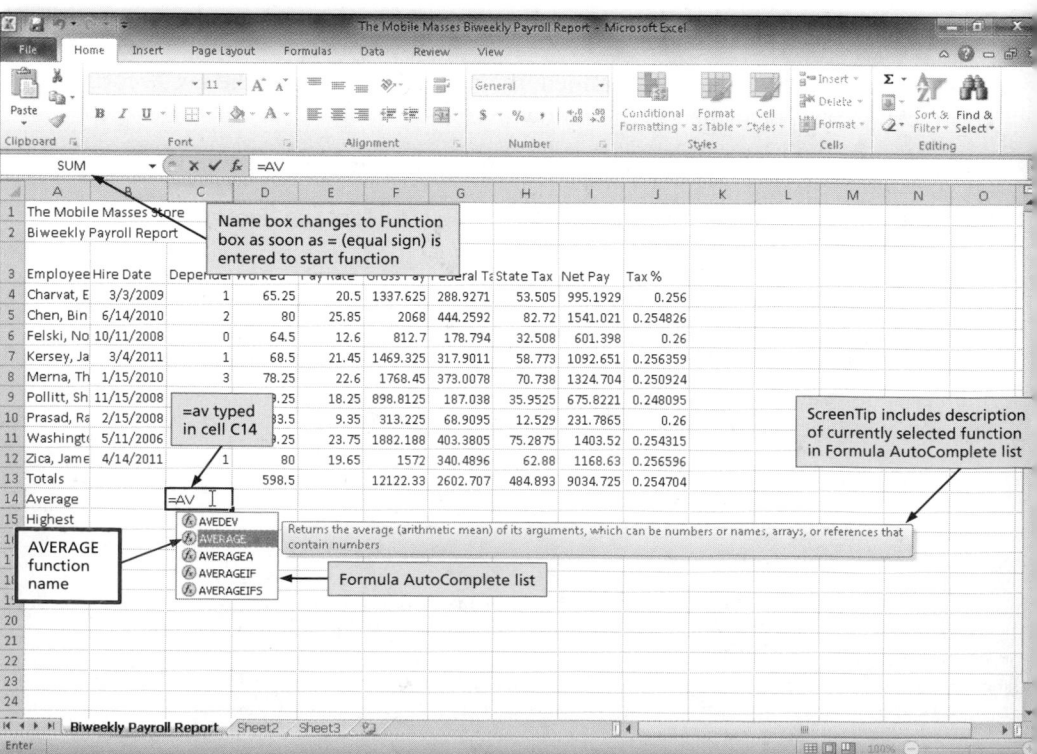

Figure 2–16

②

- Double-click AVERAGE in the Formula AutoComplete list to select the function.

- Select the range to be averaged, C4:C12 in this case, to insert the range as the argument to the function (Figure 2–17).

As I drag, why does the function in cell C14 change?

When you click cell C4, Excel appends cell C4 to the left parenthesis in the formula bar and surrounds cell C4 with a marquee. When you begin dragging, Excel appends to the argument a colon (:) and the cell reference of the cell where the mouse pointer is located.

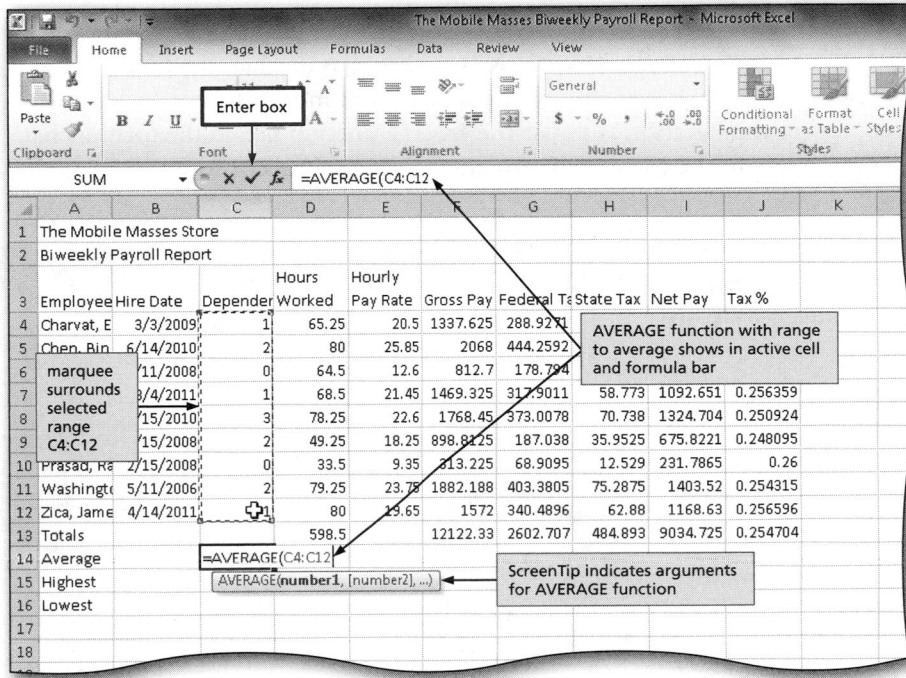

Figure 2–17

③

- Click the Enter box to compute the average of the numbers in the selected range and display the result in the selected cell (Figure 2–18).

Can I use the arrow keys to complete the entry instead?

No. When you use Point mode you cannot use the arrow keys to complete the entry. While in Point mode, the arrow keys change the selected cell reference in the range you are selecting.

What is the purpose of the parentheses in the function?

The AVERAGE function requires that the argument (in this case, the range C4:C12) be included within parentheses following the function name. Excel automatically appends the right parenthesis to complete the AVERAGE function when you click the Enter box or press the ENTER key.

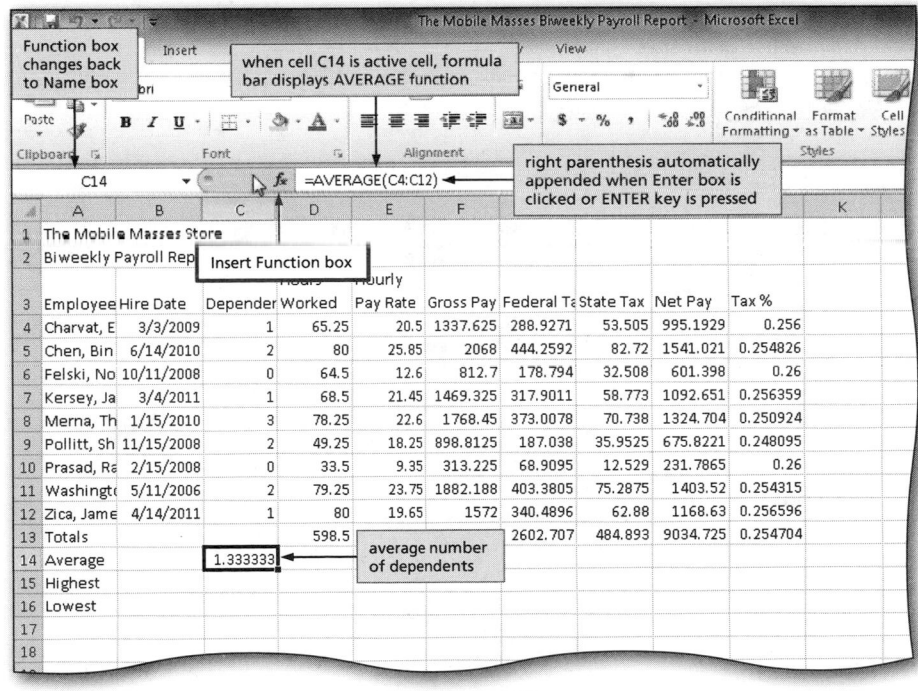

Figure 2–18

Other Ways

1. Click Insert Function box in the formula bar, click AVERAGE

2. Click Sum button arrow (Home tab | Editing group), click Average

3. Click Sum button arrow (Formulas tab | Function Library group), click Average

To Determine the Highest Number in a Range of Numbers Using the Insert Function Box

The next step is to select cell C15 and determine the highest (maximum) number in the range C4:C12. Excel includes a function called the **MAX function** that displays the highest value in a range. Although you could enter the MAX function using the keyboard and Point mode as described in the previous steps, an alternative method to entering the function is to use the Insert Function box in the formula bar. The following steps use the Insert Function box in the formula bar to enter the MAX function.

- Select the cell to contain the maximum number, cell C15 in this case.

- Click the Insert Function box in the formula bar to display the Insert Function dialog box.

- Click MAX in the 'Select a function' list (Insert Function dialog box) to select it (Figure 2–19). If the MAX function is not displayed in the 'Select a function' list, scroll the list until the function is displayed.

Figure 2–19

- Click the OK button (Insert Function dialog box) to display the Function Arguments dialog box.

- Type `c4:c12` in the Number1 box (Function Arguments dialog box) to enter the first argument of the function (Figure 2–20).

Q&A

Why did numbers appear in the Function Arguments dialog box?

As shown in Figure 2–20, Excel displays the value the MAX function will return to cell C15 in the Function Arguments dialog box. It also lists the first few numbers in the selected range, next to the Number1 box.

Figure 2–20

Click the OK button (Function Arguments dialog box) to display the highest value in the chosen range in the selected cell (Figure 2–21).

Why should I not just enter the highest value that I see in the range C4:C12 in cell C15?

In this example, rather than entering the MAX function, you visually could scan the range C4:C12,

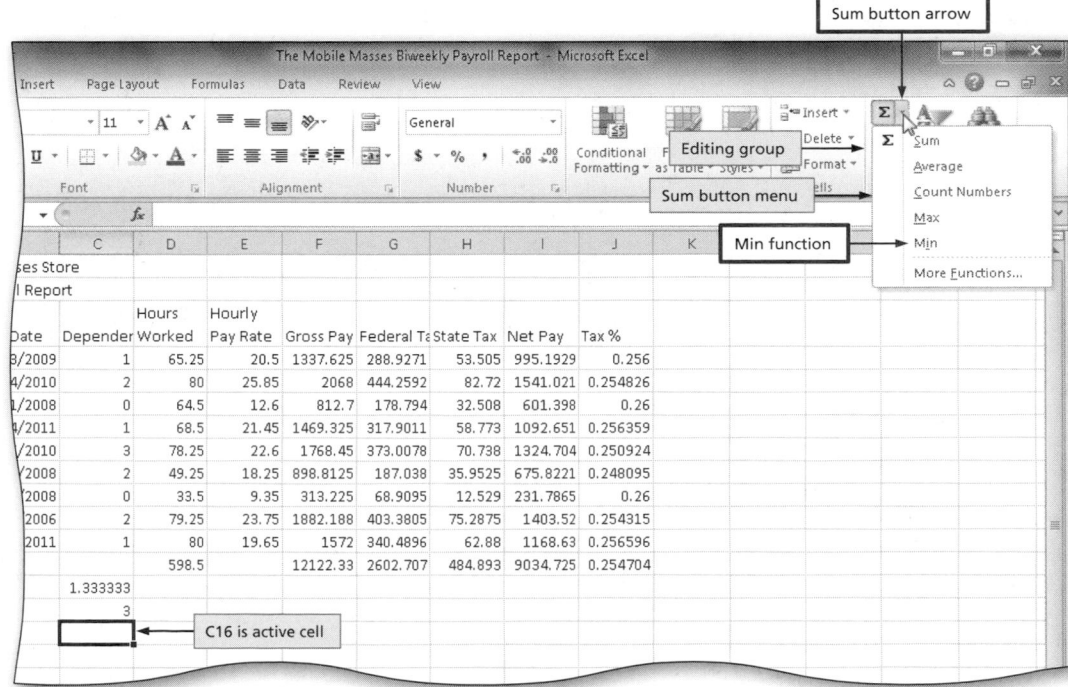

	A	B	C	D	E	F	G	H	I	J	K	L	M
	C15		fx	=MAX(C4:C12)									
1	The Mobile Masses Store												
2	Biweekly Payroll Report												
3	Employee	Hire Date	Depender	Hours Worked	Hourly Pay Rate	Gross Pay	Federal Ta	State Tax	Net Pay	Tax %			
4	Charvat, E	3/3/2009	1	65.25	20.5	1337.625	288.9271	53.505	995.1929	0.256			
5	Chen, Bin	6/14/2010	2	80	25.85	2068	444.2592	82.72	1541.021	0.254826			
6	Felski, No	10/11/2008	0	64.5	12.6	812.7	178.794	32.508	601.398	0.26			
7	Kersey, Ja	3/4/2011	1	68.5	21.45	1469.325	317.9011	58.773	1092.651	0.256359			
8	Merna, Th	1/15/2010	3	78.25	22.6	1768.45	373.0078	70.738	1324.704	0.250924			
9	Pollitt, Sh	11/15/2008	2	49.25	18.25	898.8125	187.038	35.9525	675.8221	0.248095			
10	Prasad, Ra	2/15/2008	0	33.5	9.35	313.225	68.9095	12.529	231.7865	0.26			
11	Washingto	5/11/2006	2	79.25	23.75	1882.188	403.3805	75.2875	1403.52	0.254315			
12	Zica, Jame	4/14/2011	1	80	19.65	1572	340.4896	62.88	1168.63	0.256596			
13	Totals			598.5		12122.33	2602.707	484.893	9034.725	0.254704			
14	Average		1.333333										
15	Highest		3										
16	Lowest												

MAX function determines highest value in range C4:C12

highest value in range C4:C12

Figure 2–21

determine that the highest number of dependents is 3, and manually enter the number 3 as a constant in cell C15. Excel would display the number the same as in Figure 2–21. Because it contains a constant, however, Excel will continue to display 3 in cell C15, even if the values in the range C4:C12 change. If you use the MAX function, Excel will recalculate the highest value in the range C4:C12 each time a new value is entered into the worksheet.

Other Ways

1. Click Sum button arrow (Home tab | Editing group), click Max

2. Click Sum button arrow (Formulas tab | Function Library group), click Max

3. Type **=MAX** in cell

To Determine the Lowest Number in a Range of Numbers Using the Sum Menu

The next step is to enter the **MIN function** in cell C16 to determine the lowest (minimum) number in the range C4:C12. Although you can enter the MIN function using either of the methods used to enter the AVERAGE and MAX functions, the following steps perform an alternative using the Sum button (Home tab | Editing group).

Select cell C16 to prepare to enter the next function.

Click the Sum button arrow (Home tab | Editing group) to display the Sum button menu (Figure 2–22).

Why should I use the Sum button menu?

Using the Sum button menu allows you to enter one of five often-used functions easily into a cell, without having to memorize its name or the required arguments.

Figure 2–22

2

• Click Min to display
the MIN function
in the formula bar
and in the active cell
(Figure 2–23).

Q&A

Why does Excel select
the range C14:C15?

The range C14:C15
automatically selected
by Excel is not correct.
Excel attempts to
guess which cells you
want to include in the
function by looking
for ranges that are
adjacent to the
selected cell and that
contain numeric data.

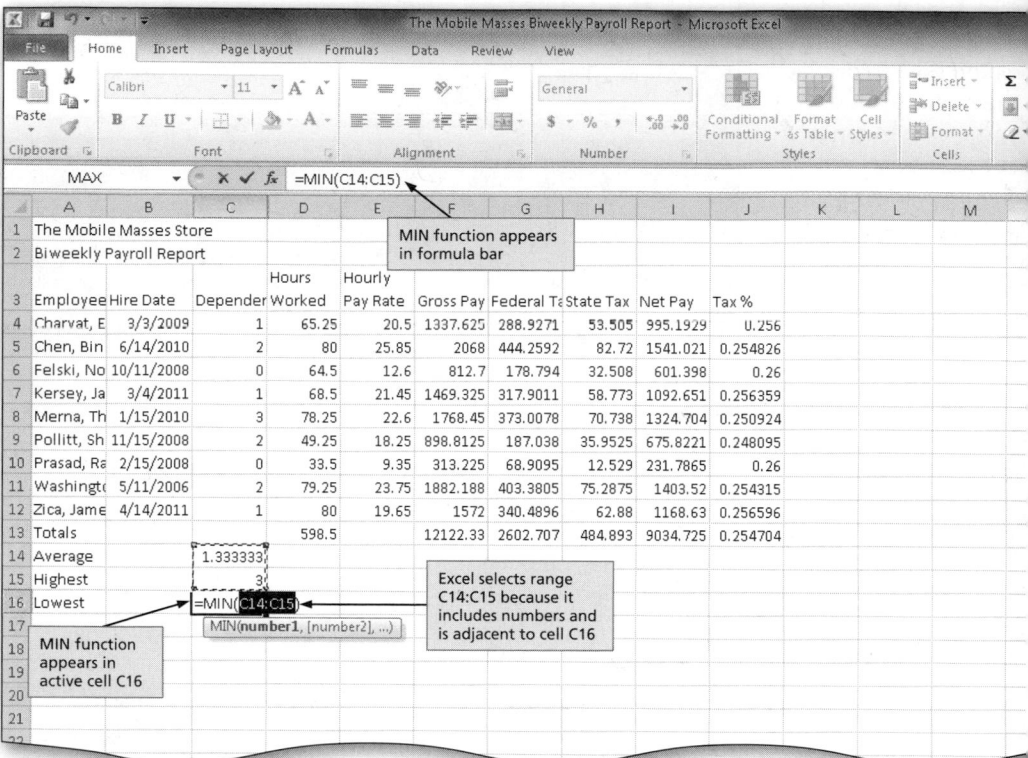

Figure 2–23

3

• Click cell C4 and then
drag through cell C12
to display the function
with the new range in
the formula bar and
in the selected cell
(Figure 2–24).

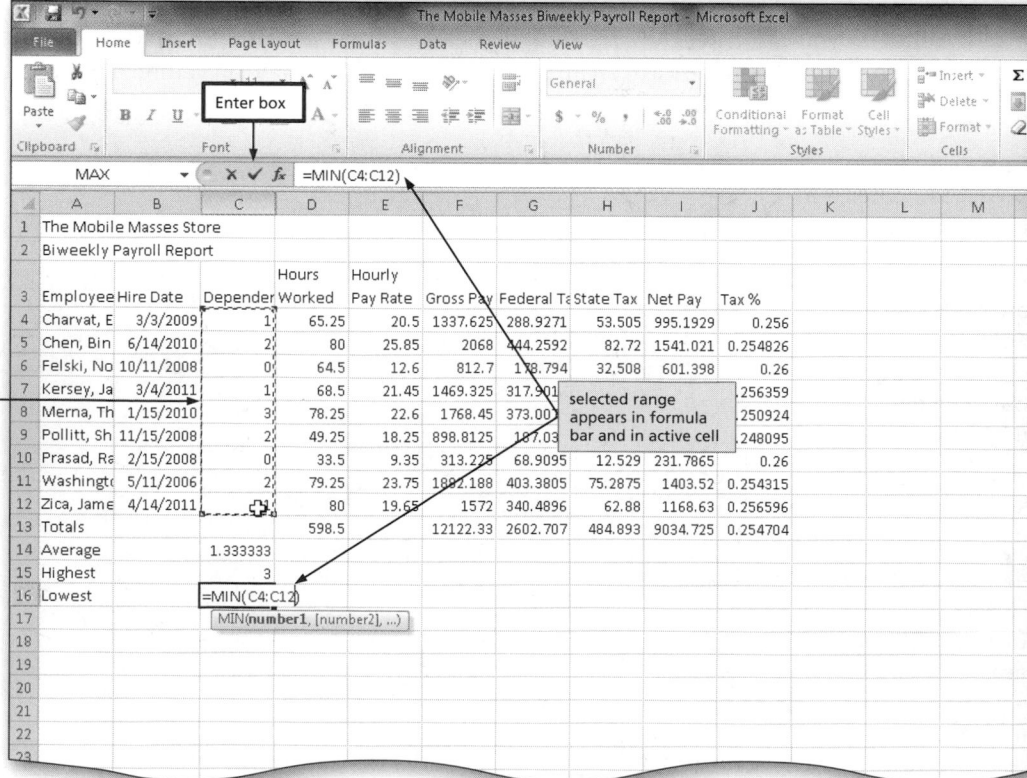

Figure 2–24

• Click the Enter box to determine the lowest value in the range C4:C12 and display the result in the formula bar and in the selected cell (Figure 2–25).

How can I learn about other functions?

Excel has more than 400 additional functions that perform just about every type of calculation you can imagine. These functions are categorized in the Insert Function dialog box shown in Figure 2–19 on page EX 86. To view the categories, click the 'Or select a category' box arrow. To obtain a description of a selected function, select its name in the Insert Function dialog box. Excel displays the description of the function below the Select a function list in the dialog box.

Figure 2–25

Other Ways
1. Click Insert Function box in the formula bar (if necessary, select Statistical category), click MIN   2. Click Sum button arrow (Formulas tab | Function Library group), click Min   3. Type =MIN in cell

To Copy a Range of Cells Across Columns to an Adjacent Range Using the Fill Handle

The next step is to copy the AVERAGE, MAX, and MIN functions in the range C14:C16 to the adjacent range D14:J16. The following steps use the fill handle to copy the functions.

• Select the source range from which to copy the functions, in this case C14:C16.

• Drag the fill handle in the lower-right corner of the selected range through cell J16 and continue to hold down the mouse button to begin a fill operation (Figure 2–26).

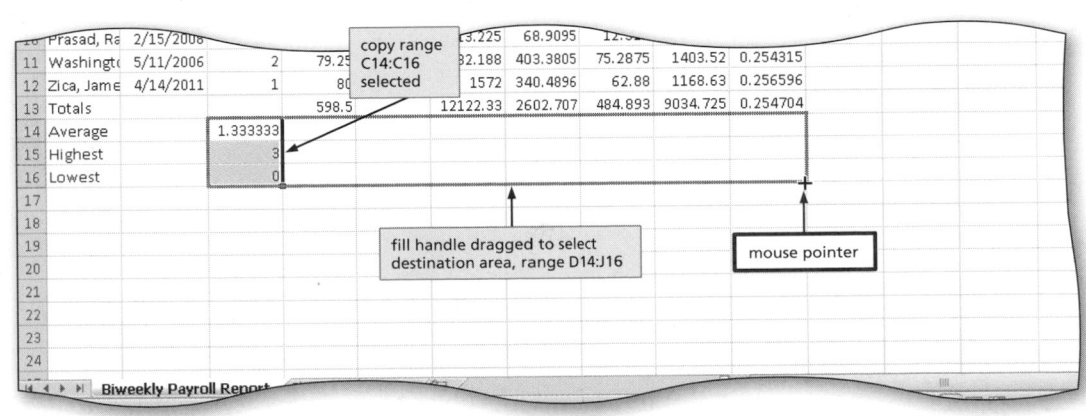

Figure 2–26

2

- Release the mouse button to copy the three functions to the selected range (Figure 2–27).

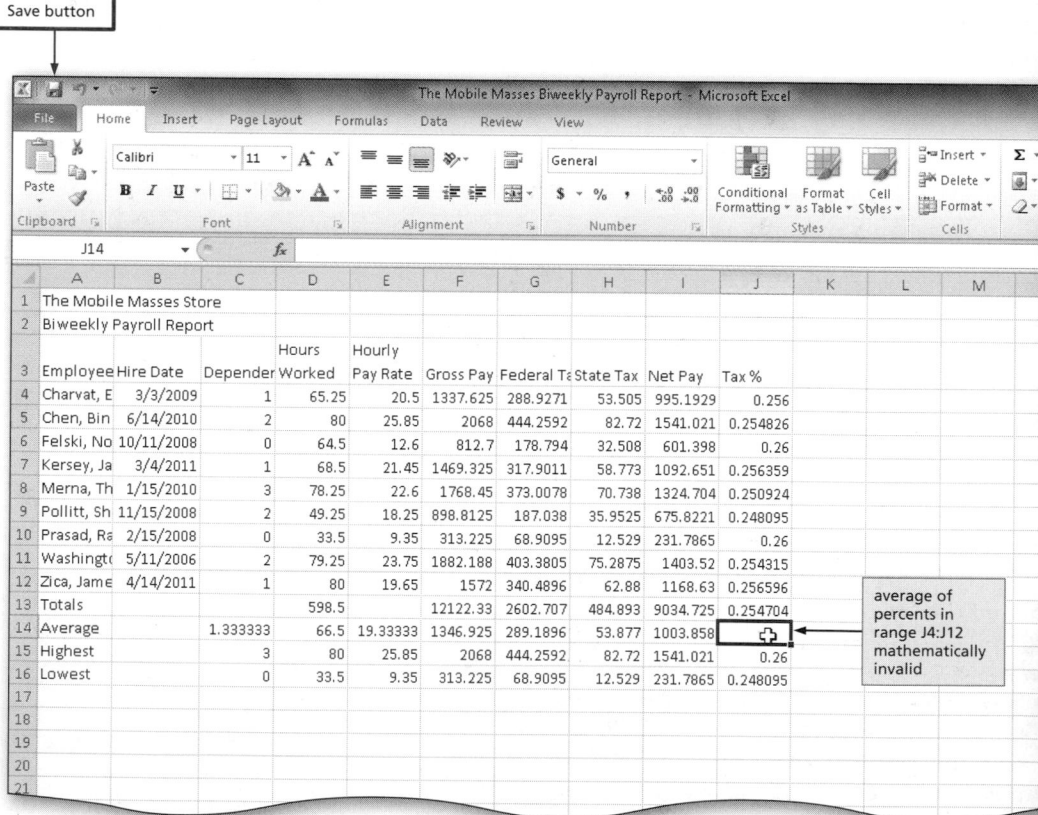

AVERAGE, MAX, and MIN functions in range C14:C16 copied to range D14:J16

9	Pollitt, Sh	11/15/2008						
10	Prasad, Ra	2/15/2008	0	33.5			.529	231.7865	0.26
11	Washingt	5/11/2006	2	79.25	23.75	1882.188	403.3805	75.2875	1403.52	0.254315
12	Zica, Jame	4/14/2011	1	80	19.65	1572	340.4896	62.88	1168.63	0.256596
13	Totals			598.5		12122.33	2602.707	484.893	9034.725	0.254704
14	Average		1.333333	66.5	19.33333	1346.925	289.1896	53.877	1003.858	0.255235
15	Highest		3	80	25.85	2068	444.2592	82.72	1541.021	0.26
16	Lowest		0	33.5	9.35	313.225	68.9095	12.529	231.7865	0.248095
17									
18									
19									
20									
21									
22									

Auto Fill Options button

Figure 2–27

How can I be sure that the function arguments are proper for the cells in range D14:J16?

Remember that Excel adjusts the cell references in the copied functions so that each function refers to the range of numbers above it in the same column. Review the numbers in rows 14 through 16 in Figure 2–27. You should see that the functions in each column return the appropriate values, based on the numbers in rows 4 through 12 of that column.

3

- Select cell J14 and then press the DELETE key to delete the average of the tax % (Figure 2–28).

Why is the formula in cell J14 deleted?

The average of the tax % in cell J14 is deleted because an average of percentages of this type is mathematically invalid.

Save button

The Mobile Masses Biweekly Payroll Report - Microsoft Excel

	A	B	C	D	E	F	G	H	I	J	K	L	M
1	The Mobile Masses Store												
2	Biweekly Payroll Report												
3	Employee	Hire Date	Dependen	Hours Worked	Hourly Pay Rate	Gross Pay	Federal Ta	State Tax	Net Pay	Tax %			
4	Charvat, E	3/3/2009	1	65.25	20.5	1337.625	288.9271	53.505	995.1929	0.256			
5	Chen, Bin	6/14/2010	2	80	25.85	2068	444.2592	82.72	1541.021	0.254826			
6	Felski, No	10/11/2008	0	64.5	12.6	812.7	178.794	32.508	601.398	0.26			
7	Kersey, Ja	3/4/2011	1	68.5	21.45	1469.325	317.9011	58.773	1092.651	0.256359			
8	Merna, Th	1/15/2010	3	78.25	22.6	1768.45	373.0078	70.738	1324.704	0.250924			
9	Pollitt, Sh	11/15/2008	2	49.25	18.25	898.8125	187.038	35.9525	675.8221	0.248095			
10	Prasad, Ra	2/15/2008	0	33.5	9.35	313.225	68.9095	12.529	231.7865	0.26			
11	Washingt	5/11/2006	2	79.25	23.75	1882.188	403.3805	75.2875	1403.52	0.254315			
12	Zica, Jame	4/14/2011	1	80	19.65	1572	340.4896	62.88	1168.63	0.256596			
13	Totals			598.5		12122.33	2602.707	484.893	9034.725	0.254704			
14	Average		1.333333	66.5	19.33333	1346.925	289.1896	53.877	1003.858				
15	Highest		3	80	25.85	2068	444.2592	82.72	1541.021	0.26			
16	Lowest		0	33.5	9.35	313.225	68.9095	12.529	231.7865	0.248095			
17													
18													
19													
20													
21													

average of percents in range J4:J12 mathematically invalid

Figure 2–28

Other Ways

1. Select source area, click Copy button (Home tab | Clipboard group), select destination area, click Paste button (Home tab | Clipboard group)

2. Right-click source area, click Copy on shortcut menu, right-click destination area, click Paste icon on shortcut menu

3. Select source area and then point to border of range; while holding down CTRL, drag source area to destination area

4. Select source area, press CTRL+C, select destination area, press CTRL+V

Save a Workbook Using the Same File Name

Earlier in this project, an intermediate version of the workbook was saved using file name, The Mobile Masses Biweekly Payroll Report. The following step saves the rkbook a second time, using the same file name.

Click the Save button on the Quick Access Toolbar to overwrite the previously saved file.

reak Point: If you wish to take a break, this is a good place to do so. You can quit Excel now. To resume at a later time, start Excel, pen the file called The Mobile Masses Biweekly Payroll Report, and continue following the steps from this location forward.

erifying Formulas Using Range Finder

e of the more common mistakes made with Excel is to include a wrong cell reference a formula. An easy way to verify that a formula references the cells you want it to erence is to use the Excel Range Finder. Use **Range Finder** to check which cells are erenced in the formula assigned to the active cell. Range Finder allows you to make mediate changes to the cells referenced in a formula.

To use Range Finder to verify that a formula contains the intended cell references, uble-click the cell with the formula you want to check. Excel responds by highlighting e cells referenced in the formula so that you can check that the cell references are correct.

BTW

Entering Functions
You can drag the Function Arguments dialog box (Figure 2–20 on page EX 86) out of the way in order to select a range. You also can click the Collapse Dialog button to the right of the Number 1 box to hide the Function Arguments dialog box. The dialog box then collapses and the Collapse Dialog button becomes an Expand Dialog box button. After selecting the range, click the Expand Dialog to expand the dialog box.

Verify a Formula Using Range Finder

The following steps use Range Finder to check the formula in cell J4.

Double-click cell J4 to activate Range Finder (Figure 2–29).

Press the ESC key to quit Range Finder and then click anywhere in the worksheet, such as cell A18, to deselect the current cell.

Figure 2–29

Formatting the Worksheet

Although the worksheet contains the appropriate data, formulas, and functions, the text and numbers need to be formatted to improve their appearance and readability.

In Chapter 1, cell styles were used to format much of the worksheet. This section describes how to change the unformatted worksheet in Figure 2–30a to the formatted worksheet in Figure 2–30b using a theme and other commands on the Ribbon. The colors and fonts that are used in the worksheet shown in Figure 2–30b are those that are associated with the Trek theme.

(a) Unformatted Worksheet

(b) Formatted Worksheet

Figure 2–30

Identify how to format various elements of the worksheet.
As you have learned, applying proper formatting to a worksheet improves its appeal and readability. The following list includes additional worksheet formatting considerations.

- **Consider using cell borders and fill colors for various portions of the worksheet.** Cell borders, or box borders, draw a border around a cell or range of cells to set the cell or range off from other portions of the worksheet. For example, worksheet titles often include cell borders. Similarly, the use of a fill color in a cell or range of cells sets off the cell or range from other portions of the worksheet and provides visual impact to draw the user's eye toward the cell or range.

- **Use good judgment when centering values in columns.** If a cell entry is short, such as the dependents in column C, centering the entries within their respective columns improves the appearance of the worksheet.

- **Consider the use of a different theme.** A **theme** is a predefined set of colors, fonts, chart styles, cell styles, and fill effects that can be applied to an entire workbook. Every new workbook that you create is assigned a default theme named Office. Excel, however, includes a variety of other themes that provide a range of visual effects for your workbooks.

- **Apply proper formatting for cells that include dates.** Excel provides a number of date formats so that date values can be formatted to meet your needs. How you decide to format a date depends on a number of factors. For example, dates that include years both before and after the year 2000 should be formatted with a four-digit year. Your organization or department may insist on the use of certain standard date formats. Industry standards also may indicate how you should format date values.

The following outlines the formatting suggested in the sketch of the worksheet in Figure 2–3 on page EX 70.

1. Workbook theme — Trek
2. Worksheet title and subtitle
   a. Alignment — center across columns A through J
   b. Cell style — Title
   c. Font size — title 18; subtitle 16
   d. Background color (range A1:J2) — Orange Accent 1, Lighter 60%
   e. Border — thick box border around range A1:J2
3. Column titles
   a. Cell style — Heading 3
   b. Alignment — center
4. Data
   a. Dates in column B — mm/dd/yy format
   b. Alignment — center data in range C4:C12
   c. Numbers in column D — Comma style and two decimal places; if a cell in range D4:D12 is greater than 70, then cell appears with background color of orange and a font color of white
   d. Numbers in top row (range E4:I4) — Accounting number format
   e. Numbers below top row (range E5:I12) — Comma style and decimal places
5. Total line
   a. Cell style — Total
   b. Numbers — Accounting number format

6. Average, highest, and lowest rows
   a. Font style of row titles in range A14:A16 — bold
   b. Numbers — Currency style with floating dollar sign in the range E14:I16

7. Percentages in column J
   a. Numbers — Percentage style with two decimal places

8. Column widths
   a. Columns A, B, and C — best fit
   b. Column H — 10.22 characters
   c. Column D, E, and J — 7.56 characters

9. Row heights
   a. Row 3 — 48.00 points
   b. Row 14 — 27.00 points
   c. Remaining rows — default

To Change the Workbook Theme

The Trek theme includes fonts and colors that provide the worksheet a professional and subtly colored appearance. The following steps change the workbook theme to the Trek theme.

1

- Display the Page Layout tab.

- Click the Themes button (Page Layout tab | Themes group) to display the Themes gallery.

- Scroll to the bottom of the gallery (Figure 2–31).

🔎 **Experiment**

- Point to several themes in the Themes gallery to see a live preview of the themes.

Q&A

Why should I change the theme of a workbook?

A company or department may standardize on a specific theme so that all of their documents have a similar appearance. Similarly, an individual may want to have a theme that sets his or her work apart from the work of others. Other Office programs, such as Word and PowerPoint, include the same themes included with Excel, meaning that all of your Microsoft Office documents can share a common theme.

Figure 2–31

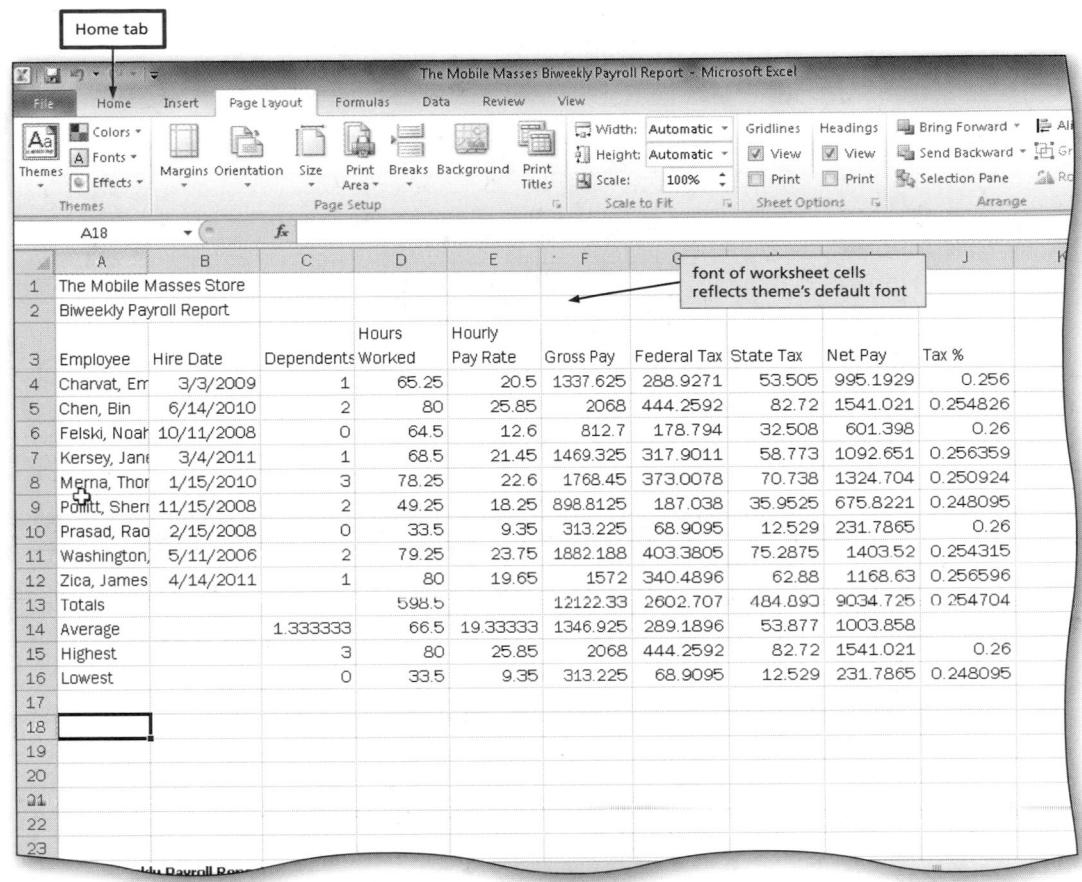

2
• Click Trek in the Themes gallery to change the workbook theme (Figure 2–32).

Figure 2–32

Why did the cells in the worksheet change?

The cells in the worksheet originally were formatted with the default font for the default Office theme. The default font for the Trek theme is different from that of the default font for the Office theme and, therefore, changed on the worksheet when you changed the theme. If you had modified the font for any of the cells, those cells would not receive the default font for the Trek theme.

To Format the Worksheet Titles

The following steps merge and center the worksheet titles, apply the Title cells style to the worksheet titles, and decrease the font of the worksheet subtitle.

1 Display the Home tab.

2 Select the range to be merged, A1:J1 in this case, and then click the Merge & Center button (Home tab | Alignment group) to merge and center the text in the selected range.

3 Select the range A2:J2 and then click the Merge & Center button (Home tab | Alignment group) to merge and center the text in the selected range.

4 Select the range to contain the Title cell style, in this case A1:A2, click the Cell Styles button (Home tab | Styles group) to display the cell styles gallery, and then click the Title cell style in the Cell Styles gallery to apply the Title cell style to the selected range.

5 Select cell A2 and then click the Decrease Font Size button (Home tab | Font group) to decrease the font size of the selected cell to the next lowest font size (Figure 2–33 on the following page).

What is the effect of clicking the Decrease Font Size button?

When you click the Decrease Font Size button, Excel assigns the next lowest font size in the Font Size gallery to the selected range. The Increase Font Size button works in a similar manner but causes Excel to assign the next highest font size in the Font Size gallery to the selected range.

Color Selection
Knowing how people perceive colors helps you emphasize parts of your worksheet. Warmer colors (red and orange) tend to reach toward the reader. Cooler colors (blue, green, and violet) tend to pull away from the reader. Bright colors jump out of a dark background and are easiest to see. White or yellow text on a dark blue, green, purple, or black background is ideal.

Figure 2–33

To Change the Background Color and Apply a Box Border to the Worksheet Title and Subtitle

The final formats assigned to the worksheet title and subtitle are the orange background color and thick box border (Figure 2–30b on page EX 92). The following steps complete the formatting of the worksheet titles.

 1

- Select the range A1:A2 and then click the Fill Color button arrow (Home tab | Font group) to display the Fill Color gallery (Figure 2–34).

Experiment

- Point to a number of colors in the Fill Color gallery to display a live preview of the color in the range A1:A2.

Figure 2–34

 2

- Click Orange, Accent 1, Lighter 60% (column 5, row 3) in the Fill Color gallery to change the background color of the range of cells (Figure 2–35).

Figure 2–35

3

- Click the Borders button arrow (Home tab | Font group) to display the Borders list (Figure 2–36).

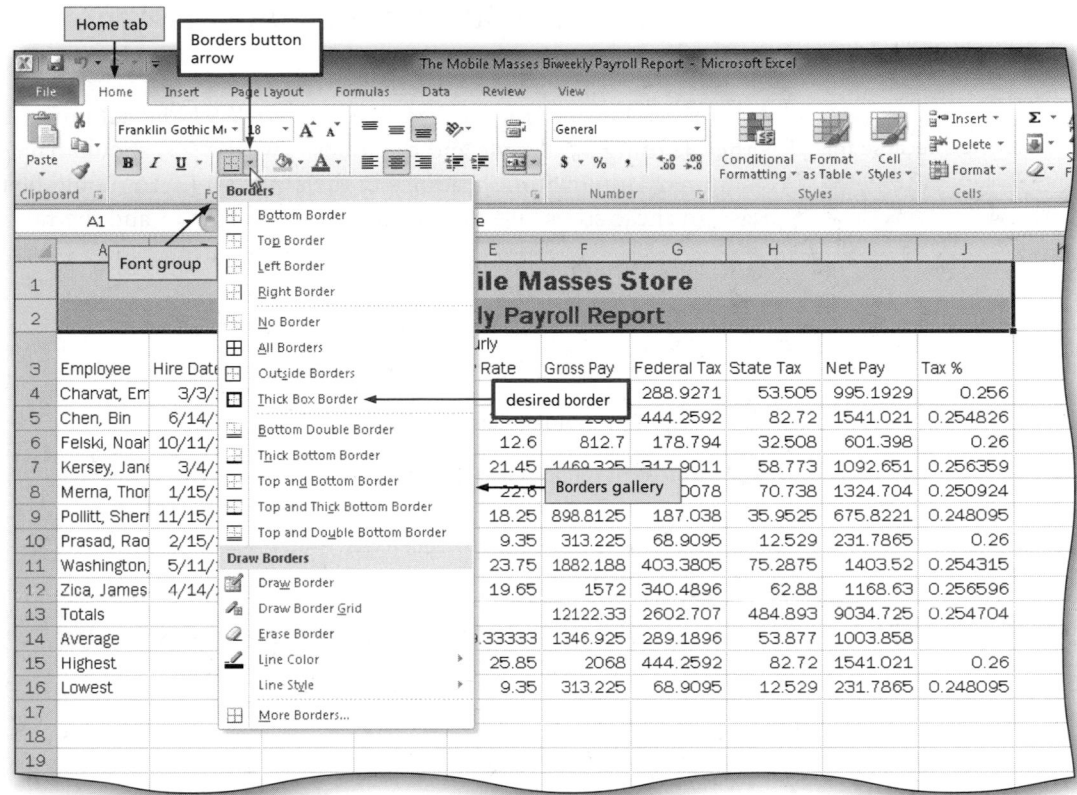

Figure 2–36

4

- Click Thick Box Border in the Borders list to display a thick box border around the selected range.

- Click anywhere in the worksheet, such as cell A18, to deselect the current range (Figure 2–37).

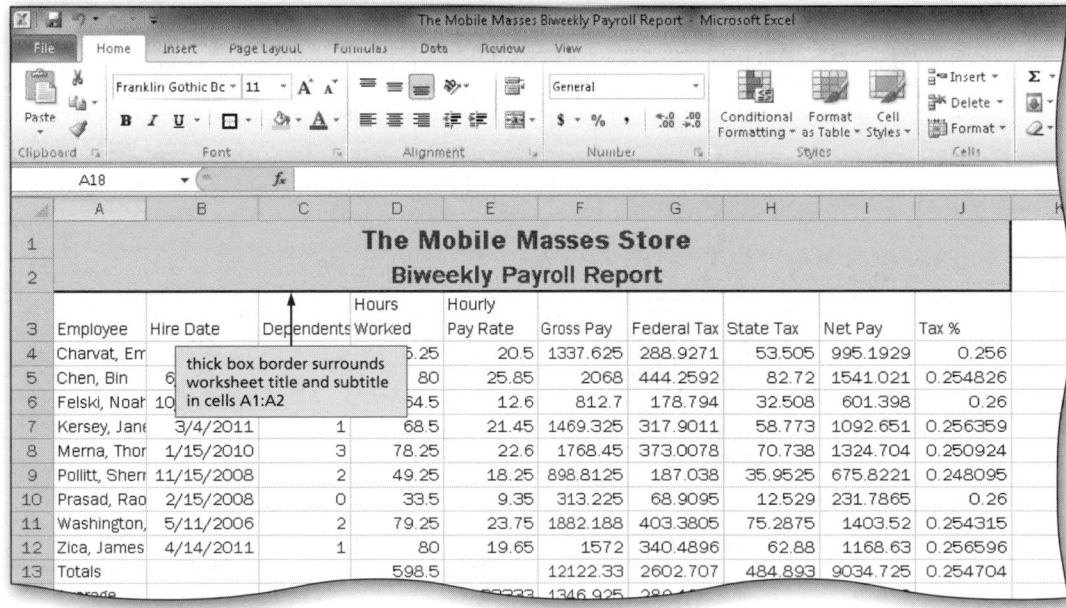

Figure 2–37

Other Ways

1. Click Format Cells Dialog Box Launcher (Home tab | Font group), click appropriate tab (Format Cells dialog box), click desired format, click OK button

2. Right-click range, click Format Cells on shortcut menu, click appropriate tab (Format Cells dialog box), click desired format, click OK button

3. Press CTRL+1, click appropriate tab (Format Cells dialog box), click desired format, click OK button

To Apply a Cell Style to the Column Headings and Format the Total Rows

As shown in Figure 2–30b on page EX 92, the column titles (row 3) should have the Heading 3 cell style and the totals row (row 13) should have the Total cell style. The summary information headings in the range A14:A16 should be bold. The following steps assign these styles and formats to row 3 and row 13 and the range A14:A16.

1 Select the range to be formatted, cells A3:J3 in this case.

2 Apply the Heading 3 cell style to the range A3:J3.

3 Click the Center button (Home tab | Alignment group) to center the column headings.

4 Apply the Total cell style to the range A13:J13.

5 Bold the range A14:A16 (Figure 2–38).

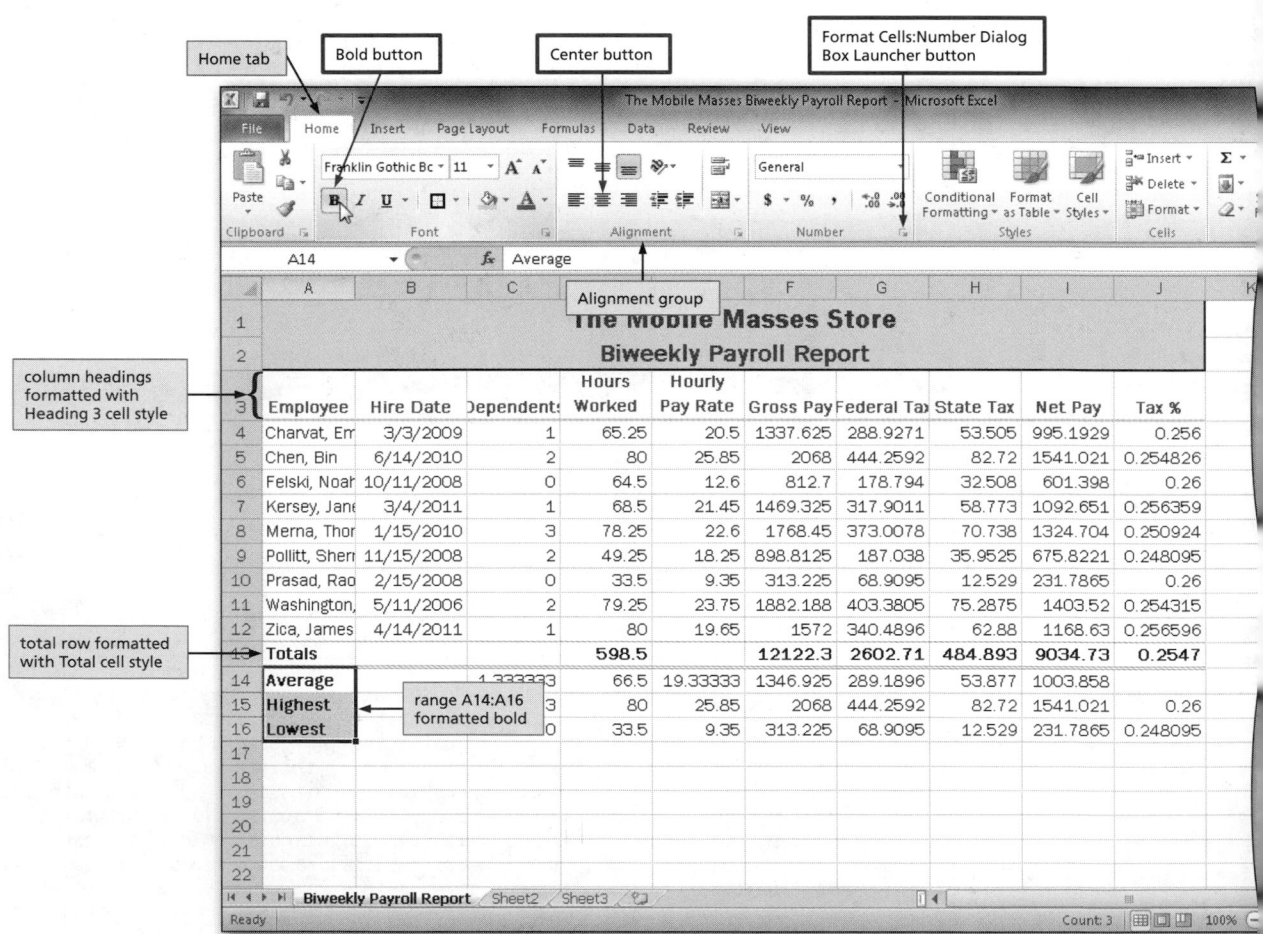

Figure 2–38

To Format Dates and Center Data in Cells

With the column titles and total rows formatted, the next step is to format the dates in column B and center the dependents in column C. The following steps format the dates in the range B4:B12 and center the data in the range C4:C12.

Select the range to contain the new date format, cells B4:B12 in this case.

Click the Format Cells: Number Dialog Box Launcher (Home tab | Number group) to display the Format Cells dialog box.

If necessary, click the Number tab (Format Cells dialog box), click Date in the Category list, and then click 3/14/01 in the Type list to choose the format for the selected range (Figure 2–39).

Figure 2-39

Click the OK button (Format Cells dialog box) to format the dates in the current column using the selected date format style.

Select the range C4:C12 and then click the Center button (Home tab | Alignment group) to center the data in the selected range.

Select cell E4 to deselect the selected range (Figure 2–40).

	A	B	C	D	E	F	G	H	I	J	K
1				**The Mobile Masses Store**							
2				**Biweekly Payroll Report**							
3	Employee	Hire Date	Dependents	Hours Worked	Hourly Pay Rate	Gross Pay	Federal Tax	State Tax	Net Pay	Tax %	
4	Charvat, Em	3/3/09	1	65.25	20.5	1337	cell E4 selected	53.505	995.1929	0.256	
5	Chen, Bin	6/14/10	2	80	25.85	2068	444.2592	82.72	1541.021	0.254826	
6	Felski, Noah	10/11/08	0	64.5	12.6	812.7	178.794	32.508	601.398	0.26	
7	Kersey, Jane	3/4/11	1	68.5	21.45	1469.325	317.9011	58.773	1092.651	0.256359	
8	Merna, Thor	1/15/10	3	78.25	22.6	1768.45	373.0078	70.738	1324.704	0.250924	
9	Pollitt, Sherr	11/15/08	2	49.25	18.25	898.8125	187.038	35.9525	675.8221	0.248095	
10	Prasad, Rao	2/15/08	0	33.5	9.35	313.225	68.9095	12.529	231.7865	0.26	
11	Washington,	5/11/06	2	79.25	23.75	1882.188	403.3805	75.2875	1403.52	0.254315	
12	Zica, James	4/14/11	1	80	19.65	1572	340.4896	62.88	1168.63	0.256596	
13	Totals			598.5		12122.3	2602.71	484.893	9034.73	0.2547	
14	Average		1.333333	66.5	19.33333	1346.925	289.1896	53.877	1003.858		
15	Highest			3	80	25.85	2068	444.2592	82.72	1541.021	0.26	
16	Lowest			0	33.5	9.35	313.225	68.9095	12.529	231.7865	0.248095	

Excel displays dates in range B4:B12 using date style format, mm/dd/yy

data centered in range C4:C12

Figure 2-40

Can I format an entire column at once?

Yes. Rather than selecting the range B4:B12 in Step 1, you could have clicked the column B heading immediately above cell B1, and then clicked the Center button (Home tab | Alignment group). In this case, all cells in column B down to the last cell in the worksheet would have been formatted to use center alignment. This same procedure could have been used to format the dependents in column C.

Other Ways

1. Right-click range, click Format Cells on shortcut menu, click appropriate tab (Format Cells dialog box), click desired format, click OK button

2. Press CTRL+1, click appropriate tab (Format Cells dialog box), click desired format, click OK button

Formatting Numbers Using the Ribbon

As shown in Figure 2–30b on page EX 92, the worksheet is formatted to resemble an accounting report. For example, in columns E through I, the numbers in the first row (row 4), the totals row (row 13), and the rows below the totals (rows 14 through 16) have dollar signs, while the remaining numbers (rows 5 through 12) in column E through column I do not.

Plan Ahead

Determine proper formatting for cells that include currency and other numeric amounts.

- To append a dollar sign to a number, you should use the Accounting number format. Excel displays numbers using the **Accounting number format** with a dollar sign to the left of the number, inserts a comma every three positions to the left of the decimal point, and displays numbers to the nearest cent (hundredths place). Clicking the Accounting Number Format button (Home tab | Number group) assigns the desired Accounting number format.

- When you use the Accounting Number Format button to assign the Accounting number format, Excel displays a **fixed dollar sign** to the far left in the cell, often with spaces between it and the first digit. To assign a **floating dollar sign** that appears immediately to the left of the first digit with no spaces, use the Currency style (Format Cells dialog box). Whether you use the Accounting number format or the Currency style format depends on a number of factors, including the preference of your organization, industry standards, and the aesthetics of the worksheet.

- The Comma style format is used to instruct Excel to display numbers with commas and no dollar signs. The **Comma style format**, which can be assigned to a range of cells by clicking the Comma Style button (Home tab | Number group), inserts a comma every three positions to the left of the decimal point and causes numbers to be displayed to the nearest hundredths.

To Apply an Accounting Number Format and Comma Style Format Using the Ribbon

The following steps assign formats using the Accounting Number Format button and the Comma Style button (Home tab | Number group). The Accounting Number format is applied to the currency amounts in rows 4 and 13. The Comma style is applied to the range E4:I12 and to column D (Hours Worked).

- Select the range to contain the Accounting Number Format, cells E4:I4 in this case.

- While holding down the CTRL key, select the range F13:I13 to select the nonadjacent range.

- Click the Accounting Number Format button (Home tab | Number group) to apply the Accounting number format with fixed dollar signs to the selected nonadjacent ranges (Figure 2–41).

Q&A

What is the effect of applying the Accounting number format?

The Accounting Number Format button assigns a fixed dollar sign to the numbers in the ranges E4:I4 and F13:I13. In each cell in these ranges, Excel displays the dollar sign to the far left with spaces between it and the first digit in the cell.

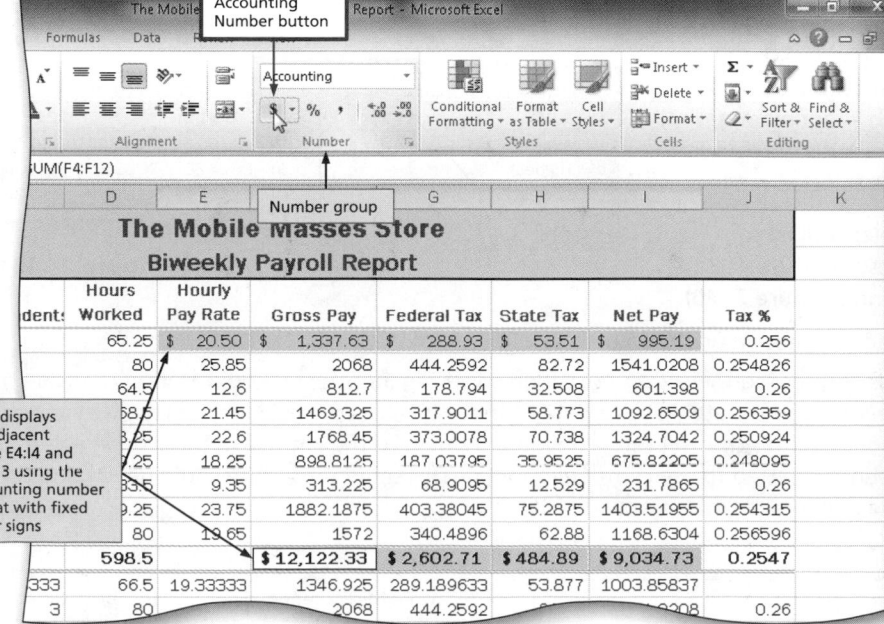

Figure 2–41

2

- Select the range to contain the Comma style format, cells E5:I12 in this case.

- Click the Comma Style button (Home tab | Number group) to assign the Comma style format to the selected range (Figure 2–42).

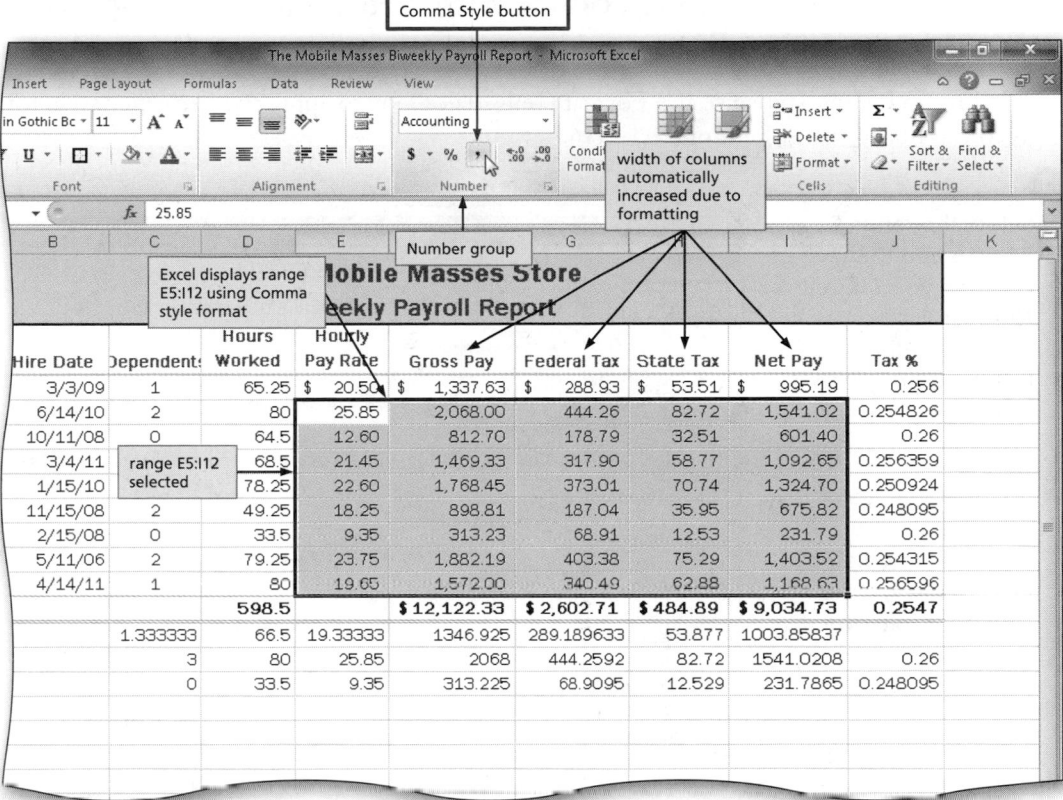

Figure 2–42

3

- Select the range to contain the Comma style format, cells D4:D16 in this case.

- Click the Comma Style button (Home tab | Number group) to assign the Comma style format to the selected range (Figure 2–43).

Figure 2–43

	Employee	Hire Date	Dependents	Hours Worked	Hourly Pay Rate	Gross Pay	Federal Tax	State Tax	Net Pay	Tax
4	Charvat, Em	3/3/09	1	65.25	$ 20.50	$ 1,337.63	$ 288.93	$ 53.51	$ 995.19	0.
5	Chen, Bin	6/14/10	2	80.00	25.85	2,068.00	444.26	82.72	1,541.02	0.254
6	Felski, Noah	10/11/08	0	64.50	12.60	812.70	178.79	32.51	601.40	0
7	Kersey, Jane	3/4/11	1	68.50	21.45	1,469.33	317.90	58.77	1,092.65	0.2563
8	Merna, Thor		3	78.25	22.60	1,768.45	373.01	70.74	1,324.70	0.2509
9	Pollitt, Sherr		2	49.25	18.25	898.81	187.04	35.95	675.82	0.2480
10	Prasad, Rao		0	33.50	9.35	313.23	68.91	12.53	231.79	0.
11	Washington,	5/11/06	2	79.25	23.75	1,882.19	403.38	75.29	1,403.52	0.2543
12	Zica, James	4/14/11	1	80.00	19.65	1,572.00	340.49	62.88	1,168.63	0.2565
13	Totals			598.50		$12,122.33	$ 2,602.71	$484.89	$ 9,034.73	0.25
14	Average		1.333333	66.50	19.33333	1346.925	289.189633	53.877	1003.85837	
15	Highest		3	80.00	25.85	2068	444.2592	82.72	1541.0208	
16	Lowest		0	33.50	9.35	313.225	68.9095	12.529	231.7865	0.248

To Apply a Currency Style Format with a Floating Dollar Sign Using the Format Cells Dialog Box

The following steps use the Format Cells dialog box to apply the Currency style format with a floating dollar sign to the numbers in the range E14:I16.

- Select the range E14:I16 and then click the Format Cells: Number Dialog Box Launcher (Home tab | Number group) to display the Format Cells dialog box.

- If necessary, click the Number tab (Format Cells dialog box) to display the Number tab (Format Cells dialog box) (Figure 2–44).

Figure 2–44

- Click Currency in the Category list to select the necessary number format category, and then click the third style ($1,234.10) in the Negative numbers list (Format Cells dialog box) to select the desired currency format for negative numbers (Figure 2–45).

Q&A

How do I select the proper format?

You can choose from 12 categories of formats. Once you select a category, you can select the number of decimal places, whether or not a dollar sign should be displayed, and how

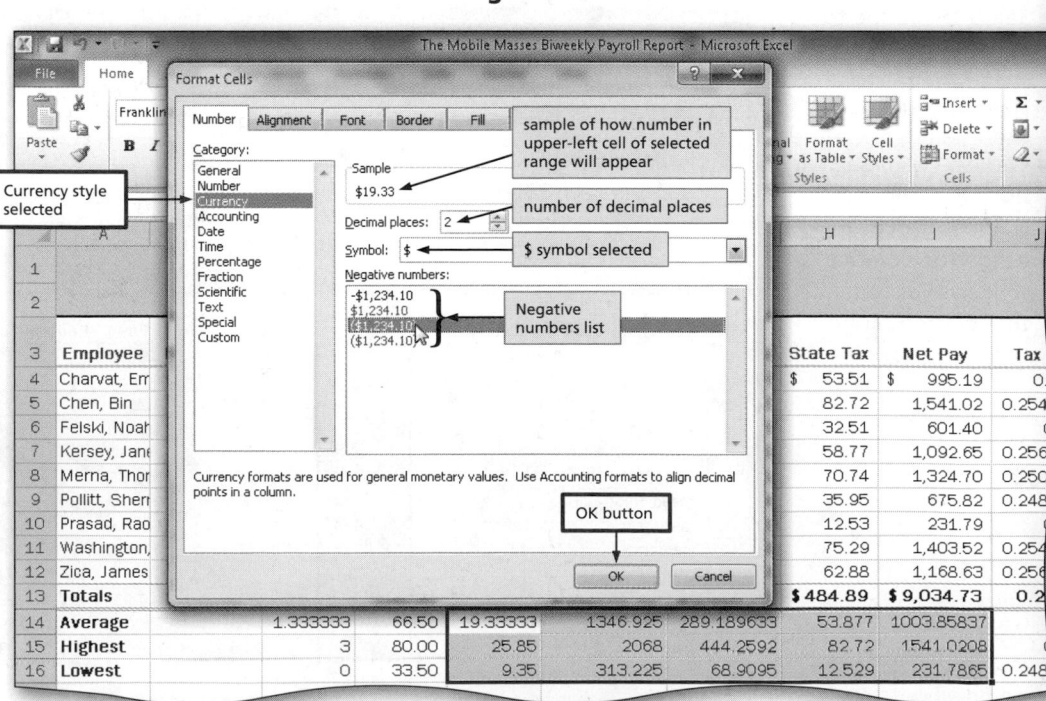

Figure 2–45

negative numbers should appear. Selecting the appropriate negative numbers format is important, because doing so adds a space to the right of the number in order to align the numbers in the worksheet on the decimal points. Some of the available negative number formats do not align the numbers in the worksheet on the decimal points.

3

- Click the OK button (Format Cells dialog box) to assign the Currency style format with a floating dollar sign to the selected range (Figure 2–46).

What is the difference between using the Accounting Number style and Currency style?

When using the Accounting Number Style button, recall that a floating dollar sign always appears immediately to the left of the first digit, and the fixed dollar sign always appears on the left side of the cell. Cell E4, for example, has a fixed dollar sign, while cell E14 has a floating dollar sign. The Currency style was assigned to cell E14 using the Format Cells dialog box and the result is a floating dollar sign.

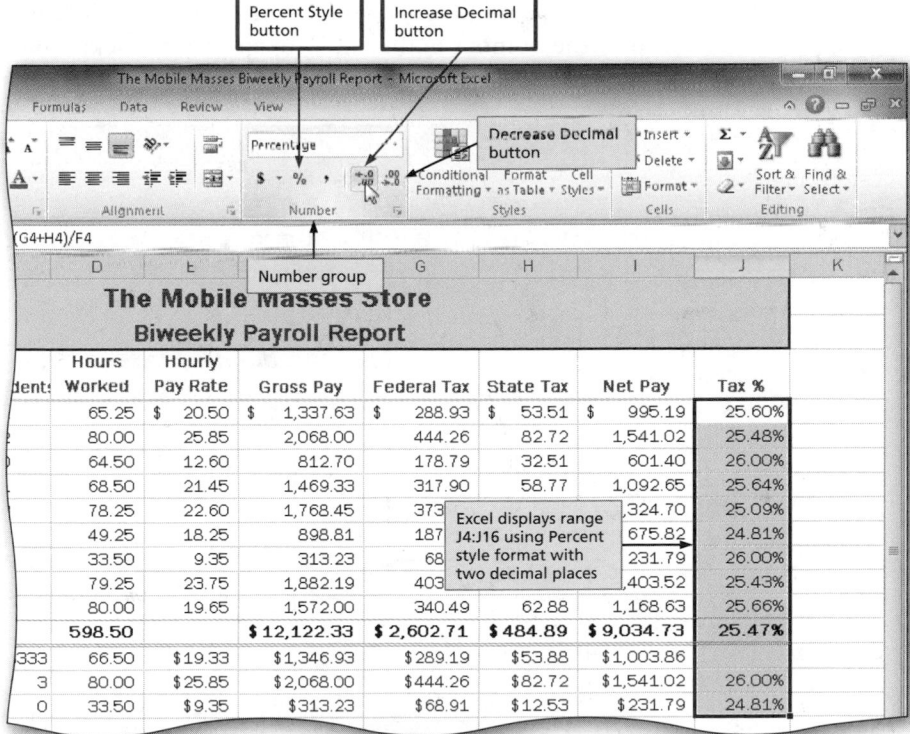

	0	33.50		68.91		0.26
11/06	2	79.25	23.75	1,882.19	403.38	75.29	1,403.52	0.254315
14/11	1	80.00	19.65	1,57?.00	340.49	62.88	1,168.63	0.256596
	8.50			$ 12,122.33	$ 2,602.71	$ 484.89	$ 9,034.73	0.2547
66.50		$19.33	$1,346.93	$289.19	$53.88	$1,003.86	
80.00		$25.85	$2,068.00	$444.26	$82.72	$1,541.02	0.26
83.50		$9.35	$313.23	$68.91	$12.53	$231.79	0.248095

Excel displays range E14:I16 using Currency style format with floating dollar signs

Figure 2–46

Other Ways

1. Press CTRL+1, click Number tab (Format Cells dialog box), click Currency
   in Category list, select format, click OK button
2. Press CTRL+SHIFT+DOLLAR SIGN ($)

To Apply a Percent Style Format and Use the Increase Decimal Button

The next step is to format the tax % in column J. Currently, Excel displays the numbers in column J as a decimal fraction (for example, 0.256 in cell J4). The following steps format the range J4:J16 to the Percent style format with two decimal places.

1

- Select the range to format, cell J4:J16 in this case.

- Click the Percent Style button (Home tab | Number group) to display the numbers in the selected range as a rounded whole percent.

What is the result of clicking the Percent Style button?

The Percent Style button instructs Excel to display a value as a percentage, determined by multiplying the cell entry by 100, rounding the result to the nearest percent, and adding a percent sign. For example, when cell J4 is formatted using the Percent Style buttons, Excel displays the actual value 0.256 as 26%.

2

- Click the Increase Decimal button (Home tab | Number group) two times to display the numbers in the selected range with two decimal places (Figure 2–47).

Figure 2–47

Other Ways

1. Right-click range, click Format Cells on shortcut menu, click Number tab (Format Cells dialog box), click Percentage
2. Press CTRL+1, click Number tab (Format Cells dialog box), click Percentage
   in Category list, select format, click OK button
   in Category list, select format, click OK button
3. Press CTRL+SHIFT+ percent sign (%)

Conditional Formatting

The next step is to emphasize the values greater than 70 in column D by formatting them to appear with an orange background and white font color (Figure 2–48).

Plan Ahead

> **Establish rules for conditional formatting.**
>
> • Excel lets you apply formatting that appears only when the value in a cell meets conditions that you specify. This type of formatting is called **conditional formatting**. You can apply conditional formatting to a cell, a range of cells, the entire worksheet, or the entire workbook. Usually, you apply conditional formatting to a range of cells that contains values you want to highlight, if conditions warrant.
>
> • A **condition**, which is made up of two values and a relational operator, is true or false for each cell in the range. If the condition is true, then Excel applies the formatting. If the condition is false, then Excel suppresses the formatting. What makes conditional formatting so powerful is that the cell's appearance can change as you enter new values in the worksheet.
>
> • As with worksheet formatting, follow the less-is-more rule when considering conditional formatting. Use conditional formatting to make cells and ranges stand out and raise attention. Too much conditional formatting can result in confusion for the reader of the worksheet.

Conditional Formatting
You can assign any format to a cell, a range of cells, a worksheet, or an entire workbook conditionally. If the value of the cell changes and no longer meets the specified condition, Excel suppresses the conditional formatting.

To Apply Conditional Formatting

The following steps assign conditional formatting to the range D4:D12, so that any cell value greater than 70 will cause Excel to display the number in the cell with an orange background and a white font color.

1

• Select the range D4:D12.

• Click the Conditional Formatting button (Home tab | Styles group) to display the Conditional Formatting list (Figure 2–48).

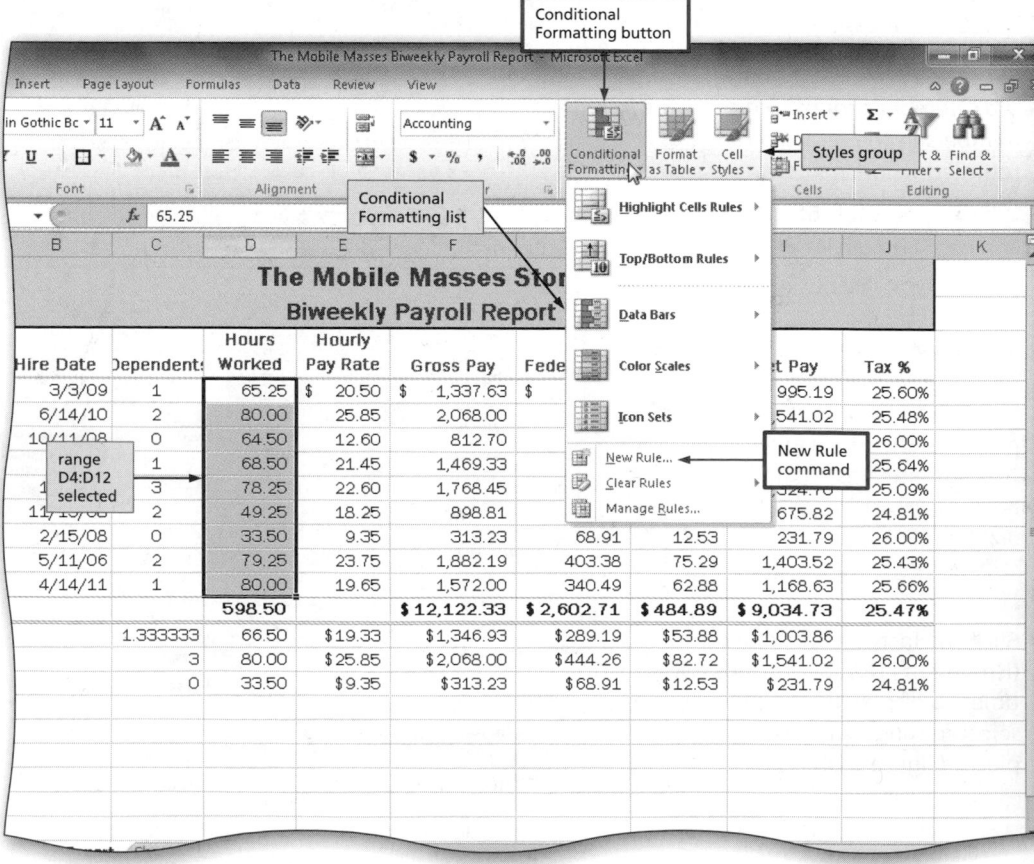

Figure 2–48

2

- Click New Rule in the Conditional Formatting list to display the New Formatting Rule dialog box.

- Click 'Format only cells that contain' in the Select a Rule Type area (New Formatting Rule dialog box) to change the 'Edit the Rule Description' area.

- In the 'Edit the Rule Description' area, click the box arrow in the relational operator box (second text box) to display a list of relational operators, and then select greater than to select the desired operator.

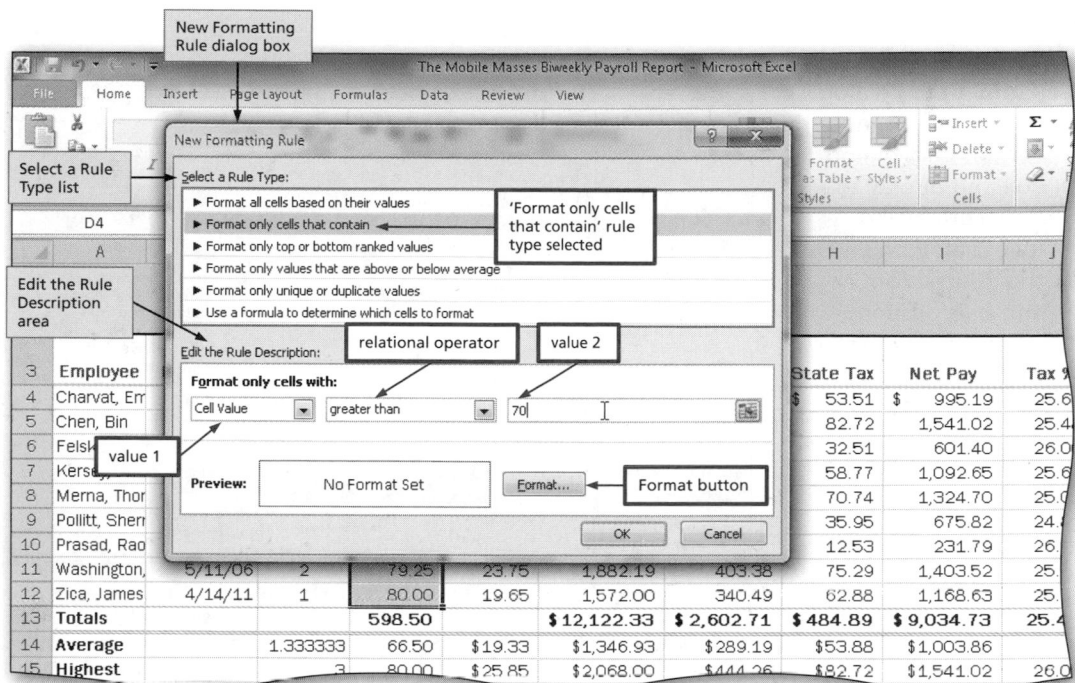

Figure 2–49

- Select the rightmost box, and then type 70 in the box in the 'Edit the Rule Description' area to enter the second value of the rule description (Figure 2–49).

What do the changes in the 'Edit the Rule Description' indicate?

The 'Edit the Rule Description' area allows you to view and edit the rules for the conditional format. In this case, reading the area indicates that Excel should conditionally format only cells with cell values greater than 70.

3

- Click the Format button (New Formatting Rule dialog box) to display the Format Cells dialog box.

- If necessary, click the Font tab. Click the Color box arrow (Format Cells dialog box) to display the Color gallery and then click White, Background 1 (column 1, row 1) in the Color gallery to select the font color.

- Click the Fill tab (Format Cells dialog box) to display the Fill sheet and then click the orange color in column 5, row 5 to select the background color (Figure 2–50).

Figure 2–50

- Click the OK button (Format Cells dialog box) to close the Format Cells dialog box and display the New Formatting Rule dialog box with the desired font and background colors displayed in the Preview box (Figure 2–51).

Figure 2–51

- Click the OK button to assign the conditional format to the selected range.

- Click anywhere in the worksheet, such as cell A18, to deselect the current range (Figure 2–52).

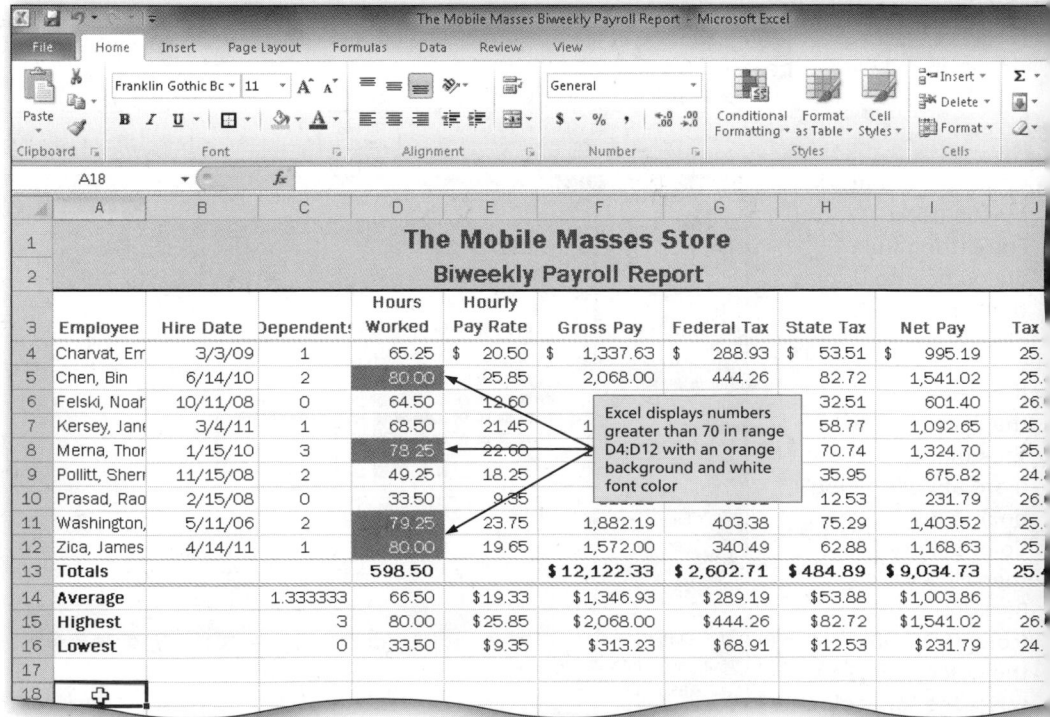

Figure 2–52

Conditional Formatting Operators

As shown in Figure 2–49 on page EX 105, the second text box in the New Formatting Rule dialog box allows you to select a relational operator, such as less than, to use in the condition. The eight different relational operators from which you can choose for conditional formatting in the New Formatting Rule dialog box are summarized in Table 2–5.

Table 2–5 Summary of Conditional Formatting Relational Operators	
Relational Operator	**Description**
between	Cell value is between two numbers.
not between	Cell value is not between two numbers.
equal to	Cell value is equal to a number.
not equal to	Cell value is not equal to a number.
greater than	Cell value is greater than a number.
less than	Cell value is less than a number.
greater than or equal to	Cell value is greater than or equal to a number.
less than or equal to	Cell value is less than or equal to a number.

Changing the Widths of Columns and Heights of Rows

When Excel starts and displays a blank worksheet on the screen, all of the columns have a default width of 8.43 characters, or 64 pixels. These values may change depending on the theme applied to the workbook. For example, in this chapter, the Trek theme was applied to the workbook, resulting in columns having a default width of 8.11 characters. A character is defined as a letter, number, symbol, or punctuation mark in 11-point Calibri font, the default font used by Excel. An average of 8.43 characters in 11-point Calibri font will fit in a cell.

Another measure of the height and width of cells is pixels, which is short for picture element. A **pixel** is a dot on the screen that contains a color. The size of the dot is based on your screen's resolution. At the resolution of 1024 x 768 used in this book, 1024 pixels appear across the screen and 768 pixels appear down the screen for a total of 786,432 pixels. It is these 786,432 pixels that form the font and other items you see on the screen.

The default row height in a blank worksheet is 15 points (or 20 pixels). Recall from Chapter 1 that a point is equal to 1/72 of an inch. Thus, 15 points is equal to about 1/5 of an inch. You can change the width of the columns or height of the rows at any time to make the worksheet easier to read or to ensure that Excel displays an entry properly in a cell.

BTW

Hidden Rows and Columns
For some people, trying to unhide a range of columns using the mouse can be frustrating. An alternative is to use the keyboard: select the columns to the right and left of the hidden columns and then press CTRL+SHIFT+) (RIGHT PARENTHESIS). To use the keyboard to hide a range of columns, press CTRL+0 (ZERO). You also can use the keyboard to unhide a range of rows by selecting the rows immediately above and below the hidden rows and then pressing CTRL+SHIFT+((LEFT PARENTHESIS). To use the keyboard to hide a range of rows, press CTRL+9.

To Change the Widths of Columns

When changing the column width, you can set the width manually or you can instruct Excel to size the column to best fit. **Best fit** means that the width of the column will be increased or decreased so that the widest entry will fit in the column. Sometimes, you may prefer more or less white space in a column than best fit provides. To change the white space, Excel allows you to change column widths manually.

When the format you assign to a cell causes the entry to exceed the width of a column, Excel automatically changes the column width to best fit. If you do not assign a format to a cell or cells in a column, the column width will remain 8.43 characters. To set a column width to best fit, double-click the right boundary of the column heading above row 1.

The steps on the following pages change the column widths: column A, B, and C to best fit; column H to 10.22 characters; and columns D, E, and J to 7.56 characters.

1

- Drag through column headings A, B, and C above row 1 to select the columns.

- Point to the boundary on the right side of column heading C to cause the mouse pointer to become a split double arrow (Figure 2–53).

Q&A

What if I want to make a large change to the column width?

If you want to increase or decrease column width significantly, you can right-click a column heading and then use the Column Width command on the shortcut menu to change the column's width. To use this command, however, you must select one or more entire columns.

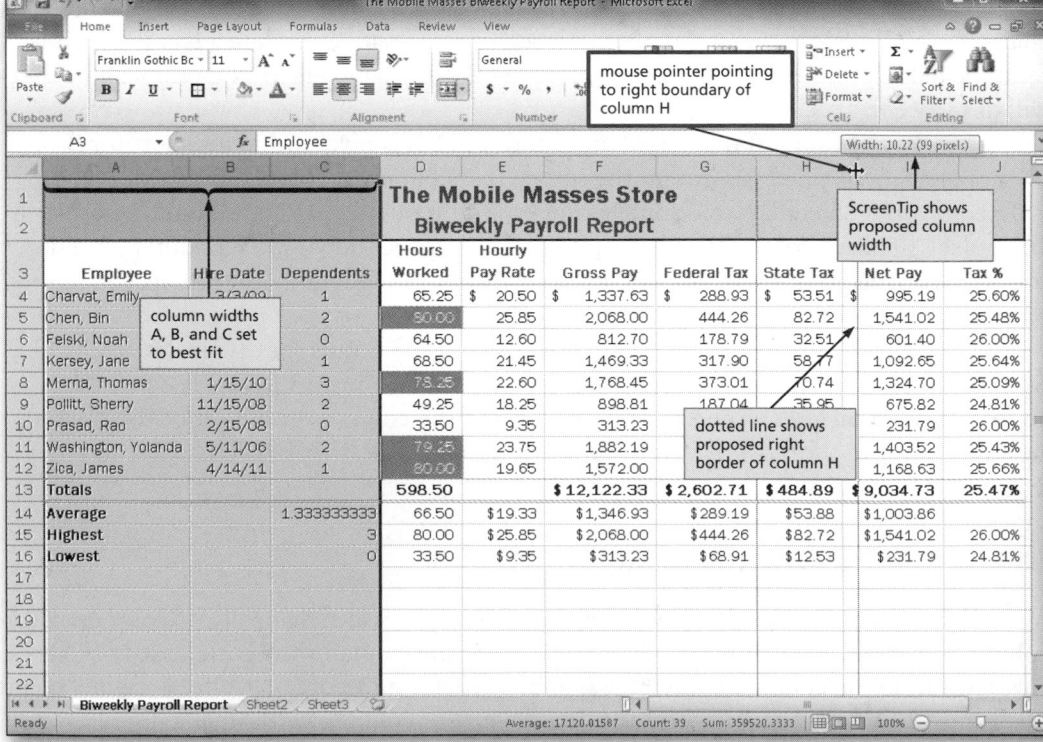

Figure 2–53

2

- Double-click the right boundary of column heading C to change the width of the selected columns to best fit.

- Point to the boundary on the right side of the column H heading above row 1.

- When the mouse pointer changes to a split double arrow, drag until the ScreenTip indicates Width: 10.22 (99 pixels). Do not release the mouse button (Figure 2–54).

Q&A

What happens if I change the column width to zero (0)?

If you decrease the column width to 0, the column is hidden. **Hiding cells** is a technique you can use to hide data that might not be relevant to a particular report or sensitive data that you do not want others to see. To instruct Excel to display a hidden column, position the mouse pointer to the right of the column heading boundary where the hidden column is located and then drag to the right.

Figure 2–54

3

- Release the mouse button to change the column width.

- Click the column D heading above row 1 to select the column.

- While holding down the CTRL key, click the column E heading and then the column J heading above row 1 so that nonadjacent columns are selected (Figure 2–55).

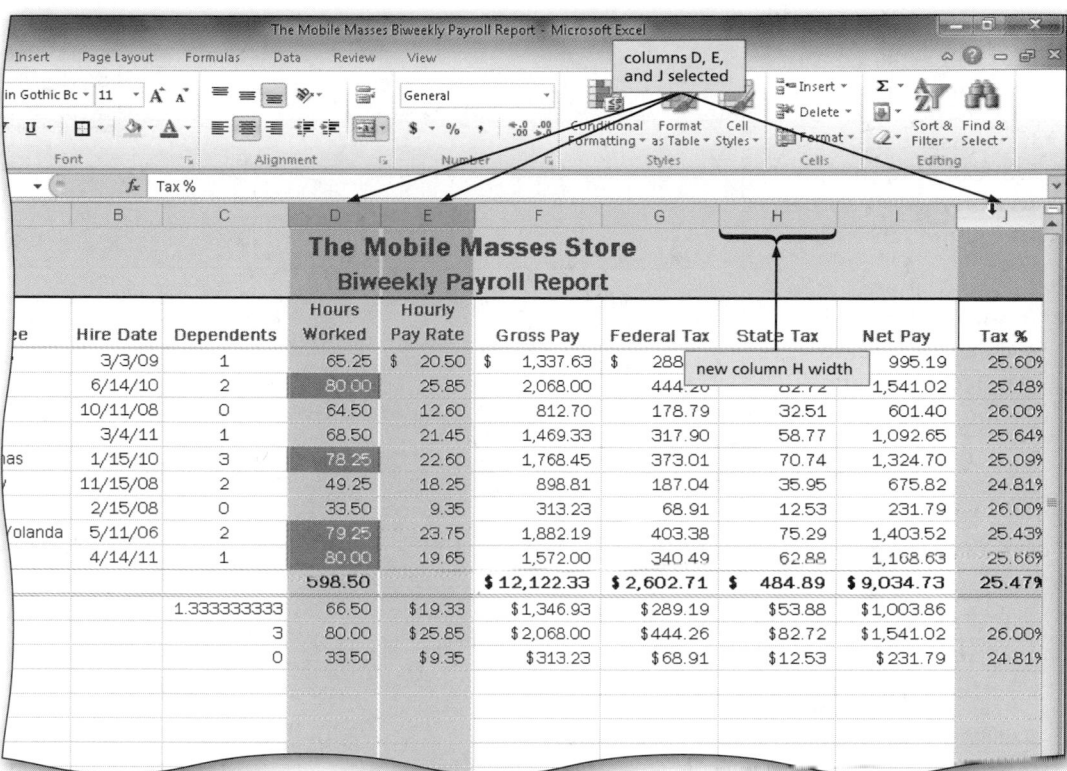

Figure 2–55

4

- If necessary, scroll the worksheet to the right so that the right border of column J is visible. Point to the boundary on the right side of the column J heading above row 1.

- Drag until the ScreenTip indicates Width: 7.56 (75 pixels). Do not release the mouse button (Figure 2–56).

Figure 2–56

- Release the mouse button to change the column widths.

- If necessary, scroll the worksheet to the left so that the left border of column A is visible.

- Click anywhere in the worksheet, such as cell A18, to deselect the columns (Figure 2–57).

Other Ways

1. Right-click column heading or drag through multiple column headings and right-click, click Column Width on shortcut menu, enter desired column width, click OK button

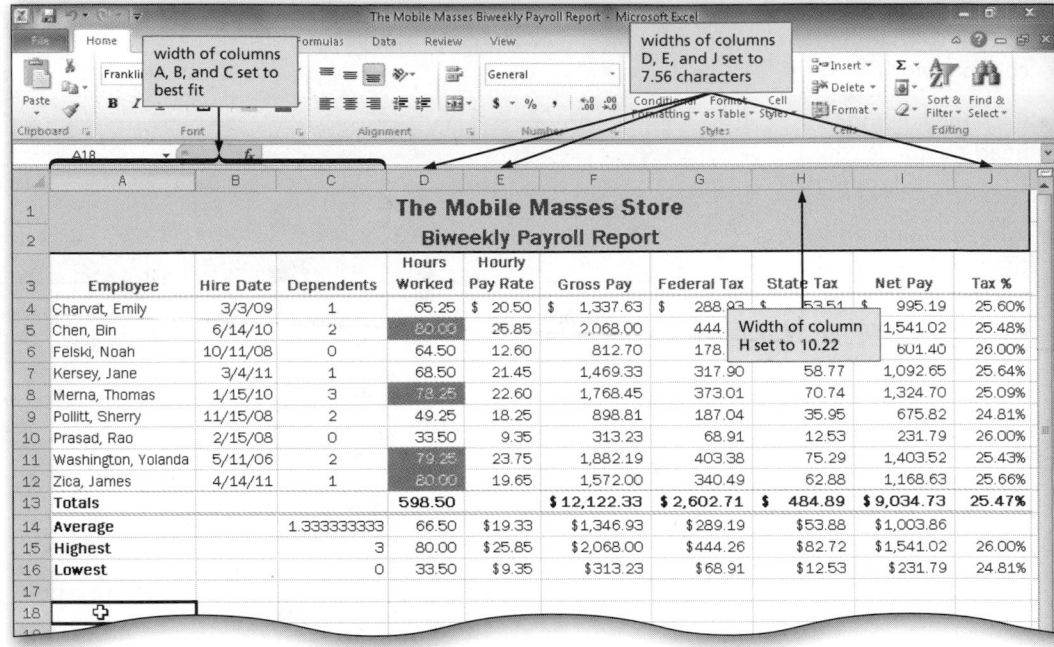

Figure 2–57

To Change the Heights of Rows

When you increase the font size of a cell entry, such as the title in cell A1, Excel automatically increases the row height to best fit so that it can display the characters properly. Recall that Excel did this earlier when multiple lines were entered in a cell in row 3, and when the cell style of the worksheet title and subtitle was changed.

You also can increase or decrease the height of a row manually to improve the appearance of the worksheet. The following steps improve the appearance of the worksheet by increasing the height of row 3 to 48.00 points and increasing the height of row 14 to 27.00 points.

- Point to the boundary below row heading 3.

- Drag down until the ScreenTip indicates Height: 48.00 (64 pixels). Do not release the mouse button (Figure 2–58).

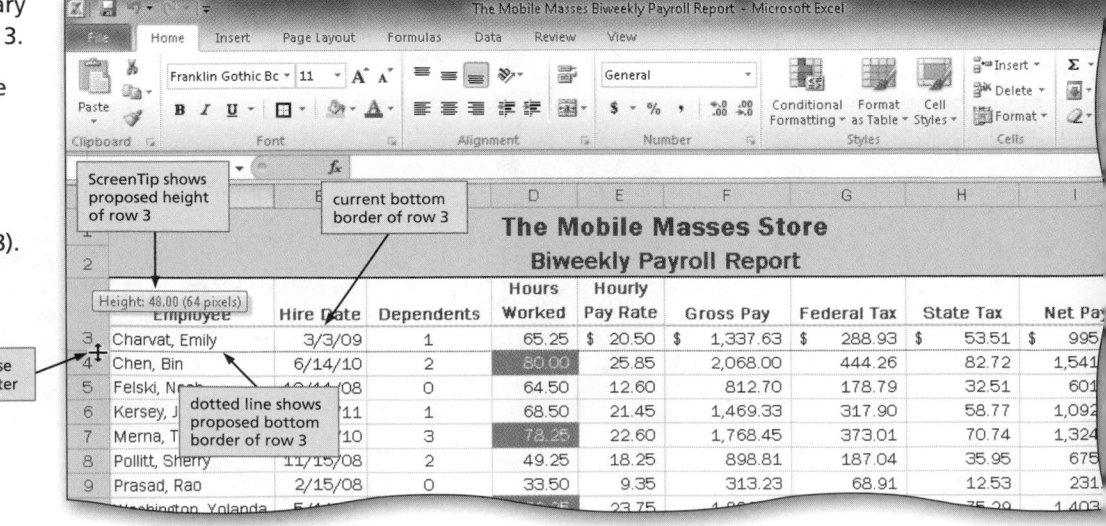

Figure 2–58

2

- Release the mouse button to change the row height.

- Point to the boundary below row heading 14.

- Drag down until the ScreenTip indicates Height: 27.00 (36 pixels). Do not release the mouse button (Figure 2–59).

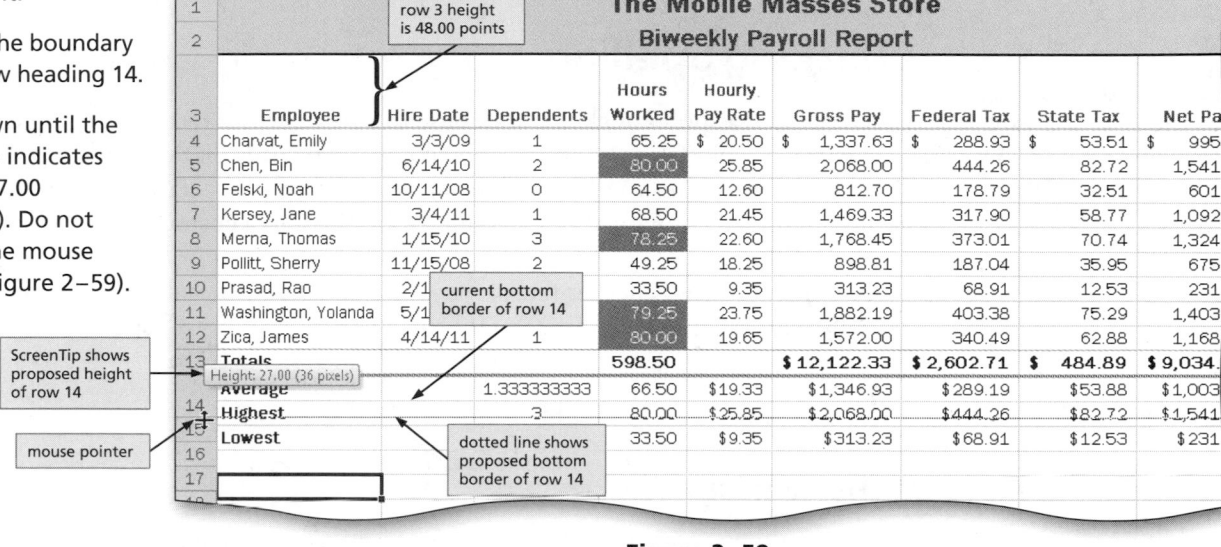

Figure 2–59

3

- Release the mouse button to change the row height.

- Click anywhere in the worksheet, such as cell A18, to deselect the current cell (Figure 2–60).

Can I hide a row?

Yes. As with column widths, when you decrease the row height to 0, the row is hidden. To instruct Excel to display a hidden row, position the mouse pointer just below the row heading boundary where the row is hidden and then drag down. To set a row height to best fit, double-click the bottom boundary of the row heading.

Figure 2–60

Other Ways

1. Right-click row heading or drag through multiple row headings and right-click, click Row Height | on shortcut menu, enter desired row height, click OK button

Break Point: If you wish to take a break, this is a good place to do so. Be sure to save the The Mobile Masses Biweekly Payroll Report file again and then you can quit Excel. To resume at a later time, start Excel, open the file called The Mobile Masses Biweekly Payroll Report and continue following the steps from this location forward.

BTW

Spell Checking
While Excel's spell checker is a valuable tool, it is not infallible. You should proofread your workbook carefully by pointing to each word and saying it aloud as you point to it. Be mindful of misused words such as its and it's, through and though, and to and too. Nothing undermines a good impression more than a professional looking report with misspelled words.

Checking Spelling

Excel includes a **spell checker** you can use to check a worksheet for spelling errors. The spell checker looks for spelling errors by comparing words on the worksheet against words contained in its standard dictionary. If you often use specialized terms that are not in the standard dictionary, you may want to add them to a custom dictionary using the Spelling dialog box.

When the spell checker finds a word that is not in either dictionary, it displays the word in the Spelling dialog box. You then can correct it if it is misspelled.

To Check Spelling on the Worksheet

To illustrate how Excel responds to a misspelled word, the following steps misspell purposely the word, Employee, in cell A3 as the word, Empolyee, as shown in Figure 2–61.

1
- Click cell A3 and then type **Empolyee** to misspell the word Employee.

- Select cell A1 so that the spell checker begins checking at the selected cell.

- Click Review on the Ribbon to display the Review tab.

- Click the Spelling button (Review tab | Proofing group) to run the spell checker and display the misspelled word in the Spelling dialog box (Figure 2–61).

Figure 2–61

Q&A

What happens when the spell checker finds a misspelled word?

When the spell checker identifies that a cell contains a word not in its standard or custom dictionary, it selects that cell as the active cell and displays the Spelling dialog box. The Spelling dialog box lists the word not found in the dictionary and a list of suggested corrections (Figure 2–61).

2

- Click the Change button (Spelling dialog box) to change the misspelled word to the correct word (Figure 2–62).

- Click the Close button (Spelling dialog box) to close the Spelling dialog box.

- If the Microsoft Excel dialog box is displayed, click the OK button.

3

- Click anywhere in the worksheet, such as cell A18, to deselect the current cell.

- Display the Home tab.

- Click the Save button on the Quick Access Toolbar to save the workbook.

Figure 2–62

What other actions can I take in the Spelling dialog box?

If one of the words in the Suggestions list is correct, click it and then click the Change button. If none of the suggestions is correct, type the correct word in the Not in Dictionary text box and then click the Change button. To change the word throughout the worksheet, click the Change All button instead of the Change button. To skip correcting the word, click the Ignore Once button. To have Excel ignore the word for the remainder of the worksheet, click the Ignore All button.

Other Ways
1. Press F7

Additional Spell Checker Considerations

Consider these additional guidelines when using the spell checker:

- To check the spelling of the text in a single cell, double-click the cell to make the formula bar active and then click the Spelling button (Review tab | Proofing group).

- If you select a single cell so that the formula bar is not active and then start the spell checker, Excel checks the remainder of the worksheet, including notes and embedded charts.

- If you select a cell other than cell A1 before you start the spell checker, Excel will display a dialog box when the spell checker reaches the end of the worksheet, asking if you want to continue checking at the beginning.

- If you select a range of cells before starting the spell checker, Excel checks the spelling of the words only in the selected range.

- To check the spelling of all the sheets in a workbook, right-click any sheet tab, click Select All Sheets on the sheet tab shortcut menu, and then start the spell checker.

- To add words to the dictionary such as your last name, click the Add to Dictionary button in the Spelling dialog box (Figure 2–61) when Excel identifies the word as not in the dictionary.

- Click the AutoCorrect button (Spelling dialog box) to add the misspelled word and the correct version of the word to the AutoCorrect list. For example, suppose that you misspell the word, do, as the word, dox. When the spell checker displays the Spelling dialog box with the correct word, do, in the Change to box, click the AutoCorrect button. Then, anytime in the future that you type the word dox, Excel automatically will change it to the word, do.

BTW

Error Checking
Always take the time to check the formulas of a worksheet before submitting it to your supervisor. You can check formulas by clicking the Error Checking button (Formulas tab | Formula Auditing group). You also should test the formulas by employing data that tests the limits of formulas. Experienced spreadsheet specialists spend as much time testing a workbook as they do creating it, and they do so before placing the workbook into production.

Changing the Header and Footer Size
To make a header or footer include more lines of text, change the top or bottom margin for the worksheet and then add the necessary lines of text to the header or footer. To make a header or footer wider, continue typing text in the header or footer area and the header or footer automatically will widen to accommodate the text. If text from adjacent header or footer areas overlaps, Excel displays the overlapped text, which will appear unreadable.

Preparing to Print the Worksheet

Excel allows for a great deal of customization in how a worksheet appears when printed. For example, the margins on the page can be adjusted. A header or footer can be added to each printed page as well. Excel also has the capability to work on the worksheet in Page Layout view. **Page Layout view** allows you to create or modify a worksheet while viewing how it will look in printed format. The default view that you have worked in up until this point in the book is called **Normal view**.

Plan Ahead

Specify how the printed worksheet should appear.

Before printing a worksheet, you should consider how the worksheet will appear when printed. In order to fit as much information on the printed page as possible, the margins of the worksheet should be set to a reasonably small width and height. While the current version of a worksheet may print on one page, you may add more data in the future that causes the worksheet to extend to multiple pages. It is, therefore, a good idea to add a page header to the worksheet that prints in the top margin of each page. A **header** is common content that prints on every page of a worksheet. Landscape orientation is a good choice for large worksheets because the printed worksheet's width is greater than its length.

To Change the Worksheet's Margins, Header, and Orientation in Page Layout View

The following steps change to Page Layout view, narrow the margins of the worksheet, change the header of the worksheet, and set the orientation of the worksheet to landscape. Often, you may want to reduce margins so that the printed worksheet better fits the page. **Margins** are those portions of a printed page outside the main body of the printed document and always are blank when printed. Recall that in Chapter 1, the worksheet was printed in landscape orientation. The current worksheet also is too wide for a single page and requires landscape orientation to fit on one page in a readable manner.

1

- Click the Page Layout button on the status bar to view the worksheet in Page Layout view (Figure 2–63).

Q&A

What are some key features of Page Layout view?

Page Layout view shows the worksheet divided into pages. A gray background separates each page. The white areas surrounding each page indicate the print margins. The top of each page includes a Header area, and the bottom of each page includes a Footer area. Page Layout view also includes a ruler at the top of the page that assists you in placing objects on the page, such as charts and pictures.

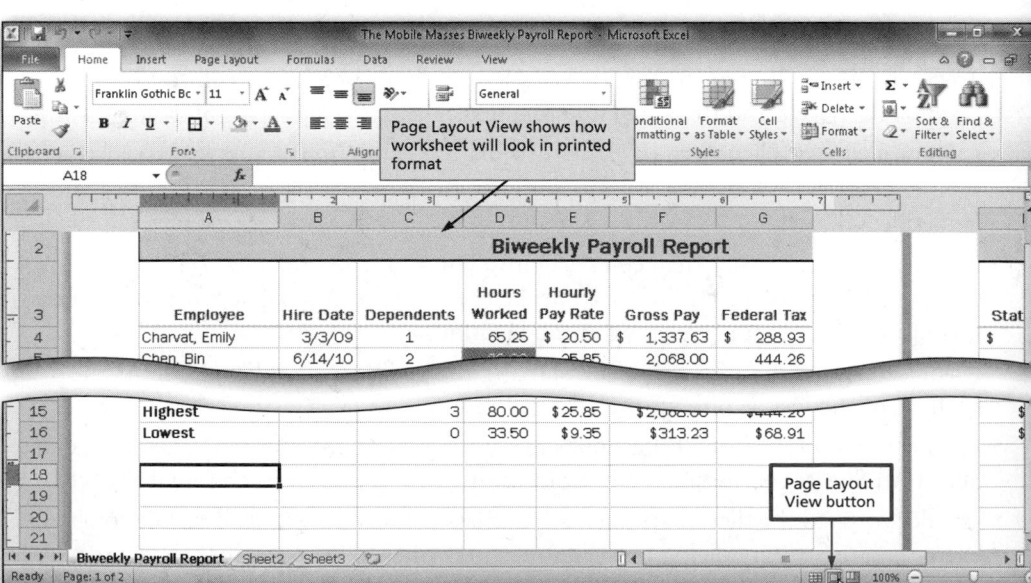

Figure 2–63

2

- Display the Page Layout tab.

- Click the Margins button (Page Layout tab | Page Setup group) to display the Margins gallery (Figure 2–64).

Figure 2–64

3

- Click Narrow in the Margins gallery to change the worksheet margins to the Narrow margin style.

- Drag the scroll bar on the right side of the worksheet to the top so that row 1 of the worksheet is displayed.

- Click above the worksheet title in cell A1 in the center area of the Header area.

- Type **Samuel Snyder** and then press the ENTER key. Type **Chief Financial Officer** to complete the worksheet header (Figure 2–65).

Figure 2–65

What else can I place in a header?

You can add text, page number information, date and time information, the file path of the workbook, the file name of the workbook, the sheet name of the workbook, and pictures to a header.

4

- Select cell B16 to deselect the header. Click the Orientation button (Page Layout tab | Page Setup group) to display the Orientation gallery (Figure 2–66).

Q&A

Why do I need to deselect the header?

Excel disables almost all of the buttons on the Ribbon as you edit a header or footer. In addition to the commands on the Design tab (Figure 2–65 on the previous page), only a few commands remain available on the Home tab on the Ribbon. To continue working in Excel, therefore, you should select a cell in the worksheet so that all of the commands on the Ribbon are available for your use.

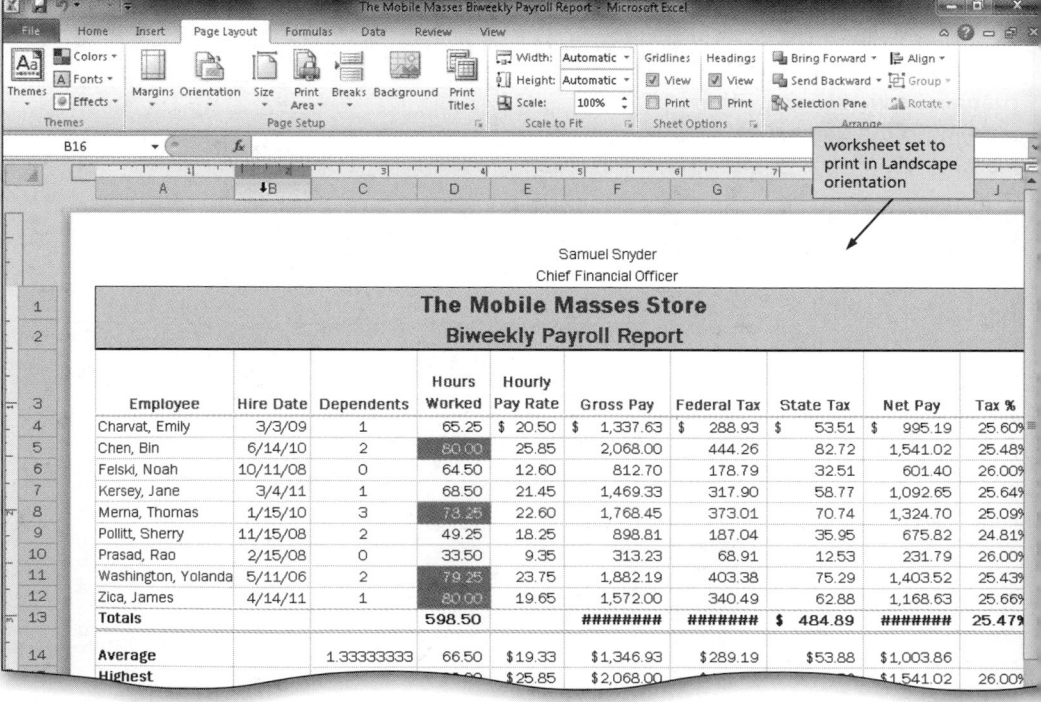

Figure 2–66

5

- Click Landscape in the Orientation gallery to change the worksheet's orientation to landscape (Figure 2–67).

Q&A

Do I need to change the orientation every time I want to print the worksheet?

No. Once you change the orientation and save the workbook, Excel will save the orientation setting for that workbook until you change it. When you open a new workbook, Excel sets the orientation to portrait.

Figure 2–67

Other Ways

1. Click Page Setup Dialog Box Launcher (Page Layout tab | Page Setup group), click Page tab (Page Setup dialog box), click Portrait or Landscape, click OK button

Printing the Worksheet

Excel provides other options for printing a worksheet. The following sections print the worksheet and print a section of the worksheet.

To Print a Worksheet

The following steps print the worksheet.

1 Click File on the Ribbon to open the Backstage view.

2 Click the Print tab in the Backstage view to display the Print gallery.

3 If necessary, click the Printer Status button in the Print gallery to display a list of available Printer options and then click the desired printer to change the currently selected printer.

4 Click the Print button in the Print gallery to print the worksheet in landscape orientation on the currently selected printer.

5 When the printer stops, retrieve the hard copy (Figure 2–68).

landscape orientation

Samuel Snyder
Chief Financial Officer

The Mobile Masses Store
Biweekly Payroll Report

Employee	Hire Date	Dependents	Hours Worked	Hourly Pay Rate	Gross Pay	Federal Tax	State Tax	Net Pay	Tax %
Charvat, Emily	3/3/09	1	65.25	$ 20.50	$ 1,337.63	$ 288.93	$ 53.51	$ 995.19	25.60%
Chen, Bin	6/14/10	2	80.00	25.85	2,068.00	444.26	82.72	1,541.02	25.48%
Felski, Noah	10/11/08	0	64.50	12.60	812.70	178.79	32.51	601.40	26.00%
Kersey, Jane	3/4/11	1	68.50	21.45	1,469.33	317.90	58.77	1,092.65	26.01%
Merna, Thomas	1/15/10	3	70.25	22.00	1,768.45	373.01	70.74	1,324.70	25.09%
Pollitt, Sherry	11/15/08	2	49.25	18.25	898.81	187.04	35.95	675.82	24.81%
Prasad, Rao	2/15/08	0	33.50	9.35	313.23	68.91	12.53	231.79	26.00%
Washington, Yolanda	5/11/06	2	79.25	23.75	1,882.19	403.38	75.29	1,403.52	25.43%
Zica, James	4/14/11	1	80.00	19.65	1,572.00	340.49	62.88	1,168.63	25.66%
Totals			598.50		$ 12,122.33	$ 2,602.71	$ 484.89	$ 9,034.73	25.47%
Average		1.333333333	66.50	$19.33	$1,346.93	$289.19	$53.88	$1,003.86	
Highest		3	80.00	$25.85	$2,068.00	$444.26	$82.72	$1,541.02	26.00%
Lowest		0	33.50	$9.35	$313.23	$68.91	$12.53	$231.79	24.81%

Figure 2–68

Conserving Ink and Toner
If you want to conserve ink or toner, you can instruct Excel to print draft quality documents by clicking File on the Ribbon to open the Backstage view, clicking Options in the Backstage view to display the Excel Options dialog box, clicking Advanced in the left pane (Excel Options dialog box), scrolling to the Print area in the right pane, placing a check mark in the 'Use draft quality' check box, and then clicking the OK button. Then, use the Backstage view to print the document as usual.

Printing Headers
Excel allows you to create different page headers for the first page of a printed worksheet and for even and odd pages of a printed worksheet. To create a custom page header for the first page or even and odd pages, select the 'Different odd and even pages' check box or the 'Different first page' check box in the Header/Footer tab of the Page Setup dialog box. When editing page headers and footers in Page Layout view, Excel will indicate whether you are editing a first page, odd page, or even page header or footer.

Printing Document Properties
To print document properties, click File on the Ribbon to open the Backstage view, click the Print tab in the Backstage view to display the Print gallery, click the first button in the Settings area to display a list of options specifying what you can print, click Document Properties in the list to specify you want to print the document properties instead of the actual document, and then click the Print button in the Print gallery to print the document properties on the currently selected printer.

To Print a Section of the Worksheet

You might not always want to print the entire worksheet. You can print portions of the worksheet by selecting the range of cells to print and then clicking the Selection option button in the Print what area in the Print dialog box. The following steps print the range A3:F16.

- Select the range to print, cells A3:F16 in this case.

- Click File on the Ribbon to open the Backstage view.

- Click the Print tab to display the Print gallery.

- Click Print Active Sheets in the Settings area (Print tab | Print gallery) to display a list of options that determine what Excel should print (Figure 2–69).

Figure 2–69

- Click Print Selection to instruct Excel to print only the selected range.

- Click the Print button in the Print gallery to print the selected range of the worksheet on the currently selected printer (Figure 2–70).

- Click the Normal button on the status bar to return to Normal view.

- Click cell A18 to deselect the range A3:F16.

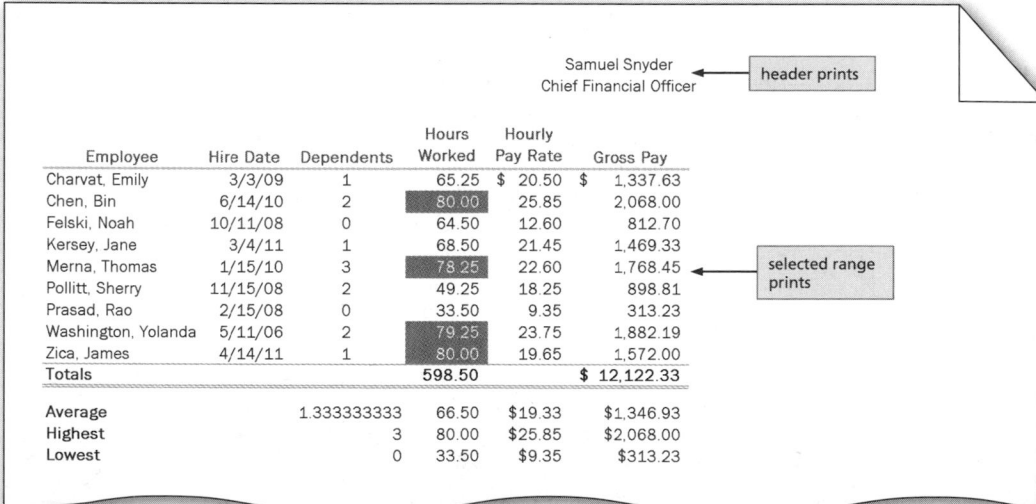

Figure 2–70

Q&A

What are my options for telling Excel what to print?

Excel includes three options to allow you to determine what should be printed (Figure 2–69). As shown in the previous steps, the Print Selection button instructs Excel to print the selected range. The Print Active Sheets button instructs Excel to print the active worksheet (the worksheet currently on the screen) or the selected worksheets. Finally, the Print Entire Workbook button instructs Excel to print all of the worksheets in the workbook.

Other Ways

1. Select range, click Print Area button (Page Layout tab | Page Setup group), click Set Print Area, click Quick Print button on Quick Access Toolbar, click Print Area, click Clear Print Area

2. Select range, click Print Area button (Page Layout tab | Page Setup group), click Set Print Area, click File tab to open Backstage view, click Print tab, click Print button

Displaying and Printing the Formulas Version of the Worksheet

Thus far, you have been working with the **values version** of the worksheet, which shows the results of the formulas you have entered, rather than the actual formulas. Excel also can display and print the **formulas version** of the worksheet, which shows the actual formulas you have entered, rather than the resulting values.

The formulas version is useful for debugging a worksheet. **Debugging** is the process of finding and correcting errors in the worksheet. Viewing and printing the formulas version instead of the values version makes it easier to see any mistakes in the formulas.

When you change from the values version to the formulas version, Excel increases the width of the columns so that the formulas and text do not overflow into adjacent cells on the right. The formulas version of the worksheet, thus, usually is significantly wider than the values version. To fit the wide printout on one page, you can use landscape orientation, which has already been selected for the workbook, and the Fit to option in the Page sheet in the Page Setup dialog box.

BTW

Values versus Formulas
When completing class assignments, do not enter numbers in cells that require formulas. Most instructors will check both the values version and formulas version of your worksheets. The formulas version verifies that you entered formulas, rather than numbers, in formula-based cells.

To Display the Formulas in the Worksheet and Fit the Printout on One Page

The following steps change the view of the worksheet from the values version to the formulas version of the worksheet and then print the formulas version on one page.

1
- Press CTRL+ACCENT MARK (`) to display the worksheet with formulas.

- Click the right horizontal scroll arrow until column J appears (Figure 2–71).

2
- Click the Page Setup Dialog Box Launcher (Page Layout tab | Page Setup group) to display the Page Setup dialog box.

Figure 2–71

3
- If necessary, click Landscape in the Orientation area to select it.

- If necessary, click Fit to in the Scaling area to select it.

4

- Click the Print button (Page Setup dialog box) to print the formulas in the worksheet on one page in landscape orientation (Figure 2–72). If necessary, in the Backstage view, select the Print Active Sheets option in the Settings area of the Print gallery.

- When Excel displays the Backstage view, click the Print button to print the worksheet.

Samuel Snyder
Chief Financial Officer

The Mobile Masses Store
Biweekly Payroll Report

Employee	Hire Date	Dependents	Hours Worked	Hourly Pay Rate	Gross Pay	Federal Tax	State Tax	Net Pay	Tax %
Charvat, Emily	39875	1	65.25	20.5	=D4*E4	=0.22*(F4-C4*24.32)	=0.04*F4	=F4-(G4+H4)	=(G4+H4)/F4
Chen, Bin	40343	2	68	25.85	=D5*E5	=0.22*(F5-C5*24.32)	=0.04*F5	=F5-(G5+H5)	=(G5+H5)/F5
Felski, Noah	39732	0	64.5	12.6	=D6*E6	=0.22*(F6-C6*24.32)	=0.04*F6	=F6-(G6+H6)	=(G6+H6)/F6
Kersey, Jane	40606	1	68.5	21.45	=D7*E7	=0.22*(F7-C7*24.32)	=0.04*F7	=F7-(G7+H7)	=(G7+H7)/F7
Merna, Thomas	40193	3	22.25	22.6	=D8*E8	=0.22*(F8-C8*24.32)	=0.04*F8	=F8-(G8+H8)	=(G8+H8)/F8
Pollitt, Sherry	39767	2	49.25	18.25	=D9*E9	=0.22*(F9-C9*24.32)	=0.04*F9	=F9-(G9+H9)	=(G9+H9)/F9
Prasad, Rao	39493	0	33.5	9.35	=D10*E10	=0.22*(F10-C10*24.32)	=0.04*F10	=F10-(G10+H10)	=(G10+H10)/F10
Washington, Yolanda	38848	2	79.25	23.75	=D11*E11	=0.22*(F11-C11*24.32)	=0.04*F11	=F11-(G11+H11)	=(G11+H11)/F11
Zica, James	40647	1	80	19.65	=D12*E12	=0.22*(F12-C12*24.32)	=0.04*F12	=F12-(G12+H12)	=(G12+H12)/F12
Totals			=SUM(D4:D12)		=SUM(F4:F12)	=SUM(G4:G12)	=SUM(H4:H12)	=SUM(I4:I12)	=(G13+H13)/F13
Average	=AVERAGE(C4:C12)	=AVERAGE(D4:D12)	=AVERAGE(E4:E12)	=AVERAGE(F4:F12)	=AVERAGE(G4:G12)	=AVERAGE(H4:H12)	=AVERAGE(I4:I12)	
Highest	=MAX(C4:C12)	=MAX(D4:D12)	=MAX(E4:E12)	=MAX(F4:F12)	=MAX(G4:G12)	=MAX(H4:H12)	=MAX(I4:I12)	=MAX(J4:J12)
Lowest	=MIN(C4:C12)	=MIN(D4:D12)	=MIN(E4:E12)	=MIN(F4:F12)	=MIN(G4:G12)	=MIN(H4:H12)	=MIN(I4:I12)	=MIN(J4:J12)

formulas instead of values printed

font size automatically reduced so that worksheet fits on one page

Figure 2–72

5

- After viewing and printing the formulas version, press CTRL+ACCENT MARK (`) to instruct Excel to display the values version.

- Click the left horizontal scroll arrow until column A appears.

To Change the Print Scaling Option Back to 100%

Depending on your printer, you may have to change the Print Scaling option back to 100% after using the Fit to option. Doing so will cause the worksheet to print at the default print scaling of 100%. The following steps reset the Print Scaling option so that future worksheets print at 100%, instead of being resized to print on one page.

1 If necessary, display the Page Layout tab and then click the Page Setup Dialog Box Launcher (Page Layout tab | Page Setup group) to display the Page Setup dialog box.

2 Click Adjust to in the Scaling area to select the Adjust to setting.

3 If necessary, type 100 in the Adjust to box to adjust the print scaling to a new percentage.

Click the OK button (Page Setup dialog box) to set the print scaling to normal.

Display the Home tab.

What is the purpose of the Adjust to box in the Page Setup dialog box?

The Adjust to box allows you to specify the percentage of reduction or enlargement in the printout of a worksheet. The default percentage is 100%. When you click the Fit to option, this percentage automatically changes to the percentage required to fit the printout on one page.

Quick Reference
For a table that lists how to complete the tasks covered in this book using the mouse, Ribbon, shortcut menu, and keyboard, see the Quick Reference Summary at the back of this book, or visit the Excel 2010 Quick Reference Web page (scsite.com/ex2010/qr).

BTW

To Save the Workbook and Quit Excel

With the workbook complete, the following steps save the workbook and quit Excel.

Click the Save button on the Quick Access Toolbar.

Click the Close button on the upper-right corner of the title bar.

Chapter Summary

In this chapter you have learned how to enter formulas, calculate an average, find the highest and lowest numbers in a range, verify formulas using Range Finder, added borders, align text, format numbers, change column widths and row heights, and add conditional formatting to a range of numbers. In addition, you learned to spell check a worksheet, print a section of a worksheet, and display and print the formulas version of the worksheet using the Fit to option. The items listed below include all the new Excel skills you have learned in this chapter.

1. Enter a Formula Using the Keyboard (EX 75)
2. Enter Formulas Using Point Mode (EX 77)
3. Copy Formulas Using the Fill Handle (EX 80)
4. Determine the Average of a Range of Numbers Using the Keyboard and Mouse (EX 84)
5. Determine the Highest Number in a Range of Numbers Using the Insert Function Box (EX 86)
6. Determine the Lowest Number in a Range of Numbers Using the Sum Menu (EX 87)
7. Copy a Range of Cells Across Columns to an Adjacent Range Using the Fill Handle (EX 89)
8. Verify a Formula Using Range Finder (EX 91)
9. Change the Workbook Theme (EX 94)
10. Change the Background Color and Apply a Box Border to the Worksheet Title and Subtitle (EX 96)
11. Format Dates and Center Data in Cells (EX 98)
12. Apply an Accounting Number Format and Comma Style Format Using the Ribbon (EX 100)
13. Apply a Currency Style Format with a Floating Dollar Sign Using the Format Cells Dialog Box (EX 102)
14. Apply a Percent Style Format and Use the Increase Decimal Button (EX 103)
15. Apply Conditional Formatting (EX 104)
16. Change the Widths of Columns (EX 107)
17. Change the Heights of Rows (EX 110)
18. Check Spelling on the Worksheet (EX 112)
19. Change the Worksheet's Margins, Header, and Orientation in Page Layout View (EX 114)
20. Print a Section of the Worksheet (EX 118)
21. Display the Formulas in the Worksheet and Fit the Printout on One Page (EX 119)

If you have a SAM 2010 user profile, your instructor may have assigned an autogradable version of this assignment. If so, log into the SAM 2010 Web site at www.cengage.com/sam2010 to download the instruction and start files.

Learn It Online

Test your knowledge of chapter content and key terms.

Instructions: To complete the Learn It Online exercises, start your browser, click the Address bar, and then enter **scsite.com/ex2010/learn** as the Web address. When the Excel 2010 Learn It Online page is displayed, click the link for the exercise you want to complete and then read the instructions.

Chapter Reinforcement TF, MC, and SA

A series of true/false, multiple choice, and short answer questions that test your knowledge of the chapter content.

Flash Cards

An interactive learning environment where you identify chapter key terms associated with displayed definitions.

Practice Test

A series of multiple choice questions that test your knowledge of chapter content and key terms.

Who Wants To Be a Computer Genius?

An interactive game that challenges your knowledge of chapter content in the style of a television quiz show.

Wheel of Terms

An interactive game that challenges your knowledge of chapter key terms in the style of the television show *Wheel of Fortune*.

Crossword Puzzle Challenge

A crossword puzzle that challenges your knowledge of key terms presented in the chapter.

Apply Your Knowledge

Reinforce the skills and apply the concepts you learned in this chapter.

Profit Analysis Worksheet

Instructions: The purpose of this exercise is to open a partially completed workbook, enter formulas and functions, copy the formulas and functions, and then format the worksheet titles and numbers. As shown in Figure 2–73, the completed worksheet analyzes the costs associated with a police department's fleet of vehicles.

	A	B	C	D	E	F	G
1			**Village of Scott Police Department**				
2			**Monthly Vehicle Cost-per-Mile Summary**				
3	**Vehicle ID**	**Miles Driven**	**Cost per Mile**	**Maintenance Cost**	**Mileage Cost**	**Total Cost**	**Total Cost per Mile**
4	670543	2,007	$ 0.49	$ 242.80	$ 983.43	$ 1,226.23	$ 0.61
5	979253	3,192	0.48	446.37	1,532.16	1,978.53	0.62
6	948173	3,802	0.65	472.47	2,471.30	2,943.77	0.77
7	837625	2,080	0.62	432.25	1,289.60	1,721.85	0.83
8	824664	2,475	0.56	369.88	1,386.00	1,755.88	0.71
9	655385	3,294	0.50	352.05	1,647.00	1,999.05	0.61
10	836417	3,640	0.70	417.80	2,548.00	2,965.80	0.81
11	993617	3,395	0.70	390.39	2,376.50	2,766.89	0.81
12	779468	4,075	0.55	442.17	2,241.25	2,683.42	0.66
13	**Totals**	**27,960**		$ 3,566.18	$ 16,475.24	$ 20,041.42	$ 0.72
14	**Highest**	4,075	$0.70	$472.47	$2,548.00	$2,965.80	$0.83
15	**Lowest**	2,007	$0.48	$242.80	$983.43	$1,226.23	$0.61
16	**Average**	3,107	$0.58	$396.24	$1,830.58	$2,226.82	$0.72

Figure 2–73

1. Start Excel. Open the workbook Apply 2-1 Village of Scott Police Department. See the inside back cover of this book for instructions for downloading the Data Files for Students or see your instructor for information on accessing the files required in this book.

2. Use the following formulas in cells E4, F4, and G4:

   Mileage Cost (cell E4) = Miles Driven * Cost per Mile or = B4 * C4

   Total Cost (cell F4) = Maintenance Cost + Mileage Cost or = D4 + E4

   Total Cost per Mile (cell G4) = Total Cost / Miles Driven or = F4 / B4

   Use the fill handle to copy the three formulas in the range E4:G4 to the range E5:G12.

3. Determine totals for the miles driven, maintenance cost, mileage cost, and total cost in row 13. Copy the formula in cell G12 to G13 to assign the formula in cell G12 to G13 in the total line. If necessary, reapply the Total cell style to cell G13.

4. In the range B14:B16, determine the highest value, lowest value, and average value, respectively, for the values in the range B4:B12. Use the fill handle to copy the three functions to the range C14:G16.

5. Format the worksheet as follows:

   a. change the workbook theme to Foundry by using the Themes button (Page Layout tab | Themes group)

   b. cell A1 — change to Title cell style

   c. cell A2 — change to a font size of 16

   d. cells A1:A2 — Rose background color and a thick box border

   e. cells C4:G4 and D13:G13 — Accounting number format with two decimal places and fixed dollar signs by using the Accounting Number Format button (Home tab | Number group)

   f. cells C5:G12 — Comma style format with two decimal places by using the Comma Style button (Home tab | Number group)

   g. cells B4:B16 — Comma style format with no decimal places

   h. cells C14:G16 — Currency style format with floating dollar signs by using the Format Cells: Number Dialog Box Launcher (Home tab | Number group)

   i. cells G4:G12 — apply conditional formatting so that cells with a value greater than 0.80 appear with a rose background color

6. Switch to Page Layout View and delete any current text in the Header area. Enter your name, course, laboratory assignment number, and any other information, as specified by your instructor, in the Header area. Preview and print the worksheet in landscape orientation. Change the document properties, as specified by your instructor. Save the workbook using the file name, Apply 2-1 Village of Scott Police Department Complete.

7. Use Range Finder to verify the formula in cell G13.

Continued >

Apply Your Knowledge *continued*

8. Print the range A3:D16. Press CTRL+ACCENT MARK (`) to change the display from the values version of the worksheet to the formulas version. Print the formulas version in landscape orientation on one page (Figure 2–74) by using the Fit to option in the Page sheet in the Page Setup dialog box. Press CTRL+ACCENT MARK (`) to change the display of the worksheet back to the values version. Close the workbook without saving it.

9. Submit the workbook and results as specified by your instructor.

Jeff Quasney
Apply 2-1 Village of Scott Police Department

Village of Scott Police Department						
Monthly Vehicle Cost-per-Mile Summary						
Vehicle ID	Miles Driven	Cost per Mile	Maintenance Cost	Mileage Cost	Total Cost	Total Cost per Mile
670543	2007	0.49	242.8	=B4*C4	=D4+E4	=F4/B4
979253	3192	0.48	446.37	=B5*C5	=D5+E5	=F5/B5
948173	3802	0.66	472.47	=B6*C6	=D6+E6	=F6/B6
837625	2080	0.62	432.25	=B7*C7	=D7+E7	=F7/B7
824664	2475	0.56	369.88	=B8*C8	=D8+E8	=F8/B8
655385	3294	0.5	352.05	=B9*C9	=D9+E9	=F9/B9
836417	3640	0.7	417.8	=B10*C10	=D10+E10	=F10/B10
993617	3395	0.7	390.39	=B11*C11	=D11+E11	=F11/B11
779468	4075	0.55	442.17	=B12*C12	=D12+E12	=F12/B12
Totals	=SUM(B4:B12)		=SUM(D4:D12)	=SUM(E4:E12)	=SUM(F4:F12)	=F13/B13
Highest	=MAX(B4:B12)	=MAX(C4:C12)	=MAX(D4:D12)	=MAX(E4:E12)	=MAX(F4:F12)	=MAX(G4:G12)
Lowest	=MIN(B4:B12)	=MIN(C4:C12)	=MIN(D4:D12)	=MIN(E4:E12)	=MIN(F4:F12)	=MIN(G4:G12)
Average	=AVERAGE(B4:B12)	=AVERAGE(C4:C12)	=AVERAGE(D4:D12)	=AVERAGE(E4:E12)	=AVERAGE(F4:F12)	=AVERAGE(G4:G12)

Figure 2–74

Extend Your Knowledge

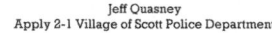

Extend the skills you learned in this chapter and experiment with new skills. You may need to use Help to complete the assignment.

Applying Conditional Formatting to Cells

Instructions: Start Excel. Open the workbook Extend 2-1 State Wildlife Department Employee Ratings. See the inside back cover of this book for instructions for downloading the Data Files for Students, or see your instructor for information on accessing the files required in this book. Perform the following tasks to apply three types of conditional formatting to cells in a worksheet:

1. Select the range C4:C18. Click the Conditional Formatting button (Home tab | Styles group) and then click New Rule in the Conditional Formatting list. Select 'Format only top or bottom ranked values' in the Select a Rule Type area (Conditional Formatting Rules Manager dialog box), as shown in Figure 2–75. Enter any value between 10 and 25 in the text box in the Edit the Rule Description (New Formatting Rule dialog box) area, and click the '% of the selected range' check box to select it. Click the Format button, and choose a blue background to assign this conditional format. Click the OK button in each dialog box and view the worksheet.

2. With range C4:C18 selected, apply a conditional format to the range that uses a green background color to highlight cells with scores that are below average.

3. With range D4:D18 selected, apply a conditional format to the range that uses an orange background to highlight cells that contain Exemplary or Exceeds Requirements.

4. With range B4:B18 selected, apply a conditional format to the range that uses a red background color to highlight cells with duplicate student names.

5. Change the document properties as specified by your instructor. Save the workbook using the file name, Extend 2-1 State Wildlife Department Employee Ratings Complete. Submit the revised workbook as specified by your instructor.

Figure 2–75

Make It Right

Analyze a workbook and correct all errors and/or improve the design.

Correcting Formatting, Functions, and Formulas in a Worksheet

Instructions: Start Excel. Open the workbook Make It Right 2-1 Dion Designwear Profit Analysis. See the inside back cover of this book for instructions for downloading the Data Files for Students, or see your instructor for information on accessing the files required for this book.

In this exercise you will learn how to correct formatting, functions, and formula problems in a worksheet (Figure 2–76).

	Product	Desciption	Cost	Profit	Units Sold	Total Sales	Total Profit	% Profit
1				**Dion Designwear**				
2				**Profit Anaylsis**				
4	4835	Coat	$247.63	$144.83	95,159	$37,346,101.14	$13,781,877.97	36.903%
5	7563	Custom	210.08	142.18	75,762	26,687,922.12	10,771,841.16	40.362%
6	8191	Dress	186.53	99.48	69,297	19,819,634.97	6,893,665.56	34.782%
7	8409	Hat	146.82	59.97	39,164	8,098,723.56	2,348,665.08	29.000%
8	5677	Jacket	140.68	85.63	38,261	8,658,846.91	3,276,289.43	37.837%
9	8985	Shirt	68.38	8.15	42,420	3,246,402.60	345,723.00	10.649%
10	5871	Slacks	144.54	30.44	68,536	11,992,429.28	2,086,235.84	17.396%
11	7796	Sleepwear	93.74	11.80	77,413	8,170,168.02	913,473.40	11.181%
12	7777	Suit	305.91	126.00	19,999	8,637,768.09	2,519,874.00	29.173%
13	8178	Sweater	112.21	9.24	61,257	7,439,662.65	566,014.68	7.608%
14	**Totals**				**587,268**	**$140,097,659.34**	**$43,503,660.12**	**31.052%**
15	Lowest		$68.38	$8.15	19,999	$3,246,402.60	$345,723.00	7.608%
16	Highest		$305.91	$144.83	95,159	$37,346,101.14	$13,781,877.97	40.362%
17	Average		$156.54	$71.77	54,679	$14,009,765.93	$3,302,420.24	25.489%

Figure 2–76

Continued >

Make It Right *continued*

Perform the following tasks:

1. Add a thick box border around the title and subtitle so that they appear more separated from the rest of the worksheet.

2. Adjust the width of column D to 8.11 pixels so that the word in the column header does not wrap. Adjust the column widths of columns F and G to best fit.

3. Spell check the worksheet and correct any spelling mistakes that are found, but ignore any spelling mistakes found with the worksheet title, document properties, and the product descriptions.

4. Center the values in the Product column.

5. The averages in several columns do not include the product in row 4. Adjust the functions in these cells so that all products are included in the calculation.

6. The total sales calculations should be:

   Total Sales = Units Sold * (Cost + Profit)

   Adjust the formulas in the range F4:F13 so that the correct formula is used.

7. The value for the lowest value in column E was entered as a number rather than as a function. Replace the value with the appropriate function.

8. The currency values in rows 4 and 14 should be formatted with the Accounting Number Format button (Home tab | Number group). They are currently formatted with the Currency format (floating dollar sign). The Accounting number format displays a fixed dollar sign.

9. Delete the function in the cell containing the average of % Profit because it is mathematically invalid.

10. Change the document properties as specified by your instructor. Save the workbook using the file name, Make It Right 2–1 Dion Designwear Profit Analysis Corrected. Submit the revised workbook as specified by your instructor.

In the Lab

Design and/or create a workbook using the guidelines, concepts, and skills presented in this chapter. Labs 1, 2, and 3 are listed in order of increasing difficulty.

Lab 1: Accounts Receivable Balance Worksheet

Problem: You are a part-time assistant in the accounting department at Aficionado Guitar Parts, a Chicago-based supplier of custom guitar parts. You have been asked to use Excel to generate a report that summarizes the monthly accounts receivable balance (Figure 2–77). A chart of the balances also is desired. The customer data in Table 2–6 is available for test purposes.

Table 2–6 Aficionado Guitar Parts Accounts Receivable Data				
Customer	**Beginning Balance**	**Credits**	**Payments**	**Purchases**
Cervantes, Katriel	803.01	56.92	277.02	207.94
Cummings, Trenton	285.05	87.41	182.11	218.22
Danielsson, Oliver	411.45	79.33	180.09	364.02
Kalinowski, Jadwiga	438.37	60.90	331.10	190.39
Lanctot, Royce	378.81	48.55	126.15	211.38
Raglow, Dora	710.99	55.62	231.37	274.71
Tuan, Lin	318.86	85.01	129.67	332.89

Instructions Part 1: Create a worksheet similar to the one shown in Figure 2–77. Include the five columns of customer data in Table 2–6 in the report, plus two additional columns to compute a service charge and a new balance for each customer. Assume no negative unpaid monthly balances.

	A	B	C	D	E	F	G
1		**Aficionado Guitar Parts**					
2		**Monthy Accounts Receivable Balance Report**					
3	Customer	Beginning Balance	Credits	Payments	Purchases	Service Charge	New Balance
4	Cervantes, Katriel	$803.01	$56.92	$277.02	$207.94	$15.24	$692.25
5	Cummings, Trenton	285.05	87.41	182.11	218.22	0.50	234.25
6	Danielsson, Oliver	411.45	79.33	180.09	364.02	4.94	520.99
7	Kalinowski, Jadwiga	438.37	60.90	331.10	190.39	1.51	238.27
8	Lanctot, Royce	378.81	48.55	126.15	211.38	6.63	422.12
9	Raglow, Dora	710.99	55.62	231.37	274.71	13.78	712.49
10	Tuan, Lin	318.86	85.01	129.67	332.89	3.39	440.46
11	Totals	$3,346.54	$473.74	$1,457.51	$1,799.55	$46.00	$3,260.84
12	Highest	$803.01	$87.41	$331.10	$364.02	$15.24	$712.49
13	Lowest	$285.05	$48.55	$126.15	$190.39	$0.50	$234.25
14	Average	$478.08	$67.68	$208.22	$257.08	$6.57	$465.83
15							
16							

Figure 2–77

Perform the following tasks:

1. Enter and format the worksheet title `Aficionado Guitar Parts` and worksheet subtitle `Monthly Accounts Receivable Balance Report` in cells A1 and A2. Change the theme of the worksheet to the Trek theme. Apply the Title cell style to cells A1 and A2. Change the font size in cell A1 to 28 points. Merge and center the worksheet title and subtitle across columns A through G. Change the background color of cells A1 and A2 to the Red standard color. Change the font color of cells A1 and A2 to the White theme color. Draw a thick box border around the range A1:A2.

2. Change the width of column A to 20.00 points. Change the widths of columns B through G to 12.00 points. Change the heights of row 3 to 36.00 points and row 12 to 30.00 points.

3. Enter the column titles in row 3 and row titles in the range A11:A14, as shown in Figure 2–77. Center the column titles in the range A3:G3. Apply the Heading 3 cell style to the range A3:G3. Apply the Total cell style to the range A11:G11. Bold the titles in the range A12:A14. Change the font size in the range A3:G14 to 12 points.

4. Enter the data in Table 2–6 in the range A4:E10.

5. Use the following formulas to determine the service charge in column F and the new balance in column G for the first customer. Copy the two formulas down through the remaining customers.

   a. Service Charge (cell F4) = 3.25% * (Beginning Balance − Payments − Credits)

   b. New Balance (G4) = Beginning Balance + Purchases − Credits − Payments + Service Charge

6. Determine the totals in row 11.

7. Determine the maximum, minimum, and average values in cells B12:B14 for the range B4:B10, and then copy the range B12:B14 to C12:G14.

Continued >

8. Format the numbers as follows: (a) assign the Currency style with a floating dollar sign to the cells containing numeric data in the ranges B4:G4 and B11:G14, and (b) assign a number style with two decimal places and a thousand's separator (currency with no dollar sign) to the range B5:G10.

9. Use conditional formatting to change the formatting to white font on a red background in any cell in the range F4:F10 that contains a value greater than 10.

10. Change the worksheet name from Sheet1 to Accounts Receivable and the sheet tab color to the Red standard color. Change the document properties, as specified by your instructor. Change the worksheet header with your name, course number, and other information as specified by your instructor.

11. Spell check the worksheet. Preview and then print the worksheet in landscape orientation. Save the workbook using the file name, Lab 2-1 Part 1 Aficionado Guitar Parts Accounts Receivable Balance Report.

12. Print the range A3:D14. Print the formulas version on another page. Close the workbook without saving the changes. Submit the assignment as specified by your instructor.

Instructions Part 2: In this part of the exercise, you will create a 3-D Bar chart on a new worksheet in the workbook (Figure 2–78). If necessary, use Excel Help to obtain information on inserting a chart on a separate sheet in the workbook.

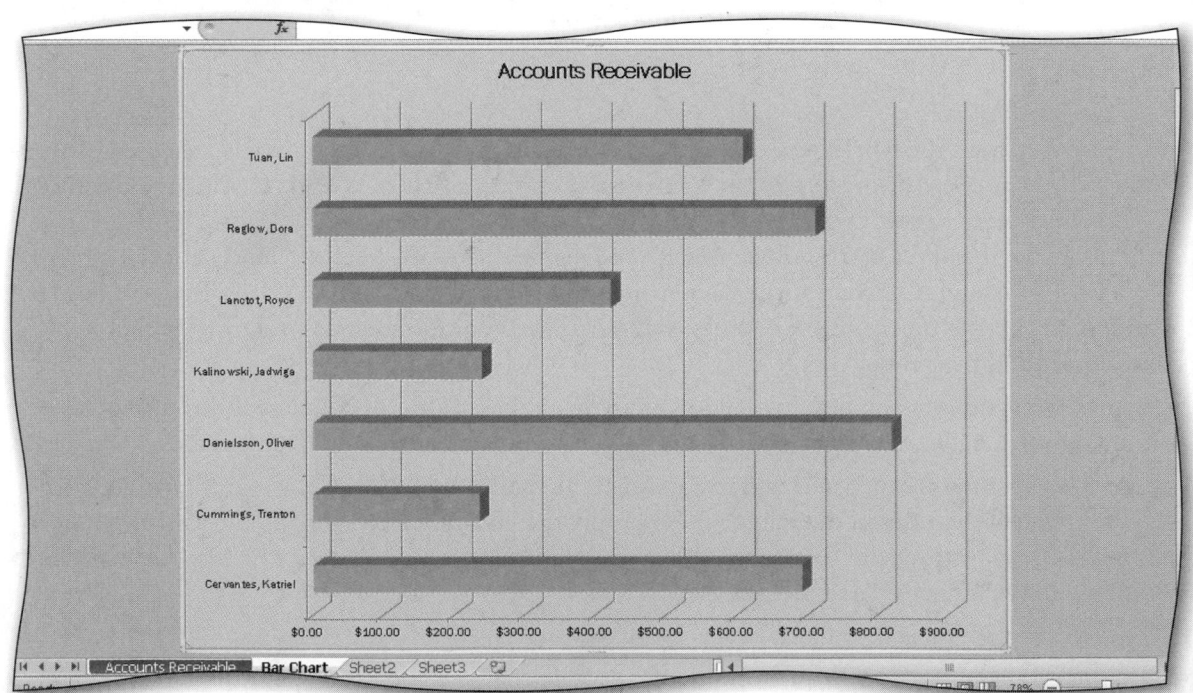

Figure 2–78

1. Open the workbook Lab 2-1 Part 1 Aficionado Guitar Parts Accounts Receivable Balance Report workbook created in Part 1. Save the workbook using the file name, Lab 2-1 Part 2 Aficionado Guitar Parts Accounts Receivable Balance Report.

2. Use the CTRL key and mouse to select the nonadjacent chart ranges A4:A10 and G4:G10. That is, select the range A4:A10 and while holding down the CTRL key, select the range G4:G10.

3. Click the Bar button (Insert tab | Charts group) and then select Clustered Bar in 3-D in the 3-D Bar area. When the chart is displayed on the worksheet, click the Move Chart button (Chart Tools Design tab | Location group). When the Move Chart dialog box appears, click New sheet and then type Bar Chart for the sheet name. Click the OK button (Move Chart dialog box). Change the sheet tab color to the Green standard color.

4. When the chart is displayed on the new worksheet, click the Series 1 series label and then press the DELETE key to delete it. Click the chart area, which is a blank area near the edge of the chart, click the Shape Fill button (Chart Tools Format tab | Shape Styles group), and then select Orange, Accent 1, Lighter 60% in the gallery (column 5, row 3). Click one of the bars in the chart. Click the Shape Fill button (Chart Tools Format tab | Shape Styles group) and then select the Green standard color. Click the Chart Title button (Chart Tools Layout tab | Labels group) and then select Above Chart in the Chart Title gallery. If necessary, use the scroll bar on the right side of the worksheet to scroll to the top of the chart. Click the edge of the chart title to select it and then type **Accounts Receivable** as the chart title.

5. Drag the Accounts Receivable tab at the bottom of the worksheet to the left of the Bar Chart tab to reorder the sheets in the workbook. Preview and print the chart.

6. Click the Accounts Receivable sheet tab. Change the following beginning balances: customer Oliver Danielsson to $702.13 and customer Lin Tuan to $482.74. The company also decided to change the service charge from 3.25% to 2.75% for all customers. After copying the adjusted formula in cell F4 to the range F5:F10, click the Auto Fill Options button and then click Fill without Formatting to maintain the original formatting in the range F5:F10. The total new balance in cell G11 should equal $3,720.82.

7. Select both sheets by holding down the SHIFT key and then clicking the Bar Chart tab. Preview and print the selected sheets. Save the workbook. Submit the assignment as specified by your instructor.

n the Lab

ab 2: Sales Summary Worksheet

roblem: You have been asked to build a orksheet for a start-up company, Electry uto, that analyzes the financing needs for ne company's first six months in business. he company plans to begin operations January with an initial investment of 500,000.00. The expected revenue and osts for the company's first six months e shown in Table 2–7. The desired orksheet is shown in Figure 2–79 on the llowing page. The initial investment is own at the starting balance for January ell B4). The amount of financing required by the company is shown as the lowest ending balance ell F12).

Table 2–7 Electry Auto Start-Up Financing Needs Data

Month	Revenue	Costs
January	105000	220000
February	82000	260000
March	200000	255000
April	250000	320000
May	325000	420000
June	510000	540000

Continued >

In the Lab *continued*

Instructions Part 1: Perform the following tasks to build the worksheet shown in Figure 2–79.

	A	B	C	D	E	F
1			**Electry Auto**			
2			Start-Up Financing Needs			
3	*Month*	*Starting Balance*	*Revenue*	*Costs*	*Net Income*	*Ending Balance*
4	January	$ 500,000.00	$ 105,000.00	$ 220,000.00	$ (115,000.00)	$ 385,000.00
5	February	385,000.00	82,000.00	260,000.00	(178,000.00)	207,000.00
6	March	207,000.00	200,000.00	255,000.00	(55,000.00)	152,000.00
7	April	152,000.00	250,000.00	320,000.00	(70,000.00)	82,000.00
8	May	82,000.00	325,000.00	420,000.00	(95,000.00)	(13,000.00)
9	June	(13,000.00)	510,000.00	540,000.00	(30,000.00)	(43,000.00)
10	*Average*	$218,833.33	$245,333.33	$335,833.33	($90,500.00)	$128,333.33
11	*Highest*	$500,000.00	$510,000.00	$540,000.00	($30,000.00)	$385,000.00
12	*Lowest*	($13,000.00)	$82,000.00	$220,000.00	($178,000.00)	($43,000.00)
13						
14						
15						
16						
17						
18						

Figure 2–79

1. Start Excel. Apply the Concourse theme to a new workbook.

2. Increase the width of column A to 10.00 and the width of columns B through F to 14.00.

3. Enter the worksheet title `Electry Auto` in cell A1 and the worksheet subtitle `Start-Up Financing Needs` in cell A2. Enter the column titles in row 3, as shown in Figure 2–79. In row 3, use ALT+ENTER to start a new line in a cell.

4. Enter the start-up financing needs data described in Table 2–7 in columns A, C, and D in rows 4 through 9. Enter the initial starting balance (cell B4) of 500000.00. Enter the row titles in the range A10:A12, as shown in Figure 2–79.

5. For the months of February through March, the starting balance is equal to the previous month's ending balance. Obtain the starting balance for February by setting the starting balance of February to the ending balance of January. Use a cell reference rather than typing in the data. Copy the formula for February to the remaining months.

6. Obtain the net income amounts in column E by subtracting the costs in column D from the revenues in column C. Enter the formula in cell E4 and copy it to the range E5:E9. Obtain the ending balance amounts in column F by adding the starting balance in column B to the net income in column E. Enter the formula in cell F4 and copy it to the range F5:F9.

7. In the range B10:B12, use the AVERAGE, MAX, and MIN functions to determine the average value, highest value, and lowest value in the range B4:B9. Copy the range B10:B12 to the range C10:F12.

8. One at a time, merge and center the worksheet title and subtitle across columns A through F. Select cells A1 and A2 and change the background color to light blue (column 7 in the Standard Colors area in the Fill Color gallery). Apply the Title cell style to cells A1 and A2. Change the worksheet title in cell A1 to 28-point white (column 1, row 1 on the Font Color gallery). Change the worksheet subtitle to the same color. Assign a thick box border to the range A1:A2.

9. Center the titles in row 3, columns A through F. Apply the Heading 3 cell style to the range A3:F3. Use the Italic button (Home tab | Font group) to italicize the column titles in row 3 and the row titles in the range A10:A12.

10. Assign a thick box border to the range A10:F12. Change the background and font color for cell F12 to the same colors applied to the worksheet title in Step 8.

11. Change the row heights of row 3 to 36.00 points and row 10 to 30.00 points.

12. Assign the Accounting number format to the range B4:F4. Assign the Comma style format to the range B5:F9. Assign a Currency format with a floating dollar sign to the range B10:F12.

13. Rename the sheet tab as Start-Up Financing Needs. Apply the Light Blue color to the sheet tab. Change the document properties, as specified by your instructor. Change the worksheet header with your name, course number, and other information as specified by your instructor. Save the workbook using the file name Lab 2-1 Part 1 Electry Auto Start-Up Financing Needs. Print the entire worksheet in landscape orientation. Next, print only the range A3:B9.

14. Display the formulas version by pressing CTRL+ACCENT MARK (`). Print the formulas version using the Fit to option button in the Scaling area on the Page tab in the Page Setup dialog box. After printing the worksheet, reset the Scaling option by selecting the Adjust to option button on the Page tab in the Page Setup dialog box and changing the percent value to 100%. Change the display from the formulas version to the values version by pressing CTRL+ACCENT MARK (`). Do not save the workbook.

15. Submit the revised workbook as requested by your instructor.

Instructions Part 2: In this part of the exercise, you will change the revenue amounts until the lowest ending balance is greater than zero, indicating that the company does not require financing in its first six months of operation. Open the workbook created in Part 1 and save the workbook as Lab 2-1 Part 2 Electry Auto Start-Up Financing Needs. Manually increment each of the six values in the revenue column by $1,000.00 until the lowest ending balance in cell F12 is greater than zero. The value of cell F12 should equal $5,000.00 All six values in column C must be incremented the same number of times. Update the worksheet header and save the workbook. Print the worksheet. Submit the assignment as specified by your instructor.

Instructions Part 3: In this part of the exercise, you will change the monthly costs until the lowest ending balance is greater than zero, indicating that the company does not require financing in its first six months of operation. Open the workbook created in Part 1 and then save the workbook as Lab 2–1 Part 3 Electry Auto Start-Up Financing Needs. Manually decrement each of the six values in the costs column by $1,000.00 until the lowest ending balance in cell F12 is greater than zero. Decrement all six values in column C the same number of times. Your worksheet is correct when the lowest ending balance in cell F12 is $5,000.00. Update the worksheet header and save the workbook. Print the worksheet. Submit the assignment as specified by your instructor.

In the Lab

Lab 3: Stock Club Investment Analysis

Problem: Several years ago, you and a large group of friends started a stock club. Each year every member invests more money per month. You have decided to create a portfolio worksheet (Figure 2–80) that summarizes the club's current stock holdings so that you can share the information with your group of friends. The club's portfolio is summarized in Table 2–8. Table 2–8 also shows the general layout of the worksheet to be created.

| A18 | | fx | | | | | | | | |

	A	B	C	D	E	F	G	H	I	J
1					**Sock-It-Away Stock Club**					
2					Summary of Investments					
3	Company	Stock Symbol	Purchase Date	Shares	Initial Price per Share	Initial Cost	Current Price per Share	Current Value	Gain/Loss	Percent Gain/Loss
4	Apple	AAPL	3/3/2007	250	$ 86.17	$ 21,542.50	$ 75.32	$ 18,830.00	$ (2,712.50)	-12.59%
5	Caterpillar	CAT	6/14/2008	200	81.74	16,348.00	69.02	13,804.00	(2,544.00)	-15.56%
6	Disney	DIS	10/11/2006	300	31.06	9,318.00	37.38	11,214.00	1,896.00	20.35%
7	General Electric	GE	3/4/2009	500	7.24	3,620.00	9.39	4,695.00	1,075.00	29.70%
8	MetLife	MET	1/15/2008	200	60.92	12,184.00	77.09	15,418.00	3,234.00	26.54%
9	Microsoft	MSFT	11/15/2006	500	29.20	14,600.00	36.30	18,150.00	3,550.00	24.32%
10	PepsiCo	PEP	2/15/2006	350	57.86	20,251.00	70.65	24,727.50	4,476.50	22.11%
11	Target	TGT	5/11/2004	450	44.11	19,849.50	44.02	19,809.00	(40.50)	-0.20%
12	Wal-Mart	WMT	4/14/2009	250	50.81	12,702.50	57.20	14,300.00	1,597.50	12.58%
13	Totals					$ 130,415.50		$ 140,947.50	$ 10,532.00	8.08%
14	Average			333.3333	$49.90	$14,490.61	$52.93	$15,660.83	$1,170.22	
15	Highest			500	$86.17	$21,542.50	$77.09	$24,727.50	$4,476.50	29.70%
16	Lowest			200	$7.24	$3,620.00	$9.39	$4,695.00	($2,712.50)	-15.56%
17										
18										
19										

Figure 2–80

Table 2–8 Sock-It-Away Stock Club

Company	Stock Symbol	Purchase Date	Shares	Initial Price per Share	Initial Cost	Current Price per Share	Current Value	Gain/ Loss	Percent Gain/ Loss
Apple	AAPL	3/3/2007	250	86.17	Formula A	75.32	Formula B	Formula C	Formula D
Caterpillar	CAT	6/14/2008	200	81.74		69.02			
Disney	DIS	10/11/2006	300	31.06		37.38			
General Electric	GE	3/4/2009	500	7.24		9.39			
MetLife	MET	1/15/2008	200	60.92		77.09			
Microsoft	MSFT	11/15/2006	500	29.20		36.30			
PepsiCo	PEP	2/15/2006	350	57.86		70.65			
Target	TGT	5/11/2004	450	44.11		44.02			
Wal-Mart	WMT	4/14/2009	250	50.81		57.20			
Totals				Formula E					
Average				Formula F					
Highest				Formula G					
Lowest				Formula H					

tructions: Perform the following tasks:

Start Excel. Enter the worksheet titles Sock-It-Away Stock Club in cell A1 and Summary of Investments in cell A2.

Enter the column titles and data in Table 2–8 beginning in row 3.

Change the column widths and row heights as follows: column A — 11.78; column C — 10.00; columns E and G — 7.44; columns F, H, and I — 13.00; column J — 8.22; row 3 — 56.25 points; row 14 — 27.00 points.

Enter the following formulas in row 4 and then copy them down through row 12:

a. Enter Formula A in cell F4: Initial Cost = Shares × Initial Price per Share

b. Enter Formula B in cell H4: Current Value = Shares × Current Price Per Share

c. Enter Formula C in cell I4: Gain/Loss = Current Value – Initial Cost

d. Enter Formula D in cell J4: Percent Gain/Loss = Gain/Loss / Initial Cost

Compute the totals for initial cost, current value, gain/loss, and percent gain loss. For the percent gain/loss in cell J13, copy cell J12 to J13 using the fill handle.

In cells D14, D15, and D16, enter Formulas F, G, and H using the AVERAGE, MAX, and MIN functions. Copy the three functions across through the range E14:J16. Delete the invalid formula in cell J14.

Format the worksheet as follows:

a. Apply the Trek theme to the worksheet.

b. Format the worksheet title with Title cell style. Merge and center across columns A through J.

c. Format the worksheet subtitle with Franklin Gothic Book font, 16 point font size, Black, Text 1 theme font color. Merge and Center across columns A through J.

d. Format the worksheet title and subtitle background with Orange, Accent 1, Lighter 60% theme color and a thick box border.

e. Format row 3 with the Heading 3 cell style and row 13 with the Total cell style.

f.   Format the data in rows 4 through 12: center data in column B; format dates in column C to the mm/dd/yyyy date format; range E4:I4 — Accounting number format style with fixed dollar sign; range E5:I12 — Comma style; range J4:J13 — Percent style with two decimal places; cells F13, H13, and I13 — Accounting Number format with fixed dollar sign.

g. Format E14:I16 — Currency format with floating decimal places; J15:J16 — Percent style with two decimal places.

h. Format J4:J12 — apply conditional formatting so that if a cell in range is less than 0, then cell appears with a pink background color.

Spell check the worksheet. Change the name of the sheet tab to Summary of Investments and apply the Orange, Accent 1, Darker 25% theme color to the sheet tab. Update the document properties, and save the workbook using the file name, Lab 2-3 Sock-It-Away Stock Club Summary of Investments. Print the worksheet in landscape orientation. Print the formulas version on one page. Close the workbook without saving changes. Submit the assignment as specified by your instructor.

Cases and Places

Apply your creative thinking and problem-solving skills to design and implement a solution.

1: Analyzing Emergency Student Loans

Academic

The Student Assistance office at your school provides emergency loans at simple interest. The data obtained from six types of loans and the desired report format are shown in Table 2–9. The required formulas are shown in Table 2–10. Use the concepts and techniques presented in this chapter to create and format the worksheet. Include total, average, maximum, and minimum values for Principal, Interest, and Amount Due.

Table 2–9 Emergency Student Loan Data and Worksheet Layout			
Loan Type	**Principal**	**Rate**	**Time in Years**
Academic Supplies	$40,000	7.5%	.4
Medical Emergency	$25,500	12%	.33
Personal Emergency	$12,750	8.25%	.5
Room and Board	$27,000	6.5%	1
Travel Expenses	$4,550	12%	.5
Tuition Reimbursement	$107,000	6%	1

Table 2–10 Emergency Student Loan Formulas
Interest = Principal × Rate × Time
Amount Due = Principal + Interest
Average = AVERAGE function
Minimum = MIN function
Maximum = MAX function

2: Analyzing Energy Consumption

Personal

Your parents believe that your late night studying sessions and household appliance usage contribute to excessive electricity bills. You have decided to try to prove them wrong by analyzing your daily and monthly electricity consumption. You research the energy consumption of your personal items and appliance usage to obtain consumption costs per hour for each item. Table 2–11 contains the data and format for the report you want to create.

Use the concepts and techniques presented in this project to create and format the worksheet. Include an embedded 3-D Pie chart that shows the cost per month. Use Microsoft Excel Help to create a professional looking 3-D Pie chart with title and data labels.

Table 2–11 Appliance Electricity Usage Costs

Appliance	Cost per Hour	Hours Used Daily	Total Cost Per Day	Total Cost per Month (30 Days)
Clothes dryer	$0.325	1		
Computer	$0.02	6		
DVD player	$0.035	1		
Light bulbs	$0.043	8		
Refrigerator	$0.035	24		
Stereo	$0.02	5		
Television	$0.04	4		
Washing machine	$0.03	2		

3: Analyzing Profit Potential

Professional

You work for HumiCorp, an online retailer of home humidifiers. Your manager wants to know the profit potential of their inventory based on the items in inventory listed in Table 2–12. Table 2–12 contains the format of the desired report. The required formulas are shown in Table 2–13. Use the concepts and techniques developed in this chapter to create and format the worksheet. The company just received 67 additional desk-sized humidifiers and shipped out 48 room-sized humidifiers. Update the appropriate cells to reflect the change in inventory.

Table 2–12 HumiCorp Inventory Profit Potential Data and Worksheet Layout

Item	Units on Hand	Unit Cost	Total Cost	Unit Price	Total Value	Potential Profit
Desk	187	27.58	Formula A	Formula B	Formula C	Formula D
Filtered home-sized	42	324.14				
Filtered room-sized	118	86.55				
Home-sized	103	253.91				
Room-sized	97	53.69				
Total	—	—	—	—	—	—
Average	Formula E					
Lowest	Formula F					
Highest	Formula G					

Table 2–13 HumiCorp Inventory Profit Potential Formulas

Formula A = Units on Hand × Unit Cost

Formula B = Unit Cost × (1 / (1 − .66))

Formula C = Units on Hand × Unit Price

Formula D = Total Value − Total Cost

Formula E = AVERAGE function

Formula F = MIN function

Formula G = MAX function

3

Microsoft **Excel 2010**

What-If Analysis, Charting, and Working with Large Worksheets

Objectives

You will have mastered the material in this chapter when you can:

- Rotate text in a cell
- Create a series of month names
- Copy, paste, insert, and delete cells
- Format numbers using format symbols
- Freeze and unfreeze rows and columns
- Show and format the system date
- Use absolute and mixed cell references in a formula
- Use the IF function to perform a logical test

- Create Sparkline charts
- Use the Format Painter button to format cells
- Create a 3-D Pie chart on a separate chart sheet
- Rearrange worksheet tabs
- Change the worksheet view
- Answer what-if questions
- Goal seek to answer what-if questions

3 | What-If Analysis, Charting, and Working with Large Worksheets

Introduction

Worksheets normally are much larger than those created in the previous chapters, often extending beyond the size of the Excel window. Because you cannot see the entire worksheet on the screen at one time, working with a large worksheet sometimes can be frustrating. This chapter introduces several Excel commands that allow you to control what is displayed on the screen so that you can view critical parts of a large worksheet at one time. One command allows you to freeze rows and columns so that Excel always displays them on the screen. Another command splits the worksheet into separate window-panes so that you can view different parts of a worksheet on the screen at one time.

When you set up a worksheet, you should use cell references in formulas whenever possible, rather than constant values. The use of a cell reference allows you to change a value in multiple formulas by changing the value in a single cell. The cell references in a formula are called assumptions. Assumptions are values in cells that you can change to determine new values for formulas. This chapter emphasizes the use of assumptions and shows how to use Excel to answer what-if questions, such as what happens to the six-month operating income i you decrease the marketing expenses assumption by 3 percent? Being able to analyze quickly the effect of changing values in a worksheet is an important skill in making business decisions

This chapter also introduces you to techniques that will enhance your ability to create worksheets and draw charts. From your work in Chapter 1, you are aware of how easily you can create charts. This chapter covers additional charting techniques that allow you to convey a message in a dramatic pictorial fashion, such as Sparkline charts and an exploded 3-D pie chart. This chapter also covers other methods for entering values in cells such as allowing Excel to enter values for you based on a pattern of values that you create, and formatting these values. In addition, you will learn how to use absolute cell references and how to use the IF function to assign a value to a cell based on a logical test.

Project — Financial Projection Worksheet with What-If Analysis and Chart

The project in the chapter follows proper design guidelines and uses Excel to create the worksheet and pie chart shown in Figures 3–1a and 3–1b. Modern Music Shops operates several stores that sell and service musical instruments. Each June and December the director of finance and accounting submits a plan to the management team to show projected monthly sales revenues, costs of goods sold, gross margin, expenses, and operating income for the next six months. The director requires an easy-to-read worksheet that shows financial projections for the next six months. The worksheet should allow for quick analysis if projections for certain numbers change, such as the percentage of expenses allocated to marketing. In addition, a 3-D pie chart is required that shows the projected operating income contribution for each of the six months.

Figure 3–1 (a) Worksheet

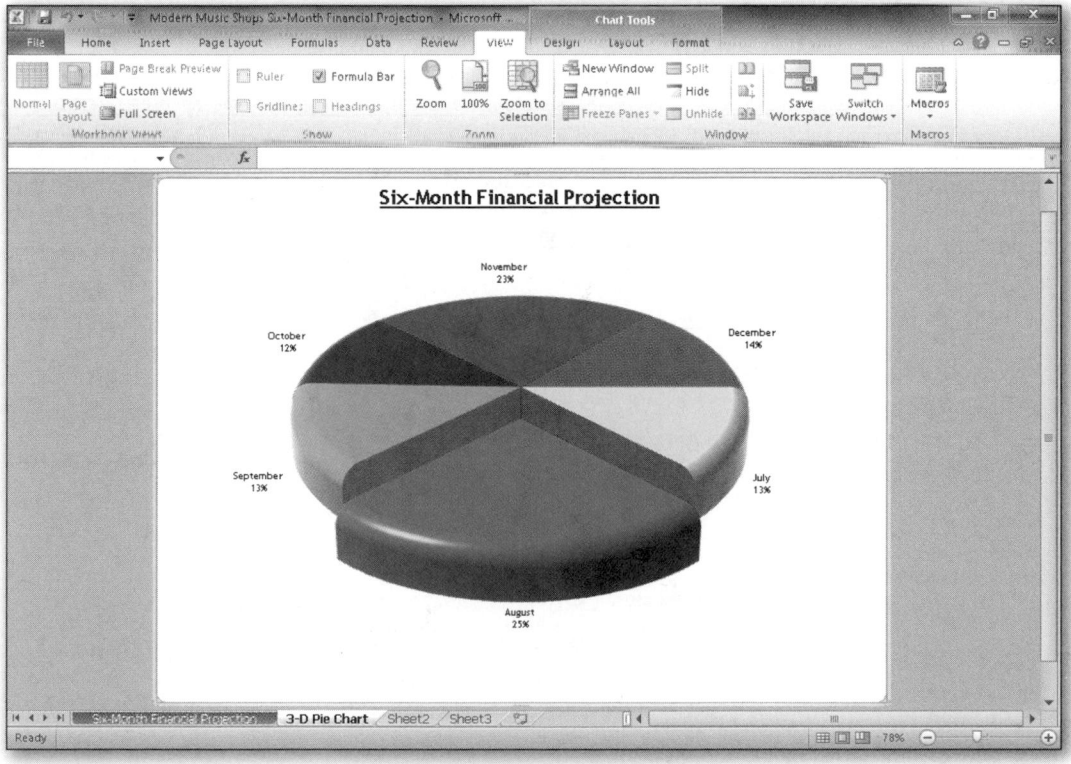

Figure 3–1 (b) 3-D Pie Chart

BTW

Correctness
Studies have shown that more than 25 percent of all business worksheets have errors. You can ensure correctness in your formulas by carefully checking them using Range Finder. The Formula Auditing group on the Formulas tab on the Ribbon also can be helpful when verifying formulas.

The requirements document for the Modern Music Shops Six-Month Financial Projection worksheet is shown in Figure 3–2. It includes the needs, source of data, summary of calculations, chart requirements, and other facts about its development.

REQUEST FOR NEW WORKBOOK

Date Submitted:	April 9, 2012
Submitted By:	Marcus Olek
Worksheet Title:	Modern Music Shops' Six-Month Financial Projection
Needs:	The needs are: (1) a worksheet (Figure 3-3a on page EX 142) that shows Modern Music Shops' projected monthly sales, cost of goods sold, gross margin, expenses, and operating income for a six-month period; and (2) a 3-D Pie chart (Figure 3-3b on page EX 142) that shows the projected contribution of each month's operating income to the six-month period operating income.
Source of Data:	The data supplied by the Finance department includes projections of the monthly sales and expenses (Table 3-1 on page EX 143) that are based on prior years. All the remaining numbers in the worksheet are determined from these 13 numbers using formulas.
Calculations:	The following calculations must be made for each month: 1. Cost of Goods Sold = Revenue − Revenue × Margin 2. Gross Margin = Revenue − Cost of Goods Sold 3. Bonus Expense = $200,000.00 if the Revenue exceeds the Revenue for Bonus; otherwise Bonus Expense = 0 4. Commission Expense = Commission Assumption × Revenue 5. Marketing Expense = Marketing Assumption × Revenue 6. Research and Development = Research and Development Assumption × Revenue 7. Support, General, and Administrative Expense = Support, General, and Administrative Assumption × Revenue 8. Total Expenses = Sum of Expenses 9. Operating Income = Gross Margin − Total Expenses
Chart Requirements:	Show Sparkline charts for Revenue and each of the items noted in the calculations area above. A 3-D Pie chart is required on a separate sheet (Figure 3-3b) to show the contribution of each month's operating income to the six-month period operating income. The chart should also emphasize the month with the greatest operating income.

Approvals

Approval Status:	X	Approved
		Rejected
Approved By:	Farah Qadir, CFO	
Date:	April 16, 2012	
Assigned To:	J. Quasney, Spreadsheet Specialist	

Figure 3–2

Overview

As you read this chapter, you will learn how to create the worksheet shown in Figure 3–1 by performing these general tasks:

- Create a series of month names
- Use absolute cell references in a formula
- Use the IF function to perform a logical test
- Create Sparkline charts in a range of cells
- Use the Format Painter button to format cells
- Create a 3-D pie chart on a separate chart sheet
- Answer what-if questions
- Manipulate large worksheets

Plan Ahead

General Project Decisions

While creating an Excel worksheet, you need to make several decisions that will determine the appearance and characteristics of the finished worksheet. As you create the worksheet required to meet the requirements shown in Figure 3–2, you should follow these general guidelines:

1. **Plan the layout of the worksheet.** Worksheets that include financial data associated with time frames typically include dates, such as months, quarters, or years, as column headers. What-if assumptions should not clutter the worksheet, but placing them in an easily located portion of the worksheet allows for quicker creation of new projections.

2. **Determine the necessary formulas and functions needed.** Often, financial calculations rely on strict definitions and commonly accepted formulas for performing the calculations. Look for such situations and always use the accepted formulas. When using a what-if section on a worksheet, make certain to create formulas that use the what-if criteria. When a requirement necessitates a calculation only under a certain condition, a function can check for the condition and make the calculation when necessary.

3. **Specify how to best utilize Sparkline charts.** Sparkline charts allow worksheet users quickly to visualize information in a small chart within a cell. The use of multiple Sparkline charts in the worksheet will provide the user with a visual comparison of the various data items for each month. The user, therefore, can see trends for each line item over time and also compare relationships among various line items.

4. **Identify how to format various elements of the worksheet.** Format separate parts of a worksheet, such as what-if assumptions, in a manner that indicates that they are separate from the main area of the worksheet. Other financial items, such as sales revenue and expenses, are distinct categories of financial data and should be separated visually. Totals and subtotals should stand out to draw the reader's attention.

5. **Specify how charts should convey necessary information.** As you have learned, different chart types convey different messages and are appropriate in different situations. For example, a 3-D pie chart is a good way to compare visually a small set of numbers. Often one or two slices of a pie chart displays as exploded, meaning that the slice appears pulled away from the cart, in order to emphasize the slice to the user. Format chart data points so that the worksheet user's eye is drawn to important information.

6. **Perform what-if analysis and goal seeking using the best techniques.** What-if analysis allows you quickly to answer questions regarding various predictions. A what-if area of a worksheet allows users of the worksheet efficiently to ask questions. Goal seeking allows you automatically to modify values in a what-if area of a worksheet based on a goal that you have for another cell in the worksheet.

When necessary, more specific details concerning the above guidelines are presented at appropriate points in the chapter. The chapter also will identify the actions you perform and decisions made regarding these guidelines during the creation of the worksheet shown in Figure 3–1 on page EX 139.

Using a sketch of the worksheet can help you visualize its design. The sketch of the worksheet consists of titles, column and row headings, location of data values, calculations, and a rough idea of the desired formatting (Figure 3–3a). The sketch of the 3-D pie chart shows the expected contribution of each month's operating income to the six-month operating income (Figure 3–3b). The assumptions will be entered at the top of the worksheet (Figure 3–3a). The projected monthly sales revenue will be entered in row 13 of the worksheet. The projected monthly sales revenue and the assumptions shown in Table 3–1 will be used to calculate the remaining numbers in the worksheet.

Figure 3–3 (a) Worksheet Sketch

Figure 3–3 (b) 3-D Pie Chart Sketch

With a solid understanding of the requirements document, an understanding of the necessary decisions, and a sketch of the worksheet, the next step is to use Excel to create the worksheet.

Table 3–1 Modern Music Shops Six-Month Financial Projections Data and What-If Assumptions	
Projected Monthly Total Sales Revenues	
July	$3,113,612.16
August	7,962,235.53
September	5,112,268.58
October	2,924,627.87
November	7,630,534.65
December	3,424,270.23
What-If Assumptions	
Bonus	$200,000.00
Commission	5.75%
Margin	57.50%
Marketing	15.00%
Research and Development	7.50%
Sales Revenue for Bonus	$3,500,000.00
Support, General, and Administrative	18.75%

To Start Excel

If you are using a computer to step through the project in this chapter and you want your screens to match the figures in this book, you should change your screen's resolution to 1024 × 768. For information about how to change a computer's resolution, refer to the Introduction to Office 2010 and Windows 7 chapter at the beginning of this book.

The following steps, which assume Windows 7 is running, start Excel based on a typical installation. You may need to ask your instructor how to start Excel for your computer. For a detailed example of the procedure summarized below, refer to the Office 2010 and Windows 7 chapter at the beginning of this book.

> For an introduction to Windows 7 and instruction about how to perform basic Windows 7 tasks, read the Office 2010 and Windows 7 chapter at the beginning of this book, where you can learn how to resize windows, change screen resolution, create folders, move and rename files, use Windows Help, and much more.

1. Click the Start button on the Windows 7 taskbar to display the Start menu.

2. Type `Microsoft Excel` as the search text in the 'Search programs and files' text box, and watch the search results appear on the Start menu.

3. Click Microsoft Excel 2010 in the search results on the Start menu to start Excel and display a new blank workbook in the Excel window.

4. If the Excel window is not maximized, click the Maximize button next to the Close button on its title bar to maximize the window.

To Enter the Worksheet Titles, Change Document Properties, Apply a Theme, and Save the Workbook

The worksheet contains two titles, initially in cells A8 and A9. In the previous chapters, titles were centered across the worksheet. With large worksheets that extend beyond the size of a window, it is best to enter titles left-aligned as shown in the sketch of the worksheet in Figure 3–3a because the worksheet prints with the title on the first page if the worksheet requires multiple pages, and the user more easily finds the worksheet title when necessary. The following steps enter the worksheet titles, change the workbook theme to Opulent, change document properties, and then save the workbook.

1 Select cell A8 and then type `Modern Music Shops` as the worksheet title.

2 Select cell A9 and then type `Six-Month Financial Projection` as the worksheet subtitle and then press the ENTER key to enter the worksheet subtitle.

3 Change the document properties as specified by your instructor.

4 Apply the Opulent theme to the workbook.

5 With a USB flash drive connected to one of the computer's USB ports, click the Save button on the Quick Access Toolbar to display the Save As dialog box.

6 Type `Modern Music Shops Six-Month Financial Projection` in the File name text box to change the file name. Do not press the ENTER key after typing the file name because you do not want to close the dialog box at this time.

7 Navigate to the desired save location (in this case, the Excel folder in the CIS 101 folder [or your class folder] on the USB flash drive).

8 Click the Save button (Save As dialog box) to save the document in the selected folder on the selected drive with the entered file name.

Rotating Text and Using the Fill Handle to Create a Series

The data on the worksheet, including month names and the What-If Assumptions section now can be added to the worksheet.

Plan Ahead

> **Plan the layout of the worksheet.**
> Excel allows you to rotate text in a cell. Rotated text often provides a strong visual appeal. Rotated text also allows you to fit more text into a smaller column width. Chapters 1 and 2 used the fill handle to copy a cell or a range of cells to adjacent cells. The fill handle also allows creation of a series of numbers, dates, or month names automatically. Using the fill handle in this way eliminates the need to type in such data, saving time and eliminating typographical errors.

To Rotate Text and Use the Fill Handle to Create a Series of Month Names

The design of the worksheet calls specifically for only six months of data. Because there always will be only six months of data in the worksheet, the months should be placed across the top of the worksheet as column headings rather than as row headings. The data for the worksheet includes more data items regarding each month than there are months, and, possibly, more expense categories could be added in the future. A proper layout, therefore, includes placing each month as column headings.

When you first enter text, its angle is zero degrees (0°), and it reads from left to right in a cell. Excel allows you to rotate text in a cell counterclockwise by entering a number between 1° and 90°.

The following steps enter the month name, July, in cell B10; format cell B10 (including rotating the text); and then use the fill handle to enter the remaining month names in the range C10:G10.

- If necessary, select the Home tab and then select cell B10 because this cell will include the first month name in the series of month names.

- Type **July** as the cell entry and then click the Enter box.

- Click the Format Cells: Alignment Dialog Box Launcher (Home tab | Alignment group) to display the Format Cells dialog box (Figure 3–4).

Figure 3–4

2

- Click the 45° point in the Orientation area (Format Cells dialog box) to move the Text hand in the Orientation area to the 45° point and to display a new orientation in the Degrees box (Figure 3–5).

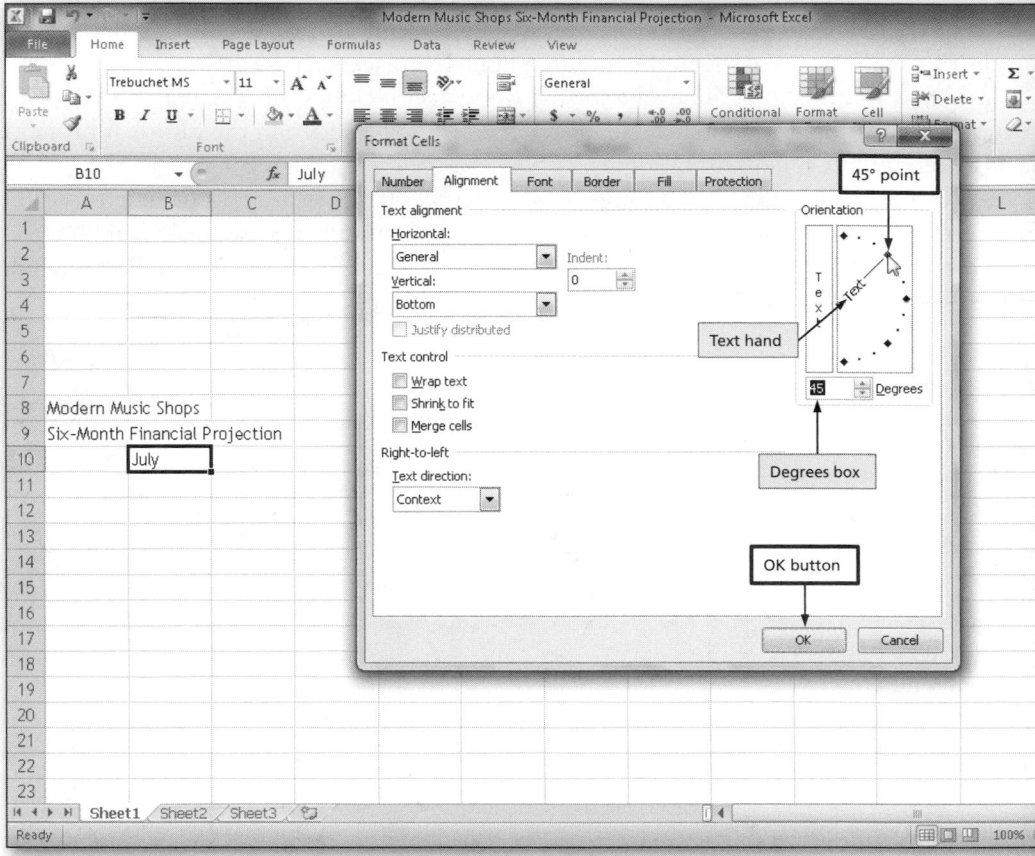

Figure 3–5

3

- Click the OK button to rotate the text in the active cell and automatically increase the height of the current row to best fit the rotated text.

- Point to the fill handle on the lower-right corner of cell B10 to display the crosshair mouse pointer in preparation of filling the month series (Figure 3–6).

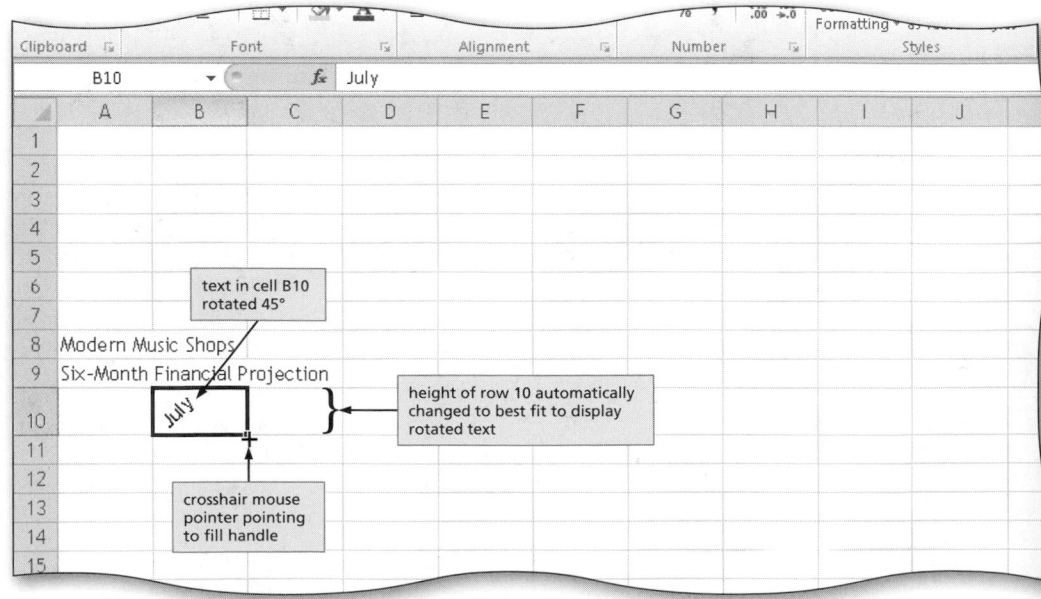

Figure 3–6

4

• Drag the fill handle to the right to select the range to fill, C10:G10 in this case. Do not release the mouse button (Figure 3–7).

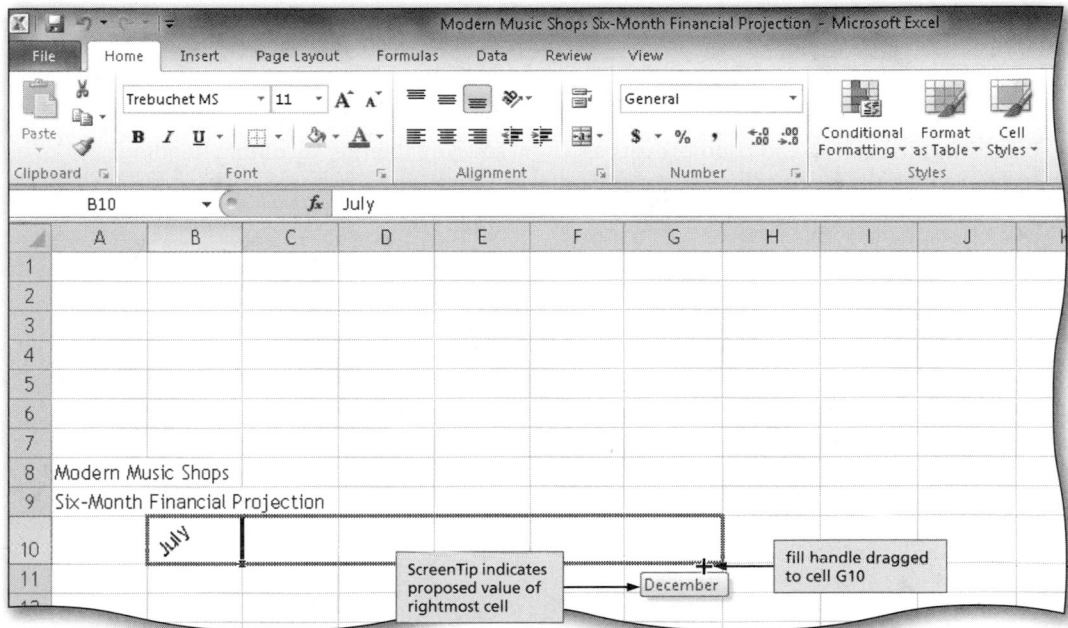

Figure 3–7

5

• Release the mouse button to create a month name series in the selected range and copy the format of the selected cell to the selected range.

• Click the Auto Fill Options button below the lower-right corner of the fill area to display the Auto Fill Options menu (Figure 3–8).

What if I do not want to copy the format of cell B10 during the auto fill operation?

In addition to creating a series of values, dragging the fill handle instructs Excel to copy the format of cell B10 to the range C10:G10. With some fill operations, you may not want to copy the formats of the

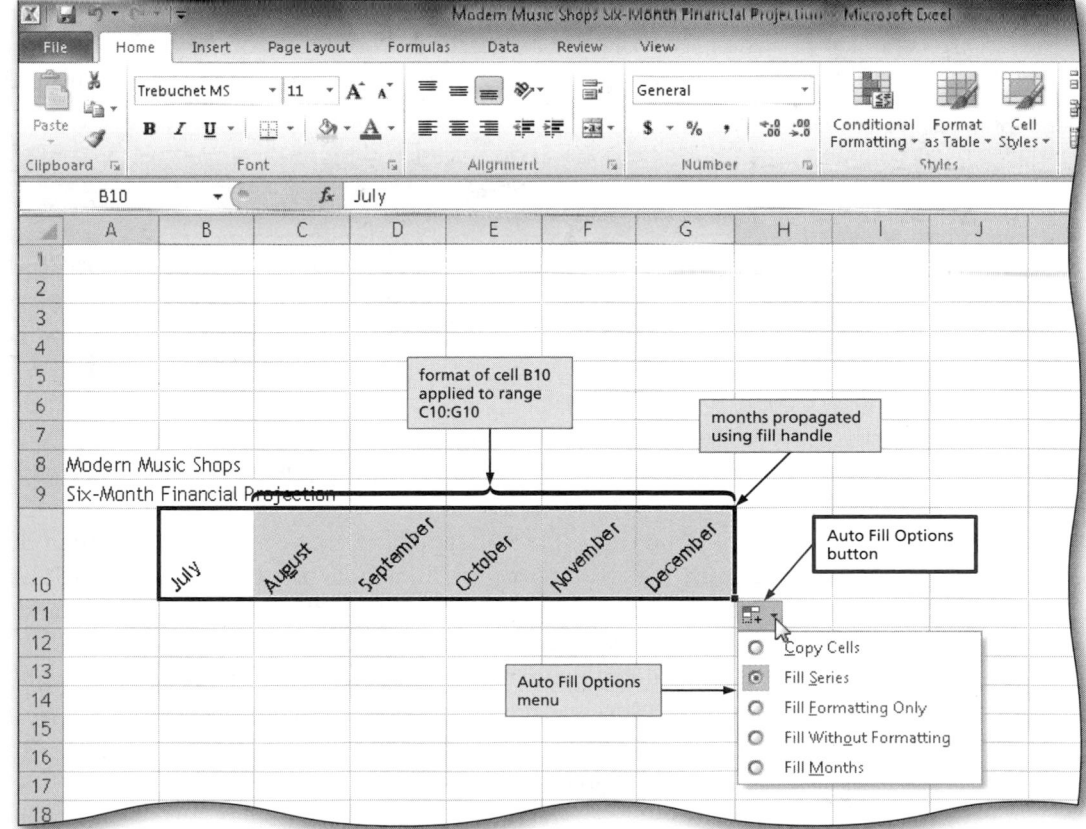

Figure 3–8

source cell or range to the destination cell or range. If this is the case, click the Auto Fill Options button after the range fills and then select the option you desire on the Auto Fill Options menu (Figure 3–8).

6

- Click the Auto Fill Options button to hide the Auto Fill Options menu.

- Select cell H10, type `Total,` and then press the RIGHT ARROW key to enter a column heading.

- Type Chart in cell I10 and then press the RIGHT ARROW key to enter a column heading.

Q&A

Why is the word Total automatically formatted with a 45° rotation?

Excel tries to save you time by automatically recognizing the adjacent cell format in cell G10 and applying it to cell H10. Such behavior also occurs when typing the column heading in cell I10.

Other Ways

1. Enter start month in cell, apply formatting, right-drag fill handle in direction to fill, click Fill Months on shortcut menu

2. Enter start month in cell, apply formatting, select range, click Fill button (Home tab | Editing group), click Series, click AutoFill

---

Using the Auto Fill Options Menu

As shown in Figure 3–8 on the previous page, Fill Series is the default option that Excel uses to fill an area, which means it fills the destination area with a series, using the same formatting as the source area. If you choose another option on the Auto Fill Options menu, then Excel immediately changes the contents of the destination range. Following the use of the fill handle, the Auto Fill Options button remains active until you begin the next Excel operation. Table 3–2 summarizes the options on the Auto Fill Options menu.

Table 3–2 Options Available on the Auto Fill Options Menu	
Auto Fill Option	**Description**
Copy Cells	Fill destination area with contents using format of source area. Do not create a series.
Fill Series	Fill destination area with series using format of source area. This option is the default.
Fill Formatting Only	Fill destination area using format of source area. No content is copied unless fill is series.
Fill Without Formatting	Fill destination area with contents, without the formatting of source area.
Fill Months	Fill destination area with series of months using format of source area. Same as Fill Series and shows as an option only if source area contains a month.

You can use the fill handle to create a series longer than the one shown in Figure 3–8. If you drag the fill handle past cell G10 in Step 4, Excel continues to increment the months and logically will repeat July, August, and so on, if you extend the range far enough to the right.

You can create several different types of series using the fill handle. Table 3–3 illustrates several examples. Notice in examples 4 through 7, 9, and 11 that, if you use the fill handle to create a series of numbers or nonsequential months, you must enter the first item in the series in one cell and the second item in the series in an adjacent cell. Excel still creates the series, however, if the first two items are in a range and the cells between the items are empty. Next, select both cells and drag the fill handle through the destination area.

Table 3–3 Examples of Series Using the Fill Handle		
Example	Contents of Cell(s) Copied Using the Fill Handle	Next Three Values of Extended Series
1	4:00	5:00, 6:00, 7:00
2	Qtr2	Qtr3, Qtr4, Qtr1
3	Quarter 1	Quarter 2, Quarter 3, Quarter 4
4	22-Jul, 22-Sep	22-Nov, 22-Jan, 22-Mar
5	2012, 2013	2014, 2015, 2016
6	1, 2	3, 4, 5
7	625, 600	575, 550, 525
8	Mon	Tue, Wed, Thu
9	Sunday, Tuesday	Thursday, Saturday, Monday
10	4th Section	5th Section, 6th Section, 7th Section
11	−205, −208	−211, −214, −217

To Increase Column Widths

In Chapter 2, you increased column widths after the values were entered into the worksheet. Sometimes, you may want to increase the column widths before you enter the values and, if necessary, adjust them later. The following steps increase the column widths.

1

• Move the mouse pointer to the boundary between column heading A and column heading B so that the mouse pointer changes to a split double arrow in preparation of adjusting the column widths.

• Drag the mouse pointer to the right until the ScreenTip displays the desired column width, Width: 36.00 (293 pixels) in this case. Do not release the mouse button (Figure 3–9).

Figure 3–9

• Release the mouse button to change the width of the column.

• Click column heading B to select the column and then drag through column heading G to select the range in which to change the widths.

• Move the mouse pointer to the boundary between column headings B and C in preparation of resizing

Figure 3–10

column B, and then drag the mouse to the right until the ScreenTip displays the desired width, Width: 14.88 (124 pixels) in this case. Do not release the mouse button (Figure 3–10).

• Release the mouse button to change the width of the selected columns.

• If necessary, scroll the worksheet so that column H is visible and then use the technique described in Step 1 to increase the width of column H to 16.00.

To Enter Row Titles

Excel allows you to indent text in cells. Often, indentation sets off titles, such as row titles, from other titles to create a hierarchy, such as you may find in a table of contents in a book. The following steps enter the row titles in column A and indent several of the row titles.

• If necessary, scroll the worksheet so that column A and row 23 are visible and then enter the row titles in the range A11:A23 but without the indents (Figure 3–11).

• Select cell A12 and then click the Increase Indent button (Home tab | Alignment group) to increase the indentation of the text in the selected cell.

• Select the range A16:A20 and then click the Increase Indent button (Home tab | Alignment group) to increase the indentation of the text in the selected range (Figure 3–11).

Figure 3–11

❷

• Select cell A1 to finish entering the row titles and deselect the current cell.

Q&A

What happens when I click the Increase Indent button?

The Increase Indent button (Home tab | Alignment group) indents the contents of a cell to the right by three spaces each time you click it. The Decrease Indent button decreases the indent by three spaces each time you click it.

Other Ways

1. To indent, right-click range, click Format Cells on shortcut menu, click Alignment tab (Format | Cells dialog box), click Left (Indent) in Horizontal list, type number of spaces to indent in Indent text box, | click OK button (Format Cells dialog box)

Copying a Range of Cells to a Nonadjacent Destination Area

The What-If Assumptions section should be placed in an area of the worksheet that is accessible easily yet does not impair the view of the main section of the worksheet. As shown in Figure 3–3a on page EX 142, the What-If Assumptions should be placed above the calculations in the worksheet. Additionally, the row titles in the Expenses area are the same as the row titles in the What-If Assumptions table, with the exception of the two additional entries in cells A4 (Margin) and A7 (Sales Revenue for Bonus). Hence, the What-If Assumptions table row titles can be created by copying the range A16:A20 to the range A2:A6 and then inserting two rows for the additional entries in cells A4 and A7. The source area (range A16:A20) is not adjacent to the destination area (range A2:A6). The first two chapters used the fill handle to copy a source area to an adjacent destination area. To copy a source area to a nonadjacent destination area, however, you cannot use the fill handle.

A more versatile method of copying a source area is to use the Copy button and Paste button (Home tab | Clipboard group). You can use these two buttons to copy a source area to an adjacent or nonadjacent destination area.

BTW

Fitting Entries in a Cell
An alternative to increasing column widths or row heights is to shrink the characters in a cell to fit the current width of the column. To shrink to fit, click Format Cells: Alignment Dialog Box Button Launcher (Home tab | Alignment group), and click Shrink to fit in the Text control area. After shrinking entries to fit in cells, consider using the Zoom slider on the status bar to make the entries more readable.

To Copy a Range of Cells to a Nonadjacent Destination Area

The Copy button copies the contents and format of the source area to the **Office Clipboard**, a reserved place in the computer's memory that allows you to collect text and graphics from an Office document and then paste them into almost any other type of document. The Paste button copies the item from the Office Clipboard to the destination area.

The following steps enter the what-if area row heading and use the Copy and Paste buttons to copy the range A16:A20 to the nonadjacent range A2:A6.

1
● With cell A1 selected, type **What-If Assumptions** as the new row title.

● Select the range A16:A20 and then click the Copy button (Home tab | Clipboard group) to copy the values and formats of the selected range, A16:A20 in this case, to the Office Clipboard.

● Select cell A2, the top cell in the destination area (Figure 3–12).

Why do I not need to select the entire destination area?

You are not required to select the entire destination area (range A2:A6) before clicking the Paste button (Home tab | Clipboard group). Excel needs to know only the upper-left cell of the destination area. In the case of a single column range, such as A2:A6, the top cell of the destination area (cell A2) also is the upper-left cell of the destination area.

Figure 3–12

2

- Click the Paste button (Home tab | Clipboard group) to copy the values and formats of the last item placed on the Office Clipboard, range A16:A20 in this case, to the destination area, A2:A6 in this case (Figure 3–13).

Q&A

What if data already existed in the destination area?

When you complete a copy, the values and formats in the destination area are replaced with the values and formats of the source area. Any data contained in the destination area prior to the copy and paste is lost. If you accidentally delete valuable data, immediately click the Undo button on the Quick Access Toolbar.

3

- Press the ESC key to remove the marquee from the source area and disable the Paste button (Home tab | Clipboard group).

Figure 3–13

Other Ways

1. Right-click source area, click Copy on shortcut menu, right-click destination area, click Paste icon on shortcut menu

2. Select source area and point on border of range; while holding down CTRL key, drag source area to destination area

3. Select source area, press CTRL+C, select destination area, press CTRL+V

BTW

Q&As
For a complete list of the Q&As found in many of the step-by-step sequences in this book, visit the Excel 2010 Q&A Web page (scsite.com/ex2010/qa).

Using the Paste Options Menu

After you click the Paste button, Excel immediately displays the Paste Options button, as shown in Figure 3–13. If you click the Paste Options button arrow and select an option on the Paste Options gallery, Excel modifies the most recent paste operation based on your selection. Table 3–4 summarizes the options available on the Paste Options gallery. When the Paste Options button is visible, you can use shortcut keys to access the paste commands available in the Paste Options gallery. Additionally, you can use combinations of the options in the Paste Options gallery to customize your paste operation. That is, after clicking one of the icons in the Paste Options gallery, you can open the gallery again to further adjust your paste operation. The Paste button (Home tab | Clipboard group) includes an arrow that, when clicked, displays the same options as does the Paste Options button arrow.

Table 3–4 Options Available in the Paste Options Gallery

Paste Option Icon	Paste Option	Shortcut Key	Description
	Paste	CTRL+P	Copy contents and format of source area. This option is the default.
fx	Formulas	CTRL+F	Copy formulas from the source area, but not the contents and format.
%fx	Formulas & Number Formatting	CTRL+O	Copy formulas and format for numbers and formulas of source area, but not the contents.
	Keep Source Formatting	CTRL+K	Copy contents, format, and styles of source area.
	No Borders	CTRL+B	Copy contents and format of source area, but not any borders.
	Keep Source Column Widths	CTRL+W	Copy contents and format of source area. Change destination column widths to source column widths.
	Transpose	CTRL+T	Copy the contents and format of the source area, but transpose, or swap, the rows and columns.
123	Values	CTRL+V	Copy contents of source area, but not the formatting for formulas.
123%	Values & Number Formatting	CTRL+A	Copy contents and format of source area for numbers or formulas, but use format of destination area for text.
123	Values & Source Formatting	CTRL+E	Copy contents and formatting of source area, but not the formula.
%	Formatting	CTRL+R	Copy format of source area, but not the contents.
	Paste Link	CTRL+N	Copy contents and format and link cells so that a change to the cells in source area updates the corresponding cells in destination area.
	Picture	CTRL+U	Copy an image of the source area as a picture.
	Linked Pictures	CTRL+I	Copy an image of the source area as a picture so that a change to the cells in source area updates the picture in destination area.

An alternative to clicking the Paste button is to press the ENTER key. The ENTER key completes the paste operation, removes the marquee from the source area, and disables the Paste button so that you cannot paste the copied source area to other destination areas. The ENTER key was not used in the previous set of steps so that the capabilities of the Paste Options button could be discussed. The Paste Options button does not appear in the screen when you use the ENTER key to complete the paste operation.

Using Drag and Drop to Move or Copy Cells

You also can use the mouse to move or copy cells. First, you select the source area and point to the border of the cell or range. You know you are pointing to the border of the cell or range when the mouse pointer changes to a block arrow. To move the selected cell or cells, drag the selection to the destination area. To copy a selection, hold down the CTRL key while dragging the selection to the destination area. You know Excel is in copy mode when a small plus sign appears next to the block arrow mouse pointer. Be sure to release the mouse button before you release the CTRL key. Using the mouse to move or copy cells is called **drag and drop**.

BTW

Cutting

When you cut a cell or range of cells using the Cut command on a shortcut menu or Cut button (Home tab | Clipboard group), Excel copies the cells to the Office Clipboard, but does not remove the cells from the source area until you paste the cells in the destination area by either clicking the Paste button (Home tab | Clipboard group) or pressing the ENTER key. When you complete the paste, Excel clears the cell's or range of cell's entries and their formats from the source area.

Using Cut and Paste to Move Cells

Another way to move cells is to select them, click the Cut button (Home tab | Clipboard group) (Figure 3–12 on page EX 151) to remove them from the worksheet and copy them to the Office Clipboard, select the destination area, and then click the Paste button (Home tab | Clipboard group) or press the ENTER key. You also can use the Cut command on the shortcut menu, instead of the Cut button.

Inserting and Deleting Cells in a Worksheet

At any time while the worksheet is on the screen, you can insert cells to enter new data or delete cells to remove unwanted data. You can insert or delete individual cells; a range of cells, rows, columns; or entire worksheets.

To Insert a Row

According to the sketch of the worksheet in Figure 3–3a on page EX 142, two rows must be inserted in the What-If Assumptions table, one between Commission and Marketing for the Margin assumption and another between Research and Development and Support, General, and Administrative for the Sales Revenue for Bonus assumption. The following steps insert the new rows into the worksheet.

1

- Right-click row heading 4, the row below where you want to insert a row, to display the shortcut menu and the Mini toolbar (Figure 3–14).

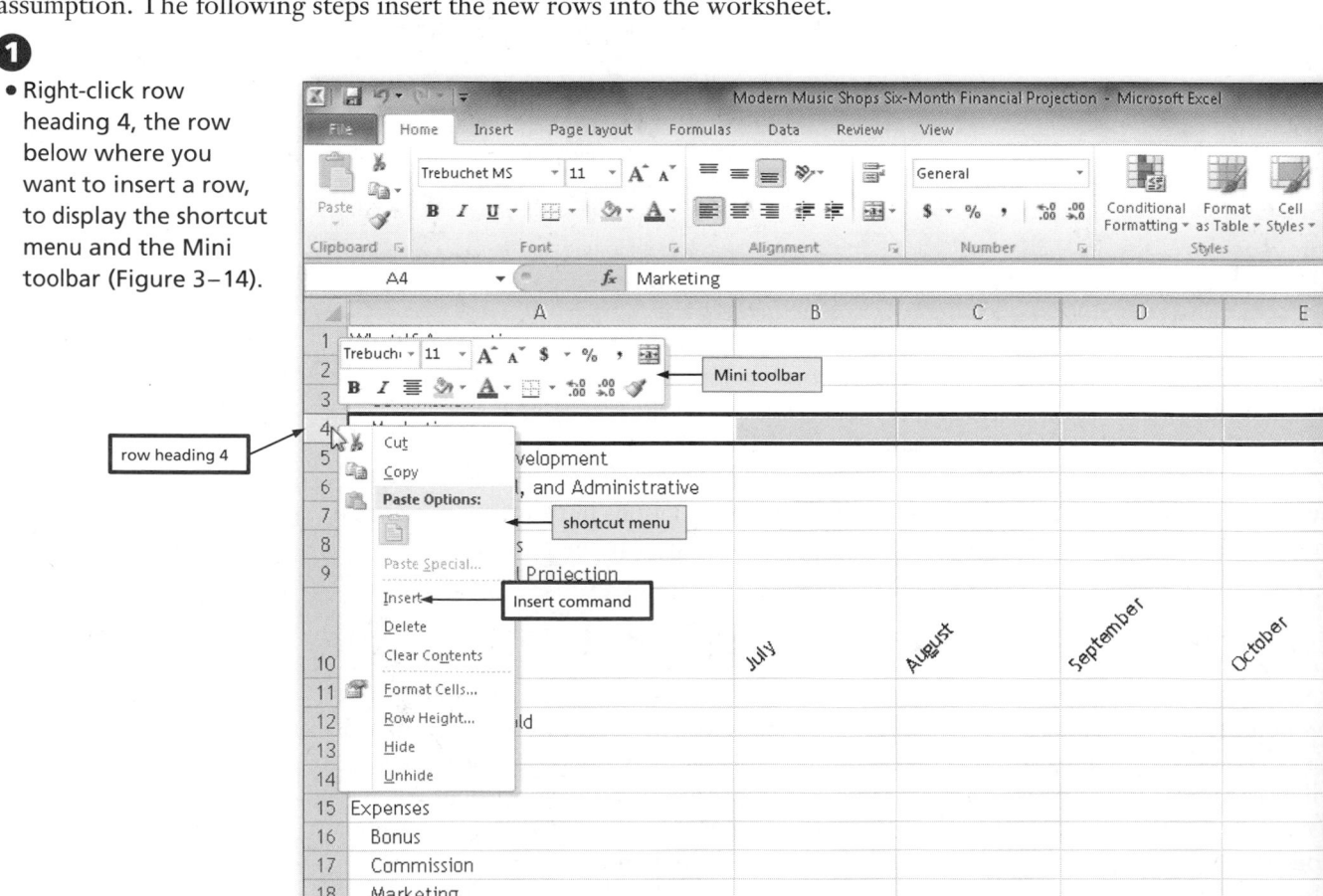

Figure 3–14

● Click Insert on the shortcut menu to insert a new row in the worksheet by shifting the selected row and all rows below it down one row.

● Select cell A4 in the new row and then enter **Margin** to enter a new row title (Figure 3–15).

What is the resulting format of the new row?

The cells in the new row inherit the formats of the cells in the row above them. You can change this behavior by clicking the Insert Options button that appears immediately below the inserted row. Following the insertion of a row, the Insert Options button allows you to select from the following options: (1) 'Format Same As Above'; (2) 'Format Same As Below'; and (3) Clear Formatting. The 'Format Same as Above' option is the default. The Insert Options button remains active until you begin the next Excel operation. Excel does not display the Insert Options button if the initial row does not contain any formatted data.

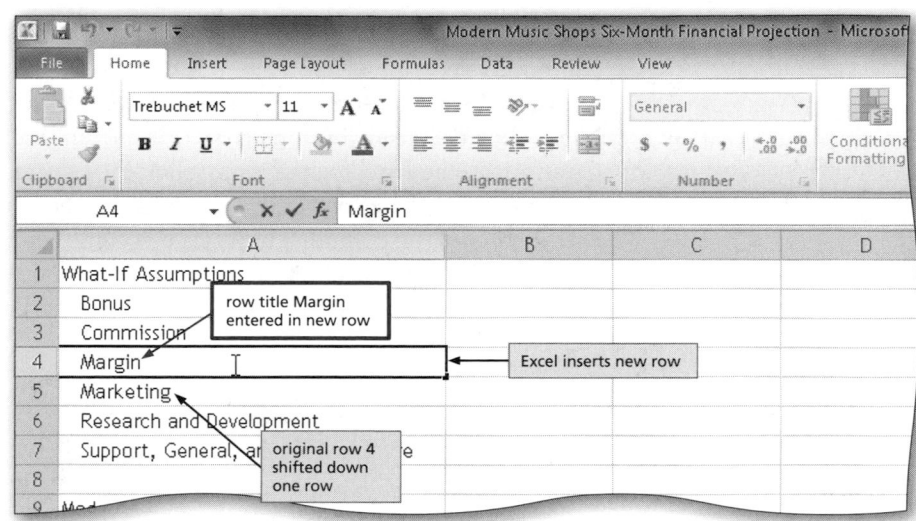

Figure 3–15

● Right-click row heading 7 to display a shortcut menu and then click Insert on the shortcut menu to insert a new row in the worksheet.

● Select cell A7 in the new row and then enter **Sales Revenue for Bonus** to enter a new row title (Figure 3–16).

What would happen if cells in the shifted rows were included in formulas?

If the rows that shift down include cell references in formulas located in the worksheet, Excel automatically would adjust the cell references in the formulas to their new locations. Thus, in Step 2, if a formula in the worksheet references a cell in row 7 before the insert, then Excel adjusts the cell reference in the formula to row 8 after the insert.

Figure 3–16

Other Ways

1. Insert (Home tab | Cells group), click Insert Sheet Rows

2. Press CTRL + SHIFT + PLUS SIGN, click Entire row, click OK button

BTW

Inserting Multiple Rows

If you want to insert multiple rows, you have two choices. You can insert a single row by using the Insert command on the shortcut menu and then repeatedly press F4 to continue inserting rows. Alternatively, you can select any number of existing rows to choose the number of rows that you want to insert. For instance, if you want to insert five rows, select five existing rows in the worksheet, right-click the rows, and then click Insert on the shortcut menu.

BTW

Dragging Ranges

You can move and insert a selected cell or range between existing cells by holding down the SHIFT key while you drag the selection to the gridline where you want to insert the selected cell or range. You also can copy and insert by holding down the CTRL+SHIFT keys while you drag the selection to the desired gridline.

BTW

Ranges and Undo

The incorrect use of copying, deleting, inserting, and moving ranges of cells have the potential to render a worksheet useless. Carefully review the results of these actions before continuing on to the next task. If you are not sure the result of the action is correct, click the Undo button on the Quick Access Toolbar.

Inserting Columns

You insert columns into a worksheet in the same way you insert rows. To insert columns, select one or more columns immediately to the right of where you want Excel to insert the new column or columns. Select the number of columns you want to insert. Next, click the Insert button arrow (Home tab | Cells group) and then click Insert Sheet Columns in the Insert list or right-click the selected column(s), then click Insert on the shortcut menu. The Insert command on the shortcut menu requires that you select an entire column (or columns) to insert a column (or columns). Following the insertion of a column, Excel displays the Insert Options button, which allows you to modify the insertion in a fashion similar to that discussed earlier when inserting rows.

Inserting Single Cells or a Range of Cells

The Insert command on the shortcut menu or the Insert Cells command on the Insert list of the Insert button (Home tab | Cells group) allows you to insert a single cell or a range of cells. You should be aware that if you shift a single cell or a range of cells, however, it no longer lines up with its associated cells. To ensure that the values in the worksheet do not get out of order, spreadsheet experts recommend that you insert only entire rows or entire columns. When you insert a single cell or a range of cells, Excel displays the Insert Options button so that you can change the format of the inserted cell, using options similar to those for inserting rows and columns.

Deleting Columns and Rows

The Delete button (Home tab | Cells group) or the Delete command on the shortcut menu removes cells (including the data and format) from the worksheet. Deleting cells is not the same as clearing cells. The Clear command, described in Chapter 1 on page EX 52, clears the data from the cells, but the cells remain in the worksheet. The Delete command removes the cells from the worksheet and shifts the remaining rows up (when you delete rows) or shifts the remaining columns to the left (when you delete columns). If formulas located in other cells reference cells in the deleted row or column, Excel does not adjust these cell references. Excel displays the error message **#REF!** in those cells to indicate a cell reference error. For example, if cell A7 contains the formula =A4+A5 and you delete row 5, Excel assigns the formula =A4+#REF! to cell A6 (originally cell A7) and displays the error message #REF! in cell A6. Excel also displays an Error Options button when you select the cell containing the error message #REF!, which allows you to select options to determine the nature of the problem.

To Enter Numbers with Format Symbols

The next step in creating the Six-Month Financial Projection worksheet is to enter the what-if assumptions values in the range B2:B8. The numbers in the table can be entered and then formatted as in Chapters 1 and 2, or each one can be entered with format symbols. When a number is entered with a **format symbol**, Excel immediately displays it with the assigned format. Valid format symbols include the dollar sign ($), comma (,), and percent sign (%).

If you enter a whole number, it appears without any decimal places. If you enter a number with one or more decimal places and a format symbol, Excel displays the number with two decimal places. Table 3–5 illustrates several examples of numbers entered with format symbols. The number in parentheses in column 4 indicates the number of decimal places.

le 3–5 Numbers Entered with Format Symbols		
rmat Symbol	Typed in Formula Bar	Displays in Cell	Comparable Format
	374, 149	374, 149	Comma(0)
	5,833.6	5,833.60	Comma(2)
	$58917	$58,917	Currency(0)
	$842.51	$842.51	Currency(2)
	$63,574.9	$63,574.90	Currency(2)
	85%	85%	Percent(0)
	12.80%	12.80%	Percent(2)
	68.4222%	68.4222%	Percent(4)

The following step enters the numbers in the What-If Assumptions table with format symbols.

nter 200,000.00 in
ell B2, 5.75% in cell B3,
7.50% in cell B4, 15.00%
n cell B5, 7.50% in cell B6,
,500,000.00 in cell B7, and
8.75% in cell B8 to display
he entries using formats based
n the format symbols entered
with the numbers (Figure 3–17).

Figure 3–17

Other Ways

1. Right-click range, click Format Cells on shortcut menu, click Number tab (Format Cells dialog box), click category in Category

 list, [select desired format], click OK button (Format Cells dialog box)

2. Press CTRL+1, click Number tab (Format Cells

 dialog box), click category in Category list, [select desired format], click OK button (Format Cells dialog box)

Freeze Column and Row Titles

Freezing worksheet titles is a useful technique for viewing large worksheets that extend beyond the window. rmally, when you scroll down or to the right, the column titles in row 12 and the row titles in column A that ine the numbers no longer appear on the screen. This makes it difficult to remember what the numbers in these s and columns represent. To alleviate this problem, Excel allows you to **freeze the titles**, so that Excel displays titles on the screen, no matter how far down or to the right you scroll.

The steps on the following page use the Freeze Panes button (View tab | Window group) to freeze the work- et title and column titles in rows 10, 11, and 12, and the row titles in column A.

1

- Scroll the worksheet to ensure that Excel displays row 10 as the first row and column A on the screen.

- Select cell B13 to select the cell on which to freeze panes.

- Display the View tab and then click the Freeze Panes button (View tab | Window group) to display the Freeze Panes gallery (Figure 3–18).

Q&A

Why should I ensure that row 10 is the first row displayed?

Before freezing the titles, it is important that Excel display the first row that you want frozen as the first row displayed. For example, if cell B13 was selected while displaying row 1, then Excel would freeze the what-if assumptions and only show a few rows of data in the Six-Month Financial Project area of the worksheet. To ensure that you can view as much data as possible, always scroll to a row that maximizes the view of your important data before freezing panes.

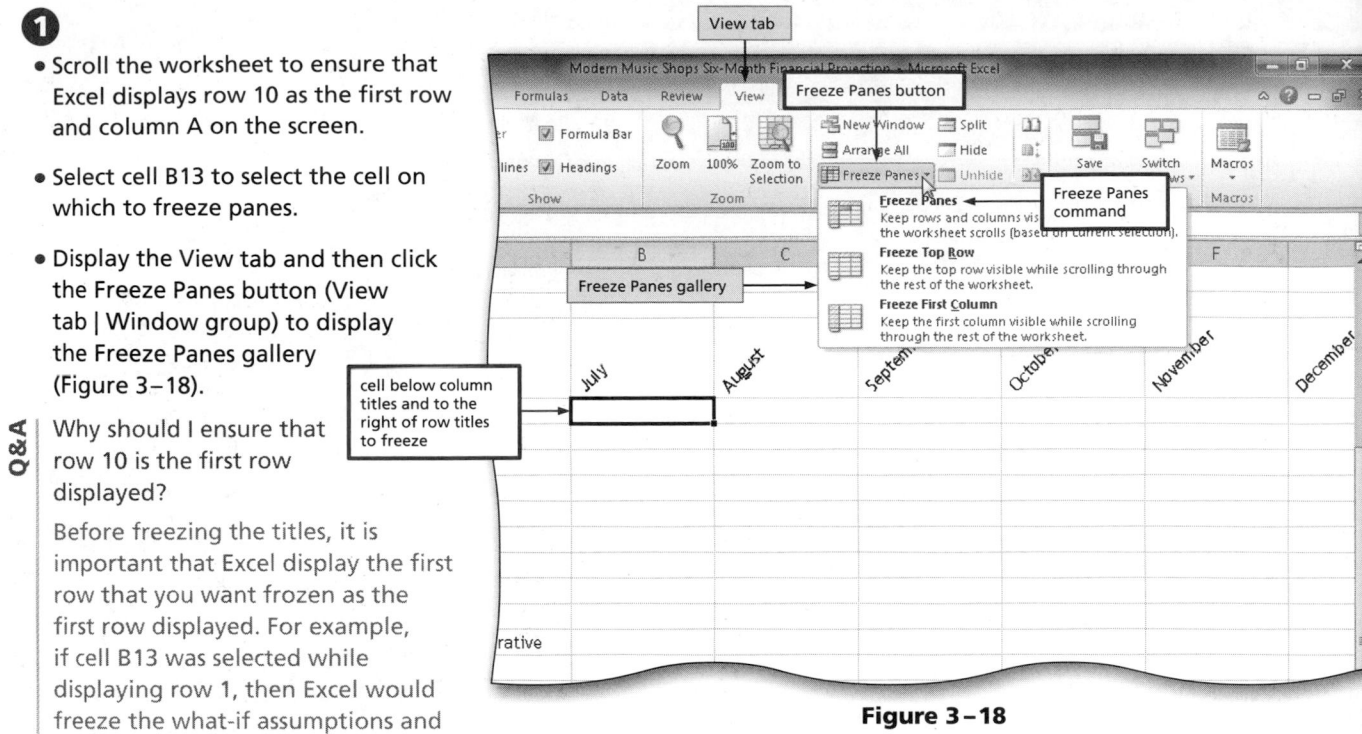

Figure 3–18

2

- Click Freeze Panes in the Freeze Panes gallery to freeze rows and columns to the left and above the selected cell, column A and rows 10 through 12 in this case (Figure 3–19).

Q&A

What happens after I click the Freeze Panes command?

Excel displays a thin black line on the right side of column A, indicating the split between the frozen row titles in column A and the rest of the worksheet. It also displays a thin black line below row 12, indicating the split between the frozen column titles in rows 10 through 12 and the rest of the worksheet (Figure 3–19).

Figure 3–19

To Enter the Projected Monthly Sales

The following steps enter the projected revenue, listed earlier in Table 3–1 on page EX 143, in row 13 and compute the projected six-month revenue in cell H13.

If necessary, display the Home tab.

Enter `3113612.16` in cell B13, `7962235.53` in cell C13, `5112268.58` in cell D13, `2924627.87` in cell E13, `7630534.65` in cell F13, and `3424270.23` in cell G13.

Select cell H13 and then click the Sum button (Home tab | Editing group) twice to create a sum in the selected cell (Figure 3–20).

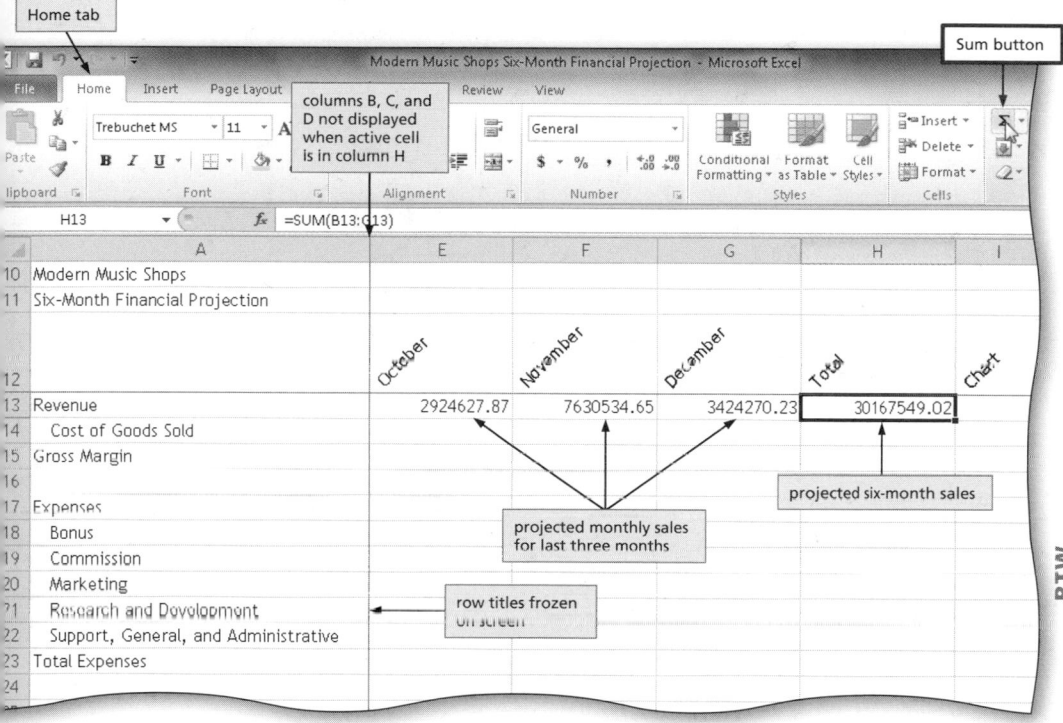

Figure 3–20

To Enter and Format the System Date

The sketch of the worksheet in Figure 3–3a on page EX 142 includes a date stamp on the right side of the heading section. A **date stamp** shows the date a workbook, report, or other document was created or the period it represents. In business, a report often is meaningless without a date stamp. For example, if a printout of the worksheet in this chapter were distributed to the company's analysts, the date stamp would show when the six-month projections were made, as well as what period the report represents.

A simple way to create a date stamp is to use the NOW function to enter the system date tracked by your computer in a cell in the worksheet. The **NOW function** is one of 22 date and time functions available in Excel. When assigned to a cell, the NOW function returns a number that corresponds to the system date and time beginning with December 31, 1899. For example, January 1, 1900 equals 1, January 2, 1900 equals 2, and so on. Noon equals .5. Thus, noon on January 1, 1900 equals 1.5 and 6 P.M. on January 1, 1900 equals 1.75. If the computer's system date is set to the current date, which normally it is, then the date stamp is equivalent to the current date.

The steps on the following pages enter the NOW function and then change the format from mm/dd/yyyy h:mm to mm/dd/yyyy.

1

- Select cell I11 and then click the Insert Function box in the formula bar to display the Insert Function dialog box.

- Click the 'Or select a category' box arrow (Insert Function dialog box) and then select Date & Time in the list to populate the 'Select a function' list with data and time functions.

- Scroll down in the 'Select a function list' and then click NOW to select the required function (Figure 3–21).

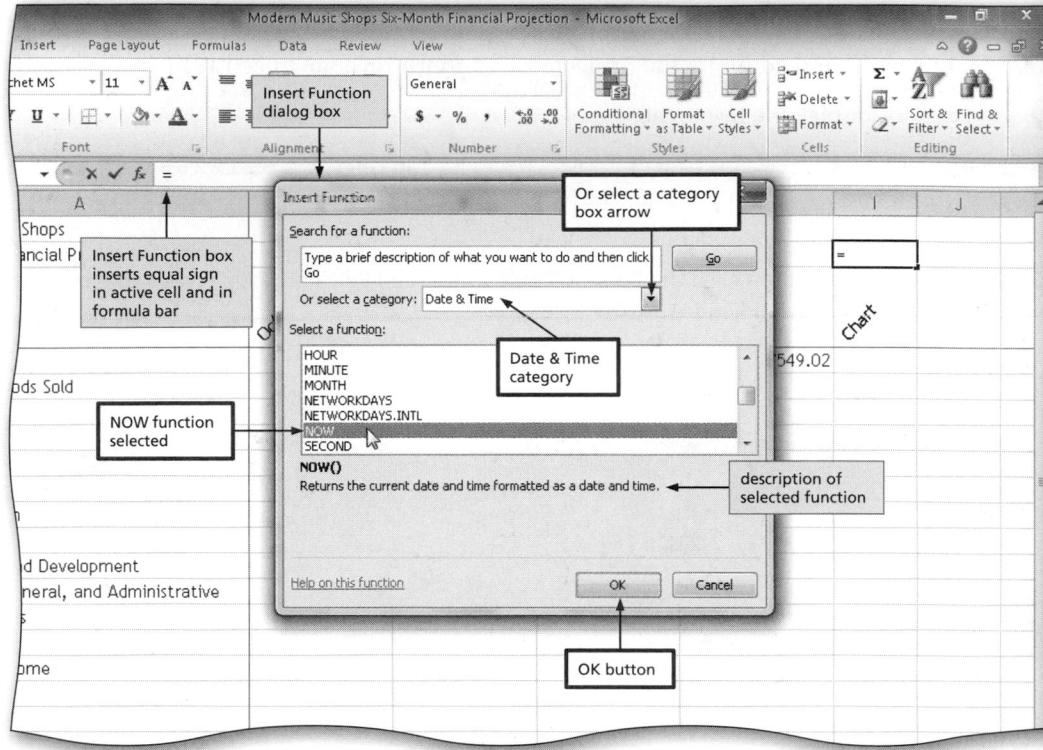

Figure 3–21

2

- Click the OK button (Insert Function dialog box) to close the Insert Function dialog box and display the Function Arguments dialog box.

- Click the OK button (Function Arguments dialog box) to display the system date and time in the selected cell, using the default date and time format mm/dd/yyyy hh:mm.

- Right-click cell I11 to display a shortcut menu and Mini toolbar (Figure 3–22).

Q&A
Why does the date appear with the mm/dd/yyyy hh:mm format?

Figure 3–22

Excel automatically formats the result of the NOW function as a date, using the date and time format, mm/dd/yyyy hh:mm, where the first mm is the month, dd is the day of the month, yyyy is the year, hh is the hour of the day, and mm is the minutes past the hour.

• Click Format Cells on the shortcut menu to display the Format Cells dialog box.

• If necessary, click the Number tab (Format Cells dialog box) to display the Number sheet.

• Click Date in the Category list (Format Cells dialog box) to display the types of date formats in the Type list. Scroll down in the Type list and then click 3/14/2001 to display a sample of the data in the active cell, I11 in this case, using the selected format in the Sample area (Figure 3–23).

Why do the dates in the Type box show March 14, 2001 instead of the current date?

The date March 14, 2001 is used as a sample date in the Format cells dialog box.

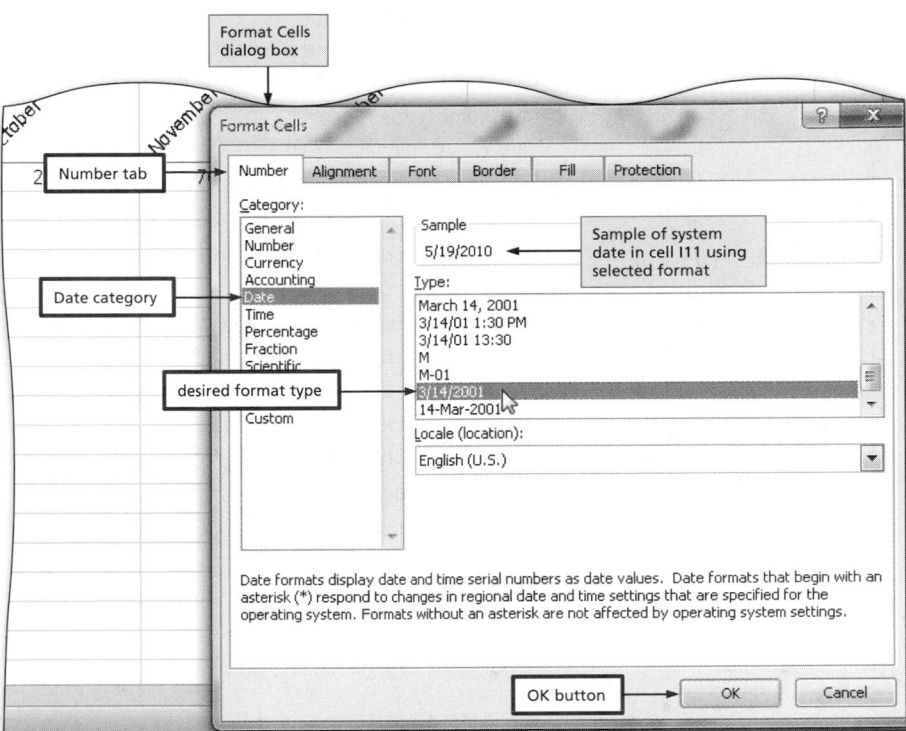

Figure 3–23

• Click the OK button (Format Cells dialog box) to display the system date in the format mm/dd/yyyy.

• Double-click the border between columns I and J to change the width of the column to best fit (Figure 3–24).

How does Excel format a date?

In Figure 3–24, the date is displayed right-aligned in the cell because

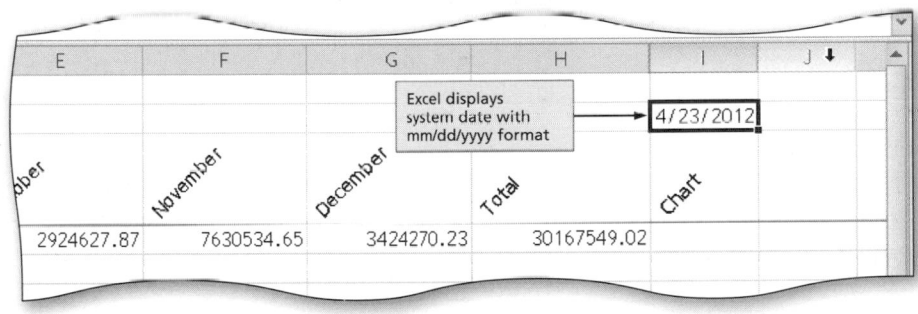

Figure 3–24

Excel treats a date as a number formatted to display as a date. If you assign the General format (Excel's default format for numbers) to a date in a cell, the date is displayed as a number with two decimal places. For example, if the system time and date is 9:00 AM on November 13, 2012 and the cell containing the NOW function is assigned the General format, then Excel displays the following number in the cell:

| 41226.375 |
| Number of days since December 31, 1899 | Time of day is 9:00 AM (Portion of day complete) |

The whole number portion of the number (41226) represents the number of days since December 31, 1899. The decimal portion of the number (.375) represents 9:00 AM as the time of day, at which point 37.5% of the day is complete. To assign the General format to a cell, click General in the Category list in the Format Cells dialog box (Figure 3–23).

Other Ways

1. Click Date & Time (Formulas tab | Function Library group), click now

2. Press CTRL + SEMICOLON (not a volatile date)

3. Press CTRL + SHIFT + # to format date to day-month-year

Break Point: If you wish to stop working through the chapter at this point, you can quit Excel now and then resume the project at a later point in time by starting Excel, opening the file called Modern Music Shops Six-Month Financial Projection, and continuing to follow the steps from this location forward.

Absolute versus Relative Addressing

The next sections describe the formulas and functions needed to complete the calculation in the worksheet.

As you learned in Chapters 1 and 2, Excel modifies cell references when copying formulas. While copying formulas, however, sometimes you do not want Excel to change cell references. To keep a cell reference constant when copying a formula or function, Excel uses a technique called absolute cell referencing. To specify an absolute cell reference in a formula, enter a dollar sign ($) before any column letters or row numbers you want to keep constant in formulas you plan to copy. For example, $B$4 is an absolute cell reference, whereas B4 is a relative cell reference. Both reference the same cell. The difference becomes apparent when they are copied to a destination area. A formula using the **absolute cell reference** $B$4 instructs Excel to keep the cell reference B4 constant (absolute) in the formula as it copies it to the destination area. A formula using the **relative cell reference** B4 instructs Excel to adjust the cell reference as it copies it to the destination area. A cell reference with only one dollar sign before either the column or the row is called a **mixed cell reference**. When planning formulas, be aware of when you need to use absolute, relative, and mixed cell references. Table 3–6 gives some additional examples of each of these types of cell references.

Table 3–6 Examples of Absolute, Relative, and Mixed Cell References		
Cell Reference	**Type of Reference**	**Meaning**
$B$4	Absolute cell reference	Both column and row references remain the same when you copy this cell, because the cell references are absolute.
B$4	Mixed reference	This cell reference is mixed. The column reference changes when you copy this cell to another column because it is relative. The row reference does not change because it is absolute.
$B4	Mixed reference	This cell reference is mixed. The column reference does not change because it is absolute. The row reference changes when you copy this cell reference to another row because it is relative.
B4	Relative cell reference	Both column and row references are relative. When copied to another cell, both the column and row in the cell reference are adjusted to reflect the new location.

The next step is to enter the formulas that calculate the following values for July: cost of goods sold (cell B14), gross margin (cell B15), expenses (range B18:B22), total expenses (cell B23), and the operating income (cell B25). The formulas are based on the projected monthly revenue in cell B13 and the assumptions in the range B2:B8.

To Enter a Formula Containing Absolute Cell References

The formulas for each column (month) are the same, except for the reference to the projected monthly revenue in row 13, which varies according to the month (B13 for July, C13 for August, and so on). Thus, the formulas for July can be entered in column B and then copied to columns C through G. Table 3–7 shows the formulas for determining the July cost of goods sold, gross margin, expenses, total expenses, and operating income in column B.

ble 3-7 Formulas for Determining Cost of Goods Sold, Margin, Expenses, Total Expenses, d Operating Income for July

ell	Row Title	Formula	Comment
4	Cost of Goods Sold	=B13 * (1 - B4)	Revenue times (1 minus Margin %)
5	Gross Margin	= B13 - B14	Revenue minus Cost of Goods Sold
8	Bonus	=IF(B13 >= B7, B2, 0)	Bonus equals value in B2 or 0
9	Commission	=B13 * B3	Revenue times Commission %
0	Marketing	=B13 * B5	Revenue times Marketing %
1	Research and Development	=B13 * B6	Revenue times Research and Development %
2	Support, General, and Administrative	=B13 * B8	Revenue times Support, General, and Administrative %
3	Total Expenses	=SUM(B18:B22)	Sum of July Expenses
5	Operating Income	=B15 - B23	Gross Margin minus Total Expenses

As the formulas are entered as shown in Table 3-7 in column B for July and then copied to columns C ough G (August through December) in the worksheet, Excel will adjust the cell references for each column tomatically. Thus, after the copy, the August Commission expense in cell C19 would be =C13 * C3. While the l reference C13 (August Revenue) is correct, the cell reference C3 references an empty cell. The formula for cell 9 should read =C13 * B3, rather than =C13 * C3, because B3 references the Commission % value in the What-If sumptions table. In this instance, a way is needed to keep a cell reference in a formula the same, or constant, when s copied.

The following steps enter the cost of goods formula = B13*(1 – $B$4) in cell B14 using Point mode. To enter absolute cell reference, you can type the dollar sign ($) as part of the cell reference or enter it by pressing F4 with e insertion point in or to the right of the cell reference to change it to absolute.

Press CTRL+HOME to select cell B13 and then click cell B14 to show cell B13 and to select the cell in which to enter the first formula.

Type = (equal sign), select cell B13, type * (1–b4 to continue entering the formula, and then press F4 to change the most recently typed cell reference, in this case cell b4, from a relative cell reference to an absolute cell reference. Type) to complete the formula (Figure 3–25).

Is an absolute reference required in this formula?

No, because a mixed cell reference could have been used. The formula in cell B14 will be copied across columns, rather than down rows. So, the formula entered in cell B14 in Step 1 could have been entered as =B13*(1–$B4), rather than =B13*(1–$B$4). That is, the formula could have included the mixed cell reference $B4, rather than the absolute cell reference $B$4. When you copy a formula across columns, the row does not change anyway. The key is to ensure that column B remains constant as you copy the formula across columns. To change the absolute cell reference to a mixed cell reference, continue to press the F4 key until you achieve the desired cell reference.

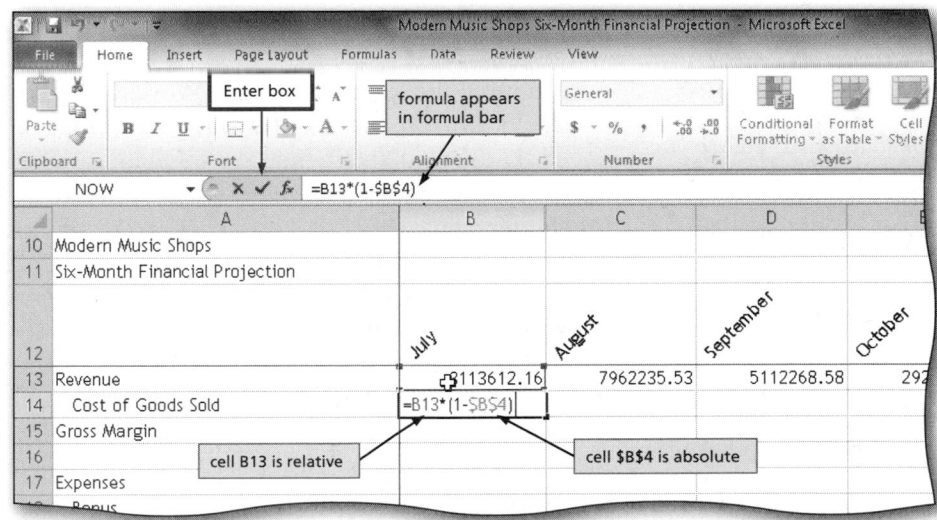

Figure 3–25

②

• Click the Enter box in the formula bar to display the result, 1323285.168, instead of the formula in B14 (Figure 3–26).

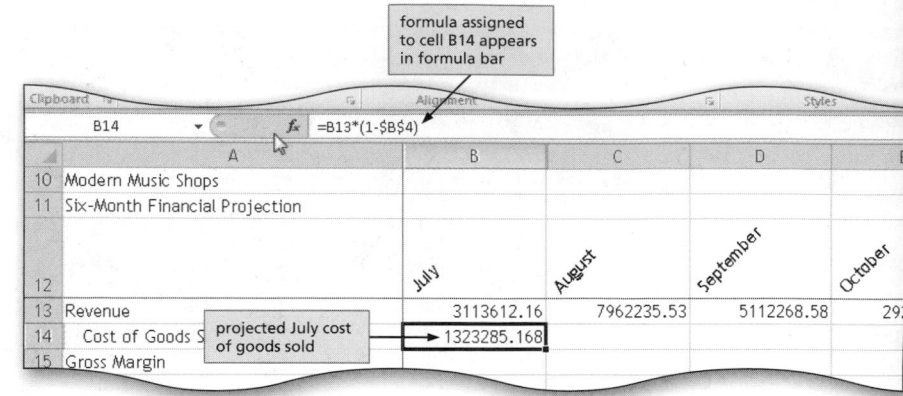

Figure 3–26

③

• Click cell B15 to select the cell in which to enter the next formula, type = (equal sign), click cell B13, type − (minus sign), and then click cell B14 to add a reference to the cell to the formula.

• Click the Enter box in the formula bar to display the result in the selected cell, in this case gross margin for July, 1790326.992, in cell B15 (Figure 3–27).

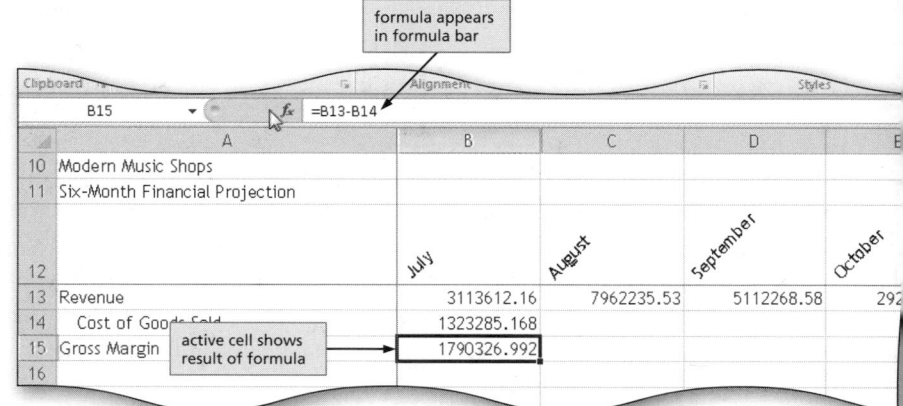

Figure 3–27

Making Decisions — The IF Function

Logical Operators in IF Functions
IF functions can use logical operators, such as AND, OR, and NOT. For example, the three IF functions =IF(AND(A1>C1, B1<C2), "OK", "Not OK") and =IF(OR(K5>J5, C3<K6), "OK", "Not OK") and =IF(NOT(B10<C10), "OK", "Not OK") use logical operators. In the first example, both logical tests must be true for the value_if_true OK to be assigned to the cell. In the second example, one or the other logical tests must be true for the value_if_true OK to be assigned to the cell. In the third example, the logical test B10<C10 must be false for the value_if_true OK to be assigned to the cell.

According to the Request for New Workbook in Figure 3–2 on page EX 140, if the projected July revenue in cell B13 is greater than or equal to the sales revenue for bonus in cell B7 (3,500,000.00), then the July bonus value in cell B18 is equal to the bonus value in cell B2 (200,000.00); otherwise, cell B18 is equal to 0. One way to assign the July bonus value in cell B18 is to check to see if the revenue in cell B13 equals or exceeds the sales revenue for the bonus amount in cell B7 and, if so, then to enter 200,000.00 in cell B18. You can use this manual process for all six months by checking the values for the corresponding months.

Because the data in the worksheet changes each time a report is prepared or the figures are adjusted, however, it is preferable to have Excel assign the monthly bonus to the entries in the appropriate cells automatically. To do so, cell B18 must include a formula or function that displays 200,000.00 or 0.00 (zero), depending on whether the projected July revenue in cell B13 is greater than, equal to, or less than the sales revenue for bonus value in cell B7.

The **IF function** is useful when you want to assign a value to a cell based on a logical test. For example, using the IF function, cell B18 can be assigned the following IF function:

$$=IF(B13>=\$B\$7, \$B\$2, 0)$$

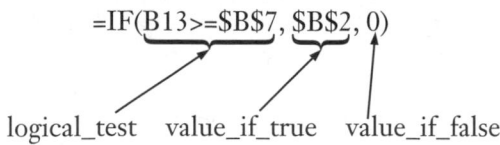

logical_test   value_if_true   value_if_false

The IF function instructs Excel that, if the projected July revenue in cell B13 is greater than or equal to the sales revenue for bonus value in cell B7, then Excel should display the value 200000 in cell B2, in cell B18. If the projected July revenue in cell B13 is less than the sales revenue for bonus value in cell B7, then Excel displays a 0 (zero) in cell B18.

The general form of the IF function is:

$$=IF(logical\_test, value\_if\_true, value\_if\_false)$$

The argument, logical_test, is made up of two expressions and a comparison operator. Each expression can be a cell reference, a number, text, a function, or a formula. Valid comparison operators, their meaning, and examples of their use in IF functions are shown in Table 3–8. The argument, value_if_true, is the value you want Excel to display in the cell when the logical test is true. The argument, value_if_false, is the value you want Excel to display in the cell when the logical test is false.

Table 3–8 Comparison Operators		
Comparison Operator	Meaning	Example
=	Equal to	=IF(B12 = 200, F3 * H4, E10 + F3)
<	Less than	=IF(G56 * Q56 < D12, $M$10, B9 ^ 5)
>	Greater than	=IF(MIN(A12:A52) > 75, 0, 1)
>=	Greater than or equal to	=IF($T$9 >= B7, P3 - H12, 1000)
<=	Less than or equal to	=IF(C9 * G2 <= 99, $T35, 350 * C9)
<>	Not equal to	=IF(G15 <> 1, "No","Yes")

To Enter an IF Function

The following steps assign the IF function =IF(B13>=$B$7,$B$2,0) to cell B18. This IF function determines whether or not the worksheet assigns a bonus for July.

1

- Click cell B18 to select the cell for the next formula.

- Click the Insert Function box in the formula bar to display the Insert Function dialog box.

- Click the 'Or select a category' box arrow (Insert Function dialog box) and then select Logical in the list to populate the 'Select a function' list with logic functions.

- Click IF in the 'Select a function list' to select the required function (Figure 3–28).

Figure 3–28

2

- Click the OK button (Insert Function dialog box) to display the Function Arguments dialog box.

- Type b13>=b7 in the Logical test box to enter a logical test for the IF function.

- Type b2 in the Value_if_true box to enter the result of the IF function if the logical test is true.

- Type 0 in the Value_if_false box to enter the result of the IF function if the logical test is false (Figure 3–29).

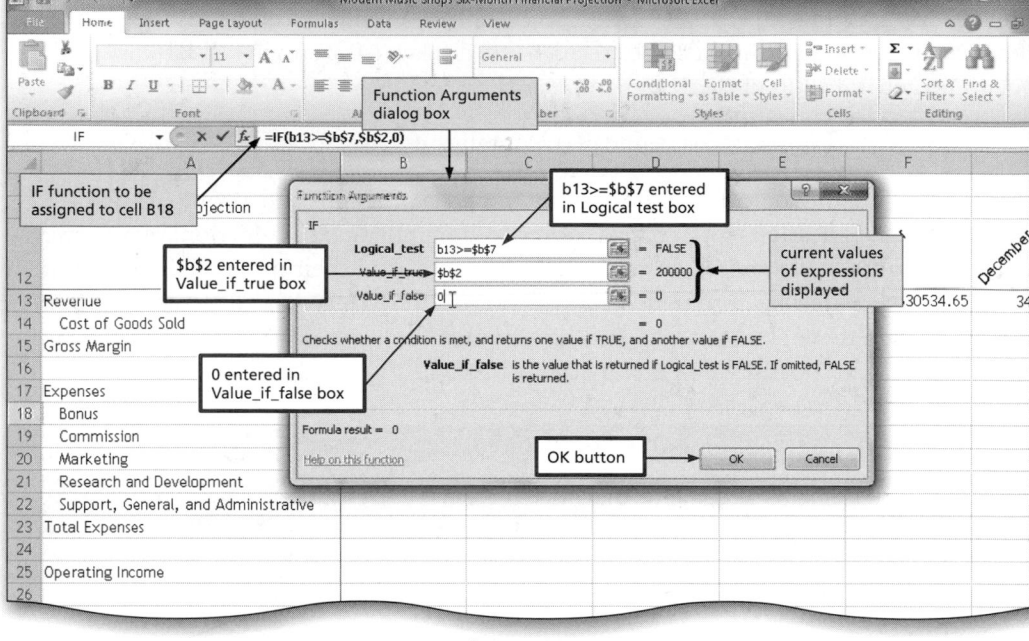

Figure 3–29

3

- Click the OK button (Function Arguments dialog box) to insert the IF function in the selected cell (Figure 3–30).

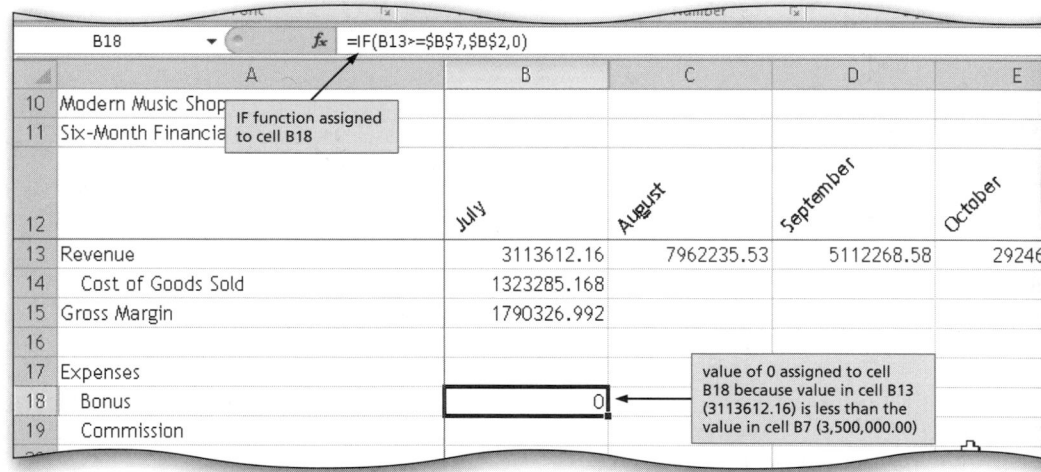

Figure 3–30

Q&A

Why is the value 0 displayed in cell B18?

The value that Excel displays in cell B18 depends on the values assigned to cells B13, B2, and B7. For example, if the value for July revenue in cell B13 is increased above 3,500,000.00, then the IF function in cell B18 will cause Excel to display 200,000.00. If you change the sales revenue for bonus in cell B7 from 3,500,000.00 to another number and the value in cell B13 is greater than or equal to the value in cell B7, it will change the results in cell B18 as well.

Other Ways

1. Click Logical button (Formulas tab | Function Library group), click IF

To Enter the Remaining July Formulas

BTW

Replacing a Formula with a Constant
By doing the following, you can replace a formula with its result so that the cell value remains constant: (1) click the cell with the formula; (2) press F2 or click in the formula bar; (3) press F9 to display the value in the formula bar; and (4) press the ENTER key.

The July commission expense in cell B19 is equal to the revenue in cell B13 times the commission assumption in cell B3 (5.75%). The July marketing expense in cell B20 is equal to the projected July revenue in cell B13 times the marketing assumption in cell B5 (5.00%). Similar formulas determine the remaining July expenses in cells B21 and B22.

The total expenses value in cell B23 is equal to the sum of the expenses in the range B18:B22. The operating income in cell B25 is equal to the gross margin in cell B15 minus the total expenses in cell B23. The formulas are short, and therefore, they are typed in the following steps, rather than entered using Point mode.

Select cell B19. Type =b13*b3 and then press the DOWN ARROW key to enter the formula in the selected cell. Type =b13*b5 and then press the DOWN ARROW key to enter the formula in the selected cell. Type =b13*b6 and then press the DOWN ARROW key to enter the formula in the selected cell. Type =b13*b8 and then press the DOWN ARROW key to enter the formula in the selected cell.

With cell B23 selected, click the Sum button (Home tab | Editing group) twice to insert a SUM function in the selected cell. Select cell B25 to prepare to enter the next formula. Type =b15-b23 and then press the ENTER key to enter the formula in the selected cell.

Press CTRL+ACCENT MARK (`) to display the formulas version of the worksheet (Figure 3–31).

When you are finished viewing the formulas version, press CTRL+ACCENT MARK (`) to display the values version of the worksheet.

Why should I view the formulas version of the worksheet?

Viewing the formulas version (Figure 3–31) of the worksheet allows you to check the formulas assigned to the range B14:B25. Recall that formulas were entered in lowercase. You can see that Excel converts all the formulas from lowercase to uppercase.

	July		August
	3113612.16		7962235.53
	=B13*(1-$B$4)		
	=B13-B14		
	=IF(B13>=$B$7,$B$2,0)	in formulas version, Excel displays formulas for July	
	=B13*$B$3		
	=B13*$B$5		
	=B13*$B$6		
nistrative	=B13*$B$8		
	=SUM(B18:B22)		
	=B15-B23		

Figure 3–31

To Copy Formulas with Absolute Cell References Using the Fill Handle

The following steps use the fill handle to copy the July formulas in column B to the other five months in columns C through G.

- Select the range B14:B25 and then point to the fill handle in the lower-right corner of the selected cell, B25 in this case, to display the crosshair mouse pointer (Figure 3–32).

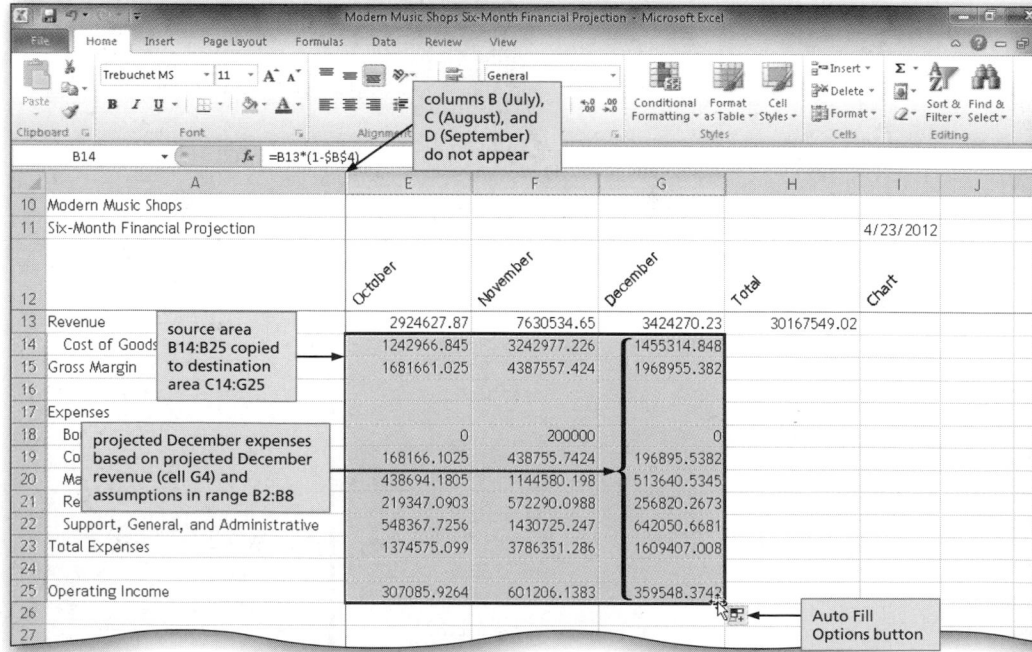

Figure 3–32

2

- Drag the fill handle to the right to copy the formulas from the source area, B14:B25 in this case, to the destination area, C14:G25 in this case, and display the calculated amounts and Auto Fill Options button (Figure 3–33).

Q&A

What happens to the formulas after performing the copy operation?

Because the formulas in the range B14:B25 use absolute cell references, the formulas still refer to the current values in the Assumptions table when the formulas are copied to the range C14:G25.

Figure 3–33

Q&A

What happened to columns B, C, and D?

As shown in Figure 3–33, as the fill handle is dragged to the right, columns B, C, and D no longer appear on the screen because column A now acts just as the row numbers do in that columns scrolled off of the visible portion of the worksheet disappear behind column A. Column A, however, remains on the screen, because the row titles were frozen earlier in this chapter.

To Determine Row Totals in Nonadjacent Cells

The following steps determine the row totals in column H. To determine the row totals using the Sum button, select only the cells in column H containing numbers in adjacent cells to the left. If, for example, you select the range H14:H25, Excel will display 0s as the sum of empty rows in cells H16, H17, and H24.

1 Select the range H14:H15. While holding down the CTRL key, select the range H18:H23 and cell H25, as shown in Figure 3–34.

2 Click the Sum button (Home tab | Editing group) to display the row totals in the selected ranges (Figure 3–34).

Error Messages
When Excel cannot calculate a formula, it displays an error message in a cell. These error messages always begin with a number sign (#). The more commonly occurring error messages are as follows: #DIV/0! (tries to divide by zero); #NAME? (uses a name Excel does not recognize); #N/A (refers to a value not available); #NULL! (specifies an invalid intersection of two areas); #NUM! (uses a number incorrectly); #REF (refers to a cell that is not valid); #VALUE! (uses an incorrect argument or operand); and ##### (refers to cells not wide enough to display entire entry).

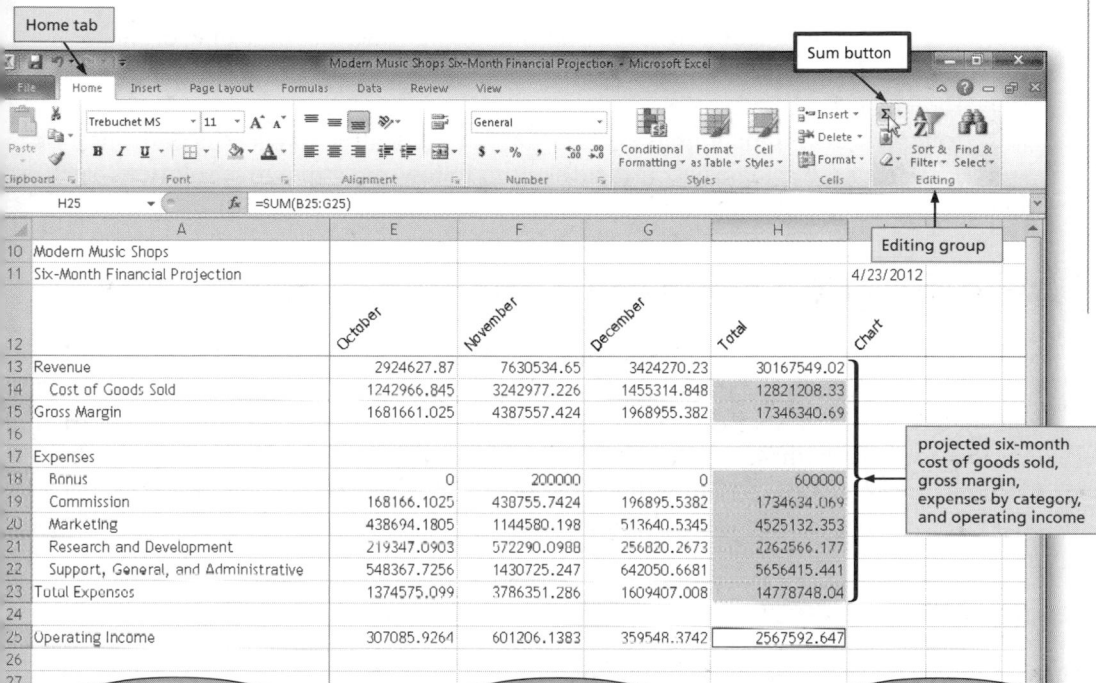

Figure 3–34

To Unfreeze the Worksheet Titles and Save the Workbook

All the text, data, and formulas have been entered into the worksheet. The following steps unfreeze the titles to allow you to work with the worksheet without frozen rows and columns, and save the workbook using its current file name, Modern Music Shops Six-Month Financial Projection.

1 Press CTRL+HOME to select cell B13 and view the upper-left corner of the screen.

2 Display the View tab and then click the Freeze Panes button (View tab | Window group) to display the Freeze Panes gallery.

3 Click Unfreeze Panes in the Freeze Panes gallery to unfreeze the frozen columns and rows.

4 Display the Home tab and then click the Save button on the Quick Access Toolbar to save the workbook.

Q&A Why does pressing CTRL+HOME select cell B13?

When the titles are frozen and you press CTRL+HOME, Excel selects the upper-left cell of the unfrozen section of the worksheet. For example, in Step 1 of the previous steps, Excel selected cell B13. When the titles are unfrozen, pressing CTRL+HOME selects cell A1.

Nested Forms of the IF Function

A **nested IF function** is one in which the action to be taken for the true or false case includes yet another IF function. The second IF function is considered to be nested, or layered, within the first. Study the nested IF function below, which determines the eligibility of a student to go on a field trip. The school permits the student to attend the field trip if the student's age is at least 14 and the student has provided a signed permission form. Assume the following in this example: (1) the nested IF function is assigned to cell L9, which instructs Excel to display one of three messages in the cell; (2) cell L7 contains a student's age; and (3) cell L8 contains a Y or N, based on whether the person provided a signed permission form.

=IF(L7>=14, IF(L8="Y","Allowed","Can Travel, but No Permission"),"Too Young to Travel")

The nested IF function instructs Excel to display one, and only one, of the following three messages in cell L9: (1) Allowed; or (2) Can Travel, but No Permission; or (3) Too Young to Travel.

You can nest IF functions as deep as you want, but after you get beyond a nest of three IF functions, the logic becomes difficult to follow and alternative solutions, such as the use of multiple cells and simple IF functions, should be considered.

Adding and Formatting Sparkline Charts

Sometimes you may want to condense a range of data into a small chart in order to show a trend or variation in the range. Excel's standard charts may be too large or extensive for your needs. An Excel **Sparkline chart** provides a simple way to show trends and variation in a range of data within a single cell. Excel includes three types of Sparkline charts: Line, Column, and Win/Loss. Because they exist in only one cell, you should use Sparkline charts to convey succinct, eye-catching summaries of the data they represent.

To Add a Sparkline Chart to the Worksheet

Each of the rows of monthly data, including those containing formulas, provides useful information easily summarized by a Line Sparkline chart. A Line Sparkline chart is a good choice because it shows trends over the six-month period for each row of data.

The following steps add a Line Sparkline chart to cell I13 and then use the fill handle to create Line Sparkline charts in the range I14:I25 that represent the monthly data in rows 13 through 25.

- Scroll the worksheet so that both columns B and I are displayed on the screen.

- Select cell I13 to prepare to insert a Sparkline chart in the cell.

- Display the Insert tab and then click Line (Insert tab | Sparklines group) to display the Create Sparklines dialog box (Figure 3–35).

Figure 3–35

2

• Drag through the range B13:G13 to select the range. Do not release the mouse (Figure 3–36).

What happened to the Create Sparklines dialog box?

When a dialog box includes a Collapse Dialog Box button (Figure 3–35), selecting cells or a range collapses the dialog box so that only the current text box is displayed. Once the selection is made, the dialog box expands back to its original size. You also can click the Collapse Dialog Box button to make your selection and then click the Expand Dialog Box button (Figure 3–36) to expand the dialog box.

Figure 3–36

3

• Release the mouse button to insert the selected range, B13:G13 in this case, in the Data Range text box.

• Click the OK button (Create Sparklines dialog box) to insert a Line Sparkline chart in the selected cell and display the Sparkline Tools contextual tab (Figure 3–37).

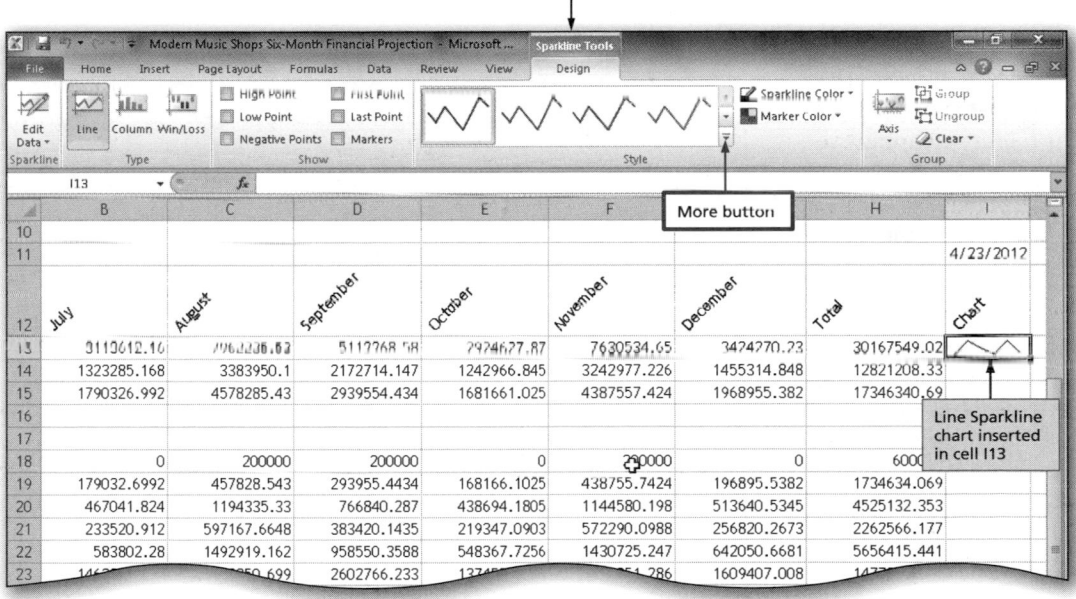

Figure 3–37

To Format and Copy the Sparkline Chart

Just as with standard charts, Excel provides formatting options for Sparkline charts. Sparkline chart formatting is restricted greatly as compared to standard charts. As shown in Figure 3–37, the Show group (Sparkline Tools Design tab) allows you to highlight various points in the chart. Markers provide a point on the chart for each cell represented in the chart. The Style group (Sparkline Tools Design tab) allows you to specify the style and color for the parts of a Sparkline chart.

The steps on the following page format the Sparkline chart in cell I13 using the Style 13 Sparkline chart style.

1

- Click the More button (Sparkline Tools Design tab | Style group) to display the Style gallery (Figure 3–38).

Figure 3–38

2

- Click Sparkline Style Accent 1, (no dark or light) in the Styles gallery to apply the style to the Sparkline chart in the selected cell, I13 in this case.

- Point to the fill handle in cell I13 and then drag through cell I25 to copy the Line Sparkline chart.

- Select cell I27 (Figure 3–39).

Q&A

Why do Sparkline charts not appear in cells I16, I17, and I24?

Excel does not draw Sparkline charts if the range for the Sparkline chart contains no data. In this case the ranges B16:G16, B17:G17, and B24:G24 do not contain data, so Excel draws no Sparkline chart. If you add data

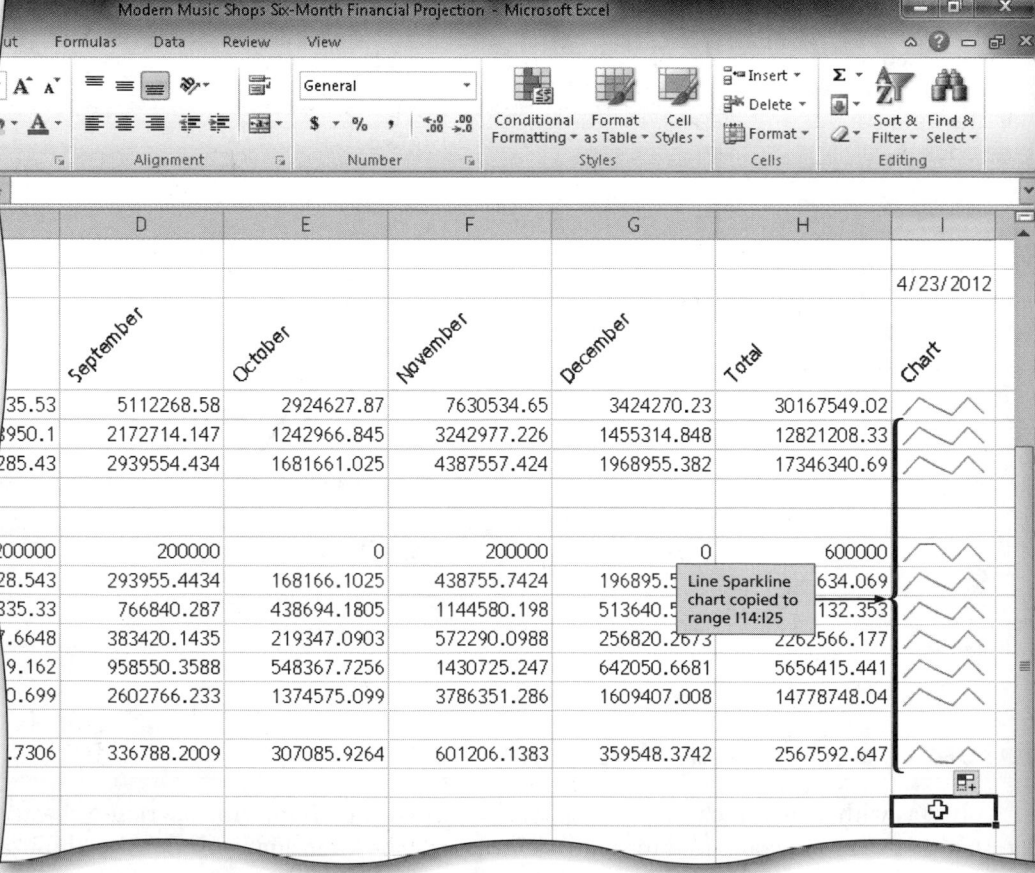

Figure 3–39

to cells in those ranges, then Excel automatically would draw Line Sparkline charts for the rows to which you added data because the Sparkline charts were defined for cells I16, I17, and I24 by the drag operation.

Formatting the Worksheet

The worksheet created thus far shows the financial projections for the six-month period, from July to December. Its appearance is uninteresting, however, even though some minimal formatting (formatting assumptions numbers, changing the column widths, formatting the date, and formatting the Sparkline chart) was performed earlier. This section will complete the formatting of the worksheet to make the numbers easier to read and to emphasize the titles, assumptions, categories, and totals as shown in Figure 3–40.

BTW

Customizing Sparkline Charts
You can customize sparkline charts in a number of ways on the Sparkline Chart Design tab. In the Show group (Sparkline Chart Design tab), you can specify values to show as markers on the chart, such as the highest value, lowest value, any negative numbers, the first point, and the last point. You can change the color of the sparkline and markers in the Style group (Sparkline Chart Design tab).

Plan Ahead

Identify how to format various elements of the worksheet.
A worksheet, such as the one presented in this chapter, should be formatted in the following manner: (1) format the numbers; (2) format the worksheet title, column titles, row titles, and total rows; and (3) format an assumptions table. Numbers in heading rows and total rows should be formatted with a currency symbol. Other dollar amounts should be formatted with a Comma style. An assumptions table should be diminished in its formatting so that it does not distract from the main calculations and data in the worksheet. Assigning the data in an assumptions table a smaller font size would set it apart from other data formatted with a larger font size.

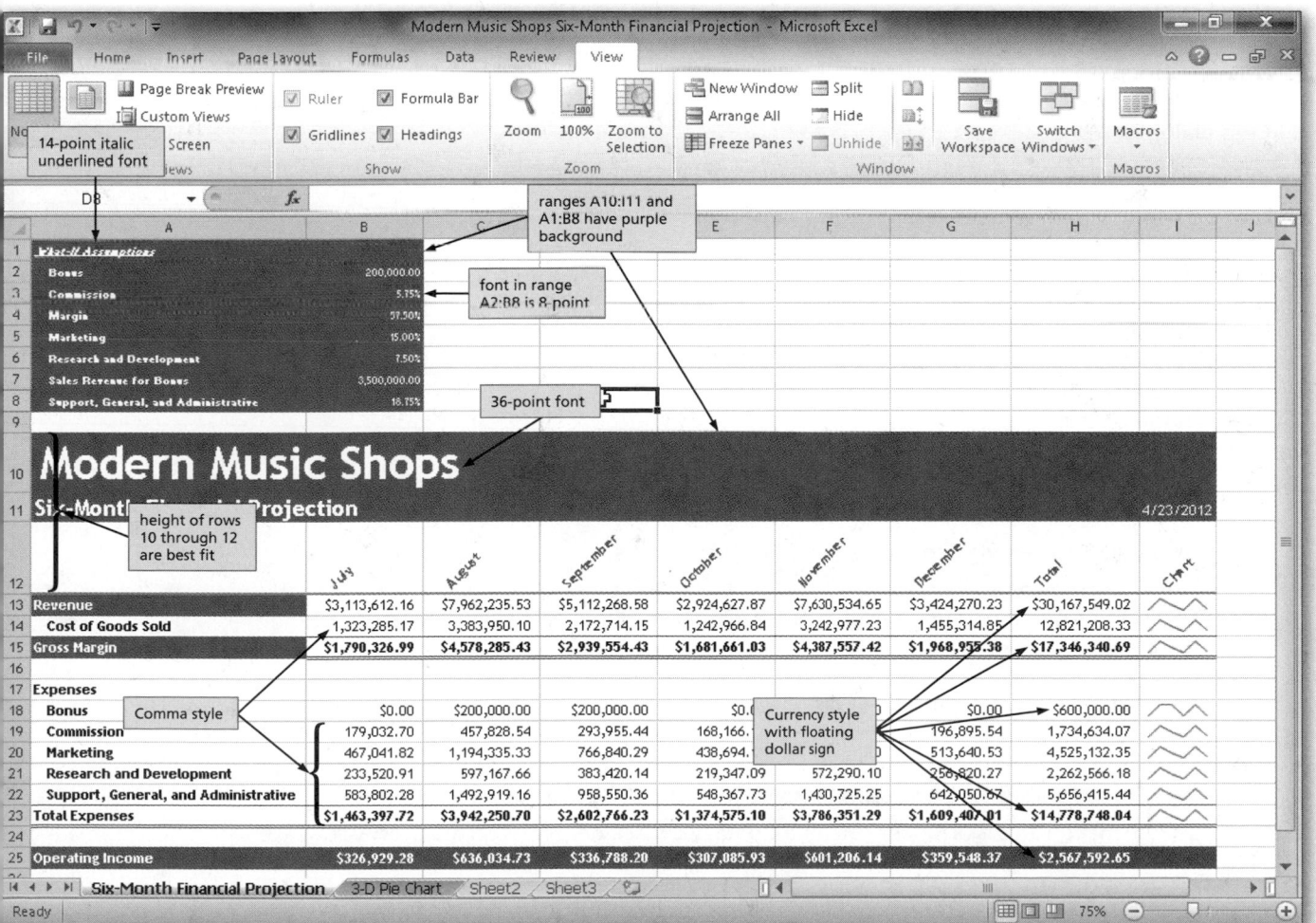

Figure 3–40

To Assign Formats to Nonadjacent Ranges

The numbers in the range B13:H25 are to be formatted as follows:

1. Assign the Currency style with a floating dollar sign to rows 13, 15, 18, 23, and 25.

2. Assign a Comma style to rows 14 and 19 through 22.

The following steps assign formats to the numbers in rows 13 through 25.

1

• Select the range B13:H13 as the first range to format.

• While holding down the CTRL key, select the nonadjacent ranges B15:H15, B18:H18, B23:H23, and B25:H25, and then release the CTRL key to select nonadjacent ranges.

• Click the Format Cells: Number Dialog Box Launcher (Home tab | Number group) to display the Format Cells dialog box.

• Click Currency in the Category list (Format Cells dialog box), if necessary select 2 in the Decimal places box, if necessary click $ in the Symbol list to ensure a dollar sign shows in the cells to be formatted, and

Figure 3–41

click the black font color ($1,234.10) in the Negative numbers list to prepare the desired Currency style for the selected ranges (Figure 3–41).

Q&A

Why was the particular style chosen for the negative numbers?

In accounting, negative numbers often are shown with parentheses surrounding the value rather than with a negative sign preceding the value. Thus, the format (1,234.10) in the Negative numbers list was clicked. The data being used in this chapter contains no negative numbers. You must select a format for negative numbers, however, and you must be consistent if you are choosing different formats in a column; otherwise, the decimal points may not line up.

Q&A

Why is the Format Cells dialog box used to create the format for the ranges in this step?

The requirements for this worksheet call for a floating dollar sign. To assign a Currency style with a floating dollar sign, use the Format Cells dialog box rather than the Accounting Style button (Home tab | Number group), which assigns a fixed dollar sign.

2

- Click the OK button (Format Cells dialog box) to close the Format Cells dialog box and apply the desired format to the selected ranges.

- Select the range B14:H14 as the next range to format.

- While holding down the CTRL key, select the range B19:H22, and then release the CTRL key to select nonadjacent ranges.

- Click the Format Cells: Number Dialog Box Launcher (Home tab | Number group) to display the Format Cells dialog box.

Figure 3–42

- Click Currency in the Category list (Format Cells dialog box). If necessary select 2 in the Decimal places box, click None in the Symbol list so a dollar sign does not show in the cells to be formatted, and click the black font color (1,234.10) in the Negative numbers list (Figure 3–42).

3

- Click the OK button (Format Cells dialog box) to close the Format Cells dialog box and apply the desired format to the selected ranges.

- Select cell B27 to select an empty cell and display the formatted numbers as shown in Figure 3–43.

Why is the Format Cells dialog box used to create the style for the ranges in Steps 2 and 3?

Figure 3–43

The Format Cells dialog box is used to assign the Comma style, because the Comma Style button (Home tab | Number group) assigns a format that displays a dash (–) when a cell has a value of 0. The specifications for this worksheet call for displaying a value of 0 as 0.00 (see cell B18 in Figure 3–40) rather than as a dash. To create a Comma style using the Format Cells dialog box, you can assign a Currency style with no dollar sign.

Other Ways

1. Right-click range, click Format Cells on shortcut menu, click Number tab (Format Cells dialog box), click category in Category list, select format, click OK button (Format Cells dialog box)

2. Press CTRL+1, click Number tab (Format Cells dialog box), click category in Category list, select format, click OK button (Format Cells dialog box)

To Format the Worksheet Titles

The following steps emphasize the worksheet titles in cells A10 and A11 by changing the font, size, and color. The steps also format all of the row headers in column A with a bold font style.

- Press CTRL+HOME to select cell A1 and then click the column A heading to select the column.

- Click the Bold button (Home tab | Font group) to bold all of the data in the selected column.

- Select cell A10, click the Font Size box arrow (Home tab | Font group), and then click 36 in the Font Size list to increase the font size of the selected cell.

- Select cell A11, click the Font Size box arrow, and then click 18 in the Font Size list to increase the font size of the selected cell (Figure 3–44).

Figure 3–44

- Select the range A10:I11 and then click the Fill Color button arrow (Home tab | Font group) to display the Fill Color gallery.

- Click Purple, Accent 2, Darker 25% (column 6, row 5) in the Fill Color gallery to add a background color to the selected range.

- Click the Font Color button arrow (Home tab | Font group) and then select White, Background 1 (column 1, row 1) in the Font Color gallery to change the font color of the selected range (Figure 3–45).

Figure 3–45

Other Ways

1. Right-click range, click Format Cells on shortcut menu, click Fill tab (Format Cells dialog box) to color background (or click Font tab to color font), click OK button

2. Press CTRL+1, click Fill tab (Format Cells dialog box) to color background (or click Font tab to color font), click OK button

To Assign Cell Styles to Nonadjacent Rows and Colors to a Cell

The next step to improving the appearance of the worksheet is to format the heading in row 12 and the totals in rows 15, 23, and 25. The following steps format the heading in row 13 with the Heading 3 cell style and the totals in rows 15, 23, and 25 with the Total cell style. Cell A13 also is formatted with a background color and font color.

1 Select the range A12:I12 and apply the Heading 3 cell style.

2 Select the range A15:I15 and while holding down the CTRL key, select the ranges A23:I23 and A25:I25.

3 Apply the Total cell style to the selected nonadjacent ranges.

4 Select cell A13, click the Fill Color button arrow (Home tab | Font group), and then click the Purple, Accent 2, Darker 25% color (column 6, row 5) in the Fill Color gallery.

5 Click the Font Color button arrow (Home tab | Font group) and then click the White, Background 1 color (column 1, row 1) in the Font Color gallery (Figure 3–46).

BTW

Toggle Commands
Many of the commands on the Ribbon, on the galleries, and the shortcut keys function as toggles. For example, if you click the Freeze Panes command on the Freeze Panes gallery, the command changes to Unfreeze Panes the next time you view the gallery. These types of commands work like on-off switches or toggles.

BTW

Work Days
Assume that you have two dates, one in cell A1 and the other in cell A2. Assume further that the date in cell A1 is your starting date and the date in cell A2 is the ending date. To calculate the work days between the two dates (excluding weekends), use the following formula: =NETWORKDAYS(A1, A2). For this function to work, make sure the Analysis ToolPak add-in is installed. You can install it on the Add-Ins page of the Excel Options dialog box.

BTW

The Fill and Font Color Buttons
You may have noticed that the color bar at the bottom of the Fill Color and Font Color buttons (Home tab | Font group) (Figure 3–45) changes to the most recently selected color. To apply this same color to a cell background or text, select a cell and then click the Fill Color button to use the color as a background or click the Font Color button to use the color as a font color.

Figure 3–46

To Copy a Cell's Format Using the Format Painter Button

Using the Format Painter, you can format a cell quickly by copying a cell's format to another cell or a range of cells. The following steps format cells A15 and the range A25:I25 using the Format Painter.

1

- If necessary, click cell A13 to select a source cell for the format to paint.

- Double-click the Format Painter button (Home tab | Clipboard group) and then move the mouse pointer onto the worksheet to cause the mouse pointer to change to a block plus sign with a paintbrush (Figure 3–47).

Figure 3–47

2

- Click cell A15 to assign the format of the source cell, A13 in this case, to the destination cell, A15 in this case (Figure 3–48).

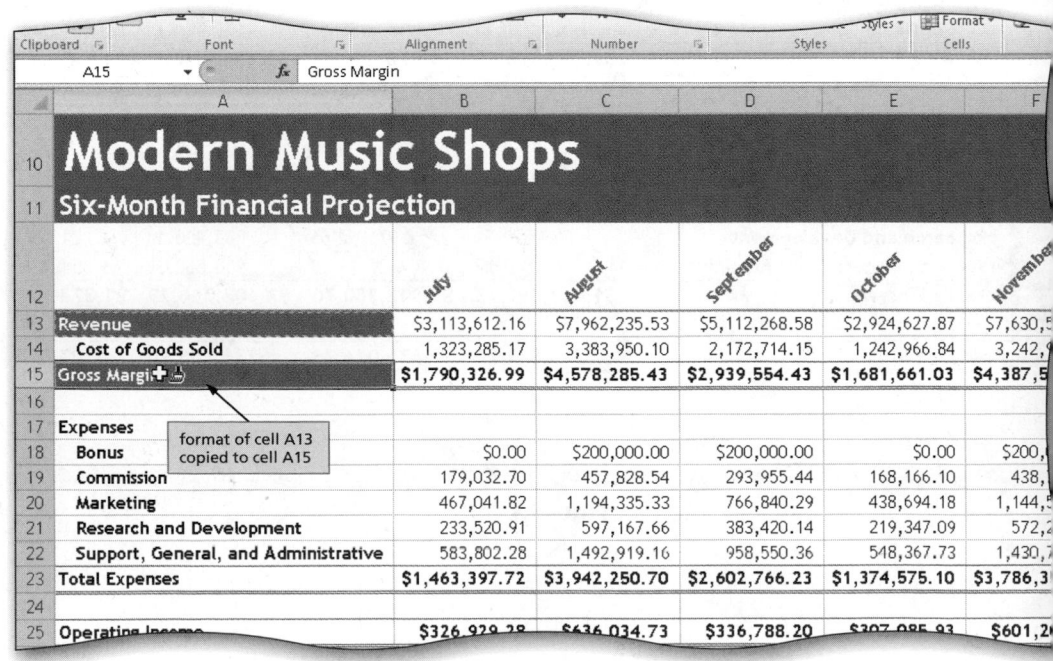

Figure 3–48

3

- With the mouse pointer still a block plus sign with a paintbrush, drag through the range A25:I25 to assign the format of the source cell, A13 in this case, to the destination range, A25:I25 in this case.

- Press the ESC key to stop the format painter.

- Apply the Currency style to the range B25:H25 to cause the cells in the range to appear with a floating dollar sign and two decimal places and then scroll the worksheet so that column A is displayed (Figure 3–49).

Figure 3–49

Why does the Currency style need to be reapplied to the range B25:H25?

Sometimes, the use of the format painter results in unintended outcomes. In this case, the changing of the background fill color and font color for the range B25:H25 resulted in the loss of the Currency style because the format being copied did not included the Currency style. Reapplying the Currency style to the range results in the proper number style, fill color, and font color.

Other Ways

1. Click Copy button (Home tab | Clipboard group), select cell, click Paste button arrow (Home tab | Clipboard group), click Formatting icon on Paste gallery

2. Right-click cell, click Copy, right-click cell, click Formatting icon on shortcut menu

To Format the What-If Assumptions Table and Save the Workbook

The last step to improving the appearance of the worksheet is to format the What-If Assumptions table in the range A1:B8. The specifications in Figure 3–40 on page EX 173 require an 8-point italic underlined font for the title in cell A1 and 8-point font in the range A2:B8. The following steps format the What-If Assumptions table.

- Press CTRL+HOME to select cell A1.

- Click the Font Size button arrow (Home tab | Font group) and then click 8 in the Font Size list to decrease the font size of the selected cell.

- Click the Italic button (Home tab | Font Group) and then click the Underline button (Home tab | Font group) to italicize and underline the text in the selected cell.

- Select the range A2:B8, click the Font Size button arrow (Home tab | Font group) and then click 8 in the Font Size list to apply a smaller font size to the selected range.

- Select the range A1:B8 and then click the Fill Color button (Home tab | Font group) to apply the most recently used background color to the selected range.

BTW

Painting a Format to Nonadjacent Ranges
Double-click the Format Painter button (Home tab | Clipboard group) and then drag through the nonadjacent ranges to paint the formats to the ranges. Click the Format Painter button (Home tab | Clipboard group) to deactivate it.

BTW

Selecting Nonadjacent Ranges
One of the more difficult tasks to learn is selecting nonadjacent ranges. To complete this task, do not hold down the CTRL key when you select the first range because Excel will consider the current active cell to be the first selection, and you may not want the current active cell in the selection. Once the first range is selected, hold down the CTRL key and drag through the nonadjacent ranges. If a desired range is not visible in the window, use the scroll arrows to view the range. You need not hold down the CTRL key while you scroll.

6 Click the Font Color button (Home tab | Font group) to apply the most recently used font color to the selected range.

7 Click cell D8 to deselect the range A1:B8 and display the What-If Assumptions table, as shown in Figure 3–50.

8 Save the workbook.

Q&A

What happens when I click the Italic and Underline buttons?

Recall that when you assign the italic font style to a cell, Excel slants the characters slightly to the right, as shown in cell A1 in Figure 3–50. The **underline** format underlines only the characters in the cell, rather than the entire cell, as is the case when you assign a cell a bottom border.

Figure 3–50

Break Point: If you wish to stop working through the chapter at this point, you can quit Excel now and then resume the project at a later point in time by starting Excel, opening the file called Modern Music Shops Six-Month Financial Projection, and continuing to follow the steps from this location forward.

BTW

Charts
When you change a value on which a chart is dependent, Excel immediately redraws the chart based on the new value. With bar charts, you can drag the bar in the chart in one direction or another to change the corresponding value in the worksheet.

Adding a 3-D Pie Chart to the Workbook

The next step in the chapter is to draw the 3-D Pie chart on a separate sheet in the workbook, as shown in Figure 3–51. Use a **pie chart** to show the relationship or proportion of parts to a whole. Each slice (or wedge) of the pie shows what percent that slice contributes to the total (100%).

The 3-D Pie chart in Figure 3–51 shows the contribution of each month's projected operating income to the six-month projected operating income. The 3-D Pie chart makes it easy to evaluate the contribution of one month in comparison to the other months.

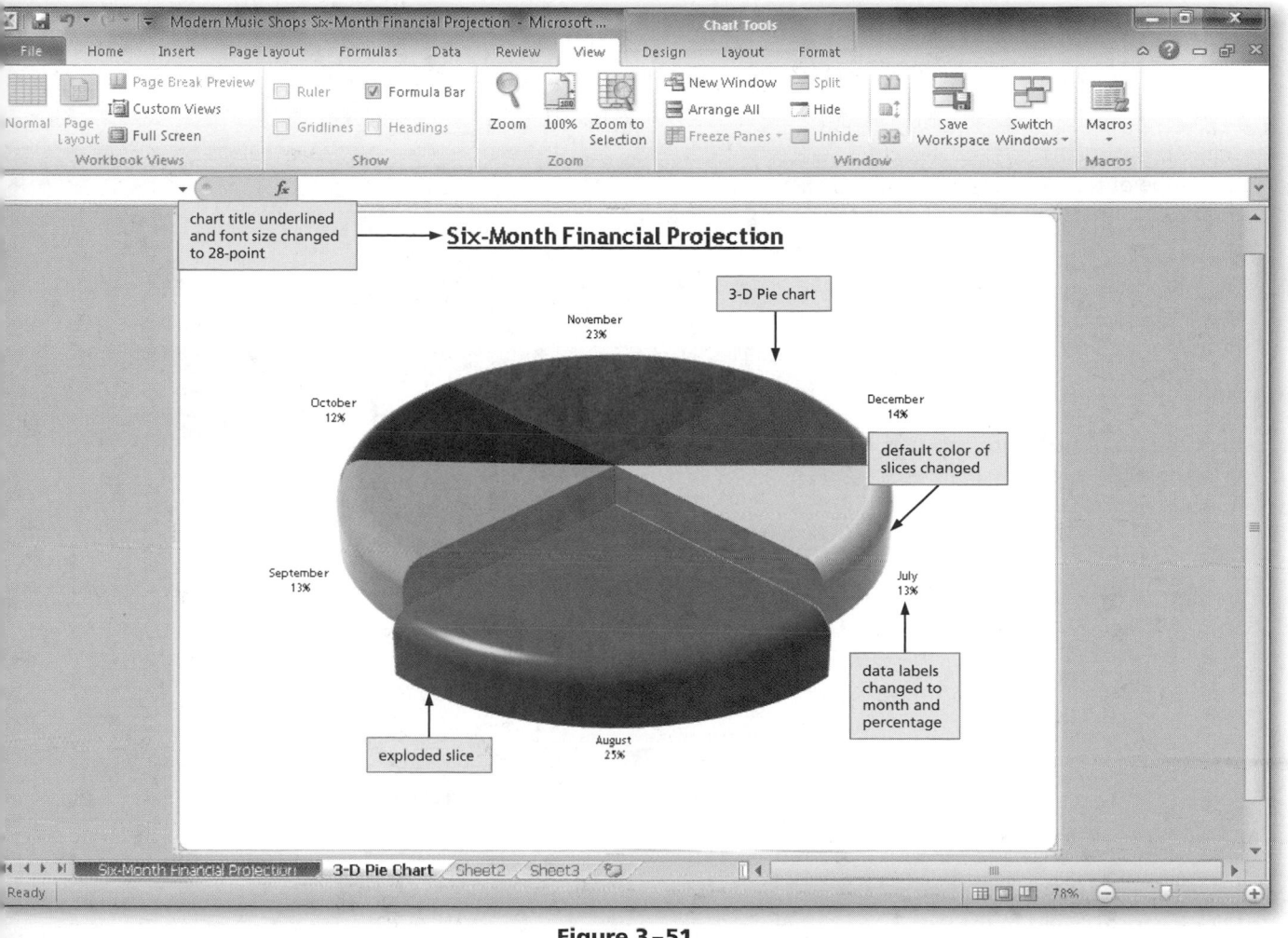

Figure 3–51

Unlike the 3-D Column chart created in Chapter 1, the 3-D Pie chart shown in Figure 3–51 is not embedded in the worksheet. Instead, the Pie chart resides on a separate sheet, called a **chart sheet**, which contains only the chart.

In this worksheet, the ranges to chart are the nonadjacent ranges B12:G12 (month names) and B25:G25 (monthly operating incomes). The month names in the range B12:G12 will identify the slices of the Pie chart; these entries are called **category names**. The range B25:G25 contains the data that determines the size of the slices in the pie; these entries are called the **data series**. Because six months are being charted, the 3-D Pie chart contains six slices.

The sketch of the 3-D Pie chart in Figure 3–3b on page EX 142 also calls for emphasizing the month of August by offsetting its slice from the main portion. A Pie chart with one or more slices offset is called an **exploded Pie chart**.

As shown in Figure 3–51, the default 3-D Pie chart also has been enhanced by rotating it, changing the colors of the slices, adding a bevel, and modifying the chart title and labels that identify the slices.

BTW

Chart Items
When you rest the mouse pointer over a chart item, such as a legend, bar, or axis, Excel displays a chart tip containing the name of the item.

BTW

Chart Templates
Once you create and format a chart to your liking, you may want to reuse the chart type and formatting for additional charts. Excel allows you to save your chart as a chart template by clicking the Save as Template button (Chart Tools Design tab | Type group). A chart template is saved in the Templates\Charts folder with a .crtx file extension. When you want to reuse the template, click the Templates folder in the Insert Chart dialog box and select your template.

To Draw a 3-D Pie Chart on a Separate Chart Sheet

The following steps draw the 3-D Pie chart on a separate chart sheet.

1

- Select the range B12:G12 to identify the range of the category name of the 3-D Pie Chart.

- If necessary, scroll the worksheet so that row 25 is displayed, and while holding down the CTRL key, select the range B25:G25.

- Display the Insert tab.

- Click the Pie button (Insert tab | Charts group) to display the Pie gallery (Figure 3–52).

Figure 3–52

2

- Click Pie in 3-D chart in the Pie gallery to select the desired chart type.

- When Excel draws the chart, click the Move Chart button (Chart Tools Design tab | Location group) to display the Move Chart dialog box (Figure 3–53).

Figure 3–53

• Click New sheet (Move Chart dialog box) and then type **3-D Pie Chart** in the 'New sheet name' text box to enter a sheet tab name for the chart sheet.

• Click the OK button (Move Chart dialog box) to move the chart to a new chart sheet with a new sheet name, 3-D Pie Chart in this case (Figure 3–54).

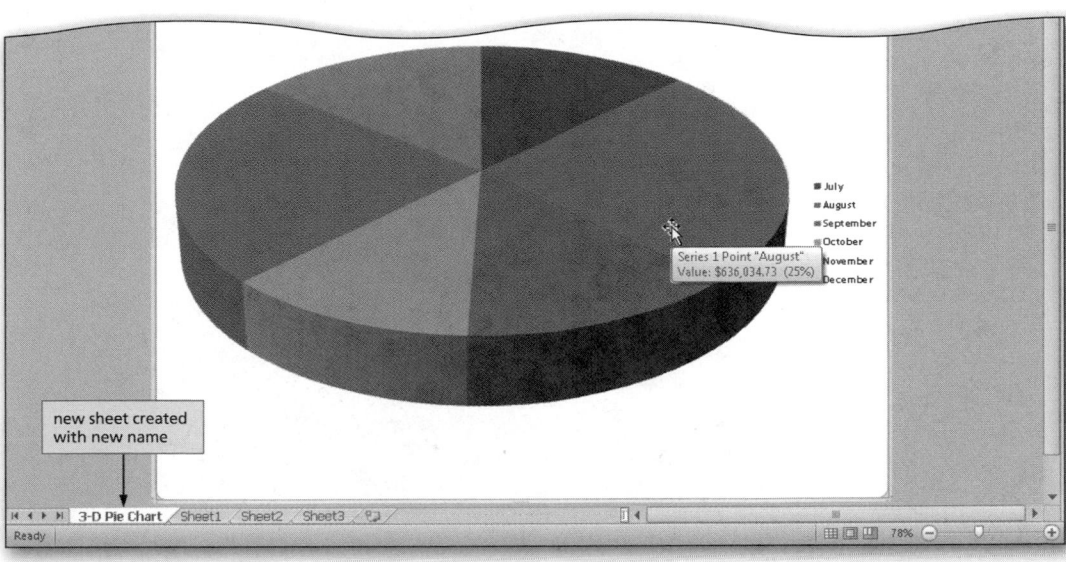

new sheet created with new name

Figure 3–54

Other Ways
1. Select range to chart, press F11

To Insert a Chart Title and Data Labels

The next step is to insert a chart title and labels that identify the slices. Before you can format a chart item, such as the chart title or data labels, you must select it. The following steps insert a chart title, remove the legend, and add data labels.

• Click anywhere in the chart area outside the chart to select the chart.

• Display the Chart Tools Layout tab and then click the Chart Title button (Chart Tools Layout tab | Labels group) to display the Chart Title gallery.

• Click the Centered Overlay Title command in the Chart Title gallery to add a chart title centered on top of the chart.

• Select the text in the chart title and then type **Six-Month Financial Projection** to add a new chart title (Figure 3–55).

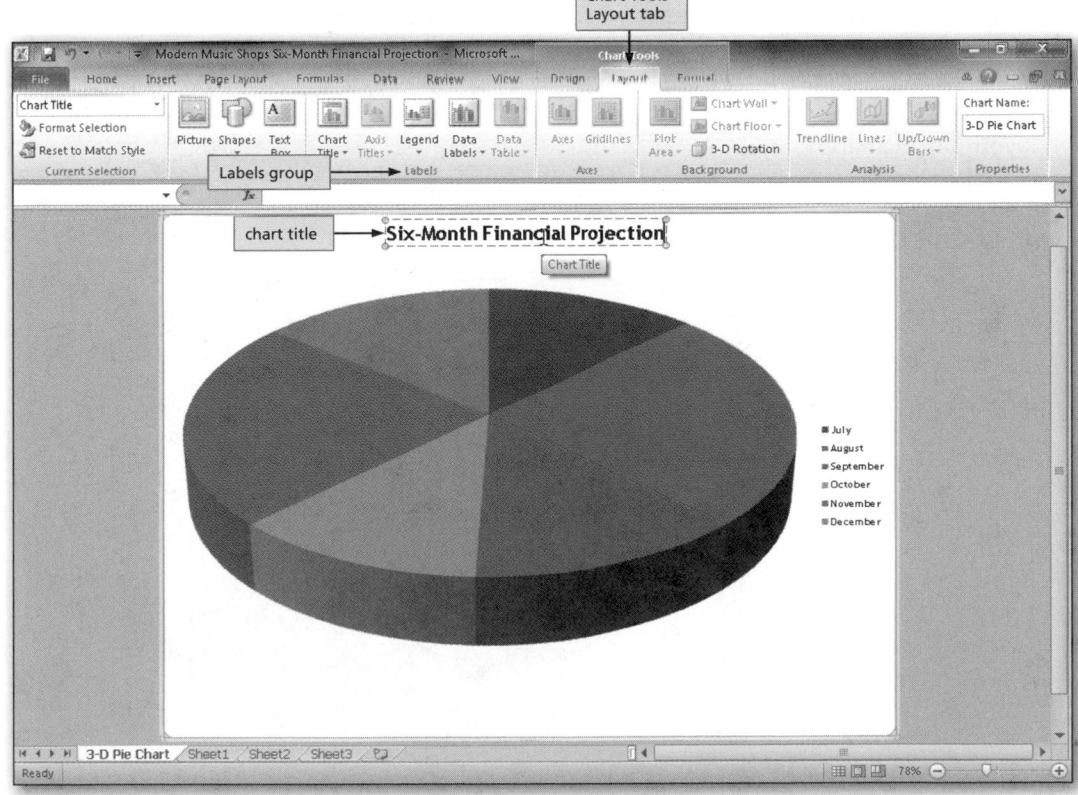

Figure 3–55

2

- Select the text in the new title and then display the Home tab.

- Click the Underline button (Home tab | Font group) to assign an underline font style to the chart title (Figure 3–56).

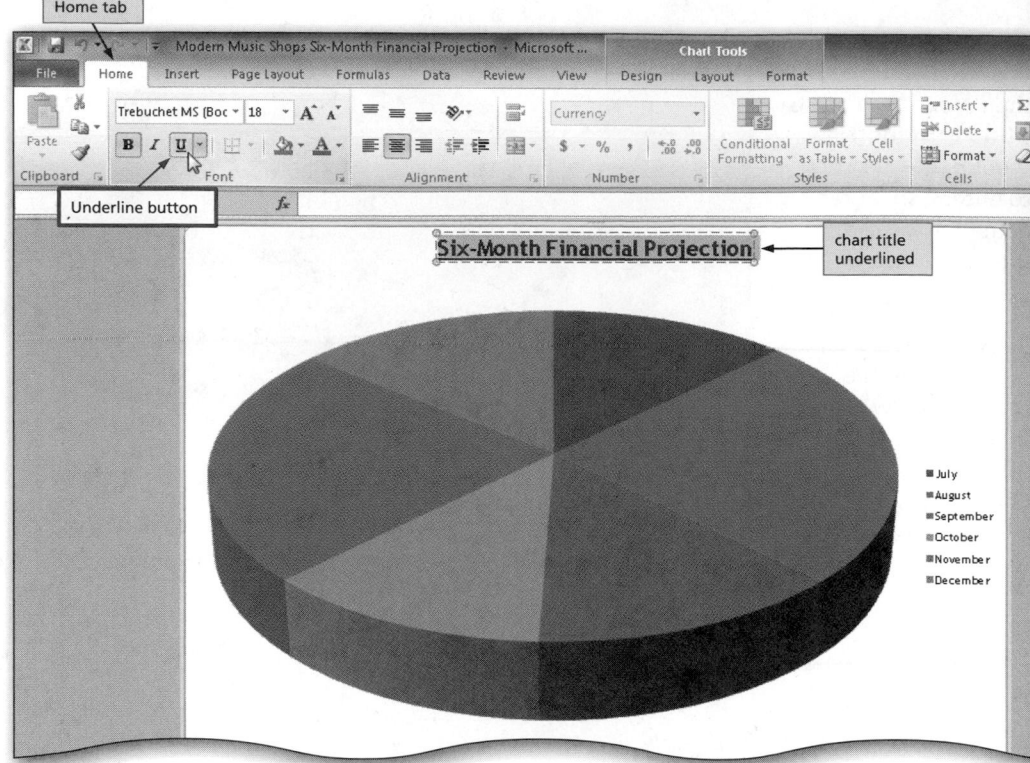

Figure 3–56

3

- Display the Chart Tools Layout tab and then click the Legend button (Chart Tools Layout tab | Labels group) to display the Legend gallery (Figure 3–57).

Figure 3–57

• Click the None Legend option in the Legend gallery to turn off the legend on the chart.

• Click the Data Labels button (Layout tab | Labels group) and then click Outside End in the Data Labels gallery to display data labels outside the chart at the end of each slice (Figure 3–58).

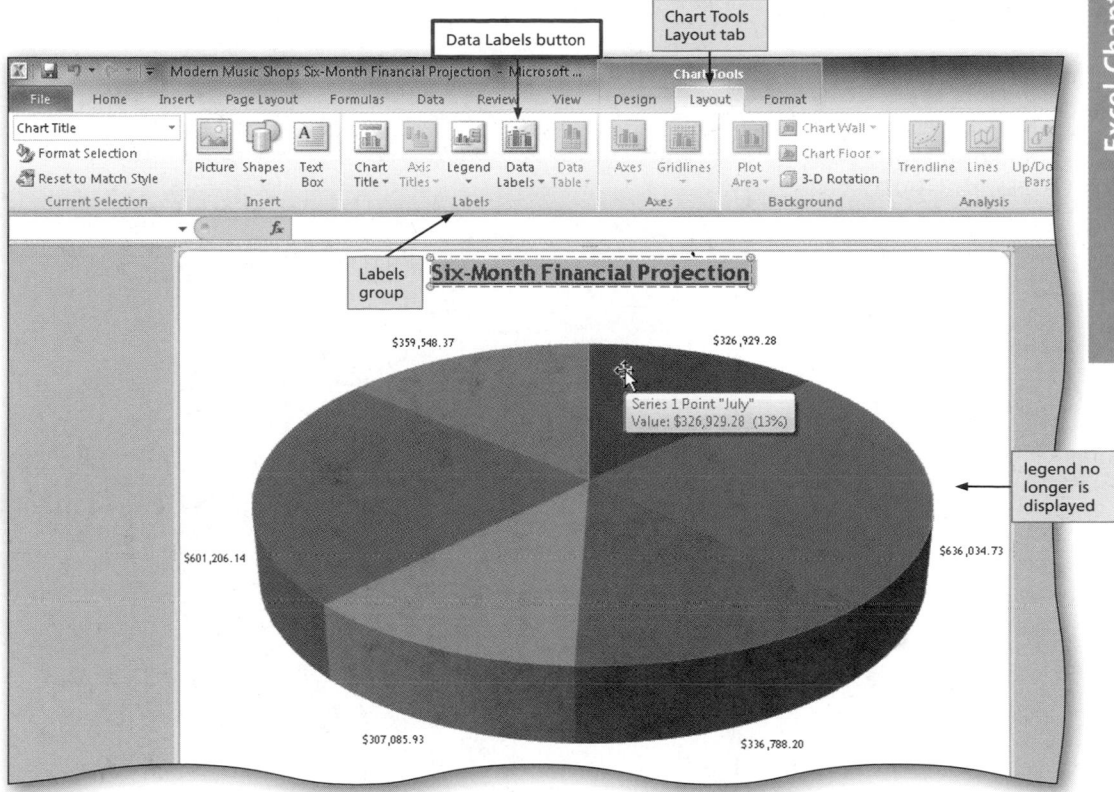

Figure 3–58

• If necessary, right-click any data label to select all of the data labels on the chart and to display a shortcut menu.

• Click the Format Data Labels command on the shortcut menu to display the Format Data Labels dialog box.

• If necessary, click the Series Name, Value, and Show Leader Lines check boxes to deselect them (Format Data Labels dialog box) and then click the Category Name and Percentage check boxes to cause the data labels to be displayed with category names and percent values, rather than currency values (Figure 3–59).

Figure 3–59

- Click the Close button to close the Format Data Labels dialog box and display the chart (Figure 3–60).

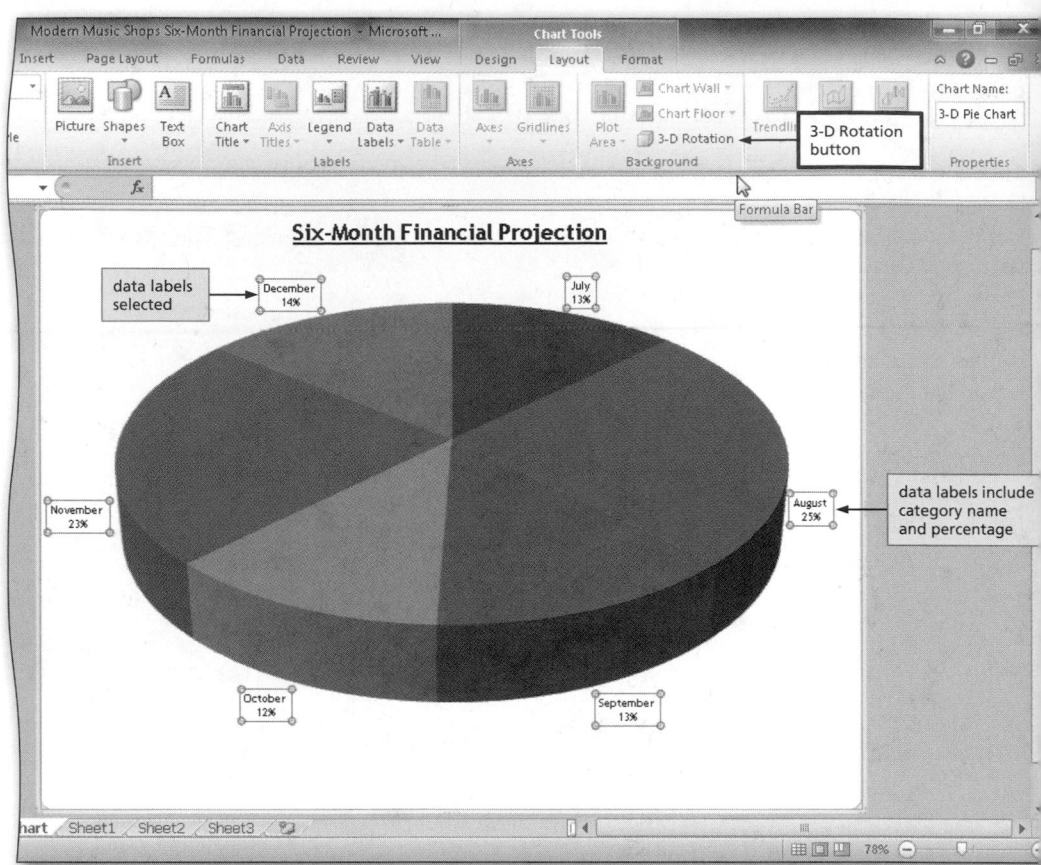

Figure 3–60

To Rotate the 3-D Pie Chart

With a three-dimensional chart, you can change the view to better show the section of the chart you are trying to emphasize. Excel allows you to control the rotation angle, elevation, perspective, height, and angle of the axes.

When Excel initially draws a Pie chart, it always positions the chart so that one of the dividing lines between two slices is a straight line pointing to 12 o'clock (or 0°). As shown in Figure 3–60, the line that divides the December and July slices currently is set to 0°. This line defines the rotation angle of the 3-D Pie chart.

To obtain a better view of the offset August slice, the largest slice, the 3-D Pie chart can be rotated 90° to the left. The following steps rotate the 3-D Pie chart.

1

• Click the 3-D Rotation button (Chart Tools Layout tab | Background group) to display the Format Chart Area dialog box.

• Click the Increase X Rotation button in the Rotation area of the Format Chart Area dialog box until the X rotation is at 90° to rotate the chart (Figure 3–61).

What happens as I click the Increase X Rotation button?

Excel rotates the chart 10° in a clockwise direction each time you click the Increase X Rotation button. The Y box in the Rotation area allows you to control the tilt, or elevation, of the chart. You can tilt the chart towards or away from your view in order to enhance the view of the chart.

Figure 3–61

2

• Click the Close button (Format Chart Area dialog box) to close the dialog box and display the rotated chart (Figure 3–62).

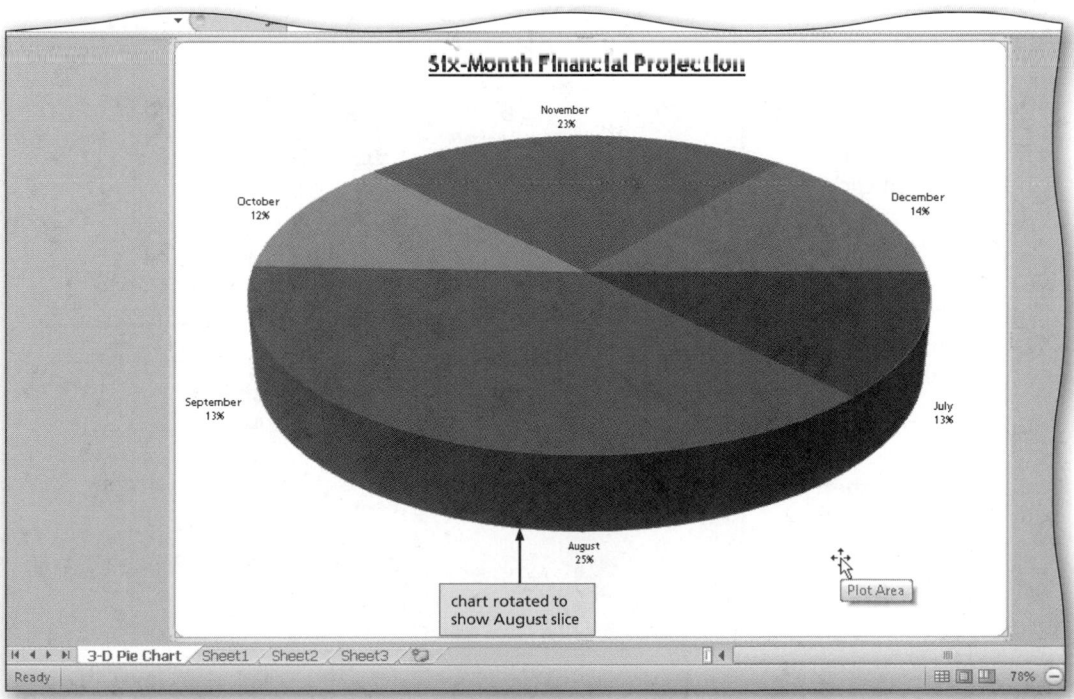

Figure 3–62

To Apply a 3-D Format to the Pie Chart

Excel allows you to apply dramatic 3-D visual effects to charts. The chart shown in Figure 3–62 could be enhanced with a bevel along the top edge. A bevel is a curve that is applied to soften the appearance of a straight edge. Excel also allows you to change the appearance of the material from which the surface of the chart appears to be constructed. The following steps apply a bevel to the chart and change the surface of the chart to a softer-looking material.

1

● Right-click the chart to display a shortcut menu and Mini toolbar (Figure 3–63).

Figure 3–63

2

● Click the Format Data Series command on the shortcut menu to display the Format Data Series dialog box and then click the 3-D Format category (Format Data Series dialog box) on the left side of the dialog box to display the 3-D Format panel.

● Click the Top button (Format Data Series dialog box) in the Bevel area to display the Bevel gallery (Figure 3–64).

Figure 3–64

3

- Click the Circle bevel button (column 1, row 1) in the Bevel gallery (Format Data Series dialog box) to add a bevel to the chart.

- Type **50 pt** in the uppermost Width box in the Bevel area (Format Data Series dialog box) and then type **50 pt** in the uppermost Height box in the Bevel area of the dialog box to increase the width and height of the bevel on the chart (Figure 3–65).

Figure 3–65

4

- Click the Material button in the Surface area (Format Data Series dialog box) to display the Material gallery (Figure 3–66).

Figure 3–66

5

- Click the Soft Edge button (column 2, row 2) in the Material gallery and then click the Close button (Format Data Series dialog box) to apply the desired material and close the Format Data Series dialog box (Figure 3–67).

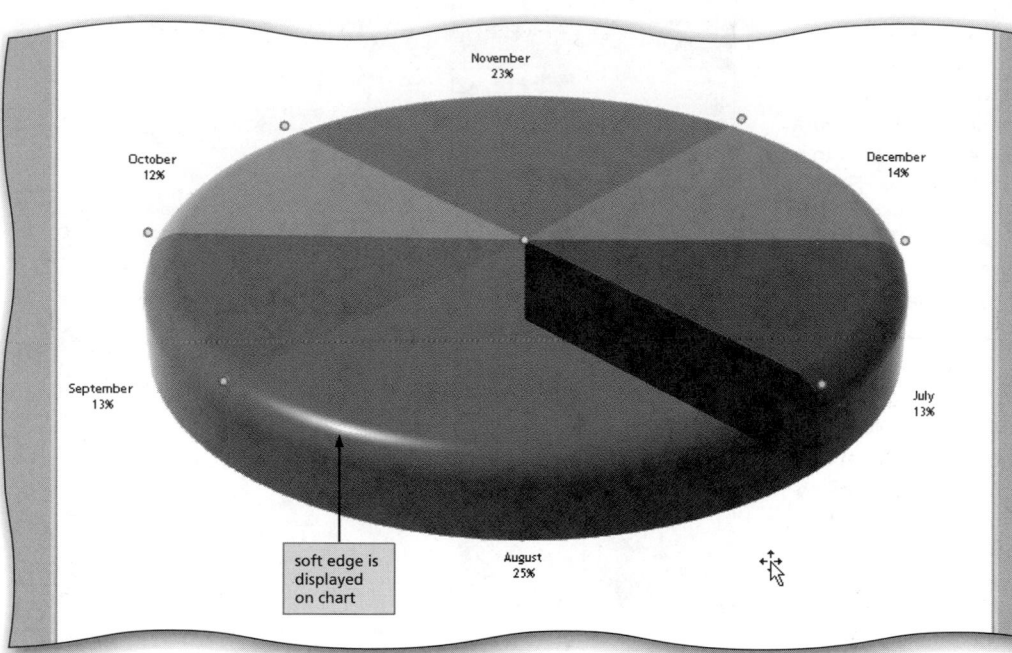

Figure 3–67

To Explode the 3-D Pie Chart and Change the Color of a Slice

The next step is to emphasize the slice representing August by offsetting, or exploding, it from the rest of the slices so that it stands out. The following steps explode the largest slice of the 3-D Pie chart and then change its color.

1

- Click the slice labeled August twice (do not double-click) to select only one slice of the 3-D Pie chart, the August slice in this case.

- Right-click the slice labeled August to display a shortcut menu and Mini toolbar (Figure 3–68).

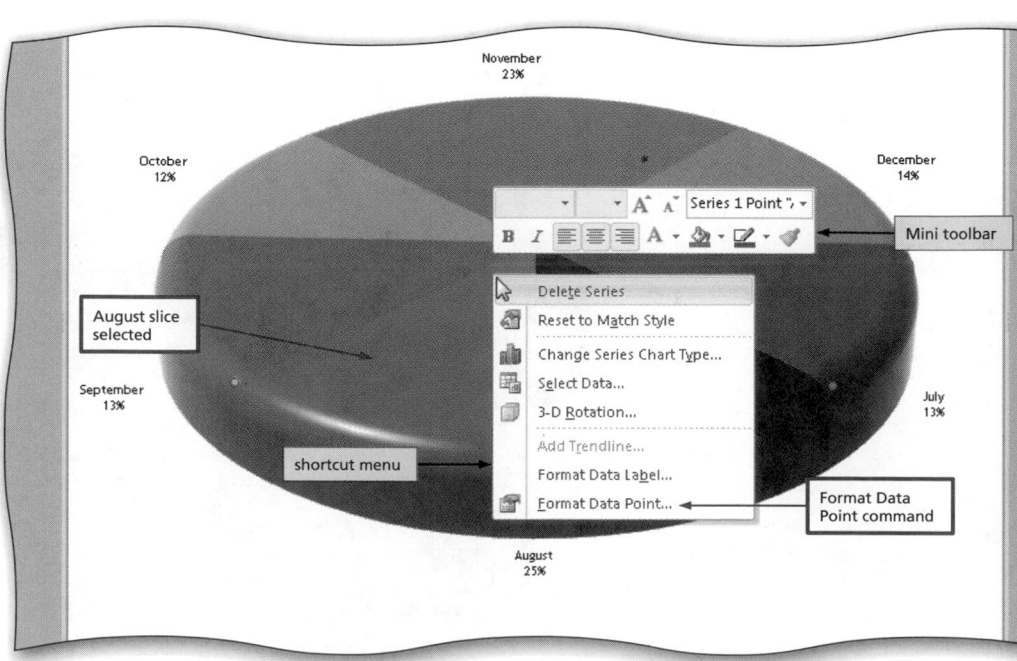

Figure 3–68

2

- Click Format Data Point on the shortcut menu to display the Format Data Point dialog box.

- Drag the Point Explosion slider (Format Data Point dialog box) to the right until the Point Explosion box reads 28% to set how far the slice in the 3-D Pie chart should be offset from the rest of the chart (Figure 3–69).

Should I offset more slices?

You can offset as many slices as you want, but remember that the reason for offsetting a slice is to emphasize it. Offsetting multiple slices tends to reduce the impact on the reader and reduces the overall size of the Pie chart.

Figure 3–69

3

- Click the Fill category (Format Data Point dialog box) on the left side of the dialog box to display the Fill panel.

- Click Solid fill to display the Fill Color area and then click the Color button to display the Color gallery.

- Click the Blue color in the Standard Colors area of the color gallery and then click the Close button (Format Data Point dialog box) to change the color of the selected slice and close the dialog box (Figure 3–70).

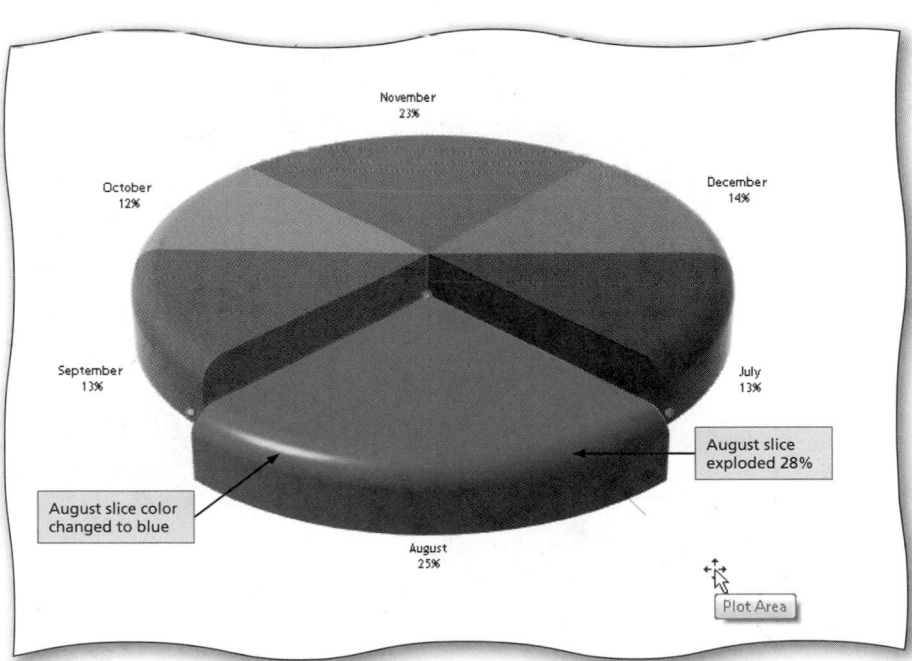

Figure 3–70

Other Ways

1. Right-click slice, click Shape Fill Color button arrow on Mini toolbar, select color

To Change the Colors of the Remaining Slices

BTW

Exploding a 3-D Pie Chart
If you click a 3-D Pie chart so that all of the slices are selected, you can drag one of the slices to explode all of the slices.

The colors of the remaining slices also can be changed to enhance the appeal of the chart. The following steps change the color of the remaining five chart slices.

1 Right-click the slice labeled July to select only the July slice, and display a shortcut menu and Mini toolbar.

2 Click the Shape Fill button arrow on the Mini toolbar to display the Color gallery.

3 Click the Yellow color in the Standard Colors area in the Color gallery to change the color of the slice.

4 Repeat Steps 1 through 3 for the remaining four slices. Assign the following colors in the Standard Colors area in the color gallery to each slice: September – Green; October – Dark Blue; November – Red; December – Purple.

5 Click anywhere outside the chart to deselect the December slice (Figure 3–71). The completed chart appears as shown in Figure 3–71.

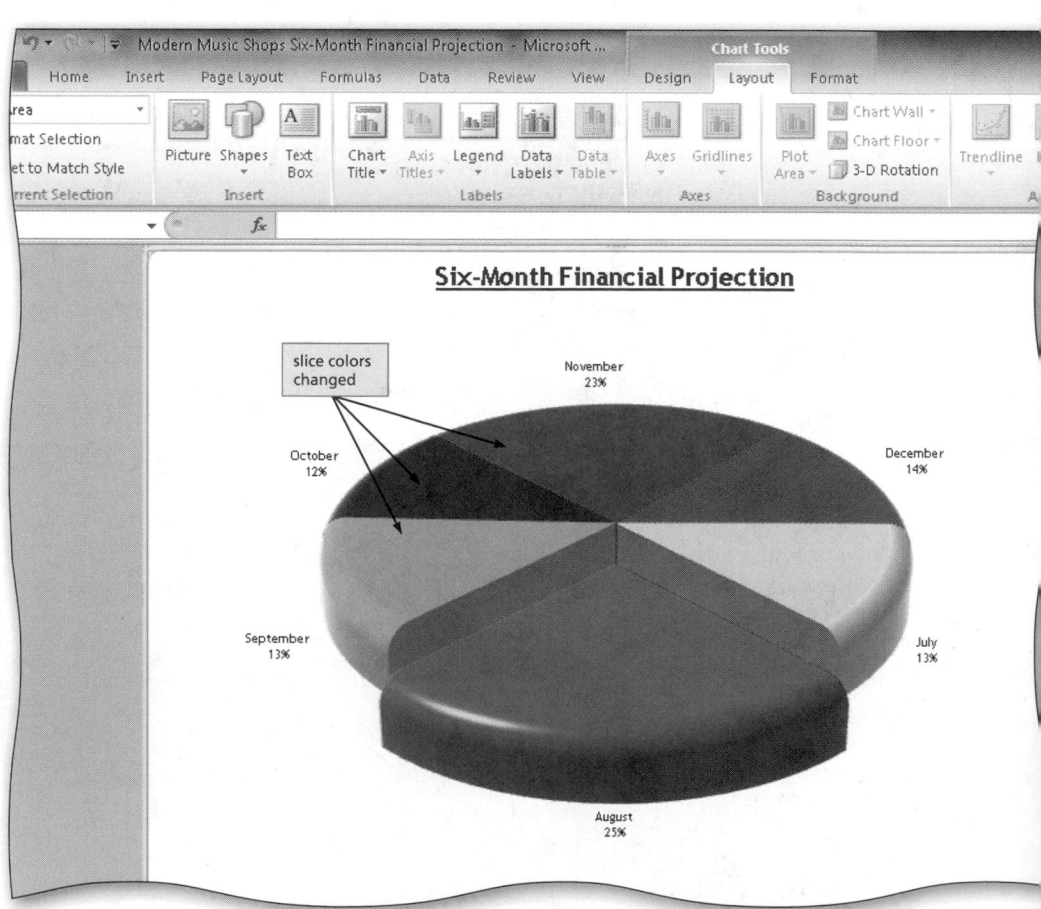

Figure 3–71

Renaming and Reordering the Sheets and Coloring their Tabs

The final step in creating the workbook is to reorder the sheets and modify the tabs at the bottom of the screen.

To Rename the Sheets and Color Their Tabs

The following steps rename the sheets and color the sheet tabs.

❶ Change the sheet tab color of the 3-D Pie Chart sheet to Orange, Accent 6 (column 10, row 1).

❷ Double-click the tab labeled Sheet1 at the bottom of the screen.

❸ Type `Six-Month Financial Projection` as the new sheet name and then press the ENTER key.

❹ Change the sheet tab color of the Six-Month Financial Projection sheet to Pink, Accent 1 (column 5, row 1) and then select cell D8 (Figure 3–72).

Figure 3–72

To Reorder the Sheet Tabs

Change the order sheets in a workbook so that they appear with the most important worksheets first. The following steps reorder the sheets so that the worksheet precedes the chart sheet in the workbook.

1

- Drag the Six-Month Financial Projection tab to the left in front of the 3-D Pie Chart tab to rearrange the sequence of the sheets (Figure 3–73).

3	Commission	5.75%
4	Margin	57.50%
5	Marketing	15.00%
6	Research and Development	7.50%
7	Sales Revenue for Bonus	3,500,000.00
8	Support, General, and Administrative	18.75%

Modern Music Shops
Six-Month Financial Projection

Six-Month Financial Projection tab moved to left of 3-D Pie Chart tab

		July	August	September	October
13	Revenue	$3,113,612.16	$7,962,235.53	$5,112,268.58	$2,924,62
14	Cost of Goods Sold	1,323,285.17	3,383,950.10	2,172,714.15	1,242,96
15	Gross Margin	$1,790,326.99	$4,578,285.43	$2,939,554.43	$1,681,66
16					
17	Expenses				
18	Bonus	$0.00	$200,000.00	$200,000.00	$

Six-Month Financial Projection / 3-D Pie Chart / Sheet2 / Sheet3

Ready

Figure 3–73

To Check Spelling in Multiple Sheets

By default, the spell checker checks the spelling only in the selected sheets. It will check all the cells in the selected sheets, unless you select a range of two or more cells. Before checking the spelling, the following steps select both sheets in the workbook so that both worksheets in the workbook are checked for spelling errors.

BTW

Checking Spelling
Unless you first select a range of cells or an object before starting the spell checker, Excel checks the entire selected worksheet, including all cell values, cell comments, embedded charts, text boxes, buttons, and headers and footers.

1 With the Six-Month Financial Projection sheet active, press CTRL+HOME to select cell A1. Hold down the CTRL key and then click the 3-D Pie Chart tab to select multiple sheets.

2 Display the Review tab and then click the Spelling button (Review tab | Proofing group) to check spelling in the selected sheets.

3 Correct any errors and then click the OK button (Spelling dialog box or Microsoft Excel dialog box) when the spell check is complete.

4 Save the workbook.

To Preview and Print the Workbook

After checking the spelling, the next step is to preview and print the sheets. As with spelling, Excel previews and prints only the selected sheets. In addition, because the worksheet is too wide to print in portrait orientation, the orientation must be changed to landscape. The following steps adjust the orientation and scale, preview the workbook, and then print the workbook.

1 Ready the printer. If both sheets are not selected, hold down the CTRL key and then click the tab of the inactive sheet.

2 Click File on the Ribbon to open the Backstage view.

3 Click the Print tab in the Backstage view to display the Print gallery.

4 If necessary, click the Portrait Orientation button in the Settings area and then select Landscape Orientation to select the desired orientation.

5 If necessary, click the No Scaling button in the Settings area and then select 'Fit Sheet on One Page' to cause the workbook to print on one page.

6 If necessary, click the Printer Status button to display a list of available Printer options and then click the desired printer to change the currently selected printer.

7 Click the Print button in the Print gallery to print the worksheet in landscape orientation on the currently selected printer.

8 When the printer stops, retrieve the printed worksheet (Figure 3–74a and Figure 3–74b on the following page).

9 Right-click the Six-Month Financial Projection tab. Click Ungroup Sheets on the shortcut menu to deselect the 3-D Pie Chart tab.

10 Save the workbook.

BTW

Conserving Ink and Toner
If you want to conserve ink or toner, you can instruct Excel to print draft quality documents by clicking File on the Ribbon to open the Backstage view, clicking Options in the Backstage view to display the Excel Options dialog box, clicking Advanced in the left pane (Excel Options dialog box), scrolling to the Print area in the right pane, placing a check mark in the 'Use draft quality' check box, and then clicking the OK button. Then, use the Backstage view to print the document as usual.

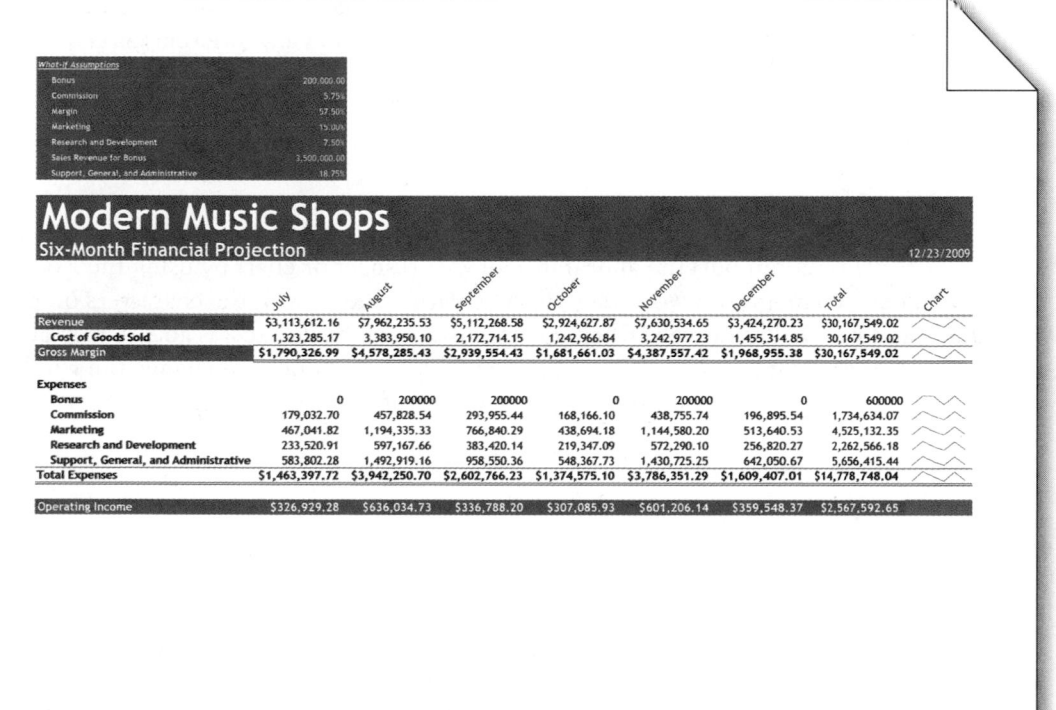

Figure 3–74 (a) Worksheet

BTW

Printing Document Properties
To print document properties, click the File on the Ribbon to open the Backstage view, click the Print tab in the Backstage view to display the Print gallery, click the first button in the Settings area to display a list of options specifying what you can print, click Document Properties in the list to specify you want to print the document properties instead of the actual document, and then click the Print button in the Print gallery to print the document properties on the currently selected printer.

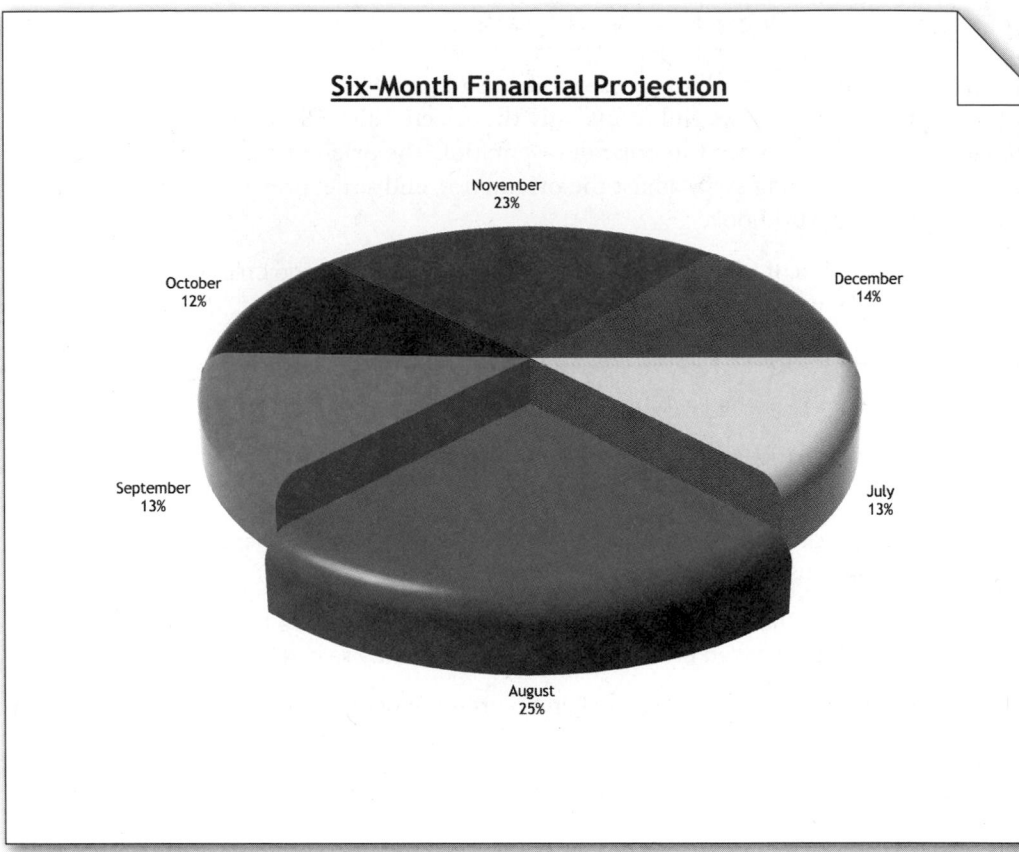

Figure 3–74 (b) 3-D Pie Chart

Changing the View of the Worksheet

With Excel, you easily can change the view of the worksheet. For example, you can magnify or shrink the worksheet on the screen. You also can view different parts of the worksheet through windowpanes.

To Shrink and Magnify the View of a Worksheet or Chart

You can magnify (zoom in) or shrink (zoom out) the appearance of a worksheet or chart by using the Zoom button (View tab | Zoom group). When you magnify a worksheet, Excel enlarges the view of the characters on the screen, but displays fewer columns and rows. Alternatively, when you shrink a worksheet, Excel is able to display more columns and rows. Magnifying or shrinking a worksheet affects only the view; it does not change the window size or printout of the worksheet or chart. The following steps shrink and magnify the view of the worksheet.

1

- If cell A1 is not active, press CTRL + HOME.

- Display the View tab and then click the Zoom button (View tab | Zoom group) to display a list of magnifications in the Zoom dialog box (Figure 3–75).

Figure 3–75

2

- Click 75% and then click the OK button (Zoom dialog box) to shrink the display of the worksheet (Figure 3–76).

Figure 3–76

- Click the Zoom In button on the status bar until the worksheet is displayed at 100% (Figure 3–77).

Figure 3–77

To Split a Window into Panes

When working with a large worksheet, you can split the window into two or four panes to view different parts of the worksheet at the same time. Splitting the Excel window into four panes at cell D13 allows you to view all four corners of the worksheet easily. The following steps split the Excel window into four panes.

- Select cell D13, the intersection of the four proposed panes, to select the cell at which to split the window.

- If necessary, display the View tab (Figure 3–78).

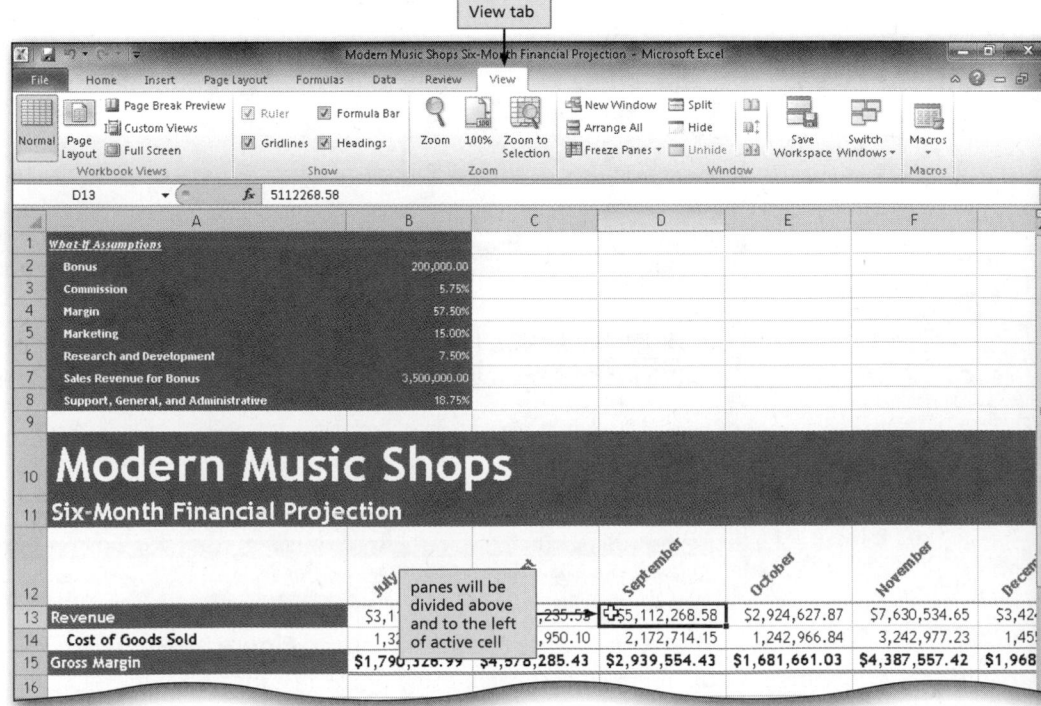

Figure 3–78

2

- Click the Split button (View tab | Window group) to divide the window into four panes.

- Use the scroll arrows to show the four corners of the worksheet at the same time (Figure 3–79).

What is shown in the four panes?

The four panes in Figure 3–79 are used to show the following: (1) range A1:C12 in the upper-left pane; (2) range G1:I12 in the upper-right pane; (3) range A19:C24 in the lower-left pane; and (4) range G19:I24

Figure 3–79

in the lower-right pane. The vertical split bar is the vertical bar going up and down the middle of the window. The horizontal split bar is the horizontal bar going across the middle of the window. If you use the scroll bars below the window and to the right of the window to scroll the window, you will see that the panes split by the horizontal split bar scroll together vertically. The panes split by the vertical split bar scroll together horizontally. To resize the panes, drag either split bar to the desired location in the window.

To Remove the Panes from the Window

1 Position the mouse pointer at the intersection of the horizontal and vertical split bars.

2 When the mouse pointer changes to a four-headed arrow, double-click to remove the four panes from the window.

What-If Analysis

The automatic recalculation feature of Excel is a powerful tool that can be used to analyze worksheet data. Using Excel to scrutinize the impact of changing values in cells that are referenced by a formula in another cell is called what-if analysis or **sensitivity analysis**. When new data is entered, Excel not only recalculates all formulas in a worksheet but also redraws any associated charts.

In the workbook created in this chapter, many of the formulas are dependent on the assumptions in the range B2:B8. Thus, if you change any of the assumption values, Excel immediately recalculates all formulas. Excel redraws the 3-D Pie chart as well, because it is based on these numbers.

Other Ways

1. Drag horizontal split box and vertical split box to desired locations

BTW
Viewing Contents in a New Window
You can open a copy of the current workbook in a new window by clicking the New Window button (View tab | Windows group).

BTW
Zooming
You can use the Zoom in and Zoom out buttons on the status bar to zoom from 10% to 400% to reduce or enlarge the display of a worksheet.

To Analyze Data in a Worksheet by Changing Values

A what-if question for the worksheet in Chapter 3 might be *what* would happen to the six-month operating income in cell H25 *if* the Bonus, Commission, Support, General, and Administrative assumptions in the What-If Assumptions table were changed as follows: Bonus $200,000.00 to $150,000.00; Commission 5.75% to 4.00%; Support, General, and Administrative 18.75% to 15.75%? To answer a question like this, you need to change only the first, second, and seventh values in the What-If Assumptions table, as shown in the following steps. The steps also divide the window into two vertical panes. Excel instantaneously recalculates the formulas in the worksheet and redraws the 3-D Pie chart to answer the question.

1

- Press CTRL+HOME to select cell A1.

- Drag the vertical split box from the lower-right corner of the screen to the left so that the vertical split bar is positioned as shown in Figure 3–80 to split the screen vertically.

- Drag the horizontal split box from the upper-right corner of the screen down so that the horizontal split bar is positioned as shown in Figure 3–80 to split the screen horizontally.

- Use the scroll arrows in the lower-right pane to view the total operating income in column H in the lower-right pane.

Figure 3–80

- Enter `150000` in cell B2, `4%` in cell B3, and `15.75%` in cell B8 (Figure 3–80), which causes the six-month operating income in cell H25 to increase from $2,567,592.65 to $4,150,551.23.

To Goal Seek

If you know the result you want a formula to produce, you can use **goal seeking** to determine the value of a cell on which the formula depends. The following steps close and reopen the Modern Music Shops Six-Month Financial Projection workbook. They then use the Goal Seek command (Data tab | Data Tools group) to determine the Support, General, and Administrative percentage in cell B8 that will yield a six-month operating income of $3,000,000.00 in cell H25, rather than the original $2,567,592.65.

1

- Close the workbook without saving the changes and then reopen it.

- Drag the vertical split box from the lower-right corner of the screen to the left so that the vertical split bar is positioned as shown in Figure 3–81 to split the screen vertically.

- Drag the horizontal split box from the upper-right corner of the screen down so that the horizontal split bar is positioned as shown in Figure 3–81 to split the screen horizontally.

- Use the scroll arrows in the lower-right pane to view the total operating income in column H in the lower-right pane.

- Select cell H25, the cell that contains the six-month operating income.

- Display the Data tab and then click the What-If Analysis button (Data tab | Data Tools group) to display the What-If Analysis menu (Figure 3–81).

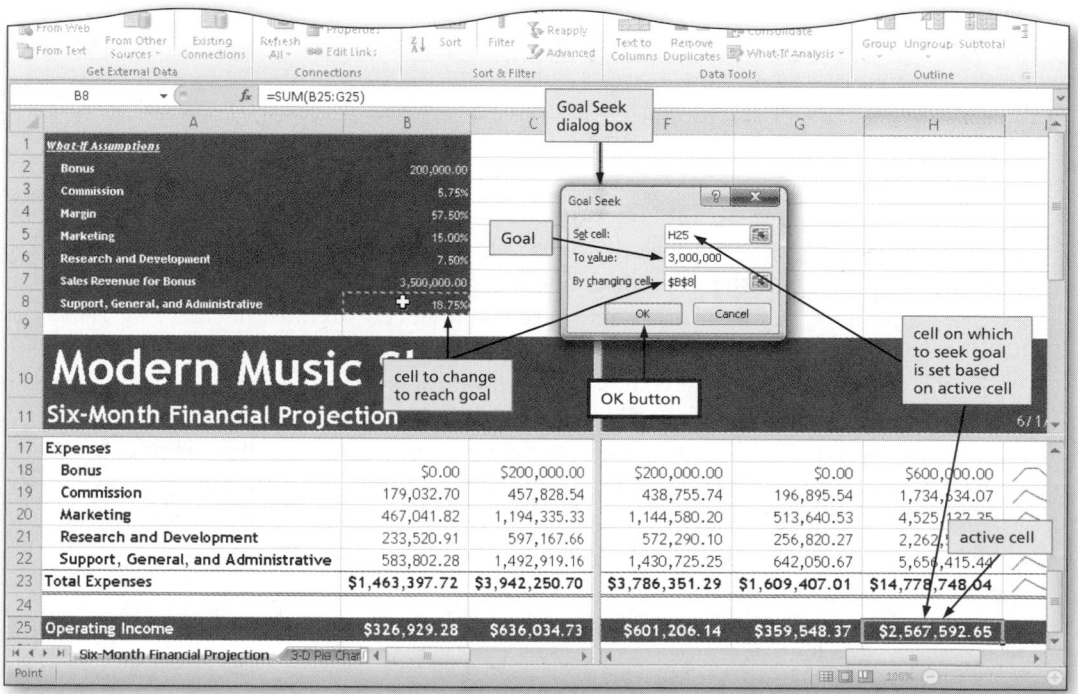

Figure 3–81

2

- Click Goal Seek to display the Goal Seek dialog box with the Set cell box set to the selected cell, H25 in this case.

- When Excel displays the Goal Seek dialog box, click the To value text box, type 3,000,000 and then click the 'By changing cell' box to select the 'By changing cell' box.

- Click cell B8 on the worksheet to assign the current cell, B8 in this case, to the 'By changing cell' box (Figure 3–82).

Figure 3–82

3

- Click the OK button (Goal Seek dialog box) to goal seek for the sought-after value in the 'To value' box, $3,000,000.00 in cell H25 in this case (Figure 3–83).

Q&A

What happens when I click the OK button?

Excel immediately changes cell H25 from $2,567,592.65 to the desired value of $3,000,000.00. More importantly, Excel changes the Support, General, and Administrative assumption in cell B8 from 18.75% to 17.32% (Figure 3–83). Excel also displays the Goal Seek Status dialog box. If you click the OK button, Excel keeps the new values in the worksheet. If you click the Cancel button, Excel redisplays the original values.

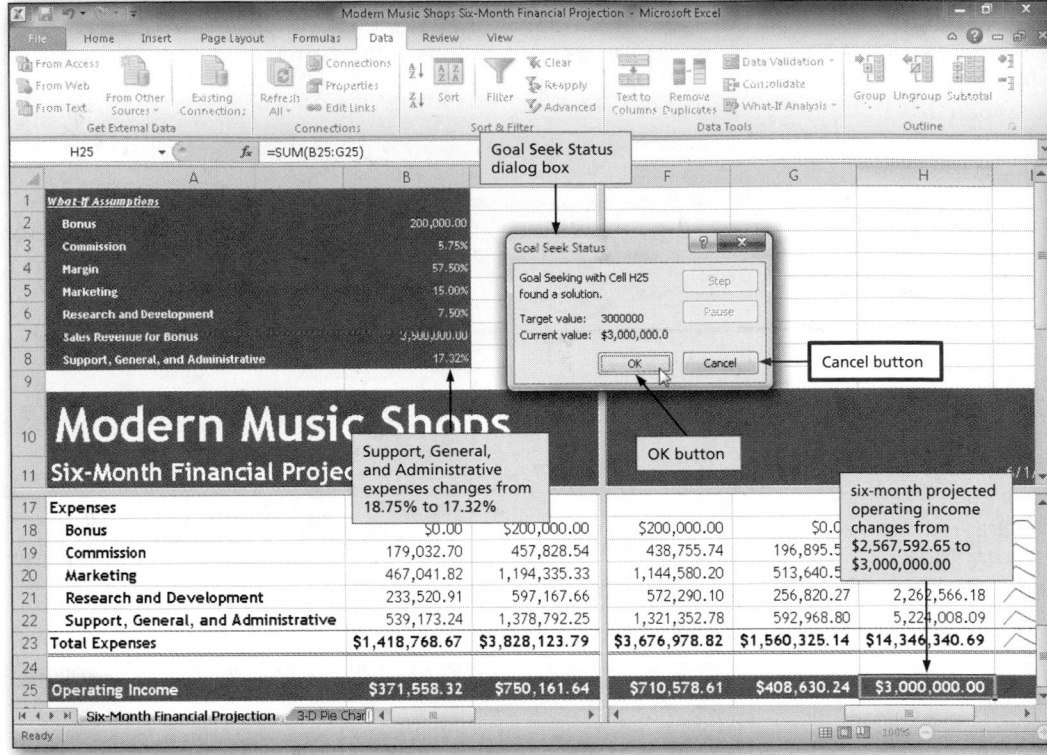

Figure 3–83

4

- Click the Cancel button in the Goal Seek Status dialog box to redisplay the original values in the worksheet.

BTW

Certification
The Microsoft Office Specialist (MOS) program provides an opportunity for you to obtain a valuable industry credential — proof that you have the Excel 2010 skills required by employers. For more information, visit the Excel 2010 Certification Web page (scsite.com/ex2010/cert).

Goal Seeking

Goal seeking assumes you can change the value of only one cell referenced directly or indirectly to reach a specific goal for a value in another cell. In this example, to change the six-month operating income in cell H25 to $3,000,000.00, the Support, General, and Administrative percentage in cell B8 must decrease by 1.43% from 18.75% to 17.32%.

You can see from this goal seeking example that the cell to change (cell B8) does not have to be referenced directly in the formula or function. For example, the six-month operating income in cell H25 is calculated by the function =SUM(B25:G25). Cell B8 is not referenced in this function. Instead, cell B8 is referenced in the formulas in rows 18 through 22, on which the monthly operating incomes in row 25 are based. Excel thus is capable of goal seeking on the six-month operating income by varying the value for the Support, General, and Administrative assumption.

To Quit Excel

With the workbook complete, the following steps quit Excel.

Click the Close button on the upper-right corner of the title bar.

If the Microsoft Excel dialog box is displayed, click the Don't Save button.

BTW

Quick Reference
For a table that lists how to complete the tasks covered in this book using the mouse, Ribbon, shortcut menu, and keyboard, see the Quick Reference Summary at the back of this book, or visit the Excel 2010 Quick Reference Web page (scsite.com/ex2010/qr).

Chapter Summary

In this chapter you learned how to work with large worksheets that extend beyond the window, how to use the fill handle to create a series, new formatting techniques, about the difference between absolute cell references and relative cell references, how to use the IF function, and how to rotate text in a cell, freeze titles, add Sparkline charts, change the magnification of the worksheet, show different parts of the worksheet at the same time through multiple panes, create a 3-D Pie chart, and improve the appearance of a 3-D Pie chart. This chapter also introduced you to using Excel to do what-if analysis by changing values in cells and goal seeking. The items listed below include all the new Excel skills you have learned in this chapter.

1. Rotate Text and Use the Fill Handle to Create a Series of Month Names (EX 145)
2. Increase Column Widths (EX 149)
3. Enter Row Titles (EX 150)
4. Copy a Range of Cells to a Nonadjacent Destination Area (EX 151)
5. Insert a Row (EX 154)
6. Enter Numbers with Format Symbols (EX 156)
7. Freeze Column and Row Titles (EX 157)
8. Enter and Format the System Date (EX 159)
9. Enter a Formula Containing Absolute Cell References (EX 162)
10. Enter an IF Function (EX 165)
11. Copy Formulas with Absolute Cell References Using the Fill Handle (EX 168)
12. Unfreeze the Worksheet Titles and Save the Workbook (EX 169)
13. Add a Sparkline Chart to the Worksheet (EX 170)
14. Format and Copy the Sparkline Chart (EX 171)
15. Assign Formats to Nonadjacent Ranges (EX 174)
16. Format the Worksheet Titles (EX 176)
17. Copy a Cell's Format Using the Format Painter Button (EX 178)
18. Draw a 3-D Pie Chart on a Separate Chart Sheet (EX 182)
19. Insert a Chart Title and Data Labels (EX 183)
20. Rotate the 3-D Pie Chart (EX 186)
21. Apply a 3-D Format to the Pie Chart (EX 188)
22. Explode the 3-D Pie Chart and Change the Color of a Slice (EX 190)
23. Reorder the Sheet Tabs (EX 194)
24. Check Spelling in Multiple Sheets (EX 194)
25. Shrink and Magnify the View of a Worksheet or Chart (EX 196)
26. Split a Window into Panes (EX 198)
27. Analyze Data in a Worksheet by Changing Values (EX 200)
28. Goal Seek (EX 200)

 If you have a SAM 2010 user profile, your instructor may have assigned an autogradable version of this assignment. If so, log into the SAM 2010 Web site at www.cengage.com/sam2010 to download the instruction and start files.

Learn It Online

Test your knowledge of chapter content and key terms.

Instructions: To complete the Learn It Online exercises, start your browser, click the Address bar, and then enter the Web address **scsite.com/ex2010/learn**. When the Excel 2010 Learn It Online page is displayed, click the link for the exercise you want to complete and then read the instructions.

Chapter Reinforcement TF, MC, and SA
A series of true/false, multiple choice, and short answer questions that test your knowledge of the chapter content.

Flash Cards
An interactive learning environment where you identify chapter key terms associated with displayed definitions.

Practice Test
A series of multiple choice questions that test your knowledge of chapter content and key terms.

Who Wants To Be a Computer Genius?
An interactive game that challenges your knowledge of chapter content in the style of a television quiz show.

Wheel of Terms
An interactive game that challenges your knowledge of chapter key terms in the style of the television show *Wheel of Fortune*.

Crossword Puzzle Challenge
A crossword puzzle that challenges your knowledge of key terms presented in the chapter.

Apply Your Knowledge

Reinforce the skills and apply the concepts you learned in this chapter.

Understanding Logical Tests and Absolute Cell Referencing
Instructions Part 1:   Determine the truth value (true or false) of the following logical tests, given the following cell values: B4 = 30; W3 = 100; H5 = 32; L2 = 25; and M8 = 15. Enter true or false.

a. M8 > B4   Truth value: _____

b. W3 = L2   Truth value: _____

c. L2 + 15 * B4 / 10 <> W3   Truth value: _____

d. H5 – L2 < B4 / M8   Truth value: _____

e. (M8 + B4) * 2 <> W3 – (M8 / 3) * 2   Truth value: _____

f. M8 + 300 > B4 * H5 + 10   Truth value: _____

g. H5 * L2 >= 2 * (W3 + 25)   Truth value: _____

h. B4 = 10 * (M8 / 5)   Truth value: _____

Instructions Part 2:   Write cell J49 as a relative reference, absolute reference, mixed reference with the column varying, and mixed reference with the row varying.

_____   _____   _____   _____

Instructions Part 3:   Start Excel. Open the workbook Apply 3-1 Absolute Cell References. See the inside back cover of this book for instructions for downloading the Data Files for Students, or see your instructor for information on accessing the files required in this book. You will re-create the numerical grid pictured in Figure 3–84.

Perform the following tasks:

1. Enter a formula in cell C7 that multiplies the sum of cells C3 through C6 times cell C2. Write the formula so that when you copy it to cells D7 and E7, Excel adjusts all the cell references according to the destination cells. Verify your formula by checking it with the values found in cells C7, D7, and E7 in Figure 3–84.

2. Enter a formula in cell F3 that multiplies cell B3 times the sum of cells C3 through E3. Write the formula so that when you copy the formula to cells F4, F5, and F6, Excel adjusts all the cell references according to the destination cells. Verify your formula by checking it with the values found in cells F3, F4, F5, and F6 in Figure 3–84.

3. Enter a formula in cell C8 that multiplies the sum of cells C3 through C6 times cell C2. Write the formula so that when you copy the formula to cells D8 and E8, cell C2 remains absolute. Verify your formula by checking it with the values found in cells C8, D8, and E8 in Figure 3–84.

4. Enter a formula in cell G3 that multiplies the sum of cells C3, D3, and E3 times cell B3. Write the formula so that when you copy the formula to cells G4, G5, and G6, cell B3 remains absolute. Verify your formula by checking it with the values found in cells G3, G4, G5, and G6 in Figure 3–84.

5. Apply the worksheet name, Cell References, to the sheet tab and apply the Red, Accent 2 theme color to the sheet tab.

6. Change the document properties, as specified by your instructor. Change the worksheet header with your name, course number, and other information as specified by your instructor. Save the workbook using the file name, Apply 3-1 Absolute Cell References Complete, and submit the workbook as requested by your instructor.

Figure 3–84

Extend Your Knowledge

Extend the skills you learned in this chapter and experiment with new skills. You may need to use Help to complete the assignment.

Nested IF Functions and More About the Fill Handle

Instructions Part 1:   Start Excel. You will use nested IF functions to determine values for sets of data.

1. Using the Insert Function dialog box, enter the following IF function in cell B1:

    IF(A1="TX", "Central", "Time Zone Error")

2. Select cell B1, select the text "Time Zone Error" in the Formula Bar, click the Logical button (Formulas tab | Function Library group), click IF, and enter the following IF function:

    IF(A1="OR", "Pacific", "Time Zone Error")

3. Select cell B1, select "Time Zone Error" in the Formula Bar, click Logical button (Formulas tab | Function Library group), click IF, and enter the following IF function:

    IF(A1="VA", "Eastern", "Time Zone Error")

4. Verify that the formula in cell B1 appears as follows:

    =IF(A1="TX","Central", IF(A1="OR","Pacific", IF(A1="VA","Eastern","Time Zone Error")))

5. Use the fill handle to copy the nested IF function down through cell B6. Enter the following data in the cells in the range A1:A6 and then write down the results that display in cells B1 through B6 for each set. Set 1: A1 = TX; A2 = NY; A3 = OR; A4 = MI; A5 = TX; A6 = VA. Set 2: A1= WI; A2 = OR; A3 = IL; A4 = VA; A5 = NJ; A6 = TX.

Set 1 Results: _____

Set 2 Results: _____

6. Save the workbook using the file name, Extend 3-1 Create Series Complete Part 1, and submit the workbook as specified by your instructor.

Instructions Part 2:   Start Excel. Open the workbook Extend 3-1 Create Series. See the inside back cover of this book for instructions for downloading the Data Files for Students, or see your instructor for information on accessing the files required in this book.

Perform the following tasks:

1. Use the fill handle on one column at a time to propagate the twelve series through row 14, as shown in Figure 3–85. For example, in column A, select cell A2 and drag the fill handle down to cell A14. In column C, hold down the CTRL key to repeat Saturday through cell C14. In column D, select the range D2:D3 and drag the fill handle down to cell D14. Likewise, in columns G through L, select the two adjacent cells in rows 2 and 3 before dragging the fill handle down to the corresponding cell in row 14.

2. Select cell D19. While holding down the CTRL key, one at a time drag the fill handle three cells to the right, to the left, up, and down to generate four series of numbers beginning with zero and incremented by one.

3. Select cell H19. Point to the cell border so that the mouse pointer changes to a plus sign with four arrows. Drag the mouse pointer down to cell H21 to move the contents of cell H19 to cell H21.

4. Select cell H21. Point to the cell border so that the mouse pointer changes to a plus sign with four arrows. While holding down the CTRL key, drag the mouse pointer to cell K21 to copy the contents of cell H21 to cell K21.

Figure 3–85

5. Select cell K19. Drag the fill handle in to the center of cell K19 so that the cell is shaded and the cell contents are deleted.

6. Apply a worksheet name to the sheet tab and apply a color of your choice to the sheet tab.

7. Select cell range H2:I14, click the Pie button (Insert tab | Charts group) to display the Pie gallery, click Pie in 3-D chart in the Pie gallery, click the Move Chart button (Chart Tools Design tab | Location group), click the New sheet option button (Move Chart dialog box), and then click the OK button (Move Chart dialog box) to move the 3-D Pie chart to a new worksheet.

8. Click the Chart Title button (Chart Tools Layout tab | Labels group), click Above Chart in the Chart Title gallery, select the title, and change the chart title to "Yearly Breakdown".

9. Click the Data Labels button (Chart Tools Layout tab | Labels group), click Outside End in the Data Labels gallery to add data points to the chart.

0. Apply a chart sheet name to the sheet tab and apply a color of your choice to the tab.

1. Change the document properties, as specified by your instructor. Change the worksheet header with your name, course number, and other information as specified by your instructor. Save the workbook using the file name, Extend 3-1 Create Series Complete Part 2, and submit the workbook as specified by your instructor.

STUDENT ASSIGNMENTS

Make It Right

Analyze a workbook and correct all errors and/or improve the design.

Inserting Rows, Moving a Range, and Correcting Formulas in a Worksheet

Instructions: Start Excel. Open the workbook Make It Right 3-1 SpeedyOfficeSupply.com Annual Projected Net Income. See the inside back cover of this book for instructions for downloading the Data Files for Students, or see your instructor for information on accessing the files required for this book. Correct the following design and formula problems (Figure 3–86a) in the worksheet.

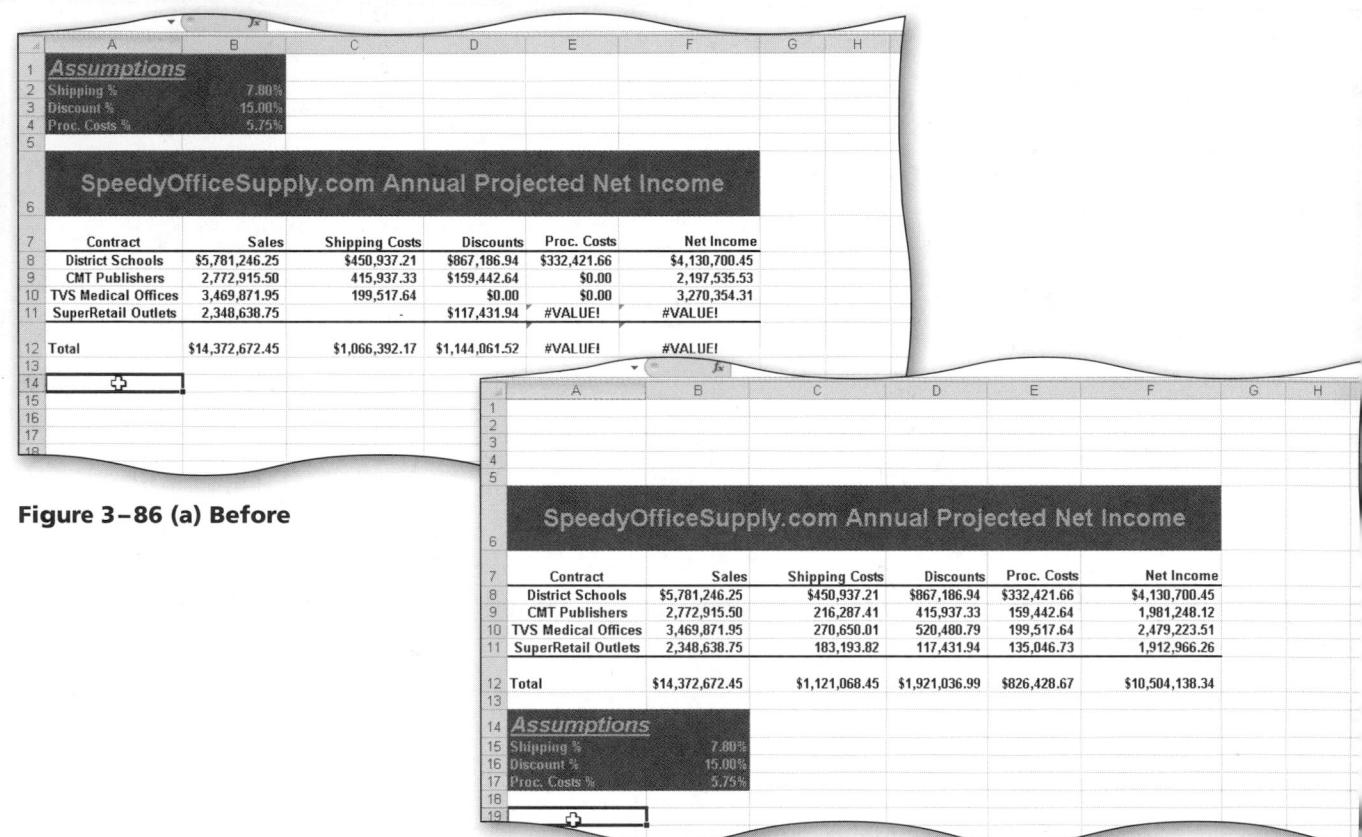

Figure 3–86 (a) Before

Figure 3–86 (b) After

1. The Shipping Cost in cell C8 is computed using the formula =B2*B8 (Shipping % × Sales). Similar formulas are used in cells C9, C10, and C11. The formula in cell C8 was entered and copied to cells C9, C10, and C11. Although the result in cell C8 is correct, the results in cells C9, C10, and C11 are incorrect. Edit the formula in cell C8 by changing cell B2 to an absolute cell reference. Copy the corrected formula in cell C8 to cells C9, C10, and C11. After completing the copy, click the Auto Fill Options button arrow that is displayed below and to the right of cell C11 and choose Fill Without Formatting.

2. The Discount amounts in cells D8, D9, D10, and D11 are computed using the IF function. The Discount amount should equal the amount in cell B3*B8 (Discount % × Sales) if the corresponding Sales in column B is greater than or equal to $2,500,000. If the corresponding Sales in column B is less than $2,500,000, then the Discount amount is 5%*B8 (5% × Sales). The IF function in cell D8

was entered and copied to cells D9, D10, and D11. The current IF functions in cells D8, D9, D10, and D11 are incorrect. Edit and correct the IF function in cell D8. Copy the corrected formula in cell D8 to cells D9, D10, and D11. After completing the copy, click the Auto Fill Options button arrow that is displayed below and to the right of cell D11 and choose Fill Without Formatting.

3. The Processing Costs in cell E8 is computed using the formula =B4*B8 (Proc. Costs % × Sales). The formula in cell E8 was entered and copied to cells E9, E10, and E11. Although the result in cell E8 is correct, the results in cells E9, E10, and E11 are incorrect. Edit and correct the formula in cell E8 by changing cell B4 to an absolute cell reference. Copy the corrected formula in cell E8 to cells E9, E10, and E11. After completing the copy, click the Auto Fill Options button arrow that displays below and to the right of cell E11 and choose Fill Without Formatting. Ensure that the range B9:E11 is formatted with the Accounting Number format.

4. Change the design of the worksheet by moving the Assumptions table in the range A1:B4 to the range A14:B17, as shown in Figure 3–86b. To complete the move drag the Assumptions table to the range A14:B17. Use Figure 3–86b to verify that Excel automatically adjusted the cell references based on the move. Use the Undo button and Redo button on the Quick Access Toolbar to move the Assumptions table back and forth while the results of the formulas remain the same.

5. Apply a worksheet name to the sheet tab and apply the Orange, Accent 3 color to the sheet tab.

6. Change the document properties, as specified by your instructor. Change the worksheet header with your name, course number, and other information as specified by your instructor. Save the workbook using the file name, Make It Right 3-1 SpeedyOfficeSupply.com Annual Projected Net Income Complete, and submit the revised workbook as specified by your instructor.

n the Lab

Create a workbook using the guidelines, concepts, and skills presented in this chapter. Labs re listed in order of increasing difficulty.

ab 1: Six-Year Financial Projection

Problem: Your supervisor in the Finance department at Med Supply Online Warehouse has asked ou to create a worksheet that will project the annual gross margin, expenses, total expenses, operating ncome, income taxes, and net income for the next six years based on the assumptions in Table 3–9. The desired worksheet is shown in Figure 3–87 on the following page. In Part 1 you will create the orksheet. In Part 2 you will create a chart to present the data, shown in Figure 3–88 on page EX 213. n Part 3 you will use Goal Seek to analyze three different sales scenarios.

Table 3–9 Med Supply Online Warehouse Financial Projection Assumptions	
Units Sold in Prior Year	1,589,712
Unit Cost	$59.50
Annual Sales Growth	4.50%
Annual Price Decrease	3.80%
Margin	38.80%

Continued >

In the Lab *continued*

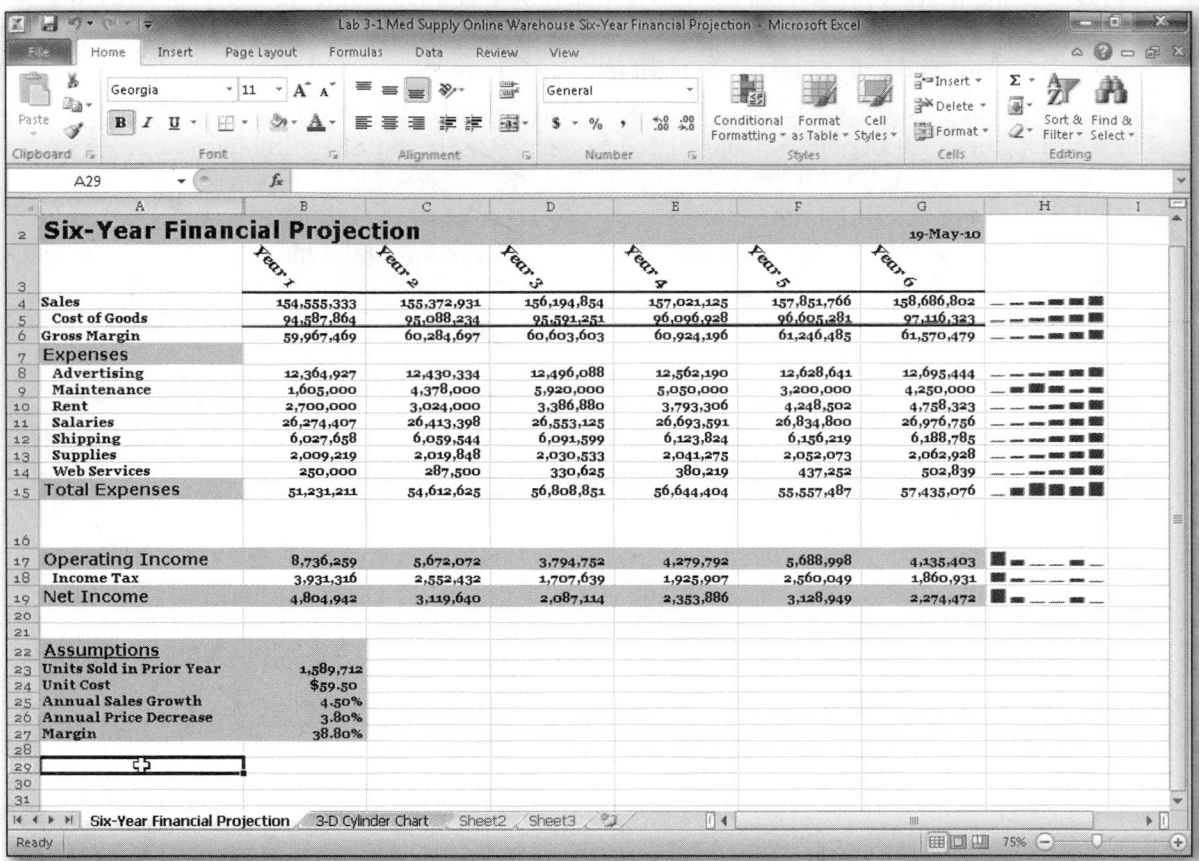

Figure 3–87

Instructions Part 1:

1. Start Excel. Apply the Civic theme to the worksheet by using the Themes button (Page Layout tab | Themes group). Bold the entire worksheet by selecting the entire worksheet and using the Bold button (Home tab | Font group).

2. Enter the worksheet title **Med Supply Online Warehouse** in cell A1 and the subtitle **Six-Year Financial Projection** in cell A2. Format the worksheet title in cell A1 to 36-point Copperplate Gothic Bold (or a similar font). Format the worksheet subtitle in cell A2 to 20-point Verdana (or a similar font). Enter the system date in cell G2 using the NOW function. Format the date to the 14-Mar-01 style.

3. Change the following column widths: A = 25.00 characters; B through H = 15.00 characters. Change the heights of rows 7, 15, 17, 19, and 22 to 18.00 points. Change the height of row 16 to 42.00 points.

4. Enter the six column titles Year 1 through Year 6 in the range B3:G3 by entering Year 1 in cell B3 and then dragging cell B3's fill handle through the range C3:G3. Format cell B3 as follows: (a) increase the font size to 14; (b) center and italicize it; and (c) angle its contents clockwise. Use the Format Painter button (Home tab | Clipboard group) to copy the format assigned to cell B3 to the range C3:G3.

5. Enter the row titles in the range A4:A19. Change the font in cells A7, A15, A17, and A19 to 14-point Verdana (or a similar font). Add thick bottom borders to the ranges B3:G3 and B5:G5. Use the Increase Indent button (Home tab | Alignment group) to increase the indent of the row titles in cell A5, the range A8:A14, and cell A18.

6. Enter the table title **Assumptions** in cell A22. Enter the assumptions in Table 3–9 on page EX 209 in the range A23:B27. Use format symbols when entering the numbers. Change the font size of the table title in cell A22 to 14-point Verdana and underline it.

7. Select the range B4:G19 and then click the Format Cells: Number Dialog Box Launcher (Home tab | Number group) to display the Format Cells dialog box. Use the Number category (Format Cells dialog box) to assign a comma style with no decimal places and negative numbers enclosed in parentheses to the range B4:G19.

8. Complete the following entries:
   a. Year 1 Sales (cell B4) = Units Sold in Prior Year * (Unit Cost / (1 – Margin)) or = B23*(B24/(1-B27))
   b. Year 2 Sales (cell C4) = Year 1 Sales * (1 + Annual Sales Growth) * (1 – Annual Price Decrease) or =B4*(1+$B$25)*(1-$B$26)
   c. Copy cell C4 to the range D4:G4.
   d. Year 1 Cost of Goods (cell B5) = Year 1 Sales * (1 – Margin) or =B4 * (1 - $B$27)
   e. Copy cell B5 to the range C5:G5.
   f. Gross Margin (cell B6) = Year 1 Sales - Year 1 Cost of Goods or =B4 – B5
   g. Copy cell B6 to the range C6:G6.
   h. Year 1 Advertising (cell B8) = 500 + 8% * Year 1 Sales or =500+8%*B4
   i. Copy cell B8 to the range C8:G8.
   j. Maintenance (row 9): Year 1 = 1,605,000; Year 2 = 4,378,000; Year 3 = 5,920,000; Year 4 = 5,050,000; Year 5 = 3,200,000; Year 6 = 4,250,000
   k. Year 1 Rent (cell B10) = 2,700,000
   l. Year 2 Rent (cell C10) = Year 1 Rent + (12% * Year 1 Rent) or =B10 + (12% * B10)
   m. Copy cell C10 to the range D10:G10.
   n. Year 1 Salaries (cell B11) = 17% * Year 1 Sales or =17%*B4
   o. Copy cell B11 to the range C11:G11.
   p. Year 1 Shipping (cell B12) = 3.9% * Year 1 Sales or =3.9%*B4
   q. Copy cell B12 to the range C12:G12.
   r. Year 1 Supplies (cell B13) = 1.3% * Year 1 Sales or =1.3%*B4
   s. Copy cell B13 to the range C13:G13.
   t. Year 1 Web Services (cell B14) = 250,000
   u. Year 2 Web Services (cell C14) = Year 1 Web Services + (15% * Year 1 Web Services) or =B14+ (15% * B14)
   v. Copy cell C14 to the range D14:G14.
   w. Year 1 Total Expenses (cell B15) = SUM(B8:B14)
   x. Copy cell B15 to the range C15:G15.
   y. Year 1 Operating Income (cell B17) = Year 1 Gross Margin - Year 1 Total Expenses or =B6-B15
   z. Copy cell B17 to the range C17:G17.

Continued >

In the Lab *continued*

    aa. Year 1 Income Taxes (cell B18): If Year 1 Operating Income is less than 0, then Year 1 Income Taxes equal 0; otherwise Year 1 Income Taxes equal 45% * Year 1 Operating Income or =IF(B17 < 0, 0, 45%*B17)

    bb. Copy cell B18 to the range C18:G18.

    cc. Year 1 Net Income (cell B19) = Year 1 Operating Income – Year 1 Income Taxes or = B17-B18

    dd. Copy cell B19 to the range C19:G19.

    ee. In cell H4, insert a Sparkline Column chart (Insert Tab | Sparklines group) for cell range B4:G4

    ff. Repeat step ee for the ranges H5:H6, H8:H15, and H17:H19

9. Change the background colors as shown in Figure 3–87. Use Teal, Accent 3, Lighter 40% for the background colors.

10. Zoom to: (a) 200%; (b) 75%; (c) 25%; and (d) 100%.

11. Change the document properties, as specified by your instructor. Change the worksheet header with your name, course number, and other information as specified by your instructor. Save the workbook using the file name, Lab 3-1 Med Supply Online Warehouse Six-Year Financial Projection.

12. Preview the worksheet. Use the Orientation button (Page Layout tab | Page Setup group) to fit the printout on one page in landscape orientation. Preview the formulas version (CTRL+`) of the worksheet in landscape orientation using the Fit to option. Press CTRL +` to instruct Excel to display the values version of the worksheet. Save the workbook again and close the workbook.

13. Submit the workbook as specified by your instructor.

Instructions Part 2:

1. Start Excel. Open the workbook Lab 3-1 Med Supply Online Warehouse Six-Year Financial Projection.

2. Use the nonadjacent ranges B3:G3 and B19:G19 to create a 3-D Cylinder chart. Draw the chart by clicking the Column button (Insert tab | Charts group). When the Column gallery is displayed, click the Clustered Cylinder chart type (column 1, row 3). When the chart is displayed, click the Move Chart button to move the chart to a new sheet.

3. Select the legend on the right side of the chart and delete it. Add the chart title by clicking the Chart Titles button (Chart Tools Layout tab | Labels group). Click Above Chart in the Chart Title gallery. Format the chart title as shown in Figure 3–88.

4. To change the color of the cylinders, click one of the cylinders and use the Shape Fill button (Chart Tools Format tab | Shape Styles group). To change the color of the wall, click the wall behind the cylinders and use the Shape Fill button to change the chart wall color. Use the same procedure to change the color of the base of the wall.

5. Rename the sheet tabs Six-Year Financial Projection and 3-D Cylinder Chart. Rearrange the sheet so that the worksheet is leftmost and color their tabs as shown in Figure 3–88.

6. Click the Six-Year Financial Projection tab to display the worksheet. Save the workbook using the same file name (Lab 3-1 Med Supply Online Warehouse Six -Year Financial Projection) as defined in Part 1. Submit the workbook as requested by your instructor.

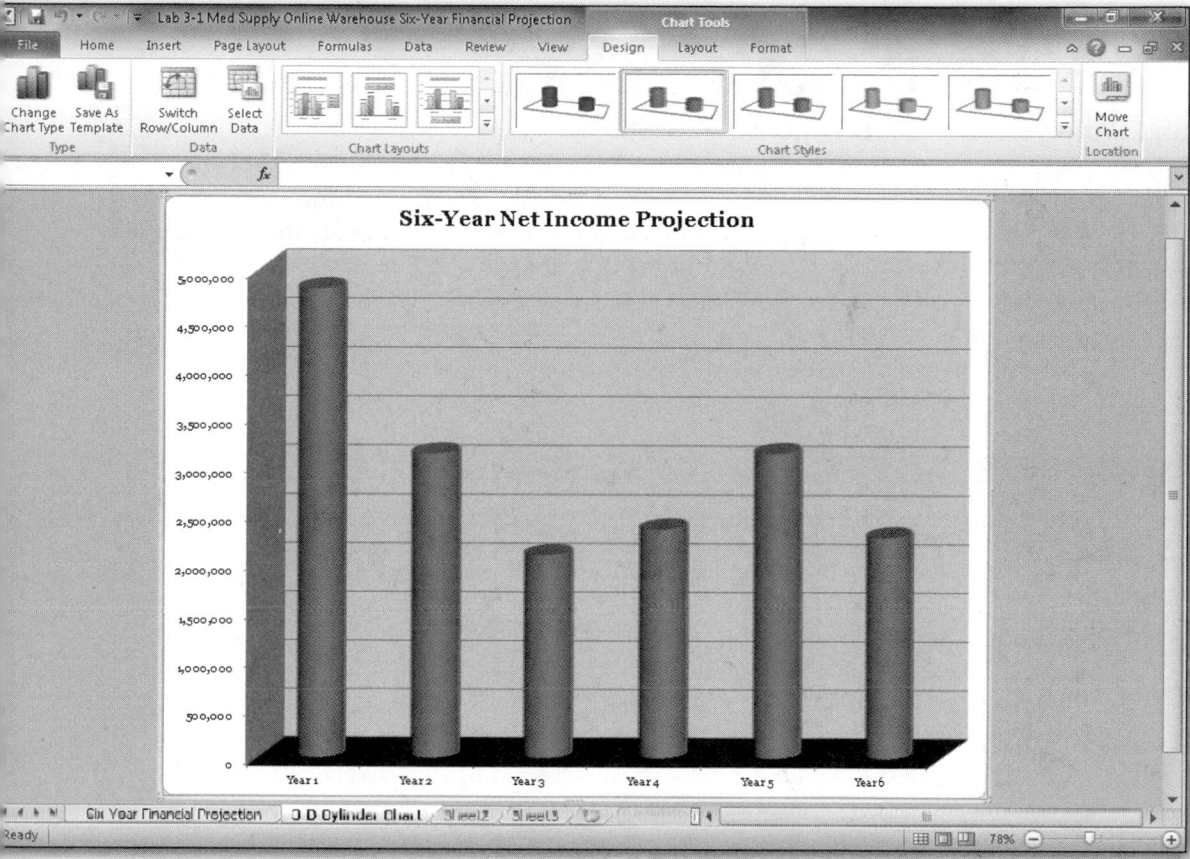

Figure 3–88

Instructions Part 3:

1. Start Excel. Open the workbook Lab 3-1 Med Supply Online Warehouse Six-Year Financial Projection. Do not save the workbook in this part of the In the Lab exercise. Divide the window into two panes by dragging the horizontal split box between rows 6 and 7. Use the scroll bars to show both the top and bottom of the worksheet. Using the numbers in columns 2 and 3 of Table 3–10, analyze the effect of changing the annual sales growth (cell B25) and annual price decrease (cell B26) on the net incomes in row 19. The resulting answers are in column 4 of Table 3–10. Submit the workbook or results of the what-if analysis for each case as requested by your instructor.

Table 3–10 Med Supply Online Warehouse Data to Analyze and Results

Case	Annual Sales Growth	Annual Price Decrease	Year 6 Resulting Net Income in Cell G19
1	8.45%	5.75%	2,925,008
2	14.75%	23.00%	(2,353,532)
3	25.50%	2.65%	14,668,149

2. Close the workbook without saving it, and then reopen it. Use the What-If Analysis button (Data tab | Data Tools group) to goal seek. Determine a margin (cell B27) that would result in a Year 6 net income of $4,000,000 (cell G19). You should end up with a margin of 40.49% in cell B27. Submit the workbook with the new values or the results of the goal seek as requested by your instructor. Do not save the workbook with the latest changes.

In the Lab

Lab 2: Analysis of Indirect Expense Allocations

Problem: Your classmate works part time as an advisor for the ReachOut Neighbors not-for-profit group. She has asked you to assist her in creating an indirect expense allocation worksheet (Figure 3–89) that will help the not-for-profit administration better evaluate the branch offices described in Table 3–11.

ReachOut Neighbors
Analysis of Indirect Expenses
19-May-10

	Chicago Branch Office	Dallas Branch Office	Houston Branch Office	Jacksonville Branch Office	Los Angeles Branch Office	New York Branch Office	Reno Branch Office	Total
Total Donations	$235,356.00	$98,190.00	$178,435.00	$212,300.00	$175,350.00	$752,900.00	$1,845,230.00	$3,997,761.00
Distributed Goods and Services	529,750.00	60,891.00	135,589.00	150,895.00	96,050.00	589,590.00	1,629,350.00	$3,192,115.00
Direct Expenses	57,550.00	22,530.00	14,750.00	25,300.00	42,670.00	58,600.00	65,000.00	286,400.00
Indirect Expenses								
Administrative	$15,175.21	$2,026.30	$3,682.28	$4,381.14	$3,618.62	$15,532.26	$38,079.18	$82,500.00
Depreciation	15,930.38	796.52	7,759.63	8,479.07	926.38	6,449.23	8,838.79	49,230.00
Energy	10,355.93	1,382.80	2,512.88	2,989.80	2,469.43	10,603.00	25,986.16	56,300.00
Insurance	4,368.48	218.42	2,122.87	2,325.16	262.75	1,768.53	2,423.80	13,500.00
Maintenance	13,632.88	681.64	6,640.53	7,256.21	835.56	5,519.12	7,564.05	42,130.00
Marketing	12,554.04	1,626.31	3,046.25	3,624.40	2,993.59	12,853.55	31,501.87	68,250.00
Total Indirect Expenses	$72,016.92	$6,781.99	$25,769.45	$29,055.77	$11,161.32	$52,730.69	$114,393.85	$311,910.00
Net Income	$76,039.08	$7,987.01	$2,326.55	$7,049.23	$25,468.68	$51,979.31	$36,486.15	$202,336.00
Square Footage	15,500	775	7,550	8,250	950	6,275	8,600	47,900
Planned Indirect Expenses								
Administrative	82,500							
Depreciation	49,230							
Energy	56,300							
Insurance	13,500							
Maintenance	42,130							
Marketing	68,250							

Indirect Expenses Analysis / 3-D Column Chart / Sheet2 / Sheet3

Figure 3–89

Table 3–11 ReachOut Neighbor Worksheet Data

	Chicago Branch Office	Dallas Branch Office	Houston Branch Office	Jacksonville Branch Office	Los Angeles Branch Office	New York Branch Office	Reno Branch Office
Total Donations	735356	98190	178435	212300	175350	752900	1845230
Distributed Goods and Services	529750	60891	135589	150895	96050	589590	1629350
Direct Expenses	57550	22530	14750	25300	42670	58600	65000
Square Footage	15500	775	7550	8250	950	6275	8600

Instructions Part 1: Do the following to create the worksheet shown in Figure 3–89.

1. Apply the Foundry theme to the worksheet. Bold the entire worksheet by selecting the entire worksheet and using the Bold (Home tab | Font group).

2. Change the following column widths: A = 30.00; B through I = 13.00; J = 20.00.

3. Enter the worksheet titles in cells A1 and A2 and the system date in cell I2. Format the date to the 14-Mar-01 style.

4. Enter the column titles, row titles, and the first three rows of numbers in Table 3–11 in rows 3 through 6. Add the column heading Total to cell I3. Center and italicize the column headings in the range B3:I3. Add a thick bottom border to the range B3:I3. Sum the individual rows 4, 5, and 6 in the range I4:I6.

5. Enter the Square Footage row as shown in Table 3–11 with the comma format symbol in row 16. Sum row 16 in cell I16. Use the Format Painter button (Home tab | Clipboard group) to format cell I16. Change the height of row 16 to 42.00. Vertically center the range A16:I16 through the use of the Format Cells dialog box.

6. Enter the remaining row titles in the range A7:A17 as shown in Figure 3–89. Increase the font size in cells A7, A14, and A15 to 14 point and indent the text in the ranges A8:A13 and A18:A23.

7. Copy the row titles in range A8:A13 to the range A18:A23. Enter the numbers shown in the range B18:B23 of Figure 3–89 with format symbols.

8. The planned indirect expenses in the range B18:B23 are to be prorated across the branch office as follows: Administrative (row 8), Energy (row 10), and Marketing (row 13) on the basis of Total Donations (row 4); Depreciation (row 9), Insurance (row 11), and Maintenance (row 12) on the basis of Square Footage (row 16). Use the following formulas to accomplish the prorating:

   a. Chicago Branch Office Administrative (cell B8) = Administrative Expenses * Chicago Branch Office Total Donations / ReachOut Neighbors Total Donations or =$B$18*B4/$I$4

   b. Chicago Branch Office Depreciation (cell B9) = Depreciation Expenses * Chicago Branch Office Square Footage / Total Square Footage or =$B$19*B16/$I$16

   c. Chicago Branch Office Energy (cell B10) = Energy Expenses * Chicago Branch Office Total Donations / ReachOut Neighbor Total Donations or =$B$20*B4/$I$4

   d. Chicago Branch Office Insurance (cell B11) = Insurance Expenses * Chicago Branch Office Square Footage / Total Square Footage or =$B$21*B16 /$I$16

   e. Chicago Branch Office Maintenance (cell B12) = Maintenance Expenses * Chicago Branch Office Square Footage / Total Square Footage or =$B$22*B16/$I$16

   f. Chicago Branch Office Marketing (cell B13) = Marketing Expenses * Chicago Branch Office Total Donations / ReachOut Neighbor Total Donations or =$B$23*B4/$I$4

   g. Chicago Branch Office Total Indirect Expenses (cell B14) = SUM(B8:B13)

   h. Chicago Branch Office Net Income (cell B15) = Total Donations - (Distributed Goods and Services + Direct Expenses + Total Indirect Expenses) or =B4-(B5+B6+B14)

   i. Copy the range B8:B15 to the range C8:H15.

   j. Sum the individual rows 8 through 15 in the range I8:I15.

9. Add a thick bottom border to the range B13:I13. Assign the Currency style with two decimal places and show negative numbers in parentheses to the following ranges: B4:I4; B8:I8; and B14:I15. Assign the Comma style with two decimal places and show negative numbers in parentheses to the following ranges: B5:I6 and B9:I13.

10. Change the font in cell A1 to 48-point Britannic Bold (or a similar font). Change the font in cell A2 to 22-point Britannic Bold (or a similar font). Change the font in cell A17 to 18-point italic Britannic Bold.

11. Use the background color Green, Accent 1, Lighter 40% and the font color Tan, Background 2, Darker 75% for cell A7 and the ranges A1:I2; A15:I15; and A17:B23 as shown in Figure 3–89.

12. Insert a Sparkline Win/Loss chart for the range B8:H8 in cell J8. Copy the cell J8 to the cell range J9:J13.

Continued >

In the Lab *continued*

13. Rename the Sheet1 sheet as Indirect Expenses Analysis and color its tab green.

14. Update the document properties with your name, course number, and name for the workbook. Change the worksheet header with your name, course number, and other information as specified by your instructor. Save the workbook using the file name, Lab 3-2 ReachOut Neighbor Analysis o Indirect Expenses.

15. Preview the worksheet. Use the Orientation button (Page Layout tab | Page Setup group) to fit the printout on one page in landscape orientation using the Fit to option. Preview the formulas version (CTRL+`) of the worksheet in landscape orientation using the Fit to option. Press CTRL+` to instruct Excel to display the values version of the worksheet. Save the workbook again and close the workbook.

16. Divide the window into four panes and show the four corners of the worksheet. Remove the four panes. Close the workbook but do not save the workbook.

Instructions Part 2:   Start Excel. Open Lab 3-2 ReachOut Neighbor Analysis of Indirect Expenses. Draw a 3-D Column Chart (Figure 3–90) on a separate sheet that shows the contribution of each category of indirect expense to the total indirect expenses. That is, chart the nonadjacent ranges A8:A1 (category names) and I8:I13 (data series). Show labels that include value of the column. Do not show the legend. Format the 3-D Column Chart as shown in Figure 3–90. Rename the chart sheet 3-D Column Chart and color the sheet tab red. Move the chart tab to the right of the worksheet tab. Save the workbook using the file name, Lab 3-2 ReachOut Neighbor Analysis of Indirect Expenses. Submit the workbook as specified by your instructor.

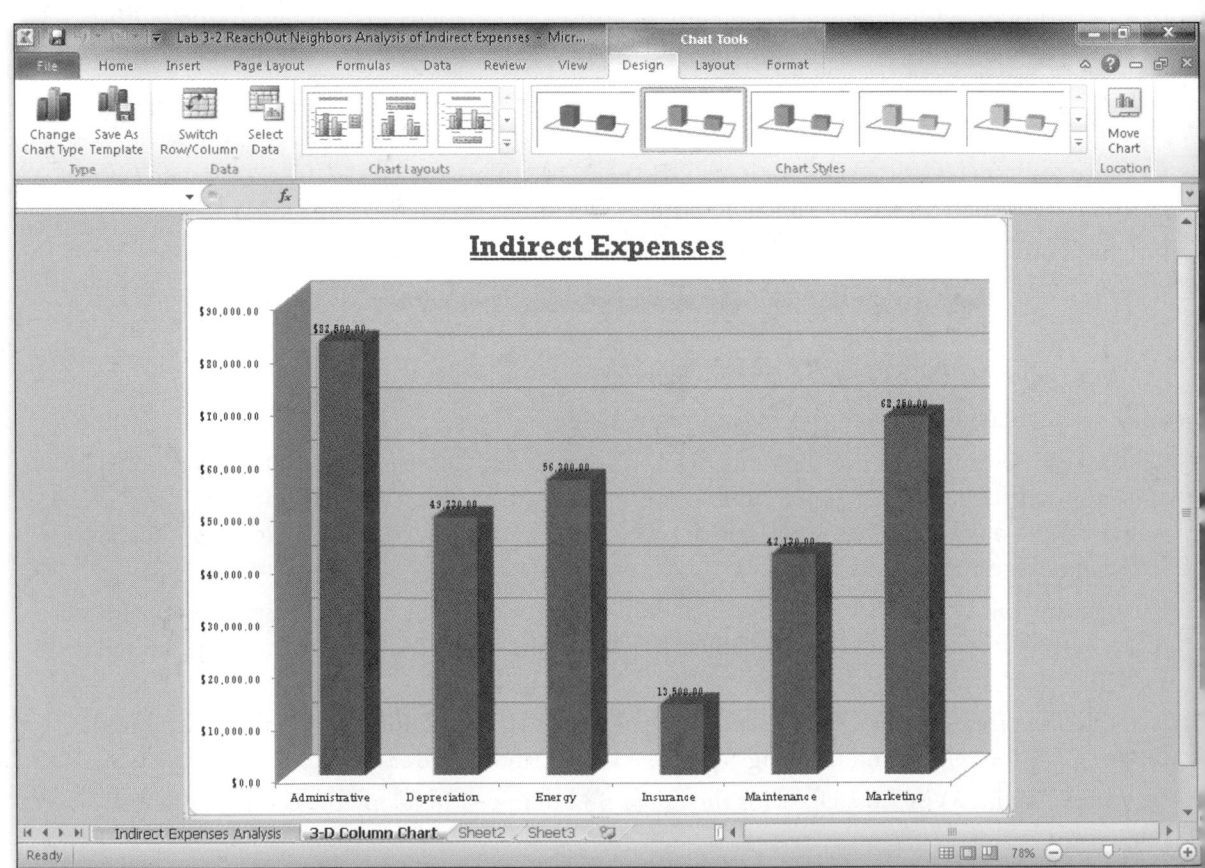

Figure 3–90

tructions Part 3:   Start Excel. Open Lab 3-2 ReachOut Neighbor Analysis of Indirect Expenses.
. Using the numbers in Table 3–12, analyze the effect of changing the planned indirect expenses in
  the range B18:B23 on the net incomes for each branch office. You should end with the following
  totals in cell I15: Case 1 = $5,846.00 and Case 2 = $124,346.00. Close the workbook without saving
  the changes. Submit the workbook or results for each case as requested by your instructor.

. Use the What-If Analysis button (Data tab | Data Tools group) to goal seek. Determine a planned
  indirect Marketing expense (cell B23) that would result in a total net income of $50,000 (cell I15).
  You should end up with a planned indirect Marketing expense of $225,586 in cell B23. Submit the
  workbook with the new values or the results of the goal seek as specified by your instructor.

ble 3–12 ReachOut Neighbor Indirect Expense Allocations What-If Data

	Case 1	Case 2
dministrative	124000	66500
epreciation	156575	75000
ergy	72525	56000
surance	46300	67000
aintenance	75000	48000
arketing	39000	82400

the Lab

b 3: Modifying a Weekly Inventory Worksheet

oblem: As a summer intern at Dinah's Candle Depot, you have been asked to modify the weekly
ventory report shown in Figure 3–91a on the following page. The workbook, Lab 3-3 Dinah's Weekly
ventory Report, is included with the Data Files for Students. See the inside back cover of this book
 instructions for downloading the Data Files for Students, or see your instructor for information on
cessing the files required for this book.

    The major modifications to the payroll report to be made in this exercise include: (1) reformatting
 worksheet; (2) adding computations of quantity to order based on reorder level and weeks to arrive;
 adding calculations to suggest changes in ordering; (4) adding current and last month sales for
ventory items; (5) adding and deleting inventory items; and (6) changing inventory item information.
 e final inventory report is shown in Figure 3–91b on the following page.

Continued >

In the Lab *continued*

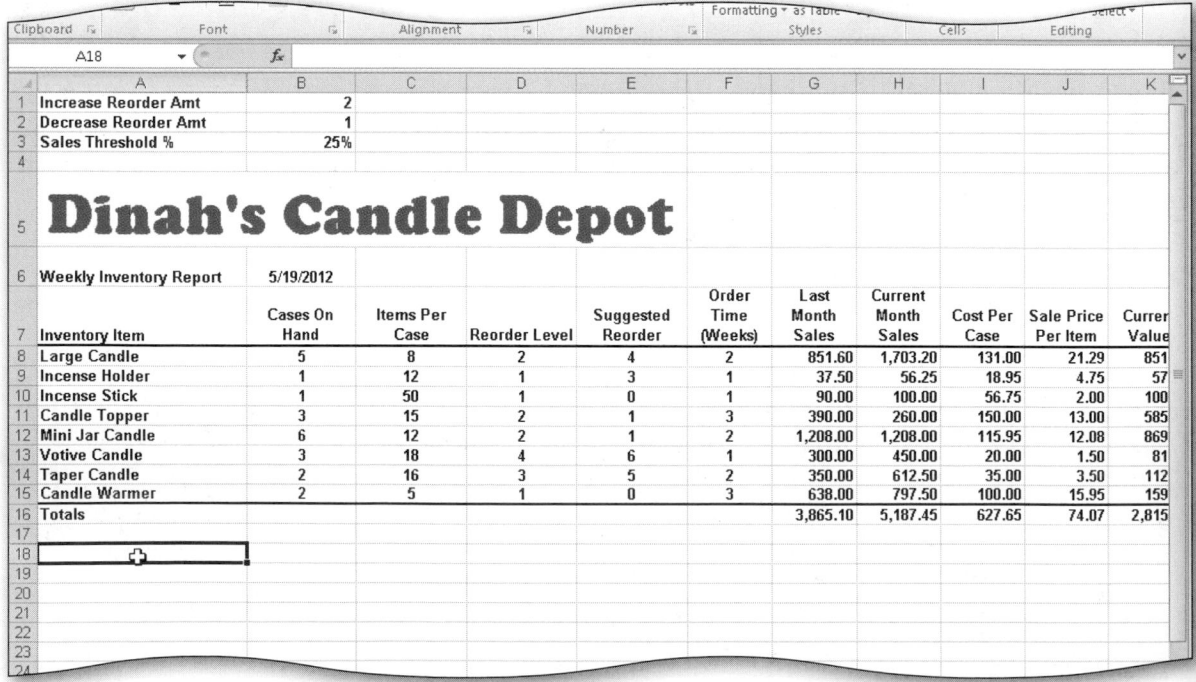

Figure 3–91 (a) Before

Figure 3–91 (b) After

Instructions Part 1:

1. Start Excel. Open the workbook, Lab 3-3 Dinah's Weekly Inventory Report and then save the workbook using the file name Lab 3-3 Dinah's Weekly Inventory Report Complete.

2. Select the worksheet by clicking the Select All button. Click the Clear button (Home tab | Editing group) and then click Clear Formats on the Clear menu to clear the formatting. Bold the entire worksheet.

3. Delete rows 11 through 13 to remove the statistics below the Totals row. Change all the row heights back to the default height (12.75).

4. Insert four rows above row 1 by selecting rows 1 through 4, right-clicking the selection, and clicking Insert on the shortcut menu.

5. Change the row heights as follows: row 5 = 48.00; row 6 = 25.50; and 7 = 38.25. For the range B7:I7, change the format so that the text wraps. Center the range B7:I7.

6. Delete column B by right-clicking the column heading and clicking Delete on the shortcut menu.

7. Insert a new column between columns D and E. Change the column widths as follows: A = 25.00; E = 13.00; and F through I = 9.71. Enter the new column E title **Suggested Reorder** in cell E7.

8. Insert two new columns between columns F and G. Enter the new column G title **Last Month Sales** in cell G7. Enter the new column H title **Current Month Sales** in cell H7.

9. Enhance the worksheet title in cell A5 by using a 36-point purple Cooper Black (or a similar font) font style as shown in Figure 3–91b.

10. Assign the NOW function to cell B6 and format it to the 3/14/2001 style.

11. Delete item Car Air Freshener (row 13). Change Mini Jar Candle's (row 12) cases on hand to 6. Change Large Candle's (row 8) items per case to 8 and cost per case to $131.00. Change Incense Stick's (row 10) sale price per item to $2.00 and Incense Holder's (row 9) sale price per item to $4.75.

12. Freeze column A and rows 1 through 7 by selecting cell B8, clicking the Freeze Panes button (View tab | Window group), and then clicking Freeze Panes on the Freeze Panes gallery.

13. In columns G and H, enter the current month and last month sales values listed in Table 3–13.

14. Insert three new rows immediately above the Totals row. Add the new items data as listed in Table 3–14.

Table 3–13 Dinah's Candle Depot Monthly Sales Values

Inventory Item	Last Month Sales	Current Month Sales
Large Candle	851.6	1703.2
Incense Holder	37.5	56.25
Incense Stick	90	100
Candle Topper	390	260
Mini Jar Candle	1208	1208

Table 3–14 Dinah's Candle Depot New Items

Inventory Item	Cases On Hand	Items Per Case	Reorder Level	Order Time (Weeks)	Last Month Sales	Current Month Sales	Cost Per Case	Sale Price Per Item
Votive Candle	3	18	4	1	300	450	20	1.5
Taper Candle	2	16	3	2	350	612.5	35	3.5
Candle Warmer	2	5	1	3	638	797.5	100	15.95

15. Center the range B8:F15. Use the Currency category in the Format Cells dialog box to assign a Comma style (no dollar signs) with two decimal places and negative numbers within parentheses to the range G8:K16. Draw a thick bottom border in the ranges A7:K7 and A15:K15.

16. As shown in Figure 3–91b, enter and format the Increase Reorder Amt (2), the Decrease Reorder Amt (1), and the Sales Threshold % (25%) information in the range A1:B3. Use format symbols where applicable.

Continued >

In the Lab *continued*

17. Remove any Totals in the range B16:F16. Update and add totals as necessary so that totals appear in the range G16:K16.

18. In cell E8, enter an IF function that applies the following logic and then copy it to the range E9:E15. If (Current Month Sales – Last Month Sales) / Current Month Sales >= Sales Threshold %, then Reorder Level + Increase Reorder Amt, otherwise Reorder Level – Decrease Reorder Amt or =IF((H8-G8)/H8 >= $B$3, D8+$B$1,D8-$B$2).

19. In cell L8, insert a Sparkline Line chart for range G8:H8. Copy cell L8 to the range L9:L16.

20. Unfreeze the worksheet by clicking the Freeze Panes button (View tab | Window group), and then clicking Unfreeze Panes on the Freeze Panes gallery.

21. Preview the worksheet. Use the Orientation button (Page Layout tab | Page Setup group) to fit the printout on one page in landscape orientation.

22. Change the document properties, as specified by your instructor. Change the worksheet header, adding your name, course number, and other information as specified by your instructor. Save the workbook.

23. Use the Zoom button (View tab | Zoom group) to change the view of the worksheet. One by one, select all the percents on the Zoom dialog box. When you are done, return the worksheet to 100% magnification.

24. Preview the formulas version (CTRL+`) in landscape orientation. Close the worksheet without saving the latest changes.

25. Submit the workbook as specified by your instructor.

Instructions Part 2:   Start Excel. Open Lab 3-3 Dinah's Weekly Inventory Report Complete. Do not save the workbook in this part. Using the numbers in Table 3–15, analyze the effect of changing the Sales Threshold in cell B3. The first case should result in a Suggested Reorder in cell E15 of 0. The second case should result in a Suggested Reorder in cell E15 of 3. Close the workbook without saving changes. Submit the results of the what-if analysis as specified by your instructor.

Table 3–15 The Dinah's Candle Depot's Sales Threshold Cases	
Case	Sales Threshold
1	30%
2	15%

Instructions Part 3:   Submit results for this part as requested by your instructor.

1. Start Excel. Open Lab 3-3 Dinah's Weekly Inventory Report Complete. Select cell E8. Write down the formula that Excel displays in the formula bar. Select the range D8:D15. Point to the border surrounding the range and drag the selection to the range E17:E24. Click cell E8, and write down the formula that Excel displays in the formula bar below the one you wrote down earlier. Compare the two formulas. What can you conclude about how Excel responds when you move cells involved in a formula? Click the Undo button on the Quick Access Toolbar.

2. Right-click the range D8:D15 and then click Delete on the shortcut menu. When Excel displays the Delete dialog box, click Shift cells left and then click the OK button. What does Excel display in cell D8? Click cell D8 and then point to the Trace Error button that is displayed to the left of the cell. Write down the ScreenTip that is displayed. Click the Undo button on the Quick Access Toolbar.

3. Right-click the range D8:D15 and then click Insert on the shortcut menu. When Excel displays the Insert dialog box, click 'Shift cells right' and then click the OK button. What does Excel display in the formula bar when you click cell F8? What can you conclude about how Excel responds when you insert cells next to cells involved in a formula? Close the workbook without saving the changes.

Cases and Places

Apply your creative thinking and problem solving skills to design and implement a solution.

: Bachelor Degree Expense and Resource Projection

Academic

Attending college with limited resources can be a trying experience. One way to alleviate some of the financial stress is to plan ahead. Develop a worksheet following the general layout in Table 3–16 that shows the projected expenses and resources for four years of college. Use the formulas listed in Table 3–17 and the concepts and techniques presented in this chapter to create the worksheet.

Table 3–16 Bachelor Degree Expense and Resource Projection

Expenses	Freshman	Sophomore	Junior	Senior	Total
Room & Board	$12,550.00	Formula A			—
Tuition & Books	16,450.00	Formula A			—
Clothes	785.00	Formula A			—
Entertainment	1,520.00	Formula A			—
Miscellaneous	936.00	Formula A			—
Total Expenses	—	—	—	—	—

Resources	Freshman	Sophomore	Junior	Senior	Total
Savings	Formula B				
Parents	Formula B				—
Job	Formula B				—
Loans	Formula B				—
Scholarships	Formula B				—
Total Resources	—	—	—	—	—

Assumptions	
Savings	10.00%
Parents	12.00%
Job	11.00%
Loans	35.00%
Scholarships	32.00%
Annual Rate Increase	8.25%

Table 3–17 Bachelor Degree Expense and Resource Projection Formulas

Formula A = Prior Year's Expense * (1 + Annual Rate Increase)

Formula B = Total Expenses for Year * Corresponding Assumption

After creating the worksheet: (a) perform what-if analysis by changing the percents of the resource assumptions; (b) perform a what-if analysis to determine the effect on the resources by increasing the Annual Rate Increase to 9.95% (answer = $149,520.41); and (c) with the original assumptions, goal seek to determine what the Annual Rate Increase would be for the total expenses to be $175,000 (answer = 10.77%). Submit the workbook and results of the what-if analysis as specified by your instructor.

Continued >

Cases and Places continued

2: Fuel Cost Analysis

Personal

You are thinking about buying a new vehicle, and you want to make sure that you get the most fuel savings you can find. You know that there are hybrid vehicles available and so you decide to research them as well as gas-only cars. Your friends also are interested in the results. Together, you decide to research the fuel costs associated with various types of vehicles. Research the gas mileage for six vehicles: three should run only on gas, and the others should be hybrid vehicles, combining gas and battery power. After you find the gas mileage for each vehicle, you will use formulas to calculate the fuel cost for 1 month, 1 year, and three years. Assume that in a typical month, you will drive 400 miles and that the average price of gas is $2.69 per gallon. Develop a worksheet following the general layout in Table 3–18 that shows the fuel cost analysis. Use the formulas listed in Table 3–19 and the concepts and techniques presented in this chapter to create the worksheet. Add a 3-D line chart showing the cost comparisons as an embedded chart.

Table 3–18 Fuel Cost Analysis

Vehicle	Miles Per Gallon	1 Month	1 Year	3 Year
Ford Expedition	17	Formula A	Formula B	Formula C
Dodge RAM 1500	20	---	---	---
Honda Civic	31	---	---	---
Chevy Silverado Hybrid	21	---	---	---
Ford Fusion Hybrid	41	---	---	---
Honda Civic Hybrid	45	---	---	---
Assumptions				
Distance per Month	400			
Price of Gas	$2.69			

Table 3–19 Fuel Cost Analysis Formulas

Formula A = (Distance per Month / Miles per Gallon)*Price of Gas

Formula B = ((Distance per Month / Miles per Gallon)*Price of Gas)*12

Formula C = ((Distance Per Month / Miles per Gallon)*Price of Gas)*36

3: Quarterly Income Projections

Professional

Notable Web Site Design is one of the largest Web site design and Web site hosting companies in the Midwest. The company generates revenue from Web site design and selling Web site hosting space on their Web servers. A fixed percentage of the total net revenue is spent on administrative, equipment, marketing, payroll, and production expenses. A bonus is expensed if the total net revenue for the quarter exceeds $14,000,000. The company's projected receipts and expenditures for the next four quarters are shown in Table 3–20.

With this data, you have been asked to prepare a worksheet similar to Figure 3–87 on page EX 210 for the next management team meeting. The worksheet should show total net revenues, total expenditures, and operating income for each quarterly period. Include a 3-D Pie chart on a separate sheet that shows the quarterly income contributions to the annual operating income. Use the concepts and techniques presented in this chapter to create and format the worksheet and chart.

During the meeting, one manager lobbied to reduce marketing expenditures by 1.25% and payroll costs by 2.75%. Perform a what-if analysis reflecting the proposed changes in expenditures. The changes should result in an operating income of $22,425,581 for the year. Using the original assumptions shown in Table 3–20, another manager asked to what extent marketing would have to be reduced to generate an annual operating income of $21,000,000. Marketing would to be reduced from 13.50% by 1.92% to 11.58%.

Submit the workbook and results of the what-if analysis as specified by your instructor.

Table 3–20 Notable Website Design Operating Income Projection by Quarter

Revenues	Quarter 1	Quarter 2	Quarter 3	Quarter 4
Site Design	12,247,999	15,234,813	16,567,102	10,619,201
Web Hosting	1,678,153	5,901,988	4,718,231	1,569,378
Expenditures				
Administrative	10.50%			
Bonus	250,000.00			
Equipment	17.75%			
Marketing	13.50%			
Payroll	22.50%			
Production	6.30%			
Revenue for Bonus	14,000,000.00			

1 Databases and Database Objects: An Introduction

Objectives

You will have mastered the material in this chapter when you can:

- Design a database to satisfy a collection of requirements
- Describe the features of the Access window
- Create a database
- Create tables in Datasheet and Design views
- Add records to a table

- Close a database
- Open a database
- Print the contents of a table
- Create and use a query
- Create and use a form
- Create and print custom reports
- Modify a report in Layout view

1 | Databases and Database Objects: An Introduction

Introduction

The term **database** describes a collection of data organized in a manner that allows access retrieval, and use of that data. Microsoft Access 2010, usually referred to as simply Access, is a database management system. A **database management system**, such as Access, is software that allows you to use a computer to create a database; add, change, and delete data in the database; ask and answer questions concerning the data in the database; and create forms and reports using the data in the database.

Project Planning Guidelines

The process of developing a database that communicates specific information requires careful analysis and planning. As a starting point, establish why the database is needed. Once the purpose is determined, analyze the intended users of the database and their unique needs. Then, gather information about the topic and decide what to include in the database. Finally, determine the database design and style that will be most successful at delivering the message. Details of these guidelines are provided in Appendix A. In addition, each project in this book provides practical applications of these planning considerations.

Project — Database Creation

Camashaly Design Group is a small company that provides custom marketing solutions for the service, nonprofit, and retail sectors. Alyssa Morgan, Camden Scott, and Ashton James started the business after they graduated from a local university. The three owners, all computer graphics design majors and business minors, worked on a service learning project during college that produced a Web site for a nonprofit organization. Alyssa, Camden, and Ashton worked well together. Upon researching the local area for competing businesses, they decided to form their own company. The company specializes in designing and maintaining Web sites and using social networking Web sites for online marketing. They also conduct market research and develop printed media. Camashaly already has received one award for its design work. Camashaly is also recognized for its efforts in providing work opportunities to individuals who want flexible schedules and to student interns.

BTW

BTWs
For a complete list of the BTWs found in the margins of this book, visit the Access 2010 BTW Web page (scsite.com/ac2010/btw).

Camashaly uses business analysts to work collaboratively with clients. Business analysts are employees who translate business requirements into marketing specifications and serve as the interface between clients and Camashaly. Business analysts are paid a base salary and can earn incentive pay for maintaining and expanding client relationships.

Camashaly charges a one-time fee for Web site development. Clients can pay for Web site maintenance by contracting for a specified number of hours or can pay for maintenance on an hour-by-hour basis. Other fees vary depending on the specific scope of work.

To ensure that operations run smoothly, Camashaly organizes data on its clients and business analysts in a database managed by Access. In this way, Camashaly keeps its data current and accurate while the owners can analyze the data for trends and produce a variety of useful reports. In this chapter, you will create the Camashaly database.

In a **relational database** such as those maintained by Access, a database consists of collection of tables, each of which contains information on a specific subject. Figure 1–1 shows the database for Camashaly Design. It consists of two tables: the Client table Figure 1–1a) contains information about the clients to whom Camashaly provides services, and the Business Analyst table (Figure 1–1b) contains information about the business analysts to whom these clients are assigned.

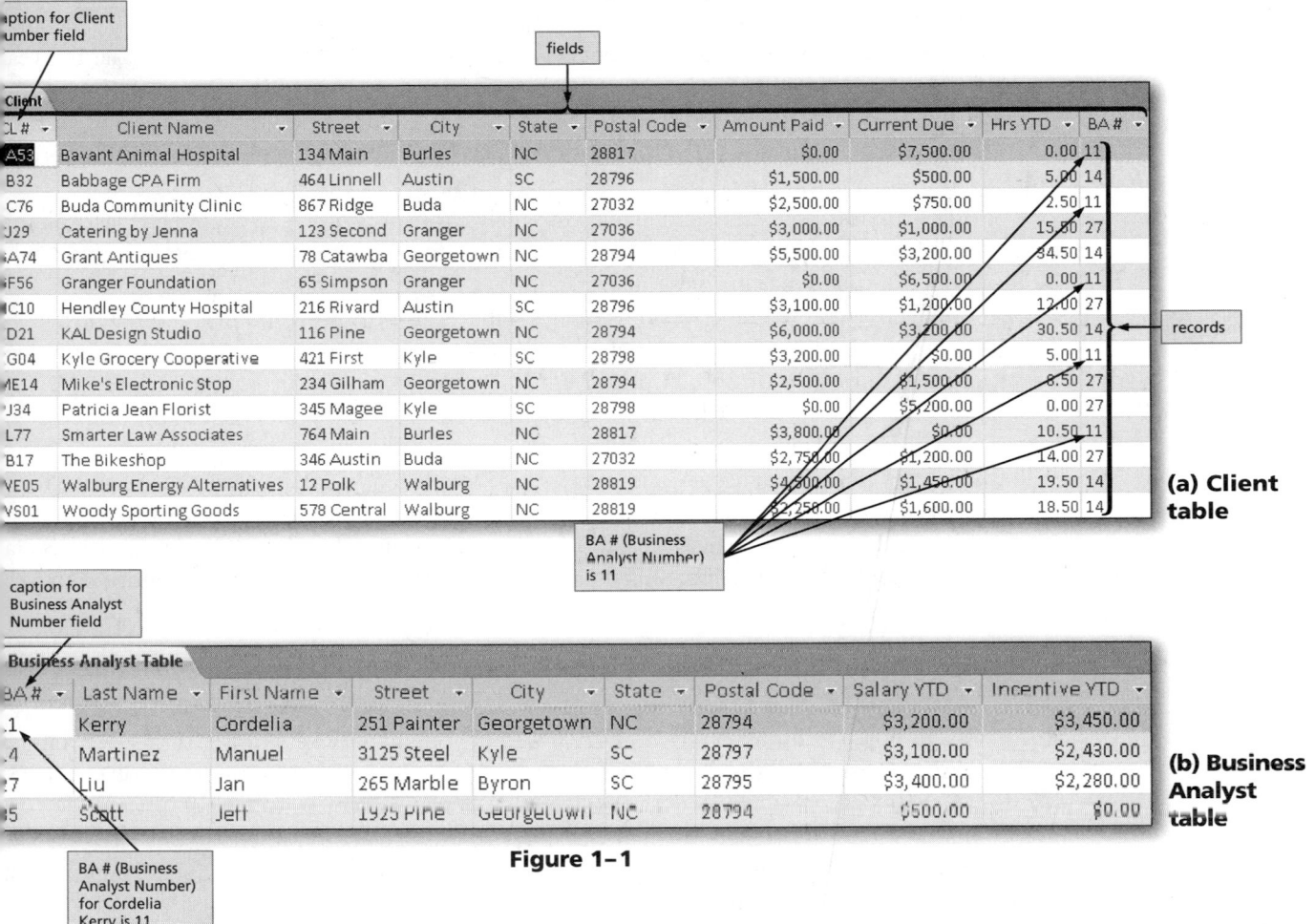

Figure 1-1

The rows in the tables are called **records**. A record contains information about a given person, product, or event. A row in the Client table, for example, contains information about a specific client, such as the client's name, address information, and other data.

The columns in the tables are called fields. A **field** contains a specific piece of information within a record. In the Client table, for example, the fourth field, City, contains the name of the city where the client is located.

The first field in the Client table is CL #, which is an abbreviation for Client Number. Camashaly Design assigns each client a client number. As is common to the way in which many organizations format client numbers, Camashaly Design calls it a number, although it actually contains letters. The Camashaly client numbers consist of two uppercase letters followed by a two-digit number.

The client numbers are unique; that is, no two clients are assigned the same number. Such a field can be used as a **unique identifier**. A unique identifier, as its name suggests, is a way of uniquely identifying each record in the database. A given client number will appear only in a single record in the table. Only one record exists, for example, in which the client number is BB32. A unique identifier also is called a **primary key**. Thus, the Client Number field is the primary key for the Client table.

The next eight fields in the Client table are Client Name, Street, City, State, Postal Code, Amount Paid, Current Due, and Hrs YTD, which is an abbreviation for Contract Hours YTD. YTD is an abbreviation for year to date. The Amount Paid column contains the amount that the client has paid Camashaly Design YTD prior to the current period. The Current Due column contains the amount due to Camashaly for the current period. The Hrs YTD column contains the number of hours the client has contracted for Web site maintenance so far this year. For example, client BB32 is Babbage CPA Firm. The address is 464 Linnell in Austin, South Carolina. The postal code is 28796. The client has paid $1,500.00 for services so far this year. The amount due for the current period is $500.00. The client has contracted for 5.00 hours of Web site maintenance.

Camashaly assigns a single business analyst to work with each client. The last column in the Client table, BA #, which is an abbreviation for Business Analyst Number, gives the number of the client's business analyst.

The first field in the Business Analyst table is also BA #, an abbreviation for Business Analyst Number. The business analyst numbers are unique, so the Business Analyst Number field is the primary key of the Business Analyst table.

The other fields in the Business Analyst table are Last Name, First Name, Street, City, State, Postal Code, Salary YTD, and Incentive YTD. The Salary YTD field gives the salary paid to the analyst thus far this year. The Incentive YTD gives the incentive for which the analyst qualified thus far this year. For example, business analyst 14 is Manuel Martinez. His address is 3125 Steel in Kyle, South Carolina. The Postal Code is 28797. So far this year, he has been paid $3,100.00 in salary. He has earned $2,430.00 in incentive pay.

The business analyst number appears in both the Client table and the Business Analyst table, and relates clients and business analysts. For example, in the Client table, you see that the business analyst number for client Babbage CPA Firm is 14. To find the name of this business analyst, look for the row in the Business Analyst table that contains 14 in the BA # column. After you have found it, you know the client is assigned to Manuel Martinez. To find all the clients assigned to Cordelia Kerry, you would first look in the Business Analyst table to find that her number is 11. You would then look through the Client table for all the clients that contain 11 in the BA # column. Her clients are BA53 (Bavant Animal Hospital), BC76 (Buda Community Clinic), GF56 (Granger Foundation), KG04 (Kyle Grocery Cooperative), and SL77 (Smarter Law Associates).

The last business analyst in the Business Analyst table, Jeff Scott, has not been assigned any clients yet; therefore, his business analyst number, 35, does not appear on any row in the Client table.

Overview

As you read this chapter, you will learn how to create the database shown in Figure 1 – 1 by performing these general tasks:

- Design the database.
- Create a new blank database.
- Create a table and add the records.
- Preview and print the contents of a table.
- Create a second table and import the records.
- Create a simple query.
- Create a simple form.
- Create and modify a report.

Database Design Guidelines

Plan
Ahead

Database design refers to the arrangement of data into tables and fields. In the example in this chapter, the design is specified, but in many cases, you will have to determine the design based on what you want the system to accomplish.

   When designing a database to satisfy a given set of requirements, the actions you take and the decisions you make will determine the tables and fields that will be included in the database. As you create a database, such as the one shown in Figure 1–1 on page AC 3, you should follow these general guidelines:

1. **Identify the tables.** Examine the requirements for the database to identify the main objects that are involved. There will be a table for each object you identify.

   In one database, for example, the main objects might be departments and employees. Thus, there would be two tables: one for departments and the other for employees. In another database, the main objects might be clients and business analysts. In this case, there also would be two tables: one for clients and the other for business analysts. In still another database, the main objects might be books, publishers, and authors. This database would require three tables: one for books, a second for publishers, and a third for authors.

2. **Determine the primary keys.** Recall that the primary key is the unique identifier for records in the table. For each table, determine the unique identifier. In a Department table, for example, the unique identifier might be the Department Code. For a Book table, the unique identifier might be the ISBN.

3. **Determine the additional fields.** The primary key will be a field or combination of fields in a table. A table typically will contain many additional fields, each of which contains a type of data. Examine the project requirements to determine these additional fields. For example, in an Employee table, the additional fields might include such fields as Employee Name, Street Address, City, State, Postal Code, Date Hired, Salary, and so on.

4. **Determine relationships between the tables.** Examine the list of tables you have created to see which tables are related. When you determine that two tables are related, include matching fields in the two tables. For example, in a database containing employees and departments, there is a relationship between the two tables because one department can have many employees assigned to it. Department Code could be the matching field in the two tables.

5. **Determine data types for the fields.** For each field, determine the type of data the field can contain. One field, for example, might contain only numbers. Another field might contain currency amounts, while a third field might contain only dates. Some fields contain text data, meaning any combination of letters, numbers, and special characters (!, ;, ', &, and so on). For example, in an Employee table, the Date Hired field would contain dates, the Salary field would contain currency amounts, and the Hours Worked field would contain numbers. The other fields in the Employee table would contain text data, such as Employee Name and Department Code.

6. **Identify and remove any unwanted redundancy.** Redundancy is the storing of a piece of data in more than one place. Redundancy usually, but not always, causes problems, such as wasted space, difficulties with update, and possible data inconsistency. Examine each table you have created to see if it contains redundancy and, if so, determine whether the redundancy causes the problems described. If it does, remove the redundancy by splitting the table into two tables. For example, you might have a single table of employees. In addition to typical employee data (name, address, earnings, and so on), the table might contain Department Number and Department Name. If so, the Department Name could repeat multiple times. Every employee whose department number is 12, for example, would have the same department name. It would be better to split the table into two tables: one for Employees and one for Department. In the Department table, the Department Name is stored only once.

7. **Determine a storage location for the database.** The database you have designed will be stored in a single file. You need to determine a location in which to store the file.

8. **Determine additional properties for fields.** Before creating the database, determine any other properties you should specify for the fields. These could include a field size, which is

(continued)

**Plan
Ahead**

(continued)

the maximum number of characters that can be stored in the field. If you want something other than the field name to appear at the top of a column (such as an abbreviation), you can change the caption to the desired heading. You also can add a description, which is a message that appears on the screen concerning a field whenever the field is selected.

9. **Determine the best method for distributing the database objects.** The traditional method of distributing database objects uses a printer to produce a hard copy of a table or report on paper. You also can distribute the table as an electronic image that mirrors the original table's appearance.

When necessary, more specific details concerning the above guidelines are presented at appropriate points in the chapter. The chapter also will identify the actions performed and decisions made regarding these guidelines during the creation of the database shown in Figure 1–1 on page AC 3.

Designing a Database

This section illustrates the database design process by showing how you would design the database for Camashaly Design from a set of requirements. In this section, you will use commonly accepted shorthand to represent the tables and fields that make up the database as well as the primary keys for the tables. For each table, you give the name of the table followed by a set of parentheses. Within the parentheses is a list of the fields in the table separated by columns. You underline the primary key. For example,

Product (<u>Product Code</u>, Description, On Hand, Price)

represents a table called Product. The Product table contains four fields: Product Code, Description, On Hand, and Price. The Product Code field is the primary key.

BTW

Determining Database Requirements
The determination of database requirements is part of a process known as systems analysis. A systems analyst examines existing and proposed documents, and examines organizational policies to determine exactly the type of data needs the database must support.

Database Requirements

The Camashaly Design database must maintain information on both clients and business analysts. The business currently keeps this data in two Word tables and two Excel workbooks, as shown in Figure 1–2. They use Word tables for address information and Excel workbooks for financial information.

Client Number	Client Name	Street	City	State	Postal Code
BA53	Bavant Animal Hospital	134 Main	Burles	NC	28817
BB32	Babbage CPA Firm	464 Linnell	Austin	SC	28796
BC76	Buda Community Clinic	867 Ridge	Buda	NC	27032
CJ29	Catering by Jenna	123 Second	Granger	NC	27036
GA74	Grant Antiques	78 Catawba	Georgetown	NC	28794
GF56	Granger Foundation	65 Simpson	Granger	NC	27036
HC10	Hendley County Hospital	216 Rivard	Austin	SC	28796
KD21	KAL Design Studio	116 Pine	Georgetown	NC	28794
KG04	Kyle Grocery Cooperative	421 First	Kyle	SC	28798
ME14	Mike's Electronic Stop	234 Gilham	Georgetown	NC	28794
PJ34	Patricia Jean Florist	345 Magee	Kyle	SC	28798
SL77	Smarter Law Associates	764 Main	Burles	NC	28817
TB17	The Bikeshop	346 Austin	Buda	NC	27032
WE05	Walburg Energy Alternatives	12 Polk	Walburg	NC	28819
WS01	Woody Sporting Goods	578 Central	Walburg	NC	28819

Figure 1–2 (a) Client Address Information (Word Table)

	A	B	C	D	E	F	G	H
1	Client Number	Client Name	Amount Paid	Current Due	Contract Hours YTD			
2	BA53	Bavant Animal Hospital	0.00	7,500.00	0			
3	BB32	Babbage CPA Firm	1,500.00	500.00	5			
4	BC76	Buda Community Clinic	2,500.00	750.00	2.5			
5	CJ29	Catering by Jenna	3,000.00	1,000.00	15.5			
6	GA74	Grant Antiques	5,500.00	3,200.00	34.5			
7	GF56	Granger Foundation	0.00	6,500.00	0			
8	HC10	Hendley County Hospital	3,100.00	1,200.00	12			
9	KD21	KAL Design Studio	6,000.00	3,200.00	30.5			
10	KG04	Kyle Grocery Cooperative	3,200.00	0.00	5			
11	ME14	Mike's Electronic Stop	2,500.00	1,500.00	8.5			
12	PJ34	Patricia Jean Florist	0.00	5,200.00	0			
13	SL77	Smarter Law Associates	3,800.00	0.00	10.5			
14	TB17	The Bikeshop	2,750.00	1,200.00	14			
15	WE05	Walburg Energy Alternatives	4,500.00	1,450.00	19.5			
16	WS01	Woody Sporting Goods	2,250.00	1,600.00	18.5			

Figure 1–2   (b) Client Financial Information (Excel Worksheet)

Business Analyst Number	Last Name	First Name	Street	City	State	Postal Code
11	Kerry	Cordelia	251 Painter	Georgetown	NC	28794
14	Martinez	Manuel	3125 Steel	Kyle	SC	28797
27	Liu	Jan	265 Marble	Byron	SC	28795
35	Scott	Jeff	1925 Pine	Georgetown	NC	28794

Figure 1–2   (c) Business Analyst Address Information (Word Table)

	A	B	C	D	E	F	G	H	I
1	Business Analyst Number	Last Name	First Name	Salary YTD	Incentive YTD				
2	11	Kerry	Cordelia	3,200.00	3,450.00				
3	14	Martinez	Manuel	3,100.00	2,430.00				
4	27	Liu	Jan	3,400.00	2,280.00				
5	35	Scott	Jeff	500.00	0.00				

Figure 1–2   (d) Business Analyst Financial Information (Excel Worksheet)

For clients, Camashaly needs to maintain address data. It currently keeps this address data in a Word table (Figure 1–2a). It also maintains financial data for each client. This includes the amount paid, current amount due, and contract hours YTD for the client. It keeps these amounts, along with the client name and number, in the Excel workbook shown in Figure 1–2b.

Camashaly keeps business analyst address data in a Word table, as shown in Figure 1–2c. Just as with clients, it keeps financial data for business analysts, including their salary YTD and incentive YTD, in a separate Excel workbook, as shown in Figure 1–2d.

Finally, it keeps track of which clients are assigned to which business analysts. Each client is assigned to a single business analyst, but each business analyst might be assigned many clients. Currently, for example, clients BA53 (Bavant Animal Hospital), BC76 (Buda Community Clinic), GF56 (Granger Foundation), KG04 (Kyle Grocery Cooperative), and SL77 (Smarter Law Associates) are assigned to business analyst 11 (Cordelia Kerry). Clients BB32 (Babbage CPA Firm), GA74 (Grant Antiques), KD21 (KAL Design Studio), WE05 (Walburg Energy Alternatives), and WS01 (Woody Sporting Goods) are assigned to business analyst 14 (Manuel Martinez). Clients CJ29 (Catering by Jenna), HC10 (Hendley County Hospital), ME14 (Mike's Electronic Stop), PJ34 (Patricia Jean Florist), and TB17 (The Bikeshop) are assigned to business analyst 27 (Jan Liu). Camashaly has an additional business analyst, Jeff Scott, whose number has been assigned as 35, but who has not yet been assigned any clients.

BTW

Additional Data for Camashaly
There are many other types of data that Camashaly could include in a database. For example, they might keep all employee information in a database as well as information on client contracts and an inventory of hardware and software.

Naming Tables and Fields

In designing your database, you must name the tables and fields. Thus, before beginning the design process, you must understand the rules Access applies to table and field names. These rules are:

1. Names can be up to 64 characters in length.
2. Names can contain letters, digits, and spaces, as well as most of the punctuation symbols.
3. Names cannot contain periods (.), exclamation points (!), accent graves (`), or square brackets ([ ]).
4. The same name cannot be used for two different fields in the same table.

The approach to naming tables and fields used in this text is to begin the names with an uppercase letter and to use lowercase for the other letters. In multiple-word names, each word begins with an uppercase letter, and there is a space between words (for example, Client Number). You should know that other approaches exist, all of which are acceptable in Access. Some people omit the space (ClientNumber). Still others use an underscore in place of the space (Client_Number). Finally, some use an underscore in place of a space, but use the same case for all letters (CLIENT_NUMBER or client_number).

Identifying the Tables

Now that you know the rules for naming tables and fields, you are ready to begin the design process. The first step is to identify the main objects involved in the requirements. For the Camashaly Design database, the main objects are clients and business analysts. This leads to two tables, which you must name. Reasonable names for these two tables are:

Client
Business Analyst

Determining the Primary Keys

The next step is to identify the fields that will be the unique identifiers, or primary keys. Client numbers uniquely identify clients, and business analyst numbers uniquely identify business analysts. Thus, the primary key for the Client table is the client number, and the primary key for the Business Analyst table is the business analyst number. Reasonable names for these fields would be Client Number and Business Analyst Number, respectively. Adding these primary keys to the tables gives:

Client (<u>Client Number</u>)
Business Analyst (<u>Business Analyst Number</u>)

Determining Additional Fields

After identifying the primary keys, you need to determine and name the additional fields. In addition to the client number, the Client Address Information shown in Figure 1–2a on page AC 6 contains the client name, street, city, state, and postal code. These would be fields in the Client table. The Client Financial Information shown in Figure 1–2b also contains the client number and client name, which are already included in the Client table. The financial information also contains the amount paid, current due, and contract hours YTD. Adding the amount paid, current due, and contract hours YTD fields to those already identified in the Client table and assigning reasonable names gives:

Client (<u>Client Number</u>, Client Name, Street, City, State, Postal Code, Amount Paid, Current Due, Contract Hours YTD)

Similarly, examining the Business Analyst Address Information in Figure 1–2c adds the last name, first name, street, city, state, and postal code fields to the Business Analyst table. In addition to the business analyst number, last name, and first name, the Business Analyst Financial Information in Figure 1–2d would add the salary YTD and Incentive YTD. Adding these fields to the Business Analyst table and assigning reasonable names gives:

Business Analyst (<u>Business Analyst Number</u>, Last Name, First Name, Street, City, State, Postal Code, Salary YTD, Incentive YTD)

Determining and Implementing Relationships Between the Tables

Plan Ahead

Determine relationships between the tables.
The most common type of relationship you will encounter between tables is the **one-to-many relationship**. This means that each row in the first table may be associated with many rows in the second table, but each row in the second table is associated with only one row in the first. The first table is called the "one" table and the second is called the "many" table. For example, there may be a relationship between departments and employees, in which each department can have many employees, but each employee is assigned to only one department. In this relationship, there would be two tables, Department and Employee. The Department table would be the "one" table in the relationship. The Employee table would be the "many" table.

To determine relationships between tables, you can follow these general guidelines:

- Identify the "one" table.
- Identify the "many" table.
- Include the primary key from the "one" table as a field in the "many" table.

According to the requirements, each client has one business analyst, but each business analyst can have many clients. Thus, the Business Analyst table is the "one" table, and the Client table is the "many" table. To implement this one-to-many relationship between business analysts and clients, add the Business Analyst Number field (the primary key of the Business Analyst table) to the Client table. This produces:

Client (<u>Client Number</u>, Client Name, Street, City, State, Postal Code, Amount Paid, Current Due, Contract Hours YTD, Business Analyst Number)
Business Analyst (<u>Business Analyst Number</u>, Last Name, First Name, Street, City, State, Postal Code, Salary YTD, Incentive YTD)

BTW

Database Design Language (DBDL)
DBDL is a commonly accepted shorthand representation for showing the structure of a relational database. You write the name of the table and then within parentheses you list all the columns in the table. If the columns continue beyond one line, indent the subsequent lines.

Determining Data Types for the Fields

Each field has a **data type**. This indicates the type of data that can be stored in the field. Three of the most commonly used data types are:

1. **Text** — The field can contain any characters. A maximum number of 255 characters is allowed in a field whose data type is Text.

2. **Number** — The field can contain only numbers. The numbers either can be positive or negative. Fields are assigned this type so they can be used in arithmetic operations. Fields that contain numbers but will not be used for arithmetic operations (such as postal codes) usually are assigned a data type of Text.

3. **Currency** — The field can contain only monetary data. The values will appear with currency symbols, such as dollar signs, commas, and decimal points, and with two digits following the decimal point. Like numeric fields, you can use currency fields in arithmetic operations. Access assigns a size to currency fields automatically.

Table 1–1 shows the other data types that are available in Access.

BTW
Data Types
Different database management systems have different available data types. Even data types that are essentially the same can have different names. The Currency data type in Access, for example, is referred to as Money in SQL Server.

Table 1–1 Additional Data Types	
Data Type	**Description**
Memo	Field can store a variable amount of text or combinations of text and numbers where the total number of characters may exceed 255.
Date/Time	Field can store dates and times.
AutoNumber	Field can store a unique sequential number that Access assigns to a record. Access will increment the number by 1 as each new record is added.
Yes/No	Field can store only one of two values. The choices are Yes/No, True/False, or On/Off.
OLE Object	Field can store an OLE object, which is an object linked to or embedded in the table.
Hyperlink	Field can store text that can be used as a hyperlink address.
Attachment	Field can contain an attached file. Images, spreadsheets, documents, charts, and so on can be attached to this field in a record in the database. You can view and edit the attached file.
Calculated	Field specified as a calculation based on other fields. The value is not actually stored.

In the Client table, because the Client Number, Client Name, Street, City, and State can all contain letters, their data types should be Text. The data type for Postal Code is Text instead of Number because postal codes are not used in arithmetic operations; you do not add postal codes or find an average postal code, for example. The Amount Paid and Current Due fields both contain monetary data, so their data types should be Currency. The Contract Hours YTD field contains a number that is not a currency amount, so its data type should be Number.

Similarly, in the Business Analyst table, the data type for the Business Analyst Number, Last Name, First Name, Street, City, State, and Postal Code fields all should be Text. The Salary YTD and Incentive YTD fields both contain monetary amounts, so their data types should be Currency.

Fields whose data type is Number often require you to change the field size, which is the storage space assigned to the field by Access. Table 1–2 shows the possible field sizes for Number fields. If the size were Byte, Integer, or Long Integer, for example, only integers could be stored. If you try to store a value that has decimal places, such as 2.50, the portion to the right of the decimal point would be removed, giving a result of 2. To address this problem, you would change to a size such as Single.

Table 1–2 Field Sizes for Number Fields	
Field Size	**Description**
Byte	Integer value in the range of 0 to 255
Integer	Integer value in the range of –32,768 to 32,767
Long Integer	Integer value in the range of –2,147,483,648 to 2,147,483,647
Single	Numeric values with decimal places to seven significant digits — requires 4 bytes of storage
Double	Numeric values with decimal places to more accuracy than Single — requires 8 bytes of storage
Replication ID	Special identifier required for replication
Decimal	Numeric values with decimal places to more accuracy than Single or Double — requires 12 bytes of storage.

Identifying and Removing Redundancy

Redundancy means storing the same fact in more than one place. It usually results from placing too many fields in a table — fields that really belong in separate tables — and often causes serious problems. If you had not realized there were two objects, clients and business nalysts, for example, you might have placed all the data in a single Client table. Figure 1–3 nows an example of a table that includes both client and business analyst information. Notice hat the data for a given business analyst (number, name, address, and so on) occurs on more han one record. The data for analyst 11, Cordelia Kerry, is repeated in the figure.

Client Table

Client Number	Client Name	Street	...	Business Analyst Number	Last Name	First Name	...
3A53	Bavant Animal Hospital	134 Main	...	11	Kerry	Cordelia	...
3B32	Babbage CPA Firm	464 Linnell	...	14	Martinez	Manuel	...
3C76	Buda Community Clinic	867 Ridge	...	11	Kerry	Cordelia	...
..	...	...	...	...	...	..	...

business analyst numbers are 11

name of business analyst 11 appears more than once

Figure 1–3

Storing this data on multiple records is an example of redundancy, which causes several roblems, including:

1. Wasted storage space. The name of business analyst 11, Cordelia Kerry, for example, should be stored only once. Storing this fact several times is wasteful.

2. More difficult database updates. If, for example, Cordelia Kerry's name is spelled wrong and needs to be changed in the database, her name would need to be changed in several different places.

3. A possibility of inconsistent data. Nothing prohibits the business analyst's last name from being Kerry on client BA53's record and Bronson on client BC76's record. The data would be inconsistent. In both cases, the business analyst number is 11, but the last names are different.

The solution to the problem is to place the redundant data in a separate table, one in hich the data no longer will be redundant. If, for example, you place the data for business ana- sts in a separate table (Figure 1–4), the data for each business analyst will appear only once.

Client Table

Client Number	Client Name	Street	...	Business Analyst Number
3A53	Bavant Animal Hospital	134 Main	...	11
3B32	Babbage CPA Firm	464 Linnell	...	14
3C76	Buda Community Clinic	867 Ridge	...	11
	...	...		

business analyst numbers are 11

Business Analyst Table

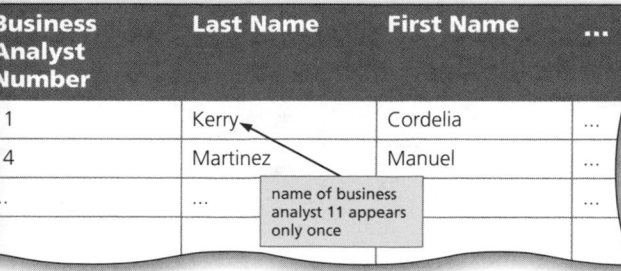

Business Analyst Number	Last Name	First Name	...
1	Kerry	Cordelia	...
4	Martinez	Manuel	...
..	...		...

name of business analyst 11 appears only once

Figure 1–4

BTW

Postal Codes
Some organizations with customers throughout the country have a separate table of postal codes, cities, and states. When placing an order, you typically are asked for your postal code (or ZIP code), rather than city, state, and postal code. You then are asked to confirm that the city and state correspond to that postal code.

Notice that you need to have the business analyst number in both tables. Without it, there would be no way to tell which business analyst is associated with which client. The remaining business analyst data, however, was removed from the Client table and placed in the Business Analyst table. This new arrangement corrects the problems of redundancy in the following ways:

1. Because the data for each business analyst is stored only once, space is not wasted
2. Changing the name of a business analyst is easy. You have only to change one row in the Business Analyst table.
3. Because the data for a business analyst is stored only once, inconsistent data cannot occur. Designing to omit redundancy will help you to produce good and valid database designs.

You should always examine your design to see if it contains redundancy. If it does, you should decide whether you need to remove the redundancy by creating a separate table

If you examine your design, you'll see that there is one area of redundancy (see the data in Figure 1–1 on page AC 3). Cities and states are both repeated. Every client whose postal code is 28794, for example, has Georgetown as the city and NC as the state. To remove this redundancy, you would create a table whose primary key is Postal Code and that contains City and State as additional fields. City and State would be removed from the Client table. Having City, State, and Postal Code in a table is very common, however, and usually you would not take such action. No other redundancy exists in your tables.

For an introduction to Windows 7 and instruction about how to perform basic Windows 7 tasks, read the Office 2010 and Windows 7 chapter at the beginning of this book, where you can learn how to resize windows, change screen resolution, create folders, move and rename files, use Windows Help, and much more.

To Start Access

If you are using a computer to step through the project in this chapter and you want your screens to match the figures in this book, you should change your screen's resolution to 1024 × 768. For information about how to change a computer's resolution, refer to the Office 2010 and Windows 7 chapter at the beginning of this book.

The following steps, which assume Windows 7 is running, start Access based on a typical installation. You may need to ask your instructor how to start Access for your computer. For a detailed example of the procedure summarized below, refer to the Office 2010 and Windows 7 chapter.

1 Click the Start button on the Windows 7 taskbar to display the Start menu.

2 Type `Microsoft Access` as the search text in the 'Search programs and files' text box and watch the search results appear on the Start menu.

3 Click Microsoft Access 2010 in the search results on the Start menu to start Access and display the Backstage view for Access.

4 If the Access window is not maximized, click the Maximize button next to the Close button on its title bar to maximize the window.

Creating a Database

In Access, all the tables, reports, forms, and queries that you create are stored in a single file called a database. Thus, you first must create the database to hold the tables, reports, forms, and queries. You can use either the Blank database option or a template to create a new database. If you already know the tables and fields you want in your database, you would use the Blank database option. If not, you can use a template. Templates can guide you by suggesting some commonly used databases.

Plan Ahead

For an introduction to Office 2010 and instruction about how to perform basic tasks in Office 2010 programs, read the Office 2010 and Windows 7 chapter at the beginning of this book, where you can learn how to start a program, use the Ribbon, save a file, open a file, quit a program, use Help, and much more.

Determine a storage location for the database.
When creating a database, you must decide which storage medium to use.

If you always work on the same computer and have no need to transport your database to a different location, then your computer's hard drive will suffice as a storage location. It is a good idea, however, to save a backup copy of your database on a separate medium in case the file becomes corrupted or the computer's hard drive fails.

If you plan to work on your database in various locations or on multiple computers, then you can consider saving your projects on a portable medium, such as a USB flash drive or CD. The projects in this book are stored on a USB flash drive, which saves files quickly and reliably and can be reused. CDs are easily portable and serve as good backups for the final versions of projects because they generally can save files only one time.

To Create a Database

Because you already know the tables and fields you want in the Camashaly Design database, you would use the Blank database option rather than using a template. The following steps assume you already have created folders for storing your files, for example, a CIS 101 folder (for your class) that contains an Access folder (for your assignments). Thus, these steps save the document in the Access folder in the CIS 101 folder on a USB flash drive using the file name, Camashaly Design. For a detailed example of the procedure summarized below, refer to the Office 2010 and Windows 7 chapter at the beginning of this book.

- With a USB flash drive connected to one of the computer's USB ports, ensure the New tab is selected in the Backstage view and that Blank database is selected in the New gallery.

- Click the Browse button in the right pane of the New gallery to display the File New Database dialog box.

- Type `Camashaly Design` in the File New Database dialog box to change the file name. Do not press the ENTER key after typing the file name.

- Navigate to the desired save location (in this case, the Access folder in the CIS 101 folder [or your class folder] on the USB flash drive).

- Click the OK button, which returns you to the New gallery. (Your screen may show Camashaly Design.accdb.)

- Click the Create button in the right pane of the New gallery to create the database on the selected drive with the entered file name (Figure 1–5).

BTW

Q&As
For a complete list of the Q&As found in many of the step-by-step sequences in this book, visit the Access 2010 Q&A Web page (scsite.com/ac2010/qa).

Q&A

The title bar for my Navigation Pane contains All Tables rather than All Access Objects, as in the figure. Is that a problem?

It is not a problem. The title bar indicates how the Navigation Pane is organized. You can carry out the steps in the text with either organization. To make your screens match the ones in the text, click the Navigation Pane arrow and then click Object Type.

Q&A

I do not have the Search bar that appears on the figure. Is that a problem?

It is not a problem. If your Navigation Pane does not display a Search bar and you want your screens to match the ones in the text, right-click the Navigation Pane title bar arrow to display a shortcut menu, and then click Search Bar.

Figure 1–5

TO CREATE A DATABASE USING A TEMPLATE

BTW

Available Templates
The Blank web database button on the New tab in the Backstage view allows you to create a database that you can publish to a SharePoint server running Access Services. Access 2010 also includes five Web-based templates. To display previously used templates, click the My templates button.

Ideally, you will design your own database, create a blank database, and then create the tables you have determined that your database should contain. If you are not sure what database design you will need, you could use a template. Templates can guide you by suggesting some commonly used databases. To create a database using a template, you would use the following steps.

1. After starting Access, be sure the Backstage view is open. If it is not, click File on the Ribbon to open it.
2. Click the New tab if it is not already selected.
3. Click Sample templates to display a list of templates stored locally or search Microsoft Office online for additional templates.
4. Click the template you want to use.
5. Enter a file name (or accept the suggested file name) and select a location for the database.
6. Click the Create button to create the database or the Download button to download the database and create the database, if necessary.

The Access Window

The Access window consists of a variety of components to make your work more efficient and documents more professional. These include the Navigation Pane, Access work area, Ribbon, shortcut menus, and Quick Access Toolbar. Some of these components are common to other Microsoft Office 2010 programs; others are unique to Access.

Navigation Pane and Access Work Area

You work on objects such as tables, forms, and reports in the **Access work area**. In the work area in Figure 1–5, a single table, Table1, is open in the work area. **Object tabs** for the open objects appear at the top of the work area. If you have multiple objects open at the same time, you can select one of the open objects by clicking its tab. To the left of the work area is the Navigation Pane. The **Navigation Pane** contains a list of all the objects in the database. You use this pane to open an object. You also can customize the way objects are displayed in the Navigation Pane.

The **status bar**, located at the bottom of the Access window, presents information about the database object, the progress of current tasks, and the status of certain commands and keys; it also provides controls for viewing the object. As you type text or perform certain commands, various indicators may appear on the status bar. The left edge of the status bar in Figure 1–5 shows that the table object is open in Datasheet view. Toward the right edge are View buttons, which you can use to change the view that currently is displayed.

Creating a Table

To create a table, you must describe the structure of the table to Access. That is, you must describe all the fields that make up the table and their characteristics. You must also indicate the primary key.

In Access, you can use two different views to create a table: Datasheet view and Design view. In **Datasheet view**, the data in the table is presented in rows and columns, similar to a spreadsheet. Although the main reason to use Datasheet view is to add or update records in a table, you can also use it to create a table or to later modify its structure. The other view, **Design view**, is only used to create a table or to modify the structure of the table.

As you might expect, Design view has more functionality for creating a table than Datasheet view. That is, there are certain actions that can only be performed in Design view. If creating your table requires such actions, you must use Design view. If not, you can choose either view. In this chapter, you will create the first table, the Business Analyst table, in Datasheet view. You will create the second table, the Client table, in Design view.

Whichever view you choose to use, before creating the table, you need to determine the names and data types of the fields that will make up the table. You already have determined the types for the Camashaly fields. You also need to determine additional properties for the fields.

BTW

The Ribbon and Screen Resolution
Access may change how the groups and buttons within the groups appear on the Ribbon, depending on the computer's screen resolution. Thus, your Ribbon may look different from the ones in this book if you are using a screen resolution other than 1024 × 768.

Plan Ahead

Determine additional properties for fields.

- **Determine if a special caption is warranted.** Normally, the field name will appear as the label for a field on a form or report and as the column name in Datasheet view. If you would rather have a different name appear, you can change the field's caption to the desired name. One common use of captions is to shorten the column heading. If the data in a column is considerably shorter than the column heading, you could change the caption to a shorter heading. This would enable you to reduce the width of the column and yet still be able to see the entire column heading.

- **Determine if a special description is warranted.** Determine whether to include a description that would appear in the status bar whenever the field is selected.

- **Determine field sizes.** For Text fields, determine the field size; that is, the maximum number of characters that can be entered in the field. Users will be prohibited from entering a value that has more characters than the field size.

- **Determine formats.** Determine whether the data in the field should be formatted in any particular way. You could, for example, specify that a number field is to be formatted with precisely two decimal places.

BTW

Naming Tables
Database users typically have their own guidelines for naming tables. Some use the singular version of the object being described while others use the prefix tbl with a table name. This book uses the singular version of the object (Client, Business Analyst) but adds the word Table to the name for the Business Analyst table to illustrate another possible approach. Including the word Table can assist visually impaired users when viewing the Navigation Pane.

The results of these decisions for the fields in the Business Analyst table are shown in Table 1–3. The table also shows the data types and field sizes of the fields as well as any special properties that need to be changed. The Business Analyst Number field has a caption of BA #, enabling the width of the Business Analyst Number column to be reduced in the datasheet.

Table 1–3 Structure of Business Analyst Table

Field Name	Data Type	Field Size	Description
Business Analyst Number	Text	2	**Primary Key** **Description:** Business Analyst Number **Caption:** BA #
Last Name	Text	15	
First Name	Text	15	
Street	Text	15	
City	Text	15	
State	Text	2	
Postal Code	Text	5	
Salary YTD	Currency		
Incentive YTD	Currency		

To Modify the Primary Key

When you first create your database, Access automatically creates a table for you. You can immediately begin defining the fields. If, for any reason, you do not have this table or inadvertently delete it, you can create the table by clicking Create on the Ribbon and then clicking the Table button (Create tab | Tables group). In either case, you are ready to define the fields.

The following steps define the first field, the Business Analyst Number field, which is the primary key. Access has already created a primary key field, which it has named ID. Thus, the steps will change the name, data type, and other properties of this field to match the Business Analyst field in Table 1–3.

- Right-click the column heading for the ID field to display a shortcut menu (Figure 1–6).

Why does my shortcut menu look different?

You right-clicked within the column instead of right-clicking the column heading.

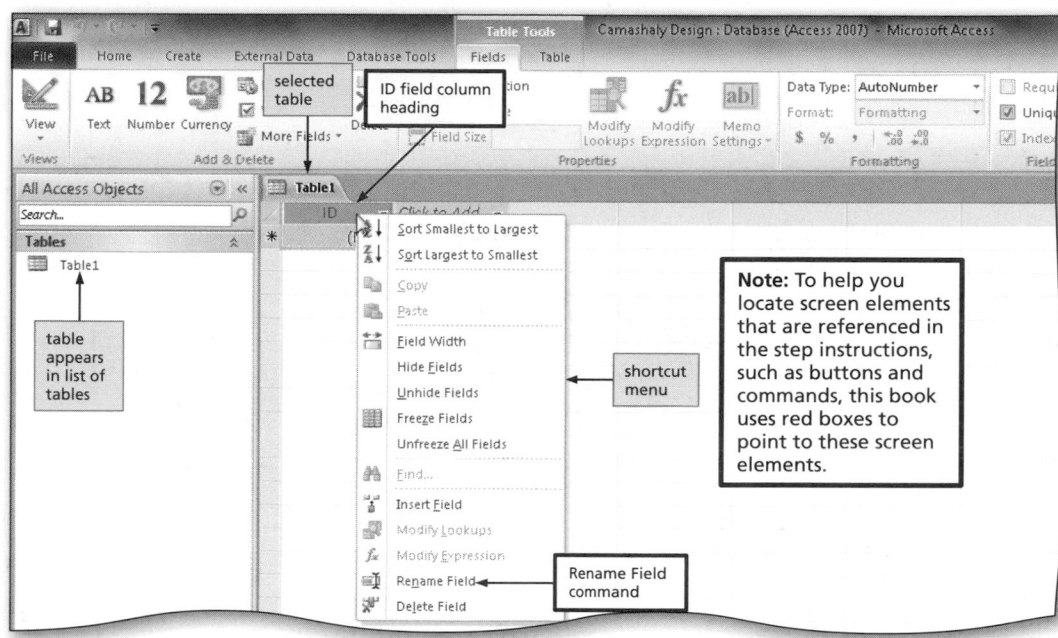

Figure 1–6

Click Rename Field on the shortcut menu to highlight the current name.

Type **Business Analyst Number** to assign a name to the new field.

Click the white space immediately below the field name to complete the addition of the field (Figure 1–7).

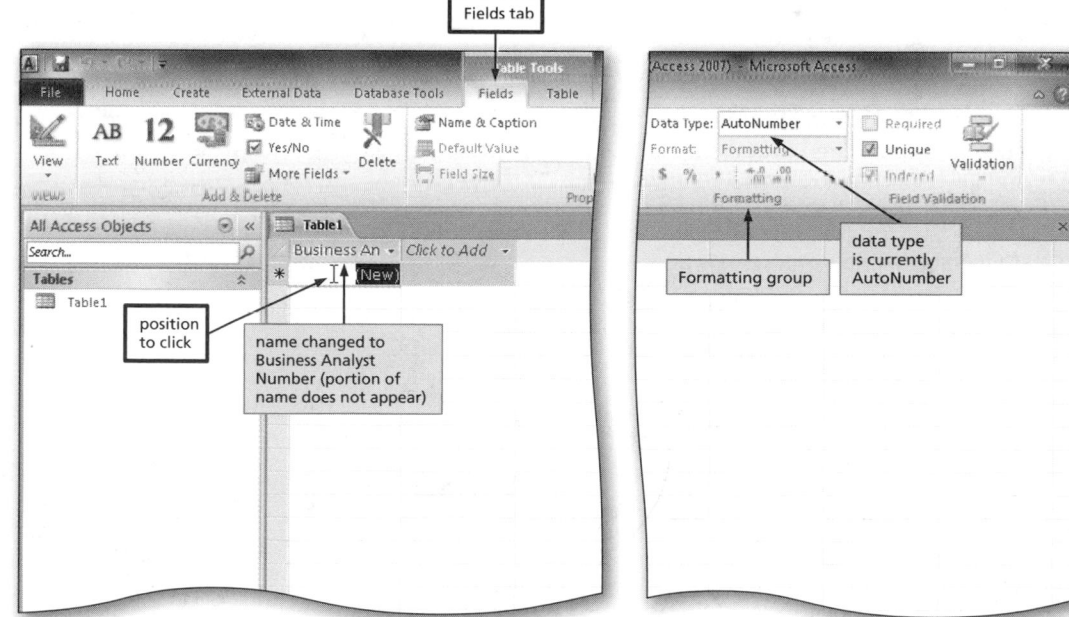

Figure 1–7

Why does the name not appear in its entirety?

The default column size is not large enough for Business Analyst Number to appear in its entirety. You will address this issue in later steps.

3

- Because the data type needs to be changed from AutoNumber to Text, click the Data Type box arrow (Table Tools Fields tab | Formatting group) to display a menu of available data types (Figure 1–8).

Figure 1–8

4

- Click Text to select the data type for the field (Figure 1–9).

Figure 1–9

5

- Click the Field Size text box (Table Tools Fields tab | Properties group) to select the current field size, use either the DELETE or BACKSPACE keys to erase the current field size, and then type 2 as the new field size.

- Click the Name & Caption button (Table Tools Fields tab | Properties group) to display the Enter Field Properties dialog box.

- Click the Caption text box (Enter Field Properties dialog box), and then type **BA #** as the caption.

Figure 1–10

- Click the Description text box, and then type **Unique identifier of business analyst** as the description (Figure 1–10).

6

- Click the OK button (Enter Field Properties dialog box) to change the caption and description (Figure 1–11).

Figure 1–11

To Define the Remaining Fields in a Table

To define an additional field, you click the Click to Add column heading, select the data type, and then type the field name. This is different from the process you used to modify the ID field, which was an existing field. The following steps define the remaining fields shown in Table 1–3 on page AC 16.

• Click the Click to Add column heading to display a menu of available data types (Figure 1–12).

Why did I follow a different process when I renamed this field?

The ID field was an existing field, created automatically by Access. For a new field, you need to click the Click to Add heading.

Figure 1–12

• Click Text in the menu of available data types to select the Text data type.

• Type Last Name to enter a field name.

• Click the white space below the field name to complete the change of the name. Click the white space a second time to select the field (Figure 1–13).

I realized after I entered the field name that I selected the wrong data type. How can I correct it?

Click the Data Type box arrow and then select the correct type.

I inadvertently clicked the white space before entering the field name. How can I correct the name?

Right-click the field name, click Rename Field on the shortcut menu, and then type the new name.

Figure 1–13

• Change the field size to 15 just as you changed the field size of the Business Analyst Number field.

• Using the same technique, add the remaining fields in the Business Analyst table. For the First Name, Street, City, State, and Postal Code fields, the Text data type is correct, but you will need to change the field size to match Table 1–3. For the Salary YTD and Incentive YTD fields, you need to change the data type to Currency. Before defining the Incentive YTD field, you may need to click the right scroll arrow to bring the column for the field to the screen (Figure 1–14).

Figure 1–14

Q&A Why does Currency appear twice?

The second Currency is the format, which indicates how the data will be displayed. For the Currency data type, Access automatically sets the format to Currency, which is usually what you would want. You could change it to something else, if desired, by clicking the arrow and selecting the desired format.

Q&A I have an extra row between the row containing the field names and the row that begins with the asterisk. What happened? Is this a problem? If so, how do I fix it?

You inadvertently added a record to the table by pressing some key. Even pressing the SPACEBAR would add a record. You now have a record you do not want. To fix it, you need to delete the record, which you will do in Step 4.

- If you have an additional record between the field names and the asterisk, press the ESC key to delete the record.

Making Changes to the Structure

When creating a table, check the entries carefully to ensure they are correct. If you discover a mistake while still typing the entry, you can correct the error by repeatedly pressing the BACKSPACE key until the incorrect characters are removed. Then, type the correct characters. If you do not discover a mistake until later, you can use the following techniques to make the necessary changes to the structure:

- To undo your most recent change, click the Undo button on the Quick Access Toolbar. If there is nothing that Access can undo, this button will be dim, and clicking it will have no effect.

- To delete a field, right-click the column heading for the field (the position containing the field name), and then click Delete Field on the shortcut menu.

- To change the name of a field, right-click the column heading for the field, click Rename Field on the shortcut menu, and then type the desired field name.

- To insert a field as the last field, click the Click to Add column heading, click the appropriate data type on the menu of available data types, type the desired field name, and, if necessary, change the field size.

- To insert a field between existing fields, right-click the column heading for the field that will follow the new field, and then click Insert Field on the shortcut menu. Right-click the column heading for the field, click Rename Field on the shortcut menu, and then type the desired field name.

- To move a field, click the column heading for the field to be moved to select the field, and then drag the field to the desired position.

As an alternative to these steps, you may want to start over. To do so, click the Close button for the table, and then click the No button in the Microsoft Access dialog box. Click Create on the Ribbon and then click the Table button to create a table. You then can repeat the process you used earlier to define the fields in the table.

To Save a Table

The Business Analyst table structure now is complete. The final step is to save the table within the database. As part of the process, you will give the table a name. The following steps save the table, giving it the name, Business Analyst Table.

- Click the Save button on the Quick Access Toolbar to display the Save As dialog box (Figure 1–15).

Figure 1–15

Type **Business Analyst Table** to change the name to be assigned to the table.

Click the OK button (Save As dialog box) to save the table (Figure 1–16).

Figure 1–16

Other Ways

1. Click File on the Ribbon, click Save in the Backstage view
2. Right-click tab for table, click Save on shortcut menu
3. Press CTRL+S

To View the Table in Design View

Even when creating a table in Datasheet view, Design view can be helpful. You should view the fields, data types, and properties to ensure you have entered them correctly. This viewing is easier to do in Design view. It is also easier to determine the primary key in Design view. The following steps view the structure of the Business Analyst Table in Design view so that you can verify the design is correct.

1
- Click the View button arrow (Table Tools Fields tab | Views group) to display the View button menu (Figure 1–17).

Could I just click the View button rather than the arrow?

Yes. Clicking the button is equivalent to clicking the command represented by the icon currently appearing on the button. Because the icon on the button in Figure 1–17 is the icon for Design view, clicking the button would display the table in Design view. If you are uncertain, you can always click the arrow and select from the menu.

Figure 1–17

2
- Click Design View on the View button menu to view the table in Design view (Figure 1–18).

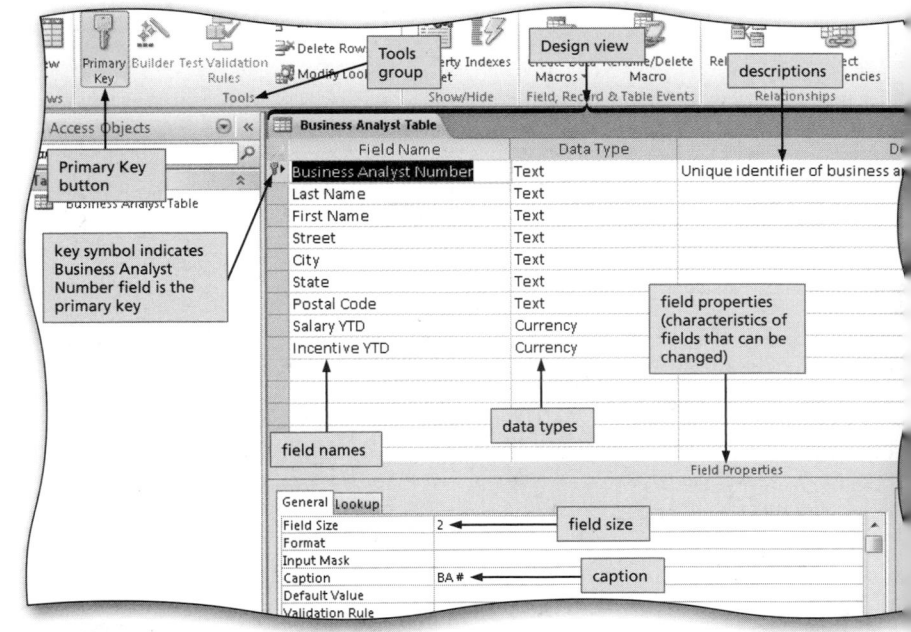

Figure 1–18

Other Ways
1. Click Design View button on status bar

Checking the Structure in Design View

You should use Design view to carefully check the entries you have made. In Figure 1–18, for example, you can see that the Business Analyst Number field is the primary key of the Business Analyst Table by the key symbol in front of the field name. If your table does not have a key symbol, you can click the Primary Key button (Table Tools Design tab | Tools group) to designate the field as the primary key. You also can check that the data type, the description, the field size, and the caption are all correct.

For the other fields, you can see the field name, data type, and description without taking any special action. To see the field size and/or caption for a field, click the field's **row selector**, the small box that precedes the field. Clicking the row selector for the Last Name field, for example, displays the field properties for the field (Figure 1–19). You then can check to see that the field size is correct. In addition, if the field has a caption, you can check to see that is correct as well. If you find any mistakes, you can make the necessary corrections on this screen. When you have finished, you would click the Save button to save your changes.

To Close the Table

Once you are sure that your entries are correct and you have saved your changes, you can close the table. The following step closes the table.

- Click the Close button for the Business Analyst Table to close the table (Figure 1–19).

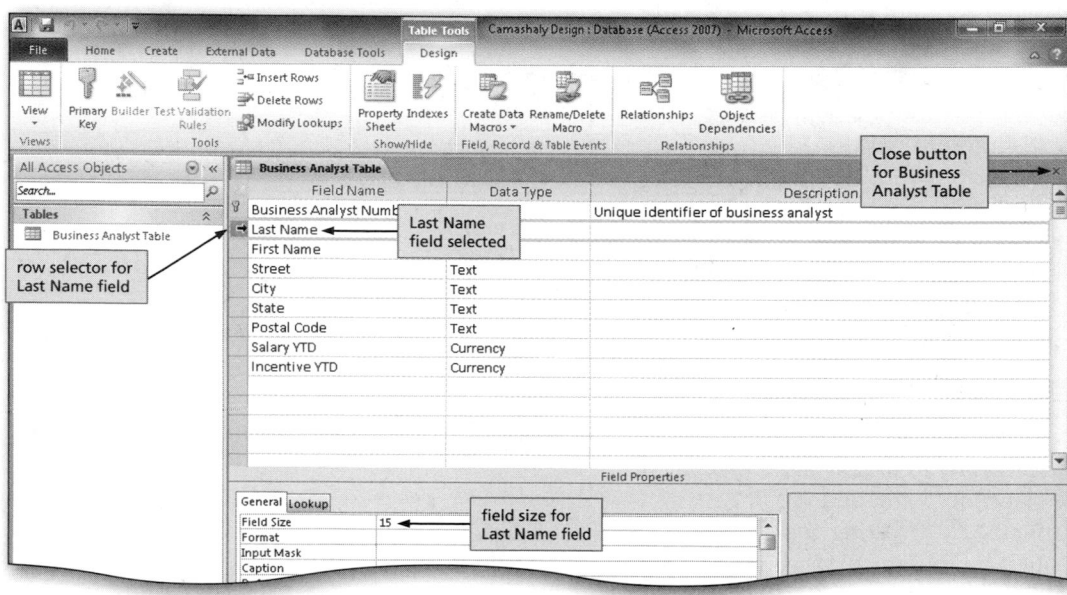

Figure 1–19

Other Ways

1. Right-click tab for table, click Close on shortcut menu

To Add Records to a Table

Creating a table by building the structure and saving the table is the first step in a two-step process. The second step is to add records to the table. To add records to a table, the table must be open. When making changes to tables, you work in Datasheet view. In Datasheet view, the table is represented as a collection of rows and columns called a **datasheet**.

You often add records in phases. For example, you might not have enough time to add all the records in one session. The following steps open the Business Analyst Table in Datasheet view and then add the first two records in the Business Analyst Table (Figure 1–20).

BA # ▾	Last Name ▾	First Name ▾	Street ▾	City ▾	State ▾	Postal Code ▾	Salary YTD ▾	Incentive YTD ▾
Business Analyst Table								
11	Kerry	Cordelia	251 Painter	Georgetown	NC	28794	$3,200.00	$3,450.00
14	Martinez	Manuel	3125 Steel	Kyle	SC	28797	$3,100.00	$2,430.00

Figure 1–20

- Right-click the Business Analyst Table in the Navigation Pane to display the shortcut menu (Figure 1–21).

Figure 1–21

2

- Click Open on the shortcut menu to open the table in Datasheet view.

Q&A

What if I want to return to Design view?

You can open Design view by clicking Design View on the shortcut menu.

- Click the Shutter Bar Open/Close Button to close the Navigation Pane (Figure 1–22).

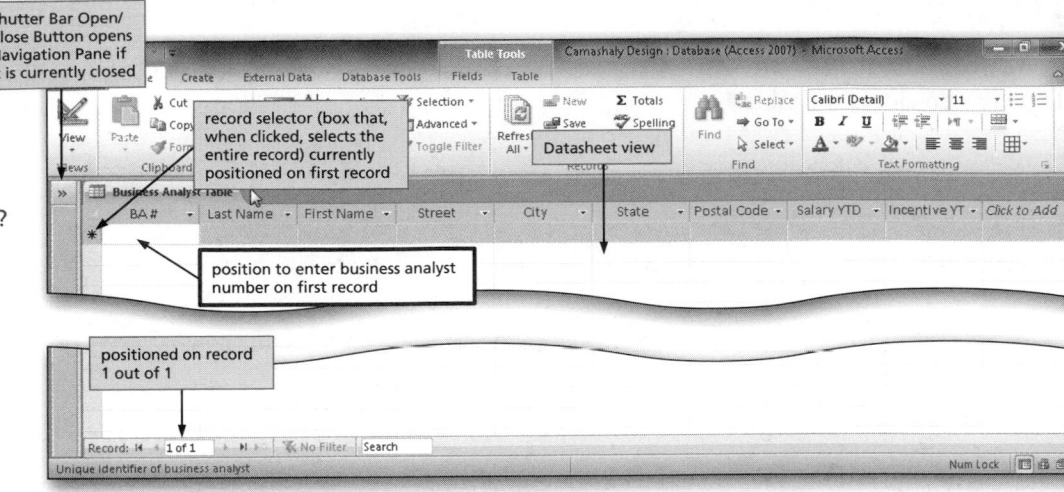

Figure 1–22

3

- Click the BA # field if necessary to display an insertion point, and type **11** to enter the first business analyst number (Figure 1–23).

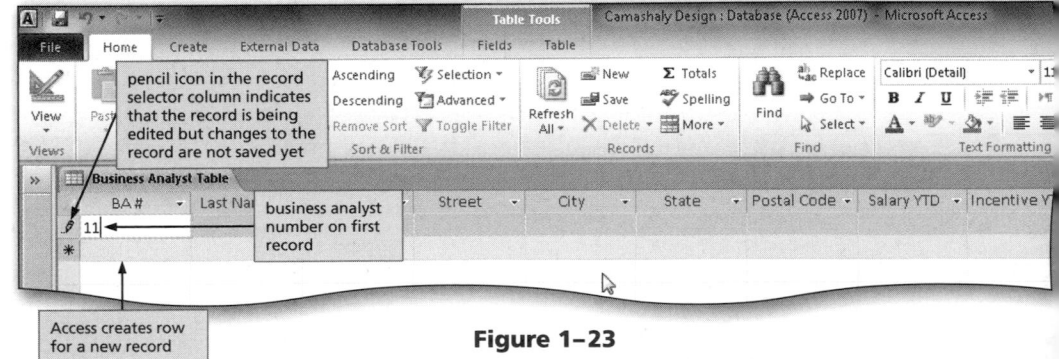

Figure 1–23

4

- Press the TAB key to move to the next field.

- Enter the last name, first name, street, city, state, and postal code by typing the following entries, pressing the TAB key after each one: **Kerry** as the last name, **Cordelia** as the first name, **251 Painter** as the street, **Georgetown** as the city, **NC** as the state, and **28794** as the postal code.

- Type **3200** in the Salary YTD field (Figure 1–24).

Figure 1–24

Q&A

Do I need to type a dollar sign?

You do not need to type dollar signs or commas. In addition, because the digits to the right of the decimal point are both zeros, you do not need to type either the decimal point or the zeros.

5

- Press the TAB key to complete the entry for the field.

- Type 3450 in the Incentive YTD field, and then press the TAB key to complete the entry of the first record (Figure 1–25).

How and when do I save the record?

As soon as you have entered or modified a record and moved to another record, the original record is saved. This is different from other applications. The rows entered in an Excel worksheet, for example, are not saved until the entire worksheet is saved.

Figure 1–25

6

- Use the techniques shown in Steps 3 through 5 to enter the data for the second record (Figure 1–26).

 Experiment

- Click the Salary YTD field on either of the records. Be sure the Table Tools Fields tab is selected. Click the Format box arrow and then click each of the

Figure 1–26

formats in the Format box menu to see the effect on the values in the Salary YTD field. When finished, click Currency in the Format box menu.

Making Changes to the Data

As you enter data, check your entries carefully to ensure they are correct. If you make a mistake and discover it before you press the TAB key, correct it by pressing the BACKSPACE key until the incorrect characters are removed, and then type the correct characters. If you do not discover a mistake until later, you can use the following techniques to make the necessary corrections to the data:

- To undo your most recent change, click the Undo button on the Quick Access Toolbar. If there is nothing that Access can undo, this button will be dimmed, and clicking it will have no effect.

- To add a record, click the New (blank) record button, click the position for the Business Analyst Number field on the first open record, and then add the record. Do not worry about it being in the correct position in the table. Access will reposition the record based on the primary key, in this case, the Business Analyst Number.

BTW

Adding Records
You can add records in any order. When you close a table and reopen it, the records will be in order by primary key.

- To delete a record, click the record selector, shown in Figure 1–26, for the record to be deleted. Then press the DELETE key to delete the record, and click the Yes button when Access asks you to verify that you do indeed want to delete the record.

- To change the contents of one or more fields in a record, the record must be on the screen. If it is not, use any appropriate technique, such as the UP ARROW and DOWN ARROW keys or the vertical scroll bar, to move to it. If the field you want to correct is not visible on the screen, use the horizontal scroll bar along the bottom of the screen to shift all the fields until the one you want appears. If the value in the field is currently highlighted, you can simply type the new value. If you would rather edit the existing value, you must have an insertion point in the field. You can place the insertion point by clicking in the field or by pressing F2. You then can use the arrow keys, the DELETE key, and the BACKSPACE key for making the correction. You also can use the INSERT key to switch between Insert and Overtype mode. When you have made the change, press the TAB key to move to the next field.

If you cannot determine how to correct the data, you may find that you are "stuck" on the record, in which case Access neither allows you to move to another record nor allows you to close the table until you have made the correction. If you encounter this situation, simply press the ESC key. Pressing the ESC key will remove from the screen the record you are trying to add. You then can move to any other record, close the table, or take any other action you desire.

To Close a Table

Now that you have created and saved the Business Analyst Table, you can close it. The following step closes the table.

1 Click the Close button for the Business Analyst Table, shown in Figure 1–26, to close the table (Figure 1–27).

Figure 1–27

To Quit Access

The following steps quit Access. For a detailed example of the procedure summarized below, refer to the Office 2010 and Windows 7 chapter at the beginning of this book.

1 Click the Close button on the right side of the title bar to quit Access.

2 If a Microsoft Access dialog box appears, click the Save button to save any changes made to the object since the last save.

Break Point: If you wish to take a break, this is a good place to do so. To resume at a later time, continue following the steps from this location forward.

Starting Access and Opening a Database

Once you have created and later closed a database, you will need to open it in the future in order to use it. Opening a database requires that Access is running on your computer.

To Start Access

1 Click the Start button on the Windows 7 taskbar to display the Start menu.

2 Type `Microsoft Access` as the search text in the 'Search programs and files' text box and watch the search results appear on the Start menu.

3 Click Microsoft Access 2010 in the search results on the Start menu to start Access.

To Open a Database from Access

Earlier in this chapter, you saved your database on a USB flash drive using the file name, Camashaly Design. The following steps open the Camashaly Design database from the Access folder in the CIS 101 folder on the USB flash drive. For a detailed example of the procedure summarized below, refer to the Office 2010 and Windows 7 chapter at the beginning of this book.

1 With your USB flash drive connected to one of the computer's USB ports, click File on the Ribbon to open the Backstage view, if necessary.

2 Click Open in the Backstage view to display the Open dialog box.

3 Navigate to the location of the file to be opened (in this case, the USB flash drive, then to the CIS 101 folder [or your class folder], and then to the Access folder).

4 Click Camashaly Design to select the file to be opened.

5 Click the Open button (Open dialog box) to open the selected file and display the opened database in the Access window.

6 If a Security Warning appears, click the Enable Content button (Figure 1–28).

BTW

Organizing Files and Folders
You should organize and store files in folders so that you easily can find the files later. For a discussion of folders and detailed examples of creating folders, refer to the Office 2010 and Windows 7 chapter at the beginning of this book.

When would I not want to enable the content?

You would want to disable the content if you suspected that your database might contain harmful content or damaging macros. Because you are the one who created the database and no one else has used it, you should have no such suspicions.

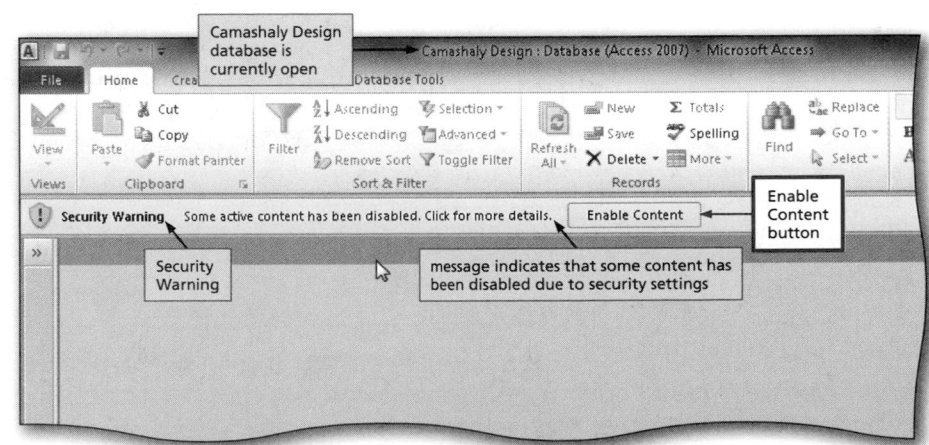

Figure 1–28

Other Ways

1. Click File on the Ribbon, click Recent in the Backstage view, click file name

To Add Additional Records to a Table

You can add records to a table that already contains data using a process almost identical to that used to add records to an empty table. The only difference is that you place the insertion point after the last record before you enter the additional data. To do so, use the **Navigation buttons**, which are buttons used to move within a table, found near the lower-left corner of the screen when a table is open. The purpose of each of the Navigation buttons is described in Table 1–4.

Table 1–4 Navigation Buttons in Datasheet View	
Button	**Purpose**
First record	Moves to the first record in the table
Previous record	Moves to the previous record
Next record	Moves to the next record
Last record	Moves to the last record in the table
New (blank) record	Moves to the end of the table to a position for entering a new record

The following steps add the remaining records (Figure 1–29) to the Business Analyst table.

Figure 1–29

- If the Navigation Pane is closed, click the Shutter Bar Open/Close Button, shown in Figure 1–27, to open the Navigation Pane (Figure 1–30).

Figure 1–30

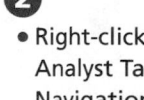

- Right-click the Business Analyst Table in the Navigation Pane to display a shortcut menu.

- Click Open on the shortcut menu to open the table in Datasheet view.

- Close the Navigation Pane by clicking the Shutter Bar Open/Close Button (Figure 1–31).

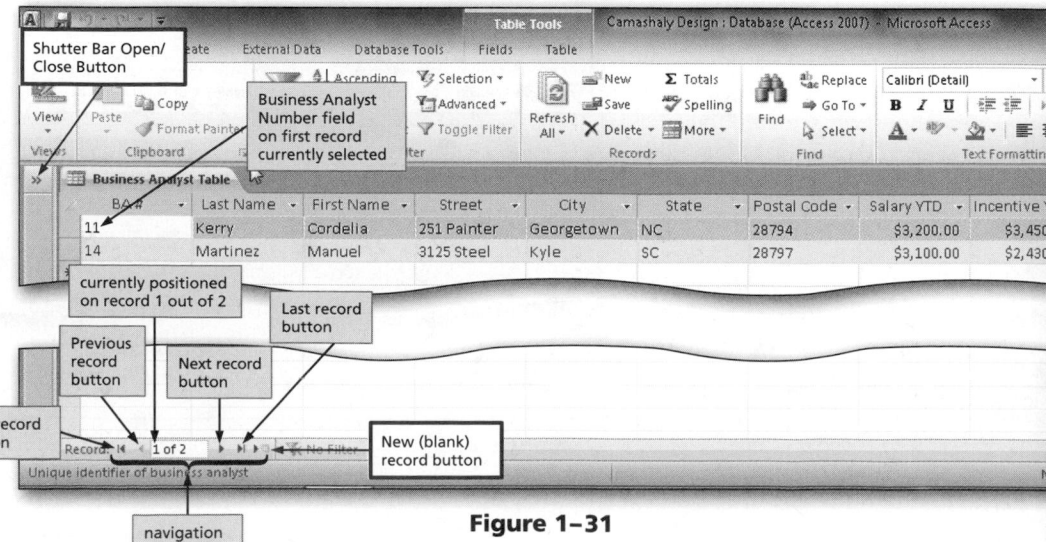

Figure 1–31

- Click the New (blank) record button to move to a position to enter a new record (Figure 1–32).

Could you just click the Business Analyst Number (BA #) on the first open record and then add the record?

Yes, but it is a good habit to use the New (blank) Record button. Once a table contains more records than will fit on the screen, it is easier to click the New (blank) record button.

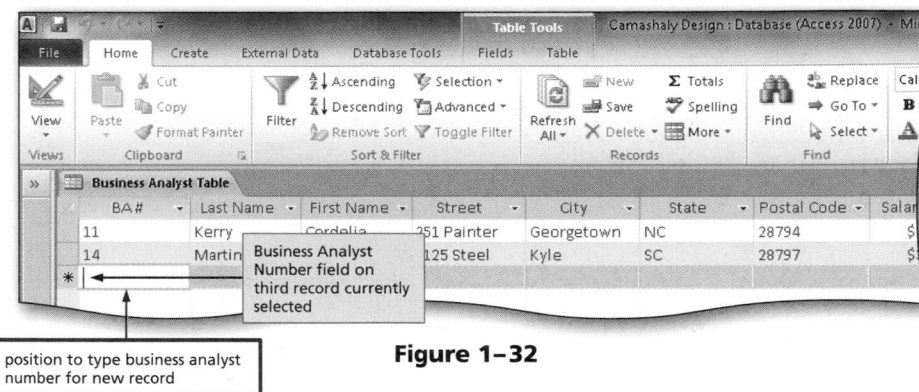

Figure 1–32

- Add the records shown in Figure 1–29, using the same techniques you used to add the first two records (Figure 1–33).

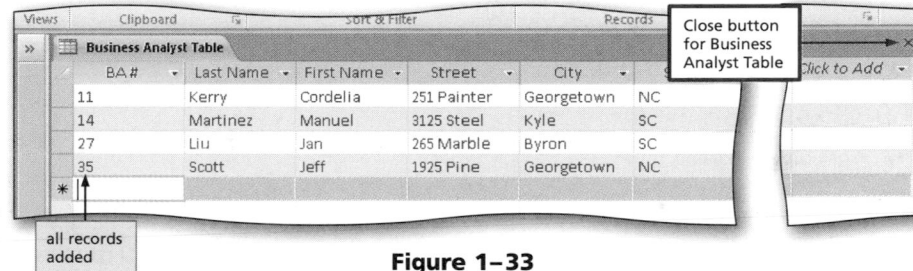

Figure 1–33

Other Ways
1. Click New button (Home tab | Records group)
2. Press CTRL+PLUS SIGN (+)

To Resize Columns in a Datasheet

Access assigns default column sizes, which do not always allow all the data in the field to appear. In some cases, the data might appear but not the entire field name. You can correct this problem by **resizing** the column (changing its size) in the datasheet. In some instances, you may want to reduce the size of a column. The State field, for example, is short enough that it does not require all the space on the screen that is allotted to it. Changing a column width changes the **layout**, or design, of a table.

The following steps resize the columns in the Business Analyst table and save the changes to the layout.

- Point to the right boundary of the field selector for the Business Analyst (BA #) field (Figure 1–34) so that the mouse pointer becomes a two-headed arrow.

Figure 1–34

2

- Double-click the right boundary of the field selector to resize the field so that it best fits the data.

- Use the same technique to resize all the other fields to best fit the data (Figure 1–35).

3

- Save the changes to the layout by clicking the Save button on the Quick Access Toolbar (Figure 1–35).

- Click the table's Close button (shown in Figure 1–33) to close the table.

Q&A What if I closed the table without saving the layout changes?
You would be asked if you want to save the changes.

Figure 1–35

Other Ways
1. Right-click field name, click Field Width

Plan Ahead

Determine the best method for distributing the database objects.
The traditional method of distributing database objects uses a printer to produce a hard copy of a table. A **hard copy** or **printout** is information that exists on a physical medium such as paper. For users who can receive fax documents, you can elect to print a hard copy on a remote fax machine. Hard copies can be useful for the following reasons:

- Many people prefer proofreading a hard copy of a document rather than viewing it on the screen to check for errors and readability.

- Hard copies can serve as reference material if your storage medium is lost or becomes corrupted and you need to re-create the document.

Instead of distributing a hard copy, users can choose to distribute the document as an electronic image that mirrors the original document's appearance. The electronic image of the document can be e-mailed, posted on a Web site, or copied to a portable medium such as a USB flash drive. Two popular electronic image formats, sometimes called fixed formats, are PDF by Adobe Systems and XPS by Microsoft. In Access, you can create PDF and XPS files through the External Data tab on the Ribbon. Electronic images of documents, such as PDF and XPS, can be useful for the following reasons.

- Users can view electronic images of documents without the software that created the original document (i.e., Access). Specifically, to view a PDF file, you use a program called Acrobat Reader, which can be downloaded free from Adobe's Web site. Similarly, to view an XPS file, you use a program called an XPS Viewer, which is included in the latest versions of Windows and Internet Explorer.

- Sending electronic documents saves paper and printer supplies. Society encourages users to contribute to **green computing**, which involves reducing the environmental waste generated when using a computer.

BTW

Changing Printers
To change the default printer that appears in the Print dialog box, click File on the Ribbon, click the Print tab in the Backstage view, click Print in the Print gallery, then click the Name box arrow and select the desired printer.

Previewing and Printing the Contents of a Table

When working with a database, you often will need to print a copy of the table contents. Figure 1–36 shows a printed copy of the contents of the Business Analyst table. (Yours may look slightly different, depending on your printer.) Because the Business Analyst table is substantially wider than the screen, it also will be wider than the normal printed page in portrait orientation. **Portrait orientation** means the printout is across the width of the page. **Landscape orientation** means the printout is across the height of the page. Thus, to

print the wide database table, you might prefer to use landscape orientation. A convenient
way to change to landscape orientation is to preview what the printed copy will look like
by using Print Preview. This allows you to determine whether landscape orientation is
necessary and, if it is, to change the orientation easily to landscape. In addition, you also can
use Print Preview to determine whether any adjustments are necessary to the page margins.

Business Analyst Table   4/12/2012

BA #	Last Name	First Name	Street	City	State	Postal Code	Salary YTD	Incentive YTD
11	Kerry	Cordelia	251 Painter	Georgetown	NC	28794	$3,200.00	$3,450.00
14	Martinez	Manuel	3125 Steel	Kyle	SC	28797	$3,100.00	$2,430.00
27	Liu	Jan	265 Marble	Byron	SC	28795	$3,400.00	$2,280.00
35	Scott	Jeff	1925 Pine	Georgetown	NC	28794	$500.00	$0.00

Figure 1–36

To Preview and Print the Contents of a Table

The following steps use Print Preview to preview and then print the contents of the Business Analyst table.

• If the Navigation Pane is closed, open the Navigation Pane by clicking the Shutter Bar Open/Close Button.

• Be sure the Business Analyst table is selected.

Why do I have to be sure the Business Analyst table is selected? It is the only object in the database.

When the database contains only one object, you do not have to worry about selecting the object. Ensuring that the correct object is selected is a good habit to form, however, to make sure that the object you print is the one you want.

• Click File on the Ribbon to open the Backstage view.

• Click the Print tab in the Backstage view to display the Print gallery (Figure 1–37).

Figure 1–37

• Click the Print Preview button in the Print gallery to display a preview of what the table will look like when printed.

• Close the Navigation Pane to free up more of the screen for the preview (Figure 1–38).

I cannot read the table. Can I magnify a portion of the table?

Yes. Point the mouse pointer, whose shape will change to a magnifying glass, at the portion of the table that you want to magnify, and then click. You can return the view of the table to the one shown in the figure by clicking a second time.

Figure 1–38

❸

- Click the mouse pointer in the position shown in Figure 1–38 to magnify the upper-right section of the table (Figure 1–39).

Q&A

My table was already magnified in a different area. How can I see the area shown in the figure?

One way is to use the scroll bars to move to the desired portion of the table. You also can click the mouse pointer anywhere in the table to produce a screen like the one in Figure 1–38, and then click in the location shown in the figure.

Figure 1–39

 ❹

- Click the Landscape button to change to landscape orientation (Figure 1–40).

- Click the Print button (Print Preview tab | Print group) to display the Print dialog box.

- Click the OK button (Print dialog box) to print the table.

- When the printer stops, retrieve the hard copy of the Business Analyst Table.

- Click the Close Print Preview button (Print Preview tab | Close Preview group) to close the Print Preview window.

Figure 1–40

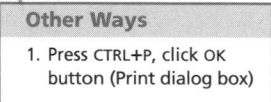

Other Ways

1. Press CTRL+P, click OK button (Print dialog box)

Creating Additional Tables

The Camashaly Design database contains two tables, the Business Analyst table and the Client table. You still need to create the Client table and add records to it. You created the Business Analyst table in Datasheet view. You will create the Client table in Design view.

Recall that the fields for the Client table are Client Number, Client Name, Street, City, State, Postal Code, Amount Paid, Current Due, Contract Hours YTD, and Business Analyst Number. The details that must be entered for these fields are shown in Table 1–5. The Client Number is the primary key. The Client Number field and the Business Analyst Number fields have both descriptions and captions. The Contract Hours YTD field has a caption.

Because the values in the Contract Hours YTD field have decimal places, only Single, Double, or Decimal would be possible field size choices. (See Table 1–2 on Page AC 10 for a description of the possible field sizes for Number fields.) The difference between these choices concerns the amount of accuracy. Double is more accurate than Single, for example, but requires more storage space. Because the rates are only two decimal places, Single is a perfectly acceptable choice.

In addition to changing the field size for the Contract Hours YTD, you will also change the format to Fixed (a fixed number of decimal places) and the number of decimal places to 2.

Table 1–5 Structure of Client Table			
Field Name	**Data Type**	**Field Size**	**Notes**
Client Number	Text	4	**Primary Key** **Description:** Client Number (two uppercase letters followed by 2-digit number) **Caption:** CL #
Client Name	Text	30	
Street	Text	15	
City	Text	15	
State	Text	2	
Postal Code	Text	5	
Amount Paid	Currency		
Current Due	Currency		
Contract Hours YTD	Number	Single	**Caption:** Hrs YTD **Format:** Fixed **Decimal Places:** 2
Business Analyst Number	Text	2	**Caption:** BA # **Description:** Business Analyst Number (number of business analyst for client)

To Create a Table in Design View

The next step in creating the table is to define the fields by specifying the required details in Design view. You will make entries in the Field Name, Data Type, and Description columns and enter additional information in the Field Properties box in the lower portion of the Table window. As you define the fields, the row selector (Figure 1–19 on page AC 23) indicates the field you currently are describing. Clicking the row selector selects the entire row. It is positioned on the first field, indicating Access is ready for you to enter the name of the first field in the Field Name column.

The following steps use Design view to define the fields in the table.

1
- Open the Navigation Pane.

- Click Create on the Ribbon to display the Create tab (Figure 1–41).

Figure 1–41

2

• Click the Table Design button (Create tab | Tables group) to create a new table in Design view (Figure 1–42).

Q&A

Could I save the table now so I can assign it the name I want, rather than Table1?

You certainly could. Be aware, however, that you will still need to save it again once you have added all your fields.

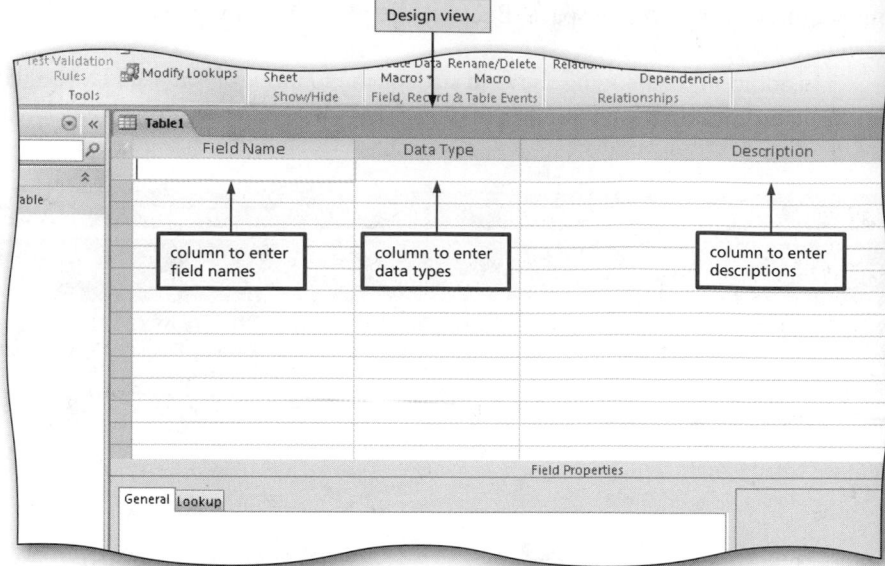

Figure 1–42

3

• Type **Client Number** (the name of the first field) in the Field Name column and then press the TAB key to accept the field name and move to the Data Type column (Figure 1–43).

Figure 1–43

4

• Because the Client Number field is the primary key, click the Primary Key button (Table Tools Design tab | Tools group) to designate the Client Number field as the primary key (Figure 1–44).

Figure 1–44

- Press the TAB key to move to the Description column, and then type `Client Number (two uppercase letters followed by a two-digit number)` as the description.

- Click the Field Size text box in the Field Properties pane to produce an insertion point, use either the BACKSPACE or DELETE key as necessary to erase the current entry (255), and then type `4` to change the field size.

- Click the Caption text box to produce an insertion point, and then type `CL #` to enter a caption (Figure 1–45).

Figure 1–45

- Click the Field Name column on the second row to produce an insertion point and then make the entries for the Client Name field.

- Use the techniques illustrated in Steps 1 through 5 to make the entries for the remaining fields in the Client table structure, shown in Table 1–5 on page AC 33, up through and including the name of the Amount Paid field.

- Click the Data Type box arrow to display a menu of available data types (Figure 1–46).

Figure 1–46

- Click Currency to select the data type.

- Enter the Current Due field and select the Currency data type.

- Enter the Contract Hours YTD field and select the Number data type (Figure 1–47).

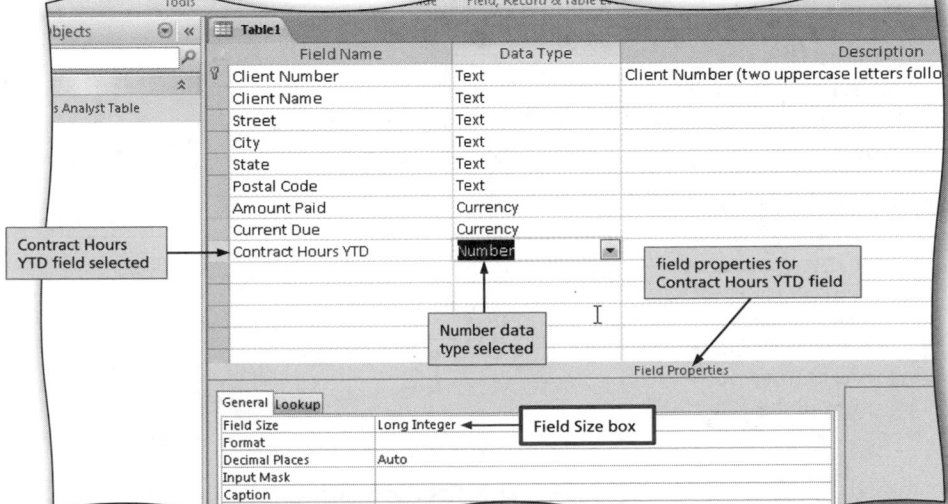

Figure 1–47

8

- Click the Field Size box to display the Field Size box arrow.

- Click the Field Size box arrow to display the Field Size box menu (Figure 1–48).

Q&A

What would happen if I left the field size set to Integer?

If the field size is Integer, no decimal places can be stored. Thus a value of 2.50 would be stored as 2. If you enter your hours and none of the values have decimal places, probably you did not change the field size.

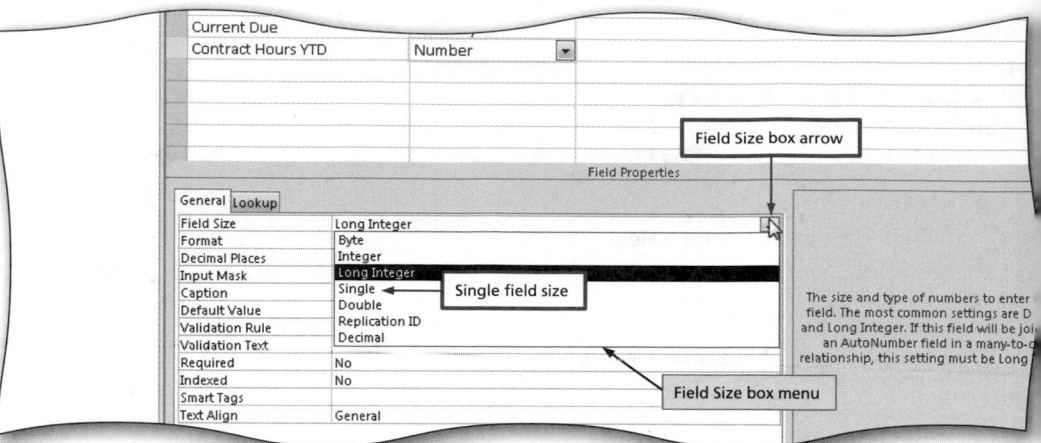

Figure 1–48

9

- Click Single to select single precision as the field size.

- Click the Format box to display the Format box arrow.

- Click the Format box arrow to display the Format box menu (Figure 1–49).

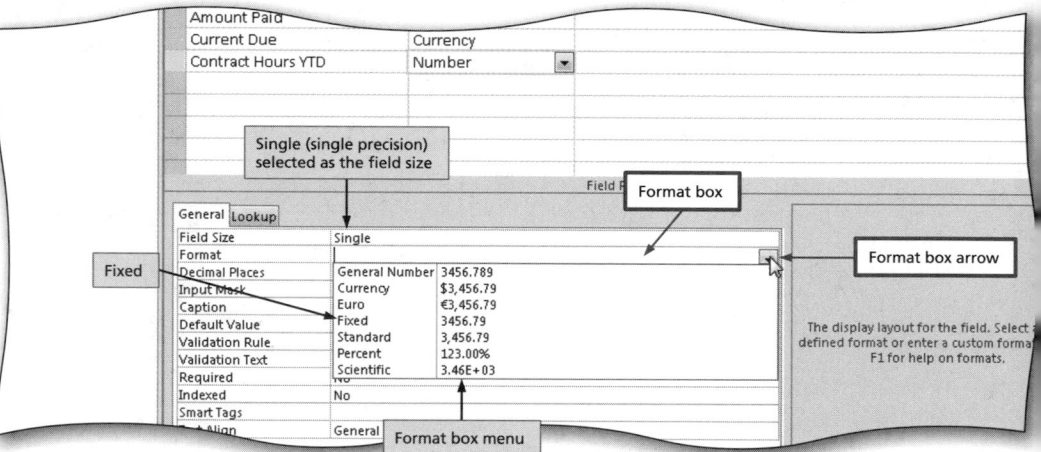

Figure 1–49

10

- Click Fixed to select fixed as the format.

- Click the Decimal Places box to display the Decimal Places box arrow.

- Click the Decimal Places box arrow to enter the number of decimal places.

- Click 2 to select 2 as the number of decimal places.

- Click the Caption text box to produce an insertion point, and then type **Hrs YTD** to enter a caption (Figure 1–50).

Figure 1–50

Figure 1–51

* Enter the Business Analyst Number field from Table 1–5. Be sure to change the description, field size, and caption to the ones shown in the table.

* Click the Save button on the Quick Access Toolbar to display the Save As dialog box, type Client as the name of the table, and then click the OK button (Save As dialog box) to save the table (Figure 1–51).

Correcting Errors in the Structure

When creating a table, check the entries carefully to ensure they are correct. If you make a mistake and discover it before you press the TAB key, you can correct the error by repeatedly pressing the BACKSPACE key until the incorrect characters are removed. Then, type the correct characters. If you do not discover a mistake until later, you can click the entry, type the correct value, and then press the ENTER key. You can use the following techniques to make changes to the structure:

* If you accidentally add an extra field to the structure, select the field by clicking the row selector (the leftmost column on the row that contains the field to be deleted). Once you have selected the field, press the DELETE key. This will remove the field from the structure.

* If you forget to include a field, select the field that will follow the field you want to add by clicking the row selector, and then press the INSERT key. The remaining fields move down one row, making room for the missing field. Make the entries for the new field in the usual manner.

* If you made the wrong field a primary key field, click the correct primary key entry for the field and then click the Primary Key button (Table Tools Design tab | Tools group).

* To move a field, click the row selector for the field to be moved to select the field, and then drag the field to the desired position.

As an alternative to these steps, you may want to start over. To do so, click the Close button for the window containing the table, and then click the No button in the Microsoft Access dialog box. Click Create on the Ribbon and then click the Table Design button to create a table. You then can repeat the process you used earlier to define the fields in the table.

BTW

AutoCorrect Feature
The AutoCorrect feature of Access corrects common mistakes when entering text in a cell. AutoCorrect corrects two capital letters by changing the second letter to lowercase and capitalizes the first letter in the names of days. It also corrects more than 400 commonly misspelled words.

BTW

Other AutoCorrect Options
Using the Office AutoCorrect feature, you can create entries that will replace abbreviations with spelled-out names and phrases automatically. To specify AutoCorrect rules, click File on the Ribbon to open the Backstage view, click Options, and then click Proofing in the Access Options dialog box.

To Close the Table

Now that you have completed and saved the Client table, you can close it. The following step closes the table.

1 Click the Close button for the Client table (see Figure 1–51) to close the table.

Importing Data from Other Applications to Access

Now that you have created the Client table, you could add the records to it just as you did with the Business Analyst table. Access provides an alternative, however, that is available because Camashaly Design has already stored the necessary data in an Excel workbook (Figure 1–52). The data is stored in the form of an Excel **list**; that is, the first row contains column headings describing the data in each of the columns, and the remaining rows contain the data. Camashaly can **import** the data, which means to make a copy of the data in a table in the Access database.

When importing data, you have two choices. You can create a new table, in which case the column headings in the worksheet become the field names in the table. Access will attempt to assign appropriate data types. You would need to review the data types, adjust field sizes, captions, descriptions, and formats after the data was imported. The other option is to add the records to an existing table. This method is appropriate if you have already created the table, provided the column headings in the worksheet match the field names in the table, as they do in the case of the Client table.

	A	B	C	D	E	F	G	H	I	J	K
1	Client Number	Client Name	Street	City	State	Postal Code	Amount Paid	Current Due	Contract Hours YTD	Business Analyst Number	
2	BA53	Bavant Animal Hospital	134 Main	Burles	NC	28817	$0.00	$7,500.00	0.00	11	
3	BB32	Babbage CPA Firm	464 Linnell	Austin	SC	28796	$1,500.00	$500.00	5.00	14	
4	BC76	Buda Community Clinic	867 Ridge	Buda	NC	27032	$2,500.00	$750.00	2.50	11	
5	CJ29	Catering by Jenna	123 Second	Granger	NC	27036	$3,000.00	$1,000.00	15.50	27	
6	GA74	Grant Antiques	78 Catawba	Georgetown	NC	28794	$5,500.00	$3,200.00	34.50	14	
7	GF56	Granger Foundation	65 Simpson	Granger	NC	27036	$0.00	$6,500.00	0.00	11	
8	HC10	Hendley County Hospital	216 Rivard	Austin	SC	28796	$3,100.00	$1,200.00	12.00	27	
9	KD21	KAL Design Studio	116 Pine	Georgetown	NC	28794	$6,000.00	$3,200.00	30.50	14	
10	KG04	Kyle Grocery Cooperative	421 First	Kyle	SC	28798	$3,200.00	$0.00	5.00	11	
11	ME14	Mike's Electronic Stop	234 Gilham	Georgetown	NC	28794	$2,500.00	$1,500.00	8.50	27	
12	PJ34	Patricia Jean Florist	345 Magee	Kyle	SC	28798	$0.00	$5,200.00	0.00	27	
13	SL77	Smarter Law Associates	764 Main	Burles	NC	28817	$3,800.00	$0.00	10.50	11	
14	TB17	The Bikeshop	346 Austin	Buda	NC	27032	$2,750.00	$1,200.00	14.00	27	
15	WE05	Walburg Energy Alternatives	12 Polk	Walburg	NC	28819	$4,500.00	$1,450.00	19.50	14	
16	WS01	Woody Sporting Goods	578 Central	Walburg	NC	28819	$2,250.00	$1,600.00	18.50	14	
17											

Figure 1–52

The process of importing into an Access database uses a wizard. Specifically, if the data is imported from an Excel worksheet, the process will use the Import Spreadsheet Wizard. The wizard takes you through some basic steps, asking a few simple questions. After you have answered the questions, the wizard will import or link the data.

To Import an Excel Worksheet

To import the data in the Camashaly Client Data workbook, you use the Import Spreadsheet Wizard to place the rows from an Excel worksheet into an existing table. The following steps import the Camashaly Client Data Excel workbook, which is provided as a data file. See the inside back cover of this book for instructions on downloading the Data Files for Students, or contact your instructor for more information about accessing the required files.

①

• Click External Data on the Ribbon to display the External Data tab (Figure 1–53).

Figure 1–53

②

• Click the Excel button (External Data tab | Import & Link group) to display the Get External Data – Excel Spreadsheet dialog box.

• Click the Browse button (Get External Data – Excel Spreadsheet dialog box) to display the File Open dialog box.

• Navigate to the USB flash drive (or the location of your data files).

• Double-click your USB flash drive, and then click Camashaly Client Data to select the file to be opened.

• Click the Open button (File Open dialog box), which will return you to the Get External Data dialog box with the Camashaly Client Data workbook selected.

③

• Click the option button to append a copy of records to a table (Figure 1–54).

What happens if I select the option button to import records into a new table?

Instead of the records being added to an existing table, they will be placed in a new table. Access will assign all the data types. You would then need to ensure they are correct. You also would need to change any field sizes, descriptions, captions, formats, or number of decimal places to the ones you want.

Figure 1–54

4

- Click the arrow to produce a menu of available tables.

- Click the Client table to select the table to which a copy of the records will be appended (Figure 1–55).

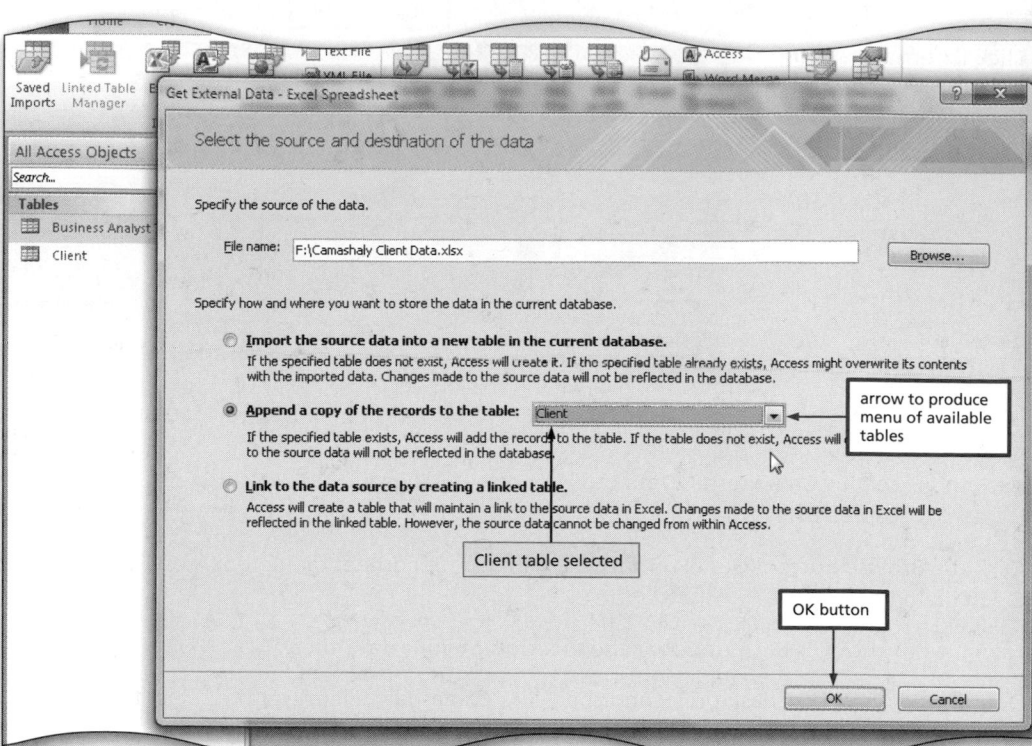

Figure 1–55

5

- Click the OK button to move to the next Import Spreadsheet Wizard screen (Figure 1–56).

Q&A

The First Row Contains Column Headings check box is checked, but it is dimmed. What if I want to remove the check mark?

When you are appending records to an existing table, the first row must contain column headings. If instead you were creating a new table, the first row might not contain column headings. In that case, you would have control over this check box.

Figure 1–56

6

- Click the Next button to move to the next Import Spreadsheet Wizard screen (Figure 1–57).

What happens if I later realize I have selected the wrong table?

If you have not yet clicked the Finish button, you can click the Back button to return to the screen where you selected the table, and then select the correct table.

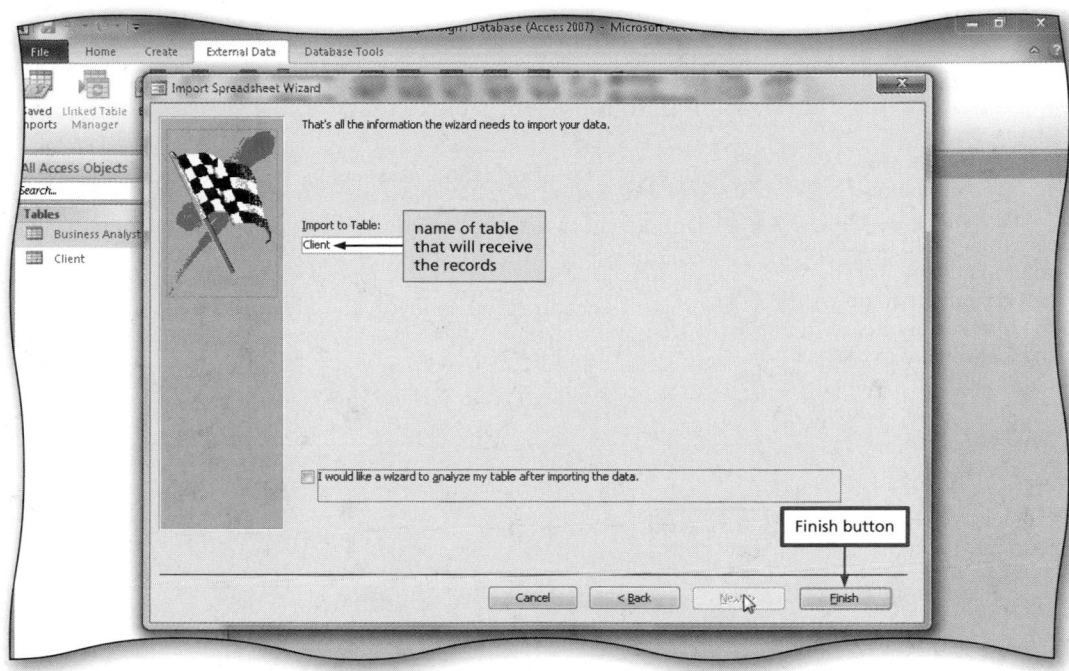

Figure 1–57

7

- Because the table name is correct, click the Finish button to import the data (Figure 1–58).

I got an error message that stated that a particular field did not exist in the Client table. What did I do wrong? How do I fix it?

When you created the table, you did not name that particular field correctly. Open the table in Design view and change the field name to the correct name. Check other field names as well. When you are done, save and close the table. Then, repeat the import process.

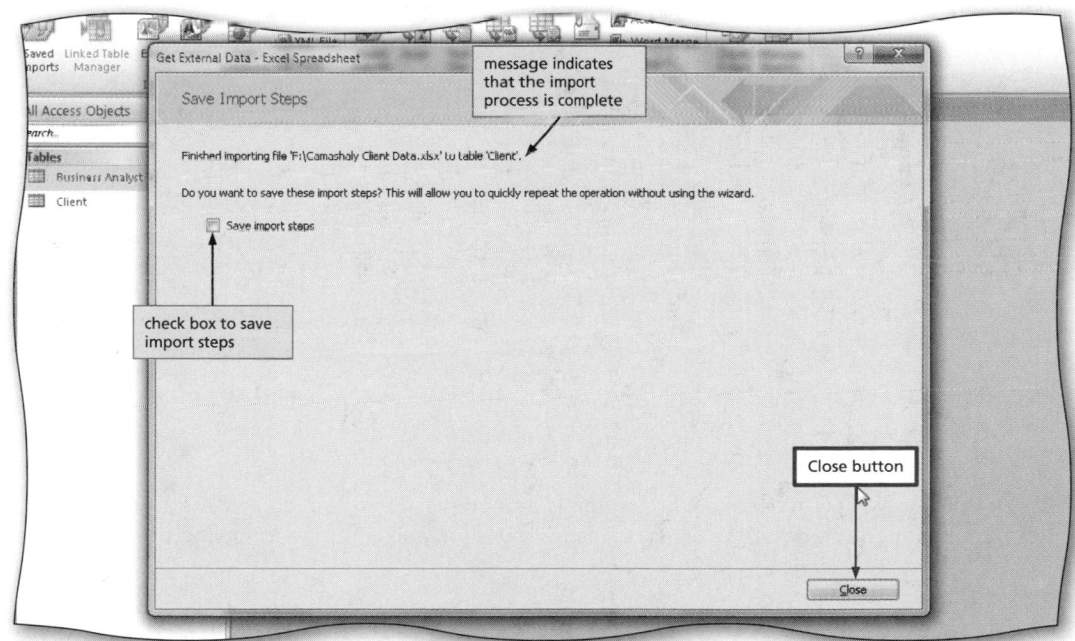

Figure 1–58

8

- Because you will not save the import steps, click the Close button.

When would I save the import steps?

If you think you might need to repeat these steps in the future, you can save time by saving the steps.

Other Ways

1. Right-click table in Navigation Pane, click Import on shortcut menu

To Resize Columns in a Datasheet

You can resize the columns in the datasheet for the Client table just as you resized the columns in the datasheet for the Business Analyst table. The following steps resize the columns in the Client table to best fit the data.

BTW

Resizing Columns
To resize all columns in a datasheet to best fit simultaneously, select the column heading for the first column, hold down the SHIFT key and select the last column in the datasheet. Then, double-click the right boundary of any field selector.

1 Open the Client table in Datasheet view and then close the Navigation Pane.

2 Double-click the right boundary of the field selectors of each of the fields to resize the columns so that they best fit the data.

3 Save the changes to the layout by clicking the Save button on the Quick Access Toolbar (Figure 1–59).

4 Close the table.

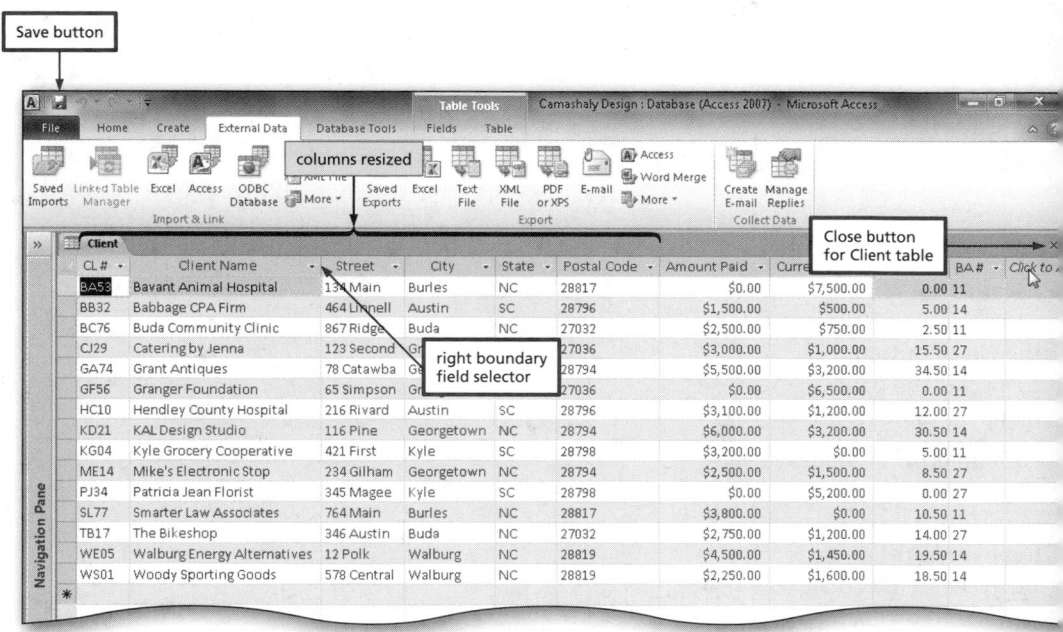

Figure 1–59

Break Point: If you wish to take a break, this is a good place to do so. You can quit Access now. To resume at a later time, start Access, open the database called Camashaly Design, and continue following the steps from this location forward.

Additional Database Objects

A computerized database such as Access contains many types of objects. Tables are the objects you use to store and manipulate data. Access supports other important types of objects as well; each of these objects has a specific purpose that assists in maximizing the benefits of a database. Through queries (questions), Access makes it possible to ask complex questions concerning the data in the database and then receive instant answers. Access also allows the user to produce attractive and useful forms for viewing and updating data. Additionally, Access includes report creation tools that make it easy to produce sophisticated reports for presenting data.

To Use the Simple Query Wizard to Create a Query

Queries are simply questions, the answers to which are in the database. Access contains a powerful query feature that helps you find the answers to a wide variety of questions. Once you have examined the question you want to ask to determine the fields involved in the question, you can begin creating the query. If there are no restrictions involved in the query, nor any special order or calculations, you can use the Simple Query Wizard.

The following steps use the Simple Query Wizard to create a query that Camashaly Design might use to obtain financial information on its clients. The query displays the number, name, amount paid, current due, contract hours YTD, and business analyst number of all clients.

❶
- If the Navigation Pane is closed, click the Shutter Bar Open/Close Button to open the Navigation Pane.

- Be sure the Client table is selected.

- Click Create on the Ribbon to display the Create tab.

- Click the Query Wizard button (Create tab | Queries group) to display the New Query dialog box (Figure 1–60).

Figure 1–60

❷
- Be sure Simple Query Wizard is selected, and then click the OK button (New Query dialog box) to display the Simple Query Wizard dialog box (Figure 1–61).

  What would happen if the Business Analyst Table were selected instead of the Client table?

  The list of available fields would contain fields from the Business Analyst Table rather than the Client table.

  If the list contained Business Analyst Table fields, how could I make it contain Client table fields?

  Click the arrow in the Tables/Queries box and then click the Client table in the list that appears.

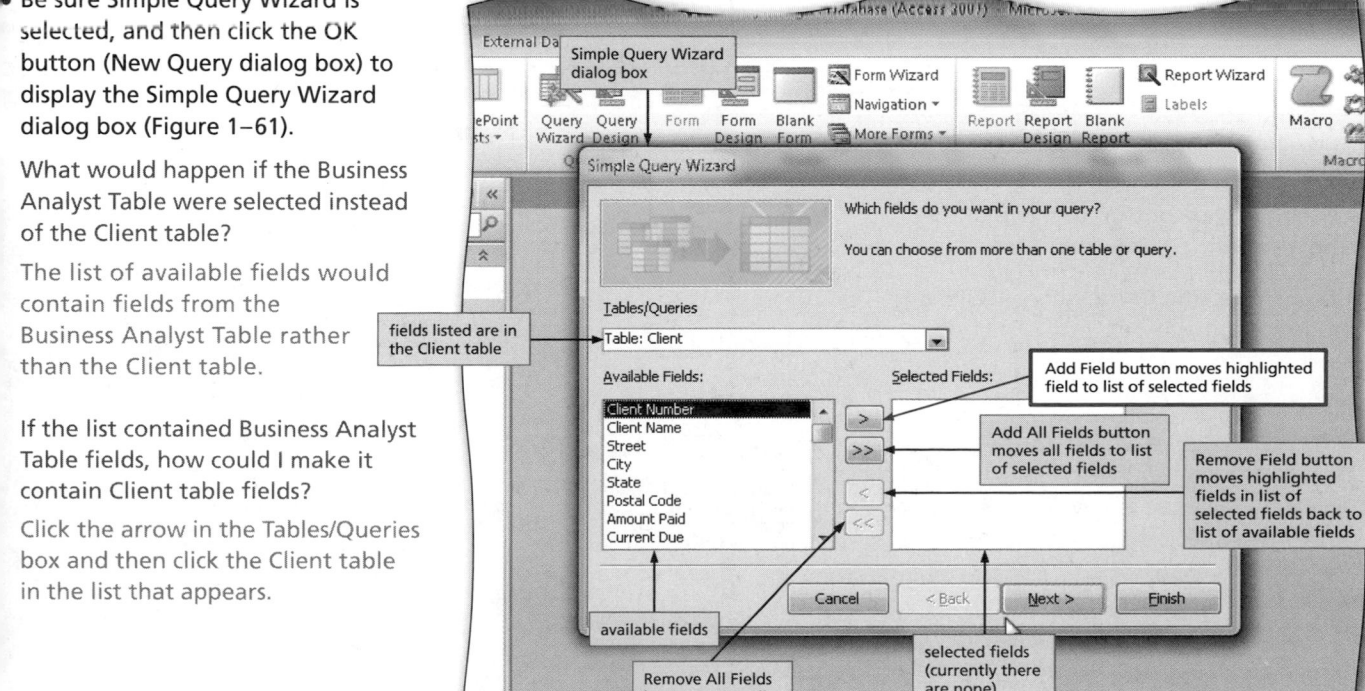

Figure 1–61

3

- With the Client Number field selected, click the Add Field button to add the field to the query.

- With the Client Name field selected, click the Add Field button a second time to add the field.

- Click the Amount Paid field, and then click the Add Field button to add the field.

- In a similar fashion, add the Current Due, Contract Hours YTD, and Business Analyst Number fields (Figure 1–62).

Figure 1–62

4

- Click the Next button to move to the next screen.

- Ensure that the Detail (shows every field of every record) option button is selected (Figure 1–63).

Q&A What is the difference between Detail and Summary?

Detail shows all the records and fields. Summary only shows computations (for example, the total amount paid).

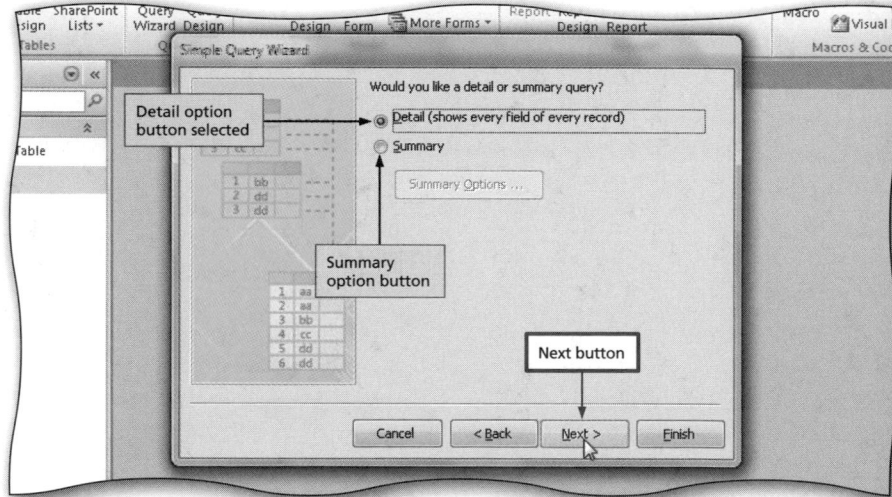

Figure 1–63

5

- Click the Next button to move to the next screen.

- Ensure the title of the query is Client Query (Figure 1–64).

Figure 1–64

6
• Click the Finish button to create the query (Figure 1–65).

• Click the Close button for the Client Query to remove the query results from the screen.

If I want to use this query in the future, do I need to save the query?

Normally you would. The one exception is a query created by the wizard. The wizard automatically saves the query it creates.

CL #	Client Name	Amount Paid	Current Due	Hrs YTD	BA #
BA53	Bavant Animal Hospital	$0.00	$7,500.00	0.00	11
BB32	Babbage CPA Firm	$1,500.00	$500.00	5.00	14
BC76	Buda Community Clinic	$2,500.00	$750.00	2.50	11
CJ29	Catering by Jenna	$3,000.00	$1,000.00	15.50	27
GA74	Grant Antiques	$5,500.00	$3,200.00	34.50	14
GF56	Granger Foundation	$0.00	$6,500.00	0.00	11
HC10	Hendley County Hospital	$3,100.00	$1,200.00	12.00	27
KD21	KAL Design Studio	$6,000.00	$3,200.00	30.50	14
KG04	Kyle Grocery Cooperative	$3,200.00	$0.00	5.00	11
ME14	Mike's Electronic Stop	$2,500.00	$1,500.00	8.50	27
PJ34	Patricia Jean Florist	$0.00	$5,200.00	0.00	27
SL77	Smarter Law Associates	$3,800.00	$0.00	10.50	11
TB17	The Bikeshop	$2,750.00	$1,200.00	14.00	27
WE05	Walburg Energy Alternatives	$4,500.00	$1,450.00	19.50	14
WS01	Woody Sporting Goods	$2,250.00	$1,600.00	18.50	14

Figure 1–65

Using Queries

After you have created and saved a query, Access stores it as a database object and makes it available for use in a variety of ways:

• To view the results of the query, open it by right-clicking the query in the Navigation Pane and clicking Open on the shortcut menu.

• To print the results with the query open, click File on the Ribbon, click the Print tab, and then click either Print or Quick Print.

• If you want to change the design of the query, right-click the query in the Navigation Pane and then click Design View on the shortcut menu to open the query in Design view.

• To print the query without first opening it, be sure the query is selected in the Navigation Pane and click File on the Ribbon, click the Print tab, and then click either Print or Quick Print.

You can switch between views of a query using the View button (Home tab | Views group). Clicking the arrow in the bottom of the button produces the View button menu. You then click the desired view in the menu. The two query views you will use in this chapter are Datasheet view (see the results) and Design view (change the design). You also can click the top part of the View button, in which case, you will switch to the view identified by the icon on the button. In the figure, the button contains the icon for Design view, so clicking the button would change to Design view. For the most part, the icon on the button represents the view you want, so you can usually simply click the button.

To Use a Criterion in a Query

After you have determined the fields to be included in a query, you will determine whether there are any restrictions on the records that are to be included. For example, you might only want to include those clients whose business analyst number is 14. In such a case, you need to enter the 14 as a **criterion**, which is a condition that the records to be included must satisfy. To do so, you will open the query in Design view, enter the criterion below the appropriate field, and then view the results of the query. The following steps enter a criterion to include only the clients of business analyst 14 and then view the query results.

- Right-click the Client Query in the Navigation Pane to produce a shortcut menu (Figure 1–66).

Figure 1–66

- Click Design View on the shortcut menu to open the query in Design view (Figure 1–67).

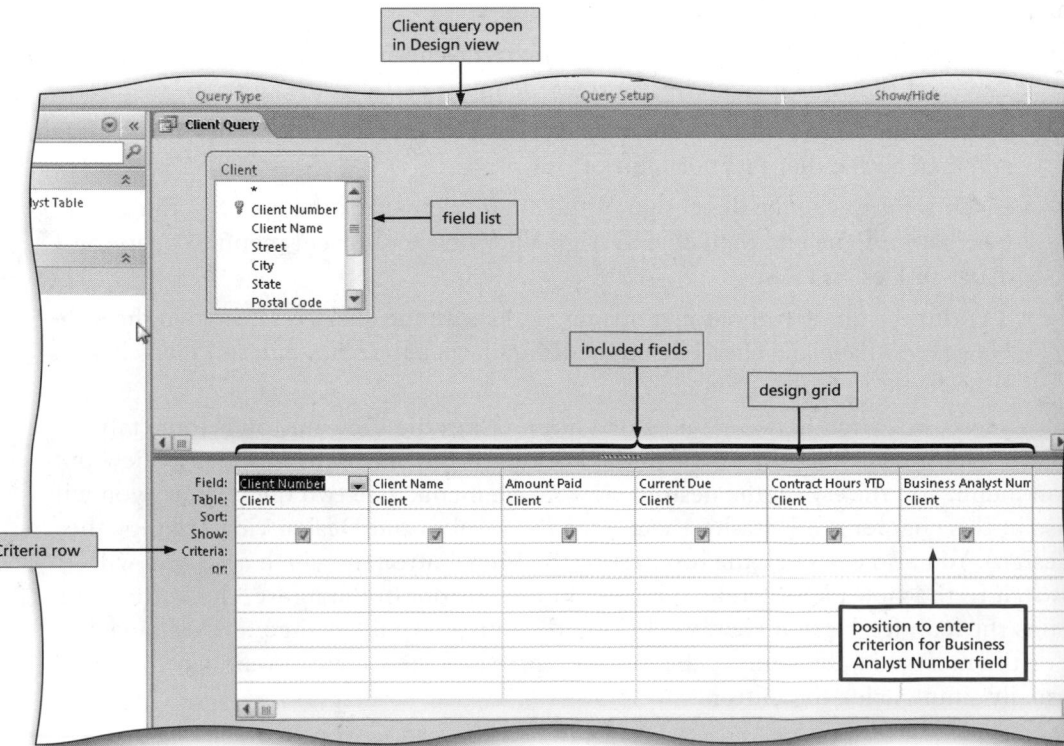

Figure 1–67

3
• Click the Criteria row in the Business Analyst Number column of the grid, and then type **14** as the criterion (Figure 1–68).

The Business Analyst Number field is a text field. Do I need to enclose the value for a text field in quotation marks?

You could, but it is not necessary, because Access inserts the quotation marks for you automatically.

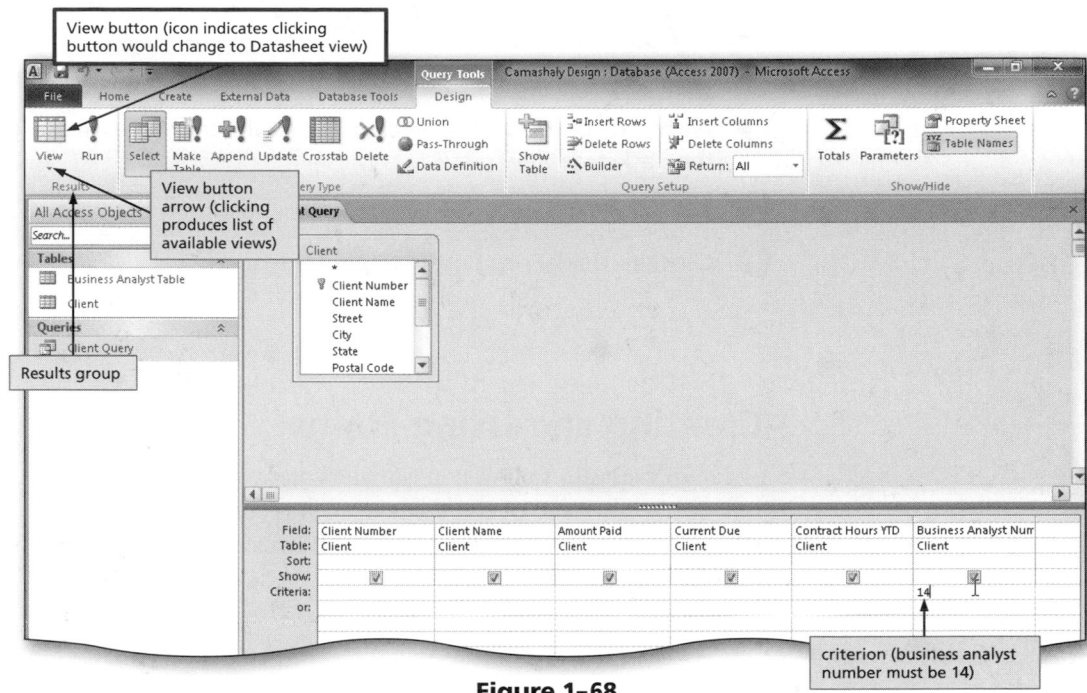

Figure 1–68

4
• Click the View button to display the query results in Datasheet view (Figure 1–69).

Could I click the View button arrow and then click Datasheet view?

Yes, if the icon representing the view you want appears on the View button; however, it is easier just to click the button.

Figure 1–69

5
• Click the Close button for the Client Query to close the query.

• When asked if you want to save your changes, click the No button.

If I saved the query, what would happen the next time I ran the query?

You would see only clients of business analyst 14.

Could I save the query with another name?

Yes. To save the query with another name, click File on the Ribbon, click Save Object As, enter a new file name in the Save As dialog box and click the OK button (Save As dialog box).

Other Ways

1. Click Run button (Query Tools Design tab | Results group)

2. Click Datasheet View button on status bar

To Print the Results of a Query

The following steps print the results of a saved query.

1 With the Client Query selected in the Navigation Pane, click File on the Ribbon to open the Backstage view.

2 Click the Print tab in the Backstage view to display the Print gallery.

3 Click the Quick Print button to print the query.

Creating and Using Forms

In Datasheet view, you can view many records at once. If there are many fields, however, only some of the fields in each record might be visible at a time. In **Form view**, where data is displayed in a form on the screen, you usually can see all the fields, but only for one record.

To Create a Form

Like a paper form, a **form** in a database is a formatted document with fields that contain data. Forms allow you to view and maintain data. Forms also can be used to print data, but reports are more commonly used for that purpose. The simplest type of form in Access is one that includes all the fields in a table stacked one above the other. The following steps create a form, use the form to view records, and then save the form.

1

- Select the Client table in the Navigation Pane.

- If necessary, click Create on the Ribbon to display the Create tab (Figure 1–70).

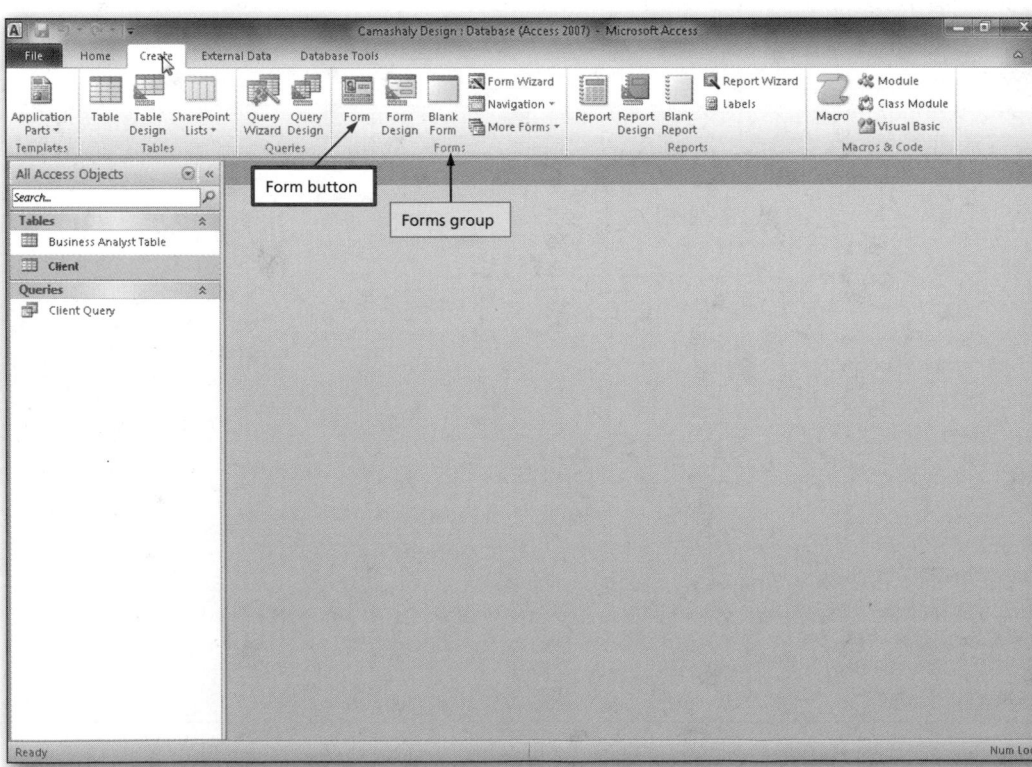

Figure 1–70

2

• Click the Form button (Create tab | Forms group) to create a simple form (Figure 1–71).

A Field list appeared on my screen. What should I do?

Click the Add Existing Fields button (Form Layout Tools Design tab | Tools group) to remove the Field list from the screen.

Figure 1–71

3

• If the form appears in Layout view, click the Form View button on the Access status bar to display the form in Form view.

How can I recognize Layout view?

Access identifies Layout view in three ways. The left side of the status bar will contain the words Layout View; there will be shading around the outside of the selected field in the form; and the Layout View button will be selected on the right side of the status bar.

• Click the Next Record button three times to move to record 4 (Figure 1–72).

Figure 1–72

4

- Click the Save button on the Quick Access Toolbar to display the Save As dialog box (Figure 1–73).

Figure 1–73

Did I have to click the Next Record button before saving?

No. The only reason you were asked to click the button was so that you could experience navigation within the form.

5

- Type **Client Form** as the form name, and then click the OK button to save the form.

- Click the Close button for the form to close the form.

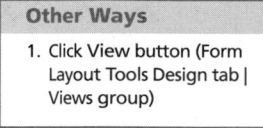

Other Ways

1. Click View button (Form Layout Tools Design tab | Views group)

Using a Form

After you have saved a form, you can use it at anytime by right-clicking the form in the Navigation Pane and then clicking Open in the shortcut menu. In addition to viewing data in the form, you can also use it to enter or update data, a process that is very similar to updating data using a datasheet. If you plan to use the form to enter or revise data, you must ensure you are viewing the form in Form view.

Break Point: If you wish to take a break, this is a good place to do so. You can quit Access now. To resume at a later time, start Access, open the database called Camashaly Design, and continue following the steps from this location forward.

Creating and Printing Reports

Camashaly Design wants to create the Client Financial Report shown in Figure 1–74. Just as you can create a form containing all fields by clicking a single button, you can click a button to create a report containing all the fields. Doing so will not match the report shown in Figure 1–74, however, which does not contain all the fields. Some of the column headings are different. In addition, some of the headings in the report in Figure 1–74 are split over multiple lines, whereas the ones in the report created by clicking the button will not be split. Fortunately, you can later modify the report design to make it precisely match the figure. To do so, you use Layout view for the report.

Client Financial Report

Thursday, April 12, 2012
5:17:00 PM

Client Number	Client Name	Amount Paid	Current Due	Hrs YTD	Business Analyst Number
BA53	Bavant Animal Hospital	$0.00	$7,500.00	0.00	11
BB32	Babbage CPA Firm	$1,500.00	$500.00	5.00	14
BC76	Buda Community Clinic	$2,500.00	$750.00	2.50	11
CJ29	Catering by Jenna	$3,000.00	$1,000.00	15.50	27
GA74	Grant Antiques	$5,500.00	$3,200.00	34.50	14
GF56	Granger Foundation	$0.00	$6,500.00	0.00	11
HC10	Hendley County Hospital	$3,100.00	$1,200.00	12.00	27
KD21	KAL Design Studio	$6,000.00	$3,200.00	30.50	14
KG04	Kyle Grocery Cooperative	$3,200.00	$0.00	5.00	11
ME14	Mike's Electronic Stop	$2,500.00	$1,500.00	8.50	27
PJ34	Patricia Jean Florist	$0.00	$5,200.00	0.00	27
SL77	Smarter Law Associates	$3,800.00	$0.00	10.50	11
TB17	The Bikeshop	$2,750.00	$1,200.00	14.00	27
WE05	Walburg Energy Alternatives	$4,500.00	$1,450.00	19.50	14
WS01	Woody Sporting Goods	$2,250.00	$1,600.00	18.50	14
		$40,600.00	$34,800.00	176.00	

Figure 1–74

To Create a Report

You will first create a report containing all fields. The following steps create and save the initial report. They also modify the report title.

- Be sure the Client table is selected in the Navigation Pane.

- Click Create on the Ribbon to display the Create tab (Figure 1–75).

Q&A

Why do I need to select the Client table prior to clicking Create on the Ribbon?

You do not need to select it at that point. You do need to select it prior to clicking the Report button at the next step because Access will include all the fields in whichever table or query is currently selected.

Figure 1–75

- Click the Report button (Create tab | Reports group) to create the report (Figure 1–76).

Q&A

Why is the report title Client?

Access automatically assigns the name of the table or query as the title. It also automatically includes the date. You can change either of these later.

Figure 1–76

3

- Click the Save button on the Quick Access Toolbar to display the Save As dialog box and then type `Client Financial Report` as the name of the report (Figure 1–77).

Figure 1–77

4

- Click the OK button (Save As dialog box) to save the report (Figure 1–78).

The name of the report changed. Why did the report title not change too?

The report title just happens to begin with the same name as the report. If you change the name of the report, Access will not change the report title. You can change it at any time to any title you like.

Figure 1–78

5

- Close the report by clicking its Close button.

Using Layout View in a Report

When working with a report in Access, there are four different ways to view the report. They are Report view, Print Preview, Layout view, and Design view. Report view shows the report on the screen. Print Preview shows the report as it will appear when printed. Layout view is similar to Report view in that it shows the report on the screen, but it also allows you to make changes to the report. It is usually the easiest way to make such changes. Design view also allows you to make changes, but it does not show you the actual report. It is most useful when the changes you need to make are especially complex. In this chapter, you will use Layout view to modify the report.

To Modify Column Headings and Resize Columns

To make the report match the one in Figure 1–74, you need to change the title, remove some columns, modify the column headings, and also resize the columns. The following steps use Layout view to make the necessary modifications to the report.

 1

- Right-click Client Financial Report in the Navigation Pane, and then click Layout View on the shortcut menu to open the report in Layout view.

- If a Field list appears, click the Add Existing Fields button (Report Layout Tools Design tab | Tools group) to remove the Field list from the screen.

- Close the Navigation Pane.

- Click the report title once to select it.

- Click the report title a second time to produce an insertion point (Figure 1–79).

Figure 1–79

Q&A

I clicked at a different position in the title and my insertion point is in the middle of Client. How do I produce an insertion point at the position shown in the figure?

You can use the RIGHT ARROW key to move the insertion point to the position in the figure or you can click the desired position.

 2

- Press the SPACEBAR to insert a space and then type **Financial Report** to complete the title.

- Click the column heading for the Street field to select it.

- Hold the SHIFT key down and then click the column headings for the City field, the State field, and the Postal Code fields to select multiple column headings.

Q&A

What happens if I do not hold down the SHIFT key?

As soon as you click the column heading, it will be the only one that is selected. To select multiple objects, you need to hold the SHIFT key down for every object after the first one.

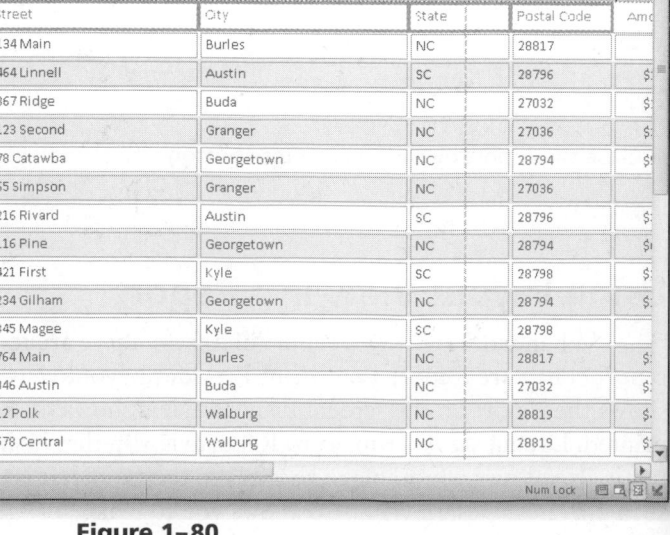

Figure 1–80

I selected the wrong collection of objects. What should I do?

You can click somewhere else on the report so that the objects you want are not selected, and then begin the process again. Alternatively, you can repeatedly click the Undo button on the Quick Access Toolbar to undo your selections. Once you have done so, you can select the objects you want.

• Click Arrange on the Ribbon to display the Arrange tab (Figure 1–80).

3

• Click the Select Column button (Report Layout Tools Arrange tab | Rows & Columns group) to select the entire columns corresponding to the column headings you selected in the previous step.

• Press the DELETE key to delete the columns.

• Click the column heading for the Client Number field twice, once to select it and the second time to produce an insertion point (Figure 1–81).

I inadvertently selected the wrong field. What should I do?

Click somewhere outside the various fields to deselect the one you have selected. Then, click the Client Number field twice.

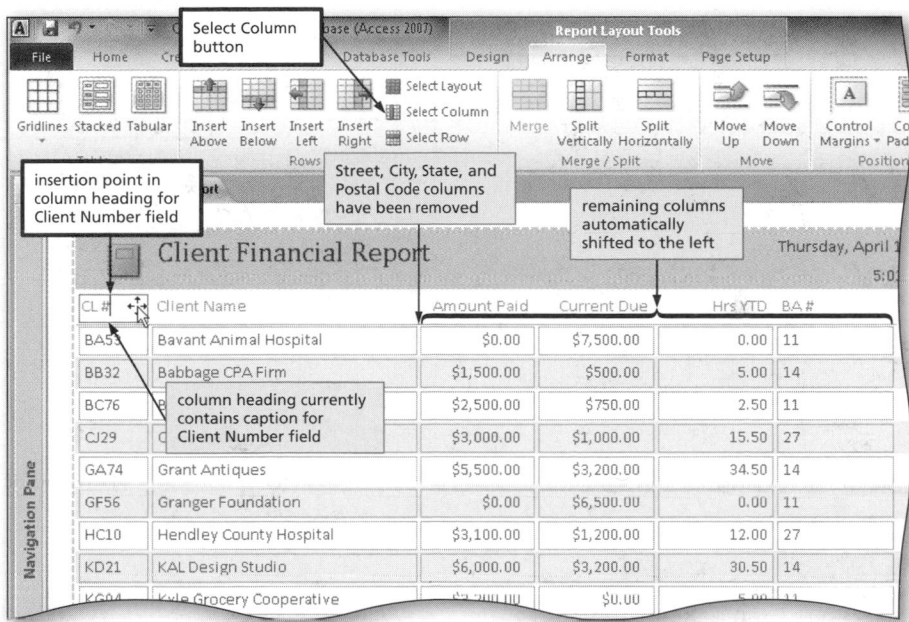

Figure 1–81

4

• Use the DELETE or BACKSPACE keys as necessary to erase the current entry and then type **Client Number** as the new entry.

• Click the heading for the Business Analyst Number field twice, erase the current entry, and then type **Business Analyst Number** as the new entry.

• Click the Client Number field heading to select it, point to the lower boundary of the heading for the Client Number field so that the mouse pointer changes to a two-headed arrow and then drag the lower boundary to the approximate position shown in Figure 1–82 to expand the column headings.

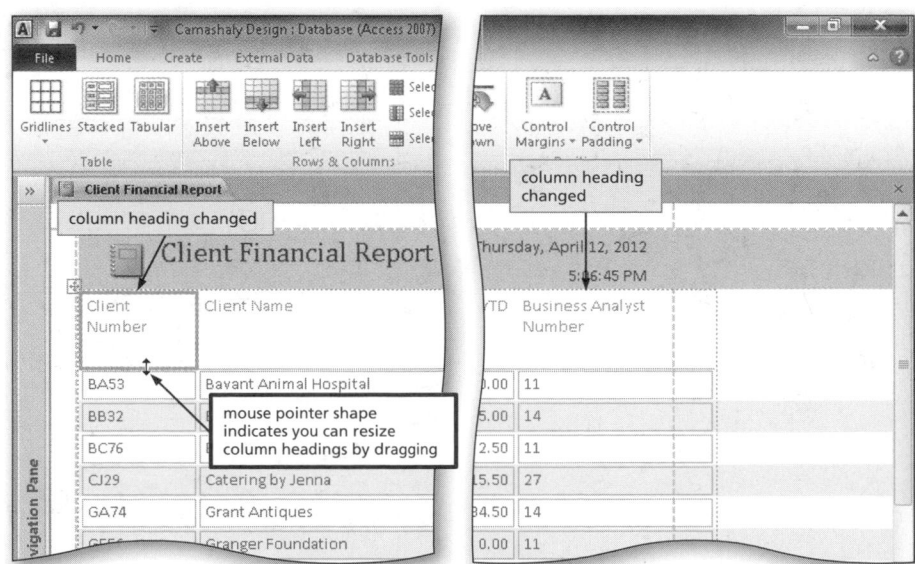

Figure 1–82

Do I have to be exact?

No. If you are in a slightly different position, your report would look a little different from the one in the figure, but the difference would not be significant.

5

- Point to the right boundary of the heading for the Client Number field so that the mouse pointer changes to a two-headed arrow and then drag the right boundary to the approximate position shown in Figure 1–83 to reduce the width of the column.

Q&A

Do I have to be exact?

No. Again, if you are in a slightly different position, the difference between your report and the one in the figure would not be significant.

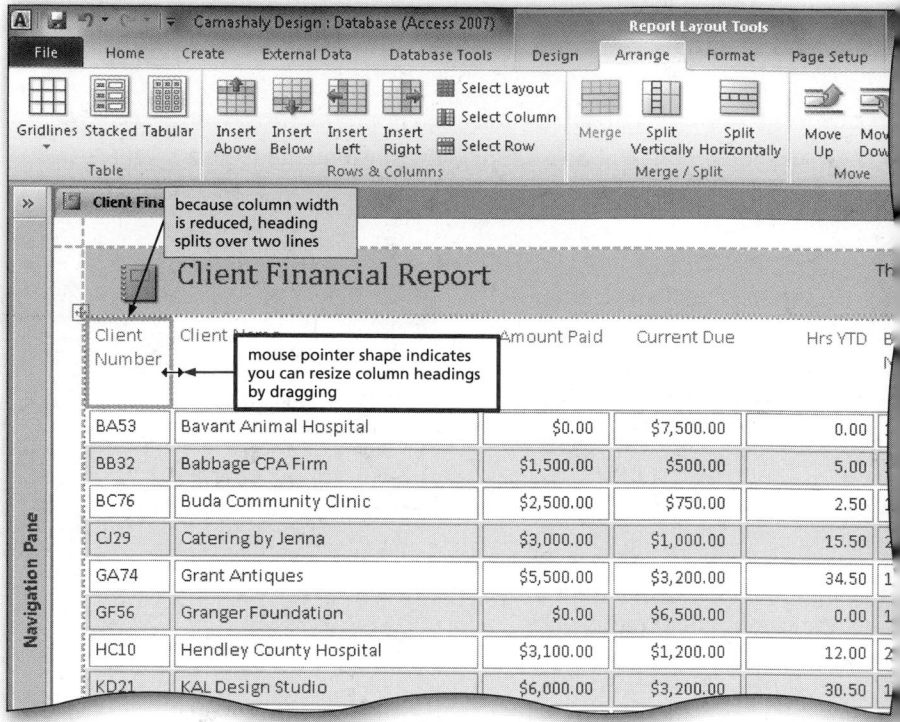

Figure 1–83

6

- Using the same technique, resize the other columns to the sizes shown in Figure 1–84.

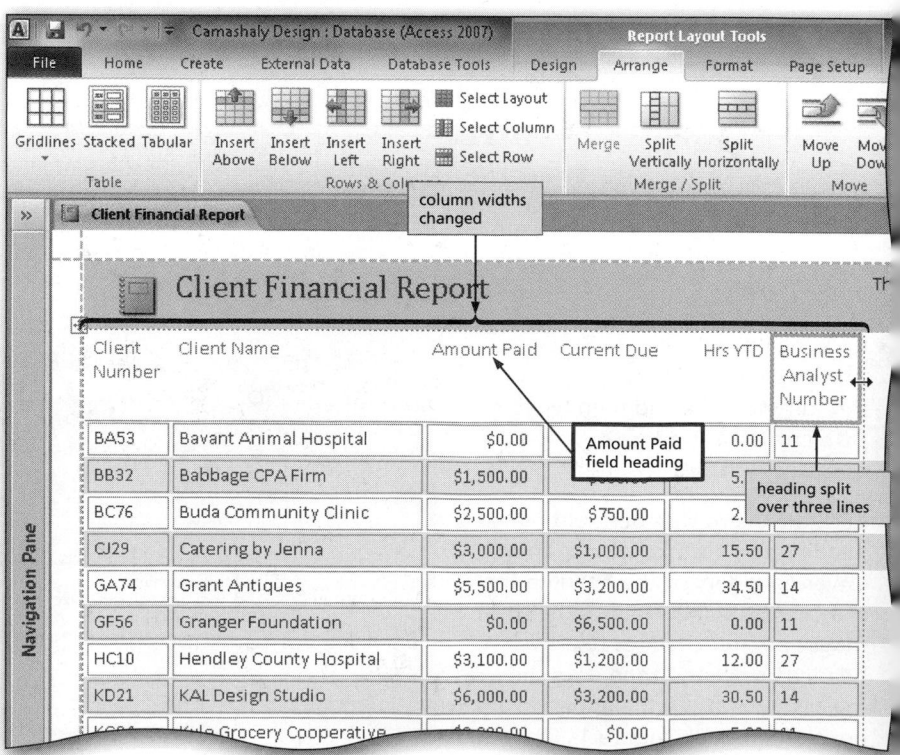

Figure 1–84

To Add Totals to a Report

The report in Figure 1–74 contains totals for the Amount Paid, Current Due, and Hrs YTD columns. You can use Layout view to add these totals. The following steps use Layout view to include totals for these three columns.

1

- Click the Amount Paid field heading (shown in Figure 1–84) to select the field.

  Do I have to click the heading? Could I click the field on one of the records?

  You do not have to click the heading. You also could click the Amount Paid field on any record.

- Click Design on the Ribbon to display the Design tab.

- Click the Totals button (Report Layout Tools Design tab | Grouping & Totals group) to display the list of available calculations (Figure 1–85).

Figure 1–85

2

- Click Sum to calculate the sum of the amount of paid values.

  Is Sum the same as Total?

  Yes.

- Using the same technique, add totals for the Current Due and Hrs YTD columns.

- Scroll down to the bottom of the report to verify that the totals are included. If necessary, expand the size of the total controls so they appear completely.

- Click the Page number to select it and then drag it to the approximate position shown in Figure 1–86.

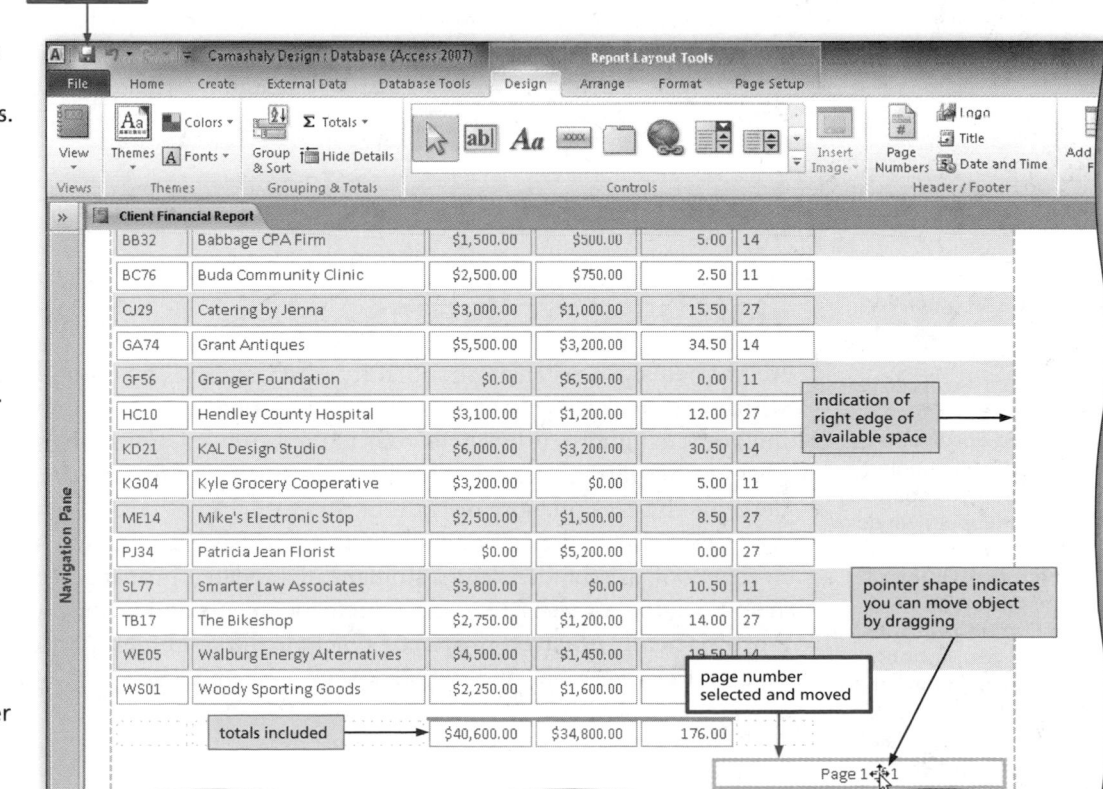

Figure 1–86

Q&A Why did I need to move the page number?

The dotted line near the right-hand edge of the screen indicates the right-hand border of the available space on the printed page, based on whatever margins and orientation are currently selected. A portion of the page number extends beyond this border. By moving the page number, it no longer extends beyond the border.

- Click the Save button on the Quick Access Toolbar to save your changes to the report layout.
- Close the report.

To Print a Report

The following steps print the report.

1 With the Client Financial Report selected in the Navigation Pane, click File on the Ribbon to open the Backstage view.

2 Click the Print tab in the Backstage view to display the Print gallery.

3 Click the Quick Print button to print the report.

Q&A How can I print multiple copies of my report?

Click File on the Ribbon to open the Backstage view. Click the Print tab, click Print in the Print gallery to display the Print dialog box, increase the number in the Number of Copies box, and then click the OK button (Print dialog box).

Q&A How can I print a range of pages rather than printing the whole report?

Click File on the Ribbon to open the Backstage view. Click the Print tab, click Print in the Print gallery to display the Print dialog box, click the Pages option button in the Print Range area, enter the desired page range, and then click the OK button (Print dialog box).

Database Properties

Access helps you organize and identify your databases by using **database properties**, which are the details about a file. Database properties, also known as **metadata**, can include such information as the file's author, title, or subject. **Keywords** are words or phrases that further describe the database. For example, a class name or database topic can describe the file's purpose or content.

Five different types of document properties exist, but the more common ones used in this book are standard and automatically updated properties. **Standard properties** are associated with all Microsoft Office documents and include author, title, and subject. **Automatically updated properties** include file system properties, such as the date you create or change a file, and statistics, such as the file size.

To Change Database Properties

The Database Properties dialog box contains areas where you can view and enter database properties. You can view and change information in this dialog box at anytime while you are working on your database. It is a good idea to add your name and class name as database properties. You also can add keywords that further describe your database. The following steps use the Properties dialog box to change database properties.

- Click File on the Ribbon to open the Backstage view.

- If necessary, click the Info tab in the Backstage view to display the Info gallery (Figure 1–87).

How do I close the Backstage view?

Click File on the Ribbon or click the preview of the document in the Info gallery to return to the Access database window.

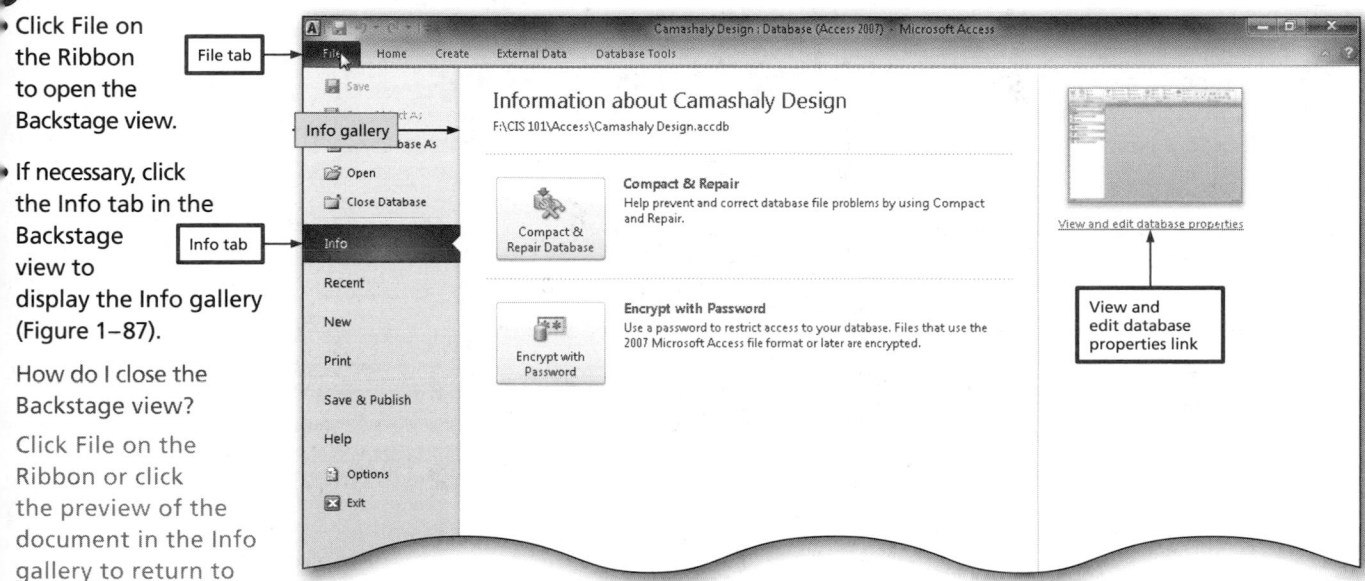

Figure 1–87

- Click the 'View and edit database properties' link in the right pane of the Info gallery to display the Camashaly Design.accdb Properties dialog box (Figure 1–88).

Why are some of the database properties in my Properties dialog box already filled in?

The person who installed Microsoft Office 2010 on your computer or network may have set or customized the properties.

Figure 1–88

3

- If necessary, click the Summary tab.

- Click the Subject text box, if necessary delete any existing text, and then type `CIS 101, Section 20` as the Subject property.

- Click the Author text box and then type `Trevor Wilkins` as the Author property. If a name already is displayed in the Author text box, delete it before typing the new name.

- Click the Keywords text box, if necessary delete any existing text, and then type `online marketing, Web site design` as the Keywords property (Figure 1–89).

Q&A

What types of properties does Access collect automatically?

Access records such details as when the database was created, when it was last modified, total editing time, and the various objects contained in the database.

Figure 1–89

4

- Click the OK button to save your changes and remove the Camashaly Design.accdb Properties dialog box from the screen.

To Quit Access

The following steps quit Access.

1 Click the Close button on the right side of the title bar to quit Access.

2 If a Microsoft Access dialog box appears, click the Save button to save any changes made to the object since the last save.

Special Database Operations

The special operations involved in maintaining a database are backup, recovery, compacting a database, and repairing a database.

Backup and Recovery

It is possible to damage or destroy a database. Users can enter data that is incorrect; programs that are updating the database can end abnormally during an update; a hardware problem can occur; and so on. After any such event has occurred, the database may contain invalid data. It even might be totally destroyed.

Obviously, you cannot allow a situation in which data has been damaged or destroyed to go uncorrected. You must somehow return the database to a correct state. This process is called recovery; that is, you **recover** the database.

The simplest approach to recovery involves periodically making a copy of the database (called a **backup copy** or a **save copy**). This is referred to as **backing up** the database. If a problem occurs, you correct the problem by copying this backup copy over the actual database, often referred to as the **live database**.

To back up the database that is currently open, you use the Back Up Database command on the Save & Publish tab in the Backstage view. In the process, Access suggests a name that is a combination of the database name and the current date. For example, if you back up the Camashaly Design database on April 20, 2012, Access will suggest the name, Camashaly Design_2012-04-20. You can change this name if you desire, although it is a good idea to use this name. By doing so, it will be easy to distinguish between all the backup copies you have made to determine which is the most recent. In addition, if you discover that a critical problem occurred on April 18, 2012, you may want to go back to the most recent backup before April 18. If, for example, the database was not backed up on April 17 but was backed up on April 16, you would use Camashaly Design_2012-04-16.

To Back Up a Database

You would use the following steps to back up a database to a file on a hard disk or high-capacity removable disk.

1. Open the database to be backed up.
2. Click File on the Ribbon to open the Backstage view, and then click the Save & Publish tab.
3. With Save Database As selected in the File Types area, click Back Up Database in the Save Database As area, and then click the Save As button.
4. Selected the desired location in the Save As box. If you do not want the name Access has suggested, enter the desired name in the File name text box.
5. Click the Save button to back up the database.

Access creates a backup copy with the desired name in the desired location. Should you ever need to recover the database using this backup copy, you can simply copy it over the live version.

Compacting and Repairing a Database

As you add more data to a database, it naturally grows larger. When you delete an object (records, tables, forms, or queries), the space previously occupied by the object does not become available for additional objects. Instead, the additional objects are given new space; that is, space that was not already allocated. To remove this wasted space from the database, you must **compact** the database. The same option that compacts the database also repairs problems that might have occurred in the database.

To Compact and Repair a Database

You would use the following steps to compact and repair a database.

1. Open the database to be compacted.
2. Click File on the Ribbon to open the Backstage view, and then, if necessary, select the Info tab.
3. Click the Compact & Repair Database button in the Info gallery to compact and repair the database.

The database now is the compacted form of the original.

BTW

Access Help
At any time while using
Access, you can find
answers to questions
and display information
about various topics
through Help. Used
properly, this form of
assistance can increase
your productivity and
reduce your frustrations
by minimizing the time
you spend learning how to
use Access. For instruction
about Access Help and
exercises that will help you
gain confidence in using it,
read the Office 2010 and
Windows 7 chapter at the
beginning of this book.

BTW

Certification
The Microsoft Office
Specialist (MOS) program
provides an opportunity
for you to obtain a
valuable industry
credential — proof that you
have the Access 2010 skills
required by employers. For
more information, visit the
Access 2010 Certification
Web page (scsite.com/
ac2010/cert).

BTW

Quick Reference
For a table that lists how
to complete the tasks
covered in this book
using the mouse, Ribbon,
shortcut menu, and
keyboard, see the Quick
Reference Summary at
the back of this book,
or visit the Access 2010
Quick Reference Web page
(scsite.com/ac2010/qr).

Additional Operations

Additional special operations include opening another database, closing a database without quitting Access, and saving a database with another name. They also include deleting a table (or other object) as well as renaming an object. Finally, you can change properties of a table or other object, such as the object's description.

When you open another database, Access will automatically close the database that previously was open. Before deleting or renaming an object, you should ensure that the object has no dependent objects; that is, other objects that depend on the object you want to delete.

TO OPEN ANOTHER DATABASE

To open another database, you would use the following steps.

1. Click File on the Ribbon to open the Backstage view.
2. Click Open.
3. Select the database to be opened.
4. Click the Open button.

TO CLOSE A DATABASE WITHOUT QUITTING ACCESS

You would use the following steps to close a database without quitting Access.

1. Click File on the Ribbon to open the Backstage view.
2. Click Close Database.

TO SAVE A DATABASE WITH ANOTHER NAME

To save a database with another name, you would use the following steps.

1. Click File on the Ribbon to open the Backstage view, and then select the Save & Publish tab.
2. With Save Database As selected in the File Types area and Access Database selected in the Save Database As area, click the Save As button.
3. Enter a name and select a location for the new version.
4. Click the Save button.

TO DELETE A TABLE OR OTHER OBJECT IN THE DATABASE

You would use the following steps to delete a database object.

1. Right-click the object in the Navigation Pane.
2. Click Delete on the shortcut menu.
3. Click the Yes button in the Microsoft Access dialog box.

TO RENAME AN OBJECT IN THE DATABASE

You would use the following steps to rename a database object.

1. Right-click the object in the Navigation Pane.
2. Click Rename on the shortcut menu.
3. Type the new name and press the ENTER key.

Chapter Summary

In this chapter you have learned to design a database, create an Access database, create tables and add records to them, print the contents of tables, create queries, create forms, and create reports. You also have learned how to change database properties. The items listed below include all the new Access skills you have learned in this chapter.

1. Start Access (AC 12)
2. Create a Database (AC 13)
3. Create a Database Using a Template (AC 14)
4. Modify the Primary Key (AC 16)
5. Define the Remaining Fields in a Table (AC 19)
6. Save a Table (AC 21)
7. View the Table in Design View (AC 21)
8. Close the Table (AC 23)
9. Add Records to a Table (AC 23)
10. Quit Access (AC 26)
11. Open a Database from Access (AC 27)
12. Add Additional Records to a Table (AC 28)
13. Resize Columns in a Datasheet (AC 29)
14. Preview and Print the Contents of a Table (AC 31)
15. Create a Table in Design View (AC 33)
16. Import an Excel Worksheet (AC 38)
17. Use the Simple Query Wizard to Create a Query (AC 43)
18. Use a Criterion in a Query (AC 46)
19. Print the Results of a Query (AC 48)
20. Create a Form (AC 48)
21. Create a Report (AC 52)
22. Modify Column Headings and Resize Columns (AC 54)
23. Add Totals to a Report (AC 57)
24. Change Database Properties (AC 59)
25. Back Up a Database (AC 61)
26. Compact and Repair a Database (AC 61)
27. Open Another Database (AC 62)
28. Close a Database without Quitting Access (AC 62)
29. Save a Database with Another Name (AC 62)
30. Delete a Table or Other Object in the Database (AC 62)
31. Rename an Object in the Database (AC 62)

 If you have a SAM 2010 user profile, your instructor may have assigned an autogradable version of this assignment. If so, log into the SAM 2010 Web site at www.cengage.com/sam2010 to download the instruction and start files.

Learn It Online

Test your knowledge of chapter content and key terms.

Instructions: To complete the Learn It Online exercises, start your browser, click the Address bar, and then enter the Web address **scsite.com/ac2010/learn**. When the Access 2010 Learn It Online page is displayed, click the link for the exercise you want to complete and then read the instructions.

Chapter Reinforcement TF, MC, and SA
A series of true/false, multiple choice, and short answer questions that test your knowledge of the chapter content.

Flash Cards
An interactive learning environment where you identify chapter key terms associated with displayed definitions.

Practice Test
A series of multiple choice questions that test your knowledge of chapter content and key terms.

Who Wants To Be a Computer Genius?
An interactive game that challenges your knowledge of chapter content in the style of a television quiz show.

Wheel of Terms
An interactive game that challenges your knowledge of chapter key terms in the style of the television show *Wheel of Fortune*.

Crossword Puzzle Challenge
A crossword puzzle that challenges your knowledge of key terms presented in the chapter.

Apply Your Knowledge

Reinforce the skills and apply the concepts you learned in this chapter.

Adding a Caption, Creating a Query, Creating a Form, and Creating a Report

Instructions: Start Access. Open the Babbage CPA Firm database. See the inside back cover of this book for instructions for downloading the Data Files for Students, or see your instructor for information on accessing the files required in this book.

The Babbage CPA Firm employs bookkeepers who maintain the books for those clients who need bookkeeping services. The Babbage CPA Firm has a database that keeps track of its bookkeepers and clients. Each client is assigned to a single bookkeeper, but each bookkeeper may be assigned many clients. The database has two tables. The Client table contains data on the clients who use the bookkeeping services of the Babbage CPA Firm. The Bookkeeper table contains data on the bookkeepers employed by Babbage CPA Firm.

Perform the following tasks:

1. Open the Bookkeeper table in Design view and add BKR # as the caption for Bookkeeper Number. Save the changes to the table.

2. Open the Bookkeeper table in Datasheet view and resize all columns to best fit the data. Save the changes to the layout of the table.

3. Use the Simple Query Wizard to create a query for the Client table that contains the Client Number, Client Name, Amount Paid, and Balance Due. Use the name, Client Query, for the query.

4. Create a simple form for the Bookkeeper table. Use the name, Bookkeeper, for the form.

5. Close the Bookkeeper form.

6. Create the report shown in Figure 1–90 for the Client table. The report includes totals for both the Amount Paid and Balance Due fields. Be sure the totals appear completely. You might need to expand the size of the controls. Move the page number so that it is within the margins.

7. Compact the database.

8. Back up the database.

9. Change the database properties, as specified by your instructor. Submit the revised database in the format specified by your instructor.

Client Number	Client Name	Amount Paid	Balance Due	Bookkeeper Number
A54	Afton Mills	$575.00	$315.00	22
A62	Atlas Suppliers	$250.00	$175.00	24
B26	Blake-Scripps	$875.00	$250.00	24
D76	Dege Grocery	$1,015.00	$325.00	22
G56	Grand Cleaners	$485.00	$165.00	24
H21	Hill Shoes	$0.00	$285.00	34
J77	Jones Plumbing	$685.00	$0.00	22
M26	Mohr Crafts	$125.00	$185.00	24
S56	SeeSaw Industries	$1,200.00	$645.00	22
T45	Tate Repair	$345.00	$200.00	34
W24	Woody Sporting Goods	$975.00	$0.00	34
C29	Catering by Jenna	$0.00	$250.00	34
		$6,530.00	$2,795.00	

Client Financial Report

Thursday, April 12, 2012
8:38:16 PM

Figure 1–90

Extend Your Knowledge

Extend the skills you learned in this chapter and experiment with new skills. You may need to use Help to complete the assignment.

Using a Database Template to Create a Students Database

Instructions: Access includes a number of templates that you can use to create a beginning database that can be modified to meet your specific needs. You will create a Students database using the Students template. The database includes sample tables, queries, forms, and reports. You will change the database and create the Student Birthdays Query, shown in Figure 1–91.

Figure 1–91

Perform the following tasks:

1. Start Access.

2. With a USB flash drive connected to one of the computer's USB ports, ensure the New tab is selected in the Backstage view and select Sample templates in the New gallery.

3. Select the Students template and create a new database on your USB drive with the file name, Students.

4. Close the Student List form and change the organization of the Navigation Pane to Tables and Related Views .

5. Delete the Student Details form.

6. Use the Query Wizard to create the query shown in Figure 1–91. Save the query as Student Birthdays Query.

7. Open the Student Phone List in Layout view and use the tools on the Format tab to make the Student Phone List title bold and change the font size to 24. Delete the control containing the time.

8. Save your changes to the report.

9. Compact the database.

0. Change the database properties, as specified by your instructor. Submit the revised database in the format specified by your instructor.

Make It Right

Analyze a database and correct all errors and/or improve the design.

Correcting Errors in the Table Structure

Instructions: Start Access. Open the Beach Rentals database. See the inside back cover of this book for instructions for downloading the Data Files for Students, or see your instructor for information on accessing the files required in this book.

Beach Rentals is a database containing information on rental properties available at a beach resort. The Rentals table shown in Figure 1–92 contains a number of errors in the table structure. You are to correct these errors before any additional records can be added to the table. The Rental Code field is a Text field that contains a maximum of three characters. The field Address was omitted from the table. The Address field is a Text field with a maximum of 20 characters. It should appear after Rental Code. Only whole numbers should be allowed in the Bedrooms and Bathrooms fields. The column heading Weakly Rental is misspelled, and the field should contain monetary values. The Distance field represents the walking distance from the beach; the field should display two decimal places. The table name should be Rental Units, not Rentals.

Change the database properties, as specified by your instructor. Submit the revised database in the format specified by your instructor.

Figure 1–92

In the Lab

Design, create, modify, and/or use a database using the guidelines, concepts, and skills presented in this chapter. Labs are listed in order of increasing difficulty.

Lab 1: Creating Objects for the ECO Clothesline Database

Problem: ECO Clothesline is a local company that designs and manufactures eco-friendly casual wear, yoga clothing, and fitness apparel. All clothes are made from earth-friendly fabrics, such as bamboo, hemp, organic cotton, and natural silk. The company recently decided to store its customer and sales rep data in a database. Each customer is assigned to a single sales rep, but each sales rep may be assigned many customers. The database and the Customer table have been created, but there is no data in the Customer table. The Sales Rep table has not been created. The company plans to import the Customer data from an Excel workbook, shown in Figure 1–93a. The other Excel workbook (Figure 1–93b) contains information on the sales representatives that ECO employs. ECO would like to finish storing this data in a database and has asked for your help.

Instructions: Perform the following tasks: Start Access and open the ECO Clothesline database. See the inside back cover of this book for instructions for downloading the Data Files for Students, or see your instructor for information on accessing the files required in this book.

1. Import the Lab 1-1 Customer Data workbook into the Customer table.

2. Add the captions Cust # to the Customer Number field and SR # to the Sales Rep Number field in the Customer table and save the changes.

3. Open the Customer table in Datasheet view and resize the columns to best fit the data. Save the changes to the layout of the table.

4. Use Datasheet view to create a table in which to store the data related to sales reps. Use the name Sales Rep for the table. The fields and the data for the Sales Rep table are shown in Figure 1–93b.

	A	B	C	D	E	F	G	H	I	J	K
1	Customer Number	Customer Name	Street	City	State	Postal Code	Balance	Amount Paid	Sales Rep Number		
2	AM23	Amy's Store	223 Johnson	Oxford	TN	37021	195.00	1,695.00	44		
3	BF34	Barbara's Fashions	1939 Jackson	Lowton	TN	37084	150.00	0.00	51		
4	BL15	Blondie's on Main	3294 Main	Oxford	TN	37021	555.00	1,350.00	49		
5	CM09	Casual by Marie	3140 Halsted	Ashton	VA	20123	295.00	1,080.00	51		
6	CY12	Curlin Yoga Studio	1632 Clark	Georgetown	NC	28794	145.00	710.00	49		
7	DG14	Della's Designs	312 Gilham	Granger	NC	27036	340.00	850.00	44		
8	EC07	Environmentally Casual	1805 Broadway	Pineville	VA	22503	0.00	1,700.00	44		
9	FN19	Fitness Counts	675 Main	Oxford	TN	37021	345.00	1,950.00	51		
10	JN34	Just Natural	2200 Lawrence	Ashton	VA	20123	360.00	700.00	49		
11	LB20	Le Beauty	13 Devon	Lowton	TN	37084	200.00	1,250.00	49		
12	NC25	Nancy's Place	1027 Wells	Walburg	NC	28819	240.00	550.00	44		
13	RD03	Rose's Day Spa	787 Monroe	Pineville	VA	22503	0.00	975.00	51		
14	TT21	Tan and Tone	1939 Congress	Ashton	VA	20123	160.00	725.00	44		
15	TW56	The Workout Place	34 Gilham	Granger	NC	27036	680.00	125.00	51		
16	WS34	Woody's Sporting Goods	578 Central	Walburg	NC	28819	1,235.00	0.00	49		
17											

(a) Customer Data (Excel Workbook to import)

	A	B	C	D	E	F	G	H	I	J
1	Sales Rep Number	Last Name	First Name	Street	City	State	Postal Code	Base Pay YTD	Comm Rate	
2	44	Jones	Pat	43 Third	Oxford	TN	37021	13,000.00	0.05	
3	49	Gupta	Pinn	678 Hillcrest	Georgetown	NC	28794	15,000.00	0.06	
4	51	Ortiz	Gabe	982 Victoria	Ashton	VA	20123	12,500.00	0.05	
5	55	Sinson	Terry	45 Elm	Walburg	NC	28819	500.00	0.04	
6										

(b) Sales Rep Data (add records to Sales Rep table)

Figure 1–93

The primary key for the Sales Rep table is Sales Rep Number. Assign the caption SR # to the Sales Rep Number field. Comm Rate is a Number field, and Base Pay YTD is a Currency data type. The field size for Sales Rep Number is 2. The State field size is 2, and the Postal Code field size is 5. All other text fields have a field size of 15.

5. Open the Sales Rep table in Design view and change the field size for the Comm Rate field to Single, the format to Fixed, and the Decimal Places to 2.

6. Add the data shown in Figure 1–93b to the Sales Rep table. Resize the columns to best fit the data. Save the changes to the layout of the table.

7. Create a query using the Simple Query Wizard for the Customer table that displays the Customer Number, Customer Name, Balance, Amount Paid, and Sales Rep Number fields. Use the name Customer Query.

8. Create and save the report shown in Figure 1–94 for the Customer table. The report should include Customer Number, Customer Name, Balance, and Sales Rep Number fields. Include a total for the Balance field.

9. Change the database properties, as specified by your instructor. Submit the revised database in the format specified by your instructor.

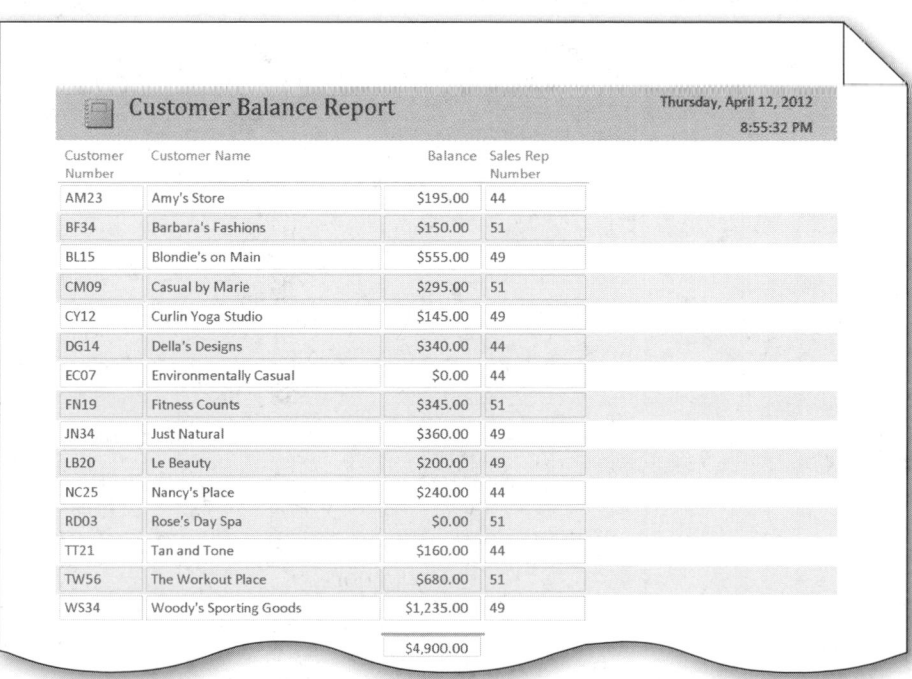

Customer Balance Report   Thursday, April 12, 2012
                                                          8:55:32 PM

Customer Number	Customer Name	Balance	Sales Rep Number
AM23	Amy's Store	$195.00	44
BF34	Barbara's Fashions	$150.00	51
BL15	Blondie's on Main	$555.00	49
CM09	Casual by Marie	$295.00	51
CY12	Curlin Yoga Studio	$145.00	49
DG14	Della's Designs	$340.00	44
EC07	Environmentally Casual	$0.00	44
FN19	Fitness Counts	$345.00	51
JN34	Just Natural	$360.00	49
LB20	Le Beauty	$200.00	49
NC25	Nancy's Place	$240.00	44
RD03	Rose's Day Spa	$0.00	51
TT21	Tan and Tone	$160.00	44
TW56	The Workout Place	$680.00	51
WS34	Woody's Sporting Goods	$1,235.00	49
		$4,900.00	

Figure 1–94

In the Lab

Lab 2: Creating the Walburg Energy Alternatives Database

Problem: Walburg Energy Alternatives is a nonprofit organization that promotes the use of energy alternatives such as solar power and wind power. The organization provides a variety of services and funds itself through donations. Recently, the organization decided to sell a small number of items in its education center to help fund programs. The store purchases the items from vendors that deal in energy-saving products. Currently, the information about the items and vendors is stored in the Excel workbook shown in Figure 1–95. Each item is assigned to a single vendor, but each vendor may be assigned many items. You volunteer part-time at the store, and the store manager has asked you to create a database that will store the item and vendor information. You have already determined that you need two tables in which to store the information: an Item table and a Vendor table.

Instructions: Perform the following tasks:

1. Design a new database in which to store all the objects related to the items for sale. Call the database Walburg Energy Alternatives.

2. Use the information shown in the Excel workbook in Figure 1–95 to determine the primary keys and determine additional fields. Then, determine the relationships between tables, the data types, and the field sizes. (*Hint:* Item Number is a text field and On Hand is a number field.)

3. Create the Item table using the information shown in Figure 1–95.

4. Create the Vendor table using the information shown in Figure 1–95. Be sure that the field size for the Vendor Code in the Item table is identical to the field size for the Vendor Code in the Vendor table. Add the caption, Phone, for the Telephone Number field.

Figure 1–95

5. Add the appropriate data to the Item table. Resize the columns to best fit the data and save the changes to the layout.

6. Add the appropriate data to the Vendor table. Resize the columns to best fit the data and save the changes to the layout.

7. Create a query for the Item table. Include the Item Number, Description, Cost, Selling Price, and Vendor Code in the query. Save the query as Item Query.

8. Open the Item Query and add a criterion to limit retrieval to those items supplied by Scryps Distributors. Save the query as Item-Scryps Query.

9. Create a simple form for the Item table. Use the name, Item, for the form.

10. Create the report shown in Figure 1–96 for the Item table. Do not add any totals.

11. Change the database properties, as specified by your instructor. Submit the database in the format specified by your instructor.

Inventory Status Report

Thursday, April 12, 2012
8:56:19 PM

Item Number	Description	On Hand	Cost
3663	Air Deflector	8	$5.45
3673	Energy Booklet	25	$2.70
4553	Energy Saving Kit	7	$42.75
4573	Faucet Aerator	20	$0.89
4583	Fluorescent Light Bulb	18	$4.50
5923	Low Flow Shower Head	11	$8.75
6185	Luminescent Night Light	12	$3.75
6234	Programmable Thermostat	3	$34.25
6345	Rain Gauge	16	$2.89
7123	Retractable Clothesline	10	$13.25
7934	Shower Timer	15	$2.45
8136	Smoke Detector	10	$6.10
8344	Toilet Tank Water Saver	18	$3.35
8590	Water Conservation Kit	8	$13.45
9458	Windows Insulator Kit	10	$4.95

Figure 1–96

In the Lab

Lab 3: Creating the Philamar Training Database

Problem: Philamar Training provides business processes and information technology training to various companies and organizations. Philamar employs trainers who work with individual companies to determine training needs and then conduct the training. Currently, Philamar keeps data on clients and trainers in two Word documents and two Excel workbooks. Philamar also keeps track of which clients are assigned to which trainers. Each client is assigned to a single trainer, but each trainer might be assigned many clients. Currently, clients BS27, FI28, and MC28 are assigned to trainer 42, Belinda Perry. Clients CE16, CP27, FL93, HN83, and TE26 are assigned to trainer 48, Michael Stevens. Clients EU28 and PS82 are assigned to trainer 53, Manuel Gonzalez. Philamar has an additional trainer, Marty Danville, who has been assigned trainer number 67, but who has not yet been assigned any clients.

Instructions: Using the data shown in Figure 1–97 and the information in the previous paragraph, design the Philamar Training database. The data shown in Figure 1–97 is included in the Data Files for Students in the following files: Lab 1-3a.docx, Lab 1-3b.docx, Lab 1-3c.xlsx, and Lab 1-3d.xlsx. Use the database design guidelines in this chapter to help you in the design process.

Client Number	Client Name	Address	City	State	Postal Code
BS27	Blant and Sons	4806 Park	Kingston	TX	76653
CE16	Center Services	725 Mitchell	San Rita	TX	78364
CP27	Calder Plastics	7300 Cedar	Kingston	TX	76653
EU28	Elba's Furniture	1445 Hubert	Tallmadge	TX	77231
FI28	Farrow-Idsen	829 Wooster	Cedar Ridge	TX	79342
FL93	Fairland Lawn	143 Pangborn	Kingston	TX	76653
HN83	Hurley National	3827 Burgess	Tallmadge	TX	77231
MC28	Morgan-Alyssa	923 Williams	Crumville	TX	76745
PS82	PRIM Staffing	72 Crestview	San Rita	TX	78364
TE26	Telton-Edwards	5672 Anderson	Dunston	TX	77893

(a) Client Address Information (Word Table)

	A	B	C	D	E
1	Client Number	Client Name	Amount Paid	Current Due	
2	BS27	Blant and Sons	$11,876.00	$892.50	
3	CE16	Center Services	$12,512.00	$1,672.00	
4	CP27	Calder Plastics	$5,725.00	$0.00	
5	EU28	Elba's Furniture	$3,245.00	$202.00	
6	FI28	Farrow-Idsen	$8,287.50	$925.50	
7	FL93	Fairland Lawn	$976.00	$0.00	
8	HN83	Hurley National	$0.00	$0.00	
9	MC28	Morgan-Alyssa	$3,456.00	$572.00	
10	PS82	PRIM Staffing	$7,500.00	$485.00	
11	TE26	Telton-Edwards	$6,775.00	$0.00	
12					

(c) Client Financial Information (Excel Workbook)

Trainer Number	Last Name	First Name	Address	City	State	Postal Code
42	Perry	Belinda	261 Porter	Burdett	TX	76734
48	Stevens	Michael	3135 Gill	Rockwood	TX	78884
53	Gonzalez	Manuel	265 Maxwell	Camino	TX	76574
67	Danville	Marty	1827 Maple	Dunston	TX	77893

(b) Trainer Address Information (Word Table)

	A	B	C	D	E
1	Trainer Number	Last Name	First Name	Hourly Rate	YTD Earnings
2	42	Perry	Belinda	$23.00	$17,620.00
3	48	Stevens	Michael	$21.00	$13,567.50
4	53	Gonzalez	Manuel	$24.00	$19,885.00
5	67	Danville	Marty	$20.00	$0.00
6					

(d) Trainer Financial Information (Excel Workbook)

Figure 1–97

When you have completed the database design, create the database, create the tables, and add the data to the appropriate tables. Be sure to determine the correct data types and field sizes.

Finally, prepare the Client Query shown in Figure 1–98 and the Client Status Report shown in Figure 1–99. The report does not include totals. Change the database properties, as specified by your instructor. Submit the database in the format specified by your instructor.

Figure 1–98

Client Status Report			Thursday, April 12, 2012	
			8:57:10 PM	

Client Number	Client Name	Amount Paid	Current Due	Trainer Number
BS27	Blant and Sons	$11,876.00	$892.50	42
CE16	Center Services	$12,512.00	$1,672.00	48
CP27	Calder Plastics	$5,725.00	$0.00	48
EU28	Elba's Furniture	$3,245.00	$202.00	53
FI28	Farrow-Idsen	$8,287.50	$925.50	42
FL93	Fairland Lawn	$976.00	$0.00	48
HN83	Hurley National	$0.00	$0.00	48
MC28	Morgan-Alyssa	$3,456.00	$572.00	42
PS82	PRIM Staffing	$7,500.00	$485.00	53
TE26	Telton-Edwards	$6,775.00	$0.00	48

Figure 1–99

Cases and Places

Apply your creative thinking and problem solving skills to design and implement a solution.

See the inside back cover of this book for instructions for downloading the Data Files for Students, or see your instructor for information on accessing the files required in this book.

1: Design and Create an Advertising Database

Academic

You are a Marketing major currently doing an internship with the Chamber of Commerce in a local city. The Chamber publishes a Newcomer's Guide that contains advertisements from local businesses. Ad reps contact the businesses to arrange for advertising. Each advertiser is assigned to a single ad rep, but each ad rep may be assigned many advertisers. The Chamber would like your help in creating a database of advertisers and advertising representatives.

Based on the information in the Case 1-1 Chamber of Commerce workbook, use the concepts and techniques presented in this chapter to design and create a database to store the data that the Chamber needs. Submit your assignment in the format specified by your instructor.

2: Design and Create a Consignment Database

Personal

You are involved in a volunteer organization that provides clothing and school supplies to needy children. Recently, the Board of Directors decided to open a consignment shop as a way to raise additional funds. In a consignment shop, individuals bring in unwanted items, and the shop sells the items. Proceeds are split between the seller and the shop. The database must keep track of the items for sale in the shop as well as maintain data on the sellers. Each item is assigned to a single seller, but each seller may be assigned many items. The Board has asked you to create a database to store information about the consignment items.

Use the concepts and techniques presented in this chapter to design and create a database to store the consignment data. Then create the necessary tables and enter the data from the Case 1-2 Consignment workbook. Create an Available Items Report that lists the item number, description, price, and seller code. Submit your assignment in the format specified by your instructor.

3: Design and Create a Senior Care Database

Professional

You are co-owner of a company, Senior Care, that provides nonmedical services to older adults who need assistance with daily living. Helpers will drive individuals to appointments, do the grocery shopping, fill prescriptions, help with personal care, and provide companionship. Each client is assigned to a single helper, but each helper may be assigned many clients. The other owners have asked you to create a database of clients and helpers. Use the concepts and techniques presented in this chapter to design and create a database to meet Senior Care needs. Then create the necessary tables and enter the data from the Case 1-3 Senior Care workbook. Create a Client Report that lists each client's client number, client last name, client first name, balance, and helper number. Submit your assignment in the format specified by your instructor.

2 | Querying a Database

Objectives

You will have mastered the material in this chapter when you can:

- Create queries using Design view
- Include fields in the design grid
- Use text and numeric data in criteria
- Save a query and use the saved query
- Create and use parameter queries
- Use compound criteria in queries
- Sort data in queries
- Join tables in queries

- Create a report and a form from a query
- Export data from a query to another application
- Perform calculations and calculate statistics in queries
- Create crosstab queries
- Customize the Navigation Pane

2 | Querying a Database

Introduction

BTW

Select Queries
The queries you create in this chapter are select queries. In a select query, you retrieve data from one or more tables using criteria that you specify and display the data in a datasheet.

One of the primary benefits of using a database management system such as Access is the ability to find answers to questions related to data stored in the database. When you pose a question to Access, or any other database management system, the question is called a query. A **query** is simply a question presented in a way that Access can process.

Thus, to find the answer to a question, you first create a corresponding query using the techniques illustrated in this chapter. After you have created the query, you instruct Access to display the query results, that is, to perform the steps necessary to obtain the answer. Access then displays the answer in Datasheet view.

Project — Querying a Database

Organizations and individuals achieve several benefits from storing data in a database and using Access to manage the database. One of the most important benefits is the capability of easily finding the answers to questions and requests such as those shown in Figure 2–1 and the following, which concern the data in the Camashaly Design database:

1. What are the number, name, amount paid, and current due for client BC76?
2. What are the number, name, amount paid, and current due for all clients whose name starts with Gr?
3. Give me the number, name, amount paid, current due, and business analyst number for all clients whose amount paid is more than $3,000 and whose business analyst number is 11.
4. List the client number, name, business analyst number, and amount paid for all clients. Sort the results by business analyst number and amount paid.
5. For each business analyst, list the number, last name, and first name. Also, list the client number and name for each of the business analyst's clients.
6. List the client number, client name, amount paid, current due, and the total amount (amount paid plus current due) for each client.
7. Give me the average amount paid by clients of each business analyst.
8. Summarize the total amount paid by city and by business analyst.

In addition to these questions, Camashaly Design managers need to find information about clients located in a specific city, but they want to enter a different city each time they ask the question. The company can use a parameter query to accomplish this task. Camashaly Design managers also want to summarize data in a specific way, and they can use a crosstab query to present the data in the desired form.

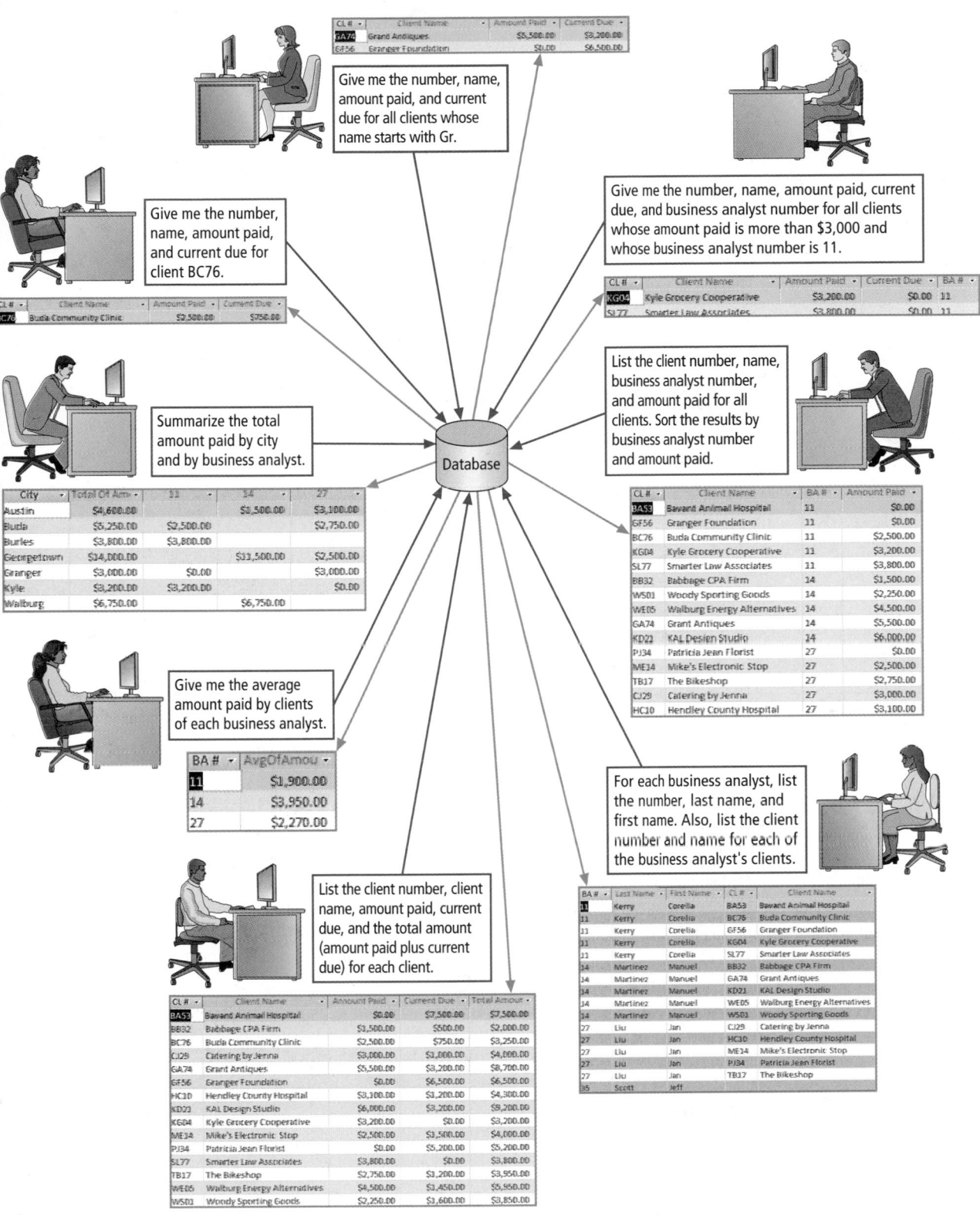

Give me the number, name, amount paid, and current due for all clients whose name starts with Gr.

Give me the number, name, amount paid, current due, and business analyst number for all clients whose amount paid is more than $3,000 and whose business analyst number is 11.

Give me the number, name, amount paid, and current due for client BC76.

List the client number, name, business analyst number, and amount paid for all clients. Sort the results by business analyst number and amount paid.

Summarize the total amount paid by city and by business analyst.

Give me the average amount paid by clients of each business analyst.

For each business analyst, list the number, last name, and first name. Also, list the client number and name for each of the business analyst's clients.

List the client number, client name, amount paid, current due, and the total amount (amount paid plus current due) for each client.

Figure 2–1

Overview

As you read this chapter, you will learn how to query a database by performing these general tasks:

- Create queries using Design view.
- Use criteria in queries.
- Create and use parameter queries.
- Sort data in queries.
- Join tables in queries.
- Create reports and forms from a query.
- Export data from a query.
- Perform calculations in queries.
- Create crosstab queries.

Query Design Decisions

When posing a question to Access, you must design an appropriate query. In the process of designing a query, the decisions you make will determine the fields, tables, criteria, order, and special calculations included in the query. To design a query, you can follow these general guidelines:

1. **Identify the fields.** Examine the question or request to determine which fields from the tables in the database are involved. Examine the contents of these fields to make sure you understand the data type and format for storing the data.

2. **Identify restrictions.** Unless the question or request calls for the inclusion of all records, determine the restrictions or the conditions records must satisfy to be included in the results.

3. **Determine whether special order is required.** Examine the question or request to determine whether the results must appear in some specific order.

4. **Determine whether more than one table is required.** If all the fields identified in Step 1 are in the same table, no special action is required. If this is not the case, identify all tables represented by those fields.

5. **Determine whether calculations are required.** Examine the question or request to determine whether, in addition to the fields determined in Step 1, calculations must be included. Such calculations include individual record calculations (for example, adding the values in two fields) or group calculations (for example, finding the total of the values in a particular field for all the records).

6. **If data is to be summarized, determine whether a crosstab query would be appropriate.** If data is to be grouped by two different types of information, you can use a crosstab query. You will need to identify the two types of information. One of the types will form the row headings and the other will form the column headings in the query results.

When necessary, more specific details concerning the decisions and/or actions are presented at appropriate points in the chapter. The chapter also will identify the use of these guidelines in creating queries such as those shown in Figure 2–1.

BTW

Designing Queries
Before creating queries, examine the contents of the tables involved. You need to know the data type for each field and how the data for the field is stored. If a query includes a state, for example, you need to know whether state is stored as the two-character abbreviation or as the full state name.

To Start Access

The following steps, which assume Windows 7 is running, start Access based on
typical installation. You may need to ask your instructor how to start Access for your
computer. For a detailed example of the procedure summarized below, refer to the
Office 2010 and Windows 7 chapter at the beginning of this book.

- Click the Start button on the Windows 7 taskbar to display the Start menu.

- Type **Microsoft Access** as the search text in the 'Search programs and files' text
  box and watch the search results appear on the Start menu.

- Click Microsoft Access 2010 in the search results on the Start menu to start Access.

- If the Access window is not maximized, click the Maximize button next to the Close button
  on its title bar to maximize the window.

For an introduction
to Windows 7 and
instruction about
how to perform basic
Windows 7 tasks, read
the Office 2010 and
Windows 7 chapter at
the beginning of this
book, where you can
learn how to resize
windows, change
screen resolution,
create folders, move
and rename files, use
Windows Help, and
much more.

To Open a Database from Access

In the previous chapter, you saved your database on a USB flash drive using the file
name, Camashaly Design. The following steps open the Camashaly Design database from
the Access folder in the CIS 101 folder on the USB flash drive. For a detailed example of
the procedure summarized below, refer to the Office 2010 and Windows 7 chapter at the
beginning of this book.

- With your USB flash drive connected to one of the computer's USB ports, click File on the
  Ribbon to open the Backstage view, if necessary.

- Click Open in the Backstage view to display the Open dialog box.

- Navigate to the location of the file to be opened (in this case, the USB flash drive, then to
  the CIS 101 folder [or your class folder], and then to the Access folder).

- Click Camashaly Design to select the file to be opened.

- Click the Open button (Open dialog box) to open the selected file and display the opened
  database in the Access window.

- If a Security Warning appears, click the Enable Content button.

For an introduction
to Office 2010 and
instruction about
how to perform
basic tasks in Office
2010 programs, read
the Office 2010 and
Windows 7 chapter
at the beginning of
this book, where you
can learn how to start
a program, use the
Ribbon, save a file,
open a file, quit a
program, use Help,
and much more.

Creating Queries

Queries are simply questions, the answers to which are in the database. Access contains a
powerful query feature. Through the use of this feature, you can find the answers to a wide
variety of complex questions.

BTW

Q&As
For a complete list of the
Q&As found in many of
the step-by-step sequences
in this book, visit the
Access 2010 Q&A Web page
(scsite.com/ac2010/qa).

Note: In this chapter, you will save each query example. When you use a query for another task, such as to create a form or report, you will assign a specific name to a query; for example, Analyst-Client Query. In situations in which you will not use the query again, you will assign a name using a convention that includes the chapter number and a query number; for example, Ch2q1. Queries are numbered consecutively.

To Create a Query in Design View

Most of the time, you will use Design view to create queries. Once you have created a new query in Design view, you can specify fields, criteria, sorting, calculations, and so on. The following steps create a new query in Design view.

- Close the Navigation Pane.

- Click Create on the Ribbon to display the Create tab.

- Click the Query Design button (Create tab | Queries group) to create a new query (Figure 2–2).

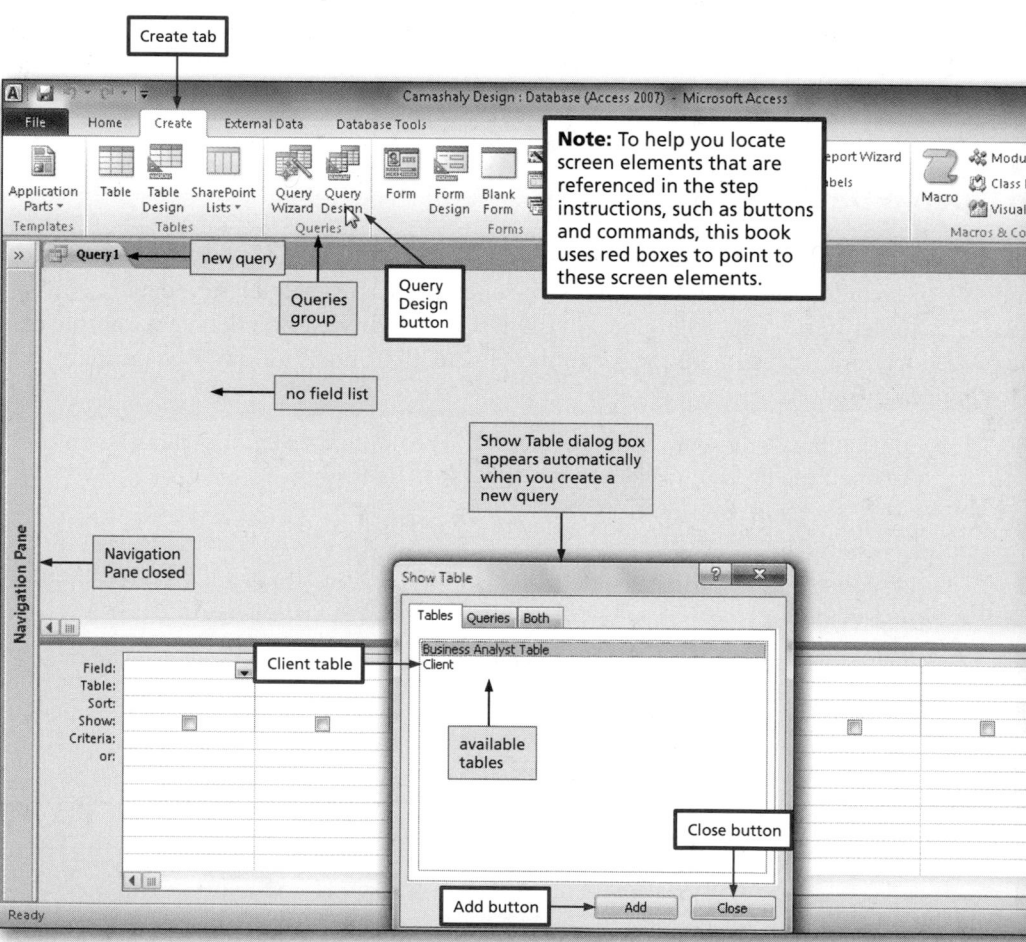

Figure 2–2

Q&A Is it necessary to close the Navigation Pane?

No. It gives you more room for the query, however, so it is usually a good practice to hide it.

2

- Click the Client table (Show Table dialog box) to select the table.

- Click the Add button to add the selected table to the query.

- Click the Close button to remove the dialog box from the screen.

What if I inadvertently add the wrong table?

Right-click the table that you added in error and click Remove Table on the shortcut menu. You also can just close the query, indicate that you do not want to save it, and then start over.

- Drag the lower edge of the field list down far enough so all fields in the table appear (Figure 2–3).

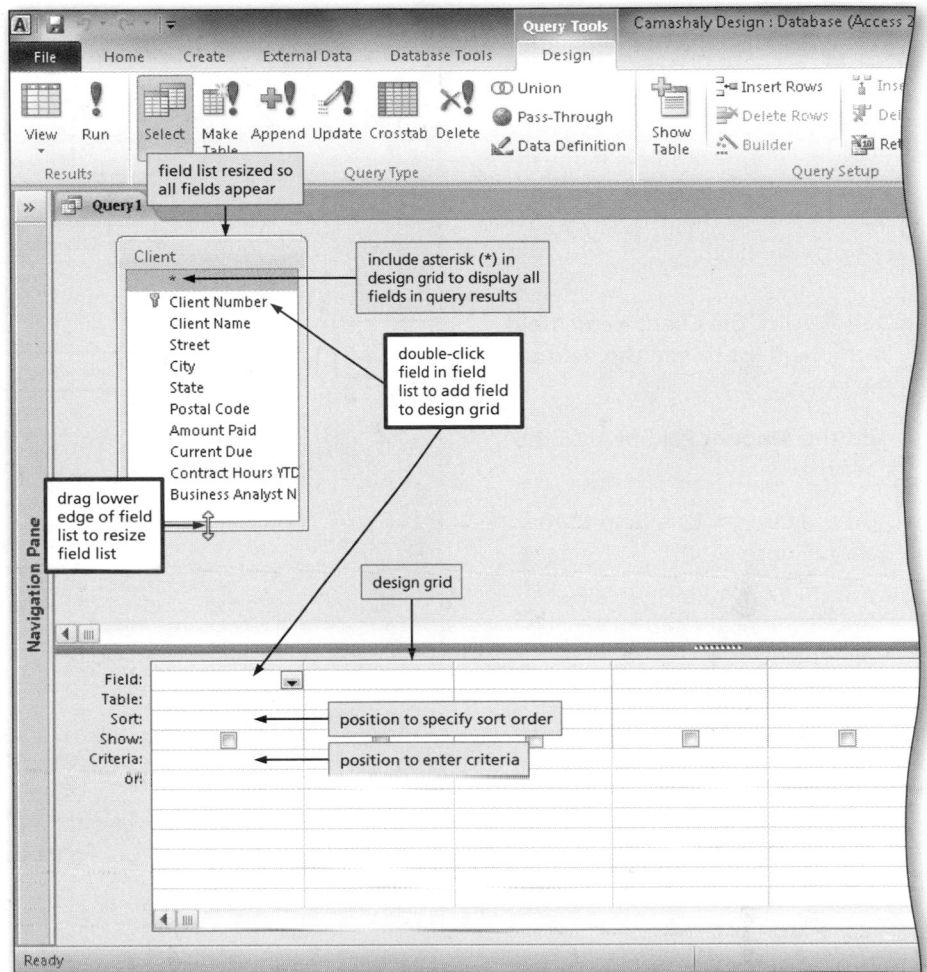

Figure 2–3

How do I drag the lower edge?

Point to the lower edge, press and hold the left mouse button, move the mouse pointer to the new position for the lower edge, and then release the left mouse button. While the mouse pointer points to the lower edge of the field list, its shape changes to a two-headed arrow.

Is it essential that I resize the field list?

No. You can always scroll through the list of fields using the scroll bar. It is usually more convenient to resize the field list so all fields appear.

To Add Fields to the Design Grid

Once you have a new query displayed in Design view, you are ready to make entries in the design grid, located in the lower pane of the window. You add the fields you want included in the query to the Field row in the grid. Only the fields that appear in the design grid will be included in the results of the query. The following steps begin the creation of a query that Camashaly Design might use to obtain the client number, client name, amount paid, and current due for a particular client. The following step selects the appropriate fields for the query.

1

- Double-click the Client Number field in the field list to add the field to the query.

Q&A

What if I add the wrong field?

Click just above the field name in the design grid to select the column and then press the DELETE key to remove the field.

- Double-click the Client Name field in the field list to add the field to the query.

- Add the Amount Paid field to the query.

- Add the Current Due field to the query (Figure 2–4).

Q&A

What if I want to include all fields? Do I have to add each field individually?

No. Instead of adding individual fields, you can double-click the asterisk (*) to add the asterisk to the design grid. The asterisk is a shortcut indicating all fields are to be included.

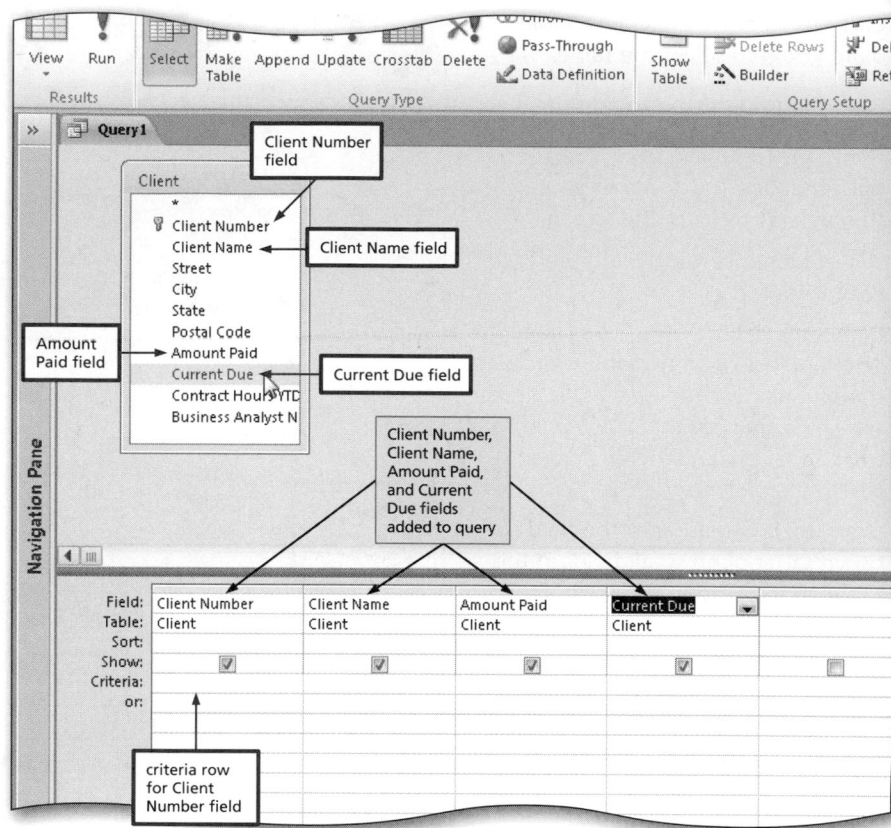

Figure 2–4

BTW

The Ribbon and Screen Resolution

Access may change how the groups and buttons within the groups appear on the Ribbon, depending on the computer's screen resolution. Thus, your Ribbon may look different from the ones in this book if you are using a screen resolution other than 1024 × 768.

Determining Criteria

When you use queries, usually you are looking for those records that satisfy some criterion. In the simple query you created in the previous chapter, for example, you entered a criterion to restrict the records that were included to those on which the business analyst number is 14. In another query, you might want the name, amount paid, and current due amounts of the client whose number is BC76, for example, or of those clients whose names start with the letters, Gr. You enter criteria in the Criteria row in the design grid below the field name to which the criterion applies. For example, to indicate that the client number must be BC76, you first must add the Client Number field to the design grid. You then would type BC76 in the Criteria row below the Client Number field.

To Use Text Data in a Criterion

To use **text data** (data in a field whose data type is Text) in criteria, simply type the text in the Criteria row below the corresponding field name. The following steps finish the creation of a query that Camashaly Design might use to obtain the client number, client name, amount paid, and current due amount of client BC76. These steps add the appropriate criterion so that only the desired client will appear in the results. The steps also save the query.

1
- Click the Criteria row for the Client Number field to produce an insertion point.

- Type **BC76** as the criterion (Figure 2–5).

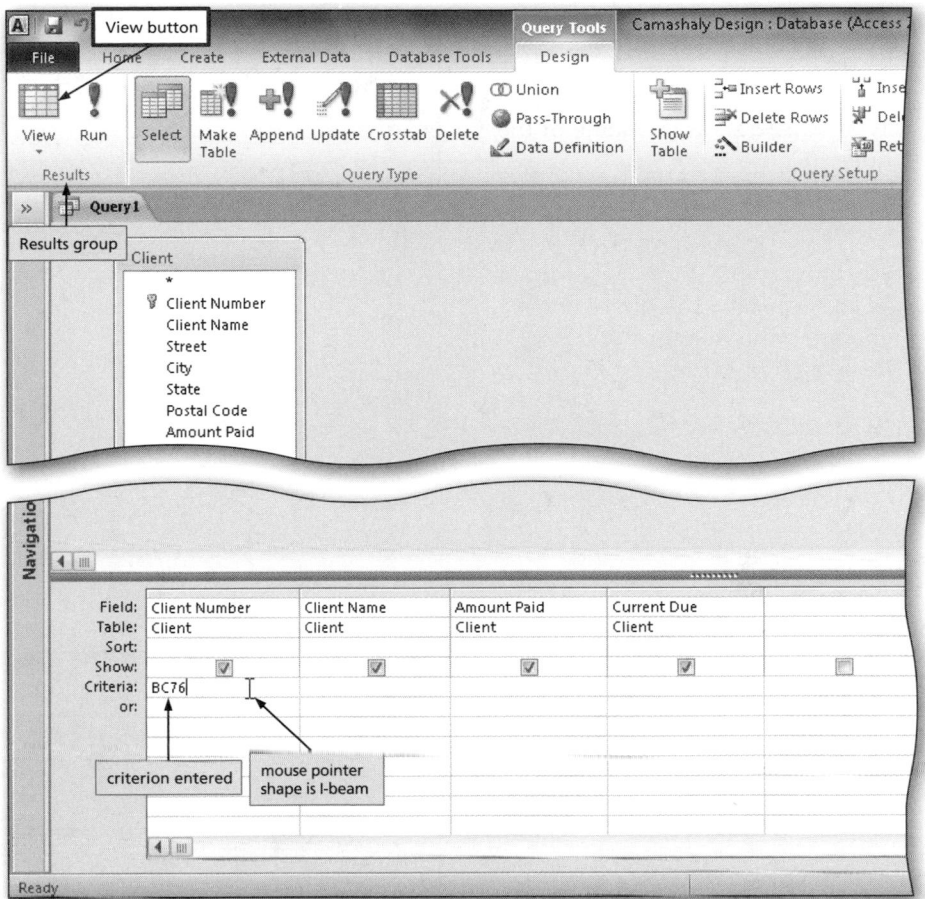

Figure 2–5

2
- Click the View button (Query Tools Design tab | Results group) to display the query results (Figure 2–6).

I noticed that there is a View button on both the Home tab and the Design tab. Do they both have the same effect?

Yes. Use whichever one you find most convenient.

Figure 2–6

- Click the Save button on the Quick Access Toolbar to display the Save As dialog box.

- Type **Ch2q1** as the name of the query (Figure 2–7).

Q&A

Can I also save from Design view?

Yes. You can save the query when you view it in Design view just as you can save the query when you view the query results in Datasheet view.

Figure 2–7

- Click the OK button (Save As dialog box) to save the query (Figure 2–8).

Figure 2–8

Other Ways

1. Right-click query tab, click Save on shortcut menu

Using Saved Queries

After you have created and saved a query, you can use it in a variety of ways:

- To view the results of the query that is not currently open, open it by right-clicking the query in the Navigation Pane and clicking Open on the shortcut menu.

- If you want to change the design of the query that is already open, return to Design view and make the changes.

- If you want to change the design of the query that is not currently open, right-click the query in the Navigation Pane and then click Design View on the shortcut menu to open the query in Design view.

- To print the results with the query open, click File on the Ribbon, click the Print tab in the Backstage view, and then click Quick Print.

- To print the query without first opening it, be sure the query is selected in the Navigation Pane and click File on the Ribbon, click the Print tab in the Backstage view, and then click Quick Print.
- You can switch between views of a query using the View button (Home tab | Views group). Clicking the arrow at the bottom of the button produces the View button menu. You then click the desired view in the menu. The two query views you use in this chapter are Datasheet view (see the results) and Design view (change the design). You can click the top part of the View button, in which case, you will switch to the view identified by the icon on the button. In the figure, the button contains the icon for Design view, so clicking the button would change to Design view. For the most part, the icon on the button represents the view you want, so you can usually simply click the button.

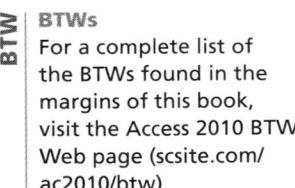

BTWs

For a complete list of the BTWs found in the margins of this book, visit the Access 2010 BTW Web page (scsite.com/ac2010/btw).

To Use a Wildcard

Microsoft Access supports wildcards. **Wildcards** are symbols that represent any character or combination of characters. One common wildcard, the **asterisk** (*), represents any collection of characters. Thus Gr* represents the letters, Gr, followed by any collection of characters. Another wildcard symbol is the **question mark** (?), which represents any individual character. Thus T?m represents the letter, T, followed by any single character, followed by the letter, m; a search might return the names Tim or Tom.

The following steps modify the previous query so that Camashaly Design can select only those clients whose names begin with Gr. Because you do not know how many characters will follow the Gr, the asterisk wildcard symbol is appropriate. The steps also save the query with a new name using the Save As command.

Click the View button (Home tab | Views group) to return to Design view.

If necessary, click the Criteria row below the Client Number field to produce an insertion point.

The text I entered now has quotation marks surrounding it. What happened?

Criteria for text data needs to be enclosed in quotation marks. You do not have to type the quotation marks; Access adds them automatically.

Use the DELETE or BACKSPACE key as necessary to delete the current entry.

Click the Criteria row below the Client Name field to produce an insertion point.

Type **Gr*** as the criterion (Figure 2–9).

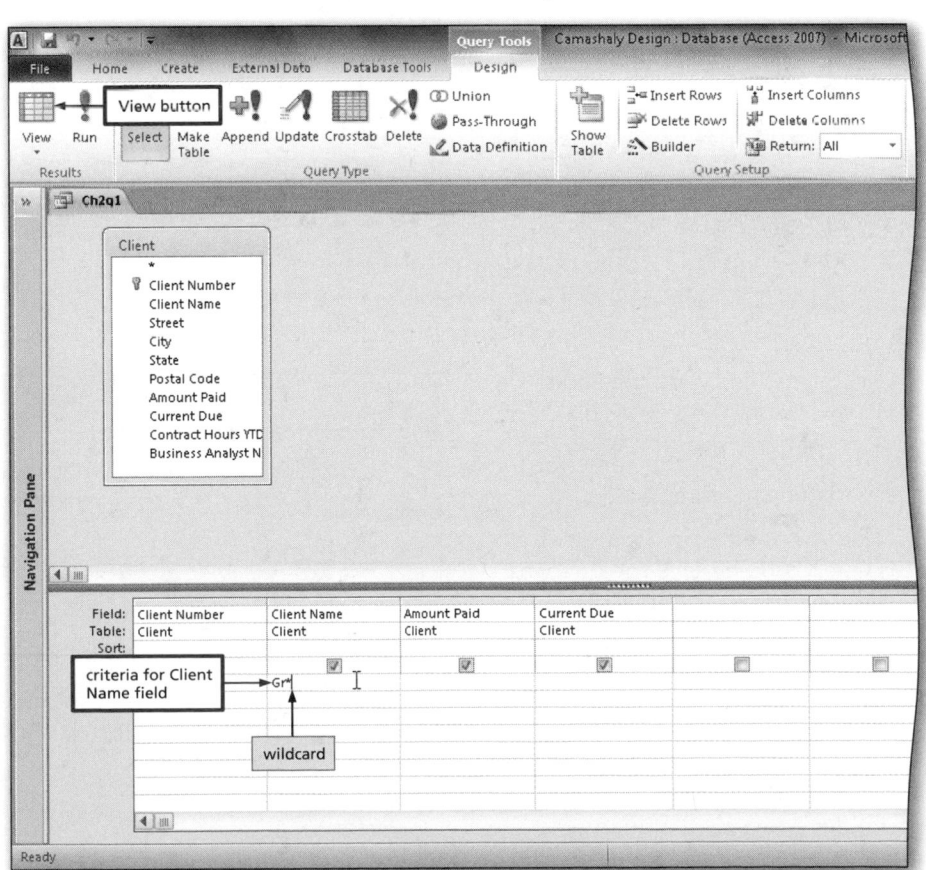

Figure 2–9

2

- View the query results by clicking the View button (Query Tools Design tab | Results group) (Figure 2–10).

🔍 **Experiment**

- Vary the case of the letters in the criteria and view the results to determine whether case makes a difference when entering a wildcard.

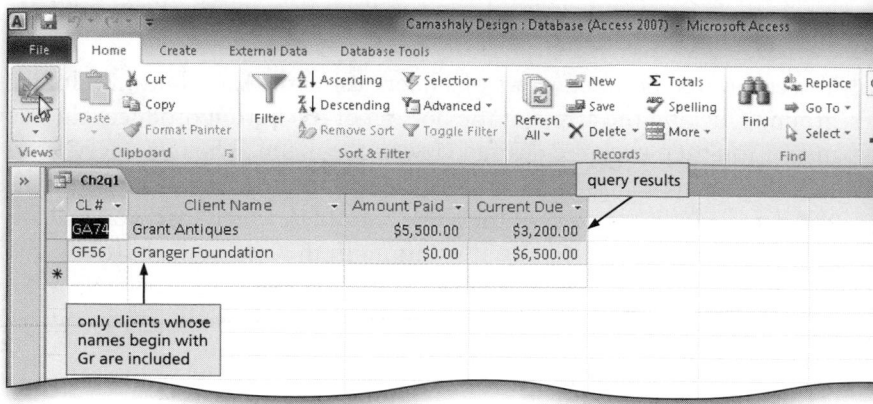

Figure 2–10

3

- Click File on the Ribbon to open the Backstage view (Figure 2–11).

Q&A Why can I not just click the Save button on the Quick Access Toolbar like I did when I saved the previous query?

If you did, you would replace the previous query with the version you just created. Because you want to save both the previous query and the new one, you need to save the new version with a different name. To do so, you must use Save Object As, which is available through the Backstage view.

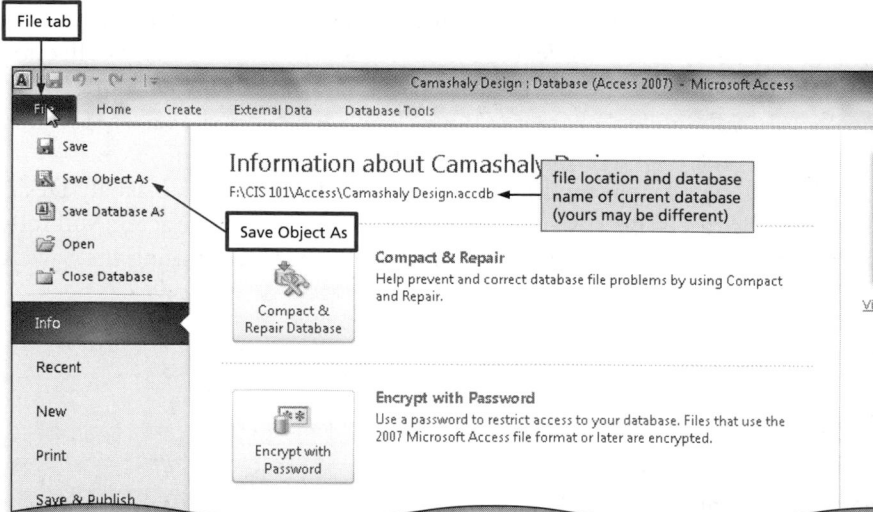

Figure 2–11

4

- Click Save Object As in the Backstage view to display the Save As dialog box.

- Type `Ch2q2` as the name for the saved query (Figure 2–12).

Q&A The current entry in the As text box is Query. Could I save the query as some other type of object?

Although you usually would want to save the query as another query, you also can save it as a form or report by changing the entry in the As text box. If you do, Access would create either a simple form or a simple report for the query.

Figure 2–12

Figure 2–13

- Click the OK button (Save As dialog box) to save the query with the new name, and then click File on the Ribbon to close the Backstage view (Figure 2–13).

How can I tell that the query was saved with the new name?

The new name will appear on the tab.

To Use Criteria for a Field Not Included in the Results

In some cases, you might require criteria for a particular field that should not appear in the results of the query. For example, you may want to see the client number, client name, address, and amount paid for all clients located in Georgetown. The criteria involve the City field, but you do not want to include the City field in the results.

To enter a criterion for the City field, it must be included in the design grid. Normally, this also would mean it would appear in the results. To prevent this from happening, remove the check mark from its Show check box in the Show row of the grid.

The following steps modify the previous query so that Camashaly Design can select only those clients located in Georgetown. Camashaly does not want the city to appear in the results, however. The steps also save the query with a new name.

- Click the View button (Home tab | Views group), shown in Figure 2–13, to return to Design view.

The text I entered is now preceded by the word, Like. What happened?

Criteria including wildcards need to be preceded by the word, Like. You do not have to type the word, Like, however. Access adds it automatically to any criterion involving a wildcard.

- Erase the criterion in the Client Name field.

- Add the City field to the query.

- Type **Georgetown** as the criterion for the City field (Figure 2–14).

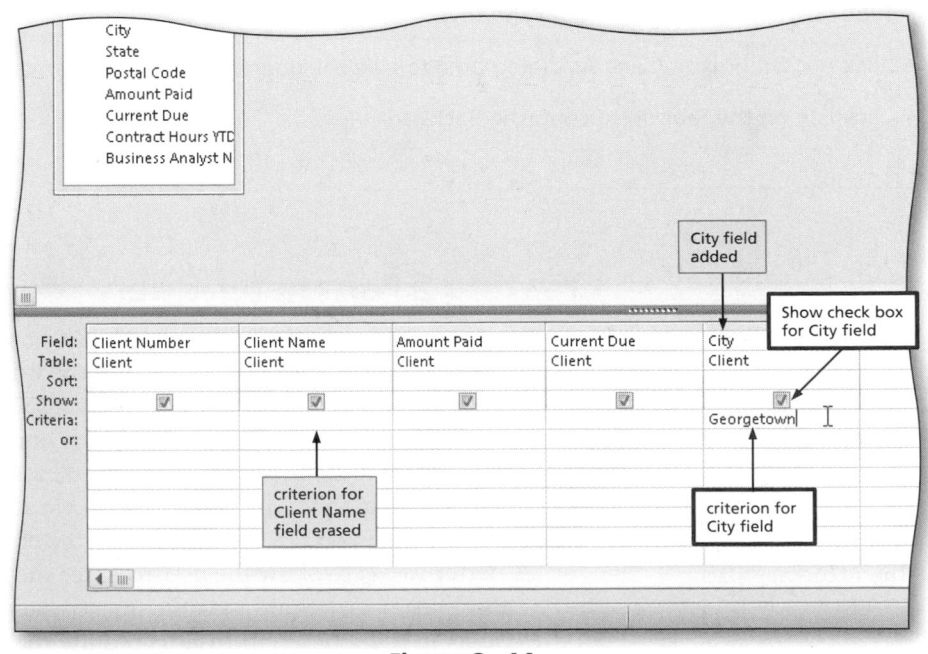

Figure 2–14

2

- Click the Show check box for the City field to remove the check mark (Figure 2–15).

Q&A

Could I have removed the check mark before entering the criterion?

Yes. The order in which you perform the two operations does not matter.

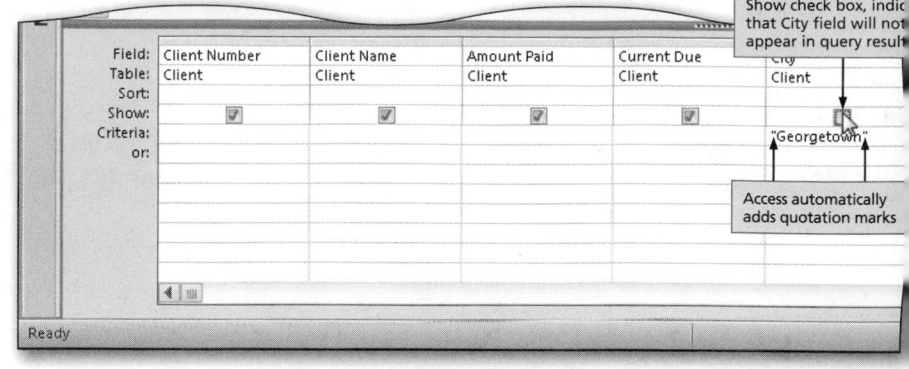

Figure 2–15

3

- View the query results (Figure 2–16).

🔍 **Experiment**

- Click the View button to return to Design view, enter a different city name, and view the results. Repeat this process with a variety of city names, including at least one city name that is not in the database. When finished, change the criterion back to Georgetown.

Figure 2–16

4

- Click File on the Ribbon to open the Backstage view.

- Click Save Object As in the Backstage view to display the Save As dialog box.

- Type **Ch2q3** as the name for the saved query.

- Click the OK button (Save As dialog box) to save the query with the new name.

- Click File on the Ribbon to close the Backstage view.

Creating a Parameter Query

BTW

Queries: Query-by-Example

Query-By-Example, often referred to as QBE, was a query language first proposed in the mid-1970s. In this approach, users asked questions by filling in a table on the screen. The Access approach to queries is based on Query-By-Example.

If you wanted to find clients located in Kyle instead of Georgetown, you would either have to create a new query or modify the existing query by replacing Georgetown with Kyle as the criterion. Rather than giving a specific criterion when you first create the query, on occasion, you may want to be able to enter part of the criterion when you view the query results and then have the appropriate results appear. For example, to include all the clients located in Kyle, you could enter Kyle as a criterion in the City field. From that point on, every time you ran the query, only the clients in Kyle would appear.

A better way is to allow the user to enter the city at the time the user wants to view the results. Thus, a user could view the query results, enter Kyle as the city, and then see all the clients in Kyle. Later, the user could use the same query but enter Georgetown as the city, and then see all the clients in Georgetown.

To enable this flexibility, you create a **parameter query**, which is a query that prompts for input whenever it is used. You enter a parameter (prompt for the user), rather than a specific value as the criterion. You create one by enclosing a value in a criterion in square brackets. It is important that the value in the brackets does not match the name of any field. If you enter a field name in square brackets, Access assumes you want that particular field and does not prompt the user for input. To prompt the user to enter the city name as the input, you could place [Enter City] as the criterion in the City field.

To Create and View a Parameter Query

The following steps create a parameter query that will prompt the users at Camashaly to enter a city, and then display the client number, name, address, and amount paid for all clients located in that city. The steps also save the query with a new name.

- Return to Design view.

- Erase the current criterion in the City column, and then type **[Enter City]** as the new criterion (Figure 2–17).

What is the purpose of the square brackets?

The square brackets indicate that the text entered is not text that the value in the column must match. Without the brackets, Access would search for records on which the city is Enter City.

Figure 2–17

What if I typed a field name in the square brackets?

Access would simply use the value in that field. To create a parameter query, you must not use a field name in the square brackets.

- Click the View button (Query Tools Design tab | Results group) to display the Enter Parameter Value dialog box (Figure 2–18).

Figure 2–18

3

- Type `Kyle` as the parameter value in the Enter City text box and then click the OK button (Enter Parameter Value dialog box) to close the dialog box and view the query (Figure 2–19).

Experiment

- Try other characters between the square brackets. In each case, view the results. When finished, change the characters between the square brackets back to Enter City.

Figure 2–19

4

- Click File on the Ribbon to open the Backstage view.

- Click Save Object As in the Backstage view to display the Save As dialog box.

- Type `Client-City Query` as the name for the saved query.

- Click the OK button (Save As dialog box) to save the query with the new name and then click File on the Ribbon (Figure 2–20).

5

- Click the Close button for the Client-City query to close the query.

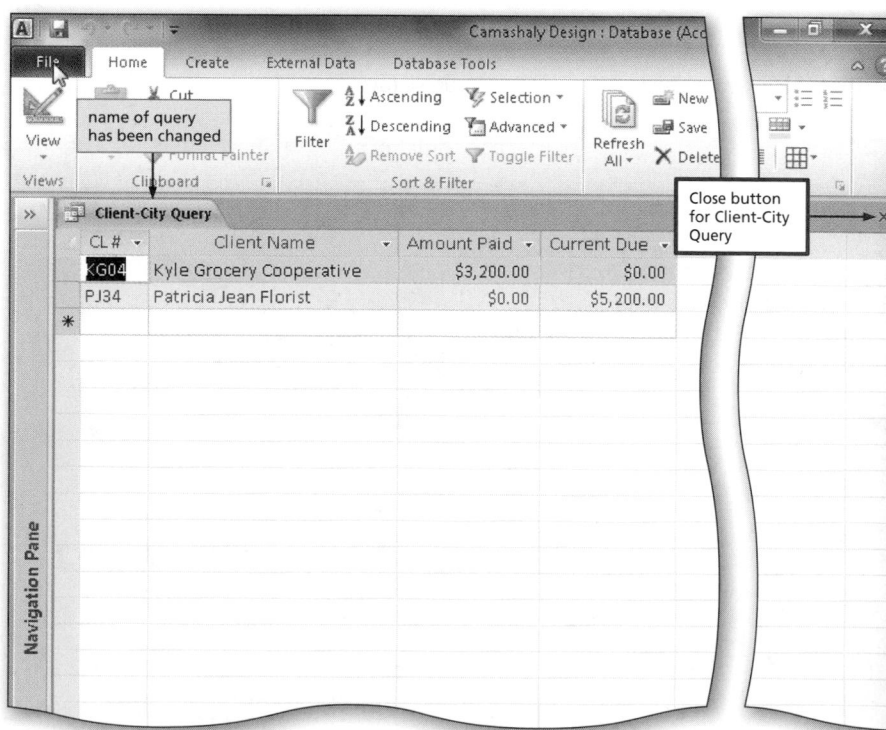

Figure 2–20

Break Point: If you wish to take a break, this is a good place to do so. You can quit Access now. To resume at a later time, start Access, open the database called Camashaly Design, and continue following the steps from this location forward.

To Use a Parameter Query

You use a parameter query like any other saved query. You can open it or you can print the query results. In either case, Access prompts you to supply a value for the parameter each time you use the query. As with other queries, the query always uses the data that is currently in the table. Thus, if changes have been made to the data since the last time you ran the query, the results of the query may be different, even if you enter the same value for the parameter. The following steps use the parameter query named Client-City Query.

- Open the Navigation Pane.

- Right-click the Client-City Query to produce a shortcut menu.

- Click Open on the shortcut menu to open the query and display the Enter Parameter Value dialog box (Figure 2–21).

  The title bar for my Navigation Pane contains Tables and Related Views rather than All Access Objects as it did in Chapter 1. What should I do?

  Click the Navigation Pane arrow and then click All Access Objects.

  I do not have the Search bar at the top of the Navigation Pane that I had in Chapter 1. What should I do?

  Right-click the Navigation Pane title bar arrow to display a shortcut menu, and then click Search Bar.

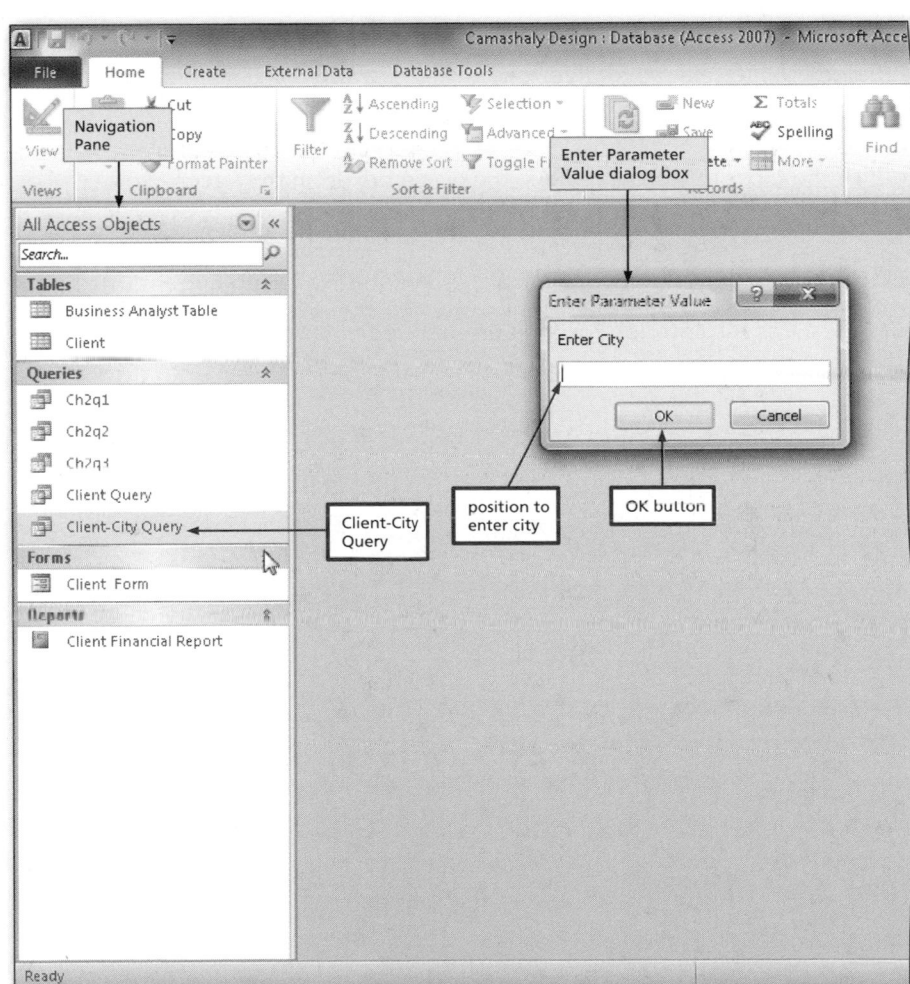

Figure 2–21

- Type **Kyle** in the Enter City text box, and then click the OK button (Enter Parameter Value dialog box) to display the results using Kyle as the city, as shown in Figure 2–20.

- Close the query.

To Use a Number in a Criterion

To enter a number in a criterion, type the number without any dollar signs or commas. The following steps create a query that Camashaly Design might use to display all clients whose current due amount is $0. The steps also save the query with a new name.

- Close the Navigation Pane.

- Click Create on the Ribbon to display the Create tab.

- Click the Query Design button (Create tab | Queries group) to create a new query.

- Click the Client table (Show Table dialog box) to select the table.

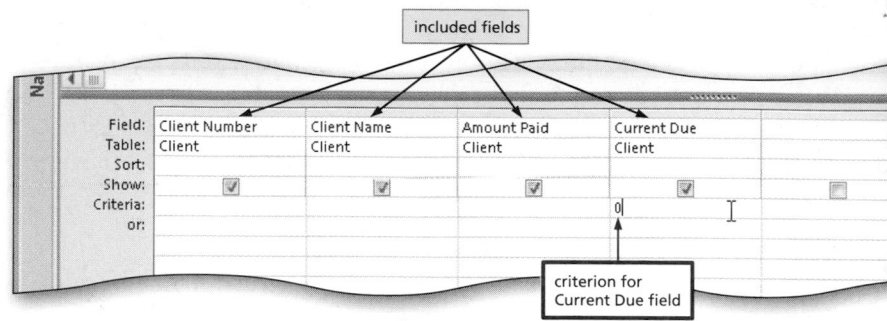

Figure 2–22

- Click the Add button to add the selected table to the query.

- Click the Close button to remove the dialog box from the screen.

- Drag the lower edge of the field list down far enough so all fields in the field list are displayed.

- Include the Client Number, Client Name, Amount Paid, and Current Due fields in the query.

- Type 0 as the criterion for the Current Due field (Figure 2–22).

Q&A Do I need to enter a dollar sign and decimal point?

No. Access will interpret 0 as $0 because the data type for the Current Due field is currency.

- View the query results (Figure 2–23).

Q&A Why did Access display the results as $0.00 when I only entered 0?

Access uses the format for the field to determine how to display the result. In this case, the format indicated that Access should include the dollar sign, decimal point, and two decimal places.

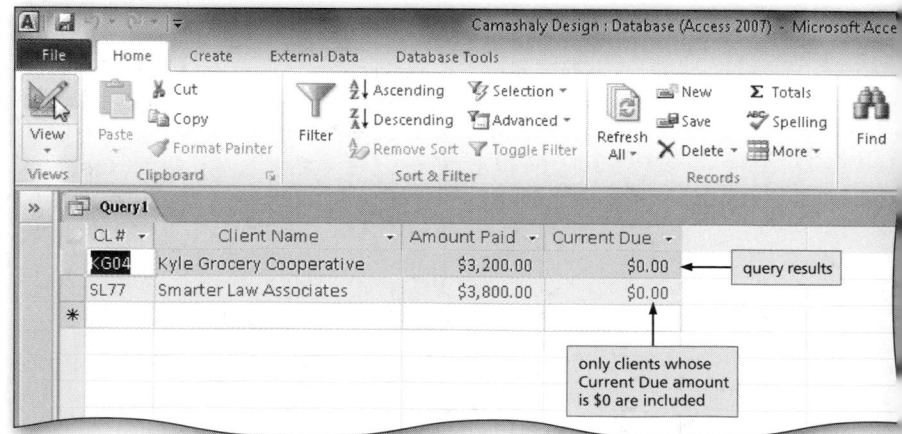

Figure 2–23

- Save the query as Ch2q4.

Q&A How do I know when to use the Save button to save a query or use the Backstage view to perform a Save As?

If you are saving a new query, the simplest way is to use the Save button on the Quick Access Toolbar. If you are saving changes to a previously saved query but do not want to change the name, use the Save button. If you want to save a previously saved query with a new name, you must use the Backstage view and perform a Save Object As.

To Use a Comparison Operator in a Criterion

Unless you specify otherwise, Access assumes that the criteria you enter involve equality (exact matches). In the last query, for example, you were requesting those clients whose current due amount is equal to 0 (zero). If you want something other than an exact match, you must enter the appropriate **comparison operator**. The comparison operators are > (greater than), < (less than), >= (greater than or equal to), <= (less than or equal to), and NOT (not equal to).

The following steps use the > operator to create a query that Camashaly Design might use to find all clients whose amount paid is more than $3,000. The steps also save the query with a new name.

- Return to Design view.

- Erase the 0 in the Current Due column.

- Type >3000 as the criterion for the Amount Paid field (Figure 2–24).

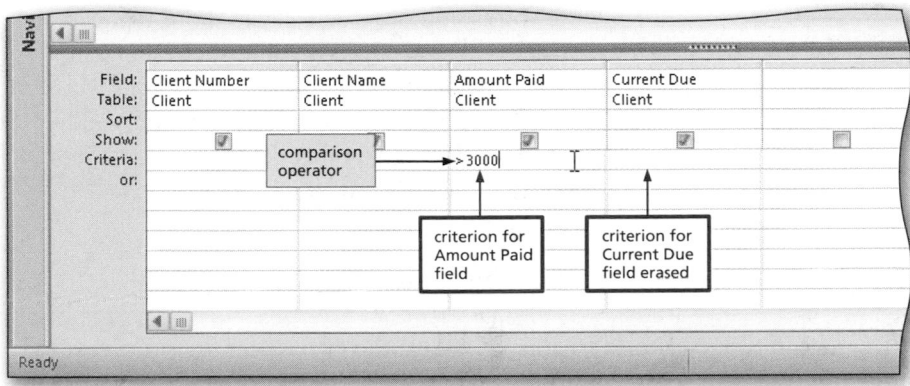

Figure 2–24

- View the query results (Figure 2–25).

Experiment

- Return to Design view. Try a different criterion involving a comparison operator in the Amount Paid field and view the results. When finished, return to Design view, enter the original criterion (>3000) in the Amount Paid field, and view the results.

- Save the query as Ch2q5.

Figure 2–25

Using Compound Criteria

Often you will have more than one criterion that the data for which you are searching must satisfy. This type of criterion is called a **compound criterion**. Two types of compound criteria exist.

In an **AND criterion**, each individual criterion must be true in order for the compound criterion to be true. For example, an AND criterion would allow you to find those clients that have an amount paid greater than $3,000 and whose business analyst is business analyst 11.

Conversely, an **OR criterion** is true provided either individual criterion is true. An OR criterion would allow you to find those clients that have an amount paid greater than $3,000 and also those clients whose business analyst is business analyst 11 — either one criterion or the other is true. In this case, any client whose amount paid is greater than $3,000 would be included in the answer, regardless of whether the client's business analyst is business analyst 11. Likewise, any client whose business analyst is business analyst 11 would be included, regardless of whether the client had an amount paid greater than $3,000.

To Use a Compound Criterion Involving AND

To combine criteria with AND, place the criteria on the same row of the design grid. The following steps use an AND criterion to enable Camashaly to find those clients whose amount paid is greater than $3,000 and whose business analyst is analyst 11. The steps also save the query with a new name.

 1

- Return to Design view.

- Include the Business Analyst Number field in the query.

- Type **11** as the criterion for the Business Analyst Number field (Figure 2–26).

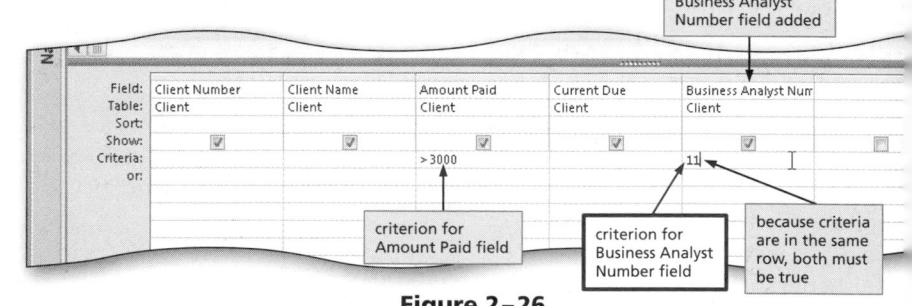

Figure 2–26

2
- View the query results (Figure 2–27).

3
- Save the query as Ch2q6.

Figure 2–27

To Use a Compound Criterion Involving OR

To combine criteria with OR, the criteria must go on separate rows in the Criteria area of the grid. The following steps use an OR criterion to enable Camashaly to find those clients whose amount paid is greater than $3,000 or whose business analyst is analyst 11 (or both). The steps also save the query with a new name.

- Return to Design view.

- If necessary, click the Criteria entry for the Business Analyst Number field and then use the BACKSPACE key or the DELETE key to erase the entry ("11").

- Click the or row (the row below the Criteria row) for the Business Analyst Number field and then type **11** as the entry (Figure 2–28).

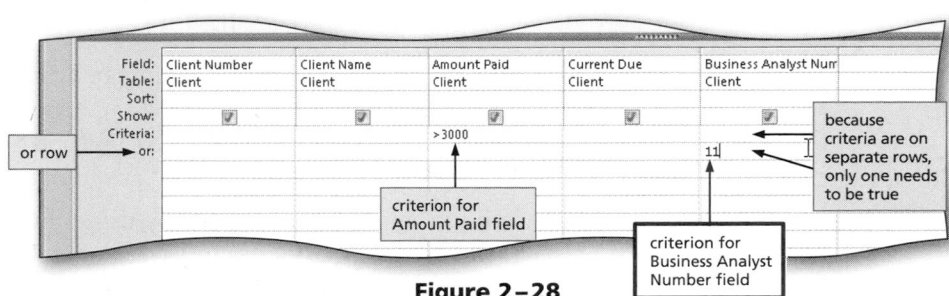

Figure 2–28

- View the query results (Figure 2–29).

- Save the query as Ch2q7.

Figure 2–29

Special Criteria

There are three special criteria you can use in queries:

1. If you want to create a criterion involving a range of values in a single field, you can use the **AND operator**. You place the word AND between the individual conditions. For example, if you wanted to find all clients whose amount paid is >= $1,000 and <= $4,000, you would enter `>= 1000 AND <= 4000` as the criterion in the Amount Paid column.

2. You can select values in a given range by using the **BETWEEN operator**. This is often an alternative to the AND operator. For example, to find all clients whose amount paid is between $1,000 and $4,000, inclusive, you would enter `BETWEEN 1000 AND 4000` as the criterion in the Amount Paid column.

3. You can select values in a list by using the **IN operator**. You follow the word IN with the list of values in parentheses. For example, to find clients whose business analyst number is 11 or 14 using the IN operator, you would enter `IN ("11","14")` as the criterion in the Business Analyst Number column. Unlike when you enter a simple criterion, you must enclose text values in quotation marks.

Sorting

BTW

Rearranging Fields in a Query
To move a field in the design grid, click the column selector for the field to select the field and drag it to the appropriate location.

In some queries, the order in which the records appear is irrelevant. All you need to be concerned about are the records that appear in the results. It does not matter which one is first or which one is last.

In other queries, however, the order can be very important. You may want to see the cities in which clients are located and would like them arranged alphabetically. Perhaps you want to see the clients listed by business analyst number. Further, within all the clients of any given business analyst, you might want them to be listed by amount paid from largest amount to smallest.

To order the records in a query result in a particular way, you **sort** the records. The field or fields on which the records are sorted is called the **sort key**. If you are sorting on more than one field (such as sorting by amount paid within business analyst number), the more important field (Business Analyst Number) is called the **major key** (also called the **primary sort key**) and the less important field (Amount Paid) is called the **minor key** (also called the **secondary sort key**).

BTW

Sorting Data in a Query
When sorting data in a query, the records in the underlying tables (the tables on which the query is based) are not actually rearranged. Instead, the DBMS determines the most efficient method of simply displaying the records in the requested order. The records in the underlying tables remain in their original order.

To sort in Microsoft Access, specify the sort order in the Sort row of the design grid below the field that is the sort key. If you specify more than one sort key, the sort key on the left will be the major sort key, and the one on the right will be the minor key.

The following are guidelines related to sorting in queries.

**Plan
Ahead**

Determine whether special order is required.

Examine the query or request to see if it contains words, such as order or sort, that would imply that the order of the query results is important. If so, you need to sort the query.

- **Determine the sort key(s).** If sorting is required, identify the field or fields on which the results are to be sorted. In the request, look for language such as ordered by or sort the results by, both of which would indicate that the specified field is a sort key.

- **If using two sort keys, determine major and minor key.** If you are using two sort keys, determine which one is the more important, or the major key. Look for language such as sort by amount paid within business analyst number, which implies that the overall order is by business analyst number. Thus, the Business Analyst Number field would be the major sort key and the Amount Paid field would be the minor sort key.

- **Determine sort order.** Words such as increasing, ascending, or low-to-high imply Ascending order. Words such as decreasing, descending, or high-to-low imply Descending order. Sorting in alphabetical order implies Ascending order. If there are no words to imply a particular order, you would typically use Ascending.

- **Determine restrictions.** Examine the query or request to see if there are any special restrictions. One common restriction is to exclude duplicates. Another common restriction is to list only a certain number of records, for example, to list only the first five records.

BTW

Clearing the Design Grid
You also can clear the design grid using the Ribbon. To do so, click the Home tab, click the Advanced button (Home tab | Sort & Filter group) to display the Advanced menu, and then click Clear Grid on the Advanced menu.

To Clear the Design Grid

If the fields you want to include in the next query are different from those in the previous query, it is usually simpler to start with a clear grid, one with no fields already in the design grid. You always can clear the entries in the design grid by closing the query and then starting over. A simpler approach to clearing the entries is to select all the entries and then press the DELETE key. The following steps return to Design view and clear the design grid.

- Return to Design view.

- Click just above the Client Number column heading in the grid to select the column.

I clicked above the column heading, but the column is not selected. What should I do?

You didn't point to the correct location. Be sure the mouse pointer changes into a down-pointing arrow and then click again.

- Hold the SHIFT key down and click just above the Business Analyst Number column heading to select all the columns (Figure 2–30).

- Press the DELETE key to clear the design grid.

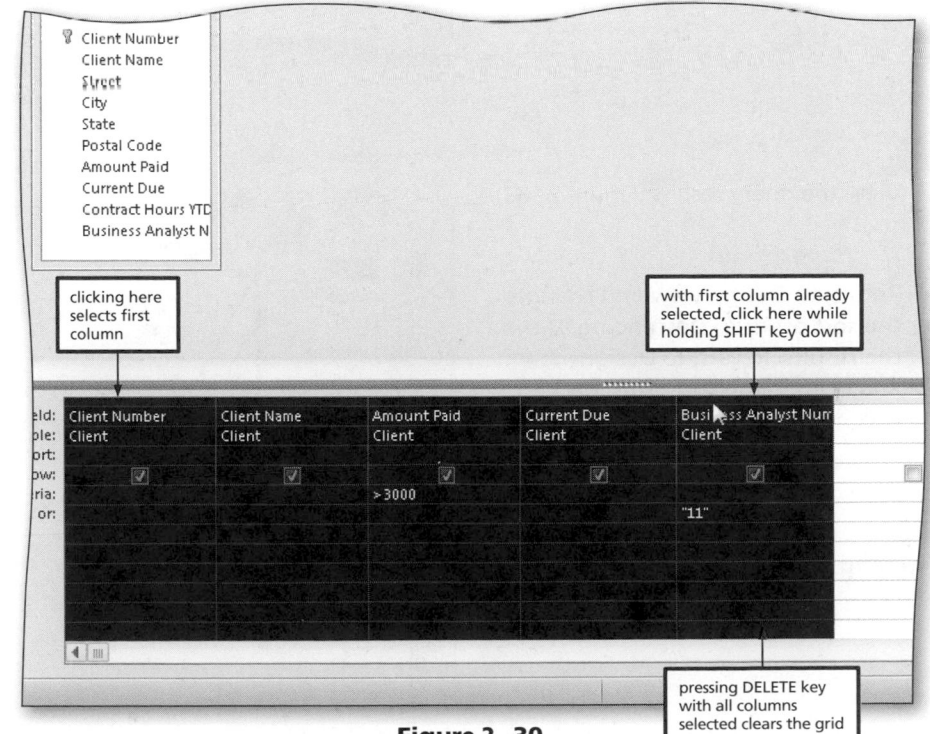

Figure 2–30

To Sort Data in a Query

After determining in the design process that a query is to be sorted, you will need to specify the sort key to Access. The following steps sort the cities in the Client table by indicating that the City field is to be sorted. The steps specify Ascending sort order.

- Include the City field in the design grid.

- Click the Sort row below the City field, and then click the Sort row arrow to display a menu of possible sort orders (Figure 2–31).

Figure 2–31

- Click Ascending to select the sort order (Figure 2–32).

Figure 2–32

- View the query results (Figure 2–33).

 Experiment

- Return to Design view and change the sort order to Descending. View the results. Return to Design view and change the sort order back to Ascending. View the results.

 Why do some cities appear more than once?

More than one client is located in those cities.

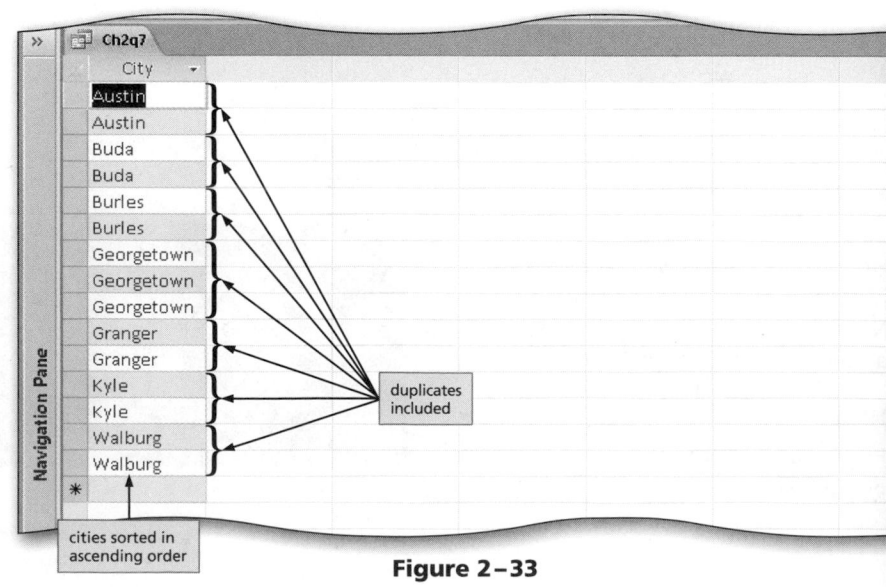

Figure 2–33

To Omit Duplicates

When you sort data, duplicates normally are included. In Figure 2–33, for example, Austin appeared twice, s did Buda, Burles, Granger, Kyle, and Walburg. Georgetown appeared three times. These duplicates do not add ny value, so you should eliminate them from the results. To eliminate duplicates, display the query's property sheet. A **property sheet** is a window containing the various properties of the object. To omit duplicates, you will use the roperty sheet to change the Unique Values property from No to Yes.

The following steps create a query that Camashaly Design might use to obtain a sorted list of the cities in the Client table in which each city is listed only once. The steps also save the query with a new name.

1
- Return to Design view.

- Click the second field (the empty field to the right of City) in the design grid.

- If necessary, click Design on the Ribbon to display the Design tab.

- Click the Property Sheet button (Query Tools Design tab | Show/Hide group) to display the property sheet (Figure 2–34).

My property sheet looks different. What should I do?

If your sheet looks different, you clicked the wrong place and will have to close the property sheet and repeat this step.

Figure 2–34

2
- Click the Unique Values property box, and then click the arrow that appears to produce a list of available choices (Figure 2–35).

Figure 2–35

- Click Yes and then close the Query Properties property sheet by clicking the Property Sheet button (Query Tools Design tab | Show / Hide group) a second time.

- View the query results (Figure 2–36).

- Save the query as Ch2q8.

Figure 2–36

Other Ways

1. Right-click second field in design grid, click Properties on shortcut menu

---

To Sort on Multiple Keys

The following steps sort on multiple keys. Specifically, Camashaly needs the data to be sorted by amount paid (low to high) within business analyst number, which means that the Business Analyst Number field is the major key and the Amount Paid field is the minor key. The steps also save the query with a new name.

- Return to Design view. Clear the design grid by clicking the first column in the grid, and then pressing the DELETE key to clear the design grid.

- In the following order, include the Client Number, Client Name, Business Analyst Number, and Amount Paid fields in the query.

- Select Ascending as the sort order for both the Business Analyst Number field and the Amount Paid field (Figure 2–37).

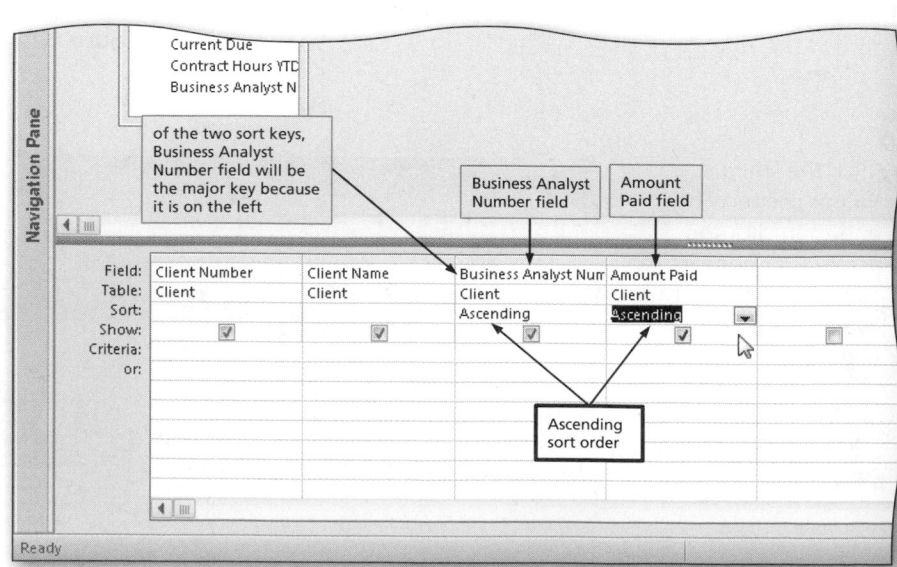

Figure 2–37

2

- View the query results (Figure 2–38).

🔍 **Experiment**

- Return to Design view and try other sort combinations for the Business Analyst Number and Amount Paid fields, such as Ascending for Business Analyst Number and Descending for Amount Paid. In each case, view the results to see the effect of the changes. When finished, select Ascending as the sort order for both fields.

What if the Amount Paid field is to the left of the Business Analyst Number field?

It is important to remember that the major sort key must appear to the left of the minor sort key in the design grid. If you attempted to sort by amount paid within business analyst number, but placed the Amount Paid field to the left of the Business Analyst Number field, your results would be incorrect.

CL #	Client Name	BA #	Amount Paid
BA53	Bavant Animal Hospital	11	$0.00
GF56	Granger Foundation	11	$0.00
BC76	Buda Community Clinic	11	$2,500.00
KG04	Kyle Grocery Cooperative	11	$3,200.00
SL77	Smarter Law Associates	11	$3,800.00
BB32	Babbage CPA Firm	14	$1,500.00
WS01	Woody Sporting Goods	14	$2,250.00
WE05	Walburg Energy Alternatives	14	$4,500.00
GA74	Grant Antiques	14	$5,500.00
KD21	KAL Design Studio	14	$6,000.00
PJ34	Patricia Jean Florist	27	$0.00
ME14	Mike's Electronic Stop	27	$2,500.00
TB17	The Bikeshop	27	$2,750.00
CJ29	Catering by Jenna	27	$3,000.00
HC10	Hendley County Hospital	27	$3,100.00

within group of clients with the same business analyst number, rows are sorted by amount paid in ascending order

overall order is by business analyst number in ascending order

Figure 2–38

3

- Save the query as Ch2q9.

To Create a Top-Values Query

Rather than show all the results of a query, you may want to show only a specified number of records or a percentage of records. Creating a **top-values query** allows you to quantify the results. When you sort records, you can limit results to those records having the highest (descending sort) or lowest (ascending sort) values. To do so, first create a query that sorts the data in the desired order. Next, use the Return box on the Design tab to change the number of records to be included from All to the desired number or percentage. The following steps create a query for Camashaly Design that shows only the first five records that were included in the results of the previous query. The steps also save the resulting query with a new name.

1

- Return to Design view.

- If necessary, click Design on the Ribbon to display the Design tab.

- Click the Return box arrow (Query Tools Design tab | Query Setup group) to display the Return box menu (Figure 2–39).

Figure 2–39

2

- Click 5 in the Return box menu to specify that the query results should contain the first five rows.

Q&A

Could I have typed the 5? What about other numbers that do not appear in the list?

Yes, you could have typed the 5. For numbers not appearing in the list, you must type the number.

- View the query results (Figure 2–40).

3

- Save the query as Ch2q10.
- Close the query.

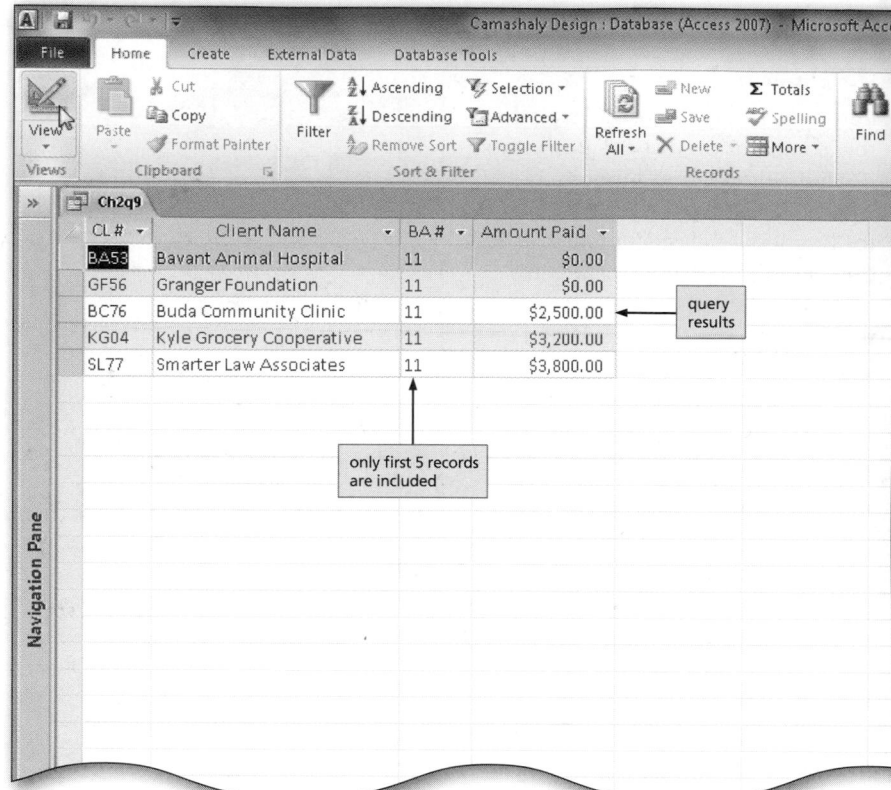

Figure 2–40

Q&A

Do I need to close the query before creating my next query?

Not necessarily. When you use a top-values query, however, it is important to change the value in the Return box back to All. If you do not change the Return value back to All, the previous value will remain in effect. Consequently, you might not get all the records you should in the next query. A good practice whenever you use a top-values query is to close the query as soon as you are done. That way, you will begin your next query from scratch, which guarantees that the value is reset to All.

Break Point: If you wish to take a break, this is a good place to do so. You can quit Access now. To resume at a later time, start Access, open the database called Camashaly Design, and continue following the steps from this location forward.

Joining Tables

In designing a query, you need to determine whether more than one table is required. If the question being asked involves data from both the Client and Business Analyst tables, for example, both tables are required for the query. For example, a query may require listing the number and name of each client along with the number and name of the client's business analyst. The client's name is in the Client table, whereas the business analyst's name is in the Business Analyst Table. Thus, this query cannot be completed using a single table; both the Client and Business Analyst tables are required. You need to **join** the tables; that is, to find records in the two tables that have identical values in matching fields (Figure 2–41). In this example, you need to find records in the Client table and the Business Analyst table that have the same value in the Business Analyst Number fields.

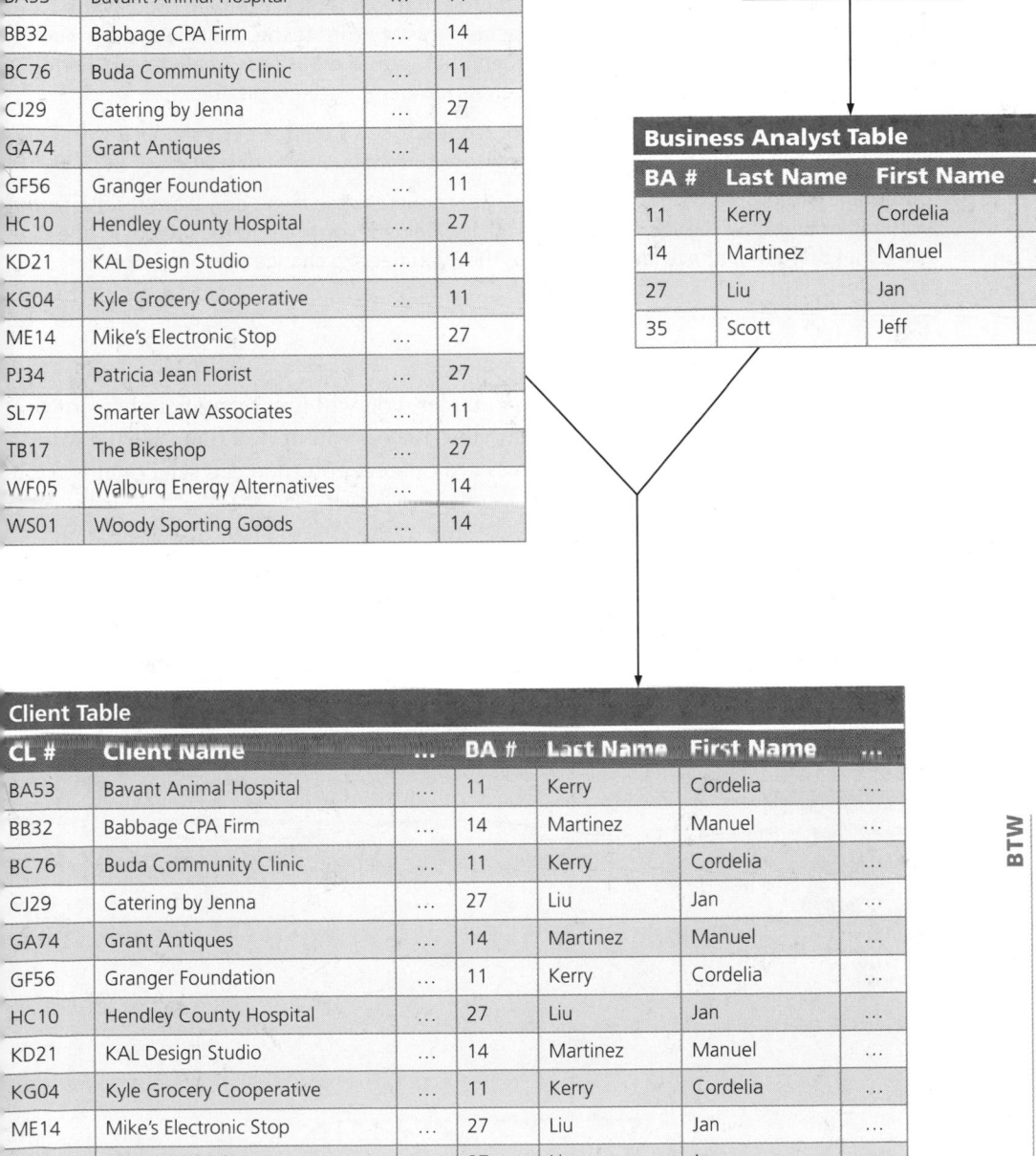

Give me the number and name of each client along with the number and name of the client's analyst.

Figure 2–41

Join Types
The type of join that finds records from both tables that have identical values in matching fields is called an inner join. An inner join is the default join in Access. Outer joins are used to show all the records in one table as well as the common records; that is, the records that share the same value in the join field. In a left outer join, all rows from the table on the left are included. In a right outer join, all rows from the table on the right are included.

The following are guidelines related to joining tables.

Plan
Ahead

Determine whether more than one table is required.
Examine the query or request to see if all the fields involved in the request are in one table. If the fields are in two (or more) tables, you need to join the tables.

- **Determine the matching fields.** If joining is required, identify the matching fields in the two tables that have identical values. Look for the same column name in the two tables or for column names that are similar.

- **Determine whether sorting is required.** Queries that join tables often are used as the basis for a report. If this is the case, it may be necessary to sort the results. For example, the Analyst-Client Report is based on a query that joins the Business Analyst and Client tables. The query is sorted by business analyst number and client number.

- **Determine restrictions.** Examine the query or request to see if there are any special restrictions. For example, the user may only want clients whose current due amount is $0.00.

- **Determine join properties.** Examine the query or request to see if you only want records from both tables that have identical values in matching fields. If you want to see records in one of the tables that do not have identical values, then you need to change the join properties.

BTW

Ad Hoc Relationships
When you join tables in a query, you are creating an ad hoc relationship, that is, a relationship between tables created for a specific purpose. In Chapter 3, you will create general-purpose relationships using the Relationships window.

To Join Tables

If you have determined in the design process that you need to join tables, you will first bring field lists for both tables to the upper pane of the Query window while working in Design view. Access will draw a line, called a **join line**, between matching fields in the two tables, indicating that the tables are related. You then can select fields from either table. Access joins the tables automatically.

The first step is to create a new query and add the Business Analyst Table to the query. Then, add the Client table to the query. A join line will appear, connecting the Business Analyst Number fields in the two field lists. This join line indicates how the tables are related, that is, linked through these matching fields. If the names of the matching fields differ from one table to the other, Access will not insert the line. You can insert it manually, however, by clicking one of the two matching fields and dragging the mouse pointer to the other matching field.

The following steps create a query that Camashaly Design might use to display information from both the Client table and the Business Analyst Table.

1

- Click Create on the Ribbon to display the Create tab.

- Click the Query Design button (Create tab | Queries group) to create a new query.

- If necessary, click the Business Analyst Table (Show Table dialog box) to select the table.

- Click the Add button (Show Table dialog box) to add a field list for the Business Analyst Table to the query (Figure 2–42).

Figure 2–42

2

- Click the Client table (Show Table dialog box).

- Click the Add button (Show Table dialog box) to add a field list for the Client table.

- Close the Show Table dialog box by clicking the Close button.

- Expand the size of the two field lists so all the fields in the Business Analyst and Client tables appear (Figure 2–43).

I did not get a join line. What should I do?

Ensure that the names of the matching fields are exactly the same, the data types are the same, and the matching field is the primary key in one of the two tables. If all of these are true and you still do not have a join line, you can produce one by pointing to one of the matching fields, pressing the left mouse button, dragging to the other matching field, and releasing the left mouse button.

Figure 2–43

3

- In the design grid, include the Business Analyst Number, Last Name, and First Name fields from the Business Analyst Table as well as the Client Number and Client Name fields from the Client table.

- Select Ascending as the sort order for both the Business Analyst Number field and the Client Number field (Figure 2–44).

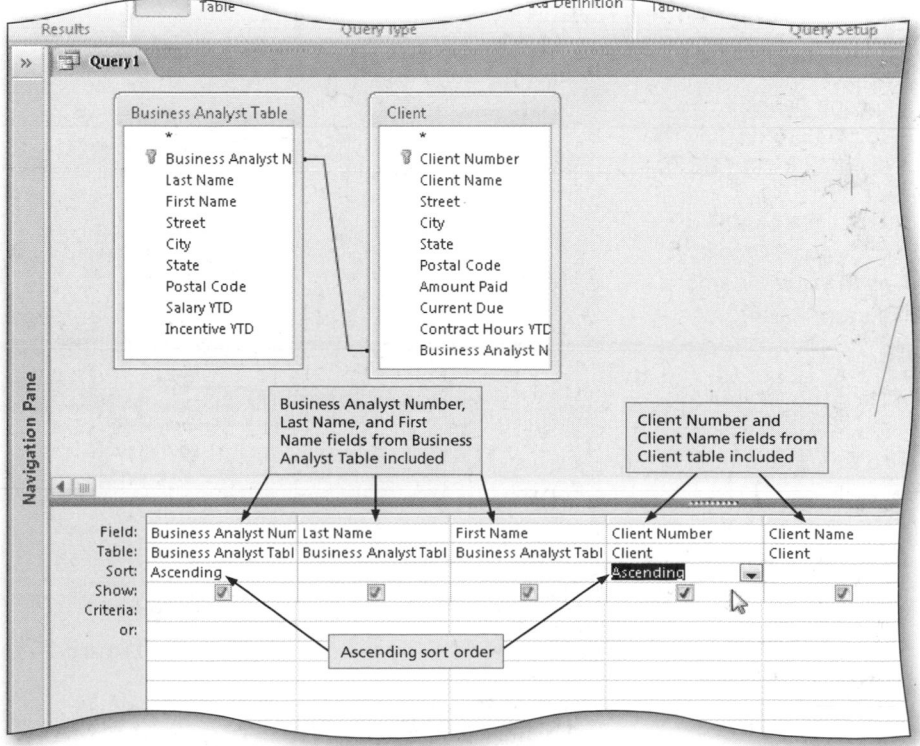

Figure 2–44

4
- View the query results (Figure 2–45).

Figure 2–45

5
- Click the Save button on the Quick Access Toolbar to display the Save As dialog box.

- Type **Analyst-Client Query** as the query name (Figure 2–46).

6
- Click the OK button (Save As dialog box) to save the query.

Figure 2–46

To Change Join Properties

Normally, records that do not match do not appear in the results of a join query. For example, a business analyst such as Jeff Scott, for whom no clients currently exist, would not appear in the results. To cause such a record to be displayed, you need to change the **join properties**, which are the properties that indicate which records appear in a join. The following steps change the join properties of the Analyst-Client Query so that Camashaly can include all business analysts in the results, rather than only those analysts who have already been assigned clients.

1

• Return to Design view.

• Right-click the join line to produce a shortcut menu (Figure 2–47).

I do not see Join Properties on my shortcut menu. What should I do?

If Join Properties does not appear on your shortcut menu, you did not point to the appropriate portion of the join line. You will need to point to the correct (middle) portion and right-click again.

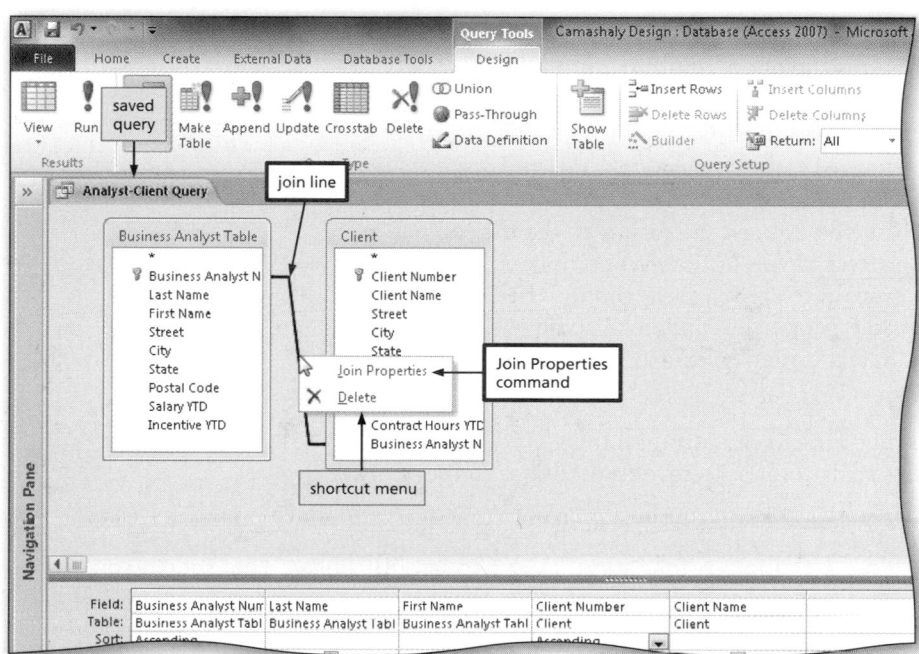

Figure 2–47

2

• Click Join Properties on the shortcut menu to display the Join Properties dialog box (Figure 2–48).

Figure 2–48

● Click option button 2 (Join Properties dialog box) to include all records from the Business Analyst Table regardless of whether they match any clients.

● Click the OK button (Join Properties dialog box) to modify the join properties.

● View the query results (Figure 2–49).

 Experiment

● Return to Design view, change the Join properties, and select option button 3. View the results to see the effect of this option. When done, return to Design view, change the Join properties, and once again select option button 2.

● Click the Save button on the Quick Access Toolbar to save the changes to the query.

● Close the Analyst-Client Query.

Q&A I see a dialog box that asks if I want to save the query. What should I do?

Click the OK button to save the query.

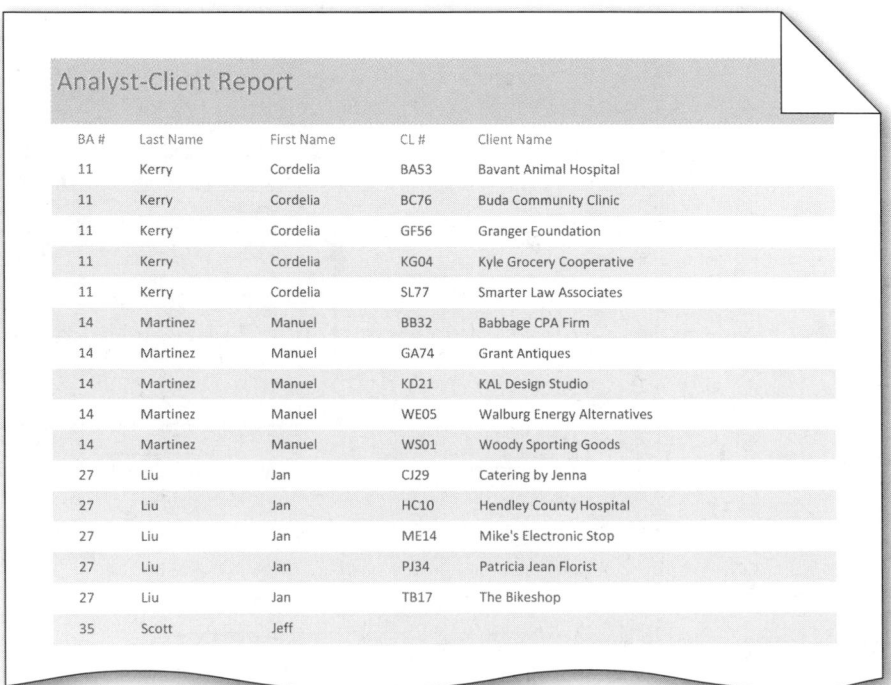

Figure 2–49

To Create a Report Involving a Join

The following steps use the Report Wizard to create the report for Camashaly Design that is shown in Figure 2–50.

Analyst-Client Report

BA #	Last Name	First Name	CL #	Client Name
11	Kerry	Cordelia	BA53	Bavant Animal Hospital
11	Kerry	Cordelia	BC76	Buda Community Clinic
11	Kerry	Cordelia	GF56	Granger Foundation
11	Kerry	Cordelia	KG04	Kyle Grocery Cooperative
11	Kerry	Cordelia	SL77	Smarter Law Associates
14	Martinez	Manuel	BB32	Babbage CPA Firm
14	Martinez	Manuel	GA74	Grant Antiques
14	Martinez	Manuel	KD21	KAL Design Studio
14	Martinez	Manuel	WE05	Walburg Energy Alternatives
14	Martinez	Manuel	WS01	Woody Sporting Goods
27	Liu	Jan	CJ29	Catering by Jenna
27	Liu	Jan	HC10	Hendley County Hospital
27	Liu	Jan	ME14	Mike's Electronic Stop
27	Liu	Jan	PJ34	Patricia Jean Florist
27	Liu	Jan	TB17	The Bikeshop
35	Scott	Jeff		

Figure 2–50

- Open the Navigation Pane, and then select the Analyst-Client Query in the Navigation Pane.

- Click Create on the Ribbon to display the Create tab.

- Click the Report Wizard button (Create tab | Reports group) to display the Report Wizard dialog box (Figure 2–51).

Figure 2–51

- Click the Add All Fields button (Report Wizard dialog box) to add all the fields in the Analyst-Client Query.

- Click the Next button to display the next Report Wizard screen (Figure 2–52).

Figure 2–52

Because you will not specify any grouping, click the Next button in the Report Wizard dialog box to display the next Report Wizard screen.

Because you already specified the sort order in the query, click the Next button again to display the next Report Wizard screen.

Make sure that Tabular is selected as the Layout and Portrait is selected as the Orientation.

Click the Next button to display the next Report Wizard screen.

Erase the current title, and then type **Analyst-Client Report** as the new title.

Click the Finish button to produce the report (Figure 2–53).

Close the Analyst-Client Report.

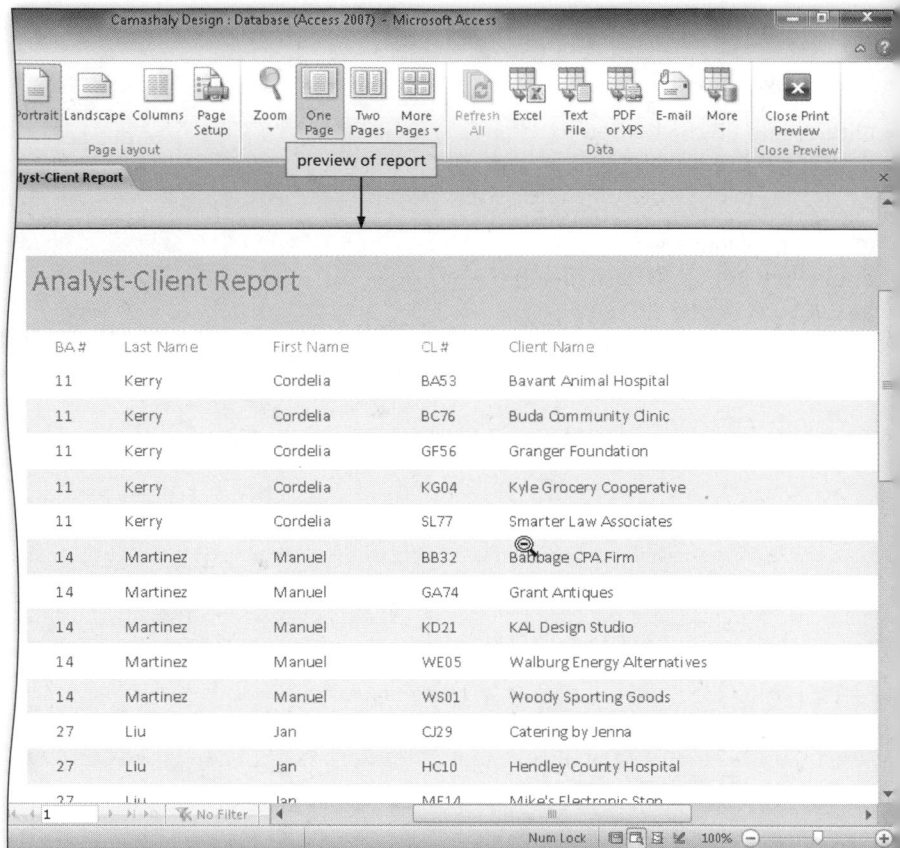

Figure 2–53

To Print a Report

The following steps print a hard copy of the report.

1 With the Analyst-Client Report selected in the Navigation Pane, click File on the Ribbon to open the Backstage view.

2 Click the Print tab in the Backstage view to display the Print gallery.

3 Click the Quick Print button to print the report.

Creating a Form for a Query

In the previous chapter, you created a form for the Client table. You also can create a form for a query. Recall that a **form** in a database is a formatted document with fields that contain data. Forms allow you to view and maintain data.

To Create a Form for a Query

The following steps create a form and then save the form.

1

- If necessary, select the Analyst-Client Query in the Navigation Pane.

- Click Create on the Ribbon to display the Create tab (Figure 2–54).

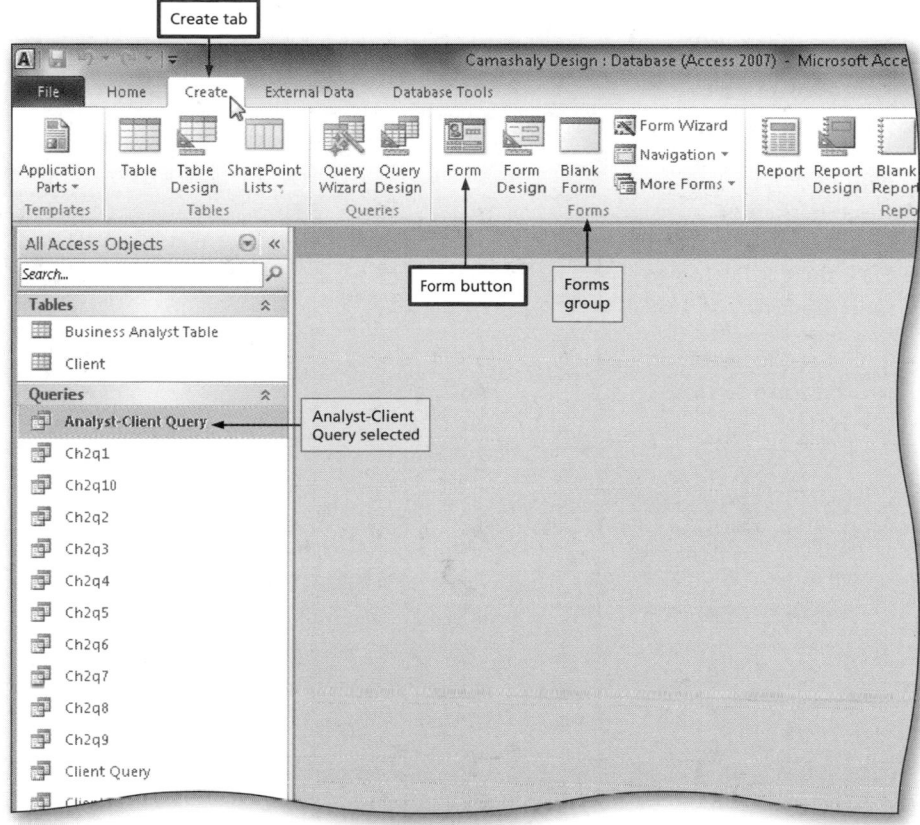

Figure 2–54

2

- Click the Form button (Create tab | Forms group) to create a simple form (Figure 2–55).

Figure 2–55

3

- Click the Save button on the Quick Access Toolbar to display the Save As dialog box.

- Type **Analyst-Client Form** as the form name (Figure 2–56).

4

- Click the OK button to save the form.

- Click the Close button for the form to close the form.

Figure 2–56

Exporting Data
You frequently need to export data so that it can be used in other applications and by other users in an organization. For example, the Accounting department might require financial data in an Excel format to perform certain financial functions. Marketing might require a list of client names and addresses in Word or RTF format for sales purposes.

Using a Form

After you have saved a form, you can use it at any time by right-clicking the form in the Navigation Pane and then clicking Open on the shortcut menu. If you plan to use the form to enter data, you must ensure you are viewing the form in Form view.

Exporting Data from Access to Other Applications

You can **export**, or copy, data from an Access database so that another application (for example, Excel or Word) can use the data. The application that will receive the data determines the export process to be used. You can export to text files in a variety of formats. For applications to which you cannot directly export data, you often can export an appropriately formatted text file that the other application can import. Figure 2–57 shows the Analyst-Client Query exported to Excel.

Figure 2–57

To Export Data to Excel

For Camashaly Design to make the Analyst-Client Query available to Excel users, it needs to export the data. To export data to Excel, select the table or query to be exported, and then click the Excel button in the Export group on the External Data tab. The following steps export the Analyst-Client Query to Excel and save the export steps. By saving the export steps, you could easily repeat the export process whenever you like without going through all the following steps. You would use the saved steps to export data in the future by clicking the Saved Exports button (External Data tab | Export group) and then selecting the steps you saved.

1

- Click the Analyst-Client Query in the Navigation Pane to select it.

- Click External Data on the Ribbon to display the External Data tab (Figure 2–58).

Figure 2–58

● Click the Excel button (External Data tab | Export group) to display the Export - Excel Spreadsheet dialog box.

● Click the Browse button (Export - Excel Spreadsheet dialog box) to display the File Save dialog box, and select your USB flash drive as the file location.

● Be sure the file name is Analyst-Client Query and then click the Save button (File Save dialog box) (Figure 2–59).

Q&A Did I need to browse?

No. You could type the appropriate file location.

Q&A Could I change the name of the file?

You could change it. Simply replace the current file name with the one you want.

Q&A What if the file I want to export already exists?

Access will indicate that the file already exists and ask if you want to replace it. If you click the Yes button, the file you export will replace the old file. If you click the No button, you must either change the name of the export file or cancel the process.

Export - Excel Spreadsheet dialog box

location of workbook to be created

name of workbook to be created

selected file format (Excel Workbook)

F:\CIS 101\Access\Analyst-Client Query.xlsx

Browse button

File format: Excel Workbook (*.xlsx)

check box to include formatting and layout

click arrow if you want to change file format

check box to open destination file after export is complete

check box to only export selected records (only valid if you have selected records prior to the export operation)

OK button

Figure 2–59

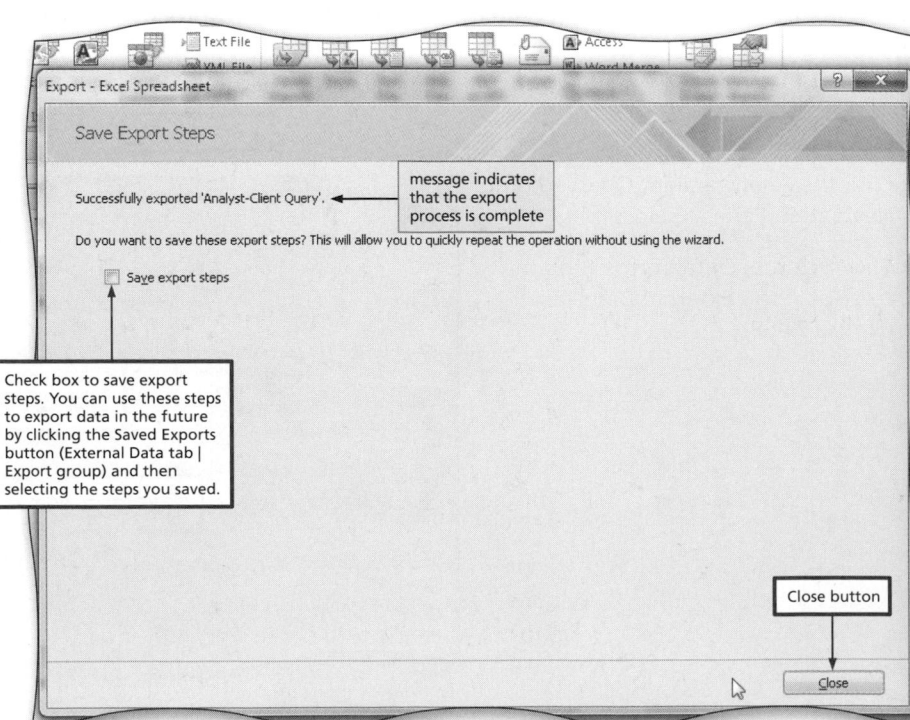

● Click the OK button (Export - Excel Spreadsheet dialog box) to export the data (Figure 2–60).

Save Export Steps

message indicates that the export process is complete

Successfully exported 'Analyst-Client Query'.

Do you want to save these export steps? This will allow you to quickly repeat the operation without using the wizard.

Save export steps

Check box to save export steps. You can use these steps to export data in the future by clicking the Saved Exports button (External Data tab | Export group) and then selecting the steps you saved.

Close button

Figure 2–60

4

- Click the 'Save export steps' check box (Export - Excel Spreadsheet dialog box) to display the Save export steps options.

- If necessary, type **Export-Analyst-Client Query** in the Save as text box.

- Type **Export the Analyst-Client Query without formatting** in the Description text box (Figure 2–61).

5

- Click the Save Export button (Export - Excel Spreadsheet dialog box) to save the export steps.

Figure 2–61

Other Ways

1. Right-click database object in Navigation Pane, click Export

To Export Data to Word

It is not possible to export data to the standard Word format. It is possible, however, to export the data as a rich text format (RTF) file, which Word can access. To export data from a query or table to an RTF file, you would use the following steps.

1. With the query or table to be exported selected in the Navigation Pane, click the More button (External Data tab | Export group) and then click Word on the More menu to display the Export - RTF File dialog box.

2. Select the name and location for the file to be created.

3. Click the Save button, and then click the OK button to export the data.

4. Save the export steps if you want, or simply click the Close button in the Export - RTF File dialog box to close the dialog box without saving the export steps.

Text Files

You also can export to text files. Text files contain unformatted characters, including alphanumeric characters, and some special characters, such as tabs, carriage returns, and line feeds.

In **delimited files**, each record is on a separate line, and the fields are separated by a special character, called the **delimiter**. Common delimiters are tabs, semicolons, commas, and spaces. You also can choose any other value that does not appear within the field contents. The comma-separated values (CSV) file often used in Excel is an example of a delimited file.

In **fixed-width files**, the width of any field is the same on every record. For example, if the width of the first field on the first record is 12 characters, the width of the first field on every other record also must be 12 characters.

TO EXPORT DATA TO A TEXT FILE

When exporting data to a text file, you can choose to export the data with formatting and layout. This option preserves much of the formatting and layout in tables, queries, forms, and reports. For forms and reports, this is the only option.

If you do not need to preserve the formatting, you can choose either delimited or fixed-width as the format for the exported file. The most common option, especially if formatting is not an issue, is delimited. You can choose the delimiter and also whether to include field names on the first row. In many cases, delimiting with a comma and including the field names is a good choice.

To export data from a table or query to a comma-delimited file in which the first row contains the column headings, you would use the following steps.

1. With the query or table to be exported selected in the Navigation Pane, click the Text File button (External Data tab | Export group) to display the Export - Text File dialog box.

2. Select the name and location for the file to be created.

3. If you need to preserve formatting and layout, be sure the 'Export data with formatting and layout' check box is checked. If you do not need to preserve formatting and layout, make sure the check box is not checked. Once you have made your selection, click the OK button in the Export - Text File dialog box.

4. To create a delimited file, be sure the Delimited option button is selected in the Export Text Wizard dialog box. To create a fixed-width file, be sure the Fixed Width option button is selected. Once you have made your selection, click the Next button.

5. a. If you are exporting to a delimited file, choose the delimiter that you want to separate your fields, such as a comma. Decide whether to include field names on the first row and, if so, click the Include Field Names on First Row check box. If you want to select a text qualifier, select it in the Text Qualifier list. When you have made your selections, click the Next button.

   b. If you are exporting to a fixed-width file, review the position of the vertical lines that separate your fields. If any lines are not positioned correctly, follow the directions on the screen to reposition them. When you have finished, click the Next button.

6. Click the Finish button to export the data.

7. Save the export steps if you want, or simply click the Close button in the Export - Text File dialog box to close the dialog box without saving the export steps.

Adding Criteria to a Join Query

Sometimes you will want to join tables, but you will not want to include all possible records. For example, you would like to create a report showing only those clients whose amount paid is greater than $3,000. In such cases, you will relate the tables and include fields just as you did before. You also will include criteria. To include only those clients whose amount paid is more than $3,000.00, you will include >3000 as a criterion for the Amount Paid field.

Saving Export Steps
Because query results are based on the data in the underlying tables, a change to an underlying table would result in a new query answer. For example, if the last name for business analyst 11 changed from Kerry to Smith, the change would be made in the Business Analyst Table. If you run the Analyst-Client Query again and export the query using the saved export steps, the Excel workbook would show the changed name.

To Restrict the Records in a Join

The following steps modify the Analyst-Client Query so that the results for Camashaly Design only include those clients whose amount paid is more than $3,000.

1

- Open the Analyst-Client Query in Design view and close the Navigation Pane.

- Add the Amount Paid field to the query.

- Type >3000 as the criterion for the Amount Paid field (Figure 2–62).

Figure 2–62

2

- View the query results (Figure 2–63).

3

- Close the query.

- When asked if you want to save your changes, click the No button.

What if I saved the changes?

The next time you used this query, you would only see clients whose amount paid is more than $3,000.

Figure 2–63

Calculations

If you have determined that a special calculation is required for a query, you then need to determine whether the calculation is an individual record calculation (for example, adding the values in two fields) or a group calculation (for example, finding the total of the values in a particular field on all the records).

Camashaly Design may want to know the total amount (amount paid and current due) from each client. This would seem to pose a problem because the Client table does not include a field for total amount. You can calculate it, however, because the total amount is equal to the amount paid plus the current due. A field that can be computed from other fields is called a **calculated field** or a **computed field**. A calculated field is an individual record calculation because each calculation only involves fields in a single record.

BTW

Expression Builder
Access includes a tool to help you create complex expressions. If you click Build on the shortcut menu (see Figure 2–64), Access displays the Expression Builder dialog box, which includes an expression box, operator buttons, and expression elements. You can type parts of the expression directly and paste operator buttons and expression elements into the box. You also can use functions in expressions.

Camashaly also may want to calculate the average amount paid for the clients of each business analyst. That is, they may want the average for the clients of business analyst 11, the average for the clients of business analyst 14, and so on. This type of calculation is called a **group calculation** because each calculation involves groups of records. In this example, the clients of business analyst 11 would form one group, the clients of business analyst 14 would be a second group, and the clients of business analyst 27 would form a third group.

The following are guidelines related to calculations in queries.

Plan Ahead

> **Determine whether calculations are required.**
> Examine the query or request to see if there are special calculations to be included. Look for words such as total, sum, compute, or calculate.
>
> - **Determine a name for the calculated field.** If calculations are required, decide on the name for the field. Assign a name that helps identify the contents of the field. For example, if you are adding the cost of a number of items, the name Total Cost would be appropriate. The name, also called an **alias**, becomes the column name when the query is run.
>
> - **Determine the format for the calculated field.** Determine how the calculated field should appear. If the calculation involves monetary amounts, you would use the currency format. If the calculated value contains decimals, determine how many decimal places to display.

To Use a Calculated Field in a Query

If you have determined that you need a calculated field in a query, you enter a name, or alias, for the calculated field, a colon, and then the calculation in one of the columns in the Field row of the design grid for the query. Any fields included in the expression must be enclosed in square brackets ([ ]). For example, for the total amount, you will type Total Amount:[Amount Paid]+[Current Due] as the expression.

You can type the expression directly into the Field row. You will not be able to see the entire entry, however, because the Field row is not large enough. The preferred way is to select the column in the Field row and then use the Zoom command on its shortcut menu. When Access displays the Zoom dialog box, you can enter the expression.

You are not restricted to addition in calculations. You can use subtraction (–), multiplication (*), or division (/). You also can include parentheses in your calculations to indicate which calculations should be done first.

The following steps create a query that Camashaly Design might use to obtain financial information on its clients including the total amount (amount paid + current due), which is a calculated field.

- Create a query with a field list for the Client table.

- Add the Client Number, Client Name, Amount Paid, and Current Due fields to the query.

- Right-click the Field row in the first open column in the design grid to display a shortcut menu (Figure 2–64).

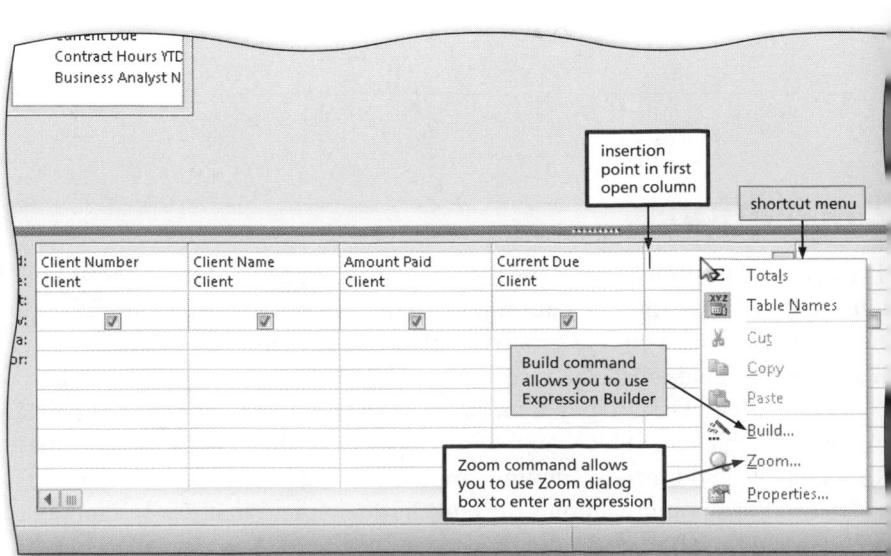

Figure 2–64

2
- Click Zoom on the shortcut menu to display the Zoom dialog box.

- Type `Total Amount: [Amount Paid]+ [Current Due]` in the Zoom dialog box (Figure 2–65).

Do I always need to put square brackets around field names?

If the field name does not contain spaces, square brackets are technically not necessary, although it is still acceptable to use the brackets. It is a good practice, however, to get in the habit of using the brackets.

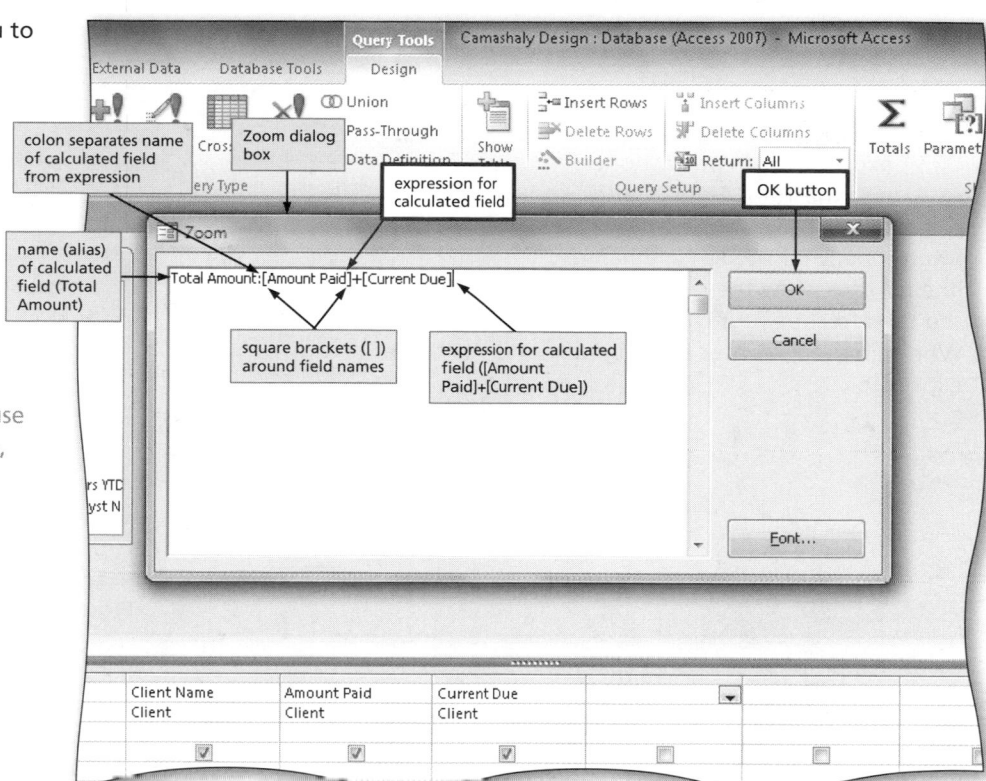

Figure 2–65

3
- Click the OK button (Zoom dialog box) to enter the expression (Figure 2–66).

Figure 2–66

- View the query results (Figure 2–67).

Experiment

- Return to Design view and try other expressions. In at least one case, omit the Total Amount and the colon. In at least one case, intentionally misspell a field name. In each case, view the results to see the effect of your changes. When finished, reenter the original expression.

CL #	Client Name	Amount Paid	Current Due	Total Amour
BA53	Bavant Animal Hospital	$0.00	$7,500.00	$7,500.00
BB32	Babbage CPA Firm	$1,500.00	$500.00	$2,000.00
BC76	Buda Community Clinic	$2,500.00	$750.00	$3,250.00
CJ29	Catering by Jenna	$3,000.00	$1,000.00	$4,000.00
GA74	Grant Antiques	$5,500.00	$3,200.00	$8,700.00
GF56	Granger Foundation	$0.00	$6,500.00	$6,500.00
HC10	Hendley County Hospital	$3,100.00	$1,200.00	$4,300.00
KD21	KAL Design Studio	$6,000.00	$3,200.00	$9,200.00
KG04	Kyle Grocery Cooperative	$3,200.00	$0.00	$3,200.00
ME14	Mike's Electronic Stop	$2,500.00	$1,500.00	$4,000.00
PJ34	Patricia Jean Florist	$0.00	$5,200.00	$5,200.00
SL77	Smarter Law Associates	$3,800.00	$0.00	$3,800.00
TB17	The Bikeshop	$2,750.00	$1,200.00	$3,950.00
WE05	Walburg Energy Alternatives	$4,500.00	$1,450.00	$5,950.00
WS01	Woody Sporting Goods			$3,850.00

results are calculated by adding the amount paid and the current due

Total Amount field

Figure 2–67

Other Ways

1. Press SHIFT+F2

To Change a Caption

You can change the way items appear in the results of a query by changing their format. You also can change a query result's heading at the top of a column by changing the caption. Just as when you omitted duplicates, you will make this change by using a property sheet. In the property sheet, you can change the desired property, such as the format, the number of decimal places, or the caption. The following steps change the caption of the Amount Paid field to Paid and the caption of the Current Due field to Due. The steps also save the query with a new name.

- Return to Design view.

- If necessary, click Design on the Ribbon to display the Design tab.

- Click the Amount Paid field in the design grid, and then click the Property Sheet button (Query Tools Design tab | Show/Hide group) to display the properties for the Amount Paid field.

- Click the Caption box, and then type **Paid** as the caption (Figure 2–68).

Q&A

My property sheet looks different. What should I do?

If your sheet looks different, you clicked the wrong place and will have to close the property sheet and repeat this step.

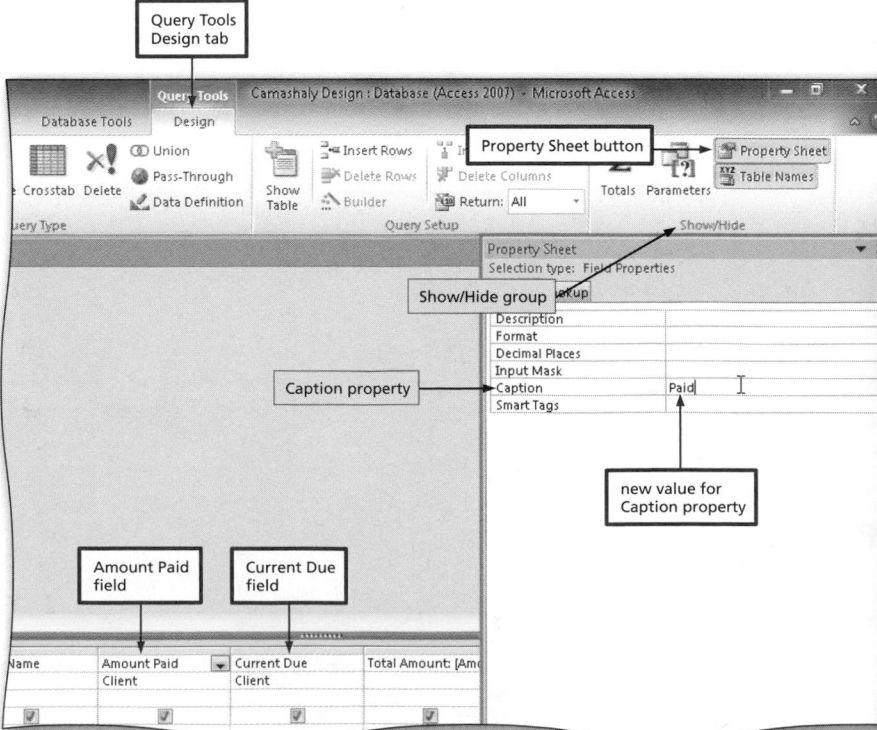

Figure 2–68

2

- Close the property sheet by clicking the Property Sheet button a second time.

- Click the Current Due field in the design grid, and then click the Property Sheet button (Query Tools Design tab | Show/Hide group).

- Click the Caption box, and then type **Due** as the caption.

- Close the Property Sheet by clicking the Property Sheet button a second time.

- View the query results (Figure 2–69).

3

- Save the query as Ch2q11.

- Close the query.

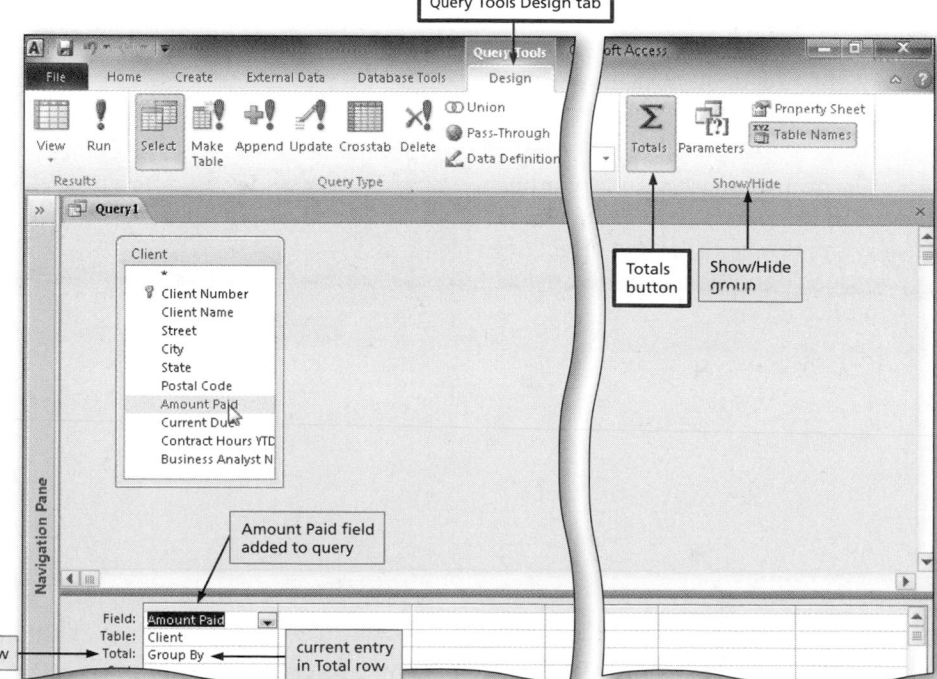

captions changed

CL #	Client Name	Paid	Due	Total Amour
BA53	Bavant Animal Hospital	$0.00	$7,500.00	$7,500.00
BB32	Babbage CPA Firm	$1,500.00	$500.00	$2,000.00
BC76	Buda Community Clinic	$2,500.00	$750.00	$3,250.00
CJ29	Catering by Jenna	$3,000.00	$1,000.00	$4,000.00
GA74	Grant Antiques	$5,500.00	$3,200.00	$8,700.00
GF56	Granger Foundation	$0.00	$6,500.00	$6,500.00
HC10	Hendley County Hospital	$3,100.00	$1,200.00	$4,300.00
KD21	KAL Design Studio	$6,000.00	$3,200.00	$9,200.00
KG04	Kyle Grocery Cooperative	$3,200.00	$0.00	$3,200.00
ME14	Mike's Electronic Stop	$2,500.00	$1,500.00	$4,000.00
PJ34	Patricia Jean Florist	$0.00	$5,200.00	$5,200.00
SL77	Smarter Law Associates	$3,800.00	$0.00	$3,800.00
TB17	The Bikeshop	$2,750.00	$1,200.00	$3,950.00
WE05	Walburg Energy Alternatives	$4,500.00	$1,450.00	$5,950.00
WS01	Woody Sporting Goods	$2,250.00	$1,600.00	$3,850.00

Figure 2–69

Other Ways

1. Right-click field in design grid, click Properties on shortcut menu

To Calculate Statistics

For group calculations, Microsoft Access supports several built-in statistics: COUNT (count of the number of records), SUM (total), AVG (average), MAX (largest value), MIN (smallest value), STDEV (standard deviation), VAR (variance), FIRST (first value), and LAST (last value). These statistics are called aggregate functions. An **aggregate function** is a function that performs some mathematical function against a group of records. To use any of these aggregate functions in a query, you include it in the Total row in the design grid. The Total row usually does not appear in the grid. To include it, click the Totals button on the Design tab.

The following steps create a new query for the Client table. The steps include the Total row in the design grid, and then calculate the average amount paid for all clients.

Query Tools Design tab

1

- Create a new query with a field list for the Client table.

- Click the Totals button (Query Tools Design tab | Show/Hide group) to include the Total row in the design grid.

- Add the Amount Paid field to the query (Figure 2–70).

Totals button

Show/Hide group

Amount Paid field added to query

Total row

current entry in Total row

Figure 2–70

• Click the Total row in the Amount Paid column to display the Total box arrow.

• Click the Total box arrow to display the Total list (Figure 2–71).

Figure 2–71

• Click Avg to select the calculation that Access is to perform (Figure 2–72).

Figure 2–72

• View the query results (Figure 2–73).

• Return to Design view and try other aggregate functions. In each case, view the results to see the effect of your selection. When finished, select Avg once again.

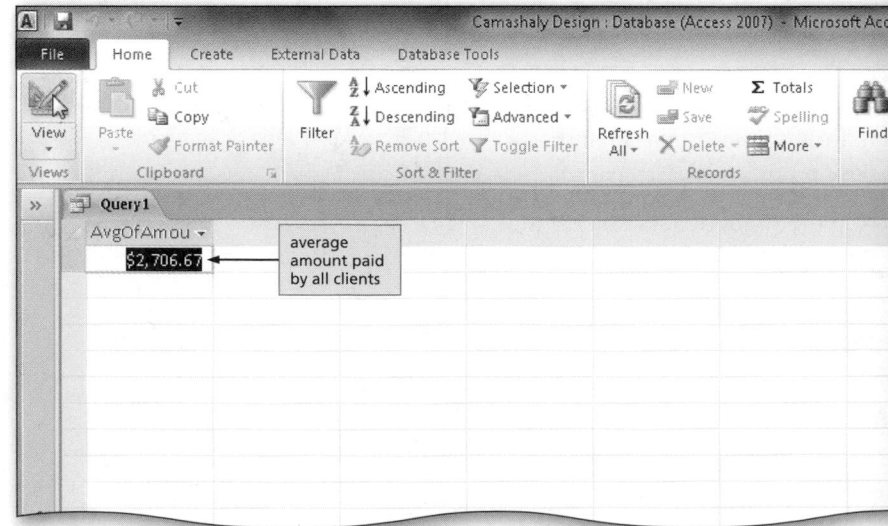

Figure 2–73

To Use Criteria in Calculating Statistics

Sometimes calculating statistics for all the records in the table is appropriate. In other cases, however, you will need to calculate the statistics for only those records that satisfy certain criteria. To enter a criterion in a field, first you select Where as the entry in the Total row for the field, and then enter the criterion in the Criteria row. The following steps use this technique to calculate the average amount paid for clients of business analyst 11. The steps also save the query with a new name.

1
- Return to Design view.

- Include the Business Analyst Number field in the design grid.

- Click the Total box arrow in the Business Analyst Number column to produce a Total list (Figure 2–74).

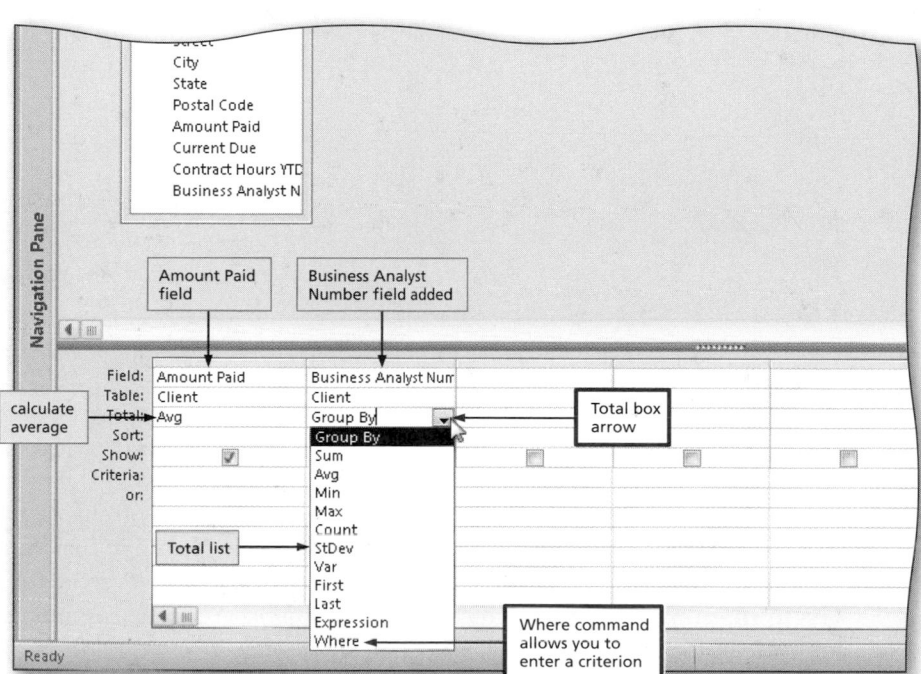

Figure 2–74

2
- Click Where.

- Type 11 as the criterion for the Business Analyst Number field (Figure 2–75).

Figure 2–75

• View the query results (Figure 2–76).

• Save the query as Ch2q12.

Figure 2–76

To Use Grouping

Another way statistics often are used is in combination with grouping; that is, statistics are calculated for groups of records. You may, for example, need to calculate the average amount paid for the clients of each business analyst. You will want the average for the clients of business analyst 11, the average for clients of business analyst 14, and so on.

Grouping means creating groups of records that share some common characteristic. In grouping by Business Analyst Number, for example, the clients of business analyst 11 would form one group, the clients of business analyst 14 would form a second, and the clients of business analyst 27 would form a third group. The calculations then are made for each group. To indicate grouping in Access, select Group By as the entry in the Total row for the field to be used for grouping.

The following steps create a query that calculates the average amount paid for clients of each business analyst at Camashaly Design. The steps also save the query with a new name.

• Return to Design view and clear the design grid.

• Include the Business Analyst Number field in the query.

• Include the Amount Paid field in the query.

• Select Avg as the calculation in the Total row for the Amount Paid field (Figure 2–77).

Q&A

Why was it not necessary for me to change the entry in the Total row for the Business Analyst Number field?

Group By, which is the initial entry in the Total row when you add a field, is correct. Thus, you did not need to change the entry.

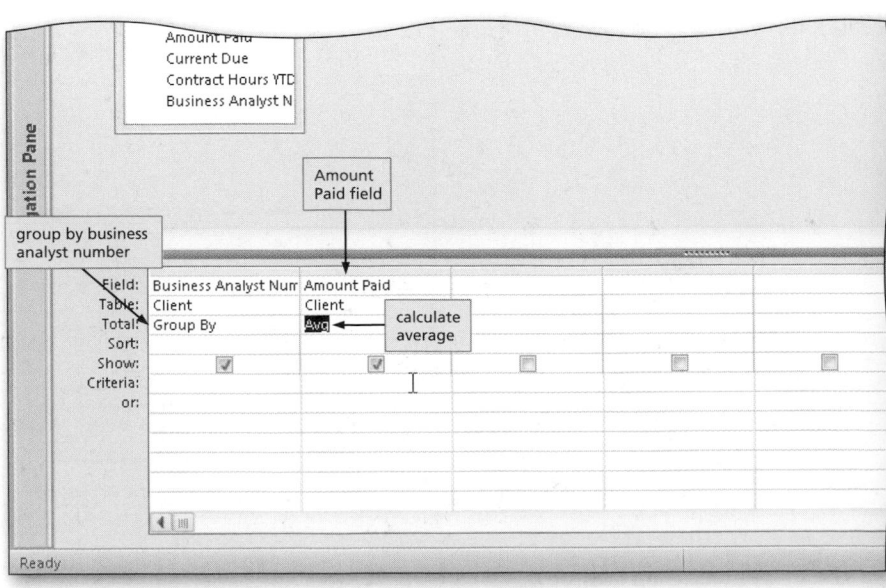

Figure 2–77

2

• View the query results (Figure 2–78).

3

• Save the query as Ch2q13.

• Close the query.

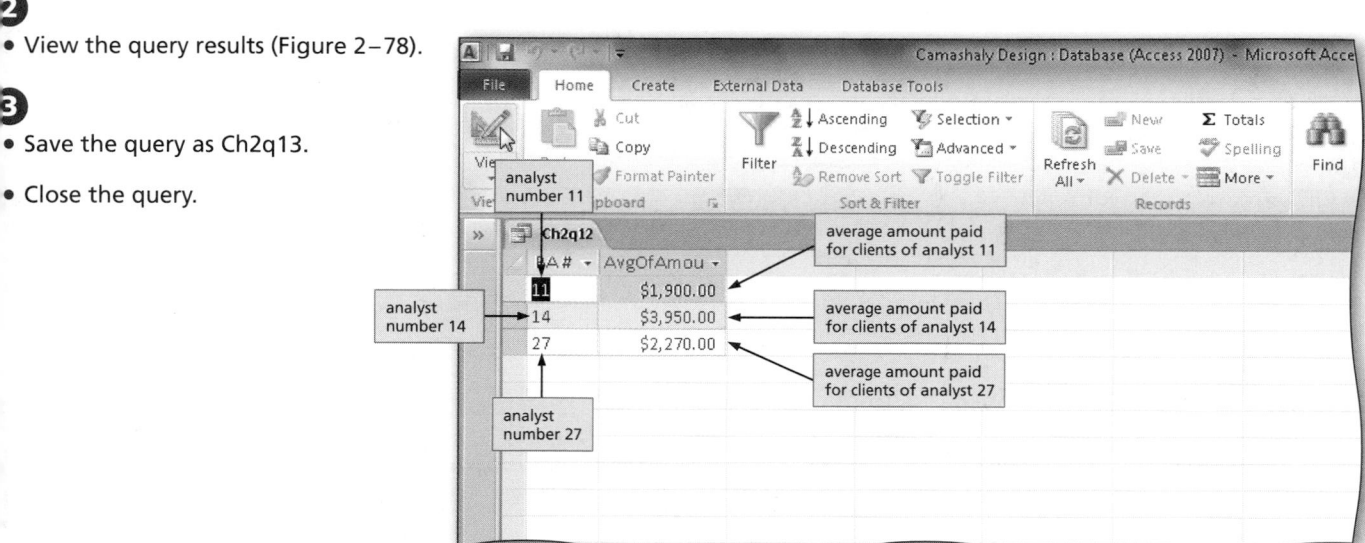

Figure 2–78

Crosstab Queries

BTW

Certification
The Microsoft Office
Specialist (MOS) program
provides an opportunity
for you to obtain a valuable
industry credential —
proof that you have the
Access 2010 skills required
by employers. For more
information, visit the
Access 2010 Certification
Web page (scsite.com/
ac2010/cert).

A crosstab query calculates a statistic (for example, sum, average, or count) for data that is grouped by two different types of information. One of the types will appear down the side of the resulting datasheet, and the other will appear across the top. Crosstab queries are useful for summarizing data by category or group.

For example, if you have determined that a query must summarize the sum of the amounts paid grouped by both city and business analyst number, you could have cities as the row headings, that is, down the side. You could have business analyst numbers as the column headings, that is, across the top. The entries within the datasheet represent the total of the amounts paid. Figure 2–79 shows a crosstab in which the total of amount paid is grouped by both city and business analyst number with cities down the left side and business analyst numbers across the top. For example, the entry in the row labeled Georgetown and in the column labeled 14 represents the total of the amount paid by all clients of business analyst 14 who are located in Georgetown.

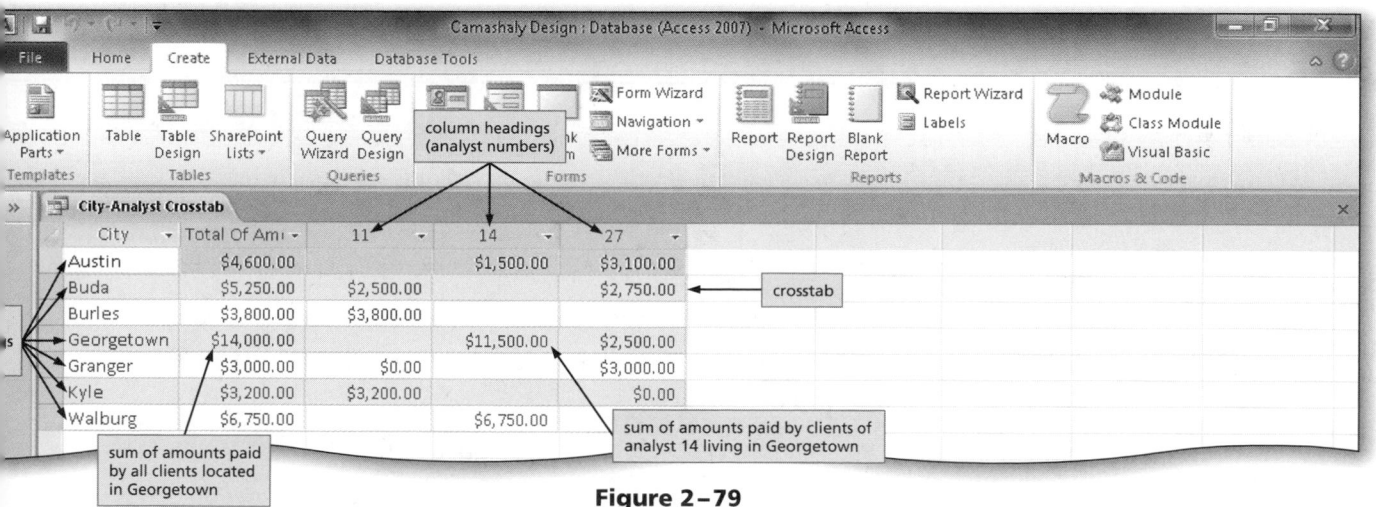

Figure 2–79

To Create a Crosstab Query

The following steps use the Crosstab Query Wizard to create a crosstab query for Camashaly Design that summarizes financial information by city and business analyst.

- Click Create on the Ribbon to display the Create tab.

- Click the Query Wizard button (Create tab | Queries group) to display the New Query dialog box (Figure 2–80).

Figure 2–80

- Click Crosstab Query Wizard (New Query dialog box).

- Click the OK button to display the Crosstab Query Wizard dialog box (Figure 2–81).

Figure 2–81

3
- With the Tables option button selected, click Table: Client to select the Client table, and then click the Next button to display the next Crosstab Query Wizard screen.

- Click the City field, and then click the Add Field button to select the City field for row headings (Figure 2–82).

Figure 2–82

4
- Click the Next button to display the next Crosstab Query Wizard screen.

- Click the Business Analyst Number field to select the Business Analyst Number field for column headings (Figure 2–83).

Figure 2–83

• Click the Next button to display the next Crosstab Query Wizard screen.

• Click the Amount Paid field to select the Amount Paid field for calculations.

• Click other fields. For each field, examine the list of calculations that are available. When finished, click the Amount Paid field again.

• Click Sum to select Sum as the calculation to be performed (Figure 2–84).

Q&A My list of functions is different. What did I do wrong?

Either you clicked the wrong field, or the Amount Paid field has the wrong data type. For example, if you mistakenly assigned it the Text data type, you would not see Sum in the list of available calculations.

Figure 2–84

• Click the Next button to display the next Crosstab Query Wizard screen.

• Type **City-Analyst Crosstab** as the name of the query (Figure 2–85).

• Click the Finish button to produce the crosstab shown in Figure 2–79 on Page AC 123.

• Close the query.

Q&A If I want to view the crosstab at some future date, can I just open the query?

Yes.

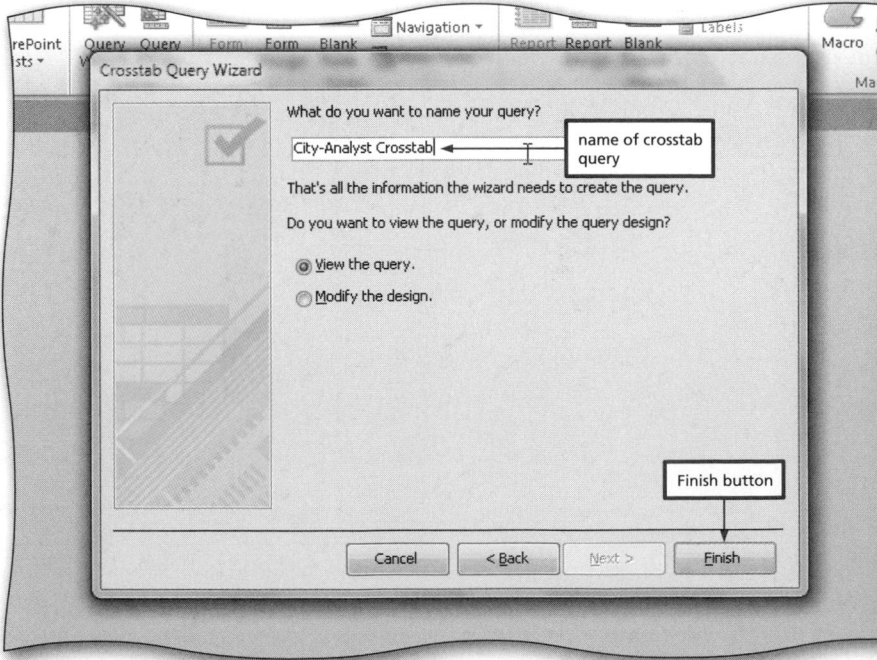

Figure 2–85

To Customize the Navigation Pane

Currently, the entries in the Navigation Pane are organized by object type. That is, all the tables are together, all the queries are together, and so on. You might want to change the way the information is organized. For example, you might want to have the Navigation Pane organized by table, with all the queries, forms, and reports associated with a particular table appearing after the name of the table. You also can use the Search bar to restrict the objects that appear to only those that have a certain collection of characters in their name. For example, if you entered the letters, Cl, only those objects containing Cl somewhere within the name will be included.

The following steps change the organization of the Navigation Pane. They also use the Search bar to restrict the objects that appear.

1
• If necessary, click the Shutter Bar Open/Close Button to open the Navigation Pane.

• Click the Navigation Pane arrow to produce the Navigation Pane menu (Figure 2–86).

2
• Click Tables and Related Views to organize the Navigation Pane by table rather than by the type of object (Figure 2–87).

3
• Click the Navigation Pane arrow to produce the Navigation Pane menu.

• Click Object Type to once again organize the Navigation Pane by object type.

Figure 2–86

Figure 2–87

Experiment

• Select different Navigate To Category options to see the effect of the option. With each option you select, select different Filter By Group options to see the effect of the filtering. When you have finished experimenting, select the Object Type Navigate To Category option and the All Access Objects Filter By Group option.

- If the Search bar does not appear, right-click the Navigation Pane and click Search Bar on the shortcut menu.

- Click in the Search bar box to produce an insertion point.

- Type **C1** as the search string to restrict the objects displayed to only those containing the desired string (Figure 2–88).

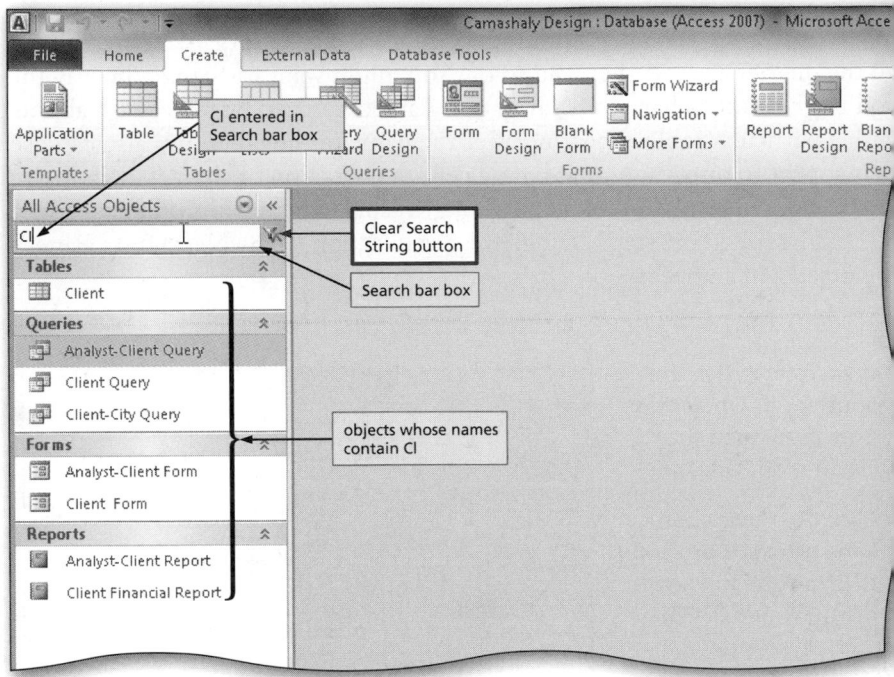

Figure 2–88

- Click the Clear Search String button to remove the search string and redisplay all objects.

Q&A

Did I have to click the button to redisplay all objects? Could I simply have erased the current string to achieve the same result?

You did not have to click the button. You could have used the DELETE or BACKSPACE keys to erase the current search string.

BTW

Quick Reference
For a table that lists how to complete the tasks covered in this book using the mouse, Ribbon, shortcut menu, and keyboard, see the Quick Reference Summary at the back of this book, or visit the Access 2010 Quick Reference Web page (scsite.com/ac2010/qr).

To Quit Access

The following steps quit Access.

1 Click the Close button on the right side of the title bar to quit Access.

2 If a Microsoft Access dialog box appears, click the Save button to save any changes made to the object since the last save.

Chapter Summary

In this chapter you have learned to create queries, enter fields, enter criteria, use text and numeric data in queries, use wildcards, use compound criteria, create parameter queries, sort data in queries, join tables in queries, perform calculations in queries, and create crosstab queries. You also learned to create a report and a form that used a query, to export a query, and to customize the Navigation Pane. The items listed below include all the new Access skills you have learned in this chapter.

1. Create a Query in Design View (AC 78)
2. Add Fields to the Design Grid (AC 79)
3. Use Text Data in a Criterion (AC 80)
4. Use a Wildcard (AC 83)
5. Use Criteria for a Field Not Included in the Results (AC 85)
6. Create and View a Parameter Query (AC 87)
7. Use a Parameter Query (AC 89)
8. Use a Number in a Criterion (AC 90)
9. Use a Comparison Operator in a Criterion (AC 91)

10. Use a Compound Criterion Involving AND (AC 92)
11. Use a Compound Criterion Involving OR (AC 93)
12. Clear the Design Grid (AC 95)
13. Sort Data in a Query (AC 96)
14. Omit Duplicates (AC 97)
15. Sort on Multiple Keys (AC 98)
16. Create a Top-Values Query (AC 99)
17. Join Tables (AC 102)
18. Change Join Properties (AC 105)
19. Create a Report Involving a Join (AC 106)

If you have a SAM 2010 user profile, your instructor may have assigned an autogradable version of this assignment. If so, log into the SAM 2010 Web site at www.cengage.com/sam2010 to download the instruction and start files.

Learn It Online

Test your knowledge of chapter content and key terms.

Instructions: To complete the Learn It Online exercises, start your browser, click the Address bar, and then enter the Web address **scsite.com/ac2010/learn**. When the Access 2010 Learn It Online page is displayed, click the link for the exercise you want to complete and then read the instructions.

Chapter Reinforcement TF, MC, and SA
A series of true/false, multiple choice, and short answer questions that test your knowledge of the chapter content.

Flash Cards
An interactive learning environment where you identify chapter key terms associated with displayed definitions.

Practice Test
A series of multiple choice questions that test your knowledge of chapter content and key terms.

Who Wants To Be a Computer Genius?
An interactive game that challenges your knowledge of chapter content in the style of a television quiz show.

Wheel of Terms
An interactive game that challenges your knowledge of chapter key terms in the style of the television show *Wheel of Fortune*

Crossword Puzzle Challenge
A crossword puzzle that challenges your knowledge of key terms presented in the chapter.

Apply Your Knowledge

Reinforce the skills and apply the concepts you learned in this chapter.

Using Wildcards in a Query, Creating a Parameter Query, Joining Tables, and Creating a Report

Instructions: Start Access. Open the Babbage CPA Firm database that you modified in Apply Your Knowledge in Chapter 1 on page AC 64. (If you did not complete this exercise, see your instructor for a copy of the modified database.)

Perform the following tasks:

1. Create a query for the Client table and add the Client Number, Client Name, City, and Amount Paid fields to the design grid. Find all clients who live in cities that start with Bu. Save the query as Apply 2 Step 1 Query.

Continued >

Apply Your Knowledge *continued*

2. Create a query for the Client table and add the Client Number, Client Name, Bookkeeper Number, and Balance Due fields to the design grid. Sort the records in descending order by Balance Due. Add a criterion for the Bookkeeper Number field that allows the user to enter a different bookkeeper each time the query is run. Save the query as Apply 2 Step 2 Query.

3. Create a query that joins the Bookkeeper and the Client tables. Add the Bookkeeper Number, First Name, and Last Name fields from the Bookkeeper table and the Client Number and Client Name fields from the Client table. Sort the records in ascending order by Bookkeeper Number and Client Number. All bookkeepers should appear in the result, even if they currently have no clients. Save the query as Bookkeeper-Client Query.

4. Create the report shown in Figure 2–89. The report uses the Bookkeeper-Client Query.

Bookkeeper-Client Report

BKR #	First Name	Last Name	CL #	Client Name
22	Johanna	Lewes	A54	Afton Mills
22	Johanna	Lewes	D76	Dege Grocery
22	Johanna	Lewes	J77	Jones Plumbing
22	Johanna	Lewes	S56	SeeSaw Industries
24	Mario	Rodriguez	A62	Atlas Suppliers
24	Mario	Rodriguez	B26	Blake-Scripps
24	Mario	Rodriguez	G56	Grand Cleaners
24	Mario	Rodriguez	M26	Mohr Crafts
34	Choi	Wong	C29	Catering by Jenna
34	Choi	Wong	H21	Hill Shoes
34	Choi	Wong	T45	Tate Repair
34	Choi	Wong	W24	Woody Sporting Goods
38	Theresa	Sinthin		

Figure 2–89

5. Submit the revised database in the format specified by your instructor.

Extend Your Knowledge

Extend the skills you learned in this chapter and experiment with new skills. You may need to use Help to complete the assignment.

Creating Crosstab Queries, Creating Queries Using Criteria, and Exporting a Query

Instructions: Start Access. Open the Natural Earthscapes database. See the inside back cover of this book for instructions for downloading the Data Files for Students, or see your instructor for information on accessing the files required in this book.

Natural Earthscapes is a small landscaping company that specializes in landscaping with native plants. The owners have created an Access database in which to store information about the customers they serve and the workers they employ. You will create the crosstab shown in Figure 2–90. You also will query the database using specified criteria.

Figure 2–90

Perform the following tasks:

1. Create the crosstab query shown in Figure 2–90. The crosstab query groups the total of customers' balances by city and worker number.

2. Create a query to find all customers who do not live in Kingston. Include the Customer Number, Last Name, Balance, and Amount Paid fields in the design grid. Save the query as Extend 2 Step 2 Query.

3. Create a query to find all customers where the customer's first name is either Frances or Francis. Include the Customer Number, Last Name, First Name, Street, and City fields in the query results. Save the query as Extend 2 Step 3 Query.

4. Create a query to find all customers where the worker number is 303 or 305 and the balance is greater than $40.00. Include the Customer Number, Last Name, First Name, Balance, and Worker Number fields in the design grid. Use the IN operator in your query design. Save the query as Extend 2 Step 4 Query.

5. Export the City-Worker Crosstab as a Word file with the name City-Worker Crosstab.rtf and save the export steps.

6. Open the Customer table and change the balance for AB10 to $90.

7. Use the saved export steps to export the City-Worker Crosstab again. When asked if you want to replace the existing file, click Yes.

8. Change the database properties, as specified by your instructor. Submit the revised database and the exported RTF file in the format specified by your instructor.

Make It Right

Analyze a database and correct all errors and/or improve the design.

Correcting Errors in the Query Design

Instructions: Start Access. Open the Retired Pet Sitters database. See the inside back cover of this book for instructions for downloading the Data Files for Students, or see your instructor for information on accessing the files required in this book.

Continued >

Make It Right *continued*

Retired Pet Sitters is a database maintained by a small pet-sitting business. The queries shown in Figure 2–91 contain a number of errors that need to be corrected before the queries run properly. The query shown in Figure 2–91a displays the query results in the proper order (Last Name, First Name, Balance, Sitter Number), but it is sorted incorrectly. The query results should be sorted by last name within sitter number in ascending order. Also, the caption for the Balance field should be Owed. Save the query with your changes.

When you try to run the query shown in Figure 2–91b, you get 0 results. You are trying to find all customers who live on Magee. Correct the error and save the query with your changes.

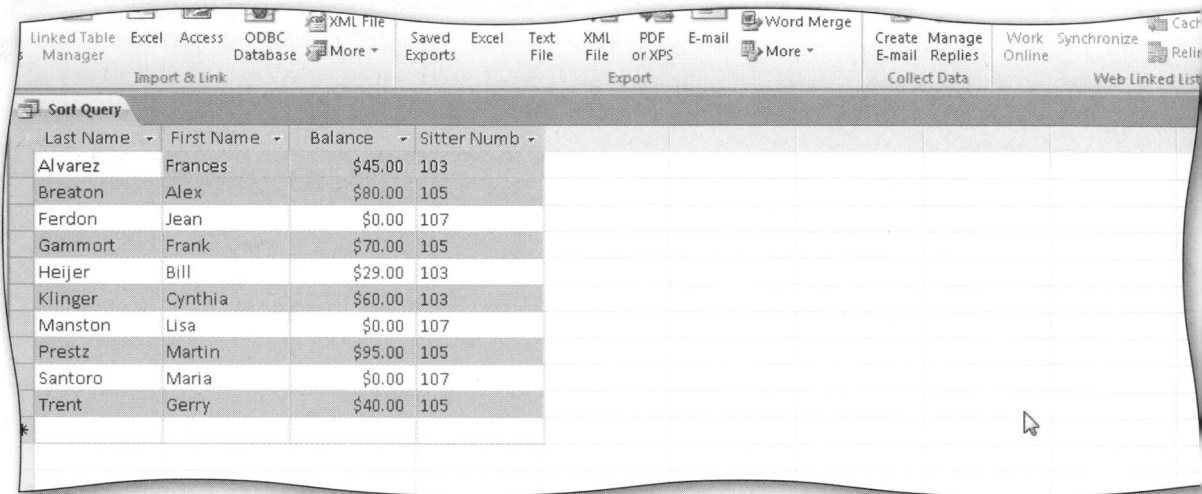

Figure 2–91 (a) Incorrect Sort Query

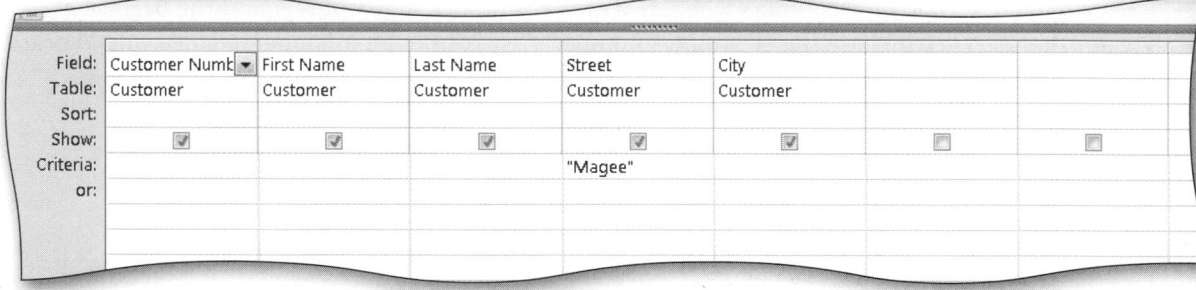

Figure 2–91 (b) Incorrect Criteria Query

Change the database properties, as specified by your instructor. Submit the revised database in the format specified by your instructor.

In the Lab

Design, create, modify, and/or use a database following the guidelines, concepts, and skills presented in this chapter. The assignments are listed in order of increasing difficulty.

Lab 1: Querying the ECO Clothesline Database

Problem: The management of ECO Clothesline has determined a number of questions it wants the database management system to answer. You must obtain answers to the questions posed by management.

Instructions: Use the database modified in the In the Lab 1 of Chapter 1 on page AC 66 for this assignment, or see your instructor for information on accessing the files required for this book.

Perform the following tasks:

1. Open the ECO Clothesline database and create a new query for the Customer table that includes the Customer Number, Customer Name, Amount Paid, and Sales Rep Number fields in the design grid for all customers where the sales rep number is 49. Save the query as Lab 2-1 Step 1 Query.

2. Create a query that includes the Customer Number, Customer Name, and Amount Paid fields for all customers located in Virginia (VA) with a paid amount greater than $1,000.00. Save the query as Lab 2-1 Step 2 Query.

3. Create a query that includes the Customer Number, Customer Name, Street, and City fields for all customers whose names begin with T. Save the query as Lab 2-1 Step 3 Query.

4. Create a query for the Customer table that lists all cities in ascending order. Each city should appear only once. Save the query as Lab 2-1 Step 4 Query.

5. Create a query for the Customer table that allows the user to enter the city to search when the query is run. The query results should display the Customer Number, Customer Name, Balance, and Amount Paid fields. Test the query by searching for those records where the client is located in Ashton. Save the query as Lab 2-1 Step 5 Query.

6. Include the Customer Number, Customer Name, and Balance fields in the design grid. Sort the records in descending order by the Balance field. Display only the top 25 percent of the records in the query result. Save the query as Lab 2-1 Step 6 Query.

7. Join the Sales Rep and the Customer table. Include the Sales Rep Number, First Name, and Last Name fields from the Sales Rep table. Include the Customer Number, Customer Name, and Balance from the Customer table. Sort the records in ascending order by sales rep's last name and customer name. All sales reps should appear in the result even if they currently have no customers. Save the query as Lab 2-1 Step 7 Query.

8. Open the Lab 2-1 Step 7 Query in Design view and remove the Sales Rep table. Add the Amount Paid field to the design grid. Calculate the total of the balance and amount paid amounts. Assign the alias Total Amount to the calculated field. Change the caption for the Balance field to Due. Use the Save Object As command to save the query as Lab 2-1 Step 8 Query.

9. Create a query to display the average balance amount for all customers. Save the query as Lab 2-1 Step 9 Query.

10. Create a query to display the average balance amount for sales rep 51. Save the query as Lab 2-1 Step 10 Query.

11. Create a query to display the average balance amount for each sales rep. Save the query as Lab 2-1 Step 11 Query.

12. Create the crosstab shown in Figure 2–92. The crosstab groups the total of customers' amount paid amounts by state and sales rep number. Save the crosstab as State-Sales Rep Crosstab.

13. Submit the revised database in the format specified by your instructor.

State ▾	Total Of Am₁ ▾	44 ▾	49 ▾	51 ▾
NC	$2,235.00	$1,400.00	$710.00	$125.00
TN	$6,245.00	$1,695.00	$2,600.00	$1,950.00
VA	$5,180.00	$2,425.00	$700.00	$2,055.00

Figure 2–92

In the Lab

Lab 2: Querying the Walburg Energy Alternatives Database

Problem: The manager of the Walburg Energy Alternatives store has determined a number of questions he wants the database management system to answer. You must obtain answers to the questions posed by the manager.

Instructions: Use the database created in the In the Lab 2 of Chapter 1 on page AC 67 for this assignment or see your instructor for information on accessing the files required for this book.

Perform the following tasks:

1. Open the Walburg Energy Alternatives database and create a query that includes all fields and all records in the Item table. There should be only one column in the design grid. Name the query Lab 2-2 Step 1 Query.

2. Create a query that includes the Item Number, Description, Cost, and Vendor Code fields for all items where the vendor code is JM. Save the query as Lab 2-2 Step 2 Query.

3. Create a query that includes the Item Number and Description fields for all items where the description starts with the letters, En. Save the query as Lab 2-2 Step 3 Query.

4. Create a query that includes the Item Number and Description fields for all items with a cost less than $4.00. Save the query as Lab 2-2 Step 4 Query.

5. Create a query that includes the Item Number and Description fields for all items with a selling price greater than $20.00. Save the query as Lab 2-2 Step 5 Query.

6. Create a query that includes all fields for all items with a vendor code of AS and where the number on hand is fewer than 10. Save the query as Lab 2-2 Step 6 Query.

7. Create a query that includes all fields for all items that have a selling price greater than $10.00 or a vendor code of JM. Save the query as Lab 2-2 Step 7 Query.

8. Join the Vendor table and the Item table. Include the Vendor Code and Vendor Name fields from the Vendor table and the Item Number, Description, On Hand, and Cost fields from the Item table. Sort the records in ascending order by item number within vendor code. Save the query as Vendor-Item Query.

9. Create the form shown in Figure 2–93. The form uses the Vendor-Item Query.

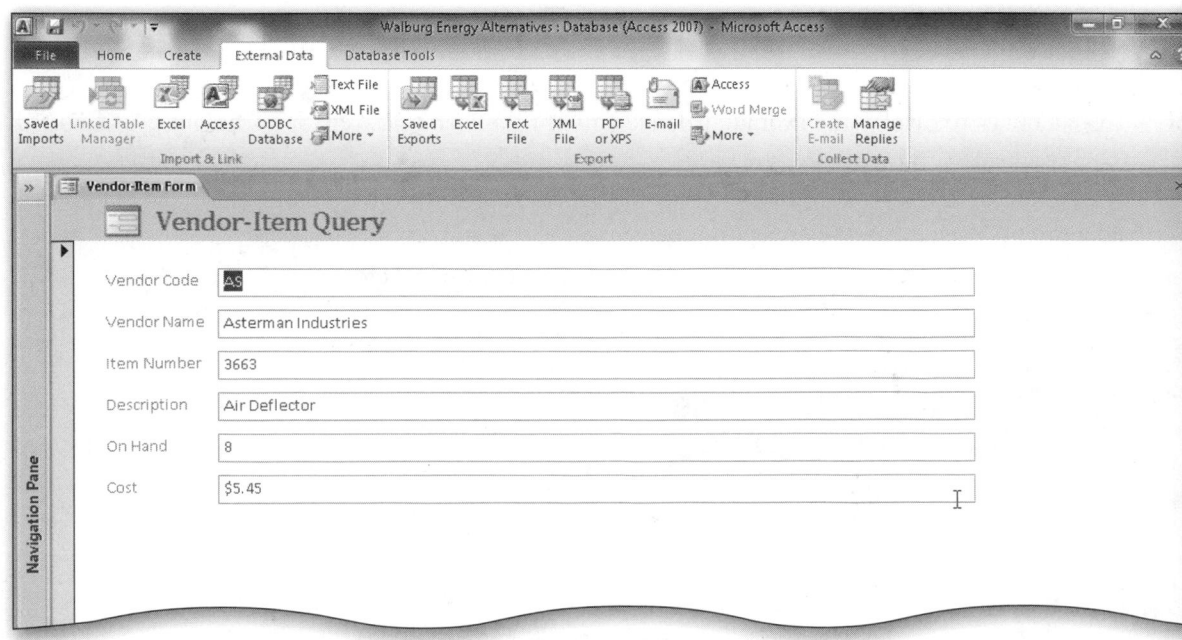

Figure 2–93

10. Create a query that includes the Item Number, Description, On Hand, and Cost fields. Calculate the inventory value (on hand*cost) for all records in the table. Assign the alias Inventory Value to the calculated field. Change the caption for the On Hand column to In Stock. Format the Inventory Value field as currency with two decimal places. Sort the records in descending order by inventory value. Save the query as Lab 2-2 Step 10 Query.

11. Create a query that calculates and displays the average cost of all items. Save the query as Lab 2-2 Step 11 Query.

12. Create a query that calculates and displays the average cost of items grouped by vendor code. Save the query as Lab 2-2 Step 12 Query.

13. Submit the revised database in the format specified by your instructor.

In the Lab

Lab 3: Querying the Philamar Training Database

Problem: The management of Philamar Training has determined a number of questions it wants the database management system to answer. You must obtain answers to the questions posed by management.

Instructions: Use the database created in the In the Lab 3 of Chapter 1 on page AC 70 for this assignment, or see your instructor for information on accessing the files required for this book. For Part 1 and Part 3, save each query using a format similar to the following: Lab 2-3 Part 1a Query, Lab 2-3 Part 3a Query, and so on. Submit the revised database and the Trainer-Client Query.xlsx file in the format specified by your instructor.

Instructions Part 1: Create a new query for the Client table and include the Client Number, Client Name, Amount Paid, and Current Due fields in the design grid. Create queries that answer the following questions: (a) Which clients' names begin with F? (b) Which clients are located in Kingston? (c) Which clients have a current due amount of $0.00? (d) Which clients have an amount paid amount between $5,000.00 and $10,000.00? (e) Which two clients have the highest current due amounts? (f) For each client, what is the total of the current due and amount paid?

Instructions Part 2: Join the Trainer and the Client table. In the design grid, include the Trainer Number, First Name, and Last Name from the Trainer table and the Client Number, Client Name, and Amount Paid from the Client table. Sort the records in ascending order by trainer number and client number. All trainers should appear in the result, even if they currently have no clients. Save the query as Trainer-Client Query. Export the query to Excel and save the export steps.

Instructions Part 3: Create queries to calculate the following statistics: (a) What is the average current due amount for clients assigned to trainer 42? (b) What is the total current due amount for all clients? (c) What is the total amount paid for each trainer?

Cases and Places

Apply your creative thinking and problem solving skills to design and implement a solution.

Note: To complete these assignments, you may be required to use the Data Files for Students. See the inside back cover of this book for instructions on downloading the Data Files for Students, or contact your instructor for information about accessing the required files.

1: Querying the Chamber of Commerce Database

Academic

Use the Chamber of Commerce database you created in Cases and Places 1 in Chapter 1 on page AC 72 for this assignment. Use the concepts and techniques presented in this chapter to create queries for the following:

a. Find the advertiser name and address of all advertisers located on Main.

Continued >

Cases and Places *continued*

b. Find the advertiser number, advertiser name, balance, and amount paid for all advertisers whose balance is greater than $300 or whose amount paid is $0.00.

c. Find the total of the balance and amount paid amounts for each advertiser. Show the advertiser number, advertiser name, and total amount. Sort the results in descending order by total.

d. Find the advertiser number, advertiser name, balance, and amount paid for all advertisers whose balance is between $200 and $500.

e. Create a parameter query for the Advertiser table that will allow the user to enter a different postal code each time the query is run. The user should see all fields in the query result.

f. Find the ad rep for each advertiser. List the ad rep number, last name, first name, advertiser number, advertiser name, and balance. Sort the results in ascending order by ad rep number and advertiser number.

g. Determine the total of the balance amounts and amount paid amounts for all advertisers.

Submit the revised database in the format specified by your instructor.

2: Querying the Consignment Database

Personal

Use the Consignment database you created in Cases and Places 2 in Chapter 1 on page AC 72 for this assignment. Use the concepts and techniques presented in this chapter to create queries for the following:

a. Find the item number and description of all items that contain the word, Table.

b. Find the item number, description, condition, and date of the item that has the earliest posting date.

c. Find the total price (price*quantity) of each item available for sale. Show the item number, item description, and total price.

d. Find the seller of each item. Show the seller's first name and last name as well as the item description, price, quantity, and date posted. Sort the results by item description within seller last name.

e. Create a report based on the query you created in Step d. Include all fields in the report.

f. Modify the query you created in Step d to restrict retrieval to those items with a price greater than $50.00.

g. Find all items posted between March 1, 2012, and March 4, 2012. The user should see all fields in the query result.

Submit the revised database in the format specified by your instructor.

3: Querying the Senior Care Database

Professional

Use the Senior Care database you created in Cases and Places 3 in Chapter 1 on page AC 72 for this assignment. Use the concepts and techniques presented in this chapter to create queries for the following:

a. Find the first name, last name, and address of all clients where the street name begins with the letter U

b. Find the client number, last name, first name, balance, and amount paid for all clients whose balance is $0.00 or whose amount paid is $0.00.

c. Find the total of the balance and amount paid amounts for each client. Show the client number, client last name, client first name, and total amount. Sort the results in descending order by total.

d. Find the helper for each client. List the helper number, helper last name, helper first name, client number, client last name, and client first name. Sort the results in ascending order by helper number and client number.

e. Create a report for the query created in Step d. Include all fields except the helper first name in the report. Create a form for the query created in Step d.

f. Export the query created in Step d as a text file.

g. Find the highest and lowest balances.

Submit the exported text file and revised database in the format specified by your instructor.

3 | Maintaining a Database

Objectives

You will have mastered the material in this chapter when you can:

- Add, change, and delete records
- Search for records
- Filter records
- Update a table design
- Use action queries to update records
- Use delete queries to delete records
- Specify validation rules, default values, and formats

- Create and use single-valued lookup fields
- Create and use multivalued lookup fields
- Add new fields to an existing report
- Format a datasheet
- Specify referential integrity
- Use a subdatasheet
- Sort records

3 | Maintaining a Database

Introduction

Once a database has been created and loaded with data, it must be maintained. **Maintaining the database** means modifying the data to keep it up to date by adding new records, changing the data for existing records, and deleting records. Updating can include mass updates or mass deletions, that is, updates to, or deletions of, many records at the same time.

Maintenance of a database also can involve the need to **restructure the database** periodically, that is, to change the database structure. Restructuring can include adding new fields to a table, changing the characteristics of existing fields, and removing existing fields. Restructuring also includes the creation of validation rules and referential integrity. Validation rules ensure the validity of the data in the database, whereas referential integrity ensures the validity of the relationships. Maintaining a database also can include filtering records, a process that ensures that only the records that satisfy some criterion appear when viewing and updating the data in a table. Changing the appearance of a datasheet is a maintenance activity.

BTW

Database Backup
If you are doing mass changes to a database, be sure to back up the database prior to doing the updates.

BTW

The Ribbon and Screen Resolution
Access may change how the groups and buttons within the groups appear on the Ribbon, depending on the computer's screen resolution. Thus, your Ribbon may look different from the ones in this book if you are using a screen resolution other than 1024 × 768.

Project — Maintaining a Database

Camashaly Design faces the task of keeping its database up to date. As the company takes on new clients and business analysts, it will need to add new records, make changes to existing records, and delete records. Camashaly believes that it can serve its clients better by changing the structure of the database to categorize the clients by type. The company will do this by adding a Client Type field to the Client table. Business analysts believe they can maintain better client relationships if the database includes the services that are of interest to clients. The company will do so by adding a Services Needed field to the Client table. Because clients may need more than one service, this field will be a multivalued field, which is a field that can store multiple values or entries. Along with these changes, Camashaly staff wants to change the appearance of a datasheet when displaying data.

Camashaly would like the ability to make mass updates, that is, to update or delete many records in a single operation. It wants rules that make sure users can enter only valid or appropriate, data into the database. Camashaly also wants to ensure that the database cannot contain the name of a client who is not associated with a specific business analyst. A final goal for Camashaly is to improve the efficiency of certain types of processing, specifically, sorting and retrieving data.

Figure 3–1 summarizes some of the various types of activities involved in maintaining the Camashaly Design database.

Figure 3–1

Overview

As you read through this chapter, you will learn how to maintain a database by performing these general tasks:

- Add, change, and delete records.
- Filter records so that only those records that satisfy some criterion appear in a datasheet or form.
- Change the structure of a table.
- Make mass changes to a table.
- Create validation rules to ensure that the database contains only valid data.
- Use single-valued and multivalued lookup fields.
- Update forms and reports to reflect changes to the table structure.
- Change the appearance of a datasheet.
- Enforce relationships by creating referential integrity.
- Order records.

Plan
Ahead

Database Maintenance Decisions

When maintaining a database in Access, you must consider how the database is being used and how it could be improved. The decisions you make will affect the modification of records, fields, default settings, formatting, and table relationships. To maintain a database, you should follow these general guidelines:

1. **Determine when it is necessary to add, change, or delete records in a database.** Decide how often updates are necessary. You might need to update the database on a regular schedule, or only as needed, depending on your needs. Also determine whether to make the updates to individual records or whether mass updates would be more efficient.

2. **Determine whether you should filter records.** For each situation where a user will be working with a table in the database, examine whether it might be desirable to have the records filtered, that is, to have only those records that satisfy some criterion appear.

3. **Determine whether additional fields are necessary or whether existing fields should be deleted.** Have there been any changes to the initial requirements that would require the addition of a field (or fields) to one of the tables? If so, you will need to add the field to the appropriate table. Also, now that the database has been in operation for a period of time, determine whether all the fields actually are being used. If some fields are not in use, verify that they are, in fact, no longer needed. If so, you can delete the field from the table.

4. **Determine whether validation rules, default values, and formats are necessary.** Can you improve the accuracy of the data entry process by enforcing data validation? What values are allowed for a particular field? For example, client name data should not be allowed in a city field. Are there some fields in which one particular value is used more than another? You can control the values that are entered in a field by modifying the table design to include default values, formats, and validation rules.

5. **Determine whether changes to the format of a datasheet are desirable.** Do you want to modify the appearance of the Datasheet view of your tables? It is a good idea to be consistent throughout all your tables except in special circumstances.

6. **Identify related tables in order to implement relationships between the tables.** Examine the database design you created earlier to identify related tables. Is there a one-to-many relationship between the tables? If so, which table is the one table? Which table is the many table? For each pair of related tables, you will need to make decisions about the implementation of the relationship between the tables.

When necessary, more specific details concerning the above decisions and/or actions are presented at appropriate points in the chapter. The chapter also will identify the use of these guidelines in database maintenance tasks such as those shown in Figure 3–1.

For an introduction to Windows 7 and instruction about how to perform basic Windows 7 tasks, read the Office 2010 and Windows 7 chapter at the beginning of this book, where you can learn how to resize windows, change screen resolution, create folders, move and rename files, use Windows Help, and much more.

To Start Access

The following steps, which assume Windows 7 is running, start Access based on a typical installation. You may need to ask your instructor how to start Access for your computer. For a detailed example of the procedure summarized below, refer to the Office 2010 and Windows 7 chapter at the beginning of this book.

1 Click the Start button on the Windows 7 taskbar to display the Start menu.

2 Type **Microsoft Access** as the search text in the 'Search programs and files' text box and watch the search results appear on the Start menu.

3 Click Microsoft Access 2010 in the search results on the Start menu to start Access.

4 If the Access window is not maximized, click the Maximize button next to the Close button on its title bar to maximize the window.

To Open a Database from Access

In Chapter 1, you created and saved your database on a USB flash drive using the file name, Camashaly Design. The following steps open the Camashaly Design database from the Access folder in the CIS 101 folder on the USB flash drive. For a detailed example of the procedure summarized below, refer to the Office 2010 and Windows 7 chapter at the beginning of this book.

1 With your USB flash drive connected to one of the computer's USB ports, click File on the Ribbon to open the Backstage view.

2 Click Open in the Backstage view to display the Open dialog box.

3 Navigate to the location of the file to be opened (in this case, the USB flash drive, then to the CIS 101 folder [or your class folder], and then to the Access folder).

4 Click Camashaly Design to select the file to be opened.

5 Click the Open button (Open dialog box) to open the selected file and display the opened database in the Access window.

6 If a Security Warning appears, click the Enable Content button.

For an introduction to Office 2010 and instruction about how to perform basic tasks in Office 2010 programs, read the Office 2010 and Windows 7 chapter at the beginning of this book, where you can learn how to start a program, use the Ribbon, save a file, open a file, quit a program, use Help, and much more.

Updating Records

Keeping the data in a database up to date requires updating records in three ways: adding new records, changing the data in existing records, and deleting existing records.

Adding Records

In Chapter 1, you added records to a database using Datasheet view; that is, as you added records, the records appeared on the screen in a datasheet. The data looked like a table. When you need to add additional records, you can use the same techniques.

In Chapter 1, you used a simple form to view records. You also can use a **split form**, a form that allows you to simultaneously view both simple form and datasheet views of the data. You can use either portion of a split form to add or update records. To add new records, change existing records, or delete records, you use the same techniques you used in Datasheet view.

BTW

Q&As
For a complete list of the Q&As found in many of the step-by-step sequences in this book, visit the Access 2010 Q&A Web page (scsite.com/ac2010/qa).

To Create a Split Form

The following steps create a split form.

- Open the Navigation Pane if it is currently closed.

- If necessary, click the Client table in the Navigation Pane to select it.

- Click Create on the Ribbon to display the Create tab.

- Click the More Forms button (Create tab | Forms group) to display the More Forms menu (Figure 3–2).

Figure 3–2

- Click Split Form to create a split form.

- Close the Navigation Pane (Figure 3–3).

Q&A

Is the form automatically saved the way the report was created when I used the Report Wizard?

No. You will need to take specific actions if you want to save the form.

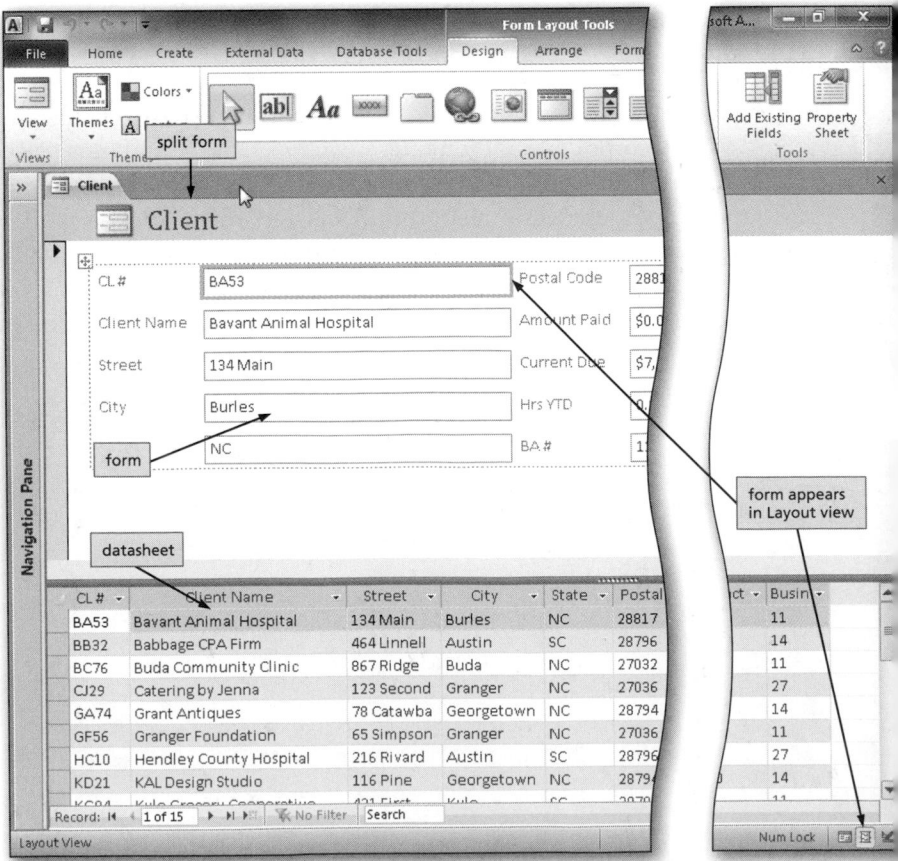

Figure 3–3

3

- If the form appears in Layout view, click the Form View button on the Access status bar to display the form in Form view (Figure 3–4).

🔎 **Experiment**

- Click the various Navigation buttons (First record, Next record, Previous record, Last record, and New (blank) record) to see each button's effect. Click the Current Record box, change the record number, and press the ENTER key to see how to move to a specific record.

Figure 3–4

4

- Click the Save button on the Quick Access Toolbar to display the Save As dialog box.

- Type **Client Split Form** as the form name (Figure 3–5).

5

- Click the OK button (Save As dialog box) to save the form.

Figure 3–5

To Use a Form to Add Records

Once a form or split form is open in Form view, you can add records using the same techniques you used to add records in Datasheet view. The changes you make on the form are automatically made on the datasheet. You do not need to take any special action. The following steps use the split form that you just created to add records.

1

• Click the 'New (blank) record' button on the Navigation bar to enter a new record, and then type the data for the new record, as shown in Figure 3–6. Press the TAB key after typing the data in each field, except after typing the data for the final field (Business Analyst Number).

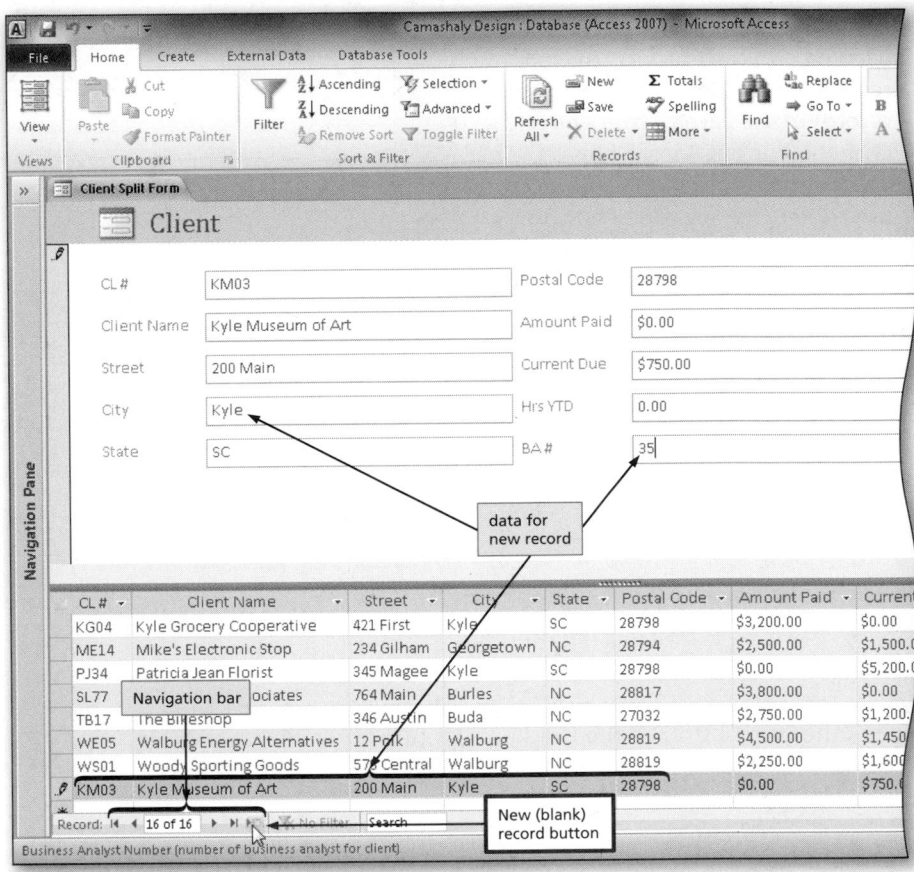

Figure 3–6

2

• Press the TAB key to complete the entry of the record.

• Close the form.

Other Ways

1. Click New button (Home tab | Records group)
2. Press CTRL+PLUS SIGN (+)

To Search for a Record

In the database environment, **searching** means looking for records that satisfy some criteria. Looking for the client whose number is GF56 is an example of searching. The queries in Chapter 2 also were examples of searching. Access had to locate those records that satisfied the criteria.

However, you can perform a search in Form view or Datasheet view without creating a query. To update client GF56, for example, first you need to find the client.

The following steps show how to search for the client whose number is GF56.

1

- Open the Navigation Pane.

- Scroll down in the Navigation Pane, if necessary, so that Client Split Form appears on your screen, right-click Client Split Form to display a shortcut menu, and then click Open on the shortcut menu to open the form in Form view.

   Which command on the shortcut menu gives me Form view? I see both Layout View and Design View, but no option for Form View.

   The Open command opens the form in Form view.

- Close the Navigation Pane (Figure 3–7).

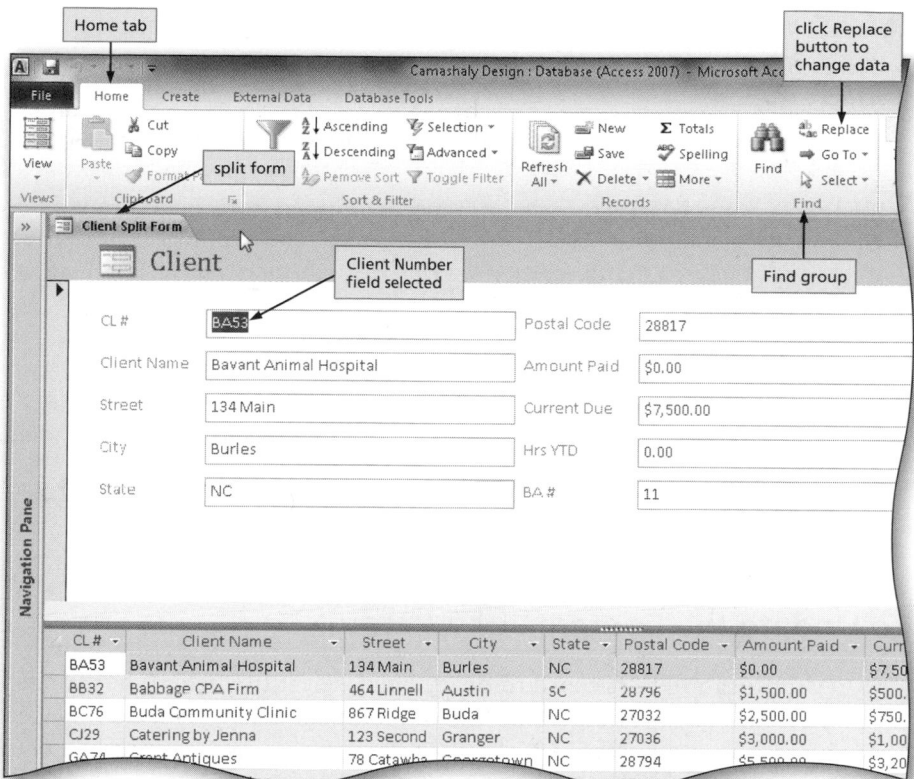

Figure 3–7

2

- Click the Find button (Home tab | Find group) to display the Find and Replace dialog box.

- Type **GF56** in the Find What text box (Find and Replace dialog box).

- Click the Find Next button to find client GF56 (Figure 3–8).

   Can I find records in Datasheet view or in Form view?

   Yes. You use the same process to find records whether you are viewing the data with a split form, in Datasheet view, or in Form view.

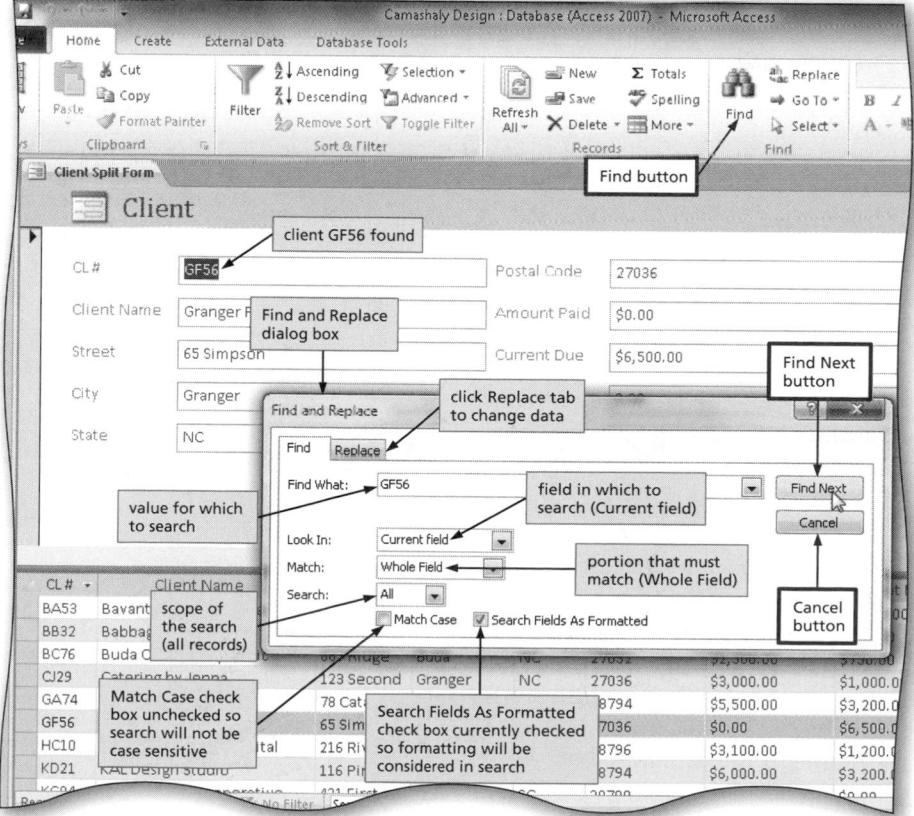

Figure 3–8

3

- Click the Cancel button (Find and Replace dialog box) to remove the dialog box from the screen.

Q&A Why does the button in the dialog box read, Find Next, rather than simply Find?

In some cases, after locating a record that satisfies a criterion, you might need to find the next record that satisfies the same criterion. For example, if you just found the first client whose business analyst number is 14, you then may want to find the second such client, then the third, and so on. To do so, click the Find Next button. You will not need to retype the value each time.

Q&A Can I replace one value with another using this dialog box?

Yes. Either click the Replace button (Home tab | Find group) or click the Replace tab in the Find and Replace dialog box. You then can enter both the value to find and the new value.

BTW

BTWs
For a complete list of the BTWs found in the margins of this book, visit the Access 2010 BTW Web page (scsite.com/ac2010/btw).

Other Ways
1. Press CTRL+F

To Update the Contents of a Record

After locating the record to be changed, select the field to be changed by clicking the field. You also can press the TAB key repeatedly until the desired field is selected. Then make the appropriate changes. (Clicking the field automatically produces an insertion point. If you use the TAB key, you will need to press F2 to produce an insertion point.)

The following step uses Form view to change the name of client GF56 from Granger Foundation to Granger Family Foundation.

1

- Click in the Client Name field in the form for client GF56 immediately to the left of the F in the word, Foundation.

- Type the word **Family** before the word, Foundation, and then press the SPACEBAR to insert a space.

- Press the TAB key to complete the change and move to the next field (Figure 3–9).

Q&A Could I have changed the contents of the field in the datasheet portion of the split form?

Yes. You will first need to ensure the record to be changed appears in the datasheet. You then can change the value just as in the form.

Q&A Do I need to save my change?

No. Once you move to another record or close this form, the change to the name will become permanent.

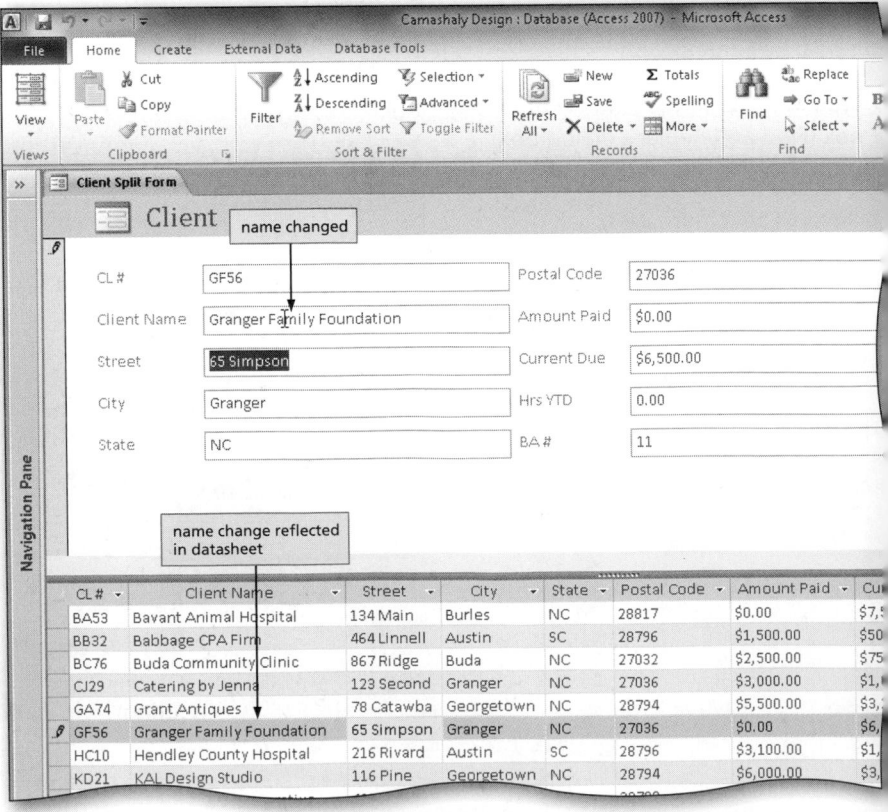

Figure 3–9

To Delete a Record

When records no longer are needed, delete the records (remove them) from the table. If client GA74 no longer is served by Camashaly Design and its final payment has been received, the record can be deleted. The following steps delete client GA74.

1

- With the Client Split Form open, click the record selector in the datasheet, the small box that appears to the left of the first field of the record on which the client number is GA74 to select the record (Figure 3–10).

  That technique works in the datasheet portion. How do I select the record in the form portion?

  With the desired record appearing in the form, click the record selector (the triangle in front of the record) to select the entire record.

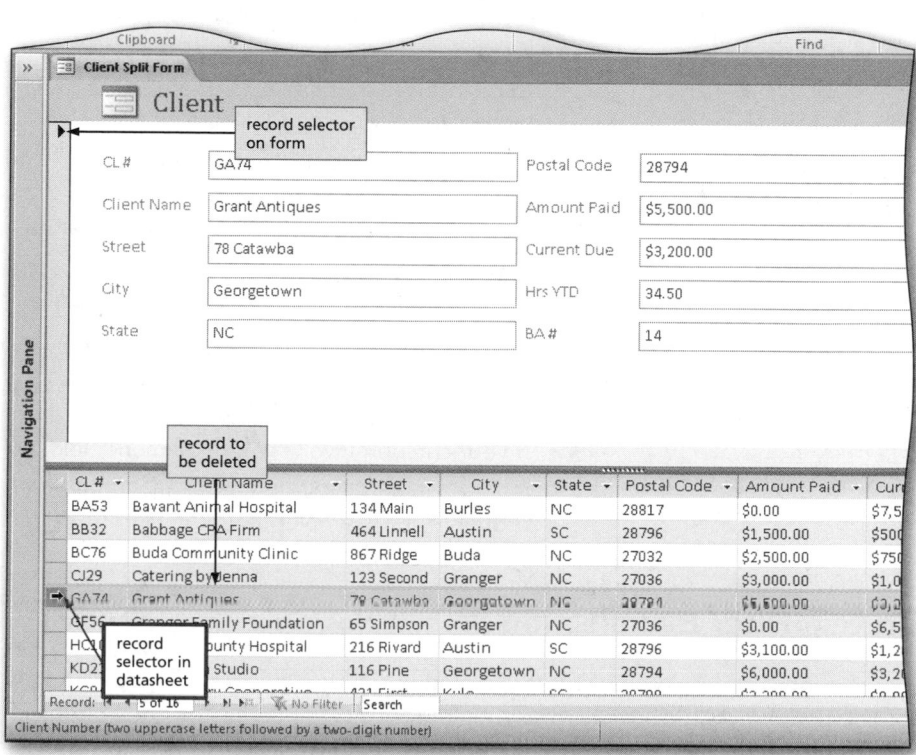

Figure 3–10

2

- Press the DELETE key to delete the record (Figure 3–11).

3

- Click the Yes button to complete the deletion.

- Close the Client Split Form.

Other Ways

1. Click Delete button (Home tab | Records group)

Figure 3–11

Filtering Records

You can use the Find button in either Datasheet view or Form view to locate a record quickly that satisfies some criterion (for example, the client number is GF56). All records appear, however, not just the record or records that satisfy the criterion. To have only the record or records that satisfy the criterion appear, use a **filter**. Four types of filters are available: Filter By Selection, Common Filters, Filter By Form, and Advanced Filter/Sort. You can use a filter in either Datasheet view or Form view.

BTW

Using the Find button
You can use the Find button (Home tab | Find group) to search for records in datasheets, forms, query results, and reports.

Plan Ahead	**Determine whether to filter records.**

If you determine that it is desirable to have only those records that satisfy some criterion appear, you have two choices: You can create a query or create a filter. The following guidelines apply to this decision.

- If you think that you will frequently want to display records that satisfy precisely this same criterion, you should consider creating a query whose results only contain the records that satisfy the criterion. To display those records in the future, simply open the query.

- If you are viewing data in a datasheet or form and decide you want to restrict the records to be included, it is easier to create a filter than a query. You can create and use the filter while you are viewing the data.

- If you have created a filter that you would like to be able to use again, you can save the filter as a query.

Once you have decided to use a filter, you need to decide which type of filter to use.

- If your criterion for filtering is that the value in a particular field matches or does not match a certain specific value, you can use Filter By Selection.

- If your criterion only involves a single field but is more complex (for example, the criterion specifies that the value in the field begins with a certain collection of letters) you can use a common filter.

- If your criterion involves more than one field, use Filter By Form.

- If your criterion involves more than a single And or Or, or if it involves sorting, you will probably find it simpler to use Advanced Filter/Sort.

Filter By Selection
If you want to search a field for a collection of characters, select the characters, and then click the Selection button arrow. For example, to find all cities in the Client table that contain the characters, ge, select the characters in the City field, click the Selection button arrow, then click Contains "ge" on the Selection button menu. Access filters the Client table and returns records where the city is either Georgetown or Granger.

To Use Filter By Selection

The simplest type of filter is called Filter By Selection. To use Filter By Selection, you give Access an example of the data you want by selecting the data within the table. You then choose the option you want on the Selection menu. For example, if you only want to display those clients located in Burles, Filter By Selection is appropriate. The following steps use Filter By Selection in Datasheet view to display only the records for clients in Burles.

1

- Open the Navigation Pane.

- Open the Client table, and close the Navigation Pane.

- Click the City field on the first record to select the city on that record as the city (Figure 3–12).

Q&A

Could I have selected the City field on another record where the city is also Burles to select the same city?

Yes. It does not matter which record you select as long as the city is Burles.

Figure 3–12

2

• Click the Selection button (Home tab | Sort & Filter group) to display the Selection menu (Figure 3–13).

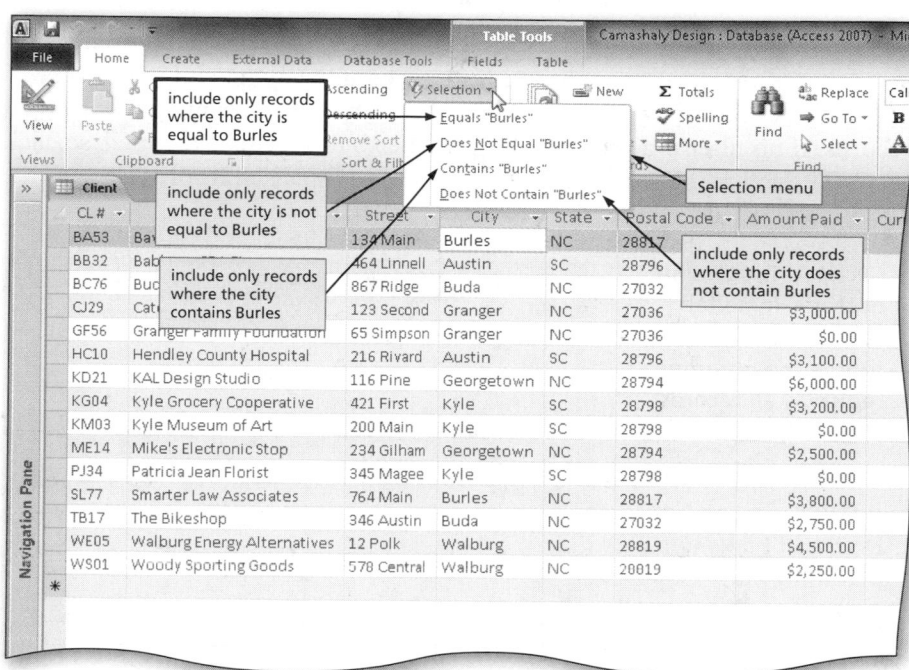

Figure 3–13

3

• Click Equals "Burles" to select only those clients whose city is Burles (Figure 3–14).

Can I also filter in Form view?

Yes. Filtering works the same whether you are viewing the data with split form, in Datasheet view, or in Form view.

🔎 **Experiment**

• Try each of the other values in the Selection menu to see their effect. When done, once again select those clients whose city is Burles.

Figure 3–14

To Toggle a Filter

The Toggle Filter button toggles between filtered and unfiltered displays of the records in the table. That is, if only filtered records currently appear, clicking the Toggle Filter button will redisplay all records. If all records are currently displayed and there is a filter that is in effect, clicking the Toggle Filter button will display only the filtered records. If no filter is active, the Toggle Filter button will be dimmed, so clicking it would have no effect.

The following step toggles the filter to redisplay all records.

1

• Click the Toggle Filter button (Home tab | Sort & Filter group) to toggle the filter and redisplay all records (Figure 3–15).

Q&A Does that action clear the filter?

No. The filter is still in place. If you click the Toggle Filter button a second time, you will again see only the filtered records.

Figure 3–15

To Clear a Filter

Once you have finished using a filter, you can clear the filter. After doing so, you no longer will be able to use the filter by clicking the Toggle Filter button. The following steps clear the filter.

1 Click the Advanced button (Home tab | Sort & Filter group) to display the Advanced menu.

2 Click Clear All Filters on the Advanced menu.

To Use a Common Filter

You can filter individual fields by clicking the arrow to the right of the field name and using one of the common filters that are available for the field. If you have determined you want to include those clients whose city begins with G, Filter By Selection would not be appropriate. You could instead use the common filter for the field that would include only those records whose city begins with a particular value. The following steps use this common filter to include only those clients whose city begins with G.

1

• Click the City arrow to display the common filter menu.

• Point to the Text Filters command to display the custom text filters (Figure 3–16).

I selected the City field and then clicked the Filter button on the Home tab | Sort & Filter group. My screen looks the same. Is this right?

Yes. That is another legitimate way to display the common filter menu.

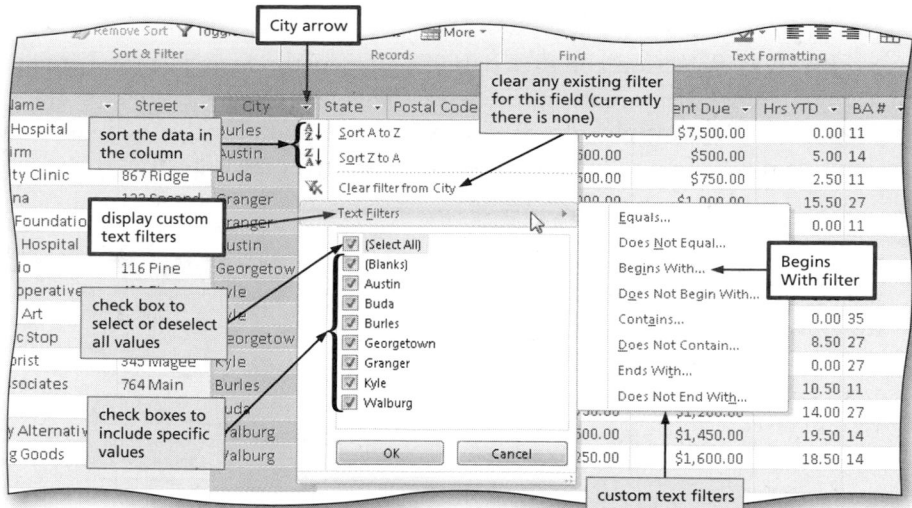

Figure 3–16

2

• Click Begins With to display the Custom Filter dialog box.

• Type **G** as the 'City begins with' value (Figure 3–17).

If I wanted certain cities included, could I use the check boxes?

Yes. Be sure the cities you want are the only ones checked.

 Experiment

• Try other options in the common filter menu to see their effects. When done, once again select those clients whose city begins with G.

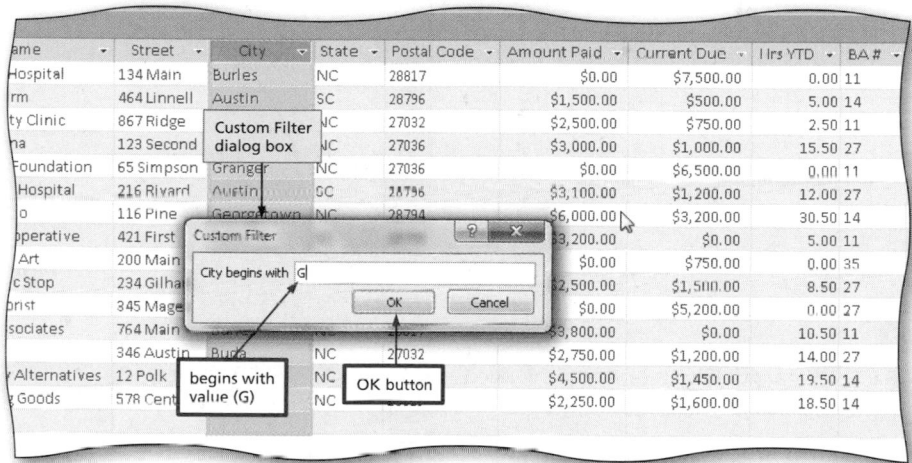

Figure 3–17

3

• Click the OK button to filter the records (Figure 3–18).

Can I use the same technique in Form view?

In Form view, you would need to click the field and then click the Filter button to display the Common Filter menu. The rest of the process would be the same.

4

• Click the Toggle Filter button (Home tab | Sort & Filter group) to toggle the filter and redisplay all records.

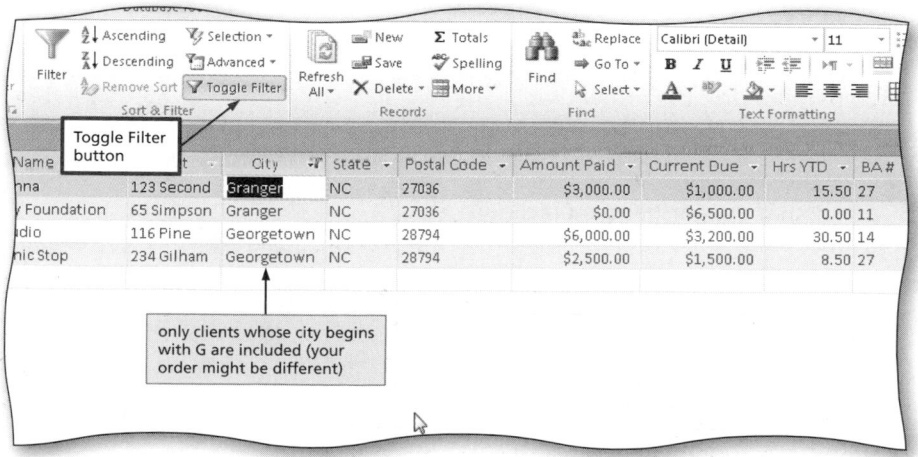

Figure 3–18

To Use Filter By Form

Filter By Selection and the common filter method you just used are quick and easy ways to filter by the value in a single field. For more complex criteria, however, these methods are not appropriate. Filter by Form allows you to filter based on multiple criteria, for example, to find only those clients whose postal code is 27036 and whose amount paid is 0. The following steps use Filter by Form to restrict the records that appear.

❶

- Click the Advanced button (Home tab | Sort & Filter group) to display the Advanced menu (Figure 3–19).

Figure 3–19

❷

- Click Clear All Filters on the Advanced menu to clear the existing filter.

- Click the Advanced button again to display the Advanced menu a second time.

- Click Filter By Form on the Advanced menu.

- Click the blank row in the Postal Code field, click the arrow that appears, and then click 27036.

- Click the Amount Paid field, click the arrow that appears, and then click 0 (Figure 3–20).

Q&A

Is there any difference in the process if I am viewing a table in Form view rather than in Datasheet view?

In Form view, you will make your entries in a form rather than a datasheet. Otherwise, the process is the same.

Figure 3–20

- Click the Toggle Filter button (Home tab | Sort & Filter group) to apply the filter (Figure 3–21).

🔍 Experiment

- Select Filter by Form again and enter different criteria. In each case, toggle the filter to see the effect of your selection. When done, once again select those clients whose postal code is 27036 and whose amount paid is $0.

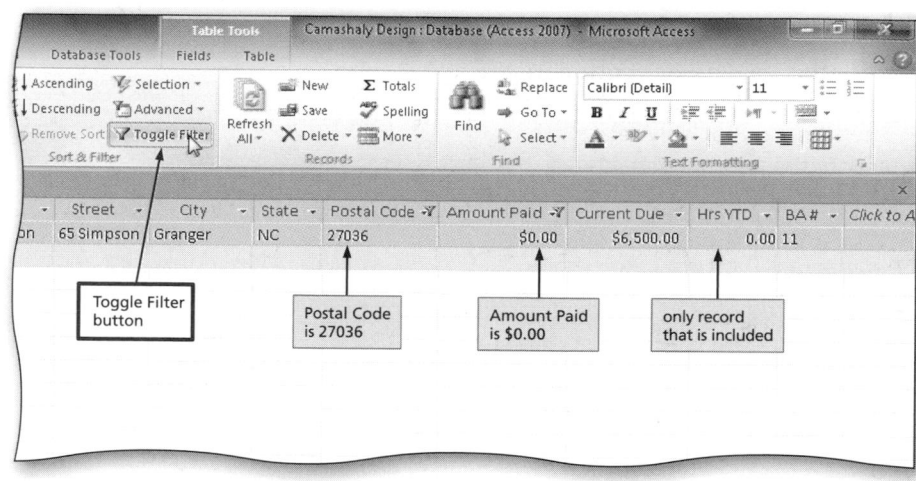

Figure 3–21

To Use Advanced Filter/Sort

In some cases, your criteria may be too complex even for Filter By Form. You might decide you want to include any client for which the postal code is 27036 and the amount paid is $0. Additionally, you might want to include any client whose amount paid is greater than $4,000, no matter where the client is located. Further, you might want to have the results sorted by name. To filter records using complex criteria, you need to use Advanced Filter/Sort, as in the following steps.

1

- Click the Advanced button (Home tab | Sort & Filter group) to display the Advanced menu, and then click Clear All Filters on the Advanced menu to clear the existing filter.

- Click the Advanced button to display the Advanced menu a second time.

- Click Advanced Filter/Sort on the Advanced menu.

- Expand the size of the field list so all the fields in the Client table appear.

- Include the Client Name field and select Ascending as the sort order to specify the order in which the filtered records will appear.

- Include the Postal Code field and enter `27036` as the criterion.

- Include the Amount Paid field and enter `0` as the criterion in the Criteria row and `>4000` as the criterion in the or row (Figure 3–22).

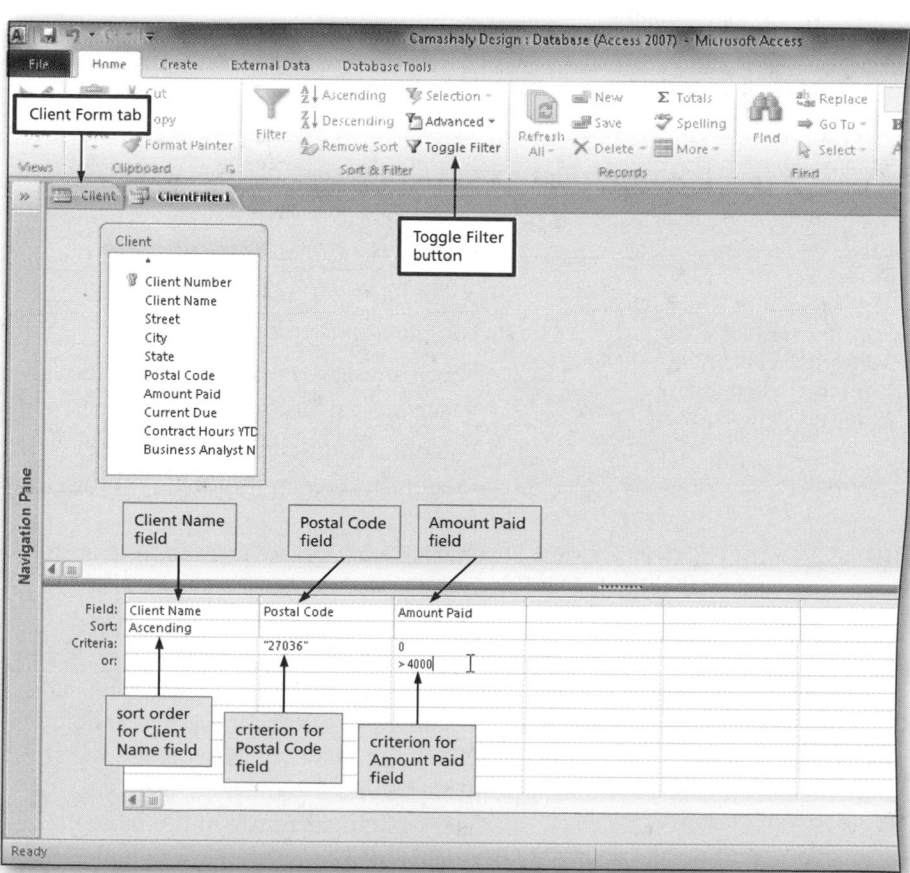

Figure 3–22

2

• Click the Toggle Filter button (Home tab | Sort & Filter group) to toggle the filter so that only records that satisfy the criteria will appear (Figure 3–23).

Why are those particular records included?

The first record is included because the postal code is 27036 and the amount paid is $0.00. The other two records are included because the amount paid is over $4,000.

 Experiment

• Select Advanced Filter/Sort again and enter different sorting options and criteria. In each case, toggle the filter to see the effect of your selection. When done, change back to the sorting options and criteria you entered in Step 1.

Figure 3–23

3

• Close the Client table. When asked if you want to save your changes, click the No button.

Should I not have cleared all filters before closing the table?

If you are closing a table and not saving the changes, it is not necessary to clear the filter. No filter will be active when you next open the table.

Filters and Queries

Now that you are familiar with how filters work, you might notice similarities between filters and queries. Filters and queries are related in three ways.

1. You can apply a filter to the results of a query just as you can apply a filter to a table.
2. When you have created a filter using Advanced Filter/Sort, you can save the filter settings as a query by using the Save as Query command on the Advanced menu.
3. You can restore filter settings that you previously saved in a query by using the Load from Query command on the Advanced menu.

Break Point: If you wish to take a break, this is a good place to do so. You can quit Access now. To resume at a later time, start Access, open the database called Camashaly Design, and continue following the steps from this location forward.

Changing the Database Structure

When you initially create a database, you define its **structure**; that is, you assign names and types to all the fields. In many cases, the structure you first define will not continue to be appropriate as you use the database.

Perhaps a field currently in the table no longer is necessary. If no one ever uses a particular field, it is not needed in the table. Because it is occupying space and serving no useful purpose, you should remove it from the table. You also would need to delete the field from any forms, reports, or queries that include it.

More commonly, an organization will find that it needs to maintain additional information that was not anticipated at the time the database was first designed. The organization's own requirements may have changed. In addition, outside regulations that the organization must satisfy may change as well. Either case requires the addition of fields to an existing table.

Although you can make some changes to the database structure in Datasheet view, it is usually easier and better to make these changes in Design view.

TO DELETE A FIELD

If a field in one of your tables no longer is needed, you should delete the field; for example, it may serve no useful purpose, or it may have been included by mistake. To delete a field, you would use the following steps.

1. Open the table in Design view.
2. Click the row selector for the field to be deleted.
3. Press the DELETE key.
4. When Access displays the dialog box requesting confirmation that you want to delete the field, click the Yes button.

To Add a New Field

You can add fields to a table in a database. Camashaly Design has decided that it needs to categorize its clients. To do so requires an additional field, Client Type. The possible values for Client Type are NON (which indicates the client is a nonprofit organization), RET (which indicates the client is a retail organization), or SER (which indicates the client is a service organization). The following steps add the Client Type field to the Client table immediately after the Postal Code field.

• If necessary, open the Navigation Pane.

• Open the Client table in Design view.

• Click the row selector for the Amount Paid field, and then press the INSERT key to insert a blank row above the selected field (Figure 3–24).

2

• Click the Field Name column for the new field.

• Type **Client Type** as the field name and then press the TAB key.

Figure 3–24

To Create a Lookup Field

Because there are only three possible values for the Client Type field, you should make it easy for users to enter the appropriate value. A **lookup field** allows the user to select from a list of values when updating the contents of the field.

The following steps make the Client Type field a lookup field.

1
- Click the Data Type column for the Client Type field, and then click the Data Type box arrow to display the menu of available data types (Figure 3–25).

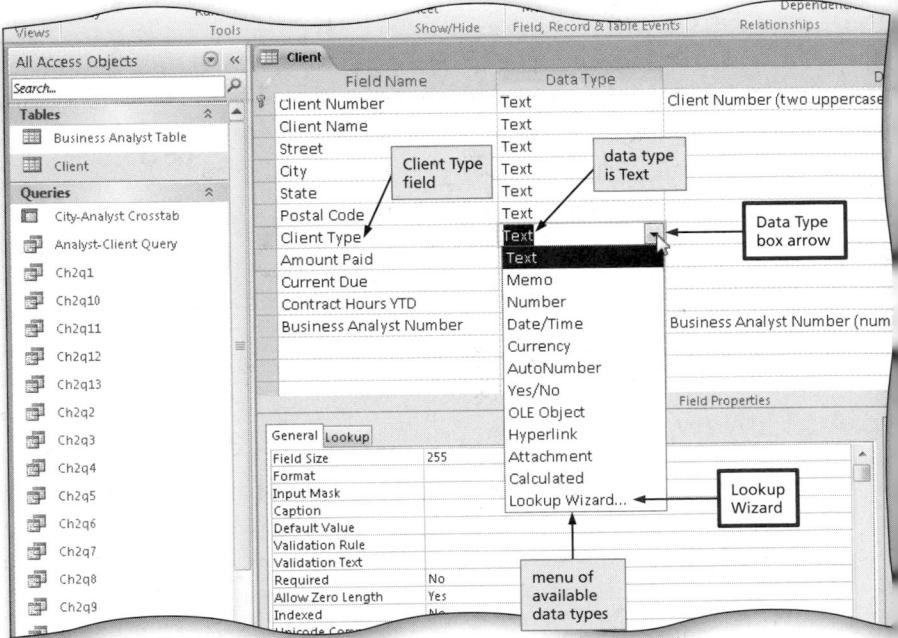

Figure 3–25

2
- Click Lookup Wizard, and then click the 'I will type in the values that I want.' option button (Lookup Wizard dialog box) to indicate that you will type in the values (Figure 3–26).

When would I use the other option button?

You would use the other option button if the data to be entered in this field is found in another table or query.

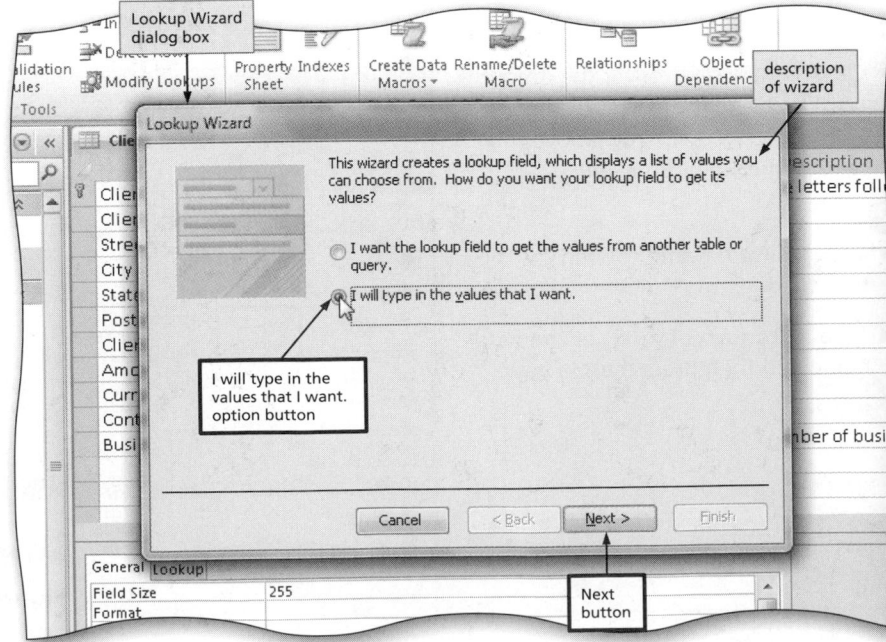

Figure 3–26

3

- Click the Next button to display the next Lookup Wizard screen (Figure 3–27).

  Why did I not change the field size for the Client Type field?

  You could have changed the field size to 3 but it is not necessary. When you create a lookup field and indicate specific values for the field, you automatically restrict the field size.

Figure 3–27

4

- Click the first row of the table (below Col1), and then type **NON** as the value in the first row.

- Press the DOWN ARROW key, and then type **RET** as the value in the second row.

- Press the TAB key, and then type **SER** as the value in the third row (Figure 3–28).

  I notice you can press either the DOWN ARROW or the TAB key to move to the second row. Can you also press the ENTER key?

  No. Pressing the ENTER key will exit the Lookup Wizard without finishing the process of adding a Lookup field.

Figure 3–28

5

- Click the Next button to display the next Lookup Wizard screen.

- Ensure Client Type is entered as the label for the lookup field and that the Allow Multiple Values check box is NOT checked (Figure 3–29).

6

- Click the Finish button to complete the definition of the lookup field.

Q&A

Why does the data type for the Client Type field still show Text?

The data type is still Text because the values entered in the wizard were entered as text.

Figure 3–29

To Add a Multivalued Field

Normally, fields contain only a single value. In Access, it is possible to have **multivalued fields**, that is, fields that can contain more than one value. Camashaly Design wants to use such a field to store the abbreviations of the various services its clients need (see Table 3–1 for the service abbreviations and descriptions). Unlike the Client Type, where each client only had one type, clients can require multiple service descriptions. One client might need Ad, Ban, Bill, and Logo (Ad Design, Banners, Billboards, and Logo Design). Another client might only need Host (Web Site Hosting).

Table 3–1 Service Abbreviations and Descriptions	
Service Abbreviation	**Description**
Ad	Ad Design
Ban	Banners
Bill	Billboards
Bus	Business Cards
ENews	Email Newsletter
Host	Web Site Hosting
Logo	Logo Design
Mkt	Marketing Research
News	Printed Newsletters
Pod	Podcasting
SE	Search Engine Visibility
Shop	Shopping Cart
Soc	Social Networking

Creating a multivalued field uses the same process as creating a lookup field, with the exception that you check the Allow Multiple Values check box. The following steps create a multivalued field.

1 Click the row selector for the Amount Paid field, and then press the INSERT key to insert a blank row.

2 Click the Field Name column for the new field, type `Services Needed` as the field name, and then press the TAB key.

3 Click the Data Type arrow to display the menu of available data types for the Services Needed field, and then click Lookup Wizard in the menu of available data types to start the Lookup Wizard.

4 Click the 'I will type in the values that I want.' option button to indicate that you will type in the values.

5 Click the Next button to display the next Lookup Wizard screen.

6 Click the first row of the table (below Col1), and then type `Ad` as the value in the first row.

7 Enter the remaining values from the first column in Table 3–1. Before typing each value, press the TAB key to move to a new row.

8 Click the Next button to display the next Lookup Wizard screen.

9 Ensure that Services Needed is entered as the label for the lookup field.

10 Click the Allow Multiple Values check box to allow the user to enter multiple values.

11 Click the Finish button to complete the definition of the Lookup Wizard field.

To Add a Calculated Field

A field that can be computed from other fields is called a **calculated field** or a **computed field**. In Chapter 2, you created a calculated field in a query that provided total amount data. With Access 2010, it is now possible to also include a calculated field in a table. Users will not be able to update this field. Instead, Access will automatically perform the necessary calculation whenever you display or use this field in any way. The following steps add a calculated field in the table.

1

• Click the row selector for the Contract Hours YTD field, and then press the INSERT key to insert a blank row above the selected field.

• Click the Field Name column for the new field.

• Type `Total Amount` as the field name and then press the TAB key.

• Click the Data Type box arrow to display the menu of available data types (Figure 3–30).

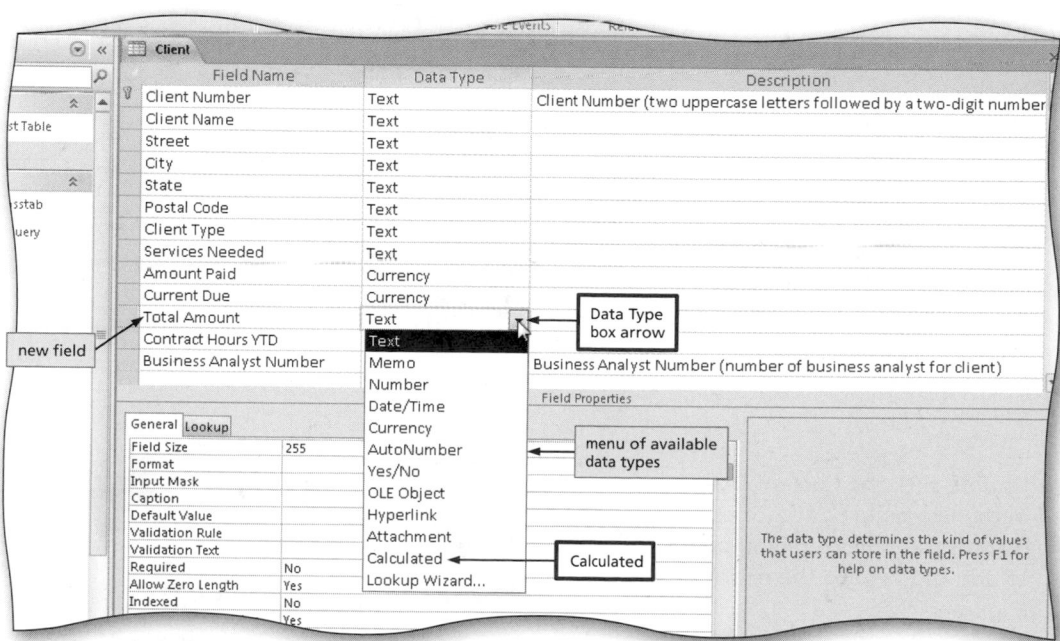

Figure 3–30

2

• Click Calculated to select the Calculated data type and display the Expression Builder dialog box (Figure 3–31).

Figure 3–31

3

• Double-click the Amount Paid field in the Expression Categories area (Expression Builder dialog box) to add the field to the expression.

Q&A I do not have the list of fields in the Expression Categories area. What should I do?

Click Client in the Expression Elements area.

• Type a plus sign (+).

Q&A Could I select the plus sign from a list rather than typing it?

Yes. Double-click Operators in the Expression Elements area to display available operators and then click the plus sign.

• Double-click the Current Due field in the Expression Categories area (Expression Builder dialog box) to add the field to the expression (Figure 3–32).

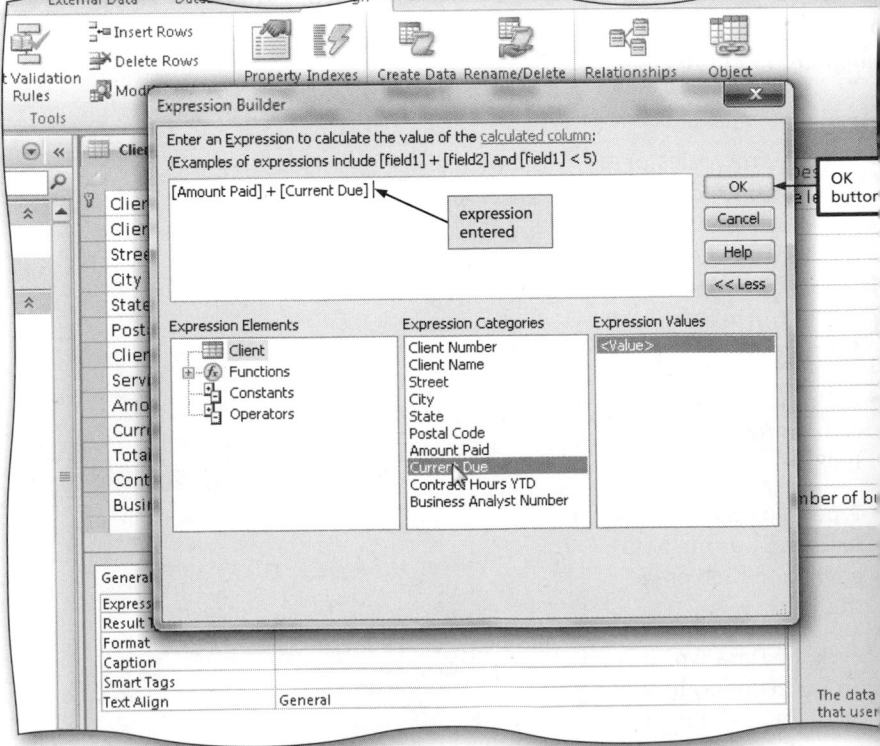

Figure 3–32

4

- Click the OK button (Expression Builder dialog box) to enter the expression in the Expression property of the selected field (Figure 3–33).

Could I have simply typed the expression in the Expression Builder dialog box rather than selecting the fields from a list?

Yes. You can use whichever technique you find more convenient.

When I entered a calculated field in a query, I typed the expression in the Zoom dialog box. Could I have used the Expression Builder instead?

Yes. To do so, you would click Build rather than Zoom on the shortcut menu.

Figure 3–33

To Save the Changes and Close the Table

The following steps save the changes; that is, they save the addition of the new fields and close the table.

1 Click the Save button on the Quick Access Toolbar to save the changes.

2 Close the Client table.

TO MODIFY SINGLE OR MULTIVALUED LOOKUP FIELDS

You may find that you later want to change the list of choices in a lookup field. If you find you need to modify a single or multivalued lookup field, you can use the following steps.

1. Open the table in Design view and select the field to be modified.
2. Click the Lookup tab in the Field Properties pane.
3. Change the list in the Row Source property to change the desired list of values.

BTW

Calculated Fields
Do not add a calculated field to a table if you plan to also use the database with Access 2007. Access 2007 does not recognize calculated fields. Also, if you modify the expression used to create the calculated field, the field may not update correctly.

Mass Changes

In some cases, rather than making individual changes to records, you will want to make mass changes. That is, you will want to add, change, or delete many records in a single operation. You can do this with action queries. Unlike the queries that you created in Chapter 2, which simply presented data in specific ways, an **action query** adds, deletes, or changes data in a table. An **update query** allows you to make the same change to all records satisfying some criterion. If you omit the criterion, you will make the same changes to all records in the table. A **delete query** allows you to delete all the records satisfying some criterion. You can add the results of a query to an existing table by using an **append query**. You also can add the query results to a new table by using a **make-table query**.

To Use an Update Query

The new Client Type field is blank on every record in the Client table. One approach to entering the information for the field would be to step through the entire table, assigning each record its appropriate value. If most of the clients have the same type, a simpler approach is available.

In the Camashaly Design database, for example, more clients are type NON. Initially, you can set all the values to NON. To accomplish this quickly and easily, you can use an **update query**, which is a query that makes the same change to all the records satisfying a criterion. Later, you can change the type for retail organizations and service organizations.

The following steps use an update query to change the value in the Client Type field to NON for all the records. Because all records are to be updated, criteria are not required.

1

- Create a new query for the Client table, and close the Navigation Pane.

- Click the Update button (Query Tools Design tab | Query Type group), double-click the Client Type field to select the field, click the Update To row in the first column of the design grid, and then type **NON** as the new value (Figure 3–34).

Q&A

Do I not have to enter a criterion?

If you only want the change to be made on some of the records, you would need to enter a criterion to identify those records. Without a criterion, the change will be made on all records, which is what you want in this update.

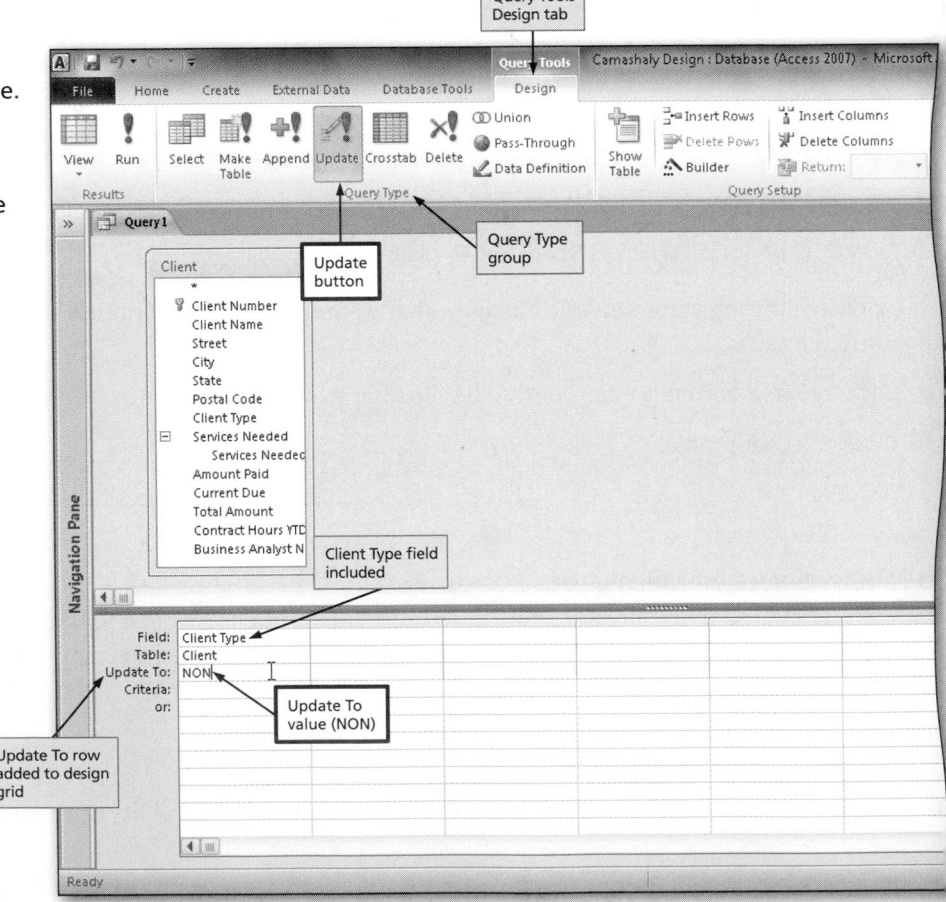

Figure 3–34

2

- Click the Run button (Query Tools Design tab | Results group) to run the query and update the records (Figure 3–35).

Why do I not click the View button to update the records?

The purpose of the View button is to simply view results. The Run button causes the updates specified by the query to take place.

Why would the dialog box not appear on my screen when I click the Run button?

If the dialog box does not appear, it means that you did not click the Enable Content button when you first opened the database. Close the database, open it again, and enable the content. Then, create and run the query again.

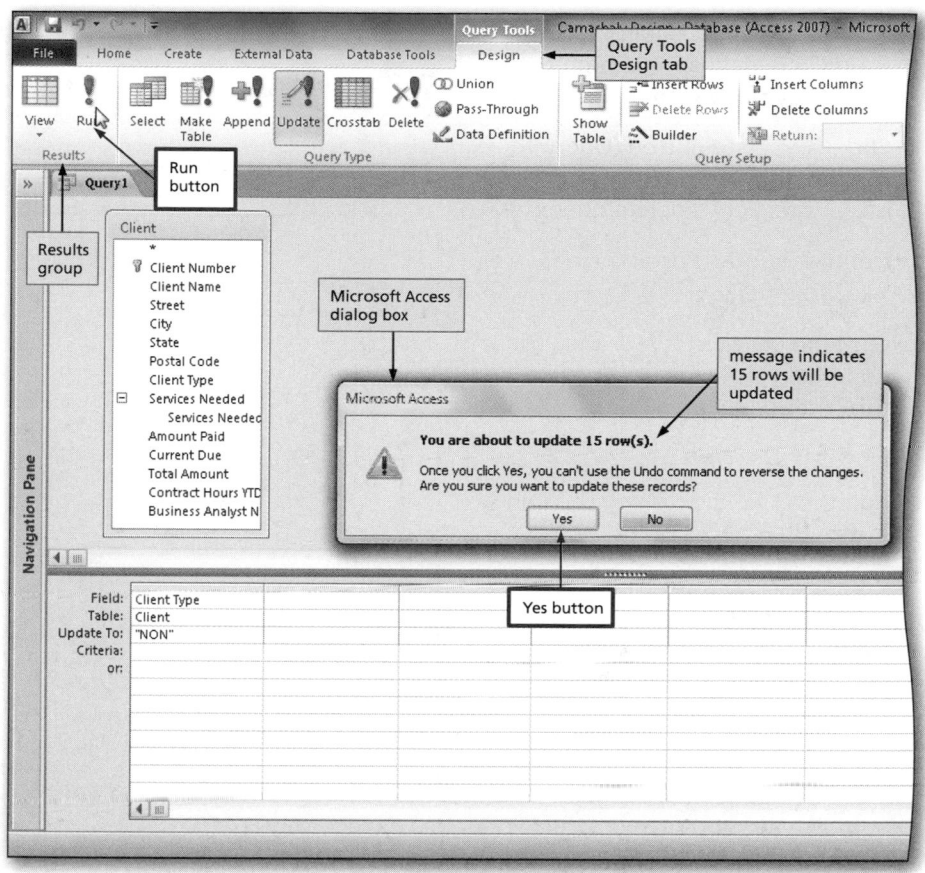

Figure 3–35

(within figure)
Query Tools Design tab

Run button

Results group

Microsoft Access dialog box

message indicates 15 rows will be updated

Microsoft Access

You are about to update 15 row(s).

Once you click Yes, you can't use the Undo command to reverse the changes. Are you sure you want to update these records?

Yes   No

Yes button

Field: Client Type
Table: Client
Update To: "NON"
Criteria:
or:

🔍 **Experiment**

- Create an update query to change the client type to RET. Enter a criterion to restrict the records to be updated, and then run the query. Open the table to view your changes. When finished, create and run an update query to change the client type to NON on all records.

3

- Click the Yes button to make the changes.

Is there any way to see the records that will be updated before performing the update, in case you are not sure you are updating the correct records?

Yes. Click the Select button (Query Tools Design tab | Query Type group) to convert the query to a select query, add any additional fields that would help you identify the records, and then view the results. Return to Design view and make any necessary corrections to the query. When you are satisfied, click the Update button to once again convert the query to an update query.

Other Ways

1. Right-click any open area in upper pane, point to Query Type on shortcut menu, click Update Query on Query Type submenu

To Use a Delete Query

In some cases, you may need to delete several records at a time. If, for example, all clients in a particular postal code are to be serviced by another firm, the clients with this postal code can be deleted from the Camashaly Design database. Instead of deleting these clients individually, which could be very time consuming in a large database, you can delete them in one operation by using a **delete query**, which is a query that will delete all the records satisfying the criteria entered in the query.

The following steps use a delete query to delete any client whose postal code is 28819. (Two such clients currently exist in the database.)

- Click the column heading for the Client Type field and then press the DELETE key to clear the grid.

- Click the Delete button (Query Tools Design tab | Query Type group) to make the query a delete query.

- Double-click the Postal Code field to select the field.

- Click the Criteria row for the Postal Code field and type 28819 as the criterion (Figure 3–36).

2

- Run the query by clicking the Run button.

- Click the Yes button when Access displays a message indicating that there are two records which will be deleted to complete the deletion.

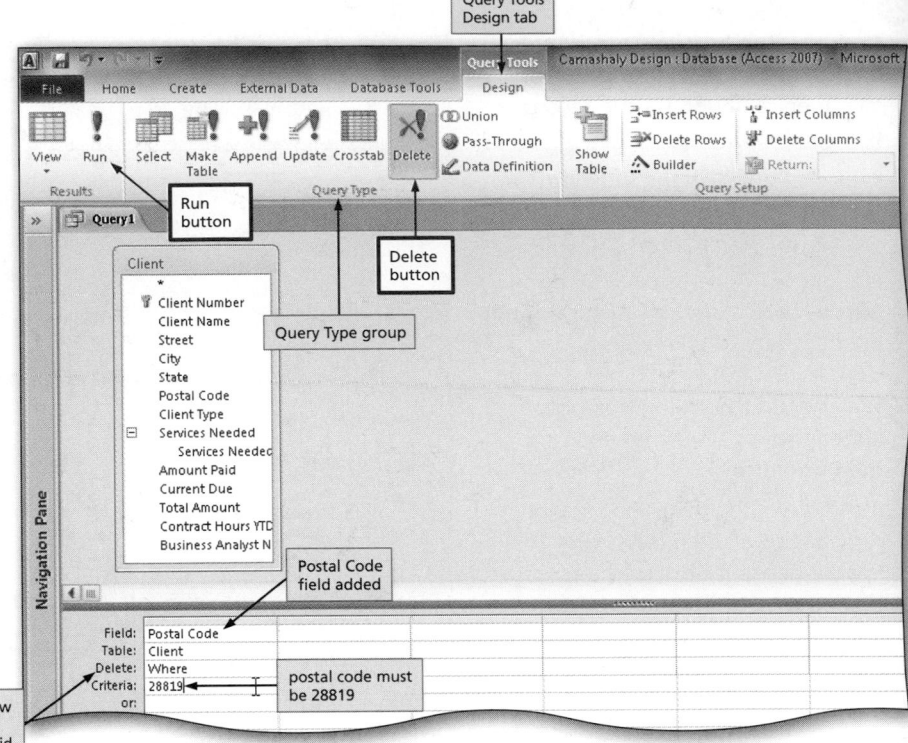

Figure 3–36

Q&A

Is there any way to see the records that will be deleted before performing the deletion, in case you are not sure you are deleting the correct records?

Yes. Prior to running the query, you would click the Select button (Query Tools Design tab | Query Type group) to convert the query to a select query, add any additional fields that would help you identify the records, and then view the results. You would then return to Design view and make any corrections to the query. When you are satisfied, click the Delete button to once again convert the query to a delete query.

- Close the Query window. Because you do not need to use this delete query again, do not save the query.

Other Ways

1. Right-click any open area in upper pane, point to Query Type on shortcut menu, click Delete Query on Query Type submenu

To Use an Append Query

An **append query** adds a group of records from one table to the end of another table. For example, suppose that Camashaly Design acquires some new clients and a database containing a table with those clients. To avoid entering all this information manually, you can append it to the Client table in the Camashaly Design database using the append query. To create an append query, you would use the following steps.

1. Create a query for the table containing the records to append.

2. In Design view, indicate the fields to include, and then enter any necessary criteria.

3. View the query results to be sure you have specified the correct data, and then return to Design view.

4. Click the Append button (Query Tools Design tab | Query Type group).

5. When Access displays the Append dialog box, specify the name of the table to receive the new records and its location. Run the query by clicking the Run button (Query Tools Design tab | Results group).

6. When Access indicates the number of records to be appended, click the OK button.

BTW

Delete Queries
If you do not specify any criteria in a delete query, Access will delete all the records in the table.

TO USE A MAKE-TABLE QUERY

In some cases, you might want to copy the records from an existing table to a new table, that is, a table that has not yet been created. If so, use a **make-table query** to add the records to a new table. To create a make-table query, you would use the following steps.

1. Create a query for the table containing the records to add.
2. In Design view, indicate the fields to include, and then enter any necessary criteria.
3. View the query results to be sure you have specified the correct data, and then return to Design view.
4. Click the Make Table button (Query Tools Design tab | Query Type group).
5. When Access displays the Make Table dialog box, specify the name of the table to receive the new records and its location. Run the query by clicking the Run button (Query Tools Design tab | Results group).
6. When Access indicates the number of records to be inserted, click the OK button.

> **BTW**
>
> **Archive Tables**
> You can use a make table query to create an archive table. An **archive table** is a table that contains data that is no longer used in operations but that might still be needed by the organization.

Break Point: If you wish to take a break, this is a good place to do so. You can quit Access now. To resume at a later time, start Access, open the database called Camashaly Design, and continue following the steps from this location forward.

Validation Rules

You now have created, loaded, queried, and updated a database. Nothing you have done so far, however, restricts users to entering only valid data, that is, data that follows the rules established for data in the database. An example of such a rule would be that client types can only be NON, RET, or SER. To ensure the entry of valid data, you create these **validation rules,** that is, rules that a user must follow when entering the data. As you will see, Access will prevent users from entering data that does not follow the rules. The steps also specify **validation text**, which is the message that will appear if a user violates the validation rule.

Validation rules can indicate a **required field**, a field in which the user actually must enter data. Validation rules can restrict a user's entry to a certain **range of values**; for example, the values in the Amount Paid field must be between $0 and $30,000. They can specify a **default value**, that is, a value that Access will display on the screen in a particular field before the user begins adding a record. To make data entry of client numbers more convenient, you also can have lowercase letters appear automatically as uppercase letters. Finally, validation rules can specify a collection of acceptable values.

> **BTW**
>
> **Database Design: Validation**
> In most organization, decisions about what is valid and what is invalid data are made during the requirements gathering process and the database design process.

To Change a Field Size

The Field Size property for text fields represents the maximum number of characters a user can enter in the field. Because the field size for the Client Number field is 4, for example, a user would not be able to enter a fifth character in the field. Occasionally, you may find that the field size that seemed appropriate when you first created a table is no longer appropriate. In the Client table, there is now a name that is longer than 30 characters. To allow this name in the table, you need to change the field size for the Client Name field to a number that is large enough to accommodate the new name. The following step changes the field size for the Client Name field from 30 to 35.

1 Ensure that the Client table is open in Design view and that the Navigation Pane is closed.

2 Select the Client Name field by clicking its row selector.

3 Click the Field Size property to select it, delete the current entry (30), and then type 3 5 as the new field size.

To Specify a Required Field

To specify that a field is to be required, change the value for the Required property from No to Yes. The following step specifies that the Client Name field is to be a required field.

1

- Ensure that the Client Name field is still selected.

- Click the Required property box in the Field Properties pane, and then click the down arrow that appears.

- Click Yes in the list (Figure 3–37).

Q&A What is the effect of this change?

Users cannot leave the Client Name field blank when entering or editing records.

Figure 3–37

To Specify a Range

The following step specifies that entries in the Current Due field must be between $0 and $30,000. To indicate this range, the criterion specifies that the amount paid amount must be both >= 0 (greater than or equal to 0) and <= 30000 (less than or equal to 30,000).

1

- Select the Current Due field by clicking its row selector, click the Validation Rule property box to produce an insertion point, and then type `>=0 and <=30000` as the rule.

- Click the Validation Text property box to produce an insertion point, and then type **Must be at least $0.00 and at most $30,000.00** as the text (Figure 3–38).

Q&A What is the effect of this change?

Users now will be prohibited from entering a current due amount that either is less than $0.00 or greater than $30,000.00 when they add records or change the value in the Current Due field.

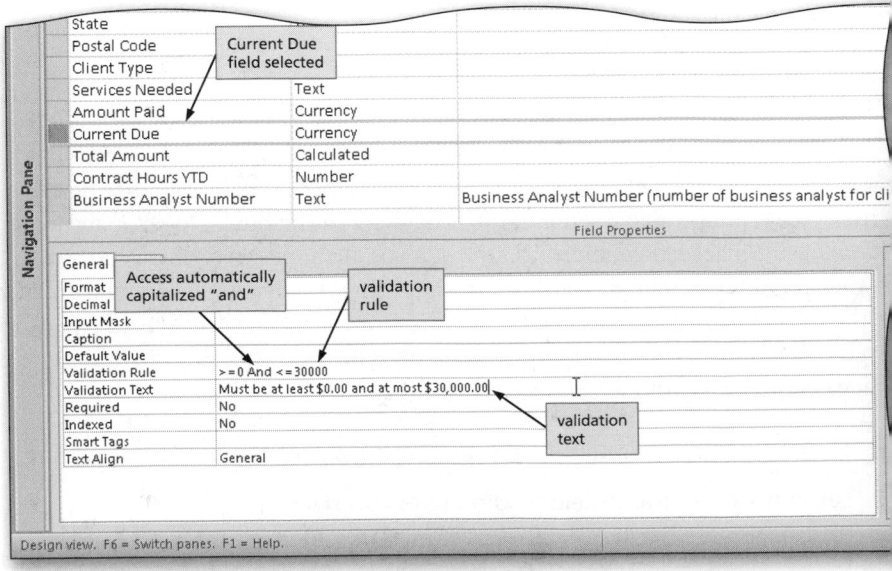

Figure 3–38

To Specify a Default Value

To specify a default value, enter the value in the Default Value property box. The following step specifies NON as the default value for the Client Type field. This simply means that if users do not enter a client type, the type will be NON.

1

- With the Client Type field selected, click the Default Value property box to produce an insertion point, and then type `=NON` as the value (Figure 3–39).

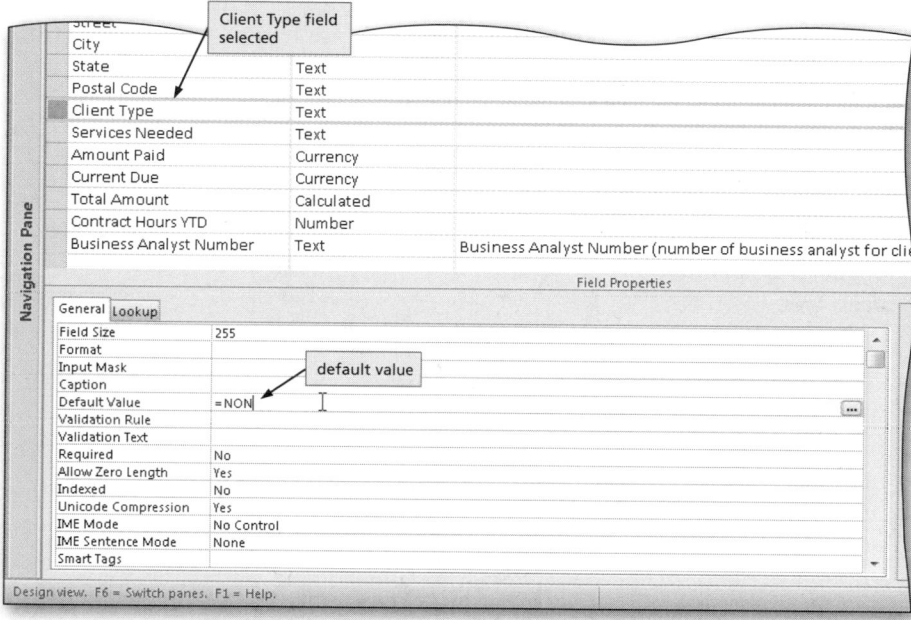

Figure 3–39

To Specify a Collection of Legal Values

The only **legal values, or allowable values,** for the Client Type field are NON, RET, and SER. An appropriate validation rule for this field prevents Access from accepting any entry other than these three possibilities. The following step specifies the legal values for the Client Type field.

- With the Client Type field selected, click the Validation Rule property box to produce an insertion point and then type `=NON or =RET or =SER` as the validation rule.

- Click the Validation Text property box and then type **Must be NON, RET, or SER** as the validation text (Figure 3–40).

What is the effect of this change?

Users now will be allowed to enter only NON, RET, or SER in the Client Type field when they add records or make changes to this field.

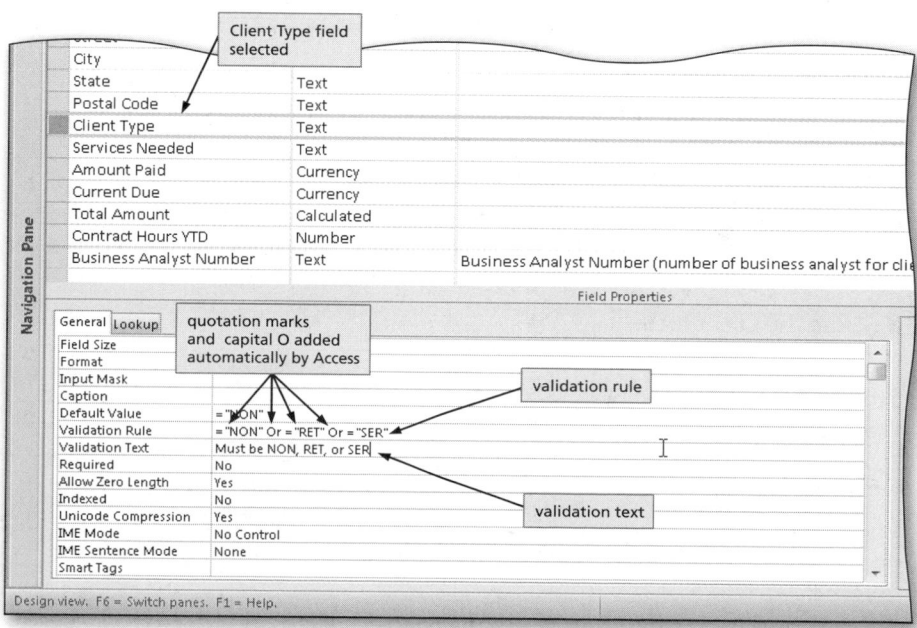

Figure 3–40

To Specify a Format

To affect the way data appears in a field, you can use a **format**. To use a format with a Text field, you enter a special symbol, called a **format symbol**, in the field's Format property box. The Format property uses different settings for different data types. The following step specifies a format for the Client Number field in the Client table and illustrates the way you enter a format. The format symbol used in the example is >, which causes Access to display lowercase letters automatically as uppercase letters. The format symbol < causes Access to display uppercase letters automatically as lowercase letters.

1

- Select the Client Number field.

- Click the Format property box and then type   > (Figure 3–41).

Q&A

What is the effect of this change?

From this point on, any lowercase letters will appear automatically as uppercase when users add records or change the value in the Client Number field.

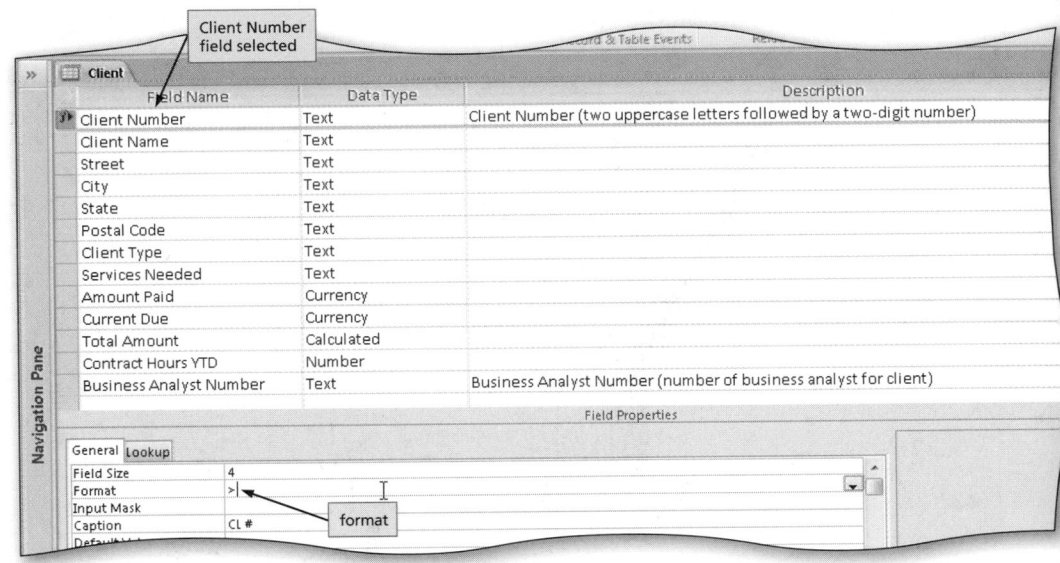

Figure 3–41

To Save the Validation Rules, Default Values, and Formats

The following steps save the validation rules, default values, and formats.

1 Click the Save button on the Quick Access Toolbar to save the changes (Figure 3–42).

2 Click the No button to save the changes without testing current data.

3 Close the Client table.

Q&A

Should I always click the No button when saving validation rules?

If this were a database used to run a business or to solve some other critical need, you would click Yes. You would want to be sure that the data already in the database does not violate the rules.

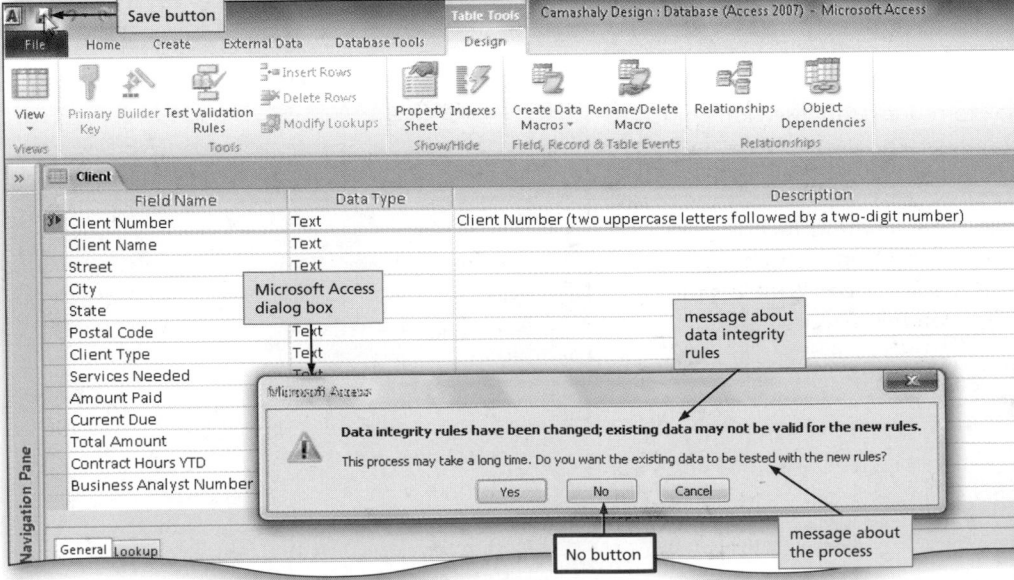

Figure 3–42

Updating a Table that Contains Validation Rules

When updating a table that contains validation rules, Access provides assistance in making sure the data entered is valid. It helps in making sure that data is formatted correctly. Entering a number that is out of the required range, for example, or entering a value that is not one of the possible choices, will produce an error message in the form of a dialog box. The database will not be updated until the error is corrected.

If the client number entered contains lowercase letters, such as wi12 (Figure 3–43), Access will display the data automatically as WI12 (Figure 3–44).

Figure 3–43

Figure 3–44

If the client type is not valid, such as xxx, Access will display the text message you specified (Figure 3–45) and prevent the data from entering the database.

BTW

Modifying Table Properties
You can change the properties of a table by opening the table in Design view and then clicking the Propery Sheet button. To display the records in a table in an order other than primary key (the default sort order), use the Order By property. For example, to display the Client table automatically in Client Name order, change the the Order By property box setting to `Client.Client Name` in the property box, close the property sheet, and save the change to the table design. When you open the Client table in Datasheet view, the records will be sorted in Client Name order.

Figure 3–45

If the amount paid value is not valid, such as 50000, which is too large, Access also displays the appropriate message (Figure 3–46) and refuses to accept the data.

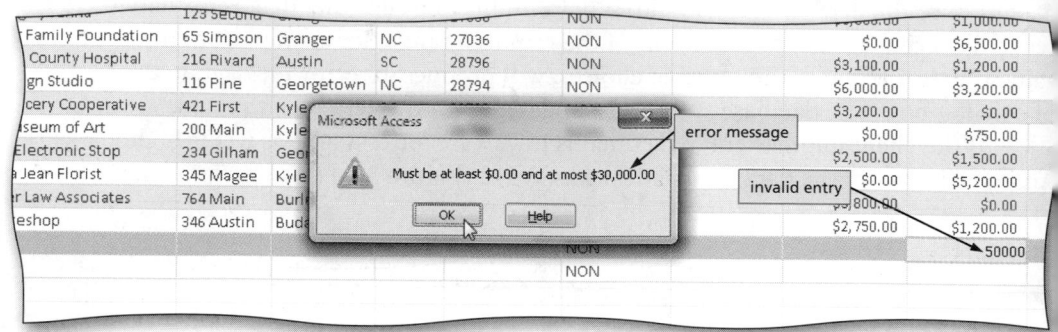

Figure 3–46

If a required field contains no data, Access indicates this by displaying an error message as soon as you attempt to leave the record (Figure 3–47). The field must contain a valid entry before Access will move to a different record.

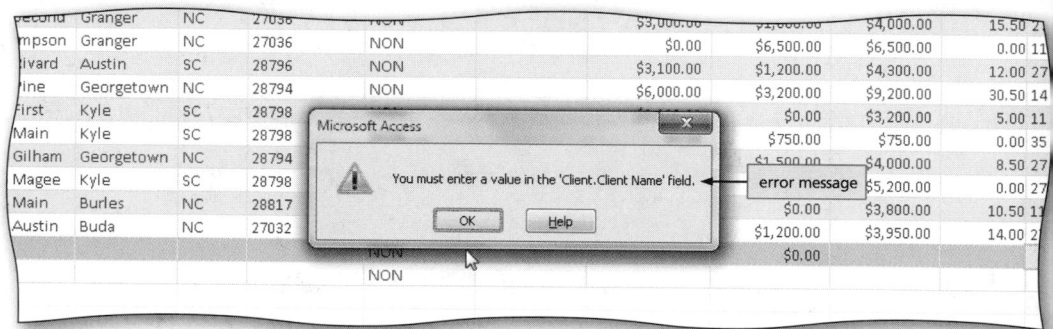

Figure 3–47

When entering data into a field with a validation rule, you may find that Access displays the error message and you are unable to make the necessary correction. It may be that you cannot remember the validation rule you created or it was created incorrectly. In such a case, you neither can leave the field nor close the table because you have entered data into a field that violates the validation rule.

If this happens, first try again to type an acceptable entry. If this does not work, repeatedly press the BACKSPACE key to erase the contents of the field and then try to leave the field. If you are unsuccessful using this procedure, press the ESC key until the record is removed from the screen. The record will not be added to the database.

Should the need arise to take this drastic action, you probably have a faulty validation rule. Use the techniques of the previous sections to correct the existing validation rules for the field.

To Change the Contents of a Field

Now that the size for the Client Name field has been increased, you can change the name for client HC10 to Hendley County Regional Hospital. Changing the field size for the field does not automatically increase the width of the corresponding column in the datasheet, however. You need to take the necessary action to resize the column, just as you resized columns in Chapter 1 on page AC 29. The following steps change the name and resize the column in the datasheet to accommodate the new name.

● Open the Client table in Datasheet view and ensure the Navigation Pane is closed.

● Click in the Client Name field for client HC10 immediately before the word, Hospital, to produce an insertion point.

● Change the name from Hendley County Hospital to Hendley County Regional Hospital by typing the word **Regional** and pressing the SPACEBAR.

2

● Resize the Client Name column to best fit the new data by double-clicking the right boundary of the field selector, that is, the column heading (Figure 3–48).

3

● Save the changes to the layout by clicking the Save button on the Quick Access Toolbar.

● Close the Client table.

Figure 3–48

To Use a Lookup Field

Earlier, you changed all the entries in the Client Type field to NON. You have created a rule that will ensure that only legitimate values (NON, RET, or SER) can be entered in the field. You also made Client Type a lookup field. You can make changes to a lookup field for individual records by clicking the field to be changed, clicking the arrow that appears in the field, and then selecting the desired value from the list.

The following steps change the Client Type values to the correct values.

1

● Open the Client table in Datasheet view and ensure the Navigation Pane is closed.

● Click in the Client Type field on the first record to display an arrow.

● Click the arrow to display the drop-down list of available choices for the Client Type field (Figure 3–49).

I got the drop-down list as soon as I clicked. I did not need to click the arrow. What happened?

If you click in the position where the arrow would appear, you will get the drop-down list. If you click anywhere else, you would need to click the arrow.

Figure 3–49

Q&A

Could I type the value instead of selecting it from the list?

Yes. Once you have either deleted the previous value or selected the entire previous value, you can begin typing. You do not have to type the full entry. When you begin with the letter, R, for example, Access will automatically add the ET.

Experiment

• Select the Client Type field on the first record. Try to change the client type by typing various values. Try to type an invalid client type (like MAN). When finished, change the value on the record to SER.

2

• Click SER to change the value.

• In a similar fashion, change the values on the other records to match those shown in Figure 3–50.

Figure 3–50

To Use a Multivalued Lookup Field

Using a multivalued lookup field is similar to using a regular lookup field. The difference is that when you drop down the list, the entries all will be preceded by check boxes. You then can check all the entries that you want. The appropriate entries are shown in Figure 3–51. As indicated in the figure, the services needed for client BA53 are Ad, Ban, Bill, and Logo.

CL #	Client Name	Services Needed
BA53	Bavant Animal Hospital	Ad, Ban, Bill, Logo
BB32	Babbage CPA Firm	Ad, Bus, ENews
BC76	Buda Community Clinic	Ban, Host, News
CJ29	Catering by Jenna	Bus, Host, Logo
GF56	Granger Family Foundation	Host
HC10	Hendley County Regional Hospital	ENews, News, Soc
KD21	KAL Design Studio	Host, Mkt, SE
KG04	Kyle Grocery Cooperative	Ad, Bill, Soc
KM03	Kyle Museum of Art	ENews, Host, Pod, Shop
ME14	Mike's Electronic Stop	Ad, Ban, Logo
PJ34	Patricia Jean Florist	Bus, Mkt, Shop
SL77	Smarter Law Associates	ENews, Pod
TB17	The Bikeshop	Ad, SE

Figure 3–51

The following steps make the appropriate entries for the Services Needed field.

1

• Click the Services Needed field on the first record to display the arrow.

• Click the arrow to display the list of available services (Figure 3–52).

All the services currently appear in the box. What if there were too many services to fit?

Access would automatically include a scroll bar that you could use to scroll through all the choices.

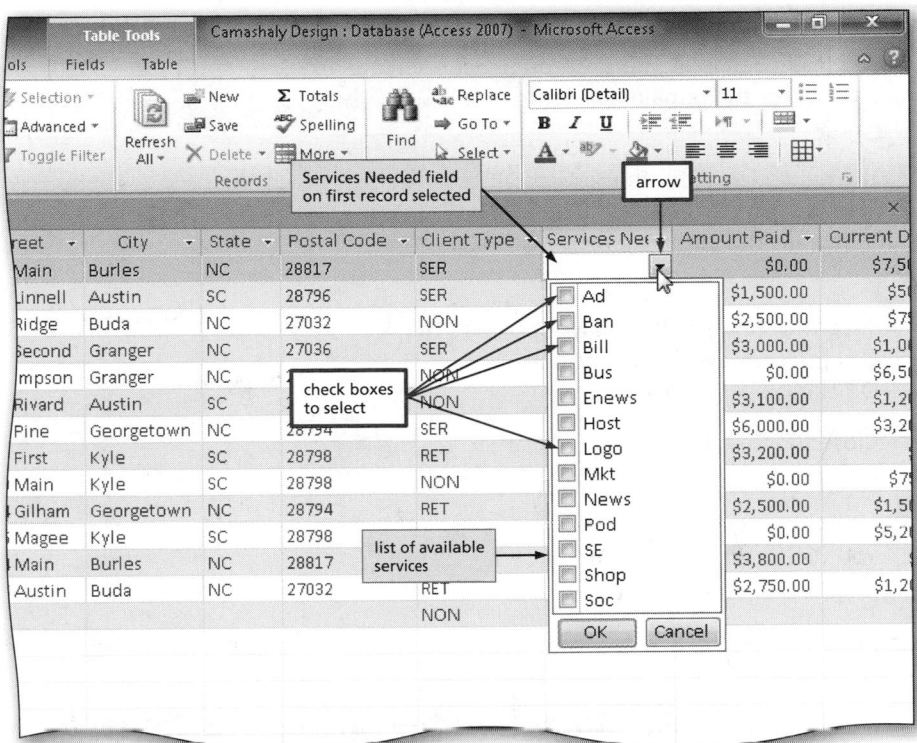

Figure 3–52

2

• Click the Ad, Ban, Bill, and Logo check boxes to select the services for the first client (Figure 3–53).

Figure 3–53

- Click the OK button to complete the selection.

- Using the same technique, enter the services given in Figure 3–51 on page AC 172 for the remaining clients.

- Double-click the right boundary of the field selector for the Services Needed field to resize the field so that it best fits the data (Figure 3–54).

- Save the changes to the layout by clicking the Save button on the Quick Access Toolbar.

- Close the Client table.

Q&A What if I closed the table without saving the layout changes?

You would be asked if you want to save the changes.

Figure 3–54

To Update a Form to Reflect the Changes in the Table

In the first chapter, on page AC 48, you clicked the Form button (Create tab | Forms group) to create a simple form that contained all the fields in the Client table. Now that you have added additional fields, the form you created, Client Form, no longer contains all the fields in the table. Because creating the form required only clicking a single button, the simplest way to include all the fields from the Client table in the form is to delete the form and create it once again. The following steps delete the Client Form and then create it a second time. The form then will contain all the fields.

- Open the Navigation Pane, and then right-click the Client Form in the Navigation Pane to display a shortcut menu.

- Click Delete on the shortcut menu to delete the selected form, and then click the Yes button in the Microsoft Access dialog box to confirm the deletion.

- Click the Client table in the Navigation Pane to select the table.

- Click Create on the Ribbon to display the Create tab.

- Click the Form button (Create tab | Forms group) to create a simple form (Figure 3–55).

Figure 3–55

2

- Click the Save button on the Quick Access Toolbar to save the form.

- Type `Client Form` as the form name, and then click the OK button to save the form.

- Close the form.

To Update a Report to Reflect the Changes in the Table

You also may want to include the new fields in the Client Financial Report you created earlier. Just as you did with the form, you could delete the current version of the report and then create it all over again. There are several steps involved in creating a report, however, so it is more complicated than the process of recreating the form. An easier way is to modify the report in Layout view. In Layout view, you easily can resize columns and add new fields. The following steps modify the Client Financial Report by resizing the Client Name field so that the entire name of Hendley County Regional Hospital appears. They also add the Client Type and Total Amount fields. Finally, to accommodate the extra fields, the steps change the orientation of the report from Portrait to Landscape.

1

- Open the Navigation Pane, if necessary, and then right-click the Client Financial Report in the Navigation Pane to display a shortcut menu.

- Click Layout View on the shortcut menu to open the report in Layout view.

- Close the Navigation Pane.

- Click the column heading for the Client Name column, point to the right-hand border of the column heading so that the mouse pointer becomes a two-headed arrow, and then drag the pointer to the approximate position shown in Figure 3–56 to resize the column.

Do I have to be exact?

No. Make sure, however, that you can see all the data in the client name for client HC10. If not, you need to drag the border further to the right.

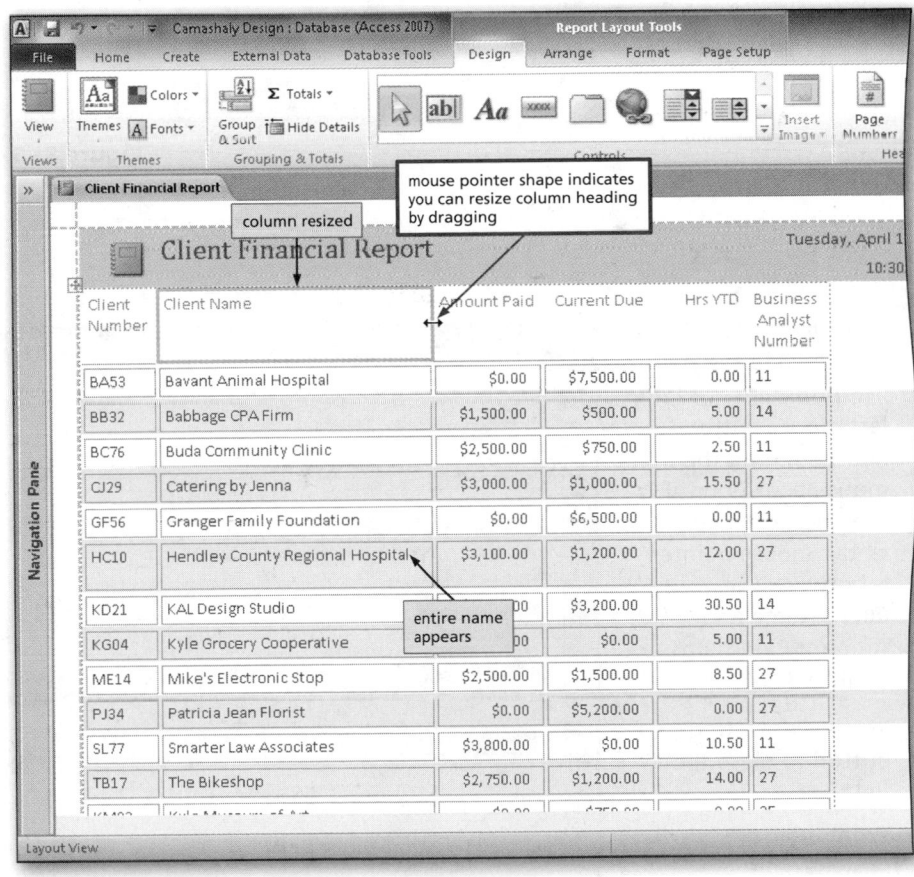

Figure 3–56

Did I have to select the column heading or could I have selected one of the entries in the column?

You could have selected any of the entries in the column.

2

- Click the Add Existing Fields button (Report Layout Tools Design tab | Tools group) to display a field list (Figure 3–57).

Q&A

Why are there two Services Needed fields in the list?

They serve different purposes. If you were to select Services Needed, you would get all the services for a given client on one line. If you were to select Services Needed.Value, each service would be on a separate line. You are not selecting either one for this report.

Figure 3–57

3

- Point to the Client Type field in the field list, press and hold the left mouse button, and then drag the mouse pointer until the line to the left of the mouse pointer is between the Client Name and Amount Paid fields (Figure 3–58).

- Release the left mouse button to place the field.

Q&A

What if I make a mistake?

You can delete the field by clicking the field and then pressing the DELETE key. You can move the field by dragging it to the correct position.

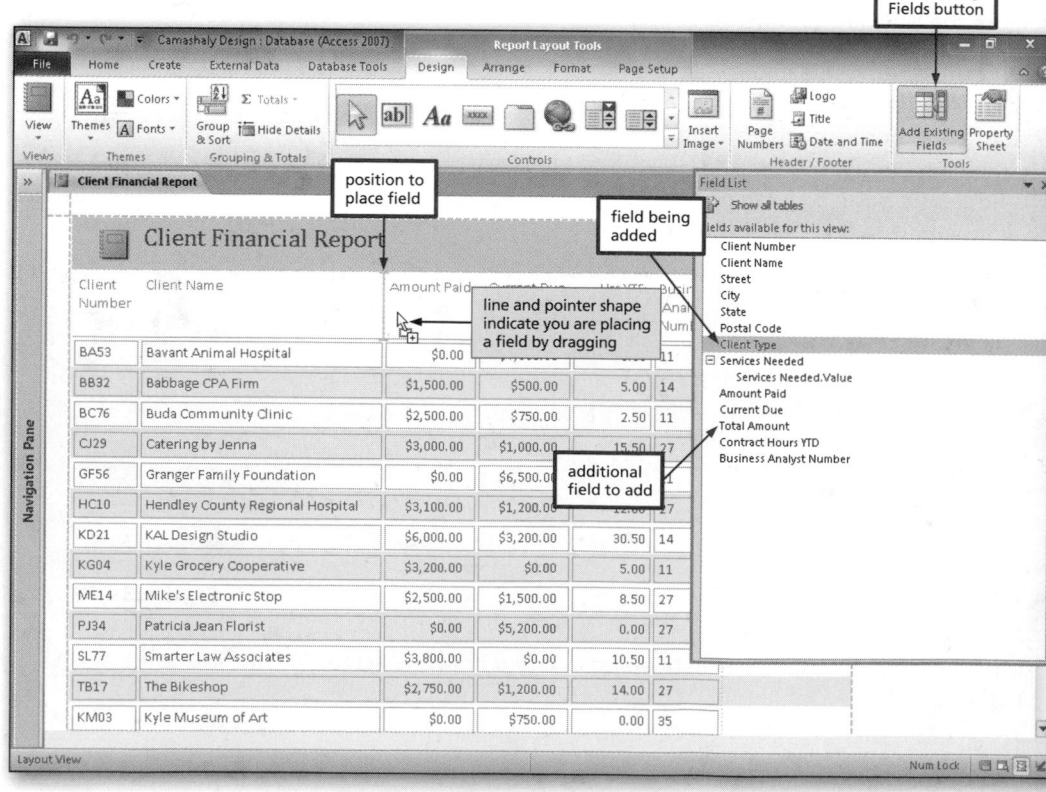

Figure 3–58

④

- Using the same technique, add the Total Amount field between the Current Due and Hrs YTD fields.

- Click the Add Existing Fields button (Report Layout Tools Design tab | Tools group) to remove the field list from the screen (Figure 3–59).

  What would I do if the field list covered the portion of the report where I wanted to insert a new field?

  You can move the field list to a different position on the screen by dragging its title bar.

- Scroll the report, if necessary, so that the entire width of the report appears on the screen.

Figure 3–59

⑤

- Click Page Setup on the Ribbon to display the Page Setup tab.

- Click the Landscape button (Report Layout Tools Page Setup tab | Page Layout group) to change the orientation of the report to Landscape.

- Click the Save button on the Quick Access Toolbar to save your changes.

- Close the report.

To Include Totals in a Datasheet

It is possible to include totals and other statistics at the bottom of a datasheet in a special row called the Total row. The following steps display the total of the salary YTD and Incentive YTD for analysts in the Total row.

1

- Open the Business Analyst Table in Datasheet view and close the Navigation Pane.

- Click the Totals button (Home tab | Records group) to include the Total row in the datasheet.

- Click the Total row in the Salary YTD column to display an arrow.

- Click the arrow to display a menu of available calculations (Figure 3–60).

Q&A

Will I always get the same list?

No. You will only get the items that are applicable to the type of data in the column. You cannot calculate the sum of text data, for example.

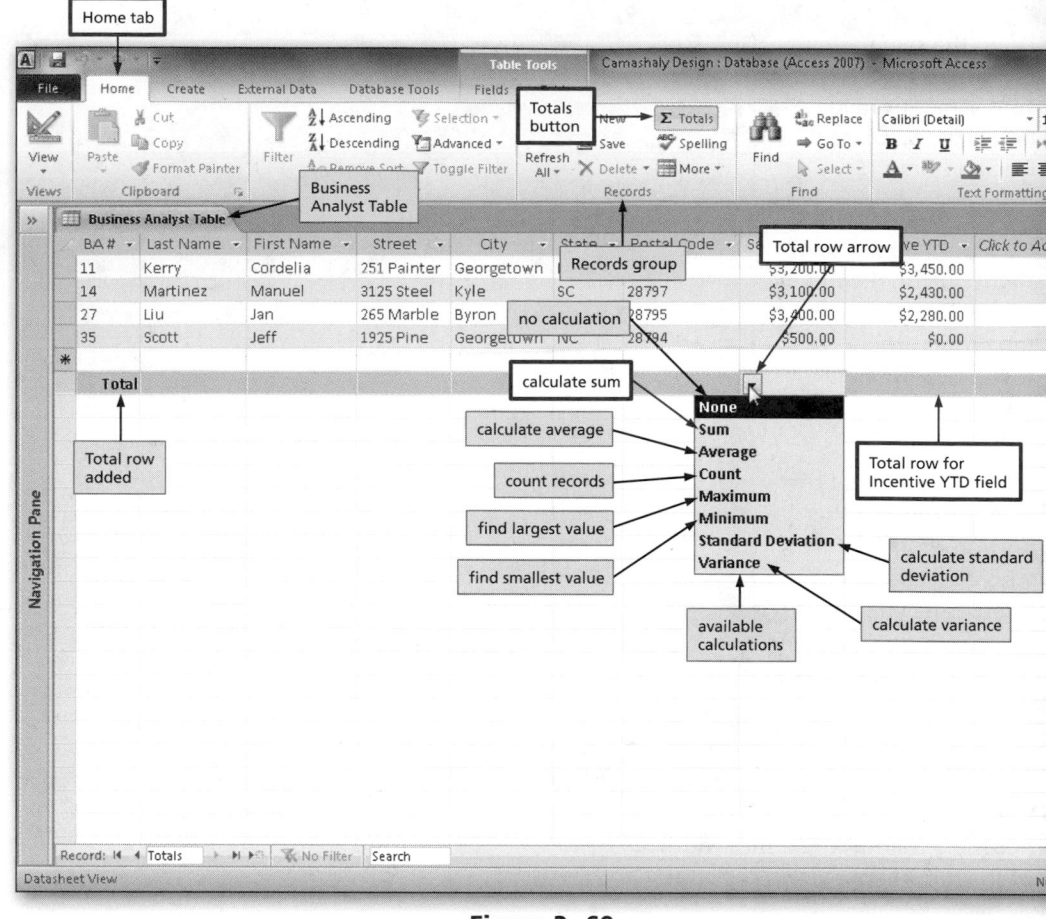

Figure 3–60

2

- Click Sum to calculate the total of the salary YTD amounts.

- Click the Total row in the Incentive YTD column to display an arrow, click the arrow to display a menu of available calculations, and then click Sum to calculate the total of the incentive YTD amounts (Figure 3–61).

Experiment

- Experiment with other statistics. When finished, once again select the sum in both columns.

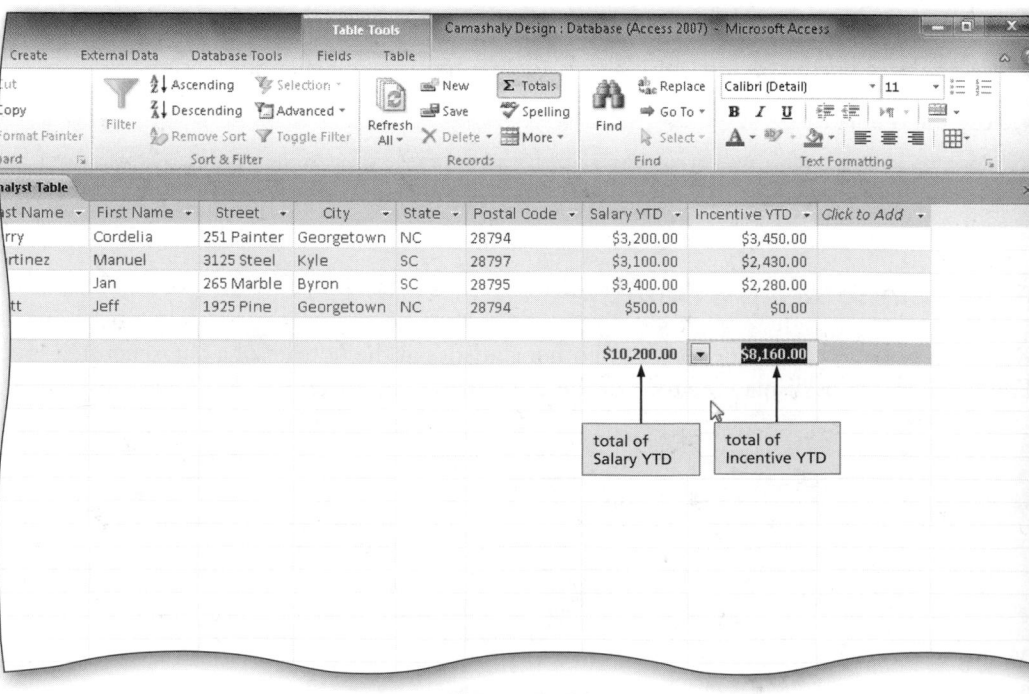

Figure 3–61

To Remove Totals from a Datasheet

If you no longer want the totals to appear as part of the datasheet, you can remove the Total row. The following step removes the Total row.

- Click the Totals button (Home tab | Records group), which is shown in Figure 3–60, to remove the Total row from the datasheet.

Changing the Appearance of a Datasheet

You can change the appearance of a datasheet in a variety of ways. For example, you can change the appearance of gridlines or change the text colors and font. Figure 3–62 shows the various buttons, found in the Text Formatting group on the Home tab, that are available to change the datasheet appearance.

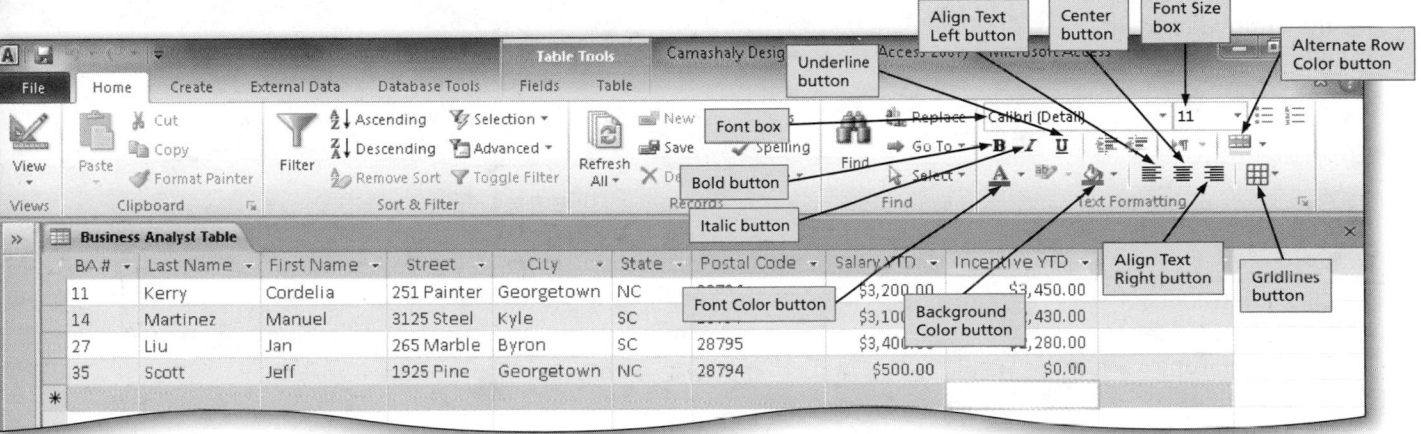

Figure 3–62

The changes to the datasheet will be reflected not only on the screen, but also when you print or preview the datasheet.

Determine whether changes to the format of a datasheet are desirable.
You need to decide if changes to the format of a datasheet would improve its appearance and/or its usefulness. The following are the decisions you would make.

- Would totals or other calculations be useful in the datasheet? If so, include the Total row and select the appropriate computations.

- Would different gridlines make the datasheet more useful? If so, change to the desired gridlines.

- Would alternating colors in the rows make them easier to read? If so, change the alternate fill color.

- Would a different font and/or font color make the text stand out better? If so, change the font color and/or the font.

- Is the font size appropriate? Can you see enough data at one time on the screen and yet have the data be readable? If not, change the font size to an appropriate value.

- Is the column spacing appropriate? Are some columns wider than they need to be? Do some columns not display all the data? Change the column sizes as necessary.

As a general guideline, once you have decided on a particular look for a datasheet, all your datasheets should have the same look, unless there is a compelling reason for one of your datasheets to differ.

Plan
Ahead

To Change Gridlines in a Datasheet

One of the changes you can make to a datasheet is which gridlines appear. You may feel that the appearance would be improved by having only horizontal gridlines. The following steps change the datasheet so that only horizontal gridlines are included.

- Open the Business Analyst Table in Datasheet view, if it is not already open.

- If necessary, close the Navigation Pane.

- Click the box in the upper-left corner of the datasheet to select the entire datasheet (Figure 3–63).

Figure 3–63

- Click the Gridlines button (Home tab | Text Formatting group) to display the Gridlines gallery (Figure 3–64).

Q&A
Does it matter whether I click the button or the arrow?

In this case, it does not matter. Either one will produce the same result.

Figure 3–64

- Click the Gridlines: Horizontal command in the Gridlines gallery to include only horizontal gridlines.

- Experiment with other gridline options. When finished, once again select horizontal gridlines.

To Change the Colors and Font in a Datasheet

You may also decide to modify the appearance of the datasheet by changing the colors and the font. The following steps change the Alternate Fill color, a color that appears on every other row in the datasheet. They also change the font color, the font, and the font size.

- With the datasheet for the Business Analyst Table selected, click the Alternate Row Color button arrow (Home tab | Text Formatting group) to display the color palette (Figure 3–65).

Does it matter whether I click the button or the arrow?

Yes. Clicking the arrow produces a color palette. Clicking the button applies the currently selected color. When in doubt, you should click the arrow.

Figure 3–65

- Click Brown in the upper-right corner of Standard Colors to select brown as the alternate color.

- Click the Font Color button arrow, and then click Red (the second color in the bottom row) in the lower-left corner of Standard Colors to select Red as the font color.

- Click the Font box arrow, scroll down in the list until Bodoni MT appears, and then select Bodoni MT as the font. (If it is not available, select any font of your choice.)

- Click the Font Size box arrow, and select 10 as the font size (Figure 3–66).

Does the order in which I make these selections make a difference?

No. You could have made these selections in any order.

 Experiment

- Experiment with other colors, fonts, and font sizes. When finished, return to the options selected in this step.

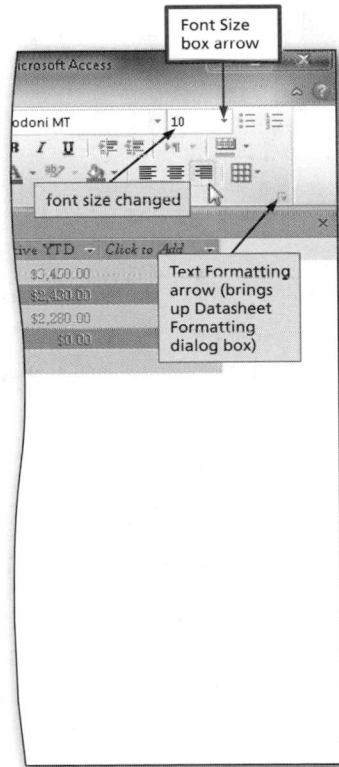

Figure 3–66

Using the Datasheet Formatting Dialog Box

As an alternative to using the individual buttons, you can click the Datasheet Formatting dialog box launcher to display the Datasheet Formatting dialog box (Figure 3–67). You can use the various options within the dialog box to make changes to the datasheet format. Once you are finished, click the OK button to apply your changes.

Figure 3–67

To Close the Datasheet without Saving the Format Changes

The following steps close the datasheet without saving the changes to the format. Because the changes are not saved, the next time you open the Business Analyst Table in Datasheet view, it will appear in the original format. If you had saved the changes, the changes would be reflected in its appearance.

1 Close the Business Analyst Table.

2 Click the No button in the Microsoft Access dialog box when asked if you want to save your changes.

Multivalued Fields in Queries

You can use multivalued fields in queries just as you can use other fields. You have a choice concerning how the multiple values appear. You can choose to have them on a single row or on multiple rows.

To Query a Multivalued Field Showing Multiple Values on a Single Row

To include a multivalued field in the results of a query, place the field in the query design grid just like any other field. The results will list all of the values for the multivalued field on a single row, just as in a datasheet. The following steps create a query to display the client number, client name, client type, and services needed for all clients.

1

• Create a query for the Client table and close the Navigation Pane.

• Include the Client Number, Client Name, Client Type, and Services Needed fields (Figure 3–68).

Figure 3–68

2

- View the results (Figure 3–69).

Q&A
Can I include criteria for the multivalued field?

Yes. You can include criteria for the multivalued field.

 Experiment

- Return to Design view and enter various criteria in the Services Needed field. Run the queries. When finished, return to the options selected in this step.

Figure 3–69

To Query a Multivalued Field Showing Multiple Values on Multiple Rows

You may want to see the multiple services needed for a client on separate rows rather than a single row. To do so, you need to use the Value property of the Services Needed field. The following steps use the Value property to display each service on a separate row.

- Return to Design view and ensure that the Client Number, Client Name, Client Type, and Services Needed fields are included in the design grid.

- Click the Services Needed field to produce an insertion point, press the RIGHT ARROW key as necessary to move the insertion point to the end of the field name, and then type a period and the word `Value` after the word, Needed, to use the Value property (Figure 3–70).

Q&A
I do not see the word, Services. Did I do something wrong?

No. There is not enough room to display the entire name. If you wanted to see it, you could point to the right boundary of the column selector and then either drag or double-click.

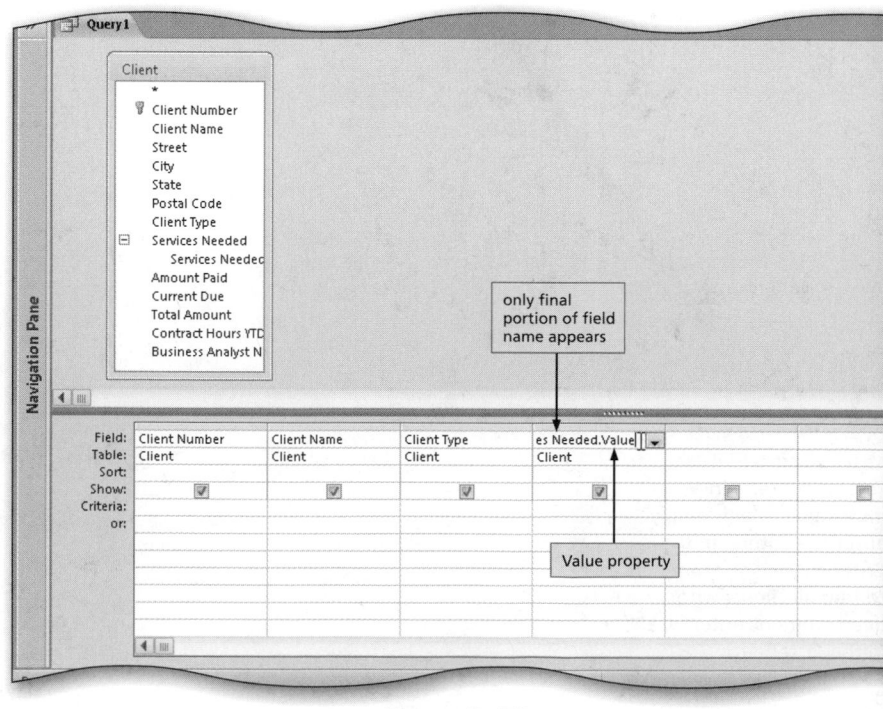

Figure 3–70

● View the results (Figure 3–71).

Can I now include criteria for the multivalued field?

Yes. You could enter a criterion just like in any other query.

● Close the query.

● When asked if you want to save the query, click the No button.

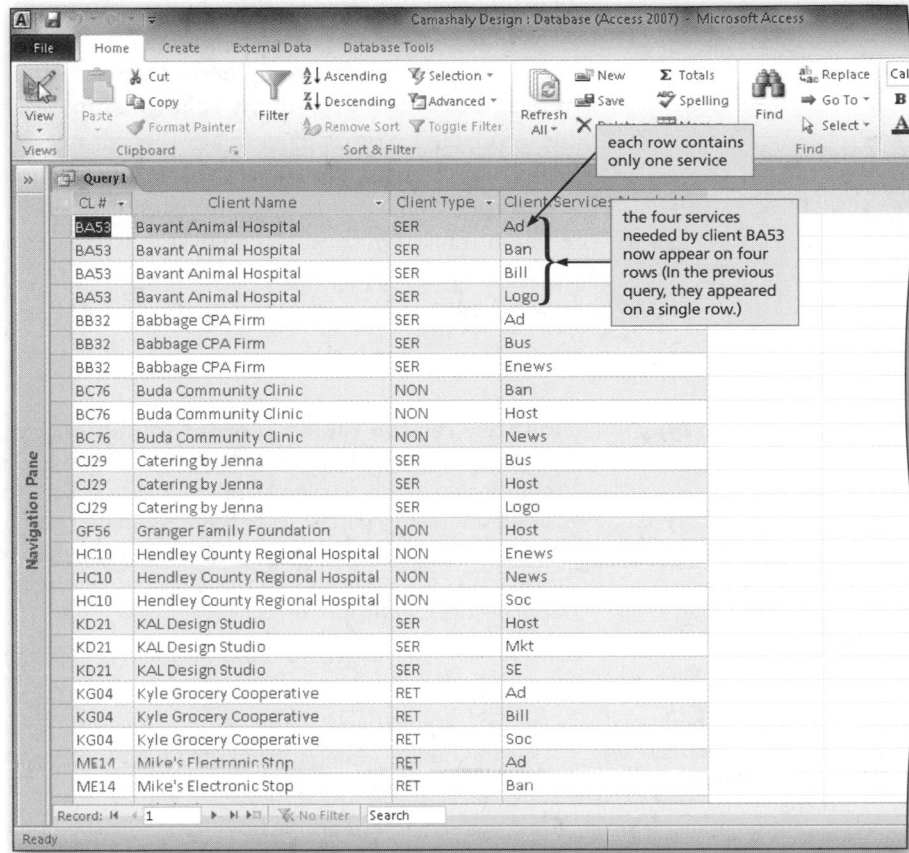

Figure 3–71

Break Point: If you wish to take a break, this is a good place to do so. You can quit Access now. To resume at a later time, start Access, open the database called Camashaly Design, and continue following the steps from this location forward.

Referential Integrity

When you have two related tables in a database, it is essential that the data in the common fields match. There should not be a client in the Client table whose business analyst number is 11, for example, unless there is a record in the Business Analyst Table whose number is 11. This restriction is enforced through **referential integrity**, which is the property that ensures that the value in a foreign key must match that of another table's primary key.

A **foreign key** is a field in one table whose values are required to match the *primary key* of another table. In the Client table, the Business Analyst Number field is a foreign key that must match the primary key of the Business Analyst Table; that is, the business analyst number for any client must be a business analyst currently in the Business Analyst Table. A client whose business analyst number is 92, for example, should not be stored because no such business analyst exists.

In Access, to specify referential integrity, you must define a relationship between the tables by using the Relationships button. Access then prohibits any updates to the database that would violate the referential integrity.

The type of relationship between two tables specified by the Relationships command is referred to as a **one-to-many relationship**. This means that *one* record in the first table is related to, or matches, *many* records in the second table, but each record in the second table is related to only *one* record in the first. In the Camashaly Design database, for example, a one-to-many relationship exists between the Business Analyst Table and the Client table. *One* business analyst is associated with *many* clients, but each client is associated with only a single business analyst. In general, the table containing the foreign key will be the *many* part of the relationship.

<table>
<tr>
<td align="right">

**Plan
Ahead**

</td>
<td>

Identify related tables in order to implement relationships between the tables.
When specifying referential integrity, you need to decide how to handle deletions. In the relationship between clients and business analysts, for example, deletion of a business analyst for whom clients exist, such as business analyst number 14, would violate referential integrity. Any clients for business analyst 14 no longer would relate to any business analyst in the database. You can handle this in two ways. For each relationship, you need to decide which of the approaches is appropriate.

- The normal way to avoid this problem is to prohibit such a deletion.

- The other option is to **cascade the delete.** This means that Access would allow the deletion but then delete all related records. For example, it would allow the deletion of the business analyst from the Client table but then automatically delete any clients related to the deleted business analyst.

You also need to decide how to handle the update of the primary key. In the relationship between business analysts and clients, for example, changing the business analyst number for business analyst 14 to 41 in the Business Analyst Table would cause a problem because some clients in the Client table have business analyst number 14. These clients no longer would relate to any business analyst. You can handle this in two ways. For each relationship, you need to decide which of the approaches is appropriate.

- The normal way to avoid this problem is to prohibit this type of update.

- The other option is to **cascade the update.** This means to allow the change, but make the corresponding change in the foreign key on all related records. In the relationship between clients and business analysts, for example, Access would allow the update but then automatically make the corresponding change for any client whose business analyst number was 14. It now will be 41.

</td>
</tr>
</table>

BTW

Relationships
You also can use the Relationships window to specify a one-to-one relationship. In a one-to-one relationship, the matching fields are both primary keys. If Camashaly maintained a company car for each analyst, the data concerning the cars might be kept in a Car table, in which the primary key is Business Analyst Number — the same primary key as the Business Analyst Table. Thus, there would be a one-to-one relationship between analysts and cars.

To Specify Referential Integrity

The following steps use the Relationships button on the Database Tools tab to specify referential integrity by specifying a relationship between the Business Analyst and Client tables. The steps also ensure that update will cascade, but that delete will not.

1
• Click Database Tools on the Ribbon to display the Database Tools tab. (Figure 3–72).

Figure 3–72

2
• Click the Relationships button (Database Tools tab | Relationships group) to open the Relationships window and display the Show Table dialog box (Figure 3–73).

Figure 3–73

3

- If necessary, click the Business Analyst Table (Show Table dialog box) and then click the Add button to add the Business Analyst Table.

- Click the Client table and then click the Add button to add the Client table.

- Click the Close button (Show Table dialog box) to close the dialog box.

- Resize the field lists that appear so all fields are visible (Figure 3–74).

Do I need to resize the field lists?

No. You can use the scroll bars. Before completing the next step, however, you would need to make sure the Business Analyst Number fields in both tables appear on the screen.

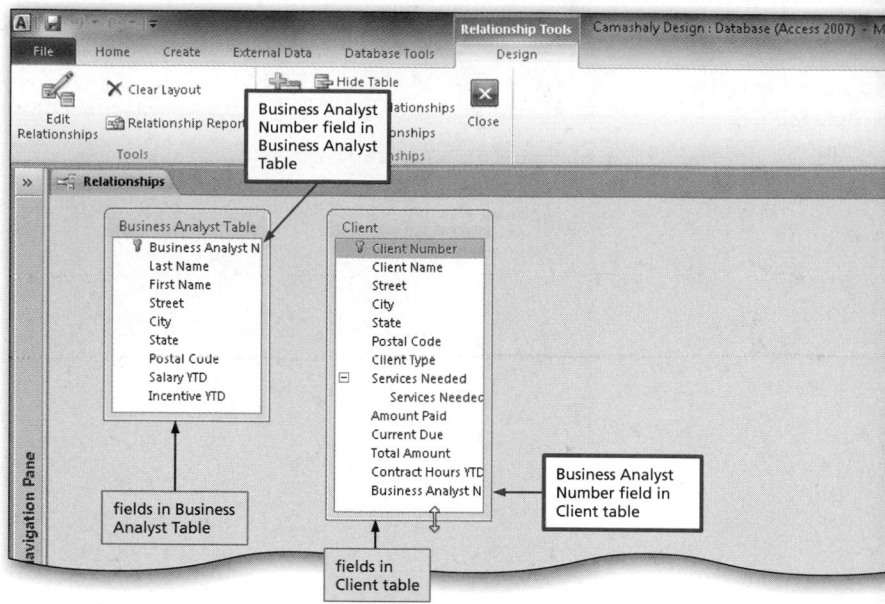

Figure 3–74

4

- Drag the Business Analyst Number field in the Business Analyst Table field list to the Business Analyst Number field in the Client table field list to display the Edit Relationships dialog box to create a relationship.

Do I actually move the field from the Business Analyst Table to the Client table?

No. The mouse pointer will change shape to indicate you are in the process of dragging, but the field does not move.

- Click the Enforce Referential Integrity check box (Edit Relationships dialog box).

- Click the Cascade Update Related Fields check box (Figure 3–75).

The Cascade check boxes were dim until I clicked the Enforce Referential Integrity check box. Is that correct?

Yes. Until you have chosen to enforce referential integrity, the cascade options are not applicable.

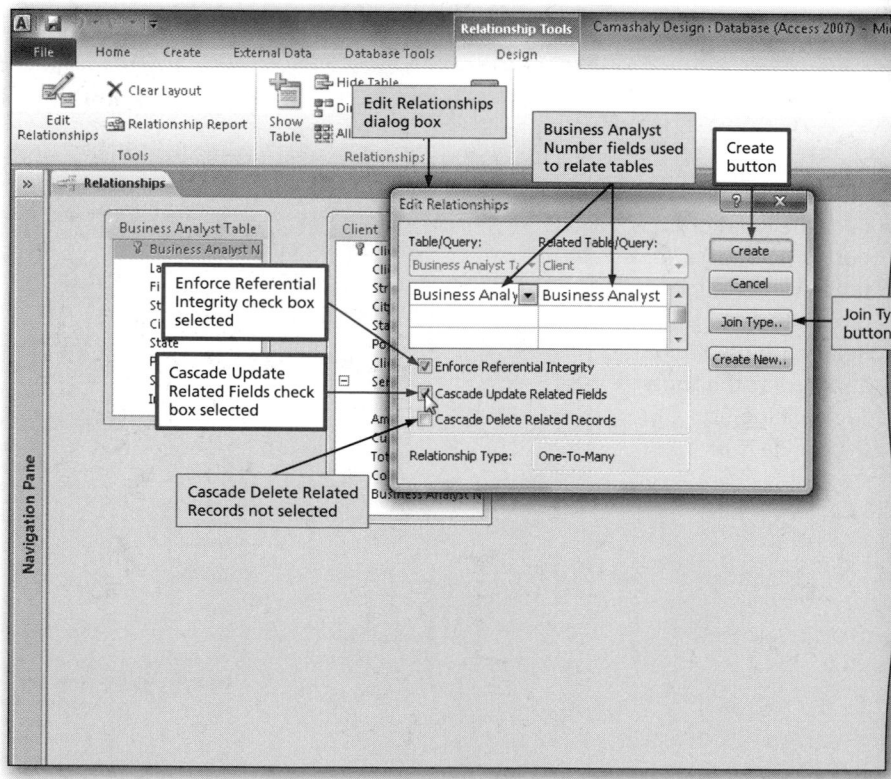

Figure 3–75

Can I change the join type like I can in queries?

Yes. Click the Join Type button in the Edit Relationships dialog box. Just as with queries, option button 1 creates an INNER join, option button 2 creates a LEFT join, and option button 3 creates a RIGHT join.

5

• Click the Create button (Edit Relationships dialog box) to complete the creation of the relationship (Figure 3–76).

What is the symbol at the lower end of the join line?

It is the mathematical symbol for infinity. It is used here to denote the "many" end of the relationship.

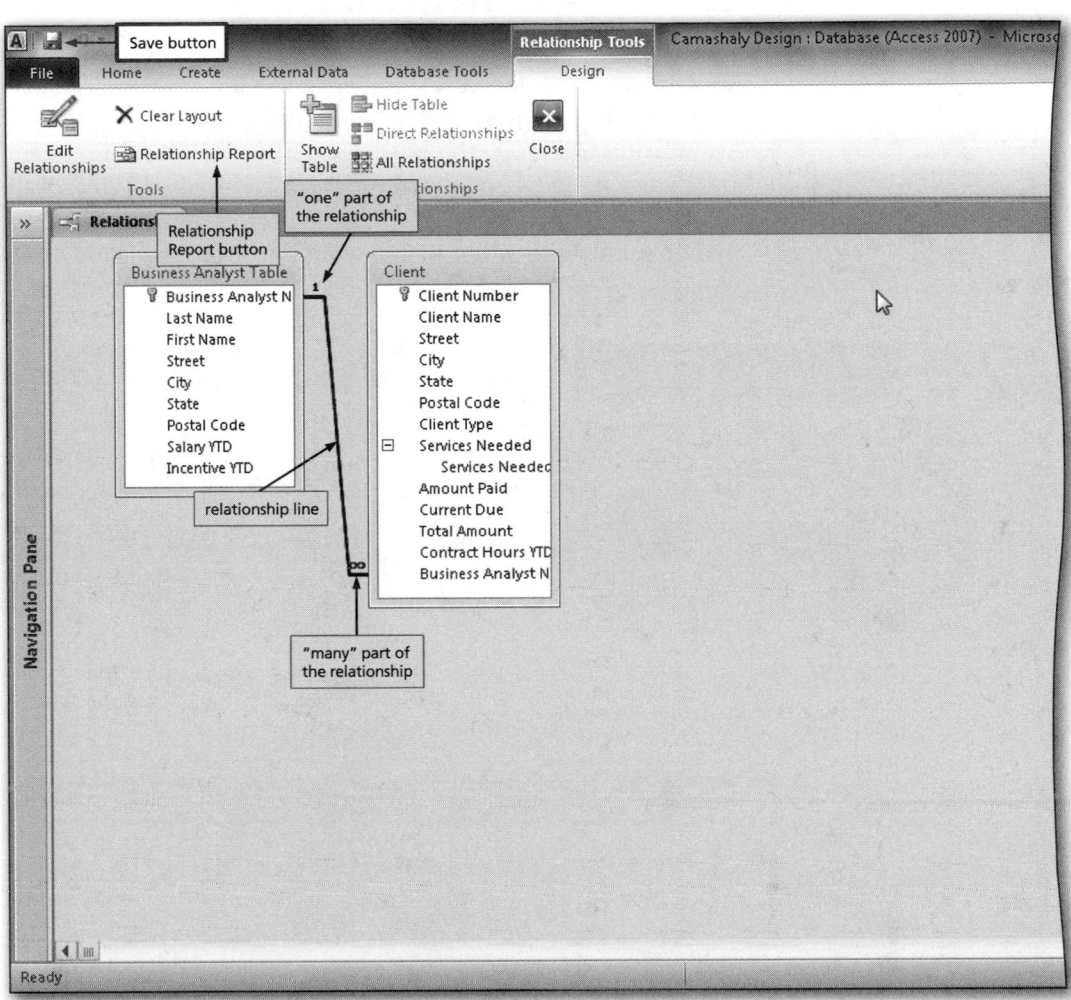

Figure 3–76

Can I print a copy of the relationship?

Yes. Click the Relationship Report button (Relationship Tools Design tab | Tools group) to produce a report of the relationship. You can print the report. You also can save it as a report in the database for future use. If you do not want to save it, close the report after you have printed it and do not save the changes.

6

• Click the Save button on the Quick Access Toolbar to save the relationship you created.

• Close the Relationships window.

Can I later modify the relationship if I want to change it in some way?

Yes. Click Database Tools on the Ribbon to display the Database Tools tab, and then click the Relationships button (Database Tools tab | Relationships group) to open the Relationships window. To add another table, click the Show Table button on the Design tab. To remove a table, click the Hide Table button. To edit a relationship, select the relationship and click the Edit Relationships button.

Effect of Referential Integrity

Referential integrity now exists between the Business Analyst and Client tables. Access now will reject any number in the Business Analyst Number field in the Client table that does not match a business analyst number in the Business Analyst Table. Attempting to change the business analyst number for a client to one that does not match any business analyst in the Business Analyst Table would result in the error message shown in Figure 3–77. Similarly, attempting to add a client whose business analyst number does not match would produce the same error message.

Figure 3–77

Access also will reject the deletion of a business analyst for whom related clients exist. Attempting to delete business analyst 11 from the Business Analyst Table, for example, would result in the message shown in Figure 3–78.

Figure 3–78

Access would, however, allow the change of a business analyst number in the Business Analyst Table. Then it automatically makes the corresponding change to the business analyst number for all the business analyst's clients. For example, if you changed the business analyst number of business analyst 14 to 41, the same 41 would appear in the business analyst number field for clients whose business analyst number had been 14.

To Use a Subdatasheet

Now that the Business Analyst Table is related to the Client table, it is possible to view the clients of a given business analyst when you are viewing the datasheet for the Business Analyst Table. The clients for the business analyst will appear below the business analyst in a **subdatasheet**. The availability of such a subdatasheet is indicated by a plus sign that appears in front of the rows in the Business Analyst Table. The following steps display the subdatasheet for business analyst 14.

1

• Open the Business Analyst Table in Datasheet view and close the Navigation Pane (Figure 3–79).

Figure 3–79

2

• Click the plus sign in front of the row for business analyst 14 to display the subdatasheet (Figure 3–80).

Q&A

How do I hide the subdatasheet when I no longer want it to appear?

When you clicked the plus sign, it changed to a minus sign. Click the minus sign.

 Experiment

• Display subdatasheets for other business analysts. Display more than one subdatasheet at a time. Remove the subdatasheets from the screen.

Figure 3–80

3

• Close the datasheet for the Business Analyst Table.

Handling Data Inconsistency

In many organizations, databases evolve and change over time. One department may create a database for its own internal use. Employees in another department may decide they need their own database containing much of the same information. For example, the Purchasing department may create a database of products that it buys and the Receiving department may create a database of products that it receives. Each department is keeping track of the same products. When the organization eventually merges the databases, they may find inconsistencies and duplication. The Find Duplicates Query Wizard and the Find Unmatched Query Wizard can assist in clearing the resulting database of duplication and errors.

TO FIND DUPLICATE RECORDS

One reason to include a primary key for a table is to eliminate duplicate records. A possibility still exists, however, that duplicate records can get into your database. The following steps illustrate how to use the Find Duplicates Query Wizard to find duplicate records.

1. Click Create on the Ribbon, and then click the Query Wizard button (Create tab | Queries group).
2. When Access displays the New Query dialog box, click the Find Duplicates Query Wizard and then click the OK button.
3. Identify the table and field or fields that might contain duplicate information.
4. Indicate any other fields you want displayed.
5. Finish the wizard to see any duplicate records.

TO FIND UNMATCHED RECORDS

Occasionally, you may want to find records in one table that have no matching records in another table. For example, you may want to determine which business analysts currently have no clients. The following steps illustrate how to find unmatched records using the Find Unmatched Query Wizard.

1. Click Create on the Ribbon, and then click the Query Wizard button (Create tab | Queries group).
2. When Access displays the New Query dialog box, click the Find Unmatched Query Wizard and then click the OK button.
3. Identify the table that might contain unmatched records and then identify the related table.
4. Indicate the fields you want displayed.
5. Finish the wizard to see any duplicate records.

Ordering Records

Normally, Access sequences the records in the Client table by client number whenever listing them because the Client Number field is the primary key. You can change this order, if desired.

To Use the Ascending Button to Order Records

To change the order in which records appear, use the Ascending or Descending buttons. Either button reorder the records based on the field in which the insertion point is located.

The following steps order the records by city using the Ascending button.

1

- Open the Client table in Datasheet view and close the Navigation Pane.

- Click the City field on the first record to select the field (Figure 3–81).

Q&A

Did I have to click the field on the first record?

No. Any other record would have worked as well.

Figure 3–81

BTW

Certification
The Microsoft Office Specialist (MOS) program provides an opportunity for you to obtain a valuable industry credential — proof that you have the Access 2010 skills required by employers. For more information, visit the Access 2010 Certification Web page (scsite.com/ac2010/cert).

2

- Click the Ascending button (Home tab | Sort & Filter group) to sort the records by City (Figure 3–82).

What if I wanted the cities to appear in reverse alphabetical order?

Click the Descending button.

🔍 **Experiment**

- Sort the records by city in reverse order. When done, sort the records by city in the original order.

Figure 3–82

- Close the Client table.

- Click the No button (Microsoft Access dialog box) when asked if you want to save your changes.

TO USE THE ASCENDING BUTTON TO ORDER RECORDS ON MULTIPLE FIELDS

Just as you are able to sort the answer to a query on multiple fields, you also can sort the data that appears in a datasheet on multiple fields. To do so, the major and minor keys must be next to each other in the datasheet with the major key on the left. (If this is not the case, you can drag the columns into the correct position. Instead of dragging, however, usually it will be easier to use a query that has the data sorted in the desired order.)

To sort on a combination of fields where the major key is just to the left of the minor key, you would use the following steps.

1. Click the field selector at the top of the major key column to select the entire column.
2. Hold down the SHIFT key and then click the field selector for the minor key column to select both columns.
3. Click the Ascending button to sort the records.

To Quit Access

The following steps quit Access.

1 Click the Close button on the right side of the title bar to quit Access.

2 If a Microsoft Access dialog box appears, click the Save button to save any changes made to the object since the last save.

BTW

Quick Reference
For a table that lists how to complete the tasks covered in this book using the mouse, Ribbon, shortcut menu, and keyboard, see the Quick Reference Summary at the back of this book, or visit the Access 2010 Quick Reference Web page (scsite.com/ac2010/qr).

Chapter Summary

In this chapter you have learned how to use a form to add records to a table, search for records, delete records, filter records, create and use lookup fields, create calculated fields, create and use multivalued fields, make mass changes, create validation rules, change the appearance of a datasheet, specify referential integrity, and use subdatasheets. The items listed below include all the new Access skills you have learned in this chapter.

1. Create a Split Form (AC 142)
2. Use a Form to Add Records (AC 144)
3. Search for a Record (AC 144)
4. Update the Contents of a Record (AC 146)
5. Delete a Record (AC 147)
6. Use Filter By Selection (AC 148)
7. Toggle a Filter (AC 150)
8. Use a Common Filter (AC 150)
9. Use Filter By Form (AC 152)
10. Use Advanced Filter/Sort (AC 153)
11. Delete a Field (AC 155)
12. Add a New Field (AC 155)
13. Create a Lookup Field (AC 156)
14. Add a Calculated Field (AC 159)
15. Modify Single or Multivalued Lookup Fields (AC 161)
16. Use an Update Query (AC 162)
17. Use a Delete Query (AC 163)
18. Use an Append Query (AC 164)
19. Use a Make-Table Query (AC 165)
20. Specify a Required Field (AC 166)
21. Specify a Range (AC 166)
22. Specify a Default Value (AC 167)
23. Specify a Collection of Legal Values (AC 167)
24. Specify a Format (AC 168)
25. Change the Contents of a Field (AC 170)
26. Use a Lookup Field (AC 171)
27. Use a Multivalued Lookup Field (AC 172)
28. Update a Form to Reflect the Changes in the Table (AC 174)
29. Update a Report to Reflect the Changes in the Table (AC 175)
30. Include Totals in a Datasheet (AC 177)
31. Remove Totals from a Datasheet (AC 179)
32. Change Gridlines in a Datasheet (AC 180)
33. Change the Colors and Font in a Datasheet (AC 181)
34. Query a Multivalued Field Showing Multiple Values on a Single Row (AC 183)
35. Query a Multivalued Field Showing Multiple Values on Multiple Rows (AC 184)
36. Specify Referential Integrity (AC 186)
37. Use a Subdatasheet (AC 191)
38. Find Duplicate Records (AC 193)
39. Find Unmatched Records (AC 193)
40. Use the Ascending Button to Order Records (AC 194)
41. Use the Ascending Button to Order Records on Multiple Fields (AC 195)

Learn It Online

Test your knowledge of chapter content and key terms.

Instructions: To complete the Learn It Online exercises, start your browser, click the Address bar, and then enter the Web address **scsite.com/ac2010/learn**. When the Access 2010 Learn It Online page is displayed, click the link for the exercise you want to complete and then read the instructions.

Chapter Reinforcement TF, MC, and SA
A series of true/false, multiple choice, and short answer questions that test your knowledge of the chapter content.

Flash Cards
An interactive learning environment where you identify chapter key terms associated with displayed definitions.

Practice Test
A series of multiple choice questions that test your knowledge of chapter content and key terms.

Who Wants To Be a Computer Genius?
An interactive game that challenges your knowledge of chapter content in the style of a television quiz show.

Wheel of Terms
An interactive game that challenges your knowledge of chapter key terms in the style of the television show *Wheel of Fortune*.

Crossword Puzzle Challenge
A crossword puzzle that challenges your knowledge of key terms presented in the chapter.

Apply Your Knowledge

Reinforce the skills and apply the concepts you learned in this chapter.

Specifying Validation Rules, Updating Records, Formatting a Datasheet, and Creating Relationships

Instructions: Start Access. Open the Babbage CPA Firm database that you modified in Apply Your Knowledge in Chapter 2 on page AC 129. (If you did not complete this exercise, see your instructor for a copy of the modified database.)

Perform the following tasks:

1. Open the Client table in Design view, as shown in Figure 3–83 on page AC 198.

2. Format the Client Number field so any lowercase letters appear in uppercase and make the Client Name field a required field.

3. Specify that balance due amounts must be between $0 and $1,200. Include validation text.

4. Save the changes to the Client table.

5. Create a split form for the Client table and find the record for M26 and change the client name to Mohr Craft Supplies.

6. Use the form to add the following record:

| L50 | Lou's Salon | 124 Fulton | Granger | 27036 | $0.00 | $325.00 | 38 |

Continued >

Apply Your Knowledge *continued*

Figure 3–83

7. Save the form as Client Split Form and close the form.

8. Open the Client table in Datasheet view and use Filter By Selection to find the record for H21. Delete the record. Remove the filter.

9. Add totals to the datasheet for the Amount Paid and Balance Due fields. Remove the gridlines from the datasheet.

10. Save the changes to the layout of the table. Close the Client table.

11. Create a relationship between the Bookkeeper table (the one table) and the Client table (the many table). Cascade the update but do not cascade the delete. Create a relationship report for the relationship. Save the report with the default report name Relationships for Babbage CPA Firm.

12. Submit the revised database in the format specified by your instructor.

Extend Your Knowledge

Extend the skills you learned in this chapter and experiment with new skills. You may need to use Help to complete the assignment.

Creating Action Queries and Changing Table Properties

Instructions: See the inside back cover of this book for instructions for downloading the Data Files for Students, or see your instructor for information on accessing the required files.

Generic Temp Services is a company that specializes in placing temporary workers in various administrative positions. Philamar Training has been approached about buying Generic Temp Services. Philamar is interested in knowing how many clients the companies have in common. Generic also needs to do some database maintenance by finding duplicates and finding unmatched records.

Perform the following tasks:

1. Open the Generic Temp Services database. Create and run a make-table query to create the Potential Clients table in the Generic Temp Services database shown in Figure 3–84. Save the query as Make Table Query.

Client Name	Street	City	Postal Code
Afton Manufac	612 Revere	Granger	27036
Atlas Distribut	227 Dandelion	Burles	28817
Blake-Scryps	557 Maum	Georgetown	28794
Dege Grocery C	446 Linton	Burles	28817
Grandston Clea	337 Abelard	Buda	27032
Hill Country Sh	247 Fulton	Granger	27036
Jones Plumbin	75 Getty	Buda	27032
Mohr Art Suppl	665 Maum	Georgetown	28794
SeeSaw Indust	31 Liatris	Walburg	28819
Tate Repair	824 Revere	Granger	27036
Woody Sportin	578 Central	Walburg	28819
Catering by Jer	123 Second	Granger	27036

Figure 3–84

2. Open the Potential Clients table, change the font size to 14, and resize the columns to best fit the data.

3. Save the changes to the layout of the table. Close the table.

4. Use the Find Duplicates Query Wizard to find duplicate information in the City field. Include the Client Name field in the query. Name the query City Duplicates Query. Close the query.

5. Use the Find Unmatched Query Wizard to find all records in the Worker table that do not match records in the Client table. Worker Number is the common field in both tables. Include the Worker Number, Last Name, and First Name in the query. Name the query Worker Unmatched Query. Close the query.

6. Submit the revised database in the format specified by your instructor.

Make It Right

Analyze a database and correct all errors and/or improve the design.

Correcting Table Design Errors

Instructions: Start Access. Open the Senior Jobbers database. See the inside back cover of this book for instructions for downloading the Data Files for Students, or see your instructor for information on accessing the required files.

Perform the following tasks:

Senior Jobbers provides a variety of small repairs and maintenance to homeowners. The owner of Senior Jobbers has decided that he could better manage the business if he added a multivalued field that lists the various types of repairs and maintenance that customers request. He created the field shown in Figure 3–85 but forgot to add Clean Gutters as one of the job types. Modify the multivalued lookup field to include Clean Gutters as a job type. By mistake, the owner also added the contact number field shown in Figure 3–85 to the Customer table. That field should be deleted.

Figure 3–85

Finally, he wanted to specify referential integrity between the Worker table and the Customer table. The relationship shown in Figure 3–86 is not correct and must be fixed. The owner does not want to cascade the update or the delete.

Figure 3–86

Submit the revised database in the format specified by your instructor.

n the Lab

Design, create, modify, and/or use a database following the guidelines, concepts, and skills presented in this chapter. Labs 1, 2, and 3 are listed in order of increasing difficulty.

ab 1: Maintaining the ECO Clothesline Database

Problem: ECO Clothesline is expanding rapidly and needs to make some database changes to handle the expansion. The company needs to know more about its customers, such as the type of business, and t needs to ensure that data that is entered is valid. It also needs to update the records in the database.

Use the database modified in the In the Lab 1 of Chapter 2 on page AC 132 for this assignment, r see your instructor for information on accessing the files required for this book.

Perform the following tasks:

1. Open the ECO Clothesline database and then open the Customer table in Design view.

2. Add a Lookup field, Customer Type, to the Customer table. This field should not allow multiple values. The field should appear after the Postal Code field. The field will contain data on the type of customer. The customer types are SAL (Salons, Studios, Fitness Clubs), SPG (Sporting Goods), and WMN (Women's Wear). Save these changes to the structure.

Continued >

In the Lab continued

3. Using a query, change all the entries in the Customer Type column to WMN. Save the query as Customer Type Update Query.

4. Open the Customer table and make the following changes. You can use either the Find button or Filter By Selection to locate the records to change:

   a. Change the customer type for customers CY12, FN19, LB20, RD03, TT21, and TW56 to SAL.

   b. Change the customer type for customer WS34 to SPG.

   c. Change the name of customer LB20 to Le Beauty Salon & Spa.

5. Change the alternate background color on the datasheet to white and remove the vertical gridlines. Save the changes to the layout of the table.

6. Create the following validation rules for the Customer table and save the changes.

   a. Specify the legal values SAL, SPG, and WMN for the Customer Type field. Include validation text.

   b. Assign a default value of WMN to the Customer Type field.

   c. Ensure that any letters entered in the Customer Number field appear as uppercase.

   d. Make Customer Name a required field.

7. Open the Customer table and use Filter By Form to find all records where the customer is located in Lowton and has a customer type of WMN, and then delete these records.

8. ECO Clothesline has signed up a sporting goods store, Ralph's (Customer Number RA21) and needs to add the record to the Customer table. Ralph's is at 72 Main in Lowton, TN 37084. Terry Sinson is the sales rep assigned to the account. To date, Ralph's has not been billed nor does the company owe for any services. Create a split form for the Customer table and use this split form to add the record. Save the split form as Customer Split Form.

9. Establish a relationship between the Sales Rep table (the one table) and the Customer table (the many table). Cascade the update but not the delete.

10. Add the Customer Type field to the Customer Balance Report. The field should follow the Customer Name field. Save the changes to the report.

11. Submit the revised database in the format specified by your instructor.

In the Lab

Lab 2: Maintaining the Walburg Energy Alternatives Database

Problem: The management of the Walburg Energy Alternatives recently acquired some items from a store that is going out of business. You now need to append these new items to the current item table. You also need to change the database structure and add some validation rules to the database.

Use the database modified in the In the Lab 2 of Chapter 2 on page AC 134 for this assignment. You also will use the More Items database from the Data Files for Students. See the inside back cover of this book for instructions for downloading the Data Files for Students, or see your instructor for information on accessing the required files.

Perform the following tasks:

1. Open the More Items database from the Data Files for Students.

2. Create a new query for the Item table and add all fields to the query.

3. Using an append query, append all records in the More Items database to the Item table in the Walburg Energy Alternatives database, as shown in Figure 3–87.

Figure 3–87

4. Save the append query as Walburg Append Query and close the More Items database.

5. Open the Walburg Energy Alternatives database and then open the Item table in Datasheet view. There should be 20 records in the table.

6. The items added from the More Items database do not have a vendor assigned to them. Assign items 1234 and 2234 to vendor JM. Assign item 2216 to vendor AS. Assign items 2310 and 2789 to vendor SD.

7. Create an advanced filter for the Item table. The filter should display records with fewer than 10 items on hand and be sorted in ascending order by Description. Save the filter settings as a query and name the filter Reorder Filter.

8. Make the following changes to the Item table:

   a. Change the field size for the On Hand field to Integer. The Format should be fixed and the decimal places should be 0.

   b. Make Description a required field.

   c. Specify that the number on hand must be between 0 and 50. Include validation text.

   d. Add a calculated field Inventory Value (On Hand*Cost) following the Cost field. Format the field as currency.

9. Save the changes to the table design. If a dialog box appears indicating that some data may be lost, click the Yes button.

10. Add the Inventory Value field to the Inventory Status Report. Place the field after the Cost field. Save the changes to the report.

11. Establish a relationship between the Vendor table (the one table) and the Item table (the many table). Cascade the update but not the delete.

12. Submit the revised More Items database and the Walburg Energy Alternatives database in the format specified by your instructor.

In the Lab

Lab 3: Maintaining the Philamar Training Database

Problem: Philamar Training is expanding rapidly and needs to make some database changes to handle the expansion. The company needs to know more about its clients, such as the type of business and the training services needed. You also are to add validation rules and update records in the database.

Use the Philamar Training database modified in the In the Lab 3 of Chapter 2 on page AC 135 for this assignment, or see your instructor for information on accessing the files required for this book. Submit the revised database in the format specified by your instructor.

Instructions Part 1: Several changes must be made to the database structure. For example, management would like a lookup field, Client Type, added to the Client table. The field should appear after the Postal Code field. The field will contain data on the type of client. The client types are MAN (Manufacturing), RET (Retail), and SER (Service). Philamar also needs a multivalued field that lists the general type of computer training of interest to each client. This knowledge can help Philamar better meet the needs of their clients. Add the field following the Client Type field. Table 3–2 lists the training abbreviations and descriptions that management would like in a Training Needed multivalued field.

Table 3–2 Training Abbreviations and Descriptions	
Training Abbreviation	**Description**
APP	Application Software
HRD	Hardware
LAN	Local Area Networks
SEC	Security
WEB	Internet and World Wide Web
WIN	Windows

Management wants to ensure that an entry always appears in the Client Name field and that any letters entered in the Client Number field appear in uppercase. It also requires that the amount in the Current Due field is never less than 0 or greater than $5,000. The only values in the Client Type field are MAN, SER, and RET. Most clients are manufacturing organizations. Make the changes to the database structure.

Instructions Part 2: Use a query to assign the client type MAN to all records in the Client table. Save the query as Update Query. Clients EU28 and FI28 are retail organizations. Clients CE16, HN83, and PS82 are service organizations. The data for the Training Needed field shown in Figure 3–88 must be added to the database. The address for PRIM Staffing is incorrect. It should be 727 Crestview. Hurley National is really Hurley National Bank. A new retail organization, Ralph's, just became a Philamar client. The address for the store is 42 Main, Crumville, TX 76745. Ralph's is interested in application software and Windows training.

Management wants to use RA10 as the client number and Marty Danville as the trainer. The new client has not yet received any training and does not owe any money to Philamar.

CL # ▾	Client Name ▾	Training Needed ▾
BS27	Blant and Sons	HRD, LAN, SEC
CE16	Center Services	APP, WEB, WIN
CP27	Calder Plastics	LAN, SEC, WEB
EU28	Elba's Furniture	APP, SEC, WEB
FI28	Farrow-Idsen	APP, WEB
FL93	Fairland Lawn	LAN, SEC, WEB
HN83	Hurley National Bank	APP, WIN
MC28	Morgan-Alyssa	HRD, LAN
PS82	PRIM Staffing	APP, WEB, WIN
RA10	Ralph's	APP, WIN
TE26	Telton-Edwards	SEC

Figure 3–88

Instructions Part 3: Management wants to make sure that clients are not assigned to a trainer who is not in the database. It also wants the ability to change a trainer number in the Trainer table and have the change applied to the Client table. Create the appropriate relationship that would satisfy management's needs.

Cases and Places

Apply your creative thinking and problem solving skills to design and implement a solution.

See the inside back cover of this book for instructions for downloading the Data Files for Students, or see your instructor for information on accessing the required files.

1: Maintaining the Chamber of Commerce Database

Academic

Use the Chamber of Commerce database you modified in Cases and Places 1 in Chapter 2 on page AC 135 for this assignment. Use the concepts and techniques presented in this chapter to modify the database as follows:

1. The chamber would like to categorize the businesses that advertise in the guide as retail, dining, or service establishments. These three types are the only valid category types. Most businesses are retail businesses.

2. Advertisers A228, C135, G346, H123, K109, M321, T167, and W456 are retail establishments. Advertisers C048, C234, D217, N007, and P124 are service establishments. The remaining advertisers are dining establishments.

3. An entry should always appear in the Advertiser Name field and any letters in the Advertiser Number field should appear in uppercase.

4. Chloe's Salon has changed its name to Chloe's Salon and Spa.

Continued >

Cases and Places *continued*

5. AAA Diner is a new restaurant in town and wants to advertise in the guide. Assign the Advertiser Number A245 to AAA Diner. The restaurant is located at 23 Berton, the postal code is 19363, and the telephone number is 555-0998. It has not yet made a payment and the balance is $75.00. Lars Tolbert is the ad rep.

6. Specify referential integrity. Cascade the update but not the delete.

7. Change the ad rep number for ad rep 26 to 22.

Submit the revised database in the format specified by your instructor.

2: Maintaining the Consignment Database

Personal

Use the Consignment database you modified in Cases and Places 2 in Chapter 2 on page AC 136 for this assignment. Use the concepts and techniques presented in this chapter to modify the database as follows:

1. Make the Condition field a lookup field. Only the current values in the database should be legal values. Most items are in good condition.

2. Update descriptions: A better description for the recliner is Leather Recliner. A better description for the bar stools is Kitchen Counter Stools.

3. The clothes hamper has been sold.

4. The minimum price of any item is $2.

5. The Description field always should contain data.

6. It would be easier to find items for sale if the default sort order for the Items table was by Description rather than by Item Number. Also, all descriptions should be displayed completely in Datasheet view.

7. Add the Condition field to the Available Items Report you created in Chapter 1. The field should follow the Description field. All descriptions should display completely.

8. Specify referential integrity. Cascade the delete but not the update.

Submit the revised database in the format specified by your instructor.

3: Maintaining the Senior Care Database

Professional

Use the Senior Care database you modified in Cases and Places 3 in Chapter 2 on page AC 136 for this assignment. Use the concepts and techniques presented in this chapter to modify the database as follows:

1. Senior Care could better serve its clients by adding a field that would list the type of services each client needs. Table 3–3 lists the service abbreviations and descriptions that should appear in the field.

Table 3–3 Service Abbreviations and Descriptions	
Service Abbreviation	**Description**
Bill	Bill/Mail/Correspondence Help
Cmp	Companionship
Hskp	Light Housekeeping
Hyg	Hygiene Assistance
Meal	Meal Planning/Preparation
Tran	Transportation/Errands

2. Add the data for this multivalued field shown in Figure 3–89 to the database.

3. This multivalued field also should appear in the Client Report you created in Chapter 1.

4. Senior Care is having trouble finding helpers willing to help with hygiene. Query the Client table to find all clients who require hygiene assistance. Save the query as Hygiene Needs Query.

5. Mike Preston has moved to assisted living and is no longer a client of Senior Care. Use Find or Filter By Selection to delete this record.

6. An entry should always appear in the client first and last name fields. Any letters in the Client Number field should appear in uppercase.

7. Specify referential integrity. Cascade the update but not the delete.

Client Number	Last Name	First Name	Services Needed
AB10	Alvarez	Francine	Bill, Cmp, Meal
BR18	Breeton	Alex	Hskp, Hyg
CH21	Chalmer	Ben	Cmp, Tran
FE47	Ferber	Jane	Cmp
GM50	Gammon	Fred	Hskp
HA15	Hammond	Lois	Bill, Hskp, Meal
HJ05	Heijer	Bill	Hyg, Tran
KL10	Klinger	Cynthia	Hskp, Meal
LA75	Last	Bill	Hyg, Tran
MA24	Manchester	Liz	Cmp, Tran
SA23	Santoro	Maria	Bill, Meal, Tran
TH41	Thomas	Albert	Bill, Tran
TR35	Trent	Jerry	Hskp, Hyg
WI87	Width	Evelyn	Cmp, Meal

Figure 3–89

Submit the revised database in the format specified by your instructor.

1 Managing E-Mail Messages with Outlook

Objectives

You will have mastered the material in this chapter when you can:

- Start and quit Outlook
- Compose, address, and send an e-mail message
- Open, read, print, and close an e-mail message
- Reply to an e-mail message
- Forward an e-mail message
- Delete an e-mail message
- Check spelling as you type an e-mail message

- Save an e-mail message in the Drafts folder
- Retrieve a saved e-mail message
- Attach a file to an outgoing e-mail message
- Copy another person when sending an e-mail message
- Preview and save a file attachment
- Create an e-mail folder
- Move and copy received e-mail messages to a folder

1 | Managing E-Mail Messages with Outlook

Introduction

E-mail (short for **electronic mail**) is the transmission of messages and files over a computer network. Today, e-mail is the primary communication method for both personal and business use. An **e-mail program**, such as Microsoft Outlook 2010, is software in the user's computer that can access the mail servers in a local or remote network. Outlook is used to compose, send, receive, store, print, and delete e-mail messages. Finally, you can organize messages so that you easily can find and respond to them later.

To use Outlook, you must have an e-mail account. An **e-mail account** is an account used to connect to an e-mail service via an Internet service provider. An **Internet service provider (ISP)** delivers Internet access to a geographic location, either regionally or nationally. An e-mail account could be set up by your employer or school, or through a Web application such as Google's Gmail, Yahoo! Mail, or Windows Live Hotmail. Outlook does not create or issue e-mail accounts; it merely provides you with access to them. You may be able to establish e-mail service through your cable or telephone company.

In Outlook, an e-mail account is contained in an e-mail profile. An **e-mail profile** includes the e-mail account(s), data files, and settings that contain information about where a user's e-mail is stored. A **personal folders file (.pst file)** is a data file that stores a user's Outlook items, including e-mail messages, on your computer. A data file is created automatically when you set up an e-mail profile in Outlook, called an Outlook profile. If you are using Outlook on a home computer and starting it for the first time, the Auto Account Setup feature starts and begins to configure e-mail account settings for the e-mail account you want to use. (The process is discussed later in this chapter.) If you are using Outlook on a classroom computer, your instructor will provide the necessary information on how to begin using Outlook.

Project Planning Guidelines

The process of composing an e-mail message that communicates specific information requires some analysis and planning. As a starting point, establish why the e-mail message is needed. Once the purpose is determined, analyze the intended readers of the e-mail message and their unique needs. Then, gather information about the topic and decide what to include in the e-mail message. Details of these guidelines are provided in Appendix A. In addition, each project in this book provides practical applications of these planning considerations.

Project — Composing and Sending E-Mail Messages

The project in this chapter follows the general guidelines for using Outlook to compose, open, and reply to e-mail messages, as shown in Figure 1–1. To communicate with individuals and groups, you typically send or receive some kind of message. Phone calls, faxes, letters, and e-mail are examples of ways to communicate a message. E-mail is a convenient way to send information to multiple people simultaneously, instantly, and inexpensively.

As a student assistant to the director of the Business and Computer Division at Condor Harbor Community College (CHCC), you use Outlook to communicate with faculty, staff, and fellow classmates. This chapter uses the communications features of

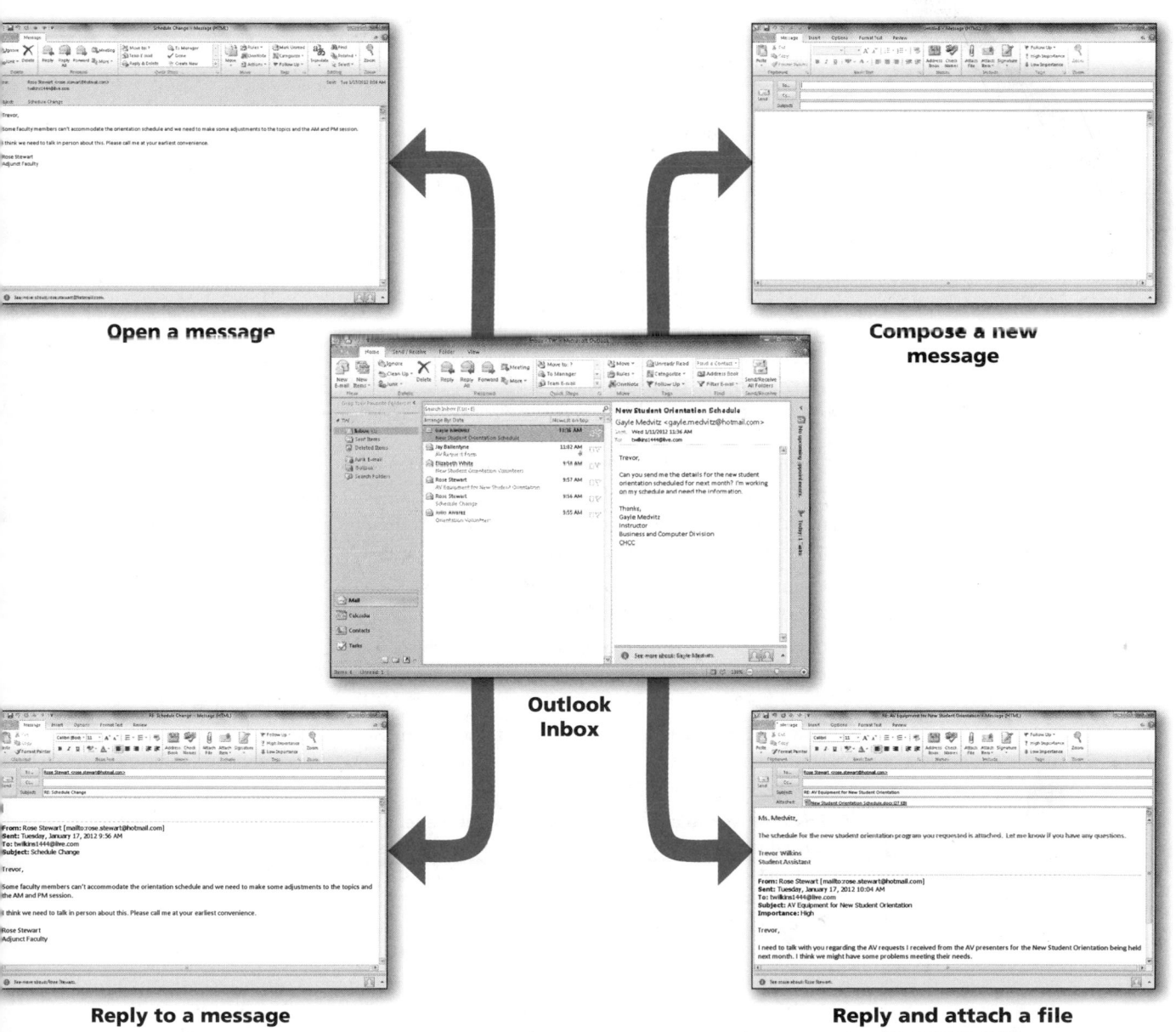

Open a message

Compose a new message

Outlook Inbox

Reply to a message

Reply and attach a file to a message

Figure 1–1

Microsoft Outlook 2010 to compose, send, read, reply to, and forward e-mail messages regarding an upcoming New Student Orientation program. Your responsibilities include collecting information from instructors who are participating in the orientation program, coordinating the resources needed, and scheduling student volunteers to work at the orientation program. Using Outlook, you open e-mail messages from instructors and students regarding these activities. You reply to e-mail messages and include a document containing the schedule that the recipient, or receiver of the e-mail message, can open. To organize messages, you create folders in which to store them.

Overview

As you read this chapter, you will learn how to communicate using e-mail by performing these general tasks:

- Compose and send an e-mail message.
- Open, read, and print an e-mail message.
- Reply to an e-mail message.
- Forward an e-mail message.
- Save an e-mail message.
- Attach a file to an e-mail message.
- Send an e-mail message to multiple recipients.
- Organize e-mail messages in folders.

Plan Ahead

General Project Guidelines

When creating an e-mail message, the actions you perform and decisions you make will affect the appearance and characteristics of the finished message. As you read, respond to, and create e-mail messages, such as those shown in Figure 1–1, you should follow these general guidelines:

1. **Determine the best method for reading e-mail messages you receive.** Although e-mail messages are sent electronically, you can read them on the computer in several ways or print them if you need a paper copy.

2. **Organize the e-mail message.** An e-mail message typically is organized into two areas: the message header and the message area.

3. **Choose the words for the subject line.** The subject line should indicate the main purpose or topic of the e-mail message. Use as few words as possible and never leave the subject line blank because it provides important information for the person receiving the e-mail message.

4. **Choose the words for the message text.** The message text should be clear and concise. Use as few words as possible to make a point. Brief or short message text is more likely to be read than lengthy text.

5. **Ensure that the content of the e-mail message is appropriate for the recipient.** An e-mail message sent to a close friend may be considerably different from one sent to an instructor, coworker, or client. Shortening words or using abbreviations (such as u for you, r for are, and 2 for to) may be appropriate for personal e-mail messages, but should be avoided when sending work-related e-mail messages. These types of abbreviations are too informal for the workplace and often are viewed as unprofessional.

6. **Alert the recipient(s) when sending large file attachments.** An **attachment** is a file, such as a document or picture, which is sent along with an e-mail message. Recipients can open attachments only if they have the appropriate software installed on their computer. Be aware when sending large file attachments that some e-mail services only allow file attachments up to a certain size.

(continued)

(continued)

**Plan
Ahead**

7. **Be aware of computer viruses and how they spread.** A **virus** is a malicious computer program that can damage files and the operating system. One way that viruses spread is through virus-infected e-mail attachments. You only should open attachments when the e-mail message is from someone you know or when you are expecting the attachment. If you receive an e-mail attachment, you should use an **antivirus program**, which is a program that checks files for viruses, to verify that the attachment is virus free.

When necessary, more specific details concerning the above guidelines are presented at appropriate points in the chapter. The chapter also will identify the actions performed and decisions made regarding these guidelines during the creation of the messages shown in Figure 1–1.

Outlook Account Settings

The first time you start Outlook on a home computer, the Auto Account Setup feature starts automatically to help you provide information that Outlook needs to send and receive e-mail messages. First, you will be prompted to provide your name, which will appear in e-mail messages that you send to other people. You also need to provide an e-mail address. An **e-mail address** identifies a user so that he or she can receive Internet e-mail. Just as you address a letter when using the postal system, you address an e-mail message with the e-mail address of the person receiving the message, or the recipient. Likewise, when someone sends you a message, he or she must have your e-mail address.

An e-mail address is divided into two parts. The first part contains a **user name**, which is a unique combination of characters, such as letters of the alphabet and numbers, which identifies a specific user. The last part is a **domain name**, which is the unique name associated with a specific Internet address and is provided by your ISP or school. In an Internet e-mail address, an @ (pronounced *at*) symbol separates the user name from the domain name. A possible e-mail address for someone named Kiley Barnhill, for example, would be kbarnhill@scsite.com, which would be read as k barnhill at s c site dot com. Figure 1–2 shows the parts of an e-mail address.

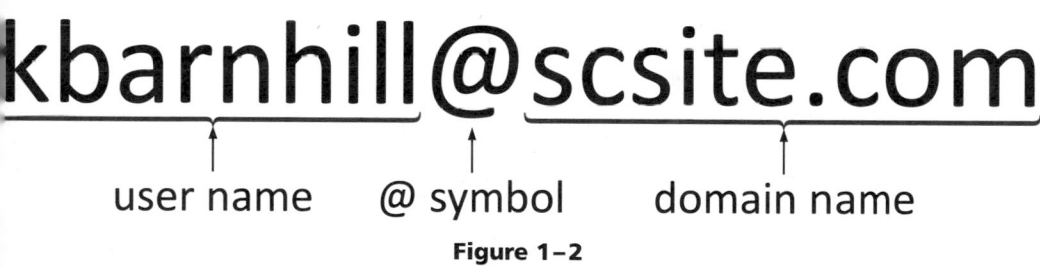

user name   @ symbol   domain name

Figure 1–2

After entering an e-mail address, you enter a password for the account. A **password** is a combination of letters, numbers, and symbols that verifies your identity. Typically, the ISP provides a password when you set up your e-mail service. Most people change the password so that they can remember it easily.

Figure 1–3 shows typical entries in the Add New Account dialog box, which is part of the Auto Account Setup feature and can be displayed by clicking File on the Ribbon to open the Backstage view and then clicking the Add Account link in the Backstage view. Notice in Figure 1–3 that the entered password is displayed as asterisks or bullets, which keeps your password private, preventing anyone from learning your password as you type it.

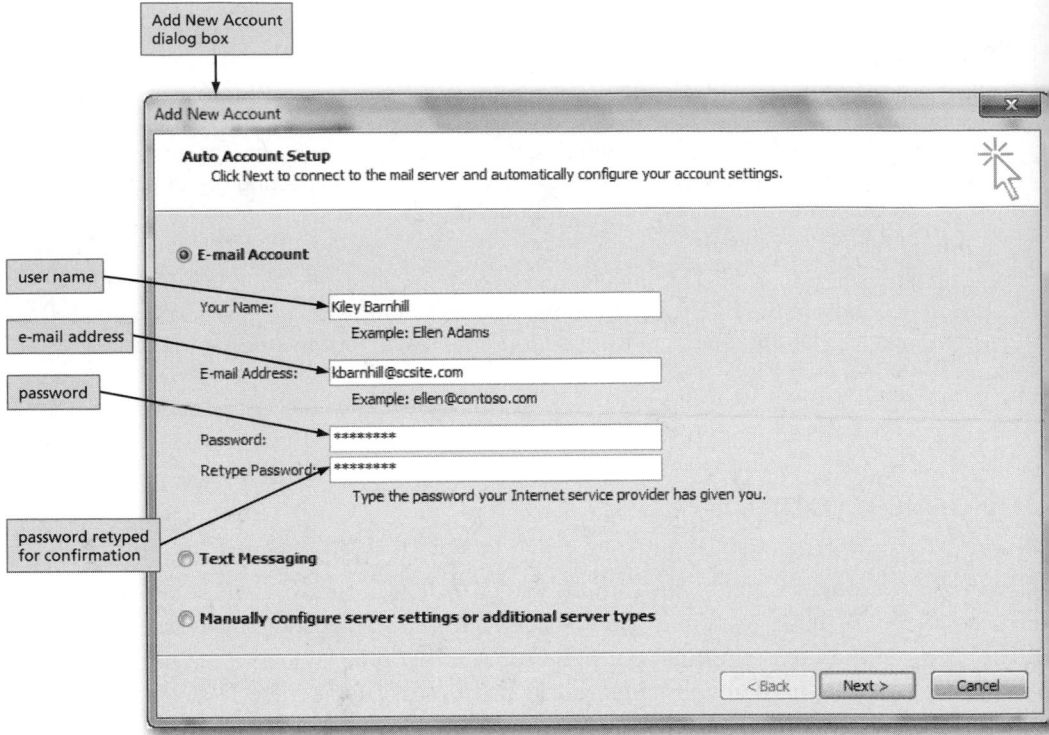

Add New Account
dialog box

Figure 1–3

For an introduction to Windows 7 and instruction about how to perform basic Windows 7 tasks, read the Office 2010 and Windows 7 chapter at the beginning of this book, where you can learn how to resize windows, change screen resolution, create folders, move and rename files, use Windows Help, and much more.

To Start Outlook

If you are using a computer to step through the project in this chapter and you want your screens to match the figures in this book, you should change your screen's resolution to 1024×768. For information about how to change a computer's resolution, refer to the Office 2010 and Windows 7 chapter at the beginning of this book.

The following steps, which assume Windows 7 is running, start Outlook based on a typical installation. You may need to ask your instructor how to start Outlook for your computer. For a detailed example of the procedure summarized below, refer to the Office 2010 and Windows 7 chapter.

1 Click the Start button on the Windows 7 taskbar to display the Start menu.

2 Type `Microsoft Outlook` as the search text in the 'Search programs and files' text box and watch the search results appear on the Start menu.

3 Click Microsoft Outlook 2010 in the search results on the Start menu to start Outlook and display the Outlook window.

4 If the Outlook window is not maximized, click the Maximize button next to the Close button on its title bar to maximize the window.

5 If the Inbox – Outlook – Microsoft Outlook window is not displayed, click the Mail button in the Navigation Pane to display your mailbox.

Q&A What does the name in the title bar mean?

The name of your window in the title bar is the name of the profile you set up when starting Outlook for the first time.

Note: If you are stepping through this project on a computer and you want your screens to appear the same as in the figures, then you should ask your instructor for assistance with opening or importing the TW.pst mailbox from the Data Files for Students. See the inside back cover of this book for instructions for downloading the Data Files for Students or see your instructor for information about accessing files for this book.

To Open an Outlook Data File

The e-mail messages you work with in this chapter are stored in a personal folders (.pst) file named TW.pst, which is an Outlook mailbox available on the Data Files for Students. See the inside back cover of this book for instructions on downloading the Data Files for Students, or contact your instructor for information about accessing the required files. The following steps show how to open this personal folders file in Outlook, display the Inbox for the TW file, and then make your TW mailbox match the figures in this chapter. In this example, the TW mailbox is located in the Chapter01 folder in the Outlook folder in the Data Files for Students folder on a USB flash drive.

1

- With your USB flash drive connected to one of the computer's USB ports, click File on the Ribbon to open the Backstage view.

- Click Open in the Backstage view to display the Open commands.

- Click Open Outlook Data File to display the Open Outlook Data File dialog box.

- Navigate to the mailbox location (in this case, the Chapter01 folder in

Figure 1–4

the Outlook folder in the Data Files for Students folder on a USB flash drive). For a detailed example of this procedure, refer to Steps 3a – 3c in the To Save a File in a Folder section in the Office 2010 and Windows 7 chapter at the beginning of this book.

- Click TW to select the file, and then click the Open button to open the TW mailbox in your Outlook window.

- Click Inbox below the TW heading in the Navigation Pane to view the TW Inbox (Figure 1–4).

What is the Navigation Pane?

The **Navigation Pane** is a pane along the left side of the Outlook window that contains shortcuts to your Outlook folders and gives you quick access to them. You use the Navigation Pane to browse all your Outlook folders using one of its views: Mail, Calendar, Contacts, or Tasks. The contents of the Navigation Pane change depending on the folder you are using.

What is the Inbox?

The **Inbox** is the Outlook folder that contains incoming e-mail messages.

For an introduction to Office 2010 and instruction about how to perform basic tasks in Office 2010 programs, read the Office 2010 and Windows 7 chapter at the beginning of this book, where you can learn how to start a program, use the Ribbon, save a file, open a file, quit a program, use Help, and much more.

2

- Right-click the Arrange By: bar in the Inbox to display the shortcut menu.

- If Date is not selected with a check mark, click Date to select it.

Q&A

My Outlook window includes an option called Date: [Conversations]. Is that the same command as Date?

Yes, the Date command and the Date: [Conversations] commands are the same.

BTW

Q&As
For a complete list of the Q&As found in many of the step-by-step sequences in this book, visit the Outlook 2010 Q&A Web page (scsite.com/out2010/qa).

- If Show in Groups is selected with a check mark, click Show in Groups to remove the check mark and deselect this command.

- If Show as Conversations is selected with a check mark, click Show as Conversations to remove the check mark and deselect this command.

Composing and Sending E-Mail Messages

Composing an e-mail message consists of four basic steps — open a new message window, enter message header information, enter the message text, and add a signature.

Plan Ahead

Organize the e-mail message.
An e-mail message typically is organized into two areas: the message header and the message area.

- The information in the **message header** routes the message to its recipients and identifies the purpose or contents of the message. The message header contains the e-mail address of the recipient(s), the primary person or persons to whom you are sending the message; it also may contain a courtesy copy or carbon copy (cc), which includes one or more additional recipients; and the **subject line**, which states the reason for the message.

- The **message area**, where you type an e-mail message, consists of a greeting line or salutation, the message text, an optional closing, and a signature line(s).

- A **greeting line** or salutation sets the tone of the message and can be formal or informal, depending on the nature of the message. You can use a comma (,) or a colon (:) at the end of the greeting line.

- The **message text** informs the recipient or summarizes or requests information.

- A **closing** signals an end to the message using courtesy words such as *Thank you* or *Regards*. Because the closing is most appropriate for formal e-mail messages, it is optional.

- A **signature line(s)** identifies the sender and may contain additional information, such as a job title and phone number(s). In a signature, the name usually is provided on one line followed by other information listed on separate lines.

BTW

The Outlook Window
The chapters in this book begin with the Outlook window appearing as it did at the initial installation of the software. Your Outlook window may look different depending on your screen resolution and other Outlook settings.

To Compose and Send an E-Mail Message

The first step in this project is to send an e-mail message to Rose Stewart, a faculty member at the college, asking her to send you the morning agenda for the new student orientation program. The following steps compose a new e-mail message to Rose Stewart.

1

- Click the New E-mail button (Home tab | New group) to open the Untitled – Message (HTML) window (Figure 1–5).

What does HTML mean in the title bar?

HTML is the format for the new e-mail message. Outlook messages can use two other formats — Rich Text Format (RTF) and Plain Text — all of these are discussed later in this chapter.

Figure 1–5

2

- If necessary, click the Maximize button in the Untitled – Message (HTML) window to maximize the window.

- With the insertion point in the To text box, type **rose .stewart@ hotmail.com** (with no spaces) to enter the e-mail address of the recipient.

- Click the Subject text box to position the insertion point in the Subject text box.

- Type **Draft Agenda** as the subject.

- Press the TAB key to move the insertion point into the message area (Figure 1–6).

Figure 1–6

What if I make an error while typing an e-mail message?

Press the BACKSPACE key until you have deleted the error and then retype the text correctly. You also can click the Undo button on the Quick Access Toolbar to undo your most recent action.

BTW

The Ribbon and Screen Resolution
Outlook may change how the groups and buttons within the groups appear on the Ribbon, depending on the computer's screen resolution. Thus, your Ribbon may look different from the ones in this book if you are using a screen resolution other than 1024 × 768.

3

- Type **Ms. Stewart,** as the greeting line.

- Press the ENTER key to move the insertion point to the beginning of the next line.

- Press the ENTER key again to insert a blank line between the greeting line and the message text.

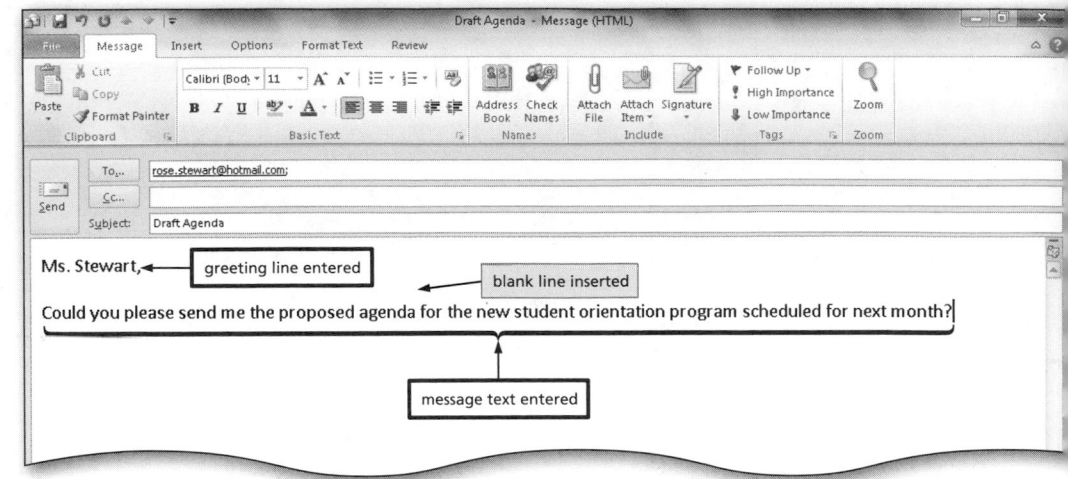

Figure 1–7

Why did a blank space appear between the greeting line and the insertion point?

Each time you press the ENTER key, Outlook creates a new paragraph. When you press the ENTER key on a line with no text, Outlook inserts blank space between the two paragraphs.

- Type **Could you please send me the proposed agenda for the new student orientation program scheduled for next month?** to enter the message text (Figure 1–7).

4

- Press the ENTER key two times to insert a blank line below the message text.

- Type **Thanks,** as the closing and then press the ENTER key to move the insertion point to the next line.

- Type **Trevor Wilkins** as signature line 1.

- Press the ENTER key to move the insertion point to the next line and then type **Student Assistant** as signature line 2 (Figure 1–8).

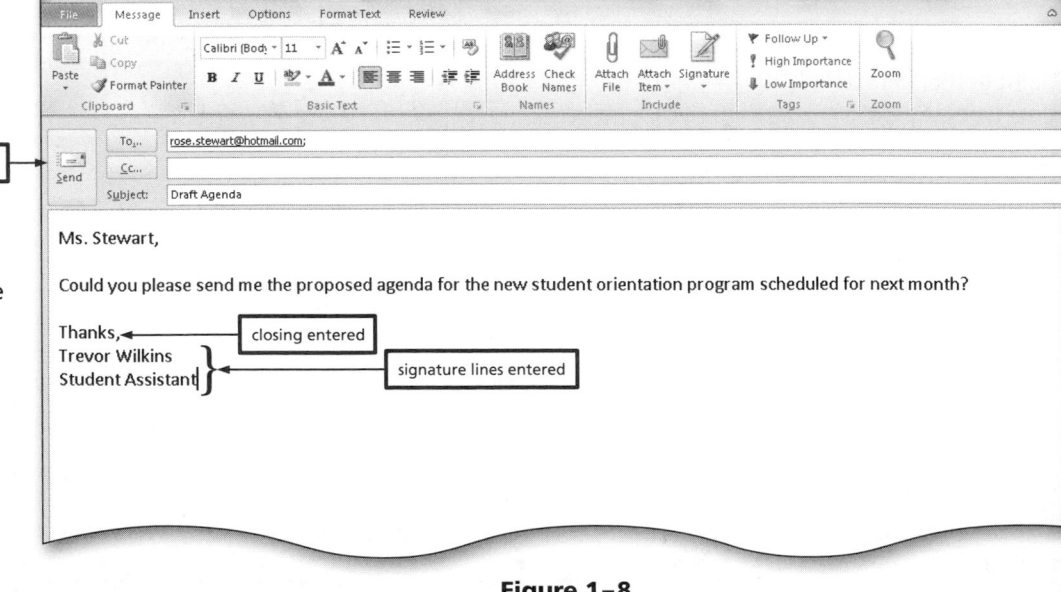

Figure 1–8

Do I always need to type my last name in the signature of an e-mail message?

No. If you and your recipient know each other, you can type only your first name as the signature.

Other Ways

1. Click Inbox folder, press CTRL+N

To Send an E-Mail Message

The message to Rose Stewart is created and ready to be sent. The following step sends the completed e-mail message to Rose Stewart.

1

• Click the Send button in the message header to send the e-mail message and close the message window.

What happened to the e-mail message?

E-mail messages are sent automatically when you click Send in a new message window.

Other Ways
1. Press ALT+S

How E-Mail Messages Travel from Sender to Receiver

When you send someone an e-mail message, it travels across the Internet to the computer at your ISP that handles outgoing e-mail messages. This computer, called the **outgoing e-mail server,** examines the e-mail address on your message, selects the best route for sending the message across the Internet, and then sends the e-mail message. Many outgoing e-mail servers use **SMTP (Simple Mail Transfer Protocol)**, which is a communications protocol, or set of rules for communicating with other computers. An e-mail program such as Outlook contacts the outgoing e-mail server and then transfers the e-mail message(s) in its Outbox to that server. If the e-mail program cannot contact the outgoing e-mail server, the e-mail message(s) remains in the Outbox until the program can connect to the server.

As an e-mail message travels across the Internet, routers direct the e-mail message to a computer at your recipient's ISP that handles incoming e-mail messages. (A **router** is a device that forwards data on a network.) The computer handling incoming e-mail messages, called the **incoming e-mail server,** stores the e-mail message(s) until your recipient uses an e-mail program such as Outlook to retrieve the e-mail message(s). Some e-mail servers use **POP3**, the latest version of **Post Office Protocol (POP)**, a communications protocol for incoming e-mail. Figure 1–9 shows how an e-mail message may travel from a sender to a receiver.

How an E-Mail Message May Travel from a Sender to a Receiver

Step 1
Using an e-mail program, you create and send a message.

Step 2
Your e-mail program contacts software on your service provider's outgoing mail server.

Step 3
Software on the outgoing mail server determines the best route for the data and sends the message, which travels along Internet routers to the recipient's incoming mail server.

Internet router

Step 4
When the recipient uses an e-mail program to check for e-mail messages, the message transfers from the incoming mail server to the recipient's computer.

Internet service provider's incoming mail server

Internet router

Figure 1–9

In most cases, the user provides Outlook information about the outgoing and incoming e-mail servers when using the Auto Account Setup feature to set up an e-mail account. You can verify these Internet e-mail settings in the Change Account dialog box, which is displayed by clicking File on the Ribbon to open the Backstage view, clicking the Account Settings button in the Backstage view, clicking Account Settings to display the Account Settings dialog box, selecting your e-mail address, and then clicking the Change button on the toolbar. Figure 1–10 shows the Change Account dialog box for Kiley Barnhill. Notice that this account uses a POP3 incoming mail server and an SMTP outgoing mail server with the same domain name as in the e-mail address. Use the Test Account Settings button to test these Internet e-mail settings, if necessary.

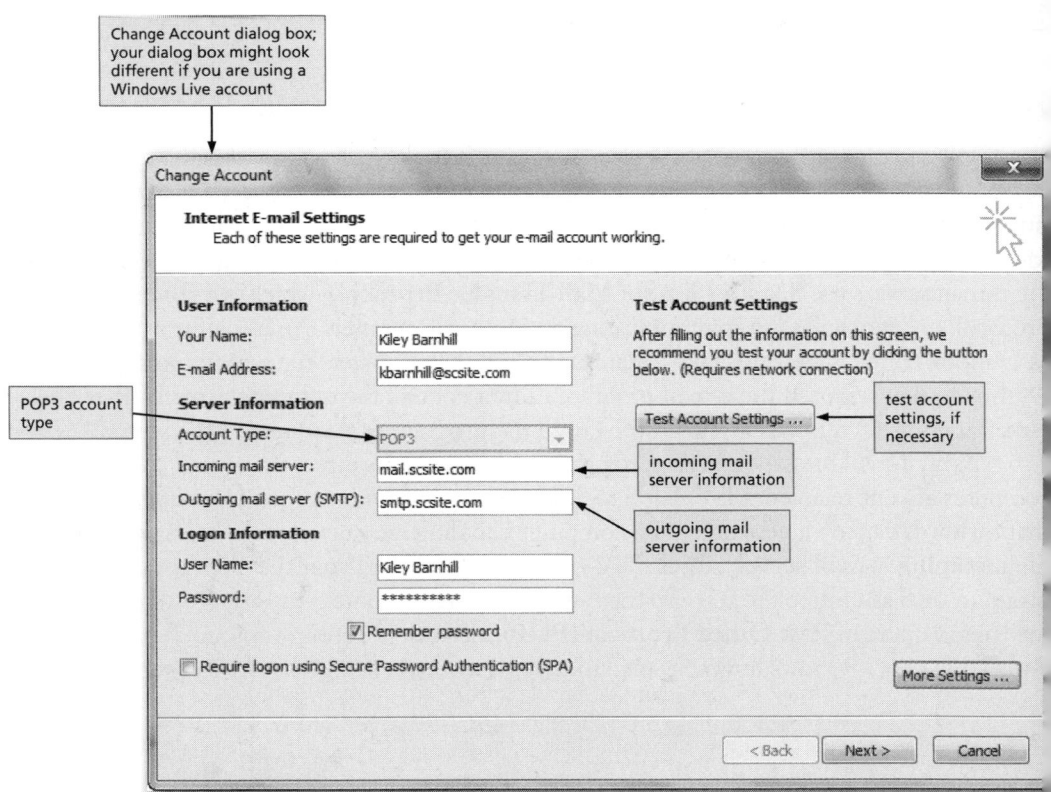

Figure 1–10

BTW

Message Notifications
If Outlook is not the active window on your desktop, it still provides a mail notification alert informing you when you receive a new message. Outlook briefly displays a closed envelope and a semitransparent ScreenTip in the notification area of the taskbar. The ScreenTip includes the sender's name, subject of the message, and the first few words of the message body.

Working with Incoming Messages

When you receive e-mail messages, Outlook directs them to the Inbox and displays them in the **message pane,** which lists the contents of the selected folder, in this case the Inbox (Figure 1–11). The list of messages displayed in the message pane is called the **message list.** A highlighted e-mail message in the message list displays the selected message header, which appears in bold with a **closed envelope icon** to the left of the e-mail message if the e-mail message is unread (unopened). An **open envelope icon** indicates a previously read (opened) message. The blue number next to the Inbox folder shows how many unread messages are stored in the Inbox. The e-mail messages on your computer may be different.

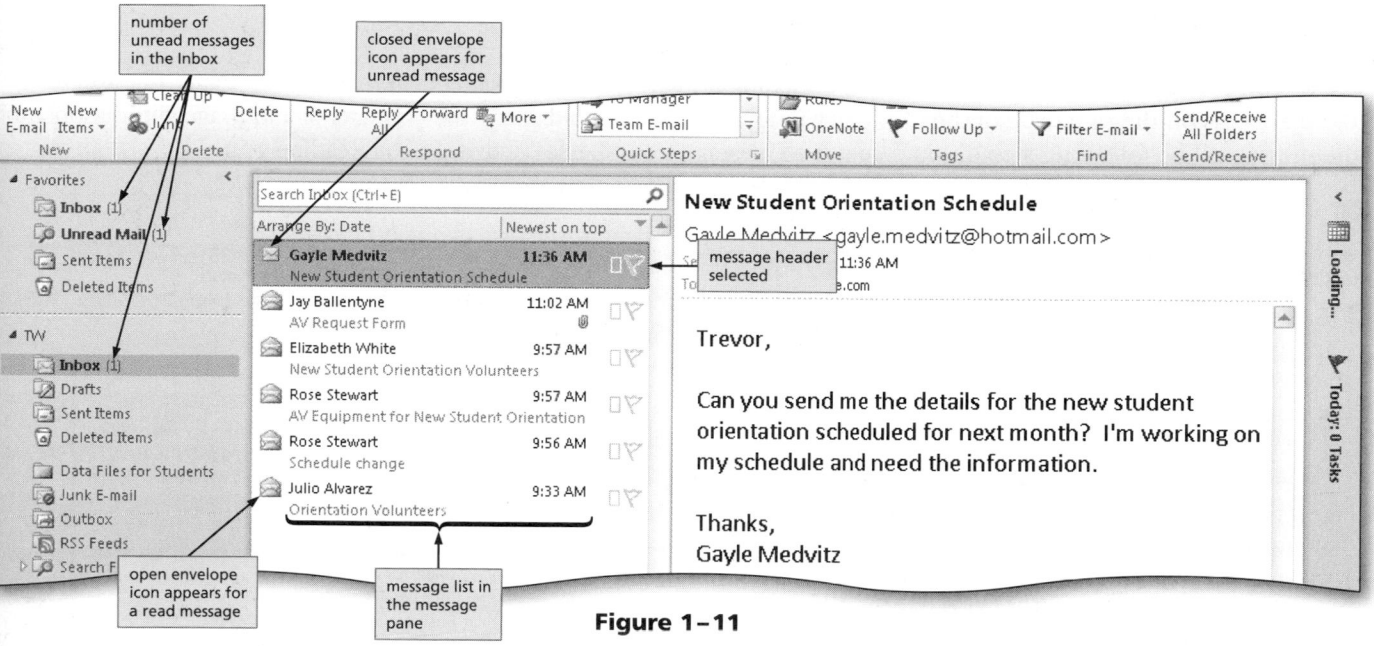

Figure 1–11

You can read incoming messages in three ways: in an open window, in the Reading Pane, or as a hard copy. A **hard copy** (**printout**) is information presented on a physical medium such as paper.

Determine the best method for reading e-mail messages you receive.
Popular methods for reading an e-mail message are to either display it in the Reading Pane or to open it in its own message window. These methods are easy and quick. Reading electronic documents also saves paper and printer supplies. You should be aware of problems, however, that can be caused by reading e-mail messages.

- **Know the sender.** If you receive an e-mail message from someone you do not know, you should not open it because it might trigger a virus. Unsolicited e-mail messages, known as **spam** or **junk e-mail**, are e-mail messages sent from an unknown sender to many e-mail accounts, usually advertising a product or service such as low-cost medication, low-interest loans, or free credit reports. Spam quickly can fill an Inbox with unwanted messages. If a suspicious e-mail message appears to come from someone you know and trust, contact them first to make sure they actually sent the e-mail message.

- **Do not click a hyperlink in an e-mail message from an unknown sender.** A **hyperlink** is a word, phrase, symbol, or picture in an e-mail message or on a Web page that, when clicked, directs you to another document or Web site. One way spammers (senders of spam) verify your e-mail address is by sending messages that request you to click a hyperlink to direct you to a Web site. After spammers know that your e-mail address is valid, they are likely to send you many more e-mail messages.

The next several pages in this chapter read and reply to an e-mail message. The following pages follow these general tasks:

1. Read an e-mail message in the Reading Pane.
2. Open, print, and close an e-mail message.
3. Reply to and forward an e-mail message.
4. Delete an e-mail message.
5. Check the spelling of an e-mail message.
6. Save an e-mail message.
7. Attach a file to an outgoing e-mail message.

Plan Ahead

BTW

Reading Pane
By default, the Reading Pane is displayed on the right side of the Outlook window. To change its position, click the Reading Pane button (View tab | Layout group), and then click the desired option.

BTW

Junk E-Mail Filters
The Outlook Junk E-mail Filter is turned on by default and evaluates whether an incoming message should be sent to the Junk E-mail folder. By scanning message information such as the content, time the message was sent, and who sent the message, this feature determines whether a message might be spam and diverts it to the Junk E-mail folder. To change junk e-mail settings, click the Junk button (Home tab | Delete group), and then click Junk E-mail Options to display the Junk E-mail Options dialog box. Choose the level of protection you want and click the OK button.

To Read an E-Mail Message in the Reading Pane

You can read an e-mail message without opening it by displaying its contents in the Reading Pane. The **Reading Pane** appears on the right side of the Outlook window by default and displays the contents of a message without opening the message. The following step displays an e-mail message from Gayle Medvitz in the Reading Pane.

- If necessary, click the message header from Gayle Medvitz in the Inbox message list to select the e-mail message and display its contents in the Reading Pane (Figure 1–12).

Q&A

What happens to the message icon when I select another message?

Outlook automatically marks messages as read after you preview the message in the Reading Pane and select another message to view. A read message is displayed in the message list with an open envelope and is not bold. An unread message is displayed with a closed envelope icon and appears in bold in the message list.

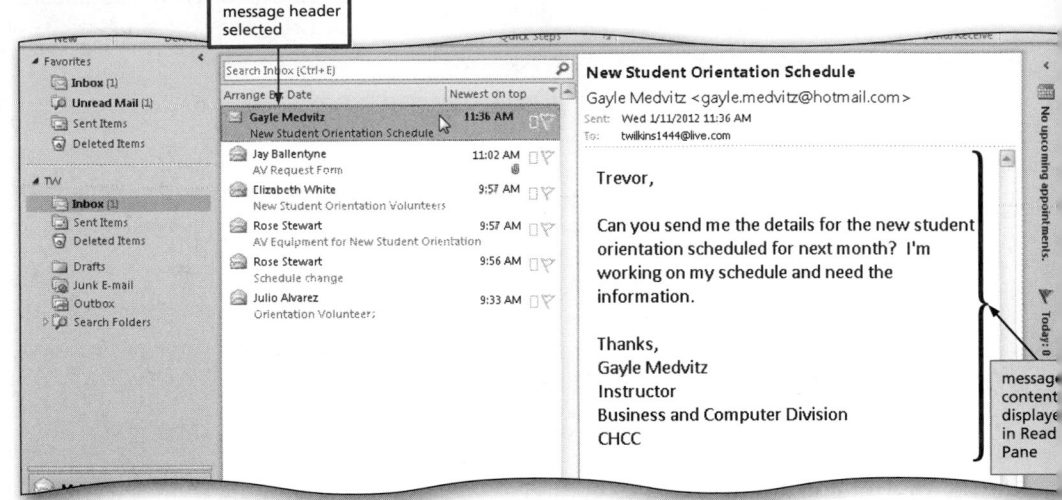

Figure 1–12

To Open an E-Mail Message in a Window

The next step is to open the message in its own window for further evaluation. The following step opens the message from Gayle Medvitz.

- Double-click the Gayle Medvitz message in the message list to display the selected e-mail message in its own window (Figure 1–13).

Q&A

Does the message header contain additional information about the e-mail message?

Yes. To view the additional information, known as the message properties, make sure the e-mail message is open in its own window, click File on the Ribbon to display the Backstage view, click the Info tab to display the Info gallery, and then click the Properties button.

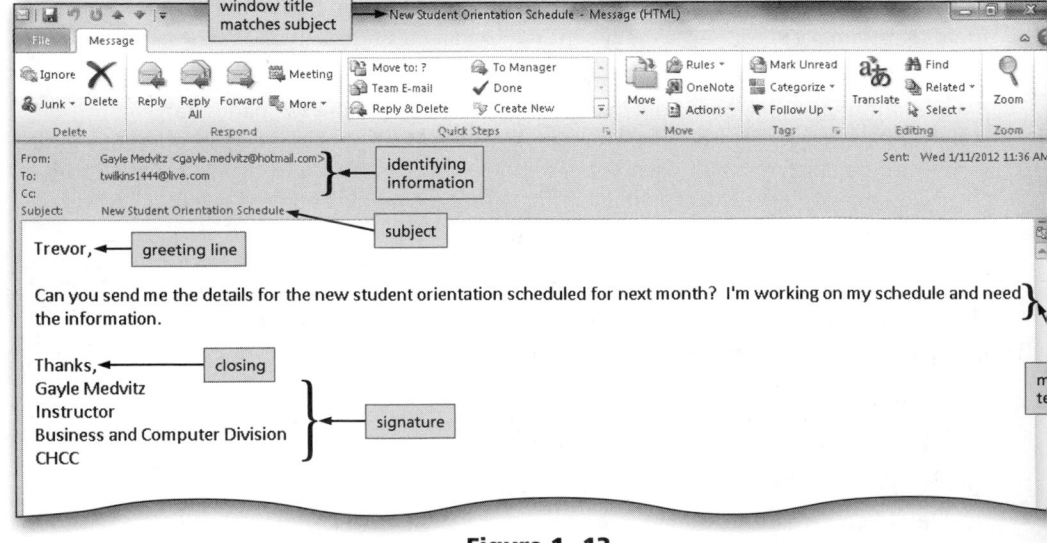

Figure 1–13

Other Ways

1. Select message header, press CTRL+O

To Close an E-Mail Message

You are finished with the e-mail message from Gayle Medvitz, so you can close it. The following steps close the New Student Orientation Schedule – Message (HTML) window.

1
- Point to the Close button on the title bar of the message window to prepare for selecting the button (Figure 1–14).

Figure 1–14

2
- Click the Close button on the title bar of the message window to close the window and display the message icon for Gayle Medvitz as an open envelope (Figure 1–15).

Can I change the message status from unread to read or from read to unread?

Yes, right-click the message you want to change and select the desired command on the shortcut menu.

Why did the number next to the Inbox folder change?

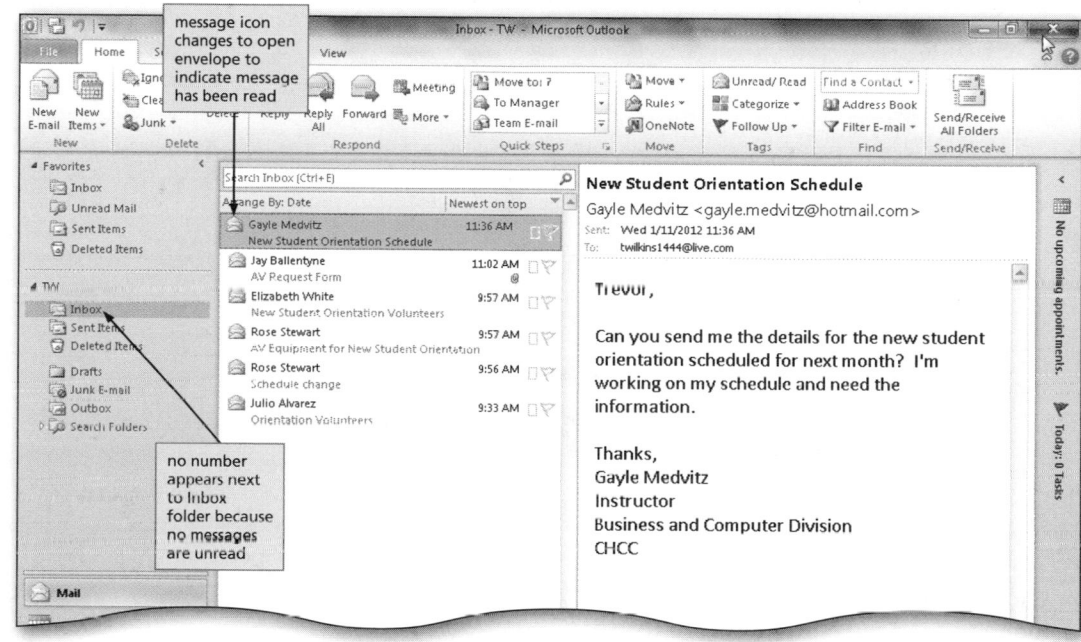

Figure 1–15

When you close a message window, the message header (Gayle Medvitz, in this case) in the message pane no longer appears in bold, the closed envelope icon changes to an open envelope icon to indicate the message has been opened, and the number next to the Inbox folder changes to reflect the number of unread messages.

Other Ways
1. Click Close (File tab)

To Print an E-Mail Message

Occasionally, you may want to print the contents of an e-mail message. A hard copy of an e-mail message can serve as reference material if your storage medium becomes corrupted and you need to re-create the message or refer to the message when your computer is not readily available. A printed copy of an e-mail message also serves as **backup**, which is an additional copy of a file or message that you store for safekeeping. You can print the contents of an e-mail message from an open message window or directly from the Inbox window.

You would like to have a hard copy of the message from Gayle Medvitz so that you can keep it with other documents relating to the orientation topic. The following steps print the e-mail message from Gayle Medvitz.

- In the message list, right-click the e-mail message from Gayle Medvitz to display a shortcut menu that presents a list of possible actions (Figure 1–16).

Figure 1–16

- Click Quick Print on the shortcut menu to send the e-mail message to the currently selected printer.

- When the printer stops, retrieve the hard copy (Figure 1–17).

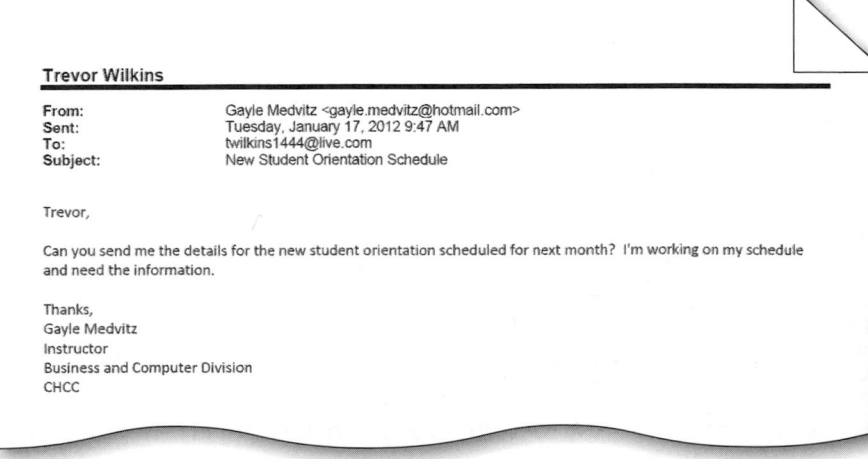

Figure 1–17

Other Ways

1. Press CTRL+P, press ENTER
2. Click File tab, click Print tab (Backstage view), click Print

TO PRINT MULTIPLE COPIES OF AN E-MAIL MESSAGE

You may need to print multiple copies of an e-mail message if you want to distribute the message to more than one person, or if you want to file one copy for later use and keep a second copy as a backup. If you wanted to print multiple copies of an e-mail message, you would follow these steps.

1. Click File on the Ribbon to open the Backstage view and then click the Print tab in the Backstage view to display the Print gallery.
2. Click the Print Options button in the Print gallery to display the Print dialog box.
3. Change the number in the 'Number of copies' box to the number of desired copies, such as a 2 for 2 copies (Print dialog box).
4. Click the Print button to print the message and close the Print dialog box.

Responding to E-Mail Messages

In this chapter, you respond to e-mail messages by replying to and forwarding them. Thus, the next step is to respond to an e-mail message that has already been received.

Ensure that the content of the e-mail message is appropriate for the recipient. An e-mail message you send to a close friend may be much less formal than one you send to an instructor, coworker, or client. For example, conversational language to a friend, such as "Can't wait to see you!" is not appropriate in professional e-mail messages. All standard grammar rules apply, however, such as punctuation, capitalization, and spelling, no matter the audience.

Plan Ahead

When responding to e-mail messages, you have three options in Outlook: Reply, Reply All, or Forward. Table 1–1 lists the response options and their actions.

Table 1–1 Outlook Response Options	
Response Option	**Action**
Reply	Opens the RE: reply window and sends a reply to the person who sent the message.
Reply All	Opens the RE: reply window and sends a reply to everyone listed in the message header.
Forward	Opens the FW: message window and sends a copy of the selected message to additional people, if you want to share information with others. The original message text is included in the message window.

BTW

Configuring Options for Replies and Forwards
Microsoft Outlook includes multiple options you can configure for replies to e-mail messages and forwarded e-mail messages. To access these options, click the Reply, Reply All, or Forward button to display the appropriate message window, and then click Options on the Ribbon to display the Options tab.

You reply to messages you already have received. You can forward an e-mail message to additional recipients to share information with others. You should receive permission from the sender before forwarding a message, in case the sender intended the original message to remain private. A message that you forward is similar to a new message in that you send the message to someone other than the original sender of the message. A reply sends the message to the person who sent the message.

To Reply to an E-Mail Message

The message from Gayle Medvitz is asking for information and requires a reply. The following steps reply to the e-mail message from Gayle Medvitz.

- If necessary, click the Gayle Medvitz message header in the message list to select it and display its contents in the Reading Pane (Figure 1–18).

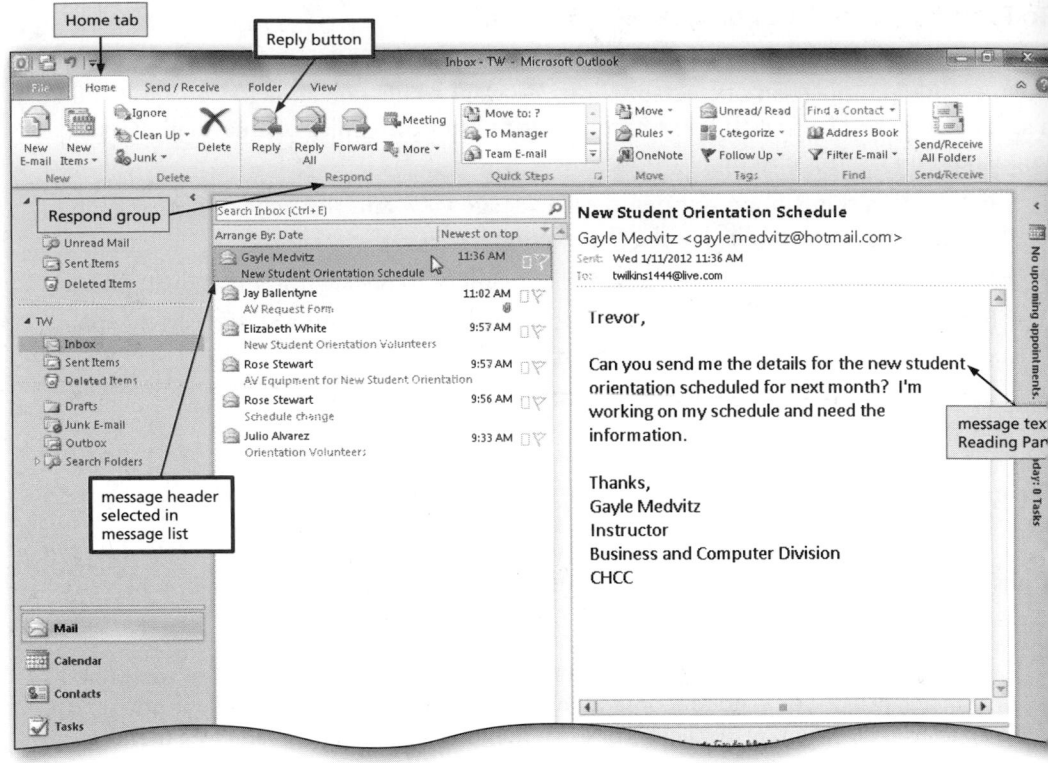

Figure 1–18

2

- Click the Reply button (Home tab | Respond group) to open the RE: New Student Orientation Schedule – Message (HTML) window.

- If the message window is not maximized, click the Maximize button next to the Close button on its title bar to maximize the window (Figure 1–19).

Q&A

Why does RE: appear at the beginning of the subject line and in the title bar?

The RE: indicates this message is a reply to another message. The subject of the original message appears after the RE.

RE: New Student Orientation Schedule – Message (HTML) reply window opened and maximized

Maximize button chan Restore Down button window is maximized

RE: inserted in Subject line

top of message area

original message appears below this line

insertion point

From: Gayle Medvitz [mailto:gayle.medvitz@hotmail.com]
Sent: Wednesday, January 11, 2012 11:36 AM
To: twilkins1444@live.com
Subject: New Student Orientation Schedule

Trevor,

Can you send me the details for the new student orientation scheduled for next month? I'm working on my schedule and need the information.

Thanks,
Gayle Medvitz
Instructor
Business and Computer Division
CHCC

Figure 1–19

- If necessary, click the message area below the message header to position the insertion point at the top of the message area.

- Type **Good morning,** as the greeting line.

- Press the ENTER key two times to place a blank line between the greeting line and the message text.

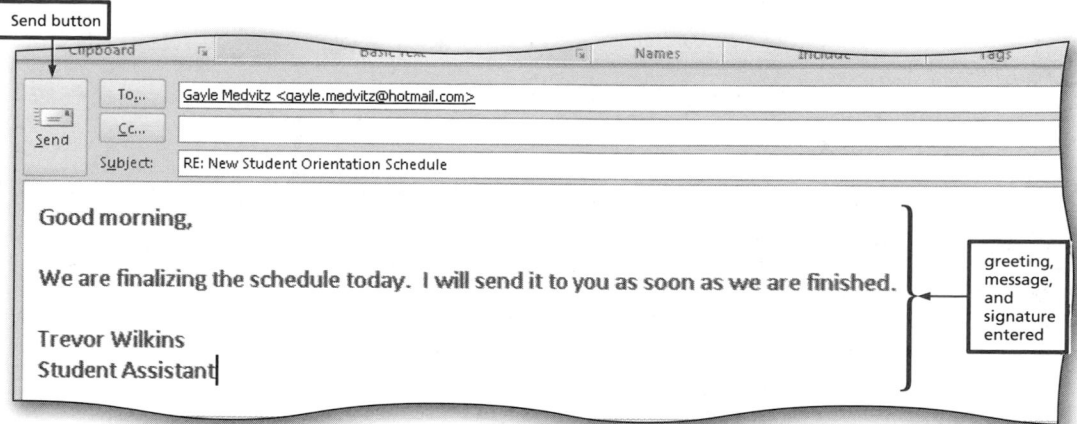

Figure 1–20

- Type **We are finalizing the schedule today. I will send it to you as soon as we are finished.** to enter the message text.

- Press the ENTER key two times to place a blank line between the message text and the signature lines.

- Type **Trevor Wilkins** as signature line 1 and then press the ENTER key to move the insertion point to the next line.

- Type **Student Assistant** as signature line 2 (Figure 1–20).

- Click the Send button in the message header to send the e-mail message and display the Inbox window.

Other Ways

1. Right-click message header, click Reply

2. Click message header, press CTRL+R

To Forward an E-Mail Message

Elizabeth White has sent you an e-mail message offering to volunteer for the New Student Orientation Program. Because she is not sure you can authorize her volunteer service, she mentions that you can forward her message to the appropriate person. In fact, Julio Alvarez is the person handling the volunteers for the program. The following steps forward Elizabeth White's message to Julio Alvarez.

- In the Inbox window, click the Elizabeth White message header in the message list to select the e-mail message (Figure 1–21).

Figure 1–21

- Click the Forward button (Home tab | Respond group) to display the FW: New Student Orientation Volunteers – Message (HTML) window.

- Type **julioa1776@ hotmail.com** (with no spaces) in the To text box as the recipient's e-mail address (unless you are stepping through this task — in that case, enter an actual e-mail address) (Figure 1–22).

FW: New Student Orientation Volunteers – Message (HTML) in subject box and title bar indicates message is being forwarded

recipient's e-mail address entered

original e-mail message

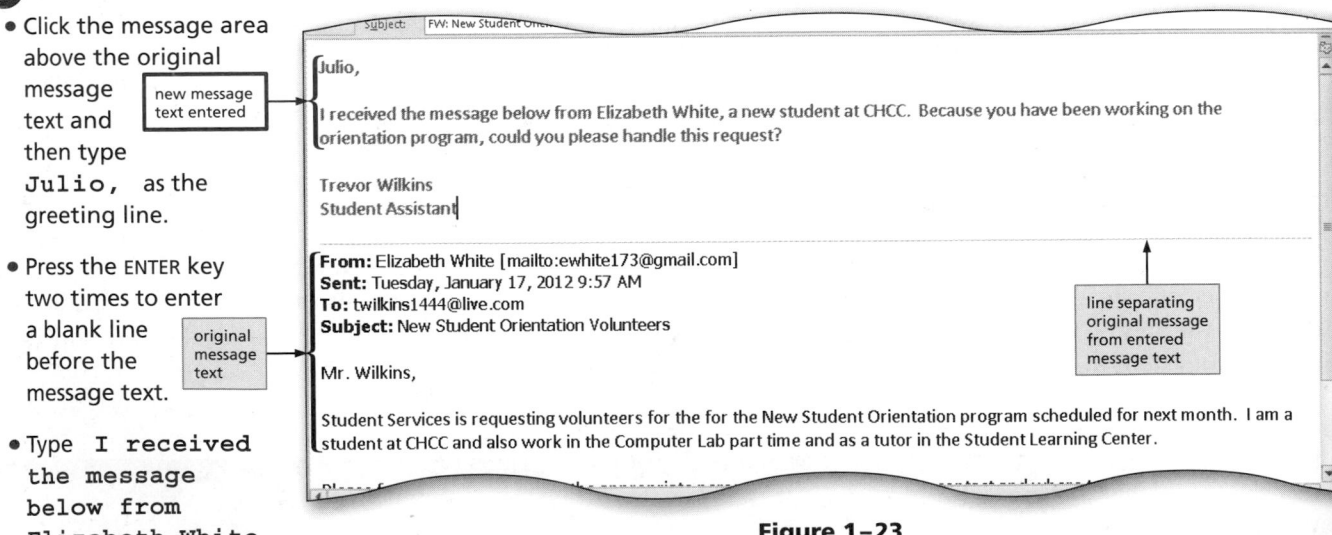

Figure 1–22

Q&A Why does the original message appear in the message area of the window?

By default, Outlook is configured to automatically display the original message below the new message area for all message replies and forwards.

- Click the message area above the original message text and then type **Julio,** as the greeting line.

- Press the ENTER key two times to enter a blank line before the message text.

- Type **I received the message below from Elizabeth White, a new student at CHCC. Because you have been working on the orientation program, could you please handle this request?** to enter the message text.

new message text entered

original message text

line separating original message from entered message text

Figure 1–23

- Press the ENTER key two times to place a blank line between the message text and the signature lines.

- Type **Trevor Wilkins** as signature line 1 and then press the ENTER key to move the insertion point to the next line.

- Type **Student Assistant** as signature line 2 (Figure 1–23).

Other Ways

1. Right-click message header, click Forward

2. Click message header, press CTRL+F

Message Formats

As shown in Figure 1–23 on the previous page, Outlook's default (preset) message format is HTML (Hypertext Markup Language), which is a format that allows you to view pictures and text formatted with color and various fonts and font sizes. **Formatting** refers to changing the appearance of text in a document such as the font (typeface), font size, color, and alignment of the text in a document.

Before you send an original e-mail message, reply to an e-mail message, or forward an e-mail message, consider which message format you want to use. A message format determines whether an e-mail message can include pictures or formatted text, such as bold, italic, and colored fonts. Select a message format that is appropriate for your message and your recipient. Outlook offers three message formats: HTML, Plain Text, and Rich Text, summarized in Table 1–2. If you select the HTML format, for example, the e-mail program your recipient uses must be able to display formatted messages or pictures.

Table 1–2 Message Formats

Message Format	Description
HTML	HTML format is the default format for new messages in Outlook. HTML lets you include pictures and basic formatting, such as text formatting, numbering, bullets, and alignment. HTML is the recommended format for Internet mail because the more popular e-mail programs use it.
Plain Text	Plain Text format is recognized by all e-mail programs and is the most likely format to be allowed through a company's virus-filtering program. Plain Text does not support basic formatting, such as bold, italic, colored fonts, or other text formatting. It also does not support pictures displayed directly in the message.
Rich Text	Rich Text Format (RTF) is a Microsoft format that only the latest versions of **Microsoft Exchange** (a Microsoft message system that includes an e-mail program and a mail server) and Outlook recognize. RTF supports more formats than HTML or Plain Text, as well as hyperlinks. A hyperlink can be text, a picture or other object that is displayed in an e-mail message.

Be aware of computer viruses and how they are spread.
Your message may be blocked by the recipient's e-mail server. Some e-mail servers are set up to automatically block messages in the HTML format using antivirus software. If you have concerns about whether the recipient's server is set up to block messages formatted as HTML, use Plain Text as the message format.

BTW

Using Plain Text Formatting to Guard Against E-Mail Viruses
Because HTML-formatted messages can contain viruses, minimize the risk of receiving a virus-infected e-mail message by changing the format of messages you read. You can configure Outlook to format all opened messages in Plain Text. Click File on the Ribbon to open the Backstage view. Click the Trust Center button in the Backstage view, and then click Trust Center Settings to display the Trust Center dialog box. Click the E-mail Security tab (Trust Center dialog box), and in the Read as Plain Text section, click the 'Read all standard mail in plain text' check box.

BTW

Inserting Hyperlinks
To insert a Web address in an e-mail message, click where you want to insert the hyperlink, and then click the Hyperlink button (Insert tab | Links group) to display the Insert Hyperlink dialog box. In the Address text box, type the Web address you want to insert as a hyperlink, and then click the OK button to insert the hyperlink into the message body.

Plan Ahead

To Change the Message Format and Send the Message

The next step in this project is to change the message format of the e-mail message before forwarding it to Julio Alvarez. You want to make sure that your reply is not blocked by an antivirus program, so you will change the message format to Plain Text. The following steps change the message format to Plain Text and then send the message.

1

- In the message window, click Format Text on the Ribbon to display the Format Text tab.

- Click the Plain Text button (Format Text tab | Format group) to select the Plain Text message format, which removes all formatting in the message (Figure 1–24).

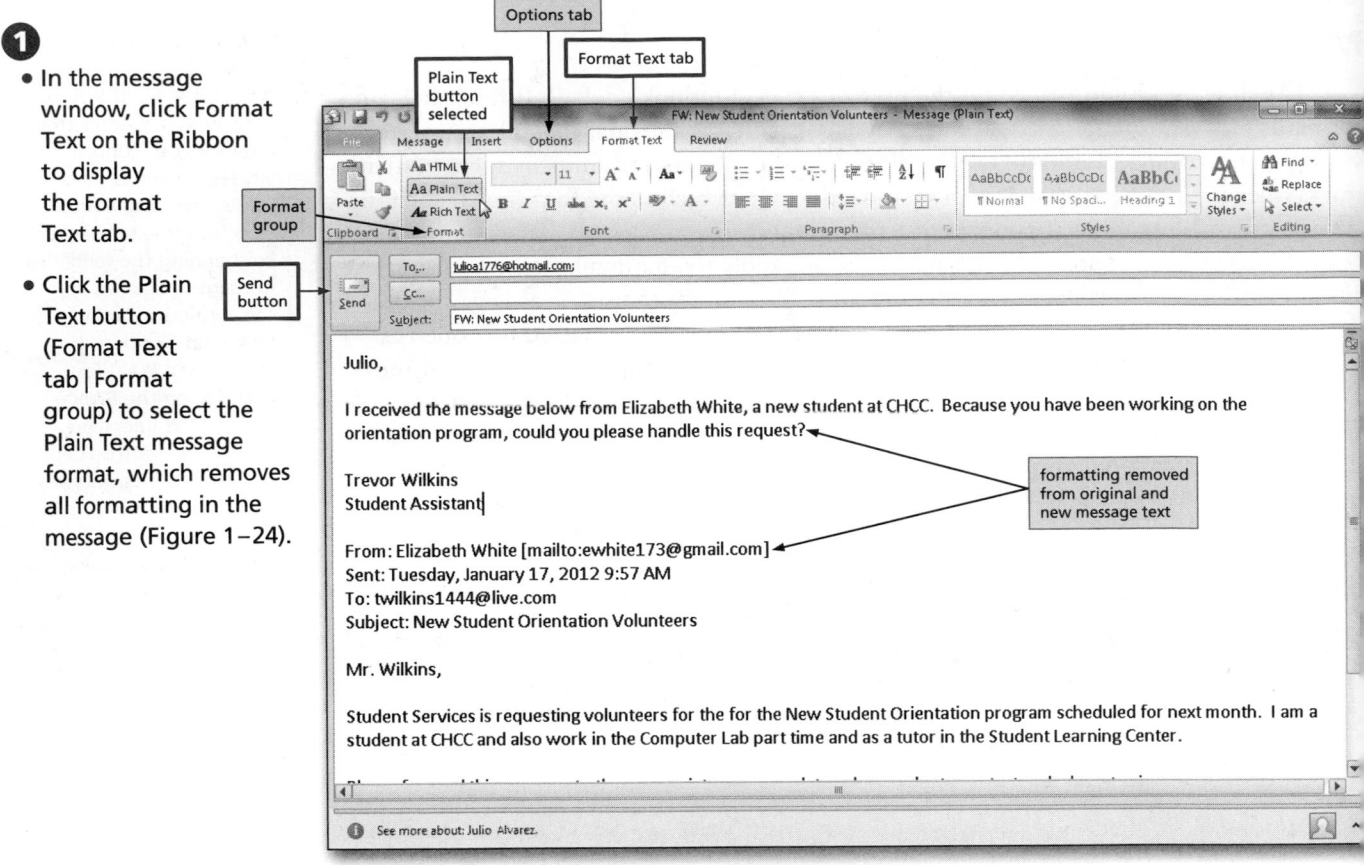

Figure 1–24

Q&A A warning message appeared after I completed Step 1. How should I respond?

Click the Continue button.

Q&A What happened to the line separating the existing message and the new message?

When Plain Text is selected as the message format, all formatting such as text color, font type, and size is removed.

Q&A Can I display additional fields in the message header?

Yes. Outlook allows you to display the From field and the Bcc field. To display these fields, click the Bcc button or the From button (Options tab | Show Fields group) to display the corresponding field(s). To hide a field, click the corresponding button again.

2

- Click the Send button in the message header to send the e-mail message and display the Inbox window.

Q&A Why did the envelope icon for this message change to an open envelope with a forward-pointing blue arrow?

The forward-pointing blue arrow indicates you forwarded the message. The status of the envelope icon represents your last action with the message.

To Delete an E-Mail Message

Now that you have forwarded Elizabeth White's message, you no longer need to keep it in your Inbox and you decide to delete it. When you delete a message from a folder, Outlook removes the message from the folder and moves it to the Deleted Items folder. The following steps delete the e-mail message from Elizabeth White.

- If necessary, click the Elizabeth White message header in the message list to select the e-mail message (Figure 1–25).

Why does the Navigation Pane contain two Deleted Items folders?

By default, Outlook automatically includes the Deleted Items in the Favorites section of the Navigation Pane.

Figure 1–25

- Click the Delete button (Home tab | Delete group) to move the e-mail message from the current folder (Inbox, in this case) to the Deleted Items folder.

- If you want to verify the location of the deleted file, click the Deleted Items folder in the Navigation Pane to display the Deleted Items message list in the message pane, which shows all deleted e-mail messages (Figure 1–26).

Is the e-mail message permanently deleted when I click the Delete button?

No, after Outlook moves the e-mail message to the Deleted Items folder, it stores the deleted e-mail message in that folder until you permanently delete the message. One way to permanently delete a message is to select the Deleted Items folder to view its contents in the message pane and then select the item to be deleted. Click the Delete button (Home tab | Delete group), and then click the Yes button in the Microsoft Office Outlook dialog box to permanently delete the selected item from Outlook.

Figure 1–26

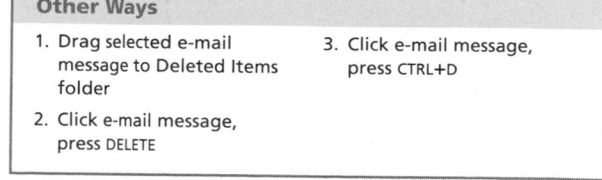

Other Ways
1. Drag selected e-mail message to Deleted Items folder	3. Click e-mail message, press CTRL+D
2. Click e-mail message, press DELETE	

Break Point: If you wish to take a break, this is a good place to do so. You can quit Outlook now (refer to page OUT 38 for instructions). To resume at a later time, start Outlook (refer to page OUT 6 for instructions), and then continue to follow the steps from this location forward.

You can quit Outlook now (refer to page OUT 38 for instructions). To resume at a later time, start Outlook (refer to page OUT 6 for instructions)

BTW

Automatic Spelling Correction

As you type an e-mail message, Outlook automatically corrects some misspelled words. For example, if you type recieve, Word automatically corrects the misspelling and displays the word, receive, when you press the spacebar or type a punctuation mark. To see a complete list of automatically corrected words, click File on the Ribbon to open the Backstage view, click Options in the Backstage view, click Mail in the left pane (Outlook Options dialog box), click the Spelling and AutoCorrect button, click the Proofing tab, and then click the AutoCorrect Options button. Scroll through the list near the bottom of the dialog box.

BTW

BTWs

For a complete list of the BTWs found in the margins of this book, visit the Outlook 2010 BTW Web page (scsite.com/out2010/btw).

Spelling and Grammar Check

As you type text in an e-mail message, Outlook checks your typing for possible spelling and grammar errors and flags any potential errors in the message text with a red, green, or blue wavy underline. A red wavy underline means the flagged text is not in Outlook's main dictionary (because it is a proper name or misspelled). A green wavy underline indicates the text may be incorrect grammatically. A blue wavy underline indicates the text may contain a contextual spelling error such as the misuse of homophones (words that are pronounced the same but have different spellings or meanings, such as one and won). Although you can check the entire message for spelling and grammar errors at once, you also can check these flagged errors as they appear on the screen.

A flagged word is not necessarily misspelled. For example, many names, abbreviations, and specialized terms are not in Outlook's main dictionary. In these cases, you instruct Outlook to ignore the flagged word. As you type, Outlook also detects duplicate words while checking for spelling errors. For example, if your e-mail message contains the phrase, to the the store, Outlook places a red wavy underline below the second occurrence of the word, the.

The following pages illustrate how to ignore a correctly typed word and correct an incorrectly typed word in a reply to an e-mail message.

To Reply to an E-Mail Message

You are ready to reply to Gayle Medvitz's e-mail message and send her a copy of the orientation schedule, which now is complete. The following steps begin the reply to the e-mail message.

1 If necessary, click the Inbox folder to display its contents in the message list.

2 Click the Gayle Medvitz message header to select the e-mail message.

3 Click the Reply button (Home tab | Respond group) to send a second reply to Gayle Medvitz.

4 Maximize the message window to provide more room to work.

To Check the Spelling of a Correctly Typed Word

As you start typing the e-mail message, you will notice that Gayle Medvitz's last name has a red wavy line below it even though it is spelled correctly, indicating the word is not in Outlook's main dictionary. The following steps ignore the error and remove the red wavy line.

1

• Type **Ms. Medvitz,** as the greeting line and then press the ENTER key, which causes Outlook to place a red wavy line below the proper name (in this case, Medvitz) (Figure 1–27).

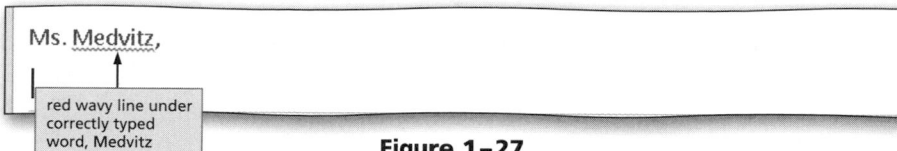

Ms. Medvitz,

red wavy line under correctly typed word, Medvitz

Figure 1–27

Why does a red wavy line appear below Medvitz even though it is spelled correctly?

Outlook places a red wavy line below any word that is not in the main dictionary when Outlook checks for spelling errors.

What if Outlook does not flag my spelling and grammar errors with wavy underlines?

To verify that the check spelling and grammar as you type features are enabled, click the File tab on the Ribbon to open the Backstage view and then click Options to display the Outlook Options dialog box. In the Compose messages section, click the Editor Options button to display the Editor Options dialog box. Click Proofing in the left pane (Editor Options dialog box). In the 'When correcting spelling in Outlook' section, ensure the 'Check spelling as you type' check box contains a check mark. Click the OK button two times to close each open dialog box.

2

• Right-click the proper name, Medvitz, to display a shortcut menu that presents a list of suggested spelling corrections for the flagged word, and then point to the Ignore command to prepare for selecting it (Figure 1–28).

What is the toolbar that appears above the shortcut menu?

The Mini toolbar appears when you right-click text by default and provides quick and easy access formatting options for the selected text.

Clipboard | Basic Text | Names | Include

To... Gayle Medvitz <gayle.medvitz@hotmail.com>

insertion point

Calibri (E ▼ 11 ▼ A˄ A˅ ≣ ≣ Jule

B *I* U ≣ aby ▼ A ▼ ⌀

Mini toolbar displayed

Ms. Medvitz,

correctly spelled proper name flagged in greeting line

Levitz

Edits

Ignore command

From: Gayle ...tmail.com]
...nt: Wedne... 12 11:36 AM
...: twilkins1...
...bject: Ne... n Schedule

Ignore

Ignore All

Add to Dictionary

AutoCorrect ▶

Language ▶

Spelling...

shortcut menu

Trevor,

Can you sen... ...he new student orientation scheduled for next mont
the informat...

Thanks,
Gayle Medvi...
Instructor
Business and
CHCC

Look Up ▶

Who Is...

Cut

Copy

Paste Options:

Additional Actions ▶

Figure 1–28

3

• Click Ignore on the shortcut menu to ignore this flagged error, close the shortcut menu, and remove the red wavy line beneath the name (in this case, Medvitz) (Figure 1–29).

Ms. Medvitz,

red wavy line removed

Figure 1–29

To Check the Spelling of Misspelled Text

In the following steps, the word, program, has been misspelled intentionally as profram to illustrate Outlook's check spelling as you type feature. If you are performing the steps in this project, your e-mail message may contain different misspelled words, depending on the accuracy of your typing. The following steps check the spelling of a misspelled word.

 1

- Press the DOWN ARROW key to move the insertion point to the blank paragraph below the greeting line.

- Press the ENTER key, type **The schedule for the new student orientation profram** to begin entering the message text, and then press the SPACEBAR so that a red wavy line appears below the misspelled word.

- Right-click the flagged word (profram, in this case) to display a shortcut menu that presents a list of suggested spelling corrections for the flagged word, and then point to program to prepare for selecting it (Figure 1–30).

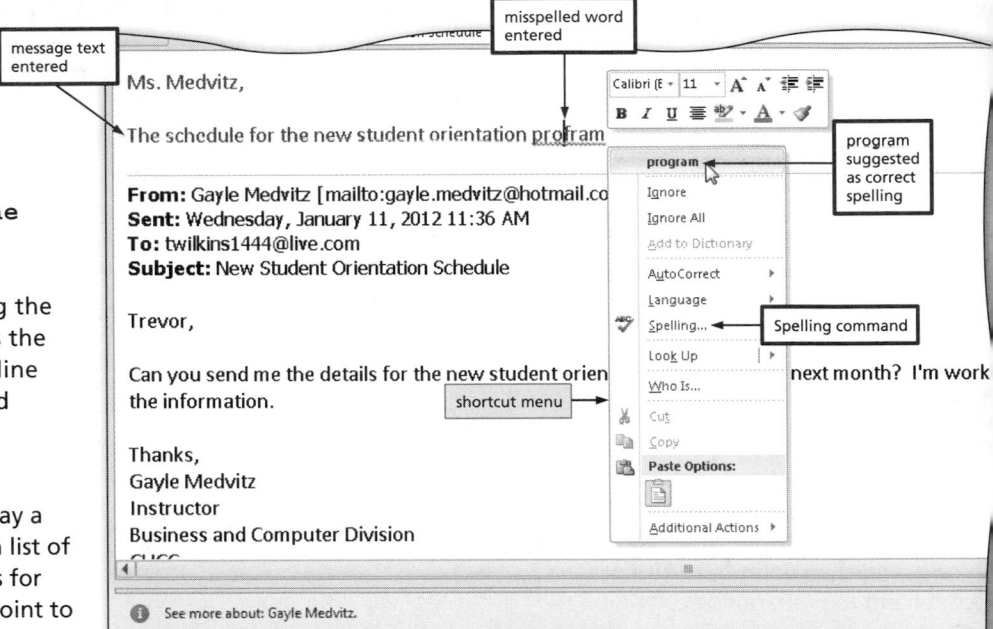

Figure 1–30

Q&A

What should I do if the correction I want to use is not in the list on the shortcut menu?

You can click outside the shortcut menu to close the shortcut menu and then retype the correct word, or you can click Spelling on the shortcut menu to display the Spelling dialog box.

 2

- Click program on the shortcut menu to replace the misspelled word in the e-mail message with a correctly spelled word (Figure 1–31).

Figure 1–31

Other Ways

1. Click Review tab on Ribbon (message window), click Spelling and Grammar button (Review tab | Proofing group)
2. Press F7

To Enter More Text

In the e-mail message, the text yet to be entered includes the remainder of the message text and the signature lines. The following steps enter the remainder of the message text and signature lines.

1 Type **you requested is attached. Let me know if you have any questions.** to continue entering the message text.

2 Press the ENTER key two times to move the insertion point one blank line below the message text.

3 Type **Trevor Wilkins** as signature line 1.

4 Press the ENTER key and then type **Student Assistant** as signature line 2 (Figure 1–32).

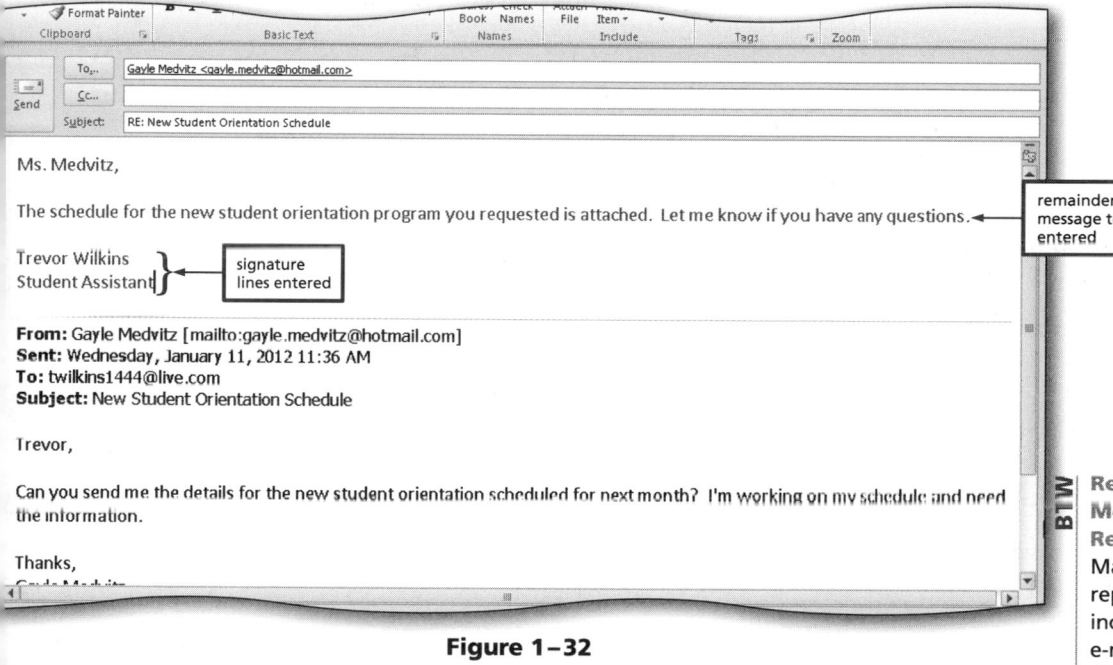

Figure 1–32

Saving and Closing an E-Mail Message

Occasionally, you begin composing a message but cannot complete the process. You may be waiting for information from someone else to include in the message, or you might prefer to complete the message later after you have time to evaluate its content. One option is to save the message, which stores the message in the Drafts folder until you are ready to send it. The Drafts folder is the default location for all saved messages.

To Save and Close an E-Mail Message without Sending It

The orientation schedule that Gayle Medvitz requested still is being drafted, so you are not ready to send the e-mail message to her. The following steps save the RE: New Student Orientation Schedule – message in the Drafts folder for completion at a later time.

BTW

Removing the Original Message When Replying
Many e-mail users prefer to reply to a message without including the original e-mail message along with their response. To remove the original message from *all* e-mail replies, click the File to open the Backstage view, and then click the Mail tab. In the Replies and forwards section, click the 'When replying to a message box' arrow, select the 'Do not include original message' option, and then click OK.

1

- Click the Save button on the Quick Access Toolbar to save the message in the Drafts folder (Figure 1–33).

Q&A How does Outlook know where to store the saved message?

The Drafts folder is the default folder where Outlook automatically stores all saved messages.

Q&A Can I save the message to a location other than the Drafts folder?

To save the message on a USB flash drive, click File on the Ribbon to open the Backstage view and then click Save As in the Backstage view to display the Save As dialog box. Click Computer to display a list of available devices and select a USB flash drive. In the File name text box, type the name of the message and then click the Save button.

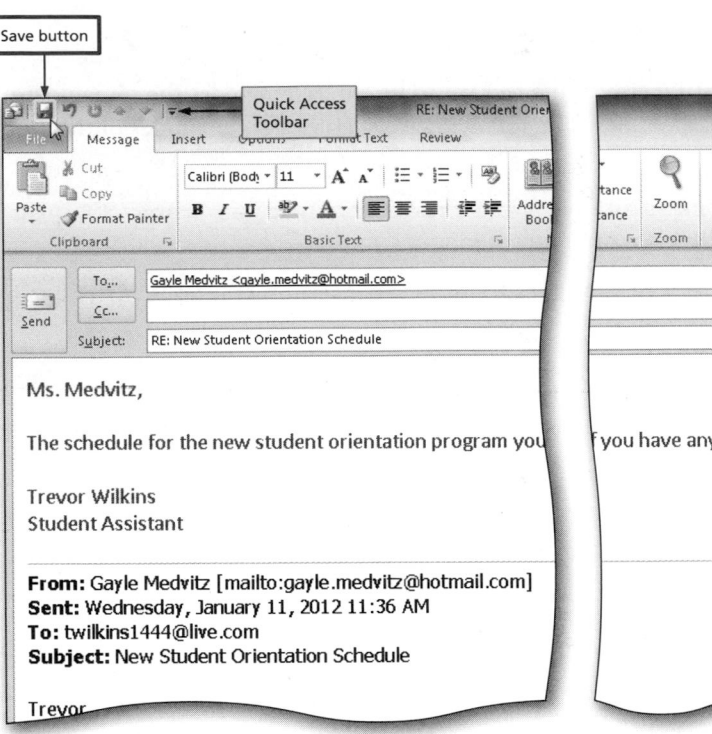

Figure 1–33

2

- Click the Close button on the title bar to close the RE: New Student Orientation Schedule - Message (HTML) window.

Q&A What happens if I click the Close button without saving the message?

If you create a message and then click the Close button, Outlook displays a dialog box asking you if you want to save the changes. If you click Yes, Outlook saves the file to the Drafts folder and closes the message window. If you click No, Outlook discards the e-mail message and closes the message window.

3

- If you want to view the saved message, click the Drafts folder to view any saved messages (Figure 1–34).

Q&A Do I need to view the messages in the Drafts folder?

No, they are stored in the Drafts folder until you need them.

Figure 1–34

Other Ways

1. Click Close button, click Yes to keep saved draft of message
2. Press F12

Opening and Modifying a Saved E-Mail Message

The Word document containing the New Orientation Schedule that Gayle Medvitz requested has been completed. The next step is to modify the saved message to Gayle Medvitz by attaching the Word file. You also want to include Rose Stewart as a courtesy copy recipient. By including her e-mail address as a courtesy copy in the message header, Rose Stewart receives a copy of the message but is not the primary recipient. As such, she neither is required to reply nor is a reply expected from her.

To Open a Saved E-Mail Message

To complete the message to Gayle Medvitz, you first must open it. The following steps open the previously saved New Student Orientation Schedule message, located in the Drafts folder.

1
• If necessary, click the Drafts folder in the Mail folder list to display the message header for the Gayle Medvitz e-mail message in the message list (Figure 1–35)

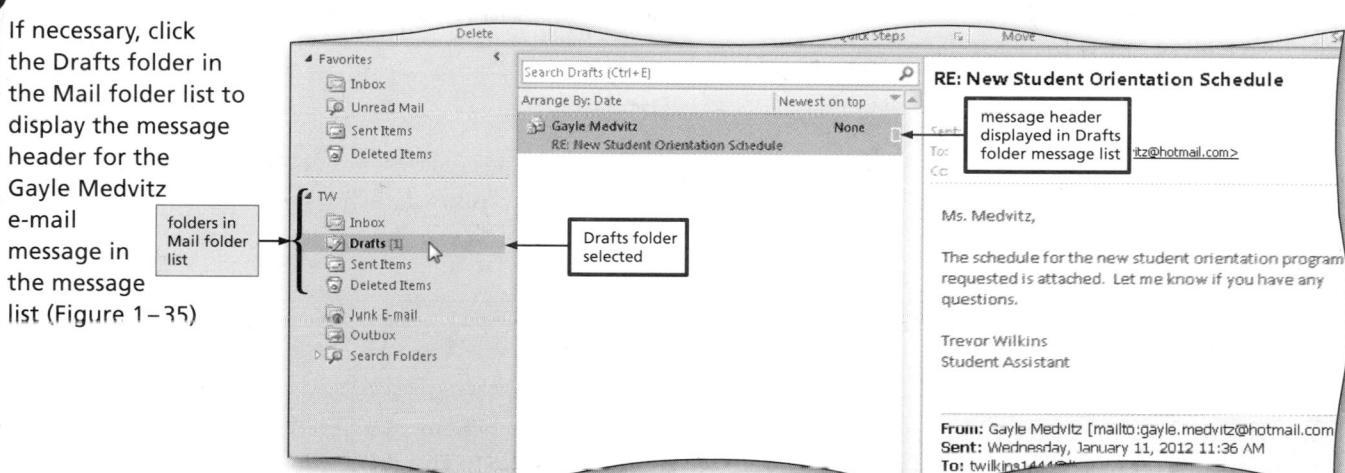

Figure 1–35

2
• Double-click the Gayle Medvitz message header in the Drafts folder to open the e-mail message (Figure 1–36).

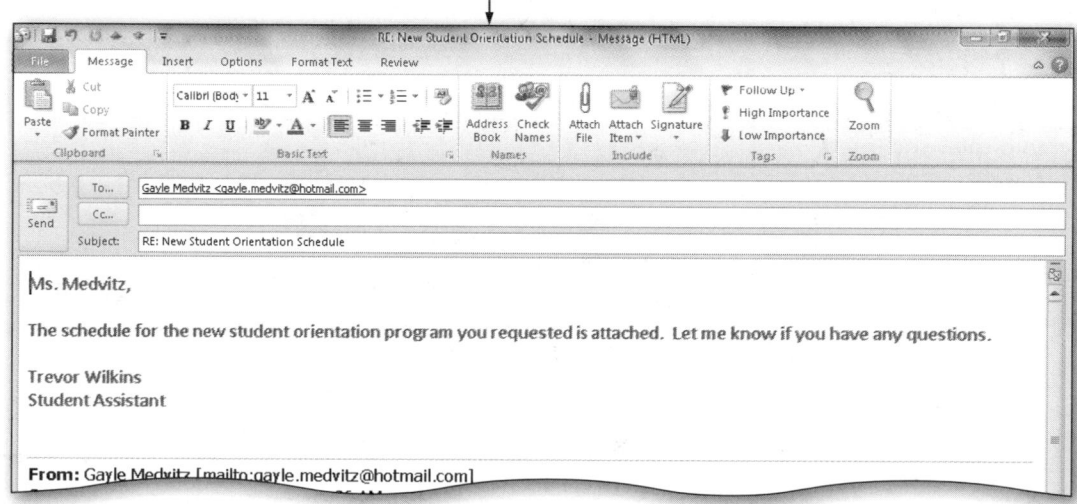

Figure 1–36

Other Ways

1. Right-click message, click Open

2. With message selected, press CTRL+O

To Include a Courtesy Copy Recipient in an E-Mail Message

The following step includes Rose Stewart as a courtesy copy recipient of the message to Gayle Medvitz.

1

• Click the Cc text box to select it and then type **rose.stewart@ hotmail.com** (with no spaces) to include a courtesy copy e-mail address in the message header (Figure 1–37).

Q&A

Why does Rose Stewart's complete e-mail address appear when I start typing the address?

As you type in the Cc text box, Outlook uses a feature called **AutoComplete**, which begins to suggest possible matches based on names you have typed before. Because you have typed Rose Stewart's e-mail address before, AutoComplete suggests the complete address before you finish typing. Press the ENTER key to add the suggested e-mail address to the Cc text box.

Figure 1–37

To Attach a File to an E-Mail Message

Many of the messages you receive and respond to are likely to contain an attachment, that is, a file such as a document or picture sent along with a message. You typically attach a file to an e-mail message to provide additional information to a recipient.

Before you send the e-mail message, you need to attach a file to the message to Gayle Medvitz to include the schedule she requested. The following steps attach a file to an e-mail message.

1

• Click the Attach File button (Message tab | Include group) to display the Insert File dialog box (Figure 1–38).

Figure 1–38

- If Computer is not displayed in the navigation pane, drag the navigation pane scroll bar (Insert File dialog box) until Computer appears.

- Click Computer in the navigation pane to display a list of available storage devices in the Insert File dialog box.

- If necessary, scroll through the Insert File dialog box until your USB flash drive appears in the list of available storage devices, and then click the USB flash drive to select it (Figure 1–39).

Figure 1–39

- Double-click your USB flash drive in the list of available storage devices to display a list of files and folders on the selected USB flash drive.

- If necessary, navigate to the folder containing the data files for this chapter, and then double-click that folder to open it and display the data files for this chapter.

- Click New Student Orientation Schedule to select the file to attach (Figure 1–40).

Why does my screen show .docx after the file name?

Windows does not display file name extensions by default, so your system has been changed to display the file extension with the name of the file. To change this, open a folder window. Press ALT+T to display the Tools menu. Click Folder options to open the Folder Options dialog box and then click the View tab. In the Advanced settings section, click the appropriate check box to hide or unhide the file extensions.

Figure 1–40

- Click the Insert button (Insert File dialog box) to attach the selected file to the e-mail message and close the Insert File dialog box (Figure 1–41).

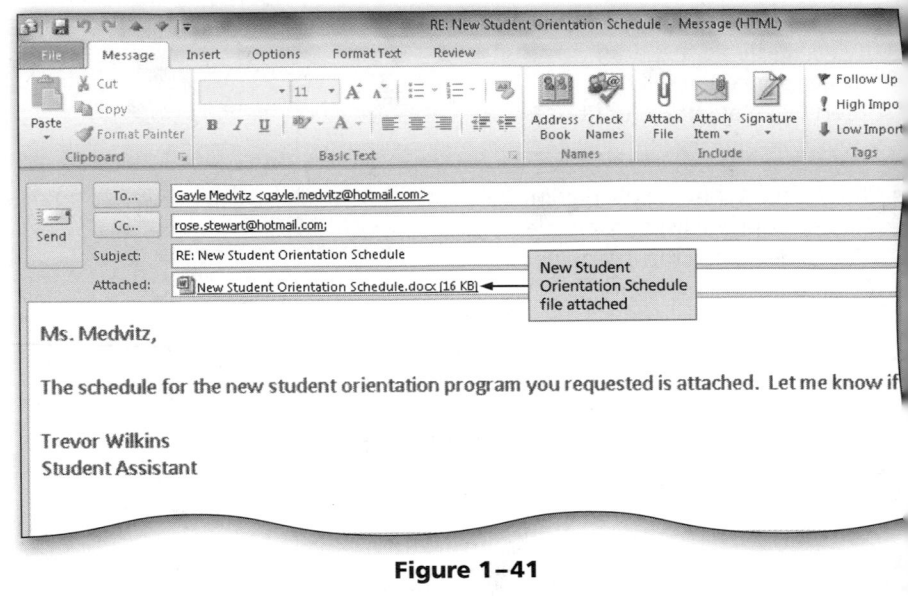

Figure 1–41

Other Ways

1. Click Insert tab, click Attach File button (Insert or Message tab | Include group)
2. Drag file to message area
3. Right-click file, click Copy, right-click message area, click Paste

To Set Message Importance for a Single E-Mail Message and Send the Message

Outlook provides the option to assign an **importance level** to a message, which indicates to the recipient the priority level of an e-mail message. The default importance level for all new messages is normal importance, but you can change the importance level to high or low, depending on the priority level of the e-mail message. A message sent with **high importance** displays a red exclamation point in the message header and indicates to the recipient that the message requires a higher priority than other messages he or she might have received. The **low importance** option displays with a blue arrow and indicates to the recipient a low priority for the message.

Your e-mail message to Gayle Medvitz and Rose Stewart requires their immediate attention so you decide to send the message with high importance. The following steps set the high importance option for a single e-mail message and then send the message.

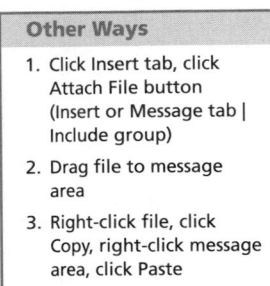

- With the message to Gayle Medvitz and Rose Stewart open, click the High Importance button (Message tab | Tags group) to add a high importance level to the e-mail message (Figure 1–42).

Q&A

How would I set a low importance to an e-mail message?

Click the Low Importance button (Message tab | Tags group).

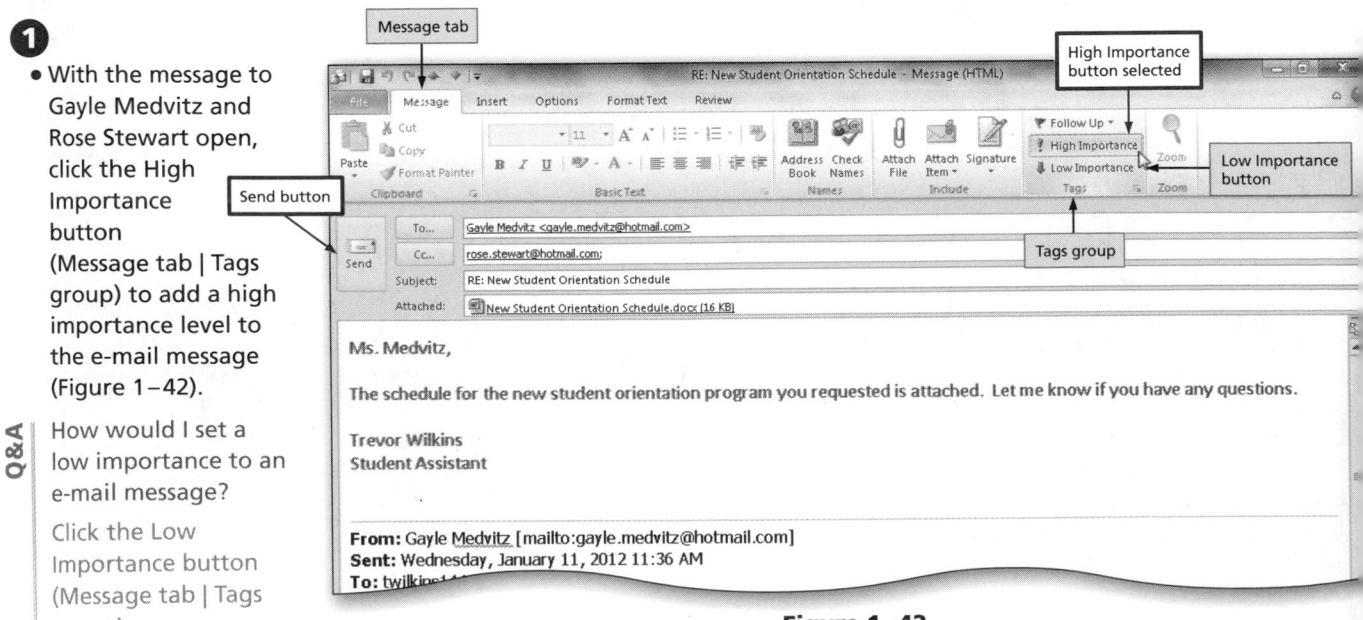

Figure 1–42

• Click the Send button in the message header to send the e-mail message.

What happens to the e-mail message I just sent?

After Outlook closes the message window, it stores the e-mail message reply in the Outbox folder while it sends the message to the two recipients. You might not see the message in the Outbox because Outlook usually stores it there only briefly. Next, Outlook moves the message to the Sent Items folder. The original message in the message list now shows an open envelope icon with a purple arrow to indicate a reply was sent.

File Attachments

Users typically attach a file to an e-mail message to provide additional information to the recipient. The **Attachment Preview** feature in Outlook allows you to preview an attachment you receive in an e-mail message from either the Reading Pane in an unopened message or the message area of an opened message.

Outlook has built-in previewers for several file types, such as other Office programs, pictures, text, and Web pages. Outlook includes attachment previewers that work with other Microsoft Office programs so that users can preview an attachment without opening it. These attachment previewers are turned on by default. To preview an attached file created in an Office 2010 application, you must have that Office application installed on your computer. For example, to preview an Excel attachment in Outlook, you must have Excel installed. Third-party software vendors may provide previewers that support additional attachment file types.

The previewers in Microsoft Office 2010 are designed to provide additional security against potentially harmful code, allowing you to preview attachments more safely. Turning off the attachment previewers removes that layer of protection. Using Attachment Preview, you quickly can see the contents of the attachment without opening it, thus eliminating the need to save the attachment. If you do not have the program that was used to create the attached file, you cannot open an attachment.

If Outlook does not have a built-in previewer for an attachment's file type, Outlook displays a message explaining why it cannot preview the attachment. It also asks if you want to save the file and open it with the program in which it was created.

You should be aware of the limitations of Attachment Preview. For example, Outlook can preview attachments in the HTML or Plain Text message format, but not attachments formatted in Rich Text. In addition, you should preview or open attachments from trustworthy sources only. Sometimes, malicious code such as scripts, macros, and Active X controls is embedded in an e-mail message. For your protection, Outlook disables this type of active content when it previews a document. The Trust Center allows you to configure the way Outlook handles attachments.

BTW

Printing Attachments
You sometimes may want to print a file attached to an e-mail message you receive. To print an attachment, right-click the attachment to display the shortcut menu, and then click Quick Print.

BTW

Outlook Help
At any time while using Outlook, you can find answers to questions and display information about various topics through Outlook Help. Used properly, this form of assistance can increase your productivity and reduce your frustrations by minimizing the time you spend learning how to use Outlook. For instruction about Outlook Help and exercises that will help you gain confidence in using it, read the Introduction to Windows 7 and Office 2010 chapter at the beginning of this book.

To Preview and Save an Attachment

When you receive a message with an attachment, you can preview an attached file without opening it to see its contents. After Trevor Wilkins receives the e-mail message and attachment from Jay Ballentyne, he previews the contents of the attached file and then saves the attachment in a folder on his computer. The following steps preview and store the attachment from Jay Ballentyne.

1
- If necessary, click Inbox to display the TW Inbox.

- In the message list, click the message header from Jay Ballentyne with the AV Request Form subject line to select the e-mail message and display its contents in the Reading Pane (Figure 1–43).

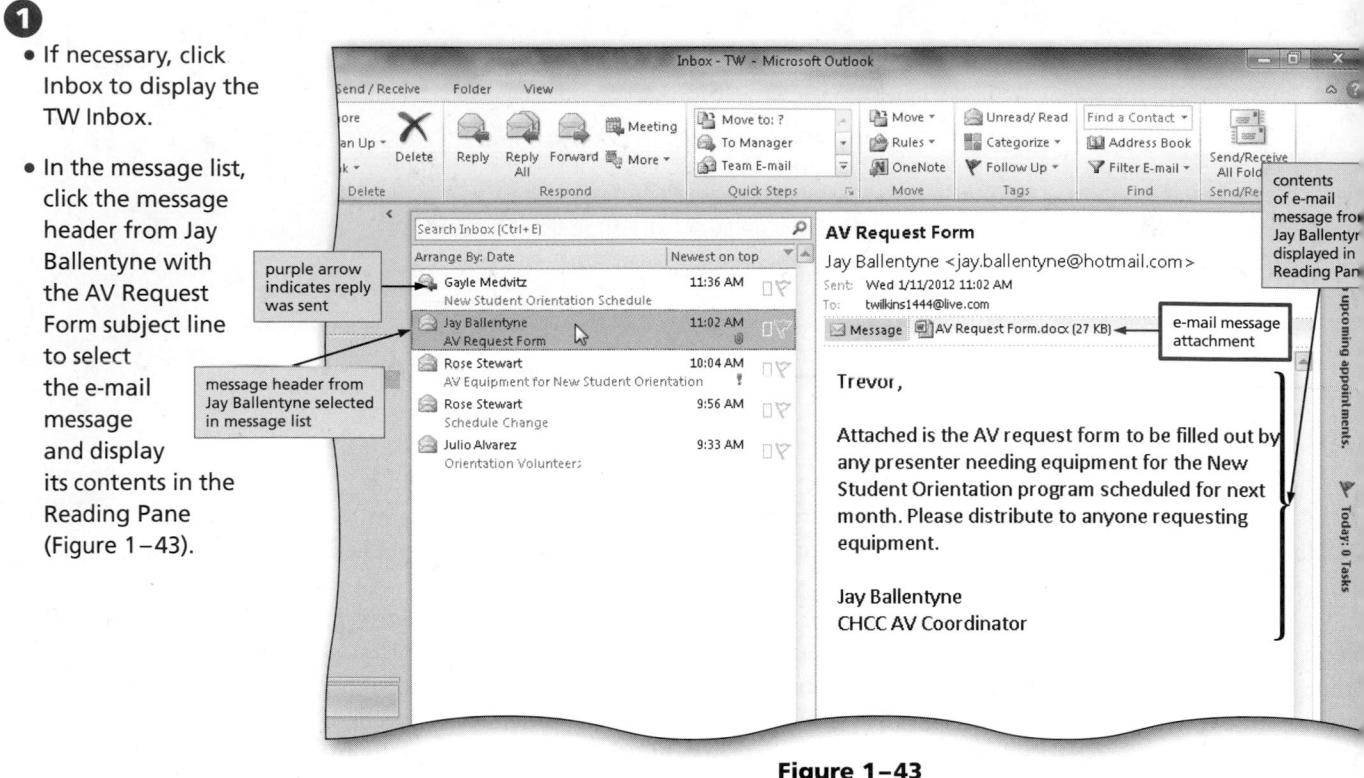

Figure 1–43

Attachment Tools Attachments tab automatically appears when attachment contents are displayed

2
- In the Reading Pane, click the attachment to preview the document in the Reading Pane and display the Attachment Tools Attachments tab (Figure 1–44).

Q&A

What if I do not have a message from Jay Ballentyne in my Inbox?

If you sent the message with the AV Request Form attachment to yourself, that message should appear in your Inbox. Otherwise, you can read but not perform these steps.

Figure 1–44

- Click the Save As button (Attachment Tools Attachments tab | Actions group) to display the Save Attachment dialog box.

- If Computer is not displayed in the navigation pane, drag the navigation pane scroll bar (Save Attachment dialog box) until Computer appears.

- Click Computer in the navigation pane to display a list of available storage devices in the Save Attachment dialog box.

- If necessary, scroll through the Save Attachment dialog box until your USB flash drive appears in the list of available storage devices.

Figure 1–45

- Double-click your USB flash drive to display a list of files and folders on the selected USB flash drive.

- If necessary, navigate to the folder containing the files for this chapter, and then double-click that folder to open it (Figure 1–45).

- Click the Save button (Save Attachment dialog box) to save the attached file and close the Save Attachment dialog box.

  After I save the attachment, is there a way to keep the e-mail message but not the attachment?

  Yes, click the attachment in the Reading Pane and then click the Remove Attachment button (Attachment Tools Attachments tab | Actions group) to remove the attachment from the e-mail message.

Other Ways

1. Right-click attachment, click Save As

Using Outlook Folders to Organize the Inbox

Keeping track of incoming messages and other Outlook items can be a challenge, especially if you receive many e-mail messages. Outlook provides a basic set of **folders**, which are containers that store Outlook items of a specific type, such as messages, appointments, or contacts. For example, the Inbox is a mail folder created to store e-mail messages. One way to organize your Outlook items is to create folders. The process for creating folders in Outlook is similar to that for creating folders in Windows.

To Create a New Folder in the Inbox Folder

You anticipate receiving several messages throughout the semester from faculty and classmates and want to create a folder in the Inbox folder, known as a subfolder, to store these e-mail messages. The following steps create a subfolder called Volunteers in Trevor Wilkins' Inbox folder.

1

- If it is not already selected, click the Inbox folder to select it.

- Click the Folder tab on the Ribbon to display the Folder tab commands.

- Click the New Folder button (Folder tab | New group) to display the Create New Folder dialog box (Figure 1–46).

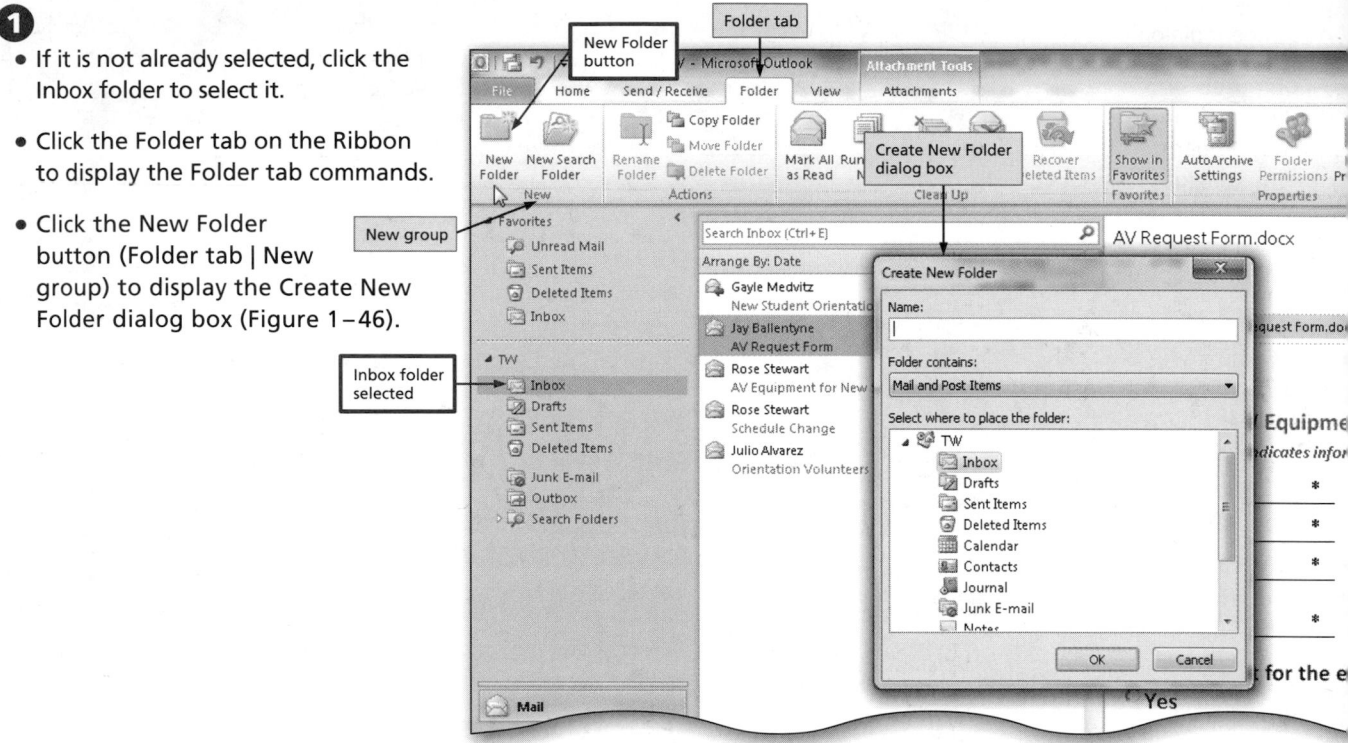

Figure 1–46

2

- Type **Volunteers** as the subfolder name in the Name text box.

- If Mail and Post Items is not already selected, click the Folder contains button arrow and then click Mail and Post Items to place only e-mail messages in the new folder.

- If necessary, click Inbox in the 'Select where to place the folder' list to place the new folder in the selected folder (in this case, Inbox) (Figure 1–47).

Figure 1–47

- Click the OK button to create the Volunteers folder and close the Create New Folder dialog box (Figure 1–48).

Why is the Volunteers folder indented below the Inbox folder?

A folder within a folder is called a subfolder. When you create a subfolder, Outlook indents the folder in the list to indicate that it is a subfolder of a main folder.

Figure 1–48

Other Ways

1. Right-click folder in Folder pane, click New Folder

To Move an E-Mail Message to a Folder

With the folder for e-mail messages regarding volunteers created, the next step is to move messages about volunteers to that folder. Specifically, you will move the message from Julio Alvarez from the Inbox folder to the Volunteers folder. In this case, the Inbox folder is called the source folder, and the Volunteers folder is called the destination folder. A **source folder** is the location of the document or message to be moved or copied. A **destination folder** is the location where you want to move or copy the file or message. The following steps move the message from Julio Alvarez to the Volunteers folder.

- Click Home on the Ribbon to display the Home tab.

- In the Inbox folder (source folder), click the message header from Julio Alvarez in the Inbox message list to select the e-mail message.

- Click the Move button (Home tab | Move group) to display the Move menu (Figure 1–49).

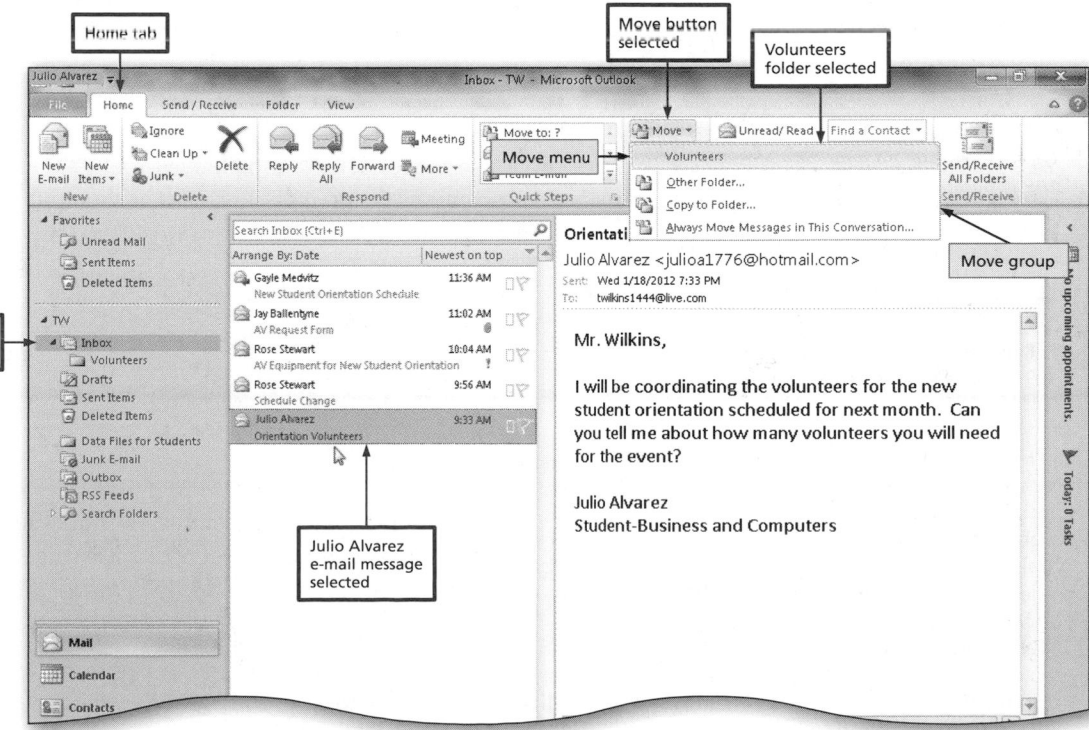

Figure 1–49

2

- Click Volunteers on the Move menu to move the selected message from the source folder (Inbox folder, in this case) to the destination folder (Volunteers folder, in this case).

- In the Navigation Pane, click the Volunteers folder to display its contents (Figure 1–50).

Figure 1–50

Q&A Can I move more than one message at a time?

Yes. Click the first message to select it. While holding the CTRL key, click additional messages to select them. Click the Move button (Home tab | Move group) and then click the destination folder to select it.

Q&A Can I copy the e-mail messages instead of moving them?

Yes. Select the message(s) to copy and click the Move button (Home tab | Move group). Click Copy to Folder on the menu to display the Copy Items dialog box. Select the destination folder (the folder you want to copy the e-mail message to) and then click the OK button to copy the selected message to the destination folder.

Other Ways

1 Right-click selected message, point to Move, click folder

BTW

Certification
The Microsoft Office Specialist program provides an opportunity for you to obtain a valuable industry credential — proof that you have the Outlook 2010 skills required by employers. For more information, visit the Outlook 2010 Certification Web page (scsite.com/ out2010/cert).

To Quit Outlook

This project now is complete. The following step quits Outlook. For a detailed example of the procedure summarized below, refer to the Office 2010 and Windows 7 chapter at the beginning of this book.

1 If you have an e-mail message open, click the Close button on the right side of the title bar to close the message window and then click the Close button on the right side of the Inbox – TW – Microsoft Outlook to close the message window and quit Outlook.

Chapter Summary

In this chapter, you learned how to use Outlook to read, open, print, reply to, forward, format, delete, save, and send e-mail messages. You viewed and saved file attachments as well as attached a file to an e-mail message. You learned how to add a courtesy copy to an e-mail message and set the importance of e-mail messages. Finally, you created a folder in the Inbox and moved an e-mail message to the new folder. The items listed below include all the new Outlook skills you have learned in this chapter.

1. Start Outlook (OUT 6)
2. Compose and Send an E-Mail Message (OUT 8)
3. Read an E-Mail Message in the Reading Pane (OUT 14)
4. Open an E-Mail Message in a Window (OUT 14)
5. Close an E-Mail Message (OUT 15)
6. Print an E-Mail Message (OUT 15)
7. Print Multiple Copies of an E-Mail Message (OUT 17)
8. Reply to an E-Mail Message (OUT 17)
9. Forward an E-Mail Message (OUT 19)
10. Change the Message Format and Send the Message (OUT 21)
11. Delete an E-Mail Message (OUT 22)
12. Reply to an E-Mail Message (OUT 24)
13. Check the Spelling of a Correctly Typed Word (OUT 24)
14. Check the Spelling of Misspelled Text (OUT 26)
15. Enter More Text (OUT 27)
16. Save and Close an E-Mail Message without Sending It (OUT 27)
17. Open a Saved E-Mail Message (OUT 29)
18. Include a Courtesy Copy Recipient in an E-Mail Message (OUT 30)
19. Attach a File to an E-Mail Message (OUT 30)
20. Set Message Importance for a Single E-Mail Message and Send the Message (OUT 32)
21. Preview and Save an Attachment (OUT 33)
22. Create a New Folder in the Inbox Folder (OUT 36)
23. Move an E-Mail Message to a Folder (OUT 37)
24. Quit Outlook (OUT 38)

Quick Reference

For a table that lists how to complete the tasks covered in this book using the mouse, Ribbon, shortcut menu, and keyboard, see the Quick Reference Summary at the back of this book, or visit the Outlook 2010 Quick Reference Web page (scsite.com/out2010/qr).

Learn It Online

Test your knowledge of chapter content and key terms.

Instructions: To complete the Learn It Online exercises, start your browser, click the Address bar, and then enter the Web address **scsite.com/out2010/learn**. When the Outlook 2010 Learn It Online page is displayed, click the link for the exercise you want to complete and then read the instructions.

Chapter Reinforcement TF, MC, and SA

A series of true/false, multiple choice, and short answer questions that test your knowledge of the chapter content.

Flash Cards

An interactive learning environment where you identify chapter key terms associated with displayed definitions.

Practice Test

A series of multiple choice questions that test your knowledge of chapter content and key terms.

Who Wants To Be a Computer Genius?

An interactive game that challenges your knowledge of chapter content in the style of the television quiz show.

Wheel of Terms

An interactive game that challenges your knowledge of chapter key terms in the style of the television show *Wheel of Fortune.*

Crossword Puzzle Challenge

A crossword puzzle that challenges your knowledge of key terms presented in the chapter.

Apply Your Knowledge

Reinforce the skills and apply the concepts you learned in this chapter.

Creating an E-Mail Message with an Attachment

Note: To complete this assignment, you will be required to use the Data Files for Students. See the inside back cover of this book for instructions on downloading the Data Files for Students, or contact your instructor for information about accessing the required files.

Instructions: Start Outlook. You are to send an e-mail addressed to selected customers of Hickory Ridge Day Care for Pets who might be interested in boarding their pets. You also attach a file named Day Care for Pets Flyer from the Data Files for Students.

Perform the following tasks:

1. Create a new e-mail message addressed to your instructor and enter `Hickory Ridge Day Care for Pets Bulletin` as the subject.

2. Enter `Greetings,` as the greeting line, checking spelling as you type.

3. Insert a blank line, and then enter `Hickory Ridge Day Care for Pets would like to acquaint you with our newly upgraded facility. We have expanded our facilities to include a climate controlled playroom and a security system to monitor our facility 24/7. Please stop by with your pet any time between 7 am and 5 pm for a visit. We would love to see you and your pet.` as the message text, checking spelling as you type.

4. Enter your name as the signature.

5. Attach the Day Care for Pets Flyer file to the e-mail message.

6. Save the e-mail message on a USB flash drive using the file name, Day Care for Pets Bulletin. Submit the e-mail message, shown in Figure 1–51, in the format specified by your instructor.

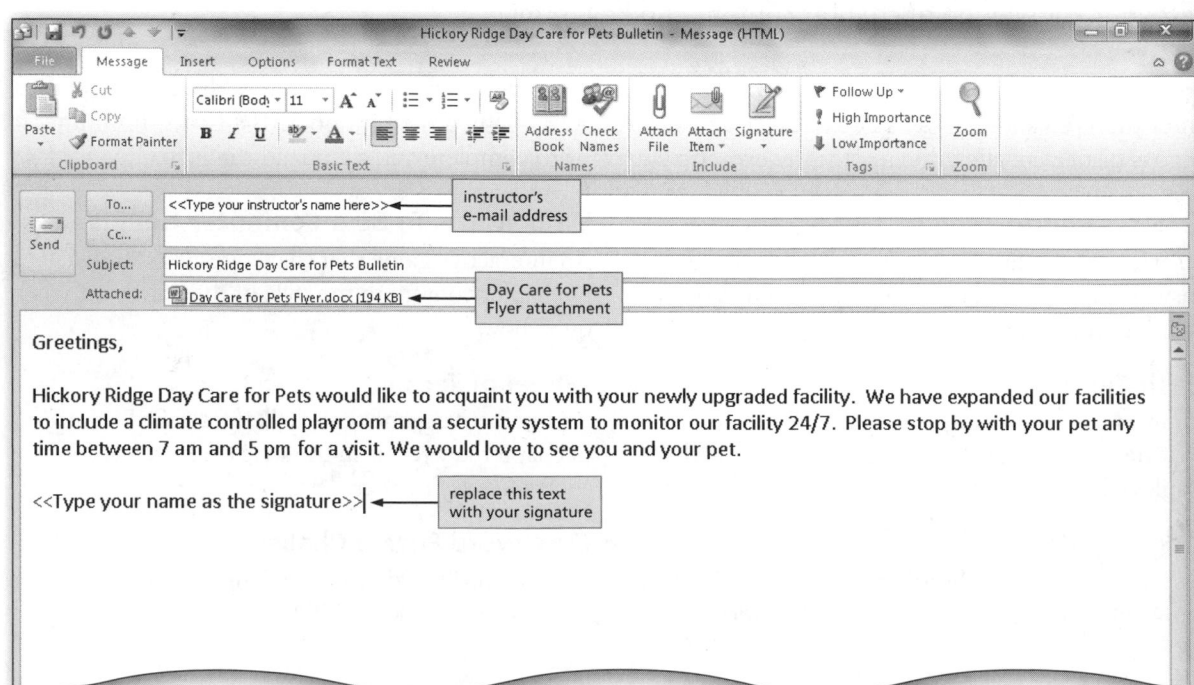

Figure 1–51

Extend Your Knowledge

Extend the skills you learned in this chapter and experiment with new skills. You may need to use Help to complete the assignment.

Managing E-Mail Messages

Note: To complete this assignment, you will be required to use the Data Files for Students. See the inside back cover of this book for instructions on downloading the Data Files for Students, or contact your instructor for information about accessing the required files.

Instructions: Start Outlook. Open the Extend 1-1.pst mailbox file from the Data Files for Students. You will create three folders, rename the folders, and then move messages into the appropriate folders. You also will apply a follow-up flag for the messages in one of the folders. Use Outlook Help to learn about how to add a flag to a message for follow-up and how to create an Outlook Data File (.pst).

Perform the following tasks:

1. Create three new subfolders in the Inbox folder. Name one folder New folder 1, another folder New folder 2, and the third folder New folder 3. Make sure that only mail items are contained in the new folders.

2. In the Navigation Pane, rename the newly created folders. Rename New folder 1 to USB Problems. Rename New folder 2 to Monitor Problems. Rename New folder 3 to Printer Problems. (*Hint:* To rename the folders, right-click the folder you want to rename in the Navigation Pane to open a shortcut menu. Select Rename Folder on the shortcut menu. Type the new name of the folder, and then press the ENTER key).

3. Based on the message headers and content of the e-mail messages in the Extend 1-1 mailbox, move each message to one of the folders you created. Figure 1–52 shows the mailbox with the messages moved to the new folders.

4. In the Monitor Problems folder, assign a flag for follow-up for next week to all messages.

5. Export the Inbox mailbox to an Outlook data file (.pst) on a USB flash drive using the file name, Extend 1-1.pst, and then submit it in the format specified by your instructor.

Figure 1–52

Make It Right

Analyze a document and correct all errors and/or improve the design.

Correcting Errors and Changing the Format of an E-Mail Message

Note: To complete this assignment, you will be required to use the Data Files for Students. See the inside back cover of this book for instructions on downloading the Data Files for Students, or contact your instructor for information about accessing the required files.

Instructions: In a folder window, open the message file, Make It Right 1-1.msg, from the Data Files for Students. Outlook starts and opens the message. The Dietary Needs for the Upcoming Conference message contains spelling errors. To see the red wavy line under the misspelled words, click at the end of the message and press the SPACEBAR. The e-mail message was sent using the HTML message format, as shown in Figure 1–53.

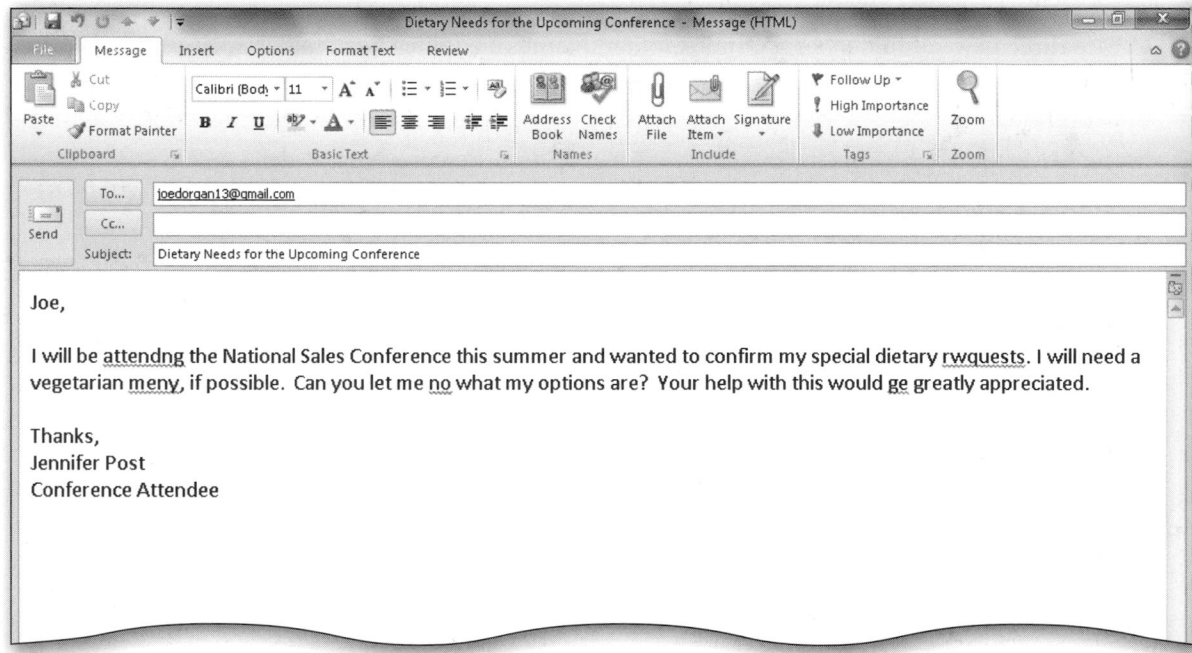

Figure 1–53

If you received the message as Plain Text, change the message format to HTML. Recheck the spelling and grammar errors by pressing F7 to open the Spelling and Grammar dialog box, clicking the Options button, clicking the Recheck E-mail button, and then clicking Yes. Then correct each spelling (red wavy underline) and grammar error (green or blue wavy underlines). In most cases, you can make the correction by right-clicking the flagged text and then clicking the appropriate correction on the shortcut menu. In some cases, however, you may need to make the correction by hand. If your screen does not display the wavy underlines, click the File tab on the Ribbon to open the Backstage view, and then click Options to display the Outlook Options dialog box. In the Compose messages section, click the Editor Options button to display the Editor Options dialog box. Click Proofing in the left pane (Editor Options dialog box). In the 'When correcting spelling in Outlook' section, ensure the 'Check spelling as you type' check box and the 'Mark grammar errors as you type' check box each contains a check mark. Click the OK button two times.

Change the format of the e-mail message to Plain Text, and then send the message to yourself. Save the message on a USB flash drive as Make It Right 1-1.msg, and then submit it in the format specified by your instructor.

In the Lab

Design and/or create an e-mail message using the guidelines, concepts, and skills presented in this chapter. Labs are listed in order of increasing difficulty.

Lab 1: Composing and Saving an E-Mail Message with High Importance

Problem: After returning from an illness that required you to miss a class at school, you need to contact your instructor. Create an e-mail message to your instructor requesting information about missed class assignments and change the message format to Plain Text. Because you need this information immediately, send the e-mail message with high importance. Also, send a Cc (courtesy copy) to yourself. Figure 1–54 shows the completed e-mail message.

Instructions: Perform the following tasks:

1. Open the Untitled – Message window to create a new e-mail message.

2. Address the e-mail message to your instructor and send a Cc (courtesy copy) to yourself.

3. Type **Missed Class Assignments** as the subject.

4. Change the format of the message to Plain Text.

5. Type the message text as shown in Figure 1–54, inserting blank lines where they appear in the figure. Use your name as the signature. If Outlook flags any misspelled words as you type, check their spelling and correct them.

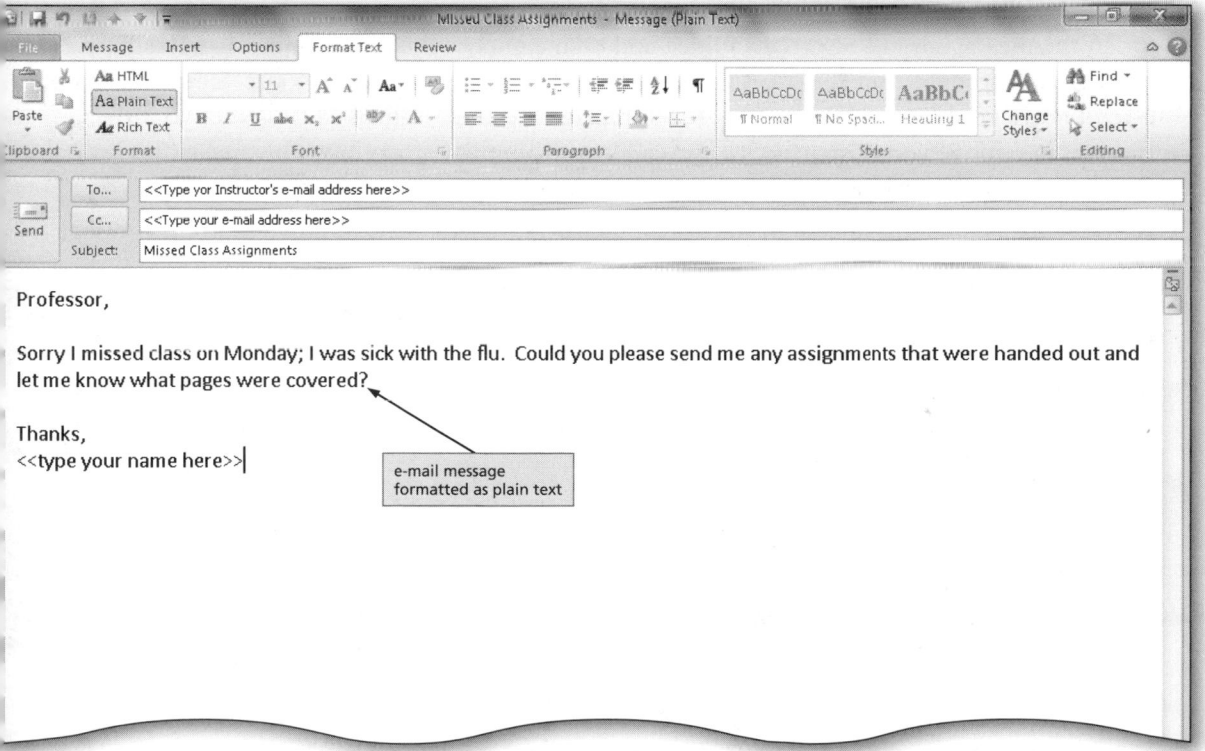

Figure 1–54

6. Apply High Importance to this message and send the message.

7. Save the message in the Drafts folder.

8. Save the message on a USB flash drive as Missed Class Assignments.msg, and then submit it in the format specified by your instructor.

In the Lab

Lab 2: Composing and Sending, and Replying to an E-Mail Message

Problem: As a part-time employee in the Computer Help Center for your school, you have been asked to compile a list of keyboard shortcuts for Outlook 2010. First, you compose the e-mail message shown in Figure 1–55, and then you attach a file. The document to be attached is named Outlook 2010 Keyboard Shortcuts.

Note: To complete this assignment, you may be required to use the Data Files for Students. See the inside back cover of this book for instructions on downloading the Data Files for Students, or contact your instructor for information about accessing the required files.

Instructions: Perform the following tasks:

1. Create a new e-mail message. Address the message to yourself with a courtesy copy to your instructor.

2. Enter the subject, message text, and signature shown in Figure 1–55a. Insert blank lines where the are shown in the figure. If Outlook flags any misspelled words as you type, check their spelling and correct them.

3. Attach the Outlook 2010 Keyboard Shortcuts file to the e-mail message.

4. Send the e-mail message with high importance and use the HTML format for the message.

5. When you receive the Keyboard Shortcuts for Outlook 2010 e-mail message, move it to a new folder in your Inbox named Shortcuts.

6. Open the message in the Shortcuts folder, and then compose the reply. Figure 1–55b shows a reply from a student named Dana Cooper to a student named Heather Moore. Copy the text of the e-mail message shown in Figure 1–55b, but replace Heather's e-mail address with your own. Be sure to remove your instructor's e-mail address from the Cc text box, if necessary. If Outlook flags any misspelled words as you type, check their spelling and correct them.

7. If necessary, change the format of the e-mail message to Plain Text, and then send the message to yourself.

8. When you receive the RE: Keyboard Shortcuts for Outlook 2010 message, move it to the Shortcuts folder in your Inbox folder.

9. Save the e-mail message on a USB flash drive using your last name plus *Lab 2* as the file name. For example, if your last name is Smith, the file name would be Smith Lab 2.msg. Submit the file in the format specified by your instructor.

Figure 1–55 (a)

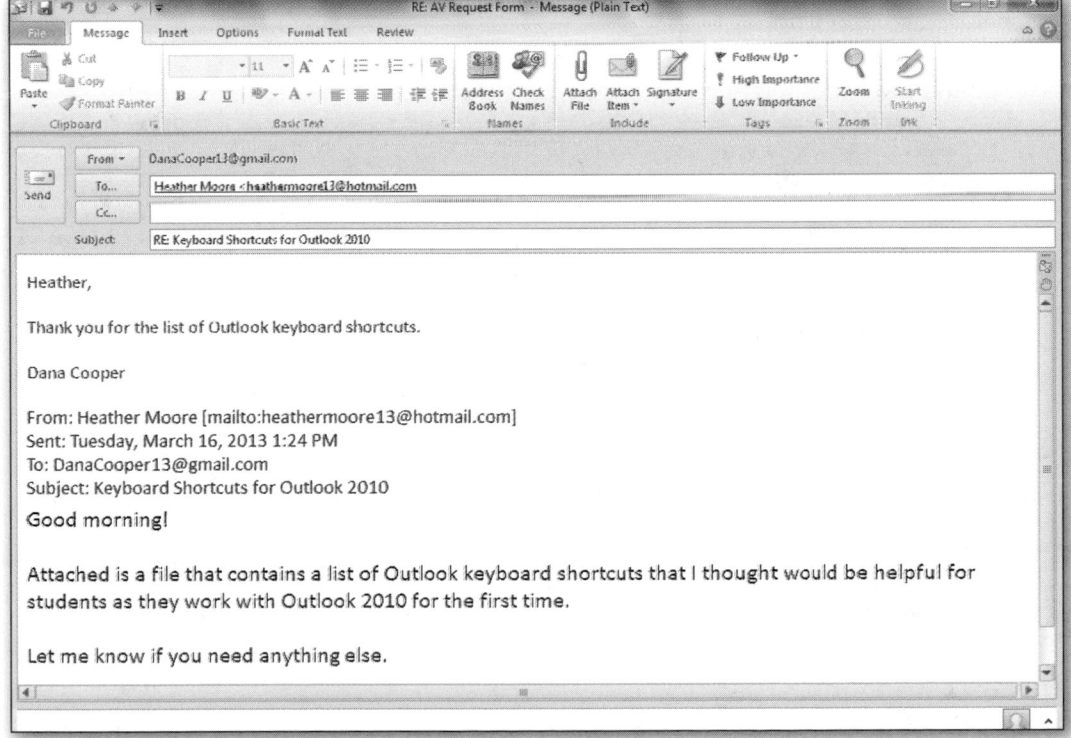

Figure 1–55 (b)

In the Lab

Lab 3: Creating and Sending an E-Mail Message to Several People

Problem: Your boss at Maple Valley Bakery has asked you to send e-mail messages to a few new customers inviting them to a pastry and coffee event the bakery is hosting. For one e-mail message, you need to attach a document named Maple Valley Bakery Flyer. You prepare the e-mail messages shown in Figure 1–56.

Note: To complete this assignment, you may be required to use the Data Files for Students. See the inside back cover of this book for instructions on downloading the Data Files for Students, or contact your instructor for information about accessing the required files.

Figure 1–56 (a)

Figure 1–56 (b)

Instructions: Perform the following tasks:

1. Create a new e-mail message. Address the message to the following recipients:

    anneclark@live.com

    laurareasons123@live.com

    janetmartin123@live.com

    vickichristof123@gmail.com

    marywilliams234@gmail.com

2. Enter your e-mail address so that you send a courtesy copy to yourself.

3. Enter the subject, message text, and signature shown in Figure 1–56a. Insert blank lines where they are shown in the figure. If Outlook flags any misspelled words as you type, check their spelling and correct them.

4. Attach the Maple Valley Bakery Flyer document to the e-mail message.

5. Save the e-mail message in the Drafts folder.

6. Send the e-mail message with high importance and use the HTML format for the message.

7. When you receive the Invitation to a Pastry and Coffee Sampling e-mail message, move it to a new folder in your Inbox named Events.

8. Select the message in the Events folder, and then forward to your instructor the message shown in Figure 1–56b. If Outlook flags any misspelled words as you type, check their spelling and correct them.

9. If necessary, change the format of the e-mail message to Plain Text, and then send yourself a courtesy copy.

10. Save the response e-mail message on a USB flash drive using your last name plus *Lab 3* as the file name. For example, if your last name is Smith, the file name would be Smith Lab 3.msg. Submit the file in the format specified by your instructor.

Cases and Places

Apply your creative thinking and problem solving skills to design and implement a solution.

Note: To complete these assignments, you may be required to use the Data Files for Students. See the inside back cover of this book for instructions on downloading the Data Files for Students, or contact your instructor for information about accessing the required files.

: Compose, Print, and Send a Message for a Campus Event

Academic

As an employee of the student union, you are responsible for creating and sending e-mail messages informing student leaders about upcoming lectures and presentations at the union. This month, the union has two lectures and one presentation scheduled. The presentation is about travel in Washington, DC. The e-mail message should include an attachment of a digital photo. The Data Files for Students contain a photo named DC.jpg or you can use your own digital photo if it is appropriate for the topic of the e-mail message. The e-mail message should be addressed to yourself and your instructor. The subject should contain the text, Spring Lectures at the Union. The message text consists of the following, in any order: The student union is sponsoring three events in its lecture series on our nation's capital this month. Enjoy a panoramic presentation about tourism in Washington, DC.

Continued >

Cases and Places *continued*

Experience the varieties of culinary offerings. Learn about the upcoming festivals and cultural events throughout the Washington, DC, metropolitan area. Use the concepts and techniques presented in this chapter to create this e-mail message. Be sure to check spelling and grammar before you send the message. Submit your assignment in the format specified by your instructor.

2: Compose an E-Mail Message to a Relative or Friend and Attach a File

Personal

Being involved with your studies, extracurricular activities, and college life in general can limit the time you have to communicate with family and friends. Compose and send an e-mail message to a close relative or friend. The e-mail message should contain information about your class schedule, activities, and new friends that you have made. Attach a picture of the school to the message. You can use the file College.jpg or you can use your own digital photo of your school. Compose the message in HTML format. The subject should be Campus Life or you can use your own subject. The message text consists of at least the following information: This semester I am taking 15 credits, so my schedule is very full. I also am involved in the Student Government Association. I met a student who went to high school in a neighboring town, and we found we have many mutual friends. Attached is a picture of one of our buildings so you can get a sense of how beautiful the campus is. Add a greeting line, closing, and other appropriate text. Use the concepts and techniques presented in this chapter to create this e-mail message. Be sure to check spelling and grammar before you send the message. Submit your assignment in the format specified by your instructor.

3: Forward an E-Mail Message to Multiple Recipients Informing Them about an Event

Professional

As an IT recruiter for local executive search firm, you receive many e-mail messages regarding job and career fairs throughout your community. You recently received an e-mail message, IT Recruitment Fair. msg, inviting you to attend an employment fair sponsored by the Chamber of Commerce and held at a local high school. The Career Fair also provides job seekers with a free résumé review service and access to a job search database. More than 100 employers representing various industries will be represented and attending would be a wonderful networking opportunity. Your schedule is full and you cannot attend. The e-mail message asks that you forward the invitation to anyone you think might be interested in attending. In a folder window, open the message file IT Recruitment Fair.msg from the Data Files for Students in the Cases and Places folder. Replace nikitanner123@gmail.com in the To box with your own e-mail address and send the e-mail message to yourself. Now you can forward the e-mail message to your coworkers.

Forward the e-mail message to three coworkers who you think might benefit from attending, telling them about the benefits of such an event. Their e-mail addresses are as follows:

davidclark@live.com

angelareasons123@live.com

marcimartin123@live.com

Send a courtesy copy to your boss, in case she might want to send additional people to the event or perhaps attend the event herself. Her e-mail address is susanwilliams234@gmail.com.

Print the forwarded message and submit it in the format specified by your instructor.

2 | Managing Calendars

Objectives

You will have mastered the material in this chapter when you can:

- Open the Calendar folder
- Describe the components of the Outlook Calendar
- Navigate the Calendar using the Date Navigator
- View specific dates on the Date Navigator
- Create a personal calendar
- Enter, save, move, edit, and delete appointments

- Set the status of and a reminder for an appointment
- Create and edit events
- Move and delete events
- Create and edit meetings and respond to meeting requests
- Display the calendar in Day, Work Week, Week, and Month views
- Print the calendar in Daily Style

2 | Managing Calendars

Introduction

Whether you are a student at a local college, an activity coordinator in your community, or a business professional, you can take advantage of the Outlook Calendar to schedule and manage appointments, events, and meetings. In particular, you can use Calendar to keep track of your class schedule and appointments, and to schedule meetings. If you are traveling and do not have electronic access to your calendar, you can print a copy to keep with you. You can use Outlook to view or print a daily, weekly, or monthly calendar.

In addition to using Calendar in your academic or professional life, you will find it helpful for scheduling personal time. Most people have multiple appointments to keep each day, week, or month. Calendar can organize activity-related information in a structured, readable manner.

Project — Appointments, Events, and Meetings in Calendar

Time management is a part of everyday life. Many people constantly are rearranging appointments, work schedules, and vacations in an attempt to use their time efficiently. Managing your schedule using a calendar can increase productivity, while maximizing free time. Outlook is the perfect tool to maintain both a professional and a personal schedule. The **Calendar** is the Outlook folder that contains your personal schedule of appointments, events, and meetings. In this project, you use the basic features of Calendar to create a calendar for appointments, classes, work schedules, and extracurricular activities for Trevor Wilkins (Figure 2–1). In addition to creating a calendar for Trevor, you will learn how to print a daily, weekly, or monthly calendar.

Overview

As you read through this chapter, you will learn how to create the calendar shown in Figure 2–1 by performing these general tasks:

- Enter appointments on specific dates.
- Create one-time and recurring appointments.
- Move appointments to new dates.
- Create one-time and recurring events.
- Schedule a meeting with others.
- Respond to a meeting request.
- View and print the calendar.

Figure 2–1

General Project Guidelines

When creating a calendar, the actions you perform and decisions you make will affect the appearance and characteristics of the finished calendar. As you create an appointment, event, or meeting to develop a schedule, you should follow these general guidelines:

1. **Determine what you need to schedule.** People use a calendar to keep track of their schedule and to organize and manage their time. For students, a class list with room numbers and class times would be a good start toward managing their school schedule. For business professionals, the calendar is a dynamic tool that requires frequent updating to keep track of appointments and meetings. You also may want to keep track of personal items, such as birthdays and family gatherings.

2. **Determine where to store your calendar items.** Any information you add to the Outlook Calendar is called a calendar item, or item for short. Outlook stores items in a folder named Calendar by default. If you are creating personal, academic, or business items, you may want to create separate calendars for each group.

3. **Determine if an activity is recurring.** A recurring activity is one that happens on a regular basis. Classes most likely recur throughout the semester. Work schedules can change week-by-week or month-by-month. Family events, such as birthdays and anniversaries, also can be recurring events on the calendar.

4. **Create an agenda before scheduling a meeting.** An agenda is a list of items to be discussed in a meeting. A poorly organized meeting may be the least productive tool in the business world, while a carefully planned meeting with a defined agenda can be a productive use of time, helping meeting participants stay focused and on schedule.

5. **Set calendar item options.** When creating items on a calendar, determine how to display the time of an appointment or event, such as busy or out of the office, so that the calendar is an accurate indication of your time. Also, decide whether to set a reminder for the item and how often it recurs, if at all.

6. **Determine the best method for distributing a calendar.** Consider whether you need to share a calendar with others. If you do, you can share calendars electronically in Outlook or print a calendar and distribute printed copies.

When necessary, more specific details concerning the above guidelines are presented at appropriate points in the chapter. The chapter also will identify the actions performed and decisions made regarding these guidelines during the creation of the calendar shown in Figure 2–1.

Plan
Ahead

For an introduction to Windows 7 and instruction about how to perform basic Windows 7 tasks, read the Office 2010 and Windows 7 chapter at the beginning of this book, where you can learn how to resize windows, change screen resolution, create folders, move and rename files, use Windows Help, and much more.

To Start Outlook

If you are using a computer to step through the project in this chapter and you want your screens to match the figures in this book, you should change your screen's resolution to 1024 × 768. For information about how to change a computer's resolution, refer to the Office 2010 and Windows 7 chapter at the beginning of this book.

The following steps, which assume Windows 7 is running, start Outlook based on a typical installation. You may need to ask your instructor how to start Outlook for your computer. For a detailed example of the procedure summarized below, refer to the Office 2010 and Windows 7 chapter at the beginning of this book.

1 Click the Start button on the Windows 7 taskbar to display the Start menu.

2 Type `Microsoft Outlook` as the search text in the 'Search programs and files' text box and watch the search results appear on the Start menu.

3 Click Microsoft Outlook 2010 in the search results on the Start menu to start Outlook with your Inbox as the default Mail folder.

4 If the Outlook window is not maximized, click the Maximize button next to the Close button on its title bar to maximize the window.

5 Click the Calendar button in the Navigation Pane to display the Calendar – TW – Microsoft Outlook window in Day view (Figure 2–2).

Q&A Why does my title bar not match the title bar in Figure 2–2?

The title bar always displays the name of the Outlook data file, which may include your name or initials.

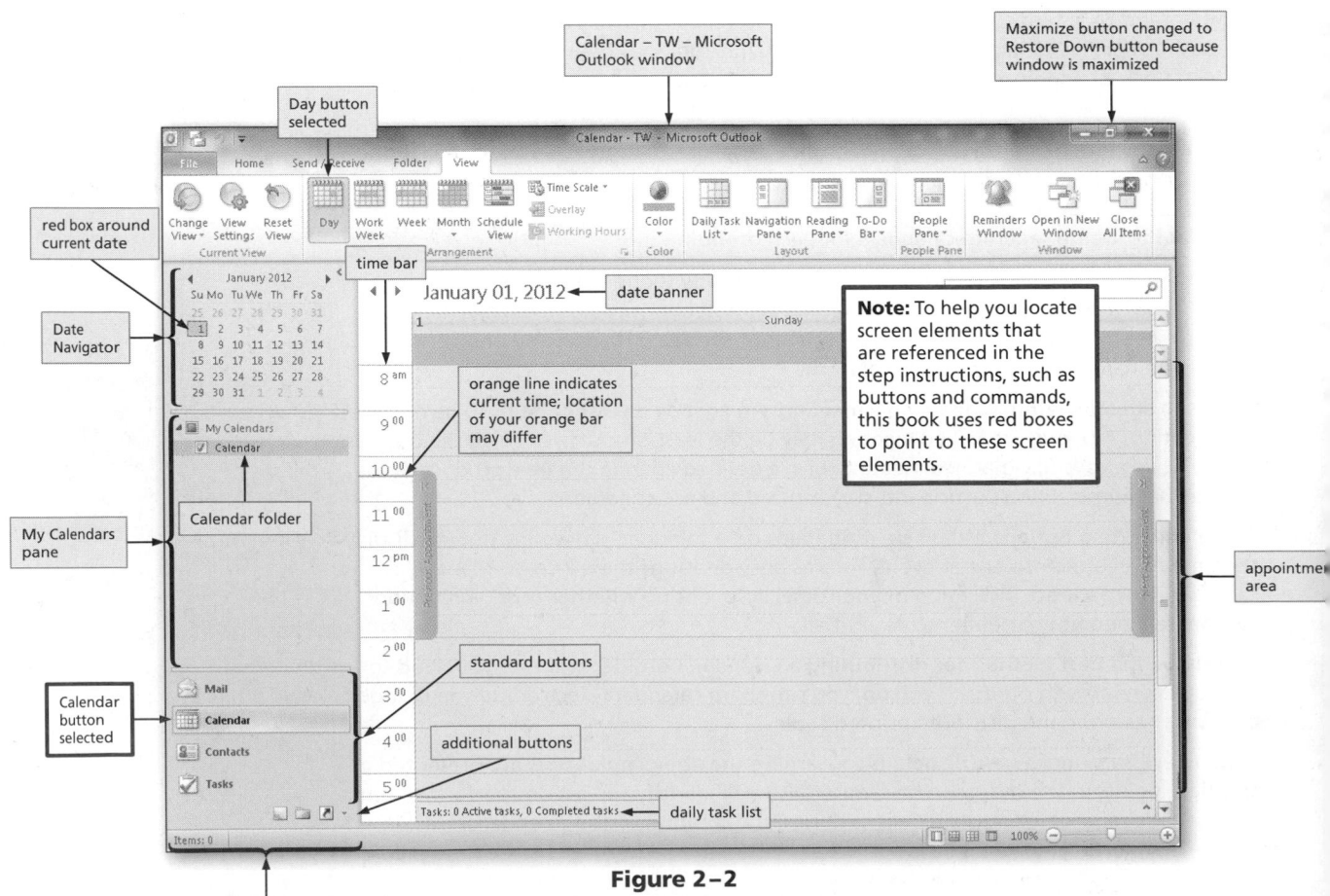

Figure 2–2

Calendar Window

The Calendar – TW – Microsoft Outlook window shown in Figure 2–2 includes a variety of features to help you work efficiently. It contains many elements similar to the windows in other Office programs, as well as some that are unique to Outlook. The main elements of the Calendar window are the Navigation Pane, the appointment area, and the Daily Task List.

The Navigation Pane includes two sets of buttons (standard and additional) and two panes: the Date Navigator and the My Calendars pane. The **Date Navigator** shows a calendar for the current month with a red box around the current date, scroll arrows to advance from one month to another, and any date on which an item is scheduled in bold. The **My Calendars pane** includes a list of available calendars where you can view a single calendar or view additional calendars side by side. The Standard folders represent shortcuts to the standard items that are part of the Microsoft Outlook mailbox: Mail, Calendar, Contacts, and Tasks. Additional folder buttons are displayed below the Standard folder buttons and represent shortcuts to other Outlook functions, such as Notes, Folder List shortcuts, and Configure buttons, which allow you to specify which folders to display. The appointment area contains a date banner, a day heading, and a time bar. The appointment area displays 30-minute time slots by default when viewing Calendar in Day, Work Week, or Week view and is not available in Month view. Similar to the time bar, the task list displays a list of current tasks, appears below the appointment area, and is only visible in Day, Work Week, and Week views.

BTW

Using Calendars
Other users can give you access to their calendars. This allows you to make appointments, check free times, schedule meetings, and refer to contact information. This is especially useful when you are scheduling meetings or events that depend on other people's schedules.

Calendar Items

An **item** is any element in Outlook that contains information. Examples of calendar items include appointments, events, and meetings. All calendar items start as an appointment. Outlook defines an **appointment**, such as a doctor's appointment, as an activity that does not involve other people or resources, such as conference rooms. Outlook defines an **event**, such as a seminar or vacation, as an activity that occurs at least once and lasts 24 hours or longer. An appointment becomes an event when you schedule it for the entire day. An annual event, such as a birthday, anniversary, or holiday, occurs yearly on a specific date. Events do not occupy time slots in the appointment area and, instead, are displayed in a banner below the day heading when viewing the calendar in Day, Work Week, or Week view. An appointment becomes a **meeting** when people and other resources, such as meeting rooms, are invited.

When you create items on your calendar, it is helpful to show your time using the appointment status information. You set the appointment status for a calendar item using the Show As button, which provides four options for showing your time on the calendar: Free, Tentative, Busy, and Out of Office. For example, if you are studying or working on a project, you might show your time as busy because you are unable to perform other tasks at the same time. On the other hand, a dental appointment or a class would show your time as Out of Office because you need to leave your home or office to attend. Table 2–1 describes the items you can schedule on your calendar and the appointment status option associated with each item. Each calendar item also can be one-time or recurring.

Table 2–1 Calendar Items		
Calendar Item	**Description**	**Show As Default**
One-time appointment	Default calendar item, involves only your schedule and does not invite other attendees or require resources such as a conference room	Busy
Recurring appointment	Occurs at regular intervals, such as weekly, biweekly, monthly, or bimonthly	Busy
One-time event	Occurs at least once and lasts 24 hours or longer, such as a vacation or conference	Free
Recurring event	Occurs at regular intervals, such as weekly, biweekly, monthly, or bimonthly, such as holidays	Free
One-time meeting	Includes people and other resources, such as meeting rooms	Busy
Recurring meeting	Occurs at regular intervals, such as weekly, biweekly, monthly, or bimonthly, such as staff meetings or department meetings	Busy

Plan Ahead

Determine where to store your calendar items.
When you schedule an appointment, Outlook adds the appointment to the Calendar folder by default. If you are creating personal, academic, and business items, you may want to create a separate calendar for each group. Users often create multiple calendars to keep personal items separate from academic or business items.

To Create a Personal Folder

As in other Outlook folders, such as the Inbox, you can create multiple folders within the Calendar folder. In certain situations, you may need to keep more than one calendar, such as one for business items and another for personal items.

The following steps create a folder to store your class and school related information, separate from your default folder, Calendar.

1

• With the Calendar – TW – Microsoft Outlook window open, click Folder on the Ribbon to display the Folder tab (Figure 2–3).

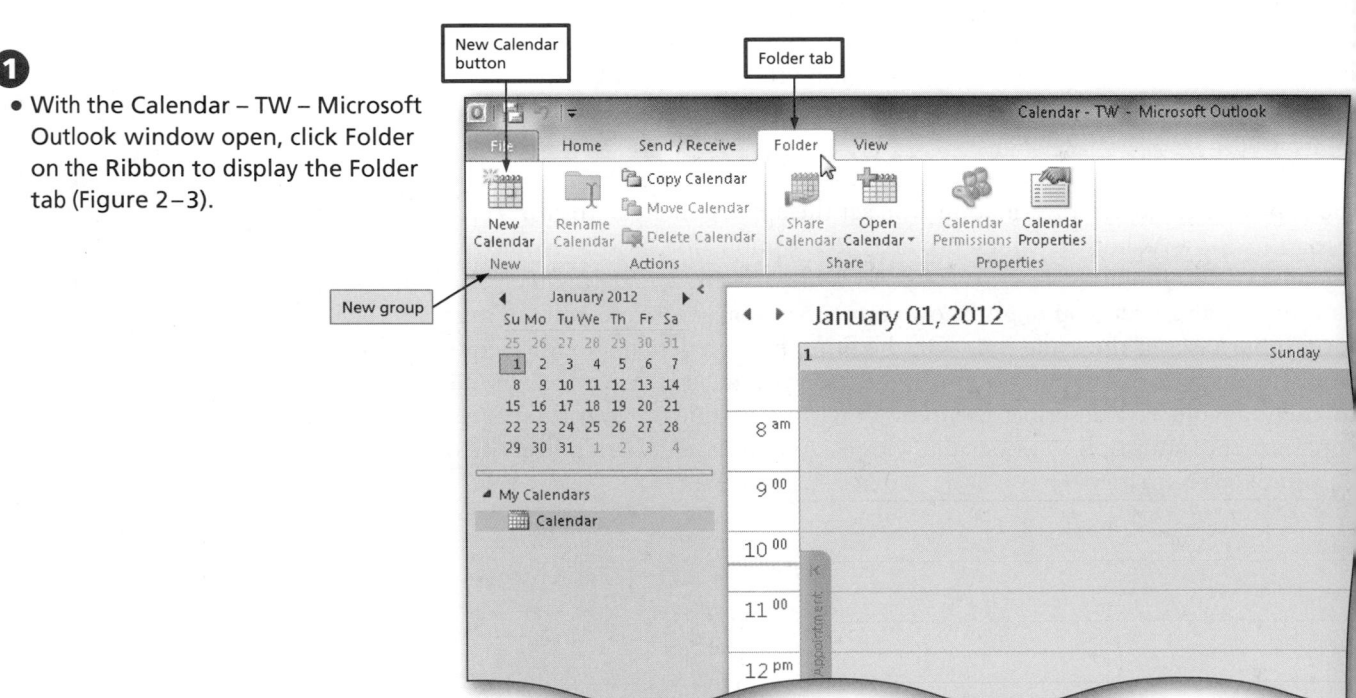

Figure 2–3

2

- Click the New Calendar button (Folder tab | New group) to display the Create New Folder dialog box.

- Type **School Calendar** in the Name text box (Create New Folder dialog box) to enter a name for the new folder.

- If necessary, click the Folder contains button to display a list of items the folder will contain.

- Click Calendar Items to specify what the folder will contain.

- If necessary, click Calendar in the 'Select where to place the folder' list to specify where the folder will be stored (Figure 2–4).

Figure 2–4

3

- Click the OK button to close the Create New Folder dialog box and add the new folder to the My Calendars list (Figure 2–5).

The School Calendar folder is not displayed after I create it. Why is that?

Outlook does not automatically display the newly created calendar.

Figure 2–5

Other Ways
1. Press CTRL+SHIFT+E

To Display a Personal Calendar

Now that the School Calendar folder has been created, the next step is to display both calendar folders in the appointment area, so that the default Calendar folder and the School Calendar folder appear side by side. The following step displays the Calendar and the School Calendar folders side by side.

1

- In the My Calendars pane, click School Calendar to place a check mark in the check box, so that both the Calendar and the School Calendar folders are selected in the calendar list and displayed in the appointment area (Figure 2–6).

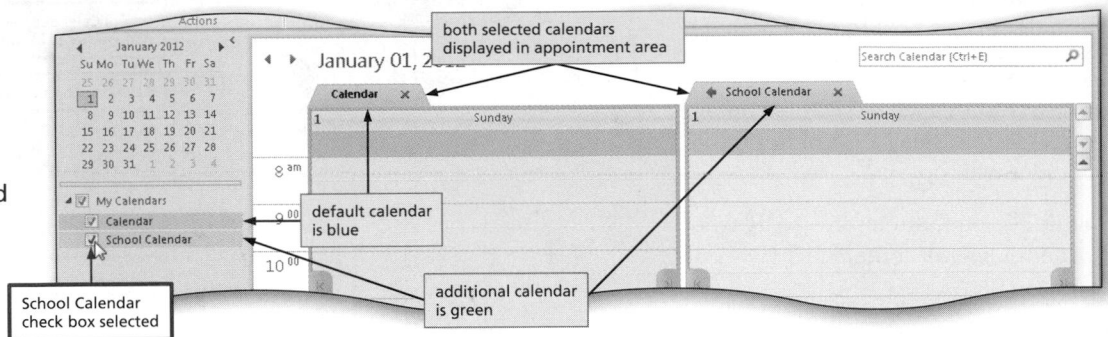

Figure 2–6

Q&A Why is the default calendar displayed in a different color from the School Calendar?

Outlook automatically assigns a different color to each new calendar you create to make it easier to distinguish one calendar from the other. Your calendar colors might be different from those shown in Figure 2–6.

Q&A What does the left pointing arrow mean on the School Calendar tab?

When the calendars are displayed side by side, the arrow allows you to view the School Calendar in overlay mode, which increases the size of the School Calendar while keeping the other calendar open. The appointments on the Calendar folder in the background still are visible on the School Calendar, allowing you to see any appointment conflicts.

To Remove the Default Calendar from the Appointment Area

While working with the School Calendar, you may want to display only that calendar in the Outlook window to avoid entering the information on the wrong calendar. The following step removes the default calendar from the appointment area.

1

- Click Calendar in the My Calendars pane to remove the check mark from the Calendar check box so that the default calendar no longer is displayed in the appointment area (Figure 2–7).

Q&A Why does my view look different from what is shown?

Figure 2–7 shows Day view, which is the default view for Calendar. If this is not the current view, click the Day button (Home tab | Arrange group).

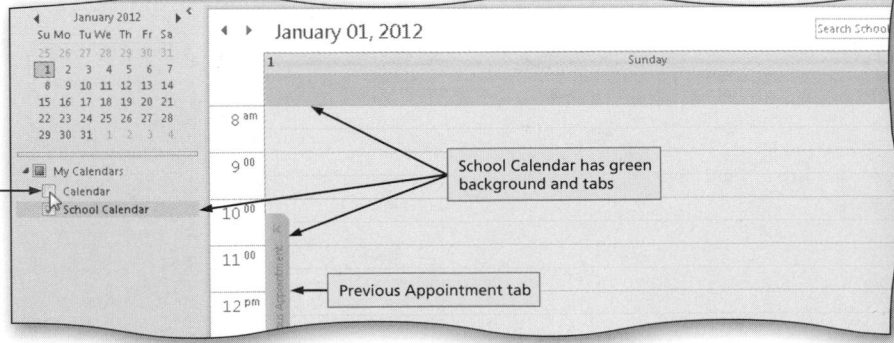

Figure 2–7

Q&A What do the green tabs in the appointment area represent?

The green tabs provide navigation to the previous and next appointments.

Viewing the Calendar

Each Microsoft Outlook 2010 folder displays the items it contains in a layout called a view. You can change the arrangement and format of the folder contents by changing the view. Recall that the default view of the Calendar folder is Day view. Some people may prefer a different view of their calendar, such as weekly or monthly. For instance, you might want to view all the items for a given month at one time, in which case Month view would work best.

In this section, you will navigate to a specific date and then examine the different ways to view a calendar. Although the Outlook window looks different in each view, you can accomplish the same tasks in each view: you can add, edit, or delete appointments, events, and meetings.

BTW

Q&As
For a complete list of the Q&As found in many of the step-by-step sequences in this book, visit the Outlook 2010 Q&A Web page (scsite.com/out2010/qa).

To Go to a Specific Date

The next step in this project is to display a date that is not visible in the current view so that you can view that date in the appointment area. One option is to use the Go To Dialog Box Launcher, which allows you to navigate to a specific date and display that date in the appointment area. The following steps display a specific date, in this case January 15, 2012, in the appointment area in a calendar.

1

• If necessary, display the Home tab, and then click the Go To Dialog Box Launcher (Home tab | Go To group) to display the Go To Date dialog box (Figure 2–8).

Figure 2–8

2

- Type 1/15/2012 in the Date box (Go To Date dialog box) to enter the date you want to display in the current calendar.

- If necessary, click the Show in button to display the list of calendar views.

- Click Day Calendar to show the calendar in Day view (Figure 2–9).

Q&A Why did 'Sun' appear next to the date in the Date box?

Outlook automatically includes the day of the week (Sunday, in this case) when you enter a date in the Date box.

Figure 2–9

3

- Click the OK button to close the Go To Date dialog box and display the current calendar with the entered date as the selected date (Figure 2–10).

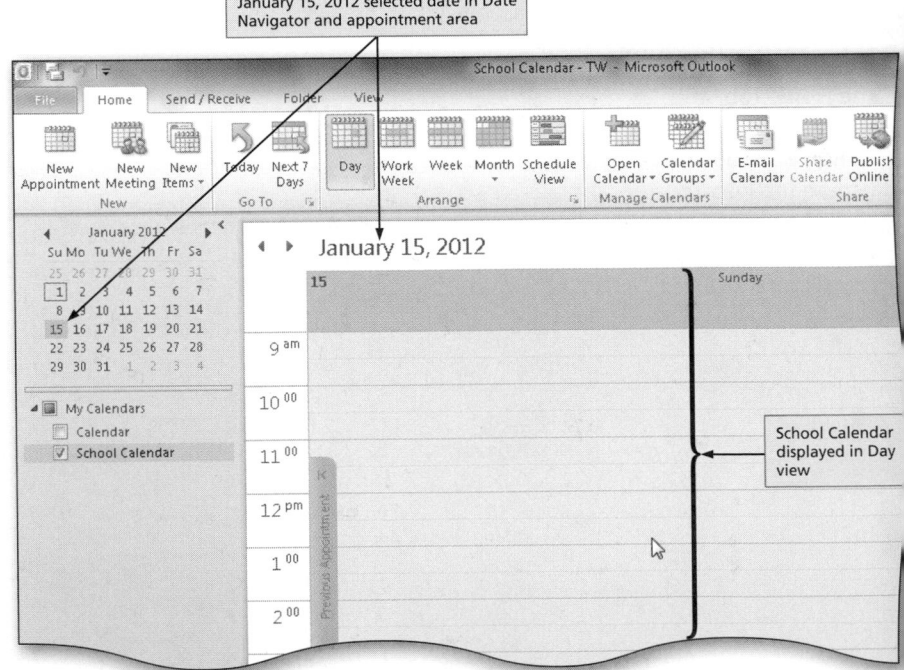

Figure 2–10

Other Ways
1. Press CTRL+G

To Display the Calendar in Work Week View

In Outlook, you can display several calendar days at once so that you can see multiple appointments at the same time. **Work Week view** shows five workdays (Monday through Friday) in a columnar style. Hours that are not part of the default workday (8:00 AM – 5:00 PM) appear shaded when viewing the calendar in Day, Work Week, and Week view. The following step displays the calendar in Work Week view.

1
- Click the Work Week button (Home tab | Arrange group) to display the work week in the appointment area for the selected date (Figure 2–11).

🔍 **Experiment**
- Scroll up and down in Day view to see how the color changes to reflect hours outside the default workday.

Why is Monday, January 16, through Friday, January 20, highlighted on the Date Navigator?

The calendar days displayed in the appointment area are highlighted on the Date Navigator.

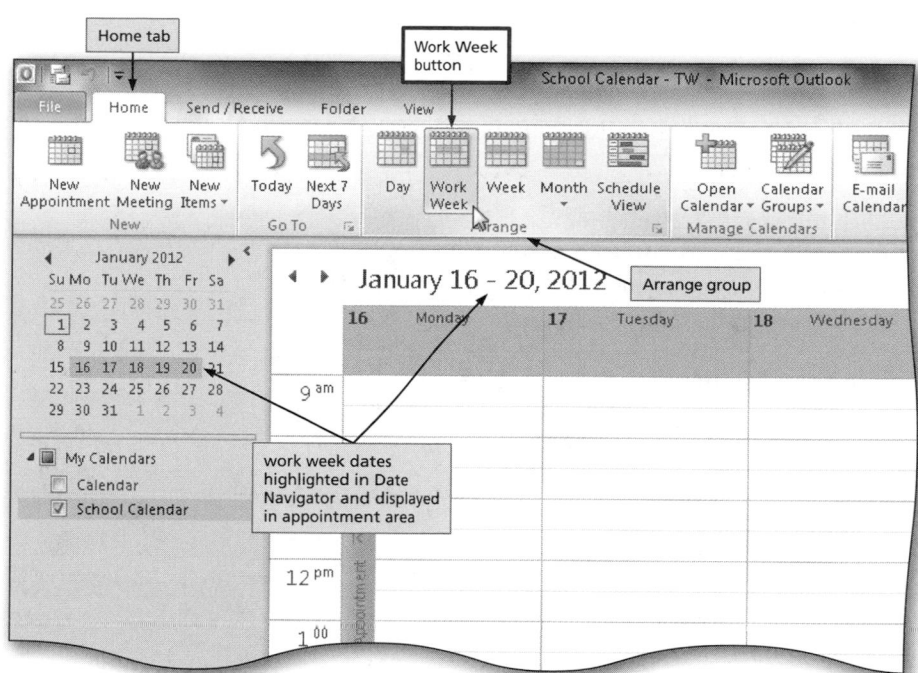

Figure 2–11

To Display the Calendar in Week View

The advantage of displaying a calendar in **Week view** is to see how many appointments are scheduled for any given week, including weekends. In Week view, the seven days of the selected week appear in the appointment area. The following step displays the calendar in Week view.

1
- Click the Week button (Home tab | Arrange group) to display the full week, including weekends, in the appointment area (Figure 2–12).

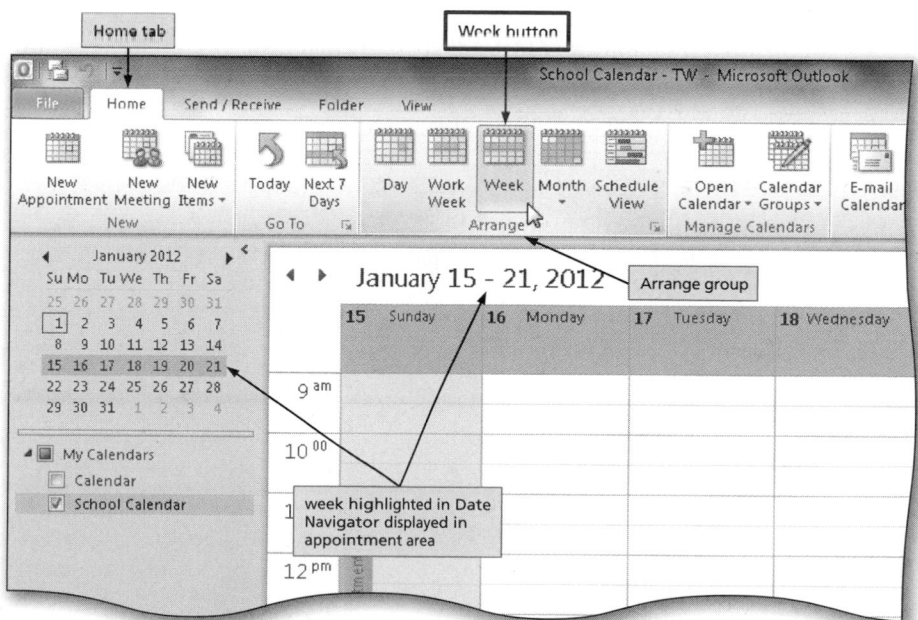

Figure 2–12

To Display the Calendar in Month View

Month view resembles a standard monthly calendar page and displays a schedule for an entire month. Appointments are listed in each date in the calendar. The following step displays the calendar in Month view.

- Click the Month button (Home tab | Arrange group) to display one full month in the appointment area (Figure 2–13).

 Experiment

- By default, Month view displays dates from the beginning to the end of a calendar month. To select several weeks across two calendar months, click the Date Navigator and then drag to select the weeks you want to view.

Q&A

What if I accidentally click the Month button arrow instead of the Month button?

Click the Month button arrow again to remove the list of options displayed when you clicked the Month button arrow.

Figure 2–13

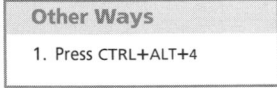

1. Press CTRL+ALT+4

To Display the Calendar in Schedule View

Schedule View, new to Outlook 2010, displays multiple calendars at the same time in a horizontal layout of the daily calendar. The following steps display the default Calendar and the School Calendar in Schedule View so that you can check for overlapping items.

- Click Calendar in the Navigation Pane to place a check mark in the check box and to display both the Calendar and the School Calendar in the appointment area (Figure 2–14).

Q&A

Why are both calendars displayed in Month view?

Outlook displays the newly displayed Calendar in the same view that the existing Calendar was displayed. In this case, the School Calendar was displayed in Month view, so the default Calendar also is displayed in Month view.

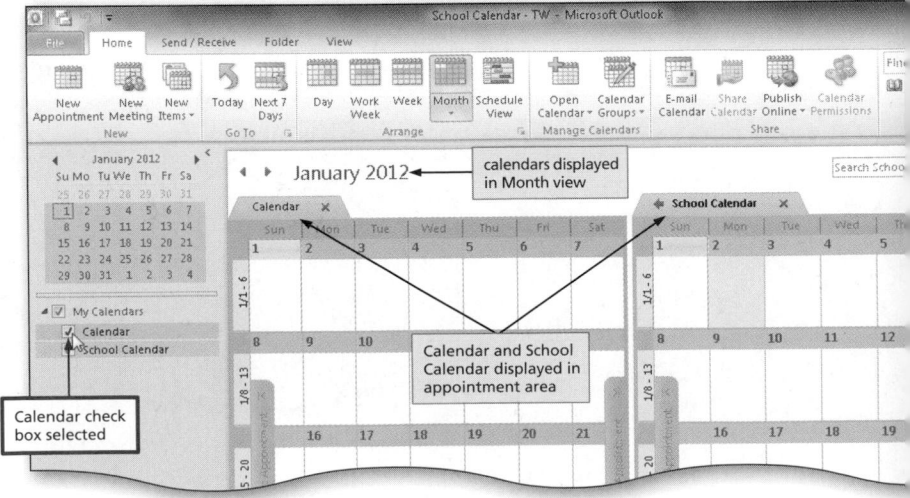

Figure 2–14

②

- Click the Schedule View button (Home tab | Arrange group) to display both calendars in Schedule View (Figure 2–15).

Why does Schedule View show a single day instead of multiple days?

Schedule View only displays one day at a time.

What does the dark blue shaded area in the calendar represent?

The dark blue shaded area represents the selected time in Day view.

Figure 2–15

Other Ways

1. Press CTRL+ALT+5

Creating and Editing Appointments

Recall that every item you schedule in Outlook Calendar begins as an appointment. In Outlook, you easily can change an appointment to an event or a meeting. This section describes how to navigate to a specific date, schedule a dental visit as a one-time appointment, and enter classes in a class schedule as recurring appointments, starting with January 1, 2012.

Determine what you need to schedule.
As mentioned previously, you can schedule appointments, events, and meetings using Outlook Calendar. You can create appointments either directly in the appointment area or use the New Appointment dialog box. One method may be more efficient than the other, depending on the item you are scheduling and how much detail you need to enter for the calendar item you are creating.

Plan Ahead

Creating Appointments in the Appointment Area

A one-time appointment, such as a lunch date, doctor's appointment, or conference call, is an appointment that occurs only once on a calendar. A recurring appointment, such as a class in a class schedule, repeats on the calendar at regular intervals. Appointments can be created in two ways: using the appointment area, where you enter the appointment directly in the appropriate time slot, or the Untitled – Appointment window, where you can enter more specific details about the appointment. This chapter examines each method.

BTW

Keeping Appointments Private
Besides setting the status of an appointment, you can designate an appointment as private so that other users cannot view or access the appointment. Use the Private button (Calendar Tools Appointment tab | Tags group) to mark an appointment as private.

To Display One Calendar in Day View

When working with your school schedule, you may want to display only the calendar with which you are working. The following step closes the Calendar folder and displays the School Calendar folder in Day view.

1

- In the My Calendars pane, click Calendar to remove the check mark from the check box, remove the Calendar from the appointment area, and display the School Calendar in Day view (Figure 2–16).

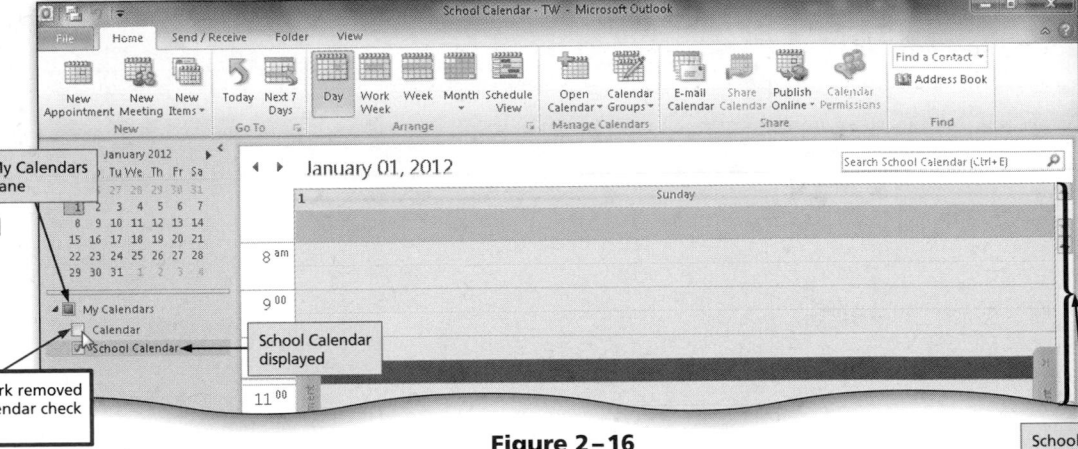

Figure 2–16

To Create a One-Time Appointment Using the Appointment Area

When you click a day on the calendar in the Navigation Pane, Outlook displays the calendar for the date selected in Day view in the appointment area. Day view shows a daily view of a specific date in half-hour increments. As mentioned previously, one way to create an appointment is to enter the information directly in the appointment area. The following steps create a one-time conference call appointment on January 16 using the appointment area.

1

- If necessary, click the Day button (Home tab | Arrange group) to display the daily view of the calendar in the appointment area.

- Click 16 in the January calendar on the Date Navigator to display the selected date in the appointment area (Figure 2–17).

Experiment

- View several dates that are not consecutive by clicking a date in the Date Navigator, holding down the CTRL key, and then clicking additional days.

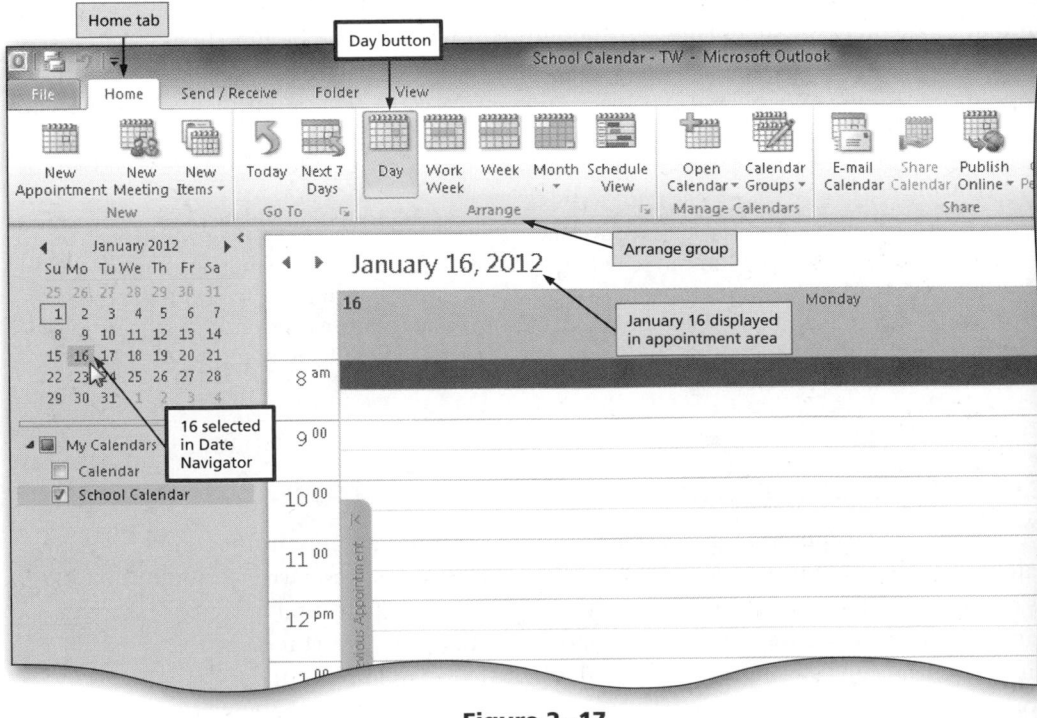

Figure 2–17

2

● Drag to select the three half-hour increments from the 10:00 AM to the 11:30 AM time slots in the appointment area (Figure 2–18).

What if I select more or fewer half-hour increments?

If you incorrectly select the appointment time, simply repeat this step to try again.

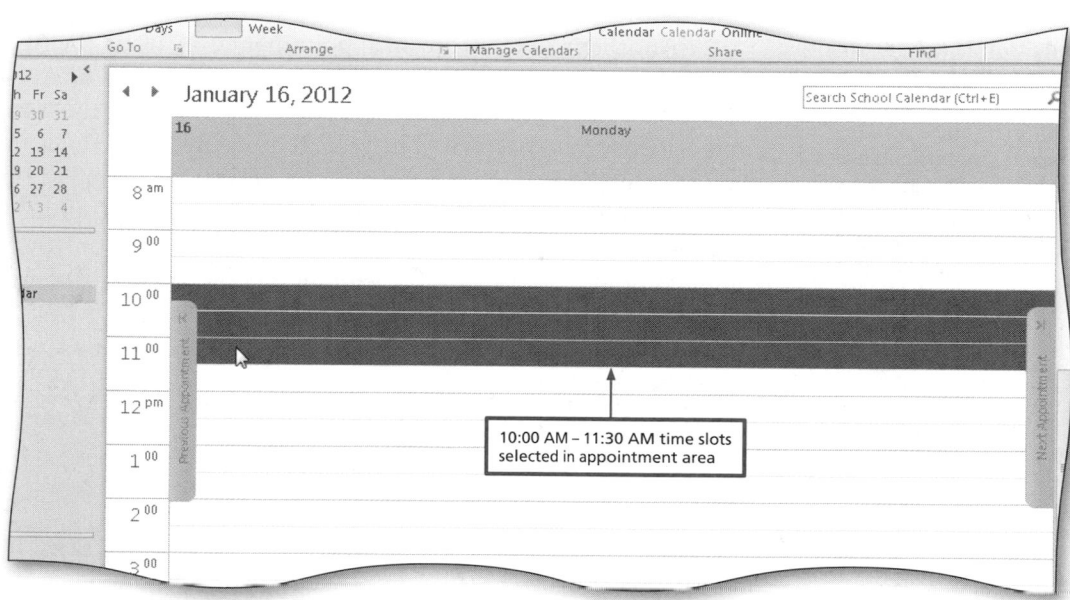

Figure 2–18

3

● Type **Conference Call** as the appointment subject and then press the ENTER key to enter the conference call appointment in the appointment area (Figure 2–19).

What are the white dots on the selected appointment, in this case, the conference call?

The white dots indicate that the appointment is selected.

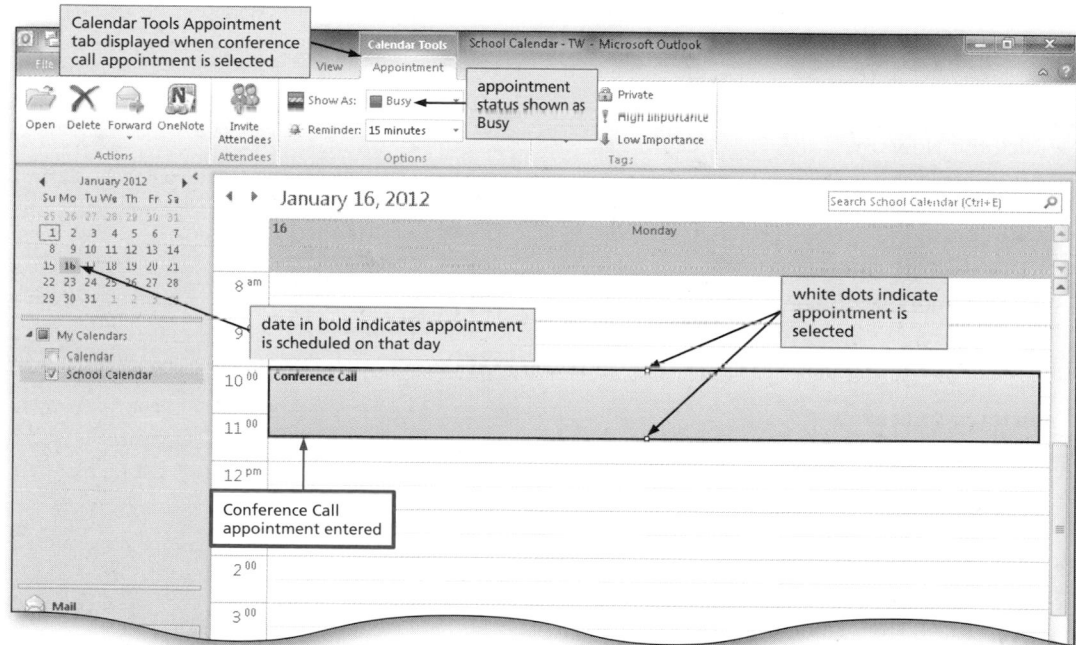

Figure 2–19

Do I have to save the appointment entry?

No, the appointment entry is saved automatically when you press the ENTER key.

Why is Busy showing in the Show As box?

When you create an appointment, Outlook assigns your time as busy by default.

Why does the date of the conference call appointment appear in bold on the Date Navigator?

Outlook displays in bold any date with a time allocated on your calendar as busy to indicate that you have something scheduled on that day.

Other Ways

1. Select beginning time slot, hold down SHIFT, click ending time slot, type appointment name, press ENTER.

Creating Appointments Using the Appointment Window

Another way to create an appointment is by using the Appointment window, which lets you enter more details than the appointment area. The Appointment window provides additional options for entering an appointment, such as the location of the appointment and a **recurrence pattern.** The recurrence pattern schedules the Outlook appointment on the calendar at regular intervals for a designated period of time.

Outlook also allows you to configure a **reminder**, similar to an alarm clock reminder, which is an alert window that briefly appears on your screen as a reminder of an upcoming appointment. Depending on how Outlook Calendar is configured, you may hear a chime or other sound as part of the reminder.

Another option when creating an appointment is to set the **appointment status**, which is how the time for a calendar item is marked on your calendar. The default appointment status setting is Busy, as indicated in the previous steps, but you can change the status to more accurately reflect your time.

To Create a One-Time Appointment Using the Appointment Window

You volunteered to work at the annual blood drive from 11:00 AM until 4:00 PM on Tuesday, January 17. Because this appointment has more detailed information than the conference call appointment, you decide to use the Appointment window to create this appointment. The following steps enter the blood drive appointment using the Appointment window.

1

- Click the New Appointment button (Home tab | New group) to open the Untitled – Appointment window.

- If necessary, maximize the appointment window to provide as much room as possible to work in the calendar.

- Type `Volunteer for Blood Drive` in the Subject text box as the appointment subject.

- Press the TAB key to move the insertion point to the Location box (Figure 2–20).

Figure 2–20

Why did the title of the window change from Untitled – Appointment to Volunteer for Blood Drive – Appointment?

The title bar displays the name of the appointment. Because the name of the appointment has changed, the name on the title bar also changes.

2

- Type **Student Activities Center** in the Location text box as the location of the event (Figure 2–21).

Why are the date and time already specified?

When you start to create a new appointment, Outlook configures the start and end times using the time selected in the appointment area.

Figure 2–21

3

- Click the first Start time box arrow to display a calendar for the current month (Figure 2–22).

Figure 2–22

- Click 17 to select the start date, in this case, January 17.

- Click the second Start time box arrow to display a list of time slots (Figure 2–23).

Why did the end time in the first Start time box change to the same date as the end time in the first End time box?

Outlook automatically sets appointments to occur during a single day.

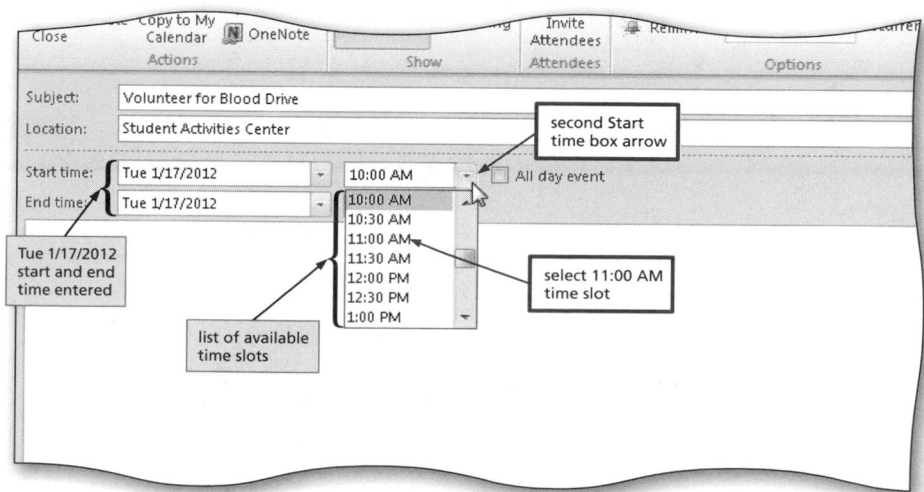

Figure 2–23

5

- Click 11:00 AM to select it as the Start time for the appointment.

- Click the second End time box arrow and then scroll to display 4:00 PM (5 hours) in the list of time slots (Figure 2–24).

Why does the second end time list have a duration next to it?

Outlook automatically sets the duration in half-hour increments next to the end time so that you know how long the appointment will take.

Figure 2–24

6

- Click 4:00 PM (5 hours) to select it as the End time for the appointment (Figure 2–25).

Why did I not have to specify an End date for the appointment?

When you specify a Start date, Outlook uses the same date for the End date by default.

Figure 2–25

Other Ways
1 CTRL+SHIFT+A

Setting Appointment Options

One advantage to creating appointments using the Appointment window is the ability to set options for an appointment.

Plan Ahead

Set Calendar item options.
When creating items on your calendar, you can set a number of options that determine how the Calendar is displayed and how it handles an appointment. Table 2–2 lists the options available when creating an item on your calendar. Consider setting one or all of the options shown in Table 2–2.

Table 2–2 Main Elements of the Calendar Window

Option	Description
Show As	Indicates your availability on a specific date and time; if you want to show others your availability when they schedule a meeting with you during a specific time, this must be set accurately
Reminder	Alerts you at a specific time prior to the item's occurrence
Recurrence	If an item on your calendar repeats at regularly scheduled intervals, set the recurring options so that you only have to enter the item once on your calendar

Outlook provides four options for indicating your availability on the Calendar, as described in Table 2–3.

Table 2–3 Calendar Item Status Options

Calendar Item Status Options	Description
Free	Shows time with a white bar in Day, Week, Work Week, or Month view
Tentative	Shows time with a slashed bar in Day, Week, Work Week, or Month view
Busy	Shows time in Day, Week, Work Week, or Month view
Out of Office	Shows time with a purple bar in Day, Week, Work Week, or Month view

The following pages illustrate how to set these various appointment options.

To Change the Status of an Appointment

To make sure your time is displayed accurately on the calendar, you change the appointment status from the default of Busy to Out of Office, meaning you are not in the office for the time of the blood drive appointment. The following steps change the status of an appointment.

- Click the Show As box arrow (Appointment tab | Options group) to display the list of appointment status options (Figure 2–26).

Figure 2–26

2

• Click Out of Office to change the appointment status from Busy to Out of Office (Figure 2–27).

Figure 2–27

To Set a Reminder for the Appointment

With the start and end date and time for the blood drive appointment set and the appointment status selected you want to schedule a reminder so that you do not forget the appointment. Recall that a reminder works similar to an alarm clock with options such as snooze and dismiss. When the reminder is displayed, you also can open the item for further review. The following steps set a 30-minute reminder for the blood drive appointment.

1

• Click the Reminder box arrow (Appointment tab | Options group) to display a list of available reminder intervals (Figure 2–28).

Q&A

What does the Sound option in the reminder list do?

In addition to a visual reminder, Outlook allows you to set an auditory alarm, much like an alarm clock. You can use the default sound or click the Sound option to select your own.

Figure 2–28

2

- Click 30 minutes to set a reminder for 30 minutes prior to the start time of the appointment (Figure 2–29).

Figure 2–29

To Save the Appointment

Recall that appointments created directly in the appointment area are saved when you press the ENTER key. When you create an appointment using the New Appointment window, you must save it manually. The following step saves the Volunteer for Blood Drive – Appointment and closes the Volunteer for Blood Drive – Appointment window.

1

- Click the Save & Close button (Appointment tab | Actions group) to save and close the Volunteer for Blood Drive – Appointment window and place the appointment on the calendar.

- Click 17 on the Date Navigator to display January 17, 2012 in the appointment area (Figure 2–30).

Do I have to click the date in the appointment area when I save an appointment?

It is not necessary to click the date in the appointment area, but it is good practice to verify your appointments to ensure the details are accurate.

Figure 2–30

To Create the Remaining One-Time Appointments and View the Calendar

BTW

Searching for Calendar Items
To find a calendar item, click the Search Calendar text box in the upper-right corner of the calendar. Type a word or phrase contained in the calendar item you are seeking. Items that contain the text you typed are listed with the search text highlighted. When you are finished, click the Close Search button (Search Tools Search tab | Close group).

With the Volunteer for Blood Drive appointment created, the next step is to add the other appointments listed in Table 2–4, which shows appointments for various student activities on campus. The following steps create the remaining one-time appointments in the Appointment window.

Table 2–4 Additional One-Time Appointments						
Subject	Location	Start Date	Start Time	End Time	Show As	Reminder
Interview for student activity position	Activity Center	1/18/2012	9:00 AM	10:30 AM	Out of Office	10 minutes
International Student Fundraiser	RFB 400	1/19/2012	11:00 AM	12:00 PM	Tentative	30 minutes
Internship Opportunities	DH 100	1/20/2012	9:30 AM	11:00 AM	Tentative	5 minutes

1 Click the New Appointment button (Home tab | New group) to open the Untitled – New Appointment window.

2 Enter the subject for the first appointment in Table 2–4 in the Subject text box and then press the TAB key to move the insertion point to the Location text box.

3 Enter the location for the first appointment in Table 2–4.

4 Click the first Start time box arrow to display a calendar of available dates, and then click the date listed in Table 2–4 to select it.

5 Click the second Start time box arrow to display a list of time slots, and then click the time the class starts.

6 Click the second End time box arrow to display a list of available time slots and then select the time the class ends.

7 Click the Show As box arrow option to change the appointment status for the first appointment as indicated in Table 2–4.

8 Click the Reminder box arrow to change the reminder for the first appointment as indicated in Table 2–4.

9 Click the Save & Close button (Appointment tab | Actions group) to save the appointment.

10 Repeat Steps 1 through 9 for the two remaining one-time appointments in Table 2–4.

11 Click the Week button (Home tab | Arrange group) to view the completed calendar (Figure 2–31).

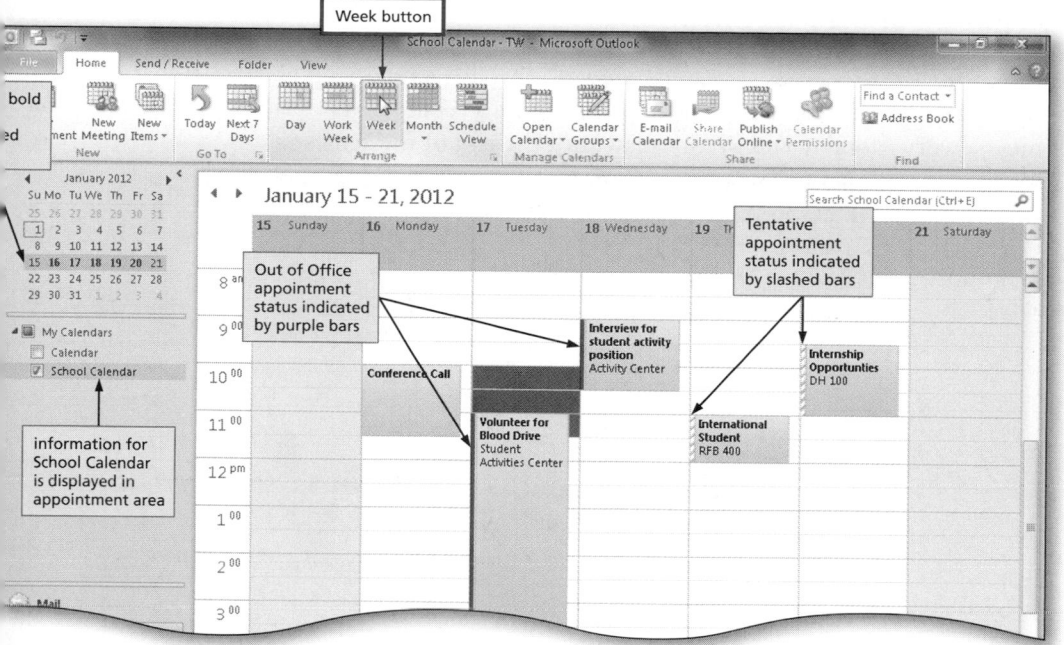

Figure 2–31

Creating Recurring Appointments

Many appointments are **recurring appointments**, meaning they happen at regular intervals for a designated period of time. For example, a class held every Monday and Wednesday from 9:00 AM to 11:00 AM is a recurring appointment. Your college classes occur two times per week, at regular weekly intervals during the semester, and entering these recurring appointments for each occurrence during the semester would be time-consuming. You want to add the classes to the calendar as recurring appointments so that you can keep track of time throughout the entire semester. Adding these classes as recurring appointments enables you to enter the appointment information one time, with it automatically recurring at a set interval for a specified period of time. You will create the appointment only once and configure the recurrence pattern to designate the rate of recurrence, in this case weekly, and on what day(s) of the week the class occurs.

To Create an Appointment Using the Appointment Window

The following steps create an appointment for the Introduction to Computers class.

- Click the New Appointment button (Home tab | New group) to open the Untitled – Appointment window.

- Type `Intro to Computers` in the Subject text box and then press the TAB key to move the insertion point to the Location text box.

- Type `DH 302` in the Location text box as the location for the class.

- Click the Start time box arrow to display a calendar of available dates, and then click 23 to select Mon 1/23/2012 as the day the first class meets.

- Click the second Start time box arrow to display a list of time slots, and then click 10:00 AM as the time the class starts.

- Click the second End time box arrow to display a list of available time slots, scroll through the list, and then click 12:00 PM (2 hours) to set the End time to 12:00 PM.

To Set Recurrence Options for an Appointment

Now that the appointment for the first class is created, you will establish a recurring pattern so that you do not have to enter the class schedule every week. The following steps configure a recurring pattern for the Introduction to Computers class, which meets every Monday and Wednesday until the end of the semester.

- Click the Recurrence button (Appointment tab | Options group) to display the Appointment Recurrence dialog box (Figure 2–32).

Figure 2–32

- If necessary, in the Recurrence pattern area, click Weekly (Appointment Recurrence dialog box) to set the recurrence pattern.

- In the Recur every text box (Appointment Recurrence dialog box), type 1 if it does not already appear in the text box to schedule the frequency of the recurrence pattern.

- Click Wednesday to place a check mark in the check box and to schedule the class two times per week (Mondays and Wednesdays) (Figure 2–33).

Q&A
Why is the Monday check box already selected in the Recurrence pattern area?

Monday is already selected because that was the date you entered for the day the class starts. If the class started on Tuesday, then the Tuesday check box would be selected when you set the recurrence pattern.

Figure 2–33

Managing Calendars **Outlook Chapter 2** **OUT** 73

Why does the Start box in the 'Range of recurrence' area contain a date?

When you display the Appointment Recurrence dialog box, Outlook automatically sets the range of recurrence with the date the appointment starts.

- In the 'Range of recurrence' area, click End by and then press the TAB key two times to select the End by box.

- Type 5/9/2012 as the day the class ends to replace the displayed end date with a new date (Figure 2–34).

What if I do not know the end date, but I know how many times the class meets?

You can click the End after option button and then type the number of times the class meets in the End after text box.

Figure 2–34

- Click the OK button to close the Appointment Recurrence dialog box and set the recurrence pattern (Figure 2–35).

Why is the value in the Reminder box (Appointment Series tab | Options group) set for 15 minutes?

The default reminder time for all calendar items is 15 minutes.

Why did the Appointment tab change to the Appointment Series tab?

When you set a recurring pattern, the tab name changes to reflect a series.

Figure 2–35

To Set a Reminder and Show As Options for an Appointment

Next, you will set a reminder 30 minutes prior to the class and mark your time as Out of Office because you will be in class during this time. The following steps set the Show As and Reminder options.

1 Click the Show As box arrow (Appointment Series tab | Options group) to display the list of appointment status options.

2 Click Out of Office to change the appointment status from Busy to Out of Office.

3 Click the Reminder box arrow (Appointment Series tab | Options group) to display a list of available reminder intervals.

4 Click 30 minutes to set a reminder for 30 minutes prior to the start time of the appointment (Figure 2–36).

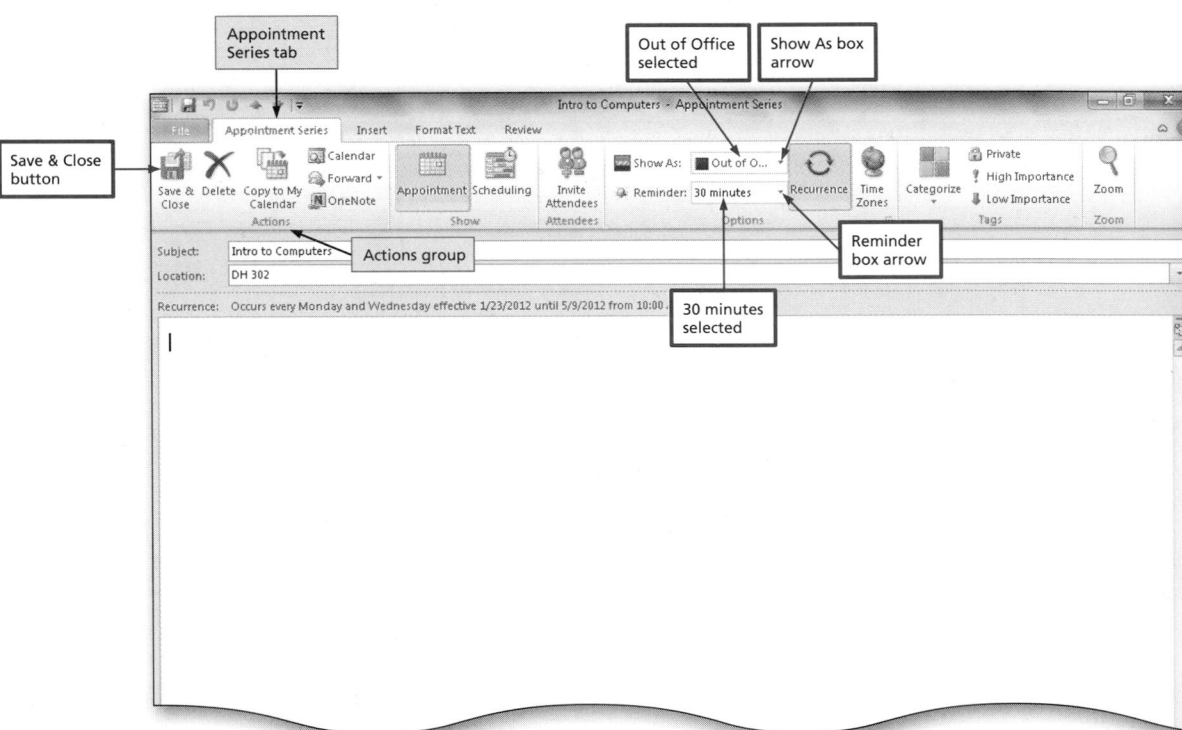

Figure 2–36

To Save the Appointment

With all the information about the Introduction to Computers class entered, you must save the appointment. The following steps save the Intro to Computers – Appointment Series and close the window.

1 Click the Save & Close button (Appointment Series tab | Actions group) to save the recurring appointment on the calendar and close the window.

2 Click 23 on the Date Navigator to display the January 23, 2012 recurring appointment in the appointment area in Week view (Figure 2–37).

Q&A Do I need to display the appointment after I save it?

No, this step was included to view the appointment on the calendar.

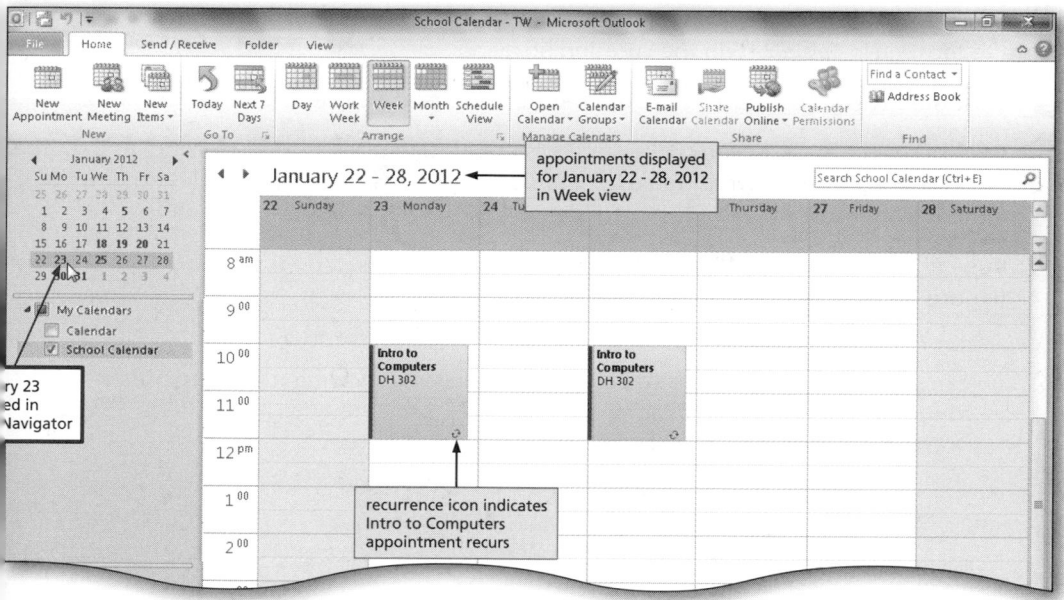

Figure 2–37

To Create the Recurring Appointments

With the Intro to Computers class appointment series created, the next step is to create recurring class appointments for the remainder of your class schedule using the appointment information in Table 2–5. The following steps create the remaining class schedule.

Table 2–5 Recurring Appointments

Appointment (Class)	Location	Start Date	End Date	Start Time	End Time	Show As	Reminder	Recurrence
Sociology	HRB 203	1/24/2012	Set in Recurrence	8:00 AM	10:00 AM	Out of Office	30 minutes	Weekly, every Tuesday and Thursday, end by Thursday, 5/3/2012
English Literature	Library 105	1/24/2012	Set in Recurrence	11:00 AM	1:00 PM	Out of Office	15 minutes	Weekly, every Tuesday and Thursday; end by Thursday, 5/3/2012

1 If necessary, click the Day button (Home tab | Arrange group) to display the daily view of the calendar in the appointment area.

2 Click 24 in the January calendar on the Date Navigator to display the selected date in the appointment area.

3 Drag to select a two-hour increment from the 8:00 AM to the 10:00 AM time slot in the appointment area.

4 Type `Sociology` as the appointment subject and then press the ENTER key to enter the appointment in the appointment area.

5 Select the appointment to display the Calendar Tools Appointment tab on the Ribbon.

6 Select the Show as box arrow to display the list of appointment status options and then click the option shown Table 2–5.

7 Select the Reminder box arrow to display the list of time slots and then click the option shown in Table 2–5.

8 Double-click the Sociology appointment to open the Appointment window, and then type the location in Table 2–5 in the Location box.

9 Click the Save & Close button to close the Appointment window.

10 Click the Recurrence button (Calendar Tools Appointment tab | Options group) and set the recurrence pattern shown in Table 2–5, and then click the OK button to close the Appointment Recurrence window.

11 Repeat Steps 1 through 10 to add the information in the second row of Table 2–5 (Figure 2–38).

Q&A

What if I have appointments that recur other than weekly?

You can set daily, weekly, monthly, or yearly recurrence patterns in the Appointment Recurrence dialog box. A recurring appointment can be set to have no end date, to end after certain number of occurrences, or to end by a certain date.

Figure 2–38

Using Natural Language Phrasing

In the previous steps, you entered dates and times in the Appointment window using standard numeric entries, such as 1/31/2012. You also can specify appointment dates and times using natural language. A **natural language phrase** is a phrase closely resembling how people speak during normal conversation. For example, you can type a phrase, such as "next Tuesday," "two weeks from yesterday," or a single word, such as "midnight," and Outlook will calculate the correct date and time, relative to the current date and time on the computer's system clock.

In addition to these natural language phrases, Outlook can convert abbreviations and ordinal numbers into complete words and dates. For example, you can type "Feb" instead of "February" or "the first of May" instead of "5/1". Outlook's Calendar also can convert words such as "yesterday" and "tomorrow" and the names of holidays that occur on the same date each year, such as Valentine's Day. Table 2–6 lists various natural language options.

Table 2–6 Natural Language Options

Category	Examples
Dates Spelled Out	• July twenty-third, March 29th, first of December • This Fri, next Sat, two days from now • Three weeks ago, next week • One month from today
Times Spelled Out	• Noon, midnight • Nine o'clock AM, five-twenty • 7 PM
Descriptions of Times and Dates	• Now • Yesterday, today, tomorrow • Next, last
Holidays	• Cinco de Mayo • Christmas Day, Christmas Eve • Halloween • Independence Day • New Year's Day, New Year's Eve • St. Patrick's Day • Valentine's Day • Veteran's Day
Formulas for dates and times	3/14/2012 + 12d converts the date to 3/26/2012; use *d* for day, *m* for month, or *y* or year and add that amount of time to any date

To Enter an Appointment Date and Time Using Natural Language Phrases

You signed up for a college trip to New York this coming Saturday and need to enter the trip information on your calendar. Buses leave from the front parking lot at 7:00 AM and will return by 11:00 PM the same day. The following steps create an appointment using natural language phrases for the date and time of the New York trip.

- Click the New Appointment button (Home tab | New group) to open the Untitled – Appointment window.

- Type **New York Trip** in the Subject text box, and then press the TAB key to move the insertion point to the Location text box.

- Type **Bus pickup in front parking lot** in the Location text box, and then press the TAB key to select the first Start time box (Figure 2–39).

Figure 2–39

2

- Type **next saturday** in the Start time box to enter the start date.

- Press the TAB key to select the second Start time box.

- Type **seven am** as the time in the second Start time box to enter the start time (Figure 2–40).

Q&A
Do I need to use proper capitalization when entering natural language phrases?

No, Outlook converts the text to the proper date or time, regardless of the capitalization.

Q&A
Why did the text change to a numeric date when I pressed the TAB key?

When you enter the date using natural language phrasing, Outlook converts typed text to the correct date format when you click or move the insertion point to a different box.

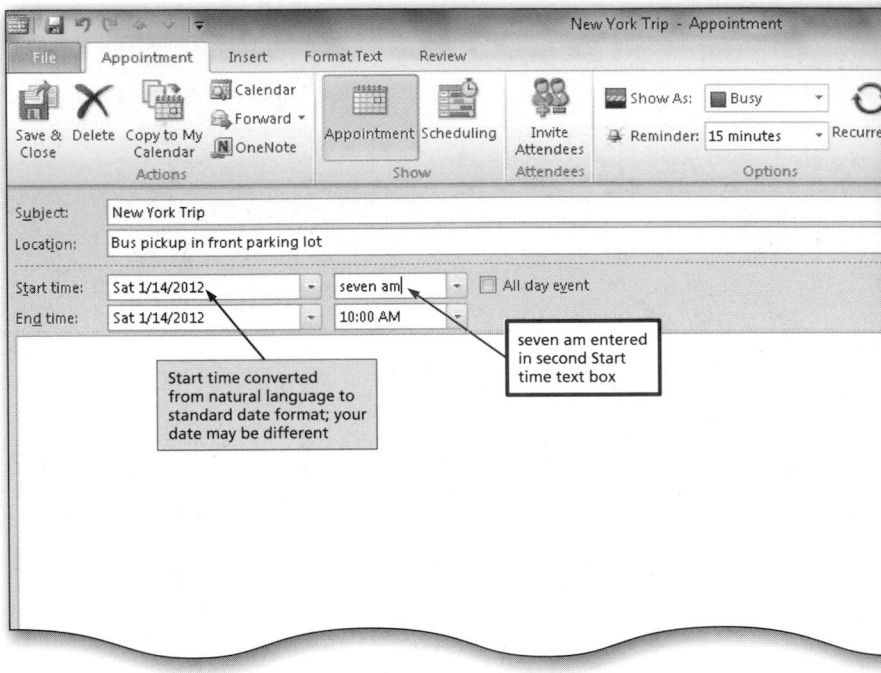

Figure 2–40

3

- Press the TAB key two times to convert the Start time entry to 7:00 AM and to select the entry in the second End time box.

- Type **eleven pm** as the time in the second End time box (Figure 2–41).

Figure 2–41

4

• Press the ENTER key to convert the end time text to 11:00 PM.

• Click the Save & Close button (Appointment tab | Actions group) to save the appointment and close the window.

• Scroll to find the date that corresponds to next Saturday's date (Figure 2–42).

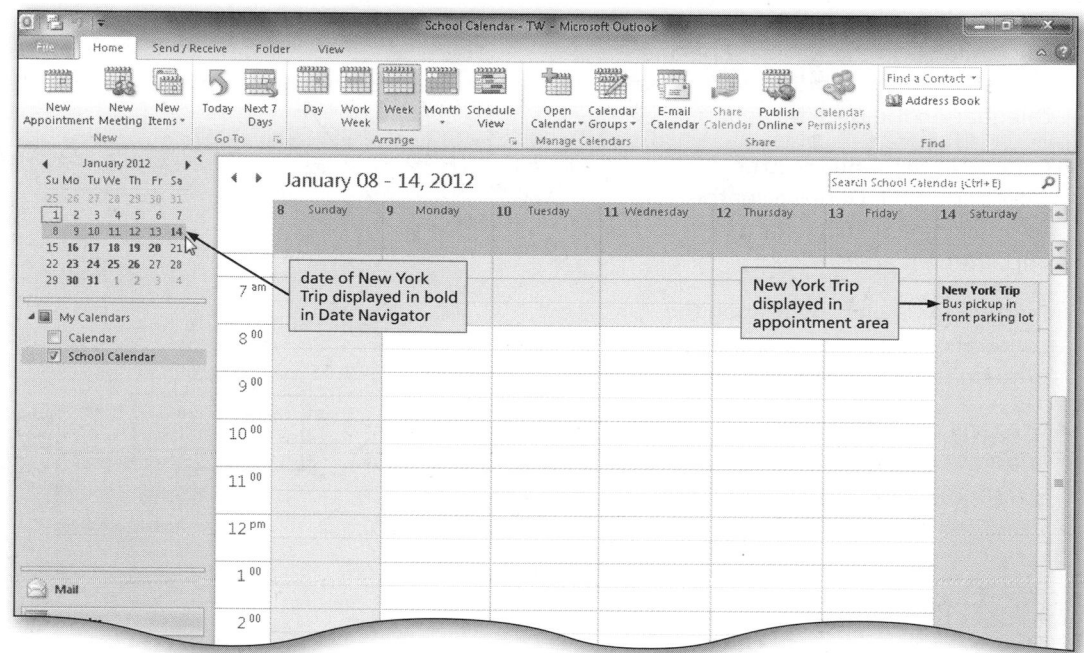

Figure 2–42

Why is it important to verify the appointment?

It is important to verify that you did not make inadvertent mistakes while adding the appointment to your calendar. Errors might cause you to miss an important appointment.

Why is the New York trip appointment scheduled for January 14 and not January 7?

In Outlook, next Saturday means the Saturday in the next full week. This Saturday means the Saturday in the current week.

Editing Appointments

Schedules often need to be rearranged, and Outlook provides several ways to edit appointments. You can change the subject and location by clicking the appointment and editing the information directly in the appointment area, or by double-clicking the appointment and making corrections using the Appointment window. You can specify whether all occurrences in a series of recurring appointments need to be changed, or a single occurrence should be altered.

To Move an Appointment to a Different Time on the Same Day

Outlook provides several ways to move appointments. Suppose, for instance, that you cannot attend the conference call appointment at 10:00 AM on Monday, January 16, 2012. The appointment needs to be rescheduled to 1:00 PM for the same amount of time (two hours, in this case). Instead of deleting and then retyping the appointment, you can drag it to a new time slot. The following step moves the conference call appointment to a new time slot.

1

- If necessary, click a scroll arrow on the Calendar in the Navigation Pane until January 2012 is displayed in the calendar on the Date Navigator.

- Click 16 in the January 2012 calendar on the Date Navigator to display the selected date in the appointment area.

- Position the mouse pointer on the conference call appointment to prepare to move the appointment.

- Drag the conference call appointment to the 1:00 PM time slot on the same day to reschedule the appointment (Figure 2–43).

Other Ways

1. Double-click appointment, change time
2. Press CTRL+O, change time

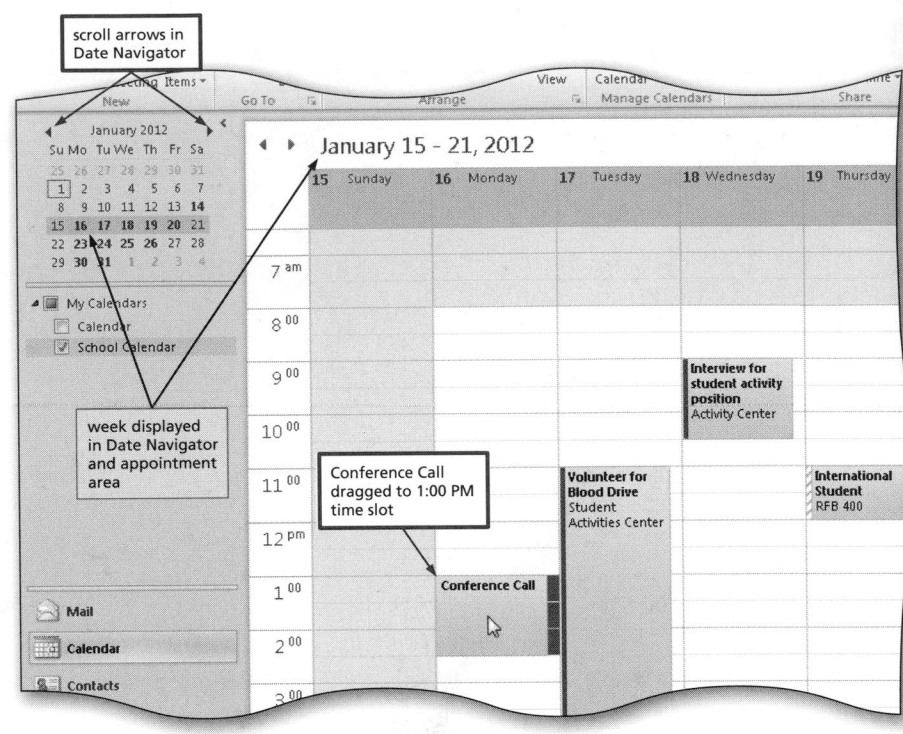

Figure 2–43

To Move an Appointment to a Different Date

If you are moving an appointment to a new date but remaining in the same time slot, you can drag the appointment to the new date on the Date Navigator. The following step moves an appointment to a new date in the same time slot.

1

- Drag the selected appointment on January 16, 2012 to the 25 in the January 2012 calendar on the Date Navigator and then release the mouse button to move the appointment to a new date (Figure 2–44).

Figure 2–44

To Move an Appointment to a Different Month

The blood drive, originally scheduled for January 17, 2012, has been rescheduled to February 3, 2012. To move an appointment to another month, you must open the Appointment window. The following steps open the Volunteer for Blood Drive appointment and move it to February 3, 2012.

1
- Click 17 in the January 2012 calendar on the Date Navigator to display the selected date in the appointment area (Figure 2–45).

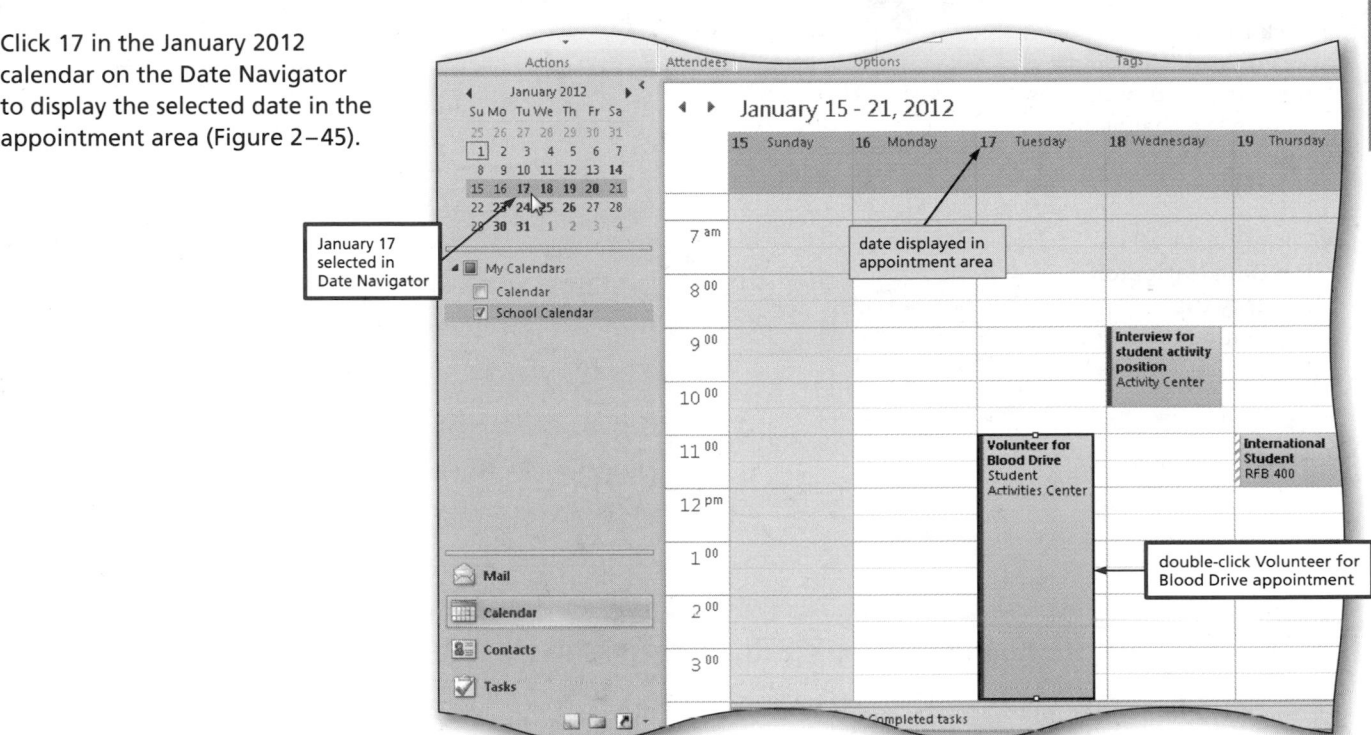

Figure 2–45

2
- Double-click the Volunteer for Blood Drive appointment in the appointment area to open the appointment window.

- Click the first Start time box arrow to display the calendar for selecting a start date.

- Click the right scroll arrow to display the calendar for February 2012 (Figure 2–46).

Figure 2–46

- Click 3 in the February calendar to display the selected date in both the first Start time and first End time boxes.

- Click the Save & Close button (Appointment tab | Actions group) to save the change to the appointment and close the window.

- Click February 3 in the Date Navigator to verify the appointment change (Figure 2–47).

Other Ways

1. Click appointment, press CTRL+O, set appointment options, click Save & Close

Figure 2–47

To Delete a Single Occurrence of a Recurring Appointment

Appointments sometimes are canceled and must be deleted from the schedule. For example, the schedule created thus far in this project contains class appointments during the spring semester. The college is closed for Spring Break from April 9 – 13, 2012 and no classes will meet during that time. The classes scheduled during Spring Break need to be deleted. The following steps delete only the classes scheduled during Spring Break.

- Click the right scroll arrow on the Date Navigator until April 2012 is displayed.

- Click 9 in the April 2012 calendar on the Date Navigator to display the selected date in the appointment area.

- Click the first appointment to be deleted, Intro to Computers, scheduled for April 9, 2012, to select the appointment and display the Calendar Tools Appointment Series tab (Figure 2–48).

Figure 2–48

2

• Click the Delete button (Calendar Tools Appointment Series tab | Actions group) to display the Delete menu (Figure 2–49).

Figure 2–49

3

• Click Delete Occurrence on the Delete menu to delete only the selected occurrence from the calendar.

4

• Repeat Steps 1 through 3 to delete the remaining classes from the week of April 9, 2012 (Figure 2–50).

Other Ways

1. Click appointment, press DELETE, click Delete Occurrence, click OK
2. Right–click appointment, click Delete on shortcut menu, click Delete Occurrence, click OK

Figure 2–50

Break Point: If you wish to take a break, this is a good place to do so. To resume at a later time, start Outlook and continue following the steps from this location forward.

Creating and Editing Events

BTW

Adding Holidays to the Calendar
To add holidays to your calendar, click the File tab, click Options, and then click Calendar. In the Calendar Options section, click the Add Holidays button. Your country is selected by default. Click the OK button.

Outlook's Calendar folder allows you to keep track of important events. Recall that events are activities that last 24 hours or longer. Examples of events include conferences, vacations, and holidays. Events can be one-time or recurring. In Outlook, events differ from appointments in one primary way — they do not appear in individual time slots in the appointment area. Instead, when you schedule an event, its description appears in a small banner below the day heading. Similar to an appointment, the event status can be indicated as time that is free, busy, tentative, or out of the office during the event. See Table 2–3 on page OUT 67 for a complete description of these options.

To Create a One-Time Event in the Appointment Window

A Computer Expo is being held at the Convention Center from May 9, 2012 through May 11, 2012 that you want to attend. Because the conference will last for several days, Outlook will schedule the conference as an event. You begin to schedule an event by creating an appointment. Because you are not certain you can attend the event, you decide to show your time as Tentative. The following steps create an event for the convention on the calendar.

1
- Click the New Appointment button (Home tab | New group) to open the Untitled – Appointment window.

- Type **Computer Expo** in the Subject text box, and then press the TAB key to move the insertion point to the Location text box.

- Type **Convention Center** as the location of the event (Figure 2–51).

Figure 2–51

2
- Click the first Start time box arrow to display the Start time calendar.

- Click the right scroll arrow until the May 2012 calendar is displayed.

- Click 9 in the May calendar to display Wed 5/9/2012 as the day the Computer Expo starts.

- Click All day event to place a check mark in the 'All day event' check box and change the appointment to an event (Figure 2–52).

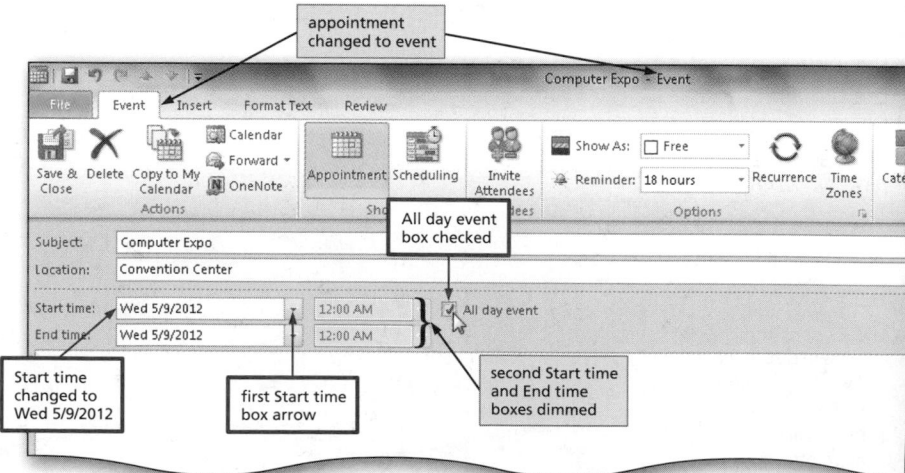

Figure 2–52

Q&A
Can I create an event without using the Untitled – Appointment window?

Yes. Click the New Items button (Home tab | New group) to display a list of items and then click All Day Event to open the Untitled – Event window.

Q&A
Why did the second Start and End time boxes become dimmed when the 'All day event' check box was checked?

An event occurs during a 24-hour time period, so the hourly time slot option is not needed.

3

• Click the first End time box arrow to display the End time calendar.

• Click 11 in the May calendar as the end date to set the end date (Figure 2–53).

Why does the Show As box display the time as Free?

The default Show As appointment status for events is Free because events do not occupy blocks of time during the day on the calendar.

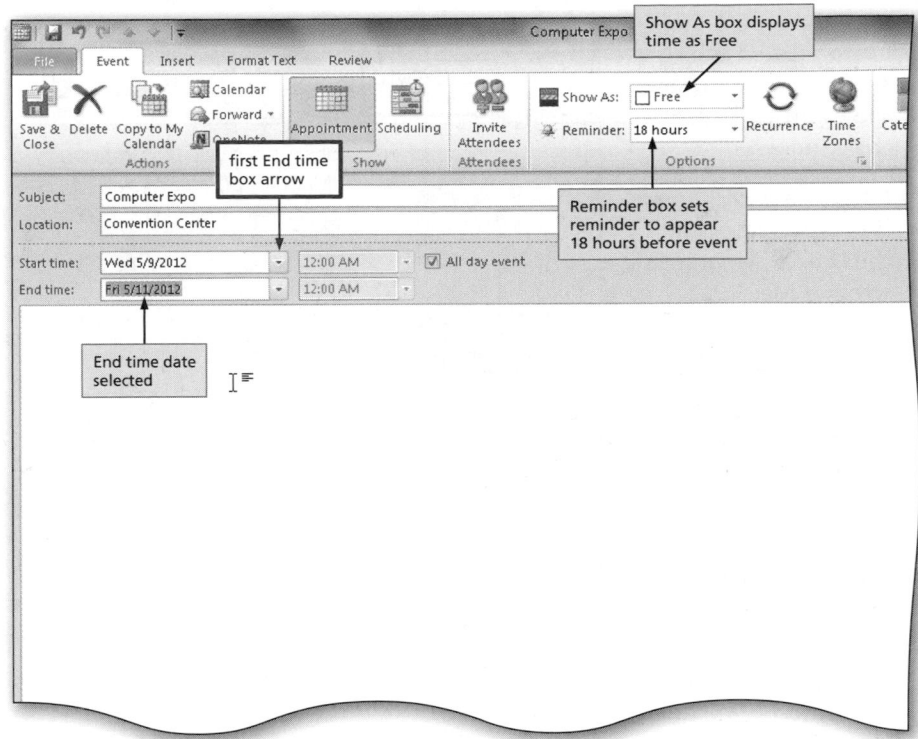

Figure 2–53

4

• Click the Show As box arrow to display a list of appointment status options.

• Click Tentative to set the appointment status.

• Click the Reminder box arrow to display the list of reminder time slots.

• Click None to set no reminder (Figure 2–54).

Why does the appointment area display dashes in the time slots?

When you show the time for an event as Tentative, the appointment displays dashes to indicate the tentative status of the time on your calendar.

Why is the event reminder set for 18 hours?

The default reminder for events is 18 hours.

Figure 2–54

- Click the Save & Close button (Event tab | Actions group) to save the event and close the window.

- If necessary, click the right scroll arrow on the Date Navigator to scroll to May 2012.

- Click 9 to display May 9, 2012 in the appointment area and to view the Computer Expo event banner (Figure 2–55).

Q&A

Why is the Computer Expo event displayed at the top of the Day view of the calendar?

Events do not occupy time slots on the Day view of the calendar, so they appear as banners at the top of the calendar on the day they occur.

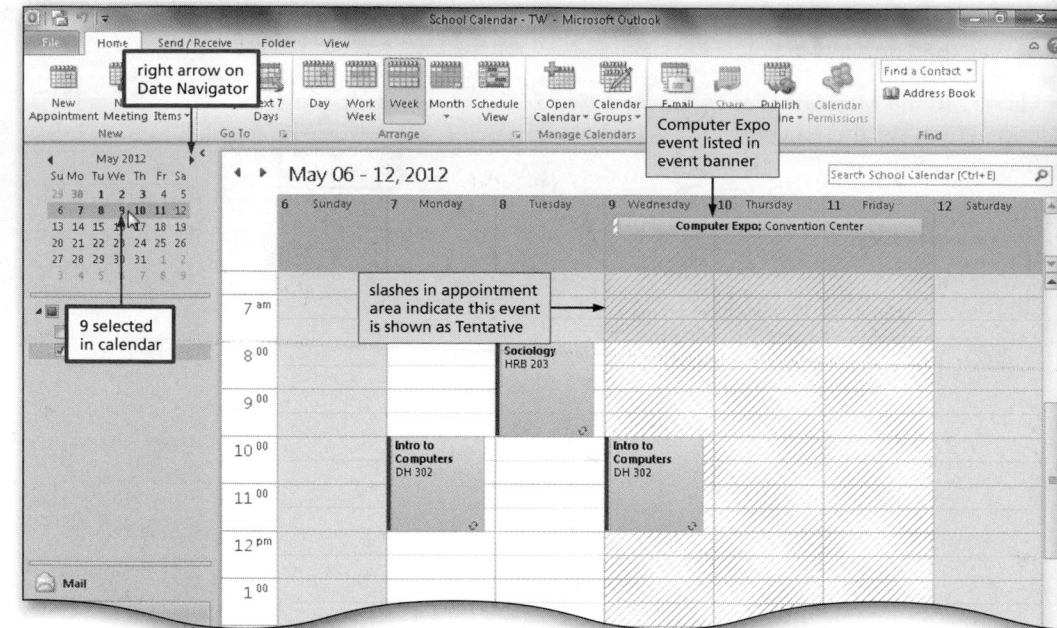

Figure 2–55

To Move a One-Time Event to a New Date and Change the Event Status

The Computer Expo, originally scheduled for May 9, has been postponed to a later date. You need to move the Computer Expo event to a new date. Because you will be off campus for the Computer Expo, you also want the calendar to show your time for the Computer Expo as Out of Office. The following steps move the one-time event to a new date and change the status to Out of Office.

1

- Double-click the Computer Expo event to open the window for the selected event (Figure 2–56).

Figure 2–56

2

- Click the first Start time box arrow to display a calendar.

- Click 11 to change the Computer Expo start time.

- Click the Show As box arrow (Event tab | Options group) to display the list of appointment status options and then click Out of Office to change the event status from Tentative to Out of Office (Figure 2–57).

Figure 2–57

Why did the end time change when I changed the start time?

Outlook automatically calculates the new end time when you change the start time.

3

- Click the Save & Close button (Event tab | Actions group) to save the changes to the selected event and close the window.

- If necessary, click 11 on the Date Navigator to display May 11, 2012 in the appointment area and view the Computer Expo event banner.

Why did the reminder not change when I changed the appointment status?

When the appointment status changes after you create the appointment, the reminder does not automatically change as it does when you create the appointment for the first time.

To Delete a One-Time Event

Because your schedule has changed, you no longer can attend the Computer Expo event. You need to delete the Computer Expo event from your calendar. The following step deletes the Computer Expo event from your calendar.

1

- If necessary, click the Computer Expo event banner in the appointment area of the calendar to select it and display the Calendar Tools Appointment tab on the Ribbon.

- Click the Delete button (Calendar Tools Appointment tab | Actions group) to delete the Computer Expo event from the calendar, and then click the 8:00 AM box for May 11 (Figure 2–58).

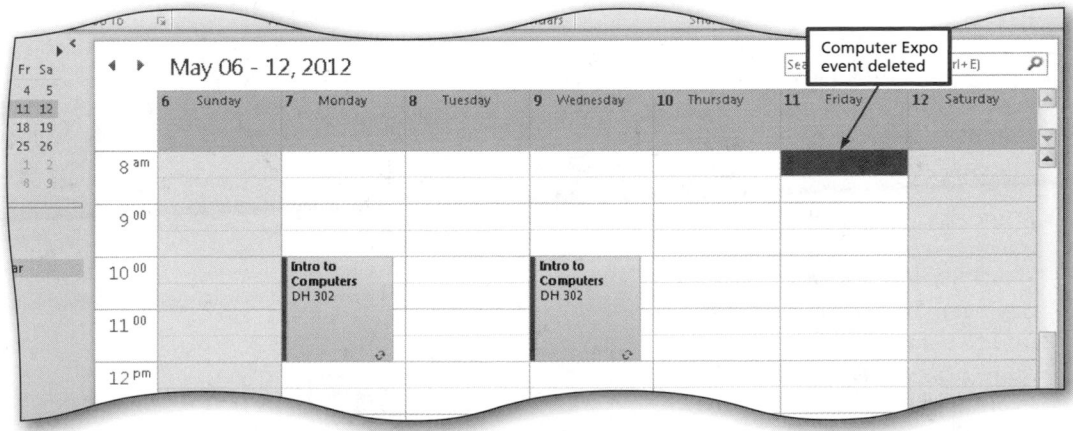

Figure 2–58

Other Ways

1. Select appointment, press DELETE

To Create a Recurring Event Using the Appointment Window

A recurring event is similar to a recurring appointment in that it occurs at regular intervals on your calendar. However, editing a recurring event is slightly different from editing one-time events. You can specify whether all occurrences in a series of recurring events need to be changed or if a single occurrence should be altered.

You want to add your pay schedule to the calendar to keep track of when you receive a paycheck. The following steps create a recurring event for your pay schedule.

- Click Home on the Ribbon to display the Home tab.

- Click the New Appointment button (Home tab | New group) to display the Untitled – Appointment window.

- If necessary, click the Maximize button on the title bar to maximize the window.

- In the Subject text box, type **Payday** as the subject.

Figure 2–59

- Press the TAB key two times to select the time in the first Start time box (Figure 2–59).

Q&A Do I need to add a location to the Payday event?

No, an event such as a payday, birthday, or anniversary does not have a location.

Q&A Why does the title bar indicate that this is an Appointment window?

The title bar and Appointment tab on the Ribbon will display the item as an appointment until you place a check mark in the 'All day event' check box. When you change the appointment to an all-day event, the title bar identifies the item as an event.

- Type **1/6/2012** as the first payday in the first Start time box.

- If necessary, click All day event to place a check mark in the 'All day event' check box and to change the appointment to an event (Figure 2–60).

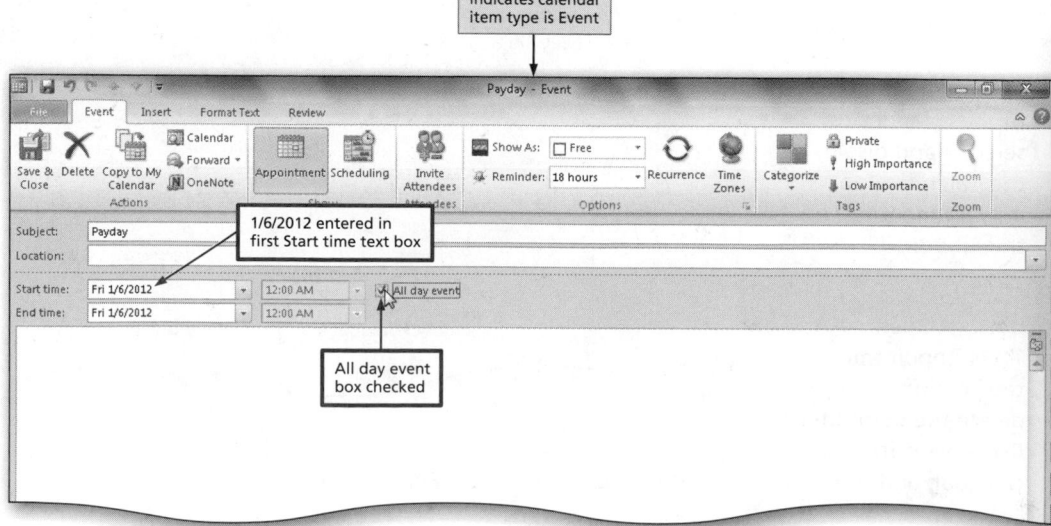

Figure 2–60

3

- Click the Recurrence button (Event tab | Options group) to display the Appointment Recurrence dialog box (Figure 2–61).

Figure 2–61

4

- If necessary, in the Recurrence pattern section, click Weekly (Appointment Recurrence dialog box) to set the Recurrence pattern to Weekly.

- In the Recur every text box, type 2 to have the event appear on the calendar every two weeks.

- If necessary, click the Friday check box to schedule the day for this event.

- If necessary, click any other selected check box in the Recur every section to remove the check marks so that only Friday is selected.

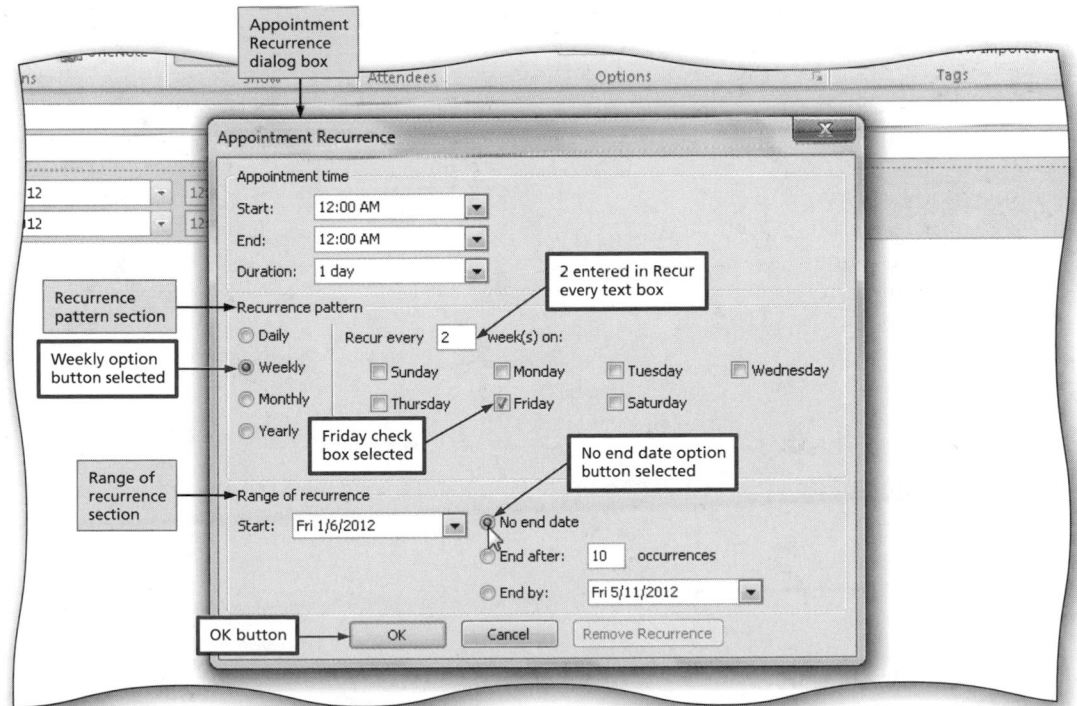

Figure 2–62

- In the 'Range of recurrence' section, click the 'No end date' option button so that the event remains on the calendar indefinitely (Figure 2–62).

5

- Click the OK button to accept the recurrence settings and close the Appointment Recurrence dialog box.

- Click the Reminder box arrow (Recurring Event tab | Options group) to display a list of reminder time slots.

- Click None to remove the reminder from the event (Figure 2–63).

Q&A

Why was the reminder removed from the event?

The Payday event does not require a reminder.

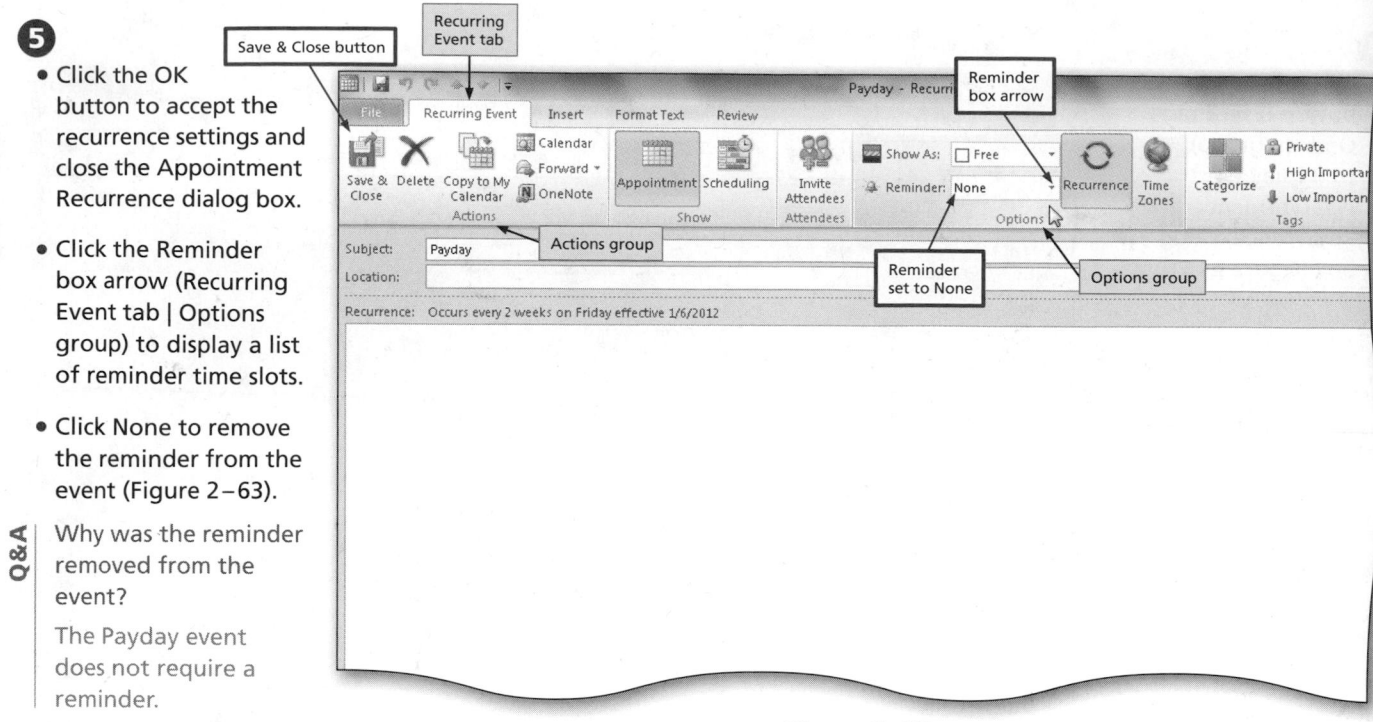

Figure 2–63

6

- Click the Save & Close button (Recurring Event tab | Actions group) to save the event and close the window.

- Click the appropriate scroll arrow on the Date Navigator to display the January 2012 calendar and the Payday event banner in the appointment area (Figure 2–64).

Experiment

- To view more pay dates at one time, click the Month button (Home tab | Arrange group) and then change the view to Week view.

Figure 2–64

To Move a Recurring Event to a Different Day

Your school is changing the day it pays employees from Friday to Thursday. Because this will affect all Payday events in the series, you will change the date in the Payday event series from Friday to Thursday. The following steps change the date for all occurrences in a series.

1

- Click 6 to display January 6, 2012 and the Payday event banner in the appointment area.

- In the appointment area, click the Payday event banner to display commands for changing the appointment series on the Calendar Tools Appointment Series tab (Figure 2–65).

Figure 2–65

2

- Click the Recurrence button (Calendar Tools Appointment Series tab | Options group) to display the Appointment Recurrence dialog box.

- Click Thursday to place a check mark in the check box.

- Click Friday to remove the check mark from the check box.

- Click the Start box arrow in the Range of Recurrence area to change the start date to Thu 1/5/2012 (Figure 2–66).

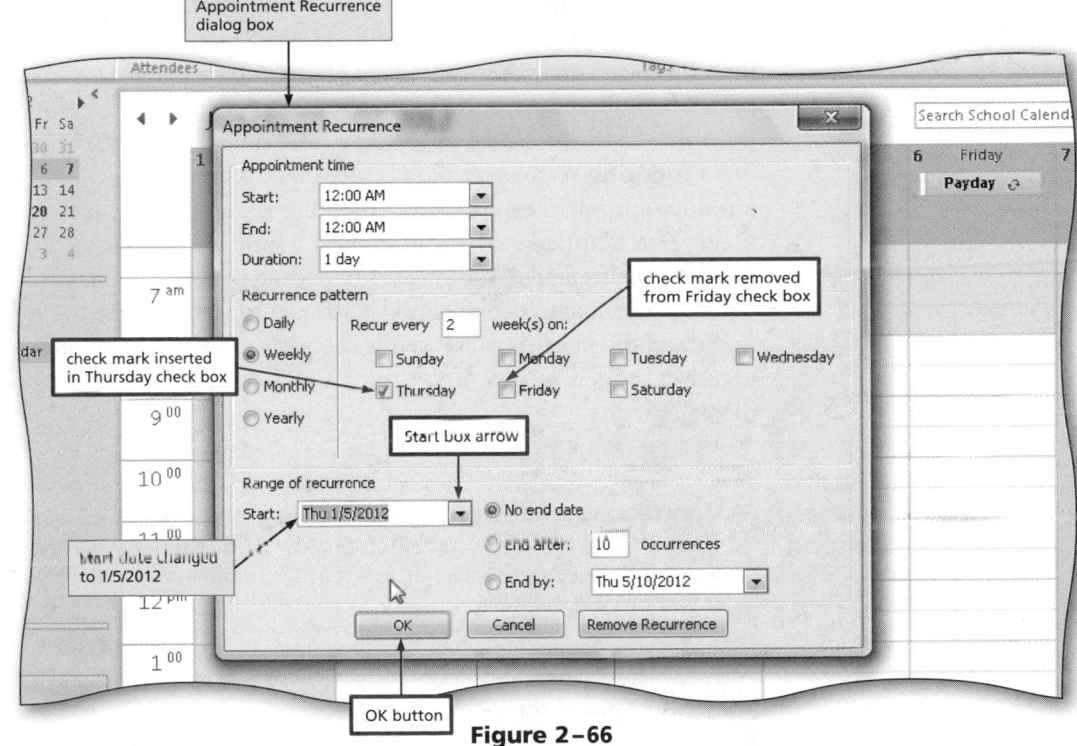

Figure 2–66

3

- Click the OK button to close the Appointment Recurrence dialog box and change the event day.

- Click 19 in the Date Navigator to view the event in the banner (Figure 2–67).

Figure 2–67

Other Ways

1. Double-click event, open series, click Recurrence button

2. Click event, press CTRL+O, click Recurrence button

Deleting Items Permanently
Items you delete, including events and e-mail messages, are stored in the Deleted Items folder until you empty this folder by right-clicking the Deleted Items folder and then clicking Empty Folder on the shortcut menu.

To Delete a Recurring Event

Deleting a recurring event is similar to deleting a recurring appointment. If you choose to delete a recurring event, you would use the following steps.

1. Click the scroll arrow on the Date Navigator to display the date of the event.
2. Click the event to display the Calendar Tools Appointment Series tab.
3. Click the Delete button (Calendar Tools Appointment Series tab | Actions group) to display the Delete menu.
4. Click Delete Series on the Delete menu to delete the event from the calendar.

Creating and Editing Meetings

Entering Locations
As you enter appointments, events, and meetings, you can include location information by entering it in the Location box. After entering one or more locations, you can click the Location box arrow and select a location from the list.

Outlook Calendar includes many items that help you manage your time in a given day, week, or month. In addition to appointments and events, you likely will have to schedule meetings with other people or reply to a meeting invitation you received indicating to the sender whether you can attend. As defined earlier, a meeting is an appointment that includes people to whom you send an invitation. A meeting also can include resources such as conference rooms. The person who creates the meeting and sends the invitations is known as the **meeting organizer**. The meeting organizer schedules a meeting by creating a **meeting request**, which is an e-mail invitation to the meeting and arrives in each attendee's Inbox. Responses to a meeting request arrive in the Inbox of the meeting organizer. The Untitled – Meeting request window is similar to the Untitled – Appointment window with a few exceptions. The meeting request window includes the To text box, where you enter an e-mail address for **attendees**, who are people invited to the meeting, and the Send button, which sends the invitation for the meeting to the attendees. When a meeting request arrives in the attendee's Inbox, it displays an icon different from an e-mail message icon.

Plan Ahead

Create an agenda before scheduling a meeting.
Have a list of topics for discussion prepared and estimate the time for each item and an ending time. When creating the agenda, consider who will attend the meeting and where it will be held.

- **Be sure you include everyone you need to attend the meeting.** Invite only those people whose attendance is absolutely necessary to ensure that all of the agenda items can be addressed at the meeting.

- **Be sure you have a location for the meeting.** Confirm that the location of the meeting is available and that the room is the appropriate size for the number of people invited. Also, make sure the room can accommodate any multimedia equipment that might be needed for the meeting, such as a projector or telephone and video conferencing capabilities.

To View the School Calendar in Overlay Mode

Before you schedule a meeting on your main calendar, you want to make sure no scheduling conflicts exist on the School Calendar. Outlook provides overlay mode, which allows you to view one calendar folder in front of another. The following steps display both calendars in overlay mode and make the Calendar folder the active folder.

1

- Click the Calendar check box to display the Calendar.

- If necessary, click the School Calendar arrow on the School Calendar tab to view the School Calendar in Overlay Mode (Figure 2–68).

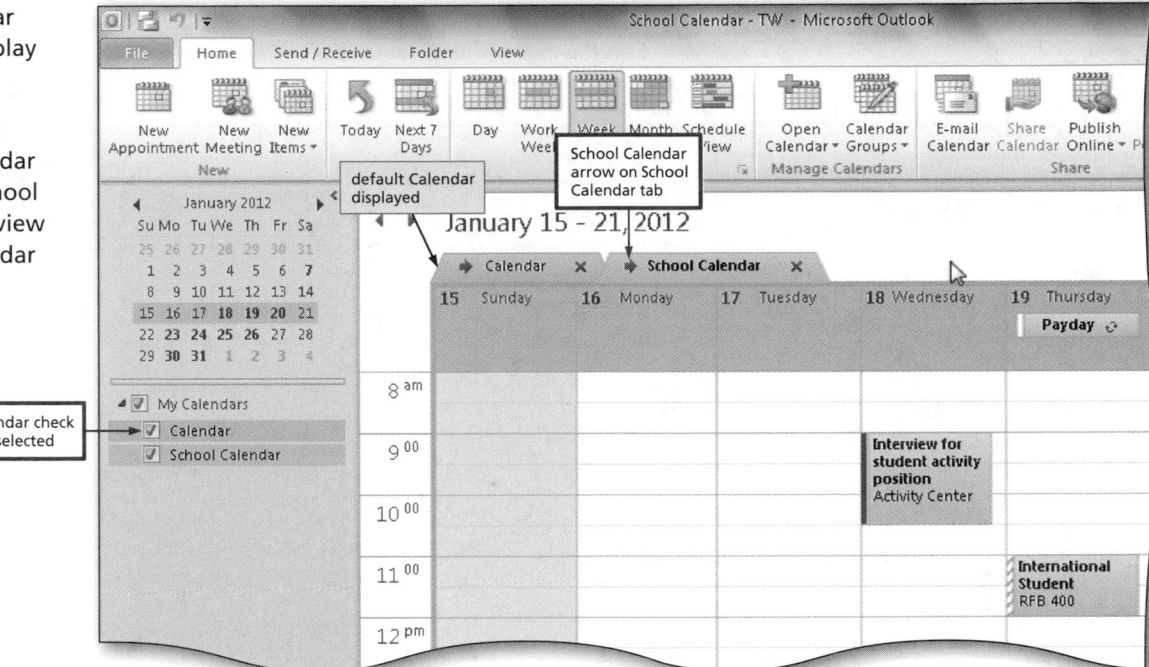

Figure 2–68

2

- Click the Calendar tab to display the Calendar in front of the School Calendar (Figure 2–69).

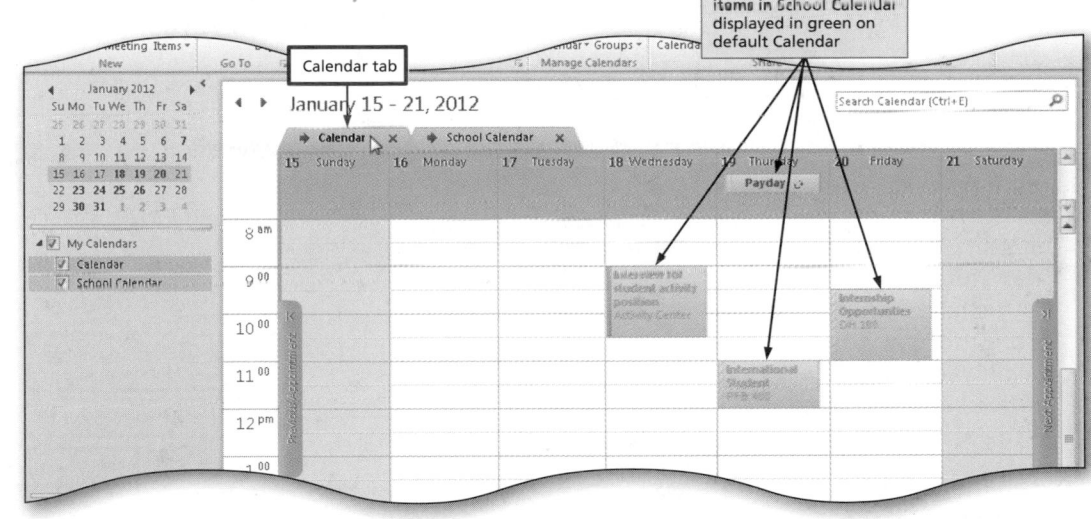

Figure 2–69

To Create and Send a Meeting Request

You want to meet with your advisor, Jay Ballentyne, to discuss your course selection for the next semester. Rather than send an e-mail message requesting the meeting, you decide to use Outlook Calendar to create this meeting. Meetings can be scheduled on your main calendar or supplemental calendars, even though meetings scheduled on your secondary calendars will be not be tallied. The following steps display the main calendar, create a meeting request, and send an invitation to your advisor. You will also use overlay mode to see if any conflicts appear on your schedule. If you are completing this project on a personal computer, use the e-mail address of your instructor instead of Jay Ballentyne's e-mail address.

1

- Click the New Meeting button (Home tab | New group) to open the Untitled – Meeting window.

- If necessary, maximize the Untitled – Meeting window to provide as much room as possible to work (Figure 2–70).

Q&A

Why does the message header include the text, "Invitations have not been sent for this meeting"?

When scheduling a meeting with other people, invitations are sent to them. This notice reminds you that you have not yet sent the invitation to the meeting.

Figure 2–70

2

- Click the To text box and then type **jay .ballentyne@ hotmail.com** (substitute your instructor's e-mail address for Jay Ballentyne's e-mail address) as the invitee to this meeting.

- Press the TAB key to move the insertion point to the Subject text box.

- Type **Course Selection for Next Semester** as the subject of the meeting.

- Press the TAB key to move the insertion point to the Location text box.

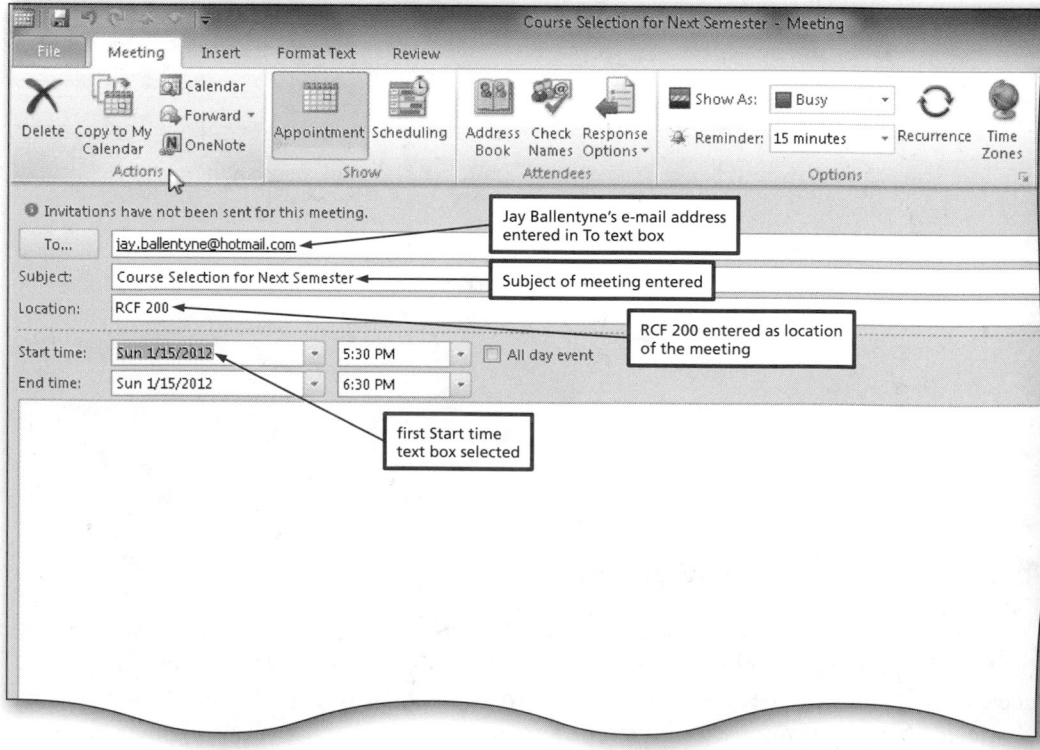

Figure 2–71

- Type **RCF 200** as the location of the meeting.

- Press the TAB key to select the date in the first Start time text box (Figure 2–71).

3
- Type 4/23/2012 as the start date of the meeting, and then press the TAB key to select the time in the second Start time box.

- Type 12:30 pm as the start time for the meeting, and then press the TAB key two times to select the time in the second End time box.

- Type 1:30 pm as the end time for the meeting (Figure 2–72).

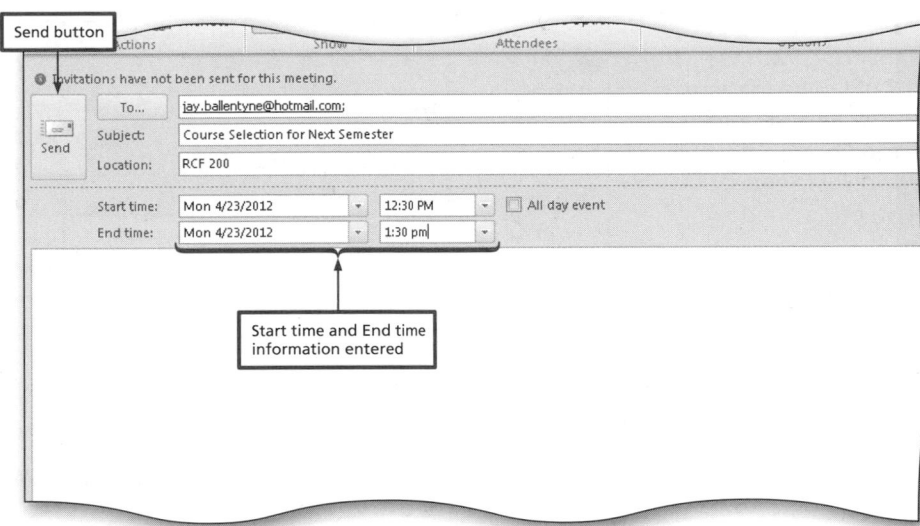

Figure 2–72

4
- Click the Send button to send the invitation to Jay Ballentyne (or your instructor) and add the meeting to the calendar.

- Click the appropriate scroll arrow on the Date Navigator to display the April 2012 calendar.

- Click April 23, 2012 on the Date Navigator to display the date in the meeting area and view the meeting (Figure 2–73).

Figure 2–73

To Change the Time of a Meeting and Send an Update

Your schedule has changed, which means you need to change the time of the meeting with Jay Ballentyne and send an update to inform her of the change. Though the invitee can propose a new time, only the originator can change or delete the meeting. Other reasons to update a meeting request may be that you have added or removed attendees or resources, changed the meeting to a recurring series, or moved the meeting to a different date or time. The following steps change the time of the meeting and send an update to the attendee.

- Double-click the meeting with Jay Ballentyne (or your instructor) to open the Course Selection for Next Semester – Meeting window.

- Click the second Start time box arrow to display a list of times.

- Click 1:30 PM as the new start time for the meeting (Figure 2–74).

Figure 2–74

- Click the Send Update button in the message header to send the new information, close the meeting request, and view the updated meeting in the appointment area (Figure 2–75).

Q&A

What if I need to cancel the meeting?

Click the meeting in the appointment area to display the Calendar Tools Meeting tab on the Ribbon, click the Cancel Meeting button (Cancel Meeting button | Actions group), and then click the Send Cancellation button to send the cancellation notice and remove the meeting from the calendar.

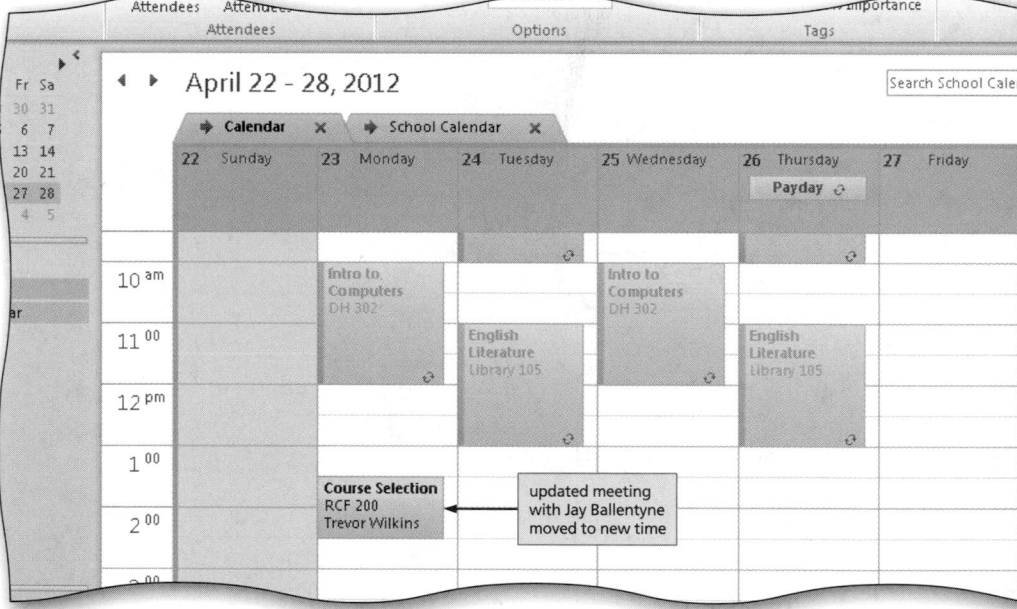

Figure 2–75

Other Ways

1. Drag meeting to new time, click 'Save changes and send update', click OK, click Send Update

To Reply to a Meeting Request

You and another student, Gillian Winston, are working on a project for your social studies class. Using Outlook Calendar, Gillian has sent you a meeting request to meet and work on the project together. You accept the invitation by replying to the meeting request from Gillian. Outlook allows you to choose from four response options: Accept, Tentative, Decline, or Propose New Time. The following steps accept the meeting request from Gillian Winston. If you do not have a meeting request from Gillian Winston, substitute another meeting request in your Inbox. If you do not have any meeting requests, read these steps without performing them.

- If necessary, click the Mail button in the Navigation Pane to display the Inbox folder.

- Open a folder window displaying the data files for this chapter to retrieve the message from Gillian Winston.

- Arrange the window so you can see both the folder window and the Outlook window.

- Drag the Work on project message from the folder window to the Inbox to import the message into the Inbox.

Figure 2–76

- If necessary, click the invitation from Gillian Winston in the message list to select the invitation (Figure 2–76).

- Double-click the Gillian Winston message header to open the invitation.

- Click the Accept button (Meeting tab | Respond group) to display the options for accepting the meeting, and then point to Send the Response Now (Figure 2–77).

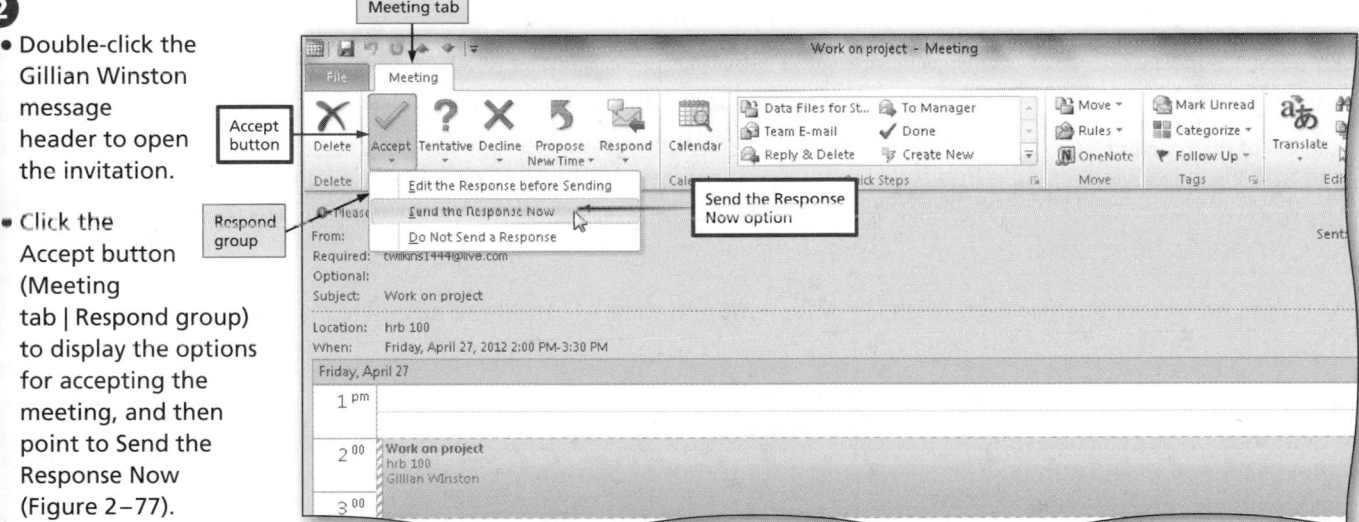

Figure 2–77

- Click Send the Response Now to send the accept response and add the meeting to the calendar.

What happened to the meeting invitation in the Inbox?

When you accept or tentatively accept a meeting request, the invitation is deleted from the Inbox and the meeting is added to your calendar. The meeting response is in the Sent Items folder.

What happens when I decline a meeting request?

When a meeting request is declined, the meeting request is removed from your Inbox and the meeting is not added to your calendar. The reply is placed in the Sent Items folder.

TO PROPOSE A NEW MEETING TIME

When you receive a meeting invitation, one thing you can do is propose a new time. When you propose a new time, a proposal is sent to the meeting originator via e-mail, indicating that you tentatively accept the request, but propose the meeting be held at a different time or on a different date. To propose a new time for a meeting, you would perform the following steps.

1. Click the appropriate meeting request to display the Calendar Tools Meeting Occurrence tab on the Ribbon.
2. Click the Propose New Time button (Calendar Tools Meeting Occurrence tab | Respond group) to display the Occurrence menu.
3. Click the Tentative and Propose New Time option to display the Propose New Time dialog box for the selected meeting.
4. Drag through the time slot that you want to propose or enter the appropriate information in the Meeting start and Meeting end boxes (Propose New Time dialog box).
5. Click the Propose time button to open the New Time Proposed – Meeting Response window.
6. Click the Send button.

TO CHANGE THE TIME OF A ONE-TIME MEETING AND SEND AN UPDATE

When someone proposes a new meeting time, it may be necessary to update the meeting request to the other potential attendees. Other reasons to update a meeting request may be that you have added or removed attendees, changed the meeting to a recurring series, or moved the meeting to a different date. To change the time of a meeting and send an update, you would perform the following steps.

1. With the Calendar window open, drag the meeting to its new time.
2. When the Microsoft Outlook dialog box is displayed, select the 'Save changes and send an update' option button.
3. Click the OK button. If the appointment opens, click the Send button.

To Cancel a Meeting

You no longer need to meet with Jay Ballentyne and want to cancel the meeting. The following steps cancel a meeting.

• Click the Course Selection for Next Semester meeting in the appointment area to select the meeting and display the Calendar Tools Meeting tab on the Ribbon (Figure 2–78).

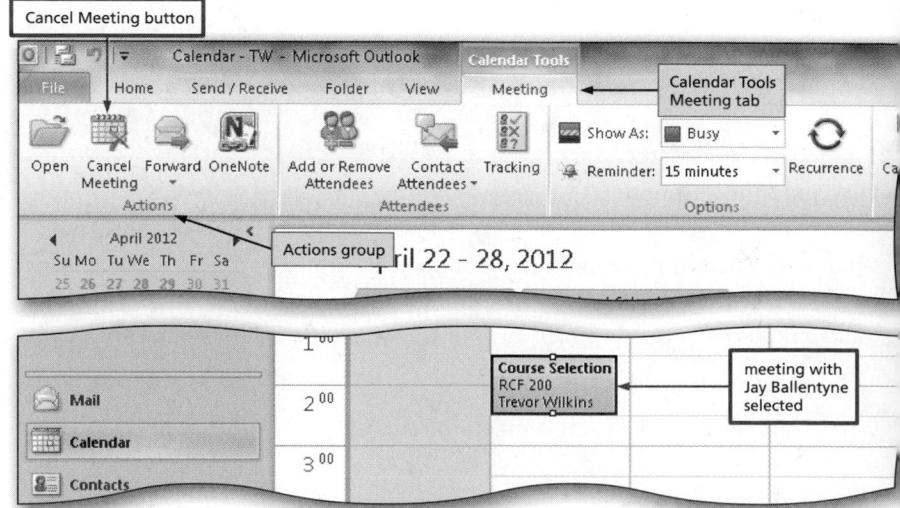

Figure 2–78

2

• Click the Cancel Meeting button (Calendar Tools Meeting tab | Actions group) to open the window for the selected meeting (Figure 2–79).

Figure 2–79

3

• Click the Send Cancellation button in the message header to send the cancellation notice and delete the meeting from your calendar (Figure 2–80).

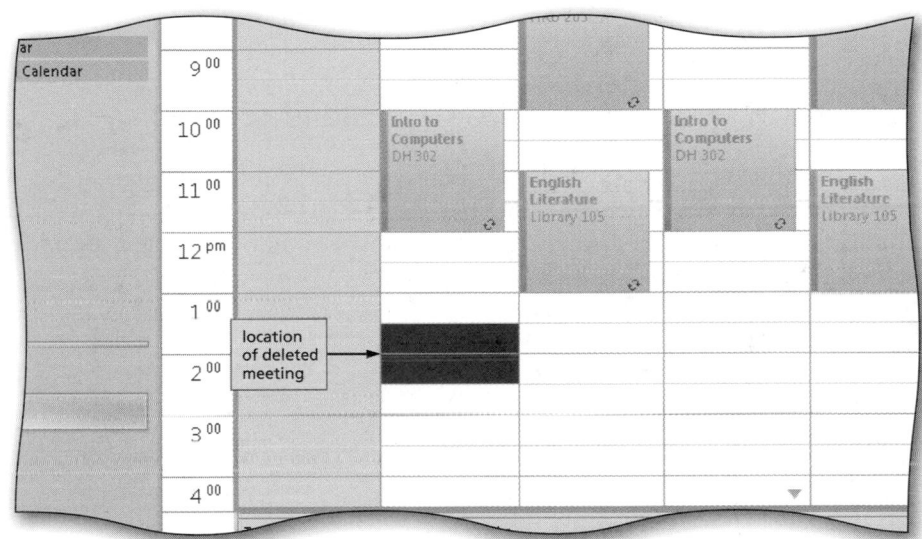

Figure 2–80

Other Ways
1. Click Delete button (Calendar Tools Meeting tab | Actions group), select option

Printing Calendars in Different Views

All or part of a calendar can be printed in a number of different views, or **print styles**. Printing a calendar enables you to distribute the calendar to others in a form that can be read or viewed, but cannot be edited. You can print a monthly, daily, or weekly view of your calendar and select options such as the date range and fonts used. You also can view your calendar in a list by changing the current view from Calendar view to List view. This section prints your calendar from Calendar view in the Weekly Calendar style, and then changes the current view to List view and prints the calendar in Table style. Table 2–7 lists the print styles available for printing your calendar from Calendar view.

Table 2–7 Print Styles for Calendar View	
Print Style	**Description**
Daily	Prints a daily appointment schedule for a specific date including one day per page, a daily task list, an area for notes, and a two-month calendar
Weekly Agenda	Prints a seven-day weekly calendar with one week per page and a two-month calendar
Weekly Calendar	Prints a seven-day weekly calendar with one week per page and an hourly schedule, similar to the Daily style
Monthly	Prints five weeks per page of a particular month or date range
Tri–fold	Prints a page for each day, including a daily task list and a weekly schedule
Calendar Details	Prints a list of calendar items and supporting details

Plan Ahead

Determine the best method for distributing a calendar.
The traditional method of distributing a calendar uses a printer to produce a hard copy. A **hard copy** or **printout** is information that exists on a physical medium such as paper. Hard copies can serve as reference material if your storage medium is lost or becomes corrupted and you need to re-create the calendar.

To Print the Calendar in Weekly Calendar Style

In this exercise, you will be working with the School Calendar, so you need to make that the active calendar and close the default calendar. Also, you want a hard copy of your first week of classes so that you can see all your appointments for the first week of the semester. The following steps display the School Calendar, and then print the calendar for the first week of classes.

1

- Click the Calendar check box to close the default Calendar and display only the School calendar.

- Click the Go To Dialog Box Launcher to display the Go To Date dialog box.

- Type 1/29/2012 to display that date in the appointment area, and then click the OK button to close the Go To Date dialog box.

- Click File on the Ribbon to open the Backstage view.

- Click the Print tab in the Backstage view to display the Print gallery.

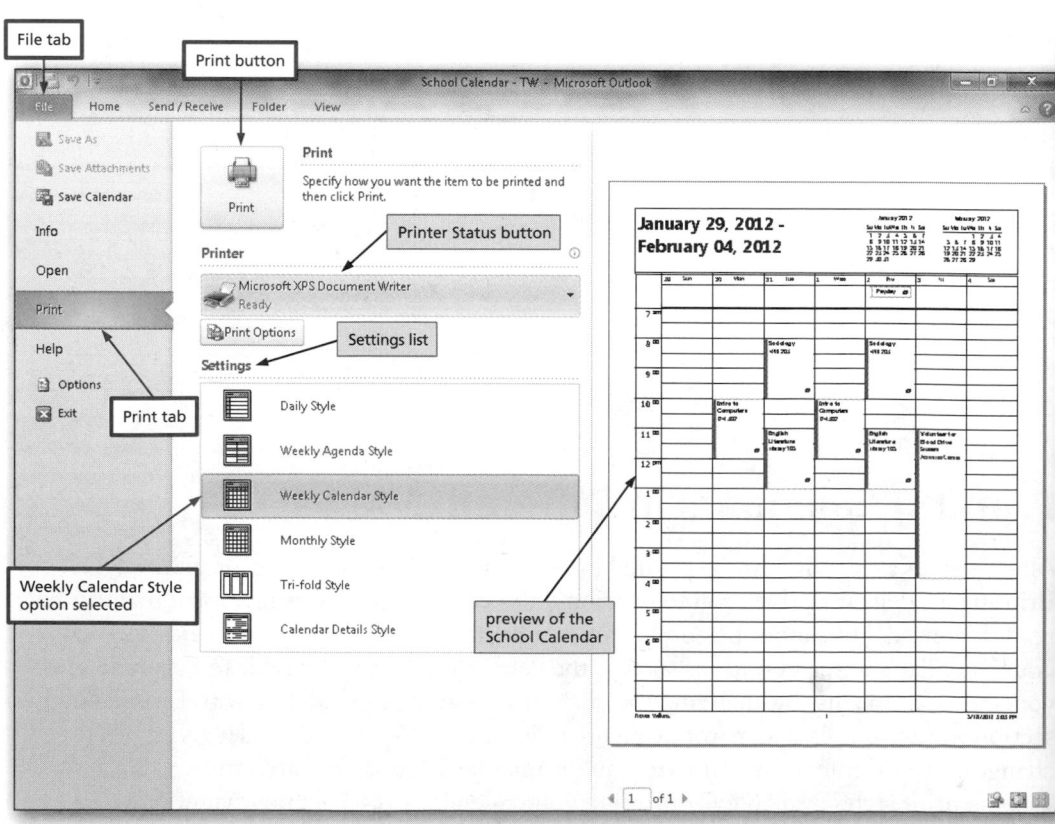

Figure 2–81

- Select Weekly Calendar Style in the Settings list to preview how the printed calendar will look in Weekly Calendar Style (Figure 2–81).

Experiment

- Click the other settings to preview the different print styles. When finished, select Weekly Calendar Style.

2

- Verify the printer name that appears on the Printer Status button will print a hard copy of the calendar. If necessary, click the Printer Status button to display a list of available printer options and then click the desired printer to change the currently selected printer.

- Click the Print button in the Print gallery to print the calendar on the currently selected printer.

- When the printer stops, retrieve the hard copy (Figure 2–82).

How can I print multiple copies of my calendar?

Click the Print Options button to display the Print dialog box, increase the number in the Number of Copies box, and then click the Print button to send the calendar to the printer and return to the calendar.

What if I decide not to print the calendar at this time?

Click File on the Ribbon to close the Backstage view and return to the calendar window.

Figure 2–82

Other Ways
1. Press CTRL+P, press ENTER

Shortcut Keys
To print a complete list of shortcut keys in Outlook, click the Microsoft Outlook Help button near the upper-right corner of the Outlook window, type `shortcut keys` in the search text box at the top of the Outlook Help window, press the ENTER key, click the Keyboard shortcuts for Microsoft Outlook link, click the Show All link in the upper-right corner of the Help window, click the Print button in the Help window, and then click the Print button in the Print dialog box.

To Change the Current View to List View

You can print a list of all your calendar items using Table style, which prints your calendar in a table format. To print a calendar in this view, you must change the current view to List view, which only is available when you change the current view from the View tab. The following steps change the view from Calendar view to List view and then print the calendar in the Table style.

1

- With the Calendar button selected in the Navigation Pane, click View on the Ribbon to display the View tab.

- Click the Change View button (View tab | Current View group) to display the Change View gallery (Figure 2–83).

Figure 2–83

2

- Click List in the Change View gallery to display a list of calendar items in the appointment area (Figure 2–84).

Figure 2–84

To Print the Calendar from List View

Now that the calendar view is displaying all your calendar items in a list, you want to print the calendar in this format. The following steps print the calendar in Table style.

1 Click File on the Ribbon to open the Backstage View.

2 Click the Print tab in the Backstage view to display the Print gallery.

3 Click the Table style option in the Settings list to preview the calendar in Table Style.

4 Verify the printer name in the Printer box will print a hard copy of the calendar in Table Style. If necessary, click the Printer box to display a list of available printer options and then click the desired printer to change the currently selected printer.

5 Click the Print button to send the list of appointments to the selected printer.

6 When the printer stops, retrieve the hard copy (Figure 2–85).

How can I modify what is included on the hard copy?

Click the Print Options button to display the Print dialog box for additional print options.

When I changed the view from List view to Calendar view, why did the Calendar display the current date and not the date I printed?

The calendar always displays the current date when you change from List view to Calendar view.

BTW

Changing Settings before Printing
To change the margins, page orientation, or paper size before printing, click the Print Options button in the Print dialog box and then click the Page Setup button to display the Page Setup dialog box.

Figure 2–85

Other Ways

1. Press CTRL+P, click Print

Exporting and Importing Folders

The calendar now is ready to be saved on a USB flash drive. Saving your work on an external storage device allows you to take your schedule to another computer where you will import the calendar for use on a secondary computer.

With many programs, a single file, such as a letter or spreadsheet, can be saved directly on an external storage device. With Outlook, each appointment, task, or contact is a separate file. Rather than saving numerous individual files, Outlook uses the **Import and Export Wizard** to guide you through the process of saving an entire folder including any subfolders, which are folders within another folder. Transferring a subfolder to a USB flash drive is called **exporting**. Adding a subfolder to your Outlook mailbox is called **importing**. Subfolders can be imported and exported from any Outlook item. When you export a folder, Outlook saves the folder and its subfolders to a USB flash drive, adding the extension **.pst** to the exported file. A .pst file is a data file that stores all Outlook items in a specific location.

To Export a Subfolder to a USB Flash Drive

The following steps export a Calendar subfolder to a USB flash drive.

1
- Connect the USB flash drive containing the Data Files for Students to one of the computer's USB ports.

- Click File on the Ribbon to display the Backstage view and then click the Open tab to display the Open options (Figure 2–86).

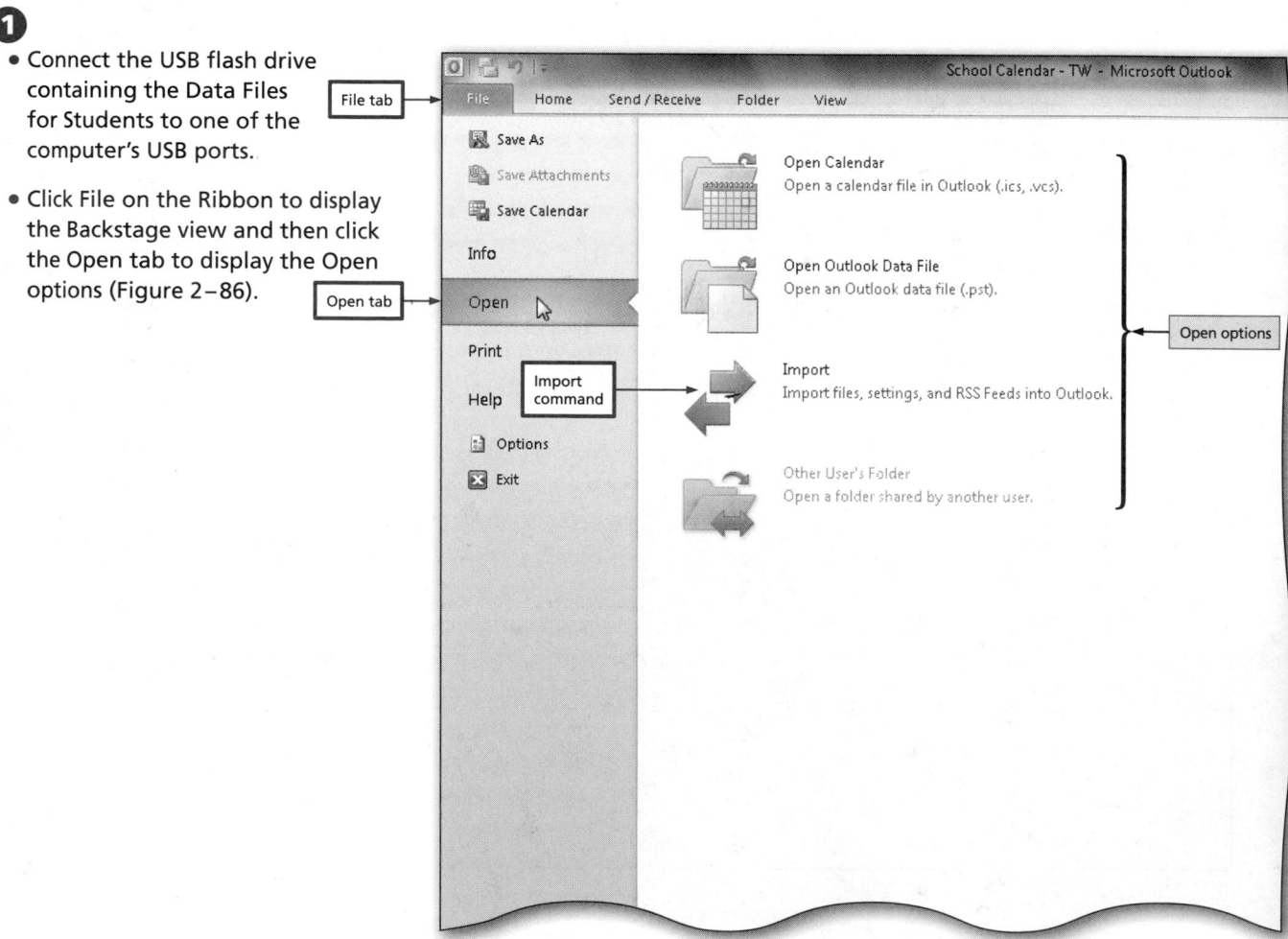

Figure 2–86

2

- Click Import to display the Import and Export Wizard dialog box (Figure 2–87).

Figure 2–87

3

- Click 'Export to a file' in the 'Choose an action to perform' list to indicate you want to export an item.

- Click the Next button to display the Export to a File dialog box.

- In the Export to a File dialog box, click Outlook Data File (.pst) to select .pst as the file type for exporting (Figure 2–88).

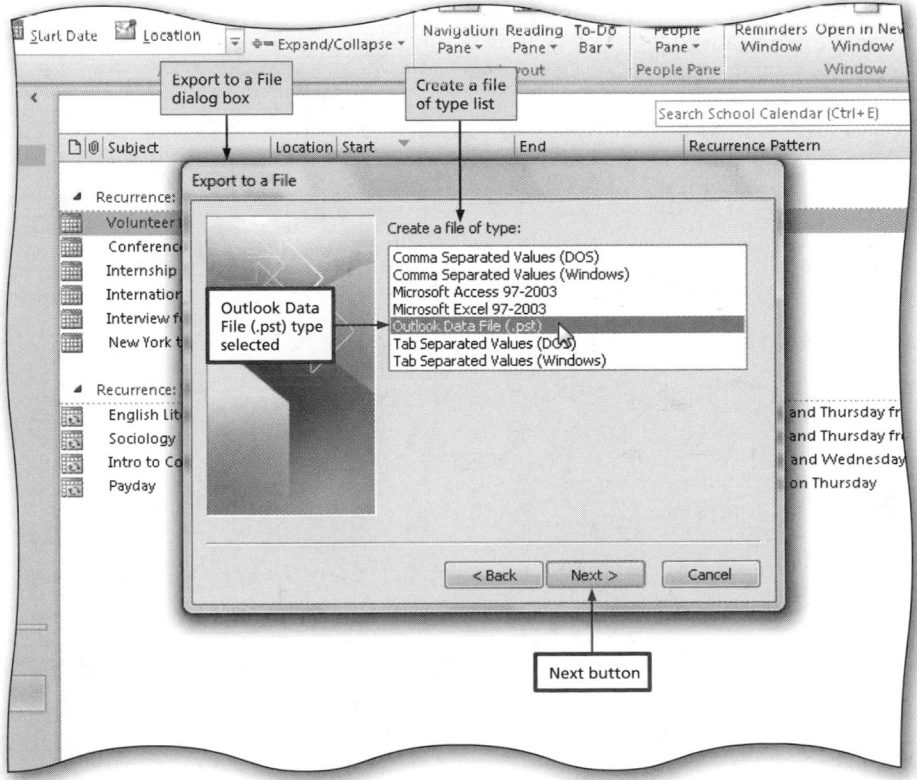

Figure 2–88

4
- Click the Next button to display the first Export Outlook Data File dialog box.

- If necessary, scroll until the Calendar folder is displayed, and then click the expand arrow to the left of the Calendar icon in the 'Select the folder to export from' list to view School Calendar in the list.

- Click School Calendar to select it as the folder to export from (Figure 2–89).

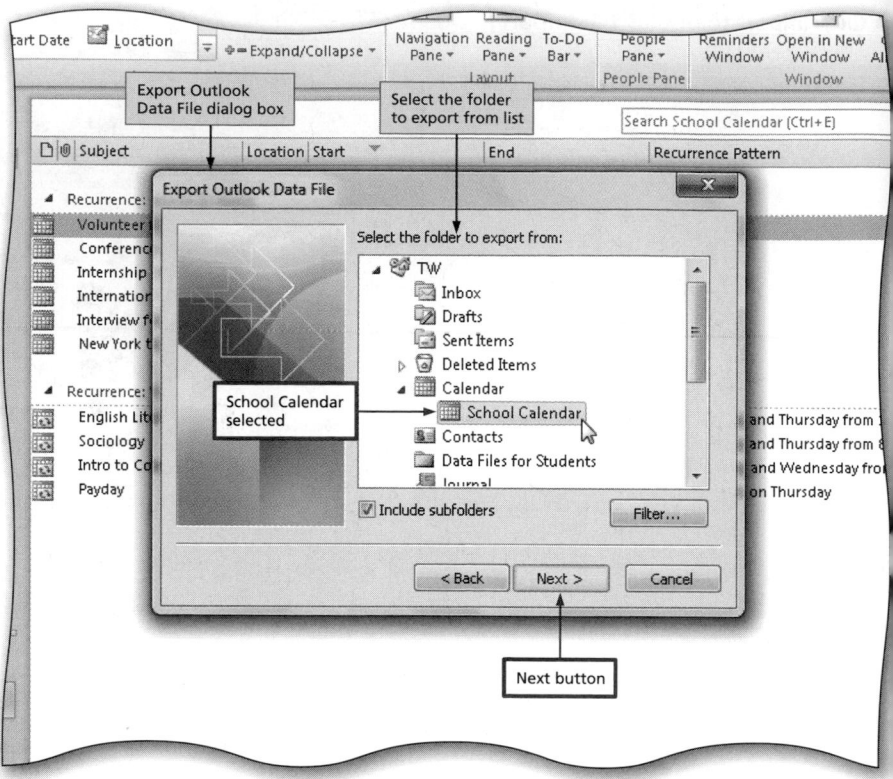

Figure 2–89

5
- Click the Next button to display the next Export Outlook Data File dialog box.

- Click the Browse button to display the Open Outlook Data Files dialog box (Figure 2–90).

Figure 2–90

5

- If necessary, click Computer in the Navigation pane to display the list of possible locations, and then double-click the drive where you store your data files, such as the REMOVABLE (G:) USB flash drive.

- Type **School Calendar** in the File name text box (Figure 2–91).

Figure 2–91

7

- Click the OK button to specify the name and location of the file, close the Open Outlook Data Files dialog box, and return to the Export Outlook Data File dialog box.

- Click the 'Replace duplicates with items exported' option button to replace any duplicate information in the School Calendar with the information in the School Calendar you are exporting (Figure 2–92).

Figure 2–92

- Click the Finish button to export the School Calendar subfolder to a .pst file.

Q&A   What should I do if I am prompted for a password?
Click the OK button to avoid associating a password with this file.

Q&A   What programs can I use to view the exported subfolder (.pst file)?
Exported subfolders (.pst files) can be viewed only in Outlook and must be opened from within Outlook.

TO IMPORT A PERSONAL SUBFOLDER

You may want to transfer your school calendar from one computer to another. For example, you may want to have your calendar on a notebook computer and a desktop computer. To do this, you need to export your calendar, as shown earlier, and then import that calendar to another computer. To import a calendar, you would perform the following steps.

1. Select the folder into which you want to import the data file.
2. Click File on the Ribbon to display the Backstage view, and then click the Open tab to display options for opening a file.
3. Click the Import button to start the Import and Export Wizard.
4. Click 'Import from another program or file' and then click the Next button.
5. Select Outlook Data File (.pst) and then click the Next button.
6. Click the Browse button in the Import Outlook Data File dialog box and then navigate to the location where the data file is stored.
7. Select the file to import and click the Open button.
8. In the Options section, select the desired option regarding duplicates and then click the Next button.
9. In the 'Select the folder to import from' box, select the appropriate folder and include subfolders if desired.
10. Select the 'Import items into the current folder' option button.
11. Click the Finish button.

To Delete a Personal Subfolder

The School Calendar subfolder now has been exported to a USB flash drive. A copy of the School Calendar.pst file still is stored on the hard disk of your computer, and appears in Outlook's Folder List. To delete a subfolder from the computer entirely, use the Delete command. The following steps delete a personal subfolder. If you did not complete the previous set of steps, do not delete the School Calendar subfolder.

- Click the School Calendar button in the Navigation Pane to display the School Calendar in the appointment area.

- Click the Delete Calendar button (Folder tab | Actions group) to display the Microsoft Outlook dialog box (Figure 2–93).

Figure 2–93

Is there a way to retrieve a deleted folder?

Yes. Outlook sends the deleted folder to the **Deleted Items** folder. If you accidentally delete a folder without first exporting it to an external storage device, you still can open the folder by double-clicking it in the Deleted Items folder in the Folder List.

Can I delete the Calendar folder below My Calendars?

The Calendar folder is the default Calendar and cannot be deleted.

- Click the Yes button in the Microsoft Outlook dialog box to delete the folder.

Other Ways
1. Right-click folder to delete, click Delete Calendar
2. Click folder to delete, press DELETE

To Quit Outlook

With the project complete, the final step is to quit the Outlook program and return to the Windows desktop. The following step quits Outlook.

1 Click the Close button on the right side of the title bar to quit Outlook.

Quick Reference

For a table that lists how to complete the tasks covered in this book using the mouse, Ribbon, shortcut menu, and keyboard, see the Quick Reference Summary at the back of this book, or visit the Outlook 2010 Quick Reference Web page (scsite.com/out2010/qr).

Certification

The Microsoft Office Specialist program provides an opportunity for you to obtain a valuable industry credential — proof that you have the Outlook 2010 skills required by employers. For more information, visit the Outlook 2010 Certification Web page (scsite.com/out2010/cert).

Chapter Summary

In this chapter, you have learned how to use Outlook to create a personal schedule by entering appointments, creating recurring appointments, moving appointments to new dates, and scheduling events. You also learned how to invite attendees to a meeting, accept a meeting request, and propose and change the time of a meeting. To review your schedule, you learned to view and print your calendar in different views and print styles. Finally, you learned how to export your personal folder to an external storage device. The following list includes all the new Outlook skills you have learned in this chapter.

1. Create a Personal Folder (OUT 54)
2. Display a Personal Calendar (OUT 56)
3. Remove the Default Calendar from the Appointment Area (OUT 56)
4. Go to a Specific Date (OUT 57)
5. Display the Calendar in Work Week View (OUT 58)
6. Display the Calendar in Week View (OUT 59)
7. Display the Calendar in Month View (OUT 60)
8. Display the Calendar in Schedule View (OUT 60)
9. Create a One-Time Appointment Using the Appointment Area (OUT 62)
10. Create a One-Time Appointment Using the Appointment Window (OUT 64)
11. Change the Status of an Appointment (OUT 67)
12. Set a Reminder for an Appointment (OUT 68)
13. Save the Appointment (OUT 69)
14. Create a Recurring Appointment Using the Appointment Window (OUT 71)
15. Set Recurrence Options for a Recurring Appointment (OUT 72)
16. Set a Reminder and Show As Options for an Appointment (OUT 74)
17. Enter an Appointment Date and Time Using Natural Language Phrases (OUT 77)
18. Move an Appointment to a Different Time on the Same Day (OUT 79)
19. Move an Appointment to a Different Date (OUT 80)
20. Move an Appointment to a Different Month (OUT 81)
21. Delete a Single Occurrence of a Recurring Appointment (OUT 82)
22. Create a One-Time Event in the Appointment Window (OUT 84)
23. Move a One-Time Event to a New Date and Change the Event Status (OUT 86)
24. Delete a One-Time Event (OUT 87)
25. Create a Recurring Event Using the Appointment Window (OUT 88)
26. Move a Recurring Event to a Different Day (OUT 90)
27. Delete a Recurring Event (OUT 92)
28. View the School Calendar in Overlay Mode (OUT 92)
29. Create and Send a Meeting (OUT 93)
30. Change the Time of a Meeting and Send an Update (OUT 95)
31. Reply to a Meeting Request (OUT 96)
32. Cancel a Meeting (OUT 98)
33. Print the Calendar in Weekly Calendar Style (OUT 100)
34. Change the Current View to List View (OUT 102)
35. Export a Subfolder to a USB Flash Drive (OUT 104)
36. Delete a Personal Subfolder (OUT 108)

Learn It Online

Test your knowledge of chapter content and key terms.

Instructions: To complete the Learn It Online exercises, start your browser, click the Address bar, and then enter the Web address `scsite.com/out2010/learn`. When the Outlook 2010 Learn It Online page is displayed, click the link for the exercise you want to complete and then read the instructions.

Chapter Reinforcement TF, MC, and SA
A series of true/false, multiple choice, and short answer questions that test your knowledge of the chapter content.

Flash Cards
An interactive learning environment where you identify chapter key terms associated with displayed definitions.

Practice Test
A series of multiple choice questions that test your knowledge of chapter content and key terms.

Who Wants To Be a Computer Genius?
An interactive game that challenges your knowledge of chapter content in the style of a television quiz show.

Wheel of Terms
An interactive game that challenges your knowledge of chapter key terms in the style of the television show *Wheel of Fortune*.

Crossword Puzzle Challenge
A crossword puzzle that challenges your knowledge of key terms presented in the chapter.

Apply Your Knowledge

Reinforce the skills and apply the concepts you learned in this chapter.

Editing a Calendar

Note: To complete this assignment, you will be required to use the Data Files for Students. See the inside back cover of this book for instructions on downloading the Data Files for Students, or contact your instructor for information about accessing the required files.

Instructions: Start Outlook. Edit the calendar provided in the file called Apply Your Knowledge 2-1 Calendar, located on the Data Files for Students. The Apply Your Knowledge 2-1 Calendar is a personal calendar with appointments for personal activities, class schedules, and events in 2012. Many of the scheduled items have changed and you now need to revise these scheduled items.

Perform the following tasks:
1. Create a folder called Apply Your Knowledge and import the Apply Your Knowledge 2-1 Calendar folder into the newly created folder.
2. Display only the Apply Your Knowledge 2-1 Calendar in the Outlook Calendar window. Use Week view to display the calendar.
3. Change Kelly's Birthday Party from February 17 to February 19. The party is at the same time.
4. Reschedule the work on February 9 to February 12. The work starts at 12:00 PM and continues until 4:00 PM.
5. Reschedule the two-hour Chemistry Study Lab on Wednesday evenings from 5:00 PM – 7:00 PM to 6:00 PM – 8:00 PM in CHM 225.
6. Change Intramural Basketball from Mondays and Wednesdays to Tuesdays and Thursdays at the same time.

Continued >

Apply Your Knowledge *continued*

7. Print the final calendar in Month view, shown in Figure 2–94, and then submit the printout to your instructor.

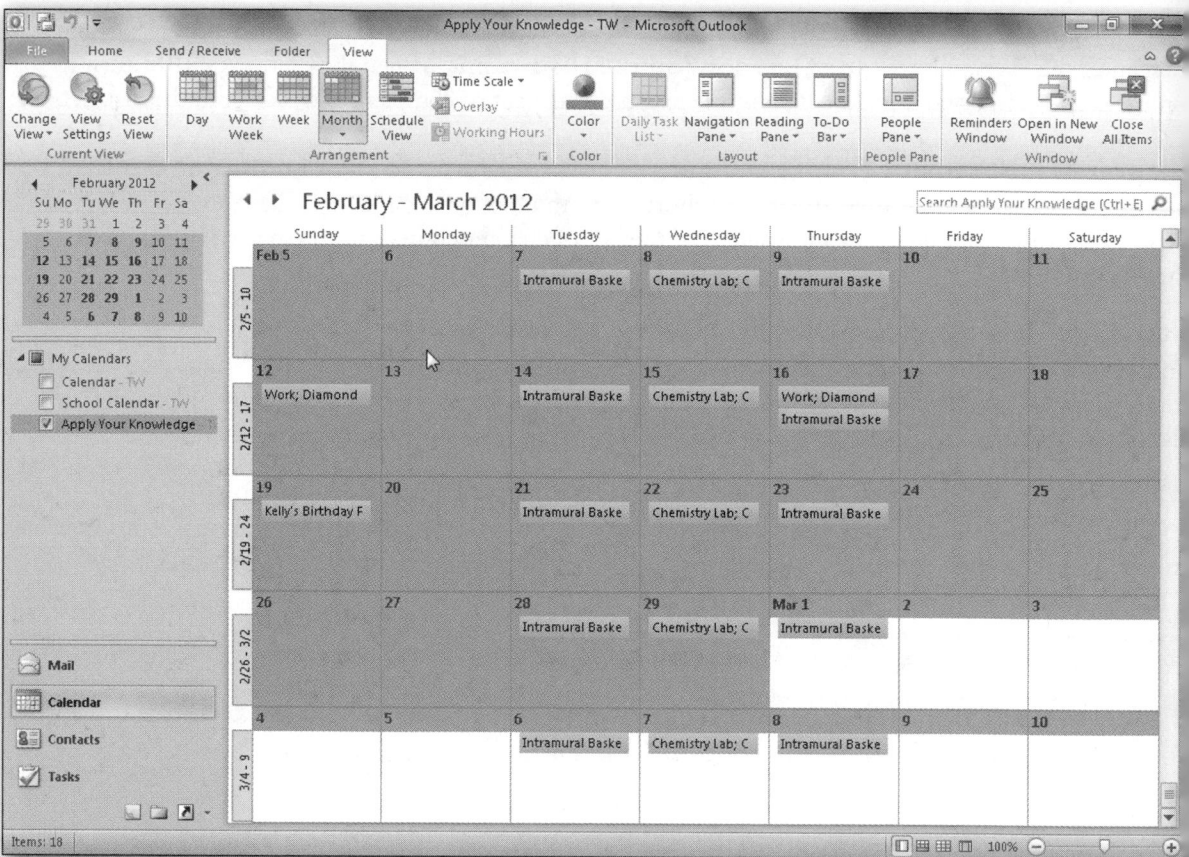

Figure 2–94

8. Export the Apply Your Knowledge 2–1 Calendar folder to a USB flash drive and then delete the folder from the hard disk.

Extend Your Knowledge

Extend the skills you learned in this chapter and experiment with new skills. You may need to use Help to complete the assignment.

Sharing and Publishing Calendars

Instructions: Start Outlook. Create a new blank calendar and then add appointments to the new calendar. You will also share the calendar with others.

Perform the following tasks:

1. Start Outlook and create a new blank calendar named Extend Your Knowledge 2-1.

2. Add three appointments to the new calendar. At least one appointment should be a weekly recurring appointment and end after six occurrences.

3. Use Help to learn about e-mailing calendars, creating a Windows Live account, and publishing a calendar online.

4. Using the E-mail Calendar button (Home tab | Share group), e-mail the calendar to your instructor. The calendar should include only the dates containing the three appointments added in Step 2. Change the e-mail layout to 'List of events.'

5. Create a Windows Live account, and then publish the calendar to Office.com (Figure 2–95). (If you are unable to create a Windows Live account, contact your instructor.) In an e-mail message, write three reasons that someone might choose to publish their calendar online.

Figure 2–95

6. Share your calendar with your instructor. When you share your calendar, request permission to view your instructor's calendar. In the e-mail message, include the answers to the following questions: What is the difference between sending a calendar as an e-mail message and sharing a calendar? What steps are required to designate who can view the calendar, as well as who can edit the calendar?

7. You decide that it no longer is necessary to share your calendar or publish it online. Configure your calendar so that it no longer is shared with anyone or published online.

8. Remove the three appointments added in Step 2.

9. Submit your answers in the format specified by your instructor.

Make It Right

Analyze a calendar and correct all errors and/or improve the design.

Correcting Appointment Times

Note: To complete this assignment, you may be required to use the Data Files for Students. See the inside back cover of this book for instructions on downloading the Data Files for Students, or contact your instructor for information about accessing the required files.

Instructions: Start Outlook. Import the Make It Right 2-1 Calendar folder in the Data Files for Students folder into Outlook. While reviewing your Outlook calendar, you realize that you created several appointments incorrectly. You will identify and open the incorrect appointments, edit them so that they reflect the correct information, and then save all changes.

Perform the following tasks:

1. Display only the Make It Right 2–1 Calendar in the Outlook Calendar window.

2. While adding a dentist appointment to the Calendar, you inadvertently recorded the appointment time as 2:00 AM instead of 2:00 PM. Edit the appointment on April 2, 2012, and change the Start time to 2:00 PM. The appointment still will last one hour.

3. The Yoga class scheduled for Wednesday, April 25, 2012 is a recurring appointment on your calendar. Change the appointment to reflect the Yoga class meeting every Thursday starting April 19, 2012 through the end of June from 7:00 PM until 9:00 PM.

4. Your monthly homeowner's association board meeting has modified their meeting schedule to meet on the second Tuesday of each month instead of on the thirteenth of each month. Update the calendar to reflect this change.

5. An appointment during the week of April 16, 2012, has been added to your calendar two times with the same start time and end time. Remove one of these appointments from the calendar.

6. Print the calendar using the Monthly style for April 8, 2012 to May 12, 2012 (Figure 2–96).

Figure 2–96

7. Export the Make It Right 2–1 Calendar folder to a USB flash drive and then delete the folder from the hard disk.

8. Submit the calendar in a format specified by your instructor.

In the Lab

Design, create, modify, and/or use a document using the guidelines, concepts, and skills presented in this chapter. Labs are listed in order of increasing difficulty.

Lab 1: Creating Recurring Events

Problem: You are a graduate assistant for the English Department at your college and have been asked to create a list of faculty birthdays. Table 2–8 lists each faculty member's birthday. Enter the birthdays as recurring events (these events should occur one time per year).

Perform the following tasks:

1. Create a personal Calendar subfolder named English Department Birthdays.

2. Create the events in the calendar, using the information listed in Table 2–8.

Table 2–8 Employee Birthday Information	
Employee Name	**Birthday**
Shannon Brown	1/6/1952
Brett Lipinski	2/17/1980
Sloan McLoughlin	3/29/1975
Joseph Kelly	5/6/1963
Emma Thompson-Wright	6/5/1979
Madelyn Judowski	8/26/1968

3. For each event, show the time as Free.

4. For each event, set the reminder to one day.

5. Set each event to recur yearly on the same day.

6. Each event should be an all-day event.

7. Print the English Department Birthdays calendar using the Calendar Details style, and submit it in a format specified by your instructor.

In the Lab

Lab 2: Creating a Calendar

Problem: You are the owner of a small hardware store. Your store has experienced rapid growth during the last several months, and with spring approaching, you need to change to regular from seasonal stock. As the owner, you also have administrative duties to perform, such as staff meetings, payroll, advertising, and sales campaigns. To make your schedule even more hectic, you coach your child's spring soccer team. You need to create a schedule of appointments to help you keep track of your various jobs and responsibilities each day (Figure 2–97).

Continued >

In the Lab *continued*

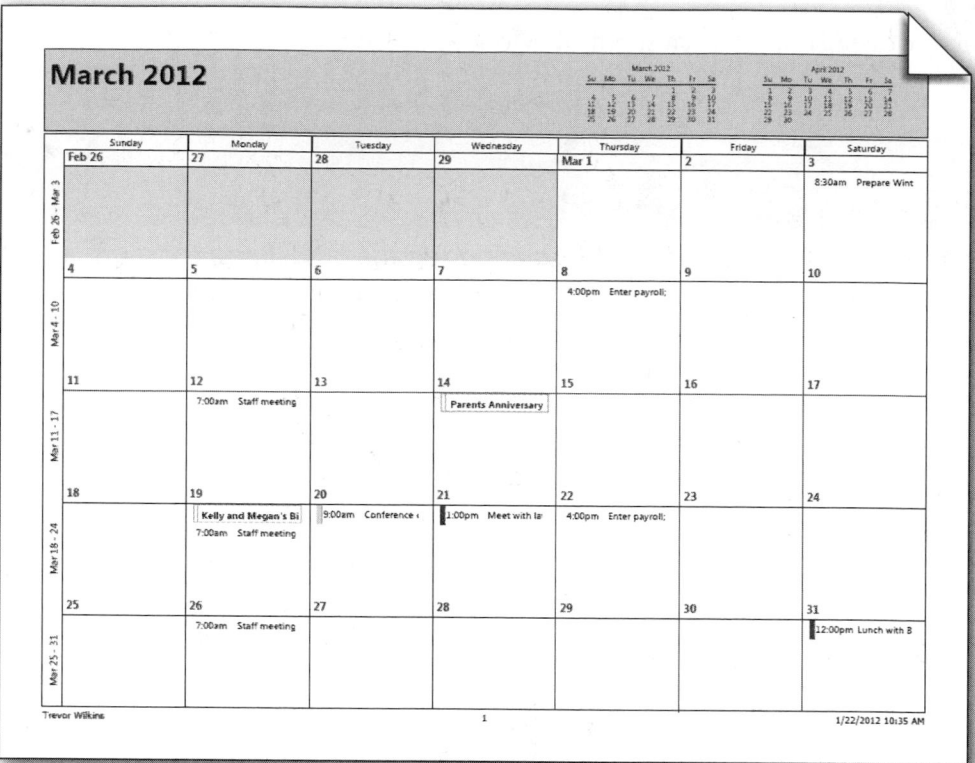

Figure 2–97

Perform the following tasks:

1. Create a personal Calendar subfolder named A-1 Hardware.

2. Enter the calendar items in the calendar, using the information listed in Table 2–9.

Table 2–9 Calendar Appointment Information

Description	Location	Date	Time	Show As	Reminder	Recurrence
Staff meeting	Lunchroom	Every Monday from March 12, 2012 – June 12, 2012	7:00 AM – 8:00 AM	Busy	30 minutes	Weekly, end by June 12, 2012
Prepare Winter Closeout Sale	Manager's Office	March 3, 2012	8:30 AM – 10:30 AM	Busy	10 minutes	None
Enter payroll	Manager's Office	Start March 8, 2012, every Thursday	4:00 PM – 5:00 PM	Busy	15 minutes	Every two weeks, no end date
Kelly & Megan's birthday		March 19, 2012	All-day event	Free	None	Yearly
Parents Anniversary		March 14, 2012	All-day event	Free	1 day	Yearly
Conference call with Liz and Greg		March 20, 2012	9:00 AM – 10:00 AM	Tentative	15 minutes	None
Meet with lawn care supplier		March 21, 2012	1:00 PM – 2:00 PM	Out of Office	30 minutes	None
Lunch with Beth		March 31, 2012	12:00 PM – 1:00 PM	Out of Office	15 minutes	None

3. Print the Appointment calendar for the month of March, and then submit the printout in the format specified by your instructor.

In the Lab

Lab 3: Creating a Schedule

Problem: Start Outlook. Create a new Calendar folder using your name as the name of the new folder. You are to create a schedule of classes and other appointments using the information in Table 2–10. This calendar is for the spring semester that begins Monday, January 30, 2012, and ends Friday, May 11, 2012. The calendar you create is shown in Figure 2–98.

Figure 2–98

Table 2–10 Appointment Information

Subject	Location	Start Date	Time	Show As	Reminder	Recurrence	End After
Doctor Appointment	Drs. office	2/3/2012	2:00 PM – 3:00 PM	Out of Office	30 minutes	None	
Work		1/31/2012	7:00 AM – 3:30 PM	Out of Office	1 hour	Weekly, T, Th, Sa	No end date
Volunteer for New Student Orientation	Student Union	1/21/2012	8:30 AM – 12:00 PM	Out of Office	15 minutes	None	
Chemistry	Science 300	1/30/2012	8:00 AM – 9:30 AM	Busy	15 minutes	Weekly, M, W	30 classes
Technical Report Writing	HRB 201	1/30/2012	11:30 AM – 1:00 PM	Busy	10 minutes	Weekly, M, W	30 classes
Marketing	HRB 300	1/31/2012	7:00 PM – 8:30 PM	Busy	30 minutes	Weekly, T, Th	30 classes

Perform the following tasks:

1. Create a one-time appointment for the first item in Table 2–10. Enter the text in the Subject column, Doctor Appointment, as the appointment subject. Enter the location, start date, and time as shown in Table 2–10. Show the time as Out of Office in your calendar and set a 30-minute reminder.

Continued >

In the Lab *continued*

2. Create a recurring appointment for the Work item in Table 2–10. Enter the subject, start date, and time as shown. Show the time as Out of Office in your calendar and set a one-hour reminder. Set the appointment to recur weekly on Tuesdays, Thursdays, and Saturdays with no end date.

3. Create a one-time appointment for the Volunteer for New Student Orientation item in Table 2–10. Enter the subject, start date, and time as shown. Show the time as Out of Office in your calendar and set a 15-minute reminder.

4. Create a recurring appointment for the Chemistry item in Table 2–10. Enter the subject, start date, and time as shown. Show the time as busy and set a 15-minute reminder. Set the appointment to recur weekly on Mondays and Wednesdays for 30 occurrences.

5. Create a recurring appointment for the Technical Report Writing item in Table 2–10. Enter the subject, start date, and time as shown. Show the time as busy and set a 10-minute reminder. Set the appointment to recur weekly on Mondays and Wednesdays for 30 occurrences.

6. Create a recurring appointment for the Marketing item in Table 2–10. Enter the subject, start date, and time as shown. Show the time as busy and set a 30-minute reminder. Set the appointment to recur weekly on Tuesdays and Thursdays for 30 occurrences.

7. Print the February 2012 calendar in Month view, and then submit it in the format specified by your instructor.

Cases and Places

Apply your creative thinking and problem solving skills to design and implement a solution.

Note: To complete these assignments, you may be required to use the Data Files for Students. See the inside back cover of this book for instructions on downloading the Data Files for Students, or contact your instructor for information about accessing the required files.

1: Create a Personal Schedule

Academic

Create a personal schedule for the next month using the information provided in Table 2–11. Include your appointments for work, classes, and study time. You also can include any extracurricular activities in which you participate. Use recurring appointments when possible. Schedule all-day activities as events. Print the calendar in Monthly Style and submit it in the format specified by your instructor.

Table 2–11 Academic Calendar Items

Description	Location	Date	Time	Show As	Reminder	Recurrence
Financial Planning Workshop	Columbia Inn	March 11, 2012	1:00 PM – 4:00 PM	Busy	30 minutes	None
Spring Fling	Quad	March 3, 2012	12:00 PM – 2:00 PM	Out of Office	10 minutes	None
Department Meeting		Every Monday	2:00 PM – 3:00 PM	Busy	5 minutes	Weekly, end after 12 occurrences
Petition to Graduate		March 15, 2012	All Day Event	Free	1 day	None
Parents Anniversary		October 20, 2012	All Day Event	Free	1 day	Yearly
NJCAA D3 Women's Lacrosse Nationals		March 6, 2012 – March 8, 2012	All Day Event	Tentative	None	None
SGA Meeting		March 21, 2012	11:30 PM – 12:30 PM	Out of Office	30 minutes	None
Work Schedule		2/28/2012	2:00 PM – 5:30 PM	Out of Office	15 minutes	Tuesdays and Thursdays

2: Create a Work Schedule for Employees

Professional

At work, you are in charge of scheduling snack bar coverage for your local athletic club for the month of May. Create a schedule of work times for four employees. Brett works Mondays, Wednesdays, and Fridays from 9:00 AM to 5:00 PM; Megan works Tuesdays, Thursdays, and Saturdays from 9:00 AM to 5:00 PM; Joe works from 12:00 PM until 9:00 PM on Mondays, Wednesdays, and Fridays. Pat completes the schedule working from 12:00 PM until 9:00 PM on Tuesdays, Thursdays, and Saturdays. Print the calendar in Monthly Style and submit it in the format specified by your instructor.

3: Create Meeting Invitations

Personal

Create a personal calendar to keep track of several items relating to your schedule outside of class or work. Use Table 2–12 to add these items to your personal calendar.

Table 2–12 Personal Calendar Items

Description	Location	Date	Time	Show As	Reminder	Recurrence
Open House at your child's new school	Jenna's School	April 3, 2012	1:00 PM – 4:00 PM	Out of Office	30 minutes	None
Annual Physical	Medical Plan	April 5, 2012	12:00 PM – 2:00 PM	Out of Office	10 minutes	None
Air Conditioning Yearly Service	Home	April 4, 2012	2:00 PM – 3:00 PM	Busy	5 minutes	Yearly, on the first Wednesday in April
Performance Evaluation	Manager's Office	April 16, 2012	All Day Event	Free	1 day	None
Car Payment Due		April 15, 2012	All Day Event	Free	1 day	Monthly, 15th day of every month

NOTES

NOTES

NOTES

NOTES

Appendix A
Project Planning Guidelines

Using Project Planning Guidelines

The process of communicating specific information to others is a learned, rational skill. Computers and software, especially Microsoft Office 2010, can help you develop ideas and present detailed information to a particular audience.

Using Microsoft Office 2010, you can create projects such as Word documents, PowerPoint presentations, Excel spreadsheets, and Access databases. Productivity software such as Microsoft Office 2010 minimizes much of the laborious work of drafting and revising projects. Some communicators handwrite ideas in notebooks, others compose directly on the computer, and others have developed unique strategies that work for their own particular thinking and writing styles.

No matter what method you use to plan a project, follow specific guidelines to arrive at a final product that presents information correctly and effectively (Figure A–1). Use some aspects of these guidelines every time you undertake a project, and others as needed in specific instances. For example, in determining content for a project, you may decide that a chart communicates trends more effectively than a paragraph of text. If so, you would create this graphical element and insert it in an Excel spreadsheet, a Word document, or a PowerPoint slide.

Determine the Project's Purpose

Begin by clearly defining why you are undertaking this assignment. For example, you may want to track monetary donations collected for your club's fund-raising drive. Alternatively, you may be urging students to vote for a particular candidate in the next election. Once you clearly understand the purpose of your task, begin to draft ideas of how best to communicate this information.

Analyze Your Audience

Learn about the people who will read, analyze, or view your work. Where are they employed? What are their educational backgrounds? What are their expectations? What questions do they have?

PROJECT PLANNING GUIDELINES

1. DETERMINE THE PROJECT'S PURPOSE
Why are you undertaking the project?

2. ANALYZE YOUR AUDIENCE
Who are the people who will use your work?

3. GATHER POSSIBLE CONTENT
What information exists, and in what forms?

4. DETERMINE WHAT CONTENT TO PRESENT TO YOUR AUDIENCE
What information will best communicate the project's purpose to your audience?

Figure A–1

Design experts suggest drawing a mental picture of these people or finding photos of people who fit this profile so that you can develop a project with the audience in mind.

By knowing your audience members, you can tailor a project to meet their interests and needs. You will not present them with information they already possess, and you will not omit the information they need to know.

Example: Your assignment is to raise the profile of your college's nursing program in the community. How much do they know about your college and the nursing curriculum? What are the admission requirements? How many of the applicants admitted complete the program? What percent pass the state board exams?

Gather Possible Content

Rarely are you in a position to develop all the material for a project. Typically, you would begin by gathering existing information that may reside in spreadsheets or databases. Web sites, pamphlets, magazine and newspaper articles, and books could provide insights of how others have approached your topic. Personal interviews often provide perspectives not available by any other means. Consider video and audio clips as potential sources for material that might complement or support the factual data you uncover.

Determine What Content to Present to Your Audience

Experienced designers recommend writing three or four major ideas you want an audience member to remember after reading or viewing your project. It also is helpful to envision your project's endpoint, the key fact you wish to emphasize. All project elements should lead to this ending point.

As you make content decisions, you also need to think about other factors. Presentation of the project content is an important consideration. For example, will your brochure be printed on thick, colored paper or posted on the Web? Will your PowerPoint presentation be viewed in a classroom with excellent lighting and a bright projector, or will it be viewed on a notebook computer monitor? Determine relevant time factors, such as the length of time to develop the project, how long readers will spend reviewing your project, or the amount of time allocated for your speaking engagement. Your project will need to accommodate all of these constraints.

Decide whether a graph, photo, or artistic element can express or emphasize a particular concept. The right hemisphere of the brain processes images by attaching an emotion to them, so audience members are more apt to recall these graphics long term rather than just reading text.

As you select content, be mindful of the order in which you plan to present information. Readers and audience members generally remember the first and last pieces of information they see and hear, so you should place the most important information at the top or bottom of the page.

Summary

When creating a project, it is beneficial to follow some basic guidelines from the outset. By taking some time at the beginning of the process to determine the project's purpose, analyze the audience, gather possible content, and determine what content to present to the audience, you can produce a project that is informative, relevant, and effective.

Appendix B

Publishing Office 2010 Web Pages Online

With Office 2010 programs, you use the Save As command in the Backstage view to save a Web page to a Web site, network location, or FTP site. **File Transfer Protocol (FTP)** is an Internet standard that allows computers to exchange files with other computers on the Internet.

You should contact your network system administrator or technical support staff at your Internet access provider to determine if their Web server supports Web folders, FTP, or both, and to obtain necessary permissions to access the Web server.

Using an Office Program to Publish Office 2010 Web Pages

When publishing online, someone first must assign the necessary permissions for you to publish the Web page. If you are granted access to publish online, you must obtain the Web address of the Web server, a user name, and possibly a password that allows you to connect to the Web server. The steps in this appendix assume that you have access to an online location to which you can publish a Web page.

TO CONNECT TO AN ONLINE LOCATION

To publish a Web page online, you first must connect to the online location. To connect to an online location using Windows 7, you would perform the following steps.

1. Click the Start button on the Windows 7 taskbar to display the Start menu.
2. Click Computer in the right pane of the Start menu to open the Computer window.
3. Click the 'Map network drive' button on the toolbar to display the Map Network Drive dialog box. (If the 'Map network drive' button is not visible on the toolbar, click the 'Display additional commands' button on the toolbar and then click 'Map network drive' in the list to display the Map Network Drive dialog box.)
4. Click the 'Connect to a Web site that you can use to store your documents and pictures' link (Map Network Drive dialog box) to start the Add Network Location wizard.
5. Click the Next button (Add Network Location dialog box).
6. Click 'Choose a custom network location' and then click the Next button.
7. Type the Internet or network address specified by your network or system administrator in the text box and then click the Next button.
8. Click 'Log on anonymously' to deselect the check box, type your user name in the User name text box, and then click the Next button.
9. If necessary, enter the name you want to assign to this online location and then click the Next button.
10. Click to deselect the Open this network location when I click Finish check box, and then click the Finish button.

11. Click the Cancel button to close the Map Network Drive dialog box.

12. Close the Computer window.

TO SAVE A WEB PAGE TO AN ONLINE LOCATION

The online location now can be accessed easily from Windows programs, including Microsoft Office programs. After creating a Microsoft Office file you wish to save as a Web page, you must save the file to the online location to which you connected in the previous steps. To save a Microsoft Word document as a Web page, for example, and publish it to the online location, you would perform the following steps.

1. Click File on the Ribbon to display the Backstage view and then click Save As in the Backstage view to display the Save As dialog box.

2. Type the Web page file name in the File name text box (Save As dialog box). Do not press the ENTER key because you do not want to close the dialog box at this time.

3. Click the 'Save as type' box arrow and then click Web Page to select the Web Page format.

4. If necessary, scroll to display the name of the online location in the navigation pane.

5. Double-click the online location name in the navigation pane to select that location as the new save location and display its contents in the right pane.

6. If a dialog box appears prompting you for a user name and password, type the user name and password in the respective text boxes and then click the Log On button.

7. Click the Save button (Save As dialog box).

The Web page now has been published online. To view the Web page using a Web browser, contact your network or system administrator for the Web address you should use to connect to the Web page.

Appendix C

Saving to the Web Using Windows Live SkyDrive

Introduction

Windows Live SkyDrive, also referred to as **SkyDrive**, is a free service that allows users to save files to the Web, such as documents, presentations, spreadsheets, databases, videos, and photos. Using SkyDrive, you also can save files in folders, providing for greater organization. You then can retrieve those files from any computer connected to the Internet. Some Office 2010 programs including Word, PowerPoint, and Excel can save files directly to an Internet location such as SkyDrive. SkyDrive also facilitates collaboration by allowing users to share files with other SkyDrive users (Figure C–1).

Figure C–1

Note: An Internet connection is required to perform the steps in this appendix.

To Save a File to Windows Live SkyDrive

You can save files directly to SkyDrive from within Word, PowerPoint, and Excel using the Backstage view. The following steps save an open Word document (Koala Exhibit Flyer, in this case) to SkyDrive. These steps require you to have a Windows Live account. Contact your instructor if you do not have a Windows Live account.

1

- Start Word and then open a document you want to save to the Web (in this case, the Koala Exhibit Flyer).

- Click File on the Ribbon to display the Backstage view (Figure C–2).

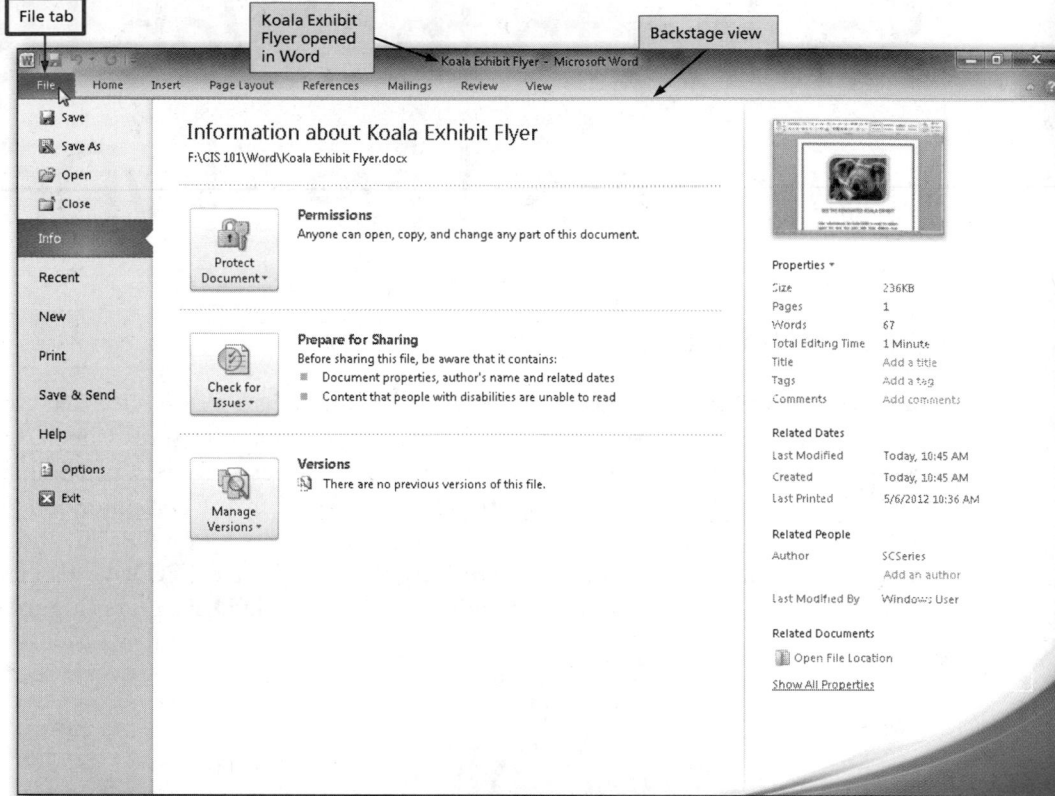

Figure C–2

2

- Click the Save & Send tab to display the Save & Send gallery (Figure C–3).

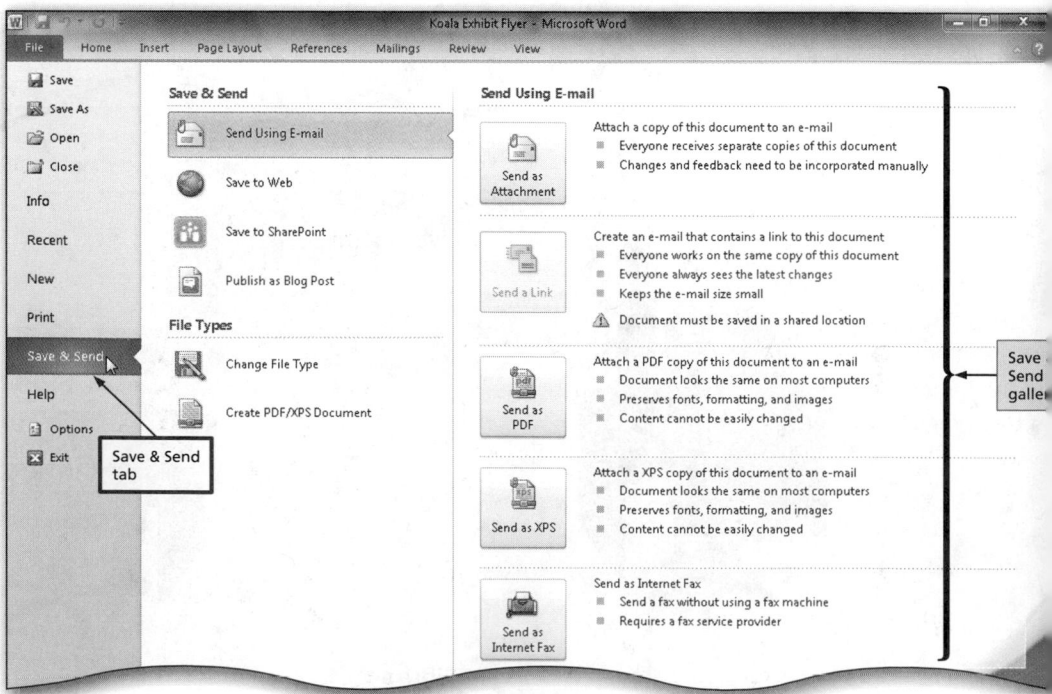

Figure C–3

3

• Click Save to Web in the Save & Send gallery to display information about saving a file to the Web (Figure C–4).

Figure C–4

4

• Click the Sign In button to display a Windows Live login dialog box that requests your e-mail address and password (Figure C–5).

What if the Sign In button does not appear?

If you already are signed into Windows Live, the Sign In button will not be displayed. Instead, the contents of your Windows Live SkyDrive will be displayed. If you already are signed into Windows Live, proceed to Step 6.

Figure C–5

5

• Enter your Windows Live e-mail address in the E-mail address box (Windows Live login dialog box).

• Enter your Windows Live password in the Password text box.

• Click the OK button to sign into Windows Live and display the contents of your Windows Live SkyDrive in the right pane of the Save & Send gallery.

• If necessary, click the My Documents folder to set the save location for the document (Figure C–6).

Figure C–6

What if the My Documents folder does not exist?

Click another folder to select it as the save location. Record the name of this folder so that you can locate and retrieve the file later in this appendix.

My SkyDrive shows personal and shared folders. What is the difference?

Personal folders are private and are not shared with anyone. Shared folders can be viewed by SkyDrive users to whom you have assigned the necessary permissions.

• Click the Save As button in the right pane of the Save & Send gallery to contact the SkyDrive server (which may take some time, depending on the speed of your Internet connection) and then display the Save As dialog box (Figure C–7).

Figure C–7

• Type **Koala Exhibit Web** in the File name text box to enter the file name and then click the Save button (Save As dialog box) to save the file to Windows Live SkyDrive (Figure C–8).

Figure C–8

Is it necessary to rename the file?

It is good practice to rename the file. If you download the file from SkyDrive to your computer, having a different file name will preserve the original file.

8

• If you have one Word document open, click the Close button on the right side of the title bar to close the document and quit Word; or if you have multiple Word documents open, click File on the Ribbon to open the Backstage view and then click Exit in the Backstage view to close all open documents and quit Word.

Web Apps

Microsoft has created a scaled-down, Web-based version of its Microsoft Office suite, called **Microsoft Office Web Apps,** or **Web Apps**. Web Apps contains Web-based versions of Word, PowerPoint, Excel, and OneNote that can be used to view and edit files that are saved to SkyDrive. Web Apps allows users to continue working with their files even while they are not using a computer with Microsoft Office installed. In addition to working with files located on SkyDrive, Web Apps also enables users to create new Word documents, PowerPoint presentations, Excel spreadsheets, and OneNote notebooks. After returning to a computer with the Microsoft Office suite, some users choose to download files from SkyDrive and edit them using the associated Microsoft Office program.

Note: As with all Web applications, SkyDrive and Office Web Apps are subject to change. Consequently, the steps required to perform the actions in this appendix might be different from those shown.

To Download a File from Windows Live SkyDrive

Files saved to SkyDrive can be downloaded from a Web browser using any computer with an Internet connection. The following steps download the Koala Exhibit Web file using a Web browser.

1

• Click the Internet Explorer program button pinned on the Windows 7 taskbar to start Internet Explorer.

• Type **skydrive.live.com** in the Address bar and then press the ENTER key to display a SkyDrive Web page requesting you sign in to your Windows Live account (Figure C–9). (If the contents of your SkyDrive are displayed instead, you already are signed in and can proceed to Step 3 on the next page.)

Why does the Web address change after I enter it in the Address bar?

The Web address changes because you are being redirected to sign into Windows Live before you can access SkyDrive.

Can I open the file from Microsoft Word instead of using the Web browser?

If you are opening the file on the same computer from which you saved it to the SkyDrive, click File on the Ribbon to open the Backstage view. Click the Recent tab and then click the desired file name (Koala Exhibit Web, in this case) in the Recent Documents list, or click Open and then navigate to the location of the saved file (for a detailed example of this procedure, refer to the Office 2010 and Windows 7 chapter at the beginning of this book).

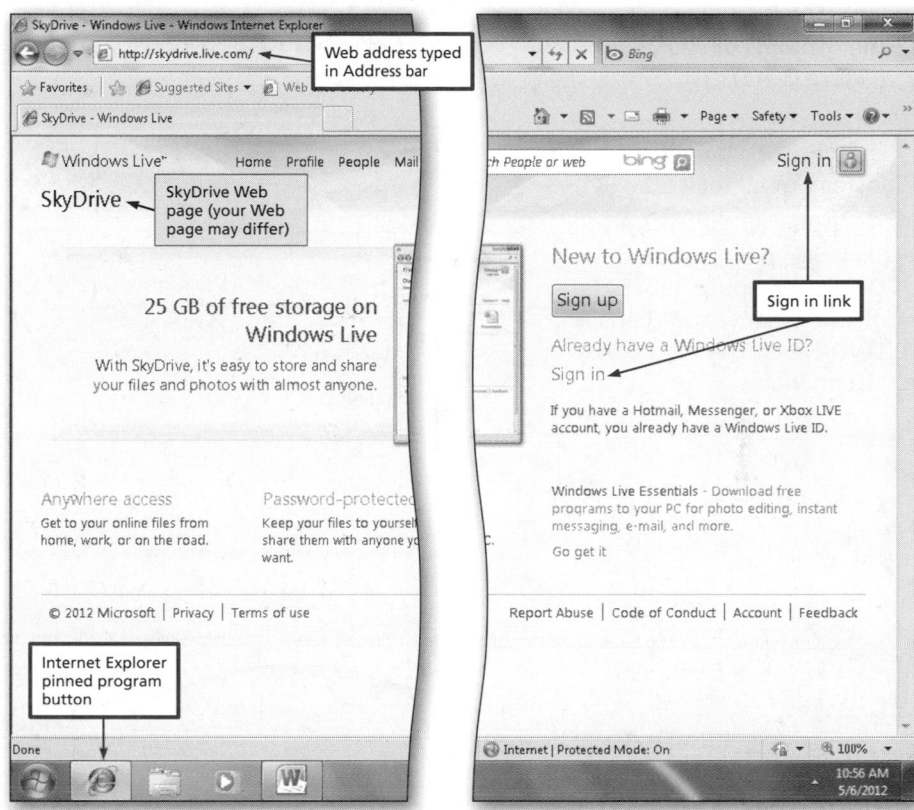

Figure C–9

2

• Click the Sign in link to display the Windows Live ID and Password text boxes (Figure C–10).

Why can I not locate the Sign in link?

If your computer remembers your Windows Live sign in credentials from a previous session, your e-mail address already may be displayed on the SkyDrive Web page. In this case, point to your e-mail address to display the Sign in button, click the Sign in button, and then proceed to Step 3. If you cannot locate your e-mail address or Sign in link, click the Sign in with a different Windows Live ID link and then proceed to Step 3.

Figure C–10

- If necessary, enter your Windows Live ID and password in the appropriate text boxes and then click the Sign in button to sign into Windows Live and display the contents of your SkyDrive (Figure C–11).

Q&A

What if my screen shows the contents of a particular folder, instead of all folders?

To display all folders on your SkyDrive, point to Windows Live in the upper-left corner of the window and then click SkyDrive on the Windows Live menu.

Figure C–11

- Click the My Documents folder, or the link corresponding to the folder containing the file you wish to open, to select the folder and display its contents (Figure C–12).

Figure C–12

• Point to the Koala Exhibit Web file to select the file and display commands associated with the file.

• Click the More link to display the More menu (Figure C–13).

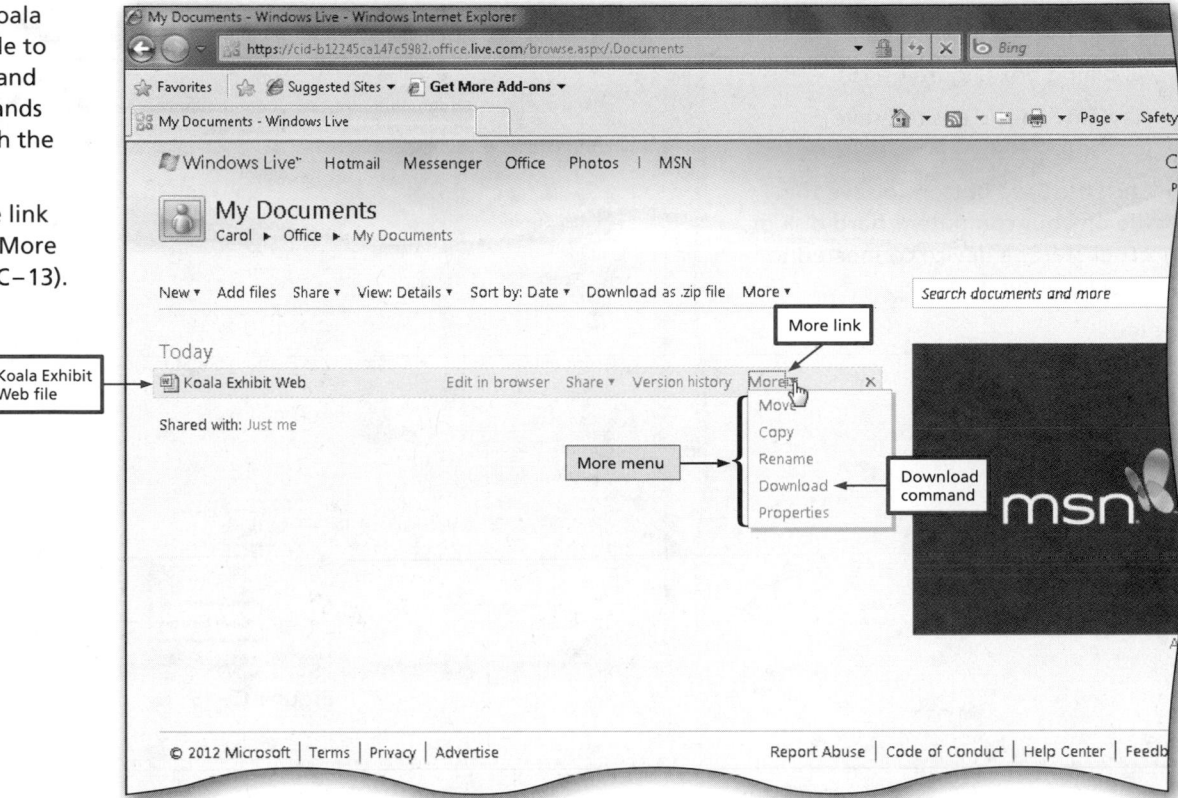

Figure C–13

• Click Download on the More menu to display the File Download dialog box (Figure C–14).

Figure C–14

7

- Click the Save button (File Download dialog box) to display the Save As dialog box (Figure C–15).

- Navigate to the desired save location.

- Click the Save button to save the file on your computer's hard disk or other storage device connected to the computer.

Figure C–15

Collaboration

In today's workplace, it is common to work with others on projects. Collaborating with the members of your team often requires sharing files. It also can involve multiple people editing and working with a certain set of files simultaneously. Placing files on SkyDrive in a public or shared folder enables others to view or modify the files. The members of the team then can view and edit the files simultaneously using Web Apps, enabling the team to work from one set of files (Figure C–16). Collaboration using Web Apps not only enables multiple people to work together, it also can reduce the amount of time required to complete a project

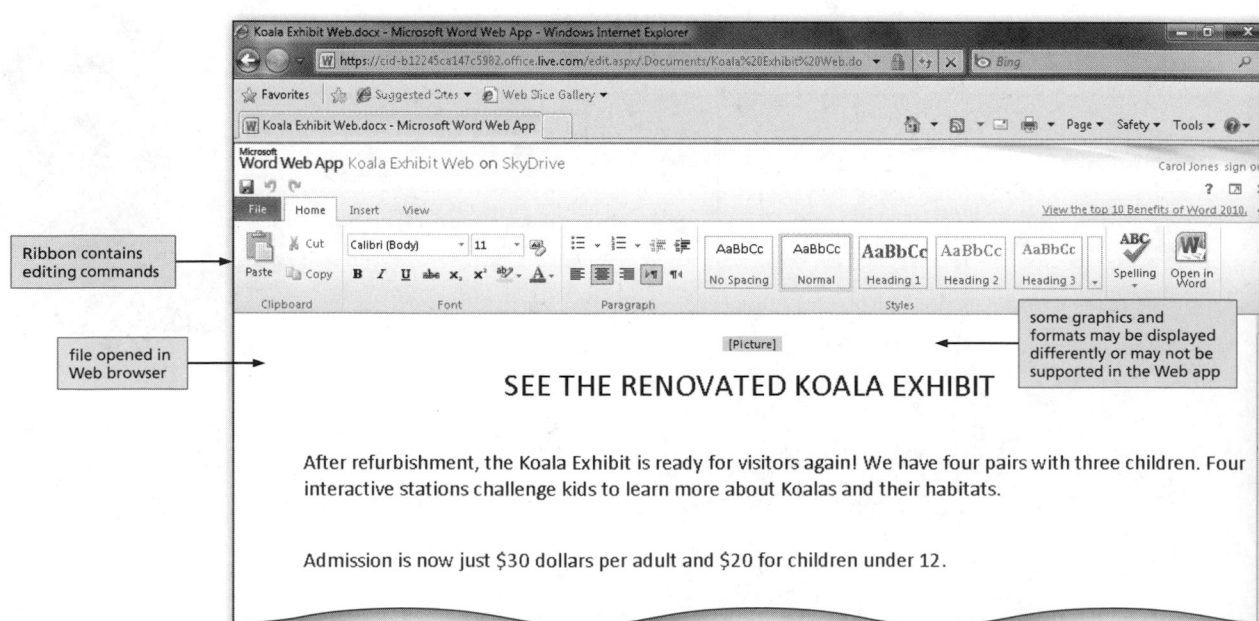

Figure C–16

Capstone Project: Wee Ones Day Care

The Capstone Project consists of an integrated, comprehensive set of problems relating to a single scenario. Students apply concepts and skills presented in this book to create solutions to the problems using Word, PowerPoint, Excel, and Access.

Wee Ones Day Care, which is located in downtown Springfield, Rhode Island, provides 24-hour day care for children ages up to 12 years old. The children's activities include arts and crafts, field trips, and organized outdoor games. As the executive assistant to the owner, Elizabeth Jordan, you provide many office support tasks to keep the day care center running.

Word Capstone Project

Creating a One-Page Flyer with a Picture and a Table

Problem: Wee Ones Day Care provides an open house to parents four times a year and distributes a flyer to announce each of these open houses. The owner of the day care center has asked you to produce the flyer for the upcoming open house.

Instructions Part 1: Change the theme colors to Opulent. Enter the text and table of the flyer and modify the text and table as shown in Figure 1–1. Locate the clip art by searching for the text, teacher, in the Clip Art pane. Change the document properties to reflect today's date and your name.

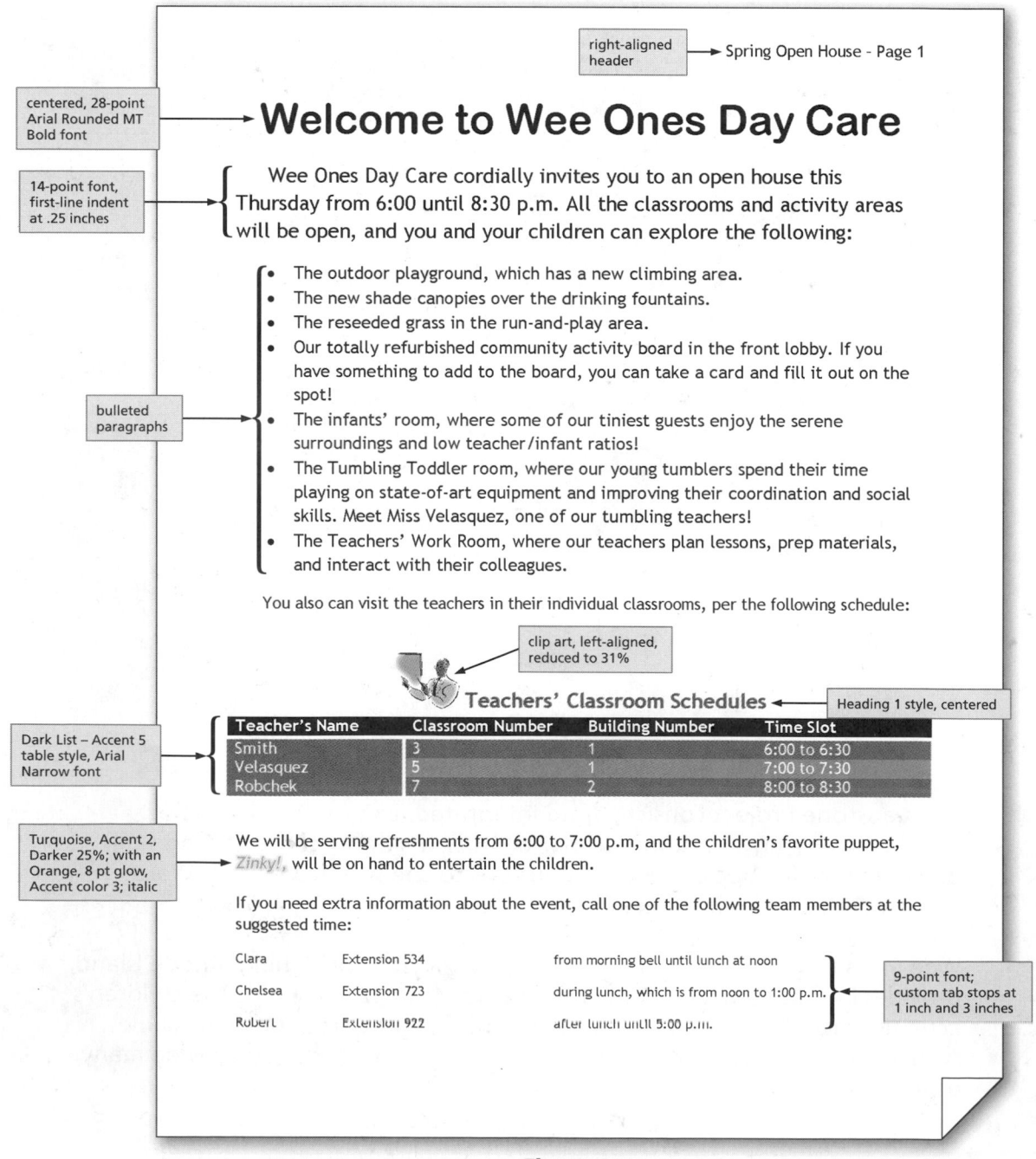

Figure 1–1

Instructions Part 2: The owner of the day care is pleased with your flyer, but she has some changes for you. Check the spelling of your document, but be sure not to change the spelling of the puppet's name. Center the table, add the first initials "R" and "S" to the teachers' names "Smith" and "Robchek," respectively, and adjust the columns to fit the table contents. Then, bold the teachers' names and italicize their respective time slots in the table. The grass area in the playground is not ready for use; as such, delete the third bullet from the bulleted list and move the first bullet so that it is the second bullet in the list. Move the clip art to the right side of the table title and set it to a Tight text wrap. Delete the tab stop at the 3-inch mark and use a comma between each of the extensions and suggested times. Change the custom tab stops for the last three lines of text so that the text is more evenly aligned across the page. Miss Velasquez will not be attending the event. Search and replace her name with "Chardon," the last name of the other tumbling teacher. Last, find a synonym for the text, tiniest, which is used within the bulleted list, and change the theme colors to Slipstream.

PowerPoint Capstone Project

Creating a Presentation with Images and a Transition

Problem: During each open house at Wee Ones Day Care, you give an orientation presentation to the parents who come to visit. The owner, Elizabeth Jordan, has asked you to ensure that the PowerPoint presentation for the upcoming open house showcases the day care and highlights its offerings.

Instructions Part 1: Use the typed notes shown in Figure 1–2 on page CAP 4 to start the presentation shown in Figure 1–3 on page CAP 5. Apply the Angles theme, change the Theme Colors to Apex, and use a Title Slide layout for Slide 1, the Two Content layout for Slide 2, and the Content with Caption layout for Slides 3 and 4.

On Slide 1, shown in Figure 1–3 (a), change the font size of the title, Welcome to Wee Ones Day Care, to 48 point, adjusting the text as shown in Figure 1–3 (a). Apply the Word Art style, Fill – Olive Green, Accent 2, Warm Matte Bevel, to the title and then italicize the text. Apply the Newsprint texture fill to the subtitle text, center the text and then change the font size to 18 point. Insert the Explosion 1 shape, position and resize it as shown in Figure 1–3 (a). Apply the Light 1 Outline, Colored Fill – Lavender, Accent 6 style to the shape, add the text, apply bold, and then change the font size to 20 point.

On Slide 2, shown in Figure 1–3 (b), in the right placeholder, click the Clip Art button and use the text, preschool, to search for the picture shown in Figure 1–3 (b). Resize the picture to approximately 6" × 4", soften the picture by 25%, increase the Saturation to 200%, and apply the Texturizer artistic effect. Then, add a Reflected Bevel, White picture style, an Aqua, Accent 3, Darker 25% picture border, and a Relaxed Inset bevel. Insert the Canvas texture fill to the background of the slide.

On Slide 3, shown in Figure 1–3 (c), adjust the title text to match the figure. Format the Craft table bullets to match the bullets in Slide 2. Insert a Striped Right Arrow and position it to point to the craft tables bullets. Add the text, Look!, and then format the text as 32 point, bold, Lavender, Accent 6, Darker 50%. Change the shape style to Subtle Effect – Lavender, Accent 6. Delete the subtitle placeholder.

On Slide 4, shown in Figure 1–3 (d), format the list as bullets, and then underline and italicize the word, Gated. Use the Format Painter button to underline and italicize the indicated words in the subsequent bullets. Delete the subtitle placeholder. Open the Format Background dialog box and use the text, preschool, to search for and insert the picture shown in Figure 1–3 (d). Set the Transparency to 40%.

Instructions Part 2: Elizabeth Jordan reviewed your presentation and has suggested a few changes. On Slide 2, change the border color of the image to Blue, Accent 4, Darker 25% as shown in Figure 1–4 (a). Then, apply the Push transition to all the slides and increase the duration to 04.00.

On the Safety slide, Slide 4, replace the text, Safety is our concern!, with Healthy Kids Are Happy Kids. Apply the Subtle Effect – Aqua, Accent 3 shape style, change the shape outline to Blue, Accent 4, and change the weight to 2¼ pt. Reposition and resize the title placeholder as shown in Figure 1–4 (c). Center the text and then apply the Stop Warp Transform text effect. Format the WordArt with the Gradient Fill – Lavender, Accent 6, Inner Shadow.

Continued >

To accommodate some last-minute content, duplicate Slide 2, position the new slide as Slide 4, delete the image, search for the giraffe and bird in tree picture shown in Figure 1–4 (b) and insert this clip art into the placeholder. Resize the clip art to approximately 5.6" × 4.32" and apply the Bevel Perspective picture style. Replace the text on the slide with the following content, formatted as bulleted text. Be sure to resize the placeholder so that each bulleted item appears on a single line.

Title: Special Events for Older Children
Field trip to the Roger Williams Zoo
Fundraisers for local charities
Carnival Night
Submit the assignment as requested by your instructor.

Slide #1

Welcome to Wee Ones Day Care

We cater to families who want the very best for their children

Slide #2

Activities for the Little Ones

Outdoors

       Playground

       Tetherball

Indoors

       Computer games

       Story nook

Nap time

       Individual mats

       Blankets and pillows

Slide #3

Adventures for the Older Children

       Supervised Internet exploration

       Writing centers

       Craft tables

          Paints

          Beading

          Pottery tools

Slide #4

Safety is our concern!

       Gated driveway

       Cameras at all entrances

       Identification process for all visitors

       Staff nurse on duty

Figure 1–2

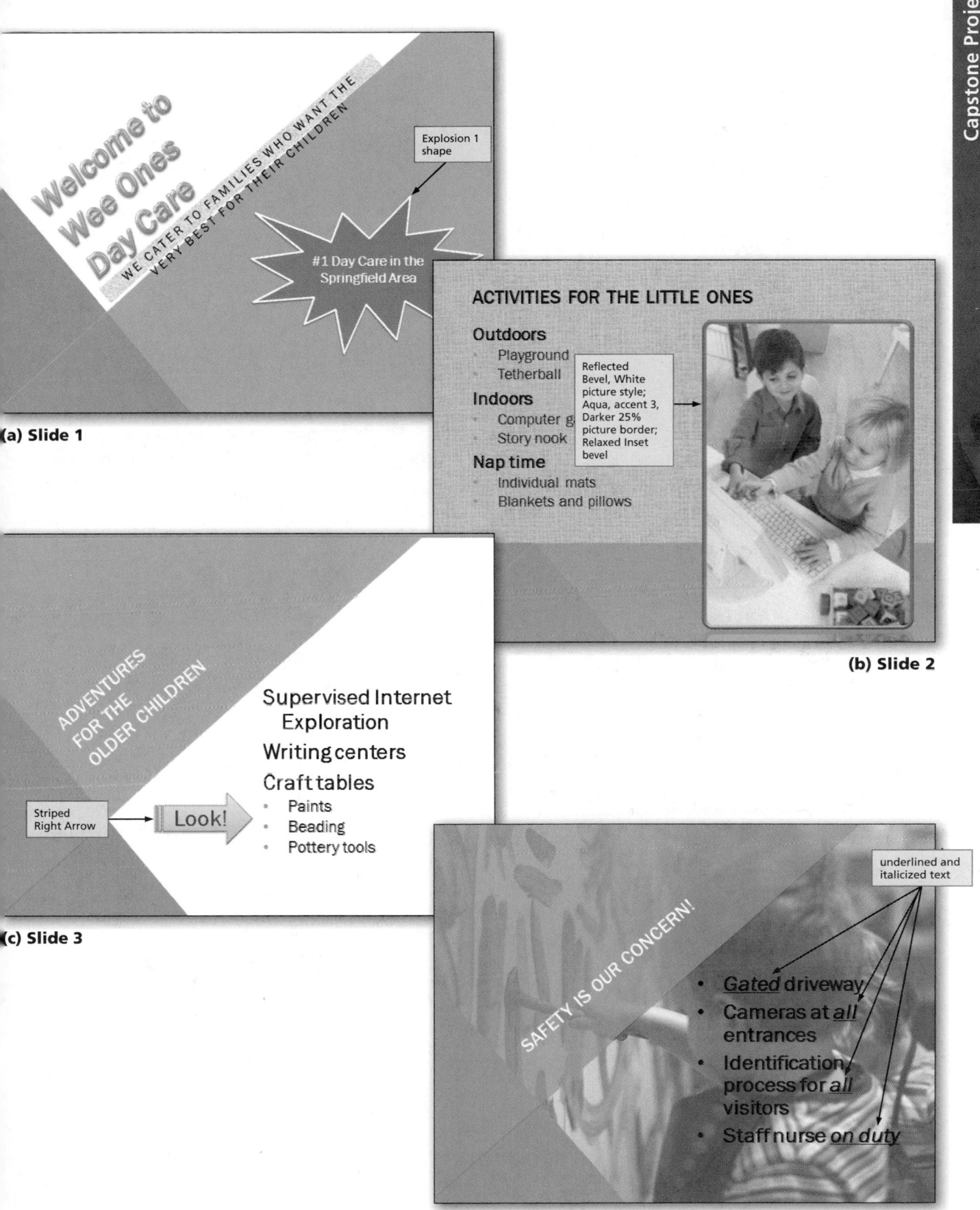

(a) Slide 1

(b) Slide 2

(c) Slide 3

(d) Slide 4

Figure 1–3

Continued >

PowerPoint Capstone Project *continued*

(a) Slide 2 (Modified)

ACTIVITIES FOR THE LITTLE ONES

Outdoors
- Playground
- Tetherball

Indoors
- Computer games
- Story nook

Nap time
- Individual mats
- Blankets and pillows

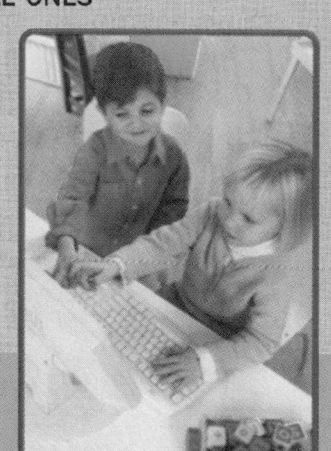

(b) Slide 4 (Duplicated and Modified Slide 2)

SPECIAL EVENTS FOR OLDER CHILDREN

- Field trip to Roger Williams Zoo
- Fundraisers for local charities
- Carnival Night

(c) Slide 5 (Original Slide 4 Modified)

Healthy Kids Are Happy Kids

- *Gated* driveway
- Cameras at *all* entrances
- Identification process for *all* visitors
- Staff nurse *on duty*

Figure 1–4

Excel Capstone Project

Analyzing and Presenting Fundraising Data

Problem: The teachers at Wee Ones Day Care have been running fundraisers throughout the year so that the day care can fund the many field trips that the children take. Over the last year, money has come in from different events, including bake sales, car washes, community book sales, and similar activities. In addition, cash donations were received from individuals and business groups, and grants were received from several government agencies in the city. The owner of the day care has asked you to organize the information about the money that has flowed from these events and prepare a basic spreadsheet, as shown in Figure 1–5, for use by the administration team.

Instructions Part 1: Start Excel and enter the text from Table 1–1. Place the text, **Events**, from the top-left of the table in cell A1. Place the remainder of the table in the adjacent rows and columns in the worksheet. Format the range B2:E2 with Currency formatting (Number group | Home tab) with floating dollar signs, and format the range B3_E7 with Accounting Number Format (Number group | Home tab). Change the column width of column A to 115 pixels. Change the width of columns B, C, D, and E to 109 pixels.

Double-click the Sheet1 tab, and rename the tab to **Fundraising Overview**. Change the tab color to Red (column 2, row 1 in the Standard Colors area).

Table 1–1 Sources of Money at Wee Ones Day Care

Events	1st Quarter	2nd Quarter	3rd Quarter	4th Quarter
Bake Sales	354	98	39	117
Car Washes	192	0	430	381
Community Book Sales	91	119	43	117
Corporate Donations	1678	891	1229	834
Individual Donations	2800	0	1500	0
Government Grants	2500	1250	3000	0

Insert two new rows above row 1. Enter the text **Fundraising at Wee Ones Day Care** in cell A1 and the text **A Year in Review** in cell A2. Merge and center the cell A1 text across columns A through E, and do the same for the cell A2 text. Format cells A1:E2 with the Title style; change the font size of the text in row 2 to 16. Format cells A3:E3 with the Heading 3 style. Apply the Equity theme to the workbook.

To align the column widths to their best fit, double-click the left column border for column B, and for columns C through F.

Instructions Part 2: In cell A10, enter **Total** and apply the Total cell style to the range A10:E10. In cell A11, enter **Lowest Funding Amount**. In cell A12, enter **Highest Funding Amount**, and in cell A13, enter **Average Funding Amount**. Bold the text in cells A10, A11, A12, and A13, and change the font in those cells to Arial Narrow, size 10 font. Increase the width of column A to 147 pixels. Change cells B4:E10 to font size 14.

In cell B10, use the Sum function to sum the values in the range B4:B9. Copy the formula in cell B10 to the range C10:E10 and apply the Currency format with fixed dollar signs to the numbers in the range B10:E10.

In cell B11, use the Insert Function button (Formulas tab | Function Library group) to insert the MIN function for the range B4:B9. Use the fill handle to copy the formula from cell B11 to the range C11:E11.

In cell B12, enter **=(max(B4:B9))**. Copy the formula in cell B12 to the range C12:E12.

Continued >

In cell B13, use the Insert Function button (Formulas tab | Function Libraries group) to insert the AVERAGE function for the range B4:B9. Use the fill handle to copy the formula from cell B13 to the range C13:E13.

Select the range B11:E13. Format the range with Accounting Number Format (Number group | Home tab). Use the Decrease Decimal button (Home tab | Number group) to remove all decimal places from the values in the cells.

If necessary, select the range B11:E13. Change the font color of the text to Dark Red, Accent 2, Darker 50%; change the font to Times New Roman; and change the font size to 12 point.

One of the school's instructors reviews the entries in the spreadsheet and asks you to change cell C8 to 350 to reflect updated records and to change the header text in the range B3:E3 to make the header text clearer. Delete the contents of cell C8, and enter `350`. Using the Find & Select button (Home tab | Editing group) to find all cells containing the word Quarter, replace all instances with the words `Fiscal Quarter`, and then use the Wrap Text button (Home tab | Alignment group) to wrap the text.

Highlight the range B3:E3, and using the Fill Color arrow (Home tab | Font group), select Orange, Accent 1, Lighter 40%. Highlight the range A4:A9. Using the Format Cells command on a shortcut menu, choose the sixth choice in the seventh row of the Background Color palette.

To create a chart to make your spreadsheet more effective, use the range A3:E9 and the Bar button (Insert tab | Charts group) to create a Clustered Bar in 3-D chart. Style the chart with a Gradient line, Mahogany Border color; a Border Style of 6 pts; and a 3-D Format of Bevel Top Slope. Double-click the Horizontal (Value) Axis of the chart, and then change the Major Unit to `1000` (Format Axis dialog box). Select the chart, make sure that the Snap to Grid command is selected (Align gallery | Format tab), and size and position the chart as shown in Figure 1–5.

Before you turn in the spreadsheet and chart for Elizabeth Jordan's first review, spell check your work and change the document properties as specified by your instructor. Save the workbook, and print your work in formula view.

Instructions Part 3: After considering your work further, you decide to make some changes before you give the spreadsheet file to Elizabeth Jordan for her final approval.

Use the Colors button (Page Layout tab | Themes group) to select the Flow color for the workbook theme. For the range A4:A9, use the Fill tab (Format Cells dialog box) to choose the fourth color in the second row of the Background Color palette.

Use the Format Painter button (Home tab | Clipboard group) to copy the formatting of cell E3 to F3. Enter the text, `Trend`, in cell F3. Use the Line button (Insert tab | Sparklines group) to create a Sparkline chart in F4 for the range B4:E4. Use the fill handle to build the same type of chart in each of the cells in the range F5:F9. Highlight the range F4:F9, and use the Sparkline Color button (Design tab | Style group) to change the Weight to 4 ½ pt.

To showcase the team's efforts in the second quarter, rename the Sheet2 tab to `Second Fiscal Quarter`. From the Fundraising Overview tab, use the range A3:A9 and the range C3:C9 to create a 2-D Pie chart (Insert tab | Charts group). Use the Move Chart command on a shortcut menu to move the chart to the Second Fiscal Quarter tab.

On the Second Fiscal Quarter tab, use the Change Chart Type command on a shortcut menu to change the chart to Pie in 3-D. Use the Themes button (Page Layout tab | Themes group) to select the Waveform theme and use the Format Data Series command on a shortcut menu to change the Pie Explosion to 10% (Format Data Series dialog box). Change the border color (Format Chart Area) to a Gradient Line, Gold color, and change the border style to 12 pts with a Join type of Bevel. Select the chart, make sure that the Snap to Grid command is selected (Align gallery | Format tab), and size and position the chart as shown in Figure 1–6.

Using the bottom row border of row 2, resize row 2 to 50 pixels. In cell A2, enter `To Be Reviewed at Next Meeting`. Select cells A2:J2, and then use the Merge & Center button (Home tab | Alignment group) to merge and center the text, and then change the font of the text to Bodoni MT, 28 pt.

To prepare a polished spreadsheet for printing, you have some final tasks to complete.

Figure 1–5

Use the Header & Footer button (Insert tab | Text group) to insert the current time and current date in the header. Next, use the Margins button (Page Layout tab | Page Setup group) to select Narrow margins and the Orientation button (Page Layout tab | Page Setup group) to select Landscape orientation.

You want to make a further good impression on your boss. Before you turn in the spreadsheet and chart for her review, spell check your work. Save the workbook, and print your work in non-formula view and then formula view.

Continued >

Excel Capstone Project *continued*

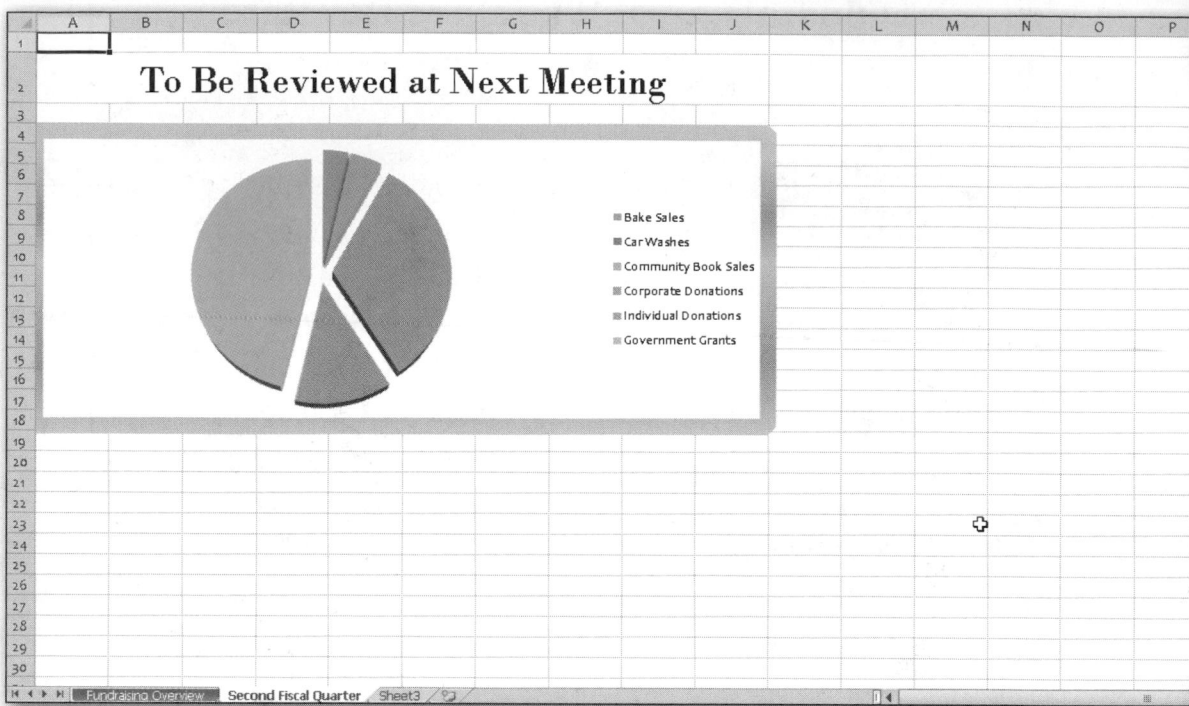

Figure 1–6

Change the document properties as specified by your instructor. Change the worksheet header with your name, course number, and other information as specified by your instructor. Save the workbook using the current file name. Close the workbook. Submit the assignment as requested by your instructor.

Access Capstone Project

Creating, Querying, and Maintaining the Wee Ones Database

Problem: Elizabeth Jordan has asked you to work on a special project for the Wee Ones Day Care. She has been keeping information about the children in the program and their parents in Word documents and Excel workbooks, and she would like you to create an Access database for storing this information, using the data shown in Figure 1–7.

Elizabeth keeps a list of the children and their enrollment details in a Word document. She maintains their tuition and fee information in an Excel workbook.

She also maintains information on the children's parents. She keeps their parents' addresses in a Word document. However, she keeps the previous and current balances for each parent in an Excel workbook, which she provides to you electronically. The parents' financial information includes the parent ID, their last and first names, previous balance, and current balance.

Elizabeth also keeps a list of which children belong to which parent. Each child has one parent listed as the 'parent of record,' but a parent or guardian may be responsible for more than one child. The following parents have one child in the program: Cho Song, Karen Leon, Mara Olivo, Mary Ann Arnold, Daniel Navarro, Addas Abdi, and Claire Montout. Allen Kwan has two children in the program. The Hunter twins' mother's name is Jennifer White. Barbara Lehmann is responsible for Emma Chao, Lucas Jordan, and Paul Lehmann. Susan Hargraves has reserved a place at Wee Ones for her child, but her child has not yet enrolled.

Instructions Part 1: Using the data shown in Figure 1–7, design and create the Wee Ones database. Use the database design guidelines provided in Chapter 1 to help you in the design process.

Child ID	Last Name	First Name	Enrollment Type
C-347	Song	Mia	Morning
C-348	Leon	Primrose	Afternoon
C-352	Olivo	Lily	Morning
C-355	Arnold	Alexander	Full day
C-357	Navarro	Sofia	Full day
C-358	Hunter	Andrew	Afternoon
C-359	Hunter	Emily	Full day
C-363	Lehmann	Paul	Full day
C 364	Jordan	Lucas	Morning
C-365	Abdi	Almen	3 Mornings
C-369	Kwan	Christie	Afternoon
C-370	Kwan	Wendy	Morning
C-371	Montout	Jean Jacques	3 Mornings
C-342	Chao	Emma	Afternoon

Figure 1–7 (a) Child Schedule Information

Continued >

Access Capstone Project *continued*

▲	A	B	C	D	E	F	G	H
1	Child ID	Last Name	First Name	Tuition (Weekly)	Other Fees			
2	C-347	Song	Mia	$90	$0			
3	C-348	Leon	Primrose	$60	$17.50			
4	C-352	Olivo	Lily	$90	$0			
5	C-355	Arnold	Alexander	$165	$12.50			
6	C-357	Navarro	Sofia	$165	$12.50			
7	C-358	Hunter	Andrew	$60	$17.50			
8	C-359	Hunter	Emily	$165	$12.50			
9	C-363	Lehmann	Paul	$165	$0			
10	C-364	Jordan	Lucas	$90	$17.50			
11	C-365	Abdi	Almen	$45	$25			
12	C-369	Kwan	Christie	$60	$17.50			
13	C-370	Kwan	Wendy	$90	$17.50			
14	C-371	Montout	Jean Jacques	$45	$25			
15	C-342	Chao	Emma	$60	$17.50			
16								

Figure 1–7 (b) Tuition Information

Parent ID	Last Name	First Name	Street	City	State	Postal Code
P-136	Song	Cho	25 Sagamore Rd.	Springfield	RI	02913
P-129	Leon	Karen	74 North Mayfair	Springfield	RI	02913
P-165	Olivo	Mara	8 Bayview Place	Greenwich	RI	02922
P-131	Arnold	Mary Ann	Crandall Dr.	Greenwich	RI	02922
P-135	Navarro	Daniel	68 Sofia St.	Springfield	RI	02913
P-155	White	Jennifer	1145 Farmington Ave.	Lincolnville	RI	02923
P-261	Lehmann	Barbara	118 Fairfax Dr.	Springfield	RI	02913
P-147	Abdi	Abbas	3 Rose Ct.	Lincolnville	RI	02923
P-187	Kwan	Allen	170 Gillooly Dr.	Lincolnville	RI	02923
P-231	Montout	Claire	39 Wales St.	Springfield	RI	02913
P-246	Hargraves	Susan	26 Maple St.	Greenwich	RI	02922

Figure 1–7 (c) Parent Address Information

	A	B	C	D	E	F	G	H
1	Parent ID	Last Name	First Name	Previous Balance	Current Balance			
2	P-136	Song	Cho	90	90			
3	P-129	Leon	Karen	120	77.5			
4	P-165	Olivo	Mara	270	90			
5	P-131	Arnold	Mary Ann	0	165			
6	P-135	Navarro	Daniel	0	165			
7	P-155	White	Jennifer	0	255			
8	P-261	Lehmann	Barbara	315	350			
9	P-147	Abdi	Abbas	0	70			
10	P-187	Kwan	Allen	185	450			
11	P-231	Montout	Claire	180	90			
12	P-246	Hargraves	Susan	0	290			
13								

Figure 1–7 (d) Parent Account Information

Using Datasheet view, create a table in which to store the data related to the children. Use the name, Child, for the table. The fields and data for the Child table are shown in Figure 1–7 (a) and (b). Be sure to determine the correct data types and field sizes. Resize the columns to best fit the data and save the changes to the layout of the table.

Using Design view, add the fields shown in Figure 1–7 (c) and Figure 1–7 (d) to the Parent table. Use the name, Parent, for the table. Be sure to determine the correct data types and field sizes, and then import the data from the Parent Account workbook. Use Datasheet view to resize the columns to best fit the data. Save the changes to the layout of the table.

Print the contents of the tables.

Use the Simple Query Wizard to create a query that displays the child's first and last names, child ID, and enrollment type. Save the query as Child Attendance Query.

Open the Child Attendance Query and add a criterion to limit attendance to those children who attend for the full day. Save the query as Child Attendance-Full day Query.

Create a simple form for the Child table. Save the form as Child Form.

Use the Report button to create a report for the Child table. The report should include Child ID, the child's first and last names, Enrollment Type, Tuition, and Other Fees fields. Do not include a total. Save the report as Child Detail Report.

Change the database properties as specified by your instructor.

Instructions Part 2: Answer the following questions, using the Parent table, and include the Parent ID, parent's first and last names, City, Previous Balance, and Current Balance fields. Save each query.

(a) Which parents are located in Springfield?

(b) Which parents' last names begin with 'L'?

(c) Which parents have a postal code of 02922? (Postal Code field should not appear in the query results.)

(d) Which parents have a current balance of $90?

(e) Which parents have a previous balance that is greater than $100 and a current balance of less than $200?

(f) Which parents are located in Lincolnville or have a current balance of $90?

(g) Sort the parents so that those with the greatest current balance appear at the top, and then display only the top 25 percent.

(h) Create a parameter query that requests a parent's last name and then displays the Parent ID, parent's first and last name, Previous Balance, and Current Balance.

Continued >

Elizabeth wants to review the children's enrollment type and current balances. Join the Parent and Child tables, including the Parent ID, the parent's first and last name, city, and Current balance, from the Parent table, and the Child ID, child's first name, and Enrollment Type from the Child table. Sort the records in ascending order by Parent Last Name, and then descending by Current balance. All parents should appear, even if they have no children currently enrolled. Save the query as Parent–Child Query. Export the Parent–Child Query to Excel, and save the export steps.

Use the Report Wizard and the Parent–Child Query to create a report that includes the following fields: Parent ID, parent last name, Current balance, Child ID, and child first name so that the report fits on the page.

Using the Child table, create a calculated field that adds the Tuition to the Other Fees. Add the caption, Total Charges, to the field.

Create queries to calculate the following statistics: (a) What is the average Current Balance for all parents? (b) What is the average Current Balance for parents who live in Greenwich? (c) What is the average Current Balance by postal code?

Using the Parent–Child Query, create a crosstab query where Enrollment Type appears as the row header and City appears as the column header. Count the number of children using the Child ID field. Save the query as Parent–Child Query Crosstab.

Instructions Part 3: Elizabeth needs to update some parent and child information. Create a split form for the Parent table. Filter the form to locate Parent ID P-131 and change their address to 1010 Florissant Rd, Lincolnville, 02923. Save the form as Parent Split Form.

Add the following data to the Child table: Charlotte Hargraves (C-381) is enrolling for all mornings (not 3 Mornings) at a tuition rate of $90, and $12.50 in other fees. Assign Parent ID P-246 to this child. Use a delete query to delete Child ID C-342 from the Child table. Save the query as Delete Child Query.

In the Parent table, specify that Last Name is a required field, use RI as the default value for the State field, and add a rule that specifies that the Current Balance must be greater than $0 and less than or equal to $500. Test the validation rules.

Elizabeth wants to add additional details about which classroom each child is in to the database. Add a lookup field named Program Details to the Child table with the following values: CAT (Caterpillar classroom, age 3), FLY (Butterfly classroom, age 4), and BLU (Bluebird classroom, age 5). Limit the lookup field to these three choices. Use an update query to assign all children to the Butterfly classroom and save the query. Then, make the following changes to the Child table:

Change the Program Details of children C-347, C-358, C-364, and C-357, to CAT.

Change the Program Details of children C-352, C-363, and C-371 to BLU.

In the Child table, make the Parent ID field a required field. Test the validation rule. Save and close the table.

After reviewing the database, the Board of Directors would like to make sure that the parent and child data meets state requirements, and wants the database to follow certain guidelines. The Board wants to ensure that no child is assigned a parent who is not in the database. They also want the ability to change a Parent ID in the Parent table and have that change applied to the Child table.

Open the Parent table and using the subdatasheet, view the children of the parent with Parent ID P-261. Enter the following information using the subdatasheet: C-374, Oliver Lehmann, enrolled for 3 mornings in the Caterpillar classroom for $45 tuition and no other fees.

For an upcoming board meeting, Elizabeth needs updated data on the children in the program. Update the Child Detail Report to include the Program Details field to the right of the Enrollment Type field. Include totals for tuition and fees. Change the orientation to landscape to fit the data. Save and close the report. Using the Parent table, add a Total row that includes the total for the previous balance and the current balance, and counts the number of parents. (*Hint*: use the Count function on the Parent ID field.)

Submit the database in the format specified by your instructor.

Index

Quick Reference Summary

Table 1: Microsoft Word 2010 Quick Reference Summary

Task	Page Number	Mouse	Ribbon	Shortcut Menu	Keyboard Shortcut
All Caps	WD 81		Change Case button (Home tab | Font group), UPPERCASE		CTRL+SHIFT+A
AutoCorrect Entry, Create	WD 86		Options (File tab), Proofing (Word Options dialog box)		
AutoCorrect Options button, Use	WD 85	Point to AutoCorrect Options button in flagged word			
Bibliographical List, Create	WD 108		Bibliography button (References tab | Citations & Bibliography group)		
Bibliography Style, Change	WD 89		Bibliography Style box arrow (References tab | Citations & Bibliography group)		
Bold	WD 28	Bold button on Mini toolbar	Bold button (Home tab | Font group)	Font, Font tab (Font dialog box)	CTRL+B
Border Paragraph	WD 160		Border button arrow (Home tab | Paragraph group)		
Building Block, Create	WD 171		Quick Parts button (Insert tab | Text group)		ALT+F3
Building Block, Insert	WD 174		Quick Parts button (Insert tab | Text group		F3
Building Block, Modify	WD 173		Quick Parts button (Insert tab | Text group), right-click building block, Edit Properties		
Bullets, Apply	WD 22		Bullets button (Home tab | Paragraph group)	Bullets	* (ASTERISK), SPACEBAR
Center	WD 14	Center button on Mini toolbar	Center button (Home tab | Paragraph group)	Paragraph, Indents and Spacing tab (Paragraph dialog box)	CTRL+E
Change Case	WD 18		Change Case button (Home tab | Font group)	Font, Font tab (Font dialog box)	SHIFT+F3
Change Spacing before or after Paragraph	WD 43		Spacing Before or Spacing After box arrow (Page Layout tab | Paragraph group)	Paragraph, Indents and Spacing tab (Paragraph dialog box)	

Table 1: Microsoft Word 2010 Quick Reference Summary *(continued)*

Task	Page Number	Mouse	Ribbon	Shortcut Menu	Keyboard Shortcut
Citation Placeholder, Insert	WD 94		Insert Citation button (References tab | Citations & Bibliography group), Add New Placeholder		
Citation, Edit	WD 91	Click citation, Citations Options box arrow, Edit Citation			
Citation, Insert	WD 90		Insert Citation button (References tab | Citations & Bibliography group), Add New Source		
Clear Formatting	WD 161		Clear Formatting button (Home tab | Font group)		CTRL+SPACEBAR, CTRL+Q
Click and Type	WD 80	Position mouse pointer until desired icon appears, then double-click			
Clip Art, Insert	WD 148		Clip Art button (Insert tab | Illustrations group)		
Color Text	WD 25	Font Color button on Mini toolbar	Font Color button arrow (Home tab | Font group)		
Copy	WD 113		Copy button (Home tab | Clipboard group)	Copy	CTRL+C
Count Words	WD 101	Word Count indicator on status bar	Word Count button (Review tab | Proofing group)		CTRL+SHIFT+G
Custom Dictionary, Set Default, View or Modify Entries	WD 120		Options (File tab), Proofing (Word Options dialog box), Custom Dictionaries button		
Date, Insert Current	WD 170		Insert Date and Time button (Insert tab | Text group)		
Document Properties, Change	WD 49		Properties button (File tab | Info tab)		
Document Properties, Print	WD 123		File tab | Print tab, first button in Settings area		
Double-Space	WD 73		Line and Paragraph Spacing button (Home tab | Paragraph group)	Paragraph, Indents and Spacing tab (Paragraph dialog box)	CTRL+2
Double-Underline	WD 81		Underline button arrow (Home tab | Font group)	Font, Font tab (Font dialog box)	CTRL+SHIFT+D
Envelope, Address and Print	WD 189		Create Envelopes button (Mailings tab | Create group), Envelopes tab (Envelopes and Labels dialog box)		
Field, Convert to Regular text	WD 110				Click field, CTRL+SHIFT+F9
Find Text	WD 115	Select Browse Object button on vertical scroll bar, Find button	Find button (Home tab | Editing group)		CTRL+F
Font Size, Change	WD 16	Font Size box arrow on Mini toolbar	Font Size box arrow (Home tab | Font group)	Font, Font tab (Font dialog box)	CTRL+D
Font Size, Decrease	WD 81	Shrink Font button on Mini toolbar	Shrink Font button (Home tab | Font group)		CTRL+SHIFT+<

Table 1: Microsoft Word 2010 Quick Reference Summary *(continued)*

Task	Page Number	Mouse	Ribbon	Shortcut Menu	Keyboard Shortcut
Font Size, Decrease 1 point	WD 81				CTRL+[
Font Size, Increase	WD 146	Grow Font button on Mini toolbar	Grow Font button (Home tab | Font group)		CTRL+SHIFT+>
Font Size, Increase 1 point	WD 81				CTRL+]
Font, Change	WD 17	Font box arrow on Mini toolbar	Font box arrow (Home tab | Font group)	Font, Font tab (Font dialog box)	CTRL+D
Footnote, Insert	WD 93		Insert Footnote button (References tab | Footnotes group)		
Formatting Marks	WD 7		Show/Hide ¶ button (Home tab | Paragraph group)		CTRL+SHIFT+*
Go to a Page	WD 117	'Browse the pages in your document' tab in Navigation Pane	Find button arrow (Home tab | Editing group)		CTRL+G
Graphic, Adjust Brightness and Contrast	WD 153		Corrections button (Picture Tools Format tab | Adjust group)	Format Picture, Picture Corrections button (Format Picture dialog box)	
Graphic, Change Border Color	WD 154		Picture Border button (Picture Tools Format tab | Picture Styles group)		
Graphic, Change Color	WD 151		Color button (Picture Tools Format tab | Adjust group)	Format Picture, Picture Color button (Format Picture dialog box)	
Graphic, Flip	WD 157		Rotate button (Picture Tools Format tab | Arrange group)		
Graphic, Move	WD 155	Drag graphic			
Graphic, Resize	WD 34	Drag sizing handle	Shape Height and Shape Width text boxes (Picture Tools Format tab | Size group)	Size and Position, Size tab (Layout dialog box)	
Graphic, Set Transparent Color	WD 152		Color button (Picture Tools Format tab | Adjust group)		
Hanging Indent, Create	WD 81	Drag Hanging Indent marker on ruler	Paragraph Dialog Box Launcher (Home tab or Page Layout tab | Paragraph group), Indents and Spacing tab (Paragraph dialog box)	Paragraph, Indents and Spacing tab (Paragraph dialog box)	CTRL+T
Hanging Indent, Remove	WD 81	Drag Hanging Indent marker on ruler	Paragraph Dialog Box Launcher (Home tab or Page Layout tab | Paragraph group), Indents and Spacing tab (Paragraph dialog box)	Paragraph, Indents and Spacing tab (Paragraph dialog box)	CTRL+SHIFT+T
Header and Footer, Close	WD 78	Double-click dimmed document text	Close Header and Footer button (Header & Footer Tools Design tab | Close group)		
Header, Switch to	WD 75	Double-click dimmed header	Header button (Insert tab | Header & Footer group)		
Hyperlink, Convert to Regular Text	WD 163	Undo Hyperlink (AutoCorrect Options menu)	Hyperlink button (Insert tab | Links group)	Remove Hyperlink	
Indent, Decrease	WD 81	Drag First Line Indent marker on ruler	Decrease Indent button (Home tab | Paragraph group)	Paragraph, Indents and Spacing tab (Paragraph dialog box)	CTRL+SHIFT+M

Table 1: Microsoft Word 2010 Quick Reference Summary *(continued)*

Task	Page Number	Mouse	Ribbon	Shortcut Menu	Keyboard Shortcut
Indent, First-Line	WD 83	Drag First Line Indent marker on ruler	Paragraph Dialog Box Launcher (Home tab or Page Layout tab | Paragraph group)	Paragraph, Indents and Spacing tab (Paragraph dialog box)	TAB
Indent, Increase	WD 81		Increase Indent button (Home tab | Paragraph group)		CTRL+M
Insertion Point, Move Down/Up One Line	WD 11				DOWN ARROW/ UP ARROW
Insertion Point, Move Down/Up One Paragraph	WD 11				CTRL+DOWN ARROW/ CTRL+UP ARROW
Insertion Point, Move Down/Up One Screen	WD 11				PAGE DOWN/ PAGE UP
Insertion Point, Move Left/ Right One Character	WD 11				LEFT ARROW/ RIGHT ARROW
Insertion Point, Move Left/ Right One Word	WD 11				CTRL+LEFT ARROW/ CTRL+RIGHT ARROW
Insertion Point, Move to Beginning/End of Document	WD 11				CTRL+HOME/ CTRL+END
Insertion Point, Move to Beginning/End of Line	WD 11				HOME/ END
Insertion Point, Move to Bottom of Document Window	WD 11				ALT+CTRL+PAGE DOWN/ ALT+CTRL+PAGE UP
Italicize	WD 24	Italic button on Mini toolbar	Italic button (Home tab | Font group)	Font, Font tab (Font dialog box)	CTRL+I
Justify Paragraph	WD 81		Justify button (Home tab | Paragraph group)	Paragraph, Indents and Spacing tab (Paragraph dialog box)	CTRL+J
Left-Align Paragraph	WD 81		Align Text Left button (Home tab | Paragraph group)	Paragraph, Indents and Spacing tab (Paragraph dialog box)	CTRL+L
Line Spacing, Change	WD 73		Line and Paragraph Spacing button (Home tab | Paragraph group)	Paragraph, Indents and Spacing tab (Paragraph dialog box)	CTRL+[number of desired line spacing, i.e., 2 fo double-spacing]
Mailing Label, Print	WD 190		Create Labels button (Mailings tab | Create group)		
Margin Settings, Change	WD 141	Drag margin boundary on ruler	Margins button (Page Layout tab | Page Setup group)		
Move Text	WD 47	Drag and drop selected text	Cut button (Home tab | Clipboard group); Paste button (Home tab | Clipboard group)	Cut; Paste	CTRL+X; CTRL+V
New File, Create from Existing	WD 165		'New from existing' button (File tab | New tab)		

Table 1: Microsoft Word 2010 Quick Reference Summary *(continued)*

Task	Page Number	Mouse	Ribbon	Shortcut Menu	Keyboard Shortcut
Nonbreaking Space, Insert	WD 175		Symbol button (Insert tab | Symbols group), More Symbols, Special Characters tab (Symbol dialog box)		CTRL+SHIFT+ SPACEBAR
Normal Style, Apply	WD 106		Normal in Quick Style gallery (Home tab | Styles group)		CTRL+SHIFT+S
Normal Style, Modify	WD 71		Styles Dialog Box Launcher (Home tab | Styles group), style box arrow, Modify	Right-click style (Home tab | Styles group), Modify	
Open a Document	WD 45		Open (File tab)		CTRL+O
Page Border, Add	WD 41		Page Borders button (Page Layout tab | Page Background group)		
Page Break, Insert	WD 106		Page Break button (Insert tab | Pages group)		CTRL+ENTER
Page Number, Insert	WD 77		Insert Page Number button (Header & Footer Tools Design tab | Header & Footer group)		
Paste	WD 113		Paste button (Home tab | Clipboard group)	Paste	CTRL+V
Paste Options	WD 156		Paste button arrow (Home tab | Clipboard group)		
Paste Options Menu, Display	WD 114	Paste Options button by moved/copied text			
Picture Style, Apply	WD 37		More button in Picture Styles gallery (Picture Tools Format tab | Picture Styles group)		
Picture Effects, Apply	WD 38		Picture Effects button (Picture Tools Format tab | Picture Styles group)	Format Picture	
Picture, Insert	WD 31		Insert Picture from File button (Insert tab | Illustrations group)		
Preview a Document	WD 124		File tab | Print tab, Next Page and Previous Page buttons		CTRL+P, ENTER
Print Document	WD 51		Print button (File tab | Print tab)		CTRL+P
Quick Style, Apply	WD 166		[style name] in Quick Style gallery (Home tab | Styles group)		CTRL+SHIFT+S, Style Name box arrow
Quit Word	WD 44	Close button on title bar	Exit (File tab)		ALT+F4
Redo	WD 23	Redo button on Quick Access Toolbar			CTRL+Y
Remove Character Formatting	WD 81				CTRL+SPACEBAR
Remove Paragraph Formatting	WD 81				CTRL+Q
Remove Space after Paragraph	WD 74		Line and Paragraph Spacing button (Home tab | Paragraph group)	Paragraph, Indents and Spacing tab (Paragraph dialog box)	CTRL+0 (zero)

Table 1: Microsoft Word 2010 Quick Reference Summary *(continued)*

Task	Page Number	Mouse	Ribbon	Shortcut Menu	Keyboard Shortcut
Replace Text	WD 116	Select Browse Object button on vertical scroll bar, Find button, Replace tab (Find and Replace dialog box)	Replace button (Home tab | Editing group)		CTRL+H
Research Task Pane, Look Up Information	WD 120	ALT+click desired word	Research button (Review tab | Proofing group)		
Right-Align	WD 76		Align Text Right button (Home tab | Paragraph group)	Paragraph, Indents and Spacing tab (Paragraph dialog box)	CTRL+R
Rulers, Display	WD 82	View Ruler button on vertical scroll bar	View Ruler check box (View tab | Show group)		
Save New Document	WD 12	Save button on Quick Access Toolbar	Save or Save As (File tab)		F12
Save Document, Same File Name	WD 30	Save button on Quick Access toolbar	Save (File tab)		CTRL+S
Scroll, Page by Page	WD 112	Previous Page/Next Page button on vertical scroll bar			CTRL+PAGE UP or CTRL+PAGE DOWN
Scroll, Up/Down One Line	WD 11	Click scroll arrow at top/bottom of vertical scroll bar			
Scroll, Up/Down One Screen	WD 11	Click above/below scroll box on vertical scroll bar			
Select Block of Text	WD 30	Click beginning, SHIFT-click end			
Select Character(s)	WD 30	Drag through characters			SHIFT+RIGHT ARROW or SHIFT+LEFT ARROW
Select Entire Document	WD 30	In left margin, triple-click	Select button arrow (Home tab | Editing group)		CTRL+A
Select Graphic	WD 30	Click graphic			
Select Group of Words	WD 27	Drag mouse pointer through words			CTRL+SHIFT+RIGHT ARROW
Select Line	WD 15	Click in left margin			SHIFT+DOWN ARROW
Select Multiple Lines	WD 21	Drag mouse pointer in left margin			SHIFT+DOWN ARROW
Select Nonadjacent Items	WD 15	Select first item, hold down CTRL key while selecting item(s)			
Select Paragraph	WD 30	Triple-click paragraph			CTRL+SHIFT+DOWN ARROW or CTRL+SHIFT+UP ARROW
Select Sentence	WD 30	CTRL-click			
Select Word	WD 30	Double-click word			CTRL+SHIFT+RIGHT ARROW or CTRL+SHIFT+LEFT ARROW
Shade Paragraph	WD 20		Shading button arrow (Home tab | Paragraph group)		
Shape, Add Text	WD 145			Add Text	

Table 1: Microsoft Word 2010 Quick Reference Summary *(continued)*

Task	Page Number	Mouse	Ribbon	Shortcut Menu	Keyboard Shortcut
Shape, Apply Style	WD 144		More button in Shape Styles gallery (Drawing Tools Format tab | Shape Styles group)	Format Shape, Color button in left pane (Format Shape dialog box)	
Shape, Insert	WD 142		Shapes button (Insert tab | Illustrations group)		
Single-Space Lines	WD 81		Line and Paragraph Spacing button (Home tab | Paragraph group)	Paragraph, Indents and Spacing tab (Paragraph dialog box)	CTRL+1
Small Caps	WD 81		Font Dialog Box Launcher (Home Tab | Font group), Font tab (Font dialog box)		CTRL+SHIFT+K
Source, Edit	WD 97		Click citation, Citation Options box arrow, Edit Source		
Source, Modify	WD 109		Manage Sources button (References tab | Citations & Bibliography group), Edit button		
Spelling and Grammar, Check at Once	WD 118	Spelling and Grammar check icon on status bar, Spelling	Spelling & Grammar button (Review tab | Proofing group)	Spelling	F7
Spelling, Check as You Type	WD 9	Click word, Spelling and Grammar Check icon on status bar		Right-click error, click correct word on shortcut menu	
Style, Update to Match Selection	WD 74		Right-click style in Quick Style gallery (Home tab | Styles group)	Styles	
Subscript	WD 81		Subscript button (Home tab | Font group)	Font, Font tab (Font dialog box)	CTRL+EQUAL SIGN
Superscript	WD 81		Superscript button (Home tab | Font group)	Font, Font tab (Font dialog box)	CTRL+SHIFT+PLUS SIGN
Symbol, Insert	WD 158		Insert Symbol button (Insert tab | Symbols group)		
Synonym, Find and Insert	WD 118		Thesaurus (Review tab | Proofing group)	Right-click word, click desired synonym on Synonym submenu	SHIFT+F7
Tab Stops, Set Custom	WD 169	Click desired tab stop on ruler	Paragraph Dialog Box Launcher (Home tab or Page Layout tab | Paragraph group), Tabs button (Paragraph dialog box)		
Table Columns, Resize to Fit Table Contents	WD 180	Double-click column boundary	AutoFit button (Table Tools Layout tab | Cell Size group)	AutoFit	
Table, Align Data in Cells	WD 182		Align [location] button (Table Tools Layout tab | Alignment group)		
Table, Apply Style	WD 179		More button in Table Styles gallery (Table Tools Design tab | Table Styles group)		
Table, Center	WD 183	Select table, Center button on Mini toolbar	Select table, Center button (Home tab | Font group)		
Table, Delete Cell Contents	WD 185		Cut button (Home tab | Clipboard group)		Select cell contents, DELETE or CTRL+X

Table 1: Microsoft Word 2010 Quick Reference Summary *(continued)*

Task	Page Number	Mouse	Ribbon	Shortcut Menu	Keyboard Shortcut
Table, Delete Entire	WD 185		Delete button (Table Tools Layout tab | Rows & Columns group)		
Table, Delete Row or Column	WD 185		Delete button (Table Tools Layout tab | Rows & Columns group)	Select row/column, Delete Rows or Delete Columns	
Table, Insert	WD 176		Table button (Insert tab | Tables group)		
Table, Insert Column	WD 185		Insert Columns to the Left/Right button (Table Tools Layout tab | Rows & Columns group)	Insert	
Table, Insert Row	WD 184		Insert Rows Above/Below button (Table Tools Layout Tab | Rows & Columns group)	Insert	
Table, Merge Cells	WD 185		Merge Cells button (Table Tools Layout tab | Merge group)	Merge Cells	
Table, Select Cell	WD 181	Click left edge of cell	Select button (Table Tools Layout tab | Table group)		
Table, Select Column	WD 181	Click top border of column	Select button (Table Tools Layout tab | Table group)		
Table, Select Entire	WD 181	Click table move handle	Select button (Table Tools Layout tab | Table group)		
Table, Select Multiple Cells, Rows, or Columns, Adjacent	WD 181	Drag through cells, rows, or columns			
Table, Select Next Cell	WD 181				TAB
Table, Select Previous Cell	WD 181				SHIFT+TAB
Table, Select Row	WD 181	Click to left of row	Select button (Table Tools Layout tab | Table Group)		
Table, Split Cells	WD 186		Split Cells button (Table Tools Layout tab | Merge group)	Split Cells	
Text Effect, Apply	WD 19		Text Effects button (Home tab | Font group)		
Text Wrapping, Change	WD 148		Wrap Text button (Drawing Tools format tab | Arrange group)	Wrap Text	
Theme Colors, Change	WD 28		Change Styles button (Home tab | Styles group)		
Underline	WD 27	Underline button on Mini toolbar	Underline button (Home tab | Font group)	Font, Font tab (Font dialog box)	CTRL+U
Underline Words, Not Spaces	WD 81		Font Dialog Box Launcher (Home tab | Font group), Font tab (Font dialog box), Underline style box arrow		CTRL+SHIFT+W
Undo	WD 23	Undo button on Quick Access Toolbar			CTRL+Z
Zoom Document	WD 33	Zoom Out or Zoom In button on status bar	Zoom button (View tab | Zoom group)		
Zoom One Page	WD 41		One Page button (View tab | Zoom group)		

Table 2: Microsoft PowerPoint 2010 Quick Reference Summary

Task	Page Number	Mouse	Ribbon	Shortcut Menu	Keyboard Shortcut
Animated GIF (Movie), Insert	PPT 174		Picture button (Insert tab | Images group)		
Audio File, Insert	PPT 167		Insert Audio button (Insert tab | Media group)		
Audio Options, Add	PPT 170		Audio Tools Playback tab | Audio Options group		
Clip Art, Insert	PPT 27	Clip Art icon in slide	Clip Art button (Insert tab | Images group)		
Clip Art, Photo, or Shape, Move	PPT 36	Drag			ARROW KEYS move selected image in small increments
Clip Art, Regroup	PPT 162		Group button, Regroup command (Drawing Tools Format tab | Arrange group)	Group, Regroup	
Clip Art, Ungroup	PPT 157		Group button, Ungroup command (Picture Tools Format tab | Arrange group), click Yes to convert to Microsoft Office drawing, click Drawing Tools Format tab, Group button, Ungroup		
Clip Object, Recolor	PPT 158		Shape Fill button (Drawing Tools Format tab | Shape Styles group)	Format Shape, Color button (Format Shape dialog box)	
Copy	PPT 108, 155		Copy button (Home tab | Clipboard group)	Copy	CTRL+C
Document Properties, Change	PPT 46		Properties button (File tab | Info tab)		
Document Theme, Change Color	PPT 81		Colors button (Design tab | Themes group)		
Document Theme, Choose	PPT 5		More button (Design tab | Themes group)		
Font Size, Decrease	PPT 104	Decrease Font Size button or Font Size box arrow on Mini toolbar	Decrease Font Size button or Font Size box arrow (Home tab | Font group)		CTRL+SHIFT+<
Font Size, Increase	PPT 11	Increase Font Size button or Font Size box arrow on Mini toolbar	Increase Font Size button or Font Size box arrow (Home tab | Font group)		CTRL+SHIFT+>
Font, Change	PPT 102	Font box arrow on Mini toolbar	Font box arrow (Home tab | Font group)	Font, Font tab (Font dialog box)	CTRL+SHIFT+F
Font, Change Color	PPT 13	Font Color button or Font Color button arrow on Mini toolbar	Font Color button or Font Color button arrow (Home tab | Font group)	Font, Font tab (Font dialog box)	CTRL+SHIFT+F
Format Painter, Use	PPT 105	Format Painter button on Mini toolbar	Double-click Format Painter button (Home tab | Clipboard group), select text with format you want to copy, select text to apply previously selected format; press ESC to turn off Format Painter		

Table 2: Microsoft PowerPoint 2010 Quick Reference Summary *(continued)*

Task	Page Number	Mouse	Ribbon	Shortcut Menu	Keyboard Shortcut
Handout, Print	PPT 184		Print button (File tab | Print tab)		
List Level, Increase	PPT 17	Increase List Level button on Mini toolbar	Increase List Level button (Home tab | Paragraph group)		TAB or ALT+SHIFT+RIGHT ARROW
List Level, Decrease	PPT 18	Decrease List Level button on Mini toolbar	Decrease List Level button (Home tab | Paragraph group)		SHIFT+TAB or ALT+SHIFT+LEFT ARROW
Next Slide	PPT 25	Next Slide button on vertical scroll bar or next slide thumbnail on Slides tab			PAGE DOWN
Normal View	PPT 153	Normal button at lower-right PowerPoint window	Normal View button (View tab | Presentation Views group)		
Open Presentation	PPT 50		Open (File tab)		CTRL+O
Paste	PPT 109		Paste button (Home tab | Clipboard group)	Paste	CTRL+V
Photo, Insert	PPT 32, 83	Insert Picture from File icon on slide or Insert Clip Art icon on slide	Picture button or Clip Art button (Insert tab | Images group)		
Picture, Add an Artistic Effect	PPT 145		Artistic Effects button (Picture Tools Format tab | Adjust group)	Format Picture, Artistic Effects (Format Picture dialog box)	
Picture, Add Border	PPT 91		Picture border button (Picture Tools Format tab | Picture Styles group)		
Picture, Correct	PPT 87		Corrections button (Picture Tools Format tab | Adjust group)	Format Picture, Picture Corrections (Format Picture dialog box)	
Picture, Recolor	PPT 143		Color button (Picture Tools Format tab | Adjust group)	Format Picture, Picture Color (Format Picture dialog box)	
Picture Border, Change Color	PPT 92		Picture border button (Picture Tools Format tab | Picture Styles group)		
Picture Effects, Apply	PPT 89		Picture Effects button (Picture Tools Format tab | Picture Styles group)	Format Picture	
Picture Style, Apply	PPT 87		More button (Picture Tools Format tab | Picture Styles group)		
Placeholder, Delete	PPT 149				Select placeholder, DELETE
Placeholder, Move	PPT 148	Drag			
Placeholder, Resize	PPT 148	Drag sizing handles			
Previous Slide	PPT 26	Previous Slide button on vertical scroll bar or click previous slide thumbnail on Slides tab			PAGE UP

Table 2: Microsoft PowerPoint 2010 Quick Reference Summary *(continued)*

Task	Page Number	Mouse	Ribbon	Shortcut Menu	Keyboard Shortcut
Print a Presentation	PPT 51		Print button (File tab | Print tab)		CTRL+P
Quit PowerPoint	PPT 50	Close button on title bar	Exit (File tab)	Right-click Microsoft PowerPoint button on taskbar, click Close window	ALT+F4
Reading View	PPT 154	Reading View button at lower-right PowerPoint window	Reading View button (View tab | Presentation Views group)		
Resize	PPT 33, 93, 148	Drag sizing handles	Enter height and width values (Picture Tools Format tab | Size group or Drawing Tools Format tab | Size group)	Format Picture or Format Shape, Size tab; or enter height and width in Shape Height and Shape Width boxes	
Save a Presentation	PPT 14	Save button on Quick Access Toolbar	Save or Save As (File tab)		CTRL+S or F12
Shape, Apply Style	PPT 110		More button or Format Shape Dialog Box Launcher in Shapes Style gallery (Drawing Tools Format tab | Shape Styles group)	Format Shape	
Shape, Insert	PPT 106		Shapes button (Home tab | Drawing group); More button (Drawing Tools Format tab | Insert Shapes group)		
Slide, Add	PPT 14		New Slide button (Home tab | Slides group)		CTRL+M
Slide, Arrange	PPT 39	Drag slide in Slides tab or Outline tab to new position, or in Slide Sorter view drag to new position			
Slide, Delete	PPT 152			Delete Slide	DELETE
Slide, Duplicate	PPT 38		New Slide arrow (Home tab | Slides group), Duplicate Selected Slides		
Slide, Format Background	PPT 95		Background Styles button (Design tab | Background group)	Format Background	
Slide, Insert Picture as Background	PPT 97		Background Styles button (Design tab | Background group)	Format Background, Picture or Texture Fill, Insert from File (Format Background dialog box)	
Slide, Select Layout	PPT 21		Layout button or New Slide arrow (Home tab | Slides group)		

Table 2: Microsoft PowerPoint 2010 Quick Reference Summary *(continued)*

Task	Page Number	Mouse	Ribbon	Shortcut Menu	Keyboard Shortcut
Slide Number, Insert	PPT 182		Insert Slide Number button (Insert tab | Text group) or Header & Footer button (Insert tab | Text group), click Slide number check box		
Slide Show View	PPT 47	Slide Show button at lower-right PowerPoint window	Slide Show button (Slide Show tab | Start Slide Show group)		F5
Slide Show, End	PPT 49	Click black ending slide		End Show	ESC or HYPHEN
Slide Sorter View	PPT 153	Slide Sorter button at lower-right PowerPoint window	Slide Sorter button (View tab | Presentation Views group)		
Speaker Notes, Add	PPT 179	In Normal view, click Notes pane and type notes			
Speaker Notes, Print	PPT 187		File tab, Print tab, click Notes Pages (Print Layout area), click Print button		
Spelling, Check	PPT 181		Spelling button (Review tab | Proofing group)	Spelling (or click correct word on shortcut menu)	F7
Stacking Order, Change	PPT 146		Bring Forward or Send Backward button (Picture Tools Format tab | Arrange group)	Send to Back or Bring to Front	
Synonym, Find and Insert	PPT 178		Thesaurus button (Review tab | Proofing group)	Right-click word, click desired synonym on Synonym submenu	SHIFT+F7
Text, Add Shadow	PPT 103		Text Shadow button (Home tab | Font group)		
Text, Align Horizontally	PPT 150	Align Text buttons on Mini toolbar	Align Text buttons (Home tab | Paragraph group)	Paragraph, Alignment box (Paragraph dialog box)	CTRL+R (right), CTRL+L (left), CTRL+E (center)
Text, Bold	PPT 20	Bold button on Mini toolbar	Bold button (Home tab | Font group)	Font, Font tab (Font dialog box)	CTRL+B
Text, Change Color	PPT 13	Font Color button or Font Color button arrow on Mini toolbar	Font Color button or Font Color button arrow (Home tab | Font group)	Font, Font tab (Font dialog box)	
Text, Delete	PPT 41		Cut button (Home tab | Clipboard group)	Cut	DELETE or CTRL+X or BACKSPACE
Text, Find and Replace	PPT 176		Replace button (Home tab | Editing group)		CTRL+H
Text, Italicize	PPT 11	Italic button on Mini toolbar	Italic button (Home tab | Font group)	Font, Font tab (Font dialog box)	CTRL+I
Text, Select Paragraph	PPT 10	Triple-click paragraph			SHIFT+DOWN ARROW or SHIFT+UP ARROW
Text, Select Word	PPT 12	Double-click word			CTRL+SHIFT+RIGHT ARROW or CTRL+SHIFT+LEFT ARROW

Table 2: Microsoft PowerPoint 2010 Quick Reference Summary (continued)

Task	Page Number	Mouse	Ribbon	Shortcut Menu	Keyboard Shortcut
Transition, Add	PPT 43		Transitions tab | Transition to This Slide group		ALT+A , T
Transparency, Change	PPT 98		Background Styles button (Design tab | Background group), Format Background, move Transparency slider	Format Background, Transparency slider	
Video File, Insert	PPT 163		Insert Video button (Insert tab | Media group)		
Video File, Trim	PPT 165		Trim Video button (Video Tools Playback tab | Editing group), drag video start/end points or edit Start Time and End Time boxes		
Video Options	PPT 166		Video Tools Playback tab | Video Options group		
Video Style, Add	PPT 172		More button (Video Tools Format tab | Video Styles group)		
WordArt, Add Text Effects	PPT 115		Text Effects button (Drawing Tools Format tab | WordArt Styles group)		
WordArt, Insert	PPT 114		WordArt button (Insert tab | Text group)		
Zoom for Viewing Slides	PPT 156	Drag Zoom slider on status bar; click Zoom In or Zoom Out button on Zoom slider; change percentage in Zoom level box on left side of slider	Zoom button (View tab | Zoom group)		

Table 3: Microsoft Excel 2010 Quick Reference Summary

Task	Page Number	Mouse	Ribbon	Shortcut Menu	Keyboard Shortcut
Accounting Number Format, Apply	100		Accounting Number Format button (Home tab | Number group)		
All data in a cell, Select	51	Double-click if there are no spaces in data			
Auto Fill	18	Drag fill handle	Auto Fill Options button (Home tab | Editing group)		
AutoCalculate	48	Select range | right-click AutoCalculate area | click calculation			
Average Function	84	Insert Function box in formula bar | AVERAGE in Select a function list | OK | range | OK	Sum button arrow (Home tab | Editing group) or Sum button arrow (Formulas tab | Function Library)		Type =av | press DOWN ARROW | ENTER

Table 3: Microsoft Excel 2010 Quick Reference Summary (continued)

Task	Page Number	Mouse	Ribbon	Shortcut Menu	Keyboard Shortcut
Background Color, Change	96		Format Cells Dialog Box Launcher (Home tab | Font group) | Fill tab | click color | click OK	Format Cells on shortcut menu	CTRL+1
Best Fit	107	Select columns | point to boundary until arrow is split double arrow | double-click			
Bold	25	Bold button on Mini toolbar	Bold button (Home tab | Font group)	Format Cells on shortcut menu | Font tab | Bold	CTRL+B
Cell Entries, Clear Selected	52	Drag fill handle from empty cell through cells with entries	Clear button (Home tab | Editing group) | Clear Contents	Clear Contents on shortcut menu	DELETE
Cell Reference, Add	78	Click cell			
Cell Style, Change	52		Cell Styles button (Home tab | Styles group)		
Cell, Highlight	19	Drag mouse pointer			
Cell, Select	34	Click cell or click Name box, type cell reference, press ENTER			Use arrow keys
Cells, Merge and Center	28	Merge & Center button on Mini toolbar	Merge & Center button (Home tab | Alignment group)	Format Cells on shortcut menu | Alignment tab	
Characters to left of insertion point, Delete	50				BACKSPACE
Characters to right of insertion point, Delete	50				DELETE
Characters, Highlight	51	Drag through adjacent characters			SHIFT+RIGHT ARROW or SHIFT+LEFT ARROW
Chart, Add	38		Charts group | Insert tab		
Color Text	27	Font Color button on Mini toolbar	Font Color button arrow (Home tab | Font group)		
Column Width	33	Drag column heading boundary		Column Width on shortcut menu	
Comma Style Format, Apply	100		Comma Style button (Home tab | Number group)		
Complete an Entry	8	Click Enter box			Press ENTER
Conditional Formatting	104		Conditional Formatting button (Home tab | Styles group)		
Copy Range of Cells	80	Select range | drag fill handle |	Copy button (Home tab | Clipboard group) |	Copy on shortcut menu	CTRL+C
Currency Style Format, Apply	100		Format Cells: Number Dialog Box Launcher (Home tab | Number group)		CTRL+1 OR CTRL+SHIFT+ DOLLAR SIGN ($)

Table 3: Microsoft Excel 2010 Quick Reference Summary *(continued)*

Task	Page Number	Mouse	Ribbon	Shortcut Menu	Keyboard Shortcut
Date, Format	98		Format Cells: Number Dialog Box Launcher on Home tab	Format Cells on shortcut menu | Number tab (Format Cells dialog box)	
Document Properties, Change	43		Properties button (File tab | Info tab)		
Document Properties, Print	45		File tab | Print tab, first box arrow (Settings area)		
Document Properties, Set or View	43		File | Info tab		
Entry, Complete	8	Click Enter box			Press ENTER
Font Color	27	Font Color box arrow on Mini toolbar	Font Color button arrow (Home tab | Font group)	Format Cells on shortcut menu | Font tab	
Font Size, Decrease	26	Font Size box arrow on Mini toolbar	Decrease Font Size button (Home tab | Font group)	Format Cells on shortcut menu | Font tab	
Font Size, Increase	26	Font Size box arrow on Mini toolbar	Increase Font Size button (Home tab | Font group)	Format Cells | Font Tab	
Font Type	24	Font box arrow on Mini toolbar	Font box (Home tab | Font group)	Format Cells | Font tab	
Font, Change	24	Font Size box arrow on Mini toolbar	Font box arrow (Home tab | Font group)	Format Cells | Font tab	
Formulas Version	119				CTRL+ACCENT MARK (`)
Highlight Cells	18	Drag mouse pointer			SHIFT+ARROW KEY
In-Cell Editing	50	Double-click cell			F2
Insert and Overtype modes, Toggle between	50				INSERT
Insertion point, Move	8	Click			Use arrow keys
Insertion point, move to beginning of data in cell	51	Point to left of first character and click			HOME
Insertion point, move to ending of data in cell	51	Point to right of last character and click			END
Margins, Change	114	Page Layout button on status bar | Page Layout tab | Margins button	Page Setup Dialog Box Launcher | Margins tab (Page Layout tab | Page Setup group)		
Max Function	86	Insert Function box in formula bar | MAX in Select a function list | OK | range | OK	Sum button arrow (Home tab | Editing group) or Sum button arrow (Formulas tab | Sum group)		
Min Function	87	Insert Function box in the formula bar | MIN in Select a function list | OK | range | OK	Sum button arrow (Home tab | Editing group) or Sum button arrow (Formulas tab | Sum group)		
New Line in Cell, Start	71				ALT+ENTER

Table 3: Microsoft Excel 2010 Quick Reference Summary *(continued)*

Task	Page Number	Mouse	Ribbon	Shortcut Menu	Keyboard Shortcut
Numbers, Format	31	Accounting Number Format, Percent Style, or Comma Style button on Mini toolbar	Cell Styles button (Home tab | Styles group) or Accounting Number Format, Percent Style, or Comma Style button (Home tab | Number group), or Format Cells: Number dialog box launcher | Accounting, or Percentage or Number Format list arrow | Accounting or Percentage		
Open a Workbook	48		Open or Recent (File tab)		CTRL+O
Percent style format	103		Percent Style button (Home tab | Number group)	Format Cells on shortcut menu | Number tab | Percentage (Format Cells dialog box)	CTRL+SHIFT+ percent sign (%)
Print Scaling Option	120		Page Setup Dialog Box Launcher (Page Layout tab | Page Setup group)		
Print Section of Worksheet	118		File | Print tab | Print Active Sheets or Print Area button (Page Layout tab | Page Setup group)		
Print Worksheet	46		File tab | Print tab		CTRL+P
Quit Excel	47	Close button on right side of title bar	Exit (File tab)		
Range Finder	91	Double-click cell			
Range, Deselect	18	Click outside range			
Range, Select	28	Drag fill handle through range			
Redo	51	Redo button on Quick Access Toolbar			CTRL+Y
Row Height	110	Drag row heading boundary		Row Height on shortcut menu	
Save Workbook	20	Save button on Quick Access Toolbar	Save (File tab | Save button)		CTRL+S
Save Workbook, New Name	20	Save button on Quick Access Toolbar			
Save Workbook, Same Name	20	Save button on Quick Access Toolbar	Save (File tab | Save button)		CTRL+S
Select Cell	7	Click cell or click Name box, type cell reference, press ENTER			Use arrow keys
Select Entire Worksheet	52	Click Select All button			CTRL+A
Select Nonadjacent Cells	100	Select first cell, hold down CTRL key while selecting second cell			
Selected characters, Delete	50		Cut button (Home tab | Clipboard group)		DELETE

Table 3: Microsoft Excel 2010 Quick Reference Summary *(continued)*

Task	Page Number	Mouse	Ribbon	Shortcut Menu	Keyboard Shortcut
Selected Chart, Delete	53				DELETE
Sheet Name, Change	42	Double-click type name		Rename on shortcut menu	
Spelling	112		Spelling button (Review tab | Proofing group)		F7
Sum	15	Click Insert Function button in formula bar | SUM in Select a function list | OK | range | OK	Sum button (Home tab | Editing group)		ALT+EQUAL SIGN (=) twice
Text, Delete after typing but before pressing the ENTER key	8	Click Cancel box in formula bar			Press ESC
Text, Delete while typing	8				Press BACKSPACE
Undo	51	Undo button on Quick Access Toolbar			CTRL+Z
Workbook Theme, Change	94		Themes button (Page Layout tab | Themes group)		
Worksheet Name, Change	42	Double-click sheet tab, type name		Rename on shortcut menu	
Worksheet, Clear	52		Select All button | Clear button (Home tab | Editing group)		CTRL A, press DELETE
Worksheet, Preview	46		File tab | Print tab		CTRL+P

Table 4: Microsoft Access 2010 Quick Reference Summary

Task	Page Number	Mouse	Ribbon	Shortcut Menu	Keyboard Shortcut
Advanced Filter/Sort, Use	AC 153		Advanced button (Home tab | Sort & Filter group), Advanced Filter/Sort		
All Fields in Query, Include	AC 79, AC 80	Double-click asterisk			
Alternate Row Colors, Change in Datasheet	AC 181, AC 182		Select table, Alternate Row Color button arrow (Home tab | Text Formatting group), select color OR Datasheet Formatting Dialog Box Launcher (Home tab | Text Formatting group)		
Append Query, Use	AC 164		Append button (Query Tools Design Tab | Query Type group)		
Ascending Button, Use to Order Records	AC 194		Select field, Ascending button (Home tab | Sort & Filter group)	Right-click field name, click Sort A to Z or Sort Z to A	
Calculated Field in Query, Use	AC 116			Right-click field row, Zoom	

Table 4: Microsoft Access 2010 Quick Reference Summary *(continued)*

Task	Page Number	Mouse	Ribbon	Shortcut Menu	Keyboard Shortcut
Calculated Field, Create	AC 159	In Design view, create new field, click Data Type box arrow, click Calculated			
Caption, Change in Query	AC 118		Property Sheet button (Query Tools Design Tab | Show/Hide group), Caption box	Right-click field in design grid, click Properties on shortcut menu, Caption box	
Close Object	AC 23	Close button for object		Right-click item, Close	
Collection of Legal Values, Specify	AC 167	In Design view, enter criterion specifying legal values in Validation Rule property box in Field Properties pane			
Column Headings, Modify	AC 54			Right-click field name, Rename Field	
Column, Resize	AC 54, AC 55	Double-click right boundary of field selector in datasheet		Right-click field name, Field Width	
Common Filter, Use	AC 150			Click arrow for field, point to Text Filters	
Comparison Operator, Use	AC 91	Create query, enter comparison operator in criterion			
Compound Criterion Involving AND, Use	AC 92				Place criteria on same line
Compound Criterion Involving OR, Use	AC 93				Place criteria on separate lines
Criteria, Use in Calculating Statistics	AC 121		Totals button (Query Tools Design Tab | Show/Hide group), Total box arrow, click calculation		
Criterion, Use	AC 46	Right-click query, Design View, Criteria row			
Crosstab Query, Create	AC 124		Query Wizard button (Create tab | Queries group), Crosstab Query Wizard		
Data, Export to Excel	AC 111		Excel button (External Data tab | Export group)	Right-click object, click Excel on Export menu	
Data, Import	AC 38		Button for imported data format (External Data tab | Import & Link group)	Right-click object, click selected format on Import menu	
Data, Sort in Query	AC 96		Select field in design grid, click Sort row, click Sort row arrow, select order		

Table 4: Microsoft Access 2010 Quick Reference Summary *(continued)*

Task	Page Number	Mouse	Ribbon	Shortcut Menu	Keyboard Shortcut
Database Properties, Change	AC 59		View and edit database properties link (File tab | Info tab)		
Database, Create	AC 13		Blank database button (File tab | New tab)		
Default Value, Specify	AC 167	In Design view, select field in upper pane, enter value in Default Value property box in Field Properties pane			
Delete Query, Use	AC 163		Delete button (Query Tools Design tab | Query Type group)	Right-click any open area in upper pane, point to Query Type on shortcut menu, click Delete Query on Query Type submenu	
Design Grid, Clear	AC 95	In Design view, select all columns, DELETE			
Duplicate Records, Find	AC 100		Query Wizard button (Create tab | Queries group), Find Duplicates Query Wizard		
Duplicates, Omit	AC 97		In Design view, click first empty field, Property Sheet button (Query Tools Design tab | Show/Hide group), click Yes in Unique Values property box	Right-click first empty field, click Properties on shortcut menu, click Yes in Unique Values property box	
Field, Add to Report	AC 175		In Layout view, Add Existing Fields button (Report Layout Tools Design tab | Tools group), drag field from field list to desired location		
Field Contents, Change	AC 146	In Datasheet view, click in field, enter data			
Field in Query, Add	AC 79	Double-click field in upper pane			
Field, Add New	AC 155		In Design view, Insert Rows button (Table Tools Design Tab | Tools group)		Design view, INSERT
Field, Delete	AC 155	In Design view, click row selector for field, DELETE	Delete Rows button (Table Tools Design tab | Tools group)		
Filter by Form, Use	AC 152		Advanced button (Home tab | Sort & Filter group), Clear All Filters, Advanced button, Filter by Form		
Filter by Selection, Use	AC 148		Selection button (Home tab | Sort & Filter group), select criterion		

Table 4: Microsoft Access 2010 Quick Reference Summary *(continued)*

Task	Page Number	Mouse	Ribbon	Shortcut Menu	Keyboard Shortcut
Filter, Clear	AC 150		Advanced button (Home tab | Sort & Filter group), Clear All Filters		
Filter, Toggle	AC 150		Toggle Filter button (Home tab | Sort & Filter group)		
Font, Change in Datasheet	AC 181		Select table, Font box arrow (Home tab | Text Formatting group), select font		
Font Color, Change in Datasheet	AC 181		Select table, Font Color button arrow (Home tab | Text Formatting group), select color		
Font Size, Change in Datasheet	AC 181		Select table, Font Size box arrow (Home tab | Text Formatting group), select size		
Form for Query, Create	AC 109		Select query, Form button (Create tab | Forms group)		
Form, Create	AC 48		Form button (Create tab | Forms group)		
Format, Specify	AC 168	In Design view, select field, type format			
Gridlines, Change in Datasheet	AC 180		Gridlines button (Home tab | Text Formatting group)		
Grouping, Use	AC 122	Create query, select Group By in Total row, select field to group by			
Join Properties, Change	AC 105			In Design view, right-click join line	
Lookup Field, Create	AC 156	In Design view, click Data Type column for field, Data Type box arrow, Lookup Wizard			
Make-Table Query, Use	AC 165		Make Table button (Query Tools Design tab | Query Type group)		
Multiple Keys, Sort on	AC 98	Assign two sort keys in design grid			
Multivalued Field, Query Showing Multiple Values	AC 183	Create query with specified fields			
Multivalued Lookup Field, Use	AC 172	In Datasheet view, click field, click check boxes, OK			
Navigation Pane, Customize	AC 127	Navigation Pane arrow			
Number Criterion, Use	AC 90	Create query, select table, enter criterion in field grid			
Open Database	AC 27		Open button (File tab)		
Open Table	AC 24	Double-click table in Navigation Pane		Right-click table in Navigation Pane, click Open in shortcut menu	

Table 4: Microsoft Access 2010 Quick Reference Summary *(continued)*

Task	Page Number	Mouse	Ribbon	Shortcut Menu	Keyboard Shortcut
Parameter Query, Create	AC 87		In Design view, type parameter in square brackets in criterion row of field grid, View button (Query Tools Design tab | Results group)		
Preview or Print Object	AC 31		Print or Print Preview button (File tab | Print tab)		CTRL+P, ENTER
Query, Create in Design View	AC 78		Query Design button (Create tab | Queries group)		
Query, Create using Simple Query Wizard	AC 43		Query Wizard button (Create tab | Queries group)		
Query, Export	AC 111, AC 113, AC 114		Select query in Navigation Pane, application button (External Data tab | Export group)	Right-click query in Navigation Pane, click Export	
Range, Specify	AC 166	In Design view, select field, enter criterion specifying range in Validation Rule property box in Field Properties pane			
Record, Add	AC 28	New (blank) record button in Navigation buttons	New button (Home tab | Records Group)		CTRL+PLUS SIGN (+)
Record, Delete	AC 147	In Datasheet view, click record selector, DELETE	Delete button (Home tab | Records group)		DELETE
Record, Search for	AC 144		Find button (Home tab | Find group)		CTRL+F
Record, Update	AC 146	In Form view, change desired data			In Datasheet, select field and edit
Records in a Join, Restrict	AC 115	In Design view, enter criterion for query			
Referential Integrity, Specify	AC 186		Relationships button (Database Tools tab | Relationships group)		
Remaining Fields in Table, Define	AC 19	In Datasheet view, click Click to Add field (Fields tab)			
Report, Create	AC 52		Report button (Create tab | Reports group)		
Report, Create Involving Join	AC 106		Select query, Report Wizard button (Create tab | Reports group)		
Required Field, Specify	AC 166	In Design view, select field, Required property box in Field Properties pane, down arrow, Yes			
Save Object	AC 21	Save button on Quick Access Toolbar	File tab, Save		CTRL+S

Table 4: Microsoft Access 2010 Quick Reference Summary *(continued)*

Task	Page Number	Mouse	Ribbon	Shortcut Menu	Keyboard Shortcut
Single or Multivalued Lookup Fields, Modify	AC 161	In Design view, select field, click Lookup tab in Field Properties pane, change list in Row Source property to desired list			
Split Form, Create	AC 142		Select table, More Forms button (Create tab | Forms group), Split Form		
Statistics, Calculate	AC 119		Create query, Totals button (Query Tools Design tab | Show/Hide group), click Total row in design grid, click Total box arrow, select calculation		
Subdatasheet, Use	AC 191	In Datasheet view, click plus sign in front of row			
Table, Create in Design View	AC 33		Table Design button (Create tab | Tables group)		
Table, View in Design View	AC 21		View button arrow (Table Tools Fields tab | Views group), Design View		
Tables, Join	AC 102		Query Design button (Create tab | Queries group), add field lists for tables to join, add desired fields to design grid, view query		
Text Data Criterion, Use	AC 80	Enter text as criterion in Criteria row of design grid			
Top Values Query, Create	AC 99		In Design view, Return box arrow (Query Tools Design tab | Query Setup group)		
Totals, Add to a Report	AC 57		Totals button (Report Layout Tools Design tab | Grouping & Totals group)		
Totals, Include in a Datasheet	AC 177		In Datasheet view, Totals button (Home tab | Records group), click Total row, click arrow		
Totals, Remove from a Datasheet	AC 179		Totals button (Home tab | Records group)		
Unmatched Records, Find	AC 193		Query Wizard button (Create tab | Queries group), Find Unmatched Query Wizard		
Update Query, Use	AC 162		Create query, Update button (Query Tools Design tab | Query Type group), select field, click Update To row in design grid	Right-click any open area in upper pane, point to Query Type on shortcut menu, click Update Query on Query Type submenu	
Wildcard, Use	AC 83	In Design view, click Criteria row in design grid, type criterion including wildcard			

Table 5: Microsoft Outlook 2010 Quick Reference Summary

Task	Page Number	Mouse	Ribbon	Shortcut Menu	Keyboard Shortcut
Appointment, Change Date for	OUT 80	Double-click appointment, change date *or* Drag appointment to different date in Date Navigator			CTRL+O, change date
Appointment, Change Time for	OUT 79	Double-click appointment, change time *or* Drag appointment to different time slot in appointment area			CTRL+O, change time
Appointment, Create	OUT 62, OUT 64	Drag to select time slots, type appointment title	New Appointment button (Home tab | New group)		CTRL+SHIFT+A
Appointment, Delete	OUT 82		Delete button (Calendar Tools Appointment Series tab | Actions group)	Delete	DELETE
Appointment, Save	OUT 69	Close button, Yes to save changes	Save & Close button (Appointment tab | Actions group)		
Appointment, Set Recurrence Options for	OUT 72		Recurrence button (Appointment tab | Options group)		
Appointment, Set Reminder for	OUT 68		Reminder box arrow (Appointment tab | Options group)		
Appointment, Set Status for	OUT 67		Show As box arrow (Appointment tab | Options group)		
Attach File to E-mail Message	OUT 30	Drag file to message area	Attach File button (Message tab | Include group or Insert tab | Include group)	Copy, right-click message area, click Paste	
Attachment, Preview	OUT 33	Click message header, click attachment			
Attachment, Save	OUT 35		Save As button (Attachment Tools Attachments tab | Actions group), Save button (Save Attachment dialog box)	Save As	
Calendar, Accept Meeting Request	OUT 96		Accept button (Meeting tab | Respond group)		CTRL+ALT+R
Calendar, Delete Personal Calendar	OUT 108		Delete Calendar button (Folder tab | Actions group)	Delete Calendar	
Calendar, Display Day View	OUT 62		Day button (Home tab | Arrange group)		CTRL+ALT+1
Calendar, Display Different Month in	OUT 80	Click left or right scroll arrow			PAGE UP or PAGE DOWN
Calendar, Display List View	OUT 102		Change View button (View tab | Current View group), click List		
Calendar, Display Month View	OUT 60		Month button (Home tab | Arrange group)		CTRL+ALT+4
Calendar, Display Personal Folder	OUT 56	Click folder check box			
Calendar, Display Schedule View	OUT 60		Schedule View button (Home tab | Arrange group)		CTRL+ALT+5
Calendar, Display Week View	OUT 59		Week button (Home tab | Arrange group)		CTRL+ALT+3

Table 5: Microsoft Outlook 2010 Quick Reference Summary (continued)

Task	Page Number	Mouse	Ribbon	Shortcut Menu	Keyboard Shortcut
Calendar, Display Work Week View	OUT 58		Work Week button (Home tab | Arrange group)		CTRL+ALT+2
Calendar, Export Subfolder	OUT 104		File | Open tab | Import | Export to a file (Import and Export Wizard)		
Calendar, Go to Specific Date	OUT 57	Click date in Date Navigator	Go To Dialog Box Launcher (Home tab | Go To group)		CTRL+G
Calendar, Import Subfolder	OUT 108		File | Open tab | Import | Import from another program or file (Import and Export Wizard)		
Calendar, Print Table Style	OUT 103		Change View button (View tab | Current View group), click List, Print button (File tab | Print| Table Style)		CTRL+P
Calendar, Print Weekly Calendar Style	OUT 100		Change View button (View tab | Current View group), click Calendar, Print button (File tab | Print | Weekly Calendar Style)		CTRL+P
Calendar, Recurrence Options, Set for Appointment/Event/Meeting	OUT 72		Recurrence button (Appointment tab | Options group)		
Calendar, Reminder, Set for Appointment/Event/Meeting	OUT 68		Reminder box arrow (Appointment tab | Options group)		
Calendar, Remove Default Calendar from Appointment Area	OUT 56	Click Calendar check box in My Calendars Pane (to remove check mark)			
Cancel Meeting	OUT 98		Cancel Meeting button (Calendar Tools Meeting tab | Actions group)		
Change Meeting Time	OUT 98	Double-click meeting, change time *or* Drag meeting to new time			
Create Appointment	OUT 62, OUT 64	Drag to select time slots, type appointment title	New Appointment button (Home tab | New group)		CTRL+N
Create Event	OUT 84		New Appointment button (Home tab | New group), click All day event		
Create Folder in Inbox	OUT 36		New Folder button (Folder tab | New group)	New Folder	
Create Meeting	OUT 93		New Meeting button (Home tab | New group)		
Create New E-mail Message	OUT 9		New E-mail button (Home tab | New group)		CTRL+N
Create Personal Folder	OUT 54		New Calendar button (Folder tab | New group)		CTRL+SHIFT+E
Date, Go to	OUT 57	Click date in Date Navigator	Go To Dialog Box Launcher (Home tab | Go To group)		Press CTRL+G

Table 5: Microsoft Outlook 2010 Quick Reference Summary *(continued)*

Task	Page Number	Mouse	Ribbon	Shortcut Menu	Keyboard Shortcut
Day View, Display in Calendar	OUT 56		Day button (View tab | Arrangement group)		CTRL+ALT+1
Default Calendar, Remove from Appointment Area	OUT 56	Click Calendar check box in My Calendars pane (to remove check mark)			
Delete Appointment	OUT 82		Delete button (Calendar Tools Appointment Series tab | Actions group)	Delete	DELETE
Delete E-mail Message	OUT 22	Drag to Deleted Items folder	Delete button (Home tab | Delete group)		DELETE or CTRL+D
Delete Event	OUT 87		Delete button (Calendar Tools Appointment tab | Actions group)		DELETE
Delete Personal Calendar	OUT 108		Delete Calendar button (Folder tab | Actions group)	Delete Calendar	DELETE
Deleted Items Folder, Move E-mail Message to	OUT 22	Drag to Deleted Items folder	Delete button (Home tab | Delete group)		DELETE or CTRL+D
Display Calendar in List View	OUT 102		Change View button (View tab | Current View group), click List		
E-mail Message, Attach File to	OUT 30		Attach File button (Message tab | Include group) or Insert tab | Include group		
E-mail Message, Change Format to Plain Text	OUT 21		Plain Text button (Format Text tab | Format button)		
E-mail Message, Check Spelling	OUT 24		Spelling & Grammar button (Review tab | Proofing group)		F7
E-mail Message, Close	OUT 15	Click the Close button	Close button (File tab | Close)		
E-mail Message, Compose New	OUT 8		New E-mail button (Home tab | New group		CTRL+N
E-mail Message, Delete	OUT 22		Delete button (Home tab | Delete group)	Delete	DELETE
E-mail Message, Forward	OUT 19		Forward button (Home tab | Respond group)		CTRL+F
E-mail Message, Mark as Read	OUT 15		Unread/Read button (Home tab | Tags group)	Mark as Read	CTRL+Q
E-mail Message, Mark as Unread	OUT 15		Unread/Read button (Home tab | Tags group)	Mark as Unread	CTRL+U
E-mail Message, Open	OUT 14	Double-click message header			CTRL+O
E-mail Message, Print	OUT 15		Print button (File tab | Print)	Quick Print	CTRL+P
E-mail Message, Read	OUT 14	Select message in message list and read in Reading Pane			
E-mail Message, Reply	OUT 17		Reply button (Home tab | Respond group)		CTRL+R
E-mail Message, Reply All	OUT 17		Reply All button (Home tab | Respond group)		CTRL+SHIFT+R

Table 5: Microsoft Outlook 2010 Quick Reference Summary *(continued)*

Task	Page Number	Mouse	Ribbon	Shortcut Menu	Keyboard Shortcut
E-mail Message, Save Response in Drafts Folder	OUT 27		Save button (Quick Access Toolbar)		CTRL+S
E-mail Message, Send	OUT 11				ALT+S or CTRL+ENTER
E-mail Message, Set High Importance for	OUT 32		High Importance button (Message tab | Tags group)		
Event, Create	OUT 84		New Appointment button (Home tab | New group), click All day event check box	New All Day Event	CTRL+SHIFT+A
Event, Delete	OUT 87		Delete button (Calendar Tools Appointment tab | Actions group)		DELETE
Event, Save	OUT 86		Save & Close button (Event tab | Actions group)		
Event, Set Recurrence Options for	OUT 88		Recurrence button (Event tab | Options group)		
Export Calendar Subfolder	OUT 104		File | Open tab | Import | Export to a file (Import and Export Wizard)		
File, Attach to E-mail Message	OUT 30		Attach File button (Message tab | Include group)		
Folder, Create in Inbox	OUT 36		New Folder button (Folder tab | New group)	New Folder	CTRL+SHIFT+E
Folder, Create Personal Calendar Folder	OUT 54		New Calendar button (Folder tab | New group)	New Calendar	
Folder, Move E-mail Message to	OUT 37	Drag e-mail message to folder	Move button (Home tab | Move group)	Move | folder name	
Forward E-mail Message	OUT 19		Forward button (Home tab | Respond group)	Forward	CTRL+F
Go to Date	OUT 57		Go To Dialog Box Launcher (Home tab | Go To group)		Press CTRL+G
High Importance, Set for E-mail Message	OUT 32		High Importance button (Message tab | Tags group)		
Import Personal Subfolder	OUT 108		File | Open tab | Import | Import from another program or file (Import and Export Wizard)		
Importance, Set to High for E-mail Message	OUT 32		High Importance button (Message tab | Tags group)		
Invite People to Meeting	OUT 94		New Meeting button (Home tab | New group), type e-mail address and subject, click Send		
List View, Display for Calendar	OUT 102		Change View button (View tab | Current View group), click List		
Meeting, Cancel	OUT 98		Cancel Meeting button (Calendar Tools Meeting tab | Actions group)		
Meeting Cancellation Notice, Send	OUT 98	Send Cancellation button in message header			
Meeting, Create	OUT 94		New Meeting button (Home tab | New group)		CTRL+SHIFT+Q

Table 5: Microsoft Outlook 2010 Quick Reference Summary *(continued)*

Task	Page Number	Mouse	Ribbon	Shortcut Menu	Keyboard Shortcut
Meeting, Invite People to	OUT 94		New Meeting button (Home tab | New group), type e-mail address and subject, click Send		
Meeting Time, Change	OUT 98	Double-click meeting, change time *or* Drag meeting to new time			
Meeting Time, Propose New	OUT 98		Propose New Time button (Calendar Tools Meeting Occurrence tab | Respond group)		
Message Format, Change to Plain Text	OUT 21		Plain Text button (Format Text tab | Format group)		
Message List, Arrange by Date	OUT 7	Click Arrange by: Date column heading		Date	
Message List, Show in Groups	OUT 8		Show In Groups button (View tab | Arrangement group | More button)	Show in Groups	
Month View, Display in Calendar	OUT 60		Month button (Home tab | Arrange group)		CTRL+ALT+4
Move E-mail Message to Folder	OUT 37	Drag e-mail message to folder	Move button (Home tab | Move group)	Move | folder name	
Open E-mail Message	OUT 14	Double-click message header			CTRL+O
Outlook Data File, Open	OUT 7		Open Outlook Data File button (File tab | Open tab), Open Outlook Data File		
Personal Calendar, Delete	OUT 108		Delete Calendar button (Folder tab | Actions group)	Delete Calendar	DELETE
Personal Folder, Create	OUT 54		New Calendar button (Folder tab | New group)		CTRL+SHIFT+E
Personal Folder, Display	OUT 56	Click check box in My Calendars pane			
Personal Subfolder, Import	OUT 108		File | Open tab | Import | Export to a file (Import and Export Wizard)		
Plain Text, Change Message Format to	OUT 21		Plain Text button (Format Text tab | Format group)		
Preview Attachment	OUT 33	Click message header, click attachment			
Print Calendar in Table Style (List View)	OUT 103		File | Print tab | Table Style		CTRL+P
Print Calendar in Weekly Style	OUT 100		File | Print tab | Weekly Calendar Style		CTRL+P
Print E-mail Message	OUT 15		Print button (File tab | Print tab)	Quick Print	CTRL+P
Propose Meeting Time	OUT 98		Propose New Time button (Calendar Tools Meeting Occurrence tab | Respond group)		
Quit Outlook	OUT 38, OUT 109	Click Close button	Exit button (File tab)		
Read E-mail Message	OUT 14	Message header in message list			

Table 5: Microsoft Outlook 2010 Quick Reference Summary *(continued)*

Task	Page Number	Mouse	Ribbon	Shortcut Menu	Keyboard Shortcut
Recurrence Options, Set for Appointment	OUT 72		Recurrence button (Appointment tab | Options group)		
Recurrence Options, Set for Event	OUT 88		Recurrence button (Event tab | Options group)		
Reminder, Set for Appointment	OUT 68		Reminder box arrow (Appointment tab | Options group)		
Reply to E-mail Message	OUT 17		Reply button (Home tab | Respond group)	Reply	CTRL+R
Save Appointment	OUT 69		Save & Close button (Appointment tab | Actions group)		
Save Attachment	OUT 33		Save As button (Attachment Tools Attachments tab | Actions group), Save button (Save Attachment dialog box)		
Save E-mail Message in Drafts Folder	OUT 27	Save button on Quick Access Toolbar	Save (File tab | Save tab)		
Save Event	OUT 86		Save & Close button (Event tab | Actions group)		
Schedule View, Display in Calendar	OUT 60		Schedule View button (Home tab | Arrange group)		CTRL+ALT+5
Send E-mail Message	OUT 8	Send button (message window)			ALT+S
Send Meeting Cancellation Notice	OUT 99	Send Cancellation button in message header			
Spelling, Check as You Type	OUT 24		Spelling & Grammar button (Review tab | Proofing group)	Right-click error, click correct word on shortcut menu	F7
Status, Set for Appointment	OUT 67		Show As box arrow (Appointment tab | Options group)		
Table Style (List View), Print Calendar in	OUT 103		File | Print tab | Table Style		CTRL+P
Undo	OUT 9	Undo button on Quick Access Toolbar			CTRL+Z
Update Changed Meeting	OUT 95	Change meeting time, click Send Update button			
Week View, Display in Calendar	OUT 59		Week button (Home tab | Arrange group)		CTRL+ALT+3
Weekly Style, Print Calendar in	OUT 100		File | Print tab | Weekly Calendar Style		CTRL+P
Work Week View, Display in Calendar	OUT 58		Work Week button (Home tab | Arrange group)		CTRL+ALT+2